FINALLY, AN OPERATIONS MANAGEMENT BOOK TO GET EXCITED ABOUT!

Operations Management: A Supply Chain Process Approach exposes students to the exciting and changing world of operations management through dynamic writing, relevant application activities, and cutting-edge examples that will keep students interested and instructors inspired!

Author **Joel Wisner** understands that today's students will be entering a highly competitive global marketplace where two things are crucial: a solid knowledge of operations management and an understanding of the importance of integrating operations and supply chain processes. With this in mind, Wisner not only provides a clear and comprehensive introduction to operations management but also gives attention to the important processes involved in linking firms' operations in a supply chain environment.

Video case studies!

Today's students prefer an entertaining learning experience. **Original, assignable video case studies** provide students with the opportunity to see the concepts they are learning about in action.

VIDEO CASE STUDY

Learn more about ***forecasting and managing demand*** from real organizations that use operations management techniques every day. Christine Keelin is CFO at MPK Foods, a small family-owned company based in Duarte, California, that produces seasoning mixes sold to grocery stores. Each year MPK is challenged with forecasting demand based on seasonal promotions and market trends. Watch this short interview to find out how they do it.

Balanced emphasis on manufacturing and service operations!

Knowing that many of his readers will work in the service industry, Wisner intentionally includes a balance of operations examples from both manufacturing companies and service providers.

MANUFACTURING SPOTLIGHT Nike's Lean and Sustainable Supply Chain

Footwear manufacturer Nike has been working with its contract manufacturers to train them in lean principles. This allows for more and quicker decision making by workers, through skill building, teamwork, and quality concepts. These traits have allowed Nike to build a more lean, green, empowered, and equitable supply chain.

Nike's corporate responsibility strategy has evolved from a risk management, philanthropic, compliance model to a long-term strategy focused on innovation and collaboration to prepare Nike to thrive in a sustainable economy. The company is increasing its focus on sustainable business and innovation (SB&I) to provide greater returns to its business, communities, factory workers, consumers, and the planet.

"Sustainability is key to Nike's growth and innovation," says Mark Parker, president and CEO. Recognizing the impacts of declining natural resources and the need to move to a low-carbon economy, Nike's goal is to achieve zero waste in the supply chain and have products and materials that can be continuously reused.

"The link between sustainability and Nike as a growth company has never been clearer," says Hannah Jones, vice president of SB&I. Today, the company is reducing waste and toxins and increasing its use of environmentally preferred materials throughout its product lines.[39]

SERVICE SPOTLIGHT Service Shop Implements Cloud ERP

Australia-based Headland Machinery recently found it needed a solution for its project management problems. As the business expanded, Headland's management team found it increasingly difficult to assign and manage projects to its growing service workforce. At one point Headland was using three systems simultaneously in order to gain organizational efficiencies. With a service team of field engineers, and office staff who all required access to the database, Headland was finding it difficult to manage customer data, schedule service calls, automate maintenance, or streamline billing. The situation was reducing productivity and creating miscommunications.

In 2011, Headland implemented NetSuite's cloud ERP system for its Australian operations and its foreign sister company, Aotea Machinery. The ERP solution provided a single, comprehensive, real-time view of its projects. Its system handles Headland's scheduling of maintenance and repair work, project installations, and breakdown support, with greater accuracy, faster response, and better problem resolution.

The system manages all account services through a single dashboard view via the Internet, with all backups, upgrades, and installations completed automatically. Mobile integration allows access via smartphone, tablet, and laptop, so field users can accept jobs, invoice from the field, and log travel times. Workforce automation capabilities create more efficient planning, scheduling, and administration for a streamlined work flow.[24]

Cutting-edge coverage!

In this groundbreaking new book, Wisner outpaces the competition by paying special attention to several critical and emerging issues in OM including customer relationships and customer service, job scheduling and vehicle routing, customer flows and work flows, and the management of information flows. In addition, each chapter includes a section describing trends and current issues that are impacting managers today including RFID, big data analytics, ethics in OM, sustainability in design, CPFR, process management automation, cloud-based systems, and more.

TRENDS IN SIX SIGMA

13.5 Explain the new applications of Six Sigma

Although the philosophy and practices of Six Sigma have been in use for over 25 years, new applications of Six Sigma are constantly being discussed and published in research journals and trade publications. Two of the most recent applications are presented here.

TRENDS IN ENTERPRISE RESOURCE PLANNING

11.5 Recall three important trends in Enterprise Resource Planning

In the years since the start of the recent global recession, businesses have had to adapt and evolve their operations to remain competitive and profitable. One area changing radically in the face of this new business environment is ERP. ERP systems have been largely characterized by companies rolling out large, in-house systems from technology giants like SAP and Oracle. The complexity of ERP systems meant that they tended to be big, expensive, and difficult or time-consuming to implement.

INSTRUCTORS: WE MAKE IT EASY FOR YOU TO BRING YOUR CLASSROOM TO LIFE!

The book is just the beginning! A full suite of online multimedia resources is available with this text to help bring operations management to life for your students.

VIDEO

- Exclusive **video case studies** follow several companies, including Rolls Royce and ThinkFoodGroup, as they make decisions, solve problems, overcome obstacles, and strategically use operational tools and techniques to create a competitive advantage.
- **50 step-by-step, problem-solving videos** accompany the examples in the text and help students understand quantitative material.
- Additional **online videos** referenced throughout the chapters make this a truly entertaining and engaging learning experience for your students!

TURN-KEY IN-CLASS AND ASSIGNMENT PROGRAM

SAGE makes your job easier! All of the dynamic resources listed below are available in an easy-to-upload SAGE coursepack specially designed for your specific learning management system. A **SAGE coursepack** is a simple and user-friendly solution for building your online teaching and course management environment.

Chapter **pre-tests** (25 multiple-choice questions) and **post-tests** (40 multiple-choice questions) and over 50 assignable homework problems per chapter (including solutions for the instructor) provide additional quantitative practice. To assist students with these problems, online Excel® templates are included for each formula presented in the book.

3–5 activities are provided for each chapter. They can be used in class and/or online, individually or in groups, and include suggestions for how each activity might be adapted for large, small, and online classes.

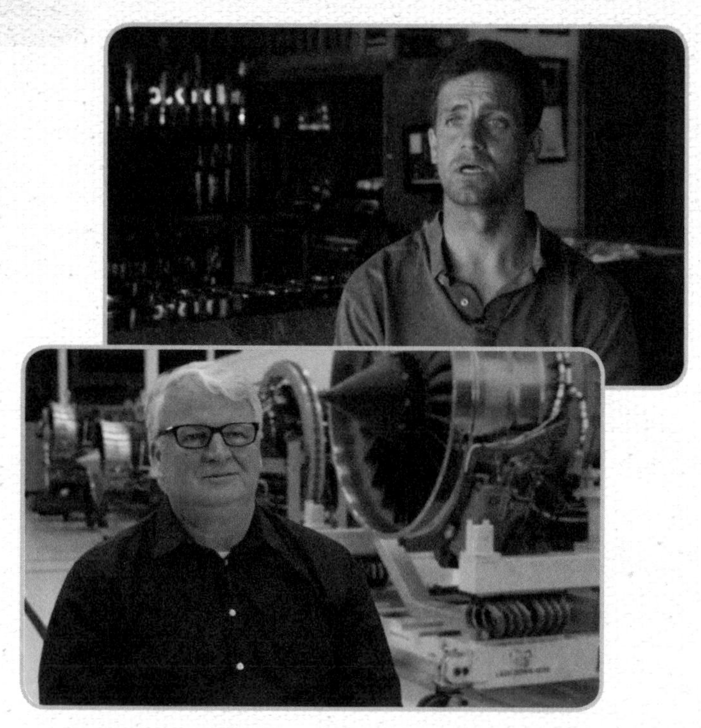

Also available to make lesson planning easier:

- **TEST BANK** built on Bloom's Taxonomy and tied to AACSB guidelines with 100 multiple-choice, 15 true-or-false, 10 fill-in-the-blank, and 5–10 essay questions per chapter
- **POWERPOINTS** with 25–35 slides per chapter that include key points and significant tables and figures from the text
- **LECTURE NOTES** that include summaries of each learning objective and an annotated chapter outline
- **CASE NOTES** including summary, analysis, and answers to the questions from the book's case studies
- **A MEDIA GUIDE** that includes hyperlinks and descriptions for all the video and web resources, as well as assessment questions for the videos
- **SAMPLE SYLLABI** for semester, quarter, and online courses
- **ANSWERS** to all in-text questions and a **SOLUTIONS MANUAL** with the answers to all assignment problems
- **SIMULATION GUIDE** for the Littlefield Technologies simulation including additional assignment ideas
- **TABLES AND FIGURES** and numbered examples from the book available in multiple file formats
- **ADDITIONAL PRACTICE PROBLEMS** for each chapter give you more assignment options

ONLINE SIMULATIONS

Your students can practice what they learn through a fun, hands-on simulation. Select chapters of the book include interactive assignments that ask students to manage **Littlefield Labs'** daily operations to test their understanding of operations and supply chain concepts. You have the flexibility to make the simulation experience as short as a one-hour assignment for use in class or as homework, or as involved as a two-week-long, out-of-class, small-group project.

Contact your SAGE sales rep for a demo!

LITTLEFIELD LABS

LITTLEFIELD LABORATORIES

Demonstrate your understanding of **process design and capacity management** at Littlefield Labs!

Littlefield Laboratories is a highly automated, state-of-the-art blood testing facility for clinics and hospitals. The lab will operate for a limited time frame lasting 210 days. You're asked to step in as the operations manager on Day 30, and are tasked with managing the capacity of the lab for the duration of its operation. Because Littlefield Labs guarantees results within a specific time frame, delays in testing and processing times can cost you money. Based on historic data and predicted demand patterns, you must buy or sell machines in order to optimize capacity and maximize the lab's profits.

Compete against your classmates to prove your understanding of the chapter concepts:

- LO 4-1: Describe the different types of processes and the types of outputs they create
- LO 4-2: Create a process flowchart and describe how it is used
- LO 4-3: Explain the relationship between capacity, capacity utilization, and process design

The team with the most cash in hand at the end of the 210-day time frame wins!

SAGE GIVES YOU OPTIONS

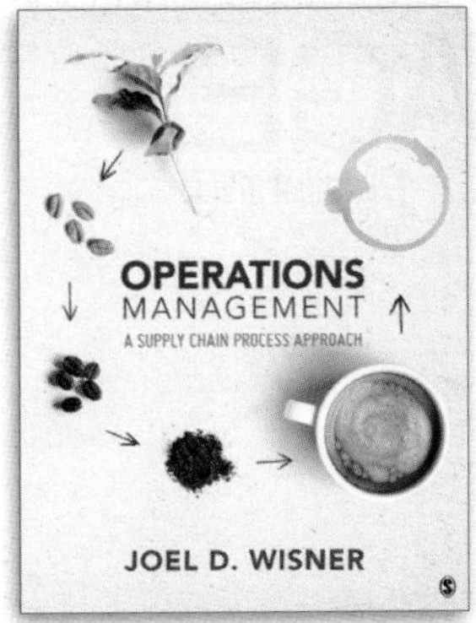

Order the loose-leaf version of this text and save! **ISBN 978-1-5063-6115-4**

To make it even easier to integrate this dynamic online content, consider adopting the **Interactive eBook!** The **IEB** includes interactive icons that link to multimedia resources and notetaking tools. Use the following ISBN to give your students the print book and accompanying Interactive eBook at no extra cost: **978-1-5063-5557-3**

 video resources

 sample spreadsheets

 audio resources

 web content

 whiteboard example videos

SAGE PUBLISHING: OUR STORY

Founded in 1965 by 24-year-old entrepreneur Sara Miller McCune, SAGE remains committed to fostering **creativity**, **innovation**, and **entrepreneurial mindsets** around the world. We believe in creating fresh, innovative content to help you prepare your students to compete in the modern business world.

- By partnering with **top business authors** with just the right balance of research, teaching, and industry experience, we bring you the most current and applied content.
- As a **student-friendly publisher**, we keep our prices affordable, our resources open-access and free, and provide multiple formats of our textbooks so your students can choose the option that works best for them.
- We remain majority-owned by our founder who has ensured we will remain permanently **independent** and fiercely committed to publishing the highest-quality resources for you and your students.
- SAGE means **BUSINESS**! Explore our new Business & Management titles, video collections, case collections, and more at **www.sagepub.com** or by contacting your sales representative.

To my wife, C. J., and to our children, Hayley and Blake.

OPERATIONS MANAGEMENT

A SUPPLY CHAIN PROCESS APPROACH

JOEL D. WISNER

University of Nevada, Las Vegas

Los Angeles | London | New Delhi
Singapore | Washington DC | Melbourne

FOR INFORMATION:

SAGE Publications, Inc.
2455 Teller Road
Thousand Oaks, California 91320
E-mail: order@sagepub.com

SAGE Publications Ltd.
1 Oliver's Yard
55 City Road
London, EC1Y 1SP
United Kingdom

SAGE Publications India Pvt. Ltd.
B 1/I 1 Mohan Cooperative Industrial Area
Mathura Road, New Delhi 110 044
India

SAGE Publications Asia-Pacific Pte. Ltd.
3 Church Street
#10-04 Samsung Hub
Singapore 049483

Printed in Canada.

Library of Congress Cataloging-in-Publication Data

Names: Wisner, Joel D., author.

Title: Operations management : a supply chain process approach / Joel D. Wisner, University of Nevada, Las Vegas.

Description: Thousand Oaks, California : SAGE Publications, Inc., 2017. | Includes bibliographical references and index.

Identifiers: LCCN 2016005419 | ISBN 978-1-4833-8306-4 (hardcover : alk. paper)

Subjects: LCSH: Business logistics. | Operations research.

Classification: LCC HD38.5 .W 569 2017 | DDC 658.5—dc23 LC record available at http://lccn.loc.gov/2016005419

Acquisitions Editor: Maggie Stanley
Development Editor: Abbie Rickard
Editorial Assistant: Neda Dallal
eLearning Editor: Katie Ancheta
Production Editor: Olivia Weber-Stenis
Copy Editor: Talia Greenberg
Typesetter: C&M Digitals (P) Ltd.
Proofreader: Jennifer Grubba
Indexer: Sheila Bodell
Cover Designer: Gail Buschman
Marketing Manager: Ashlee Blunk

This book is printed on acid-free paper.

16 17 18 19 20 10 9 8 7 6 5 4 3 2 1

BRIEF CONTENTS

DETAILED CONTENTS

LIST OF FEATURES

CHAPTER-OPENING VIGNETTES

SERVICE SPOTLIGHT

MANUFACTURING SPOTLIGHT

SPOTLIGHT ON OM TRENDS

CASE STUDIES

/ PREFACE /

Welcome to *Operations Management: A Supply Chain Process Approach.* Operations management (OM) is a key set of activities guiding the efficiency of organizations, giving managers the tools necessary for firms to be competitive in the marketplace. This textbook describes in detail how firms buy, make, and deliver goods and services around the globe, and provides students with a solid foundation of operations management concepts and techniques. While there are many operations management textbooks available, they tend to share some common problems: They cover the same traditional concepts as every other text, and they lack context for applying these concepts in real-world settings. Because of this, students tend to find operations management topics boring or challenging. They are not offered a broader perspective of how these concepts contribute to a firm's overall success, and they are not shown what their role in OM looks like in the real world.

Operations Management: A Supply Chain Process Approach addresses these shortcomings by covering foundational and cutting-edge OM topics and concepts, discussing current trends in the field including sustainability and working in the global marketplace, and providing numerous real-world examples and engaging exercises that enable students to put themselves in the shoes of real OM professionals. Written for today's students and the exciting and fast-changing marketplace they will enter, *Operations Management: A Supply Chain Process Approach* is the text that will bring OM into the modern era.

APPROACH

STUDENT-FRIENDLY STYLE

The primary objective of this textbook is to engage, enlighten, and entertain students while providing them with the knowledge and tools they will need on the job. Chapters are written in a student-friendly style and include a variety of photos, figures, and graphics to keep students interested. Step-by-step guides to using formulas and solving problems break down quantitative concepts for students and enable them to grasp challenging topics. Real-world examples, dynamic original video, and exercises and projects in each chapter give students several ways to engage with the material.

TOPICAL COVERAGE THAT REFLECTS THE CURRENT MARKETPLACE

Another objective of the book is to make readers think about how operations management impacts the internal processes of the firm as well as its external supply chain trading partners, and to illustrate how managers can create a competitive advantage by employing the practices described throughout the text. Every chapter delivers current examples of real companies using analytic tools in decision-making situations, explained in ways that make the topics interesting, easy to follow, and relatable to students' experiences. Chapters also contain discussions of emerging trends in operations such as sustainability, customer relationships, and quality management. As many students will work in the service industry, chapters carefully and intentionally include a balance of operations examples from both manufacturing and service industries as well.

SUPPLY CHAIN PROCESS INTEGRATION

Since all organizations are members of one or more supply chains, topics are presented within the context of key supply chain processes. These include:

- product development
- customer relationship management
- customer service management
- demand management
- order fulfillment
- manufacturing flow management
- supplier relationship management, and
- returns management.

Successful firms and their trading partners must frequently collaborate and share resources to maximize product value for customers. Coordinating efforts in this way can occasionally create problems, and for this reason, operations management students should learn the importance of process integration in supply chains, and how to identify integration problems and create solutions. Discussing operations in a supply chain context will give students a better understanding of how specific roles and functions contribute to a firm's overall success.

TARGET AUDIENCE

This textbook is best suited for the undergraduate Introduction to Operations Management course offered in most business schools. Undergraduate business students can find this class challenging, since many have little business experience and can find quantitative topics to be very demanding. This book is written with this student in mind. Students and professors alike will benefit from the numerous chapter examples, video links, and practice opportunities in each chapter when covering quantitative material inside and outside of class. Junior- or senior-level business students, beginning MBA students, as well as practicing managers can also benefit from reading and using this text. In many MBA curricula, a basic knowledge of operations management concepts and tools is required. Since this textbook approaches topics from the ground up, students will find the information enjoyable and understandable, regardless of their background or experience level.

ORGANIZATION OF THE BOOK

The topics in this book are arranged from a strategic to a tactical perspective, starting with foundational concepts and ending with broader discussions of managing supply chains. Operations management begins with top management strategic decisions impacting how the firm intends to compete. Operations decisions then translate corporate strategies into the more tactical, short-term decisions, such as how to manage inventories, assess quality, and purchase goods. Since all firms are members of one or more supply chains, the text ends with discussions of outward-facing topics such as supply management and logistics management.

PART I: DEVELOPING OPERATIONS STRATEGIES

Top managers decide how an organization will compete. Operations strategies and tactics support the organization's strategies, and these decisions are presented in this section.

- **Chapter 1: Operations Management, Processes, and Supply Chain Management** defines operations management, processes, and supply chain management, and describes their importance to the firm. The eight key supply chain processes, operations management in services, and important developments in operations management are also discussed.
- **Chapter 2: Corporate Strategy, Performance, and Sustainability** describes the development of corporate strategies and the alignment of operations strategies. The important roles of ethics and sustainability in developing operations strategies are also presented. A discussion of operations performance is also included.
- **Chapter 3: New Product and Service Design** presents the topics of product design and development for goods and services. The product development process,

environmental aspects of product design, and the latest trends in product design are included.

- **Chapter 4: Process Design and Capacity Management** presents process design and capacity management for services and manufacturers. Discussions of process analysis and flowcharting, capacity, break-even analysis, and sustainability in process design are included.
- The final chapter in Part I is **Chapter 5: Customer Relationships and Customer Service**, which is a discussion of the management of customer relationships and customer service, and their importance to all organizations. Discussions of the design of customer relationship programs, auditing customer service, and measuring customer service quality are included.

PART II: MANUFACTURING AND SERVICE FLOWS

In organizations, the flows of materials, customers, employees, and information coming into, through, and out of companies enable them to provide goods and services effectively. The following chapters present these topics.

- **Chapter 6: Demand Management, Forecasting, and Aggregate Planning** presents the topics of forecasting and aggregate planning. Forecasting techniques, forecast accuracy, collaborative planning and forecasting, and aggregate planning techniques are discussed.
- **Chapter 7: Independent Demand Inventory Management** discusses independent demand inventory management topics, including the types, functions, and costs of inventory, and measuring inventory management performance.
- **Chapter 8: Material Flow Analysis and Facility Layouts** describes the analysis of material flows and facility layouts. Material flow mapping, the theory of constraints, layout analysis, and layout trends are discussed in this chapter. Chapter 8 also includes the **Supplement: Job Scheduling and Vehicle Routing**, which presents a number of techniques for scheduling jobs in organizations and for routing of delivery vehicles.
- **Chapter 9: Lean Systems** presents discussions of the Toyota Production System, lean systems in manufacturing and services, lean supply chains, and current issues with lean systems.
- **Chapter 10: Managing Customer and Work Flows** presents topics associated with customer and work flows. Customer flow mapping, service delivery system design, managing customer queues, and managing work flows are presented and discussed.
- **Chapter 11: Managing Information Flows—MRP and ERP** describes how information is managed, including the concepts of material requirements planning, enterprise resource planning, business process management, and business process reengineering.
- **Chapter 12: Managing Projects** discusses the tools of project management, including project planning, project management techniques, managing project risk, and project management trends.
- **Chapter 13: Six Sigma Quality Management** describes Six Sigma quality and its origins, elements, and current trends. Chapter 13 also includes the **Supplement: Statistical Quality Control**, which presents techniques for controlling quality in variable and attribute data environments.

PART III: MANAGING SUPPLY CHAINS

All organizations are members of one or more supply chains, and the chapters in this section present concepts and tools used in managing supply chain trading partners.

- **Chapter 14: Global Supply Management** includes discussions of the purchasing cycle, make-or-buy decisions, supplier relationship management, ethical and sustainable sourcing, and e-procurement.

- **Chapter 15: Location, Logistics, and Product Returns** includes discussions of logistics, location analysis, warehouse and returns management, and logistics sustainability.
- **Chapter 16: Integrating Processes Along the Supply Chain** is the concluding chapter. It discusses the integration of key supply chain processes and managing supply chain risk and security.

FEATURES

Each chapter of the textbook contains a number of features to assist in teaching an introductory course in operations management and to keep students interested in the material.

CHAPTER-OPENING FEATURES

- **Chapter-opening quotes** by CEOs, directors, and well-known business personalities provide students evidence of the value of the content covered in each chapter, and initially interest students in reading the material.
- **Learning objectives** highlight the key topics of each chapter and summarize the skills students will develop after completing each chapter. The learning objectives are tied to the main topics of each chapter.
- **Chapter-opening "spotlights"** of services or manufacturers will offer initial interest to students about a major topic of the chapter and will immediately demonstrate the real-world relevance of the content. The profiles are summaries of best practices of real companies taken from well-known business periodicals.

IN-CHAPTER FEATURES

- **Key terms** are highlighted in the margins of pages where the terms are discussed, and defined at the end of each chapter, to aid students in finding and learning key term definitions.
- **Spotlight boxes** are boxed features throughout each chapter highlighting real service providers, manufacturers, and organizations solving real problems or utilizing techniques discussed in the chapter. Like the chapter-opening spotlights, these examples show students how real companies use OM concepts in their daily operations.
- **Example boxes** show students how to use and solve formulas, including both step-by-step and graphic solutions, where applicable. Excel spreadsheets related to certain examples are included on the SAGE edge website for students' reference.
- **Whiteboard videos** are live illustrations with narration that accompany each example box. These videos dive into challenging quantitative material and give students step-by-step instructions on how to use complex formulas and equations.
- **Marginal video icons** indicate to students that there is a YouTube video on the SAGE edge site that illustrates chapter concepts. Related Point-and-Click video questions on the site ask students to answer questions related to each video to check their understanding.

END-OF-CHAPTER FEATURES

- **Chapter summaries** give a quick wrap-up of the topics discussed in the chapter.
- **Lists of key terms**, including page references to their placement in the chapter, offer students a quick guide for reviewing key terms and concepts.
- **Formula reviews** in quantitative chapters list the key formulas covered in the chapter.
- **Solved problems** show students a step-by-step guide on how to use key formulas and concepts from the chapter.
- **Review questions** give students the opportunity to check their understanding by asking them to recall information, define key terms, or discuss chapter concepts.

- **Discussion questions** encourage students to think critically about how chapter topics can be applied to a real business. They require students to integrate a number of topics and explain how these would apply to real-world scenarios.
- **Exercises and projects** can be used as term projects, extra-credit assignments, or more advanced, in-depth chapter homework questions.
- **Problems** associated with each quantitative example are included at the end of each chapter to enable students to demonstrate their mastery of quantitative topics.
- **Case studies** illustrating chapter concepts appear at the end of each chapter, with discussion questions that can be assigned as course requirements or to prepare students for in-class discussions.
- **Original video case studies** featuring interviews, plant tours, and other company-specific information keep students engaged in the chapter material with demonstrations of how OM concepts are used in the real world.

I think my SAGE team and I have compiled a very interesting operations management textbook that will keep readers engaged, and I hope you enjoy it. I welcome your comments and suggestions for improvement. Please direct all comments and questions to Dr. Joel Wisner, at: Joel.Wisner@unlv.edu.

AACSB STATEMENT

The Association to Advance Collegiate Schools of Business (AACSB) is a global association that provides business schools with accreditation standards for the advancement of management education. Dr. Wisner and SAGE Publishing understand the value of these accreditation standards to the success of business students and have tied test bank and pre- and post-test questions that accompany Operations Management: A Supply Chain Process Approach to the general knowledge and skill areas identified by AACSB.

STUDENT AND INSTRUCTOR RESOURCES

http://edge.sagepub.com/wisner

SAGE edge offers a robust online environment featuring an impressive array of tools and resources for review, study, and further exploration, keeping both instructors and students on the cutting edge of teaching and learning.

SAGE edge for Students helps students accomplish their coursework goals in an easy-to-use learning environment.

- A complete online **action plan** allows you to track your progress and enhance your learning experience
- **Learning objectives with summaries** reinforce the most important material
- Downloadable **chapter outlines** facilitate note-taking as you study
- Mobile-friendly **eFlashcards** strengthen understanding of key terms and concepts
- Mobile-friendly practice **quizzes** allow for independent assessment by students of their mastery of course material
- **Video and multimedia content** includes original SAGE videos that appeal to students with different learning styles
- Meaningful **web readings** facilitate further exploration of topics
- **Excel templates** for formulas assist with practice problems

SAGE edge for Instructors supports teaching by making it easy to integrate quality content and create a rich learning environment for students.

- **Test banks** built on Bloom's Taxonomy provide a diverse range of pre-written options as well as the opportunity to edit any question and/or insert personalized questions to effectively assess students' progress and understanding
- Editable, chapter-specific **PowerPoint® slides** offer complete flexibility for creating a multimedia presentation for the course
- **Lecture notes** summarize key concepts by chapter to ease preparation for lectures and class discussions
- **Teaching notes for the cases** include sample answers to case questions, as well as summaries and analyses
- Additional **homework problems** for each chapter help students practice applying key concepts
- A **solutions manual** for problems in the book and **sample answers to questions in the text** provide an essential reference
- **Sample course syllabi** for semester and quarter courses provide suggested models for structuring one's course
- **Video and multimedia content** includes original SAGE videos that appeal to students with different learning styles
- **Excel templates** for formulas assist with practice problems
- Meaningful **web readings** facilitate further exploration of topics
- A **Course cartridge** provides easy LMS integration

/ ACKNOWLEDGMENTS /

I am grateful to the initial and steady members of my SAGE team: Acquisitions Editor, Maggie Stanley, and Development Editor, Abbie Rickard. They have provided invaluable assistance and encouragement in bringing this title to a pleasant close. I'd also like to thank the remaining members of my SAGE team: Editorial Assistant, Neda Dallal; eLearning Editor, Katie Ancheta; Senior Marketing Manager, Ashlee Blunk; Marketing Communications Management Manager, Christina Fohl; Copy Editor, Talia Greenberg; Associate Marketing Manager, Jill Oelsen, and Marketing Associate, Georgia McLaughlin for their assistance.

I also want to thank the case writers, Rick Bonsall, Jeff Fahrenwald, Brian Hoyt, Stella Hua, Jack Sapsanguanboon, and Tobias Schoenherr, identified at the ends of cases throughout the textbook. For their terrific work on creating the instructor and student ancillaries, I would like to thank Rick Bonsall, Asoke Dey, Jason Gurtovoy, Stephen Hill, and C. J. Wisner. A number of reviewers provided thoughtful comments that were very helpful to me throughout the writing process. I would like to thank the following reviewers who contributed to the quality of the book:

Ajay Aggarwal, Henderson State University

M. Khurrum S. Bhutta, Ohio University

Jerry K. Bilbrey Jr., Clemson University

Rick Bonsall, McKendree University

Mustafa S. Canbolat, SUNY, Brockport

Moula Cherikh, Winston-Salem State University

Asoke Dey, University of Akron

Art Duhaime, Nichols College

Jeff Fahrenwald, Rockford University

R. Ray Gehani, University of Akron

Jason Gurtovoy, Embry-Riddle University

Samuel K. Gyapong, Fort Valley State University

Stephen Hill, University of North Carolina–Wilmington

Mark Jacobs, University of Dayton

Navneet Jain, Maine Maritime Academy

Pam Janson, Stark State University

Jian-yu "Fisher" Ke, California State University, Dominguez Hills

Rajkumar Kempaiah, Mount Saint Vincent

Patrick Lee, Fairfield University

Jon H. Marvel, Western Carolina University

John E. Michaels, California University of Pennsylvania

Kishore Pochampally, Southern New Hampshire University

Antonios Printezis, Arizona State University

Gioconda Quesada, College of Charleston

Pedro Reyes, Baylor University

Tobias Schoenherr, Michigan State University

Rao Tummala, Eastern Michigan University

Lisa Weber, Carroll University

I am also very appreciative of the following instructors who participated in market development activities:

Henry Aigbedoo, Oakland University

Leslie Bobb, Baruch College–CUNY

Salem Boumediene, Montana State University Billings

Sebastian Brackhaus, Weber State University

Janice Cerveny, Florida Atlantic University

Norma Davis, Pepperdine University

Greg DeYong, Southern Illinois University

Mark Hanna, Georgia Southern University

Faizul Huq, Ohio University

Burcu B. Keskin, University of Alabama

Sang-Heui Lee, Pittsburg State University

Yulong Li, Simmons College

Chris McCart, Roanoke College

Katrina Moskalik, Milwaukee School of Engineering

Scott Nadler, University of Central Arkansas

Ravi Narayanaswamy, University of South Carolina Aiken

Vafa Saboori, Dominican University of California

Samia Siha, Kennesaw State University

Feng Tian, Governors State University

Lisa Walters, SUNY Fredonia

Scott Webb, Brigham Young University

Allen White, Bacone College

Lifang Wu, Xavier University

Linda (Xiaowei) Zhu, West Chester University of Pennsylvania

Special thanks to my wife, C. J., who also teaches operations management, for her assistance in reviewing aspects of chapters, writing and answering questions, and allowing me the time to work on this textbook. Additionally, I want to thank Dr. Linda Stanley, a friend and coauthor, for helping me think through some of the topics contained in this book. I'd also like to thank my colleagues for their understanding and for allowing me to skip lunches and close my office door at times, to work on this book. Finally, I'd like to thank my students for their feedback and encouragement.

ABOUT THE AUTHOR

Joel D. Wisner is Professor of Supply Chain Management at the University of Nevada, Las Vegas (UNLV). He earned his BS in Mechanical Engineering from New Mexico State University in 1976 and his MBA from West Texas State University in 1986. During that time, Dr. Wisner worked as an engineer for Union Carbide at its Oak Ridge, TN, facility and then worked in the oil industry in the Louisiana Gulf Coast and West Texas areas. In 1991, he earned his PhD in Supply Chain Management from Arizona State University. He holds certifications in transportation and logistics (CTL) and in purchasing management (C.P.M.).

Dr. Wisner is currently teaching undergraduate and graduate courses in operations management and supply chain management at UNLV. He has been a visiting scholar in Brazil, Finland, Indonesia, Italy, New Zealand, and Spain. His research interests are in process assessment and improvement strategies along the supply chain, and he has authored or coauthored over 100 articles, cases, conference presentations, and monographs. Dr. Wisner's research has appeared in numerous leading journals, including the *Business Case Journal, Journal of Business Logistics, Journal of Operations Management, Journal of Supply Chain Management, Journal of Transportation,* and *Production and Operations Management Journal.* Dr. Wisner has also written two other textbooks: *Principles of Supply Chain Management* and *Process Management.* He is the founder and past executive editor of the *International Journal of Integrated Supply Management* and serves on several major journal review boards.

PART I
DEVELOPING OPERATIONS STRATEGIES

iStock/PeopleImages

1. Operations Management, Processes, and Supply Chain Management
2. Corporate Strategy, Performance, and Sustainability
3. New Product and Service Design
4. Process Design and Capacity Management
5. Customer Relationships and Customer Service

Carolyn Franks/Alamy

When you think about production schedules, engineering changes, production planning, our global supply chain, they are all changing and they change rapidly. And what everyone's had to do across manufacturing is share information across the globe as quickly and effectively as possible. Global architectures are driving a global supply base and it's added another level of complexity that has to be managed. We're all dealing with that today.

—**BILL HURLES,** executive director of global supply chain operations, General Motors[1]

Part of what you need to do in the supply chain is to help your company anticipate events, and understand the environment you operate in—physical, political, economic—around the globe.

—**FRANCES TOWNSEND,** former Homeland Security advisor to U.S. president George W. Bush[2]

OPERATIONS MANAGEMENT, PROCESSES, AND SUPPLY CHAIN MANAGEMENT

LEARNING OBJECTIVES

After completing this chapter, you should be able to:

1.1 Define and discuss operations management
1.2 Define processes and supply chains
1.3 Explain the value of viewing operations management from a process and a supply chain perspective
1.4 Describe the eight key processes linking organizations along the supply chain
1.5 Discuss the importance of operations management in services
1.6 Summarize a number of the important developments in operations management

Master the content.

edge.sagepub.com/wisner

WALMART USES ITS SUPPLY CHAIN TO REDUCE COSTS AND IMPROVE PROFITABILITY

Walmart is huge. When it moves, lots of things move with it, and these include many of its more than 100,000 worldwide suppliers. In 2006, Walmart set its sights on sustainability when it announced its Packaging Scorecard. This scorecard is designed to be a key element in the company's commitment to reduce packaging globally. Several criteria included in the scorecard are closely related to cost reduction. These include product/package ratio, cube utilization, and transportation.

Walmart is doing what any good business should do: using its supply chain to help it reduce costs and improve profitability. With sustainability, it can also gain the goodwill of knowledgeable customers. With such a significant undertaking, it is not surprising that additional business opportunities are popping up to support implementation of the scorecard.

June Anderson is a partner with Packaging Knowledge Group, a consultant providing custom solutions in the packaging arena and in sustainable supply chain practices. Anderson gives credit to Walmart for its focus on packaging sustainability. "I believe the Walmart sustainability initiative and the introduction of its Sustainable Packaging Scorecard is what started the sustainability revolution in packaging, as well as other industries," she says. "Because of it, a lot of people, companies, and industries started to initiate programs and set goals and objectives that would not have otherwise happened. It will be a corporate and company advantage moving into the future for those people implementing sustainable programs."

According to a Walmart Global Sustainability report, packaging information has been collected for about 329,000 items since the scorecard's initial rollout in 2007. Material light-weighting is one method that can achieve positive results. For a recent Sustainable Packaging Expo held by Walmart, Anderson says that one of the new requirements for exhibitors was to include a success story that had a positive impact on sustainability and the scorecard. "One in particular was a package change that light-weighted the material of the current package, and because of that light-weighting process, the greenhouse gas emissions were cut in half from the original package," she reports.

Whether or not Walmart should be given credit for starting the sustainability revolution in packaging is open to debate. What should not be debated is the significance of the effort and results that have been and will be achieved because of use of the scorecard.[3]

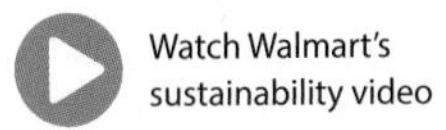

Watch Walmart's sustainability video

INTRODUCTION

In today's highly competitive global marketplace, organizations must continually assess, adjust, and redefine themselves to win new customers, please existing ones, and remain competitive. In recent years, markets for goods and services have opened up in China and Russia, for instance, and many smaller markets in developing countries are continually opening and growing as social and political climates change. Many foreign organizations are coming to the United States and other highly developed nations and adding competition, while domestic firms are constantly seeking ways to expand into new product areas and new markets to improve their profits. In the recent global recession, depressed economic conditions further complicated the competitive landscape. Suddenly, firms were faced with trying to reduce costs, while needing to keep their current customers and find new ones as well. Additionally, in 2011, after Japan suffered through the devastating Tohoku earthquake and tsunami, many manufacturers doing business with Japanese suppliers were unable to get parts and supplies through their supply chains and were forced to shut down until substitute suppliers could be located. These dynamic conditions create a need for organizations to be continually searching markets for the best suppliers, reducing operating costs, and improving quality and customer service, while listening to customers so their desires can be translated into new, innovative products. For most organizations, becoming and then staying successful is like hitting a moving target. Managers study their firms' markets and then forecast what their customers and potential customers' needs will be in the future. Managers then use strategies to develop new product and process capabilities or adjust current ones to provide goods and services to meet these forecasted needs.

Processes, by the way, can be found throughout all organizations and represent unique ways of providing goods and services. Organizations manage their processes by successfully managing inventories; hiring knowledgeable employees; creating long-lasting and mutually beneficial partnerships with suppliers and customers; establishing effective information and communication systems; and instituting cost, quality, and process management programs to create and deliver the goods and services customers want, for the prices they want to pay.

Operations managers who take a strictly inward-facing view of the organization ignore the value suppliers and customers bring to the firm in terms of shared information and knowledge of markets, products, and technologies. The most successful organizations collaborate with their trading partners, blending functional groupings and firm boundaries to find the most effective solutions to a host of issues facing the firm. Managing operations processes along a firm's many supply chains improves the competitiveness of all participating organizations. Thus, successful operations management requires knowledge of the firm's supply chains and the key processes linking the firm to its supply chains.

These topics, among other related operations management topics, will be addressed in detail in this and other chapters of the textbook. This chapter presents the foundation for the remainder of the text, leading the reader through short discussions of many topics explored more fully in the remaining chapters in the textbook. Let's begin by defining several important terms.

OPERATIONS MANAGEMENT DEFINED

Define and discuss operations management

operations The set of activities associated with purchasing, making, delivering, and returning (or recycling) goods and services.

good Any tangible product, like an automobile.

service An intangible product such as the delivery of automobiles to the dealership, or the repair of automobiles once they are sold.

operations management The effective planning, organizing, and controlling of the many value-creating activities of the firm.

The term **operations** refers to the set of activities associated with purchasing, making, delivering, and returning (or recycling) goods and services. A **good** refers to any tangible product like an automobile, while a **service** refers to an intangible product such as the delivery of automobiles to the dealership, or the repair of automobiles once they are sold. In other words, products refer to both goods and services. **Operations management** (OM) refers to the effective planning, organizing, and controlling of the many value-creating activities of the firm. While operations management might vary somewhat from firm to firm, particularly when comparing manufacturing and service firms, the sizes and locations of firms, or the products firms sell, there are still many similar operations responsibilities. Effective management of operations creates value for organizations' products. In many organizations, an Operations, Production, or Manufacturing VP reports directly to the president or CEO, as shown for three organizations in Figure 1.1.[4] Note the high level of importance placed on operations in all three organization charts.

Watch a discussion about OM jobs

Firms purchase goods and services. They might store many of the goods in warehouses; at some point, these goods are transported to the firm's manufacturing or retail locations. Once at the manufacturing facility, purchased materials, parts, and components are transformed into finished products, where again they might be stored in warehouses or distribution centers. In a timely fashion, products are delivered to customers, some of whom are end-product consumers while others might be businesses in foreign locations. Finally, some products are returned for repair or replacement, and companies must consider alternatives for handling these returns.

So it can be seen here that the **basic operations activities** can be summarized as purchasing, storage, transformation, distribution, and product returns. To make these activities come together successfully, a number of other associated activities also fall under the responsibility of operations managers, including quality assessment and improvement, forecasting, inventory management, performance measurement, supplier and customer relationship management, information systems management, and product and process design.

Operations activities and their management have been around for quite some time. In ancient Rome, for instance, competent facilities managers were hired for public bath houses, the most complicated organization in Rome at the time. The structures were designed to provide a year-round warm indoor climate, and aqueducts were constructed to supply a continual source of water. The design of early Roman manufacturing facilities could also be sophisticated—large bakeries in the third century CE had a production line layout; marble workshops were also laid out in an assembly-line fashion.[5] Whenever an entrepreneur tries to make and sell a product or service, operations management is needed—from finding a suitable location, designing a needed product, buying the right materials, assembling a high-quality product, delivering it on time to customers, and finally, performing warranty and product return services.

Operations managers help the organization perform correctly, and for that reason, they are highly sought after and rewarded. "Operations really is the heart of most companies, because the operations department actually gets the job that the company needs to get done, done," says Eric Schaudt, manager of operations programs at Virginia-based aerospace company Northrop Grumman. The Bureau of Labor Statistics projects operations management employment growth of 12.4% between 2012 and 2022, and today, operations managers have one of the highest-paying occupations in the United States. These professionals earned a median income of $95,000 in 2012, with the highest-paid 10% earning more than $187,000 per year. The Association for Operations Management (APICS) offers certification programs in production and inventory management, and also certifies employees as supply chain professionals. "A lot of companies use these certifications as search criteria and filter their candidates as whether they are certified or not certified," Schaudt adds.[6]

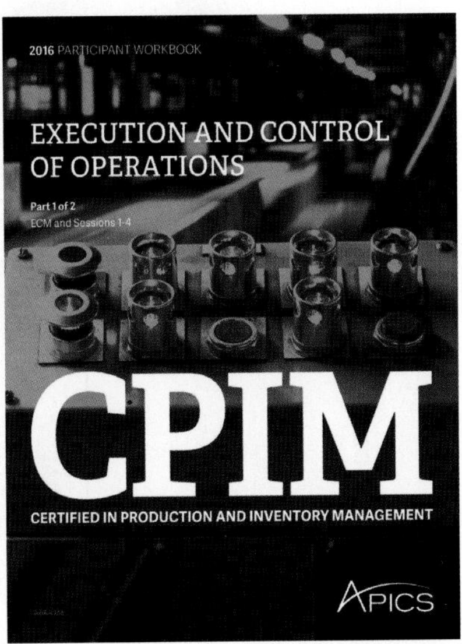

APICS

The APICS CPIM certification has been earned by more than 100,000 professionals since 1973.

PROCESSES AND SUPPLY CHAINS

1.2 Define processes and supply chains

WHAT IS A PROCESS?

Our individual and work lives are filled with processes that need to be managed, from getting up in the morning, getting the kids off to school, and arriving to work on time, to hiring the right individual for an open position, organizing a meeting, making products customers will buy, and delivering products to customers in a timely fashion. Simply put, a **process** is a method for getting work done. A process consists of a series of steps that turn inputs (such as experience, equipment, materials, time, and money) into outputs (goods, services, effective meetings, and educated kids). Many processes are trivial and require minimal time and effort

basic operations activities Purchasing, storage, transformation, distribution, and product returns.

process Methods for getting work done. Processes consist of a series of steps that turn inputs into outputs.

Figure 1.1 Organizational Chart Examples

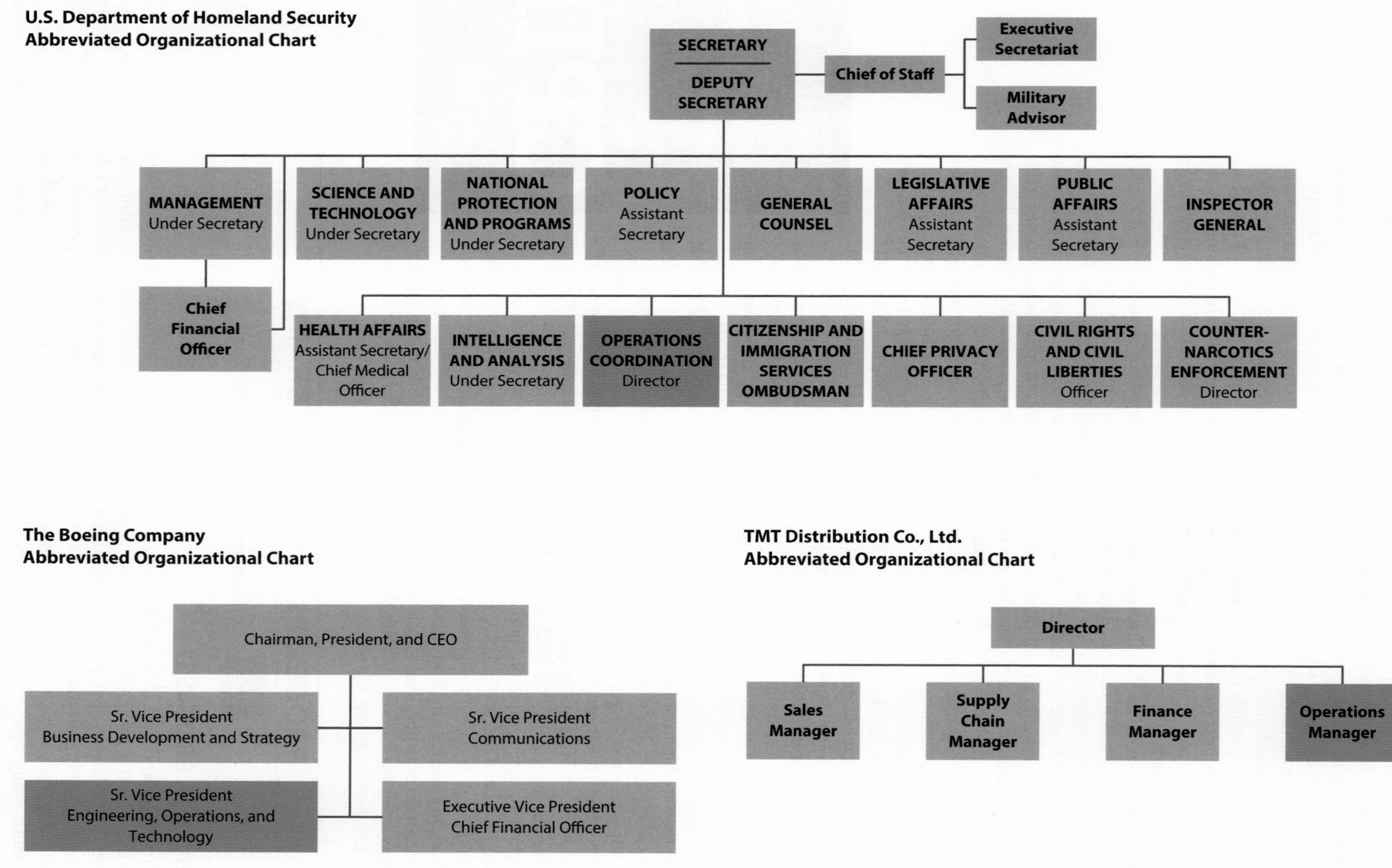

Figure 1.2 Generic Business Process Elements

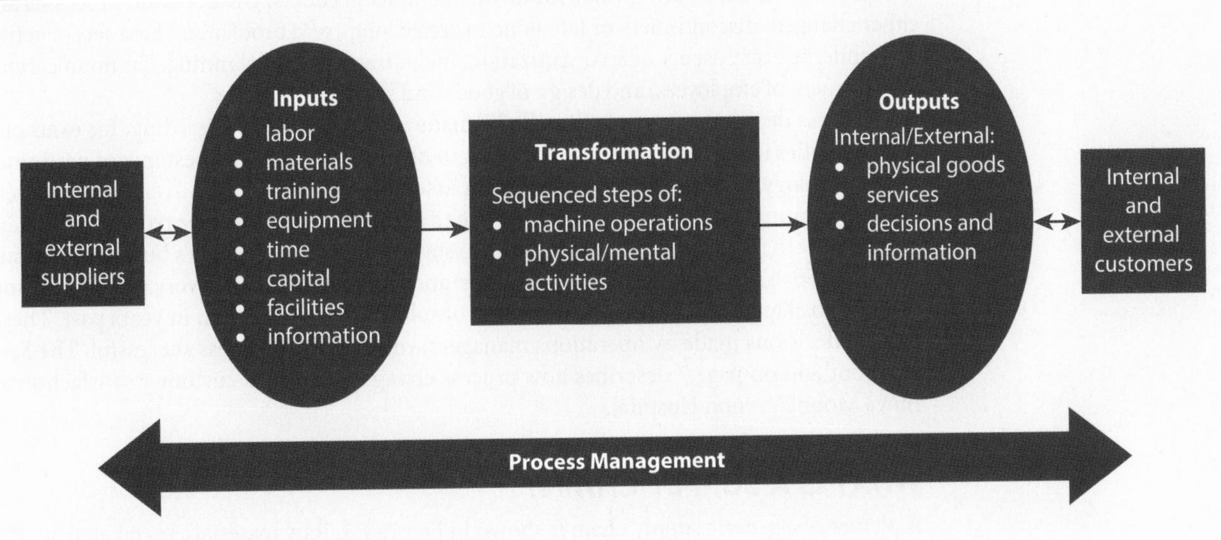

to be managed, while others can be monumental, requiring significant effort and resources over long periods of time to be managed successfully. In this text, we will be concerned with processes within the firm and processes linking businesses and their trading partners. Most operations activities are sets of business processes that are managed by operations managers. Two business process definitions are shown here:

- "The collection of activities and operations involved in transforming inputs, which are the physical facilities, materials, capital, equipment, people, and energy, into outputs, or the goods and services."[7]
- "A collection of activities and decisions that produce an output for an internal or external customer."[8]

As shown in Figure 1.2, a business process consists of a set of linked activities or elements designed to create valued goods, services, and decisions for internal and external customers. Collectively, these processes *are* the business, and they need to be managed. Process activities may be performed, for instance, by suppliers, employees, customers, manufacturing

SERVICE SPOTLIGHT

Process Improvement at Inova Mount Vernon Hospital

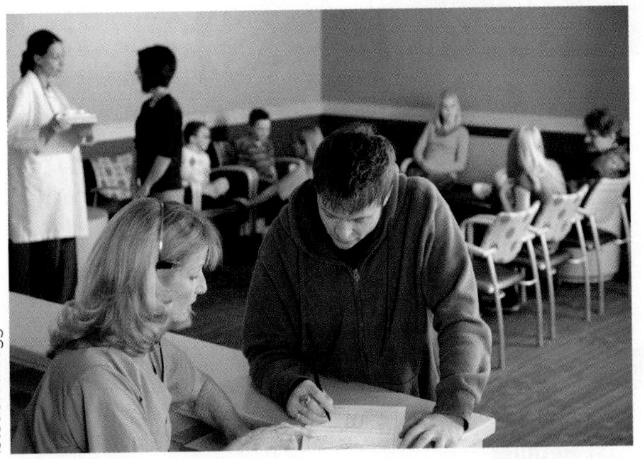
iStock/RichLegg

Inova Mount Vernon hospital in Mount Vernon, Virginia, was experiencing patient dissatisfaction with its emergency room. Simply put, patients were being kept too long prior to discharge. Hospital managers recognized this as a problem and communicated it throughout the hospital. They studied what other hospitals were doing and established goals for treating and discharging ER patients. They started tracking key length-of-stay performance information and shared the data with the staff. Activities in need of improvement were identified. Improvement ideas were implemented, and eventually, the average emergency room length of stay was reduced from 266 minutes to 150 minutes. Patient satisfaction rose dramatically as a result.[9]

equipment, and computers. Successful processes ultimately keep employees, stockholders, and customers satisfied, creating value for the firm and its products. Unsuccessful processes are either changed, discontinued, or left alone to create long-term problems. These sets of activities underlie every aspect of an organization, including top-level planning, communication, management of employees, and design of goods and services.

Process decisions must continually be made in organizations regarding, for example, what activities to perform in-house and what to obtain elsewhere; the best mix of personnel and technology; how to improve an existing assembly process when current quality levels are deteriorating; implementing a new service to accommodate customer requests; or determining how to reduce manufacturing costs to stay competitive. In today's business environment, materials, technologies, customer tastes, and competition change very rapidly, causing demand to change and processes to become obsolete much faster than in years past. These process decisions made by operations managers will keep the business successful. The Service Spotlight on page 7 describes how process changes improved customer satisfaction at Inova Mount Vernon Hospital.

WHAT IS A SUPPLY CHAIN?

A picture of a generic supply chain is shown in Figure 1.3. Raw materials are taken from the earth (oil, wood, iron ore), wherein a supplier turns these into parts or manufacturing materials (such as plastics, lumber, sheet steel, steering wheels). These items are delivered to manufacturers, which produce finished goods and distribute these to retailers, which then sell them to end-consumers. The final step in the supply chain involves recycling of the worn-out goods (this step is not shown in Figure 1.3).

As can be seen in Figure 1.3, a number of companies are involved in this supply chain, from oil companies, lumber mills, and raw material manufacturers, to end-product manufacturers, transportation companies, warehousing companies, and labeling, packaging, and retailing companies, to finally, the recycling companies. Behind the scenes, there are also support services like maintenance, janitorial, and office supply companies.

supply chain The network of companies eventually making goods and services available to consumers, including all of the functions enabling the purchasing, production, delivery, and recycling of materials, components, and end-goods.

Thus, the network of companies eventually making goods and services available to consumers, including all of the functions enabling the purchasing, production, delivery, and recycling of materials, components, and end-products, is called a **supply chain**. Companies with multiple products have multiple supply chains. All goods and services reach customers via some type of supply chain—some much larger, longer, and more complex than others. Some may also involve foreign suppliers, subsidiaries, and markets. Keith Oliver, a British logistics consultant, is credited with coining the term *supply chain* in a 1982 interview with the *Financial Times*.[10]

Figure 1.3 Generic Supply Chain

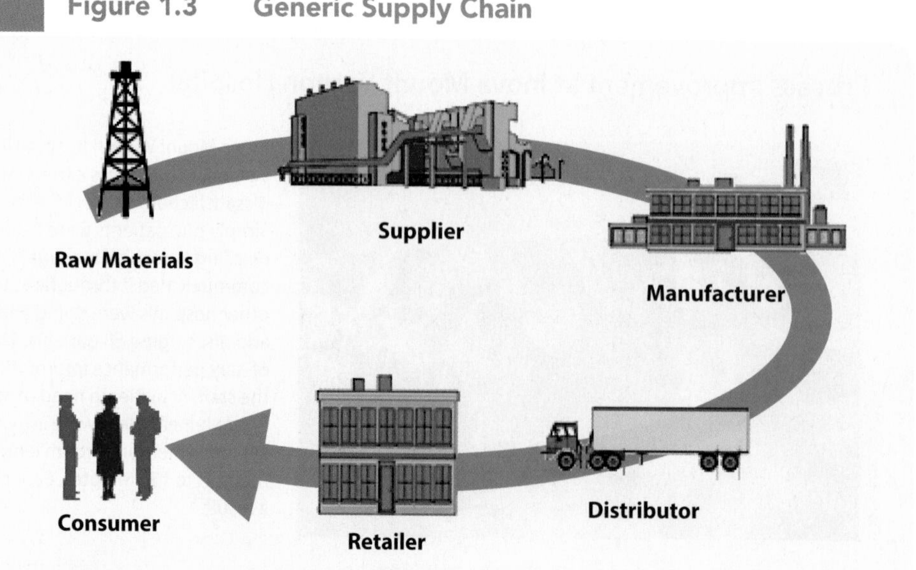

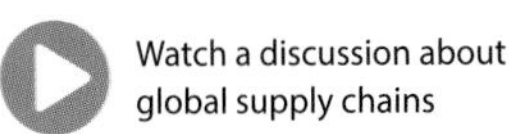
Watch a discussion about global supply chains

Gary Miller, a supply chain manager at global plastics supplier A. Schulman, Inc., for example, is charged with leveraging the company's worldwide purchasing power, reducing materials inventories, eliminating waste, and improving supply chain efficiencies. The company has 35 facilities globally, with nearly 70% of its revenues coming from its European markets. "We have global customers that we service around the world," says Miller. "Europe is a very large region for us, so we have deep relationships with our customers there. As those customers expand around the world, they're also looking for us to come with them." For instance, Schulman has some large customers in the German automotive market who are opening facilities in China. Consequently, Schulman is following its customers into China to manufacture and supply the same plastics products that are being used in Germany. "Now we can continue to supply them our products from Germany if we want to, but the advantage is that if they're in China and we have manufacturing in China, then we can transfer our manufacturing technology to China and provide those parts on a local basis," Miller adds.[11]

A SUPPLY CHAIN VIEW OF THE ORGANIZATION

1.3 Explain the value of viewing operations management from a process and a supply chain perspective

Widespread and frequent changes in consumer demand beginning in the 1980s, due in many cases to rapid technological changes and competitive pressures, has prompted organizations to move from an internal focus to more of an external focus, sharing and coordinating key processes with trading partners as products move along their supply chains. The quest for cheaper operating costs has also led to more geographically dispersed or global supply chains. **Business process integration**, or the sharing and coordination of key processes between companies in a supply chain, begins with a firm's primary goods and service suppliers (or its **first-tier suppliers**) and extends to the firm's most valued direct customers (its **first-tier customers**). These joint efforts or collaborations allow each participant within the supply chain to learn the actual purchase plans of its customers; to share new product design and development plans with suppliers; to jointly develop better ways to purchase, build, and deliver products; to reduce stockout costs, inventory carrying costs, and delivery costs; and finally, to improve customer service and satisfaction. Thus, sharing information and coordinating processes improves planning and performance. Process integration is further discussed in Chapter 16.

When firms decide to focus more of their attention on their internal competencies (what they do best), then other, less important activities might cease to be performed in-house. This leads to **outsourcing**, or buying goods and services from suppliers instead of making them in-house. This results in a greater reliance on outside suppliers to keep product costs low while providing high levels of service and product quality. One proven way to ensure this is to foster long-term, mutually beneficial buyer–supplier relationships. Thus, organizations begin to realize the importance and potential benefits of jointly managing business processes with their supply chain partners in order to improve quality, supplier responsiveness, and final product delivery to meet the needs of customers at a reasonable cost.

Outsourcing the information technology (IT) function is something organizations have been wrestling with for a number of years. Many large businesses have outsourced at least some of their IT operations to low-cost service providers such as Indian companies Tata Consultancy Services, Infosys, and Wipro. Recently, however, wage inflation in India has reduced opportunities for negotiating based on cost. Some manufacturers, including Apple, Motorola, and Lenovo, have announced plans to shift some of their IT operations back to the United States. Occasionally, outsourcing can be troublesome if companies give up control of a core process. For instance, in 2004, J. P. Morgan announced it was terminating a seven-year IT outsourcing deal with IBM. J. P. Morgan decided to take its tech services back because the services had become strategically too important to leave to an outsider.[12]

The integration of key business processes concerning the flow of materials from raw material suppliers to the final customer has today developed into the concept known as **supply chain management**. Business process integration is thus the foundation of supply

business process integration The sharing and coordination of key processes between companies in a supply chain.

first-tier suppliers The firm's primary goods and service suppliers.

first-tier customers The firm's most valued direct customers.

outsourcing Buying goods and services from suppliers instead of making them in-house.

supply chain management The integration of key business processes concerning the flow of materials from raw material suppliers to the final customer.

chain management. Today, operations managers are working harder than ever to integrate processes with their firms' direct suppliers and customers. Some large firms have both a supply chain manager and an operations manager. In these cases, operations managers deal most often with internal operations activities while supply chain managers work with external integration activities involving direct and second-tier suppliers and customers.

Watch an employee talking about supply chain management

Managing and coordinating business processes within a network of supply chain trading partners requires a great deal of trust and cooperation. Walmart's adept supply chain management capabilities, for example, enable it to deliver a diverse assortment of products to customers around the world at low prices. It recently committed to further reducing its supply chain costs by 15%, in part by shifting from distributors to direct purchasing for private-label goods and fresh foods. Walmart is also becoming increasingly responsive to local markets by setting up a global sourcing partnership with Li & Fung, the Hong Kong–based supply chain management company for consumer goods.[13]

The Global Supply Chain Forum, a supply chain management research group at The Ohio State University, identified eight key processes that are typically integrated among trading partners in successful supply chains.[14] The following section presents and discusses in more detail these primary supply chain processes.

THE EIGHT KEY SUPPLY CHAIN PROCESSES

1.4 Describe the eight key processes linking organizations along the supply chain

Identifying which business processes should be jointly managed along a supply chain is an important issue. To achieve successful supply chain process integration and all of the associated benefits, supply chain partners must reach a shared understanding of the key supply chain processes. Table 1.1 lists the eight supply chain processes identified by the Global Supply Chain Forum. The processes are briefly discussed here.

Table 1.1 Eight Key Supply Chain Processes

Process	Description	Associated Activities
Customer Relationship Management	Creating and maintaining customer relationships	Identify and categorize key customers; tailor goods and services to meet the needs of customer groups.
Customer Service Management	Interacting with customers to maintain customer satisfaction	Manage product and service agreements with customers; design and implement customer response procedures.
Demand Management	Balancing customer requirements with supply chain capabilities	Forecast demand; plan or adjust capacity to meet demand; develop contingency plans for imbalances.
Order Fulfillment	Satisfying customer orders	Design distribution network to deliver goods on-time.
Manufacturing Flow Management	Making goods to satisfy target markets	Design mfg. processes to create goods customers want.
Supplier Relationship Management	Creating and maintaining supplier relationships	Identify key suppliers; establish formal relationships; further develop key suppliers.
Product Development and Commercialization	Developing new products frequently and getting them to market effectively	Develop sources for new ideas; develop cross-functional product teams, including customers and suppliers.
Returns Management	Managing product returns and disposal effectively	Develop guidelines for returns and disposal; develop returns network.

Source: See for example, Croxton, K., S. García-Dastugue, D. Lambert, and D. Rogers, "The Supply Chain Management Processes," *The International Journal of Logistics Management* 12 (2), 2001: 13-36.

THE CUSTOMER RELATIONSHIP MANAGEMENT PROCESS

This process provides the structure for creating and maintaining successful relationships with customers and is discussed in detail in Chapters 5 and 10. Firms that know their customers, and understand which ones are the most important, can design strategies and assign resources to maximize value for these key customers, and in turn, maximize the firm's profitability. The general idea of **customer relationship management** (CRM) is to manage the firm's customer base so they remain satisfied and continue to purchase goods and services. Since customers are not all the same, firms segment their customers and provide different sets of goods and value-enhancing services to each segment to maximize long-term profitability. A successful CRM program is both simple and complex: It is simple in that it involves treating customers right; it is complex in that it also means finding ways to identify the firm's customers and their needs, and then designing strategies so that customer contact activities are geared toward creating customer satisfaction and loyalty.

The market for CRM software has remained strong even through the recent global recession. For example, global CRM software revenues grew at a 6.5% pace in 2010 coming out of the recession and totaled $16.5 billion, according to International Data Corp.[15] In 2012, for example, the CRM software market experienced a 12% growth, three times the average of all other enterprise software applications, according to a report by Gartner, a business research company.[16] CRM is the topic of Chapter 5.

THE CUSTOMER SERVICE MANAGEMENT PROCESS

Today, poor customer service is almost expected when visiting many businesses, and represents one area where organizations can create a significant competitive advantage, provided customer service processes are designed and managed correctly. The **customer service management** process attends to customer needs before, during, and after the sale. Companies develop appropriate response procedures for anticipated questions and complaints. Then information systems, software, and websites are designed to relay information to customers, and customer service employees are trained to provide information and services that customers want. Customer service management might also include carrying safety stock to avoid stockout situations and using excess service capacity to avoid long customer wait times (**capacity** can be defined here as the maximum amount of goods and/or services that a system can produce over a set period of time, and is discussed in detail in Chapter 5).

In a 2013 survey of 1,500 U.S. consumers conducted by MSN Money and JZ Analytics, respondents were asked to rate the overall customer service capabilities of 150 companies in 15 industries. The top five customer service providers were Amazon.com, Marriott Hotels, Hilton Hotels, UPS, and FedEx. At the bottom of the heap were Bank of America, Comcast, Dish Network, Citigroup, and Wells Fargo. For several of the top companies, business has responded so favorably to customer service levels that advertising is no longer needed.[17] Customer service is further discussed in Chapter 5.

THE DEMAND MANAGEMENT PROCESS

The **demand management** process seeks to balance customer requirements with supply chain capabilities. To accomplish this goal, firms forecast demand and then translate these forecasts into desired levels of purchasing, production, and distribution activities. Forecasts can be short- or long-term oriented, simple or complex, and qualitative or quantitative. To minimize forecast error and use of safety stock, customers can share their planned future purchase quantities, actual sales data, or promotion and new product plans with their suppliers. The Service Spotlight on page 12 describes demand management activities at the 2010 Winter Olympic Games.

Once decisions have been made, based on forecasts, demand management is used to develop contingency plans for the occasions when demand and capacity imbalances exist. Organizations can try to reduce excess demand during busy periods, for instance, by raising prices to curtail or move some demand to less busy periods, or by segmenting demand to facilitate better service (for instance, express versus regular checkout counters). When

customer relationship management Managing the firm's customer base so they remain satisfied and continue to purchase goods and services.

customer service management Attending to customer needs before, during, and after the sale.

capacity The maximum amount of goods and/or services that a system can produce over a set period of time.

demand management The process that balances customer requirements with supply chain capabilities.

SERVICE SPOTLIGHT

Demand Management at the 2010 Olympic Winter Games

The Vancouver, Canada, 2010 Olympic Winter Games were the largest-ever test of that city's transportation network. TransLink, the South Coast British Columbia Transportation Authority, was responsible for the entire transportation system during the Games.

TransLink benchmarked five previous Olympic Games to identify successful practices that could be used in Vancouver. Ultimately, the transportation investments prior to the Games included a rapid transit line between Vancouver and the airport, additional units on existing transit lines, a new SeaBus connecting the North Shore area to downtown Vancouver, and more than 100 new city buses. TransLink's rail system operated longer service hours, resulting in higher capacity during the Games. The rail system was advertised as the best option for accessing the transit network, and all rail lines connected the major venues in downtown Vancouver. Additional bus service was provided throughout the region, primarily on a flexible, on-demand basis dispatched by transit authorities.

iStock/heyengel

TransLink received very positive feedback regarding transportation during the Games. Record transit ridership was achieved, and overall customer transportation experiences were considered excellent. *Time* magazine even called the system "scarily efficient."[18]

demand is low, firms can stimulate demand through use of off-peak reduced pricing and aggressive marketing campaigns. In manufacturing and service environments, firms can also adjust capacity by hiring or laying off employees and cross-training employees; service providers might also use customers to perform part or all of a service. Complete coverage of demand management and forecasting is included in Chapter 6.

THE ORDER FULFILLMENT PROCESS

The **order fulfillment** process provides for the on-time delivery of goods and services to customers. This requires the internal integration of marketing, manufacturing, and distribution so that customers get what they want on time, at a competitive price. Successful firms know their customer requirements and have a good distribution network, so that products are delivered where and when they are needed, at a low cost. The distribution network potentially consists of warehousing facilities and the transportation modes utilized by an organization. Facility sizes and locations, customer locations, and the modes of transportation used all impact the ability to deliver goods and services to customers.

Transportation is what allows goods to move from point-of-origin to point-of-consumption throughout the supply chain. For international supply chains, the transportation function is even more critical. Providing adequate transportation and storage, getting items through customs, delivering goods to foreign locations in a timely fashion, and transportation pricing can all impact the ability of a firm and its supply chain to serve a foreign market competitively. Collectively, these transportation, storage, and related activities are referred to as **logistics**. In many cases, firms use outside agents or **third-party logistics services** (3PLs) to move items domestically or into foreign locations effectively. Supplier and customer locations impact where production facilities, warehouses, and retail facilities are located. Using foreign suppliers and entering foreign markets can greatly complicate the order fulfillment process. Order fulfillment and related topics are covered in Chapter 15.

order fulfillment The on-time delivery of goods and services to customers.

logistics Transportation, storage, and related activities.

third-party logistics services Outside agents that move items domestically or into foreign locations.

One of the most successful delivery services is in Mumbai, India, where over 5,000 delivery men, or *dabbawalas*, pick up more than 150,000 hot lunches every day from residences for a small fee, then deliver these on time, to the correct people working in the city. Each dabbawala makes about 8,000 rupees (or \$130) per month. The dabbawalas have a complex system of sorting, coding, handing off, and delivering the lunches using bicycles, trains, and foot traffic to make the system work. The dabbawala supply chain in Mumbai has been in existence for more than 100 years, and has been studied by many of the world's top business schools. Unbelievably, an incorrect delivery occurs about one time every two months, which equates to approximately 8 million deliveries.[19]

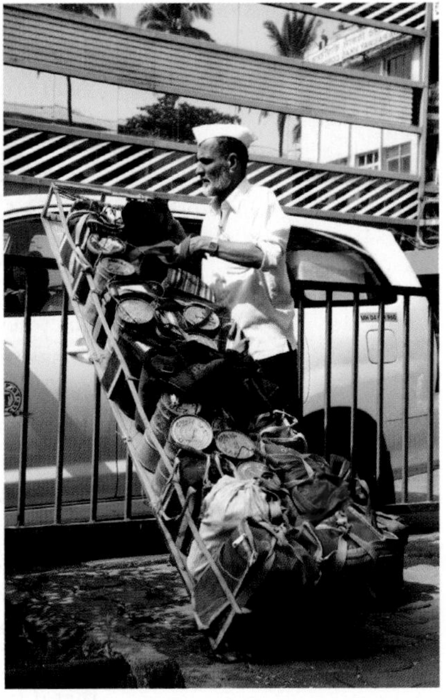
iStock/JHMimagine

The intricate supply chain system utilized by dabbawalas in India has been in use for over 100 years.

THE FLOW MANAGEMENT PROCESS

The **flow management** process is responsible for making the product or service and managing production inventories. This involves designing the manufacturing or service processes to achieve the desired flexibility to meet changing customer requirements. Flow management decisions include how and where to store and move incoming and work-in-process materials, how to design and manage customer queues, how to schedule goods and service attendants, the type of processing equipment to use, the level of technology to employ, and how and where to store finished goods. Aiding in all of these decisions is the use of information systems; thus, information flow is also included in the very broad topic of flow management. Other issues impacting flow management decisions include personnel hiring and training, quality procedures, manufacturing postponement, outsourcing, environmental compliance, automation, product and service customization, reverse logistics, and customer service goals. The topics of flow management are discussed at length in the chapters in Part II of this text.

Decisions within the flow management process are coordinated with other internal processes such as customer service management, order fulfillment, and supplier relationship management. Most firms, for instance, know how long customers are willing to wait once an order is placed, and the level of product quality and customization desired. Manufacturing and customer processing requirements will also impact purchase order frequency and supplier selection. Aside from actual warehouses, online retailer Amazon.com uses a data warehouse to get a single view of its business. "Amazon can understand and manage its entire global business at any level from enhancing customers' experiences, to managing product flow, to providing business intelligence," says Mark Dunlap, director of data warehousing for Amazon.com.[20]

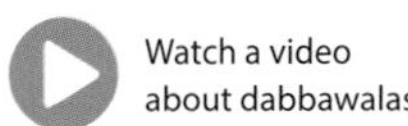
Watch a video about dabbawalas

THE SUPPLIER RELATIONSHIP MANAGEMENT PROCESS

Top-level managers today are realizing the importance of developing win–win, long-term relationships with a relatively small number of key suppliers. It is critical that firms develop strategic relationships with their suppliers, and then manage these relationships to create value for all participants in the supply chain. These activities constitute the supplier relationship management (SRM) process and are primarily discussed in Chapter 14. Successful partnerships with key suppliers can contribute to product innovations, cost containment, and quality improvement, and have the potential to create long-term competitive advantage for the firm. Selecting the right supply partners and successfully managing these relationships over time is thus strategically important, and as it is sometimes stated, "A firm is only as good as its worst suppliers."

Most firms operate with too many suppliers; in fact, many newly employed purchasing managers and executives reduce their supplier bases to increase leverage on the remaining, best-performing suppliers, resulting in lower prices along with better quality and service levels. For example, Carlos Ghosn, named CEO of Nissan Motor Co. in 2001, halved the number of suppliers to cut purchasing costs as part of his revival plan to return Nissan to profitability. In just one year, Nissan's profit climbed to $2.1 billion, compared to a loss of $6.1 billion the previous year.[21] Working with fewer suppliers also allows companies to spend more time building relationships with their best suppliers.

Watch an interview about managing supply chain relationships

Successful SRM requires firms to establish performance criteria to rank suppliers. The best suppliers are then used, while the suppliers not performing well receive little, if any, further business. Companies can further develop their suppliers through training and knowledge sharing, developing compatible information systems, and including supplier representatives on new product development teams. Suppliers are also typically reevaluated on a periodic basis to achieve continuous improvements in cost, quality, and service.

flow management Making the product or service and managing production inventories.

Companies develop performance measures to assess and improve all their important processes, including supplier relationship management. The topic of performance measurement is discussed in Chapter 2.

THE PRODUCT DEVELOPMENT AND COMMERCIALIZATION PROCESS

Designing and producing new products that customers want, and doing it frequently and efficiently, is today a requirement for continued success in competitive industries. Product lifecycles are constantly shortening, as customers demand new products and better versions of old ones. The **product development and commercialization** process, discussed in Chapters 3 and 16, looks to the CRM process as a source for new product and product improvement ideas. Operations managers are typically involved in new product development, along with representatives of other internal functions, thus enabling **concurrent engineering**. In this way, designing the manufacturing process or service delivery system simultaneously with the design of the product enables firms to reduce new product development cycles, design the distribution infrastructure and marketing plans, and reduce time to market. A relatively new development in improving new product design is the simultaneous design of product, process, and supply chain configuration, referred to as **three-dimensional concurrent engineering** (3-DCE). The reason for the use of 3-DCE is that it further reduces the time from new product design to purchase and use by customers, while also reducing cost and potentially improving product quality.

THE RETURNS MANAGEMENT PROCESS

While often overlooked, managing product returns effectively can reduce disposal costs and also be a source of additional customer satisfaction. In many cases, proper disposal of product returns may also be a legal requirement. Close contact with product development and commercialization, and manufacturing flow management is necessary to provide feedback from product returns due to quality defects and poor fit with customer expectations. Managing the **returns management** process is today becoming a significant concern. For example, product returns today cost U.S. suppliers more than $100 billion per year, or a loss in profit of about 3.8%.[22] Returns management is discussed in Chapter 15.

Finding the right product return strategy can result in real benefits to the firm. Online retailer Zappos.com, for example, has a very liberal return policy, and it uses this strategy to improve customer service and sales.[23] Retailers, for instance, can share product return and complaint data with manufacturers, with the aim of improving future product offerings and customer satisfaction. Another objective of returns management should be to ultimately reduce or eliminate product returns. The firm must therefore develop a performance measurement system that effectively tracks returns, warranty repairs, product dispositions, and customer complaints. This information can be used to find and fix product and service problems.

Decisions within the product returns process include how to receive, inspect, process, dispose, and route a product return. Possible process actions include repairing, remanufacturing, recycling or reselling goods, or disposing them in an environmentally acceptable manner. While the eight key supply chain processes discussed in this section include a number of operations management tools and activities, there remain a number of important operations topics to explore. These are summarized in the next section, and are discussed in detail throughout the text.

product development and commercialization Designing and producing new products that customers want, and doing it frequently and efficiently.

concurrent engineering Designing the manufacturing process or service delivery system simultaneously with the design of the product.

three-dimensional concurrent engineering The simultaneous design of the product, the process, and the supply chain.

returns management The movement, storage, and processing of returned goods.

OPERATIONS MANAGEMENT IN SERVICES

1.5 Discuss the importance of operations management in services

While manufacturers make physical or tangible goods, services make intangible products, which may also include some tangible elements. For example, Southwest Airlines provides a transportation service that also includes drinks, the use of a seat (and the airplane), and of course, peanuts. In many cases, determining whether or not a business is actually a service may be difficult—is McDonald's a service or a manufacturer? Many go there for the fast service or the kids' play area; these are definitely service components. Others go for the food, a manufactured component.

According to the U.S. Standard Industry Classification System, the U.S. economy is separated into two sectors. These are the goods-producing sector, comprised of agriculture, forestry, fishing, mining, construction, and manufacturing; and the service sector, which includes transportation, communications, utilities, wholesale trade, retail trade, finance, insurance, real estate, public administration, and a number of what it simply refers to as "services" such as hotels, churches, private education, and personal, business, repair, entertainment, healthcare, legal, social, and consulting services.[24]

iStock/Vallarie

Southwest Airlines is an example of a service provider that also includes tangible elements.

Operationally, services can be classified based on customer contact. **Customer contact** refers to the amount or percentage of time customers are in contact with the service system while the service is being provided. In high contact services, the service processes are more difficult to manage—customers require more and customized services, such as with a beauty parlor. Customers are heavily involved in the service and may impact service quality. Servers require more training, and may be more difficult to find in the first place. With low contact services, such as an online self-service stock broker, most of the actual work is done behind the scenes, and is highly automated. Service workers are mainly skilled technicians trained to operate computer software and equipment. Managing this type of system is much more straightforward.

While discussions of services and service issues are covered in a balanced fashion throughout this text, this segment is intended to familiarize students with services and service processes.

THE DIFFERENCES BETWEEN MANUFACTURERS AND SERVICES

As shown in Table 1.2, one primary distinction between manufacturers and services is that a service provides a mostly *intangible product*, while a manufacturer provides one that is mostly *tangible*. This can present somewhat of a problem for services—customers, for example, typically cannot try out a service prior to its purchase. Services also must provide their products in a decentralized fashion, since most services require some degree of customer interaction. This also means that services must be in an easy-to-find location. Manufacturers, on the other hand, can make their goods in a low-cost or centralized location, and then simply ship the goods to their designated markets.

customer contact The amount or percentage of time customers are in contact with the service system while the service is being provided.

Table 1.2 Characteristics of Manufacturers and Services

Manufacturers	Services
Tangible product	Intangible product
Centralized location	Decentralized location
Location based on low cost	Location based on customer traffic
Quality based on product design	Quality based on customer perceptions
Goods can be inventoried, sold later	Services can't be inventoried; unused service is lost
Customers can compare competitors' products relatively easily	Service products vary widely between competitors

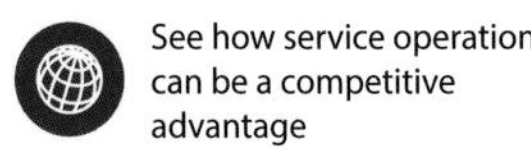

See how service operations can be a competitive advantage

Another important distinction is that *service quality varies* from server to server, and customer to customer. Server attitudes and customer whims can play a large role in service quality, making service quality difficult to measure. A poor service in many cases cannot be repaired (such as a bad haircut or poor musical performance), and it can result in a permanent loss of customers. Goods, on the other hand, can be made to very strict design specifications, resulting in specific and measureable quality characteristics. Additionally, when a defective unit of product is produced, it can be repaired, replaced, or scrapped.

Unlike goods, *services cannot be inventoried*—they generally are produced and consumed simultaneously. Many goods can be placed in a warehouse for lengthy periods of time prior to their sale or use, so a manufacturer producing too many units in one period can simply store units of product for sale at a later time. On the other hand, scheduling many servers in anticipation of high demand (such as in a restaurant when a nearby convention is held) can result in excess labor costs and lost productivity if demand fails to materialize.

Finally, while competing goods are often very similar, *service products can vary widely* from one similar service company to the next, depending on the **goods–service package** offered. The goods–service package is defined by the:

- *Explicit service* (travel from point A to point B, the haircut, the stock purchase);
- *Implicit service* (server attitudes, safety and security, convenience, atmosphere);
- *Facilitating goods* (the goods accompanying the service such as food or TV in a restaurant); and the
- *Supporting facility* (the airplane, the bank building, and the layouts).

Depending on how the goods–service package is designed and delivered, one service might be provided for a lower price than another or might be considered much higher quality than a competitor's similar service. For example, when comparing two airlines offering essentially the identical service (air transportation), British Airways and JetBlue, one sees that company philosophies are quite different. British Airways is typical of larger carriers, with its focus on the customer limited by the realities of routes, unions, policies and procedures, infrastructure, and the price of fuel. Because of its fleet size, British Airways can provide various (and costly) amenities to its first class and business class customers. These amenities help to differentiate British Airways from its competition. JetBlue, in contrast, offers a slimmed-down fleet, and instead of first class amenities, it places a greater emphasis on managing

goods–service package
The explicit service, implicit service, facilitating goods, and the supporting facility.

SERVICE SPOTLIGHT

Phone.com Succeeds With Outstanding Customer Service

Phone.com's customer service team, run by Jeremy Watkin, is focused on supporting the unique needs of small businesses and entrepreneurs. Phone.com provides cost-effective access to VoIP and cloud-based telephone services needed to run a global business. It operates its own private cloud for hosting and telephony. According to Watkin, "It is really all about making our product accessible to the customer, making our website simple and easy to use."

Phone.com differentiates itself from others because it focuses on being fun, with real people talking to real people. "We don't overly script our customer service processes. We want to connect with our customers and find real solutions for them and be honest enough with them so that if [we] don't have a solution for them we tell them," explained Watkin.

Over the years, Phone.com's customer service capabilities have significantly grown. Recently, the company started the Communicate Better Blog, dedicated to discussing customer service, learning about customer service, and introspecting on how

iStock/OJO Images

Phone.com is improving its customer service, as well as networking with other people in customer service. "We are just trying to make a difference in the world of customer service, which definitely needs it," Watkin added.[25]

its customer relationships. The company founder, David Neeleman, emphasized the need to build customer relationships continuously, above all. Labeling every employee a crewmember, he emphasized the importance of everyone, from the check-in clerk to the baggage handler, in the company's CRM and financial success.[26] The Service Spotlight on page 16 describes Phone.com's emphasis on customer service to differentiate itself from its competition.

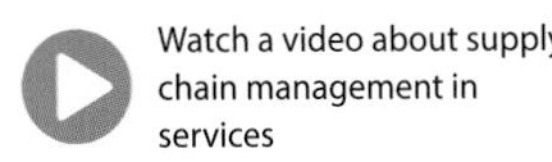
Watch a video about supply chain management in services

GLOBAL SERVICE ISSUES

The growth and export of services are occurring everywhere as the demand for services increases. Even during the recent periods of global economic recession, services are finding ways to stay profitable and expand. DineEquity, for example, owner of the IHOP and Applebee's restaurants, has grown to over 3,400 global locations to become the world's largest full-service restaurant company, and retailer Uniqlo, the largest clothing retailer in Japan, is doubling its overseas operations each year.[27]

Successfully managing services as they expand into foreign markets involves a number of issues, including:

- *Labor, facilities, and infrastructure support.* Cultural differences, education, and expertise levels can prove to be problematic for firms unfamiliar with local human resources. Firms must also become adept at locating the most appropriate support facilities, suppliers, transportation providers, communication systems, and housing.
- *Legal and political issues.* Local laws may restrict foreign competitors, limit use of certain resources, attach tariffs to prices, or otherwise impose barriers to global service expansion. Some countries require foreign companies to form joint ventures with local businesses.
- *Domestic competitors and the economic climate.* Managers must be aware of the local competitors, the services they offer, their pricing structures, and the current state of the local economy.
- *Identifying global customers.* Perhaps most important, firms must find out where their potential global customers are, through use of the Internet, foreign government agencies, trading partners, or foreign trade intermediaries. Once potential customers are identified, services can modify their products to meet the needs of these customers.

IMPORTANT DEVELOPMENTS IN OPERATIONS MANAGEMENT

1.6 Summarize a number of the important developments in operations management

Over the years, a large number of concepts, tools, and practices have come into use in operations, providing many opportunities for operations managers to create value for their organizations. A few of these are briefly reviewed here. These and others are discussed in detail throughout the text.

LEAN THINKING AND SIX SIGMA QUALITY

The concept of **lean thinking** refers to a collection of processes and philosophies emphasizing the reduction of waste, along with continuous improvement, and the synchronization of material flows within the organization and between supply chain trading partners. Central to the lean philosophy is the **Just-in-Time** (JIT) concept, and today the two terms are synonymous. With JIT systems, supplies and assemblies are "pulled" through the system when and where they are needed. When problems are encountered, processes are stopped until the problem is solved. Lean is a very important aspect of supply chain management since, in effect, supply chain management seeks to incorporate lean elements across the entire supply chain, to get products where they are needed on time, at the desired quality and price. Lean thinking is discussed in Chapter 9.

lean thinking An operating philosophy encompassing the objectives of high quality, fast response, and low waste within the organization and between supply chain trading partners.

Just-in-Time Systems in which supplies and assemblies are "pulled" through the system when and where they are needed.

While Henry Ford initially used and discussed manufacturing activities that are today referred to as parts of the overall lean philosophy,[28] Taiichi Ohno and several of his colleagues at Toyota are given credit for developing many aspects of lean production and the Just-in-Time concept, and widely communicating the practices to other manufacturing organizations beginning in the 1970s.

As with lean thinking, quality management—also termed **total quality management** (TQM), and more recently Six Sigma, although there are several differences between the two concepts—is a philosophy encompassing a collection of processes that seek to improve quality continuously to please customers, reduce costs, and ultimately create competitive advantage for the firm. Quality management is also an integral part of all lean production programs, since waste-free production requires high-quality parts and finished goods. Ultimately, all quality management programs involve the coordinated efforts of the firm and its supply chain partners to achieve incoming and outbound product quality.

Motorola, the originator of the registered (and capitalized) term, *Six Sigma*, has seen many benefits over the years with its use. "Six Sigma projects at Motorola have had a bottom-line impact of more than $18 billion. Motorola University, Motorola's external Six Sigma training division, has trained thousands of 'belts' in recent years, having an impact on profitability for hundreds of companies," says Jeff Summers, Six Sigma Master Black Belt at Motorola.[29] Six Sigma, including the use of colored belts to indicate the level of training, is discussed in Chapter 13.

MATERIAL REQUIREMENTS PLANNING AND ENTERPRISE RESOURCE PLANNING

Operations managers are continuously involved in resource and operations planning to balance capacity and planned production. Too much capacity means high production costs per unit due to idle workers and machinery. Too little capacity means overworked employees, leading to quality problems. Starting with the Black & Decker company in 1964, **material requirements planning** (MRP) software applications were developed to try and balance part purchases and plant capacities with production requirements. Later, as computing capabilities grew, **manufacturing resource planning** (MRP-II) software systems were designed to allow firms to perform forward-looking *what-if analyses* of plant capacities. Eventually, MRP-II systems evolved into much more complex **enterprise resource planning** (ERP) systems in the 1990s. The concepts of MRP, MRP-II, and ERP are discussed in Chapter 11.

Enterprise resource planning is a multimodule software application for managing a firm's functional activities, suppliers, and customers. Initially, ERP software focused on integrating the internal business activities of a multifacility organization. With the onset of supply chain management, ERP vendors today are designing their products to include the capabilities of managing suppliers and customers. ERP utilizes the idea of a centralized and shared database system to tie the entire organization together.

PROJECT MANAGEMENT

Project management is concerned with the planning, scheduling, and controlling of resources (such as capital, people, materials, and equipment) to meet the specific goals (such as the completion date, budgeted cost, and required performance) of a project. Project goals are usually tied to the client's requirements such as when the project needs to be completed, how the completed project will perform, and what constitutes completion.

While project construction techniques have been around for quite some time (dating back to the Great Pyramids of thousands of years ago), it has only been in the past 50 years that project management tools and techniques have been developed and used for complex projects. The modern project management era started in 1958 with the development of CPM (the critical path method) and PERT (program evaluation and review technique). Back then, it was the U.S. Department of Defense that utilized project management principles and tools to manage large-budget, schedule-driven projects.[30] Environmental conditions today require project managers to more carefully assess risk and security, and consequently develop failure probabilities and contingency plans for many projects. Additionally, technological advances such as cloud-based computing and open-source software have allowed for better project planning options and reduced costs for many companies. Project management is the topic of Chapter 12.

total quality management A philosophy that seeks to improve quality continuously to please customers, reduce costs, and ultimately create competitive advantage for the firm.

material requirements planning Software applications that were developed to try to balance part purchases and plant capacities with production requirements.

manufacturing resource planning Software systems that were designed to allow firms to perform forward-looking *what-if analyses* of plant capacities.

enterprise resource planning (ERP) A multimodule software application for managing a firm's functional activities, suppliers, and customers.

project management The planning, scheduling, and controlling of resources to meet the specific goals of a project.

RADIO FREQUENCY IDENTIFICATION

Radio frequency identification (RFID) technology enables a device to read data stored on chips at a distance, without requiring line-of-sight scanning. While this technology has existed for quite some time, recent cost decreases, technology advances (which have greatly reduced their size), and the required use by suppliers of large customers like Walmart have enabled many supply chain participants to start thinking about or testing the use of RFID tags, such as the one shown here. The potential benefits include greater product visibility across the supply chain, better inventory management, easier product tracing and recalls, and reduced product tampering. Getting the right data onto RFID tags in the first place and then deploying middleware to access or filter the data as products move along the supply chain is also a significant problem. The topic of RFID is discussed further in Chapter 15.

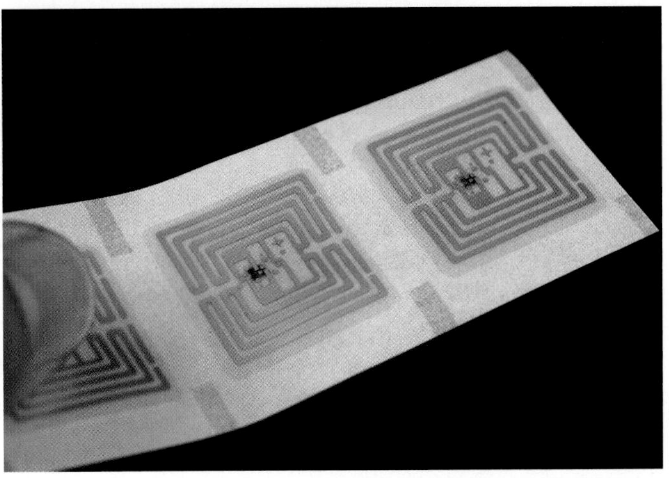
iStock/albin

Today, RFID tags are used more commonly due to their decreased size and cost.

BUSINESS ETHICS AND SUSTAINABILITY

With respect to operations, **business ethics** is the application of ethical principles to business situations, a rapidly growing trend. Ethical actions recognize the rights of others and the duties those rights impose on the ones performing the actions. Today, the practice of business ethics is referred to as **corporate social responsibility** (CSR). Whether firms practice CSR because they are forced to do it, feel obliged to do it, or want to do it, is a matter for debate. However, it is indeed being practiced; many firms have formal CSR policies and initiatives under way. Ethical purchasing practices, for instance, include promoting diversity by intentionally buying from small firms, ethnic minority businesses, and women-owned enterprises. Japan automaker Nissan uses a steering committee to monitor its progress in key CSR areas. "Over time, we made the house strong enough to weather external storms like the financial crisis of recent years and the natural disaster of 2011," says CEO Carlos Ghosn. "But a company is only as strong as the society around it. At Nissan, we support the people and society around us. This is our CSR."[31]

While the notion of protecting the Earth's environment has been a topic of concern for many years, it has more recently become a popular topic of debate as politicians and voters have made global warming an election issue. Indeed, businesses today are discovering that significant additional profits can be realized from acting environmentally responsible. **Sustainability** as applied to supply chains is a broad term that includes green purchasing, some aspects of social responsibility, as well as financial performance. Consequently, sustainability is often linked to what is termed the triple bottom line, or people, planet, and profits. Sustainability can more formally be defined as the ability to meet the needs of current supply chain members without hindering the ability to meet the needs of future generations in terms of economic, environmental, and social challenges. For businesses and their trading partners, sustainability is seen today as doing the right things in ways that make economic sense. Ethics and sustainability are further discussed in Chapters 2 and 14.

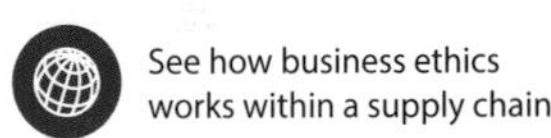
See how business ethics works within a supply chain

radio frequency identification A small, data storage device that allows data to be read at a distance, without requiring line-of-sight scanning.

business ethics The application of ethical principles to business situations.

corporate social responsibility The practice of business ethics.

sustainability The ability to meet the needs of current supply chain members without hindering the ability to meet the needs of future generations in terms of economic, environmental, and social challenges.

Visit edge.sagepub.com/wisner to help you accomplish your coursework goals in an easy-to-use learning environment.

- Mobile-friendly eFlashcards
- Mobile-friendly practice quizzes
- A complete online action plan
- Chapter summaries with learning objectives
- Excel templates to assist with practice problems
- Original video case studies that demonstrate chapter concepts in action

SUMMARY

This chapter has introduced the concepts of operations, operations management, processes, supply chains, and supply chain management. Decision making in operations management requires knowledge of these areas and the management of suppliers and customers in maintaining a competitive organization. Eight generally recognized supply chain processes were described, along with the role these processes play in the organization and its supply chains. The topic of service operations was also introduced in this chapter, and a number of differences between services and manufacturing firms were discussed. Finally, a number of important developments in operations management were introduced, all of which comprise major portions of this text.

KEY TERMS

Basic operations activities, 5
Business ethics, 19
Business process integration, 9
Capacity, 11
Concurrent engineering, 14
Corporate social responsibility, 19
Customer contact, 15
Customer relationship management, 11
Customer service management, 11
Demand management, 11
Enterprise resource planning, 18
First-tier customers, 9
First-tier suppliers, 9
Flow management, 13
Good, 4
Goods–service package, 16
Just-in-Time, 17
Lean thinking, 17
Logistics, 12
Manufacturing resource planning, 18
Material requirements planning, 18
Operations, 4
Operations management, 4
Order fulfillment, 12
Outsourcing, 9
Processes, 5
Product development and commercialization, 14
Project management, 18
Radio frequency identification, 19
Returns management, 14
Service, 4
Supply chain, 8
Supply chain management, 9
Sustainability, 19
Third-party logistics services, 12
Three-dimensional concurrent engineering, 14
Total quality management, 18

REVIEW QUESTIONS

1. What is operations management? Define the term, identify the basic activities, and provide an example.
2. Define the terms process, supply chain, and supply chain management.
3. What is process integration? What does it have to do with the management of supply chains?
4. What is meant by first-tier and second-tier suppliers and customers?
5. List and briefly describe the eight key supply chain processes.
6. Define concurrent engineering.
7. What is the difference between a good and a service? A manufacturer and a service producer?
8. What is a goods–service package?
9. What is customer contact, and how does it impact service management?
10. What is lean thinking, and what does it have to do with operations management?
11. What are the historical developments of ERP?
12. What is project management?
13. What marks the beginning of modern project management?
14. What is RFID, and how is it used?
15. Describe sustainability and the triple bottom line. What is the difference between sustainability, corporate social responsibility, and being green?

DISCUSSION QUESTIONS

1. Describe all of the processes you employ to come to class each day.
2. Describe a supply chain for a library. Would a library have any second-tier suppliers or customers? Explain.
3. Describe a number of customer relationship management and customer service management activities for your college or university.
4. Do you think it is a good idea to use only a small number of (really good) suppliers? Why?
5. Discuss the demand management activities you would find at a fast-food restaurant.
6. What sorts of customer contact do you see at McDonald's? A fancy restaurant? A bank?
7. Describe the goods–service package for an exercise facility; a college bookstore; a radio station.
8. What impact should effective operations management have on costs? Profits? Productivity? Customer service? Quality?
9. Which is more important: customer relationship management or supplier relationship management?

EXERCISES AND PROJECTS

1. In your place of employment or an organization to which you belong, describe all of the processes you come in contact with on a frequent basis, their inputs and outputs, how each process works, and how successful the processes are.
2. In your place of employment or an organization to which you belong, describe its supply chains as accurately as you can, and construct a figure showing the relevant supply chains. Also, describe any foreign members of these supply chains.
3. In your place of employment or an organization to which you belong, describe as much as you can regarding the eight key supply chain processes, and how each one of these functions.

CASE STUDY

CASE 1: Organ Mountain Vegan Restaurant

John Kohl, the owner of Organ Mountain Vegan Restaurant, had just completed a painful meeting with his employees talking about problems and what to do. It had been two years since John had opened his restaurant and he thought that by now, he should be enjoying himself and making a decent living. For a number of years, John had taken business classes at his local university and saved money, with the goal of opening his own restaurant. Now, though, he felt overwhelmed with all the problems the restaurant faced.

Company Background

John had opened his restaurant in downtown Las Cruces, a town in southern New Mexico with a population of about 80,000, in 2013. He had grown up in Las Cruces and learned the restaurant business from his father, who was a chef at a Las Cruces hotel. John had worked summers in the hotel's restaurant and had developed a taste for the vegetarian dishes offered there. A space downtown had become available when a barbecue restaurant had gone out of business, so John leased it and eventually opened his restaurant. He hired a chef to work Wednesday through Sunday from lunchtime through dinner, while John took reservations, did office work, other behind-the-scene jobs, and anything else required to operate the restaurant. John also hired another part-time cook, three waiters, and one kitchen helper.

Since the business was small, John had no formal purchasing, inventory management, or quality control systems. The chef and one waiter were allowed to purchase food, alcohol, and supplies as they required, from several local distributors. Over the past two years, inventory problems had cropped up—there were frequent times when various food items on the menu would be stocked out, while other items took up too much room in the storage area or had to be thrown out because they were spoiled. On other occasions, the restaurant would run out of things like napkins or ketchup, requiring John to rush down to the local Walmart to buy these items at a higher price. Several times, when John looked, he could not tell where things were stored, or how many items were in stock. The full-time chef, while a good cook, would take cigarette breaks at the most inopportune times, and he always seemed to be fighting with the kitchen helper and the part-time cook. In fact, several helpers and one part-time cook had quit in the two years they had been open. There also were days when customer traffic seemed very light—so much so that John was wondering if he should lay off one of the waiters. On other days, though, there were so many customers that wait times were long and John had noticed some customers leaving before their names were called. Recently, John had begun getting customer complaints about the food and the service when he walked around, asking customers how they liked their meals.

The Meeting

John decided to call a meeting on Tuesday morning to discuss the various problems with the restaurant. Unfortunately, the meeting turned into a finger-pointing complaint session, and John quickly felt it getting out of control. So he thanked everyone for attending and adjourned the meeting. He had a lot of things to consider.

QUESTIONS

1. Identify the operations and/or supply chain problems that John is facing at his restaurant.
2. Discuss the reasons or potential causes for the problems listed in question 1.
3. What is the restaurant's supply chain? Which of the key supply chain processes should be of concern to John? Describe how each of these processes is affected.
4. What could John have done differently to avoid the problems listed in question 1?
5. Going forward, what should John do to solve his problems and create a more successful restaurant?

Note: This case was prepared solely to provide material for class discussion. It does not intend to illustrate either effective or ineffective handling of a managerial situation.

VIDEO CASE STUDY

Learn more about ***managing supply chains*** from real organizations that use operations management techniques every day. Amy Keelin and Christine Keelin are COO and CFO (respectively) at MPK Foods, a small family-owned company based in Duarte, California, that produces seasoning mixes sold to grocery stores. MPK works with a number of suppliers in order to get their products on the shelves. Watch this short interview to find out how they do it.

iStock/Elenathewise

We were very optimistic about the world. And then we have this [global economic] meltdown. Most really great companies try to set up strategies and come out stronger than when they went in. We did a lot of that, but there were some very painful things involved.

—**FREDERICK SMITH,** chairman and CEO, FedEx[1]

GE's commitment to high standards of integrity and social and environmental performance, as well as our ability to innovate, position us as a natural partner in helping solve the world's toughest problems.

—**JEFF IMMELT,** chairman and CEO, GE[2]

CORPORATE STRATEGY, PERFORMANCE, AND SUSTAINABILITY

LEARNING OBJECTIVES

After completing this chapter, you should be able to:

2.1 List the properties of a mission statement and how corporate strategies are developed

2.2 Describe how companies create operations strategies for competitive advantage

2.3 Explain the trade-offs in operations strategies

2.4 Discuss a number of operations performance measures and potential measurement problems

2.5 Demonstrate how corporate ethics and sustainability impact corporate and operations strategies

Master the content.

edge.sagepub.com/wisner

DOW CHEMICAL'S USE OF ETHICS AND SUSTAINABILITY

The Dow Chemical Company's core values revolve around ethical behavior, and this influences how company employees treat one another, their customers, and their suppliers. According to Andrew Liveris, president, chairman, and CEO of Dow Chemical, the company recently entered into its "Phase 3" of ethics and sustainability. The three phases are described here:

Phase 1—*The Great Awakening*. This began in the 1970s when company CEOs started getting pressure from the public to change their operating philosophies of using any means to make profits. Public outcries served as a wake-up call for businesses to reassess their processes and ways of doing business. Dow developed its Code of Business Conduct during this time. This was a commitment to using business practices that included integrity, respect for people, and protecting the planet.

Phase 2—*The Triple Bottom Line*. In 1988, Dow began thinking in terms of the triple bottom line: the economic, environmental, and social impact of Dow's operations. Dow began promoting its concept of "responsible care," which is a global initiative encouraging all chemical companies to work together to improve stakeholder health, safety, and environmental performance. Dow became more involved in the communities where it operates; it began promoting volunteerism, recycling, diversity, and education initiatives.

Phase 3—*The Great Integration*. To sustain its growth, Dow Chemical felt it necessary to integrate the triple bottom line across its business strategies. Ethical behavior became a central part of its business activities, and Dow made sustainability and corporate responsibility part of its corporate DNA. A number of global challenges in the areas of health care, energy, and transportation are seen as opportunities for Dow not only to make a difference using triple bottom line thinking, but to make a profit as well.[3]

INTRODUCTION

The recent global economic recession has hastened many organizations' plans to institute various strategies to reduce costs, delivery times, and carbon footprints while improving quality, customer service, and ethical reputations. The overall goals of these transformations are to improve competitiveness, market share, and financial performance. Indeed, the increasing number of global competitors, demands by customers for companies to become more ethically and environmentally focused, rising costs of fuel and materials, and the desire to deliver more innovative products more frequently and cheaply than competitors, have also combined to place added pressures on firms to achieve optimal performance. Today, these trends have become the drivers of corporate strategy initiatives.

This chapter presents discussions of mission statements and how these impact organizations' competitive strategies. Once these have been set, they become the impetus behind the formation of various functional strategies. Eventually, these strategies result in short-term tactics for process improvements aimed at meeting these strategies. Obviously, there will be trade-offs the firm's managers will need to resolve along the way. For instance, pursuing a high-quality strategy may mean higher prices for purchased goods and services.

This chapter also includes a discussion of operations performance measurement. Achieving company objectives and improving key processes can only be a guessing game if performance characteristics are not monitored. Think about it: If you weren't told your test scores for this class, could you determine if you were successfully completing the class, and what you needed to do differently to prepare for the next test? Today, many firms are using scorecards to help them track the right performance measures, and this topic is also discussed.

Finally, emerging trends in operations strategy development include the use of socially responsible and environmentally friendly strategies. Used the right way, these can create a competitive advantage and even reduce costs for the organization, but they may also prove elusive. Many firms have successfully developed these strategies, though, as evidenced by Dow Chemical in the chapter-opening Manufacturing Spotlight. Creating and implementing strategies to support ethical and sustainable operations is a growing practice, but it can ultimately fail due to misaligned strategies, lack of commitment, and unrealized goals.

CORPORATE STRATEGY DEVELOPMENT

List the properties of a mission statement and how corporate strategies are developed

An organization's **strategy** is a description of how it intends to compete, or provide value to its customers, both now and into the future. Executives in the firm must address two questions when developing the firm's overall strategy: "Who are we now?" and "What do we want to be?" The process of determining a firm's long-term goals, plans, and policies is called **strategic planning**.

The firm's vision or **mission statement** provides direction for its strategic plan and should address both of the questions above. It might include descriptions of the company's goods and services, the processes employed, the markets where the company competes, its potential customers, and its distinctive competencies. The mission statement might be something very direct and simple, such as that of CVS Pharmacy:

> We will be the easiest pharmacy retailer for customers to use.[4]

It might also be a detailed set of statements providing guidance for a number of the firm's activities, such as FedEx's:

> FedEx will produce superior financial returns for shareowners by providing high value-added supply chain, transportation, business and related information services through focused operating companies. Customer requirements will be met in the highest quality manner appropriate to each market segment served. FedEx will strive to develop mutually rewarding relationships with its employees, partners and suppliers. Safety will be the first consideration in all operations. Corporate activities will be conducted to the highest ethical and professional standards.[5]

The strategic plan addresses how the firm intends to achieve its mission.

While strategic plans are periodically revisited and potentially revised, typically annually, mission statements are changed far less often—only when a change in culture or direction is needed. In one extreme example, New York–based software systems company CA Technologies hired a new CEO in 2004 in hopes of transforming the company, following a $2 billion accounting fraud and insider trading fiasco perpetrated by the former CEO and

strategy A description of how the firm intends to compete, or provide value to its customers, both now and into the future.

strategic planning The process of determining a firm's long-term goals, plans, and policies.

mission statement A statement that provides direction for the firm's strategic plan. It might include descriptions of its goods and services, the processes it employs, the markets where it competes, its potential customers, and its distinctive competencies.

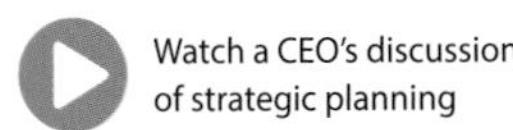

others in the organization. Over a several-year period, the new management team changed the company's name (its original name was Computer Associates International), rewrote its mission statement, revised its core values to reflect the new mission, and developed or revised systems throughout the entire organization to be consistent with its new mission. Today, CA Technologies is one of the largest software companies in the world. (Ultimately, the former CEO and chairman, Sanjay Kumar, received a 12-year prison sentence for orchestrating the frauds.)[6]

STRATEGY CHOICES

Firms compete using some combination of **the three competitive dimensions**: cost, quality, and customer service. When consumers buy products, some choose the low-cost alternative; others may prefer instead to buy the higher-priced, higher-quality product; and still others may base their purchases on various service attributes of the product or retailer. Each of these dimensions is briefly discussed here.

Cost

Almost any product line includes a low-cost alternative, from cars to bread to financial services. Competing on cost requires attention to reducing the costs of purchases, labor, equipment, manufacturing, overhead, and other cost items included in the products and services sold to customers. Retailers like Walmart, for example, sell items for low prices in part because they purchase in very large quantities, which reduces purchase costs per unit. Walmart also has its own distribution centers and trucks; helps its supply chain members to reduce their costs, which means lower purchase prices for Walmart; and offers little in the way of assistance to customers in the retail stores, which minimizes labor costs.

Automated services such as Redbox maintain extremely low video rental rates using self-service video rental kiosks at about 35,000 locations in the United States. Customers can locate specific movies and games online, go and rent the disks, and then return them to any kiosk. Their very low cost and high customer service model has proven extremely successful.[7]

the three competitive dimensions Cost, quality, and customer service.

economies of scale Conditions that are created when purchasing and manufacturing in bulk to reduce per-unit costs.

Manufacturers, too, can compete using a low-cost strategy by producing very large quantities of no-frills products with automated equipment, which reduces the per-unit cost. Purchasing and manufacturing in bulk to reduce per-unit costs is also referred to as creating **economies of scale**. Additionally, manufacturers seek locations in countries with low labor costs, low taxes, and plentiful suppliers. These savings can then be passed along to customers. Recently, as labor costs have risen in Asian countries, electronics manufacturers such as Foxconn and Sharp have expanded production in Mexico. In Western Europe, the United Kingdom has emerged as one of the lowest-cost manufacturing locations. "Many companies are beginning to see the world in a new light," says Harold Sirkin, a Boston Consulting Group senior partner. "They are finding that many old perceptions of low-cost and high-cost countries are out of date, and they are starting to realign their global sourcing and production networks accordingly."[8]

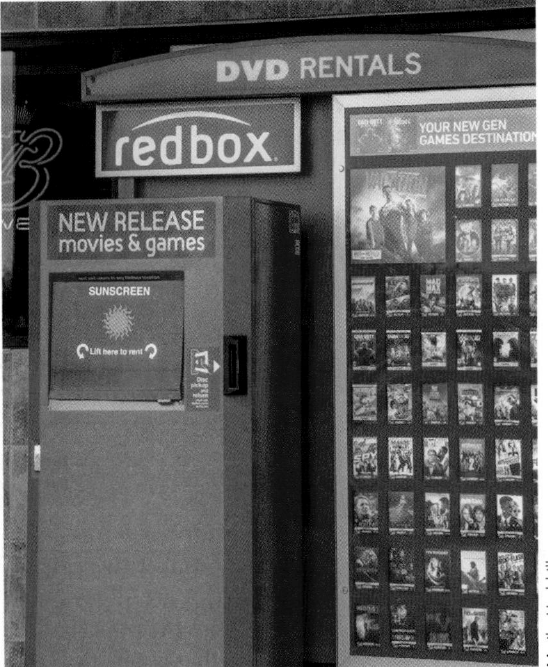

MarilynHaddrill

By utilizing self-service kiosks, Redbox keeps operating costs low.

Quality

Competing using quality typically means providing a great or unique product or service. Quality, though, has many elements, including the product's design or features, reliability, performance, safety, and warranty package. Additionally, consumers might have varying perceptions of quality—some might argue, for instance, that Southwest Airlines is high quality because of its historically high 82% on-time arrival performance,[9] while others might argue that Southwest is low quality because of its lack of food and first-class and reserved seating. Higher-quality goods and services generally

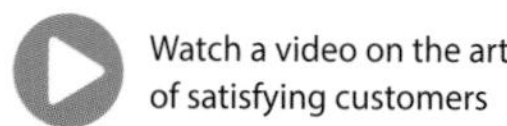
Watch a video on the art of satisfying customers

command higher prices to cover the costs of higher-quality parts, closer attention to meeting design specifications, better-trained personnel, and use of better equipment and technology. Building a reputation for high quality is also the focus of most of these companies. For these reasons, high-quality products command higher profit margins.

Annually, the Reputation Institute, a global consulting firm based in New York City, uncovers the world's most reputable companies, based on customer surveys and interviews regarding trust, innovation, governance, corporate citizenship, and other variables. In 2015, the top five companies were BMW Group, Google, Daimler, Rolex, and LEGO Group. Other companies scoring high on the list included Apple, Sony, Microsoft, and Volkswagen.[10]

iStock/killerbayer

Amazon.com is consistently rated as having one of the best customer service programs in the United States.

Customer Service

Customer service includes a number of aspects such as delivery speed, flexibility, reliability, product support, server knowledge and empathy, and service recovery. *Speed* refers to the ability to complete the service quickly. *Flexibility* refers to the firm's ability to respond to a wide variety of customer expectations; it can also mean the firm can accommodate varying demand levels. In customer service terms, *reliability* refers to delivering a good or service as promised. When products are sold such as a computer, customers want to know something about the after-sales *product support*—can the firm provide useful operating information, software support, and periodic upgrades? When talking to sales associates or service representatives, customers want to feel assured that the salesperson is knowledgeable about the firm's products and truly understands or feels *empathy* for the customer. And finally, when things go wrong—the product fails to operate correctly, or the restaurant's food is cold—customers expect an equitable compensation or arrangement. This capability is also known as **service recovery**.

In the Zogby Analytics 2015 survey of 2,500 adults in the United States regarding customer service, Amazon.com was the highest-rated company. In fact, Amazon has been number one in this survey for five consecutive years. Trader Joe's, Chick-fil-A, and UPS also scored high in the survey. As the largest online shopping site in the world, Amazon.com offers a level of convenience that is difficult for other businesses to match. The company's roots in technology also help its customer service capabilities. Amazon.com maintains its customers' purchase histories as part of an extremely valuable pool of customer behavior data, which is used to make purchase suggestions.[11]

Companies utilize strategic combinations of low cost, high quality, and great customer service as a way to create customer value and compete. Obviously, offering high levels of all three would be great; in practice, however, this is very hard to achieve. High levels of quality and customer service generally lead to higher product costs. Usually, firms decide to concentrate on one or two, while providing adequate levels of the remaining dimension(s).

Once the mission and competitive strategy have been decided upon, functional area strategies and tactics are identified and implemented to support the firm's overall strategy choices. These decisions within operations are discussed next.

ALIGNING OPERATIONS STRATEGIES FOR COMPETITIVE ADVANTAGE

2.2 Describe how companies create operations strategies for competitive advantage

service recovery An equitable compensation or arrangement to compensate for a service failure.

operations strategies The set of decisions made within the operations function to support the overall mission and strategy of the firm.

Competitive advantage can be achieved when the operations function creates strategies that are aligned with the overall mission and strategy of the firm. **Operations strategies** are thus the set of decisions made within the operations function to support the overall mission and strategy of the firm. These decisions define how the operations function will contribute to the firm's ability to compete, and collectively, these are considered core competencies of the firm.

SERVICE SPOTLIGHT

Delivering Happiness at Zappos

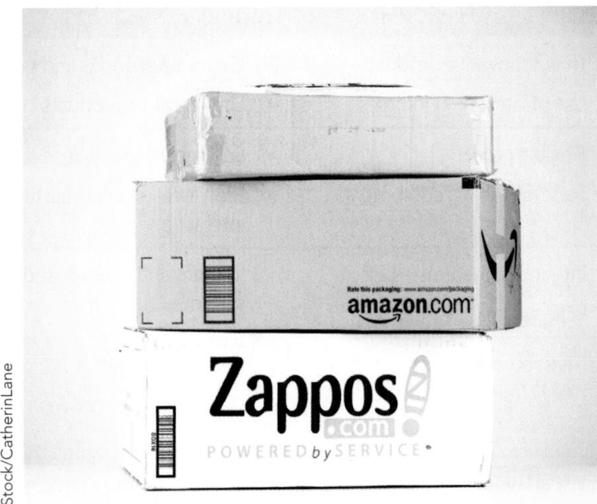

iStock/CatherinLane

Internet shoe retailer Zappos, under the leadership of CEO Tony Hsieh, delivers heavy doses of happiness to its customers—it stores and ships all its inventory from a warehouse in Kentucky strategically located near a UPS shipping hub. This allows customers to get their orders quickly. From its corporate offices in Las Vegas, Nevada, Zappos cultivates a company culture that encourages employees to grow and be happy. It carefully hires and trains employees to fit into the company's culture—in fact, after a four-week training period, employees are offered $2,000 to resign if they don't think they fit the Zappos mold.

Most Zappos employees work in its call center and are under no pressure to end customer calls quickly. If Zappos doesn't have what a caller is looking for, the employee will find it for them at another retailer. It also offers free deliveries and returns. This attention to customer service has resulted in a heavy growth in sales, even during a depressed economy.[12]

CORE COMPETENCIES

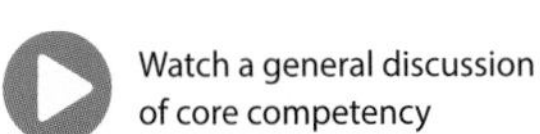
Watch a general discussion of core competency

Core competencies are the collective capabilities or skill sets possessed by the firm that distinguish it from its competitors. Core competencies create competitive advantage. Walmart's knowledge and practice of supply chain management and cost reduction strategies allow it to be a successful low-cost retailer. Apple uses its design capabilities to create easy-to-use and unique communication and computing products. And, as described in the Service Spotlight above, the online shoe and accessory retailer Zappos uses its unique ability to hire and motivate employees in order to deliver high levels of service to its customers.

Core competencies are also dynamic—as customer tastes, competition, and technologies change, a firm's core competencies must also change to continue to provide an advantage for the firm. In the 1970s, Polaroid instant cameras were extremely popular because prints were available instantly. Today, the digital age has forced Polaroid to reinvent itself. Now, its instant digital camera has a miniature built-in, color printer that prints cropped and filtered images and has the ability to save images with the camera's memory chip.[13]

Finally, core competencies should be difficult to imitate. This is what makes a competitive advantage sustainable. Patent portfolios are used to protect core technologies and can be used to block competitors from entering a market. When patents are not possible, implementing policies and procedures to protect trade secrets is also important.

OPERATIONS STRATEGY CHOICES

Operations strategies will vary based on the firm's overall strategic plan. Operations strategy decisions will comprise the topics covered in this text: product design, process design, production control systems, facility location, facility layout, purchasing, logistics, quality, inventory, and customer service. Table 2.1 lists the operations strategy categories and illustrates how operations strategies align with the firm's strategic plan. These topics will be covered in detail throughout the text.

Aligning Operations With a Low-Cost Strategy. Firms competing using a low-cost strategy, for example, will require operations to focus their efforts on creating competencies that achieve low costs, such as copying successful products instead of designing unproven products; purchasing and manufacturing in large quantities to reduce per-unit costs; and using

core competencies The collective capabilities or skill sets possessed by the firm that distinguish it from its competitors.

Table 2.1 Aligning Operations Strategies with the Firm's Strategies

Operations Strategy Categories	Cost Strategy	Quality Strategy	Customer Service Strategy
Product design	• Copy other successful products • Improve older products	• New, innovative products • Use of latest technologies	• Customized goods and services • Low leadtime products
Process design	• High-volume processes • Automated processes	• Flexible processes • State-of-the-art equipment	• Self-service processes • High level of server-customer interaction
Production control system	• Legacy systems—MRP • Manual 2-bin systems	• Integrated systems—ERP • RFID system	• Internet and cloud-based systems
Facility location	• Low labor-cost or lowest total cost location • Centralized location	• Near sources of innovation or highly trained personnel	• Near the customers • Decentralized locations
Facility layout	• Maximum use of floor space and height	• Visual layout • Integrated flow of products	• Layouts to reduce customer queues • Layouts that occupy customers
Purchasing	• Low cost (foreign) suppliers • Buy in bulk	• High-quality suppliers • Require ISO quality certification	• Buy from local suppliers • Frequent deliveries of supplies
Logistics	• Use centralized distribution centers • Lowest-cost transportation mode	• Deliver when needed using best mode • Use 4PL provider	• Use decentralized distribution centers • Delivering on time is priority
Quality	• Cost is priority • Quality is minimum to meet requirements	• Quality is priority • Use of SQC and continuous improvement	• Service is priority • Quality is minimum to meet requirements
Inventory	• Low inventories • Use of backorder system for stockouts	• Use of ERP systems for inventory control • Use of lean thinking	• High inventories to avoid stockouts
Customer service	• Minimal—barely meets customer expectations	• Moderately exceeds customer expectations	• *Wow* factor • Strong warranties • 24-hour call center

low-cost, relatively unskilled labor. Other cost-driven operation strategies might include finding good deals on location sites, using low-cost transportation alternatives, and offering minimally acceptable quality and customer service levels.

Aligning Operations With a High-Quality Strategy. When firms compete using product quality as their priority, operations managers must seek out high-quality suppliers, through use of quality certifications such as the ISO 9000 family of standards. Additionally, the company makes use of statistical process control techniques and continuous improvement tools such as Six Sigma. These firms also use highly qualified personnel and state-of-the-art equipment, and may incorporate ethical and sustainable operating practices.

Aligning Operations With a High Customer Service Strategy. With this type of strategy, customer satisfaction is of the utmost importance. Deliveries must be on time, which may require use of air transportation and decentralized distribution centers that are close to each market served. Layouts should keep customers occupied and use fair queuing systems. Most important, companies should attempt to *wow* customers by exceeding expectations, using strong warranties, and maintaining 24-hour call centers.

OPERATIONS STRATEGY TRADE-OFFS

2.3 Explain the trade-offs in operations strategies

Strategy trade-offs occur in operations and other functional areas when doing more of one activity requires doing less of something else. When this occurs, compromise solutions must be found. Referring again to Table 2.1, it is very likely that a manufacturing firm using high-volume, automated processes to reduce per-unit costs would find it difficult to be very flexible as well, in terms of the types of products it makes. A compromise solution in this case might be offering a family of similar products capable of being produced on the same production platforms, with careful attention placed on quick equipment setups for each product, to allow multiple product runs per day. Additionally, buying products in bulk from cheap foreign suppliers to reduce purchasing costs will also tend to lengthen inbound delivery times, make rush deliveries very expensive, and increase inventory carrying costs.

Read more about the strategy of Southwest Airlines

Southwest Airlines, generally regarded as a low-cost carrier, can be used to illustrate several operations strategy trade-offs. Southwest primarily flies one model of airplane to reduce pilot training and maintenance costs. It also flies point-to-point to many smaller, regional airports to reduce landing fees. It typically offers no meals, exclusively uses its website for reservations, and offers no assigned or first-class seating, which reduces costs and speeds passenger loading. While these characteristics act together to reduce total costs and keep planes in the air, hauling more passengers than its competitors, Southwest must forgo other things that can cause it to lose favor with those customers who like pampering, meals, close-in airports, and business- or first-class and reserved seating.[14]

MEASURING OPERATIONS PERFORMANCE

Discuss a number of operations performance measures and potential measurement problems

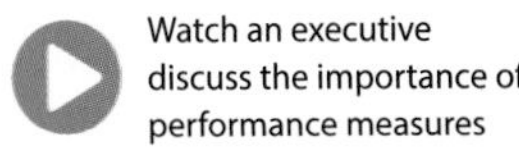

Watch an executive discuss the importance of performance measures

Operations managers make decisions that enable their organizations to better satisfy customers, reduce costs, improve quality and sustainability, and make better use of resources. Performance information tells operations managers about the processes in need of attention, and also provides feedback regarding how well a process had been corrected. Simply put, companies operate better when managers and other employees monitor process performance. To get a clear picture of overall performance, firms should develop an organization-wide system of **performance measures** linked to the firm's strategies. Managers need to know how the company is doing, and what needs to be fixed to enable the firm to accomplish its objectives. Indeed, in a report by the Conference Board of Strategic Performance Management, companies measuring performance were more likely to achieve leadership positions in their industry and were almost twice as likely to handle a major change successfully.[15]

Performance measurement systems can vary substantially from one company to the next, and even from one issue to the next, as shown in the Manufacturing Spotlight on Frito-Lay on page 32. For example, some firms concentrate solely on monitoring their costs and profits. While these measures are certainly important, managers must realize that financial performance alone gives no indication of the *underlying causes of the performance*. Designing a suite of performance measures and then monitoring the many key operations processes that impact costs and profits can provide much better information for decision-making purposes.

strategy trade-offs When doing more of one activity requires doing less of something else, creating the need for a compromise.

performance measures Criteria that tell managers how the company is doing, and what needs to be fixed to enable the firm to accomplish its objectives.

MANUFACTURING SPOTLIGHT Frito-Lay Analyzes a Performance Problem

In 2005, Frito-Lay faced a productivity problem with its route sales representatives (RSRs). Consequently, a team of Frito-Lay managers designed a plan for studying the problem.

Executives thought that compensation issues could be inhibiting performance. One idea was that compensation shortfalls were responsible for low morale, productivity, and retention. Some business leaders might have been tempted to raise compensation to solve the problem; however, the team decided to look for root causes.

Data for the analysis came from a survey of the RSRs and their supervisors. The survey measured factors related to attraction, retention, and motivation, and also included questions about respondents' previous experience.

The analysis found that for low-volume routes, differences in sales task skills were the main influence on sales performance. Also, RSRs with more prior experience had greater sales than workers with less experience. On the high-volume routes, differences in driving and delivery task skills were a stronger differentiator of sales performance. A separate analysis showed that prior sales experience was a predictor of sales for all routes.

iStock/Spauln

Thus, the emphasis on sales training was validated. To take advantage of the positive impact of prior sales experience, hiring practices were modified to emphasize prior sales experience.[16]

During the recent global recession, managers worked hard to drive costs out of their supply chains while trying to keep revenues from falling. According to a survey of global business managers, three of the activities receiving the most attention during this period were purchasing, logistics, and performance measurement.[17] Walmart, for example, decided to purchase up to 80% of its private label merchandise directly from suppliers (instead of distributors), potentially saving it billions of dollars each year.[18]

Even for companies like Walmart, low-cost performance alone is not enough to guarantee success. Products must be on the shelves when needed, and at acceptable levels of quality. For any company, becoming successful requires managers to make decisions to create goods and services customers want, and then distribute them in ways that will satisfy customers. This requires careful monitoring of a number of cost, quality, customer service, productivity, ethics, and sustainability performance measures. Table 2.2 lists a number of useful performance measures in these areas. These can vary based on industry norms, company experiences, and customer requirements. Each of the performance areas is described next.

iStock/cabania

High gas prices for consumers can mean windfall profits for oil companies.

PERFORMANCE MEASURES

Financial

As mentioned earlier, financial performance measures don't tell the whole story. Windfall profits occurring when industry prices rise, as seen over the years in the oil industry, say nothing about how effectively an oil company's processes are being managed. When demand exceeds supply in the oil industry, then airlines and other transportation companies experience higher costs and reductions in profits, while oil companies see suddenly rising profits. In 2011, for instance, ExxonMobil made $41.1 billion in profits, or almost $5 million in profits per hour.[19] These profits were not necessarily the result of something the firm's managers did particularly well; they were caused in large part by uncontrollable environmental conditions. Thus, changes in cost and profit statistics may not

Table 2.2 Some Common Operations Performance Measures

Performance Category	Measures
Financial	• Net profit margin (net income after taxes/net sales) • Current ratio (current assets/current liabilities) • Inventory turnover (cost of goods sold/average inventory value) • Total cost compared to standard or desired cost (purchase, labor, manufacturing, and transportation cost; e.g., purchasing efficiency = actual purchases/purchase goal)
Productivity	• Single-factor productivity (outputs/labor \$; outputs/material \$) • Multiple-factor productivity (outputs/(labor \$ + material \$ + energy \$))
Quality	• Number of defects per unit, or number of complaints per customer • Cost of poor quality (scrap losses + warranty costs + rework costs + return costs) • Average time between product failures • Product returns per units sold; warranty claims per units sold • Number of work centers/processes using statistical process control • Number of employees with quality training • Number of quality awards received • Percent of suppliers with quality certifications
Customer Service	• Order delivery time accuracy; order quantity accuracy • Customer satisfaction score • Complaint resolution time • Number of customer services available • Time needed to change delivery schedules, to change a customer's order • Number of stockouts per period • Completeness of website • Number of "friends" on social websites • Call center capabilities • Number of service awards received
Ethics/Sustainability	• Number of business ethics and sustainability initiatives adopted • Percent of purchases from small, minority, or women-owned suppliers • Percent reduction in greenhouse gas emissions (carbon footprint) • Number of fair trade products purchased • Percent of waste recycled • Percent of suppliers that are ISO 14000 certified • Number of ethics/sustainability awards received

accurately reflect the true, underlying capabilities of the firms. Nevertheless, financial measures should always be an integral part of any performance measurement portfolio. Several financial ratios are shown in Table 2.2, along with an efficiency indicator.

Productivity

A commonly used performance measure is productivity, an index calculated as:

$$\text{Productivity} = \left[\frac{\text{outputs}}{\text{inputs}}\right].$$

As this index grows, it means the firm is using fewer inputs per unit of output, which is generally considered good. **Multiple-factor productivity** measures such as:

$$\text{Overall productivity} = \left[\frac{\text{outputs}}{\text{costs of (labor + capital + energy + materials)}}\right]$$

and **single-factor productivity** measures such as:

$$\text{Labor productivity} = \left[\frac{\text{outputs}}{\text{cost of labor}}\right]$$

are useful but can have problems similar to the use of financial performance measures. These measures allow firms to view the impact of one or more of the firm's inputs (such as the cost of labor) on the firm's outputs (such as units produced or customers served), but do not allow the firm to determine the actual performance of any of the processes behind these elements. Hasty decisions to increase productivity may actually prove to increase a firm's costs and reduce quality or output in the long term, in effect *reducing* productivity. For example, a business manager might be tempted to increase output levels to increase productivity; however, this action could increase inventories and hence inventory carrying costs. It is also likely to increase labor and materials costs. Or a manager might lay off workers while buying cheaper materials to decrease input costs, with the aim of improving productivity, but instead create an adverse impact on the firm's product quality, customer service, and employee morale. In these ways, productivity measures can prove to be damaging.

A good case in point is the global mining industry. Encouraged by strong global demand that pushed up coal prices, many mining companies ramped up production as quickly as possible during the past decade. Costs for labor and materials rose sharply, which ultimately had a negative impact on productivity. Additionally, ramping-up mines made them more difficult to manage. "The industry thought bigger was going to be better and it has not always worked out that way," says Paul Mitchell, global mining advisory leader at business consultancy EY. "It is bad enough managing a mine with 100 people on site; with 1,000 it becomes much more complex."[20]

In many cases, there is a paradox when it comes to improving productivity. Productivity improvement efforts, while initially successful, can eventually reach a plateau, particularly if the efforts involve investments in technology. New technologies take time to absorb, refine, and fully utilize. Computer software can be reprogrammed quickly. Humans can't. Back in 1986, observing a productivity plateau on the heels of the PC revolution, MIT economist Robert Solow said, "You can see the computer age everywhere but in the productivity statistics."[21] This brought rise to the term, the *Solow productivity paradox.*

The **productivity growth rate** from one period to the next is also occasionally determined to gauge an investment's success. This can be calculated as:

$$\text{Growth rate \%} = \frac{P_2 - P_1}{P_1}(100)$$

where:

P_1 = Productivity in period 1, and
P_2 = Productivity in period 2.

Example 2.1 illustrates the use of several financial and productivity performance measures.

multiple-factor productivity A ratio of outputs to multiple inputs.

single-factor productivity A ratio of outputs to one input.

productivity growth rate A calculation of the change in productivity from one period to the next, divided by the original productivity.

Quality

Recall that quality was discussed as one of the three competitive dimensions earlier in this chapter. An in-depth treatment of quality management and control is provided in Chapter 13 and its supplement. Measures of quality performance should be viewed as extremely important for organizations in all industries. Several quality-oriented performance measures are shown in Table 2.2, and these may vary considerably depending on the firm's definitions of product and service quality, and the competitive nature of the firm.

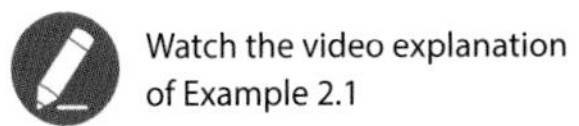

Example 2.1
Financial and Productivity Measures at Ultra Ski Company

Watch the video explanation of Example 2.1

The Ultra Ski Company makes top-of-the-line custom snow skis for high-end ski shops and employs 15 people. The owner wants to track several financial and productivity performance measures using the data shown here.

Financial Information	2013 Results
Net sales	$205,000
Cost of goods sold (purchased items)	$32,000
Net income after taxes	$28,200
Current assets	$68,000
Current liabilities	$22,000
Avg. inventory value	$4,500
Inputs and Outputs	
Skis produced	1,000
Labor hours	10,800
Lease payments	$24,000

Financial Performance

Net profit margin = $28,200/$205,000 = 0.138

Current ratio = $68,000/$22,000 = 3.09

Inventory turnover = $32,000/$4,500 = 7.11

Purchasing efficiency = $32,000/$35,000 = 91.4% (for a 2013 purchasing goal of $35,000).

Single-Factor Productivities

Labor productivity: 1,000 skis/10,800 hours = 0.093 skis per labor hour

Material productivity: 1,000 skis/$32,000 = 0.031 skis per material $

Lease productivity: 1,000 skis/$24,000 = 0.042 skis per lease $

Multiple-Factor Productivity (given an average wage of $17/hour)

1,000 skis/[(10,800)($17) + $32,000 + $24,000] = 0.0042 skis per dollar

Productivity Growth

If, for example, the 2012 multiple-factor productivity was 0.0040 skis per dollar, then productivity in 2013 grew by: (0.0042 – 0.0040)(100)/0.0040 = 5%. This could have been due to greater ski output through better use of technology or training, fewer labor hours, reduced purchasing cost, lower lease cost, or some combination of all of these.

The productivity ratios can be computed using a spreadsheet, as shown here. Note that the cells in columns C and D are formatted as numbers.

(Continued)

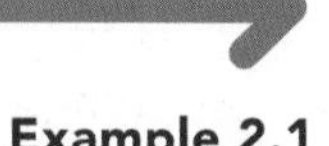

Example 2.1
(Continued)

Use Excel spreadsheet templates to find the solution

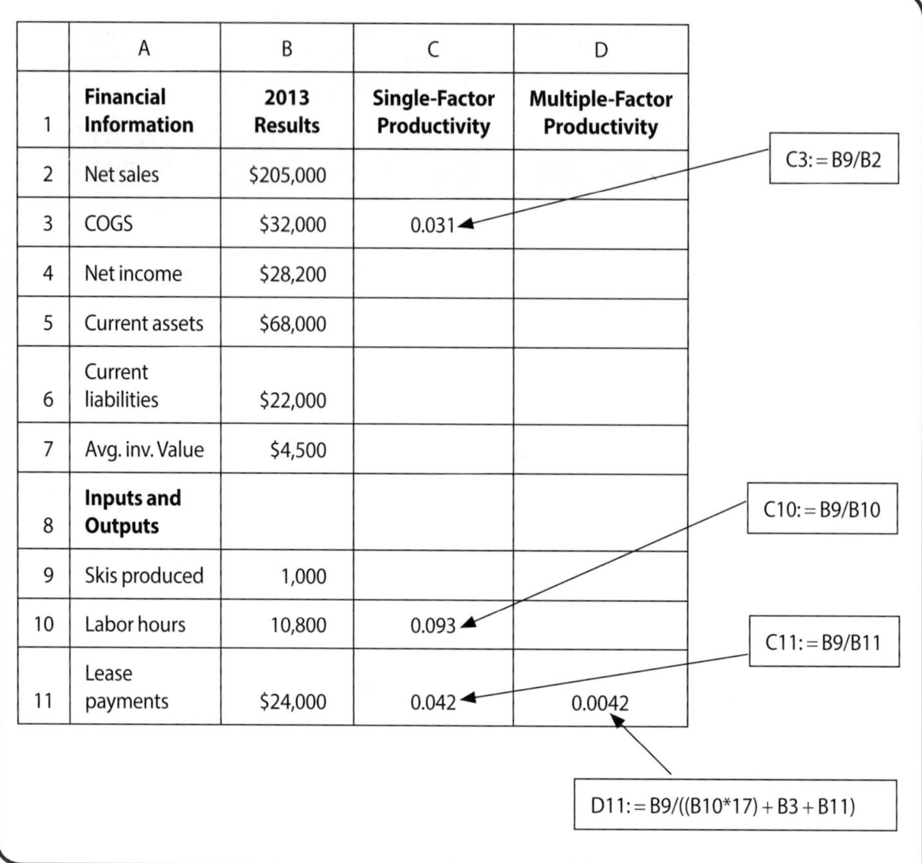

	A	B	C	D
1	**Financial Information**	**2013 Results**	**Single-Factor Productivity**	**Multiple-Factor Productivity**
2	Net sales	$205,000		
3	COGS	$32,000	0.031	
4	Net income	$28,200		
5	Current assets	$68,000		
6	Current liabilities	$22,000		
7	Avg. inv. Value	$4,500		
8	**Inputs and Outputs**			
9	Skis produced	1,000		
10	Labor hours	10,800	0.093	
11	Lease payments	$24,000	0.042	0.0042

C3: = B9/B2
C10: = B9/B10
C11: = B9/B11
D11: = B9/((B10*17) + B3 + B11)

For goods-producing firms, quality measures like the average number of defects per unit, the average time between product failures, the total cost of poor quality, and the number of warranty claims per units sold would likely be used. Services might be more interested in quality measures like the average number of complaints per customer. All firms would potentially be interested in tracking the number of employees receiving quality training, the number of quality awards received, and the number of suppliers used with quality certifications.

Customer Service

Customer service was also discussed earlier in this chapter as one of the three competitive dimensions, and should be viewed as important to most organizations. Customer service is also a major topic of Chapters 5 and 10. Studies show that successful companies care about their customers. A study of over 600 organizations by the Institute for Corporate Productivity found that 86% of high-performing companies said they kept their promises to customers, while only 64% of low-performing companies did the same.[22] Obviously, organizations need customers, and growth in customers or market share is usually a major concern for firms; so tracking and improving customer service performance becomes a way to gauge and improve a firm's success. Table 2.2 lists a number of customer service performance measures for both goods-producing firms and services.

Customer service covers a wide range of activities, from website design to call center capabilities to on-time delivery. A number of these are shown in Table 2.2. Services likely have a number of customer-facing issues to deal with in a continuing fashion, while some manufacturers deal with only a few customers or distributors. Still, all organizations should be monitoring performance in serving and satisfying customers.

Ethics and Sustainability

As consumers, governments, and business leaders begin to address the need for protecting the environment and reducing greenhouse gas emissions, the demand for goods

SERVICE SPOTLIGHT

Scorecarding at Global Workplace Solutions

Ohio-based Global Workplace Solutions, provider of specialized business services, decided in 2006 that it needed to use a performance scorecard to help it improve its operations. For example, after auditing a number of its customers, the company found it was compiling reports on over 500 service delivery measures each month! That realization led it to develop its Global Performance Scorecarding System to reduce time spent on performance reports and to create some standardization of measures.

A project team ultimately came up with standardized measures for service delivery and internal measures for human resources, safety, finance, and customer satisfaction. Ultimately, its 500+ delivery measures were reduced to just 12.

Today, more than 500 Global Workplace Solutions managers use the company scorecard to track key performance indicators. The system lets the company see which locations are best at managing various characteristics. Periodically, executives delivering the best performance meet with those who need to improve.[23]

and services will change, along with regulations impacting how companies operate. As a result, operations performance must begin to include assessments of environmental performance.

The reaches of corporate ethics and sustainability extend across the organization to its trading partners, and include the processes involved in purchasing, manufacturing, and distribution. Perhaps the world's largest sustainability effort underway today is by Walmart and its Sustainability Consortium, a collaborative venture involving a number of companies and universities with the objective of greening Walmart's (and therefore its suppliers') products. The environmental requirements that Walmart has distributed to its suppliers have already triggered changes in packaging, distribution, and performance tracking.[24]

The design of effective ethical and sustainable performance measures should be discussed by all key process personnel. The ISO 14000 environmental management standards, typically associated with one organization's environmental compliance, can be a good starting point. Managers are all beginning to realize that green operations provide cost savings and cheaper prices to customers. For these reasons, use of environmental sustainability assessments is a concept that is gaining in popularity. Several ethical and sustainable performance measures are shown in Table 2.2. The development of ethical and sustainable operations strategies is discussed further later on in this chapter.

THE BALANCED SCORECARD

Drs. Robert Kaplan and David Norton, the developers of the **balanced scorecard** for performance measures, suggest that use of 20 to 30 performance measures, balanced across four categories, is sufficient to assess organizational performance. In contrast, one study of U.S. businesses using performance measurement systems, found the average number of performance measures used was 132![25] The four balanced scorecard categories are financial, internal business, customer, and learning and growth, which have been shown to improve managerial decision making when used.[26] Figure 2.1 is an example of the balanced scorecard model.

Watch Dr. Kaplan discussing his balanced scorecard model

Also referred to as simply **scorecarding**, 80% of large U.S. businesses are either using it now or have previously used it. The Service Spotlight above describes the use of a performance scorecard system at Global Workplace Solutions. Web-based scorecards are also used and are referred to as **dashboards**. All of these kinds of report-card performance systems provide a common goal and starting place for discussions among department personnel.

Many companies have reported notable successes with the use of scorecards. According to Shell Canada's human resource director, John Hofmeister, "It gives us better and better alignment (between all operating units) and focuses attention on what's important and on results. In addition, the group's reward structure is linked directly to the scorecard."[27]

balanced scorecard Developed by Drs. Robert Kaplan and David Norton, a performance scorecard using 20 to 30 performance measures, balanced across four categories.

scorecarding Using some form of balanced scorecard.

dashboards Web-based scorecards.

Figure 2.1 The Balanced Scorecard Model

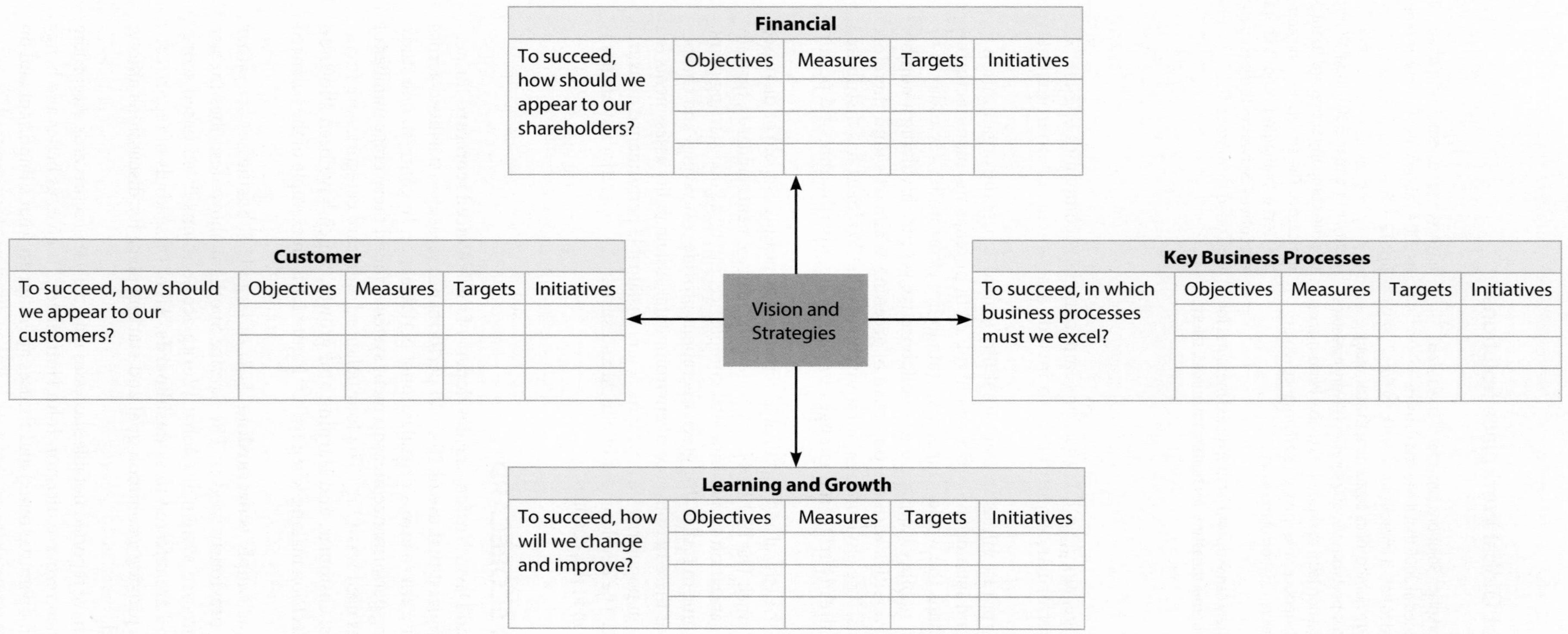

Financial

To succeed, how should we appear to our shareholders?	Objectives	Measures	Targets	Initiatives

Customer

To succeed, how should we appear to our customers?	Objectives	Measures	Targets	Initiatives

Vision and Strategies

Key Business Processes

To succeed, in which business processes must we excel?	Objectives	Measures	Targets	Initiatives

Learning and Growth

To succeed, how will we change and improve?	Objectives	Measures	Targets	Initiatives

Source: Adapted from "Linking the Balanced Scorecard to Strategy," by R. Kaplan and D. Norton, 1996, *California Management Review, 39*(1), 53–79.

EMERGING ISSUE IN PERFORMANCE: BIG DATA ANALYTICS

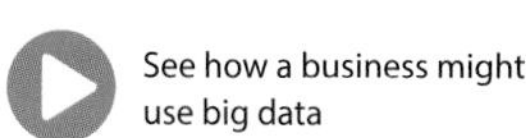
See how a business might use big data

Discussions of the use of big data and big data analytics are appearing frequently these days in business journals and trade magazines. Big data is making it possible for managers to know much more about their businesses; and this knowledge is leading to improved decisions, lower costs, and better performance. **Big data** is generally defined as large volumes of data collected (often in real time or near real time), using information technologies, from a number of sources including social networks, website clicks, emails, sales information, insurance information, billing information, and warranty information, just to name a few. When organizations analyze this huge (or "big") array of data using predictive modeling techniques to help uncover problems or opportunities to create value, this is referred to as **big data analytics**. Vastly improved computer memory and speed over the past 10 years has allowed big data analytics to gather momentum. In many cases, big data analytics is being used by marketing departments to predict what customers will buy or need in the future.

Early users of big data were large retailers like Amazon and Target. Amazon used customers' past purchases to create other product recommendations for carefully segmented customers. Target began with a simple question: How can we identify pregnant women before other retailers do? The answer was through analyzing Target's own credit card sales data. Today, use of big data is growing exponentially. In a 2014 study of marketing professionals by London-based Circle Research, 43% said they were already using big data, while an additional 40% expected to use it within the next three years. Furthermore, 61% of the respondents said data acquisition was their top internal marketing priority.[28]

Many industries are beginning to discover ways to benefit from big data analytics. For example, according to Tarek Elsawy, chief medical officer for the Cleveland (Ohio) Clinic's Community Physician Partnership and Quality Alliance, "Data are the currency that drives improvements. The ultimate goal is accurate and actionable data—not data that are three months old, but data that can be made available to providers in real time. The ability to integrate large amounts of clinical, financial, and demographic data will get us much closer to that goal."[29] Big data has had a large impact on the agricultural industry according to Mark Green, VP at RevCo, a software provider for the agricultural retail sector. "We used to ask a customer, 'What's keeping you up at night?' Thanks to the intelligence provided by big data, this has been replaced by the statement, 'Here's what should be keeping you up at night,'" says Green.[30]

A few years ago, retailer Sears tried to tailor personalized promotions to customers using huge amounts of customer, product, and promotional data concerning its Sears, Craftsman, and Lands' End brands. The company found it took about eight weeks to generate these promotions, at which point they were no longer optimal. Since these data were housed in separate databases and data warehouses maintained by the different brands, it simply took too long to integrate the data. Sears then invested in a cluster of servers coordinated by specialized software to collect, combine, and analyze data from all sources. It now takes less than a week to generate even better-personalized promotions than before.[31]

In 2012, farm products producer John Deere began using software that allowed equipment, owners, operators, dealers, and agricultural consultants to share data with one another, which helps farmers enhance productivity and efficiencies. Sensors on equipment help the farmers manage their fleets, decreasing downtime and saving fuel. This information, combined with historical and real-time data of weather predictions, soil conditions, and crop features, is collected, analyzed, and made available to farmers and other users on John Deere's MyJohnDeere.com Internet portal. Farmers can share information directly with advisors for remote advice while in the field, using an iPhone.[32]

Big data is being used to enhance security as well. Hewlett-Packard says users of its security information and event management systems can now integrate all of the data collected with HP's content analytics engine. According to HP, "This combination automatically recognizes the context, concepts, sentiments, and usage patterns related to how users interact with all forms of data," giving businesses a better way to translate raw security data into more actionable intelligence. This will allow security managers to better track individual users' behavior patterns and spot signs of unusual activity.[33]

And finally, there is a growing demand for real-time big data analytics offered as a service in the cloud. Some organizations are experimenting with big data analytics tools, but

big data Large volumes of data collected using information technologies from a number of sources including social networks, website clicks, emails, sales information, insurance information, billing information, and warranty information, just to name a few.

big data analytics When organizations analyze a huge array of data using predictive modeling techniques to help pinpoint problems or opportunities to create value.

find that costs can be high and implementation requires specialized skills. With companies such as Virtustream's secure cloud, combined with Metamarkets' real-time analytics and Skilled Analysts' consulting services, organizations can have access to tailored big data solutions that can be run on demand with professional services as needed. A large number of these cloud service arrangements are now available. "Enterprises need real-time analytics to take full advantage of big data, and we are excited to provide a cloud environment that is secure and scalable for their large-scale data projects," says Rodney Rogers, chairman and CEO of Virtustream. "Big data analytics delivered from our cloud give these enterprises flexible, real-time data solutions to make better business decisions," he adds.[34]

TRENDS IN OPERATIONS STRATEGIES: THE GROWING IMPORTANCE OF ETHICS AND SUSTAINABILITY

2.5 Demonstrate how corporate ethics and sustainability impact corporate and operations strategies

Along with ongoing plans to implement strategies to reduce costs, while improving quality and customer service, many organizations are finding it necessary to improve their environmental and ethical reputations. The demands by many customers today for greater ethical and environmental performance are placing added pressures on firms to improve in these areas. Recall that this was the topic of the Manufacturing Spotlight on Dow Chemical and was briefly mentioned in Chapter 1.

Today, these trends have become the drivers of many operations management initiatives in the key areas of purchasing, manufacturing, and finished goods delivery. This can include, for example, the use of ethical and sustainable purchasing policies, ethical hiring practices, recycling and other green manufacturing initiatives, and fuel-efficient delivery vehicles. Developing socially responsible and environmentally friendly operations strategies that also create a competitive advantage is no easy task. However, it is being done successfully.

BUSINESS ETHICS

Business ethics can be described as the application of ethical principles to business situations, and has been very widely studied. Generally speaking, there are two approaches to deciding whether or not an action is ethical. The first approach is known as **utilitarianism**. It maintains that an ethical act creates the greatest good for the greatest number of people. The second approach is known as **rights and duties**. It states that some actions are simply right, without any regard to the consequences. This approach maintains that ethical actions recognize the rights of others and the duties those rights impose on the ones performing the actions.

utilitarianism An ethical act that creates the greatest good for the greatest number of people.

rights and duties Some actions are simply right, without any regard to the consequences.

As discussed in Chapter 1, the practice of business ethics is also referred to as corporate social responsibility (CSR). Much of the discussion regarding corporate social responsibility argues that corporations should act ethically, just as individuals should. Today, many firms have formal CSR initiatives that are integral parts of their hiring, purchasing, logistics, and manufacturing practices. One such example is discussed in the Service Spotlight below.

SERVICE SPOTLIGHT

CSR at Standard Chartered Bank

London-based Standard Chartered Bank partners with blindness charities worldwide as a way to reduce preventable blindness, and it has found many other added benefits coming from this effort. The firm's culture and brand have changed—its CSR efforts motivate employees to volunteer and lend technical assistance to local charities, the bank has introduced talking ATMs, and it also hires blind individuals to work in its call centers. Standard Chartered finds its employees are becoming more motivated, creative, and engaged at work as a result of their volunteering efforts.[35]

The purchase of **fair trade products** is an activity that is becoming increasingly popular, as firms seek to demonstrate a more ethical approach to purchasing. A fair trade product refers to one that is manufactured or grown by a disadvantaged producer in a developing country who received a fair price for the goods. More likely than not, the term *fair trade* refers to farm products such as coffee, cocoa, sugar, tea, and cotton that are produced in developing countries and exported to large firms in developed countries.

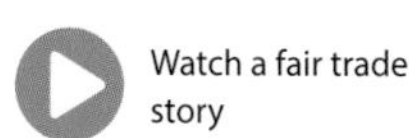
Watch a fair trade story

Starbucks Coffee Company takes a comprehensive approach to ethical sourcing, using responsible purchasing practices; farmer support; economic, social, and environmental standards; industry collaboration; and community development programs. The cornerstone of the company's approach are the Coffee and Farmer Equity (C.A.F.E.) Practices, one of the coffee industry's first set of sustainability standards. Developed in collaboration with Conservation International (CI), C.A.F.E. Practices has helped Starbucks create a long-term supply of high-quality coffee while positively impacting the lives of coffee farmers and their communities.[36]

Protecting the Earth's environment has been a topic of concern for many years, and it has more recently become a popular topic of debate as politicians and voters have made global warming an election issue. Former U.S. vice president and longtime environmentalist Al Gore, for example, was the focus of the award-winning 2006 global warming documentary *An Inconvenient Truth*. Many others, such as David Bower, longtime director of the Sierra Club; Eileen O'Neill, head of the Discovery Channel's Planet Green multimedia initiative; and Patrick Moore, director and cofounder of Greenpeace International, have played major roles in championing the modern environmental movement.[37]

SUSTAINABILITY

In Chapter 1, **sustainability** was defined as a broad term that includes "being green" as well as some aspects of CSR, and financial performance. Simply put, sustainability means doing the right social and environmental things in ways that make economic sense. The objectives, then, are not only to sustain the world we live in, but to sustain the organization as well. The idea of sustainability is certainly not new, as evidenced by the way early Native Americans thought and lived, and as Gifford Pinchot, the first chief forester of the U.S. Forest Service, wrote in an article in 1908:

> Are we going to protect our springs of prosperity, our raw material of industry and commerce and employer of capital and labor combined; or are we going to dissipate them? According as we accept or ignore our responsibility as trustees of the nation's welfare, our children and our children's children for uncounted generations will call us blessed, or will lay their suffering at our doors.[38]

fair trade products Products that are manufactured or grown by a disadvantaged producer in a developing country who received a fair price for the goods.

sustainability Doing the right social and environmental things in ways that make economic sense.

triple bottom line A firm's efforts to provide social, environmental, and economic benefits to stakeholders. Also referred to as the "three P's," which stands for *people, planet,* and *profit.*

Recently, the term **triple bottom line** has been coined to describe a firm's efforts to provide social, environmental, and economic benefits to stakeholders. This has also been referred to as the "three P's," which stands for *people, planet,* and *profit.* The EarthView program at Pennsylvania-based hotel operator Hersha Hospitality Management is a good example of implementing the triple bottom line. Housekeepers collect unused soaps and shampoo and donate them to the nonprofit group Clean the World, which then repackages and distributes the items to developing countries. This allows people to wash their hands more frequently, reducing infections and associated illnesses; 90 tons of Hersha's waste annually is diverted from landfills; and communication of this program to Hersha's guests differentiates the firm from its competitors, creating more repeat business.[39]

iStock/fatido

When businesses care about environmental stewardship and social progress, economic growth occurs, benefitting everyone.

Kroger, the largest grocery retailer in the United States, started its triple bottom line food recycling program in 2008. It rescues edible but no longer saleable produce, then donates it to food banks. By 2011, more than 90% of Kroger's stores nationwide were participating in the program. As part of the effort, Kroger works with Feeding America, a hunger relief charity, to help spread the word to other grocery retailers. Kroger donates 50 million pounds of food annually to local food banks. This also means 50 million pounds of food waste diverted from landfills and incinerators, saving Kroger $1.5 million in disposal fees. Through Kroger's sharing of its program, 1 billion meals have been served using food once destined for dumpsters.[40]

ETHICAL AND SUSTAINABLE OPERATIONS STRATEGIES

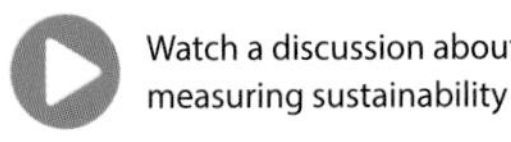
Watch a discussion about measuring sustainability

Traditionally, operations management strategies have focused on supporting cost, quality, or customer service strategies at the corporate level. Many corporate executives will argue that acting ethically and sustainably can also support these traditional strategies in ways that customers and trading partners prefer. Consequently, ethical and sustainable strategies have become relevant and useful tools for operations managers, as they make plans to support the firm's overall strategic goals.

Today, Walmart has adopted a strategy of sustainability, integrated throughout its supply chains, to achieve zero operations waste by the year 2025. Ninety years ago, the Ford Motor Company also provided a tremendous example of the way sustainable and ethical operations could be used to support a low-cost corporate strategy: Wooden boxes used to ship purchased parts to Ford's River Rouge, Michigan, assembly plant were used for the Model T's floorboard; any leftover wood was used to supply charcoal for Henry Ford's Kingsford Charcoal business. Additionally, Ford set wages to a relatively high $5 per day, creating dedicated and motivated employees who also had enough money to buy a Model T.[41]

The American Society for Quality (ASQ) released an executive study in 2011 entitled "CSR and Quality: A Powerful and Untapped Connection," which described the many linkages between CSR and quality. For example, since quality generally can be defined as excelling in all goods and services important to customers, and if CSR performance is important to customers, then this should fall under the "quality" umbrella for the organization. Also, achieving high performance in either quality or CSR requires the same approaches and resources within the firm. Both require a systems approach, the establishment of clear outcomes, and the alignment of processes to achieve those outcomes.[42]

A similar case can be made for the linkages between sustainability and customer service. If customers require firms to provide evidence of sustainability (or CSR, for that matter), then high performance in these areas becomes part of providing good customer service. The CEO of Illinois-based Deere and Company, for example, stated that sustainability helped the company achieve better customer service performance.[43]

SAGE edge™

Visit edge.sagepub.com/wisner to help you accomplish your coursework goals in an easy-to-use learning environment.

- Mobile-friendly eFlashcards
- Mobile-friendly practice quizzes
- A complete online action plan
- Chapter summaries with learning objectives
- Excel templates to assist with practice problems
- Original video case studies that demonstrate chapter concepts in action

SUMMARY

This chapter introduced the interrelated topics of mission statements, corporate strategy, operations strategy, performance measurement, and ethics and sustainability. Mission statements provide the competitive direction for the firm, and corporate and operations strategies are derived from and support the mission. Firms need performance measures to be able to track progress toward the firm's goals and for the firm to understand its strengths and weaknesses. Financial and productivity performance measures are discussed, including the problems occurring when using only these as performance measures. An emerging issue is big data analytics, which can generate useful, real-time information for firms, improving decision making and performance. Ethics and sustainability are also important current topics in operations, which impact mission and strategy formulations.

KEY TERMS

Balanced scorecard, 37
Big data, 39
Big data analytics, 39
Core competencies, 29
Dashboards, 37
Economies of scale, 27
Fair trade products, 41
Mission statement, 26
Multiple-factor productivity, 33
Operations strategies, 28
Performance measures, 31
Productivity growth rate, 34
Rights and duties, 40
Scorecarding, 37
Service recovery, 28
Single-factor productivity, 34
Strategic planning, 26
Strategy, 26
Strategy trade-offs, 31
Sustainability, 41
The three competitive dimensions, 27
Triple bottom line, 41
Utilitarianism, 40

FORMULA REVIEW

Net profit margin $= \dfrac{\text{net income after taxes}}{\text{net sales}}$

Current ratio $= \dfrac{\text{current assets}}{\text{current liabilities}}$

Inventory turnover $= \dfrac{\text{cost of good sold}}{\text{average inventory value}}$

Purchasing efficiency $= \dfrac{\text{actual purchase cost for year}}{\text{purchase cost goal for year}}$

Productivity $= \dfrac{\text{outputs}}{\text{inputs}}$

Single-factor productivity (such as labor productivity) =

$$\frac{\text{units of output}}{\text{cost of labor}}$$

Multiple-factor productivity (for example) =

$$\frac{\text{units of output}}{\text{costs of (labor + captial + energy + material)}}$$

Productivity growth rate % $= \dfrac{P_2 - P_1}{P_1}(100)$,

where P_1 and P_2 are productivities in periods 1 and 2.

SOLVED PROBLEMS

1.

	2012	2013
Output (books sold)	25,466	27,299
Inputs:		
Labor cost	53,482	57,242
Materials cost	4,286	4,930
Lease cost	12,000	12,600
Energy cost	4,250	4,105

Answer:

Single-factor productivities:

$$\text{Labor} = \frac{25466}{53482} = 0.476 \text{ books/labor \$ (2012)};$$

$$\frac{27299}{57242} = 0.477 \text{ (2013)}$$

$$\text{Materials} = \frac{25466}{4286} = 5.942 \text{ books/materials \$ (2012)};$$

$$\frac{27299}{4930} = 5.537 \text{ (2013)}$$

$$\text{Lease} = \frac{25466}{12000} = 2.122 \text{ books/lease \$ (2012)};$$

$$\frac{27299}{12600} = 2.167 \text{ (2013)}$$

$$\text{Energy} = \frac{25466}{4250} = 5.992 \text{ books/energy \$ (2012)};$$

$$\frac{27299}{4105} = 6.650 \text{ (2013)}$$

Multiple-factor productivity:

$$\frac{25466}{(53482+4286+12000+4250)} = 0.344 \text{ books/\$ (2012);}$$

$$\frac{27299}{78877} = 0.346 \text{ (2013)}$$

Productivity growth rates (2012 to 2013):

$$\text{Labor} = \frac{0.477-0.476}{0.476}(100) = 0.2\%$$

$$\text{Materials} = \frac{5.537-5.942}{5.942}(100) = -6.8\%$$

$$\text{Lease} = \frac{2.167-2.122}{2.122}(100) = 2.1\%$$

$$\text{Energy} = \frac{6.650-5.992}{5.992}(100) = 11.0\%$$

2. Net sales $526,485

Cost of goods sold (purchased items)	$128,116
Net income after taxes	$ 58,226
Current assets	$416,198
Current liabilities	$383,655
Average inventory value	$114,523

Answer:

Financial measures:

$$\text{Net profit margin} = \frac{58226}{526485} = 0.111 = 11.1\%$$

$$\text{Current ratio} = \frac{416198}{383655} = 1.08$$

$$\text{Inventory turnover} = \frac{128116}{114523} = 1.19$$

$$\text{Purchasing efficiency} = \frac{128116}{150000} = 0.854 = 85.4\%$$

REVIEW QUESTIONS

1. Define mission statement and corporate strategy.
2. What are the three competitive dimensions firms use to compete?
3. What are economies of scale?
4. Define the seven aspects of customer service.
5. What are operations strategies, and how are they different from corporate strategies?
6. What do operations strategies have to do with core competencies?
7. How can operations align its strategies with that of the corporation?
8. What does performance measurement have to do with corporate strategy?
9. What is a balanced scorecard?
10. How is a dashboard different from a scorecard?
11. What is big data? Big data analytics?
12. What is business ethics? How does that differ from corporate social responsibility?
13. What is a fair trade product?
14. What is sustainability? Is this a new concept?
15. To what does the triple bottom line refer?

DISCUSSION QUESTIONS

1. What would be a good mission statement for your university?
2. How would you rank, in order of importance, the three competitive dimensions for your university? For your favorite restaurant?
3. Explain economies of scale using a manufacturing firm; your university.
4. Using a bank and then a fast-food outlet, describe all of the seven customer service aspects.
5. What is the core competency of McDonald's? Southwest Airlines? Can they do it better than any of their competitors?
6. Strategy trade-offs must be considered in operations. Describe what these might be for a high-quality bicycle manufacturer and then a low-cost bicycle manufacturer.
7. Why are performance measures so important to the organization?
8. How can financial and productivity measures be both good and bad for tracking a firm's performance?
9. Using the formula for labor productivity, describe all the ways a firm could increase labor productivity.
10. Using Table 2.2, list a number of performance measures you might use for a sandwich shop.
11. How could a balanced scorecard help to improve a firm's performance measurements? Design one for your performance as a student.
12. Why is big data analytics becoming so important now?
13. Could a small business use big data analytics? Explain.
14. Are there any fair trade producers in the United States today?
15. How could your university use the triple bottom line? Is it already using it?

EXERCISES AND PROJECTS

1. Go online and find the mission statements of three organizations not mentioned in this chapter and analyze them for completeness. See if you can improve each mission statement. Which of the three strategies does each organization use to compete? Defend your answer.
2. Go online to www.zappos.com and pretend you are looking for some shoes or clothing for a graduation ceremony or party. Be picky. Don't buy anything. Report on how long it took before you were talking to someone; how friendly the employee was; how willing they were to help you; how long you had them on the phone. Tell them at the end you were doing this as a school project and report on what they said.
3. If you work, or are a member of some organization, find out how managers measure performance. Compare it to Table 2.2 and describe what they could do to improve their use of performance measurements. Are they using a scorecard? If so, describe it. If not, see if you can develop one for the organization.
4. Find a fair trade product not discussed in this chapter and report on how it is produced, where it is produced, and who it benefits.

PROBLEMS

Use the following information for Problems 1 and 2:

During the past month, the Blakester Lounge served 1,500 customers with very few complaints. Its labor cost was $3,000; material cost was $800; energy cost was $200; and building lease cost was $1,500. For the month prior to that, its customers served was 1,320, with labor cost of $2,900; material cost $860; energy cost $185; and building lease cost $1,500.

1. Calculate the single-factor productivities and the overall multiple-factor productivities for each of the two months.
2. Calculate the productivity growth for each productivity measure in Problem 1, from the first to the second month.
3. During the past four months, the units produced and the labor hours are as shown here. Compute the monthly labor productivities and productivity growth for the periods.

	March	April	May	June
Units produced	1260	1340	1293	1324
Labor hours	328	332	321	318

4. Jim and Rachel are concerned about their company's desired annual productivity growth rate. For the upcoming three years and the expected labor hours, determine the production output required to maintain a four-percent annual productivity growth rate.

	2016	2017	2018	2019
Units produced	42,240			
Labor hours	20,000	21,500	21,700	22,000

5. Calculate the single-factor productivities and the total productivity, given the information here.

Output	Inputs
325,000 units	6400 labor hours @ $15.00 per hour
Sales price = $1249.00/unit	Material cost = $40,625,000
	Utilities cost = $4,400

6. For the previous month, the C. J. Lounge served 1,500 customers with very few complaints. Its labor cost was $3,000; material cost was $800; energy cost was $200; and building lease cost was $1,500. Calculate the single-factor productivities and the overall multiple-factor productivity. How could it improve the productivity?

7. George's Ski Shop rents snow skis during the winter season, and employs five people. The owner wants to track productivity performance measures using the data shown here. Determine the single-factor productivities and multiple-factor productivities for the two years. Discuss potential problems that you find.

Inputs and Outputs	2014
Ski rental revenue	$66,000
Labor cost	$10,800
Lease payments	$24,000
Inputs and Outputs	**2015**
Ski rental revenue	$69,500
Labor cost	$11,600
Lease payments	$24,500

8. Use the following information to analyze the financial information and inputs and outputs of the organization from 2015 to 2016:

Financial Information	2015 Results	2016 Results
Net sales	$1,372,000	$1,416,400
Cost of goods sold (purchased items)	$622,000	$681,000
Net income after taxes	$29,400	$34,800
Current assets	$822,000	$841,000
Current liabilities	$628,000	$679,000
Average inventory value	$288,500	$312,000
Inputs and Outputs		
Units produced	22,000	24,870
Labor costs	$228,200	$242,000
Lease payments	$24,000	$26,500
Energy costs	$18,300	$18,900

Use the following information for Problems 9 and 10:

The Hayley-Girl Soup Co. operations manager wants to calculate a number of performance statistics for an upcoming meeting using the information shown here:

Net sales = $1,450,627	Cost of goods sold (purchases) = $675,860
Current assets = $327,176	Current liabilities = $86,904
Rent = $144,000	Average inventory value = $163,465
Labor cost = $226,693	Annual production = 2,608,184 cans
Net income after taxes = $94,153	

9. Calculate the profit margin, current ratio, inventory turnover, and purchasing efficiency (given an annual purchasing cost goal of $600,000).

10. Calculate the single-factor and multiple-factor productivities.

11. Given the information here, calculate the financial performance.

Net sales = $10,187,125	Cost of goods sold (purchases) = $4,325,219
Current assets = $12,427,000	Current liabilities = $2,432,804
Average inventory value = $209,398	Net income after taxes = $1,745,286

12. Mary Jane's Beauty Shop has recently invested money to add more equipment to enable more services to be offered at the shop. Given the following information, evaluate its investment.

2014	2015
net income = $752,000	equipment investment = $28,000
labor cost = $152,000	net income = $763,000
energy cost = $18,000	labor cost = $154,000
material cost = $32,000	energy cost = $18,800
	material cost = $33,500

CASE STUDIES

CASE 1: Blue Nile—A Passion for Perfection

When Mark Vadon, a Stanford MBA, searched for an engagement ring in 1998, he came across a small Internet diamond retailer. Just months later, he purchased the company and named it Blue Nile, which is now the largest online retailer of diamonds.[1] The company, based in Seattle, Washington, has less than 200 employees. It has a fulfillment center in Dublin, Ireland, but no brick-and-mortar retail stores. Over the last 15 years, Blue Nile has been recognized by the *Seattle Times, Forbes, BusinessWeek,* and *Wall Street Journal* for its unique online business model and rapid growth.[2] By the end of 2013, Blue Nile had reached a net sales of $450 million, 84% of which was in the United States.[3] More than 67% of the U.S. sales, or $255.8 million, were engagement ring orders. Blue Nile ships to 45 different countries in North America, Asia, Europe, and the Middle East, and accepts 25 currencies for payment. Its overseas sales revenue contribution was $14 million in 2013, a 30% growth from 2011. Harvey Kanter, CEO of the company since 2012, predicts continued growth in the international market, especially in China, where about 10 million couples get married each year (five times that of the United States).[4]

The jewelry industry has three major players, which accounted for more than 20% of the total market in 2013.[5] Signet Jewelers Ltd. acquired the Zales Corporation in May 2013, and the combined company has $6.2 billion in revenues and more than 3,600 locations.[6] Tiffany & Co. has an annual sales of $4.03 billion (more than nine times that of Blue Nile), and 289 stores.[7] Helzberg Diamonds has an annual sales of $692 million[8] and more than 240 stores. Blue Nile trails these competitors and has established its unique position in the industry by selling exclusively online and maintaining a low profit margin (18.8%[4] compared to Tiffany's 59% and Signet's 29%[9]).

The online model allows Blue Nile to display almost 200,000 diamonds for sale without purchasing the inventory upfront, while traditional jewelry retailers usually carry up to 70,000 items, or a year's worth of inventory. Blue Nile understands customers' frustrations of not knowing what to look for in luxury jewelry and offers online education and tutorials for diamond, gemstone, pearl, and metal items. Blue Nile provides customizations of many products—for the diamonds, for instance, customers can specify the shape, cut, color, clarity, and carat, and can get cost comparisons before making their purchases. According to the trade publication *Jewelers Circular Keystone*, Blue Nile's typical engagement ring buyer spends $5,600, compared with a national average of $3,200. Wikipedia quotes an average carat weight of 0.90, while the largest purchase was a 10-carat diamond sold for $1.5 million. However, some customers may hesitate to purchase jewelry worth over $5,000 without seeing and testing it. To set customers' minds at ease, Blue Nile provides insurance, diamond price match guarantees, a lifetime diamond upgrade, and free FedEx shipping and return on all orders. In addition, Blue Nile launched virtual try-on for iPhones in October 2014.[10] Customers take a picture of their hands and then try on different engagement rings.

Blue Nile is committed to ethical sourcing. It purchases diamonds only through suppliers who follow the Kimberley Process, which was established by the United Nations in 2003 to monitor diamond production and trade, and to ensure that diamond purchases are not financing rebel movements and their allies. Blue Nile also makes sure that its suppliers meet human rights, social, and environment standards. It currently does not source diamonds from Zimbabwe due to reports of human rights violations. It is also committed to sourcing gold from recycled and secondary sources.

DISCUSSION QUESTIONS

1. How does Blue Nile compete with traditional brick-and-mortar jewelers? What is its competitive advantage? Should it build brick-and-mortar stores?
2. What are the challenges ahead for Blue Nile?
3. What could it do to expand its overseas markets?
4. In addition to ethical sourcing, what other areas of corporate sustainability could Blue Nile consider?

Note: Written by Stella Hua, PhD, C.P.I.M., Western Washington University, Bellingham, WA. This case was prepared solely to provide material for class discussion. The author does not intend to illustrate either effective or ineffective handling of a managerial situation.

Sources:

1. "When Buying a Diamond Starts With a Mouse," by G. Rivlin, 2007, *New York Times*, http://www.nytimes.com/2007/01/07/business/yourmoney/07nile.html?ref=bluenileinc&_r=1&
2. Blue Nile awards are found at: http://www.bluenile.com/blue-nile-awards
3. Blue Nile 2013 Annual Report, http://investor.bluenile.com/annuals.cfm
4. "Why This Company Is the Best Play on the Affordable Luxury Theme," by M. Lin, 2014, http://www.fool.com/investing/general/2014/06/13/why-this-company-is-the-best-play-on-the-affordabl.aspx
5. Jewelry Stores Market Research Report, October 2014, "Jewelry Stores in the US: Market Research Report," NAICS 44831.
6. "Signet Jewelers Completes Acquisition of Zale Corp," by D. Abril, May 29, 2014, *Dallas Business Journal*, http://www.bizjournals.com/dallas/news/2014/05/29/signet-jewelers-completes-acquisition-of-zale-corp.html?s=print
7. Tiffany & Co. Annual Report, January 2014.
8. Hot 100 Retailers, https://nrf.com/resources/top-retailers-lists/hot-100-retailers/hot-100-retailers-2013
9. TIF Gross Profit Margin Benchmark, http://ycharts.com/companies/TIF/gross_profit_margin
10. "Blue Nile Adds Virtual Engagement Ring Try-on to Mobile App," by E. Winters, October 13, 2014, Price Scope, http://www.pricescope.com/blog/blue-nile-adds-virtual-engagement-ring-try-mobile-app

CASE 2: The Woods Coffee

The Woods Coffee is a family-run coffee shop chain, started in Lynden, Washington, in 2002. It is currently opening its 17th store in Western Washington, which Starbucks, Seattle's Best Coffee, and Tully's also call home. Wes Herman, the owner of The Woods Coffee shops, created the business with the help of his four teenage children, who frequently spent an average of $150 to $200 per month on coffee.[1] They helped to pick the business name, which fits perfectly with the Pacific Norwest community and lifestyle, and designed the company logo. The family is still actively involved in the business. Their efforts have paid off—The Woods Coffee was named "the Best Coffee Shop in Western Washington" in 2010 and 2011, by *Evening Magazine,* among more than 300 coffee shops nominated.[2]

The Woods Coffee offers a limited selection of fair-trade-certified (FTC) organic and Direct Trade coffees. It serves a variety of blends such as Brown Bear, Swiss Water Decaf, Espresso Blend, and Viking Blend, and started serving its own in-house roasted coffee in all stores in May 2014.[3] The coffee is roasted at its headquarters in Lynden and delivered to each store daily. The Woods has also been baking all of its bakery items in-house since 2011. It uses ingredients from local businesses whenever possible, including Edaleen Dairy, Maberry Berries, and Shepherd's Grain.[3] All of The Woods Coffee locations feature river rocks, open beams, and fireplaces, which are reflections of the Northwest. The shops are built to LEED green standards and use local materials and local laborers in their construction processes.

The Woods Coffee gives back to the community in a variety of ways. The company organizes different fund-raising events to support orphans and underprivileged children. It is also the official coffee for the annual Ski to Sea race in Bellingham. The Woods Coffee has made a long-term commitment in partnering with Western Washington University by developing and selling the WWU-branded "Viking Blend" coffee, with one dollar from every sale of the 100% FTC coffee going directly to WWU scholarships.[4] The Woods Coffee also regularly sponsors various campus and off-campus events and has become a well-recognized member of its community.

DISCUSSION QUESTIONS

1. How does The Woods Coffee compete with Starbucks or other major coffee chains?
2. Suggest some other things The Woods Coffee could do to compete.
3. Should the company expand its locations outside of the Western Washington area? Why?

Note: Written by Stella Hua, PhD, C.P.I.M., Western Washington University, Bellingham, WA. This case was prepared solely to provide material for class discussion. The author does not intend to illustrate either effective or ineffective handling of a managerial situation. Printed with permission from The Woods Coffee.

Sources:

1. Interview with Wes Herman, owner; also see The Woods Coffee story, http://vimeo.com/1653526
2. See The Woods Coffee Blog, http://woodscoffee.tumblr.com
3. See The Woods Coffee website, http://www.thewoodscoffee.com
4. "Wes Herman and Woods Coffee Receive WWU Community Volunteer Award," *PRweb*, May 31, 2013, http://www.prweb.com/releases/2013/5/prweb10782907.htm

CASE 3: Viking Sensors—The Triple Bottom Line

Viking Sensors manufactures switches and sensors for industrial equipment in Western Washington. It is also a community leader embracing the triple bottom line sustainability strategy (enhancing the 3P's, or *people, planet,* and *profit*). Throughout the past decade, it has embedded this culture in every way it conducts business.

Viking Sensors cares a great deal about the health and wellness of its employees. Before moving to the current facility, Viking looked for a facility with many windows and skylights to maximize the natural light. It added indoor plants and trees, and made sure the entire facility was ergonomically friendly. It provided chairs designed to increase employees' comfort and prevent them from injury. Each employee is cross-trained within the different cells to prevent boredom and reduce the repetitiveness of doing the same tasks. Viking Sensors provides tuition and workday scheduling accommodations to employees who wish to pursue further education.

Viking's core values support the sustainability of the planet. It has a LEED Gold Certified building. It partnered with Puget Sound Energy to add solar panels to its facility. The solar panel implementation will generate enough electricity to cover its needs, and the extra electricity will be sold back to Puget Sound Energy. It also plans on adding a 10,000 gallon rainwater cistern to bring in nonpotable water. It recycles 80% of its scrap and reuses 15%. Lean principles such as Jidoka and Poka-Yoke have been utilized to reduce overall process-related defects. Viking actively seeks out local suppliers with similar philosophies and maintains long-term partnerships with them. In addition, it keeps minimum inventories on the floor through use of blanket purchase orders and its JIT programs.

All of the products manufactured by Viking are made-to-order. This requires minimal raw materials, components, and finished goods inventories, and finished products are pulled through the manufacturing process using kanbans. As a result, Viking is able to maintain product flow with minimal cash tied up in inventory. Another practice Viking utilizes to maintain profits is inspecting for quality throughout the manufacturing process, allowing it to detect defects early in the process.

Bill Spencer, chief operating officer, is pondering what's next as it continues to preserve the triple bottom line culture. Should it move to a Platinum certified building? Obtain ISO 14000 certification? Pursue the Benefit Corporation (B-Corp) designation? (A benefit corporation is a new class of corporation that voluntarily meets higher standards of corporate purpose, accountability, and transparency.) Viking is considering the impact of its decisions on workers, the community, and the environment, in addition to shareholders.

DISCUSSION QUESTIONS

1. What is triple bottom line? How should it integrate with corporate and operations strategies?
2. How does Viking Sensors incorporate the triple bottom line into its business practices?
3. Among the future initiatives Bill Spencer is considering, which do you think the company should pursue? Why?
4. Discuss some other sustainability practices and certifications Viking could consider.

Note: Written by Stella Hua, PhD, C.P.I.M., Western Washington University, Bellingham, WA. This case was based on a student team project and prepared solely to provide material for class discussion. The author has disguised names and other identifying information to protect confidentiality and does not intend to illustrate either effective or ineffective handling of a managerial situation.

VIDEO CASE STUDY

Learn more about ***strategy*** from real organizations that use operations management techniques every day. Craig Nielsen is a Principal at Digital Benefit Advisors, a national employee benefits firm. Craig decided long ago that he wanted his company to be a service organization, focusing on their clients over the bottom line, which continues to inform corporate strategy and mission statement to this day. Watch this short interview to find out more.

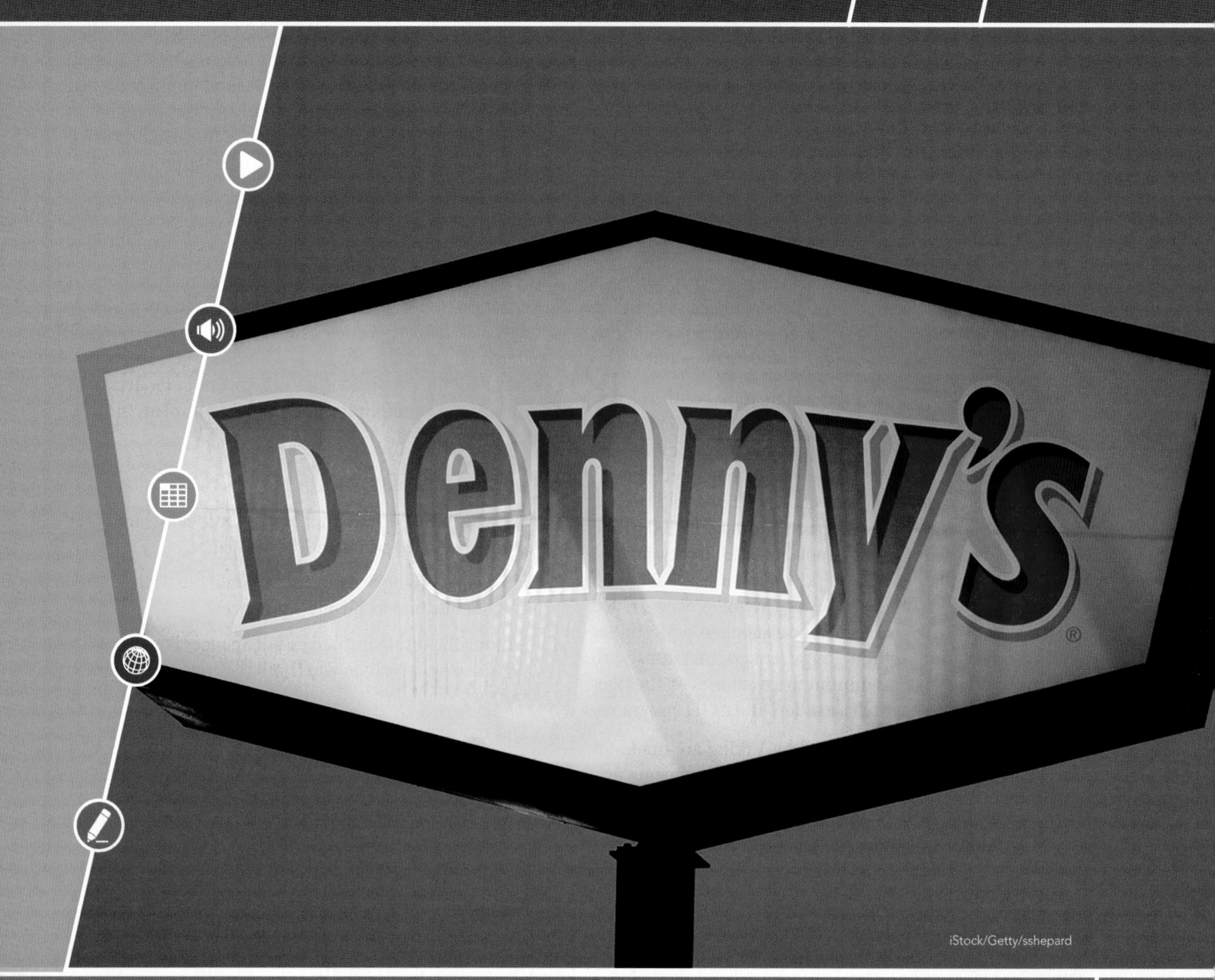

Design is intelligence made visible.

—**ALINA WHEELER,** business consultant, author, speaker[1]

A lot of times, people don't know what they want until you show it to them.

—**STEVE JOBS,** founder and former CEO, Apple, Inc.[2]

Above all else, align with customers. Win when they win. Win only when they win.

—**JEFF BEZOS,** founder and CEO, Amazon.com[3]

NEW PRODUCT AND SERVICE DESIGN

LEARNING OBJECTIVES

After completing this chapter, you should be able to:

3.1 Explain how new product ideas are generated, analyzed, selected, designed, and then manufactured
3.2 Summarize the steps in the product development process
3.3 Explain the practices used to reduce product development lead times
3.4 Describe how sustainability impacts product designs
3.5 Describe and critique some of the latest trends in product design

Master the content.

edge.sagepub.com/wisner

PRODUCT DESIGN AT DENNY'S

When South Carolina–based restaurant chain Denny's developed its late-night menu, customers were brought to the company's test kitchen at night to help the company develop its late-night dishes. "We did it at 11 o'clock at night," says Mark Chmiel, chief marketing and innovation officer for Denny's. "It had the vibe of what late night is all about."

These days, restaurant operators are becoming more adept at determining whether or not new products and promotions should be rolled out system-wide. Restaurant test marketing strategies include a thorough analysis of ideas before they ever leave corporate test kitchens and carefully selected market test sites. Most restaurant executives agree that product testing is necessary to avoid costly failures and potential loss of customers.

Because of the high level of competition, Denny's decided that actual customer testing of its breakfast items was necessary. "The number one thing they're looking for is new product ideas," Chmiel says. "They're looking for variety, they're looking for choice."

Using customer testing, Denny's found that customers were looking for a complete breakfast on the to-go menus, instead of just handheld breakfast sandwiches. Customers commented they could get these from fast-food restaurants. Once Denny's rolled out its new to-go menu, sales of the complete breakfasts exceeded its initial projections.

Typically, when testing new menu foods, Denny's market tests employ the same media as used with an actual system-wide launch. However, when it tested a menu line called Sizzlin' Breakfast Skillets in the spring of 2007, live-media weren't used, since the concept was entirely new and Denny's wanted to be first-to-market if the test proved successful. The skillet dishes tested very enthusiastically at a key location in Boise, Idaho, and then were rolled out system-wide soon afterward.[4]

INTRODUCTION

Developing new goods and services quickly is a source of competitive advantage for many firms. In fact, in many industries more than 40% of revenues are generated from new products introduced during the previous year. Companies that are first in the marketplace with new products can generate high revenue streams initially and make it tough for competitors to find any market share when their products are introduced. To be successful over the long haul, companies must be able to find out what customers want and then integrate these requirements into goods and services designs.

The product development process is complex because firms must consider a number of things, including product design and production time and costs, production capacity constraints, supply and distribution channels, and cost and quality goals. These, in turn, are impacted by existing products and processes, budgets, customers, and competitor products.

The most successful companies have their core competencies, plants, and equipment—as well as effective new product development processes—already in place, and they can "hit the ground running" whenever new product ideas emerge.

To remain competitive, companies must understand their local markets, as well as how their products can be adapted in other regional and global markets. They must observe, survey, and listen to their customers; benchmark their competitors; incorporate new technologies as they arise; and utilize supplier suggestions to design goods and services customers will want.

This chapter builds on the initial discussion of products from Chapter 1, including discussions of the environmental aspects affecting product design discussed in both Chapters 1 and 2. Additionally, discussions of some of the latest trends in the design of goods and services are presented.

DESIGN OF GOODS AND SERVICES

3.1 Explain how new product ideas are generated, analyzed, selected, designed, and then manufactured

Great product designs are created by great companies, as can be seen by looking, for instance, at iPhones and Apple, the Prius and Toyota, and Internet search and Google. These companies invested a large amount of time and effort in finding great employees, talking to potential and existing customers, and making things customers would want to use. The engineers who design Apple products, for example, make products *they want to use*. The products have to be intuitive, easy to understand, and easy to use.[5] Toyota just keeps roaring back, even after some product design problems led to tragic losses of life several years ago. Today, it sells more cars in the United States and around the world than any other car maker. Fifteen years ago, the Toyota Prius was dismissed by other automobile companies as a curiosity—today, most other car makers have hybrids, but over 60% of the hybrids sold in North America are still the Prius.[6] Google lives by a credo of 10 things, several of which are: focus on the user and all else will follow; do one thing really, really well; fast is better than slow; you can make money without being evil; and great just isn't good enough.[7] Product design has played a major role in the successes of these companies.

Product design is the process of making decisions about the characteristics, features, and performance of a company's goods and services. Product design must take into account how the item will be used and what functions will be required. Additionally, the product must perform safely and reliably, and be made economically, while still being attractive to potential customers. Poor goods and services designs will mean excess costs due to warranty repairs and product returns, as well as lower sales, and ultimately lost customers. The next section discusses a firm's core competency, followed by sections on goods design, services design, strategic fit, and contract manufacturers and services.

product design The process of making decisions about the characteristics, features, and performance of a company's product.

iStock/Sjoerdvander

Great products like the Toyota Prius are created by great companies.

CORE COMPETENCY

For continued success, firms must be good at doing something, and this should be reflected in the goods and services they sell. This refers to a firm's core competency. Specifically, a company's core competency is a capability that distinguishes it from its competitors. It is a unique expertise or skill set that cannot easily be reproduced or imitated by other companies. It is something a company does very well. One or more core competencies are what can create a competitive advantage for the firm, if they are translated effectively into the products the company sells. Over time, successful firms make continuous improvements to their core competencies through further training, use of technology, and continued top management support. Some examples of core competencies are shown in Table 3.1.

Table 3.1 Core Competency Examples

Company	Core Competency
McDonald's	Fast, standardized, inexpensive food; fun play areas for kids.
Walmart	Large selection of moderately priced goods; convenient locations.
Walt Disney Co.	Animation, themed attractions, and storytelling.
FedEx	Fast delivery anywhere in the world.

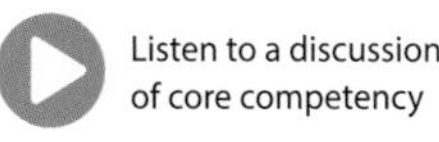
Listen to a discussion
of core competency

Blockbuster and Netflix provide good examples of how core competencies need to continue changing and improving to keep companies successful. Blockbuster, a video rental chain that began in 1985, grew to about 9,000 stores worldwide by 2004 and was the leader in movie rentals. Netflix began in 1997 as a movie rental-by-mail company, capitalizing on the popularity of DVDs, and the desire of customers to shop on the Internet, have more movie choices, and use the convenience of mail delivery. Netflix went public in 2002, with stock selling for $15 per share. At the same time, Blockbuster's share price was about $22. By 2005, Netflix had over 4 million subscription customers and was growing by 60–70% each year. Its mid-year share price was about $20. That same year, Blockbuster's share price had fallen to about $4. In 2007, Netflix introduced video streaming, which quickly began to replace DVD mailers. In 2009, Netflix partnered with consumer electronics companies to offer video streaming on Internet-connected TVs and other devices. By 2010, Netflix had 20 million subscription customers worldwide and had completely decimated the outdated Blockbuster rental service, forcing it to reorganize. By March 2010, Blockbuster's shares were selling for 25 cents, with a market cap of just $55 million. In comparison, Netflix shares in 2013 reached $400, with a market cap of about $23 billion. By the end of 2013, all Blockbuster stores were closed. Netflix was able to change its competencies over time to remain successful, while Blockbuster did very little to its original business model.[8]

GOODS DESIGN

As discussed in the next few pages of this chapter, the design of any product begins with an idea. While designs of both goods and services must consider a number of things, including competitor designs, financial resources, and customer desires, the design of goods must also consider processing equipment, factory workers and their skill sets, and the availability of equipment, land, and transportation. Another issue is the product's life cycle—the life of a good is continually shrinking, due to changing tastes, more competition, cheaper materials, and changes in technology. This means that product development process times—from idea to finished product—must also shrink. The product development process is discussed later in this chapter. The Manufacturing Spotlight on page 54 describes a number of design issues with Powerski's Jetboard.

SERVICES DESIGN

Today, a growing portion of the U.S. economy is service-oriented. Service products and processes have several unique aspects setting them apart from manufactured goods and their processes. First, customers are typically involved in service design and delivery processes that can introduce variabilities in process times and perceived service quality. For example, customers select cleaning services from a janitorial service company and might then stipulate when and for how many hours the company works for the customer. Additionally, customers might modify their service requests during the service, causing the service provider to take too long or fail to perform some of the agreed-upon services. These types of variabilities must be addressed in order to keep costs down and customers satisfied.

MANUFACTURING SPOTLIGHT

Designing Powerski's Jetboard

Francisco Galvex/Notimex/newscom

In 1995, Bob Montgomery founded Powerski International and hired engineers to design a light engine for an idea he had—a motorized surfboard. Montgomery designed the hull, with a hollow space beneath the rider's feet for the engine. "I wanted the engine to be low-profile," says Montgomery. "Surfboards are flat. They don't have big humps on them. There was no engine out there to fit that profile."

There were a number of problems. "There's a host of design and engineering challenges when you design a surfboard and add an engine," says Montgomery. "Water intrusion was one of them. When you sit on the board, it sinks. We had to make it not sink." Eventually, they began using a computer-aided design (CAD) package due to the complexity of the product.

Montgomery eventually built about 30 prototypes of the board. "But as I sit here today, I don't have a single blister on my hands," he says. "Because now we're designing the whole board in CAD." CAD enables engineers to work out the early kinks in their designs, without huge investments of time and money.

When a prototype was ready for water trials, Montgomery and his team placed sensors on the board and the engine, to transmit data about water flow, hydrodynamics, ignition, and fuel injection. They transmitted the data to a mobile workstation they took with them to the beach.

Montgomery soon found the company growing and the design changing, as the team tried to come up with better designs. He soon needed a way to track design changes and keep in touch with parts suppliers. Powerski International eventually began using a product data management system to store information, track change orders, and act as a collaboration system.

The Jetboard design puts the center of gravity under the rider's feet, rather than behind or in front of the rider. Controls under the bottom of the hull also put the pivot point directly under the rider's feet, for high-speed planing and turning.[9]

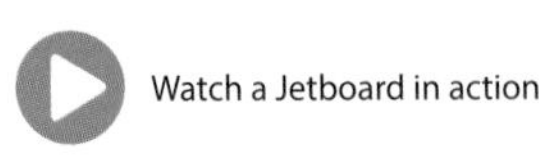
Watch a Jetboard in action

New services tend to require redesign after implementation since the roles and capabilities of servers, and the integration of customers into the new service delivery processes, are critical. In the case of a new course offered at a university, students make decisions regarding the class based on the topic of the class, when it is offered, and the class's instructor. During the years they are pursuing their degree programs, students have continual involvement in managing their degree plans. Universities, too, must consider when to schedule classes, which textbooks to use, and whether or not to change schedules, textbooks, and instructors, based in part on student feedback. These issues are true for many services.

Service organizations today are also trying to modify their service designs using technology. Advances in technology have created multiple service delivery options for consumers, and in many cases, improved quality perceptions. By then end of 2013, for example, Apple listed about 1,000,000 iPhone apps in its App Store; Amazon was offering its cloud capability for storing customers' Kindle books; and some car owners could simply press a button to parallel park their cars.

STRATEGIC FIT

strategic fit The alignment of product designs with the operational capabilities and policies of the firm (*internal fit*) and with the condition of the market and desires of customers (*external fit*).

Some new products fail due to a lack of **strategic fit** with their internal or external environment. Strategic fit refers to the alignment of designs with the operational capabilities and policies of the firm (*internal fit*) and with the condition of the market and desires of customers (*external fit*).[10] Conversely, successful products exhibit good strategic fit. The chapter-opening Service Spotlight on Denny's, for example, mentions the desire of customers for "to-go" foods. Lately, this service has become quite popular at traditional sit-down restaurants like Denny's, Applebee's, and Chili's. These services have good external fit. If, however, a restaurant offered to-go service but failed to deliver it quickly or complete, the service would eventually fail due to poor internal fit. A poor choice of service location would indicate lack of external fit with the marketplace, which might also be a cause for service failure.

The same holds true for manufactured goods. A company might be extremely good at designing and manufacturing a certain product (good internal fit) but fail at providing a product customers want. For example, Apple's Newton MessagePad, introduced in 1993, was one of the first products to offer basic computing functions in a handheld device. Its technology was revolutionary for its time (good internal fit). Unfortunately, the Newton failed to catch on, mostly because the $700 price tag was more than consumers wanted to pay. This is an example of poor external fit.[11]

CONTRACT MANUFACTURERS AND SERVICES

Sometimes firms will use **contract manufacturers** to produce parts or entire products for them, if their competencies are not in those areas. A contract manufacturer is a firm that custom manufactures parts or products for another firm, under the buying firm's label or brand. The contract manufacturer may be given a general product idea or a specific set of specifications. Pharmaceutical makers, clothing companies, food producers, and electronics companies often outsource the actual production of various goods to contract manufacturers. **Contract services** can also be used in the same way. Hotels might contract out services for housekeeping, maintenance, and landscaping.

Use of contract manufacturers has changed the competitive nature of many industries. The automobile industry was one of the first to embrace contract manufacturing. Today, parts suppliers for the automobile industry routinely design, develop, engineer, test, assemble, package, and deliver a majority of vehicle components and systems. The automakers design the cars and perform the final assembly. The reason for this is fairly simple—the contract manufacturers ideally specialize in the parts they supply; thus, they should be very good at it. They can make the parts faster, cheaper, and at higher quality levels than the automobile manufacturers, provided the right controls are in place.

In the United States in the 1990s, as Toyota began taking away market share from U.S. automakers, its use of contract manufacturers was seen as a way to reduce costs and become more competitive. The Boeing Company also has used contract manufacturers, many from foreign locations. For Boeing, it was not solely to reduce costs, but also to buy parts from foreign companies where the company desired to do business. Unfortunately, outsourcing can have adverse impacts—as Toyota sought to overtake GM in total units sold worldwide in 2008, it began to outsource more parts in order to speed production. In 2010, it was forced to make massive recalls for unintended accelerations due to a faulty contract-manufactured part.[12] With Boeing, its desire to outsource 70% of the components to speed its 787 Dreamliner to market caused a very serious problem with overheating of the lithium-ion battery system in 2012. This created several very expensive problems and delivery delays of the planes.[13]

THE PRODUCT DEVELOPMENT PROCESS

3.2 Summarize the steps in the product development process

There are several stages in the product development process, as shown in Figure 3.1. Typically, multiple functions in an organization are involved in the development and launching of new goods and services, including design engineers and personnel from marketing, finance, and operations. The process begins with the generation of a product idea or the rethinking of an existing product.

contract manufacturers Firms that custom manufacture parts or products for other firms, under the buying firm's label or brand.

contract services Firms that provide custom services for other firms, such as services for housekeeping, maintenance, and landscaping at a hotel.

Figure 3.1 The Product Development Process

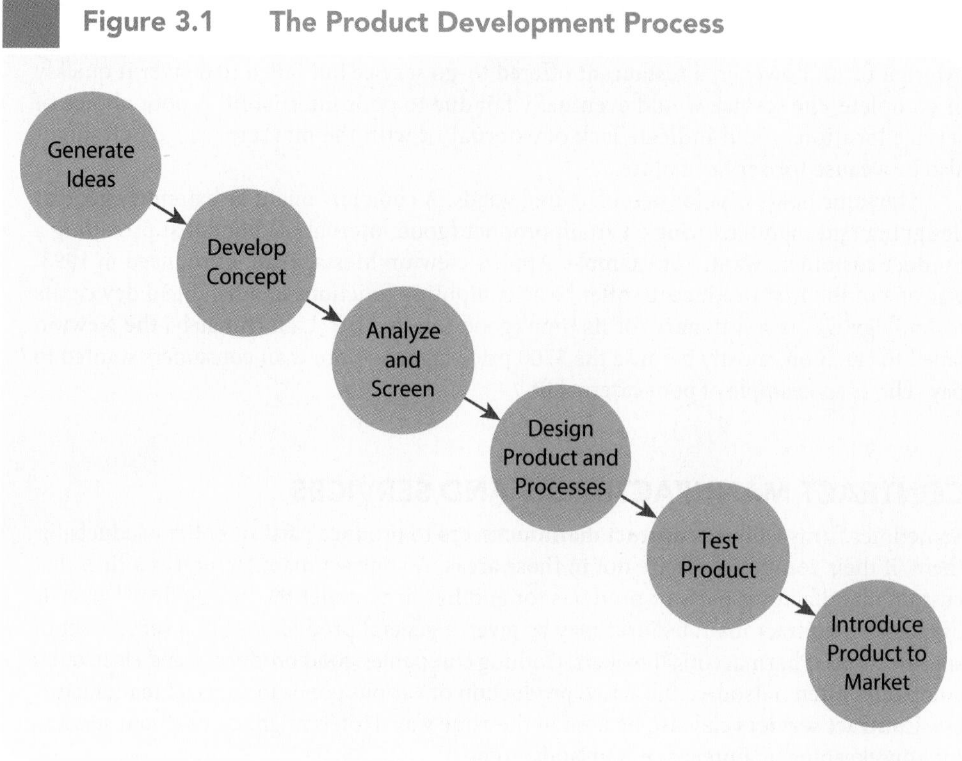

GENERATING PRODUCT IDEAS

Most large manufacturing and service organizations have research and development teams devoted to what's known as **basic research**—discovering new phenomena or new ways of looking at things. The idea is then to take these new discoveries and convert them into new commercial applications. IBM and Microsoft, for instance, spend billions of dollars annually on research and development, including things like cloud computing, nanotechnology, and computational biology. Companies are also increasingly reaching out to universities, suppliers, customers, and others in a move toward research collaboration, or what's termed **open innovation**. This openness generates many ideas from both inside and outside the firm, and can help speed new and sometimes better products to the marketplace. Since so many ideas are often generated, it is more likely that a very good idea can be found. Since 2010, General Electric, for example, has hosted the "Ecomagination Challenge," which uses a $200 million fund for identifying and investing in cutting-edge ideas and business models in the areas of renewable energy and energy consumption. GE created an online system through which academics, entrepreneurs, and others could submit their ideas. Within the first six months of the first challenge, the company attracted more than 60,000 participants and received more than 5,000 ideas and business plans from 85 countries. So far, GE and its partners have invested more than $134 million into the ideas received.[14]

Watch Steve Jobs discussing innovation

Open innovation can also create some problems. For example, PepsiCo, the food and beverage giant, created a controversy in 2011 when an open-sourced entry into its Super Bowl ad contest, posted online, featured tortilla chips being used in place of sacramental wafers during Holy Communion. Similarly, Kraft Foods Australia ran into challenges when it launched a new Vegemite-based cheese snack in conjunction with a public naming contest. The name Kraft initially chose from the submissions, iSnack 2.0, encountered widespread ridicule, and Kraft eventually abandoned it.[15]

basic research Discovering new phenomena or new ways of looking at things.

open innovation Collaborating with universities, suppliers, customers, and others to generate product ideas.

Company acquisitions and benchmarking practices are also good sources of new product ideas. Acquiring another company allows the buyer to gain quick access to existing products, as well as new personnel with new ideas, and new processing capabilities. Indian manufacturer Dynamatic Technologies, for example, acquired German automotive

MANUFACTURING SPOTLIGHT

Enterprise Social Networking at SAS Institute

Employees for the North Carolina–based business software producer SAS Institute use an enterprise social network called the Hub to connect employees and share ideas both down the hall and around the world. Even though SAS already had other communication systems in place, the Hub caught on much better than any of its other systems. The Hub proved to be great for browsing topic areas and employee messages, and connecting globally with other SAS employees.

SAS launched the Hub in January 2011 and had almost 8,000 of its 12,000 employees using it by the end of the year. For divisions like R&D, use of the Hub is nearly 100%. SAS used the Hub to launch its "Innovation Day" to brainstorm new product ideas, for example, and received suggestions from employees for months afterward. In another example, employees used the Hub to express their desire to change how customer questions were answered. Originally, these questions were routed to Technical Support personnel. Through these discussions, SAS decided to empower all employees to handle customer questions within their fields of expertise.[16]

Kris Tripplaar/Sipa USA/newscom

component manufacturer Eisenwerke in 2010, giving it new products, access to new customers, patented technologies, and one of the finest ferrous foundries in Europe.[17]

Benchmarking is the practice of copying what others do best. Often, noncompeting companies have benchmarking agreements that allow them to copy aspects of one another's processes. In other cases, it might include posing as a customer to see what a competitor is doing or buying a competitor's product, then taking it apart to see how it's designed. A number of trade organizations conduct "best practice" studies to identify organizations worth benchmarking, and then publish what these firms do best. The APQC (American Productivity and Quality Center), for example, has over 8,500 best practice studies for use by its members.

Employees, suppliers, and customers are also good sources of product ideas. In a 2011 survey of the U.S. beverage industry, 95% of the respondents stated their firms used teams of employees including those from sales, marketing, R&D, and upper management to generate new product ideas. Almost 50% said they also included customers on their teams, and about a third included supplier representatives.[18] North Carolina–based SAS Institute, for example, uses an enterprise social network called the Hub, to help turn employee ideas into new goods and services, as described in the Manufacturing Spotlight above.

For decades, marketing departments have relied on customer surveys and focus groups to gather information on what customers want. Every year, thousands of focus groups and many tens of thousands of customer surveys are organized in these efforts at a cost of many billions of dollars. Sometimes this results in successful products; however, by some estimates, 80% of new products fail. The high failure rate, combined with technological breakthroughs, has spawned the use of **neuroscience** to tap into the subconscious minds of consumers. California-based NeuroFocus uses neuroscience to make connections between consumers' brains and their buying behavior. Companies like Google, HP, Microsoft, ESPN, and many others have already used NeuroFocus to help them better understand their customers. Frito-Lay hired NeuroFocus to study customers' attitudes toward one of its products—Cheetos—and found its customers actually liked the orange sticky mess on their fingers; it triggered a sense of subversion for them. Frito-Lay leveraged this knowledge into its advertising and found that sales improved.[19]

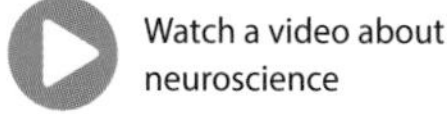

DEVELOPING THE CONCEPT

If an idea appears to be a good "fit" with a company's mission, strategy, core capabilities, and financial picture, it is generally further developed. Traditional methods have focused more

benchmarking The practice of copying what others do best.

neuroscience Exploring the subconscious minds of consumers to uncover new product ideas.

on the capabilities of the design engineers and less on the customer. One technique developed in the 1960s that bridges this gap and which is commonly used in manufacturing today is **quality function deployment** (QFD). QFD helps companies create designs that are more customer-focused. Many companies use QFD, including Toyota, Ford, Proctor & Gamble, AT&T, 3M, and Hewlett-Packard.

quality function deployment A method that helps companies create designs that are more customer-focused.

house of quality Part of quality function deployment, it shows the relationships among customer requirements, product attributes, and design specifications. It helps evaluate how competitive the product will be, and is used as a benchmarking evaluation tool of the product against its competitors.

The QFD process begins with identifying, listening to, and surveying customers. The results are analyzed and a list of customer requirements, ranked in order of importance, is developed during the concept development stage. The company's product design team can then begin creating a product document called the **house of quality**, which shows the relationships among customer requirements, product attributes, and design specifications. Additionally, the house of quality helps evaluate how competitive the product will be, and is used as a benchmarking evaluation tool of the product against its competitors. Figure 3.2 shows a house of quality figure for a car door.

At the top of the house is a "roof," which indicates the correlations among a product's technical characteristics. The technical characteristics are design elements created for one or more of the customer requirements. Design target values are design goals put in place to better meet customer requirements. A competitive comparison of the firm and two of its competitors is shown on the right side of the house, and a technical evaluation is at the bottom of

Figure 3.2 House of Quality for a Car Door

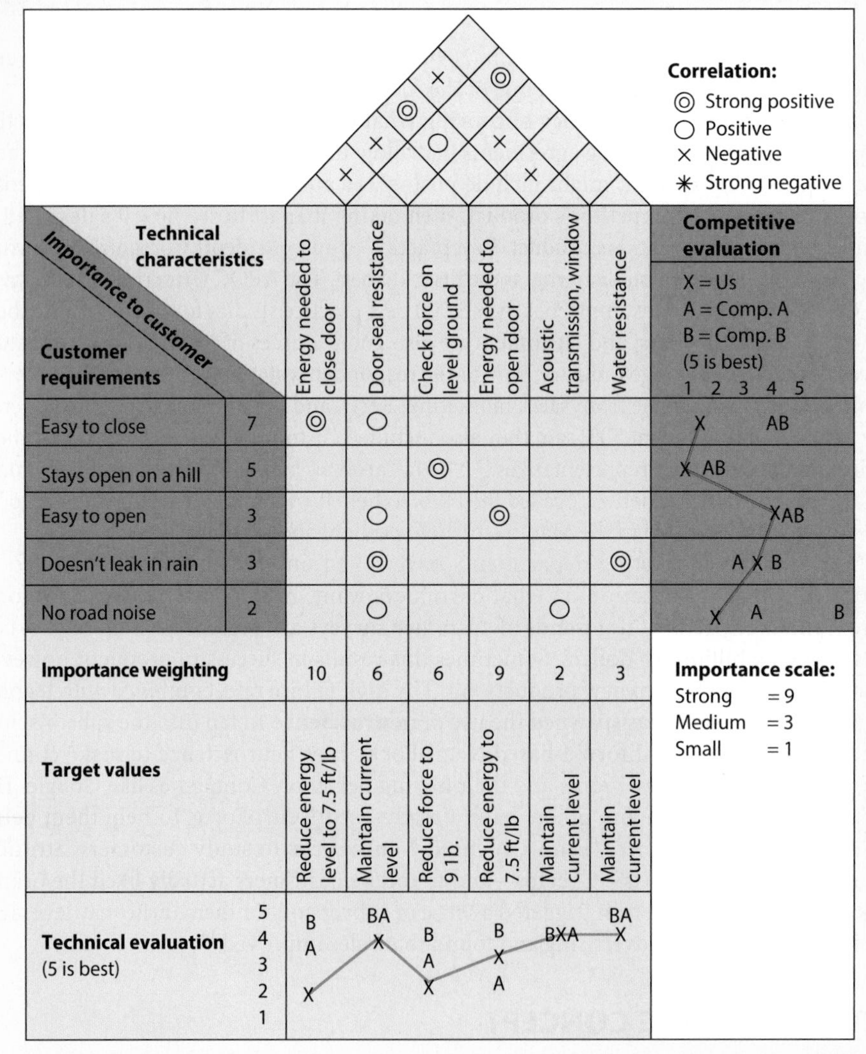

Source: Based on J. R. Hauser and D. Clausing, May/June 1988, "The House of Quality," *Harvard Business Review*, pp. 62–73.

the house. In the figure, the focal firm (Firm X) is doing poorly on the two most important customer requirements ("easy to close" and "stays open on a hill"). The "no road noise" requirement also appears to be a problem; in fact, none of the design elements has a strong positive association with the "no road noise" customer requirement. Future door design efforts should then concentrate on these three customer requirements.

PRODUCT ANALYSIS AND SCREENING

Once a product concept is more fully developed, it is reviewed by a product screening team, or the firm's executives. An analysis is presented, including information on the expected size of the target market, an environmental analysis, projected demand trends, a competitor analysis, and the product's financial analysis.

Many issues must be considered before the product idea moves on to the final product and process design phase. Screeners will generally consider three categories of issues, as shown in Table 3.2: the product, the competition, and the financials. The product should be something the company can sell; it should be in line with what the company does best; and there should be no costly barriers to entry, such as design patents or trademark protections. Ideally, the product can be distributed similarly to other products the firm sells.

Table 3.2 Product Screening Issues

The Product

- What unmet needs will this product satisfy?
- Is this product a good fit with our overall strategy?
- What are the barriers to entry for this product?
- What technologies and processes will be required?
- Are the preliminary product design specifications established?
- What is the expected product life?
- How will we distribute the product?

The Competition

- Who is the competition?
- What are our product's competitive strengths?
- How will we compete? (cost, quality, customer service)
- Can we sustain a competitive advantage?

The Financials

- Do we have realistic sales and cost estimates?
- What are the product development, production, and distribution costs?
- What is the break-even point?
- What is the expected net present value and return-on-investment?
- What is the expected profit?

The firm should also know the product's competition. What will this product do that the competition doesn't? Will this product compete on price, quality, or customer service? And finally, can this product meet the firm's financial requirements? Product concepts not performing well with respect to many of these issues will typically be dropped from further consideration.

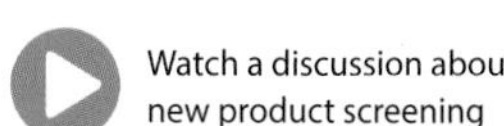
Watch a discussion about new product screening

New Product Financials

Managers typically review a new product's projected **net present value** or **internal rate of return** when deciding to invest in new product ideas. As an example, in using net present value (NPV) to screen a new product idea, consider Company A and its new product idea—product X. Company A estimates that the future cash flows generated by product X, discounted at a rate of 10%, would yield an NPV of $20 million. If product X requires a total initial investment of $15 million, then the total NPV of product X would be $5 million ($20 million minus the $15 million initial investment). If this value meets Company A's minimum profit criteria for an investment of this size, then Company A would likely invest in product X. But Company A might also want to know the projected internal rate of return (IRR) that would be generated by this investment. To determine the IRR, Company A calculates the discount rate that would make the product's NPV equal to zero. This is product X's IRR. The value of IRR depends on the projected cash flows and the lifetime of the product. Let us assume that in this example the IRR of product X is 15%. If Company A's minimum acceptable projected IRR for new products is 12%, then it would probably invest in product X. Example 3.1 provides a financial analysis for a new product.

In Example 3.1, the NPV calculation uses the following formula:

$$\text{NPV} = \frac{(\text{Cash flow year 1})}{(1+\text{discount rate})^1} + \frac{(\text{Cash flow year 2})}{(1+\text{discount rate})^2} + \ldots + \frac{(\text{Cash flow year Y})}{(1+\text{discount rate})^Y},$$

where Y = the year number.

net present value The sum of a stream of future cash flows, discounted using the firm's desired discount rate.

internal rate of return The discount rate that makes a project's net present value equal to its investment cost.

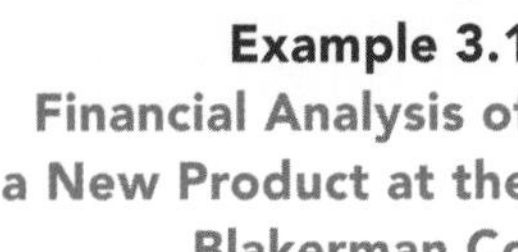

Example 3.1 Financial Analysis of a New Product at the Blakerman Co

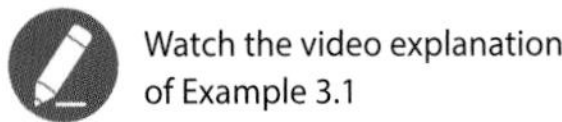

Watch the video explanation of Example 3.1

The management at the Blakerman Co. has been shown the projected cash flows (below) for a new skateboard product. The expected life of the product is five years. The projected product and process design costs are $750,000. Blakerman management uses a discount rate of 8% for all new product financials and wants to see both the projected NPV and IRR.

Year	Projected Cash Flows ($)	Net Present Value of Cash Flows ($)
1	250,000	$250{,}000/(1.08)^1 = 231{,}481$
2	300,000	$300{,}000/(1.08)^2 = 257{,}202$
3	350,000	$350{,}000/(1.08)^3 = 277{,}841$
4	200,000	$200{,}000/(1.08)^4 = 147{,}006$
5	100,000	$100{,}000/(1.08)^5 = 68{,}058$
	Total NPV	$981,588 − $750,000 = $231,588

Using the NPV formula, the total NPV for the new skateboard product is found to be $231,588 and the payback is slightly less than three years (found by adding the discounted cash flows for the first three years). These appear to be positive signs for the $750,000 investment. To find the product's projected IRR, the NPV formula is solved iteratively, to make the NPV = $750,000. We first try 15%:

$$\$750{,}000 = \frac{(250{,}000)}{(1.15)^1} + \frac{(300{,}000)}{(1.15)^2} + \frac{(350{,}000)}{(1.15)^3} + \frac{(200{,}000)}{(1.15)^4} + \frac{(100{,}000)}{(1.15)^5}$$

$$= 217{,}391 + 226{,}843 + 230{,}131 + 114{,}351 + 49{,}718 = \$838{,}434.$$

The IRR is too low, so next we try 20%:

$$\$750{,}000 = \frac{(250{,}000)}{(1.20)^1} + \frac{(300{,}000)}{(1.20)^2} + \frac{(350{,}000)}{(1.20)^3} + \frac{(200{,}000)}{(1.20)^4} + \frac{(100{,}000)}{(1.20)^5}$$

$$= 208{,}333 + 208{,}333 + 202{,}546 + 96{,}451 + 40{,}188 = \$755{,}851.$$

This is quite close; however, the IRR is still too low, so we next try 21%:

$$\$750{,}000 = \frac{(250{,}000)}{(1.21)^1} + \frac{(300{,}000)}{(1.21)^2} + \frac{(350{,}000)}{(1.21)^3} + \frac{(200{,}000)}{(1.21)^4} + \frac{(100{,}000)}{(1.21)^5}$$

$$= 206{,}612 + 204{,}904 + 197{,}566 + 93{,}301 + 38{,}554 = \$740{,}937.$$

Now the IRR is too high. Using interpolation, the IRR is found to be approximately 20.4%. Since this exceeds the firm's discount rate of 8%, this is also a good sign.

The previous example can also be computed using a spreadsheet, as shown here.

Use Excel spreadsheet templates to find the solution

	A	B
1	**Year**	**Cash Flows ($)**
2	0	−750,000
3	1	250,000
4	2	300,000
5	3	350,000
6	4	200,000
7	5	100,000
8		$231,588.70
9		20.39%

B8: NPV(0.08,B3:B7) + B2

B9: IRR(B2:B7)

Finding the IRR requires using the same NPV equation, however, solving for the discount rate that makes the sum of the discounted cash flows equal to the initial investment, or:

$$\text{Initial investment} = \frac{(\text{Cash flow year 1})}{(1+\text{IRR})^1} + \frac{(\text{Cash flow year 2})}{(1+\text{IRR})^2} + \ldots + \frac{(\text{Cash flow year Y})}{(1+\text{IRR})^Y},$$

where Y = the year number. The equation can be solved iteratively.

The question may arise: Which is better for comparing several products or projects, NPV or IRR? In general terms, the IRR makes no distinctions between the sizes of the projects or the financial impacts. Therefore, a small project with a small total NPV can have a higher IRR than a large, long-term project with a sizeable total NPV. When any doubt arises, managers typically choose products/projects with the greatest financial impact—the highest NPV. For similar products with similar investments, managers may choose to invest in the product with the highest IRR.

PRODUCT AND PROCESS DESIGN

If a product concept meets all of the screening requirements and is approved by management, it goes into a product and process design phase, where design engineers develop detailed specifications, drawings, and processing steps for the new product. Designers then build prototypes, which can be either actual physical models or computer models. Finally, tests are undertaken to simulate actual use of the product and to potentially refine the product's design. At the same time, tools and equipment are built, purchased, and tested to create the required production steps. This concept is known as concurrent engineering (discussed in the next section) and can save a great deal of time if the production process is developed as the product design progresses (note that Chapter 4 is dedicated to process design).

David Freers/Transtock/Corbis

Prototypes, like the one for the Toyota Fun Vii shown here, are built after the product and process design phase.

For service providers, concurrent engineering would mean that the service delivery system is developed at the same time the new service is designed. As described in the chapter-opening Service Spotlight on Denny's, service customers can be utilized for feedback on whether the new service idea is easily understood, satisfying, and if the customer will actually buy the service. Various pricing options may also be tested to determine the salability of the service.

Service blueprinting, a type of flowcharting method, is often used when designing and evaluating a new service or improving an existing one. A service blueprint lays out the direct and indirect activities occurring between the service provider and the customer, and the noncontact activities that don't involve the customer, such as bookkeeping and other office activities. Figure 3.3 provides a blueprinting example of a typical experience at an automobile quick lube shop, with each service activity mapped on the blueprint. Below the "line of visibility" are those activities not generally seen by customers. Service blueprinting considers both customer requirements and company requirements. A service blueprint can be used as the starting point for designing the service delivery process. The Service Spotlight on page 62 describes a company's use of service blueprinting.

service blueprinting A flowcharting method, used when designing and evaluating a new service or improving an existing service. It lays out the direct and indirect activities occurring between the service provider and the customer, and the noncontact activities that don't involve the customer.

FINAL PRODUCT TESTING AND REFINEMENT

The product testing phase continues as final product and process designs are refined. Feedback from employees, suppliers, customer panels, and test markets may indicate improvements in the product's design that are necessary to meet product design goals, customer requirements, and suppler capabilities. Nissan North America, for example, has engineers climb into 3-D virtual automobiles, with simulated passengers. The engineers get in and out of seats, load and unload luggage, and view ergonomic placement of dashboard

Figure 3.3 Service Blueprinting for a Quick Lube Shop

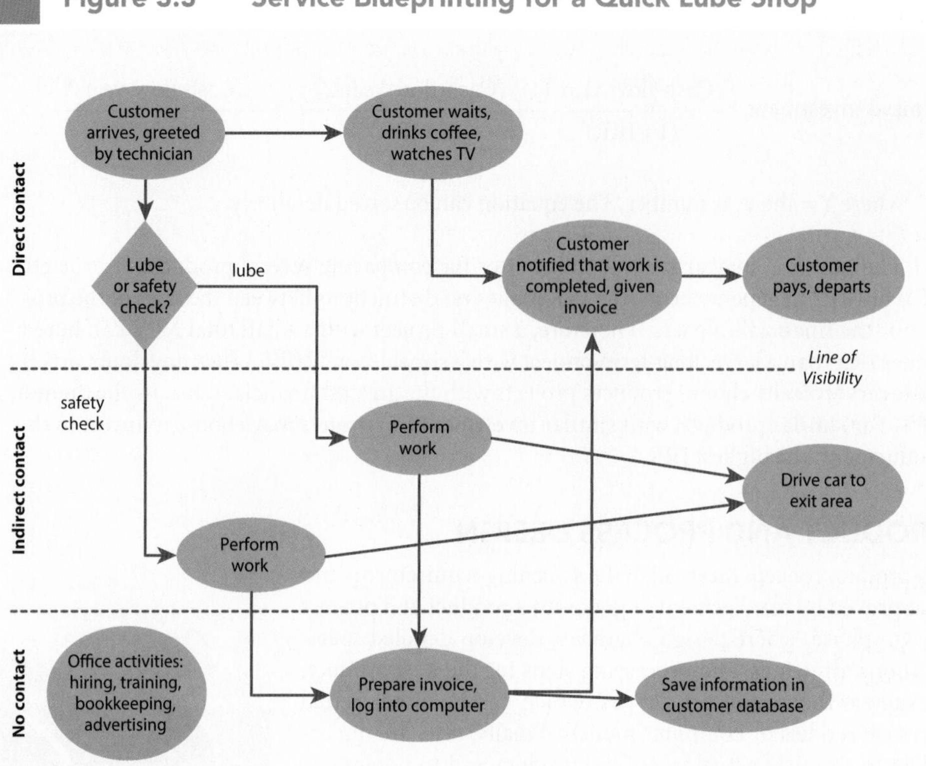

SERVICE SPOTLIGHT

Aramark's Use of Service Blueprinting

Several years ago, Pennsylvania-based Aramark noticed a disturbing trend at its Lake Powell, Arizona, houseboat resort: People were visiting once and not coming back. To find out why, executives employed service blueprinting to help them understand what their customers *actually experienced* during their stay, and how that experience compared to other resort experiences. Aramark created two blueprints—one mapped out the typical houseboat experience at Lake Powell, while the other portrayed a typical experience at another resort using houseboats.

The results were striking: Lake Powell visitors experienced high levels of stress using a houseboat. Customers began their vacations with a trip to the grocery store to pick up supplies, but then faced the challenge of lugging all their purchases to the houseboat. Additionally, many novices had difficulty maneuvering or anchoring the boats. In all, the experience for Lake Powell visitors was a lot of work. Finally, customers described the resort as comparatively run down.

As a result, Aramark executives added services such as grocery-buying for customers, and onboard chefs. They started offering flexible pickup and return times, complimentary map and itinerary planning, help with loading groceries and other supplies onto the boats, and assistance guiding the houseboats into open water.

iStock/brians101

The improvements made an immediate impact: Aramark reported an impressive 50% drop in complaints, repeat business jumped 12% and customer satisfaction increased as well.[20]

indicators. It can then use this information for redesign purposes. Virginia-based Northrup Grumman used a similar 3-D simulation on a massive scale to develop the design for the CVN 78 U.S. Navy aircraft carrier.[21] And finally, U.S. retailer Sam's Club uses employee volunteers in a corporate test kitchen and sensory lab to ensure products have the taste, texture, and appearance that will result in customer acceptance.[22]

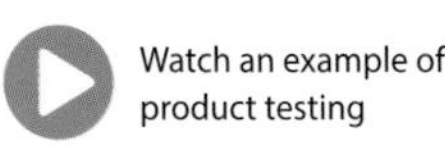
Watch an example of product testing

PRODUCTION RAMP UP AND PRODUCT INTRODUCTION

Pilot manufacturing often occurs once the design-build-test phase is successfully completed. At this point, the product is manufactured on a limited basis to determine if the production equipment can reliably manufacture the good, and if full-scale production is possible. Once successful pilot production is complete, production is "ramped-up" slowly until a consistent level of quality is maintained; then volumes are increased to a full-scale launch of the product. Texas-based Freescale Semiconductor used pilot manufacturing to certify its redistributed chip manufacturing technology for MP3 players for several of its customers. Later, it moved to full-scale production.[23] Ultimately, actual demand dictates if and when production is ramped up. Washington-based Boeing, for example, continues to increase production of its 777 aircraft as the demand for fuel-efficient passenger jets increases.[24]

Similarly, new services are rolled out to limited markets until the company is satisfied that a full-scale market rollout or introduction is warranted. This was mentioned, for example, in the chapter opener on Denny's. For Massachusetts-based Dunkin' Donuts, the Dallas, Las Vegas, and Nashville markets were used to test touchscreen self-ordering kiosks. Dunkin' Donuts saw throughput increases of more than 30% during peak operating hours, and also found the kiosks increased order accuracies while reducing customer walk-offs.[25]

REDUCING PRODUCT DEVELOPMENT LEAD TIME

3.3 Explain the practices used to reduce product development lead times

Due to ever-increasing demand for new products from customers and growing levels of competition, manufacturers have adopted a number of practices to reduce the time from new product idea generation to market introduction. Several of these are described here.

CONCURRENT ENGINEERING

The concept known as **concurrent engineering**, or the simultaneous design of products and their manufacturing and support processes, has been around since the 1980s, although some historians point out that even Henry Ford's original production facility practiced concurrent engineering in the early 1900s (although it was never called concurrent engineering). Prior to this time, the manufacturing method of choice was referred to as linear or sequential manufacturing. In the mid-1980s, as Japanese automobile and electronics manufacturers were rapidly gaining ground in world markets, business scholars and competitors began searching out the reasons for this competitive advantage. What emerged from these efforts were the characteristics now collectively referred to as concurrent engineering. One of the primary advantages of concurrent engineering is the reduced product development and production lead times, as shown in Figure 3.4.

The term *concurrent engineering* was coined in a U.S. Department of Defense research paper in 1988.[26] The definition of concurrent engineering used in the paper was:

> Concurrent engineering is a systematic approach to the integrated, concurrent design of products and their related processes, including manufacturing and support. This approach is intended to cause the developers from the outset to consider all elements of the product life cycle from conception to disposal, including quality cost, schedule, and user requirements.

pilot manufacturing After the design-build-test phase is successfully completed, the product is manufactured on a limited basis to determine if the production equipment can reliably manufacture the good, and if full-scale production is possible.

concurrent engineering Designing the manufacturing process or service delivery system simultaneously with the design of the product.

Figure 3.4 Linear Manufacturing and Concurrent Engineering

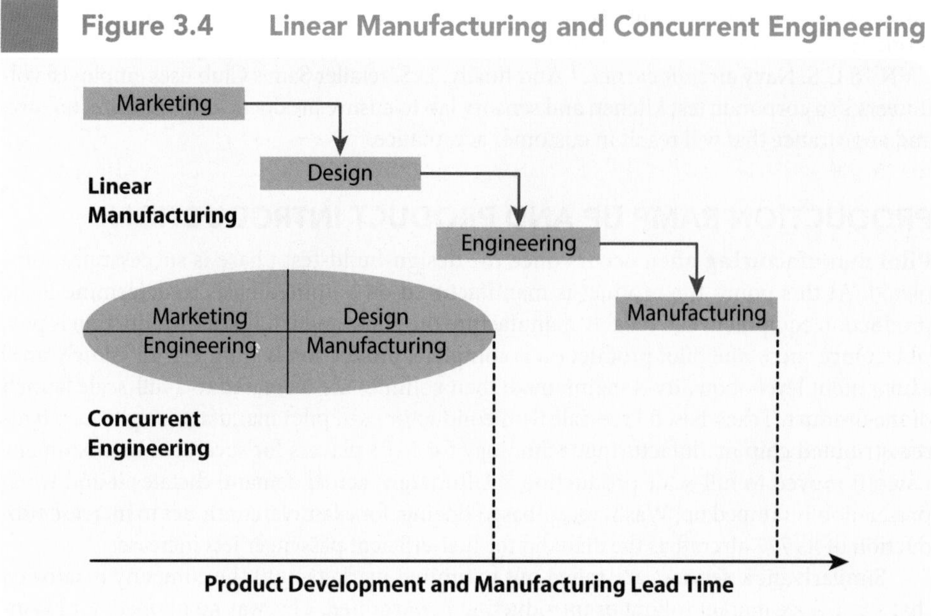

Source: Figure is based on a similar figure found at: http://www.ispangle.com/Communication.html

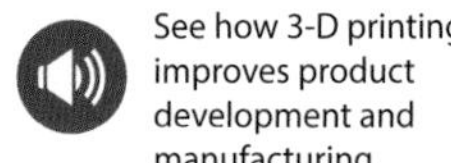
See how 3-D printing improves product development and manufacturing

The characteristics of concurrent engineering are summarized here:

- Cross-functional new product development teams, including members of engineering, R&D, marketing, operations, finance, quality control, and sometimes supplier and customer representatives.
- A high level of autonomy granted to the team to allow free flow of information, cross-fertilization of ideas, and self-organization.
- Overlapping of the product and process design phases, which tends to reduce costs and lead times while improving consistency between customer requirements and product attributes and performance.
- Fewer product design, processing, and operating problems due to the high level of team member participation in all phases of design and production.

At about the same time, these practices were also referred to as the **sashimi system** in Japan, and a paper discussing these principles was published later in the *Journal of Knowledge Management* in 2004.[27]

These early practices have today developed worldwide into a much more integrated, nonlinear form of new product development and manufacturing process. Fuji Xerox in Japan, for example, embarked on a corporate-wide effort to incorporate concurrent engineering in 1995. By 2003, it was able to cut new copier development lead times in half and was ranked first in customer satisfaction for color copiers by J. D. Power Asia.[28] In another example, the European Airbus Industrie Corp. used concurrent engineering to beat out Boeing with a wide-body jet by several years in the early 1990s.[29]

sashimi system An early Japanese version of concurrent engineering.

early supplier involvement The practice of inviting supplier representatives to participate on new product design teams.

value engineering Reducing a new product's cost through use of readily available parts instead of custom-designed parts, and use of cheaper materials and simpler designs, provided the changes have no effect on the product's use or performance.

The practice of concurrent engineering has spawned a number of activities widely used in product design today. **Early supplier involvement** (ESI) has become a commonly recognized practice of inviting supplier representatives to participate on new product design teams, since their knowledge of parts and materials design, availability, and pricing has proved invaluable in the design process. Likewise, the tem **value engineering** has become known as the practice of reducing a new product's cost through use of readily available parts instead of custom-designed parts, and use of cheaper materials and simpler designs, provided the changes have no effect on the product's use or performance.

Today, the practice of concurrent engineering is so widespread, it is no longer considered a significant competitive advantage. Furthermore, as the practice of supply chain management advanced in the 1990s, some companies coupled supply chain practices and concurrent engineering into what is termed *three-dimensional concurrent engineering*, or 3DCE. In 3DCE, the design of the product, process, and supply chain occurs simultaneously.[30] Since in many new product design teams, supplier and customer representatives are already members, the logical extension of process and product design would be the design of the new product's supply chain. Companies like Intel and Chrysler have successfully used 3DCE to further reduce their lead times from product conception to market penetration.

DESIGN FOR MANUFACTURE AND ASSEMBLY

As computer technology and software applications for use in product design grew during the 1990s, the ability to refine, test, and improve product designs also improved. Software could be used to consolidate parts and essentially simplify product designs, thus reducing assembly cost. Additionally, software was used to help designers examine alternate material, part, and process choices to judge the cost of design and material trade-offs. These practices became known as **design for manufacture and assembly** (DFMA).

Reducing the number of parts used, and the use of existing part designs, contributes to the reduction of manufacturing costs—fewer items in need of storage, less chance of things going wrong, fewer suppliers to manage, and less time required to design and then assemble products. New Hampshire–based plasma-cutter manufacturer Hypertherm provides a great example of a firm's use of DFMA to weather the recent economic downturn. Hypertherm used DFMA software to slash its costs by about 45% while reducing its assembly times by 50%. DFMA has allowed Hypertherm to cut material costs and assembly times without adversely impacting product performance.[31] Several very simple examples of DFMA are shown in Figure 3.5. Notice that in the examples, the improved designs use fewer parts and result in easier, quicker assembly times.

design for manufacture and assembly Software applications that consolidate parts and essentially simplify product designs, thus reducing assembly cost. The software helps designers examine alternate material, part, and process choices to judge the cost of design and material trade-offs.

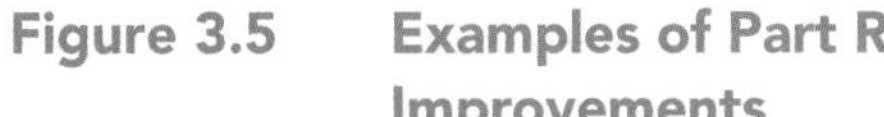

Figure 3.5 Examples of Part Reductions and Assembly Improvements

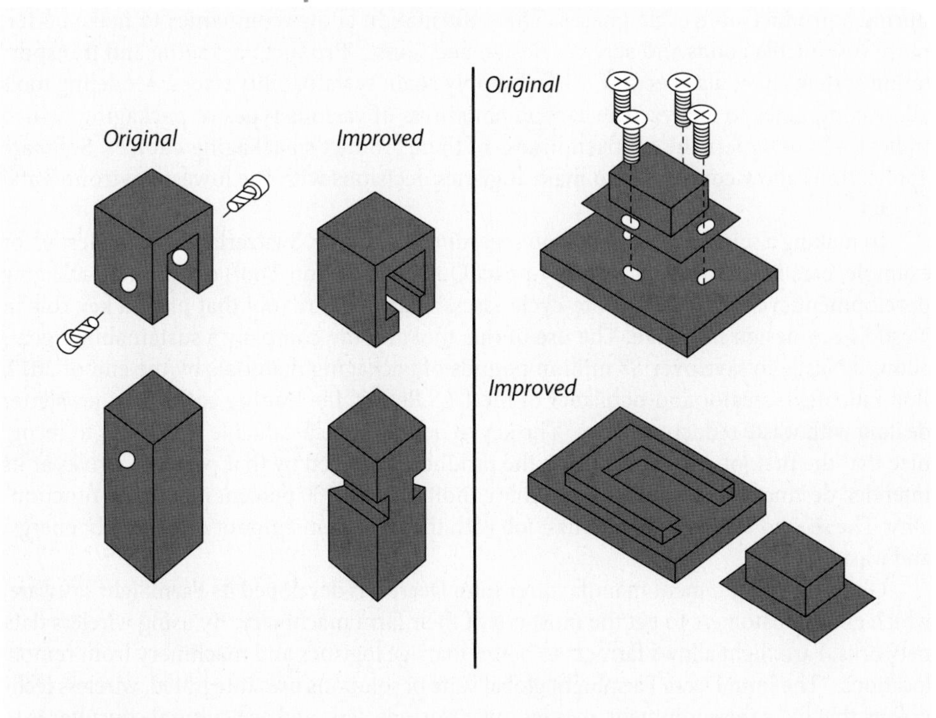

Source: Graphic design by Cody Russell. Used with permission.

SUSTAINABILITY IN PRODUCT DESIGN

3.4 Describe how sustainability impacts product designs

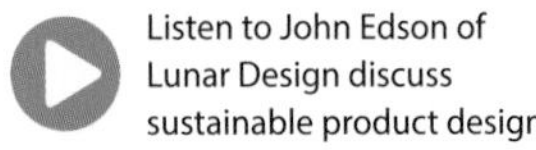

Listen to John Edson of Lunar Design discuss sustainable product design

One issue receiving attention these days is the incorporation of sustainability elements into the design, operation, and disposal stages for goods and services. **Sustainable product and process design** integrates and improves the economic, environmental, and social/ethical performance of products, processes, manufacturers, and services. Sustainability in businesses encourages consumers to buy products from innovative companies that have policies to reduce waste and energy, recycle old products into new ones, and create pleasant and productive workplaces for employees and customers.

Customers today want to know if the products they are buying use recycled materials; if businesses employ a diverse workforce or employ child laborers; if products conserve energy; and if products can be efficiently disposed of, reused, or recycled. Additionally, existing and potential employees want to know if the company has socially responsible values and a culture of collaboration. In many cases, sustainability issues provide firms with a competitive advantage in terms of lower costs, better productivity, and product or process design elements desired by consumers. Several of these issues are discussed in the following section.

ENVIRONMENTAL IMPACT

All goods and services have an environmental impact. Thus, producers must consider where purchased materials, parts, finished products, and associated items came from, how purchased items were produced and how much water used, as well as how far items are to be transported and how to dispose of products. Additionally, managers must consider the energy consumed over a product's life, the ease of product assembly, the product's durability, the potential re-use of the product at the end of its normal life, and finally, the associated environmental impacts of the goods and the service delivery systems.

Product design systems today enable engineers to perform cradle-to-grave analyses of products' environmental impacts, also known as **life cycle assessments**, which include the carbon footprint, energy usage, air acidification impact, and water contamination profile during a product's life cycle phases. This information allows companies to make better, more sustainable goods and services design decisions.[32] Product packaging and transportation systems have also become critical supply chain sustainability issues. Modeling tools allow companies to analyze the carbon emissions of various types of packaging, which indicates to designers the ecofriendliness of their product's packaging choices. Software applications allow companies to make logistics decisions with the lowest environmental impact.

In making a science-based decision regarding packaging, Switzerland-based Nestlé, for example, uses PIQET (the Packaging Impact Quick Evaluation Tool) early in its packaging development cycle. PIQET is a life-cycle assessment software tool that plays a key role in Nestlé's eco-design initiative. The use of this tool and the company's sustainability goals allowed Nestlé to save over 88 million pounds of packaging materials by the end of 2012. Bob Lilienfeld, creator and publisher of the *ULS Report*, the leading consumer newsletter dealing with waste reduction, says, "The key to designing a sustainable package is to recognize that the first job is to ensure that the product contained by that package arrives at its intended destination in 100 percent usable condition with 100 percent maximum functionality. The second task is to do that first job with the minimum amount of materials, energy, and waste."[33]

sustainable product and process design The incorporation of sustainability elements into the design, operation, and disposal stages for goods and services. Improves the economic, environmental, and social/ethical performance of products, processes, manufacturers, and services.

life cycle assessments Cradle-to-grave analyses of products' environmental impacts, including assessments of the carbon footprint, energy usage, air acidification impact, and water contamination profile.

Global farm equipment manufacturer John Deere has developed its FarmSight software, which allows customers to get the most out of their farm machinery. By using wireless data networks, FarmSight allows farmers to better manage logistics and machinery from remote locations. "The John Deere FarmSight global suite of solutions uses integrated, wireless technology that links the equipment, owners, operators, dealers, and agricultural consultants to provide even more productivity to a farm or business," says Jerry Roell, director of coordinated farm and worksite for John Deere. "We are investing in networking tools that will help

MANUFACTURING SPOTLIGHT

Sustainability at Burt's Bees

Every year, employees at North Carolina–based personal care product manufacturer Burt's Bees sort through two weeks of the company's trash. CEO John Replogle believes it gives employees a chance to identify missed recycling opportunities while also building a culture of sustainability.

In 2006, the company began considering sustainability goals and how to collect data on energy consumption, water use, and waste. When it began monitoring its trash in 2007, managers found the firm was creating 40 tons of waste per month. Therefore, in 2008, Burt's created a goal of being a zero-waste, zero-carbon company, operating in renewable energy–certified buildings by 2020. By the end of 2009, it had achieved the zero-waste goal.

Andrew Walters/Alamy

To continue toward its 2020 goals, the company required 100% employee engagement in Burt's sustainability activities. For example, workers on the production line suggested that the company use steam to clean the production containers rather than washing them with water. This reduced water use for cleaning by more than 90%. Following another employee suggestion, Burt's extended the paper label on its popular lip balm so it could also serve as a tamper-proof seal, eliminating the need for 900 miles of shrink wrap for every 20 million units of lip balm produced. It also has saved over 3,300 kilowatt-hours of electricity and $300,000 annually.[34]

producers manage data and information from their machinery easily and efficiently to assist in making better decisions for their operations."[35]

SUSTAINABILITY IN PRODUCT DISPOSAL

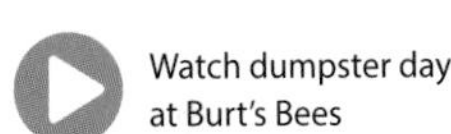
Watch dumpster day at Burt's Bees

For many companies, product reuse and recycling generate significant revenues and have a very high level of customer visibility. Products that can easily be recycled create positive impressions among consumers. Manufacturing companies like Coca-Cola and Burt's Bees, and even services like the Melbourne Cricket Ground are leading the way in using sustainable practices in product disposal.

In a recent survey, 79% of consumers agreed they preferred buying products from companies they thought were helping the environment. Coca-Cola, for example, is launching branded recycling bins in various countries, along with advertising campaigns encouraging customers to recycle. "Sustainability is at the heart of everything we do. Without sustainable, healthy communities we won't have a sustainable business. Which is why, as well as taking action ourselves, we're committed to helping consumers to do their bit as well," says Coke Great Britain president Sanjay Guha.[36] The Melbourne Cricket Ground (MCG) serves more than 4 million food and beverage products each year, and has introduced several innovative product recycling programs. Its polystyrene beer cups, for instance, were found to be its largest contributor to nonrecyclable waste. The cup was replaced with a recyclable one, and now MCG recycles 100% of its beer cups. Additionally, it now recycles over 72% of all waste generated at the facility.[37] The Manufacturing Spotlight above highlights personal product manufacturer Burt's Bees and its efforts in sustainability.

TRENDS IN PRODUCT DESIGN

3.5 Describe and critique some of the latest trends in product design

Every year, product designers entice consumers to continue purchasing products because of a new innovation, an eye-catching design, a new use for an existing design, lower energy use, better use of technology, better performance, or simply a cheaper price. Companies doing

iStock/mtreasure

Advances in automated factories and cellular technology has led to a greater variety of cellphone products available, including wearable technology.

a better job of anticipating customer desires for new products become first-to-market with their products, and enjoy higher profit margins until other companies create copycat versions of the same product. Just a few selected product design trends are discussed in the following sections, and several examples of innovative products are also presented.

CELL PHONE TRENDS

Automated factories today are becoming flexible and reconfigurable, so that a much wider variety of personalized products such as cell phones can be produced. Instead of producing millions of identical smartphones, manufacturers can build phones to customer specifications. Additionally, mobile broadband speeds are exploding. Phones are coming with much more RAM, so buffering will soon become a thing of the past. With almost 2 billion cell phones sold per year globally, cell phones are the highest-selling consumer electronics product by far. New cell phone products like the wearable phone shown in the image and multi-use phones that have become entertainment and financial transaction centers are becoming more commonplace. Personal health applications allow cell phone users to connect to a number of health management activities. The Nike+ Fuelband and a Bluetooth-connected cell phone allow users to get constant feedback regarding their activities.[38]

PACKAGING TRENDS

In the pharmaceutical industry, packaging is playing a key role in fighting counterfeiting and tampering, while aiding traceability. Unique, item-level code numbers on all prescription medicines, along with a feature showing that the outer packaging has not been tampered with, will soon be required. Germany-based August Faller, a pharmaceutical packaging manufacturer, is getting ready by developing barcodes and alphanumeric codes for the serial coding of pharmaceuticals.[39]

The use of standup pouches as shown here is another recent packaging trend. These first gained popularity with their use for children's juice drinks, but today there are a number of other uses for standup pouches, and they can hold more than five pounds. Examples are pouches for pet food, yogurt, shredded cheese, candy, coffee, chemicals, and liquids. These pouches can reduce container weight by 95%, compared to rigid containers (reducing transportation costs); they are recyclable; and they can also reduce store shelf footprints by 10%.

Sleeve labels are another very fast-growing trend in packaging. They are quickly replacing adhesive labels, since they can both shrink and stretch to fit most tube-type containers like drink containers and hair care, beauty, and cosmetic containers. Since sleeve labels can cover almost 100% of the container, the label advertising can significantly improve a product's shelf impact.[40]

iStock/inkspotts

Though they first came into popular use with children's juice drinks, standup pouches are now commonly used for packaging a number of foods and liquids.

WORKPLACE DESIGN TRENDS

Office construction is continuing to grow in the United States, by about 4%–6% per year. Office buildings need workplace designs and these are changing rapidly today, as Millenials (people born between 1980 and 2000) begin to make up a majority of office personnel. Today's office designs are driven by changing work styles, mobile technology, and the desire to encourage creativity and teamwork. Perimeter offices are disappearing, floor plans are opening up, and trendy breakout areas are appearing. Mobile technology allows work to happen anywhere, 24/7. "More than ever, we see young companies owned or dominated by Millenials gravitating to historic downtown buildings, where they're installing sustainable, laid-back interiors with adaptable furniture systems and a surprisingly high finish quality," says Barry Fires, CEO of contractor B. R. Fries & Associates.[41]

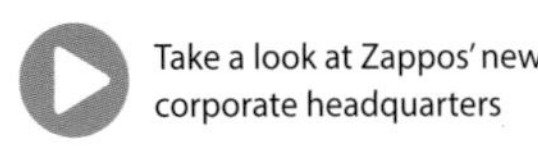
Take a look at Zappos' new corporate headquarters

Hierarchy and seniority are no longer the key factors in workplace design. Surveys by architecture firm LPA Inc. show that employees are more productive when given a variety of places to work. Knowledge workers spend just 40% of their time at their desks, as teamwork tasks have increased to about 80% of the workday. Current workspace concepts attempt to create neighborhoods that are not necessarily departmental. The idea is to give workers a feeling of membership in a club and not simply ownership of a desk. "Employee costs are the largest expense for any company, so making staff comfortable benefits the bottom line," says Rick D'Amato, an LPA principal.[42]

A FEW INNOVATIVE NEW PRODUCT EXAMPLES

The Edison Awards, established in 1987 by the American Marketing Association, annually recognize some of the most innovative goods and services in the world. Each year, nominations are sought from product and service innovators in 15 categories. The nominations are vetted by members of the Edison Awards Steering Committee, who then present a slate of finalists to the Edison Awards Panel of Judges. The panel is comprised of more than 3,000 senior U.S. business executives and academics who assess each finalist across four criteria—concept, value, delivery, and impact. The Edison Awards are named after Thomas A. Edison (1847–1931), whose extraordinary new product development methods garnered him 1,093 U.S. patents and made him a household name across the world. The 2015 award winners included:[43]

- *SCiO™, by Consumer Physics.* SCiO is the world's first molecular sensor that fits in the palm of your hand! With SCiO you can scan materials and get instant relevant information directly to your smartphone. It is a nonintrusive, no-touch sensor that provides a seamless user experience.
- *THESBOT, by HiBot Corporation.* THESBOT is a snake-like robot developed for pipe inspection. Its innovative concept allows it to autonomously climb vertical pipes and negotiate elbows, u-bends, and T-joints in pipes as small as 3 inches. While acquiring real-time images, THESBOT may carry other specialized sensors, providing invaluable information for predictive plant maintenance.
- *DAQRI Smart Helmet, by DAQRI.* DAQRI's Smart Helmet is a professional-grade hardhat that uses 4D augmented reality technology to connect workers to their environments. The head-mounted display improves productivity, safety, and efficiency by allowing work instructions to be seen through the helmet in the context of the job being done.
- *LDG Light Bulb™, by Parhelion Incorporated.* LDG (Laser Diffraction Grating) Light Bulb. LDG is a laser-based light with passive cooling. It features combined blue light wavelength and a beam-splitting optical component, able to shine through fire, smoke, fog, and mist without the blinding fog. The light uses 1 watt, 38 Lumens, for 10,000 hours, reaching deep without loss of intensity.
- *Rave Panic Button™, by Rave Mobile Safety.* With the single press of a button, the Rave Panic Button smartphone app immediately connects users to 9-1-1 and simultaneously warns other onsite personnel of an emergency, thereby accelerating response and notifying others who either may be in danger or could provide faster intervention.
- *Talkitt®, by Voiceitt.* Talkitt is the only solution that enables people that have speech disabilities due to motor, speech, and language disorders to easily communicate using their own voice. The Voice2Voice application translates unintelligible pronunciation into understandable speech and runs on any mobile or wearable device, allowing the person to communicate freely, anywhere.

- *myLINGO, by myLINGO.* myLINGO is a mobile application that allows theatergoers to enjoy movies in their language of choice, using their smartphone and earphones. Audio plays through the earphones in perfect sync with the film, making the in-theater experience more accessible and bringing multilingual families together at the movies.

SUMMARY

The development of new goods and services is a complex issue, involving the firm's core competencies, its customers, its competitors, and a product's financial requirements. Successful products will help to ensure that firms maintain their profits and competitive advantage. New product and process teams take new ideas that have completed a thorough screening process and decide how best to design these products and processes to meet customer requirements. The product development process was discussed, along with activities to reduce new product development lead times. Environmental considerations also impact the way products and processes are designed, and this topic was explored in the chapter. Finally, some innovative new products were described.

KEY TERMS

Basic research, 56
Benchmarking, 57
Concurrent engineering, 63
Contract manufacturers, 55
Contract services, 55
Design for manufacture and assembly, 65
Early supplier involvement, 64
House of quality, 58
Internal rate of return, 59
Life cycle assessments, 66
Net present value, 59
Neuroscience, 57
Open innovation, 56
Pilot manufacturing, 63
Product design, 52
Quality function deployment, 58
Sashimi system, 64
Service blueprinting, 61
Strategic fit, 54
Sustainable product and process design, 66
Value engineering, 64

FORMULA REVIEW

Net present value, NPV $= \frac{(\text{Cash flow year 1})}{(1+\text{discount rate})^1} + \frac{(\text{Cash flow year 2})}{(1+\text{discount rate})^2} + \ldots + \frac{(\text{Cash flow year Y})}{(1+\text{discount rate})^Y}$,

where Y = the year number.

Internal rate of return, IRR, solve iteratively → Initial investment $= \frac{(\text{Cash flow year 1})}{(1+\text{IRR})^1} + \frac{(\text{Cash flow year 2})}{(1+\text{IRR})^2} + \ldots + \frac{(\text{Cash flow year Y})}{(1+\text{IRR})^Y}$, where Y = the year number.

SOLVED PROBLEMS

1. Given the following end-of-year cash flows, find the net present value of the two projects using a 12% discount rate:

   Project 1: Initial investment—$52,000. Cash in-flows: Year 1—$61,000; Year 2—$22,000; Year 3—$7,500; Year 4—$4,100.

   Project 2: Initial investment—$47,000. Cash in-flows: Year 1—$46,000; Year 2—$27,000; Year 3—$13,500; Year 4—$6,200.

Answer:

For Project 1, the Year 1 NPV $= \frac{(61{,}000)}{(1.12)^1} = \$54{,}464$.

The Year 2 NPV $= \frac{(22{,}000)}{(1.12)^2} = \$17{,}538$. The NPVs are shown here.

Year	Cash in-flows$_1$	NPV$_1$	Cash in-flows$_2$	NPV$_2$
1	$61,000	$54,464	$46,000	$41,071
2	22,000	17,538	27,000	21,524
3	7,500	5,338	13,500	9,609
4	4,100	2,606	6,200	3,940
Total		$79,946		$76,144
Initial Investment		–$52,000		–$47,000
Total Value		$27,946		$29,144

2. For Problem 1, about how long will it take to recover the initial investments?

Answer:

Project 1: Approximately $\frac{52{,}000}{54{,}464}$ of first year, or 0.95 years, or 11.5 months.

Project 2: Approximately $1 + \frac{(47{,}000 - 41{,}071)}{21{,}524}$ years, or 1.28 years, or 15.4 months.

3. Given the data in Problem 1, determine the IRRs for the two projects. Which one do you think is the better investment?

Answer:

Project 1: Must iteratively solve $52{,}000 = \frac{61{,}000}{1+\text{IRR}} + \frac{22{,}000}{(1+\text{IRR})^2} + \frac{7{,}500}{(1+\text{IRR})^3} + \frac{4{,}100}{(1+\text{IRR})^4}$

We know the IRR is more than the 12% discount rate; let's guess 40%:

$52{,}000 = 43{,}571 + 11{,}224 + 2{,}733 + 1{,}067 = 58{,}595$. Too low; try 50%:

$52{,}000 = 40{,}667 + 9{,}778 + 2{,}222 + 810 = 53{,}477$. Now it's close; let's try 55%:

$52{,}000 = 39{,}355 + 9{,}157 + 2{,}014 + 710 = 51{,}236$. A bit too high, so the IRR is slightly less than 55%.

Project 2: Must iteratively solve $47{,}000 = \frac{46{,}000}{1+\text{IRR}} + \frac{27{,}000}{(1+\text{IRR})^2} + \frac{13{,}500}{(1+\text{IRR})^3} + \frac{6{,}200}{(1+\text{IRR})^4}$

Again, we know the IRR is more than 12%; let's guess 40%:

$47{,}000 = 32{,}857 + 13{,}776 + 4{,}920 + 1{,}614 = 53{,}167$. Too low; try 50%:

47,000 = 30,667 + 12,000 + 4,000 + 1,225 = 47,892. Very close; try 52%:

47,000 = 30,263 + 11,686 + 3,844 + 1,161 = 46,954. Close enough; the IRR is approximately 52%.

Project 1 has a lower payback time and a higher IRR, while Project 2 has a higher total value. Since the projects are similar, it is likely that Project 1 would be seen as slightly better.

REVIEW QUESTIONS

1. What is product design, and what things should be considered for a good product design?
2. What is core competency, and what does it have to do with product design?
3. What are some of the different considerations when designing services instead of goods?
4. Why is variability an important issue in new service design?
5. What is strategic fit? Explain the differences between internal fit and external fit.
6. Define basic research and open innovation, and then explain what they have to do with the new product development process.
7. What is the house of quality matrix, and how is it used?
8. What is pilot manufacturing, and during which phase of the new product development process is it used?
9. What is concurrent engineering, and how is it different from the sashimi system? How do these reduce product development lead times?
10. What is value engineering, when is it used, and how is it used in new product design efforts?
11. Define three-dimensional concurrent engineering.
12. What is design for manufacture and assembly (DFMA)? What activity is closely associated with DFMA?

DISCUSSION QUESTIONS

1. Why would a firm want to use a contract manufacturer or service instead of making a good or service in-house?
2. How could benchmarking help to generate new product ideas?
3. Explain how your college or university could use the house of quality matrix to improve its degree programs.
4. Use Table 3.2 to analyze a new undergraduate degree in Supply Chain Management at a business school.
5. How does the net present value of a project differ from its internal rate of return? When would you prefer one over the other?
6. Design a service blueprint for the lunch buffet or a food counter at your school.
7. Describe how three-dimensional concurrent engineering might be used if your local sandwich restaurant decided it needed to start making pizza.
8. How might design for manufacture and assembly (DFMA) be used at a fast-food restaurant?
9. What are some considerations when including environmental aspects in product design? Use an example in your discussion.
10. How do product designers gauge the environmental impacts of their product designs?
11. Why should firms worry about disposal issues when designing new products?

EXERCISES AND PROJECTS

1. Compare and contrast the Apple cell phone and the Nokia cell phone, along with the histories of both companies. How successful are these companies today? Do you think their success had something to do with product designs?
2. Research the development of the Tesla Model S electric vehicle using Figure 3.1 as a guide. Describe Tesla's core competency and strategic fit. Is Tesla successful today?
3. Construct a service blueprint for one of your favorite restaurants, and describe all of the elements in the blueprint. Explain how you might make some improvements based on the blueprint.

PROBLEMS

Use the following information for Problems 1, 2, and 3.

The management at Luke Products Inc. is looking at the financials for an innovative new diaper-changing station. The expected life cycle for the product is four years. The initial projected product design costs are $500,000. Management typically uses a discount rate of 10% for all new product financials.

Year	Projected Cash In-Flows ($)
1	130,000
2	250,000
3	300,000
4	100,000

1. Calculate the projected NPV.
2. Calculate the payback time.
3. Calculate the IRR.
4. The product design costs are $250,000. Use a discount rate of 9% for the projected cash in-flows. Assume a five-year lifespan. Calculate the projected NPV, the payback time, and the IRR.

Year	Projected Cash In-Flows ($)
1	120,000
2	90,000
3	75,000
4	50,000
5	20,000

5. For the two projects here and using a discount rate of 12%, decide which one should receive the investment funds.

Year	Projected Cash Flows$_1$ ($)	Projected Cash Flows$_2$ ($)
Cost	– $325,000	– $285,000
1	138,000	112,000
2	225,000	188,000
3	240,000	154,000
4	55,000	86,000

6. Using a discount rate of 6%, determine the NPV, the payback time, and the IRR.

Year	Projected Cash Flows ($)
Cost	– $405,000
1	174,000
2	128,000
3	110,000
4	102,000
Salvage	50,000

7. Which product project would be the best, using a discount rate of 8%?
   a. Estimated investment cost of $185,000; annual cash in-flows of $26,000 for 10 years, with a salvage value of $2,500.
   b. Estimated investment cost of $82,000; annual cash in-flows of $6,000 for 25 years, with no salvage value.
   c. Estimated investment cost of $249,000; annual cash in-flows of $80,000 for four years, with a salvage value of $16,000.

Use the following information for Problems 8 and 9.

Year	Cash Flows ($)	Year	Cash Flows ($)
0	–845,000	3	300,000
1	450,000	4	140,000
2	365,000	5	–25,000

8. Find the NPV and the IRR for the cash flows by hand, using a discount rate of 10%.
9. Using your spreadsheet software, find the NPV and the IRR for the cash flows, using a discount rate of 10%.
10. Find the NPV and the IRR for the following cash flows by hand, and then using your spreadsheet software. Use a discount rate of 12%.

Year	Cash Flows ($)	Year	Cash Flows ($)
0	–425,000	5	425,000
1	–250,000	6	280,000
2	–55,000	7	150,000
3	220,000	8	40,000
4	365,000		

CASE STUDIES

CASE 1: Sustainability at New Belgium Brewing Company

New Belgium Brewing Company is on the fast track when it comes to understanding and reducing its impact on the environment. As part of New Belgium's strategy planning process it used a balanced scorecard to measure its success in achieving its goals. Its balanced scorecard has five segments: Environmental Sustainability, Customer/Marketplace, Internal Process, Financial, and Co-workers and Culture. The components of the balanced scorecard tie back to the company's core values and beliefs.[1] For example, environmental stewardship has been a core value since it began as a company. It supported this effort by establishing a Sustainability Management System (SMS) where it made the planet a core value for the stakeholders. Two pertinent questions New Belgium managers asked were, "What are we trying to achieve with our sustainability strategy?" and "How might we achieve it?" They understood that for the SMS to be effective they must establish targets for environmental metrics. New Belgium established Key Performance Indicators (KPIs) for the following areas: greenhouse gas emissions, waste diversion, energy intensity, and water intensity.[2]

Water intensity is measured in the amount of hectoliters (HL) of water used to make one hectoliter of beer. A barrel of beer (U.S.) holds approximately 1.17 HL. At one time, New Belgium water intensity was 4.31 HL of water to produce one HL of beer. The key to achieving a reduction was to install water submeters to help it understand how it was using water. These measurements clarified which activities and brews were the most water-intensive.[3] Consequently, New Belgium could analyze the brewing process and determine areas for improvement in water usage. In 2006, the amount of water used to produce one HL of beer was 3.99

HL. By 2014, it had reduced it to 3.96 HL. The goal for 2015 was to reduce it to 3.50 HL.[4]

New Belgium took a big-picture approach to greenhouse gas emission reduction. It collected data in three areas: direct emissions, occurring from sources owned or controlled by New Belgium; indirect emissions, emissions created by the production of electricity used by New Belgium; and other indirect emissions, a result of activities by New Belgium but occurring from sources not owned or controlled by the company. One area it measured was the amount of kilograms (kg) of carbon dioxide (CO2) emitted per hectoliter of beer packaged. Again, after analyzing the data, New Belgium was able to reduce the amount of CO2 emissions.[3] It has used a similar methodology for each KPI, thus enabling it to improve sustainability.

DISCUSSION QUESTIONS

1. Product development is a reiterative process. Discuss the stages of the product development process New Belgium Brewing Company must routinely revisit to ensure it achieves its sustainability goals.
2. Do you think New Belgium's sustainability program is a strategic fit? Does it matter if sustainability is a strategic fit? Why?
3. What are the environmental impacts of the brewing process at New Belgium? Review the 2015 New Belgium Sustainability Report at: http://www.newbelgium.com/files/sustainability/New_Belgium_Sustainability_Brochure.pdf?pdf=sustainabilityreport

Note: Written by Rick Bonsall, D. Mgt., McKendree University, Lebanon, IL. This case was prepared solely to provide material for class discussion. The author does not intend to illustrate either effective or ineffective handling of a managerial situation.

Sources:

1. Sustainability in Strategic Alignment, http://www .newbelgium.com/Sustainability/Environmental-Metrics/strategic-alignment.aspx
2. New Belgium Brewing Company Inc., 2009, Sustainability Management System Version, http://www.newbelgium.com/Files/SMS% 203rd%20 edition,%202009%20for%20external%20release.pdf
3. New Belgium Sustainability Report, 2015, http://www.newbelgium.com/files/sustainability/New_Belgium_Sustainability_Brochure.pdf?pdf=sustainabilityreport
4. Water, http://www.newbelgium.com/Sustainability/Environmental-Metrics/Water.aspx

CASE 2: Target's Failure in Canada

Target stores have been a destination point for Canadians on shopping excursions to the United States.[1] As the number two retailer behind Walmart, Target wanted to expand its market in order to stay competitive and maintain growth. As the senior management team developed ideas, the idea of entering the Canadian market took hold. The question Target considered was, How could it provide the same level of service as it did in the United States?

One concept Target developed was the idea of getting Canadians accustomed to "one-stop shopping." Another part of its plan to expand services into Canada was to be aggressive in rolling out stores in the first year, 2013. As Target analyzed the situation, it discovered that Canada had a shortage of desirable retail space. To overcome this problem, Target decided to follow Walmart's lead and do what Walmart did 20 years ago.[1] Target decided that part of the expansion process was to buy the locations of an ailing discount chain. It approached Zellers, the last major Canadian discount chain, and negotiated a deal for leases of approximately 220 locations. The locations had about 100,000 square feet on average, which was about half the size of a Target store in the United States.[1] In addition, as part of the expansion process, Target gutted and rebuilt many of the locations. Target invested about $4 billion in its Canadian expansion. In 2013, it aggressively opened 124 stores.[1]

In 2014, Target abruptly announced it would shut down its Canadian stores.[3] Target suffered a $2 billion loss in its failed Canadian expansion plan.[4] The problems that led to this disaster were many. Target misread the market and made a false assumption about Canadians' preferred buying habits. Unlike their American neighbors, Canadians are not as interested in the "one-stop shopping" experience as Target had assumed. Consumers in Canada were also disappointed that the prices in Target's Canadian stores were higher than in its U.S. stores.[2] Furthermore, Target had significant supply chain issues. The stores often had empty shelves. In other situations they had excess inventories, resulting in major clearance sales. Finally, Walmart didn't stand by and let Target simply expand into Canada. It cut prices and expanded its number of stores.[2]

DISCUSSION QUESTIONS

1. Using the Product Development Process, in which stages did Target fail? Explain what it did wrong in those stages.
2. In its product analysis and screening, what questions did Target fail to answer concerning its retail service operations? Explain how it failed to answer these questions.

3. Also in its product analysis and screening, what questions did Target fail to answer concerning the competition? Explain where it went wrong.

4. Explain how use of the house of quality may have prevented this failure. Which "rooms" or areas of the house would have helped in the product analysis and screening stage?

Note: Written by Rick Bonsall, D. Mgt., McKendree University, Lebanon, IL. This case was prepared solely to provide material for class discussion. The author does not intend to illustrate either effective or ineffective handling of a managerial situation.

Sources:

1. "Target Push Into Canada Stumbles," by I. Austin, 2014, *New York Times*, http://www.nytimes.com/2014/02/25/business/international/target-struggles-to-compete-in-canada.html

2. "Five Reasons Target Came Up Short in Canada," by B. Marotte, 2013, *The Globe and Mail*, http://www.theglobeandmail.com/report-on-business/five-reasons-target-came-up-short-in-canada/article15561013/

3. "Why Target Lost Its Aim," 2015, *The Economist*, http://www.economist.com/news/business/21645218-discount-store-chain-which-forgot-its-formula-success-why-target-lost-its-aim

4. "5 Reasons Target Failed in Canada," by H. Peterson, 2015, *Business Insider*, http://www.businessinsider.com/why-target-canada-failed-2015-1

CASE 3: Expanding Educational Opportunities

Dr. Musgrove, department chair in the School of Business, was concerned about the competitiveness of Hogwood University. He was confident that the quality of the education at Hogwood University could stand up against any university its size; however, customers were changing and he felt Hogwood needed to change as well. Dr. Musgrove's primary concern was that his university was stagnating in the way it delivered learning opportunities to its customer—students. His analysis of the current trends in higher education indicated that because of the tremendous strides in technology, online education was an essential educational delivery methodology. However, Hogwood had no program to meet the needs of those who preferred online classes. Dr. Musgrove discussed this with Dean Flummery, and the dean told him to present his argument next week for developing an online degree program.

Dr. Musgrove believed understanding the customer was critical to providing the expected level of service; therefore, he addressed the following questions: Why would students take an online class instead of a face-to-face class? What are their needs or requirements? He discovered there were several reasons why students preferred online over face to face. First, there was flexibility. Students could work on their courses at any time, thus enabling them to work around their busy schedules. Plus, the accessibility of online classes enabled disabled students to take the course; total cost was reduced; there was no need to commute; often e-textbooks are less expensive, and in some cases free; and printing costs go away since all assignments are electronic. Engagement is yet another reason why students take online courses. Those who may be shy and hesitant to speak up in a face-to-face class are more comfortable posting their ideas and comments to a discussion board. Students value online classes because they enhance student-to-student, student-to-instructor, and instructor-to-student interactions by reducing the intimidation factor. Furthermore, online classes allow students time to formulate their thoughts, an opportunity not always possible in face-to-face classes. Students see an online class as an opportunity to obtain the equivalent content of a face-to-face class while satisfying their other needs. They expect online classes to be as rigorous and challenging—and therefore as valuable and beneficial—as face-to-face instruction. Because of the nature of the online environment, students expect that various types of technology will be used. Many seek out this environment in order to enhance their networking and technology skills, thereby increasing their marketability to employers.

Dr. Musgrove determined that the components of the skill set required for either online or face-to-face classes were the same; however, the degree of skill or competency required is much greater for online students. Online students must have a high computer literacy—they must be familiar with the functions of a computer, use of browsers for Internet access, and software applications. Additionally, students must be able to navigate the learning management system (such as Blackboard) that the university uses. This includes the ability to utilize discussion boards, chats, blogs, and wikis. Furthermore, since online courses are both reading and writing intensive, students must be strong in both these skills. Time management is an essential skill since most online courses are asynchronous, and therefore have no specific date and time to attend. Consequently, Dr. Musgrove determined that to ensure the success of the online student and the online program, a mandatory online orientation course must be provided. This mandatory course would "test" students to determine if they possessed the required skill set to be successful in online classes.

Dr. Musgrove's revelation of the need for an online orientation course drove him to investigate online course designs. Just as the customer requirements are different for online classes, the design of the course tends to be different as well.

Unlike a face-to-face class, where the planned instruction can be changed on the spur of the moment, online class design is less flexible. Since classes are asynchronous and students sign on at different times, changing assignment requirements for the coming week can result in disaster and dissatisfaction. Consequently, the course must be well organized in modules and lessons. Links to material outside of the specific learning management system must be tested to ensure the link's function. Videos, blogs, and podcasts must be incorporated into the course design. Discussion questions must be thought-provoking in order to promote an active dialogue among the students. Instructions for assignment must be as concise as possible while still being clear. Feedback on assignments must be timely. Activities must be designed in a manner that permits and encourages student involvement and interaction.

Dr. Musgrove felt prepared for his meeting with Dean Flummery. He understood the customers' requirements and the product design criteria for an online business degree program.

DISCUSSION QUESTIONS

1. Has Dr. Musgrove followed the initial stages of the product development process? If Dean Flummery agrees with Dr. Musgrove, what is the next step in the product development process?

2. Would the house of quality be an effective tool in the development of an online degree program? Discuss your answer.

3. Product analysis and screening is a critical stage in the product development process. What questions about the product, the competition, and the financials should Hogwood University address?

Note: Written by Rick Bonsall, D. Mgt., McKendree University, Lebanon, IL. The people and institution are fictional and any resemblance to any person or any institution is consequential. This case was prepared solely to provide material for class discussion. The author does not intend to illustrate either effective or ineffective handling of a managerial situation.

VIDEO CASE STUDY

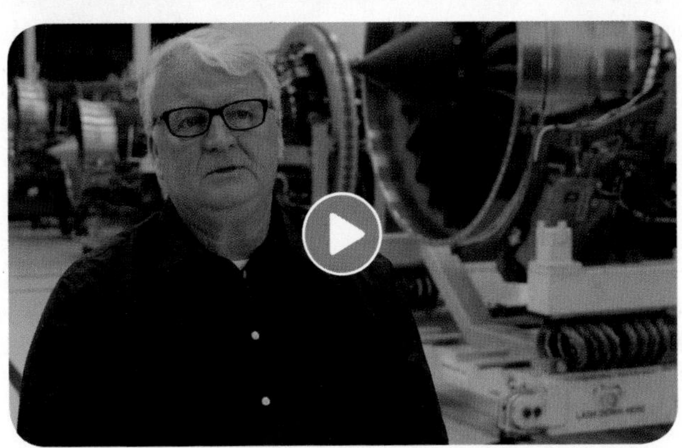

Learn more about ***designing and developing new products*** from real organizations that use operations management techniques every day. Chris Fultz is the Director of the Program Management Office for Rolls-Royce's defense business in Indianapolis, Indiana. Rolls-Royce is the world's second-largest provider of defense aero-engine products and services; developing new products keeps them in high demand. Watch this short interview to find out how they do it.

If you don't like something change it; if you can't change it, change the way you think about it.

—**MARY ENGELBREIT,** illustrator, founder and CEO, Mary Engelbreit Studios[1]

Organizations are becoming more involved in green initiatives by adopting sustainable processes and practices, adapting products and services to the low-carbon economy and innovating in all areas of their business.

—**JOHN GARRETT,** CEO, Facilities Management Advisors[2]

PROCESS DESIGN AND CAPACITY MANAGEMENT

4

LEARNING OBJECTIVES

After completing this chapter, you should be able to:

4.1 Describe the different types of processes and the types of outputs they create
4.2 Create a process flowchart and describe how it is used
4.3 Explain the relationships among capacity, capacity utilization, and process design
4.4 Illustrate how break-even analysis is used to compare potential investments in make-versus-buy decisions
4.5 Summarize the benefits of sustainability in process designs

Master the content.

edge.sagepub.com/wisner

MASS CUSTOMIZATION IN CAMPUS DINING HALLS

College students at a number of campuses across the United States are getting a taste of mass customized meals. Food on Demand (FoD) blends the customization and food quality of a restaurant with the speed and efficiency that students expect from a campus dining hall. Guests place their orders at touch-screen kiosks, watch their food being prepared, and are alerted on their smartphones when their food is ready. "It has dynamically changed the dining experience for the guest," says Jeff Pente, senior director of brand management for Maryland-based Sodexo, which operates the concept. "Before, students dropped their books and went online. Now, students come in, place their order on a touch screen, and then drop their books and hang out a few minutes before they are buzzed that their food is ready. Nobody is doing anything like this in the [college campus] marketplace," adds Pente.

The FoD program, which debuted in 2010, features daily selections from a library of more than 400 recipes that run the gamut from healthful vegetable pita plates to bar food such as onion rings. More than 80 countries' cuisines are represented, including exclusive menus by chef-restaurateurs Mai Pham, who created a Vietnamese and Thai menu, and Roberto Santibanez, who designed high-end Mexican dishes. "It's like the Food Network on campus compared to what was there before," Pente says.

There is no additional cost for students on meal plans to visit FoD rather than conventional dining halls. The concept serves an average of 500 diners each meal, and the average ticket time is six to seven minutes, including the three minutes or so it takes to cook a student's meal. "The dining halls feel like mass-produced meals, but [with FoD], every meal you get is made to order," says Shannon Hitchcock, an assistant dean who works at New York's Rensselaer Polytechnic, one of the schools using FoD.

FoD does not cost any more to operate than a conventional college dining operation, according to Tom Post, Sodexo division president. Additionally, food waste is reduced because students are getting only what they request. While most campus dining halls are in the 10,000 square-foot range, FoD requires a footprint of one fourth that size. FoD also requires a smaller staff. Finally, FoD allows staff to interact more with students. "Long gone are the days when the chefs are hiding behind the doors," says Jackie Baldwin, executive chef of the FoD program at Rensselaer. "You're right there engaging with the students. You're there asking, 'What did you like?' or 'What changes would you like to see?'"[3]

INTRODUCTION

As product designs are created and approved, companies must also consider how these goods and services are to be created. Depending on the firm's resources and the tooling, worker expertise, and technologies available, the manufacturing processes utilized might be highly automated or depend more on labor and their expertise. Government policy might even play a role in process design—in developing countries like Vietnam and Indonesia, for example, many factories use limited automation in order to employ as many people as possible.

Managers typically must consider the types of processes, the goods and services to be produced, the existing and the required process capacities, the competition, and the environmental impact of the various processes being considered. Managers must also understand how various processes work in order to achieve the required capacities. Additionally, managers must be able to design processes to fit with the organization's products, in order to maximize competitiveness. A poorly designed process can add costs and thus reduce a firm's ability to compete.

Processes can be found in any part of the organization—they take inputs and turn them into outputs. Some might be fast and inexpensive, while others might be slow and very costly. Good processes in one period might become bad ones in the next. For this reason, performance measures are employed to monitor processes. Processes in manufacturing might consist of robotic welding machines, automated assembly lines, stamping machines, and conveyors. Processes in services might include examinations, mortgage approvals, airline travel, warehousing, and legal defense. In every case, outputs can be produced well or poorly. These topics and more are discussed in this chapter.

TYPES OF PROCESSES

4.1 Describe the different types of processes and the types of outputs they create

Ideally, as described in Chapter 3, the processes for manufacturing a good or delivering a service are designed concurrently with the new product. Organizations generally match production processes to the product based on two criteria:

- The desired production volume
- The variety of goods or services desired

As the desired output for a process increases, automation and standardization requirements also tend to increase, which may mean fewer product or service variations or customizations. If high levels of variety are desired, this typically means lower output, since product or service customizations require additional equipment setups and longer production times. Some processes, though, still try to offer both volume and variety.

Banks, for example, provide ATMs for customers requiring high speed, but these offer limited services. Inside the bank, customers might use teller services, obtain access to safe-deposit boxes, open new accounts, and apply for loans, but all at much slower service speeds. Thus, as product variety increases, production output levels and speed tend to decrease. Additionally, with greater product variety come more special-purpose equipment and requirements for employees with greater levels of special equipment operating skills. As shown in Table 4.1, production processes can be separated into four basic types, as described in the following sections.

Table 4.1 Process Categories and Their Characteristics

	Job Shop	Batch	Assembly Line	Continuous
Output Volume	Very Low	Low-Medium	High	Very High
Product Variety	Very High	High	Low-Medium	Very Low
Equipment Flexibility	Very High	Medium	Low	Very Low
Employee Skills	Very High	Medium-High	Medium-Low	Low
Manufacturing Example	Auto Repair	Candy Making	Auto Assembly	Oil Refinery
Service Example	Mortgage Banking	Lasik Eye Surgery	Cafeteria	Website

JOB SHOP PROCESSES

iStock/fatihhoca

Skilled workers, work-in-process, raw materials, and scrap items are found in most machine shops.

Job shop processes are used when organizations offer custom products or services. Output volumes are typically low, unit prices are high, waiting time can be long, and production flexibility to accommodate customer requirements is high. The production area is characterized by departments where similar processing equipment or specialties are housed. As work (or service customers) makes its way through the facility, some departments may be very busy, causing queues to develop, while others might not, depending on the processing required. Workers are generally highly skilled on one or more pieces of equipment, and the equipment used in the processes is flexible.

Several standard inventory items might be held in these facilities as raw materials; however, job shops generally wait until customers arrive and jobs are generated, prior to purchasing materials and parts. Therefore, most job shop inventories are work-in-process. A visit to a large job shop (or machine shop) would reveal a number of jobs in various stages of completion, a number of others scheduled to begin, and queues of jobs waiting to be processed on busy machines or processes. Pallets of jobs, boxes of parts, tools, and scrap materials might also be found. As jobs are completed, they are delivered to customers. Machine shops, printing shops, engineering consultants, auto repair garages, physicians' offices, and beauty salons are examples of job shop environments. (Chapter 8 and its supplement discuss job shop layouts and job scheduling.)

Watch a job shop in action

At the extreme, a **project process** is a type of job shop process where one unique product is created, requiring one unique set of processes. Projects are highly customized, and project process output is very low. Project examples include office buildings, swimming pools, luxury yachts, medical procedures, and artwork. (More on projects can be found in Chapter 12.)

job shop processes Facilities with departments where similar processing equipment or specialties are housed, offering custom products or services. Output volumes are low, unit prices are high, waiting time is long, and production flexibility to accommodate customer requirements is high.

project process A type of job shop process where one unique product is manufactured requiring one unique set of processes.

batch processes Processes allowing moderate customization and higher output volume. Batch production occurs when a limited number of units are created stage by stage over a series of workstations.

assembly line processes Processes that produce high output volumes, with low unit prices, but with little production flexibility.

BATCH PROCESSES

Batch processes are found in organizations where moderate customization and higher volume are required by customers. Batch production occurs when a limited number of units are created stage by stage over a series of workstations. Batch production is commonly found in bakeries, paint facilities, semicustom furniture manufacturers, and LASIK eye surgery. In the manufacture of paint, a technique called a color run is used. A color run occurs when the lightest color is made first, followed by increasingly darker colors until reaching black. For batch manufacturers, less flexibility is needed, the equipment is more automated, and finished product completion times are shorter than in a job shop. Workers also may have fewer equipment skills than those in a job shop setting.

ASSEMBLY LINE PROCESSES

Assembly line processes produce high output volumes and low unit prices, but with little production flexibility. Customers take deliveries from finished goods inventories, so no wait time is involved. Equipment is arranged in sequence according to the product's required processing steps, and must have a high degree of precision; this requires significant automation. Part assemblies are done in stations, which are designed to achieve a particular output. Final assembly is completed on a moving assembly line. The line workers have limited tasks, such as equipment maintenance and product quality control. Assembly lines typically have relatively high levels of raw material inventories compared to job shops. Automobiles, televisions, cell

iStock/bugphai

Most assembly lines use high levels of automation, as seen here. This allows for little production flexibilty, but keeps costs low and output volumes high.

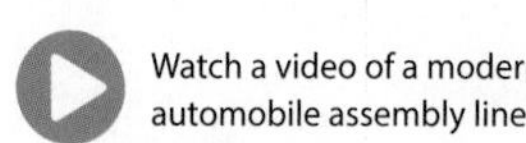
Watch a video of a modern automobile assembly line

phones, and restaurant buffets use an assembly line–type approach. (More on assembly lines can be found in Chapter 8.)

CONTINUOUS PROCESSES

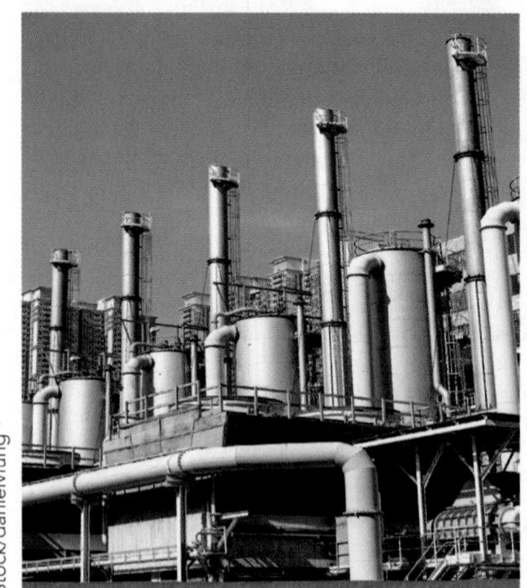
iStock/danielvfung

Continuous processes are highly automated and designed to make large quantities of one type of product. Chemical plants like the one shown here use continuous processes.

Continuous processes provide little or no product variety, and equipment is highly automated and dedicated to one specific task. The product flow is continuous with high volumes produced per day, as with electric generating stations, oil refineries, soft drink bottling facilities, and company websites. The labor generally consists of maintenance and production-monitoring personnel. Driving past one of these facilities might reveal no movement of product or people.

An oil refinery is one type of continuous process. A typical large refinery costs billions of dollars to build and millions more to operate each year. It runs around the clock and occupies up to several hundred acres of land. A refinery can process up to several hundred thousand barrels of crude oil per day, breaking it down into various components, which are then changed into gasoline, diesel, and other refined petroleum products. This process takes place inside a maze of pipes and vessels. The refinery is operated from a highly automated control room.

In each of the four processes described here, a trade-off exists—if companies make custom goods and services, they give up speed and volume (or capacity). The more speed and volume companies want, the less product customization they tend to provide. The Process Customization—Volume Relationship (also referred to as the Product—Process Matrix) illustrates this relationship, and is shown in Figure 4.1. Likewise with service providers, higher customer volume (and more sales) means less customer contact and fewer service customizations. One notable exception to this is the mass customization process, which is discussed in the following section.

MASS CUSTOMIZATION

The **mass customization process** is a hybrid process, combining several aspects of the job shop and assembly line processes. The term may sound like an oxymoron, since the objective of mass customization is to create a high volume of customized products. Combining product variety and high volume allows more consumers to find what they want at reasonable prices, as highlighted in the chapter opener on Food on Demand. It also moves companies from a mass marketing strategy to one of relationship marketing. As customers tell the company what they want, the company meets these needs while also learning something about the customers. Creating these relationships with customers hopefully leads to repeat sales later on. Maine-based CedarWorks, a wooden playset manufacturer, uses mass customization and high levels of customer interaction to offer affluent customers a once-in-a-lifetime playset with quick turnaround times, high quality, and acceptable prices. Its 98% customer satisfaction rating generates referrals that account for about one-third of its business.[4]

continuous processes Processes with almost no product variety and equipment that is highly automated and dedicated to one task. The product flow is continuous.

mass customization process A hybrid process combining several aspects of the job shop and assembly line processes to create high volume production of customized products.

Figure 4.1 Process Customization and Volume Relationship

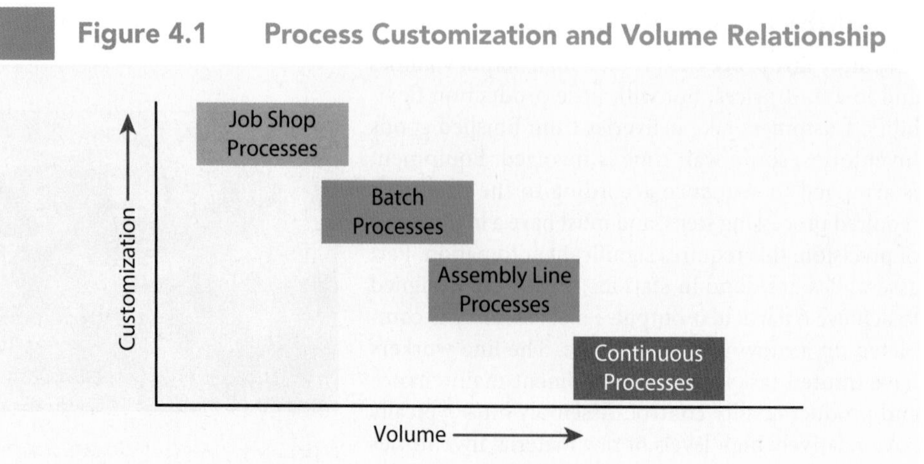

Firms can accomplish mass customization using **postponement**. If a company can first postpone and then customize the final assembly of a mass-produced product when the specific customer orders are received, then mass customization can be achieved. Texas-based Dell Computers was one of the first computer companies to utilize the concept of mass customization. Dell takes phone and Internet orders from customers, then builds a customized product using mass-produced, preexisting components. The computer then lands at the customer's doorstep in a few days.[5] Today, consumers can customize their M&M candies by selecting colors, messages, and packaging; build custom Nike shoes through the company's NikeId site; or custom build one of five Toyota Scion models, just to name a few examples.

iStock/20fifteen

Nike allows for mass customization of their shoes through postponement. Customers can pick from a wide range of colors and designs to create shoes to their own specification.

Today, technological advances and the proliferation of social media have created consumers who expect companies to cater to their every whim. Evidently, Burger King had it right 40 years ago with its slogan, "Have it your way." Recently, it revised the slogan to be even more consumer-centric; now it's "Be your way."[6] Massachusetts-based business research company Forrester Research recently predicted that mass customization would be an enduring consumer trend: "Higher shopper expectations, the dawn of tablets and apps, and the rise of cheaper, more advanced web technologies will make the phenomenon take off in the next decade."[7]

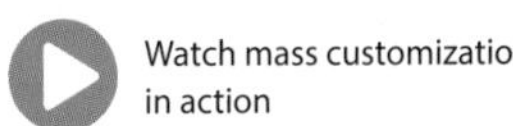
Watch mass customization in action

PROCESS CLASSIFICATION BASED ON OUTPUTS

Another way to think about processes is by the way the outputs are produced. Products can be produced on make-to-order, make-to-stock, or assemble-to-order processes. Each of these is discussed in the following sections.

Make-to-Order (MTO) Processes

Make-to-order processes create custom products, as described previously, from job shops, projects, and some batch facilities. Customers arrive at the firm with an idea, a blueprint, or a design for a product, and the firm is tasked with finding materials, parts, and suppliers, then arranging the sequence of processes to build the products as designed. Consequently, completion times are generally quite long, unit costs are relatively high, and output levels are relatively low. Many specialty services fall into the MTO category—a beauty salon, a fine-clothing tailor, a surgeon, and a gourmet restaurant would be examples.

Make-To-Stock (MTS) Processes

Make-to-stock processes create stock products in anticipation of demand, such as might be found on a shelf at a retailer. Assembly lines, continuous producers, and some batch producers would fall into the MTS category. The idea is to remove customization to enable high volume production and low unit costs. Customers select from finished products on the shelf or in a catalog, so there is only minimal customer order lead time. Unit costs are relatively low, since output levels are high. Services such as retailers, buffet restaurants, television shows, and airline flights fall into this category.

Assemble-to-Order (ATO) Processes

Mass customization producers utilize **assemble-to-order processes**. Dell, Nike, and Toyota Scion were described earlier as firms that make use of mass customization and thus assemble products once orders are received. In this way, companies can stock large quantities of parts, enabling quantity-discounted purchase costs, and configure final assemblies quickly to accommodate customer requirements. Customers choose from limited sets of parts, colors,

postponement A mass customization term, occurring when the final assembly is postponed until the specific customer orders are received.

make-to-order processes Processes that create custom products from job shops, projects, and some batch facilities.

make-to-stock processes Processes that create stock products in anticipation of demand.

assemble-to-order processes Processes that make use of mass customization and thus assemble products once orders are received.

and assemblies shown in catalogs or websites, and then wait for final assembly and shipment. ATO products are usually less costly than similar MTO products, since little design work is required. ATO products also have lower customer order lead times than similar MTO products; however, product configurations are more limited. Figure 4.2 illustrates the relationship among process classification, unit prices, and customer order lead times.

PROCESS FLOWCHARTING AND ANALYSIS

4.2 Create a process flowchart and describe how it is used

Some processes are actually groups of many other processes. An assembly line is designed with a number of interrelated processing activities or stations making a large quantity of standardized items; a job shop is a set of individual departmentalized processes designed to make smaller quantities of customized goods. Taken as a whole, these sets of many processes define the organization, and how successful it can be, relative to its competitors. The Service Spotlight on page 85 describes how Intermountain Healthcare analyzed its organization's processes to concentrate on the few processes accounting for most of its work.

A firm is thus a large collection of processes, some small and relatively simple, and others complex and key to the firm's operations and success. Recall there are eight key processes linking a firm to its trading partners. Besides manufacturing, there are internal processes in purchasing, advertising, accounting, distribution, marketing, and many others. A firm's personnel must know what its processes are, how they work, and when broken, how they can fix and improve them. Over time, processes change as requirements dictate; they evolve as product designs and markets change; and, if ignored, they can deteriorate and harm the organization.

A retailer frequently purchases merchandise from trusted suppliers based on accurate demand forecasts, then receives the items and displays them in an effective manner. Sales personnel help customers find what they want, make suggestions regarding other items, and then correctly charge them for what they purchase. They provide deliveries if needed, and after the sale, the firm offers services to customers so that they remain satisfied, return for further purchases, and tell others of their experiences. This story highlights a number of processes, and the firm has a good chance of being successful, provided it adequately manages its many processes and customers remain satisfied.

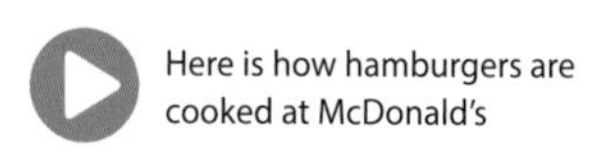

Here is how hamburgers are cooked at McDonald's

Let's compare the processes of several well-known fast-food restaurants—McDonald's, Wendy's, and Burger King. Obviously, all three sell pretty much the same thing, such as hamburgers and french fries, but what sets them apart from one another? Wendy's has one (and sometimes two) cashier(s) but only one queue; Burger King has the same queue arrangement, while McDonald's typically has multiple cashiers, each with a separate queue. McDonald's makes many of its products as stock items using quite a bit of automation. Some of the McDonald's food is MTS and sold from warming trays, while both Wendy's and Burger King use an ATO strategy. In some restaurants, Wendy's has soda machines behind the counter,

Figure 4.2 Process Classification and Customer Order Lead Time Relationship

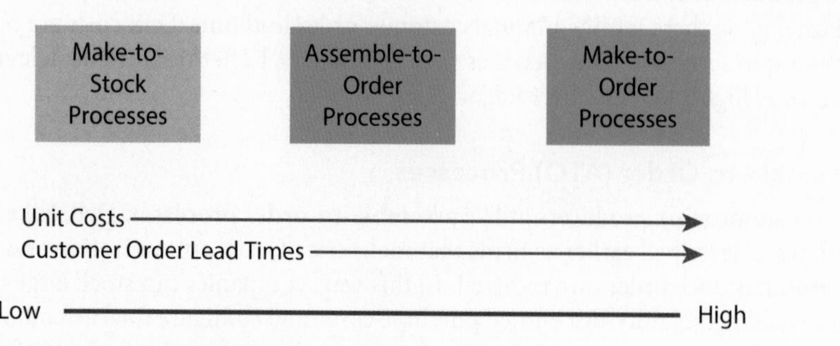

Process Analysis at Intermountain Healthcare

SERVICE SPOTLIGHT

Using key process analysis, Utah-based Intermountain Healthcare identified four major categories of key processes: treating clinical conditions, delivering clinical support services (such as radiology, nursing, or pharmacy), managing service quality, and administrative processes. Initially, it focused on clinical care delivery. It looked at more than 1,400 condition-related clinical processes. Of those, 104 processes accounted for 95% of its care delivery. This was the Pareto principle at work—technically, 7% of its clinical processes accounted for 95% of the work.

Next, Intermountain attacked clinical processes in size order. For example, management identified the two highest-volume clinical processes: pregnancy, labor, and delivery, and the management of heart disease. During the next year, it focused on those two processes.

The most challenging step was building the data systems needed to manage and track the clinical processes. Intermountain's current systems were not sufficient to manage clinical processes. It was missing 30 to 50% of the critical data elements and essentially had to build these data systems from scratch.

After building the data systems, Intermountain hired physicians and nurses for leadership positions in which they would be accountable for new clinical budgets. That is how physicians philosophically got on board. The strategy involved not only identifying leaders, but also making leaders effective.[8]

forcing customers to ask for a refill, while Burger King and McDonald's have their soda machines in the customer seating areas. Many McDonald's have play areas for children, while most Wendy's and Burger Kings do not. Recently, all three have expanded their menu offerings, although McDonald's has expanded the most. This has created some inefficiencies at McDonald's, which has seen increases in its average customer wait times. In many locations, McDonald's is adding a third service window to its drive-through lanes to reduce service times. Wendy's has tried to pay more attention to food quality, such as offering pretzel buns.

Which is the most successful? McDonald's by far is the largest of the three in terms of the number of locations. Furthermore, it takes in an average of $2.6 million per location per year in the United States, while Wendy's and Burger King have annual sales of about half that per unit. Over time, the processes at all three restaurants keep changing, as consumer tastes change, product offerings change, and the size of consumer pocketbooks change.[9] In the next section, we will look at how processes can be analyzed.

PROCESS FLOWCHARTING

process flowchart or process map A diagram showing the sequence of steps involved in a process, used to help users understand how a process works and where problems might be found.

A **process flowchart**, sometimes also referred to as a **process map**, is a diagram showing the sequence of steps involved in a process. It is a visual tool that helps users and designers understand or communicate how a process works and where problems might be found. They are also useful for documenting how work gets done. Process flowcharts can be used by personnel in both services and manufacturing, and for major as well as minor processes. A good way to begin analyzing a process is to construct a process flowchart, showing the tasks involved, the sequence of the tasks, and decisions within the process.[10] Table 4.2 shows the symbols used in a typical process flowchart.

Table 4.2 Process Flowchart Symbols

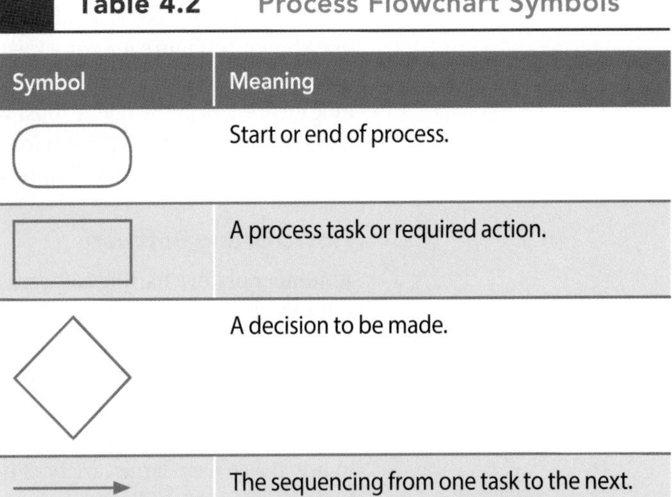

Symbol	Meaning
	Start or end of process.
	A process task or required action.
	A decision to be made.
	The sequencing from one task to the next.

While flowcharting a process, designers should brainstorm the process, asking questions such as:

- What happens or should happen next?
- Does this need an approval prior to a decision?
- Does a decision need to happen here?
- Can this task be deleted or combined with another?

Designers step through the entire process, thinking about what activities and decisions are integral parts of the process, using arrows to show

Figure 4.3 Component Assembly Process Flowchart

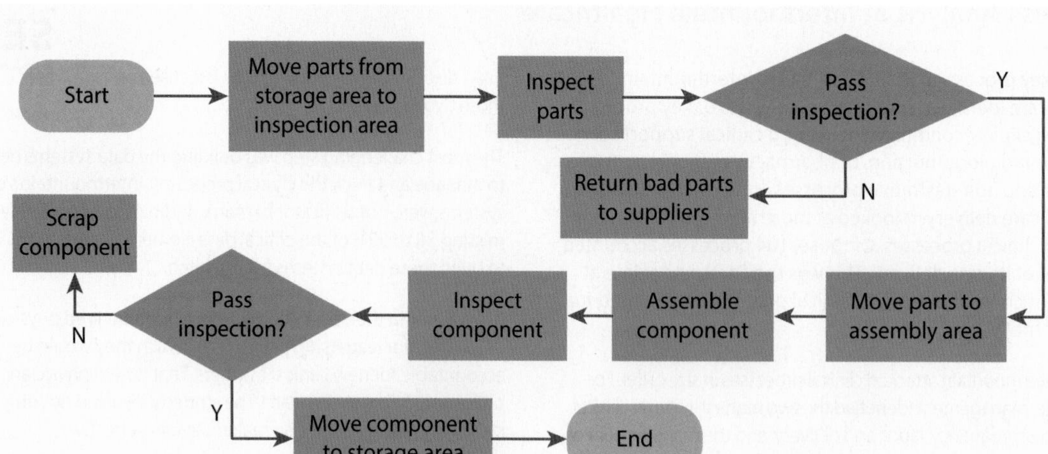

the process flow. Also, designers think about the outcomes of each decision, and what has to happen with each of the outcomes. They study each part of the flowchart, asking where delays or other problems might occur, and where value is not being created. Designers think about equipment or tasks or pathways that should be added or deleted from the process. Perhaps the wrong people or too many people are doing some of the tasks; perhaps automation could help to reduce task times; or perhaps the sequence could be changed to improve flows in the process. Thus, flowcharts can aid managers in designing a better process, and in collecting data to test current process designs. Figure 4.3 is an example of a component assembly process flowchart.

In the flowchart shown in Figure 4.3, a number of steps are required to assemble parts into a component. In viewing the flowchart, some of the steps appear to be unnecessary—for instance, suppliers could be directed to deliver parts directly to the first inspection area, instead of a storage area. Alternately, suppliers could be required to furnish inspection reports for all parts and then be directed to deliver parts directly to the component assembly area. Furthermore, finished and inspected components could be moved to the next assembly area instead of a storage area. The improved component assembly process flowchart might then look like what is shown in Figure 4.4.

Comparing Figures 4.3 and 4.4, it is seen that the number of action steps or tasks in the process has been reduced from eight to four. Consequently, the lead time required to complete the component assembly has most likely been reduced substantially, along with a reduction in labor hours, inventory carrying cost, and floor space.

Process flowcharts can also be used to design, assess, and improve services, such as the one shown in Figure 4.5 for a customer service department in an organization. Managers using this flowchart might want to know how frequently callers are placed in a queue, how long customers in the queue must wait to be served, how often callers get tired of waiting and hang up, and how long it takes for a response to be generated. (More on services and service processes can be found in Chapters 5 and 10.)

Flowcharting Software

A number of flowcharting software applications are available. Microsoft's Visio is the leader in software design features for both beginners and professionals. It has an exceptional tool set and an easy-to-use interface. Visio also includes real-time collaboration capabilities. SmartDraw is a bit cheaper and includes quick-start templates for more than 70 different kinds of charts, diagrams, and other visuals. Additionally, users get thousands of examples that can easily be edited. A significantly cheaper alternative is Edraw, which has a familiar layout and is simple to use. It also has a large variety of diagramming, text, and graphic tools. There are also several free flowcharting applications such as Lucidchart, which is ideal for the single user or student.

Figure 4.4 Improved Component Assembly Process Flowchart

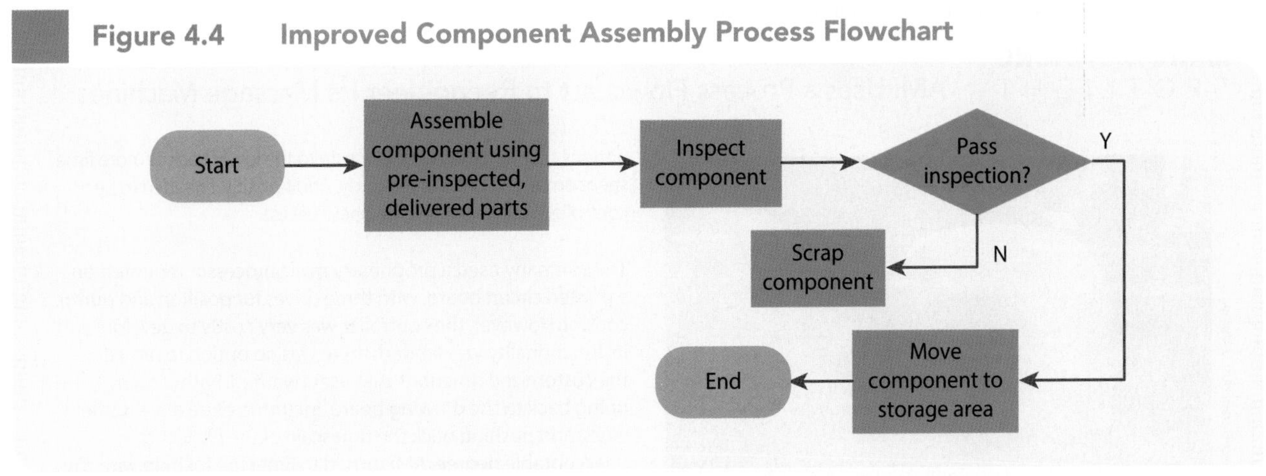

Flowcharts can also be found in reengineering efforts, where they can be used to make significant process improvements. This topic is discussed in the following section.

BUSINESS PROCESS REENGINEERING

Business process reengineering (BPR), generally defined as the fundamental rethinking and redesign of a process to achieve dramatic improvements in efficiency and effectiveness, has followed an up-and-down life cycle for the past 20 years. In the early 1990s, Michael Hammer and James Champy's very popular book, *Reengineering the Corporation: A Manifesto for Business Revolution,* combined with the many statements from notable business experts like Peter Drucker along the lines of "Reengineering is vital to success and it has to be done," creating a fervor at the time among managers seeking some sort of magic pill or easy method for making their businesses successful.[11] Unfortunately, like so many other management fads, most of the BPR efforts at the time failed to live up to the hype and expectations, causing many to claim by the latter 1990s that reengineering was dead.[12]

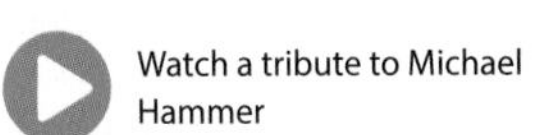

More recently, though, other business leaders have recognized that BPR has significant merit. In the Manufacturing Spotlight on page 88, for example, AMI contracted with Emerson to reengineer its dry water-massage machines with use of a process flowchart to guide its efforts. Managers are realizing that if used correctly (instead of as an excuse for downsizing, for instance), BPR requires employees to think creatively and realistically about how to bring value to customers through process redesigns.

BPR today involves making continual process improvements over time. "If you think back to traditional reengineering, there was the 'as is' and 'to be' implementation plan. There was a lot of thinking up front about the end state," says Scott Hicar, CIO at DigitalGlobe, a supplier of space imagery and geospatial content. "In today's world, growth happens so fast and technology is so pervasive and evolving at such an incredible rate that anybody who thinks they can step back and guess the end state five years from now is probably going to have a very high error rate."[14]

business process reengineering The fundamental rethinking and redesign of business processes to improve efficiency and effectiveness.

Figure 4.5 Process Flowchart for a Customer Service Department

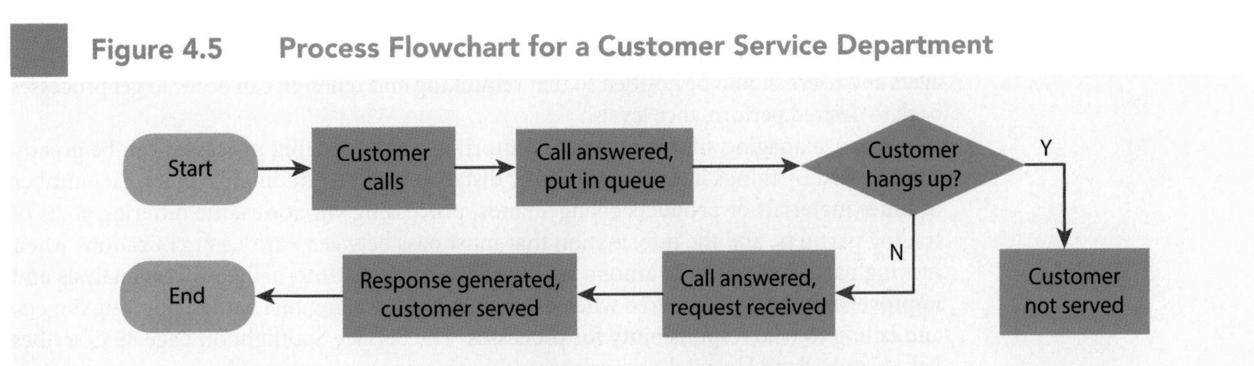

MANUFACTURING SPOTLIGHT

AMI Uses a Process Flowchart to Reengineer Its Massage Machines

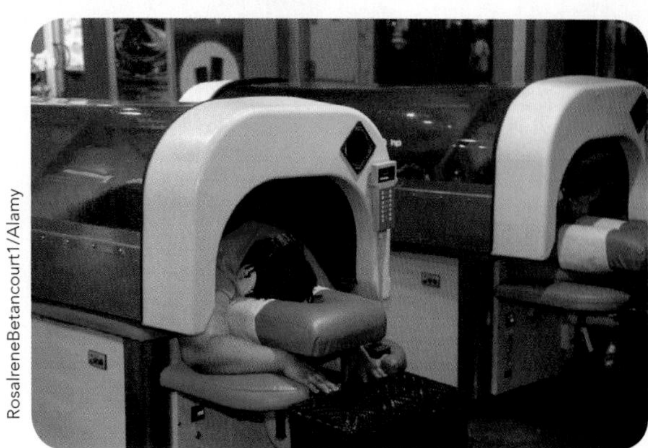

RosalreneBetancourt1/Alamy

Leisure products manufacturer Aqua Massage International (AMI), based in Connecticut, found itself having a problem with its dry water-massage machines, which deliver massages by pumping water against a membrane that lays against the user's body. Customers wanted a machine with customized controls to provide varied pulsation and pressure across 12 massage zones, including options such as extra water pressure to the lower back or more time spent on certain parts of the body. Additionally, it needed to be controlled using a simple, handheld device.

The company used a proprietary microprocessor mounted on a printed circuit board, with three drives for position and pump control. However, the controller was very costly to develop, and its functionality was limited; there was no option to provide the customized functions that users wanted. Rather than going back to the drawing board, incurring extra development costs, and pushing back the timescale of the project to an unacceptable degree, AMI turned to Emerson for help with the problem.

Emerson's Control Techniques Division received a process flowchart from AMI with a request for a solution. With a timescale of three weeks, the team devised a system that used four modules to provide the full functionality that AMI required. The system automatically provides a gentle start and run-down of water pressure and pulsation, along with the automated opening and closing of the unit's canopy at the beginning and end of treatment, and a full usage log for each user.[13]

Today, as illustrated in Figure 4.6, BPR employs a systematic approach to process analysis and change, starting with a vision, assessing current processes using flowcharts and data collection, rethinking and redesign of processes, implementation of process changes, evaluation of the new process, and continuing process assessments and improvements. At Colorado-based Lincoln Trust, a provider of trust and custodial services, CIO Helen Cousins realized the company had some need for process improvement. "When I came to Lincoln Trust Company it was pretty obvious to the entire company that we were drowning in paperwork," she recalls. "We were getting more than 100,000 documents a month. We had to institute a solution—the ultimate goal was to be paperless, which we pretty much are now." Since implementing a process reengineering effort in 2007, the company has reduced its paper-based workload by 90%, Cousins reports, adding that its new automated workflow system allows employees to track documents throughout any process. This automation has also contributed to a 90% reduction in client complaints about delays and lost paperwork.[15]

MONITORING PROCESS PERFORMANCE

The ultimate goal in process analysis is to design a system whereby process performance will be continuously monitored, and when performance is found to be lacking, improvements can be designed and implemented. When processes do not achieve desired outcomes, managers and users should be notified so that rethinking and redesign can occur to get processes back to desired performance levels.

When managing supply chains, monitoring and improving processes can be greatly complicated by things like the geographic distance between trading partners, the number of times materials or products change hands, processing variations, the differing goals of trading partners, and the information that must pass between various organizations when moving parts and products among supply chain partners. Internally, process analysis and improvement can be hampered when departments are waging turf battles, pointing fingers, and failing to take responsibility for processes. The Service Spotlight on page 89 describes Lake Cumberland Hospital's experiences with process monitoring and improvement.

Figure 4.6 Business Process Reengineering

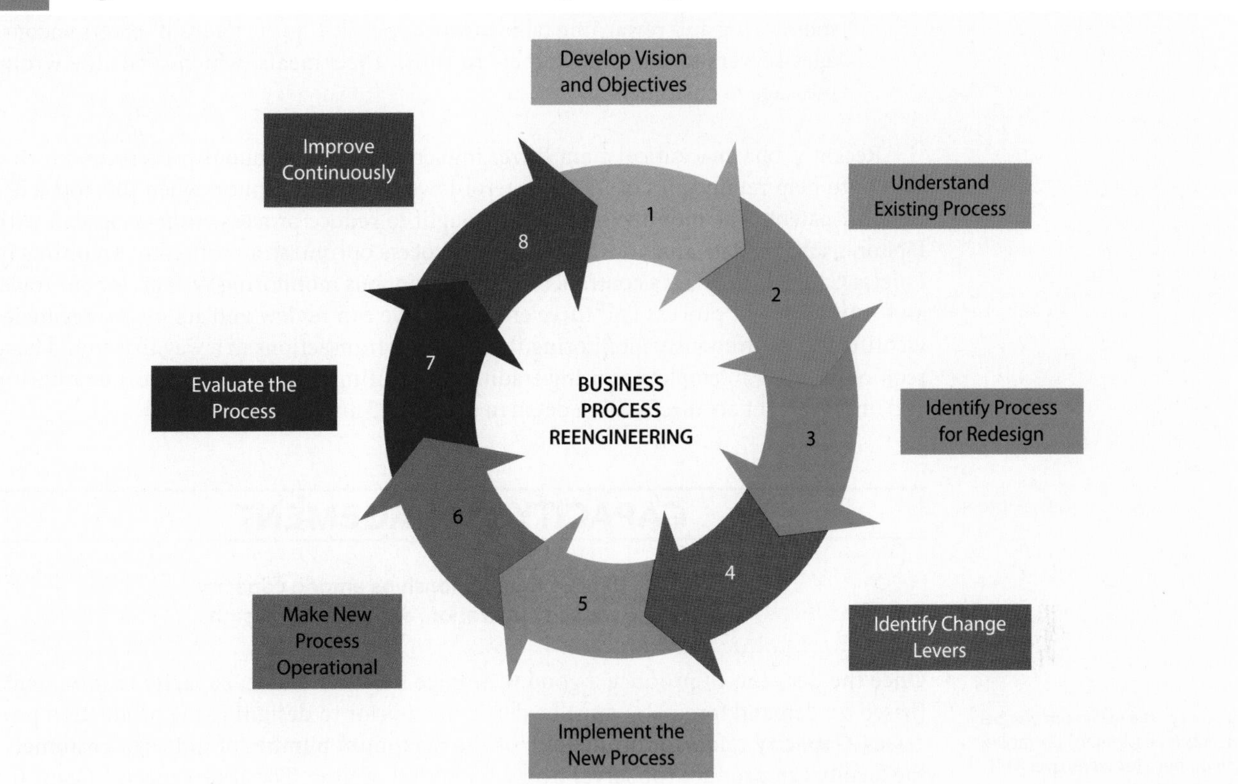

While the use of performance measurements was presented and discussed in Chapter 2, several points to consider can be mentioned here for designing performance measures for processes:[16]

1. Performance measures should support firm goals and tie process improvements to things that are important to the firm.
2. Performance measures should tie process performance to customer requirements whenever possible.
3. Performance measures should monitor the quality, cost, timing, and volume of outputs to get a complete picture of a process.

SERVICE SPOTLIGHT

Process Monitoring and Improvement at Lake Cumberland Hospital

Since August 2011, the emergency room at Kentucky-based Lake Cumberland Regional Hospital has put patients on a much faster track: Length of stay is down by more than 40 minutes; wait time for a physician is down by 75%; and patient satisfaction scores have hit an all-time high.

Plagued by inefficiencies and discouraged by failed past attempts to reform its processes, the ER's nurses, physicians, and staff gave it another try by using data analysis to identify process problems. Solutions included sending patients immediately to a bed upon being registered, providing walkie-talkies to staff to improve communication, and regularly monitoring process performance data. These and other efforts resulted in winning an award for process improvement.

"We had historically struggled with trying to get our satisfaction scores up," says Linda Hunter, senior director of emergency care services. "The comments from patients were that we were too slow, they spent too much time, and it took too long to be seen."

The ER hadn't been keeping track of performance until the initiative began. "The data was so valuable," says Hunter. "That's when we started seeing the progress, when we started posting the data. It started a competition, a little bit, and it let (staff) know that we were watching, and that it was important."[17]

4. Performance measures should be concerned with methods, or the way things get done, in addition to how much or how often something gets done. For example, monitoring and rewarding table turnover per shift for restaurant servers encourages servers to hurry customers to finish their meals, which sends the wrong message to customers.

Recently, pharmaceutical giant Pfizer implemented a continuous process monitoring system to help retain sales of its cholesterol-lowering giant, Lipitor, when this top seller went off-patent. The monitoring strategy sought to reduce process costs associated with Lipitor, using big data analytics and business process optimization software. According to Loretta Cangialosi, Pfizer's controller, "With continuous monitoring systems for our travel and entertainment process and three employees, we can review and act on discrepancies identified by continuously monitoring thousands of transactions in a way that would have required at least 30 employees using traditional auditing methods."[18] Process monitoring and improvement are discussed in detail in Chapter 13 and its supplement.

CAPACITY MANAGEMENT

4.3 Explain the relationships among capacity, capacity utilization, and process design

capacity The maximum number of units (or customers) the facility can produce (or serve) over a set period of time.

design capacity A maximum sustainable output per period.

effective capacity, or best operating level Once a production facility is completed, this lower maximum sustainable throughput will most likely be achieved, due to demand fluctuations, equipment breakdowns, worker inconsistencies, and other unforeseen circumstances.

capacity utilization The amount of effective capacity actually used.

Once the decision to produce a good or service has been made, capacity requirements (based on demand forecasts) must be determined prior to designing the production processes. **Capacity** refers to throughput, or the maximum number of units (or customers) the facility can produce (or serve) over a set period of time. Too little capacity means the facility will be overburdened, production completion times will be long, mistakes will be made, and customers might be lost to competitors. Too much capacity means that fixed costs will be too high, creating higher unit production costs and consequently higher product prices. Both situations can lead to lower sales and profits.

When processes and facilities are designed, a maximum sustainable capacity is established; this is referred to as the **design capacity**. In practice, though, and once a production facility is completed, a lower maximum sustainable throughput will most likely be achieved, due to demand fluctuations, equipment breakdowns, worker inconsistencies, and other unforeseen productivity problems. This actual throughput level is referred to as the **effective capacity,** or **best operating level**.

One measure of production system performance is the **capacity utilization**. Capacity utilization is defined as the amount of effective capacity actually used, or:

Tass/Zuma/newscom

When McDonald's opened its first restaurant in Moscow in 1990, its capacity was obviously heavily utilized.

$$\text{Capacity utilization} = \frac{\text{actual output}}{\text{effective capacity}}$$

If, for example, a restaurant was originally designed to handle 1,000 customers per day, but over time it was found to have an actual sustainable throughput of 800 customers per day, and furthermore, for the past month it had averaged 650 customers per day, then the capacity utilization would be:

$$\text{Capacity utilization} = \frac{650\,\text{customers / day}}{800\,\text{customers / day}} = 0.8125$$
$$= 81.25\%$$

For the following month, if the restaurant handled an average of 620 customers per day, the new utilization would be:

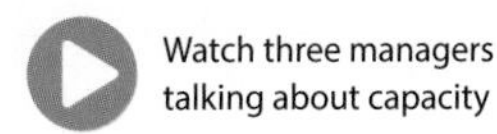

$$\text{Capacity utilization} = \frac{620\,\text{customers / day}}{800\,\text{customers / day}} = 0.775 = 77.5\%$$

and the change in utilization from one month to the next would be:

$$\text{Change, \%} = \frac{\text{Utilization}_2 - \text{Utilization}_1}{\text{Utilization}_1}(100) = \frac{0.775 - 0.8125}{0.8125}(100) = -4.62\ \%$$

Capacity planning activities typically occur over three time horizons:

Short-range planning—less than three months. This includes determining worker schedules and overtime, scheduling jobs to be completed, and allocating equipment to the jobs.

Intermediate-range planning—three months to one year. Capacity planning activities here include hiring or laying off personnel, purchasing tools or minor equipment, adding a work shift, and subcontracting work.

Long-range planning—longer than one year. Long-range capacity planning includes purchasing or building facilities and making major equipment purchases.

Modifying capacity can be fairly easy in the short run (such as hiring additional workers); however, only modest changes can be achieved. If required capacity changes are large, capacity costs and the time frame for implementing the changes can be quite significant (such as building a larger facility).

VARYING CAPACITY TO MATCH DEMAND

Depending on management's propensity for risk, the funding available, and confidence in its demand forecast, the firm may opt to use short- to intermediate-range capacity additions or the more expensive and risky long-range capacity additions. Additionally, as forecasted demand becomes a reality over time, the firm may choose to add long-term capacity to its facilities in small increments or large increments, depending again on its willingness to take risks and ability to fund capacity additions, as illustrated in Figure 4.7.

In Las Vegas, Nevada, for example, the Rio Hotel and Casino opened in 1990. As demand for rooms at the hotel increased, the hotel added a 20-story expansion tower in 1993. Demand at the hotel continued to increase, so the company added another hotel tower

Figure 4.7 Capacity Expansion Approaches

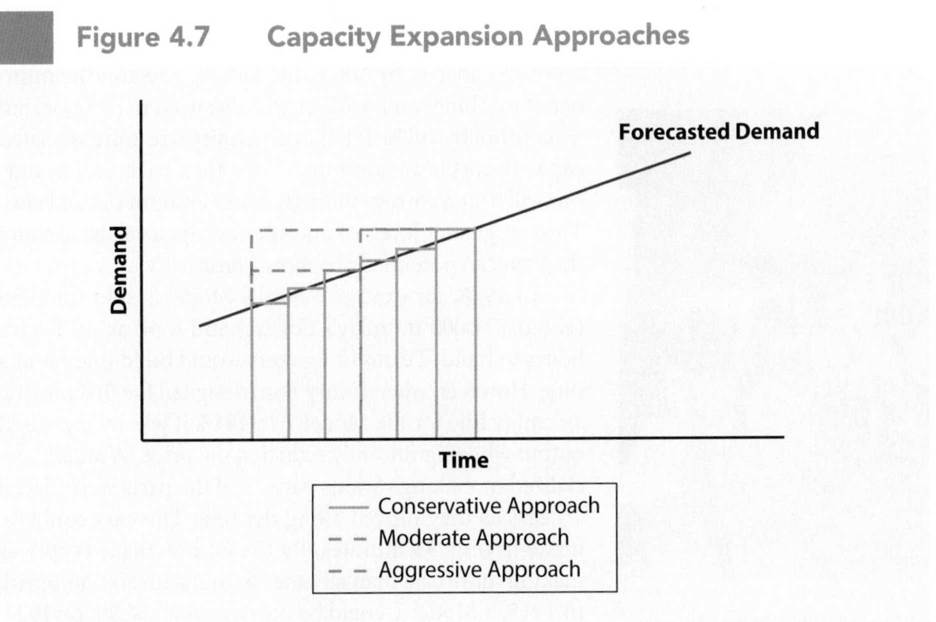

Ethan Miller/Getty

The vacant Las Vegas Fountainebleau Hotel was a victim of bad timing and high hopes.

in 1997.[19] This expansion strategy would be considered a *conservative approach to adding capacity*. An *aggressive approach to adding capacity* would have been to build all three towers at once—the total cost undoubtedly would have been less; however, if the demand had not materialized quickly, the Rio Hotel may have had difficulty servicing its initial large amount of debt and could have been put out of business.

This is precisely what happened to the Fontainebleau Hotel, also in Las Vegas. As a result of some overly optimistic demand forecasting, bad timing, and the desire simply to build a tremendously large hotel all at once, the mostly complete, 4,000-room luxury Fontainebleau declared bankruptcy in 2009. The developers had already spent over $2 billion constructing about 75% of the hotel when the recession hit Las Vegas and the investment money dried up. As room occupancy rates fell in Las Vegas during the recession in 2009, so too did the value of the Fontainebleau. Finally, in 2010, billionaire investor Carl Icahn bought the unfinished hotel for about $150 million. Today, it still sits, unfinished and vacant.[20]

Two other alternatives for adding capacity involve less risk—outsourcing and **capacity sharing**. As discussed in Chapter 1, outsourcing simply means buying instead of, or in addition to, making units of product. During the major floods in Thailand in the fall of 2011, a number of manufacturers were forced to outsource their production requirements until they could get their facilities up and running again. Lately, companies like Caterpillar, Ford, and GE have ceased some of their outsourcing of manufactured components in foreign countries due in part to increases in the costs of labor and transportation.[21] Capacity sharing occurs among companies when additions to capacity are expensive and when demand is highly variable. Hotels, for example, frequently overbook their room reservations and may share capacity with other hotels in the area when too many customers show up to claim their reservations. Airlines also practice capacity sharing, termed *code sharing*, when booking passengers on participating carriers to destinations they don't serve.

ECONOMIES OF SCALE

capacity sharing The distribution of capacity among companies when additions to capacity are expensive and when demand is highly variable.

As discussed in Chapter 2, economies of scale occur whenever a firm's marginal costs of production decrease. They can result from changes in plant and equipment, and are the reason for many capacity decisions. As a facility's capacity and thus the number of units produced per period increases, the average unit cost of production decreases. Generally speaking, to increase capacity by 100%, the facility size and the number of machines and workers will also need to increase, but usually not by 100%. If the extra facility size and associated capacity cost is an additional 70%, then each unit of output will bear a correspondingly lower amount of fixed cost. Thus, at greater levels of output, unit costs will be less and the firm can potentially be more competitive.

Heritage Images/Corbis

When Model Ts were assembled on moving assembly lines starting in 1913, their output dramatically improved, while the auto's cost decreased.

In 1908, for example, Ford's Model T sold for $850 (about $21,000 in today's dollars) and took about twelve hours to build. Teams of workers would build one car at a time. However, when Henry Ford designed the first moving assembly line for the Model T in 1913, it greatly increased output while significantly reducing the price. Workers specialized in making various parts, and the parts were placed on cars as they moved along the line. The cars could be made in only 93 minutes. By the end of 1914, Ford was making more cars than all other manufacturers combined. In 1915, a Model T could be purchased for $290. By 1924, through further improvements in manufacturing, Model Ts

Figure 4.8 Economies and Diseconomies of Scale

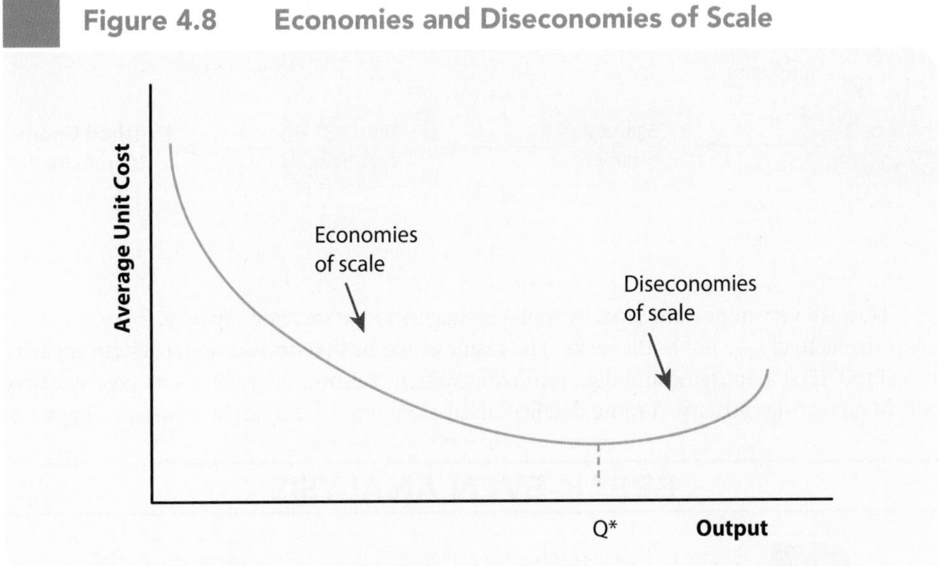

were selling for about $240.[22] Modern assembly lines seek precisely the same types of economies of scale.

At some point, though, trying to exceed a sustainable capacity for an extended period of time might lead to **diseconomies of scale**. As companies grow and hire more workers, for example, duplication of effort can occur; firms can also become top heavy with managers and supervisors, leading to lower overall company productivity (i.e., the right hand doesn't know what the left hand is doing). Costs begin rising faster than production, causing higher unit costs. This is why large firms sometimes have trouble competing with smaller firms, due to these diseconomies of scale. Figure 4.8 shows the relationship between average unit cost and output. Ideally, firms operate at output levels of Q*, as shown in Figure 4.8.

THE THEORY OF CONSTRAINTS

When multiple processes work together as part of a larger production system, operations managers must consider the capacity of each process, and how it will impact the total capacity of the system. Constraints or bottlenecks within the system can adversely impact a process's capacity, and if that process feeds units or customers to other processes, the entire facility can be impacted. A **bottleneck** occurs when a process, tool, or person limits the output of a system. Bottlenecks can adversely impact the effective capacity of an entire organization if allowed to continue.

Figure 4.9 illustrates a bottlenecked, three-stage assembly process. Stage 1 feeds partially completed units of product to Stage 2, which performs additional assembly work and then feeds units to Stage 3, where the units of product are completed. The capacities of each stage are shown. In its current state, the maximum effective capacity of the entire assembly process would be 10 units per hour, causing Stages 2 and 3 to have unused capacities. Stage 1 is the slowest, and is the capacity constraint, or bottleneck. If management added four units per hour capacity to Stage 1, the new capacity constraint would be Stage 2 and the effective capacity of the new assembly process would be 12 units per hour. A further two units per hour capacity would have to be added to Stage 2 to increase the effective capacity of the assembly process to 14 units per hour.

Identifying and managing system constraints to optimize performance (or, in this case, capacity) is the essence of the **Theory of Constraints** (TOC). The general TOC philosophy is that a system is only as good or strong as its weakest part. In manufacturing, this means that capacity is constrained by bottlenecks in the system. The simple yet brilliant concept of the TOC originated with a business-oriented novel entitled *The Goal*, written by Dr. Eliyahu Goldratt, an Israeli physicist, in 1984.[23] Managers can use the TOC by identifying the capacity constraint within a system, implementing a plan to overcome the constraint (such as more training, better tooling, or more workers), then continuing to identify new system constraints and additions until a desired system capacity is achieved.

diseconomies of scale When too much size and capacity lead to increases in unit costs.

bottleneck A constraint caused by a process, tool, or person that limits the output of a system.

Theory of Constraints A general philosophy stating that a system is only as good or strong as its weakest part.

Figure 4.9 Three-Stage Assembly Process

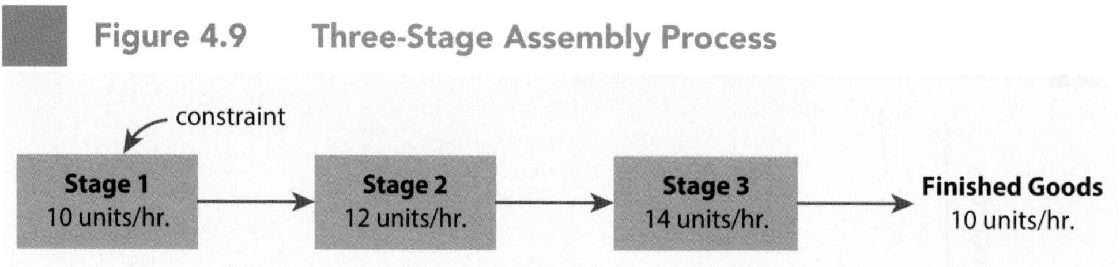

TOC is a very important capacity tool—managers might increase capacity, for example, in areas that actually are not bottlenecks. The result would be that no additional system capacity is realized. First identifying and then removing system constraints can be a very cost-effective way of increasing capacity. A more detailed discussion of the TOC can be found in Chapter 8.

BREAK-EVEN ANALYSIS

4.4 Illustrate how break-even analysis is used to compare potential investments in make-versus-buy decisions

During the new product analysis and screening phase, management generally considers the financial feasibility of the potential new product as described in Chapter 3. From an operations perspective, when new products are approved, managers must decide whether to use existing technologies and equipment, purchase entirely new equipment and/or technologies, or outsource production to an outside supplier.

These decisions are often based on the cost trade-offs among the various options, and **break-even analysis** is one technique used when considering potential new goods and services. To perform a break-even analysis, managers must have access to certain information, including:

- Expected level of production needed, based on forecasted sales;
- Projected fixed and variable costs for each option; and
- Expected sales price of the new product or service.

Fixed costs include depreciable assets like plant and equipment costs and variable costs include labor and material costs, which vary based on output. The primary assumption in a break-even analysis is that revenues and variable costs increase linearly with output. The objective of the analysis is to determine the volume of sales where management expects to begin earning a profit, defined as the **break-even point**, where total revenues equal total costs. The formula used to find the break-even point is:

$$\text{Total Revenues} = \text{Total Costs, or TR} = \text{TC}.$$

Letting:

P = sales price X = output produced

F = fixed costs V = variable costs

then:

$$TR = P \times X, \text{ and } TC = F + (V \times X).$$

Setting TR = TC and solving for X, the output:

$$P \times X = F + (V \times X) \text{ or } (P \times X) - (V \times X) = F, \text{ or } X = \frac{F}{(P - V)}$$

Example 4.1 illustrates the use of a break-even analysis when evaluating a new product, and Figure 4.10 is a graphical representation of the problem.

break-even analysis When cost trade-offs are analyzed among the various options to determine which option is best.

break-even point The point in a break-even analysis where total revenues equal total costs.

Example 4.1
Break-Even Analysis

Robert's Burgers has decided to begin making and selling hot dogs. Management has estimated the additional fixed costs to be $10,000 and has decided a sales price of $3 is needed to be competitive. The extra labor and material costs per unit have been estimated to be $0.75. Management wants to know how many hot dogs Robert's has to sell to break even.

Answer:

$(P \times X) = F + (V \times X)$ or $3X = 10{,}000 + 0.75X$ or $2.25X = 10{,}000$

Solving for X:

$X = 10{,}000/2.25 = 4445$ units (rounding up). Robert's Burgers must sell 4445 hot dogs to start earning a profit. This equates to a total break-even revenue of $3(4445) = $13,335.

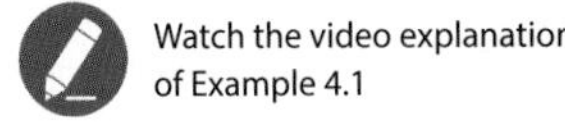

Watch the video explanation of Example 4.1

Figure 4.10 Graphical Solution to Example 4.1

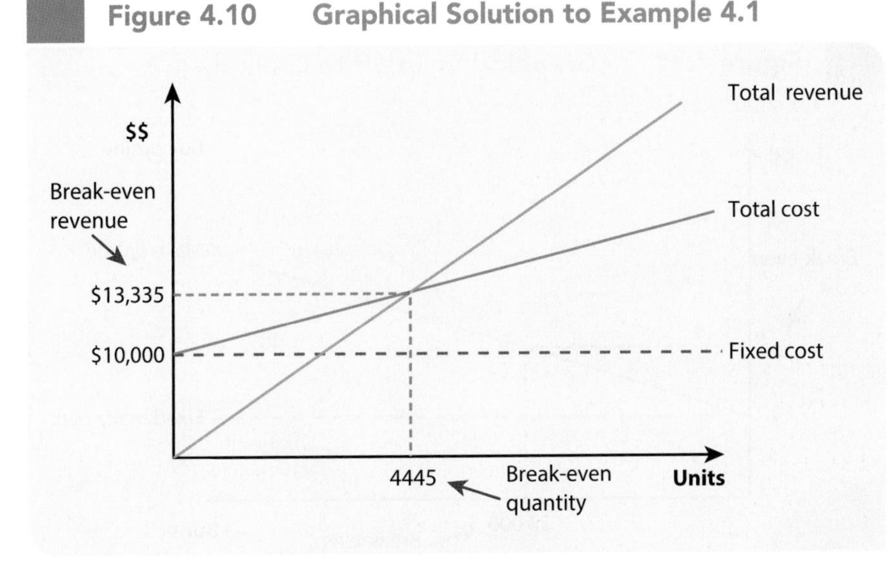

Two alternatives can also be compared using a break-even analysis. As mentioned earlier, one alternative to manufacturing a product in-house would be to outsource that product to a supplier. If it costs less, provides more flexibility, and is not a core capability, then outsourcing would be an option to consider. In this case, the break-even point is found by setting the cost of making equal to the cost of buying and then comparing the break-even quantity to the quantity required, as shown here:

$$\text{Make Cost} = \text{Buy Cost, or } MC = BC$$

Letting:

U = unit purchase price

X = quantity produced or purchased

$F_{m,b}$ = fixed costs (making or buying)

$V_{m,b}$ = variable costs (making or buying)

then:

$$MC = F_m + (V_m \times X) \text{ and } BC = F_b + (V_b \times X)$$

Setting the two equal and solving for x:

$$F_m + (V_m \times X) = F_b + (V_b \times X) \text{ or } F_m - F_b = (V_b \times X) - (V_m \times X) \text{ or}$$

$$X = (F_m - F_b)/(V_b - V_m).$$

Example 4.2
Make Versus Buy, Break-Even Analysis

Robert's Burgers is considering making hamburger buns in-house instead of buying them from its supplier. It has estimated the fixed costs for a used oven to be $7,000 and the variable costs for the buns to be $0.25. It purchases buns for $0.50 each, and there are no fixed purchase costs. Its annual demand for buns is forecasted to be 15,000. Robert's wants to know how many buns it has to make, to break even.

Answer:

$$F_m + (V_m \times X) = F_b + (V_b \times X) \text{ or } 7{,}000 + 0.25X = 0 + 0.50X$$

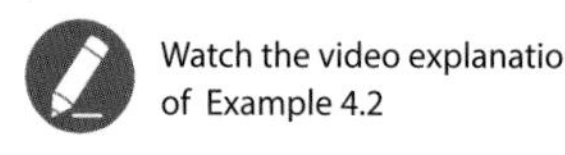

Watch the video explanation of Example 4.2

Solving for X:

0.25X = 7,000 or X = 28,000 buns. Robert's must make 28,000 buns to break even. This equates to (28,000/15,000 per year) or about 1.9 years to break even. The total break-even cost would be $7,000 + ($0.25)28,000 = $14,000.

Figure 4.11 Graphical Solution to Example 4.2

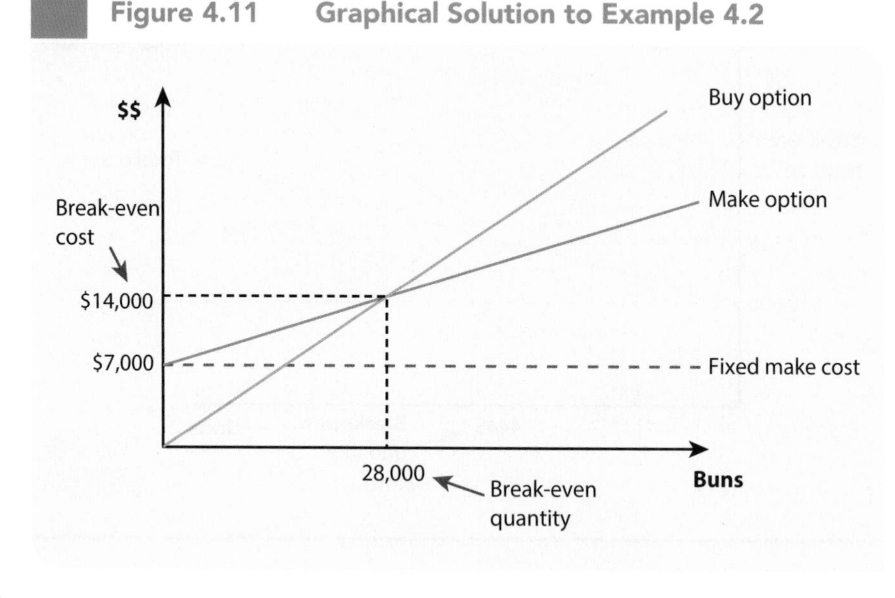

Example 4.2 illustrates the use of break-even analysis for the make versus buy comparison, and Figure 4.11 presents a graphical solution to Example 4.2. In Example 4.2, the **make versus buy analysis** indicates that it would be preferable to make the buns in-house, provided the 1.9 years to break even met Robert's investment requirements.

SUSTAINABILITY IN PROCESS DESIGN

4.5 Summarize the benefits of sustainability in process designs

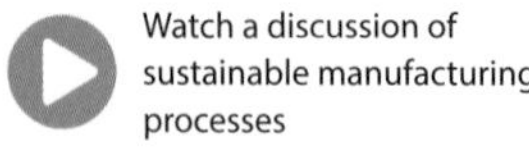

Watch a discussion of sustainable manufacturing processes

According to the Paris-based International Energy Agency, industries around the world collectively now account for one-third of total global energy use and about 22% of the world's total carbon emissions. While many firms have had environmental responsibility programs in place for years, the attention to sustainability issues by consumers and governments has never been greater. Consequently, the pressure on firms to conform to the wider topic of sustainability will only escalate. Firms today need to consider the energy use, carbon emissions, waste created, and water requirements associated with their production facilities and what operating improvements must take place to achieve new performance targets. The design of **sustainable processes** may require significant changes to business strategies, process design, plant maintenance, and supply chain management. Specifically, sustainable processes provide outputs for the organization in an environmentally acceptable manner. In Japan, Nissan has changed its focus from site-based energy saving to plant

make versus buy analysis A specific type of break-even analysis where the firm is considering two alternatives—making a product in-house or buying it from suppliers.

sustainable processes Processes that provide outputs for the organization in an environmentally acceptable manner.

floor-based savings. This has allowed it to more proactively control and reduce energy usage. It has initiated small group initiatives to pursue continuous conservation improvements.[24]

In 2015, Coca-Cola Enterprises (CCE) began a research partnership with the United Kingdom's Cranfield University entitled Sustainable Manufacturing for the Future. The project also included CCE's plans to invest £66 million into its operations, bringing total sustainability investment by the business in the United Kingdom to nearly £300 million. The study will investigate the current sustainability landscape across CCE's supply chains, investigating topics such as resource security, sustainable technologies, and waste management. It will also look to the future, forming a vision of what a sustainable factory will look like in 2050.[25]

Gary Braasch/Zuma/newscom

Chicago's City Hall was the first LEED-certified municipal building. The green roof prevents storm water runoff and creates an insulator which reduces heating and cooling costs.

In office settings, sustainability is today becoming a reality, as companies discover the added benefits to employee productivity, operating costs, waste reductions, and adaptability. Open-office environments, modular workstations, and demountable walls contribute to use of daylighting and natural ventilation strategies while providing flexibility. Colorado-based Van Gilder Insurance, for example, is housed in a 60,000 square foot office building and is using sustainability characteristics. "Van Gilder set out to create an office atmosphere that would not only be visually appealing, but also functional in attracting and retaining employees and clients," says CEO Michael Van Gilder. "Operating in a green environment has definitely been a stepping stone to helping achieve this."[26]

One of the newer sustainable process initiatives is the attainment of the Leadership in Energy and Environmental Design (LEED) certification. Developed by the U.S. Green Building Council, LEED provides independent, third-party verification that a building was designed and built using strategies aimed at achieving high performance in key areas of human and environmental health, including sustainable site development, water savings, energy efficiency, material selection, and indoor environmental quality. As Lloyd Snyder, vice president of Maine-based Woodard & Curran, an engineering firm supporting the beverage industry, notes about LEED certification:

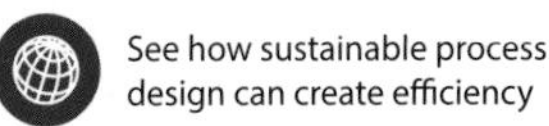

See how sustainable process design can create efficiency

> One of the benefits of that is that it helps take probably a core function within beverage-makers and helps you focus environmental benefits on the way you use water within your facility and the way you optimize your water processes. A lot of beverage-makers use it also for their clients—a lot of clients are asking them to be more environmentally sustainable and, therefore, they're getting pushed into trying to create environmentally sustainable processes within their facilities.[27]

Visit edge.sagepub.com/wisner to help you accomplish your coursework goals in an easy-to-use learning environment.

- Mobile-friendly eFlashcards
- Mobile-friendly practice quizzes
- A complete online action plan
- Chapter summaries with learning objectives
- Excel templates to assist with practice problems
- Original video case studies that demonstrate chapter concepts in action

SUMMARY

This chapter discussed several important concepts associated with production processes in an organization. After describing the basic types of processes found in organizations, the chapter presented process flowcharting and how it could be used in analyzing process effectiveness. Since the type of processes used impact the capacity of an organization, this topic was explored, including how capacity is added or supplemented. Many capacity decisions include alternatives to be considered, and break-even analysis is a tool used to address these alternatives. Finally, sustainability often impacts process decisions, a topic that also was discussed.

KEY TERMS

FORMULA REVIEW

Capacity utilization $= \dfrac{\text{actual output}}{\text{effective capacity}}$

Change in utilization, % $= \dfrac{\text{Utilization}_2 - \text{Utilization}_1}{\text{Utilization}_1}(100)$

Break-even cost is found when TR = TC, or total revenue = total cost, or $P \times X = F + (V \times X)$, where F = fixed cost, P = unit price, V = variable cost, and X = break-even units.

Break-even units, $X = \dfrac{F}{(P - V)}$

For the make-versus-buy analysis, the break-even cost is found when MC = BC, or make cost = buy cost, or $F_m + (V_m \times X) = F_b + (V_b \times X)$, where F_m = fixed cost of making, F_b = fixed cost of buying, V_m = variable cost of making, V_b = variable cost of buying, X = break-even units.

Break-even units, $X = \dfrac{(F_m - F_b)}{(V_b - V_m)}$

SOLVED PROBLEMS

1. Classroom effective capacity = 480 students per day

   Actual classroom enrollments (term 1) = 452 students per day

   Actual classroom enrollments (term 2) = 471 students per day

   Find the capacity utilization in both periods and the utilization growth.

Answer:

$$\text{Capacity utilization (term 1)} = \frac{\text{actual output}}{\text{effective capacity}} = 452/480 = 0.942 = 94.2\%$$

$$\text{Capacity utilization (term 2)} = \frac{\text{actual output}}{\text{effective capacity}} = 471/480 = 0.981 = 98.1\%$$

$$\text{Capacity growth (from term 1 to term 2)} = \frac{\text{Utilization}_2 - \text{Utilization}_1}{\text{Utilization}_1} = (0.981 - 0.942)/0.942 = 0.041 = 4.1\%$$

2. If the projected sales price for a new product is \$25.99, with fixed costs = \$225,000 and variable costs = \$12 per unit, find the break-even quantity.

Answer:

To find the break-even quantity, use: 25.99X = 225,000 + 12X, or 13.99X = 225,000. Then X = 16,083 units to break even.

Graphing:

So, if the firm expects to sell more than 16,083 units, the project looks okay. The break-even revenues would be: 16,083($25.99) = $417,997.

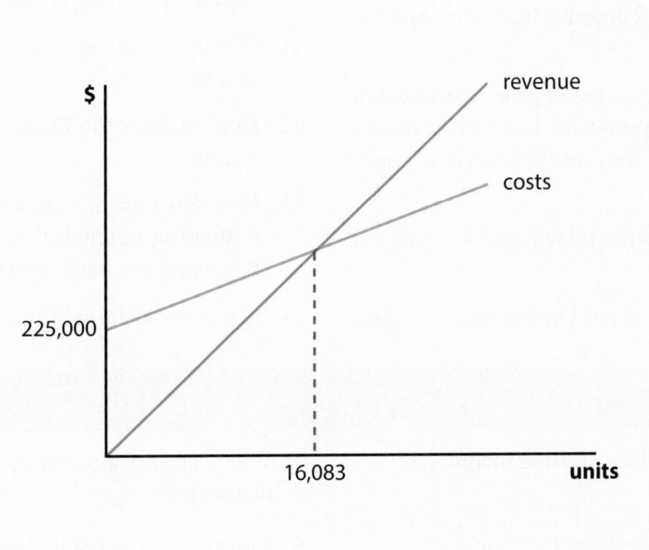

3. If the fixed costs to buy = $50, the variable costs to buy = $149, the fixed costs to make = $142,000, and the variable costs to make = $21, find the break-even quantity.

Answer:

Use the formula: Make costs = buy costs, or 142,000 + 21X = 50 + 149X, or 128X = 141,950, or X = 1109 units.

Graphing:

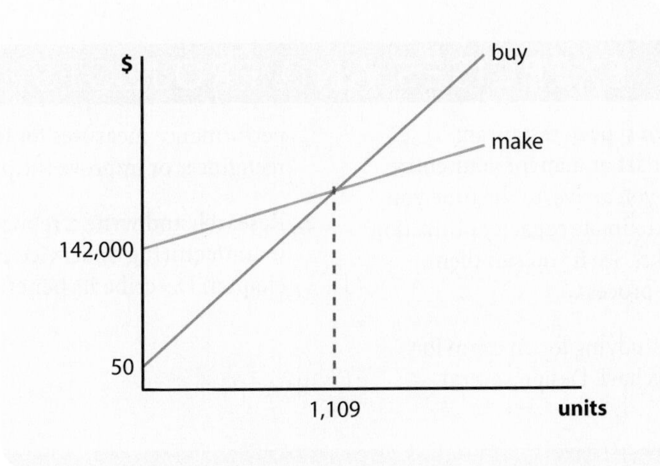

So, if the firm expects to use or sell more than 1109 units, it should make the item. The break-even cost is: $50 + 1109($149) = $165,291.

REVIEW QUESTIONS

1. What is the relationship among production output and automation and standardization?
2. List and describe the four basic types of processes.
3. What is mass customization, and why is it considered a hybrid process?
4. Define postponement and describe how it is related to mass customization.
5. List and describe the three types of processes based on the way that outputs are produced. In which of these categories would you put the process types discussed earlier in this chapter?
6. What is a process flowchart, and why would you want to construct one?
7. What is process reengineering? Do you think it's dead?
8. How can flowcharts be used in process reengineering?
9. What is design capacity? Effective capacity? Best operating level?
10. You wish to hire three part-time workers. What sort of capacity planning is this?
11. What is meant by economies and diseconomies of scale?
12. Describe how the Theory of Constraints works. Use an example.
13. How can a break-even analysis be used when evaluating a potential new product? How can it be used in a make-or-buy decision?
14. What is a sustainable process?

DISCUSSION QUESTIONS

1. Make a process flowchart for enrolling in and completing this class.
2. Discuss why managers should want to monitor process performance.
3. If you wanted to improve the process of enrolling in and completing this class, what performance measures would you monitor?
4. What is the design capacity of your classroom? What is its effective capacity? What is the typical capacity utilization of your classroom?
5. Your firm is experiencing high demand, some of which cannot be satisfied with current capacity. What capacity alternatives are available to meet demand?
6. Can an economy of scale situation turn into a diseconomy of scale? How could your university experience diseconomies of scale?
7. Discuss how a broken machine in one department can reduce an entire facility's capacity.
8. Why should managers care about sustainable processes? Can it increase profits?
9. What are the things managers should assess to make their processes more sustainable? Is your college or university acting in a sustainable way?

EXERCISES AND PROJECTS

1. Go to a traditional sit-down type of restaurant. Construct a process flowchart or map for your entire experience, from the time you arrive, to the time you depart. What was the approximate capacity utilization? Where were the bottlenecks? See if you can then improve or streamline the process.
2. Describe your process for studying for an exam for this class. Construct a flowchart. Design several performance measures for the process. See if you can reengineer or improve the process for the next exam.
3. Research and write a report on a sustainable manufacturing or service process not listed in this chapter. Describe its benefits as completely as possible.

PROBLEMS

Use the following information for Problems 1 and 2:

Sally's Ice Creamery served an average of 115 customers per day during August. Its maximum sustainable throughput was 140 customers per day. In September, it hired another worker and sent advertisements out to nearby neighborhoods. For that month, Sally's served an average of 132 customers per day, with a maximum sustainable throughput of 180 customers per day.

1. Calculate Sally's capacity utilization for August and September.
2. Calculate the percentage change in utilization at Sally's for the two months.
3. Village Plumbing can normally accommodate 25 customers per day. For the past 50 weeks, Village has served 5,500 customers. If the shop is open five days per week, what was its capacity utilization over the 50-week period?
4. A manufacturing company's effective capacity is 1 unit every 1.5 minutes. The actual output for August was 6,000 units and the actual output for September was 6,250 units. If the company was open eight hours per day and 22 days for each month, find the capacity utilization in both periods and the utilization growth.
5. A company's effective capacity is 12,000 units per day. If it normally produces 9,500 units per day, find the capacity utilization and the utilization growth necessary to produce 10,500 units per day.
6. A local bakery had a design capacity of 1,000 loaves per day, and an effective capacity of 700 loaves per day. During a three-day period, the bakery made 850 loaves per day. Calculate the capacity utilizations for the bakery's normal operating characteristics, and for the three-day period. Do you think the three-day output is sustainable?

Use the following information for Problems 7 and 8:

A machine shop has the following assembly processes for one of the products it makes:

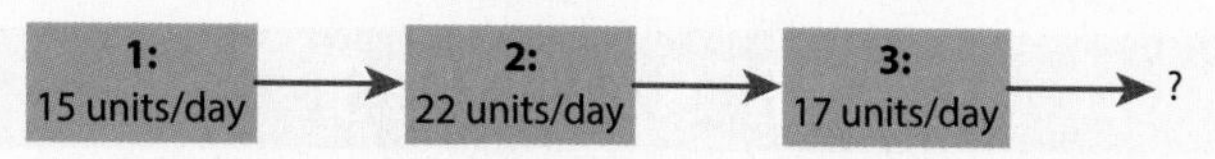

Process 1 feeds a completed part to Process 2; Process 2 feeds a completed assembly to Process 3; and Process 3 does the finish work. The capacities of each process are shown above.

7. How many finished units per day can the current assembly process produce? Where are the bottlenecks?
8. If the assembly processes needed to make 18 units per day, what should you do?
9. A specialty fabrication shop has the following assembly processes for one of the products it makes:

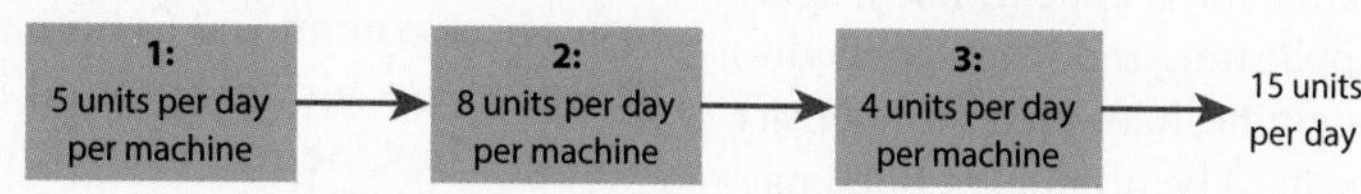

Process 1 feeds a completed component to Process 2; Process 2 feeds a completed assembly to Process 3; and Process 3 does the final finish work and packaging. The capacities of each process are shown above for each machine at each stage. The shop has plenty of excess labor and equipment.

a. How many finished units per day can the current assembly process produce, assuming one machine is running at each stage? Where are the bottlenecks?
b. Assuming each machine requires one operator, how many machines and operators are required in each stage to produce the required output shown above?

Use the following information for Problems 10 through 15:

Maggie Mae's has approved a new soft drink to be distributed with its other flavored soft drinks. Management has estimated the additional fixed costs for its new soft drink line to be $140,000 and its standard wholesale price of $0.55 per unit will be applied. The associated labor and material costs per unit have been estimated to be $0.25.

10. Management wants to know how many units it has to sell to break even.
11. Management also wishes to see a graphical representation of your answer to Problem 10.
12. Management also would like to know the break-even revenues.

13. Management can instead contract out to a soft drink bottler which can make the soft drink for a purchase price of $0.35. They expect to sell 250,000 units per year. How many years will it take Maggie Mae's to break even when comparing making versus buying the soft drink?

14. Show the answer to Problem 13 graphically. Do you think they should make or buy?

15. What is the make or buy break-even cost?

16. Jonnie Faith, a buyer for Global Metrics, is determining the make or buy quantity for a new instrument. She can have them made for $1,200 each with an equipment investment of $80,000, or Global could buy them for $1,800.

    a. Determine the break-even quantity and break-even cost.

    b. Graph your answer.

    c. If they needed 180, what should they do?

17. A firm can purchase whozits for $18 and sell them for $29. If the firm purchases 5,000 units, how many units does it have to sell to break even? The firm could buy a whozits machine for $30,000 and make whozits for $12 per unit. At what point is buying the units the same as making them?

18. Blake's Donuts can make donuts for $0.25 each with its current equipment. It could purchase a different fryer for $12,000, which would reduce the costs to $0.20 each. Or it could buy a bigger fryer for $42,000 and decrease the cost to $0.17 each. Find the break-even points and graph your answer. Over what output range would each option be preferred?

CASE STUDIES

CASE 1: The New Headache Remedy

Josh Walker sat in his office wondering what do to next. Josh's company, No Pain Solutions, was about six months old. Josh, a neurologist by training, had recently developed what he believed was a breakthrough product for people suffering from migraine headaches. He had obtained a patent for a product that could help decrease the intensity of the migraines. The product resembled in appearance a "glue stick" or a solid deodorant applicator, and when applied to the temples at the onset of a migraine, it lowered the intensity and the duration of the headache. The product is 100% natural and has been clinically proven to work. It is FDA compliant, meaning all the ingredients are approved by the FDA, and the product will be created in an FDA-approved facility.

At this point, Josh needed to decide how to manufacture the product. He believed demand for the product would be small the first year, but then grow steadily. He was currently in talks with some large regional and smaller national drug store chains, and he fully expected to win a national drug store chain placement about midway through the second year of production. Josh planned on manufacturing the product in two sizes to begin with. Over time, he envisioned the product being created in various size and color containers to meet the needs of a diverse group of consumers.

Josh planned on manufacturing the plastic containers using an injection molding machine capable of producing both sizes of containers. As long as the color didn't change, the only changeover time was for changing the molds. The product itself could be mixed in 30 gallon batches. Each batch made enough to fill 1,900 small containers or 950 large containers. Once the containers were filled, labels were applied and the product was packed in cases of 48 small or 24 large containers, which were then ready to ship.

Josh's background was as both a chemist and a doctor, and he was aware his background in operations was not very strong. Thus, he has come to you for recommendations regarding how best to manufacture the product.

DISCUSSION QUESTIONS

1. Using Table 4.1 in the book as support, what do you feel would be the best recommendation for how the product should be manufactured? Why do you feel this is a better option than the others presented?

2. Do you feel there is a potential for this process to change in 12 to 18 months? If not, why? If so, what should Josh be doing now to prepare for this possibility?

3. What are the benefits and risks of changing from one type of production process to another?

4. Should Josh outsource the entire process to contract manufacturers and simply focus on marketing? Why, or why not?

Note: Written by Jeffrey W. Fahrenwald, MBA, Rockford University, Rockford, IL. This case was prepared solely to provide material for class discussion. The author does not intend to illustrate either effective or ineffective handling of a managerial situation.

CASE 2: Safety Training at ABC Industries

Jacklyn Summers is the operations manager for ABC Industries. ABC Industries is a small manufacturer of metal storage boxes, with about 120 employees. Until now, ABC Industries has not had a formal safety program. Jacklyn has been asked to develop and coordinate the implementation of a new safety program as a part of her job as operations manager. The program she is setting up will consist of five modules, as shown here:

Introduction to Safety. This module discusses general workplace safety and how a safe environment improves morale, lowers turnover, and improves the overall performance of the organization.

Lock-Out Tag-Out. This module focuses on the correct processes or equipment to shut down and shut off for maintenance and repair.

Personal Protective Gear (PPG). This module focuses on safety glasses, hard hats, steel toe shoes, and hearing protection, and why they are beneficial to employees and the organization.

Correct Lifting Techniques. This module focuses on the reduction of back injuries due to poor lifting techniques.

Preventing Injuries on the Job. This module addresses potential safety concerns in the workplace and how to minimize injuries through reduction of risks and increased awareness.

Jacklyn decided that each module would be two hours in length and would be a yearly training program. The other managers understand the importance of providing this training, but they have requested that Jacklyn minimize the disruption to production output, since the plant is currently operating at full capacity. Additionally, the marketing department projects an increased demand for ABC's products over the next 24 months. After this initial round of training to get everyone up to speed, the yearly updates can be done in whatever way Jacklyn determines. One thing she is concerned about is how to get new hires up to speed regarding the various safety topics.

All employees will be required to attend the introduction to safety module to begin the training. The remainder of the training will be based on job classification, as shown in the following table.

Job	Number of Employees	Lock-Out Tag-Out	PPG	Correct Lifting	Preventing Injuries
Machinist	30	X			X
Material handler	16			X	X
Assembler	50			X	
Maintenance	10	X		X	X
Supervisor	14		X	X	X

After the introductory module all the other modules can be delivered in any order, but due to ease of record keeping and further developing the learning modules, the HR manager has requested the training be delivered in the same order sequence. Jacklyn has determined that no more than half of an employee job classification can be in training on any given day, and that there can be no more than 20 participants in any module at one time. Also, because of the size of ABC Enterprises and the impact that having people out of production has on productivity and delivery times, no more than 60 people can be trained in any given week. Additionally, no one can attend more than one module per week. Finally, because there is only a single training room and a setup is required for each module, only one module can be offered during any given week. Jacklyn's goal is to have all the training conducted in six weeks.

The schedule that Jacklyn has proposed is as follows:

Weeks 1 – 2	Week 3	Week 4	Week 5	Week 6
Introduction	Correct lifting	Lock-out tag-out	PPG	Preventing injuries

DISCUSSION QUESTIONS

1. What do you think of the proposed schedule and the stipulations put on the training?
2. Where are you likely to see bottlenecks in the process, given the proposed schedule?
3. Can you propose a process to Jacklyn that would be more effective for finishing the initial round of training?
4. What are your recommendations to Jacklyn for conducting training after the initial round?

Note: Written by Jeffrey W. Fahrenwald, MBA, Rockford University, Rockford, IL. This case was prepared solely to provide material for class discussion. The author does not intend to illustrate either effective or ineffective handling of a managerial situation.

CASE 3: Turner's Burgers, Dogs n' More

In 2012, Dave Turner retired and decided to do what he loved best—cook. He leased a small shop that had previously been a Mexican food restaurant, in an out-of-the-way corner of a small strip center along a fairly busy neighborhood street. It had a fully equipped kitchen and room for two small tables. When Dave opened his restaurant, his menu featured Kobe beef hamburgers and Angus beef hot dogs, which were delivered daily from a butcher shop he had been using personally for years. He also had 20 garnishes customers could select to customize their burgers and dogs. Dave's menu also featured hand-cut french fries and onion rings, along with coleslaw and potato salad, which Dave made from scratch, using recipes he had perfected at home over the years. Dave envisioned making mainly "to-go" orders for neighborhood customers, and was initially open from 11 a.m. to 7 p.m. He had no other employees.

At first, business was steady, and Dave used the afternoons to prepare most of his food items for the dinner crowd and his next day's lunch business. Life was good, and Dave's customers constantly raved about his great food and modest prices. Within a few months, though, Dave found that business had grown substantially. He started coming to the shop early in the morning and staying late in the evening to keep up with things. Soon, Dave simply couldn't keep up, so he hired Debbie, a neighbor of his, to help serve customers, take their money, and perform other tasks around the shop. Dave kept making the food and cooking, and the customers kept coming.

By the end of the first year, Dave had hired two more employees, taught Debbie how to make his coleslaw and potato salad, put three more tables outside on the sidewalk, and had raised his prices to pay for his increased labor costs. His business was literally bursting at the seams. People were occasionally complaining about the long waits and had started asking for home deliveries and later closing times. The space next to Turner's Burgers, Dogs n' More, had become available. This would allow Dave to add considerably more tables, and he was wondering if this might be a good way to serve more customers. One evening, Dave went home dog tired (no pun intended) and wondered what he should do. Maybe it was time to retire for real.

DISCUSSION QUESTIONS

1. When looking at Turner's outputs produced, would you describe his business as make-to-order, make-to-stock, or assemble-to-order? Justify your answer.
2. What alternatives does Dave Turner have for satisfying his capacity problem? Discuss each one.
3. Some customers are asking for home delivery and staying open later. How should Dave respond to these requests?
4. What performance measures could Dave use to monitor performance at his restaurant?

VIDEO CASE STUDY

Learn more about ***managing capacity*** from real organizations that use operations management techniques every day. Amy Keelin and Christine Keelin are COO and CFO (respectively) at MPK Foods, a small, family-owned company based in Duarte, California that produces seasoning mixes sold to grocery stores. A major part of MPK's daily operations involves planning and managing the capacity of their suppliers and manufacturing operations to meet varying levels of demand. Watch this short interview to find out how they do it.

LITTLEFIELD LABS

LITTLEFIELD LABORATORIES

Demonstrate your understanding of **process design and capacity management** at Littlefield Labs!

Littlefield Laboratories is a highly automated, state-of-the-art blood testing facility for clinics and hospitals. The lab will operate for a limited time frame lasting 210 days. You're asked to step in as the operations manager on Day 30, and are tasked with managing the capacity of the lab for the duration of its operation. Because Littlefield Labs guarantees results within a specific time frame, delays in testing and processing times can cost you money. Based on historic data and predicted demand patterns, you must buy or sell machines in order to optimize capacity and maximize the lab's profits.

Compete against your classmates to prove your understanding of the chapter concepts:

- LO 4-1: Describe the different types of processes and the types of outputs they create
- LO 4-2: Create a process flowchart and describe how it is used
- LO 4-3: Explain the relationship between capacity, capacity utilization, and process design

The team with the most cash in hand at the end of the 210-day time frame wins!

iStock/sturti

Companies are no longer just in the business of selling goods and services; they are in the business of selling a customer experience.

—**MARK JOHNSON,** CEO, Loyalty 360[1]

The customer's perception is your reality.

—**KATE ZABRISKIE,** business owner, speaker, and business consultant[2]

There is only one boss. The customer. And he can fire everybody in the company from the chairman on down, simply by spending his money somewhere else.

—**SAM WALTON,** founder, Walmart Stores, Inc.[3]

CUSTOMER RELATIONSHIPS AND CUSTOMER SERVICE

5

LEARNING OBJECTIVES

After completing this chapter, you should be able to:

5.1 Explain the value of customer relationships and customer service
5.2 Review the design and improvement of a customer relationship program
5.3 Explain how customer service audits are conducted and how customer service quality is measured and improved

Master the content.

edge.sagepub.com/wisner

SAGE edge™

THE IMPORTANCE OF BUILDING RELATIONSHIPS AT BYRNE INDUSTRIAL SOLUTIONS

Missouri-based Byrne Industrial Solutions provides B2B services for small and industrial-sized heating and air-conditioning units. Eric Byrne, the owner, knows the importance of focusing on the customer. According to Byrne, it means giving customers what they pay for and treating them right. "The key thing is focusing on the needs and wants of every client," he explains. Byrne attributes the success of his firm to its emphasis on building friendly relationships with clients. "It benefits us quite a bit," he explains. "It is going back to the old school of business with a handshake." Showing the firm's commitment to customers means taking customer calls at any time. "Our competitors take the easy calls," says Byrne.

Byrne's employees are skilled in different services, enabling the company to diversify its capabilities, ranging from the mining industry to the power generation industry. Consequently, during the recent economic downturn, the company's growth did not slow down at all. Additionally, its focus on relationship building is not limited to customers. "Our vendors are key elements of our business," says Byrne. Competitiveness depends in part on reasonable prices and the quality of parts, and Byrne's suppliers play a major role in helping the company provide both high quality and low prices to clients. "We stay loyal to our vendors and they stay loyal to us," explains Byrne. "We pick our vendors carefully, so that we are sure to offer the best possible product and price to our customers."[4]

INTRODUCTION

Customers are behind most of what operations managers do, for without customers, firms would cease to exist. For this reason, it can be argued that Chapter 5 is the most important chapter of this text. Frequent studies of customers are necessary for operations managers to understand what customers want, and then to determine how the firm will supply goods and services to remain competitive. Recall that two of the eight key supply chain processes as originally described in Chapter 1 are the customer relationship and customer service processes. Customer relationships are the result of ongoing interactions between the firm and its customers, while customer service refers to taking care of customer needs before, during, and after the sale. Both are closely related, since the firm's customer service activities can impact customer relationships.

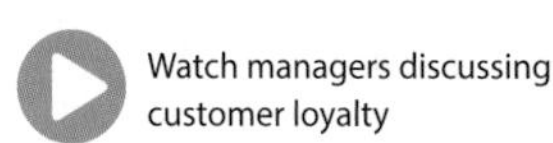
Watch managers discussing customer loyalty

All businesses want to satisfy their customers, make profits, and grow their customer base by identifying new customers. Thus, many successful companies seek to accurately identify their customers, determine their goods and service needs, then use internal resources to satisfy those needs, therefore creating satisfied customers. Consequently, satisfied customers return and tell others. As illustrated in the chapter opener, businesses doing the best job of managing customer relationships and providing customer service create a competitive advantage, making the job of finding and keeping customers much easier.

Since the mid-1990s, a number of studies have confirmed that small increases in customer retention often result in large increases in profits. This has spawned a tremendous interest among firms today in investing time and money in the management of customer relationships and customer service.

Lately, managing customer relationships has also become associated with software applications known as customer relationship management (CRM) applications. Often, firms pay high prices for these products in hopes they will generate greater sales and more profits. In fact, the global **CRM applications** market was about $23.2 billion in 2014 and growing by about 13% per year.[5] Many of these applications, though, have failed to accomplish the desired results. For instance, if managers purchase CRM applications to improve sales, but then neglect the activities their customers regard as value enhancing, this can spell trouble. Many firms have learned the true meaning of CRM the hard way—that technology alone can't endear customers to a product or company; employees and their actions do.

Customer service can be one of those things like product quality—as consumers, we may not be very good at defining what it is, but we know when we don't get it. Companies today spend a great deal of time, money, and effort trying to deliver great, or at least acceptable, customer service. Consumers see this occurring in most of the maturing markets around the world, as technologies create faster, more efficient ways to deliver various customer service activities.

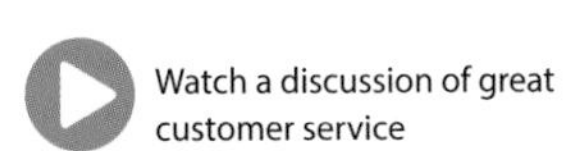

Companies delivering great customer service receive benefits in terms of competitive advantage and financial rewards. Most of us, though, can vividly recall too many examples of poor customer service, from the cashier who contentedly discusses the previous night's reality TV show with his fellow employee while disgruntled customers wait to pay for their purchases, to the physician who overloads her appointment schedule with no regard for the time patients must wait to be seen. In the United States, mediocre customer service is a problem for a number of companies. The American Customer Satisfaction Index (ACSI) produced by the Ross School of Business at the University of Michigan shows that overall customer satisfaction in the United States over the past 15 years has been stuck in the mid-70s on a 100-point scale.[6]

AP/Michael Dwyer

Trader Joe's builds customer relationships in part by stocking stores with products requested by the local community.

Delivering great customer service can be one of the key success factors for businesses. If designed and delivered well, customer service creates opportunities for long-term customer loyalty. Most successful companies are good at providing customer service because they have managed the customer service process well—they've identified their customers along with their service expectations, worked hard at developing the skills to deliver these services, thought about how technology can enhance customer service, and developed effective methods for tracking and improving customer service over time. This chapter provides a framework for designing, implementing, and improving the customer relationship and customer service processes.

CUSTOMER RELATIONSHIPS AND CUSTOMER SERVICE DEFINED

5.1 Explain the value of customer relationships and customer service

CUSTOMER RELATIONSHIPS

CRM applications Software applications used in managing customer relationships.

customer relationship process The infrastructure that motivates valuable customers to remain loyal and buy again.

The elements involved in the **customer relationship process** can vary based on the industry, the market, and the size of the company. Two definitions are provided here:

- "The infrastructure that enables the delineation of, and increase in, customer value, and the correct means by which to motivate valuable customers to remain loyal—indeed to buy again."[7]

- "Managing the relationships among people within an organization and between customers and the company's customer service representatives in order to improve the bottom line."[8]

Companies seek to create and manage customer relationships in order to improve the customer experience, make customers loyal, and sell more goods and services, resulting in long-term success and economic benefits. Unfortunately, many companies today are failing to adequately manage customer relationships. Perhaps this is because managers don't understand or simply don't care about what their customers want. In one example, a researcher talked to hundreds of employees at a large organization that had branded its customer relationship program a failure after three years and a $300 million software system investment. He found that only 24% of the employees had even heard of their company's program! Furthermore, only 15% of those involved with the program's implementation had been asked to provide any input, and the key employees had not received any training.[9]

Though corporations may collect customers' purchase, credit, and personal information, place it in a database, and use it to initiate some type of direct marketing activity, substantive efforts are also needed to create customer trust and loyalty—*to build customer relationships*. Consider this—how often, as a customer, have you been made to feel valued? How frequently do you feel neglected when dealing with business representatives?

Many companies today delegate customer relationship building and management to consulting services or internal IT departments whose goals might be to design databases and use models to predict consumer buying patterns. Though it is a potentially valuable support element, data mining alone does not build customer relationships. A number of years ago, Jessica Keyes, a well-known information system author and consultant, stated in an interview in the magazine *Infotrends*, "Technology does not beget a competitive advantage, any more than paint and canvas beget a Van Gogh."[10]

Since customers are not identical, firms building customer relationships first identify and segment their customers, then provide different sets of desired goods and services to each segment. As noted consultant Barton Goldenberg has been telling clients for many years, a successful customer relationship initiative is 50% people, 30% process, and 20% technology.[11]

Peter Endig/dpa/Corbis

Amazon.com is testing the use of drones for small-package deliveries to its customers.

The services of e-tailer Amazon.com are very simple for the consumer, for example, though some very complicated tasks take place behind the scenes. "I think what ensured that Amazon was a dotcom winner was being dedicated to the initial principle of focusing on the customer," says Rakhi Parekh, group product manager at Amazon.co.uk. "We started off by passing-on the cost advantage of the model to consumers, with low prices, then extended that to clever use of their data so that we could work out what else they might enjoy."[12]

CUSTOMER SERVICE

For the firm, a good working definition of the **customer service process** can create a solid foundation and direction for the design and delivery of high-value customer service activities. Several customer service definitions follow:

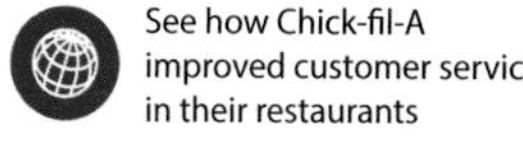
See how Chick-fil-A improved customer service in their restaurants

- The degree of assistance and courtesy granted those who patronize a business.[13]
- The collection of activities performed in filling orders and keeping customers happy, or creating in the customer's mind the perception of an organization with which it is easy to do business.[14]

These definitions clearly demonstrate that customer service is a process designed to take care of customer needs before, during, and after the sale (also referred to as pre-transaction, transaction, and post-transaction elements of customer service). Table 5.1 lists a number of these elements.

customer service process The design and delivery of high-value customer service activities.

Table 5.1 Customer Service Elements and Activities

Customer Service Elements	Activities
Pre-transaction elements	**Customer service policies.** Defines customer service for the customer, including guarantees, warranties, and return policies; sets performance standards.
	Customer service communication. Communication of policies to customers through websites, mail, TV, and other media.
	Customer service authority. Determines customer service decision-making authority at all levels in the firm.
	Information system deployment. Selection of software applications to store, analyze, and use customer information to meet customer needs.
	Personnel. Hiring and training of customer service personnel and the structures (such as call centers) associated with these employees.
Transaction elements	**Safety stock and excess service capacity.** Enables timely delivery of goods and services during periods of unforeseen demand increases.
	Substitute products. Allows firms to satisfy customers when the desired product is unavailable.
	Order entry. Enables correct order entry and communication to production.
	Order status. Determines status of orders and relays information to customers.
	Order expediting. Hastens the manufacturing and/or delivery processes, to reduce order cycle time.
	Warehousing and product delivery. Determines the most effective and efficient distribution of product or service to customer.
Post-transaction elements	**Warranty and maintenance services.** Enables repair and maintenance of goods during and after warranty period.
	Product operating information. Provides operating and troubleshooting information to customers, and updates as needed.
	Parts and installation. Enables order and installation of new and replacement parts.
	Follow-up, complaints, and returns. Enables after-sales communications, resolutions of customer complaints, and handling of product returns.

Source: Based on *Strategic Logistics Management*, by J. Stock, and D. Lambert, 2001. New York: McGraw-Hill.

Pre-transaction customer service elements occur within the firm prior to, or apart from, the sale of goods and services. These elements include the development of customer service policies, how they will be deployed and monitored within the firm, and then how these policies will be communicated to customers. Also included in this category are the assignment of decision-making responsibility for customer service, and the selection of software applications that enable customer service policies and directives to be followed. Finally, the hiring, training, and use of customer service personnel are included among the pre-transaction elements. The overall objective of the pre-transaction elements is to prepare the firm for effective customer service.

pre-transaction customer service elements The customer service elements occurring within the firm prior to, or apart from, the sale of goods and services.

transaction elements of customer service The customer service elements occurring during the order cycle.

order cycle The time from initiation of the customer order until the product or service is delivered to the customer

The **transaction elements of customer service** are associated with and occur during the **order cycle,** defined as the time from initiation of the customer order until the product or service is delivered to the customer. Transaction elements assist the firm in the successful delivery of purchased goods and services. These elements include the decisions to hold work-in-process and finished goods safety stock to reduce stockouts, policies to provide excess service capacity to enable the firm to respond quickly to unexpected demand, the carrying of substitute goods for times when stockouts do occur, the determination of a customer's order status, and the activities of order entry, order expediting, warehousing, and delivery. The objectives of customer service transaction elements are to provide service flexibility and to consistently deliver orders that are correct, on time, and damage free.

Post-transaction customer service elements are activities that occur after the product or service has been sold. These activities include the provision of warranty and maintenance services, product operating information, parts, and installation. It also refers to following up with customers after the sale and dealing with customer complaints and product returns. The objective of the post-transaction elements is to create an ongoing and successful after-sale relationship with customers. Many of these activities mark the beginning of the customer relationship process.

Customer Service Failures

When any of the customer service activities as described in Table 5.1 is neglected or performed poorly, a **customer service failure** is likely, which can lead to additional costs and possibly loss of goodwill, loss of customers, and reduced future sales revenues. Examples of customer service failures include stockouts, unwillingness to honor customer service policies, lost orders, late deliveries, employee indifference to customer needs, and unsatisfactory resolution of customer complaints.

Some of the more obvious ways organizations can try to minimize customer service failures are through more effective hiring practices, increasing general communication training of customer contact personnel, and better design and management of other activities in the three customer service categories shown in Table 5.1. Regardless of the level of preparation, though, customer service failures will occur, making it necessary for firms to be proactive and have well-thought-out recovery plans in all processes involving customers.

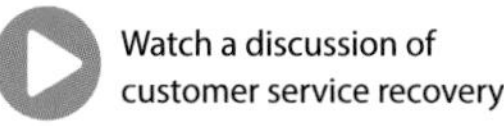
Watch a discussion of customer service recovery

Once a service failure is detected, company personnel in a position to remedy the situation need to show empathy toward the customer, while taking effective and quick actions to fix the situation. It is imperative that organizations anticipate and prepare for service failures and design the proper service recovery actions into each customer service element. Business author Maribeth Kuzmeski discusses the value of a good service recovery plan in several of her books. "Without a good service recovery plan, you can easily lose the disgruntled customer, everyone she knows, and possibly a lot of people she doesn't know if she takes her tale to cyberspace," she warns.[15]

THE CUSTOMER RELATIONSHIP PROCESS

5.2 Review the design and improvement of a customer relationship program

Once a firm has identified its key competencies, competitive strengths, and products as presented in Chapters 2, 3, and 4, it can begin considering how these can be leveraged by the customer relationship process. Loss of customers and market share might simply be the result of adopting ideas without understanding the impact they will have on customers. For instance, reducing the time taken to handle customer requests at a call center (discussed later in this chapter) may reduce call center costs, but have a negative effect on customer satisfaction.

In their book *CRM Unplugged: Releasing CRM's Strategic Value*, Philip Bligh and Douglas Turk recommend that companies answer three questions prior to implementing any customer experience improvement idea:[16]

1. What is the value being added, and for which customers?
2. Does it strengthen or dilute the firm's competitive strategy?
3. What is the expected effect on the firm's profitability?

The litmus test thus encompasses three requirements—customers must perceive value in any customer-oriented initiative, the initiative must support or advance the firm's strategy, and any investment must pay for itself by reducing costs or improving revenues. Activities that address all three requirements in a positive manner have the best chance of keeping the most profitable customers satisfied and coming back, keeping the firm focused on achieving its strategic objectives, and developing a long-term competitive advantage for the firm.

post-transaction customer service elements The customer service elements occurring after the product or service has been sold.

customer service failure Occurs when any of the customer service activities is neglected or performed poorly.

Figure 5.1 The Customer Relationship Process

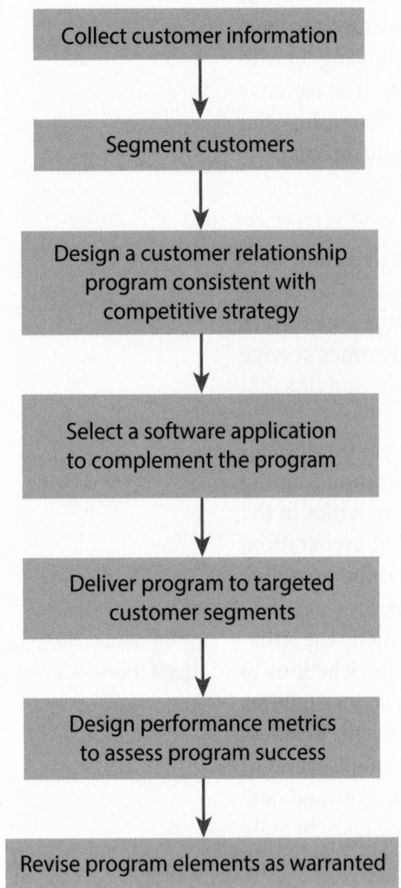
Collect customer information
Segment customers
Design a customer relationship program consistent with competitive strategy
Select a software application to complement the program
Deliver program to targeted customer segments
Design performance metrics to assess program success
Revise program elements as warranted

A formal customer relationship process should look similar to the model shown in Figure 5.1. Discussions of each element shown in the model follow.

COLLECT CUSTOMER INFORMATION

Identifying customers and constructing a customer database are necessary prior to implementing any specific relationship activity. Collecting customer information requires searching internal sources such as customer service, accounting, field sales, catalogue sales, marketing, and warranty or repair services. Information should be collected and aggregated on each of the following over time:[17]

- *Customer transactions*—purchase and return histories
- *Customer contacts*—sales calls and service requests
- *Demographic information*—examples are age, education, and profession
- *Response to marketing stimuli*—customer responses to marketing promotions

Firms having direct contact with end-customers such as retailers and banks generally have the easiest time collecting and organizing customer information, while companies with little or no direct contact with end-customers such as manufacturers have a more complicated data collection and organization problem. Manufacturers, for example, might require one database for direct business customers and yet another for end-product consumers.

SEGMENT CUSTOMERS

Obviously, firms try very hard to market products to people so they will make purchases. **Customer segmentation,** or grouping customers within a firm's existing customer database, allows the company to design specific initiatives that will satisfy customers, provide personalized services to the most profitable customers, and target specific sets of customers. The Service Spotlight on the next page describes the segmenting of customers at a credit union.

Understanding what connects customers to products or segments is extremely important, while categorizing customers based on age, gender, or income level can be problematic. A 19-year-old, single, female college student working part-time at a sandwich shop and living in a shared apartment, for instance, has seemingly nothing in common with a 47-year-old, married, male engineer with two kids, who lives at a country club housing development. But both buy U2 CDs, eat sushi, enjoy bike riding, and shop at Target. For these two customers, then, segmenting them based on their similarities might be much more effective than other segmentation techniques.

Satisfying and marketing to profitable customers, while reducing the costs of serving unprofitable or low-profit customers, is a primary objective of most customer relationship initiatives, and thus is an important way to segment customers. Another type of segmentation identifies customers with similar needs, geographical locations, buying attitudes, or buying habits. This has also been referred to as **niche segmentation.**

customer segmentation Grouping customers so the company can design specific initiatives to satisfy the groups and provide personalized services to the most profitable groups.

niche segmentation A type of segmentation that groups customers with similar needs, geographical locations, buying attitudes, or buying habits.

profitable customer A customer who yields a higher revenue stream than the company's cost of attracting, selling, and servicing that customer.

Segmenting Customers by Profitability

Philip Kotler, a leading marketing authority, defines a **profitable customer** as "a person, household, or company that over time yields a revenue stream that exceeds by an acceptable amount the company's cost stream of attracting, selling, and servicing that customer."[18] An automobile buyer, for instance, might represent tens of thousands of dollars in car purchase and maintenance profits over the buyer's lifetime, to an automobile manufacturer. Similarly, an

Using Predictive Analytics to Segment Customers

SERVICE SPOTLIGHT

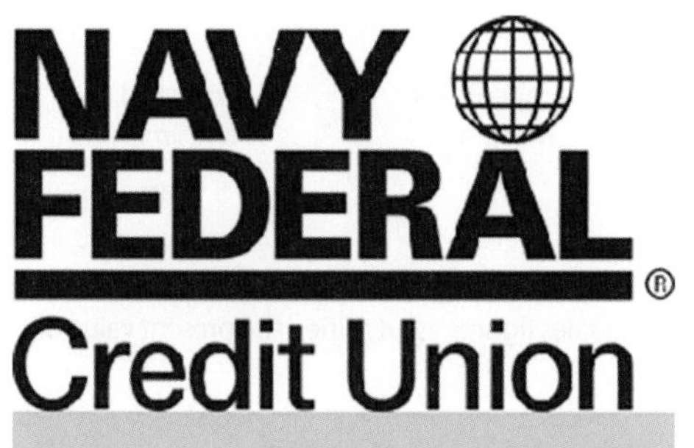

Navy Federal Credit Union, one of the largest credit unions in the United States, uses predictive analytics to segment and predict the future buying habits of its members. The credit union's CRM application allows it to segment members according to the specific service products they use, so it can create lower-cost, targeted promotions. Predictive analytics thus allows Navy Federal Credit Union to understand its customers better, by knowing what services its members are interested in and how they use these services. It can then predict its customers' immediate needs and how they will likely respond to future promotional efforts.[19]

individual credit card user might represent thousands of dollars in profit value over that user's lifetime, to the issuing company. Thus, segmenting customers based on profitability makes sense when deciding which customers the company should pursue, satisfy, and try to retain.

The term **customer lifetime value** (CLV) can be used to segment customers based on their current and projected future profitabilities.[20] Calculating CLV is based on a projection of customers' lifetime purchases, the average profit margin on the items they purchase, and the net present value of their projected profits. Essentially, the CLV can be calculated as the net present value of an annuity, as shown here:

$$NPV_A = P\left[\frac{1-(1+i)^{-n}}{i}\right]$$

where:

A = customer A

P = average annual profit, or (annual sales × profit margin)

i = annual discount rate

n = expected lifetime in years

Example 5.1 illustrates this calculation.

Use of profitability information, though, can potentially cause poor decisions to be made regarding some customers. For instance, customers who are marginally profitable now may become more profitable later. A health club, for instance, may have some unmarried members who rarely make other purchases at the club but frequently visit and use the facility. Though these members may be seen as only slightly profitable, it is likely that if they are satisfied with the club, they will tell others; and at some point they may marry and upgrade to a family membership. Firms may also be unknowingly directing resources to customers who are actually unprofitable. For instance, in a study by consultant and database marketing author Arthur Middleton Hughes, he described how Boston-based Fleet Bank's marketing staff were working hard trying to retain customers who were actually unprofitable. In fact, half of Fleet's customers were deemed unprofitable, with the bottom 28% consuming 22% of the bank's total annual profits.[21]

customer lifetime value The net present value of the customer's lifetime projected profits.

Segmenting Customers by Niche

Organizations can also identify and target a number of market niches for tailoring their customer relationship efforts. These might include niches based on industry, firm size, geography, or customer behavior. Some firms identify customers based on geography, such as in local or **neighborhood marketing**, where customer segments can be viewed as having similar

neighborhood marketing Identifying customers based on geography, where customer segments can be viewed as having similar income levels or ethnic traits.

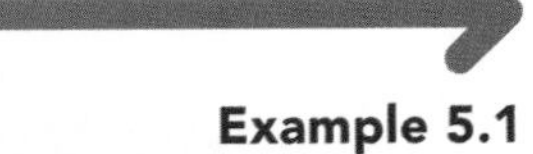

Example 5.1
Comparing Customer Lifetime Values

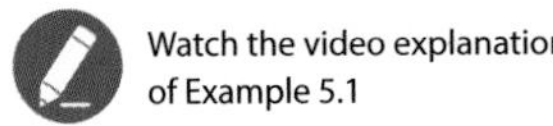

Watch the video explanation of Example 5.1

The Kentucky Bluegrass Seed Company sells grass seed and other Kentucky-area plant seeds to area plant nurseries. It has decided to begin calculating the expected lifetime profitability of each of its nursery customers in order to design differential grass and plant seed promotions. Its top two customers have the following characteristics:

	Average Annual Sales	Average Profit Margin	Expected Lifetime
Nursery A:	$22,000	20%	5 years
Nursery B:	$16,000	15%	15 years

Using a discount rate of 8%, and treating the average sales figures as annuities, the present value of the two nursery lifetime values is:

$$NPV_A = P[\frac{1-(1+i)^{-n}}{i}] = \$22,000(.20)[\frac{1-(1+.08)^{-5}}{.08}] = \$4,400[\frac{0.319}{.08}] = \$17,568$$

$$NPV_B = P[\frac{1-(1+i)^{-n}}{i}] = \$16,000(.15)[\frac{1-(1+.08)^{-15}}{.08}] = \$2,400[\frac{0.684}{.08}] = \$20,542$$

Based on these calculations, Nursery B is the more important customer because of the higher expected lifetime value.

The customer lifetime value comparison can also be performed using a spreadsheet as follows:

Use Excel spreadsheet templates to find the solution

	A	B	C	D	E	
1	**Annual Sales ($)**	**Profit Margin**	**Lifetime (years)**	**Discount Rate**	**NPV ($)**	
2	22,000	0.2	5	0.08	17,567.92	E2: = PV(D2, C2, A2*B2)
3	16,000	0.15	15	0.08	20,542.75	E3: = PV(D3, C3, A3*B3)

income levels or ethnic traits. Banks, fast-food outlets, and grocery stores, for instance, might offer different goods and services that appeal to these neighborhood segments. The East West Bank, for example, a full-service commercial bank in California, grew quickly by concentrating on serving ethnic Chinese and Koreans in their Californian communities. Employees speak Chinese and English, all interactive systems are trilingual (Mandarin, Cantonese, and English), and most employees come from Chinese backgrounds.[22]

Segmenting markets by gender is common but can often lead to problems—do it wrong, and firms risk offending or alienating customers. Many firms, though, are doing it successfully. Home Depot, for instance, invested considerable effort in understanding its women customers, who account for about 50% of sales. One thing management found through its research was that women focused more on projects and outcomes, and less on specific goods and their features. Consequently, Home Depot installed design showrooms and trained its sales clerks to check that customers had everything they needed for a project.[23]

DESIGN A CUSTOMER RELATIONSHIP PROGRAM CONSISTENT WITH COMPETITIVE STRATEGY

As mentioned in previous chapters, the three primary competitive strategies are low cost, high quality, and good customer service. Since one of the primary objectives of customer relationship programs is to achieve high levels of customer satisfaction and loyalty, these programs should support or advance the firm's competitive strategy while satisfying and retaining key customers. Several customer-oriented initiatives are shown in Table 5.2 and are discussed in the section that follows.

Table 5.2 Customer Relationship Program Initiatives

Initiative	Description
Customer Loyalty Program	Rewards repeat customers with discounts or other items depending on the frequency of the purchases.
Product Customization	Allows customers to customize goods and services to create a uniqueness to the product.
Customer Communities	Firms can create customer communities using company websites and social networks like Facebook in order to facilitate communication or the exchange of ideas between customers and company personnel.
Engaging Customers Using Social Media	Social media (such as Facebook and Twitter) present a number of opportunities for companies to build, maintain, and strengthen relationships with customers.

Customer Loyalty Programs

Customer loyalty programs (also called frequency programs, or company clubs) reward repeat customers with discounts, credits, cash, and prizes, depending on the value and frequency of the repeat purchases. Customer loyalty programs have become widespread among even the smallest of businesses, as firms have realized that repeat purchases can create brand loyalty and long-term customer relationships. Loyal customers generate more sales for businesses through frequent word-of-mouth advertising; additionally, loyal customers often buy a wide range of the firm's products. These initiatives can be a powerful way to attract potential high-value, long-term customers and gather purchase data over time, while keeping customers coming back.

iStock/Nadalinna

Customer loyalty cards help to keep customers coming back.

For a small business such as a barbershop, a punch-card system might be used to track customer purchases, with a reward of a free haircut on the tenth visit. At the other end of the spectrum might be a casino that uses a registered loyalty card to track customer expenditures, with product offerings, discounts, and gifts automatically generated when certain casino spending hurdles are reached.

Harrah's Entertainment, for instance, is one of the world's largest casino operators. Its loyalty card customers swipe its cards 100 million times per day from dozens of globally dispersed casinos. This information is fed to a computer in Memphis, Tennessee, and each morning, Harrah's knows which customers should be rewarded with free show tickets, dinner vouchers, or room upgrades. "We can see how much money is going through a machine, how frequently it pays out, how much it pays out, and what type of player is on it, male or female, and what age they are," says Tim Stanley, an executive at Harrah's in Las Vegas. "We're trying to figure out which products sell and we're trying to increase our customer loyalty."[24]

Product Customization

Allowing customers to customize the goods and services they buy creates a uniqueness that many find appealing. Thus, unwanted product attributes can be avoided, while the desired functions can be retained for each individual customer, creating greater feelings of ownership and, consequently, satisfaction. This is quite easy for services, and getting easier for manufacturers as well.

For many forms of information services, this is also called **versioning**. Using the latest digital printing presses, catalogue and magazine publishers can offer versioning to personalize their publications and appeal to individuals or very small market niche segments. Starbucks does a great job of offering customized coffee drinks, and it encourages employees to use their own discretion when customizing services for customers. This type of tailored service engages customers and creates very positive word-of-mouth advertising.

For many manufacturing companies, mass customization (discussed in Chapter 4) enables firms to offer customized goods while keeping production costs and product lead

customer loyalty programs Rewarding repeat customers with discounts, credits, cash, and prizes.

versioning Personalizing catalogues to appeal to individuals or very small market niche segments.

times under control. While some initial attempts at mass customization were unsuccessful, such as Levi's custom-fitted jeans and Mattel's customized "Friends of Barbie" dolls, companies like Lands' End and Nike appear to be succeeding at custom-ordered goods manufacturing. Even though the garments cost more at Lands' End, for instance, and take longer to arrive than standardized equivalent goods, about 40% of Lands' End shoppers choose customized garments, and their reorder rates are 34% higher than for buyers of standard-sized clothing.[25]

Building Customer Communities

Today, firms can create **customer communities**, using company websites and social networks like Facebook to facilitate communication or the exchange of ideas between customers and company personnel. This helps to foster relationships between customers and the company, creating more of a personal or family environment. Engaging customers in these communities also makes it harder for customers to "leave the family." For instance, Harley-Davidson has developed its Harley Owners Groups, or HOGs, on its website, so Harley owners can share their experiences and ideas and so Harley-Davidson can communicate directly with its customers. Harley-Davidson also has a Facebook page, a Twitter address, and YouTube videos to connect with its customers. This direct online information sharing is also sometimes referred to as **viral marketing**, or bottom-up branding.[26]

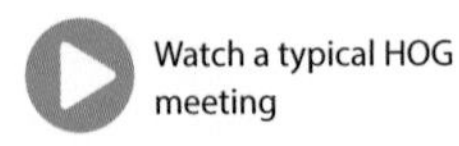
Watch a typical HOG meeting

As we've seen here, businesses can use a number of relationship initiatives that have proven to be quite successful in building and maintaining valuable customer relationships. Some can be implemented for very little cost, while others can require very large expenditures for training, computer systems, and other equipment. As companies begin identifying customers and their purchase habits, the appropriate customer relationship activities can be utilized. Along with these activities, customer relationship software applications should also be considered, and this topic follows.

Engaging Customers Using Social Media

Social media (such as Facebook and Twitter) present a number of opportunities for companies to build, maintain, and strengthen relationships with customers. Successful customer engagement turns customers into fans—fans who will continue coming back and purchasing goods and services. Additionally, fans will tell their friends. Social media have the ability to establish conversations with customers, to build more meaningful and sustainable interactions between the company and its customers, and to better satisfy customers' needs.

Connecting with a brand or business is a lot like communicating with people—trying to talk to someone who doesn't make eye contact or smile can be difficult. On the other hand, having a conversation with someone who smiles, responds, and looks at you is far more pleasant and memorable. Customers communicate with companies the same way. It is up to the company to create a good environment for customer engagement. Over the years, customer expectations have increased, and today, customers prefer using alternative means of communication with companies, and they expect companies to provide these other methods, such as social media. Raley's, for example, a privately held California and Nevada supermarket chain, rolled out a social media rewards program called Extra Friendzy in 2014. The program provides customers with offers, through social media channels, to strengthen customer engagement and draw consumers to Raley's customer rewards program.[27]

Massachusetts-based cloud computing service provider EMC employs a "social champion" in each of its product marketing departments. It has helped the company create several new marketing initiatives, including virtual social product launches, a social listening command center, and promoted tweets that far exceed EMC's current banner ad performance. EMC's social launches augment traditional product launches, and make use of the social listening command center. When the command center sees a relevant conversation on one of the EMC social platforms, the lead is routed to a social selling team within the telesales department. EMC has conducted dozens of virtual product launches. When it launched VF Cache, it was held in a small venue but broadcasted worldwide. It was promoted via email, tweets, a Facebook game, Facebook ads, and mentions throughout EMC's own community network. The event made use of social selling, with five subject matter experts from product management engaged

customer communities Using company websites and social networks to facilitate communication or the exchange of ideas between customers and company personnel.

viral marketing Direct online information sharing between the company and its customers.

in an online Q&A with the audience via its community network. That launch received 19,000 views in a short period of time, compared to 50 or 100 people in a launch venue.[28]

SELECT A SOFTWARE APPLICATION TO COMPLEMENT THE PROGRAM

Depending on the number of customers a firm has, the profit contributions of each customer, and the competitive strategy employed, customer relationship software applications will vary. Walmart, for example, has no desire to contact each of its millions of customers individually; however, it can use the Walmart website to express its appreciation, ask for feedback, and initiate customer-oriented programs. On the other hand, a custom home builder communicates directly with customers and may utilize a software application to enable customers to visualize certain home design alternatives.

The common term used for customer relationship software today is a familiar one: *customer relationship management* (CRM). Firms should consider the most appropriate CRM application, after a customer relationship initiative has been identified. Implementing a CRM application, though, can be both expensive and time consuming (purchasing and customizing the software, training users), while potentially doing a poor job of operationalizing a good customer-oriented idea.

CRM applications have matured over the past 20 years, but implementation failure rates remain high—as much as 75%, according to the Meta Group, an information technology research and consulting company. Some of the reasons for failure include:

- The inability to create an enterprise-wide customer relationship strategy
- The difficulty in integrating CRM applications with legacy systems
- A lack of an approach to analytics[29]

Companies with many disparate CRM applications are now trying to integrate these throughout their organizations, to allow better internal communications and to present one face to the customer. Additionally, some companies suffer from not knowing what to do with all of the customer information floating around in their organizations.

This lack of an **approach to analytics** has caused firms to miss out on some marketing or customer service opportunities. Furthermore, managers must always remember that CRM applications are only enablers, not substitutes for a well-designed and delivered customer relationship initiative. If a plan does not allow the firm ultimately to serve customers better, then the best technology implementation in the world will probably not help the firm much.

approach to analytics Knowing what to do with all of the customer information available to the firm.

SERVICE SPOTLIGHT

CRM Success at the University of South Florida

iStock/Chris Schmidt

Originally, the University of South Florida had little success with CRM. According to Christopher Akin, the associate director of IT, it had spent a lot of money on the CRM application, and the software just didn't work. Ultimately, it had to threaten legal action to get its money back and get out of the contract.

It decided to give RightNow Technologies' CRM system a try, since it could be implemented very quickly, gave the university room for growth, and was Web-based. It was able to streamline the help desk's self-help knowledge base, and the software allowed it to track email and phone queries. Within a few months, it was able to get rid of all its backlogged emails and phone messages. The self-help knowledge base was later expanded to 100 answers, which reduced calls and emails to the help desk. This allowed the university eventually to eliminate two full-time help desk positions, even though enrollments were up by 10%.

These successes led to the design of "Ask USF" by RightNow, which answers a much wider range of questions. Over a three-year period, the system answered 450,000 questions, saving an estimated $500,000. Next for the university is another application to help it better market and recruit graduate business students.[30]

While it has already been mentioned that CRM software failure rates are quite high, there certainly have been many successful implementation examples. The University of South Florida provides an example of both program failure and success, and is described in the Service Spotlight on page 117.

DELIVER THE PROGRAM TO TARGETED CUSTOMER SEGMENTS

Following segmentation activities, firms must decide which customers to target with which communications, promotional materials, and marketing programs, along with the most appropriate communication channels to use. A firm's best (most profitable) customers, for example, purchase the most profitable goods and services, while costing the firm the least in terms of selling and servicing or maintenance costs. Thus, customer relationship initiatives for these customers should focus on maintaining and cultivating these relationships over the long run, through careful attention to providing services and materials customers want, while seeking to increase sales of additional goods and services to them. On the other hand, a firm's worst customers (least profitable) purchase only low-profit-margin products and require high maintenance or service costs. Efforts for this group should focus on "firing" these customers diplomatically. For customers falling somewhere in between these two extremes, relationship efforts should focus on moving customers toward more profitable products or reducing servicing costs.

Watch a discussion of firing customers

A good rule of thumb to apply here is a version of the 80/20 rule—most of the firm's profits are generated by a relatively small group of customers; these customers are the ones who should then receive the most attention. Texas-based GHX Inc., a hose and accessories distributor, closed about half of its open accounts to focus specifically on its profitable customers. "It's a dramatic change in your business when you find out that 90 percent of your profit comes from 150 customers out of 2,000, but those customers made up 40 percent of your transaction costs. That means more than 60 percent of what you were doing accounted for 10 percent of your profit," says GHX president Dan Ahuero. Today, business and customer satisfaction are both up.[31]

Targeting customer segments typically involves use of the Internet, telemarketing, direct mail, and direct sales. These topics are discussed next.

Using Email to Target Customer Segments

Targeted email marketing campaigns cost very little for the firms doing them and the results are all too evident each day as we access our home and business email accounts. The very low cost of distribution is attractive to businesses, even though response rates to marketing emails can be extremely low. If customers are first asked to "opt-in," or agree to receive marketing messages, then this can be an effective way to target customers without alienating them.

Besides the cost advantage, there is also a time advantage when using email advertising. Peter Larsen, a managing director at mobile specialist Enpocket, explains that while it may take six weeks to design and deploy a piece of direct mail, it only takes a few hours to do the same thing using email. "This has a total advantage in terms of cost. Ease of deployment is a major advantage, as is ease of personalization," he says.[32] Another advantage is the ease of response for first-time and repeat customers.

One complication with email communications is that most people have multiple email addresses and utilize spam-blockers, resulting in messages that either don't reach the target audience, or reach them multiple times, aggravating customers and causing response emails to unsubscribe or opt-out. A number of messages can also be incorrectly identified as spam and blocked, creating **false positive blocking**. For instance, DoubleClick sends out billions of emails per quarter, and its research shows that 19% do not reach the intended recipients.[33]

false positive blocking When spam-blockers incorrectly identify an email as spam and block it.

Using Telemarketing to Target Customer Segments

telemarketing When salespeople use the telephone to identify potential new customers.

Telemarketing refers to salespeople who use the telephone to identify potential new customers. Telemarketing strategies can be employed to sell goods and services to these potential customers and also to cross-sell the firm's other products. Telemarketers can contact many more people per day compared to a field salesperson (perhaps 50 versus 5 customers). They can be used to give more attention to neglected accounts, and they can follow-up on other sales leads obtained through other sources. Today, the telemarketing industry accounts for well over $100 billion in annual sales in the United States.

As technologies advance and as customers become more accustomed to doing business over the phone and Internet, telemarketing systems may play a larger role in customer relationship programs. Medienhaus, a leading Austrian media company, has determined that it costs only about one tenth as much to cross-sell services to customers using telemarketing when compared to direct marketing or door-to-door selling. Telemarketing can be twice as successful if handled correctly.[34]

Telemarketing, though, has some very negative connotations. People often view phone contact from salespeople as intrusive, and in the United States this has resulted in the National Do-Not-Call Registry, initiated in late 2003. Enforced by the U.S. Federal Trade Commission, the national registry was created to make it easier for consumers to avoid telemarketing calls. Consumers can get more information and register a phone number online at www.donotcall.gov, and within 31 days most telemarketing calls will stop.

Using Direct Mail to Target Customer Segments

Direct mail involves sending an announcement, offer, or some other type of hard-copy communication to potential customers' addresses. Direct mail is used to produce prospective customer leads, to sell to existing customers, to enhance customer relationships, and to inform or educate recipients. Auto repair shops send out reminders for oil changes, grocery stores send out their latest advertisements, department stores mail tailored catalogues to customers, and hotels mail advertisements for reduced room prices. Direct mail, while expensive, allows firms to more closely target various market segments and to personalize offers sent to specific customers. For 2010, the response rate for consumer direct mail was about 3.4%.[35]

As discussed in this section, building relationships with the right customers using personalized emails, telephone calls, and direct mail has been shown to be much more effective than simply talking "at" large audiences using mass-marketing channels, and is the foundation for all successful customer relationship programs.

DESIGN PERFORMANCE METRICS TO ASSESS PROGRAM SUCCESS

Measuring the performance of customer relationship initiatives is extremely important, given the historically poor performance that many firms have experienced in this area. Since initial monetary outlays can be high, training and implementation activities can require significant time investments, and damage to customer relationships can result from poorly designed or executed initiatives, performance monitoring should be viewed as a necessary program element.

Performance metrics should measure customer satisfaction and customer loyalty associated with use of the particular program element. Initially, companies should establish baseline measurements to serve as a basis for comparison once the various program initiatives are in place. Then, as the program matures, periodic assessments can help identify program weaknesses.

In his book *Beyond Customer Satisfaction to Customer Loyalty,* Keki Bhote, one of the instrumental people behind Motorola's Six Sigma program and its winning of the prestigious Malcolm Baldrige National Quality Award (Motorola won in 1988 and again in 2002), recommends that companies generate customer information prior to embarking on any customer loyalty program.[36] He suggests use of focus groups and one-on-one, in-depth, key customer interviews. **Focus groups** are an assembled group of customers giving their opinions to company personnel regarding various proposed program initiatives. This activity and key customer interviews can provide valuable insights and ideas regarding customer relationship initiatives, as well as feedback on goods and services.

direct mail When a hard-copy marketing communication is sent to potential customers' addresses.

focus groups Assembled groups of customers giving their opinions regarding various proposed program initiatives.

Table 5.3 Customer Relationship Program Performance Metrics

Performance Metric	Description
Program return on investment	(additional profit generated)/($ program investment)
Conversion efficiency	(# new customers generated)/($ program investment)
Maintenance ratio	(# customers retained)/(# customers lost)
Customer loss rate	(# customers lost)/(total # customers)
Senior management commitment	Senior management time spent on initiatives
Key customer metrics	Can be measured using: # key customers (those exceeding an annual profitability value) (# key customers)/(total # of customers) Average key customer annual profitability Average key customer longevity Average key customer satisfaction survey rating Percent of key customer complaints successfully resolved Percent of key customers lost per period

Once program initiatives have been designed and implemented, use of interviews, surveys, and information captured using information technologies are recommended to determine levels of customer satisfaction and customer loyalty. Mail surveys can be used and are inexpensive and fast; however, they tend to suffer from poor response rates and are biased toward those customers who are dissatisfied. Telephone surveys are more effective than mail surveys, although they are more expensive, time consuming, and prone to customer hang-ups. Additionally, call center comments, customer emails, trade show customer comments, and prepaid survey postcards contained in product packages can be used to gauge customer satisfaction.

Table 5.3 presents several metrics that can be useful for measuring customer relationship program success. Measuring the performance of customer relationship programs and finding positive results will help create a more proactive, customer-centric organization, and will enable the firm to justify further program investments.

REVISE PROGRAM ELEMENTS AS WARRANTED

Inevitably, organizations will find at least a few initiatives falling short of initial program expectations. According to Patrick Harris, director of Information Technology at Sealing Devices, a manufacturer of goods in the aerospace, defense, and electronics industries and also a customer relationship program award winner, "You can't just install, train, and expect everything to work flawlessly. You need to continually reevaluate your sales processes and continually tweak the CRM system to support the processes."[37] Companies also find they must continually revise and improve their customer relationship programs just to stay even with the competition.

Revising a program involves monitoring program performance, comparing the results to desired objectives or standards, and then making changes when the standards are not met. The customer relationship revision process should identify and prioritize innovative ideas that can be tested and evaluated. Sufficient resources must be applied to smaller-scale tests, to evaluate an idea and its applicability to a larger-scale implementation. These small-scale tests can produce valuable insights into ways of improving customer relationships and profitability. Some of the ideas may fail, but they can still provide valuable insights about what will and will not work.

THE CUSTOMER SERVICE PROCESS

5.3 Explain how customer service audits are conducted and how customer service quality is measured and improved

Customer service is subject to interpretation by customers, and is not unlike hitting a moving target with each customer interaction. Managers might try various customer service initiatives but find the actual impact on the bottom line to be less than anticipated. By viewing customer service as a process, then, businesses can create a framework for managing and improving their customer service performance.

Figure 5.2 represents the customer service process framework. Organizations must prepare for providing effective customer service by evaluating (and improving, if need be) internal employee satisfaction, since this plays such a key role in good customer service.

EVALUATE AND IMPROVE EMPLOYEE SATISFACTION

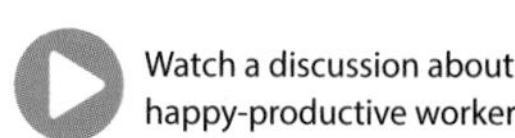

Watch a discussion about happy-productive workers

Employee satisfaction is derived from the internal work environment, including comfort factors, hiring and training practices, motivational factors, and the reward system.

For years now, the impact of employee satisfaction on customer service performance and productivity has been the subject of many research efforts. Among other things, the research has found strong evidence that overall job satisfaction is a critical link to employee performance, including their customer service performance. This is sometimes referred to as the **happy-productive worker hypothesis.**[38] Reuters, a London-based global information provider, introduced an employee satisfaction improvement initiative in 2003, in an effort to turn around the company's fortunes following a difficult year. Workers could nominate coworkers

happy-productive worker hypothesis Overall job satisfaction is a critical link to employee performance and customer service performance.

Figure 5.2 The Customer Service Process Framework

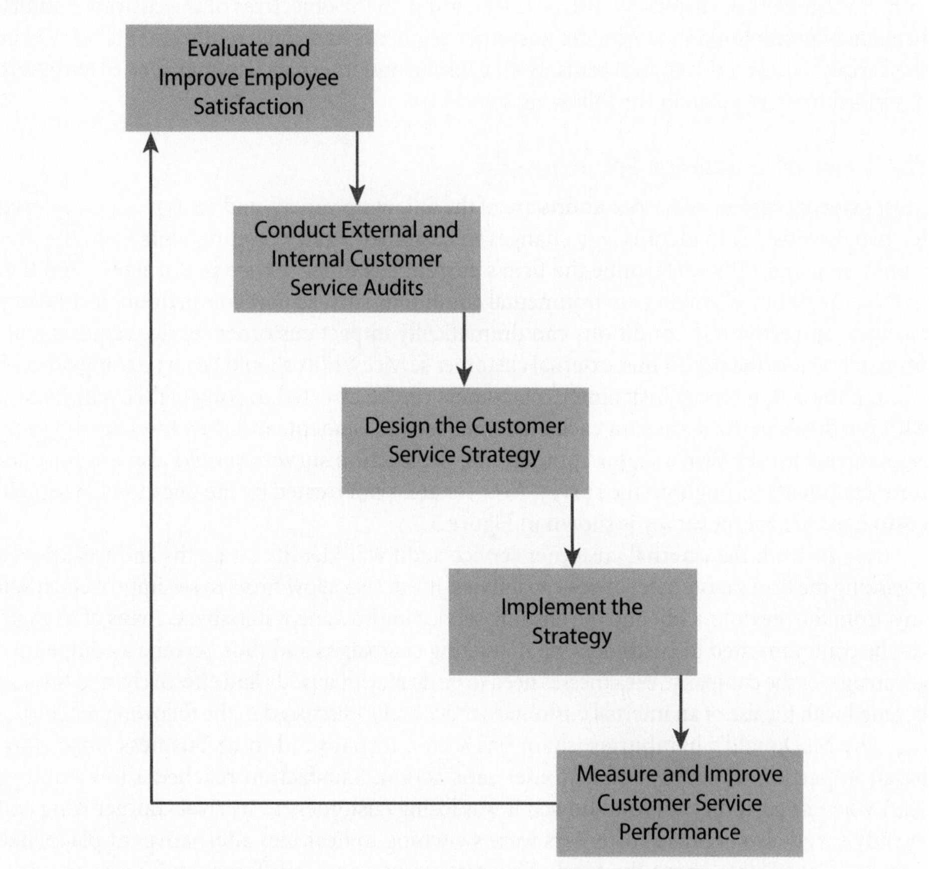

to receive merchandise and travel awards for demonstrating commitment to four characteristics: being fast, accountable, service driven, and team oriented. As a result of the recognition program, Reuters' share price, revenues, and customer satisfaction all improved.[39]

Employee satisfaction surveys are a useful tool for evaluating an organization's efforts to achieve high levels of job satisfaction. Additionally, the surveys can themselves create higher levels of satisfaction. According to research completed in the hotel industry, more than 20% of hotels administering employee surveys experienced an improvement in employee satisfaction by more than 10% for the following year.[40] Figure 5.3 provides an example of a typical Web-based employee satisfaction survey.

CONDUCT CUSTOMER SERVICE AUDITS

Once the firm is satisfied with its work environment, it can begin identifying customer service requirements. This can be accomplished with customer focus groups, interviews, and/or surveys. Customer service requirements can also be gathered from existing customer information databases, such as records of complaints, repair work, call center comments, and comment card information. This initial external audit is necessary to identify service characteristics that are important to customers as well as their performance expectations for each characteristic. Once a number of valued service characteristics and performance expectations are identified, the firm can then determine customers' overall satisfaction with each of these identified service characteristics. This is accomplished through use of follow-up customer service audits. Internal customer service audits are also necessary to review the firm's current customer service policies and practices. Once both the external and internal audits are completed, organizations will be able to identify gaps between the services customers require and the services the firm is providing. These gaps would then be used to guide any improvement activities.

One final topic to consider in customer service audits is the type of customer surveyed. Does the firm want to survey all customers, the most profitable ones, or some other segment, such as women customers? Perhaps the firm should choose to ignore the assessments of unprofitable customers, and concentrate on providing the desired service elements of one or more segments of customers instead. Depending on the objectives of the customer audits, firms may prefer looking at specific customer segments and their requirements, as well as the average customer's requirements. Both external and internal customer service audits are described in more detail in the following sections.

The External Customer Service Audit

Most **external customer service audits** are of the follow-up variety, and are typically employed for two reasons: (1) to identify any changes in customer service requirements from the previous audit, and (2) to determine the firm's current customer service performance and that of its competitors. Changing environmental conditions such as new competition, technology changes, and economic conditions can dramatically impact customer service requirements from one year to the next. Thus, external customer service audits should be an ongoing process.

On the actual survey instrument, customers can be directed to convey their satisfaction with the firm's performance on each customer service element, and then to make the same assessments for the firm's major competitors. Satisfaction surveys should also ask for free-form comments throughout the survey, to cover areas not treated by the questions. A sample customer satisfaction survey is shown in Figure 5.4.

Results from the external customer service audit will identify strengths and weaknesses regarding the firm's customer service capabilities. It will also allow firms to see improvements, if any, from the previous audit and the ensuing service improvement initiatives. Areas of strength can be communicated to customers via marketing campaigns and thus become a competitive advantage for the company. Weaknesses need to be dealt with quickly and effectively, and this can be aided with the use of an internal customer service audit (discussed in the following section).

external customer service audits Identifying changes in the service requirements of customers and determining the firm's current customer service performance and that of its competitors.

The McDonald's hamburger chain has seen a turnaround in its business since 2001, based in part on its surveys of customer satisfaction. Satisfaction reached a low point in 2001 when its customer surveys showed it was losing customers to its rivals Burger King and Wendy's, and also because customers were switching to healthier alternatives at places like Subway. Complaints about the food, dirty restaurants, and indifferent staff were growing,

Figure 5.3 Web-Based Employee Satisfaction Survey

1) Please describe your position with the company:

2) How long have you worked for the company?

-- Select Here --

Please indicate how much you agree or disagree with each of the following statements:

	Strongly Disagree	Disagree	Undecided	Agree	Strongly Agree
3) I have full access to the information and tools I need to get my job done.	○	○	○	○	○
4) I am familiar with the mission statement of the company.	○	○	○	○	○
5) I am familiar with the mission statement of my department.	○	○	○	○	○
6) I participate in decision-making that affects my job.	○	○	○	○	○
7) Management has created an open and comfortable work environment.	○	○	○	○	○
8) I know my job requirements and what is expected of me on a daily basis.	○	○	○	○	○
9) I have received the training I need to do my job efficiently and effectively.	○	○	○	○	○
10) I receive additional training to enable me to do my job better.	○	○	○	○	○
11) Management recognizes my contributions and makes good use of my abilities and skills.	○	○	○	○	○
12) I am treated with respect by management and the people I work with.	○	○	○	○	○
13) I am encouraged to develop new and more efficient ways to do my work.	○	○	○	○	○
14) I and my fellow employees work well together and get the job done.	○	○	○	○	○
15) Management is flexible and understands the importance of balancing my work and personal life.	○	○	○	○	○
16) I would recommend that others work for this company.	○	○	○	○	○
17) I am rewarded well for the work I do for the company.	○	○	○	○	○
18) Overall, I am a satisfied employee.	○	○	○	○	○

19) What changes, if any, do you feel need to be made in your department to improve working conditions?

20) What changes, if any, do you feel need to be made in the company to improve working conditions?

Source: Based in part on employee satisfaction surveys found at surveyconsole.com, questionpro.com, and surveyshare.com

Figure 5.4 Customer Satisfaction Survey

Dear Customer: Please help us serve you better by telling us about your purchase and the service that you have received so far.

1. **Thinking about your most recent customer service experience with our company, the quality of service you received was:**

   _____ **Poor** _____ **Unsatisfactory** _____ **Satisfactory** _____ **Very Satisfactory** _____ **Superior**

   If you indicated that the customer service was poor or unsatisfactory, would you please describe what happened?

   The process for getting your concerns resolved was (check one):

   _____ **Poor** _____ **Unsatisfactory** _____ **Satisfactory** _____ **Very Satisfactory** _____ **Superior**

   If you indicated that the problem resolution was poor or unsatisfactory, would you please describe what happened?

2. **Now please think about the quality (features, benefits) and cost of your recent purchase from our company. Which characteristic best describes your feelings about the product?**

   _____ **Poor** _____ **Unsatisfactory** _____ **Satisfactory** _____ **Very Satisfactory** _____ **Superior**

   If you are not at least satisfied, would you please tell us why?

3. **Customer Service Representative – The following items pertain to the customer service representative you spoke with most recently. Please indicate whether you agree or disagree with the following statements:**

	Strongly Agree	Agree	Neutral	Disagree	Strongly Disagree
The customer service representative was very courteous					
The customer service representative handled your question quickly					
The customer service representative was very knowledgeable					

   Are there any other comments about the customer service representative you would like to add?

4. **Our Competition – The following questions pertain to the company that you think is our best competitor. Please indicate whether you agree or disagree with the following statements.**

Name of our best competitor:	Strongly Agree	Agree	Neutral	Disagree	Strongly Disagree
Our customer service is better than our competitor's.					
The product you purchased is better than our competitor's.					
Our customer service representatives are better than our competitor's.					

5. **Overall satisfaction.**

	Very Satisfied	Somewhat Satisfied	Neutral	Somewhat Dissatisfied	Very Dissatisfied
Considering our total package of customer service, product quality, and cost, how satisfied are you?					

Thank you very much for your feedback. We sincerely appreciate your honest opinion and will take your input into consideration when providing goods and services in the future.

Sources: Based in part on survey templates available at SurveyConsole.com, QuestionPro.com, and SurveyShare.com.

along with general concerns about obesity and junk food. Based on this feedback, McDonald's added salads and other lighter meal options, and remodeled existing locations.[41]

The Internal Customer Service Audit

The **internal customer service audit** allows the organization to review its current customer service measures, policies, and practices. The internal customer service audit should provide information on the following topics:

- *Measures.* How does the firm actually measure customer satisfaction? Do these measures support the external customer service characteristics? How are these measures reported and communicated to employees?
- *Policies.* What customer service policies exist? How are they communicated to customers and employees? Are they related to the external customer service requirements? Have these policies contributed to improvements in customer satisfaction?
- *Practices.* How often are external customer service audits performed? Are the audit findings used in the firm's reward systems? Are the external audit findings communicated throughout the firm? Are improvement initiatives designed and implemented based on the audit results? Are resources available to support the customer service improvement initiatives? Are these activities supported and encouraged by top management?

The overall objective of the internal customer service audit is to identify any inconsistencies between the firm's practice of customer service and the actual requirements of its customers. Integrating the two can be problematic. Managers and their employees, for instance, might think the firm's customer service attributes are very good, when in fact customers are saying something entirely different. In other cases, employees may simply have no idea of their company's customer service performance or the cost of providing it. All of these disconnects between the company and its customers are likely to be identified with an effective audit of the firm's customer service measures, policies, and practices. When identified, these problems can then be resolved through the design of the right customer service strategy.

Internal customer service audit information is likely to highlight inconsistencies in how customer service is regarded in different departments and how polices are carried out and communicated to customers. It is very important for the firm to present a unified face to the customer, and audits can be the first step in that direction. The following section discusses the formation of customer service strategies, based on information obtained during the external and internal customer service audits.

DESIGNING THE CUSTOMER SERVICE STRATEGY

Effective customer service strategies are based on the knowledge of how customers define service, their perceptions of current customer service levels, and the experiences of the firm in designing and delivering customer service. The objective of all customer service strategies should be to create value through optimum service levels, leading to long-term competitive advantage. The optimum service level may not be the highest attainable, nor the most expensive, but a level that will satisfy customers. The most profitable customers, for example, should receive the highest levels and the most frequent customer service, while others receive the same or less.

In general, as shown in Table 5.4, effective customer service strategies deliver high-quality customer service and value, they foster achievement within the organization, and they are aligned with the company's mission. These are briefly discussed in the following section.

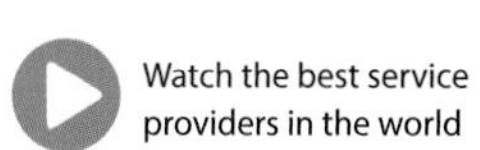

Watch the best service providers in the world

Delivering High-Quality Customer Service

Delivering **high-quality customer service** is achieved through attention to four basic service principles:

1. *Reliability.* Companies keep their promises; services are accurate and dependable.
2. *Recovery.* Companies fix customer problems in a quick, meaningful way when they occur.

internal customer service audit Reviewing the firm's current customer service measures, policies, and practices.

high-quality customer service Using the four basic service principles—reliability, recovery, fairness, and wow factor.

Table 5.4 Customer Service Strategy Elements

Element	Description
High-quality customer service	Achieved through attention to reliability, recovery, fairness, and the wow factor.
Creating value with customer service	Accomplished when customer service meets or exceeds customer expectations.
Fostering achievements in customer service	Customer service strategies should include employee training to develop customer service skills.
Mission-aligned customer service	Mission statements contain language pertaining to customer service.
Customer service departments	Customer service departments can be the drivers for creating a service culture in the organization.
Customer contact centers	These have become the focal point for developing, monitoring, and improving customer service strategies.
Customer participation and self-service	Allowing customers to participate in the service provides service customization. It also links customers with the company.
Web-based customer service applications	Company websites enable customers to receive additional information, eliminating the need for interaction with customer service personnel.
Customer service outsourcing	Can be a way to reduce costs and improve customer service.

3. *Fairness.* Companies respect customers and treat them in a fair and ethical way.
4. *Wow factor.* Companies add unexpected touches to the service, meant to impress customers, as in "Wow! This is great!"

Find companies delivering excellent customer service and you'll most likely find ample evidence of all four of these service quality principles. The Service Spotlight of Bern's Steak House is one such example. Company culture should encourage these beliefs and reward and otherwise support employees who deliver service performance in these areas. Commitment to these four principles is what creates high-quality customer service.

SERVICE SPOTLIGHT

Bern's Keeps 'Em Coming Back

Florida-based Bern's Steak House, the creation of Bern Laxer, is one of a kind. For instance, patrons can select from menu items featuring 62 cuts of steak and 21 types of caviar. After dinner, they can relocate to the dessert room. Laxer also built one of the largest wine cellars in the world, with half a million bottles. What keeps customers returning, though, is the excellent customer service.

One tradition still intact at Bern's is the long training period for the waiters. They must complete training in the kitchen, at Bern's farm, and in the wine cellar, which allows them to speak knowledgeably to customers regarding every aspect of their meal. Waiters know most of the regulars' names, and they are trained to interpret customers' needs. If customers want talk, servers are engaging; if it's a business meeting, servers are there but are almost unseen.

Zuma/Alamy

For over 50 years, Bern's has been at the top of its game. Employees love working there, they have a say on how things are done, and management's door is always open.[42]

Creating Value With Customer Service

What were the top customer service companies of 2015? Watch here

When customer service meets or exceeds customer expectations, it makes customers feel they are getting their money's worth and perhaps even more. They want to return and make future purchases. This sense of value provides firms with a competitive advantage, and in many cases, can be very easy to provide to customers. For instance, a quick-change oil business that provides magazines, a TV, and free coffee to customers while they wait, is providing extra value to the actual service. Additionally, if the company does extra things like checking the air filter and wiper blades, and washing the windows, then service value is increased even more. Finally, since many people view waiting time as lost earning potential, getting customers in and out quickly also creates service value.

Fostering Achievements in Customer Service

Service strategies should include employee training to develop customer service skills. Managers can allow employees to use creativity when solving service problems, without first getting approvals. Additionally, successful service experiences should be communicated throughout the organization. Finally, successful, innovative customer service activities exhibited by employees should be rewarded.

Aligning Customer Service With the Mission

Firms need to be serious about providing great customer service. As Leonard Berry says in his book *On Great Service*, firms must live their service strategies. Hiring and training the right people, providing the right technologies, and using effective performance measures and reward systems give life to service strategies.[43] Mission statements should contain language pertaining to customer service, and this commitment should filter down through the firm's hierarchy. Here are two examples of company missions that contain customer service language:

1. From the AGCO Corp., a Georgia-based agricultural equipment manufacturer: *Profitable growth through superior customer service, innovation, quality, and commitment.*
2. From Sainsbury's, a leading UK food retailer with banking interests:

   Our number one job is to serve our customers well. This means we must look to provide a consistent level of good customer service across all our activities whether this is customer contact, product availability, food quality, or banking services.

In both cases, the commitment to customer service is clearly stated.

A customer service strategy for a firm is made up of the collective customer service practices and policies in place, derived from the company's mission, customer requirements, and previous experiences with customer service initiatives. It is an organizing principle that directs employees to provide services that benefit customers. As competition increases and goods and services change, customer requirements also change, and consequently, customer service strategies must change. As part of an overall customer service strategy, a number of commonly used practices have been employed. Several of these are described in the following section.

Customer Service Departments

While **customer service departments** have existed for many years and may at one time have been repositories for disgruntled employees armed with a company policy manual, a curt smile, and not much else, today's customer service departments are staffed with a collection of innovative and knowledgeable people. Customer service departments create a focal point for service assessment and improvement, and can be the drivers for creating a service culture in the organization. The customer service department can create and maintain an emphasis on service quality, and add a sense of formality to the firm's customer service strategy.

customer service departments Create and maintain an emphasis on service quality, and add a sense of formality to the firm's customer service strategy.

Innovative customer service departments provide direction and coordination to customer service assessment and improvement efforts. They oversee the internal and external customer service audits, create the strategic service plan, and establish funding, timelines, and responsibilities for implementation of service activities. They also help set up project teams for specific customer service improvement initiatives, and serve as the collection point for service improvement ideas that come from customers and employees. When initiatives are implemented, the customer service department helps design performance metrics and then assists in monitoring actual performance, while taking appropriate actions to further refine and improve performance.

Temporary **customer service teams** can also be created with the help of the customer service department, and can consist of executives, department managers, design engineers, and other personnel, to react to a significant customer service problem. For example, while GE had not made appliances since the early 1980s, news of old GE coffeemakers causing fires created the need for a very innovative customer service solution, involving customers in both North and South America. GE formed a cross-functional team of GE managers to study the problem and implemented a meaningful solution that would satisfy its customers. It conducted a media blitz to publicize a toll-free phone number consumers could call to see if their coffeemaker was hazardous. When a hazardous coffeemaker was found, postage-free packaging was delivered to the consumer. Customers were also paid $10 for their inconvenience when the repaired or replaced coffeemakers were returned. "The part of the program that makes this recall unique is that from the customer standpoint, the process costs nothing and it's completely hassle-free," says Chip Keeling, GE's spokesperson for the recall. "They don't have to pay for a phone call, provide packaging, or go to the post office. In terms of customer service, we're seeing a higher level of customer satisfaction than we expected, based on previous recalls."[44]

Customer Contact Centers

Today, customer call centers are more aptly named **customer contact centers** because they integrate all of the methods customers can use to contact a business, including telephone, mail, comment cards, email, and website messages and chat rooms. For most large firms, these contact centers are open 24/7. In some cases, contact center automation technologies allow a small staff to handle a large volume of customer calls, and in cases where most customers are asking for similar information, firms have found it more efficient to add automated systems such as interactive voice response, speech recognition, and call routing systems.

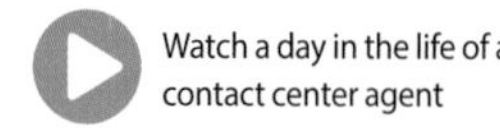

Watch a day in the life of a contact center agent

In many organizations today, the customer contact center has become the focal point for developing, monitoring, and improving customer service strategy—in essence, replacing the customer service department discussed in the previous section. And the recognized value of contact centers is increasing rapidly. For instance, a 1% increase in first-call resolution can improve customer satisfaction by 6%; and one hour of contact center training can drop the cost per customer contact by more than three cents.[45] When these savings are multiplied by many thousands of customers, the impact can be significant.

Customer contact center personnel can proactively seek out customer feedback and solve problems by making follow-up calls to customers who have recently purchased a product or service, or who complained at an earlier time and were given assurances that their complaint would be resolved. New technologies, better training, and full-enterprise awareness of the value of a well-managed customer contact center are allowing businesses today to differentiate themselves from their competitors, create loyal customers, and find new ones.

customer service teams Can consist of executives, department managers, design engineers, and other personnel, to react to a significant customer service problem.

customer contact centers Allows integration of all of the methods customers can use to contact a business, including telephone, mail, comment cards, email, website messages, and chat rooms.

customer participation approach Use of self-service.

Customer Participation and Self-Service

Allowing customers to participate in the service itself provides customers with the opportunity to somewhat customize their service. Customer participation also links the customer to a greater degree with the company, increases the productivity of service providers, and can improve customer satisfaction. Services that involve customers are becoming more common as firms try to find ways to reduce labor costs.

Self-service is one form of the **customer participation approach**. It requires a standardized service that can be administered with little or no company assistance. Examples of self-service processes include automated bank teller machines, automated information obtained during customer telephone calls, website purchases and queries, refueling at gas stations, and self-checkout stations at retailers. Self-service can be very appealing to customers, since it allows them to decide when to access the service, how long to interact, and the precise service desired. However, customer training or indoctrination may be needed, and this will involve careful thought when designing printed directions. It may also have to involve a company employee to monitor customers during the self-service.

Nevada Wier/Corbis

India remains a favored country for call center outsourcing.

Web-Based Customer Service Applications

In many cases, a well-designed company website can enable customers to obtain answers to their questions or receive additional information, eliminating the need for interaction with customer service personnel. Companies commonly post answers to frequently asked questions and provide catalogue and installation, assembly, operating, and troubleshooting manuals on their websites. Other e-service solutions can respond to customer queries by interpreting questions and then delivering answers from a knowledge database. These automated services largely eliminate emails, cost much less than providing traditional call center employees, and can raise customer satisfaction levels. Additionally, they can handle up to 90% of the typical customer queries received by companies. Good website management can also make use of e-service records to see what customers are asking for, and further develop customer relationships.[46]

Web-based customer service has also opened up opportunities for technology-assisted selling. Today, the role of the field salesperson provides added value as a customer service representative by enabling current information to be provided about the company's goods and services in the field, and by allowing company resources such as marketing information, training, logistics information, diagnostic information, and collaborative planning initiatives to be made available to customers.

Outsourcing Customer Service

When customer contact centers and other customer support personnel represent a significant expense for the organization, outsourcing is occasionally considered as a way to reduce costs and even improve customer service performance. If customer service is considered a competitive priority, companies will pay handsomely to firms with a reputation for providing high-quality customer service for their clients. In Canada, for example, many of the largest electric and gas utilities have outsourced their entire customer service functions. Accenture Business Services is one of the primary customer service providers—it lists as clients Canadian utilities such as BC Gas, BC Hydro, and Enmax. BC Hydro claims it will save $250 million over a 10-year period while improving customer satisfaction, by turning over its customer service responsibilities to Accenture.[47]

Other companies, though, remain unconvinced of the value of **outsourcing customer service**. For instance, Nationwide Building Society in the United Kingdom lists commitment to its employees, the high value of customer service, and risk to its reputation as the three main reasons why it has decided against customer service outsourcing.[48]

Lately, there has been much discussion in the press regarding outsourcing of call center activities to offshore companies, particularly to service companies located in India or Mexico. Indian IT service provider Infosys Technologies, for instance, has a large number of employees providing call center services to U.S. clients. Meta Group Inc., a U.S. research firm, estimates that offshore outsourcing by U.S. businesses has been growing by about 20% per year for the past decade.[49]

Another form of customer service outsourcing involves the creation of a **virtual call center**. With this type of arrangement, an organization's call center agents can be located anywhere, usually in their homes, while the center is managed as a single entity. Using the virtual call center model allows staffing resources to be optimized, employee retention and satisfaction to increase, call center costs to decline, and perhaps most important, allows management control to be retained. For example, My Twinn, a personalized doll manufacturer, created its virtual call center in 2000. That year, 30% more inquiry calls were converted to

web-based customer service Enabling information to be provided to customers about the company's goods and services in the field, as well as marketing information, training, logistics information, diagnostic information, and collaborative planning initiatives.

outsourcing customer service Using a third-party customer service provider.

virtual call center Locating the organization's call center agents anywhere, while the center is managed as a single entity.

orders, employee turnover decreased 88%, and 90% fewer calls had to be transferred to a higher-level employee, compared to 1999.[50]

Hopefully, the firm is able to identify a customer service strategy that is a good match between what their customers want, what the firm is capable of providing, and what competitors are not currently doing very well. A well-designed and implemented customer service program can serve the company well for a very long time, requiring only minor technical adjustments over time, for continued effectiveness.

IMPLEMENTING THE CUSTOMER SERVICE STRATEGY

Referring again to Figure 5.2, once the firm has decided on a customer service strategy and the activities to be included in this strategy, the necessary resources must be committed to implementing the activities, including the hiring and training of personnel, procurement of equipment and software applications, and assignment or construction of facility space. Obviously, management must support the overall customer service strategy, be willing to provide the resources required, and be committed to the strategy through the implementation phase. Several program implementation suggestions are discussed next.

Start With a Pilot Project

Depending on the required investment and probability of success, the firm may choose to start small, with a **customer service pilot project**. Piloting enables management to assess the impact of the initiative on customer satisfaction, the real costs involved, and the changes in organizational structure required. A number of problems will likely surface, allowing employees to work out solutions prior to any organizational customer service strategy rollout. Surveys can be used to assess customer and employee satisfaction after the pilot project is implemented. It is during this time that the required resources, costs, benefits, and merits of the customer service strategy will become clear, allowing the firm to make a final decision regarding whether or not to go ahead with a full system implementation.

Provide the Necessary Training, Equipment, and Leadership

Training is one of the more critical issues with any new customer service strategy. While service delivery personnel may be skilled in several functions, they may also be required to perform others, using unfamiliar equipment and software. Education and equipment training needs must be assessed and provided. Supervisory roles must be established along with a transitioning period for jobs that will change. The firm must decide who is going to teach, who is going to coach, and who is going to make decisions and solve problems when they arise.

MEASURING AND IMPROVING CUSTOMER SERVICE PERFORMANCE

The final step in implementing a customer service strategy is to develop performance standards and the accompanying measurements to assess ongoing performance. Management sets service performance standards for all of the activities that make up the service strategy based on factors such as the customers' service requirements, the distribution channel, and the product or service involved. Recall from discussions in Chapter 2 that standards for each service activity should be quantitative and measurable. Performance standards must then be communicated to the service activity providers.

Measuring customer service performance should be done frequently and compared to existing standards. Ideally, performance should be measured each time a service is provided. The time required to answer a telephone call and handle customer requests, for instance, can be monitored using automated applications. Measuring every customer's satisfaction at a restaurant, though, can be time consuming and impractical. In this case, random monitoring is typically employed. Performance can thus be collected, averaged over time, and compared to service standards. When negative variances are found between actual performance and the standard, corrective actions can be taken. Some potential customer service measures are shown in Table 5.5, and are organized according to the classifications shown in Table 5.1. Each measure should have a performance standard that is determined and periodically revised as conditions merit.

customer service pilot project Enables management to assess the impact of an initiative on customer satisfaction, the real costs involved, and the changes in organizational structure required, prior to any organizational customer service strategy rollout.

Table 5.5 Customer Service Performance Measures

Pre-transaction Measures	Percentage of queries answered satisfactorily
	Time to answer customer query
	Number of sales calls made
	Number of technical skills acquired
	Hours of training completed
	Number of new product/service meetings attended
	Number of existing goods/services reviewed
	Number of customer service improvements implemented
	Safety stock levels for each product
Transaction Measures	Time to seat customer
	Time to acknowledge customer order
	Time to fill customer order
	Number of deliveries made
	Order cycle time
	Percentage of on-time deliveries
	Percentage of orders unfilled (stockouts)
	Percentage of shipments with errors
	Percentage of orders expedited
	Number of orders traced
	Percentage of customers complaining during transaction
	Percentage of emergency orders handled satisfactorily
Post-transaction Measures	Percentage of invoices with errors
	Percent returns/adjustments
	Number of product/service complaints
	Percentage of shipments damaged
	Number of warranty services performed
	Number of service requests
	Percentage of operating queries answered satisfactorily

Source: Based in part on *Fundamentals of Logistics Management*, by J. Stock, D. Lambert, and L. Ellram, 1998. New York: McGraw-Hill, p. 66.

Measuring customer service performance should incorporate several methods, including use of complaint forms or suggestion systems, customer satisfaction surveys, ghost or mystery shoppers, and customer interviews. Firms should make it easy for customers to provide feedback, complaints, or suggestions, such as providing space for comments on company websites, placing feedback cards where customers regularly interact with service personnel, providing surveys with invoices or products, calling customers who recently purchased a good or service, and establishing a toll-free customer service hotline. Use of mystery shoppers can also be used, and is described next.

USING MYSTERY SHOPPERS TO MONITOR SERVICE PERFORMANCE

Many companies hire professional **mystery shoppers** who pose as customers to assess the customer service performance of employees. Mystery shoppers gather performance information and document employee behaviors, and then create summary reports that are sent to management. These reports indicate, for example, how long the customer had to wait for service, the type of greeting used, the willingness of servers to answer questions or solve

mystery shoppers Professionals who pose as customers to assess the customer service performance of employees.

problems, and the server's knowledge of the goods and services. While mystery shoppers conduct covert observations, employees are typically told in advance about the likelihood of mystery shopper visits, and how the information collected will be used. This enables the firm to maintain employee trust.

Mystery observations can yield a full picture of job performance and the work environment, and can be an ideal method for identifying the underlying causes of poor customer service. Skilled observers can uncover workplace tools and other items that help to create superior job performance, as well as things that hinder performance. Ineffective work flows, processes, and communication patterns can also be identified. Additionally, observers can assess employees' mastery of training regimens and uncover differences in behaviors among service employees.

Mystery shoppers have been used for decades in the restaurant business; however, they are gaining popularity today for gathering information on customer contact centers, hotels, conference facilities, office environments, and many other service functions and businesses. The Mystery Shoppers Providers Association based in Dallas, Texas, estimates that 70–80 percent of quick-service operators are using some type of anonymous visitor program. A 25-unit chain, for example, will spend from $15,000 to $25,000 annually on a program involving one visit per store per month. While this may sound expensive, most participating companies insist that the programs are worth the investment.[51]

Visit edge.sagepub.com/wisner to help you accomplish your coursework goals in an easy-to-use learning environment.

- Mobile-friendly eFlashcards
- Mobile-friendly practice quizzes
- A complete online action plan
- Chapter summaries with learning objectives
- Excel templates to assist with practice problems
- Original video case studies that demonstrate chapter concepts in action

SUMMARY

As evidenced in this chapter, the customer relationship and customer service processes are extremely important areas of concern for many organizations. Customer-oriented programs typically involve the hiring and training of personnel and the investment of significant sums of money to implement customer-focused initiatives and software applications. This chapter concentrated primarily on the customer relationship process as shown in Figure 5.1, which includes segmenting customers, designing a customer relationship program, selecting CRM software, and delivering the program to targeted segments; and in Figure 5.2, the customer service process framework, which includes conducting internal and external service audits, and designing and implementing the service strategy. Once the programs have been implemented, performance metrics can be developed to monitor success and guide continuous improvements. A number of examples were provided throughout the chapter to help illustrate the concepts.

KEY TERMS

Approach to analytics, 117
CRM applications, 108
Customer communities, 116
Customer contact centers, 128
Customer lifetime value, 113
Customer loyalty programs, 115
Customer participation approach, 128
Customer relationship process, 108
Customer segmentation, 112
Customer service departments, 127
Customer service failure, 111
Customer service pilot project, 130
Customer service process, 109
Customer service teams, 128
Direct mail, 119
External customer service audits, 122
False positive blocking, 118
Focus groups, 119
Happy-productive worker hypothesis, 121
High-quality customer service, 125

Internal customer service audit, 125
Mystery shoppers, 131
Neighborhood marketing, 113
Niche segmentation, 112
Order cycle, 110
Outsourcing customer service, 129
Post-transaction customer service elements, 111
Pre-transaction customer service elements, 110
Profitable customer, 112
Telemarketing, 118
Transaction elements of customer service, 110
Versioning, 115
Viral marketing, 116
Virtual call center, 129
Web-based customer service, 129

FORMULA REVIEW

Customer lifetime value: $NPV_A = P\left[\frac{1-(1+i)^{-n}}{i}\right]$, where A = customer, P = average annual profit, or (annual sales × profit margin), i = annual discount rate, and n = expected lifetime in years.

SOLVED PROBLEMS

1. Which customer is preferred?

	Average Annual Sales	Average Profit Margin	Expected Lifetime
Customer A:	$8,000	11%	15 years
Customer B:	$5,000	9%	22 years

Answer:

Using a discount rate of 6% and treating the average sales figures as annuities, the customer lifetime values are:

$$NPV_A = P\left[\frac{1-(1+i)^{-n}}{i}\right] = 880\left[\frac{1-(1.06)^{-15}}{0.06}\right] = 880\left[\frac{0.583}{0.06}\right] = \$8547$$

$$NPV_B = P\left[\frac{1-(1+i)^{-n}}{i}\right] = 450\left[\frac{1-(1.06)^{-22}}{0.06}\right] = 450\left[\frac{0.722}{0.06}\right] = \$5415$$

Based on these findings, Customer A is preferred.

REVIEW QUESTIONS

1. What is the customer service process?
2. What are the three elements of customer service? Which one do you think is the most important?
3. What causes a customer service failure?
4. How is customer relationship management different from CRM software applications?
5. What is customer segmentation, and why is it important?
6. What is the objective of the customer relationship process?
7. What sort of customer information is typically collected when segmenting customers, and how is this information obtained?
8. Define niche segmentation.
9. Discuss the term *profitable customer* and why it is so important when segmenting customers or designing marketing campaigns.
10. What is customer lifetime value, and how can it be used in the design of marketing initiatives?
11. Discuss the meaning of neighborhood marketing, and provide some examples of firms in your area.
12. Describe versioning and how it might be used in a customer relationship program.
13. What is bottom-up branding, and how can this be a helpful concept for a firm?
14. Why do CRM technology investments have relatively high failure rates?

15. Can firing customers be a good practice? Can it be bad for business?
16. How does false-positive blocking affect relationship management efforts?
17. Compare telemarketing to the use of field sales personnel for relationship management purposes.
18. How should performance metrics be used in customer relationship program implementations?
19. What is the happy-productive worker hypothesis, and what does it have to do with customer service?
20. Why do firms conduct external customer service audits, and how do they do it?
21. How do firms conduct an internal customer service audit? Why do they do it?
22. How does a firm achieve high-quality customer service?
23. What advantages and disadvantages does the customer participation approach to customer service have? What are some examples of this approach?
24. When would outsourcing customer service be a good idea? When would it be a bad idea?
25. What are mystery shoppers, and what do they do? Do you think this is a useful concept?

DISCUSSION QUESTIONS

1. Discuss how you would segment students at your school. Does the Student Union do this?
2. Why do you think so many customer relationship initiatives fail? Describe some relationships you have with businesses. Are they successful?
3. Can segmenting markets by gender be done successfully? Explain.
4. Critique the customer satisfaction survey shown in Figure 5.4.
5. What would be a good mission statement for your university or college?
6. Does your school have a customer contact or call center? Is it doing a good job?
7. When would you recommend performing a pilot customer service project?
8. Provide some examples of customer service performance measures your school could use.

EXERCISES AND PROJECTS

1. Go to a retailer or restaurant and buy some things. Identify the pre-transaction, transaction, and post-transaction customer service elements. Do something to potentially create a service failure (i.e., complain about something). Report on how the service recovery was handled.
2. Go to a small business with which you are familiar. Identify any existing customer *relationship* elements the business has in place. Discuss these and any new elements you would create for it. Design some performance measures for the program.
3. Search the Internet for a firm with a customer relationship management program. Discuss the strengths and weaknesses of its program. Do not use a firm spotlighted in this chapter.
4. Go to a small business with which you are familiar. Identify any existing customer *service* elements the business has in place. Discuss these and any new elements you would create for it. Additionally, design and discuss a customer service survey.
5. Find the websites of six large organizations and identify their mission statements. See if any of these have mission statement elements relating to customer service.

PROBLEMS

1. Sally's Mountaineering Supply sells hiking and climbing equipment to sporting goods and specialty hiking retailers. It recently began ranking its customers based on their expected lifetime profitability in order to segment customers for various customer relationship initiatives. Three of its customers are shown in the following table.

	Average Annual Sales	Average Profit Margin	Expected Lifetime
Customer A	$108,000	18%	6 years
Customer B	$82,000	22%	15 years
Customer C	$29,000	31%	26 years

Use a discount rate of 4% and treat the average sales figures as annuities.

a. Calculate the customer lifetime values for the three customers.

b. Which customer is the most valued? Should Sally's segment the customers?

2. Using the customer information in Problem 1, recalculate the lifetime values using a discount rate of 10%. Answer parts a and b again. Has anything changed?

3. Using the customer information in Problem 1, recalculate the lifetime values using average profit margins of 9%, 11%, and 15%, respectively, and a discount rate of 4%. Answer parts a and b again. Has anything changed?

4. Tire manufacturer Stonebridge sells tires to retail Firm A. The average annual sales to Firm A are $55,000. Its average profit margin is 15%. The expected lifetime of Firm A is 10 years. Using a discount rate of 10%, calculate the customer lifetime value of Firm A.

5. Using the information in the table that follows, rank the two customers in terms of customer lifetime value.

	Average Annual Sales	Average Profit Margin	Expected Lifetime
Customer A	$3,500	15%	10 years
Customer B	$4,000	14%	8 years

Use a discount rate of 8% and treat the average sales figures as annuities.

6. Using the information in Problem 5, what would the average profit margins have to be, in order to have both customer lifetime values equal $4,000?

7. Using the information in Problem 5, how much longer would the company have to hold onto Customer B in order for the two customers to have the same lifetime values?

CASE STUDIES

CASE 1: Louie's Hardware Store

Louie's Hardware is a third-generation, locally owned hardware retailer with two locations in a greater population area of approximately 250,000. Louie's has been experiencing relatively flat growth while all the other independent hardware stores in the market area have closed. Competing big box home improvement stores in the area include Lowes, Menards, and a newly opened Home Depot. The closest leading hardware store, Ace Hardware, is about 30 miles away. Louie's ownership and leadership team is at the end of a five-year planning cycle and wants the next five-year planning cycle strategy to focus on customer segments that will be profitable for the hardware store and can withstand the competitive pressures from home improvement stores. The leadership group is in consensus that the next strategic plan must emphasize the customer relationship process.

When evaluating key industry benchmarks, Louie's is just a bit below industry averages for hardware stores, with two stores at 9,000 square feet and total annual sales of $2,500,000. It has a total of 10 employees and the stores average $16 per transaction, with a net profit margin of 1.8%. Comparable benchmark averages for this-size store are total annual sales of $2,900,000, with 10 employees per store, $18 per transaction, and a net profit margin of 2.1%.

The large home improvement retailers make up almost 66% of the consumer market sales of $221 billion.[52] Large chains of hardware stores such as Ace Hardware, Do It Best, and True Value make up another 11% of the consumer market. The balance is an eclectic group made up of independent hardware stores/chains and lumber yards with regional or locally based markets. Both the professional sector and consumer sector in the home improvement market have historically trended with national economic indexes. Economic downturns impact home improvement market share negatively with revenue and profit challenges. Economic growth impacts the home improvement market with strong revenue and profit gains. Other key economic indicators include employment gains/losses, wage stagnation/growth, gasoline prices, and housing market activity including housing starts, home sales, refinancing, and major remodeling.

Hardware stores, after going through a major thinning out at the hands of the big box home improvement stores, have settled into a mature industry growth market (0–2.5%). Despite improved economic conditions, hardware stores have not experienced the same growth in consumer markets and have not been major players in the professional markets (contractors, builders, and tradespeople). Contributing factors to the decline in hardware sector growth have been the reluctance to invest in technology, missed consumer buying trends, and limited product lines.

High-profit hardware stores (the benchmark leaders for hardware stores) outperform the average hardware stores in several areas. High-profit stores have greater sales per transaction resulting in 18% greater average sales. Net profit margins are three times greater. Additionally, improved internal controls result in greater cash flow, reduced inventories, and greater inventory turns (2.2 compared to 1.8).

Louie's can't compete head to head with the big box stores, so it needs to take advantage of its position as hardware suppliers for the do-it-yourself (DIY) consumers. As it moves into the next strategic planning phase, the focus is on marketing to and satisfying profitable customers and leaving low-profit customers for the big box stores.

A recent industry association research report highlights the DIY customer: they value saving money on home repair, and home projects are done by hobbyists, budding weekend warriors, single parents, new landlords of rental property, home flippers, home sellers preparing for a sale, and are generally male, in their 40s to 50s, and with some trade skills. Using guidance from a university business class, Louie's used its CRM system software to determine what "Most Profitable" customer patterns existed. Its first step in collecting customer information and segmenting the most-profitable customers included reviewing sales records from the company's customer relationship management system (it uses store "loyalty" cards). Data were collected over the past two years and input into an Excel spreadsheet. Data were categorized by type of purchase, including products purchased, purchase frequency, transaction amount, and product purchase sequence. Data were also collected on the type of purchaser, including gender, age, address, transaction type (cash, check, credit card), and telephone number. The data were first used to calculate an average customer profile based on consumer sales behavior in dollars, products purchased, and frequency, and then used to determine a most-profitable customer profile. As part of constructing average customer and most-profitable customer profiles, customer lifetime values were calculated for both. The average lifetime for the most-profitable customer was two years, with three years for the average customer. Using an internal rate of return of 4%, the annual profit margin for the average customer was 1.8% and 5% for the most-profitable customer. The team calculated the CLV for the average customer as $124,919 and the CLV for the most-profitable customer as $94,346.

DISCUSSION QUESTIONS

1. What is the potential benefit for Louie's Hardware in using the customer relationship process model as a strategic planning framework/foundation?
2. What strategic approach can Louie's use to capitalize on the market research findings and the first look at its "typical customer"?
3. If loyalty can be quantified, how can it also be used to predict profitability in the future?
4. Using the two calculated CLVs in the case, what statements could you make about the potential for segmentation of the most-profitable customers, and what recommendations could be made relative to additional data analysis using the CRM system?

Note: Written by Brian Hoyt, Management Professor, Ohio University. This case was prepared solely to provide material for class discussion. The author does not intend to illustrate either effective or ineffective handling of a managerial situation.

CASE 2: High-Quality Service Audit at U-fit

U-fit is a boutique store that specializes in athletic workout, running, and biking apparel. U-fit opened five years ago and experienced immediate success as a high-end apparel retailer, with greater than 25% growth each year. Its current year-to-date sales are sluggish, though, and projections for the remainder of the year are flat. The owner, concerned that U-fit will lose competitive advantage over other stores that carry workout and athletic apparel, is searching for answers to the recent decline in sales and profit.

The Retail Institute's annual state of the industry report revealed important findings of interest to U-fit as it plans strategically for the next five years. Consumer survey responses indicated that while price was still the most important factor in deciding between department store workout apparel and boutique stores, another important factor was customer service excellence. The survey showed that consumers would consider switching retailers and travel up to 35 miles for workout apparel purchases if the service was excellent.

U-fit's owner teamed with several management interns from a local university to determine U-fit's level of service quality excellence using a customer service survey. The purpose was to assess the firm's service quality, compared to a local workout apparel store and a large sporting goods store. Another objective was to identify opportunities for improvement that would provide competitive advantage, and ultimately restimulate growth and profitability.

The project team used a high-quality customer service model as a framework for building and sustaining relationships with customers. Companies who seek to survive in highly competitive environments must strive to excel, and that requires knowledge of the business, customers, and competition. An emphasis on high-quality service areas can be assessed by listening, learning, reacting, and responding to the voices of the consumers, a requirement for a service audit analysis. The student team designed the service quality survey, the data collection and analysis plan, and a database template in Excel that could be imported into U-fit's CRM system. The survey results are shown in the table below. A total of 200 customers were surveyed.

DISCUSSION QUESTIONS

1. How can the quality measures observed in the service quality survey (based on the high-quality customer service principles) add value to the customer experience at U-fit?
2. How can data on high-quality customer service excellence help to guide U-fit's strategic direction?
3. Examine the table provided with data collected from U-fit and its competitors and discuss the service excellence strengths and opportunities for improvement for U-fit.

Note: Written by Brian Hoyt, Management Professor, Ohio University. This case was prepared solely to provide material for class discussion. The author does not intend to illustrate either effective or ineffective handling of a managerial situation.

Service Quality Survey	U-fit	Competitors
Wow Segment		
Is the store layout attractive and easy to navigate?	3.3	4.37
Variety of products and brands	2.67	4.17
Are there product trial opportunities?	2.96	3.7
Wow average score	2.98	4.08
Fairness Segment		
Level of straight talk: factual and need-based?	4.53	3.27
Customer advocacy: usage and return policy explained?	3.37	2.93
Price: as advertised? Price discussion?	4.43	3.6
Fairness average score	4.11	3.27
Reliability Segment		
Sales-person: adequate product knowledge?	4.37	3.37
Customer service representatives: provide adequate assistance?	4.03	2.33
After-sales service: helpful and adequate?	4.07	2.3
Reliability average score	4.16	2.67
High Quality grand average	3.75	3.34

Note: Survey used a 5-point scale, where 1 = poor, 3 = adequate, and 5 = excellent.

CASE 3: A Bike Shop CRM System

A local bike shop competing with big box sports departments at retailers such as Dick's Sporting Goods, K-Mart, and Walmart is committed to optimizing its loyal customer base. The immediate question posed by the bike shop owner was framed as, "What does our most loyal customer look like?" The bike shop partnered with a local university student project team to analyze data from its CRM system to find a "best customer profile" (BCP).

Upon completion of the customer lifetime value calculations it was evident that the most profitable customer segment was not populated with customers who were loyal to the bike shop. The owner deliberated as to whether a customer profile that represented a more loyal customer existed. If a BCP could be identified, customer characteristics could be used as data and be quantified and used in a new CLV calculation and direct marketing efforts. The CLV for the average customer was calculated as $124,919, with an average annual profit of $45,016 and 3 years average lifetime length. The CLV for the best customer was calculated as $250,402, with an average annual profit of $22,508 and 15 years average lifetime length.

The CRM system was mined for data with queries searching for patterns depicting a BCP based on measures of above averages in total expenditures per year, above-average dollars per transaction, number of items purchased, items purchased with high profit margins, number of years as a customer, and the sequence of products/product lines purchased. Data from the customer referral program were also added. A matrix was conceptualized that first weighted each customer characteristic's importance as best customer criteria (i.e., purchasing patterns over five years were weighted highest, purchasing of higher profit margins had a higher weight than general frequency of purchases/number of store visits, and customers who participated in a referral program). Each purchasing characteristic was "awarded" points as it related to average. Points were multiplied by the weighting factor, and then weighted points could be summed for each customer and represented as total customer value points.

The customer database was then divided into those customers who exhibited below-average and above-average total customer value points. Those customers who had scores above average were examined for purchasing patterns not exhibited by below average customers (i.e., variety of product categories, first purchase above $250, and purchase of bike equipment and supplies). Those customers who had scores above average in total customer value points were designated as "best customers" and were identified by customer address and used as a "tracer" to segment best customers geographically. The geographic segmentation, using U.S. Census databases, could then be used to add neighborhood characteristics to the BCP such as lot size, home square footage, median household income, and family structure.

DISCUSSION QUESTIONS

1. How could the bike shop use the CRM system to develop loyalty programs to strengthen its core customer segment?
2. How could the bike shop use the Internet to target loyal customers?
3. What recommendations could you make to the bike shop's strategic planning and efforts to compete with big box companies with large sporting goods departments?

Note: Written by Brian Hoyt, Management Professor, Ohio University. This case was prepared solely to provide material for class discussion. The author does not intend to illustrate either effective or ineffective handling of a managerial situation.

CASE 4: Customer Satisfaction at Spirit Airlines

According to a CNNMoney report in 2015, Spirit Airlines ranked dead last among airlines in the latest travel report from the American Customer Satisfaction Index, with a score of 54. The travel report is based on responses from over 7,500 customers of airline, hotel, and Internet travel industries during the January to February time period each year. JetBlue Airways was the most satisfying airline, with a score of 81, while Southwest ranked just below, with a score of 78.

Spirit Airlines is known for its low prices, but it adds fees for things like printing a boarding pass at the airport or carrying on a bag. Customer satisfaction within the airline industry increased about 3% from 2014 to 2015. Spirit was added to the list in 2015. While passenger satisfaction is at its highest level since 1994, the industry only outperformed three other industries: Internet service providers, subscription television, and health insurance.

The travel survey asks 12 questions about customers' flying experiences, including on-time arrival, boarding and baggage experiences, seat comfort, and flight schedules. The industry average satisfaction score was 71 in 2015. Seat comfort received the lowest overall score for all airlines, while the quality of in-flight food and entertainment received high marks.

Along with Spirit Airlines, Alaska Airlines, Allegiant Air, and Frontier were added to the index in 2015. Alaska debuted at third, with a score of 75, and Frontier ranked just above Spirit, with a score of 58.[1]

QUESTIONS:

1. How could Spirit go about improving its customer relationships?
2. How would you suggest that Spirit improve the elements of customer service?
3. Retrieve the latest American Customer Satisfaction Index, and see how Spirit has done lately: http://www.theacsi.org/the-american-customer-satisfaction-index.

[1] CNN.com, http://money.cnn.com/2015/04/20/pf/airline-customer-satisfaction-report/

VIDEO CASE STUDY

Learn more about ***customer service*** from real organizations that use operations management techniques every day. Matt Henriksen is the General Manager of Bart's Books, a used bookstore in Ojai, California. Since a used bookstore client base has a wide range of needs and requests, having a highly trained staff is paramount to Bart's providing a positive customer experience. Watch this short interview to see how they do it.

PART II
MANUFACTURING AND SERVICE FLOWS

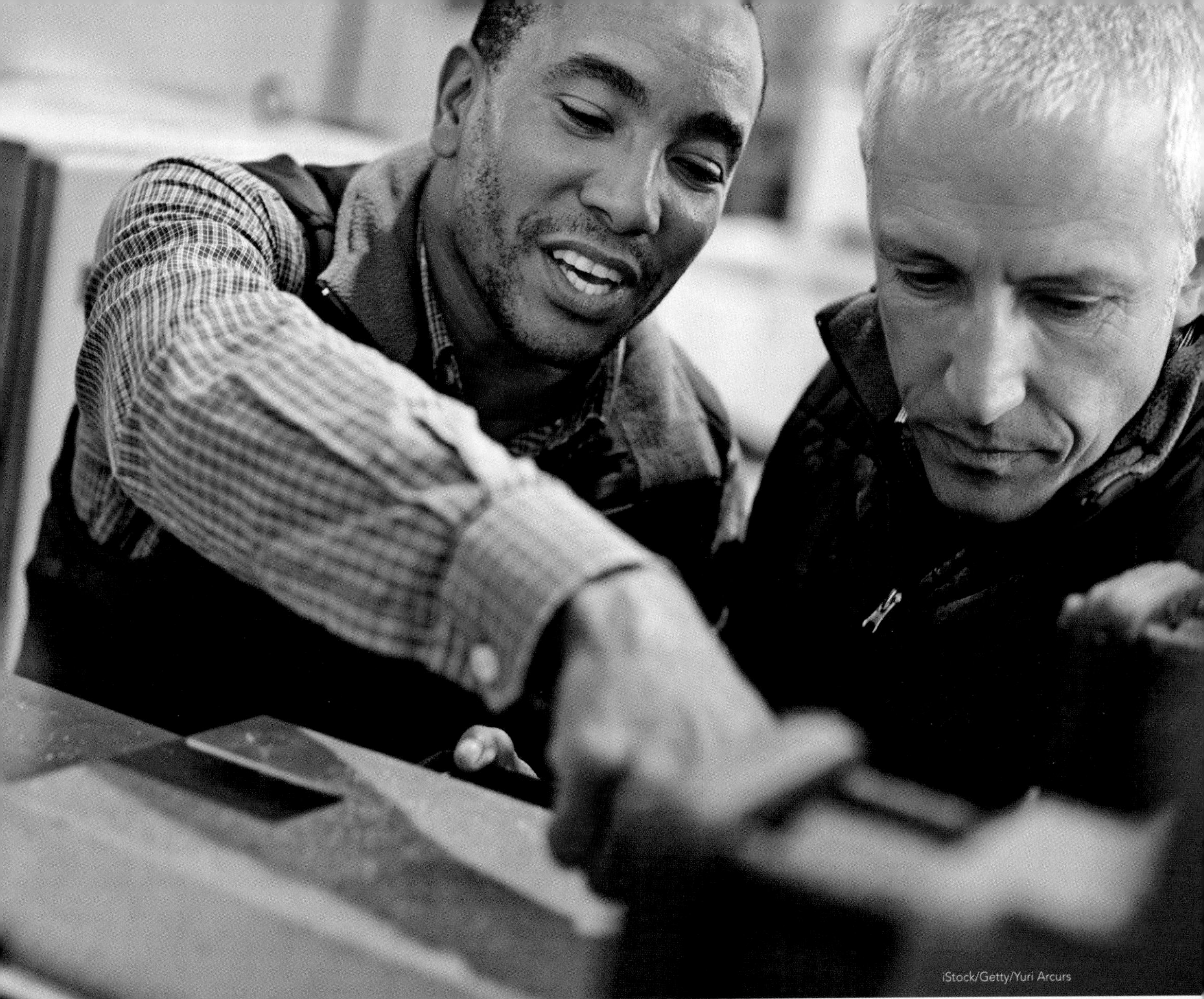
iStock/Getty/Yuri Arcurs

Deborah Jaffe/Corbis

Prediction is very difficult, especially if it's about the future.

—**NIELS BOHR,** 1922 Nobel laureate in physics

In these volatile times, it's important to respond quickly to shifts in consumer preferences and control costs. Improving forecast accuracy enables Unilever to produce the right product mix, decrease costs, and better serve our customers.

—**DOUG SLOAN,** Director of Supply Chain Support for Unilever U.S.[1]

In college, I was a weather anchor for the local news. I would "borrow" my forecast from The Weather Channel.

—**EMILY PROCTER,** American actress[2]

DEMAND MANAGEMENT, FORECASTING, AND AGGREGATE PLANNING

LEARNING OBJECTIVES

After completing this chapter, you should be able to:

6.1 Describe the demand management, forecasting, and aggregate planning processes
6.2 Explain why forecasts are necessary and how they are used
6.3 Compare the accuracies of forecasting techniques
6.4 Describe the collaborative planning, forecasting, and replenishment process
6.5 Explain how aggregate planning is used to meet the objectives of the firm

Master the content.

edge.sagepub.com/wisner

BETTER DEMAND FORECASTING SAVES MONEY FOR LEE MEMORIAL HEALTH SYSTEM

Florida-based Lee Memorial Health System (LMHS) saves millions of dollars each year, using demand forecasts. Demand forecasting means better demand planning and use of fewer temporary nurses. Additionally, it means better hospital bed management, which has led to a 20% increase in beds filled, compared to earlier years.

In 2000, the number of temporary nurses hit an all-time high at LMHS. High seasonal demand in Florida contributed to the gradual increase in temporary nurses. This was a problem, since each temporary nurse cost about twice as much as a permanent nurse. Additionally, directors tended to overstaff their units with temporary nurses, to guard against sick calls and demand spikes. To improve, LMHS needed to start doing a better job of forecasting demand.

Today, the LMHS forecasting model uses historical trends to forecast the following month's demand. LMHS collects patient data from 50 units at its five hospitals to generate forecasts. On a monthly basis, a forecast is used to determine staffing needs and the ideal number of beds to keep open in all units. The goals are to maximize productivity and efficiency, while meeting demand fluctuations.

Today, bed placements are based on each unit's forecast. Hospital bed coordinators open beds in a specific order each month. Surgical units admit patients until their demand forecasts are reached. If there are additional admissions, one unit is chosen to accept new patients and bring in additional staff. The strategy is to fill all open beds in one unit before the next unit opens additional beds.

Using forecasts of patient demand by shift and day of the week required a significant change of thinking across LMHS. Unit directors determine staffing needs based on forecasts, instead of average daily demand. About four weeks prior to the start of a schedule, unit directors receive their forecasts and staffing needs from central staffing. Directors review the forecasts and suggest changes based on any new information. For example, a director might point out that a physician will be on vacation during the forecast period, which would reduce capacity and nurses needed for that period. The demand forecast would then be revised for all units in order to balance the forecasts with available capacities. Reports indicating a balancing of each unit's schedule are then distributed by central staffing.[3]

INTRODUCTION

In today's highly competitive environment, organizations are creating more flexible supply chains to respond rapidly to shifting demand. Customers want the right products, in the right quantities, at the right price, and they want them *now*. If organizations can't forecast demand accurately, then customers will look for other organizations that can better meet their demands. Thus, poor forecasting and production planning can have a tremendously negative impact on sales, profitability, and customer relationships.

There are several ways that firms can more closely match supply to demand. One way is for the firm to hold plenty of finished goods inventory for delivery at any time. This approach, while minimizing stockouts, can be very expensive due to the cost of carrying inventory and the possibility of inventory write-downs at the end of the selling seasons. Use of flexible pricing is another approach. During heavy demand periods, prices can be raised to reduce peak demand. Price discounts can be used to increase sales during periods with excess inventory or slow demand. This pricing strategy can result in lost sales as well as stockouts, and thus cannot be considered a customer-friendly approach to satisfying demand.

Companies can also use overtime, subcontracting, or temporary workers to modify capacity during high-demand periods, then reduce these things during low-demand periods. Ultimately, while using temporary workers might suffice for unexpected demand fluctuations, firms may lose sales as workers get on-the-job training, and reputations can suffer if these employees don't do a good job of representing the company. Product quality might also suffer if unproven subcontractors are used to make products.

Managing fluctuating demand can prove to be very challenging, and firms must develop their purchasing, production, marketing, and workforce strategies within this changing environment. To aid in these planning efforts, managers must first try to create accurate forecasts while understanding the likelihood of forecast error and the impacts a bad forecast can create. All organizations must rely on forecasts to some degree for planning purposes—as a result, forecasts have an effect not only on the inventory levels of both finished goods and raw materials, but also on manufacturing and delivery lead times, the hiring of personnel, and ultimately customer satisfaction.

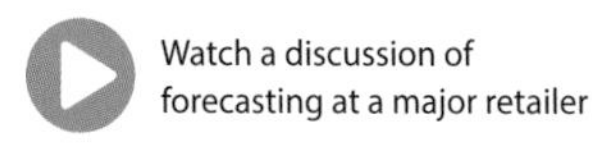

Watch a discussion of forecasting at a major retailer

When managers under-forecast, products may be in short supply and service personnel work hours may be reduced, causing customers to leave unhappy. Conversely, over-forecasting results in excess inventories with the associated higher costs of carrying inventory, along with excessive hiring and unneeded expansions, which can also result in unnecessary costs. Both types of forecast errors are costly.

Inaccurate forecasts can occur for a number of reasons, including use of the wrong forecasting tools, inability to predict mitigating circumstances, or use of distorted information. For example, company representatives might rely on guesswork instead of a proven forecasting method, resulting in a bad forecast. Or customers might over-order when trying to meet their own firms' forecasted demand. In fact, in a recent survey of forecasting practices, about two-thirds of the companies were unable to accurately forecast (within 5%) earnings or sales for the next quarter.[4] Nokia retailers in Europe, for example, started running out of cell phones one year, due to high levels of unexpected consumer demand. As a result, they ordered large quantities of phones to fill their shelves. Nokia's manufacturing arm then heavily over-produced, based on its forecast from the high retailer orders instead of actual retailer point-of-sales data. The result was that Nokia produced far too many cell phones for the upcoming period.[5]

Some companies (such as Walmart) try to reach a forecast consensus with their suppliers in an effort to reduce excess inventories and purchase prices. For instance, if Walmart planned to sell bedspreads at a discount in September, that information would then be shared with its bedspread suppliers. Walmart and its bedspread suppliers would then develop a joint forecast for bedspreads and develop production and purchasing plans based on this forecast. The advantage of this collaborative forecasting effort is that Walmart's suppliers would not allow an unusually high demand period to then skew their future forecasts. This activity has come to be known as collaborative planning, forecasting, and replenishment, and will be covered later in the chapter.

This chapter will first focus on the role of the demand planning and forecasting processes in an organization. Several forecasting methods will be introduced, along with some ways to measure and compare forecast accuracies. Once the forecasting process is complete, aggregate planning efforts can proceed, which typically govern the firm's hiring and expansion (or contraction) activities. The aggregate planning process will conclude the chapter.

DEMAND MANAGEMENT DEFINED

6.1 Describe the demand management, forecasting, and aggregate planning processes

Demand management has been defined, in a broad sense, as "the process that balances customer requirements with supply chain capabilities."[6] As mentioned in this chapter's introduction, some of the traditional ways companies have tried to balance demand and supply have been to carry high finished goods inventories, use variable pricing, and employ overtime and temporary workers to increase capacity to meet demand. For instance, department stores usually hire temporary workers for the busy Christmas season. Firms can also try to manage customers' demand patterns by using discounted prices to increase demand during slow periods. Restaurants, for example, offer "early bird specials" to entice people to dine during off-peak hours. Many services such as airlines, doctors, and dentists also use reservation systems to smooth the flow of customers during the day. The simplest way of dealing with customers is to let them stand in queues. These are all demand management activities.

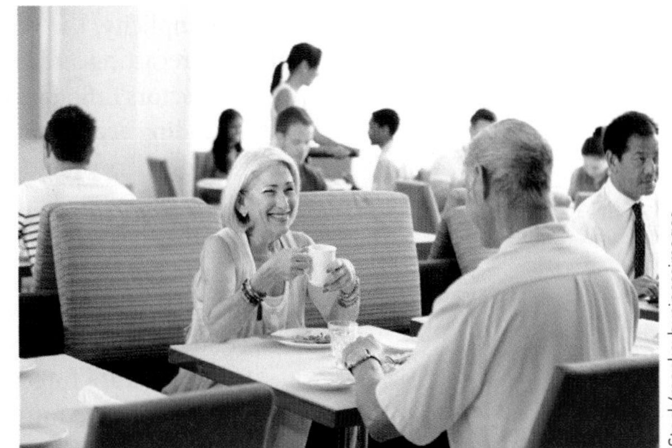

iStock/monkeybusinessimages

Buffet restaurant Golden Corral attracts seniors by using early bird special pricing from 2 pm to 4 pm.

Forecasting is also an integral part of demand management. In many respects, as forecast accuracy improves, the reactive demand management techniques described previously become less needed. Firms use forecasts to plan their operations, and once the planning stages are complete, common everyday activities take place, including order entry, communicating delivery dates to customers, and confirming the status of current orders. As described in Table 6.1, demand management can impact activities in several key departments.

The next sections will further explain the demand management process beginning with a general discussion of forecasting methods, followed by a discussion of forecast accuracy.

demand management The process that balances customer requirements with supply chain capabilities.

Table 6.1 Demand Management Activities in Various Departments

Department	Demand Management Activities
Field Sales	The sales staff provides projections for next year's sales to management for planning purposes and as input to the forecasting process.
Marketing	New product introductions, promotions, and pricing are the responsibility of marketing, and these impact demand forecasts. Marketing also has information on the competition, in terms of similar product launches and promotions, and this information can impact production planning.
Supply Management	Supply management oversees the procurement of materials, parts, and components for the organization. These staff are also responsible for determining any supply risks or opportunities, and this information should be an input to the demand management process.
Operations	Operations personnel manage the production of goods and services. They know current machine and labor capacities, which are inputs to the demand management process. Operations uses forecasts to add shifts or plan overtime, and to purchase additional equipment.
Distribution	The responsibility of distribution is to fill customer orders, monitor finished goods inventories, and to ensure on-time deliveries. Distribution uses demand forecast information to arrange warehouse inventories in advance of actual customer orders and to arrange transportation schedules with internal and contract transportation services.

THE FORECASTING PROCESS

6.2 Explain why forecasts are necessary and how they are used

Forecasts provide, among other things, estimates of future demand, supply prices, and labor availabilities, and are the basis for sound operations planning decisions. Since all organizations deal with an unknown future, some error between a forecast and the actual item being forecast is bound to occur. The goal of a good forecaster, then, is to minimize this error by using a reliable forecasting technique, while monitoring the error going forward. For the sake of simplicity, the remainder of this chapter will use demand forecasting to illustrate various forecasting and error measurement techniques.

The factors influencing demand must be considered when developing an accurate forecast, including economic conditions, new competition, and emerging markets. In addition, buyers and sellers should share relevant information to generate a consensus forecast so that the correct decisions on supply and demand can be made. Accurate demand forecasts benefit both the focal company and its supply chain trading partners in that the right amount of products can be purchased, manufactured, and delivered. Ultimately, the benefits of better forecasts are lower inventories, reduced stockouts, smoother production plans, reduced costs, and improved customer service.

Since accurate forecasts depend not only on use of the right forecasting method but also on unknowable future economic conditions, changes in the competition, and market dynamics, it is virtually impossible to achieve 100% forecast accuracy. Thus, firms must also make *contingency plans* to deal with unforeseen environmental changes and forecast errors. The impact of inaccurate forecasts resonates all along the supply chain, as mentioned earlier.

iStock/compassandcamera

MGM Mirage's City Center may not have had so much difficulty securing funds had they used a different forecasting technique combined with strategic contingency plans.

Numerous examples exist showing the problems that companies encountered when their sales forecasts did not match actual demand. For instance, Apple experienced preorders for 600,000 units of its new iPhone 4 in one day. Apple's iPhone 4 preorder sales were 10 times higher than the first day of preordering for the iPhone 3GS. Due to the high preorder rate, Apple's order system suffered many order and approval malfunctions, which delayed the delivery of the phones by at least one month.[7] When Nevada-based resort and casino MGM Mirage began working on its massive $9 billion Las Vegas CityCenter project in the mid-2000s, business in Las Vegas was booming, and all of the local forecasts predicted this would surely continue. Just a few years later, though, the global economic recession had begun, Las Vegas tourism had tanked, and banks were reluctant to loan MGM Mirage enough money to finish the CityCenter. MGM had no contingency plan in place for this situation and had nearly gone bankrupt when it finally secured financing from the Dubai government to finish the project.[8] Using the right forecasting technique, combined with demand management activities and strategic contingency plans, can help to reduce these types of problems. A number of forecasting techniques are discussed next.

qualitative forecasting techniques Forecasts that are based on guesswork, intuition, or opinions, and are generally used when data are unavailable or too old to be of much use.

quantitative forecasting techniques Forecasts that make use of mathematical models and relevant historical data to generate forecasts. The quantitative methods can be further divided into two groups: time series and associative models.

The two basic forecasting classifications are qualitative and quantitative techniques. **Qualitative forecasting techniques** are based on opinions and intuition, whereas **quantitative forecasting techniques** make use of mathematical models and relevant historical data to generate forecasts. The quantitative methods can be further divided into two groups: time series and associative models.

QUALITATIVE FORECASTING TECHNIQUES

Qualitative techniques are based on guesswork, intuition, and opinions, and are generally used for the following conditions:

Table 6.2 Qualitative Forecasting Techniques

Forecast	Description
Sales force estimates	Field sales personnel provide estimates of customer needs.
Consumer surveys	Marketing departments use focus groups to gather opinions of products and product ideas, and then analyze the information to create a demand forecast.
Delphi method	Experts determine individual forecasts, then share these with the group. Participants then modify their forecasts based on the collective input. This continues until the group converges on a forecast.
Jury of executive opinion	The jury of executive opinion uses a group of senior executives to discuss and develop a demand forecast.

- When data do not exist, as with a new product introduction
- When data are too old to be of much use, as with a demand forecast five years in the future

The chapter-opening quote by Emily Procter is an example of using a very simple qualitative forecast. While in some cases a qualitative forecast can be very low cost and quick, it can also be quite time consuming and expensive, as described in the section on the Delphi method. The effectiveness of a qualitative forecast depends to a large extent on the knowledge of the participants and the amount of relevant information available. Aside from simple guesswork forecasting, four of the most common qualitative forecasting techniques are listed in Table 6.2, and are further described in the following sections.

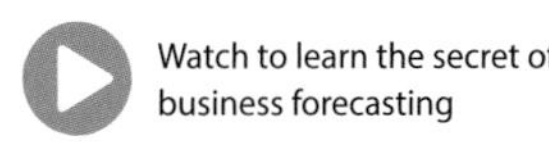

Watch to learn the secret of business forecasting

Sales Force Estimates

Field sales personnel are closest to the markets and therefore can provide good **sales force estimates** of customer needs. However, forecasts may be politically motivated or based on performance expectations. For example, if bonuses are paid when actual sales exceed the forecast, there is a tendency for the sales force to underestimate demand.

Consumer Surveys

Marketing departments and others develop surveys and use focus groups to gather consumer opinions of existing products and new product ideas, their expected future buying habits, and their opinions of competitor products. The results are then analyzed to arrive at a forecast. In the beverage industry, for example, producers use **consumer surveys** when determining new beverage choices or flavors for the upcoming year. According to U.S. trade publication *Beverage Industry*'s 2011 beverage producer survey, the latest trends are for more "natural" flavors and energy-boosting drinks.[9] As another example, in the United States, the National Multi-Housing Council surveys renters each quarter to forecast the overall demand for apartments. This information is particularly useful for mortgage bankers and apartment builders.[10]

Delphi Method

Developed by the RAND Corporation in the 1950s, the **Delphi method** uses a series of questionnaires to establish a consensus among a group of experts for situations when relevant data are not readily accessible.[11] When used in forecasting, these experts, drawn from internal and external sources, answer questionnaires to arrive initially at their individual forecasts. The results are then compiled, and a summary of all forecasts is returned to each participant. The participants are then allowed to modify their initial forecasts based on the collective input. This process is repeated until the group converges on a forecast. The advantage of the Delphi method is that participants do not physically meet, thus avoiding the risk of "group think." The obvious disadvantage is the time required and the large expense of using a number of outside experts.

sales force estimates When field sales personnel provide estimates of future customer demand. These forecasts may be politically motivated or based on performance expectations.

consumer surveys When marketing departments and others develop surveys and use focus groups to gather consumer opinions of existing products and new product ideas to generate a forecast.

Delphi method Developed by the RAND Corporation in the 1950s, a series of questionnaires are used to establish a forecast consensus among a group of experts for situations when relevant data are not readily accessible.

SPOTLIGHT ON OM TRENDS

A Delphi Forecast of Business Trends in China

To forecast future business trends in China, a Delphi technique was used with a group of global experts. The experts were academics, consultants, researchers, and executives with business experience in China.

The forecast was conducted over three rounds of email surveys. In the first round, respondents were asked to identify important trends thought likely to affect China business over the coming decade (2007–2017), in five broad categories: economic, legal, political, sociocultural, and technological. After the completion of the first round, a content analysis identified 61 common items.

In the second round, respondents provided initial estimates of the trends of the 61 items using a five-point scale.

The second round results were analyzed statistically, and the results revealed a high degree of consensus for 52 of the 61 items.

For the remaining nine items, respondents were told to consider the results of the second round and to provide fresh estimates for the nine items. The final results indicated that substantial increases were expected in the following: the quality of China's banking system; the relative share of gross domestic product (GDP) from services; the global influence of Chinese corporations; the value of the *yuan* relative to the U.S. dollar; the probability that China will reform its tax system; China's contribution to global technological innovation; the effectiveness of capital markets; and China's global competitiveness.[12]

In 2005 in northern Spain, for example, Catalan grape growers had seen grape prices falling steadily over the years. To help growers understand the long-term implications of falling prices and facilitate better planning, a Delphi study was conducted with a panel of 27 wine industry experts. Ultimately, the panel thought the grape surplus and low market prices were going to be a permanent problem, since there was a general lack of coordination and poor vertical integration in the Catalan wine sector.[13] In another example, a Delphi study was conducted by four business professors to forecast a number of economic trends likely to occur in China. This description is shown in the Spotlight on OM Trends above.

Jury of Executive Opinion

The **jury of executive opinion** technique uses a group of senior executives who are knowledgeable about the firm's products, markets, competitors, and the general business environment, to develop a demand forecast. This technique has the advantage of collective knowledge regarding the firm and its products, but if one member's views dominate the discussion, then the value and reliability of the outcome can be diminished.

jury of executive opinion A forecasting technique that uses a group of senior executives who are knowledgeable about the firm's products, markets, competitors, and the general business environment to develop a demand forecast.

time series forecasts Quantitative forecasting techniques based on the assumption that the future is an extension of the past; thus, historical demand can be used to predict future demand.

associative forecasts Quantitative forecasting techniques that assume that one or more factors (independent variables) are related to demand, and therefore can be used to predict future demand.

trend variations Demand variations caused by gradually increasing or decreasing movements over time, due to factors such as population growth and age, cultural changes, and income shifts.

QUANTITATIVE FORECASTING TECHNIQUES

Quantitative forecasting techniques are math formulations that make use of historical data and can also include causal variables to forecast demand. Several quantitative techniques will be discussed here: **time series forecasts** are based on the assumption that the future is an extension of the past; thus, historical demand can be used to predict future demand. **Associative forecasts** assume that one or more causal (or independent) variables are related to demand, and therefore can be used to predict future demand.

Since quantitative forecasts rely solely on past demand data, all quantitative methods become less accurate as the forecast's time horizon increases. Thus, quantitative methods are most useful for short- to medium-term forecasts. For long-term forecasts, qualitative techniques are recommended.

Components of Time Series

Creating a time series requires breaking down past demand and projecting it forward into the future. A time series typically has four components that must be analyzed—the trend, cyclical, seasonal, and random variations.

1. **Trend variations** represent gradually increasing or decreasing demand movements over time due to factors such as population growth and age, cultural changes, and income shifts.

2. **Cyclical variations** are demand patterns that occur every several years and are influenced by macroeconomic and political factors. One example is the **business cycle**; this refers to economic fluctuations (recessions or expansions), which are actually not very predictable. Recent business cycles in the United States have been affected by global events such as the 1973 oil embargo; the September 11, 2001, terrorist attacks; and the most recent global banking and real estate crises.
3. **Seasonal variations** are patterns that repeat over a consistent interval such as days, weeks, months, or seasons. Due to seasonalities, companies might do well in certain months and not as well in other months. Snow ski equipment sales are better in the fall and winter, but taper off in the spring and summer months. Restaurants tend to do better business on the weekends, while hotels experience higher demand during traditional holidays and vacation periods.
4. **Random variations** are due to unexpected events such as natural disasters (hurricanes, tornadoes, fire), labor strikes, economic recessions, and wars. Random variations are what cause even the best forecasts to contain error. These variations follow no pattern and thus cannot be predicted. Because of these random variations, managers typically have contingency plans to accompany important forecasts. One extreme example of a random variation is the devastating earthquake and tsunami that occurred in Japan on March 11, 2011. The Tohoku earthquake was the most powerful earthquake ever to hit Japan, triggering a tsunami that traveled six miles inland, tragically killing some 16,000 people and completely destroying 129,000 buildings and businesses, while causing heavy structural damage to roads and railways. Supply chains worldwide were disrupted for many weeks. The World Bank estimated the economic cost to be $235 billion, making it the most expensive natural disaster in world history.[14]

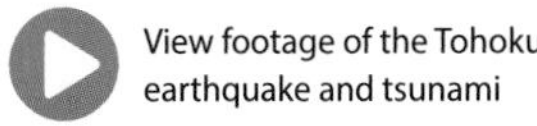
View footage of the Tohoku earthquake and tsunami

cyclical variations Demand patterns that occur every several years and are influenced by macroeconomic and political factors.

business cycle Refers to economic fluctuations (recessions or expansions), which are actually not very predictable. Recent business cycles in the United States have been affected by various global events.

seasonal variations Demand patterns that repeat over a consistent interval such as days, weeks, months, or seasons.

random variations Demand variations due to unexpected events such as natural disasters (hurricanes, tornadoes, fire), strikes, and wars. Random variations are what cause even the best forecasts to contain error.

Table 6.3 lists the quantitative forecasting techniques, and they are described further in the following sections.

Time Series Forecasting Techniques

As discussed earlier, time series forecasts are dependent on the availability of historical data. Forecasts are estimated by extrapolating past data into the future. In general, time series demand forecasts are used in planning for procurement, inventories, and human resource scheduling. Some of the most commonly used time series forecasts are simple moving average, weighted moving average, and exponential smoothing. These are discussed next.

Table 6.3 Quantitative Forecasting Techniques

Times Series Forecasting Techniques	Description
Simple moving average forecast	Uses the average of recent historical demand to generate a forecast.
Weighted moving average forecast	Calculates a weighted average of *n*-period observations, using varied weights.
Exponential smoothing forecast	The next period's forecast is the current forecast adjusted by a weighted difference between the current period's actual data and the forecast.
Associative Forecasting Techniques	**Description**
Linear trend forecast	In a linear trend forecast, the independent variable is time and the dependent variable is the actual data (such as demand).
Simple linear regression forecast	In simple linear regression forecasts, a causal variable is identified, which is a predictor of demand. Linear regression is used to identify the forecast equation.
Multiple regression forecast	Multiple regression forecasting is used when there are several independent variables used together, to predict demand.

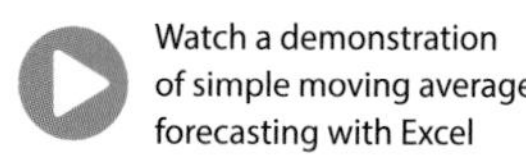

Watch a demonstration of simple moving average forecasting with Excel

The Simple Moving Average Forecast

The **simple moving average forecast** uses an average of recent historical demand to generate a forecast and is fairly reliable when the demand is stable over time. The formula for the n-period simple moving average forecast is shown here:

$$F_{t+1} = \frac{\sum_{i=t-n+1}^{t} A_i}{n} = \frac{A_t + A_{t-1} + A_{t-2} + \ldots + A_{t-n+1}}{n}$$

where F_{t+1} = forecast for period t+1

n = number of periods used to calculate moving average, and

A_i = actual demand in period i

Example 6.1
Calculating Three-Week and Six-Week Simple Moving Average Forecasts

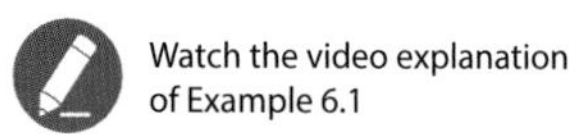

Watch the video explanation of Example 6.1

When calculating the first three-week forecast, we assume that the demands in weeks 1-3 have already occurred and we seek a forecast for week 4. The forecast for week 4 is then (1600+2200+2000)/3 = 1933. Similarly, the actual demands in weeks 2-4 are averaged to find the forecast for week 5. Note that the forecasts have been rounded off to the nearest whole number in this example, and that the week 12 actual demand has not been used.

Week	Demand	3-Week	6-Week
1	1600		
2	2200		
3	2000		
4	1600	1933	
5	2500	1933	
6	3500	2033	
7	3300	2533	2233
8	3200	3100	2517
9	3900	3333	2683
10	4700	3467	3000
11	4300	3933	3517
12	4400	4300	3817

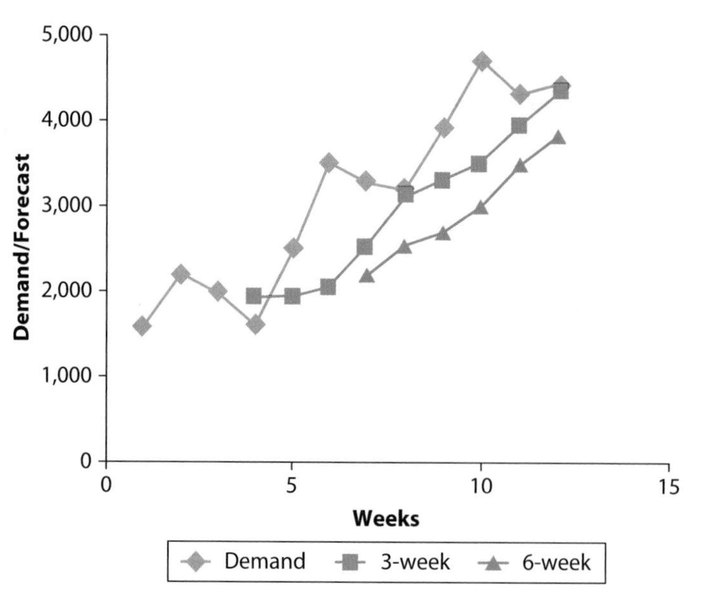

simple moving average forecast A technique that uses recent historical demand to generate a forecast and is fairly reliable when the demand is stable over time.

For the six-week simple moving average forecast, the demands in weeks 1-6 are averaged to find the forecast for week 7, and the demands in weeks 2-7 are averaged to find the forecast for week 8. Note in the graph how both forecasts lag the trend in the actual demand. Also note how the six-week forecast is smoother than the three-week forecast.

The simple moving average forecasts can also be calculated using a spreadsheet, as shown here:

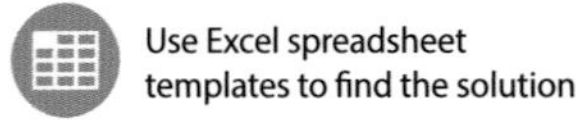

	A	B	C
1	Demand	3-Week	6-Week
2	1600		
3	2200		
4	2000		
5	1600	1933	
6	2500	1933	
7	3500	2033	
8	3300	2533	2233
9	3200	3100	2517
10	3900	3333	2683
11	4700	3467	3000
12	4300	3933	3517
13	4400	4300	3817

B5: = AVERAGE(A2:A4)

B6: = AVERAGE(A3:A5)

C8: = AVERAGE(A2:A7)

C13: = AVERAGE(A7:A12)

Note that copying cell B5 once it is designed and formatted, and then pasting it to cells B6 to B13, allows the forecasts to be quickly calculated.

Also note that the graph shown above can be generated using a spreadsheet by highlighting the three columns of data, then clicking on Insert, Line, then Line with Markers.

The simple moving average tends to be more responsive if fewer periods are used to compute the average. However, the time series components can impact the average adversely, causing the decision maker to balance the cost of responding too slowly to any demand variations. The advantage of this technique is that it is simple to use and easy to understand. A weakness of the simple moving average is its inability to respond to changes quickly. Example 6.1 illustrates the simple moving average forecast.

The Weighted Moving Average Forecast

When using the simple moving average forecast, each of the past period demands is weighted equally ($1/n$). However, forecasters may prefer to weight the more recent periods more heavily to take into consideration recent changes in the data. An n-period **weighted moving average forecast** is the weighted average of the n-period observations, using varied weights. The only restrictions are that the weights be nonnegative and sum to 1. The forecast is calculated using the following formula:

$$F_{t+1} = \sum_{i=t-n+1}^{t} w_i A_i = w_1 A_1 + w_2 A_{t-1} + w_3 A_{t-2} + \ldots + wA_{t-n+1}$$

where F_{t+1} = forecast for period t+1

n = number of periods used in determining the moving average

A_i = actual demand in period i

w_i = weight assigned to period i, and

$$\Sigma w_i = 1$$

weighted moving average forecast Similar to simple moving average forecast; however, it allows the user to weight the more recent periods more heavily to take into consideration recent changes in the data. This forecast is the weighted average of the n-period observations, using varied weights.

Example 6.2 illustrates the weighted moving average forecast.

While forecasters are free to apply weights in any fashion to any number of periods, the largest weight is typically placed on the most recent observation. In this case, the weighted moving average forecast would react more rapidly than the simple moving average forecast to actual demand changes. Although this forecast is more responsive to underlying data changes, it still lags the actual data and thus does not do a good job of tracking trend or other component changes in the data.

exponential smoothing forecast A slightly more sophisticated form of weighted moving average forecast, in which the forecast for the next period is the current period's forecast adjusted by a weighted difference between the current period's actual data and forecast. This approach requires fewer calculations than the weighted moving average forecast because only two data points are needed.

smoothing constant A weight used in the exponential smoothing forecast. The weight must be between 0 and 1.

The Exponential Smoothing Forecast

The **exponential smoothing forecast** is a slightly more sophisticated form of weighted moving average forecast, in which the forecast for the next period is the current period's forecast adjusted by a weighted difference between the current period's actual data and forecast. The weight is called the **smoothing constant** and must be between 0 and 1. This approach requires fewer calculations than the weighted moving average forecast because only two data points are needed.

The concept of exponential smoothing was first developed by Robert G. Brown during World War II while he was working as a statistical analyst for the U.S. Navy. One of his early applications was in forecasting the demand for spare parts in Navy inventory systems.[15] Due to its simplicity and minimal data requirement, exponential smoothing is one of the more widely used forecasting techniques. This model, like the other time series models, is suitable for demand that is relatively constant.

Example 6.2 Calculating Three-Week and Six-Week Weighted Moving Average Forecasts With Weights (0.5, 0.3, 0.2) and (0.3, 0.2, 0.2, 0.1, 0.1, 0.1)

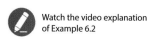

Watch the video explanation of Example 6.2

Week	Demand	3-Week	6-Week
1	1600		
2	2200		
3	2000		
4	1600	1980	
5	2500	1840	
6	3500	2130	
7	3300	2820	2450
8	3200	3200	2770
9	3900	3290	2930
10	4700	3570	3230
11	4300	4160	3760
12	4400	4340	4010

The three-week forecast uses a weighted average of the previous three weeks. Thus, the weighted moving average forecast for week 4 is $(0.5 \times 2000) + (0.3 \times 2200) + (0.2 \times 1600) = 1980$. Note that in the typical case, the largest weight is applied to the most recent week.

The six-week forecast uses a weighted average of the previous six weeks. Note again in the graph how both forecasts lag the trend in the actual demand, and how the six-week forecast is smoother than the three-week forecast.

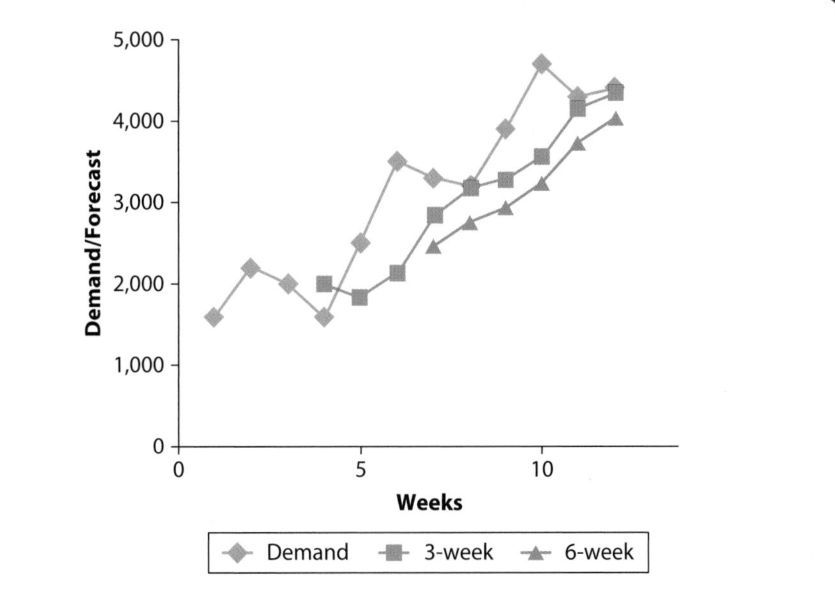

The weighted moving average forecasts can be calculated using a spreadsheet as shown here:

Use Excel spreadsheet templates to find the solution

	A	B	C
1	Demand	3-Week	6-Week
2	1600		
3	2200		
4	2000		
5	1600	1980	
6	2500	1840	
7	3500	2130	
8	3300	2820	2450
9	3200	3200	2770
10	3900	3290	2930
11	4700	3570	3230
12	4300	4160	3760
13	4400	4340	4010

B5: = A2*.2+A3*.3+A4*.5

B6: = A3*.2+A4*.3+A5*.5

C8: = A2*.1+A3*.1+A4*.1+A5*.2+A6*.2+ A7*.3

C13: = A7*.1+A8*.1+A9*.1+A10*.2+ A11*.2+A12*.3

Note that copying cells B5 and C8, once they are designed and formatted, and then pasting them to cells B6 – B13 and C9 – C13 allows the forecasts to be quickly calculated.

Also note that the graph shown above can be generated using a spreadsheet by highlighting the three columns of data, then clicking on Insert, Line, then Line with Markers.

The exponential smoothing forecast formula is:

$$F_{t+1} = F_t + \alpha\,(A_t - F_t) \text{ or } F_{t+1} = \alpha A_t + (1 - \alpha)F_t$$

where F_{t+1} = forecast for period t+1

F_t = forecast for period t

A_t = actual demand for period t;

α = smoothing constant ($0 \le \alpha \le 1$).

Note that as the smoothing constant is increased, the forecast becomes more responsive to changes in the previous period's demand (when $\alpha = 1$, the forecast is simply equal to the previous period's demand). When α has a low value, more weight is placed on the previous period's forecast, and the model responds more slowly to changes in the most recent period's demand (when $\alpha = 0$, the forecast is constant and equal to F_1). In general, the forecast will lag any trends in the actual demand, as with the other time series forecasts.

The initial or first period's forecast will need to be estimated using a qualitative method or by simply setting the first forecast equal to the first period's actual demand. Example 6.3 illustrates the exponential smoothing forecast.

Associative Forecasting Techniques

Simple linear regression can be used in time series forecasting to estimate a trend, and for cases when the forecaster finds a causal relationship between demand and another variable. Multiple regression forecasts are statistically more complex and are used when several causal variables are used to predict demand. These are discussed next.

Linear Trend Forecasts

When preparing a linear trend forecast, the independent variable is time and the dependent variable is the actual data (such as demand). The relationship between the forecasted variable (Y) and time (X) is shown by the equation for a line:

$$Y = a + bX$$

where Y = the forecast variable (demand)

X = time

a = vertical axis intercept of the line, and

b = slope of the line.

linear trend forecast A linear regression forecast, where one variable is time (the independent variable) and the other variable is the actual data (such as demand).

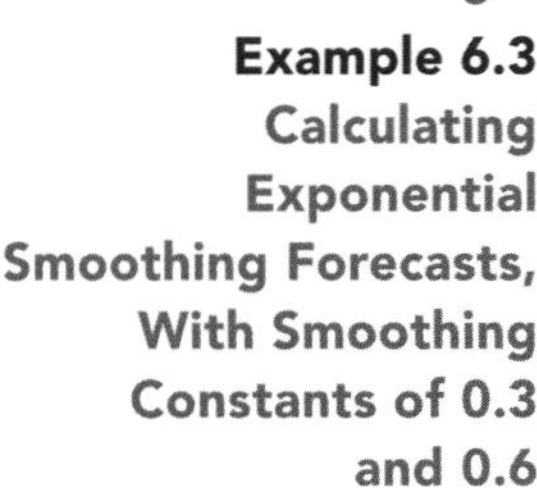

Example 6.3 Calculating Exponential Smoothing Forecasts, With Smoothing Constants of 0.3 and 0.6

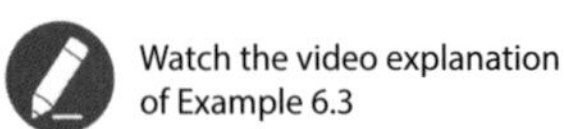

Watch the video explanation of Example 6.3

Week	Demand	$\alpha = 0.3$	$\alpha = 0.6$
1	1600	1600.0	1600.0
2	2200	1600.0	1600.0
3	2000	1780.0	1960.0
4	1600	1846.0	1984.0
5	2500	1772.2	1753.6
6	3500	1990.5	2201.4
7	3300	2443.4	2980.6
8	3200	2700.4	3172.2
9	3900	2850.3	3188.9
10	4700	3165.2	3615.6
11	4300	3625.6	4266.2
12	4400	3827.9	4286.5

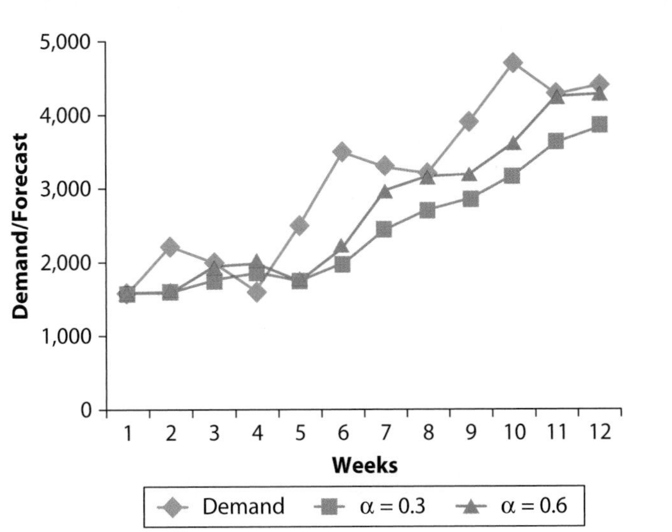

To begin, the exponential smoothing forecast for Week 1 is simply set equal to the actual demand for Week 1. There are no changes for the Week 2 forecasts, since from the formula, $F_2 = F_1 + \alpha(A_1 - F_1) = 1600 + \alpha(1600 - 1600) = 1600$. Using $\alpha = 0.3$, the Week 3 forecast is $1600 + 0.3(2200 - 1600) = 1780$. Using $\alpha = 0.6$, the Week 3 forecast is $1600 + 0.6(2200 - 1600) = 1960$. The forecasts were rounded off to one decimal place to maintain accuracy, since each forecast was used to determine the following forecast.

Note in the graph how the ($\alpha = 0.6$) forecast reacts more rapidly to changes in demand. Also note that since F_1 was set equal to A_1, the first few forecasts would be biased and unreliable.

The exponential smoothing forecasts can be calculated using a spreadsheet as shown here:

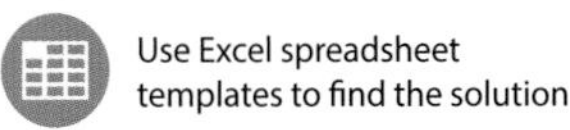
Use Excel spreadsheet templates to find the solution

	A	B	C
1	Demand	α = 0.3	α = 0.6
2	1600	1600.0	1600.0
3	2200	1600.0	1600.0
4	2000	1780.0	1960.0
5	1600	1846.0	1984.0
6	2500	1772.2	1753.6
7	3500	1990.5	2201.4
8	3300	2443.4	2980.6
9	3200	2700.4	3172.2
10	3900	2850.3	3188.9
11	4700	3165.2	3615.6
12	4300	3625.6	4266.2
13	4400	3827.9	4286.5

B3: = B2+.3*(A2-B2)

C3: = C2+.6*(A2-C2)

B13: = B12+.3*(A12-B12)

C13: = C12+.6*(A12-C12)

Note that using the copy and paste functions as described in the previous example allows the forecasts to be quickly calculated. The graph shown above can also be generated using a spreadsheet as shown in the previous example.

Using the ordinary least squares method and a number of (*X, Y*) data points, the coefficients, (a) and (b), are calculated as follows:

$$b = \frac{n\sum(XY) - \sum X \sum Y}{n\sum X^2 - (\sum X)^2}$$

$$a = \frac{\sum Y - b\sum X}{n}$$

where n = number of observations.

Example 6.4 illustrates the calculations of coefficients (a) and (b) and a linear trend forecast using the formulas above.

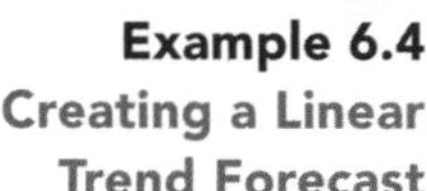

Example 6.4
Creating a Linear Trend Forecast

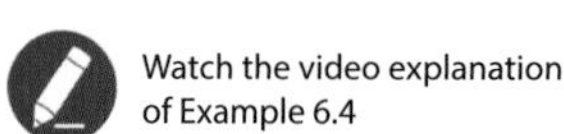

Watch the video explanation of Example 6.4

Week (X)	Demand (Y)	X^2	Y^2	XY
1	43	1	1849	43
2	42	4	1764	84
3	39	9	1521	117
4	45	16	2025	180
5	51	25	2601	255
6	48	36	2304	288
7	54	49	2916	378
8	50	64	2500	400
9	56	81	3136	504
10	58	100	3364	580
11	64	121	4096	704
12	62	144	3844	744
$\sum X = 78$	$\sum Y = 612$	$\sum X^2 = 650$	$\sum Y^2 = 31920$	$\sum XY = 4277$

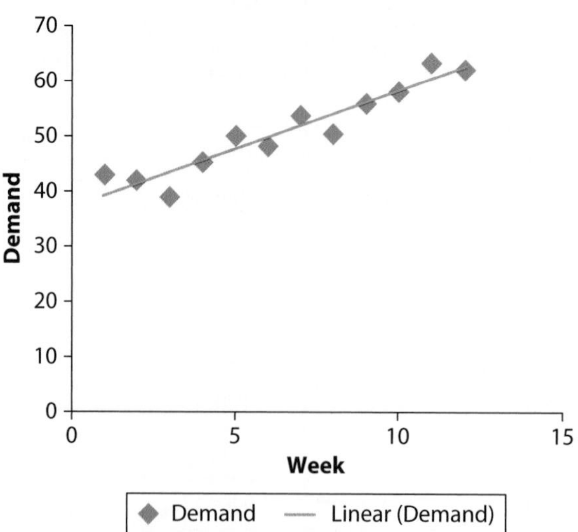

$$b = \frac{n\sum(XY) - \sum X \sum Y}{n\sum X^2 - (\sum X)^2} = \frac{12(4277) - (78)(612)}{12(650) - (78)^2} = 2.09, \text{ and } a = \frac{\sum Y - b\sum X}{n} = \frac{612 - 2.09(78)}{12}$$

$$= 37.42$$

The trend line is then $Y = 37.42 + 2.09X$, and the forecast for week 13 would be calculated as:

$37.42 + 2.09(13) = 64.58$. A plot of the trend line is shown in the graph here, where the coefficient (a) is the y-axis intercept and the coefficient (b) is the slope of the trend line.

Note that the data and trend line can be graphed as shown here, using a spreadsheet. The weeks and demand data are placed on a spreadsheet and highlighted; then the user clicks Insert, Scatter, and Scatter with only markers. Then under Chart Tools, the user clicks Layout, Analysis, Trendline, and Linear Trendline.

Simple Linear Regression Forecasts

In **simple linear regression forecasts**, one variable (a **causal variable**) is identified that is a predictor of demand. Because we are assuming that changes in the causal variable predict changes in demand, we refer to demand as the dependent variable and the causal variable as the independent variable. For example, the demand for new homes is dependent upon variables such as family income, interest rates, and the homebuilders' advertising expenditures. It may be that these factors are not very good predictors of demand, so it is necessary to look at statistics that test the strength of the relationship between the dependent and independent variables.

Several measures are used to test the relationship between the independent and dependent variables. The **sample correlation coefficient**, R, is a measure of the strength and direction of the relationship between the independent variable and the dependent variable. It ranges from −1 to +1; if the value of R is positive, it means *increases* in the independent variable result in *increases* in the dependent variable (and the relationship becomes stronger as R approaches 1). The opposite is true if the value of R is negative—*decreases* in the independent variable result in *increases* in the dependent variable (and this relationship becomes stronger as R approaches −1). If $R = 0$ (or is close to 0), there is no relationship between the independent and dependent variables, so use of this independent variable should be avoided.

The **sample coefficient of determination**, R^2, is a measure of the variation in the dependent variable that can be explained by the independent variable. Simply put, it is a measure of how good the regression line fits the data. The value of R^2 falls between 0 and 1. As the value of R^2 approaches 1, it indicates that variations in the dependent variable and the regression line (the forecast) are closely related. The value of R^2 is calculated by squaring the sample correlation coefficient.

The equations are identical to the ones used for the linear trend forecast. Example 6.5 provides an illustration of a linear regression forecast using spreadsheet software, with sales demand as the dependent variable and advertising expenditures as the independent variable.

simple linear regression forecasts A causal variable is identified, which is a predictor of demand. Linear regression is used to identify the causal relationship and the forecast equation.

causal variable A predictor of the dependent variable demand.

sample correlation coefficient R, it is a measure of the strength and direction of the relationship between the independent variable and the dependent variable. It ranges from −1 to +1; if the value of R is positive, it means *increases* in the independent variable result in *increases* in the dependent variable.

sample coefficient of determination R^2, it is a measure of the variation in the dependent variable that can be explained by the independent variable. Simply put, it is a measure of how good the regression line fits the data. The value of R^2 falls between 0 and 1. As the value of R^2 approaches 1, it indicates that variations in the dependent variable and the regression line (the forecast) are closely related.

multiple regression forecasting A regression forecast that is used when there are several independent variables used together, to predict the dependent variable (i.e., demand).

Multiple Regression Forecasts

Multiple regression forecasting is used when there are several independent variables used together, to predict demand. The multiple regression forecast equation is:

$$Y = a + b_1X_1 + b_2X_2 + b_3X_3 \ldots + b_nX_n$$

where X_n = nth independent variable

a = constant

b_n = regression coefficient of the nth independent variable X_n.

While solving for the coefficients is more complex compared to simple linear regression, software programs such as Excel can still be used. Multiple regression forecasting requires identification of multiple causal variables and more data collection and testing to determine predictability, so this must be weighed against any potential improvements in the forecast.

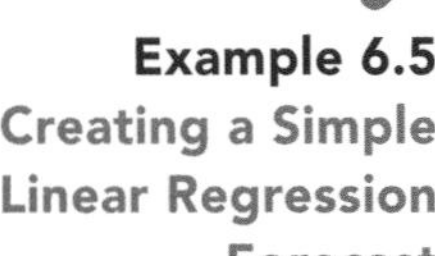

Example 6.5 Creating a Simple Linear Regression Forecast

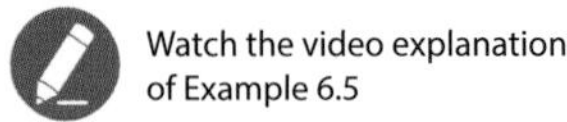

Watch the video explanation of Example 6.5

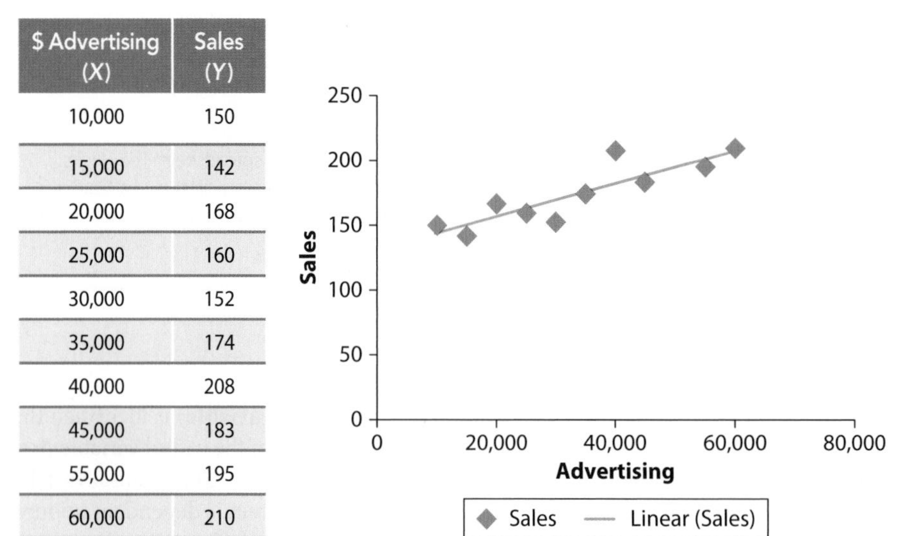

$ Advertising (X)	Sales (Y)
10,000	150
15,000	142
20,000	168
25,000	160
30,000	152
35,000	174
40,000	208
45,000	183
55,000	195
60,000	210

Output from the linear regression:

Coefficients—a = 131.8, b = 0.0012

$R = 0.869$, $R^2 = 0.755$

Since R is positive and close to 1, we conclude that sales and advertising expenditures are positively correlated—increases in advertising expenditures will likely produce increases in sales. With an R^2 of 0.755, the regression line fits the data quite well. The graph also confirms this. The linear regression sales forecast equation is: Sales = 131.8 + 0.0012(Advertising $). If we wish to spend $32,500 on advertising, our sales forecast would then be 131.8 + 0.0012(32,500) = 171 units.

Here are the steps for performing the regression using a spreadsheet:

Place the advertising data in the A-column and sales data in the B-column. Go to a cell in the C-column and click the f_x button. Select the LINEST function; for the known Y's, use B1:B10; for the known X's, use A1:A10. The function returns the Y-intercept, a, and the slope, b, of the regression line.

For the sample correlation coefficient, R, click the f_x button, select the CORREL function, and use B1:B10 for array 1, and A1:A10 for array 2. The function returns R.

To obtain the graph shown here:

Highlight the advertising and sales data, then click Insert, Scatter, then Scatter with only Markers. Then click Layout, Analysis, Trendline, and Linear Trendline.

FORECAST ACCURACY

6.3 Compare the accuracies of forecasting techniques

forecast bias A type of forecast error that occurs when a forecast has a tendency to be either consistently higher or lower than the actual demand.

While forecasts in general will *almost always be wrong* due to unforeseen random variations, managers still must try to find relatively unbiased and low-error, or fairly accurate forecasts so they can purchase, produce, and hire correctly. **Forecast bias** occurs when a forecast has a tendency to be either consistently higher or lower than the actual demand. When forecasts are too low, lost sales occur when inventory levels are too low, resulting in customer dissatisfaction and a loss of goodwill. When the forecasts are too optimistic, firms spend more money holding needless inventories. Unfortunately, in a recent survey, about 40% of the responding managers said their forecasts were less than 70% accurate, and many did not even measure forecast accuracy. Additionally, the common finding was that firms held one month or more in safety stock to guard against forecast inaccuracies—an expensive safeguard.[16]

Watch a discussion of forecasting and accuracy

To mitigate these problems, companies need to test (with a series of historical demand) a number of forecasting models while measuring the forecast error, to find the "one best" forecasting model. Since demand varies over time, this forecasting model testing process needs to continue, since demand changes would impact forecast accuracies and the choice of a forecasting model. The **forecast error** for a given time period is simply the difference between the actual demand and the forecast for that period, or:

$$e_t = A_t - F_t$$

where e_t = forecast error for period t

A_t = actual demand for period t

F_t = forecast for period t

Thus, a *negative error* means the forecast was too high, while a *positive error* means the forecast was too low. Both result in costs to the firm, as described earlier. To compare forecasting methods, managers must use a historical demand series to calculate forecasts and determine accuracy.

The most common method for comparing forecasting techniques is the **mean absolute deviation** (MAD), which averages the absolute value of the errors over a given period of time. Absolute values are used so that negative errors do not "cancel out" positive ones, when averaging the errors. As a result, errors are equally considered (which makes sense, since both types are costly). When comparing forecasting techniques, the one with the lowest MAD is then considered the best.

Another commonly used error testing method is the **mean absolute percentage error** (MAPE). This method provides an estimate of the magnitude of forecast error. To calculate the MAPE, the monthly absolute forecast error divided by actual demand is summed, then divided by the number of months used in the forecast and multiplied by 100 to derive an average percentage error.

The **running sum of forecast error** (RSFE) provides a measure of forecast bias. When the RSFE is positive, it indicates that the forecast is generally underestimating demand, resulting in stockouts and disgruntled customers. On the other hand, a negative RSFE indicates an overestimating situation, resulting in excess inventory carrying costs. A RSFE of zero indicates an unbiased forecast over time (but not necessarily an accurate one).

These forecast accuracy measures are shown here:

$$MAD = \frac{\Sigma |e_t|}{n}$$

$$MAPE = \frac{100}{n} \Sigma \frac{|e_t|}{A_t}$$

$$RSFE = \Sigma e_t$$

Where $|e_t|$ = absolute value of the forecast error for period t

e_t = forecast error for period t

A_t = actual demand for period t

n = number of periods in the evaluation.

forecast error For a given time period, it is simply the difference between the actual demand and the forecast for that period.

mean absolute deviation The most common method for comparing forecasting techniques; it averages the absolute value of the errors over a given period of time.

mean absolute percentage error This method provides an estimate of the magnitude of forecast error. The monthly absolute forecast error divided by actual demand is summed, then divided by the number of months used in the forecast and multiplied by 100 to derive an average percentage deviation.

running sum of forecast error Provides a measure of forecast bias. When the RSFE is positive, it means the forecast is generally underestimating demand. When it is negative, the RSFE indicates an overestimating demand situation.

The **tracking signal** is used for determining if the RSFE is within acceptable limits. It can also be used as a running check on the accuracy of a forecasting technique. To calculate the tracking signal, the following formula is used:

$$\text{TS} = \frac{RSFE}{MAD}$$

The acceptable limits for a forecasting technique in use are the number of desired "MADs" above or below zero. If the tracking signal falls outside these limits, it may be time to use a different forecasting method. For example, a manager may decide to set the limits based on +/– 4 MAD. As the accuracy of the forecasts improve, the limits might be reduced. Acceptable tracking signal limits depend on the item forecast. Higher volume and higher revenue items might be monitored more frequently, with tighter tracking signal limits. However, whenever the control limits are more narrowly set, personnel must spend more time investigating poor tracking signal causes. Example 6.6 illustrates the use of the accuracy measures shown here, and Example 6.7 compares several forecasting techniques using the MAD.

tracking signal Used for determining if the RSFE is within acceptable limits. It can also be used as a running check on the accuracy of a forecasting technique.

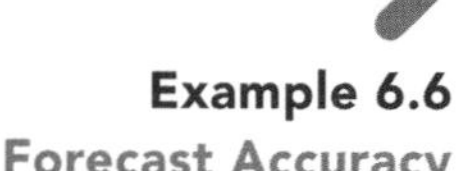

Example 6.6
Forecast Accuracy Measures

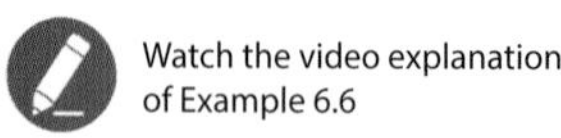

Watch the video explanation of Example 6.6

Period	Demand (*A*)	Forecast	Error (*e*)	|e|	$\frac{\|e\|}{A}(100)$	$\frac{RSFE}{MAD}$
1	1600	1523	77	77	4.8	1.0
2	2200	1810	390	390	17.7	2.0
3	2000	2097	–97	97	4.9	2.0
4	1600	2383	–783	783	48.9	–1.2
5	2500	2670	–170	170	6.8	–1.9
6	3500	2957	543	543	15.5	–0.1
7	3300	3243	57	57	1.7	0.1
8	3200	3530	–330	330	10.3	–1.0
9	3900	3817	83	83	2.1	–0.8
10	4700	4103	597	597	12.7	1.2
11	4300	4390	–90	90	2.1	0.9
12	4400	4677	–277	277	6.3	0.0
		Totals	0	3494	133.9	
		Means		**291.2**	**11.16**	**TRKG**
			RSFE	**MAD**	**MAPE**	**SGNL**

The results indicate no bias in the forecasts and a MAD of 291 or about 11% error each period. The running tracking signal (final column) is within a limit of +/- 2, which is reasonable. The MAD, however, indicates an error level that may not be acceptable. Management might consider evaluating other forecasting techniques.

A spreadsheet can also be used to calculate the accuracy measures as shown following:

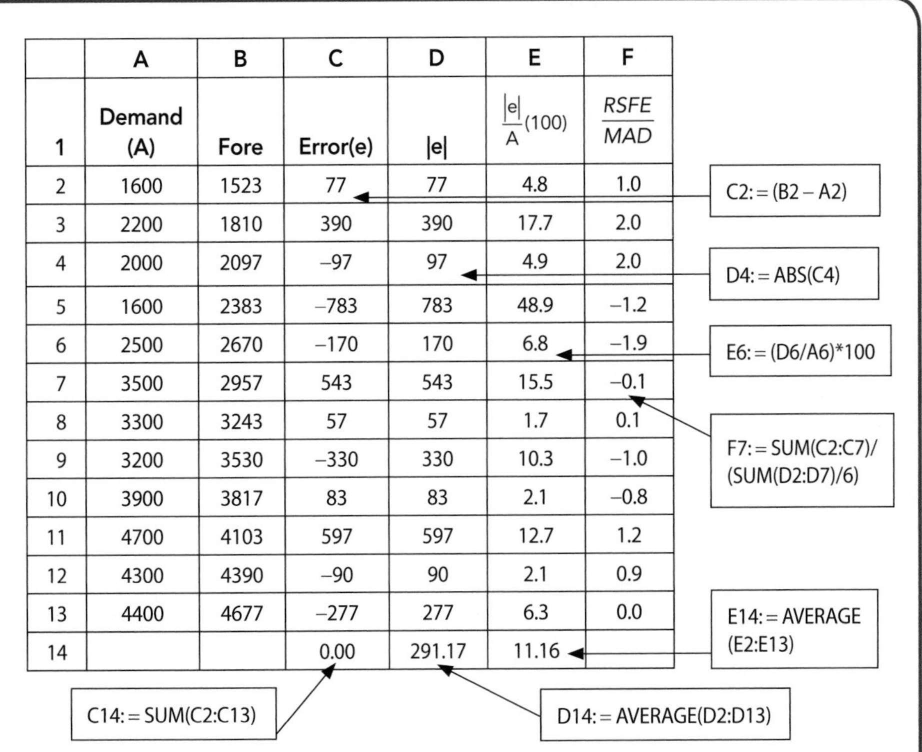

	A	B	C	D	E	F
1	Demand (A)	Fore	Error(e)	|e|	$\frac{\|e\|}{A}(100)$	$\frac{RSFE}{MAD}$
2	1600	1523	77	77	4.8	1.0
3	2200	1810	390	390	17.7	2.0
4	2000	2097	−97	97	4.9	2.0
5	1600	2383	−783	783	48.9	−1.2
6	2500	2670	−170	170	6.8	−1.9
7	3500	2957	543	543	15.5	−0.1
8	3300	3243	57	57	1.7	0.1
9	3200	3530	−330	330	10.3	−1.0
10	3900	3817	83	83	2.1	−0.8
11	4700	4103	597	597	12.7	1.2
12	4300	4390	−90	90	2.1	0.9
13	4400	4677	−277	277	6.3	0.0
14			0.00	291.17	11.16	

C2: = (B2 − A2)
D4: = ABS(C4)
E6: = (D6/A6)*100
F7: = SUM(C2:C7)/(SUM(D2:D7)/6)
E14: = AVERAGE (E2:E13)
C14: = SUM(C2:C13)
D14: = AVERAGE(D2:D13)

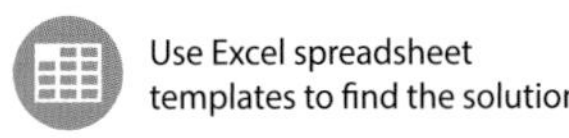

Use Excel spreadsheet templates to find the solution

Week	Demand	3-WK SMA	|e|	Exp.Sm ($\alpha = 0.3$)	|e|	Exp.Sm ($\alpha = 0.6$)	|e|
1	1600			1600.0	0.0	1600.0	0.0
2	2200			1600.0	600.0	1600.0	600.0
3	2000			1780.0	220.0	1960.0	40.0
4	1600	1933.3	333.3	1846.0	246.0	1984.0	384.0
5	2500	1933.3	566.7	1772.2	727.8	1753.6	746.4
6	3500	2033.3	1466.7	1990.5	1509.5	2201.4	1298.6
7	3300	2533.3	766.7	2443.4	856.6	2980.6	319.4
8	3200	3100.0	100.0	2700.4	499.6	3172.2	27.8
9	3900	3333.3	566.7	2850.3	1049.7	3188.9	711.1
10	4700	3466.7	1233.3	3165.2	1534.8	3615.6	1084.4
11	4300	3933.3	366.7	3625.6	674.4	4266.2	33.8
12	4400	4300.0	100.0	3827.9	572.1	4286.5	113.5
		MAD	**611.1**		**707.5**		**446.6**

Example 6.7
Comparing the Three-Week Simple Moving Average and Two Exponential Smoothing Forecasts Using the MAD

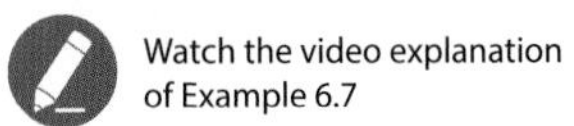

Watch the video explanation of Example 6.7

The MADs for all three forecasting techniques indicate the need to continue searching for a technique with less error. Of the three, the exponential smoothing forecast with an α = 0.6 is best, although its errors are quite high. Note that the first three errors for both exponential smoothing forecasts were not used in the MAD calculation since the first forecast was set equal to the first week's demand. It also makes sense to compare the same number of periods for all three techniques.

As shown in Example 6.6, a spreadsheet can be used to calculate each of the forecast elements.

SELECTING THE BEST NUMBER OF PERIODS, WEIGHTS, AND α'S TO USE

As shown in Examples 6.6 and 6.7, there are several ways to assess the ability of a forecasting technique to be accurate. These same accuracy measures can also tell the forecaster how many periods to use (i.e., a 3-period or a 4-period moving average forecast), what magnitude weights to use (i.e., weights of 0.5, 0.3, and 0.2, or weights of 0.4, 0.3, and 0.3), and what α to use (i.e., 0.3, 0.5, or 0.7). The simplest way to do this is to lay out all of the various forecasting techniques, weights, and α's on a spreadsheet along with a historical series of actual demand, then compute the forecasts, and finally compare the associated MADs. The one technique (along with its periods, weights, and/or α) having the lowest overall MAD, should be selected. On a smaller scale, this is what was done in Example 6.7. In other words, comparing the MADs will lead forecasters to the best technique, periods, weights, or α's.

CONTINGENCY PLANNING

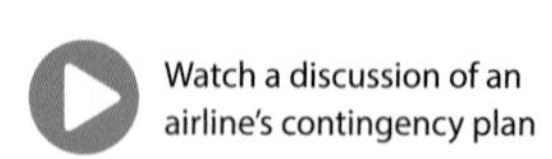

Watch a discussion of an airline's contingency plan

Regardless of the time and costs associated with forecasting, there will *always* be errors in forecasts (possibly very large ones), due to unforeseen circumstances. Thus, organizations need to develop **contingency plans** that can protect the firm and its customers when actual demand varies significantly from the forecast. For example, airlines offer to pay customers to take a later flight when seats are overbooked and too many customers show up for the flight; retailers hold safety stocks of high-demand items; resorts have lists of part-time, on-call workers who can fill in on a moment's notice when demand is greater than expected; farmers buy futures contracts to reduce the risk of product price fluctuations; manufacturers have secondary suppliers for times when their primary suppliers are out of stock; and grocery chains offer in-store specials to move unsold perishable products. Recall our discussion of the MGM CityCenter project at the beginning of this chapter. If it had secured contingency funding prior to the start of the project, in case its demand forecasts were too optimistic (which they were), the cost for this funding would likely have been less. These are all forms of contingency plans.

Sometimes, organizations seek to reach joint decisions with suppliers regarding their demand forecasts to avoid excess safety stocks. This is referred to as a **collaborative planning, forecasting, and replenishment** (CPFR) process, and is discussed further in the next section.

COLLABORATIVE PLANNING, FORECASTING, AND REPLENISHMENT

6.4 Describe the collaborative planning, forecasting, and replenishment process

contingency plans Insurance-type activities that are performed to protect the firm and its customers for times when actual demand varies significantly from the forecast. For example, airlines offer to pay customers to take a later flight when seats are overbooked and too many customers show up for the flight; retailers hold safety stocks of high-demand items; resorts have lists of part-time, on-call workers who can fill in on a moment's notice when demand is greater than expected.

collaborative planning, forecasting, and replenishment Information shared between suppliers and retailers aids in planning, forecasting, and satisfying customer demands through shared information. This allows for continuous updating of inventory and upcoming requirements, resulting in less safety stock.

As implied in the name of the process, collaboration in CPFR is a key element for developing a demand forecast, which is then used in the production and purchasing decisions of cooperating retailers and their suppliers. CPFR was first developed by the Voluntary Interindustry Commerce Solutions (VICS) Association, which merged with GS1 US in 2012.[17] The Council of Supply Chain Management Professionals describes CPFR as:

> A concept that aims to enhance supply chain integration by supporting and assisting joint practices. CPFR seeks cooperative management of inventory through joint visibility and replenishment of products throughout the supply chain. Information shared between suppliers and retailers aids in planning and satisfying customer demands through a supportive system of shared information. This allows for continuous updating of inventory and upcoming requirements, essentially making the end-to-end supply chain process more efficient. Efficiency is also created through the decreased expenditures for merchandising, inventory, logistics, and transportation across all trading partners.[18]

Due to collaboration, less safety stock is needed to protect against uncertain demand, lead times are reduced because less unnecessary product is manufactured, and sales tend

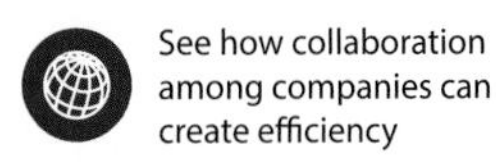

to increase because the correct amount of product is available. Ultimately, profits should be higher and costs lower. Today, more than 300 companies have formally implemented CPFR—reports from these firms show a 2–8% reduction in stockouts, accompanied by inventory reductions of 10–40%.[19]

In short, the buyer and supplier collaborate on forecasts of demand for the buyer's end-products, then agree on how much the supplier should produce and consequently, how much the buyer should purchase for a given time period. For example, if a buyer works with a trusted supplier and agrees to purchase exactly 1,000 units of a part over the upcoming quarter, then the supplier knows *exactly* how many units to produce for the buyer—no safety stock is required. Consequently, a lower-than-normal purchase price results, since no safety stock is produced. This also means that no forecasting or safety stock is required for the supplier's supplier. Additionally, the buyer knows that the supplier will deliver exactly the agreed-upon number of units and can plan accordingly.

See how collaboration among companies can create efficiency

Companies like Walmart, Procter & Gamble, Warner-Lambert, Kimberly Clark, Del Monte Foods, and Nabisco have proven that forecasting collaboration reduces costs along supply chains. In 2006, California-based Del Monte Foods wanted to involve customers when developing its forecasts. Del Monte began tapping into Walmart's and other retailers' databases and storing that information into its own data repository. That information was eventually fed into a demand-planning system that provided statistical modeling based on the retailers' forecasts and Del Monte's marketing consumption forecast. "That gives us the ability to look at all of those, have a discussion across the business and determine what our view of the future is going to look like," says CIO Marc Brown.[20]

Walmart has been a leader in CPFR efforts and encourages others in the retail sector to adopt similar practices. Partly because of Walmart's efforts, a set of consumer goods industry guidelines was developed and adopted by VICS in 1996.[21] VICS updated its CPFR model in 2004, which divides CPFR into four stages: strategy and planning, demand and supply management, execution, and analysis.

The strategy and planning stage involves two steps:

1. *Collaboration arrangement.* Includes setting goals for the relationship, setting parameters for the scope of the collaboration, and determining roles and responsibilities.
2. *Joint business plan.* Names any important events that will affect the planning process, such as store openings/closings, product promotions, product introductions, or inventory policy changes.

The demand and supply management stage includes:

1. *Sales forecasting.* Customer demand is forecasted using point-of-sale data and other available information. The forecast is generated and agreed upon by the supply chain partners.
2. *Order planning/forecasting.* Product ordering and delivery needs are set based on the sales forecast, current inventory levels, and lead times.

The third stage, execution, involves:

1. *Order generation.* The demand forecast is translated into committed orders by the purchasing/supply management department.
2. *Order fulfillment.* Orders are produced, shipped, delivered, and stocked.

Lastly, the analysis stage includes:

1. *Exception management.* The review of any situations that fall outside the current conditions.
2. *Performance assessment.* Analyzing the achievement of the joint goals, uncovering trends, and developing alternative strategies based on key performance metrics.

SERVICE SPOTLIGHT

Retailer West Marine Finds Success With CPFR

Boating supply retailer West Marine opened its first location in California in 1975. By 2001, it had hundreds of stores, selling thousands of products. At this point, it began noticing supplier order fill and delivery problems that were causing West Marine to carry too much inventory. Consequently, it began its first CPFR pilot program.

West Marine decided to make a significant commitment to work with its suppliers. For instance, most promotions were planned and entered into its forecasting system months in advance so suppliers could approve the forecast and fill the orders. Furthermore, West Marine guaranteed suppliers it would purchase the supply items based on the forecasts. All of West Marine's collaborative suppliers joined its quarterly meetings to discuss supply chain collaboration and sales and marketing planning. As a matter of fact, a number of suppliers placed sales associates at West Marine's facilities.

At last count, West Marine had more than 70 of its best suppliers loading the West Marine collaborative forecast directly into its production planning systems. Stockout rates have remained close to 4% in every store every week, forecast accuracy has climbed to 85%, and on-time shipments have improved from a dismal 30% to more than 80%.[22]

Melissa Lyttle/Zuma/newscom

In other words, trading partners must *together* develop an effective set of practices for managing demand. A process should also be implemented to match supply with demand each month. This involves determining the production level needed for a product family in order to meet the demand forecast, given the organizational strategy and any resource constraints. Teamwork between sales and operations is required to optimize this planning process. The Service Spotlight above provides a good example of CPFR experiences at a boating supply retailer.

Additionally, to allow CPFR to work, trading partners must share important information. For example, the retailer provides feedback on such things as plans for advertising and promotional campaigns and new store openings or store closures. Suppliers provide information on new product introductions and new technology investments. With access to this type of information, companies are able to improve their planning processes. Trading partners initially develop their demand forecasts independently, and if significant discrepancies occur, negotiations ensue to reach the final demand forecasts.

Lastly, performance must be measured on a regular basis. Performance information should be shared and then adjustments made for improvement. Metrics may include inventory turnover, stockout percentage, forecast accuracy, on-time deliveries, and others. There are, of course, challenges to adopting a CPFR arrangement because the process requires frequent communications, trust, information sharing, possible changes to operations, and some additional costs. The final step, once forecasting is complete, is to make annual production plans, and this topic is discussed next.

AGGREGATE PLANNING

6.5 Explain how aggregate planning is used to meet the objectives of the firm

aggregate planning Planning that occurs when firms consider their long-term business plans (such as new market expansion), forecast the intermediate- and long-term demand for their end-products, then translate this information into production, capacity, human resource, purchasing, logistics, and financial plans three to 18 months into the future.

Firms consider their long-term business plans (such as new market expansion), forecast the intermediate- and long-term demand for their end-products, then translate this information into production, capacity, human resource, purchasing, logistics, and financial plans three to 18 months into the future. Taken together, this is called **aggregate planning**. Operations managers use this information to set production schedules, production rates, labor levels and overtime, purchasing and logistics needs, inventory levels, and subcontractor usage. In general terms, the objective of aggregate planning is to *meet forecasted demand while* *minimizing costs and maximizing customer service over the planning periods.* Typically, each quarter, organizations reassess and potentially revise their aggregate plans.

For manufacturers, aggregate planning involves tying the forecast and growth information to production plans, while for services, the emphasis is more closely associated with workforce scheduling. Manufacturing aggregate planning is discussed first, followed by aggregate planning in services.

AGGREGATE PLANNING FOR MANUFACTURERS

Aggregate planning is a hierarchical process that translates annual business plans and demand forecasts into a production plan for all manufactured products. Once the production plan is completed, workforce, purchasing, and logistics plans can be determined so that the production plan can be achieved.

Aggregate production plans are typically stated in terms of product families. A **product family** consists of different products that share similar characteristics, components, or manufacturing processes. For example, a bicycle manufacturer that produces both three-speed and ten-speed options can group the two different bikes together, if the only difference between them is the gearing option. Production processes and labor and material requirements for the two bikes would be very similar.

The planning horizon for the aggregate plan is at least one year, and is typically extended forward by three months at the end of each quarter. This allows the operations manager to see the requirements at least one year ahead on a quarterly basis. Costs relevant to the aggregate planning process include inventory cost, setup cost, machine operating cost, hiring cost, firing cost, training cost, overtime cost, and costs incurred for hiring part-time and temporary workers to meet peak demand. There are three **production planning strategies** for meeting the aggregate plan:

1. *Chase strategy.* Production is varied to match demand. The firm hires and lays off workers each month as the demand varies. Since the workforce fluctuates from month to month, a pool of easily accessible and easily trained workers is necessary. Worker morale might be a problem if layoffs are frequent.
2. *Level strategy.* Production output is constant, resulting in shortages and inventory surpluses while demand varies. This type of strategy is more suited for firms requiring highly skilled labor, where hiring and training costs are high; however, customer service might suffer if shortages are frequent.
3. *Mixed strategy.* Maintains a stable core workforce while using overtime, temporary, or part-time workers to manage high-demand fluctuations. This strategy avoids the frequent layoff and stockout problems of the other two strategies.

Developing the Aggregate Plan

The common steps used when developing the aggregate plan are:

1. Identify the production planning strategy that best matches the company's objectives.
2. Determine the production rate, using the production planning strategy. For example, if the chase strategy is used, the production rate is set to match demand each month. Workers are hired and laid off frequently. Capacity requirements will vary each month. A level strategy means that production is constant and set to match the average monthly demand. Hiring is performed once, and no layoffs are needed. A mixed strategy normally tries to vary the workforce somewhat to reduce inventory shortages and surpluses, while having only a moderate need to hire and lay off workers.
3. Calculate the workforce requirement. Depending on the production plan, a level or varying workforce is needed.
4. Test the aggregate plan. Using the production rate and workforce levels, calculate end-of-period inventory levels, shortages, employees to be hired and laid off, and the overtime and part-time labor requirement.
5. Evaluate the aggregate plan's impact on cost, customer service, and human resources.

product family Consists of different products that share similar characteristics, components, or manufacturing processes.

production planning strategies Sets of activities in operations management for meeting the aggregate plan. These consist of the chase, level, and mixed strategies.

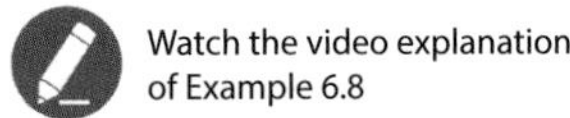

Example 6.8
Production Planning Strategies at Speedy Bike

Watch the video explanation of Example 6.8

The Speedy Bike Company makes bicycles. The 12-month aggregate production plan is determined for the chase, level, and mixed strategies. The table shows the forecast, production output, size of workforce, and monthly ending inventories from January to December, using the chase, level, and mixed production strategies. On average, one worker can assemble 20 bikes per month (or 1 bike every 8 hours). One month consists of 20 eight-hour days. Notice how the workforce and inventory vary each month for each strategy. Using a chase strategy minimizes end-of-period inventories and inventory carrying costs, but results in higher training and layoff costs. The level strategy builds inventory during the low-demand months, then draws down the inventory during the high-demand months, which can cause stockouts and high inventory carrying costs but lower training and layoff costs. The mixed strategy in this case determines the workforce size by averaging demand every four months with a maximum of 25 full-time workers. Up to two hours of overtime per worker per day are allowed, or 40 hours per month. If additional units are still needed to meet production goals, part-time workers are used up to four hours per worker per day. This strategy has moderate inventory carrying, stockout, hiring/training, and layoff costs. To determine the worker requirement in May, for example, using the mixed strategy, 675 units/20 units per worker = 33+ workers. So the maximum 25 workers are used for 500 units. With maximum overtime, 25 workers can make 25 × 2 hrs. per day × 20 days = 1,000 hrs, or 1,000/8 hrs. per unit, or 125 units. This still leaves 50 units requiring 400 hours to be performed by part-timers. One part-timer can work 80 hrs./mo., so five part-time workers in May are needed.

Month	Forecast Demand (units)	Chase Strategy (units)	Workers Needed	End Inven. (units)	Level Strategy (units)	Workers Needed	End Inven. (units)	Mixed Strategy (units)	Workers Needed	End Inven. (units)
Jan.	120	120	6	0	420	21	300	245	12+OT	125
Feb.	100	100	5	0	420	21	620	245	12+OT	270
Mar.	300	300	15	0	420	21	740	245	12+OT	215
Apr.	460	460	23	0	420	21	700	245	12+OT	0
May	600	600	30	0	420	21	520	675	25+OT+PT	75
Jun.	700	700	35	0	420	21	240	675	25+OT+PT	50
Jul.	760	760	38	0	420	21	−100	675	25+OT+PT	−35
Aug.	640	640	32	0	420	21	−320	675	25+OT+PT	0
Sept.	580	580	29	0	420	21	−480	340	17	−240
Oct.	400	400	20	0	420	21	−460	340	17	−300
Nov.	200	200	10	0	420	21	−240	340	17	−160
Dec.	180	180	9	0	420	21	0	340	17	0
	5040	5040			5040			5040		

Example 6.8 illustrates the three production planning strategies.

The three production plans illustrated in Example 6.8 result in three aggregate plans with production outputs, inventories, shortages, and labor hired, trained, and laid off. Labor overtime and part-time workers are also needed with the mixed strategy. The mixed strategy shown in Example 6.8 is only one of many mixed strategies. The firm might decide, for instance, to use more full-time employees, which would mean less overtime and fewer part-time workers.

In order to evaluate the three plans, cost data are needed, and Table 6.4 provides these costs. The cost comparison of each of the aggregate plans is then shown in Table 6.5.

For the chase strategy in February, for example, 5 workers were employed for a cost of (5 workers×160 hrs./mo.×$20/hr. = $16,000). One worker was laid off, for a cost of $750. Furthermore, 100 units were purchased for $10,000. For the level strategy in January, 21 workers were employed for a cost of (21 workers×160 hrs./mo.×$20/hr. = $67,200). There were 21 workers hired for a cost of $21,000. Additionally, 420 units were purchased for $42,000. The ending inventory was 300 units for a cost of $1,500. For the mixed strategy

Table 6.4 Cost Data

Permanent labor cost per hour	$20	Layoff cost per full-time employee	$750
Overtime labor cost per hour	$30	Layoff cost per part-time employee	$0
Part-time labor cost per hour	$15	Inventory holding cost per unit per period	$5
Hiring/training cost per full-time employee	$1000	Shortage cost per unit per period	$10
Hiring/training cost per part-time employee	$500	Material cost per unit	$100

in May, 25 workers were employed for a cost of (25 workers×160 hrs./mo.×$20/hr. = $80,000). The 25 workers also worked 20 hrs./week overtime for a cost of (25 workers×40 hrs./mo.× $30/hr. = $30,000). Five part-timers were employed for a cost of (5 workers×80 hrs./mo. ×$15/hr. = $6000). Also, 13 full-time and 5 part-time workers were hired for a cost of $13,000+$2500 = $15,500. Finally, 675 units were purchased for a cost of $67,500. The ending inventory was 75 units for a cost of $375.

Given the cost structures shown in Table 6.4, the lowest-cost aggregate plan is the level strategy. The high cost of hiring/training, layoffs, overtime, and part-time workers tended to make the other two plans less desirable.

AGGREGATE PLANNING FOR SERVICES

Since most services cannot use inventories as a buffer against periods of high demand, scheduling the workforce becomes the top priority, and a level production strategy simply cannot be used. For low labor cost, high worker availability businesses like fast-food services, a chase production strategy can be used, and for higher labor cost professional services like banking

Table 6.5 Cost Comparisons for the Aggregate Plans in Example 6.8

	Chase Strategy				Level Strategy				
Periods	Wages	Hiring	Layoff	Purch.	Wages	Hiring	Purch.	Holding	Shortage
Jan.	19200	6000		12000	67200	21000	42000	1500	
Feb.	16000		750	10000	67200		42000	3100	
Mar.	48000	10000		30000	67200		42000	3700	
Apr.	73600	8000		46000	67200		42000	3500	
May	96000	7000		60000	67200		42000	2600	
Jun.	112000	5000		70000	67200		42000	1200	
Jul.	121600	3000		76000	67200		42000		1000
Aug.	102400		4500	64000	67200		42000		3200
Sept.	92800		2250	58000	67200		42000		4800
Oct.	64000		6750	40000	67200		42000		4600
Nov.	32000		7500	20000	67200		42000		2400
Dec.	28800		750	18000	67200		42000		
Totals, $	806400	39000	22500	504000	806400	21000	504000	15600	16000
Grand Totals			$1,371,900					$1,363,000	

(Continued)

Table 6.5 (Continued)

Mixed Strategy								
Periods	**Wages**	**Over time**	**Part-time**	**Hiring**	**Layoff**	**Purch.**	**Holding**	**Shortage**
Jan.	38400	1200		12000		24500	625	
Feb.	38400	1200				24500	1350	
Mar.	38400	1200				24500	1075	
Apr.	38400	1200				24500	0	
May	80000	30000	6000	15500		67500	375	
Jun.	80000	30000	6000			67500	250	
Jul.	80000	30000	6000			67500		350
Aug.	80000	30000	6000			67500	0	
Sept.	54400				6000	34000		2400
Oct.	54400					34000		3000
Nov.	54400					34000		1600
Dec.	54400					34000	0	
Totals, $	691200	124800	24000	27500	6000	504000	3675	7350
Grand Total							$1,388,525	

and accounting firms, a mixed production strategy is normally used. In all services, accurate daily demand forecasts, workforce scheduling, and use of demand management techniques are the critical tools for meeting demand, minimizing queuing problems, and enabling the firm to meet its customer service objectives. Successful service production planning activities include:

- Forecasting demand and scheduling workers on an hour-to-hour basis throughout the day to meet fluctuating demand
- Using part-time workers and overtime during heavy demand periods; cross-training workers to shift capacities among service processes as demand dictates

SERVICE SPOTLIGHT

Workforce Scheduling at BB&T

North Carolina–based financial holding company BB&T had acquired more than 175 banks over the past 20 years and allowed its teller scheduling process to become ineffective, resulting in over- and understaffing at its teller windows. BB&T had been relying on data collected at its more than 1,600 branches to determine the teller schedules; however, there was no forecasting or system-wide scheduling performed. Obviously, BB&T needed to do something. The objectives were to optimize teller scheduling while maintaining desired customer service levels.

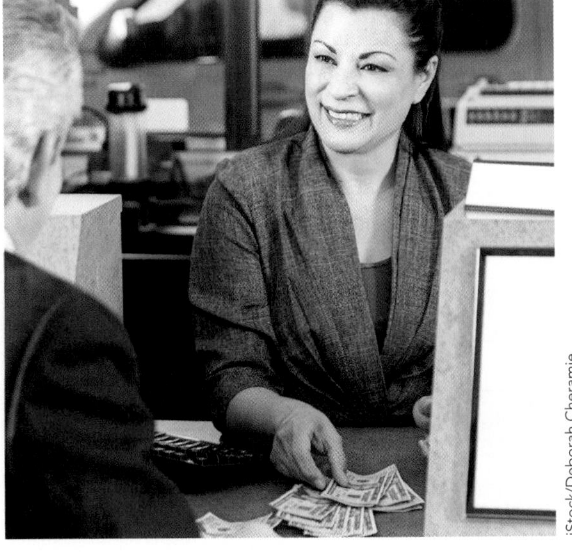

iStock/Deborah Cheramie

BB&T purchased a Web-based workforce management and forecasting application in 2007, based on its ease of use and ability to integrate with BB&T's information system. The application was tested for several weeks and was then rolled out to all of the branches. By the end of 2008, the bank had achieved effective teller scheduling, lower teller turnover, and a 50% reduction in teller overtime pay, while maintaining its high levels of customer service.[23]

- Using technology wherever possible to minimize service times and maximize productivity
- Using reservations to smooth demand, if possible

During the recent economic recession, workforce management has been a real concern for service managers. An increase in use of forecasting and labor scheduling software has been employed to keep a lid on costs. The Service Spotlight on the previous page illustrates the advantages of these technologies at a U.S. bank.

Additionally, use of part-time and temporary workers, also referred to as **contingent workers**, has escalated to 30–50% of the workforce for many companies. Prior to the recent recession, the average was 13%. Many service industry analysts now see this as a fundamental shift in the service workforce strategy. Furthermore, companies are not just using contingent workers for low-skill jobs. "More and more we are seeing requests for professional skills: engineers, information technicians, health care workers, specialists in accounting and finance. Companies are starting to look at really using a portion of contingent labor in even the more highly skilled positions," says Joanie Ruge, senior VP of staffing company Adecco Group North America.[24]

contingent workers Part-time and temporary workers.

SUMMARY

This chapter provided a look at the related topics of demand management, forecasting, and aggregate planning, and the important roles played by these subjects in the success of an organization. The objectives for all organizations are to satisfy demand in cost-effective ways that maintain desired levels of customer service. Using demand management, forecasting, and aggregate planning techniques helps organizations meet these objectives.

Forecasting is a demand management activity; however, many other demand management activities work to influence demand when forecasts contain errors. These activities were also discussed in the chapter. Forecasts can use historical data; these methods are considered quantitative in nature, and were presented in the chapter. Qualitative forecasting methods can also be used when no reliable data exist, and a number of these methods were presented. All forecasts contain at least some error, and error measurement techniques were presented and discussed. These techniques were then used to compare forecasting techniques.

In a supply chain setting, firms may desire to collaboratively arrive at a forecast of end-product demand, then use the forecast to make purchasing and production decisions among, for instance, a retailer and its suppliers. This tends to reduce the need for safety stock along a supply chain, and is termed collaborative planning, forecasting, and replenishment. This topic was also discussed.

Finally, once the firm has arrived at medium- and long-term forecasts, these are used to make workforce and production plans for the coming quarters and year. These aggregate planning activities for both manufacturing and service firms were discussed.

KEY TERMS

Aggregate planning, 164
Associative forecasts, 148
Business cycle, 149
Causal variable, 157
Collaborative planning, forecasting, and replenishment, 162
Consumer surveys, 147
Contingency plans, 162
Contingent workers, 169
Cyclical variations, 149
Delphi method, 147
Demand management, 145

Exponential smoothing forecast, 152
Forecast bias, 158
Forecast error, 159
Jury of executive opinion, 148
Linear trend forecast, 154
Mean absolute deviation, 159
Mean absolute percentage error, 159
Multiple regression forecasting, 157
Product family, 165
Production planning strategies, 165
Qualitative forecasting techniques, 146
Quantitative forecasting techniques, 146
Random variations, 149
Running sum of forecast error, 159
Sales force estimates, 147
Sample coefficient of determination, 157
Sample correlation coefficient, 157
Seasonal variations, 149
Simple linear regression forecasts, 157
Simple moving average forecast, 150
Smoothing constant, 152
Time series forecasts, 148
Tracking signal, 160
Trend variations, 148
Weighted moving average forecast, 151

FORMULA REVIEW

The simple moving average forecast:

$F_{t+1} = \frac{\sum_{i=t-n+1}^{t} A_i}{n} = \frac{A_t + A_{t-1} + A_{t-2} + ... + A_{t-n+1}}{n}$, where F_{t+1} = forecast for period t+1, n = number of periods used to calculate moving average, and A_i = actual demand in period i.

The weighted moving average forecast:

$F_{t+1} = \sum_{i=t-n+1}^{t} w_i A_i = w_1 A_1 + w_2 A_{t-1} + w_3 A_{t-2} + \ldots + wA_{t-n+1}$, where F_{t+1} = forecast for period t+1, n = number of periods used in determining the moving average, A_i = actual demand in period i, w_i = weight assigned to period i, and $\sum w_i = 1$.

The exponential smoothing forecast:

$F_{t+1} = F_t + \alpha (A_t - F_t)$ or $F_{t+1} = \alpha A_t + (1 - \alpha)F_t$, where F_{t+1} = forecast for period t+1, F_t = forecast for period t, A_t = actual demand for period t, and α = smoothing constant ($0 \leq \alpha \leq 1$).

The linear trend forecast:

$Y = a + bX$, where Y = the forecast dependent variable (demand), X = independent time variable, a = vertical axis intercept of the line, and b = slope of the line.

The coefficients, (a) and (b), for the linear trend forecast:

$b = n \frac{\Sigma(XY) - \Sigma X \Sigma Y}{n\Sigma X^2 - (\Sigma X^2)}$ and $a = \frac{\Sigma Y - b\Sigma X}{n}$, where n = number of observations.

The linear regression forecast:

$Y = a + bX$, where Y = the forecast dependent variable (demand), X = independent predictor variable, a = constant and vertical axis intercept of the regression line, and b = regression coefficient and slope of the regression line.

The multiple regression forecast:

$Y = a + b_1 X_1 + b_2 X_2 + b_3 X_3 .... + b_n X_n$, where X_n = nth independent predictor variable, a = constant, b_n = regression coefficient of the nth independent predictor variable X_n.

Forecast error:

$e_t = A_t - F_t$, where e_t = forecast error for period t, A_t = actual demand for period t, and F_t = forecast for period t.

Forecast accuracy measures:

$MAD = \frac{\Sigma|e_t|}{n}$, $MAPE = \frac{100}{n}\Sigma\frac{|e_t|}{A_t}$, $RSFE = \Sigma e_t$, where $|e_t|$ = absolute value of the forecast error for period t, e_t = forecast error for period t, A_t = actual demand for period t, and n = number of periods in the evaluation.

Tracking signal, $TS = \frac{RSFE}{MAD}$.

SOLVED PROBLEMS

Use the data below for Questions 1–5.

Period	Demand
1	1256
2	1602
3	2376
4	1844

Period	Demand
5	2231
6	2716
7	1793

1. Calculate a 4-period simple moving average forecast for periods 5–7.

Answer:

Period	Demand	4 – Pd. SMA
1	1256	
2	1602	
3	2376	
4	1844	
5	2231	(1256+1602+2376+1844)/4 = 1769.5
6	2716	(1602+2376+1844+2231)/4 = 2013.3
7	1793	(2376+1844+2231+2716)/4 = 2291.8

2. Calculate a 4-period weighted moving average forecast for periods 5–7 using the weights 0.4, 0.3, 0.2, and 0.1.

Answer:

Period	Demand	4 – Pd. WMA
1	1256	
2	1602	
3	2376	
4	1844	
5	2231	(1256x.1)+(1602x.2)+(2376x.3)+(1844x.4) = 1896.4
6	2716	(1602x.1)+(2376x.2)+(1844x.3)+(2231x.4) = 2081.0
7	1793	(2376x.1)+(1844x.2)+(2231x.3)+(2716x.4) = 2362.1

3. Calculate an exponential smoothing forecast for periods 5–7 using $\alpha = 0.2$ and a starting forecast for period 4 of 1741.

Answer:

Period	Demand	Exponential Smoothing
1	1256	
2	1602	
3	2376	
4	1844	1741 (given)
5	2231	1741+.2(1844–1741) = 1761.6
6	2716	1761.6+.2(2231–1761.6) = 1855.5
7	1793	1855.5+.2(2716–1855.5) = 2027.6

4. Calculate a linear trend forecast for periods 5–7 using the formulas provided in the text.

Period (X)	Demand (Y)	X^2	Y^2	XY	Trend Forecast
5	2231	25	4,977,361	11,155	3560.7 – (219×5) = 2465.7
6	2716	36	7,376,656	16,296	3560.7 – (219×6) = 2246.7
7	1793	49	3,214,849	12,551	3560.7 – (219×7) = 2027.7

$\Sigma X = 18 \quad \Sigma Y = 6740 \quad \Sigma X^2 = 110 \quad \Sigma Y^2 = 15{,}568{,}866 \quad \Sigma XY = 40{,}002$

$$b = \frac{n\Sigma(XY) - \Sigma X \Sigma Y}{n\Sigma X^2 - (\Sigma X)^2} = \frac{3(40002) - 18(6740)}{3(110) - 18^2} = \frac{-1314}{6} = -219$$

$$a = \frac{\Sigma Y - b\Sigma X}{n} = \frac{6740 - (-219)(18)}{3} = 3560.7$$

Answer:

Thus, Y = 3560.7 – 219(X) is the forecast equation. The trend forecasts are shown above for the three periods.

5. Compare the four forecasts in 1–4 above using the MAD, MAPE, RSFE, and TS for periods 5–7. Which forecast technique is the best?

Period	Demand	SMA	error	WMA	error	Ex Sm	error	Trend	error
5	2231	1769.5	461.5	1896.4	334.6	1761.6	469.4	2465.7	–234.7
6	2716	2013.3	702.7	2081.0	635.0	1855.5	860.5	2246.7	469.3
7	1793	2263.7	–470.7	2362.1	–569.1	2027.6	–234.6	2027.7	–234.7
	MAD		545.0		512.9		521.5		312.9**
	MAPE		24.3%		23.4%		21.9%		13.6%**
	RSFE		693.5		400.5		1095.3		–0.1**
	TS		1.27		0.78		2.10		0.0**

Answer:

The linear trend forecast is the best in all performance categories.

6. For the following forecast of demand, determine:

(a) The level, chase, and mixed strategies with labor hours, inventories, shortages, and workers required. Assume that each unit requires 7 labor hours of assembly time, and workers on average work an 8-hour day and 20 days per month. Round up to the nearest whole number of workers. Use 3-month averages for the mixed strategy, with a maximum permanent workforce of 135. The mixed strategy workers can work 4 hours of overtime each day, and part-timers can work 4 hours each day.

Answer:

Month	Demand Forecast (Units)	Level Strategy (Units)	Inven. (Units)	Labor Hours	Workers Required	Chase Strategy (Units)	Labor Hours	Workers Required
Jan.	2820	2940	120	20,580	129	2820	19,740	123
Feb.	2100	2940	960	20,580	129	2100	14,700	92
Mar.	3250	2940	650	20,580	129	3250	22,750	142
Apr.	3460	2940	130	20,580	129	3460	24,220	151
May	3600	2940	–530	20,580	129	3600	25,200	158
June	2790	2940	–380	20,580	129	2790	19,530	122
July	2760	2940	–200	20,580	129	2760	19,320	121

Month	Demand Forecast (Units)	Level Strategy (Units)	Inven. (Units)	Labor Hours	Workers Required	Chase Strategy (Units)	Labor Hours	Workers Required
Aug.	2640	2940	100	20,580	129	2640	18,480	116
Sept.	2580	2940	460	20,580	129	2580	18,060	113
Oct.	2900	2940	500	20,580	129	2900	20,300	127
Nov.	3200	2940	240	20,580	129	3200	22,400	140
Dec.	3180	2940	0	20,580	129	3180	22,260	139
	35,280	35,280		246,960		35,280	246,960	

Month	Demand Forecast (Units)	Mixed Strategy (Units)	Inven. (Units)	Labor Hours	Overtime Hours	Workers Required
Jan.	2820	2724	-96	20,300		127
Feb.	2100	2724	528	20,300		127
Mar.	3250	2724	2	20,300		127
Apr.	3460	3300	−158	21,600	1500	135+OT
May	3600	3300	–458	21,600	1500	135+OT
June	2790	3300	52	21,600	1500	135+OT
July	2760	2660	–48	18,620		117
Aug.	2640	2660	−28	18,620		117
Sept.	2580	2660	52	18,620		117
Oct.	2900	3093	245	21,600	51	135+OT
Nov.	3200	3093	138	21,600	51	135+OT
Dec.	3180	3093	51	21,600	51	135+OT
	35,280	35,331		246,360	4653	

Level: Sum demand forecasts, then divide annual requirement by 12 to get level output. Then multiply monthly output by 7 hours to get labor hours needed. Then divide by 160 hours worked per month to get workers required.

Chase: Make output each month the same as the forecast. Multiply output by 7 to get the labor hours needed. Divide by 160 to get the workers required.

Mixed: Sum the demand forecasts, then divide by 3 every 3 months to get average output. Multiply by 7 to get total hours required. Divide by 160 to get worker requirement. If required workers are greater than 135, then use overtime. No part-timers were needed.

(b) The total cost for each strategy, given the cost structure in the table below.

Cost Data			
Permanent labor cost per hour	$40	Layoff cost per full-time employee	$4,000
Overtime labor cost per hour	$60	Layoff cost per part-time employee	$0
Part-time labor cost per hour	$15	Inventory holding cost per unit per period	$5
Hiring/training cost per full-time employee	$5000	Shortage cost per unit per period	$20
Hiring/training cost per part-time employee	$2000	Material cost per unit	$50

Answer:

Month	Level Strategy Wages	Hiring	Purch.	Holding	Shortage	Chase Strategy Wages	Hiring	Layoff	Purch.
Jan.	823200	645000	147000	600		789600	615000		141000
Feb.	823200		147000	4800		588000		124000	105000
Mar.	823200		147000	3250		910000	250000		162500
Apr.	823200		147000	650		968800	36000		173000
May	823200		147000		10600	1008000	28000		180000
June	823200		147000		7600	781200		144000	139500
July	823200		147000		4000	772800		4000	138000
Aug.	823200		147000	500		739200		20000	132000
Sept.	823200		147000	2300		722400		12000	129000
Oct.	823200		147000	2500		812000	70000		145000
Nov.	823200		147000	1200		896000	65000		160000
Dec.	823200		147000	0		890400		4000	159000
Totals	9878400	645000	1764000	15800	22200	9878400	1064000	308000	1764000
Grand Totals					**$12,325,400**				**$13,014,400**

Month	Mixed Strategy Wages	Overtime	Hiring	Layoff	Purch.	Holding	Shortage
Jan.	812000		635000		136200		1920
Feb.	812000				136200	2640	
Mar.	812000				136200	10	
Apr.	864000	90000	40000		165000		3160
May	864000	90000			165000		9160
June	864000	90000			165000	260	
July	744800			72000	133000		960
Aug.	744800				133000		560
Sept.	744800				133000	260	
Oct.	864000	3060	90000		154650	1225	
Nov.	864000	3060			154650	690	
Dec.	864000	3060			154650	255	
Totals	9854400	36180	765000	72000	1766550	5340	15760
Grand Total							**$12,515,230**

Thus, using the cost structure given, the level strategy resulted in the lowest cost. The hiring and layoff costs hurt the other two strategies.

REVIEW QUESTIONS

1. What is demand management?
2. Describe the various qualitative forecasting techniques.
3. What are the time series forecasts discussed in this chapter? Explain when you would use each one.
4. What is forecast error? What are the costs of forecast error?
5. What is collaborative planning, forecasting, and replenishment? How does it differ from other forecasting methods?
6. What is aggregate planning? Do all firms practice some form of it?
7. What are the three production planning strategies, and when would you use each one?
8. What are contingent workers?

DISCUSSION QUESTIONS

1. Explain the role of demand management in forecasting.
2. Describe some demand management activities, using examples.
3. How would logistics plans be impacted by demand forecasts?
4. Why do companies perform forecasting? What are the effects of a poor forecast?
5. Why is good forecasting so difficult? Is it an art or a science?
6. What sort of qualitative forecasting do you think the MGM Mirage probably did, prior to the start of its CityCenter project? Could it have done any quantitative forecasting prior to the project?
7. Given that your firm has several years of historical demand data, would there ever be a situation where you would still prefer to use a qualitative forecasting method? Why?
8. Describe the role that random variations play in time series forecasting. Can you guard against random variations?
9. What happens to the exponential smoothing forecast when $\alpha = 0$? When $\alpha = 1$? Would you ever want to use either of these forecasts? Explain.
10. What is the difference between a linear trend forecast and a simple linear regression forecast?
11. Explain the difference between forecast bias and forecast error.
12. What is a contingency plan used with forecasting, and when would you want to formulate one? When would you use it?
13. Describe the advantages and disadvantages of using CPFR. Do you think the advantages outweigh the disadvantages? What firms would get the greatest benefits from using CPFR?
14. Could a business successfully exist without doing aggregate planning? Explain.
15. Describe several manufacturers and service companies that would use each of the three production planning strategies, and how they would use them.
16. Why do you think more and more firms these days are using contingent workers?

EXERCISES AND PROJECTS

1. Describe the forecasting methods and the items forecast at a specific large business. How do the methods compare to those discussed in this chapter? (Hint: Search the Internet using "Forecasting practices at . . . " to find company examples.)
2. Use the Dow Jones or some other daily stock market indices as data, and then take 30 days of data to start your forecasting project. Find the one best forecasting method over this period from among the ones discussed in this chapter and using several forecast accuracy measures. Then, for an upcoming week, track the performance of this method. Discuss your findings.
3. Write a report on an organization's use of CPFR and its experiences with this technique (it is also sometimes simply referred to as "collaborative forecasting"; you might also try using the same hint as described in Exercise 1).

PROBLEMS

Use the data provided here for Problems 1–6.

Period	Demand (units)	Period	Demand (units)
1	22	5	19
2	16	6	28
3	25	7	22
4	27		

1. Calculate a 3-period simple moving average forecast for periods 4–8.
2. Calculate a 3-period weighted moving average forecast for periods 4–8 using the weights 0.6, 0.3, and 0.1.
3. Calculate an exponential smoothing forecast for periods 2–8 using $\alpha = 0.3$ and an initial forecast for period 1 of 22.
4. Calculate by hand, a linear trend forecast for periods 4–7.
5. Calculate a linear regression forecast for periods 1–8 using Excel or some other spreadsheet application. What are the sample correlation coefficient and sample coefficient of determination? Do you think the forecast looks reliable? Why?
6. Compare the techniques in problems 1–3 here using the MAD, MAPE, RSFE, and TS for periods 4–7. Which forecast technique is the best? Why?
7. Monthly demand and two forecasts are shown below. Which forecast is better? Why?

Month	Demand (units)	Forecast 1 (units)	Forecast 2 (units)
Jan.	1200	1086	1421
Feb.	1160	1120	1082
March	1232	1090	1141
April	1095	1240	995
May	1250	1326	1185
June	1310	1140	1243
July	1190	1092	1072
August	1265	1141	1342

8. Using whatever methods you choose, find the best forecasting technique for the following data. Justify your answer.

Period	Demand (units)	Period	Demand (units)
1	126	5	155
2	162	6	143
3	144	7	172
4	138	8	166

9. Which is the best forecasting method to use for the following data—a 3-period weighted moving average forecast with weights of (0.5, 0.3, 0.2) or an exponential smoothing forecast with an $\alpha = 0.25$ (compare the last 5 periods only and use 1081 for the exponential smoothing forecast in period 1). Justify your answer.

Period	Demand (units)	Period	Demand (units)
1	1081	5	1291
2	1655	6	1386
3	1422	7	1224
4	1387	8	1166

Use the data shown here for monthly umbrella sales and the average monthly predicted chance of rain for Problems 10–12.

Month	Chance of Rain (%)	Umbrella Sales (units)
January	22	1420
February	26	1380
March	32	1440
April	41	1635
May	36	1744
June	32	1486
July	28	1208
August	34	1145
September	38	1337
October	44	1388
November	32	1456
December	38	1684

10. Plot the data. Do the two variables look correlated?

11. Either calculate the regression coefficients by hand, or perform a linear regression using your spreadsheet software. What is the correlation coefficient? Are the data correlated?

12. Calculate the forecasts for each month using your regression formula and then determine the MAD. Would you use this forecast if you sold these umbrellas? Why, or why not?

13. Using the umbrella sales data from 10-12, calculate forecasts using the 3-period weighted moving average with weights of (0.5, 0.3, 0.2) and using exponential smoothing with an $\alpha = 0.3$ and a period 1 forecast of 1420. Compare the MADs of these two methods using errors for months April through December, and decide which one is the better forecast.

14. Develop a chase, level, and mixed production plan for the following data. Assume that each unit produced requires 4 hours labor time, workdays are 8 hours, workweeks are 40 hours, and workers work 20 days per month. Round up for the number of workers each month. For the mixed plan, use 3-period demand averages. Use full-time workers as much as possible, up to a full-time workforce of 4 workers. Allow up to 10 hours overtime per worker per week prior to hiring any part-time workers. Part-timers can work up to 10 hours per week.

Month	Forecast of Demand (units)	Month	Forecast of Demand (units)
Jan.	200	July	40
Feb.	100	Aug.	65
March	120	Sept.	70
April	75	Oct.	120
May	50	Nov.	275
June	45	Dec.	380

15. Using the data in Problem 14 and the three production plans created, determine the total cost of each plan according to the following cost considerations. Which one is least costly?

Cost Data			
Permanent labor cost per hour	$30	Layoff cost per full-time employee	$1000
Overtime labor cost per hour	$45	Layoff cost per part-time employee	$0
Part-time labor cost per hour	$20	Inventory holding cost per unit per period	$6
Hiring/training cost per full-time employee	$4000	Shortage cost per unit per period	$20
Hiring/training cost per part-time employee	$2000	Material cost per unit	$300

CASE STUDIES

CASE 1: The Animal Shelter Director

The recently hired director of a city's animal shelter was facing several immediate operational issues that threated future funding for the shelter. The revenue streams were not adequate to cover recent increases in operating costs. Moreover, capacity utilization of kennels and key operating systems (the adoption process, intake procedures, and information systems) had not been very effective. The shelter's revenue came from the city's budget, yearly license fees, and adoption fees.

Paralleling national trends, the animal shelter has been steadily increasing the amount of medical treatments given to dogs prior to adoption. This helped the agency improve public relations within the community and increased the perception that a high-quality pet could be obtained through the shelter. When a pet was adopted, it was fully vaccinated, microchipped, altered, and given a health certificate. These services had raised costs by 30%.

After six months on the new job, the director was faced with increasingly incompatible operating pressures. The shelter was recording large budget overruns based on the increased cost of new medical screenings, food, and supplies for an increasing number of dogs housed at the shelter. There had been less predictable revenue streams from adoption fees based on the mix of dogs at the shelter each month (some breeds were adopted quickly, while other breeds remained longer). The shelter had also experienced capacity issues based on the number of dogs requiring boarding and the fluctuation of the amount of time a dog is in a kennel before adoption (length of stay, or LOS).

City officials and the local community have been supportive of the direction the new director has taken with staff, operating systems, and a data analysis approach to making decisions. Recent discussions of the increasing costs, fluctuating revenues, and capacity issues at city council meetings and public forums have generated support for the director to request more money to make a number of changes. The process required a formal proposal submitted to city officials with a description of the current problems, evidence of continued financial and service pressures, and recommendations for future improvements including new funding requirements.

The animal shelter director expects that several forecasts will be needed to accompany her proposal to increase the county budget allocation and to communicate to the community the need to raise adoption and license fees. The shelter has plenty of monthly data on costs, revenue streams from adoptions and licenses, LOS for all breeds, LOS for "hard-to-adopt" breeds, capacity utilization of kennels, and monthly adoptions. The shelter director has been struggling with how the current data can be used to estimate cost overruns and capacity issues.

DISCUSSION QUESTIONS

1. Explain the forecasting options that would be best for the director to use in her proposal. Should she use qualitative or quantitative forecasts, or both?

2. Based on the historical data available, the director noticed that the most recent months are more reflective of the increased LOS for dogs and also capacity trends. Which forecasting techniques can be used that would be more responsive to the latest month's data?

3. What operational method could the director use to determine which forecasting technique is the most accurate?

Note: Written by Brian Hoyt, Management Professor, Ohio University. This case was prepared solely to provide material for class discussion. The author does not intend to illustrate either effective or ineffective handling of a managerial situation.

CASE 2: New Hiring Predictions and Operating Costs

A local apparel manufacturer of licensed spirit wear (college shirts, hats, and sweatshirts), with 40 employees, has orders and sales forecasts that require hiring additional employees to meet increasing demand. The current calculations require the hiring of 12 new employees. In addition to the demand and capacity issues, the company must address new operating costs. Health insurance is not presently provided for the 40 employees.

The Affordable Care Act (ACA) is a government mandate for companies with over 50 employees to provide health insurance. Although the law was to be enacted in 2014 there have been numerous delays. The reprieves have run out. Small and medium-size businesses will be required to offer health insurance to most of its employees in 2016. The act was delayed a year to allow businesses with 50 to 99 full-time workers more time to comply. Small businesses have less bargaining power to negotiate less expensive insurance plans, and the underwriting costs for employees with preexisting conditions can result in premiums that are higher than in larger businesses. Penalties will be assessed if the calculations done by the government in 2014 and 2015 show more than 50 employees with no paid health insurance. During the delay, some employers have been allocating money for employees to purchase their own plans. This approach may be liable for an excise tax per day for each employee, or a dollar amount per year per applicable individual.

The company is now reviewing the balance of the important considerations of capacity and demand, along with new health care cost factors. The operations manager has suggested that several alternatives should be analyzed as part of the decision to hire. The options were listed as:

- Hire full-time employees with health insurance benefits
- Hire part-time employees with no benefits (20 hours per week)
- Hire subcontractors (not employees and no benefits)
- Do nothing/do not hire any new employees

The operations manager provided additional information necessary to review each alternative and compute a projected profit for each alternative that considered demand, capacity, costs, and projected revenues. Data were retrieved from accounting and production records, and assumptions were presented to analyze each hiring type alternative. Assumptions were categorized for full-time, part-time, and contract employees, and included wages, payroll taxes, benefits, new health care costs, productivity, and revenues based on mixed model production. In addition, chance events and probabilities were calculated based on the historical differences in productivity rates of full-time employees as the standard and the likelihood that part-time employees and contract workers would achieve the standard productivity rates.

The human resources manager added another very interesting perspective on type of hire and productivity that would adjust the probability of temporary/contract worker productivity. The manager participated in a regional (tri-state) survey of manufacturers who used both full-time and temporary employees (contract workers). The findings of this yearlong study reported that certain pre-hire demographic profiles could be strong predictors of work performance and unproductive behaviors (tardiness, absenteeism, unsafe behaviors, and poor-quality work). The study examined independent factors of gender, length of time on previous contract assignments, length of time between contract assignments, willingness to work "off shifts," and sharing wage expectation information. The dependent variable was a measure of productivity and unproductive behaviors.

DISCUSSION QUESTIONS

1. Describe the three production-planning strategies as possible directions for this apparel manufacturing company. Which strategy could provide the most flexibility in addressing Affordable Care Act constraints?

2. How would simple linear regression forecasting aid in selecting an appropriate staffing approach considering the ACA mandate?

3. Discuss any other factors that the apparel manufacturer should consider to help determine their next course of action.

Note: Written by Brian Hoyt, Management Professor, Ohio University. This case was prepared solely to provide material for class discussion. The author does not intend to illustrate either effective or ineffective handling of a managerial situation.

CASE 3: The New Sales Manager

An OEM storage equipment manufacturer recently hired a new sales manager from outside the company. The new sales manager had experience in selling storage bins, racks, and conveyors, most recently as the leading sales representative for a major competitor. His first three weeks on the job was spent with engineering and the sales team to familiarize himself with products and sales operations (quotes/estimates, order taking, distribution/warehouse, and customer service). The next three weeks were spent traveling to all the U.S. regional sales offices to meet the sales staff and ride along with sales representatives to meet key customers in each sales territory.

Sales have been flat for the past 18 months, for the largest product lines of storage bins and storage racks that make up 73% of sales. Replacement parts and service have been the only profitable items for the current year to date, but these only represent 7% of total revenues. The remaining 20% of revenue comes from an exclusive distribution contract and partnership with a manufacturer in Mexico.

The past two weeks have been spent gathering storage equipment industry growth data as well as growth data that reflect customer segments. The company sells directly to very large users of storage equipment (racks and bins), including independent retail distribution centers, warehouse operations, and corporations with their own corporate vertical marketing systems. It also sells to large storage equipment resellers, who then sell to large and small users of material management equipment. Additionally, the company sells to small resellers who specialize in maintenance, repair, and operating (MRO) items, and also to small users of storage and MRO items. Finally, the company's storage equipment products are sold through equipment and storage catalogs (some MRO resellers use these as well) and to manufacturing representatives in specialized geographic areas (specific cities or geographic areas not covered by the company's present sales force). The sales force is assigned sales responsibilities based on geographic territories (i.e., East Coast) and/or account type (i.e., MRO accounts).

The new sales manager was hired to boost lagging sales and must have a sales plan for the next 12 months on the CEO's desk in three months from his hiring date. With two months already passed, it is time to put some numbers to the sales forecast and then complete the required sales and marketing plan to present to the executive team at the end of the month. The sales manager has scheduled a sales team retreat to put together next year's sales forecast. He is bringing sales reports from the past two years and has asked all company sales representatives and contract manufacturer representatives to bring specific information, data, and insights from their sales territories to use in constructing a corporate sales forecast. The sales manager is planning to use a variety of qualitative and quantitative approaches for forecast for the next two years.

DISCUSSION QUESTIONS

1. The sales manager is considering using qualitative forecasting methods at the upcoming sales meeting. Explain the four qualitative forecasting techniques, including how qualitative forecasting can add value to quantitative approaches. Also address the challenges relative to using a qualitative technique in forecasting sales for the next two years. Which qualitative approach do you think would be best for the sales manager to use?
2. The sales manager had previous experience with the Delphi method of forecasting and is planning on discussing that method in the retreat. Identify several groups that the sales manager could use with this method. Using today's technology, briefly describe the steps that could be taken to survey a group of experts.
3. The sales manager has been working with the company's information systems team for a full quantitative analysis of historical sales performance to be used to forecast future sales. How could the qualitative forecasting approaches improve the data analysis to be done by the Information Systems team?

Note: Written by Brian Hoyt, Management Professor, Ohio University. This case was prepared solely to provide material for class discussion. The author does not intend to illustrate either effective or ineffective handling of a managerial situation.

VIDEO CASE STUDY

Learn more about ***forecasting and managing demand*** from real organizations that use operations management techniques every day. Amy Keelin and Christine Keelin are COO and CFO (respectively) at MPK Foods, a small family-owned company based in Duarte, California, that produces seasoning mixes sold to grocery stores. Each year MPK is challenged with forecasting demand based on seasonal promotions and market trends. Watch this short interview to find out how they do it.

LITTLEFIELD LABS

LITTLEFIELD LABORATORIES

Demonstrate your understanding of **demand management, forecasting, and aggregate planning** at Littlefield Labs!

Littlefield Laboratories is a highly automated, state-of-the-art blood testing facility for clinics and hospitals. The lab will operate for a limited time frame lasting 210 days. You're asked to step in as the operations manager on Day 30, and are tasked with managing the capacity of the lab with regards to product pricing. Contract prices can be determined on a case-by-case basis and the number of orders accepted at any given time can also be adjusted. Based on historic data, you must buy or sell machines, prioritize queueing, manage the flow of orders, and adjust contract prices in order to optimize capacity and maximize the lab's profits.

Compete against your classmates to prove your understanding of the chapter concepts:

- LO 6-1: Describe the demand management, forecasting, and aggregate planning processes
- LO 6-2: Explain why forecasts are necessary and how they are used
- LO 6-5: Describe the collaborative planning, forecasting, and replenishment process

The team with the most cash in hand at the end of the 210-day time frame wins!

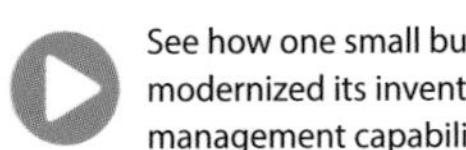
See how one small business modernized its inventory management capabilities

Every company carrying inventories must consider their impact on the firm—too little inventory can lead to stockouts, plant shutdowns, and disgruntled customers. Too much inventory can mean storage problems, inventory write-downs, and excess inventory carrying costs. Thus, inventories can be considered good, but they can also mean higher costs. Operations managers seek to find an optimal balance, then, between inventory effectiveness and cost.

Consequently, managers need to develop effective inventory control procedures. The chapter begins with a discussion of inventory terms, and then presents a number of inventory control topics and procedures. Over time, companies must seek to continuously improve competitiveness through improvements in these inventory management activities. It then becomes necessary to design inventory management performance measures, and these are discussed as the final topic of the chapter.

TYPES OF INVENTORIES

7.1 Describe the types of inventory

As shown in Table 7.1 and described here, inventories can be classified as either raw materials, work-in-process, finished goods, or maintenance, repair, and operating (MRO) supplies.

Most companies have some or all of the following types of inventories. **Raw materials** consist of purchased parts and other materials that are delivered by suppliers and used in the manufacture of finished products or services. Raw materials might include lumber, automobile assemblies, nuts and bolts, plumbing supplies, and hamburger buns. They can be delivered to warehouses or stock areas located within the facility. **Work-in-process** (WIP) inventories are items in some intermediate stage of processing at the firm. When raw materials are put into the production process, they become WIP inventories. They can be stored on the factory floor or possibly on automated overhead racks that move throughout the facility. **Finished goods** are completed products ready for delivery to customers. When WIP inventories are completed, they become finished goods and can be stored at the firm or in geographically dispersed distribution centers. **Maintenance, repair, and operating supplies** (MRO) are purchased items consumed in-house or used to support manufacturing and service processes. Examples include machine tools and maintenance supplies, cleaning supplies, and office supplies.

raw materials Purchased parts and materials that are delivered by suppliers and used in the manufacture of finished products or services.

work-in-process Items in some intermediate stage of processing by the firm.

finished goods Completed products ready for delivery to customers.

maintenance, repair, and operating supplies Purchased items consumed in-house or used to support manufacturing and service processes.

Each of these inventories creates costs, but they can also add significant value for the firm. All four play important roles in the production of high-quality, low-cost products, smoothly running equipment, and satisfied employees and customers. The objective of inventory management, then, should be to find an optimal on-hand quantity for each inventory item, considering its cost, availability, and importance. The various functions of inventory are described next.

Table 7.1 Types of Inventories

Type	Description
Raw materials	Purchased items used in manufactured products or services.
Work-in-process	Items in some intermediate stage of processing at the firm.
Finished goods	Completed products ready for delivery to customers.
Maintenance, repair, and operating supplies	Purchased items consumed in-house or used to support manufacturing and service processes.

FUNCTIONS OF INVENTORY

7.2 Explain the functions of inventory

While inventories keep factories and services running and ensure high levels of customer service, managers must decide how much inventory is enough and which functions of inventory are required. Table 7.2 lists the functions of inventory, and these are described here.

LITTLEFIELD LABS

Demonstrate your understanding of **demand management, forecasting, and aggregate planning** at Littlefield Labs!

Littlefield Laboratories is a highly automated, state-of-the-art blood testing facility for clinics and hospitals. The lab will operate for a limited time frame lasting 210 days. You're asked to step in as the operations manager on Day 30, and are tasked with managing the capacity of the lab with regards to product pricing. Contract prices can be determined on a case-by-case basis and the number of orders accepted at any given time can also be adjusted. Based on historic data, you must buy or sell machines, prioritize queueing, manage the flow of orders, and adjust contract prices in order to optimize capacity and maximize the lab's profits.

Compete against your classmates to prove your understanding of the chapter concepts:

- LO 6-1: Describe the demand management, forecasting, and aggregate planning processes
- LO 6-2: Explain why forecasts are necessary and how they are used
- LO 6-5: Describe the collaborative planning, forecasting, and replenishment process

The team with the most cash in hand at the end of the 210-day time frame wins!

Inventory is money sitting around in another form.

—**RHONDA ADAMS,** president of The Planning Shop and author of books for entrepreneurs[1]

One could argue that inventory management principles can be traced back at least to biblical times as evidenced by the story of Joseph interpreting the Pharaoh's dream as being seven years of plentiful harvests followed by seven years of crop failures and his associated advice to the Pharaoh to stockpile enough harvested grain during the plentiful years to ensure adequate food during the subsequent famine.

—**EDWARD SILVER,** professor emeritus in operations management, University of Calgary[2]

INDEPENDENT DEMAND INVENTORY MANAGEMENT

7

LEARNING OBJECTIVES

After completing this chapter, you should be able to:

7.1 Describe the types of inventory
7.2 Explain the functions of inventory
7.3 Interpret the costs, risks, and value of inventory
7.4 Calculate the EOQ and reorder point under various demand and lead time conditions
7.5 Discuss the importance of inventory management performance measures

Master the content.

edge.sagepub.com/wisner

MANAGING INVENTORY IN THE CLOUD AT USA CYCLING

In 2009, Colorado-based USA Cycling, the official governing body for all U.S.-member competitive cycling, decided to switch from a manual inventory system to an on-demand, cloud-based system. Today, USA Cycling can track the movement of all its inventories among the group's 66,000 members around the world. Keeping track of bikes and associated equipment is not easy. "From our headquarters in Colorado Springs, we were always trying to figure out how much clothing we needed to have in Belgium and Italy and where to pull those items from," says Gregory Cross, director of USA Cycling. "It wasn't unusual for us to get a call from a rider in Europe, asking us what we wanted him to do with a set of racine wheels that he'd had for a few months because we'd lost track of them."

Up until mid-2009, USA Cycling used spreadsheets to record incoming and outgoing items and then shared the information with employees via email. Once the company made the decision to change to the cloud-based system, it brainstormed with employees and surveyed the applications on the market. "We talked to quite a few of the coaches and found out what they wanted and needed," says Cross. "We also worked closely with our director of athletics to brainstorm ideas and figure out how we wanted this system to behave and operate." In the end, it selected an on-demand system due to its customization capabilities and ease of use.

With no previous system in place, USA Cycling started from scratch. To ensure accuracy with its new system, Cross and his team had to count everything and enter each item into the system. "Getting the information into the system for the first time was the hardest part of the implementation—in fact, we're still finding items [around the world] that need to be accounted for," explains Cross. "An athlete will say 'Oh, I have this bike or piece of clothing' and we have to go enter it into the system manually."

Today, when shipments arrive in Colorado Springs, the items are sorted and the information is uploaded to the system. Staff members around the world can immediately view the information and place orders. The time savings compared to the old system are huge. "Now they can just pull up the system, log in, and see where everything is," says Cross.

When a team is prepping for a race, Cross can create shipments of desired clothing and nutritional items. He knows exactly where everything is, how many items USA Cycling has, and can ship whatever the team needs when it needs it, with minimal time investment.[3]

INTRODUCTION

For most organizations, inventory represents a sizeable investment in both time and money. It can also be an extremely complex issue for most manufacturers, as well as their supply chain trading partners. In many cases, businesses may not even be aware of the impact their products and product deliveries have on their customers' products and inventory levels. Thus, managing inventory in the right ways can have beneficial impacts on customer service, competitiveness, and costs.

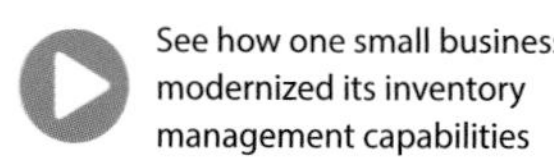
See how one small business modernized its inventory management capabilities

Every company carrying inventories must consider their impact on the firm—too little inventory can lead to stockouts, plant shutdowns, and disgruntled customers. Too much inventory can mean storage problems, inventory write-downs, and excess inventory carrying costs. Thus, inventories can be considered good, but they can also mean higher costs. Operations managers seek to find an optimal balance, then, between inventory effectiveness and cost.

Consequently, managers need to develop effective inventory control procedures. The chapter begins with a discussion of inventory terms, and then presents a number of inventory control topics and procedures. Over time, companies must seek to continuously improve competitiveness through improvements in these inventory management activities. It then becomes necessary to design inventory management performance measures, and these are discussed as the final topic of the chapter.

TYPES OF INVENTORIES

7.1 Describe the types of inventory

As shown in Table 7.1 and described here, inventories can be classified as either raw materials, work-in-process, finished goods, or maintenance, repair, and operating (MRO) supplies.

Most companies have some or all of the following types of inventories. **Raw materials** consist of purchased parts and other materials that are delivered by suppliers and used in the manufacture of finished products or services. Raw materials might include lumber, automobile assemblies, nuts and bolts, plumbing supplies, and hamburger buns. They can be delivered to warehouses or stock areas located within the facility. **Work-in-process** (WIP) inventories are items in some intermediate stage of processing at the firm. When raw materials are put into the production process, they become WIP inventories. They can be stored on the factory floor or possibly on automated overhead racks that move throughout the facility. **Finished goods** are completed products ready for delivery to customers. When WIP inventories are completed, they become finished goods and can be stored at the firm or in geographically dispersed distribution centers. **Maintenance, repair, and operating supplies** (MRO) are purchased items consumed in-house or used to support manufacturing and service processes. Examples include machine tools and maintenance supplies, cleaning supplies, and office supplies.

raw materials Purchased parts and materials that are delivered by suppliers and used in the manufacture of finished products or services.

work-in-process Items in some intermediate stage of processing by the firm.

finished goods Completed products ready for delivery to customers.

maintenance, repair, and operating supplies Purchased items consumed in-house or used to support manufacturing and service processes.

Each of these inventories creates costs, but they can also add significant value for the firm. All four play important roles in the production of high-quality, low-cost products, smoothly running equipment, and satisfied employees and customers. The objective of inventory management, then, should be to find an optimal on-hand quantity for each inventory item, considering its cost, availability, and importance. The various functions of inventory are described next.

Table 7.1 Types of Inventories

Type	Description
Raw materials	Purchased items used in manufactured products or services.
Work-in-process	Items in some intermediate stage of processing at the firm.
Finished goods	Completed products ready for delivery to customers.
Maintenance, repair, and operating supplies	Purchased items consumed in-house or used to support manufacturing and service processes.

FUNCTIONS OF INVENTORY

7.2 Explain the functions of inventory

While inventories keep factories and services running and ensure high levels of customer service, managers must decide how much inventory is enough and which functions of inventory are required. Table 7.2 lists the functions of inventory, and these are described here.

Inventories are held and used by the firm for a number of reasons. **Anticipation inventories** allow demand to be met during periods of expected high demand, such as the busy Christmas selling season or the period of time following a big advertising promotion. **Cycle inventories** are created when the firm purchases or produces in quantities large enough to last until the next purchase or production period. If a company purchases a month's worth of components, this is a cycle inventory. Another example of a cycle inventory would be the economic order quantity, which will be discussed later in this chapter. **Hedge inventories** are used when companies stockpile items to protect against price increases or supply shortages. Airlines, for example, might stockpile fuel if they think the prices are going up. The United States continues to stockpile oil in the Strategic Petroleum Reserve for the same reason. The United States started the reserve in 1975 after the 1973–1974 oil embargo, and as of September 2014, there were 691 million barrels of oil held underground in the reserve's salt dome formations near the Gulf of Mexico. This represents approximately 37 days of oil and $65 billion at 2014 consumption rates and market prices.[4] **Safety stocks** enable the firm to satisfy demand when unforeseen supplier or manufacturing problems occur or when demand is higher than expected. Firms might hold safety stocks of raw materials, WIP, finished goods, or MRO items. And finally, **transportation inventories** are inventories owned by the firm that are in-transit either in-bound to the firm or out-bound to the firm's customers. If a firm purchases parts from a supplier, for example, and chooses to use its own vehicle to transport the shipment to the firm, then the parts become transportation inventory.

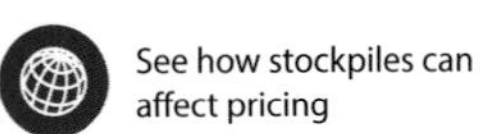
See how stockpiles can affect pricing

Table 7.2 The Functions of Inventory

Function	Description
Anticipation inventories	Allows demand to be met during periods of expected high demand.
Cycle inventories	Created when the firm purchases or produces a quantity large enough to last until the next purchase or production period.
Hedge inventories	Used when companies stockpile items to protect against price increases or supply shortages.
Safety stocks	Held to satisfy demand when unforeseen supplier or manufacturing problems occur, or when demand is higher than expected.
Transportation inventories	Owned by the firm and in-transit, either in-bound to the firm or out-bound to the firm's customers.

As shown here, inventories can serve several functions, all of which create inventory carrying costs. To reduce these costs, operations managers look to reduce any excess inventories within these various functions. Inventory costs are further discussed in the next section.

anticipation inventories These are held so that demand can be met during periods of expected high demand.

cycle inventories Created when the firm purchases or produces a quantity large enough to last until the next purchase or production period.

hedge inventories Used when companies stockpile inventories to protect against price increases or supply shortages.

safety stocks These inventories are held to satisfy demand when delivery or production problems occur, or when demand is higher than expected.

transportation inventories These inventories are owned by the firm and are in-transit either in-bound to the firm or out-bound to the firm's customers.

INVENTORY COSTS, RISKS, AND VALUE

7.3 Interpret the costs, risks, and value of inventory

Inventory costs are considerable for many organizations, such as manufacturing firms and big-box retailers like Walmart. Particularly during the recent economic recession, reducing inventory costs became a financial necessity at many businesses, since as inventory costs are reduced, profits are increased on a dollar-for-dollar basis (but *only* if stockout costs are avoided). Unfortunately, the risk of stockouts does tend to increase as inventory levels are reduced, due to the uncertainties of customer demand and supplier deliveries. Inventory costs can be broken down, as shown in Table 7.3, and are described here.

Order costs are the administrative costs associated with purchasing items. These include the labor and paperwork costs to select a supplier, write a purchase order, process it through the company, transmit it to the supplier, receive the order, inspect it, and then

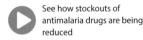

Table 7.3 The Costs of Inventory

Type of Cost	Description
Order cost	The administrative costs associated with purchasing items.
Inventory carrying cost	The costs associated with storing inventories.
Stockout cost	The cost of a lost sale, lost goodwill, or damage to the firm's reputation, as well as lost future sales, and possibly the cost to process a backorder, when no stock is available.
Purchase cost	The actual cost of the items bought from suppliers.

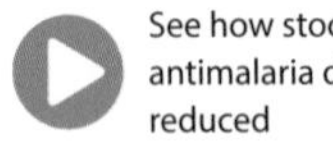
See how stockouts of antimalaria drugs are being reduced

process the invoice. In a recent survey of government offices by the U.S. General Services Administration, it was determined that the average order costs of the respondents were about $111. Interestingly, the same study also found that average order costs were only $29 when office credit cards (or p-cards) were used, and the time required to process paperwork transactions was reduced by two to six weeks.[5] **Inventory carrying costs** are the costs associated with storing inventories. These include warehouse rent or depreciation costs, maintenance and energy costs, warehouse personnel costs, handling costs, equipment depreciation costs, and shrinkage costs. These costs can be quite large for firms with a network of company-owned warehouses or distribution centers. Additionally, inventory carrying costs include lost opportunity costs and capital costs, which are what the firm gives up by having capital tied up in inventory and warehouses. For example, if the firm normally makes a 15% return on its invested capital, then this would be included in the inventory carrying costs. **Stockout costs** occur when the internal or external demand for items cannot be met. Stockout costs include the current lost sale, lost goodwill, or damage to the firm's reputation, lost future sales, and possibly the cost to process a backorder. Backordering incurs administrative costs, expediting costs, and shipping costs. Stockout costs can be very costly to both the buyer and the supplier, particularly if the item is a critical part needed by a highly valued buyer. Generally, stockout costs can be very difficult to estimate, since damage to a firm's reputation and the potential for lost future sales cannot easily be determined. Because of this, managers often resort to using trial-and-error methods when setting safety stock levels. Finally, **purchase cost** is the actual cost of the items bought from suppliers. In many inventory examples, the purchase cost per unit is considered constant. However, when suppliers offer a pricing discount for large-quantity purchases, then the purchase cost becomes variable and is a function of the order quantity. The impact of quantity discounts on inventory policies is discussed later in the chapter.

order costs The administrative costs associated with purchasing items.

inventory carrying costs The costs associated with storing inventories.

stockout costs Encountered when the internal or external demand for items cannot be met.

purchase cost The actual cost of the items bought from suppliers.

iStock/tbabasade

Carrying excess inventories can create a number of problems for the organization.

INVENTORY RISK AND VALUE

As we have somewhat alluded to already, holding too little inventory increases the risk of a stockout and its associated costs. To reduce this risk, the firm can employ more accurate forecasting techniques and use collaborative planning and forecasting techniques with customers to reduce demand uncertainties and the corresponding need to carry safety stock. Ultimately, managers must compare the cost of carrying safety stock to the cost of stocking out.

On the other hand, carrying more inventory means that more customers will be serviced in a timely fashion, creating happy customers and repeat sales. This is then the value of inventory, and cannot be taken lightly. Too often, it seems, managers become fixated on reducing inventory costs as part of a firm-wide cost reduction effort, only to find that stockouts have then increased and customers have started complaining. Today, average retail stockout rates are about 8%, and recent surveys of shoppers indicate that stockouts are the number one shopping annoyance.[6] Firms that can do a good job of managing their inventories—using better forecasts, better communication with customers and suppliers, and better delivery systems—can reduce the cost of inventories without increasing stockouts.

THE BULLWHIP EFFECT

In a supply chain, one potential costly problem associated with forecasting and the use of safety stock is the **bullwhip effect**. Manufacturers producing goods based on demand forecasts will in some cases add safety stock to their planned production schedules to reduce the risk of stockouts. This, in turn, means additional purchases of parts and assemblies from suppliers. Suppliers then unknowingly create their forecasts based on these inflated sales numbers while also adding their own safety stock to their production schedules. In this way, inventories and order sizes continue to become amplified as one moves further back in the supply chain. This inventory amplification problem can add significant costs to all of a supply chain's members, resulting in more expensive end-items for consumers. Additionally, overstock situations are likely to occur, forcing markdowns to unload slow-moving products, and production slowdowns and smaller purchases to reduce inventories. These activities then increase the risk of stockouts. Better planning, information, and inventory management practices will help to reduce these boom-and-bust cycles of the bullwhip effect.

The costs associated with the bullwhip effect can be significant. These include the costs of idle capacity, excess inventory, stockouts, and inflated purchase prices. Several years ago, office supply retailer Staples admitted carrying extra products in its warehouses to fill in for unexpected lapses in deliveries from its suppliers, or for unexpected demand surges. Additionally, Staples' suppliers carried their own levels of safety stock to be able to respond to Staples' demands, as well as all of the demand from other major office supply retailers. Staples and its suppliers found they were losing millions in extra inventory holding costs and lost sales each year.[7]

In the U.S. oil industry, the volatility of oil prices and hence demand over the past 15 years has induced the bullwhip effect. The demand changes cause reverberations in drilling, production, and capacity, which impact demand and storage of oil and gas equipment, turbines, motors, generators, engine electrical equipment, iron castings, and steel. The bullwhip effect costs the oil industry about $2 billion per year. When extrapolated to all oil and gas industry purchases, this "bullwhip tax" adds approximately 10% to the cost of every barrel of oil produced. Equipment and component suppliers bear even more of this cost than oil companies.[8]

INDEPENDENT DEMAND INVENTORY MODELS

7.4 Calculate the EOQ and reorder point under various demand and lead time conditions

Independent demand refers to the external demand for a firm's finished products. The firm forecasts this demand, and then translates these forecasts into aggregate production plans and purchase plans. If the firm is a retailer, then the independent demand forecasts translate directly into purchase plans. When making purchase plans, the firm must decide *when to order* and *how much to order*, and these and other related inventory management topics are covered in the following section.

If the firm is a manufacturer, then the independent demand forecasts are translated internally into all of the parts, assemblies, and materials comprising the finished item. These items are referred to as **dependent demand** items, because their quantities are completely dependent on the quantities of the finished goods produced. For example, if a bicycle manufacturer forecasts an annual bicycle demand of 10,000 units (independent demand), this means it must manufacture 20,000 bicycle rims and purchase 10,000 bicycle seats (dependent

bullwhip effect Forecasts of demand combined with additions of safety stock that tend to amplify purchases from suppliers. As suppliers then make forecasts and also add safety stock, inventories become still more amplified as we move back up the supply chain. This inventory amplification problem can add significant costs to the supply chain.

independent demand The external demand for a firm's finished products.

dependent demand Parts that are required to build end-items and are *dependent* on the external demand of the finished product.

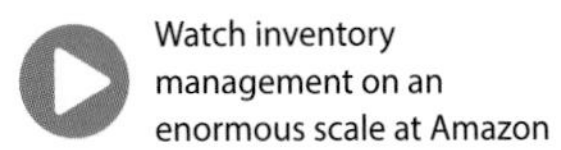
Watch inventory management on an enormous scale at Amazon

demand items). Managing this transformation process and the many dependent demand items are discussed in Chapter 11.

DECIDING HOW MUCH AND WHEN TO ORDER

Management's decision regarding *how many* units to order at one time is based on a knowledge of **total annual inventory costs** (which are the sum of the annual inventory carrying costs, order costs, stockout costs, and purchase costs). The general idea is to find an order quantity that will minimize total annual inventory costs. The decision of *when* to order is based on knowledge of how long orders take to arrive once an order has been placed (the **order lead time**), and how many units are likely to be demanded during the order lead time period. One very basic model in use that provides information for these decisions is the economic order quantity, or fixed order quantity model. The second basic inventory model is the fixed time period model. These are reviewed next.

THE ECONOMIC ORDER QUANTITY MODEL

The basic **economic order quantity** (EOQ) model derives the order quantity that will minimize the sum of the annual inventory holding cost and the annual order cost. The model uses the following assumptions:

- Daily demand is constant.
- Each purchase order arrives in a single delivery at a known delivery date (there are no stockouts).
- The purchase order lead time (the number of days from order until receipt) is known and constant.
- Order costs are known and constant.
- Inventory carrying costs per unit are known and constant.
- There are no purchase quantity discounts (purchase price is constant).

Using these assumptions, it is easy to see that the firm would know *exactly* when its stock levels would be depleted, and know with certainty that a purchasing order would be delivered *exactly* when it is expected. Also, since there are no purchase quantity discounts allowed with the basic EOQ model, then the annual purchase cost will remain constant regardless of the quantity ordered each time. Thus, the relevant total annual inventory cost reduces to the sum of the annual inventory carrying cost and the annual order cost. While these assumptions are obviously unrealistic, many firms still use the EOQ calculation when ordering from suppliers, due to its simplicity and ability to result in an order quantity that comes fairly close to minimizing inventory costs, even in real-world situations. Figure 7.1 shows the important EOQ model information.

As shown in Figure 7.1, the constant economic order quantity, Q, arrives every Q/d days (where d is the constant daily demand), and is depleted at the constant daily demand rate. The order lead time is constant and equal to L. The **reorder point**, or ROP, is the inventory on-hand needed to satisfy demand during the order lead time period, and is equal to $d \times L$. No safety stock is required, since the new order is timed to arrive exactly when the inventory on-hand reaches zero. Finally, the average inventory level is $Q/2$, which is the average of the maximum inventory, Q, and the minimum inventory, zero. With this information, it is then possible to calculate the annual order cost, O, which is:

$$O = \frac{D}{Q}S,$$

where D = annual demand (units/year),

Q = purchase order quantity (units), and

S = cost of one purchase order ($).

Note also that D/Q = the number of orders per year, and that Q/d = the number of days between orders.

total annual inventory costs The sum of the annual inventory carrying costs, order costs, stockout costs, and purchase costs.

order lead time The time from order receipt to delivery to the customer.

economic order quantity The order quantity that will minimize the sum of the annual inventory holding cost and the annual order cost.

reorder point The inventory on-hand needed to satisfy demand during the order lead time period.

Figure 7.1 The EOQ Model

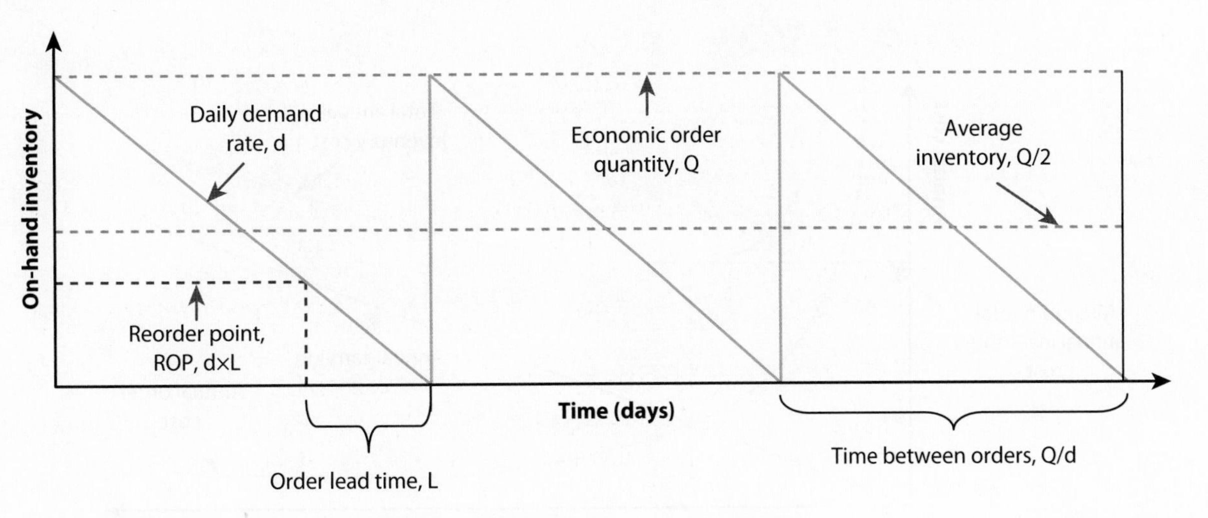

The annual inventory carrying cost, *I*, is:

$$I = \frac{Q}{2} iC,$$

where Q = purchase order quantity (units),

i = carrying cost rate per unit per year (%/year), and

C = purchase cost of one unit ($/unit).

The relevant total annual inventory cost for the EOQ model is then $O + I$. Figure 7.2 shows the relationship between the annual order cost, the annual inventory carrying cost, and the total annual inventory cost.

As shown in Figure 7.2, the minimum total annual inventory cost and the EOQ are found at the point where the annual order cost equals the annual inventory carrying cost. Thus, the expression for the EOQ can be found by setting the annual order cost equal to the annual inventory carrying cost, as follows:

$$\frac{D}{Q} S = \frac{Q}{2} iC, \text{ or}$$

$$Q^2 = \frac{2SD}{iC}, \text{ or}$$

$$\text{EOQ} = \sqrt{\frac{2SD}{iC}}.$$

Note also the flatness of the total inventory cost curve around the minimum point in Figure 7.2. This characteristic is what allows managers to use the EOQ even though demand, order lead time, order cost, and carrying cost may not necessarily be constant. Due to this flatness of the total inventory cost curve around the minimum point, the EOQ model is said to be a **robust model**. Example 7.1 provides a general inventory problem for a company such as a retailer, illustrating all of the relevant inventory equations.

robust model Refers to the flatness of the total inventory cost curve, which means the EOQ model can be used in a variety of situations.

Knowing how much to order from suppliers and when to order is certainly important, since having too much inventory is costly from a carrying cost perspective, and having too

Figure 7.2 Inventory Costs and the EOQ

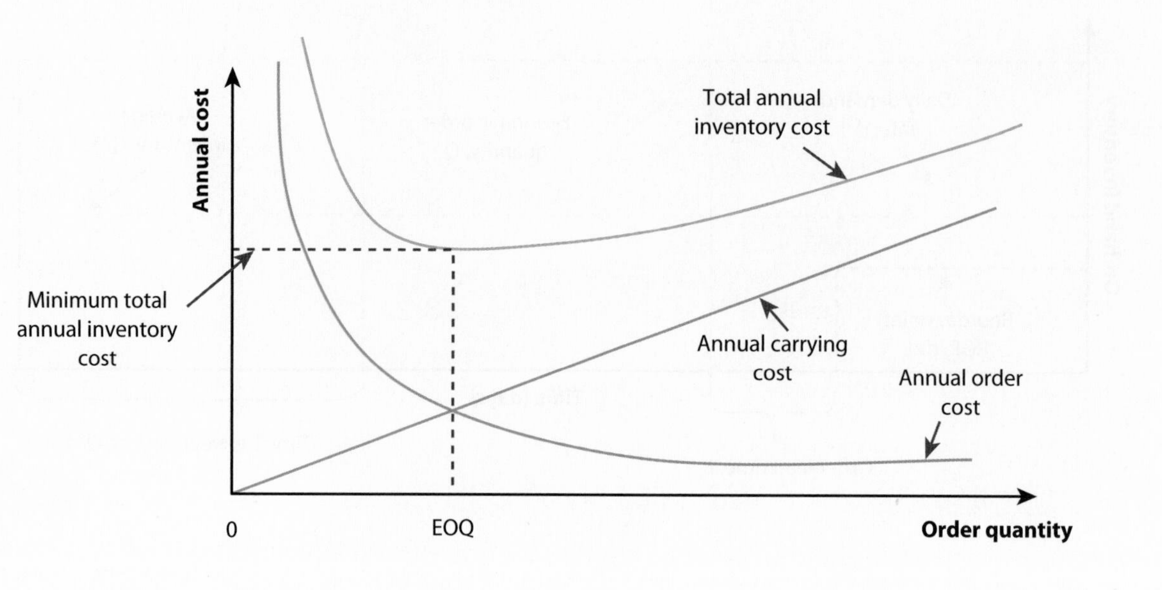

little results in stockouts and lost sales. It is also important from a supply chain management perspective, since being unable to supply a key business customer can result in stockouts for them and potentially a plant shutdown. Furthermore, ordering in an unpredictable or random fashion from key suppliers can worsen the bullwhip effect. Recall that the order fulfillment process is considered one of the key supply chain processes described in Chapter 1. The following segment discusses several extensions of the EOQ model.

Example 7.1
Solving a Standard Inventory Problem at a Retailer

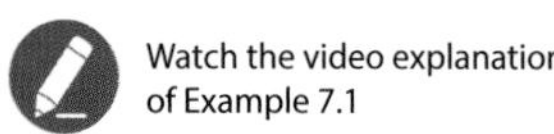
Watch the video explanation of Example 7.1

The Hayley-Girl Beret Shop would like to determine optimal inventory policies for ordering berets from its beret supplier. The owner assumes that annual beret demand is a constant 5,000 berets. The order cost is \$100, the carrying cost rate is 30% per year, the purchase cost is \$40 per beret, and the order lead time is seven days. The optimal order quantity in whole units is:

$$\text{EOQ} = \sqrt{\frac{2SD}{iC}} = \sqrt{\frac{2(100)(5000)}{.3(40)}} = \sqrt{83{,}333.3} = 289 \text{ units}$$

The annual order cost is:

$$\text{O} = \frac{D}{Q}S = \frac{5000}{289}(100) = \$1{,}730.10$$

The annual inventory carrying cost is:

$$\text{I} = \frac{Q}{2}iC = \frac{289}{2}.3(40) = \$1{,}734.00.$$

Note here that O and I are not equal, because the EOQ has been rounded off to a whole number of units, as would be the case in a real situation involving an order of hats. The relevant total annual inventory cost is:

$$\text{T} = \text{O} + \text{I} = \$1730.10 + \$1734 = \$3464.10.$$

This does not include the annual purchase cost of \$200,000, which remains constant regardless of the order policy. The number of orders the Hayley-Girl Beret Shop will make per year are:

$$n = \frac{D}{EOQ} = \frac{5000}{289} \approx 17 \text{ orders.}$$

The number of days between orders is:

$$t = \frac{EOQ}{d} = \frac{289}{5000/365} \approx 21 \text{ days}$$

The reorder point is:

$$\text{ROP} = d \times L = \frac{500}{365}(7) \approx 96 \text{ units.}$$

So, the optimal order policy is for the owner to order 289 berets whenever the on-hand inventory reaches 96 berets. Seven days later the order will arrive, just as the stock of berets is running out. The owner should check on-hand inventory and potentially order every 21 days.

A spreadsheet can also be used to calculate the statistics as shown here:

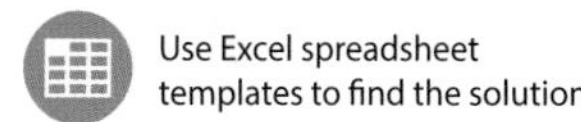

Use Excel spreadsheet templates to find the solution

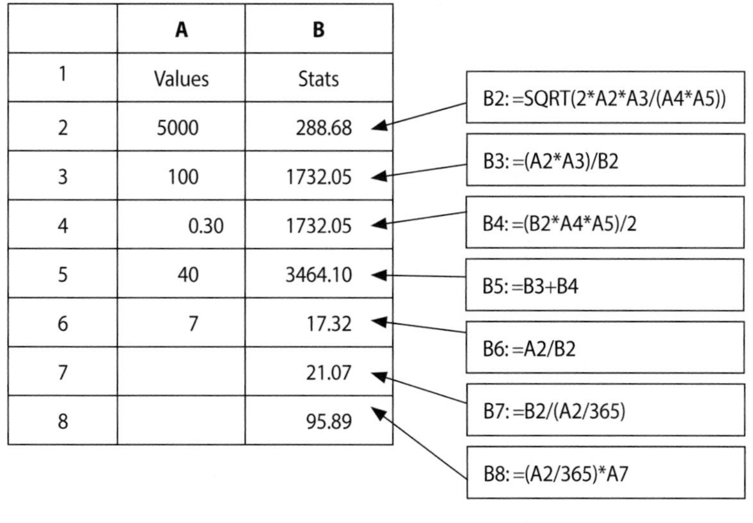

	A	B
1	Values	Stats
2	5000	288.68
3	100	1732.05
4	0.30	1732.05
5	40	3464.10
6	7	17.32
7		21.07
8		95.89

B2: =SQRT(2*A2*A3/(A4*A5))

B3: =(A2*A3)/B2

B4: =(B2*A4*A5)/2

B5: =B3+B4

B6: =A2/B2

B7: =B2/(A2/365)

B8: =(A2/365)*A7

EXTENSIONS OF THE EOQ MODEL

Allowing Purchase Price to Vary

One of the common extensions of the EOQ is when the purchase price is allowed to vary—for instance, when quantity discounts are offered by a supplier. In this case, the **quantity discount model** can be used, and is illustrated in Figure 7.3. The supplier may offer several discounted prices, depending on the purchase quantity, resulting in several total cost curves, shown in Figure 7.3. Operations managers must then consider each of the purchase prices, along with the impact on total annual costs when determining the optimal order policy. With a varying purchase price, the relevant equation for the total annual inventory cost becomes:

$$T = O + I + P,$$

where O = annual order cost,

I = annual inventory carrying cost, and

P = annual purchase cost.

quantity discount model
An extension of the EOQ to be used when the purchase price is allowed to vary—for instance, when quantity discounts are offered by a supplier.

Figure 7.3 The Quantity Discount Model

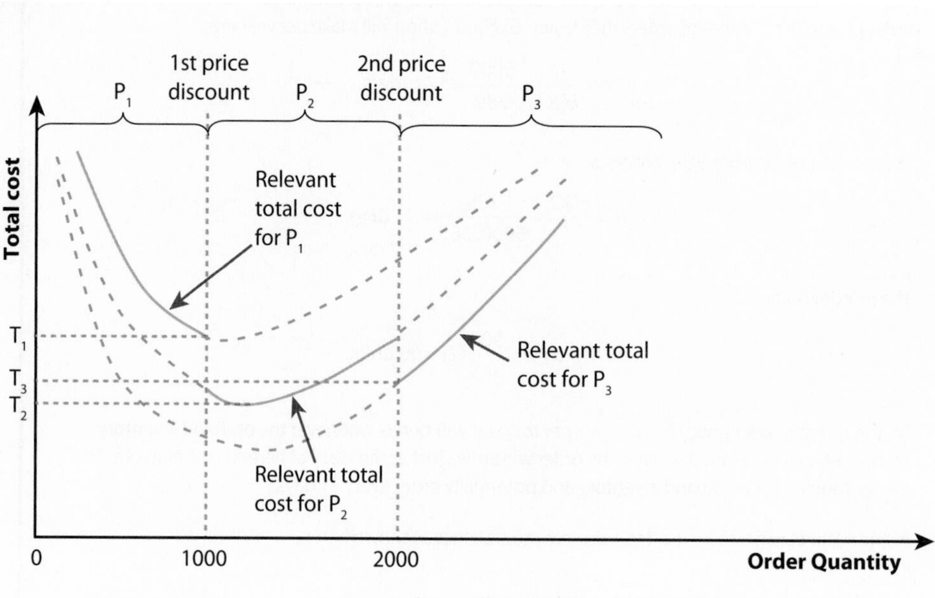

A final note here regarding discounted pricing might be warranted. Firms may opt to purchase fewer items and forgo a quantity discount to reduce obsolescence costs and theft, or perhaps because they don't want to use precious storage space. Also, suppliers today are moving toward greater use of "everyday low pricing" to avoid inventory buildups and sell-offs, which also reduces the bullwhip effect. Recently, retailer J. C. Penney moved to everyday low pricing in part to reduce expenditures on promotions—it expects to save about $75 million per year on promotions with its "fair and square" pricing approach.

As shown in Figure 7.3, two discounts are offered, resulting in three potential purchase prices—P1 is the purchase price if fewer than 1,000 units are purchased; P2 corresponds to a purchase quantity between 1,000 and 1,999 units; and P3 is the price paid when ordering 2,000 or more units at one time. Thus, three total cost curves are shown, with the solid orange lines corresponding to the actual total annual inventory costs when various quantities are ordered. Note that T1, T2, and T3 represent the minimum total annual inventory costs associated with each of the three purchase prices. Also note that if more than 2,000 units are ordered, the corresponding EOQ for that price cannot be used, since that quantity would fall at the minimum point of the curve, which is between 1,000 and 2,000. Instead, the minimum total inventory cost when paying P3 would fall at the minimum quantity to get that discount.

Example 7.2 illustrates the determination of the optimal order quantity, using several purchase quantity discounts. Note that in this example, the optimal purchase quantity was not one of the calculated EOQs. Instead, the buyer would prefer purchasing 500 units at a time, in order to pay $65 per unit. In this case, the savings in annual purchase cost more than offset the additional carrying cost when using the discounted price of $65 per unit and ordering 500 units at a time.

probabilistic demand reorder point model When variable demand exists, this model assumes the purchase lead time to be constant; however, the time between orders would vary. The model says to order the EOQ whenever the inventory on-hand reaches the reorder point level.

ALLOWING DEMAND TO VARY

If demand is allowed to vary, then the possibility of a stockout exists, and inventory policies must include the use of safety stocks. Demand in this case must be specified using a probability distribution. Managers can still calculate an EOQ using the average annual demand, and this quantity can still be ordered; however, the reorder point, or ROP, will have to include safety stock. Figure 7.4 presents the **probabilistic demand reorder point model**,

Example 7.2
Finding the Optimal Order Quantity When Quantity Discounts Are Offered

Watch the video explanation of Example 7.2

The Ceejay Software Company purchasing agent needs to determine the lowest total annual cost order quantity for a particular high-selling software product. The manufacturer is offering several pricing incentives to encourage bulk-buying. The pricing alternatives are:

- $75 per unit for 1–499 units purchased,
- $65 per unit for 500–999 units purchased, and
- $60 per unit for 1,000 or more units purchased.

Ceejay's average order cost is $75 per order, the forecasted annual demand for the product is 850 units, and the inventory carrying cost rate is 35% per year. The Ceejay purchasing agent first calculates the EOQ for each of the three purchase prices:

$$EOQ_1 = \sqrt{\frac{2(850)(75)}{0.35(75)}} = 70 \text{ units}$$

$$EOQ_2 = \sqrt{\frac{2(850)(75)}{0.35(65)}} = 75 \text{ units}$$

$$EOQ_3 = \sqrt{\frac{2(850)(75)}{0.35(60)}} = 78 \text{ units}$$

Since only EOQ_1 is a valid order quantity (both of the other EOQs are below the minimum to get a discount), the purchasing agent must use EOQ_1 to calculate T_1, the total annual inventory cost for the $75 per unit alternative, and then use the minimum order quantities when calculating the other two annual inventory costs. The total annual inventory costs are then:

$$T_1 = O_1 + I_1 + P_1 = \frac{850(75)}{70} + \frac{70(0.35)(75)}{2} + 850(75) = \$911 + \$919 + \$63{,}750 = \$65{,}580,$$

$$T_2 = O_2 + I_2 + P_2 = \frac{850(75)}{500} + \frac{500(0.35)(65)}{2} + 850(65) = \$128 + \$5{,}688 + \$55{,}250 = \$61{,}066, \text{ and}$$

$$T_3 = O_3 + I_3 + P_3 = \frac{850(75)}{1000} + \frac{1000(0.35)(60)}{2} + 850(60) = \$64 + \$10{,}500 + \$51{,}000 = \$61{,}564.$$

So it is seen that the lowest cost inventory policy is to purchase 500 units each order, and the purchase price will be $65 per unit, resulting in a total annual inventory cost of $61,066.

This problem can also be solved using a spreadsheet:

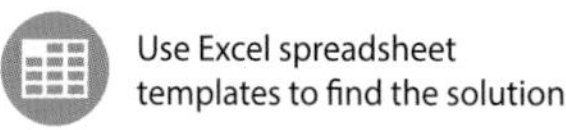
Use Excel spreadsheet templates to find the solution

	A	B	C	D
1	Data	EOQ Calcs	Order Sizes	Total Inventory Costs
2	75	69.69	70	65579.46
3	65	74.86	500	61065
4	60	77.92	1000	61563.75
5	850			
6	75			
7	0.35			

B2: = SQRT(2*A5*A6/(A7*A2))

D3: = (A5*A6/C3)+(C3*A7*A3/2)+(A5*A3)

where a variable demand situation is illustrated. This model still assumes the purchase order lead time to be constant; however, the time between orders would vary, since orders are made whenever the inventory on-hand reaches the reorder point level. The order policy for this situation thus becomes: *order the EOQ whenever the reorder point is reached.*

Figure 7.4 The Probabilistic Demand Reorder Point Model

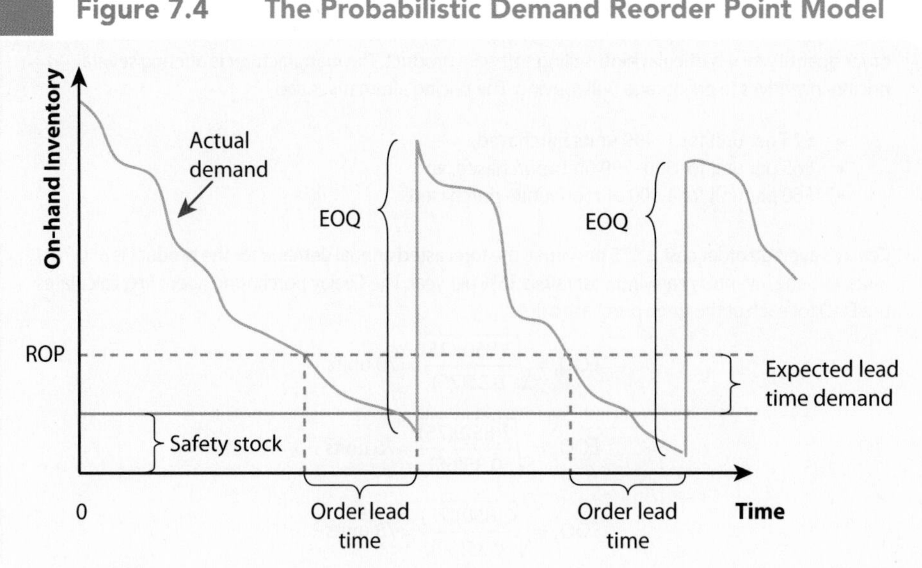

The probabilistic demand ROP is determined by the following:

$$\text{ROP} = \text{lead time demand} + \text{safety stock} = \bar{d}(\text{L}) + \text{Z}(\sigma_{\text{L}})$$

where $\bar{d}$ = average daily demand,

L = purchase order lead time,

Z = number of standard deviations required for a desired service level, and

σ_L = standard deviation of lead time demand.

Note that this formulation for the ROP is somewhat different than the ROP used with the classical EOQ model. In the classical model, the ROP is set equal to the lead time demand. Now, with variable demand, a safety stock component must be added to the ROP, to help ensure that the firm will not stockout while waiting on an order to be delivered from the supplier. The following segment describes how to find *Z*.

Figure 7.5 Variable Demand, the ROP, Safety Stock, and the Service Level

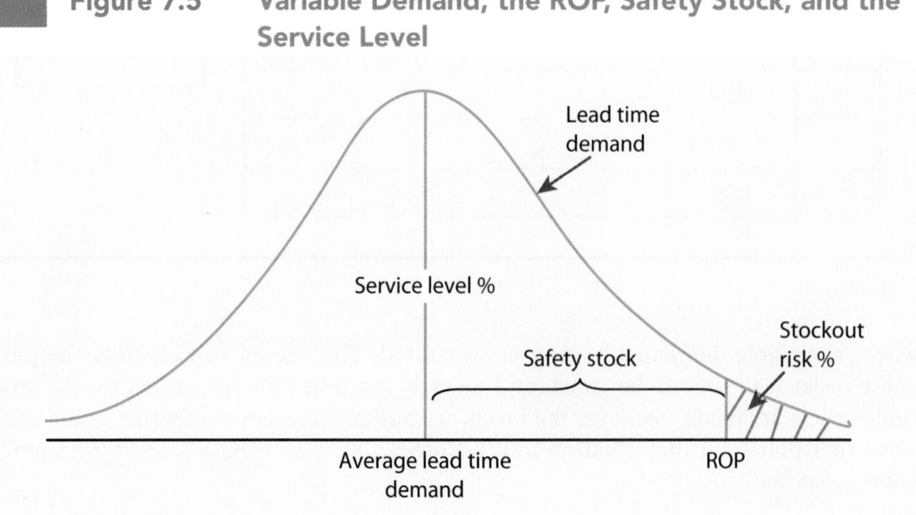

Determining Z

The level of safety stock used depends on the desired **service level**. Service level is generally defined as the percent of time the firm does not want to stockout during the order lead time period, or the area under the demand distribution that is covered by, or to the left of, the ROP, as shown in Figure 7.5. The value for Z is determined based on this desired service level. Assuming a normal distribution of lead time demand, Table 7.4 can be used to find the appropriate Z for a desired service level. Note that if the ROP from the classical EOQ was used with varying demand, the corresponding service level would only be 50%, and the firm would expect to become stocked out 50% of the time, while waiting on an order to be delivered. Example 7.3 provides the calculations for the probabilistic demand ROP.

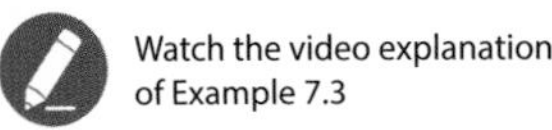

Example 7.3
Calculating the Probabilistic Demand ROP

John and Janie's Hawg Heaven store sells Harley-Davidson accessories, and it wants to calculate an appropriate ROP for many of its items. Its Harley T-shirts are one such example. The annual forecast for these T-shirts is 4,500 shirts. The lead time for T-shirt purchases is always six days. The daily demand for Harley T-shirts varies, and John and Janie's has calculated the standard deviation of lead time demand to be approximately 15 shirts. The store desires to have a 95% service level. Assuming it is open 300 days per year, then:

$$\text{ROP} = \bar{d}(L) + Z\sigma = \frac{4500}{300}(6) + 1.64(15) = 90 + 24.6 = 115 \text{ shirts.}$$

The Z-value is found using Table 7.4, and searching for an area under the curve as close as possible to 0.95 (the service level). The Z is 1.64, and thus the safety stock corresponding to a 95% service level is 25 units. The store's order policy should then be to order the EOQ whenever the stock of T-shirts falls to 115. It would expect that 5% of the time, the store would be stocked out of T-shirts when the supplier arrives.

Watch the video explanation of Example 7.3

Allowing Both Demand and Lead Time to Vary

In an even more realistic model, both demand and purchase order lead times are assumed to vary and be normally distributed. Combining demand variability with lead time variability greatly increases the variance of the joint distribution along with the safety stock needed to ensure a given service level. The new ROP will need to include this safety stock increase. The expected demand during the order lead time is then the average daily demand multiplied by the average lead time, and the variance of lead time demand is the sum of the variances of the daily demand and the lead time. The standard deviation of the lead time demand is then:[9]

$$\sigma_{dLT} = \sqrt{\bar{L}\sigma_d^2 + \bar{d}^2\sigma_L^2}$$

where $\bar{L}$ = average order lead time,

$\bar{d}$ = average daily demand,

σ_d^2 = variance of daily demand, and

σ_L^2 = variance of order lead time.

The **probabilistic demand and lead time reorder point model** can then be expressed as:

$$\text{ROP} = \bar{d}(\bar{L}) + Z\sqrt{\bar{L}\sigma_d^2 + \bar{d}^2\sigma_L^2}\,.$$

The Z-value in the ROP calculation is again found in Table 7.4, given a desired service level. Example 7.4 provides a calculation of the probabilistic demand and lead time ROP.

service level The percentage of time the firm does not want to stockout during the order lead time period, or the area under the demand distribution that is covered by, or to the left of, the ROP.

probabilistic demand and lead time reorder point model When variable demand and variable lead time exist, the model says to order the EOQ whenever the inventory on-hand reaches the reorder point level.

Table 7.4 Z-Values for Areas Under the Normal Curve

Z	00	.01	.02	.03	.04	.05	.06	.07	.08	.09
.5	.69146	.69497	.69847	.70194	.70540	.70884	.71226	.71566	.71904	.72240
.6	.72575	.72907	.73237	.73536	.73891	.74215	.74537	.74857	.75175	.75490
.7	.75804	.76115	.76424	.76730	.77035	.77337	.77637	.77935	.78230	.78524
.8	.78814	.79103	.79389	.79673	.79955	.80234	.80511	.80785	.81057	.81327
.9	.81594	.81859	.82121	.82381	.82639	.82894	.83147	.83398	.83646	.83891
1.0	.84134	.84375	.84614	.84849	.85083	.85314	.85543	.85769	.85993	.86241
1.1	.86433	.86650	.86864	.87076	.87286	.87493	.87698	.87900	.88100	.88298
1.2	.88493	.88686	.88877	.89065	.89251	.89435	.89617	.89796	.89973	.90147
1.3	.90320	.90490	.90658	.90824	.90988	.91149	.91309	.91466	.91621	.91774
1.4	.91924	.92073	.92220	.92364	.92507	.92647	.92785	.92922	.93056	.93189
1.5	.93319	.93448	.93574	.93699	.93822	.93943	.94062	.94179	.94295	.94408
1.6	.94520	.94630	.94738	.94845	.94950	.95053	.95154	.95254	.95352	.95449
1.7	.95543	.95637	.95728	.95818	.95907	.95994	.96080	.96164	.96246	.96327
1.8	.96407	.96485	.96562	.96638	.96712	.96784	.96856	.96926	.96995	.97062
1.9	.97128	.97193	.97257	.97320	.97381	.97441	.97500	.97558	.97615	.97670
2.0	.97725	.97784	.97831	.97882	.97932	.97982	.98030	.98077	.98124	.98169
2.1	.98214	.98257	.98300	.98341	.98382	.98422	.98461	.98500	.98537	.98574
2.2	.98610	.98645	.98679	.98713	.98745	.98778	.98809	.98840	.98870	.98899
2.3	.98928	.98956	.98983	.99010	.99036	.99061	.99086	.99111	.99134	.99158
2.4	.99180	.99202	.99224	.99245	.99266	.99286	.99305	.99324	.99343	.99361
2.5	.99379	.99396	.99413	.99430	.99446	.99461	.99477	.99492	.99506	.99520
2.6	.99534	.99547	.99560	.99573	.99585	.99598	.99606	.99621	.99632	.99643
2.7	.99653	.99664	.99674	.99683	.99693	.99702	.99711	.99720	.99728	.99736
2.8	.99744	.99752	.99760	.99767	.99774	.99781	.99788	.99795	.99801	.99807
2.9	.99813	.99819	.99825	.99831	.99836	.99841	.99846	.99851	.99856	.99861
3.0	.99865	.99869	.99874	.99878	.99882	.99886	.99889	.99893	.99896	.99900

In all of the models discussed so far, the order quantity has been constant and equal to the EOQ. Even though the EOQ was derived assuming constant demand, constant lead time, constant pricing, and the other assumptions listed earlier, the EOQ can nevertheless be used in more real-world situations as illustrated in Example 7.4. In these realistic cases, the order policy has been to order the EOQ whenever the reorder point is reached. This assumes that the inventory manager is continuously tracking inventory levels, using, for example, bar codes on units of product and scanners linked to computers, which keep a running tally of inventory. This may not always be feasible. Let's now explore the periodic review model.

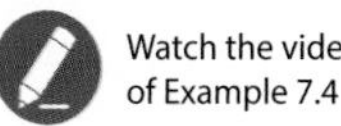

Example 7.4
Calculating the Probabilistic Demand and Lead Time ROP

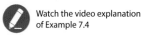

Watch the video explanation of Example 7.4

The Jay and Stella T-Shirt Depot desires to use an ROP for the various T-shirts it sells. The purchase order lead time varies, with an average of six days and a standard deviation of two days. The daily demand also varies, with an average of 15 shirts per day and a standard deviation of 3 shirts per day. It would like to maintain a 95% service level. The corresponding Z-value is 1.64, and the ROP is:

$$\text{ROP} = \bar{d}(\bar{L}) + Z\sqrt{\bar{L}\sigma_d^{\,2} + \bar{d}^2\sigma_L^{\,2}}$$

$$= 15(6) + 1.64\sqrt{6(3)^2 + (15)^2(2)^2} = 90 + 1.64(30.89) \approx 141 \text{ shirts}$$

The safety stock for this situation is 51 shirts, and the order policy is to order the EOQ whenever the stock level gets down to 141 shirts.

THE PERIODIC REVIEW MODEL

In some cases, it is more practical to order variable quantities at some fixed time interval. For instance, a supplier representative might visit a retailer on a weekly or monthly basis, count inventories of the various products the supplier sells, then order a quantity large enough to satisfy demand until the next visit by the sales representative. For relatively stable demand, low-profit items, or cases when stockout costs are fairly low, it may make sense to forgo the costs of bar codes, scanners, and computers to continually track inventories so as to identify the ROP.

Consider, for example, a vending machine operator. She visits the machines weekly and fills each item to some predetermined level based on demand histories, so that inventories will last until the following week. This is essentially describing the **periodic review model**. Assuming variable demand, this model uses a variable order quantity at fixed reorder periods (whereas the reorder point model uses a fixed order quantity at variable reorder periods). Additionally, safety stocks for the periodic review model are higher when compared to the reorder point model. When using the reorder point model, stock levels are monitored continuously, and an order is placed when the ROP is reached. Thus, the only time a stockout can occur is during the order lead time period. With the periodic review model, inventory is counted only at the specified review period, when an order is then placed. If demand were to be unexpectedly large soon after the order was placed, then a stockout could occur and go unnoticed until the next review period. Thus, a stockout could occur during the review period or the order lead time period. Consequently, more safety stock must be utilized for the periodic review model.

Deriving the Periodic Review Model Calculations

Figure 7.6 illustrates the periodic review model using a review period of P, an order lead time of L, varying order quantities of Q_i, an order-up-to or target quantity T, and probabilistic demand. Note in the figure that inventory is depleted, creating a stockout prior to the arrival of Q_2.

The Review Period

The **optimal review period** is found by using the average daily demand and the EOQ, then calculating P as:

$$P = \frac{\text{EOQ}}{\bar{d}}$$

Where P = review period (in days), and

$\bar{d}$ = average daily demand.

Recall this equation was used in the EOQ section to calculate days between orders. A review period of this magnitude should result in low inventory monitoring and stockout costs (note here that the EOQ is still being used, which further supports the importance of the EOQ).

periodic review model Assuming variable demand, this model uses a variable order quantity at fixed reorder periods. Requires higher safety stock levels than the reorder point models.

optimal review period Used for the periodic review model. It is found by dividing the EOQ by the average daily demand.

Figure 7.6 The Periodic Review Model

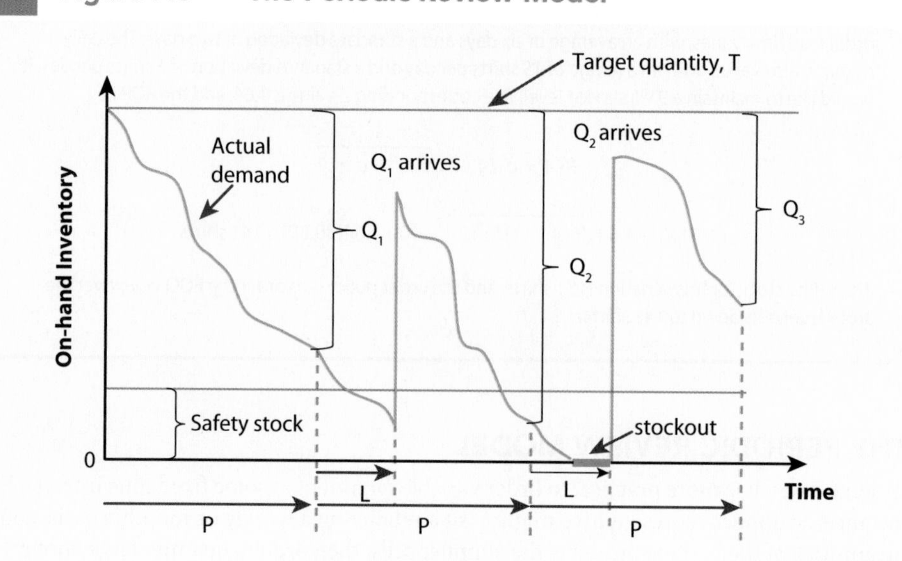

Safety Stock

Using the periodic review model, inventory is counted every P days, an order Q_i is placed, and the order arrives in L days. Since a stockout can occur at any time during the P+L period, the safety stock required is:

$$\text{Safety stock} = Z(\sigma_{P+L})$$

where Z = number of standard deviations required for a desired service level,

P = review period,

L = purchase order lead time, and

σ_{P+L} = standard deviation of (fixed review period + lead time) demand.

Normally, the standard deviation of the daily demand distribution is readily available. This can be used to generate σ_{P+L}, by assuming that the variance of the demand during the P+L days of time will be the sum of the variances of the P+L identical and independent daily distributions of demand, or:

$$\sigma_1^2 + \sigma_1^2 + \sigma_1^2 + \ldots = (P+L)\,\sigma_1^2$$

where σ_1^2 = variance of daily demand. Finally, the standard deviation of demand during P+L days of time is:

$$\sigma_{P+L}\sqrt{(P+L)\sigma_1^2} = \sqrt{(P+L)}\sigma_1$$

Target Quantity

The inventory manager must determine an order-up-to or **target inventory level** using the average daily demand and its standard deviation, so that a stockout situation can be avoided most of the time. Using the above-defined variables, this target quantity can be expressed as:

$$T = \bar{d}\,(P+L) + Z(\sigma_{P+L})$$

Order Quantity

target inventory level The order-up-to level when using the periodic review model.

The order quantity Q_i, varies based on the inventory on-hand when each review period occurs. Thus, to determine the order quantity, the current inventory level is counted and subtracted from the target quantity T:

$$Q_i = T - K_i$$

Where Q_i = order quantity in review period i, and

K_i = inventory on-hand in review period i.

Example 7.5 illustrates the use of the periodic review model.

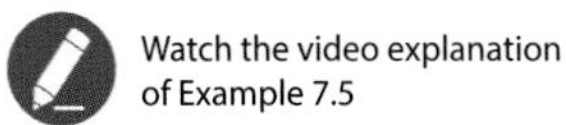

Example 7.5 Using the Periodic Review Model

Watch the video explanation of Example 7.5

The Budget T-Shirt store wants to use a periodic review system for its basic T-shirt. The shirt has an annual demand forecast of 4,500 shirts. Its order cost is \$50, and its inventory carrying cost is 15% per dollar per year. The cost of each shirt is \$10. The purchase order lead time is six days and the average daily demand is 15 shirts, with a daily standard deviation of 3 shirts. They wish to use the optimal review period. Budget T-Shirt would like to maintain a 95% service level (the corresponding Z-value is 1.64, from Table 7.4).

The $EOQ = \sqrt{\frac{2SD}{iC}} = \sqrt{\frac{2(50)(4500)}{.15(10)}} = 548; P = \frac{EOQ}{\bar{d}} = \frac{548}{15} \approx 37$ days. Its target inventory level is:

$$T = \bar{d}(P+L) + Z(\sigma_{P+L}) = 15(43) + 1.64\sqrt{43}(3) = 645 + 32.3 \approx 677$$

Therefore, Budget T-Shirt's periodic review policy should be to count its basic T-shirts every 37 days, then order (677 – K) shirts. Six days later, its order will arrive.

ABC INVENTORY CLASSIFICATION

ABC inventory classification An approach used to help companies manage their independent demand inventories. The idea is to pay closer attention to items accounting for a larger percentage of the firm's annual spend. The Class A items (the most important) represent about 20% of inventory SKUs and account for perhaps 80% of the firm's annual spend.

The **ABC inventory classification** approach is used to help companies manage their independent demand inventories. The idea is to pay closer attention to items accounting for a larger percentage of the firm's annual spend. Typically, the Class A items (the most important) represent about 20% of inventory SKUs and account for perhaps 80% of the firm's annual spend. These items should be monitored closely (counted often) and have adequate levels of safety stock, to ensure the highest service levels. Class B items account for

SERVICE SPOTLIGHT

Managing Inventories Is Like ABC at Metso

iStock/gornostaj

Brazilian energy company Petrobras recently agreed to let Finland-based valve manufacturer Metso manage Petrobras's valve and spare parts inventories. The deal reflects a growing interest in reducing costs, and inventory represents a large source of tied-up capital for many companies. Since starting its service, Metso has secured about 100 clients.

Metso produces and then stores the inventories and can typically reduce average inventory levels for its clients by about 50% within a year. Customers pay a monthly service fee and a capital fee based on the size of the inventories. Metso holds the inventories at its regional facilities, and delivers on demand at pre-agreed prices.

The agreement allows for different delivery times, based on the criticality of the part. The classifications are Class A—same-day delivery critical items; Class B—next-day delivery; Class C—four- to five-day delivery; and Class D—factory delivery, for remaining parts.

All projects start with an analysis of the client's valve assemblies to establish adequate inventories for every valve in the facility. In many cases, even though a firm may have a large valve inventory at the start of a project, it might stock out of 40–50% of the valves used, particularly if unexpected events occur. It also might find many older valve models in inventory. Over time, Metso replaces these with the latest models. Typically, after the first year, valve inventories are down significantly.[10]

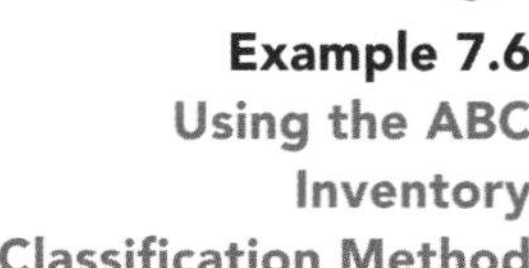

Example 7.6
Using the ABC Inventory Classification Method

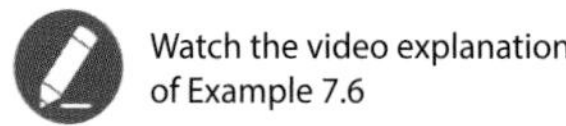

Watch the video explanation of Example 7.6

Blake's Music Emporium had a number of inventory items, and the owner wanted to make sure he had the right inventory policies in place for each item. The 10 items shown here are a representative group of stock items.

Item SKU	Cost/Unit ($)	Forecasted Annual Demand	Projected Annual Spend ($)	Percent of Spend (Class)
000325	26.45	3750	99,187.50	33.1 (A)
001026	12.40	2500	31,000.00	10.3 (B)
000977	4.35	6240	27,144.00	9.1 (B)
000265	2.79	260	725.40	0.2 (C)
001236	145.99	150	21,898.50	7.3 (B)
000635	345.00	300	103,500.00	34.5 (A)
000079	87.35	30	2,620.50	0.9 (C)
001166	146.80	50	7,340.00	2.4 (C)
000439	55.20	100	5,520.00	1.8 (C)
000237	37.16	25	929.00	0.3 (C)
			Total: $299,864.90	

Based on these findings for the upcoming year, Blake classified items 000325 and 000635 as A items; 001026, 000977, and 001236 as B items; and 000265, 000079, 001166, 000439, and 000237 as C items. Blake then decided to increase the safety stocks of the A items and count them more frequently, while doing away with the safety stock of the C items.

The ABC analysis shown above can also be performed using a spreadsheet, as shown here:

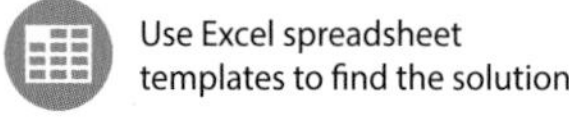

Use Excel spreadsheet templates to find the solution

	A	B	C	D
1	**Cost/Unit**	**Annual Demand**	**Annual Spend**	**% of Spend**
2	26.45	3750	99187.5	33.1
3	12.4	2500	31000.0	10.3
4	4.35	6240	27144.0	9.1
5	2.79	260	725.4	0.2
6	145.99	150	21898.5	7.3
7	345	300	103500.0	34.5
8	87.35	30	2620.5	0.9
9	146.8	50	7340.0	2.4
10	55.2	100	5520.0	1.8
11	37.16	25	929.0	0.3
12		Total	299864.9	

C2: = A2*B2

D2: = C2/C12

D9: = C9/C12

C11: = A11*B11

C12: = SUM(C2:C11)

approximately 15% of annual spend and represent about 30% of inventory SKUs. The B items are moderately important and can be monitored less closely, with lower levels of safety stock. Class C items are the least important to the firm, representing about 50% of the inventory SKUs while accounting for only about 5% of spend. Service levels can be low for these items, and this group represents an area where large savings in inventory carrying costs can be realized. Class C items should only be checked periodically, and safety stock levels should be very low or zero. Many companies today use the ABC method to reduce safety stock inventories and to get rid of slow-moving items. The Service Spotlight on page 199 shows how an ABC system is used by Metso to manage inventories.

Example 7.6 illustrates the ABC inventory classification approach. Notice that the inventory SKU and spend breakdowns do not exactly represent the percentages mentioned in this section. The percentages are only used as guidelines. While this is a managerial decision, it should be fairly obvious in which category each inventory item is placed.

ORDER QUANTITIES AND SAFETY STOCK AMONG SUPPLY CHAIN PARTNERS

In the previous section, the general objective was to minimize the focal firm's total annual inventory costs for a desired service level, which led to the use of the EOQ, the periodic order quantity, and several reorder point formulations, depending on assumptions regarding demand, review period, and order lead time. Safety stock was held to help the firm avoid stockouts when demand was larger than expected, when order lead times were longer than expected, and when the inventory review was not continuous. Each firm acted independently to minimize its annual inventory costs.

When supply chain partners such as the firm's key suppliers and customers are considered, though, the inventory objectives and strategies may be altered somewhat. Safety stock levels tend to be significantly less, since supply chain partners use collaborative planning, forecasting, and replenishment (as discussed earlier, in Chapter 6). Order lead times and demand quantities tend to be more predictable and reliable, which reduces the need for safety stock. In essence, the general idea behind actively managed supply chains is that cooperation, information sharing, inventory visibility, and collaborative planning cause demand and lead time to behave closer to the assumptions used with the classical EOQ model. The final topic of this chapter is tracking inventory management performance, discussed next.

MEASURING INVENTORY MANAGEMENT PERFORMANCE

Discuss the importance of inventory management performance measures

No discussion of inventory management would be complete without considering the tracking of **inventory management performance**. Given the earlier general presentation of operations performance in Chapter 2 and the examination of inventories in this chapter, the performance dilemma associated with inventories should be obvious—the presence of inventories helps to create good customer service, but inventory carrying costs can account for a very large portion of a firm's costs. This balancing act is one that successful firms have mastered—in a recent survey conducted by APQC, a nonprofit, member-based organization specializing in performance analytics and best practices, firms on average spend about 10% of the value of their inventories on carrying costs each year. Interestingly, the most profitable firms spend only 7%, while the least profitable firms spend about 16.5%. These excess carrying costs can amount to millions of dollars each year in lost profits.[11]

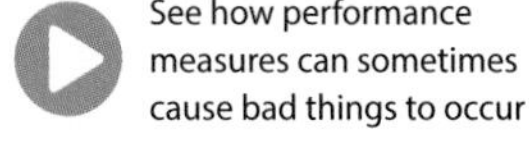

See how performance measures can sometimes cause bad things to occur

Inventory performance measures should assess performance both inside and outside the firm. The dual objectives of maximizing customer service while minimizing inventory costs require close and frequent attention to the policies and tools used when purchasing, processing, and distributing goods and services. Stockouts and excessive carrying costs can become

inventory management performance Measures of how well companies are creating good customer service while keeping inventories low.

MANUFACTURING SPOTLIGHT

Designing a Performance Measurement System at Talan

iStock/Dreef

While a number of fairly common industry performance measures can be found in many successful companies, no standard set of measure exists that is right for every company. Each company must consider what it is looking for, and what it can track that can help it achieve its objectives.

Ohio-based metal stamping firm Talan Products, for example, began forming a set of performance measures when managers and key personnel brainstormed questions like, "What do we need to get better at?" and included discussions of each measure prior to the team making a final selection. In all, it took Talan Products about 12 hours over several days to arrive at a set of performance measures. Its measures included direct labor versus budget, indirect material costs versus budget, inventory turns, controllable costs versus budget, an efficiency measure, scrap costs by workcenter, outbound on-time deliveries, and inbound on-time deliveries.

Over time, Talan Products' measures have changed somewhat, with some dropping out, new ones added, and some staying the same. The company has also started using 12-month moving averages to monitor progress on the measures. The measures are reviewed monthly, with declining measures getting attention. As the company meets performance targets, new ones are set. Use of the performance measurement system has given Talan management a better understanding of the company.[12]

a financial burden to all sizes and types of organizations, and represent an even greater concern for companies trying to maintain and improve competitiveness.

A study performed by Pennsylvania-based Strategic Value Analysis in Healthcare found that for at least one-third of U.S. hospitals, inventories were excessive for a number of reasons. These included the stocking of out-of-date items and low-usage items, carrying too much safety stock, lengthy order lead times, double stocking, and poorly determined EOQs. One of the hospital clients established an inventory reduction program—it generated a list of products that hadn't moved in three months, then held on to the more critical ones while disposing of or returning the rest. Items that were stored for only one department were transferred to the using departments. It analyzed usage patterns and discovered it could order many items more often and in smaller quantities. As a result, the hospital was able to reduce inventories by over $92,000 in the first three months without impacting its customer service capabilities.[13]

As inventory management performance improves, the firm should notice improvements in customer retention, competitiveness, and economic success. The Manufacturing Spotlight above describes how a tooling company designed a useful and company-specific set of performance measures that proved to be very beneficial for the company. A number of useful inventory-oriented performance measures are shown in Table 7.5.[14]

All of the measures shown in Table 7.5 are directly or indirectly related to the firm's ability to manage inventories. The final measure, cash-to-cash cycle time, provides an overall view of the number of days of working capital tied up in managing inventories. For this measure, inventory days of supply (IDS) can be calculated as:

$$\text{IDS} = \frac{(Avg.\ Inventory\ \$)}{(Annualized\,COGS\,/\,365)},$$

the days of receivables outstanding (DRO) can be calculated as:

$$\text{DRO} = \frac{(Avg.\ Receivables\,\$)}{(Annualized\,Credit\ Revenues\,/\,365)},$$

and the days of payables outstanding (DPO) can be calculated as:

$$DPO = \frac{(Avg.\ Payables\$)}{(Annualized\ Materials Costs / 365)}.$$

To interpret the results, the **inventory days of supply** tell management about how long inventory will be held before it is sold. A high IDS indicates too much inventory is being held, which will cause high inventory carrying costs. A low IDS indicates that not enough inventory is being held, which can create stockouts. Some analysts might recommend an IDS of about 40, but this varies based on industry norms.

The **days of receivables outstanding** (also called days of sales outstanding) is used to measure the average number of days it takes a company to collect what is owed to it after a credit sale has been completed. Put in fewer words, it is the average collection period. A low DRO is good, since the faster a company collects cash, the faster it can reinvest that cash to make more sales. Thus, a company with an increasing DRO over time is becoming less efficient, while a company with a decreasing DRO over time is becoming more efficient. A DRO of 40 to 50 might be considered normal.

Days payable outstanding tells about how long it takes a company to pay its creditors, such as suppliers. The longer the firm takes to pay its creditors, the more money the company has on-hand, but the less happy creditors will be. They may refuse to extend credit in the future, or they may offer less favorable payment terms. Again, the DPO varies by industry, but a DPO of about 30 is considered normal.

Cash-to-cash cycle time is commonly viewed as one of the best overall measures of inventory performance. It encompasses a number of contributing activities such as inventory speed, quality, and cost. The CCCT (also called the cash conversion cycle) indicates how long cash is tied up in the main cash-producing and cash-consuming areas: receivables, payables, and inventory. Normally, the lower the CCCT, the better, but too low can indicate low inventories and potential service issues, and very high days might indicate potential supplier issues.

inventory days of supply An inventory performance measure that tells management how long inventory is held before it is sold.

days of receivables outstanding An inventory performance measure that indicates the average number of days it takes a company to collect what is owed to it after a credit sale has been completed.

days payable outstanding An inventory performance measure that tells about how long it takes a company to pay its creditors, such as suppliers.

cash-to-cash cycle time An inventory performance measure indicating how long cash is tied up in the main cash-producing and cash-consuming areas of receivables, payables, and inventory.

Table 7.5 Inventory-Oriented Performance Measures

Performance Measure	Description
Delivery Performance	(Total on-time and full orders)/(Total orders)
Order Fulfillment Lead Time	Average time from customer authorization of sales order to receipt of product
Stockouts	(Number of backorders or stockout complaints)/(Total orders)
Back Order Duration	Average order fulfillment lead time for customer orders not filled in full
Other Lead Time Measures:	
Manufacturing Lead Time	Average manufacturing order start date to order ship date
Warehouse Lead Time	Average warehouse order receipt date to ship date
Shipment Lead Time	Average warehouse ship date to customer receipt date
Response Time	Average time to respond to an unplanned 20% increase or decrease in demand
Total Inventory Management Cost	Includes order management, customer service, warehousing, transportation, purchasing, supplier management, supply/demand planning, inventory holding, and returns/warranty management costs
Cash-to-Cash Cycle Time	(inventory days of supply + days of receivables outstanding) – days of payables outstanding

SUMMARY

This chapter introduced a wide range of inventory management topics, all of which are very important to the continued success of firms and their supply chain trading partners. The chapter discussed the processes, benefits, and challenges of inventory management, beginning with a general discussion of the types and functions of inventory, continuing with discussions of independent demand inventory management methods, and ending with a discussion of monitoring inventory management performance. Effective inventory management practices can enable the firm to reduce costs, while still providing high levels of customer service.

KEY TERMS

ABC inventory classification, 199
Anticipation inventories, 185
Bullwhip effect, 187
Cash-to-cash cycle time, 203
Cycle inventories, 185
Days payable outstanding, 203
Days of receivables outstanding, 203
Dependent demand, 187
Economic order quantity, 188
Finished goods, 184
Hedge inventories, 185
Independent demand, 187
Inventory carrying costs, 186
Inventory days of supply, 203
Inventory management performance, 201
Maintenance, repair, and operating supplies, 184
Optimal review period, 197
Order costs, 186
Order lead time, 188
Periodic review model, 197
Probabilistic demand and lead time reorder point model, 195
Probabilistic demand reorder point model, 192
Purchase cost, 186
Quantity discount model, 191
Raw materials, 184
Reorder point, 188
Robust model, 189
Safety stocks, 185
Service level, 195
Stockout costs, 186
Target inventory level, 198
Total annual inventory costs, 188
Transportation inventories, 185
Work-in-process, 184

FORMULA REVIEW

Annual order cost:

$O=\frac{D}{Q}S$, where D = annual demand (units/year), Q = purchase order quantity (units), and S = cost of one purchase order ($).

Number of orders per year = D/Q.

Number of days between orders = Q/d, where d = daily or average daily demand.

Annual inventory carrying cost:

$I=\frac{Q}{2}iC$, where Q = purchase order quantity (units), i = carrying cost rate per unit per year (%/year), and C = purchase cost of one unit ($/unit).

Economic order quantity:

$EOQ=\sqrt{\frac{2SD}{iC}}$, where S, D, i, C are defined as above.

Constant demand reorder point:

ROP = d(L), where d = constant daily demand and L = purchase order lead time.

Probabilistic demand, constant lead time reorder point:

ROP = $\bar{d}$ (L) + Z(σ_L), where $\bar{d}$ = average daily demand, Z = number of standard deviations required for a desired service level, and σ_L = standard deviation of lead time demand.

Probabilistic demand and lead time reorder point:

$ROP = \bar{d}(\bar{L}) + Z\sqrt{\bar{L}\sigma_d^2 + \bar{d}^2\sigma_L^2}$, where $\bar{L}$ = average order lead time, σ_d^2 = variance of daily demand, and = σ_L^2 variance of order lead time.

Optimal review period for the periodic review model:

$P = \frac{EOQ}{\bar{d}}$, where P = review period (in days), $\bar{d}$ = average daily demand.

Target inventory level for the periodic review model:

$T = \bar{d}(P + L) + Z(\sigma_{P+L})$, where σ_{P+L} = standard deviation of (fixed review period + lead time) demand.

Order quantity for periodic review model:

$Q_i = T - K_i$, where K_i = inventory on-hand in review period i.

Inventory days of supply:

$$IDS = \frac{(Avg.\ Inventory\ \$)}{(Annualized\ COGS / 365)}$$

Days receivables outstanding:

$$DRO = \frac{(Avg.\ Receivables\ \$)}{(Annualized\ Revenues / 365)}$$

Days payables outstanding:

$$DPO = \frac{(Avg.\ Payables\ \$)}{(Annualized\ Materials\ Costs / 365)}$$

Cash-to-cash cycle time:

CCCT = IDS + DRO − DPO

SOLVED PROBLEMS

1. The annual demand forecast at Nena's Shoes is 12,000 pairs. If the order cost is \$50, the average purchase price is \$22, the carrying cost is 25% per year, and the purchase order lead time is 10 days, then:

   a. What is the EOQ size of each order?
   b. How many orders per year will be made?
   c. What is the time between each order?
   d. What is the reorder point?
   e. What is the total annual inventory cost?
   f. What is the order policy?

Answer:

a. $EOQ = \sqrt{\frac{2SD}{iC}} = \sqrt{\frac{2(50)(12000)}{0.25(22)}} = 467$ pairs

b. No. orders per year $= \frac{D}{EOQ} = \frac{12000}{467} = 25.7$ orders

c. Time between orders $= \frac{EOQ}{d} = \frac{467}{12000/365}$
$= 14.2$ days

d. ROP = d × L = (12,000/365)10 = 328.8 pairs.

e. $TIC = O + I = \frac{D}{EOQ}(S) + \frac{Q}{2}iC = 25.7(50)$
$+ \frac{467}{2}(0.25)(22) = 1{,}285 + 1{,}284$
$= \$2{,}569$

f. Order policy is to order 467 pairs of shoes every 14 days or when there are 329 pairs of shoes in stock.

2. The manager at Robert's Cigars wants to determine the lowest cost order policy given the following purchase discounts offered: Cigar costs are \$4 each for orders less than 500; \$3.50 each for orders of 500 – 1,000; and \$3.25 each for orders greater than 1,000. The order cost = \$75; annual demand forecast = 5,500 cigars; inventory carrying cost = 30% per year.

Answer:

Step 1. Determine the 3 EOQs—for \$4 cigars,

$EOQ = \sqrt{\frac{2(75)(5500)}{0.3(4)}} = 829$ (infeasible, since the EOQ must be < 500). For \$3.50 cigars,

$EOQ = \sqrt{\frac{2(75)(5500)}{0.3(3.50)}} = 886$ (feasible range, since EOQ > 500 but < 1000). For \$3.25 cigars,

$$EOQ = \sqrt{\frac{2(75)(5500)}{0.3(3.25)}} = 920 \text{ (infeasible, since}$$

EOQ < 1,000, so must order 1,001 to get the discount).

Step 2. Calculate the total annual inventory costs for the \$3.50 and the \$3.25 cigars:

$$TIC_{3.50} = O + I + P = \frac{D}{EOQ}(S) + \frac{Q}{2}iC +$$
$$D \times C = \frac{5500}{886}(75) + \frac{886}{2}(.3)(3.50)$$
$$+ 5{,}500(3.50) = \$465.58$$
$$+ \$465.15 + \$19{,}250 = \$20.180.73$$

$$TIC_{3.25} = O + I + P = \frac{5500}{1001}(75) + \frac{1001}{2}(.3)(3.25)$$
$$+5500(3.25) = \$412.09 + \$487.99 +$$
$$\$17{,}875 = \$18{,}775.08$$

So the lowest cost order policy is to order 1,001 cigars at a time.

3. Jaimie's Pizza-to-Go makes and delivers pizzas and wants to know the reorder point for pizza boxes, given the following information: Average daily demand is 125 pizzas, with a daily standard deviation of 22 pizzas. The lead time for pizza box purchases is four days. It wants a 98% service level.

Answer:

$$ROP = \bar{d}(L) + Z(\sigma_L) = 125(4) + 2.06(22)(\sqrt{4})$$
$$= 500 + 90.6 = 591$$

4. Taylor's Pizza-Down-and-Dirty makes and delivers pizzas. It wants to know the reorder point for pizza boxes, given the following information: Average daily demand is 125 pizzas, with a daily standard deviation of demand of 22 pizzas; average lead time for pizza boxes is four days, with a lead time standard deviation of two days. It wants a 98% service level.

Answer:

$$ROP = \bar{d}(\bar{L}) + Z\sqrt{\bar{L}\sigma_d^2 + \bar{d}^2\sigma_L^2} = 125(4) +$$
$$2.06\ \sqrt{4(22) + 125^2(2^2)} = 500 +$$
$$2.06(250.2) = 1015$$

5. Luke's Speedy Pizzas uses a pizza box supplier that has a sales rep come by weekly to order boxes. Luke wants a 98% service level. Its average daily demand is 125 pizzas, with a daily standard deviation of demand of 22 pizzas; lead time for pizza boxes is four days. If there are 420 pizza boxes when the rep comes by, how many boxes should be ordered?

Answer:

$$T = \bar{d}(P{+}L) + Z(\sigma_{P+L}) = 125(7+4) + 2.06\left(\sqrt{11}\right)(22) = 1525$$

So the rep should order 1,525 – 420 = 1,105 boxes.

6. Given the information shown in the table below, separate the inventory items using the ABC inventory classification approach.

Answer:

The answer is shown in the orange column of the table shown here. The A-items constitute 58.8% of the annual spend, the B-items were a total of 36.8%, and the C-items were 4.4% of annual spend.

Item SKU	Cost/Unit (\$)	Forecasted Annual Demand	Projected Annual Spend (\$)	Percent of Spend (Class)
108	116.50	322	37,513	2.7 (C)
102	112.40	1500	168,600	12.2 (B)
197	24.13	4922	118,768	8.6 (B)
126	422.95	875	370,081	26.7 (A)
136	240.99	1850	445,832	32.1 (A)
125	555.00	400	222,000	16.0 (B)
179	187.25	120	22,470	1.6 (C)
116	6.80	235	1,598	0.1 (C)
			1,386,862	

7. For the following information, what are the inventory days of supply, days receivables outstanding, days payables outstanding, and cash-to-cash cycle time?

   Inventory on-hand at beginning of the year = \$1.75 million; inventory on-hand at end of the year = \$2.15 million; annual cost of goods sold = \$11.25 million; average annual accounts receivable = \$526,000; annual credit sales = \$15.45 million; beginning of year accounts payable = \$1.3 million; end of year accounts payable = \$1.08 million; total annual purchases = 14.2 million

Answer:

$$\text{IDS} = \frac{(Avg.Inventory\ \$)}{(Annualized\ COGS/365)} = \frac{(1.75+2.15)/2}{11.25/365} = 63.3 \text{ days}$$

$$\text{DRO} = \frac{(Avg.\ Receivables\ \$)}{(Annualized\ Credit\ Revenues/365)} = \frac{526{,}000}{15{,}450{,}000/365} = 12.4 \text{ days}$$

$$\text{DPO} = \frac{(Avg.\ Payables\ \$)}{(Annualized\ Materials\ Costs/365)} = \frac{(1.3+1.08)/2}{14.2/365} = 30.6 \text{ days}$$

$$\text{CCCT} = \text{IDS} + \text{DRO} - \text{DPO} = 63.3 + 12.4 - 30.6 = 45.1 \text{ days}$$

REVIEW QUESTIONS

1. Your boss tells you to buy a one-year supply of toilet paper for the company. What type of inventory is this?
2. List and describe the five functions of inventory.
3. What are all of the various types of inventory costs?
4. List some of the causes of stockouts.
5. Define the bullwhip effect and its impact on supply chain inventories.
6. Define independent and dependent demand, and provide some examples of each.
7. What items are included in total annual inventory costs?
8. Why is the EOQ model described as "robust"?
9. Explain the assumptions of the EOQ model.
10. How do changes in demand, order cost, and carrying cost affect the EOQ?
11. What determines the level of safety stock to be used in the probabilistic demand reorder point model?
12. How is the EOQ used in the periodic review model?
13. What is the ABC inventory classification, and how is it used?
14. Why are inventory management performance measures important?

DISCUSSION QUESTIONS

1. Why do you think inventory is considered a "necessary evil" in organizations?
2. How would you reduce stockout risk at a hospital? At a high-end retailer? At Walmart?
3. Discuss the relationship between the bullwhip effect and supply chain inventories, and what can be done to manage it.
4. Why does the EOQ only seek to minimize annual order cost and annual inventory carrying cost? What happened to stockout cost and purchase cost?
5. How does the quantity discount model differ from the EOQ model? Is the EOQ still used?
6. Why might it be cheaper to order a large quantity of price-discounted merchandise from a supplier rather than the appropriate EOQ amount? Won't the annual carrying cost be prohibitively high?
7. Explain the order policy used when demand is assumed to be variable. Is the EOQ still useful here?
8. In looking at the ROP formula with variable demand, what is the expected service level when Z is zero? What is the safety stock level when Z is zero? What is the maximum value of Z?
9. When both demand and purchase lead time vary, why is the required safety stock higher when compared to the variable demand ROP model, for the same service level?
10. Describe several cases when a periodic review model would be preferred to an ROP model.
11. What can be said about order lead times and safety stocks in actively managed, successful supply chains?
12. Could cash-to-cash cycle time be negative? How? Would that be good?
13. What would be some good inventory management performance measures for a fast-food company? A bicycle repair shop? A big-box retailer?

EXERCISES AND PROJECTS

1. Write a paper on managing the bullwhip effect, and provide examples of companies that have successfully managed theirs.
2. Search the Internet and write a report on five common inventory problems and how companies can avoid these problems.
3. Search the Internet for a publicly held firm with annual reports. Find the balance sheets and income statements, and then calculate and discuss the IDS, DRO, DPO, and CCCT.

PROBLEMS

Use the following information for Problems 1 through 5:

> Kathy owns a neighborhood hot dog stand, and wants to determine some good order policies for hot dogs. She estimates her annual demand to be constant and equal to 10,000 hot dogs. Her order cost is $20, the carrying cost rate is 40% per year, the purchase cost is $0.20 per hot dog, and the order lead time is two days.

1. What is the optimal order quantity?
2. What is the annual order cost?
3. What is the annual inventory carrying cost and the relevant total annual inventory cost?
4. How many orders per year will Kathy make? How many days will there be, between orders?
5. What is the reorder point? What is Kathy's optimal order policy?
6. Using the information in Problem 1, if Kathy's carrying cost rate dropped by half, to 20% per year, how would this impact Problems 1 through 5?
7. Using the information in Problem 1, if Kathy's order cost increased to $100, how does this impact Problems 1 through 5?
8. Find the economic order quantity and the reorder point for the following information: annual demand is 22,500 units; order cost is $70 per order; annual inventory carrying cost is $5 per unit; the order lead time is 10 days; and the business operates 300 days per year.

Use the following information for Problems 9 and 10:

> Grebby's Rodeo Tack & Boots sells gear to rodeo industry customers and has been offered discounts for the purchase of some alligator-hide boots from its longtime boot supplier. The pricing alternatives for the alligator boots are: $62 per pair for 1–299 pair purchased; $57 per pair for 300–599 units purchased; and $54 per pair for 600 or more units purchased. Grebby's average order cost is $25 per order; the forecasted annual demand for alligator boots is 1,200 pair; and the inventory carrying cost rate is 24% per year.

9. Calculate the EOQ for each of the three purchase prices. Which EOQs are valid?
10. Which purchasing alternative should Grebby's take? What are the total annual inventory costs for the valid alternatives?
11. The Big Cheese Pizza Parlor buys lots of pizza boxes. It normally pays $1 per box when ordering from its supplier. Based on its annual forecast for pizza demand, its demand for boxes is estimated to be 10,000 units for the year. It costs $25 to place an order, and its holding cost for boxes is 25% of the cost of a box per year. The supplier tells the Big Cheese Pizza buyer that she can sell the boxes for $0.95 each if the restaurant buys a minimum of 5,000 at a time. Should it take the discount, and what is the total cost?
12. Average demand is 2,500 units per year; order cost is $50 per order; holding cost rate is 20% of the purchase cost per unit per year; and the cost of one unit is $42. What is the total inventory cost per year? If a cost reduction per unit of $1 can be achieved by buying 1,000 at a time, should the buyer take the discount? Justify your answer.
13. The average demand is equal to 10 units per day, the order lead time is 7 days, and the standard deviation of the lead time demand is 4 units. If a 95% service level is desired, what is the reorder point?
14. Roy and Gayle's Fix-It Shop purchased a new automated inventory control software application, and it wanted to put ROPs on all of its purchased tools and supplies. After forecasting the demand for items for the upcoming

year, it was ready to start calculating ROPs. Three of the items are shown here, along with the forecasted annual demands, purchase lead times, lead time demand standard deviation levels, and desired service levels. Calculate the ROPs for the three items and their safety stock levels. Assume the store is open 365 days per year.

Item	Annual Demand	Lead Time	Std. Dev. Lead Time Demand	Required Serv. Level
Duct Tape	2300 rolls	12 days	6 rolls	99%
Super Glue	1800 bottles	6 days	4 bottles	90%
Hammer	650 hammers	21 days	3 hammers	80%

15. Phyllis was just hired as the new purchasing manager at Rich Furniture. She decided to recalculate all of its ROPs, since she noticed that many of the suppliers' delivery times varied substantially from one order to the next. Phyllis asked Mary Jane, her buyer, to recalculate the first one (a desk), to make sure it was done correctly. Phyllis also wanted to know the safety stock required. The upcoming annual demand forecast was 950 desks. The purchase order lead times varied, with an average of 18 days and a standard deviation of 6 days. The daily demand also varied, with an average of three units per day, and a standard deviation of five desks per day. Phyllis would like to maintain a 98% service level.

Use the following information for Problems 16 through 18:

The manager at Skyler's Pet Supplies decides to order catnip treats from a supplier that visits whenever the manager calls, and then makes orders. The annual demand for cat treats is 8,000, with a daily standard deviation of 6 treats. The store is open 365 days per year. Their order cost is $35, the treats are $1.25 each, and the carrying cost rate is 28% per year. The order lead time is always 5 days. The manager wants a 95% service level.

16. What is the EOQ?
17. What is the optimal review period?
18. What is the target quantity or order-up-to-level? If there were 225 cat treats in inventory when the supplier visited, what would be the order size?
19. Tom uses a fixed review period inventory system in his store. He counts his inventory every 30 days and then makes an order. Ten days later his order shows up from the supplier. On one ordering occasion, he counts and finds 81 units in inventory. If the average daily demand is 10 units, the standard deviation of the (review period + lead time) demand is 17 units, and he desires a probability of not stocking out of 96%, how many units should Tom order?
20. Classify the following items using the ABC inventory classification approach. Which items should be monitored most closely, and which ones should have the least amount of safety stock?

Item	Cost/Unit ($)	Forecasted Annual Demand
1	6.40	1,700
2	7.80	7,500
3	17.49	6,240
4	44.00	260
5	105.99	150
6	345.00	300

21. Mennitt's Bowlarama wants to determine its inventory management performance during its past year of operations. Calculate its inventory days of supply, days receivables outstanding, days payables outstanding, and cash-to-cash cycle time, and then assess its performance. Use the following information: Inventory on-hand at beginning of the year = $156,000; inventory on-hand at end of the year = $145,000; annual cost of goods sold = $895,000; average annual accounts receivable = $26,000; annual credit sales = $68,000; beginning of year accounts payable = $130,000; end of year accounts payable = $186,000; total annual purchases = $1.05 million.

CASE STUDIES

CASE 1: Inventory Problems at Three Spoons Market

Randy is the owner of Three Spoons Market. Three Spoons is an upscale tapas restaurant in a town of about 200,000 people. According to both Yelp and Trip Advisory, it is the highest-rated restaurant in town. Randy had been having trouble with inventory management (he runs out of some items while others go bad) and has brought you in as a consultant to help, due to your background in inventory management. The menu at the restaurant changes monthly, and there are daily specials.

Randy follows what other restaurant owners are doing to improve their bottom line—he reads trade publications and online blogs. He also tries to keep up with trends in other industries that may help him manage better. He recently read about the success small-job shops have had with managing inventory by classifying inventory as A, B, or C. As Randy thinks about his business, it is really a job shop, since food is prepared after the customer orders from the menu. The food is prepared to customer tastes and requirements. He is not exactly sure if an ABC inventory plan will work for his restaurant, but has hired you to provide a recommendation. All the ingredients used in the dishes are either dried or fresh. Nothing frozen or processed is put in the food. Customers can request alterations in menu items during ordering. A detail of the inventories at the restaurant are as follows:

- *Condiments.* Used for additional flavoring of foods at the table. Can be stored for long periods of time. There are five different condiments available, and multiple tables may need the same condiments at the same time. These items represent less than 0.5% of food costs.
- *Spices and dried fruits.* Used in most dishes, and can be stored for long periods of time without compromising the taste of the items. There are about 50 different spices and fruits that are stocked. Some can be substituted for others. These items represent less than 5% of the food costs for the various dishes.
- *Oils.* Used to prepare items and as an ingredient in some dishes. Have shelf lives of one week to one month. There are 10 different oils that are stocked. Two or three can be substituted, but the others have a unique taste. These items represent about 10–15% of the food costs and preparation costs of the various dishes.
- *Fresh vegetables and herbs.* Have a shelf life of two days to one week. These items are delivered in a truck that comes twice a week, but in some cases have to be ordered a week in advance. In an emergency, these items can be found at a local grocery store. These items represent between 10–70% of the food costs of the various dishes, depending on if the dish contains meat.
- *Fresh fruits.* Have a shelf life of two to four days. These items are unique to the dishes on the menu. They are not usually found in a local grocery store, but in a pinch someone can drive an hour to a distributor to pick them up, if in stock. These items are delivered twice per week. They represent about 10% of the food costs.
- *Meats.* Have a shelf life of two to four days. These items are unique to the dishes on the menu. They are not usually found in the local grocery store, but are available from a distributor, if in stock. These items are delivered twice a week. They represent up to 60% of the food costs.
- *Dairy.* Have a shelf life of one week. These items are usually delivered three times per week and can also be found locally at a grocery store. The items represent less than 5% of the costs of the food items.

DISCUSSION QUESTIONS

1. What are the advantages and disadvantages of having an ABC inventory plan at the restaurant?
2. What items would you classify in each category?
3. Are stockouts acceptable in this this type of business? Why, or why not?
4. Would the creation of more work-in-process or finished goods inventory be beneficial to the owner? Why, or why not?

Note: Written by Jeffrey W. Fahrenwald, MBA, Rockford University, Rockford, IL. This case was prepared solely to provide material for class discussion. The author does not intend to illustrate either effective or ineffective handling of a managerial situation.

CASE 2: Inventory Management at Protech Logistics

Pat is the newly hired manager of warehouse operations for Protech Logistics, a distributor that sells MRO (maintenance, repair, and operating) items to various governmental and nongovernmental organizations throughout the United States. She has been asked by the president of Protech to do a study of various types of inventory systems. The report should contain an evaluation of how Protech currently manages its inventory, along with recommendations (if applicable) for improving the system.

Historically, the company has simply ordered items four times a year based on past sales. This system has served the company well (it has been profitable for the past 20 years), but with increased competition and tightening margins, the president is fearful that in the future, this type of inventory system could hurt organizational financial performance and customer service. The organization stocks over 10,000 different items (SKUs). Costs of the items range from about $0.50 to $10,000. Sales of items run from one or two per year to hundreds of thousands per year. Currently, there are about 100 SKUs in the warehouse, with a total procurement cost of $50,000, that have not sold a single unit in more than two years.

Most (at least 80%) of the items in the warehouse that cost over $5,000 could be drop shipped directly to the customer from the supplier. Currently, this is only done for about 25% of the orders. There would be an additional cost for a drop ship; however, this cost could be offset against the cost of holding the item in the warehouse and the opportunity perhaps to downsize the warehouse.

The president would like to know more about various types of systems that could be available and wants Pat to make an evaluation of the current Protech system. She has read about various ABC and EOQ models and is not sure either model will work for an MRO supplier. She sees the ABC and EOQ models "at odds" with each other; however, she also thinks both models have the potential for saving money. On the other hand, the inventory system in place at Protech is simple and logical, and makes the process of ordering product routine. The president has also asked Pat to come up with a strategy to clear out items that have not sold for over two years, but does not want to sell these items at less than the procurement cost.

DISCUSSION QUESTIONS

1. What are the strengths and weaknesses of the current system?
2. Would the use of EOQ potentially improve the system? Why, or why not?
3. Would some sort of ABC system be suitable for this type of operation? Explain.
4. How should Pat respond to the president with regard to selling the items that have not sold for the past two years?

Note: Written by Jeffrey W. Fahrenwald, MBA, Rockford University, Rockford, IL. This case was prepared solely to provide material for class discussion. The author does not intend to illustrate either effective or ineffective handling of a managerial situation.

VIDEO CASE STUDY

Learn more about ***managing inventory*** from real organizations that use operations management techniques every day. Johnny Garcia is the Distribution Manager at Sage Publishing, an independent academic publisher based in Thousand Oaks, California. In order to provide their clients with the books they need, when they need them, Sage must keep track of all book orders, shipments, and returns. Watch this short interview to find out how they do it.

LITTLEFIELD LABS

LITTLEFIELD LABORATORIES

Demonstrate your understanding of **independent demand inventory management** at Littlefield Labs!

Littlefield Laboratories is a highly automated, state-of-the-art blood testing facility for clinics and hospitals. The lab will operate for a limited time frame lasting 210 days. You're asked to step in as the operations manager on Day 30, and are tasked with managing the inventory levels of the lab for the duration of its operation. Improper inventory management can cost you money: Having too few kits can cause delays in processing, and having too many kits ties up cash due to holding costs.

Based on historic data, you must set a raw materials order quantity and reorder point and also buy or sell machines in order to optimize capacity and maximize the lab's profits.

Compete against your classmates to prove your understanding of chapter concepts:

- LO 7-2: Explain the functions of inventory
- LO 7-3: Interpret the costs, risks, and value of inventory

The team with the most cash in hand at the end of the 210-day time frame wins!

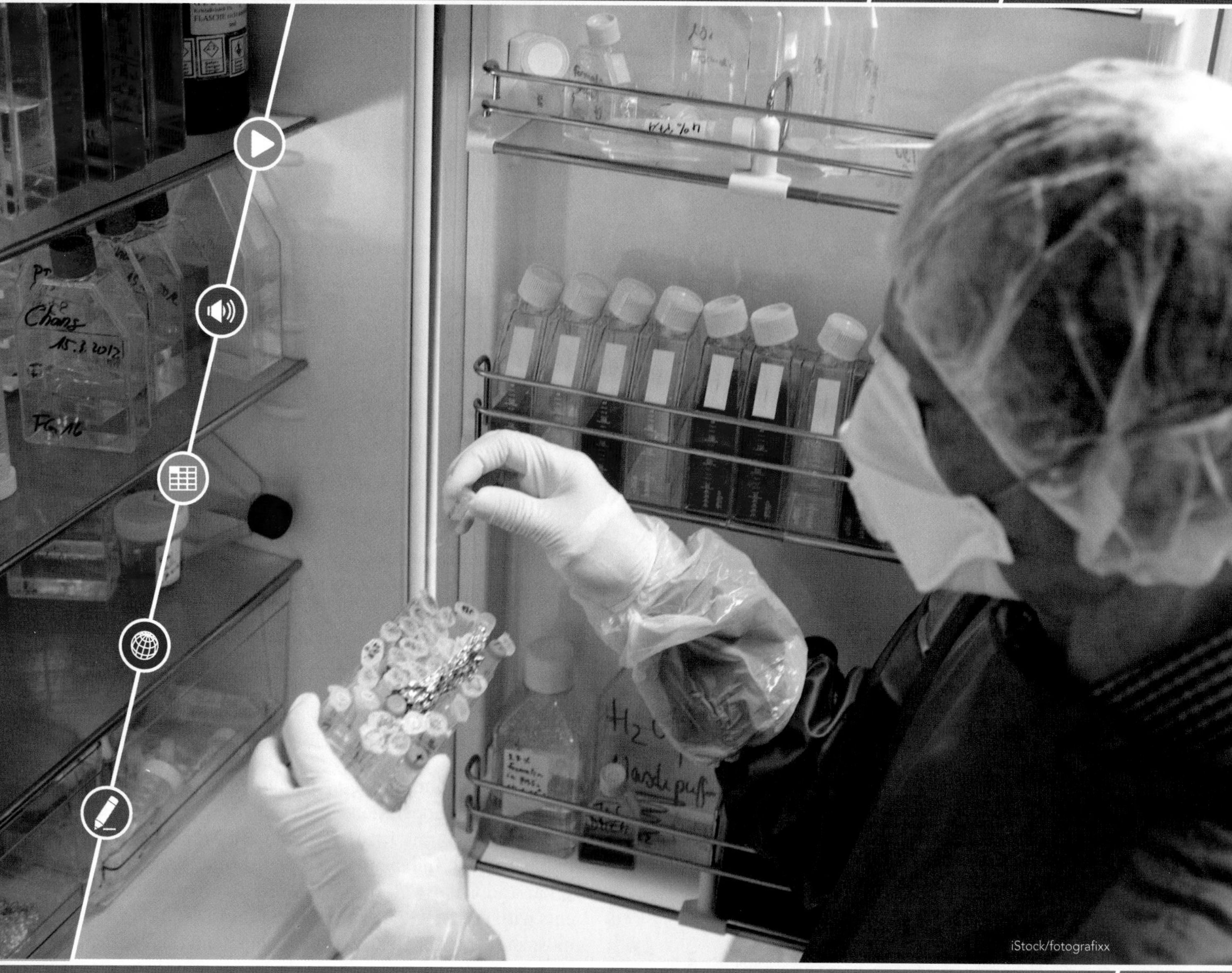

iStock/fotografixx

Our experience has been that many times the process is not completely thought through, or the building is a series of additions, which does not work well for the product or the people. A lean design expert could give you an accounting for how much money can be wasted if 50 people are required to walk an extra 200 feet five times per day, for example.

—**GARY JAMES,** engineering director, Frankfort Short Bruza[1]

It's like a steel chain with one plastic link. Tell me what you are going to do by improving any one of those steel links without doing something about the plastic one. I use my lean toolbox once I find my constraint. Theory of Constraints leads me to the core problem.

—**BOB BUCKLEY,** owner, True32 Custom Cabinetry[2]

MATERIAL FLOW ANALYSIS AND FACILITY LAYOUTS

LEARNING OBJECTIVES

After completing this chapter, you should be able to:

8.1 Explain the importance of material flows
8.2 Analyze material flows and their impact on the organization
8.3 Apply the Theory of Constraints in an organization
8.4 Explain why manufacturing flexibility is important
8.5 Critique product- and process-focused, group technology, and project layouts
8.6 Discuss some of the latest trends in layout design

VALUE STREAM MAPPING AT THERMO FISHER SCIENTIFIC

Massachusetts-based equipment manufacturer Thermo Fisher Scientific has found significant benefits from the use of value stream mapping. At one of its facilities in North Carolina, for example, a value stream team literally followed the entire process from customer orders, back to the planning of production schedules, and then on to actual production. Team members walked through the shop floor to actually see how orders moved through the plant.

The team members represented a large cross-section of the organization, including a production supervisor, a buyer, a manufacturing engineer, a process manager, a maintenance supervisor, and a quality engineer. The cross-functional team enabled workers to understand how their processes affected other areas.

One example involved Thermo Fisher's refrigeration line at its North Carolina plant. Specifically, the value stream team sought to improve order lead times, on-time deliveries, and WIP inventory levels on the refrigeration line. The team identified a number of key bottlenecks and devised a plan to implement solutions to reduce the bottlenecks. Within three months, the plant had eliminated 40% of the excess WIP inventories, reduced order lead times from 14 to 7 days, and improved on-time deliveries from 70 to 90%.

The plant eventually implemented a kanban system to further reduce excess inventories. Additionally, it realized from the value stream mapping process that workloads on the production floor were not balanced—some workers had excess downtime while others had none. Eventually, Thermo Fisher was able to implement solutions to balance its production line.[3]

INTRODUCTION

Various types of flow occur continuously in all organizations. When a company's purchasing agent buys a product from a supplier, a purchase order flows to the supplier via fax, email, or the Internet. The supplier accepts the order, then schedules the order to be manufactured for the buyer. While the order is being completed, the buyer waits for delivery. When completed, the product is delivered and the buyer pays the supplier. Five different types of flow are represented in this short example. Completing a purchase order constitutes work flow; transmitting and receiving the purchase order involves information flow; manufacturing and delivering a product constitutes material flows; waiting for the product involves customer flow; and paying for purchases creates cash flows. In each of these cases, managing flow effectively can reduce costs while improving quality, lead time, capacity, flexibility, and customer service.

At manufacturing facilities, the idea of managing material flow has been around for a long time. Henry Ford used the idea of material flow management in the early 20th century to help revolutionize automobile manufacturing. Much more recently, Toyota established a leadership position in the automobile industry by managing material flows using lean system concepts to create reliable and flexible manufacturing processes (lean systems are discussed in Chapter 9). Customer and work flows are topics discussed in Chapter 10.

Generally speaking, raw materials, parts, and assemblies are scheduled for processing at manufacturing facilities according to a desired sequence of operations, the desired delivery date, the packaging requirements, and the distribution arrangements. At service facilities, customers are part of the process and must be sequenced or placed in queues to await their services. Customer orders are processed based on each order's service requirements, service personnel capabilities, and available server capacity. As products and customers flow through these production systems, information is collected, manipulated, and communicated, to assist in the handling of goods and people.

These common flows are evident in most organizations, and are of greatest concern to organizations seeking to improve how goods and services are made and delivered to customers. Successful organizations manage these flows to create production flexibilities, to minimize inventories and wait times, and to keep customers occupied as they move through a service system. When problems arise, evidence of flow problems of one sort or another can usually be found. Any non-value-adding element that interrupts flow is a problem that must be identified and managed or eliminated. This is the essence of flow management. The material flow issues are described in this chapter and the chapter supplement.

MATERIAL FLOW MAPPING

8.1 Explain the importance of material flows

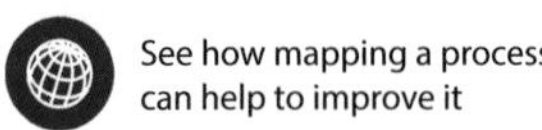

See how mapping a process can help to improve it

Chapter 7 provided a more general discussion of inventory management, and this chapter assumes readers possess an understanding of those concepts. To effectively manage material flows, an initial understanding of these flows must first be developed. A good place to start is the mapping of material flows within a process or set of processes. The chapter-opening Manufacturing Spotlight provides an interesting example of process mapping at manufacturing company Thermo Fisher Scientific.

Mapping material flows within a process is the first step in understanding how a process works and integrates with other processes. Understanding material flows is also necessary when considering strategies to improve a process. There are a number of terms used to describe **material flow mapping**, namely, **process mapping**, **process flowcharting**, and **value stream mapping**. All of these terms essentially mean the same thing and have the same objective: to understand material flows within a process, identify the current sequence of activities making up the process, identify and manage or eliminate the activities that are not adding value, and then improve the remaining process activities.

material flow mapping A method for identifying the current sequence of activities making up the process, to understand material flows. The objective is to identify and evaluate or eliminate the activities that are not adding value, and then improve the remaining process activities.

process mapping *See* Material flow mapping.

process flowcharting *See* Material flow mapping.

value stream mapping *See* Material flow mapping.

Constructing a material flow map should include the people directly involved in a process—managers, supervisors, front-line workers, and possibly supplier representatives and customers. Material flow mapping can also help identify how employees fit into or contribute to a process, and how customers interact with a process. When a material flow map is completed it can be used to identify where performance should be measured; how the process layout could be altered; where capacity imbalances and delays are occurring; and where quality, cost, and productivity problems might exist.

A number of standard symbols are generally used when constructing a material flow map to improve the map's readability and visual impact, and these are shown in Table 8.1. Additionally, a simple process map for manufacturing a hypothetical testing instrument is shown in Figure 8.1. The testing instrument consists of a purchased sensor board, and also a metal box and lid, which are fabricated from purchased sheet metal in

Workcenters 1, 2, and 3. The box, lid, and sensor board are assembled in Workcenter 4, and the final product is inspected and tested in quality assurance (Workcenter 5). If the product passes inspection and testing, it is packaged and labeled in Workcenter 6 and sent to finished goods storage until finally, the product is distributed to customers. Units that do not pass the quality assurance stage are discarded as scrap.

There is one inventory decision in the manufacturing process shown in Figure 8.1, and this decision node is shown as a diamond:

- If the assembled test instrument passes quality inspection and testing, then finished units are sent to Workcenter 6; otherwise, the units are discarded.

The triangles denote places where WIP or finished goods inventories are stored for varying lengths of time. Initially, sheet metal and sensor boards are purchased and stored in the warehouse. As each step in the manufacturing process is completed, the WIP inventories are stored on the shop floor until needed by the next step in the process (shown as triangles in Figure 8.1). When the finished testing instrument is packaged and labeled, it is stored until a batch of packaged instruments is distributed to retail or other customers. The material flow map is then complete and ready for analysis.

A material flow map of a machine shop is shown in Figure 8.2. The same symbols are used to indicate the movement of materials and storage areas. This figure illustrates the relative location of the machines and the most frequent material flows through the six-machine shop.

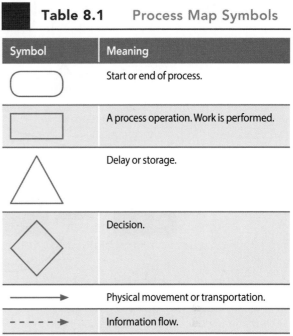

Table 8.1 Process Map Symbols

Symbol	Meaning
	Start or end of process.
	A process operation. Work is performed.
	Delay or storage.
	Decision.
	Physical movement or transportation.
	Information flow.

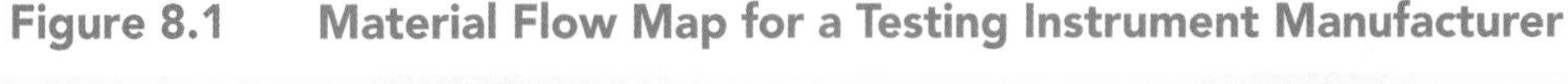

Figure 8.1 Material Flow Map for a Testing Instrument Manufacturer

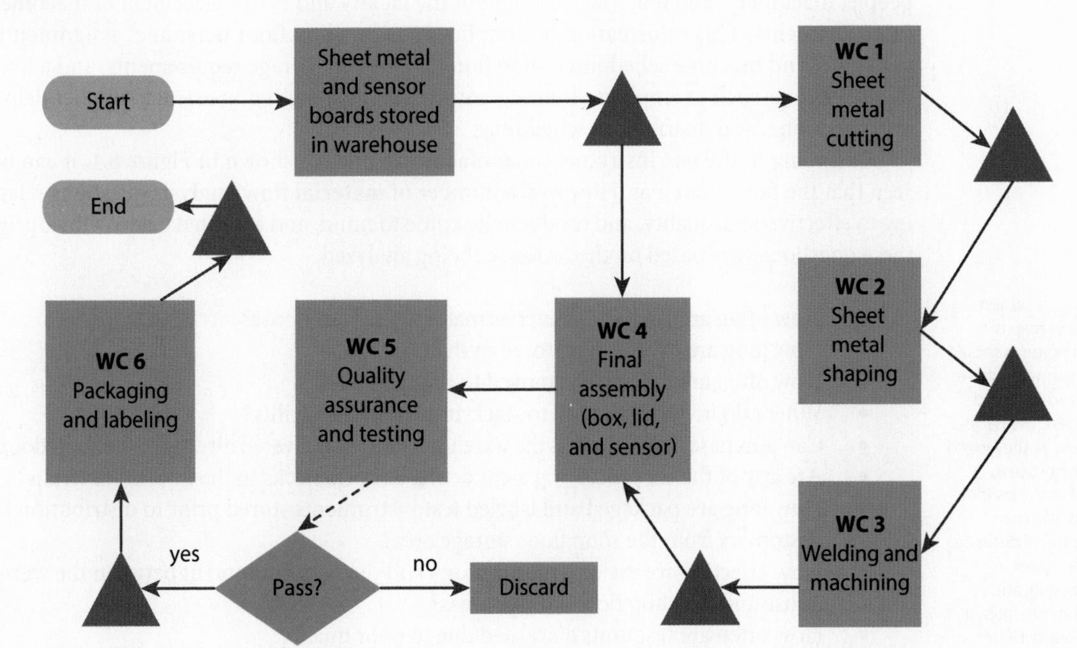

Figure 8.2 Frequent Material Flows at a Machine Shop

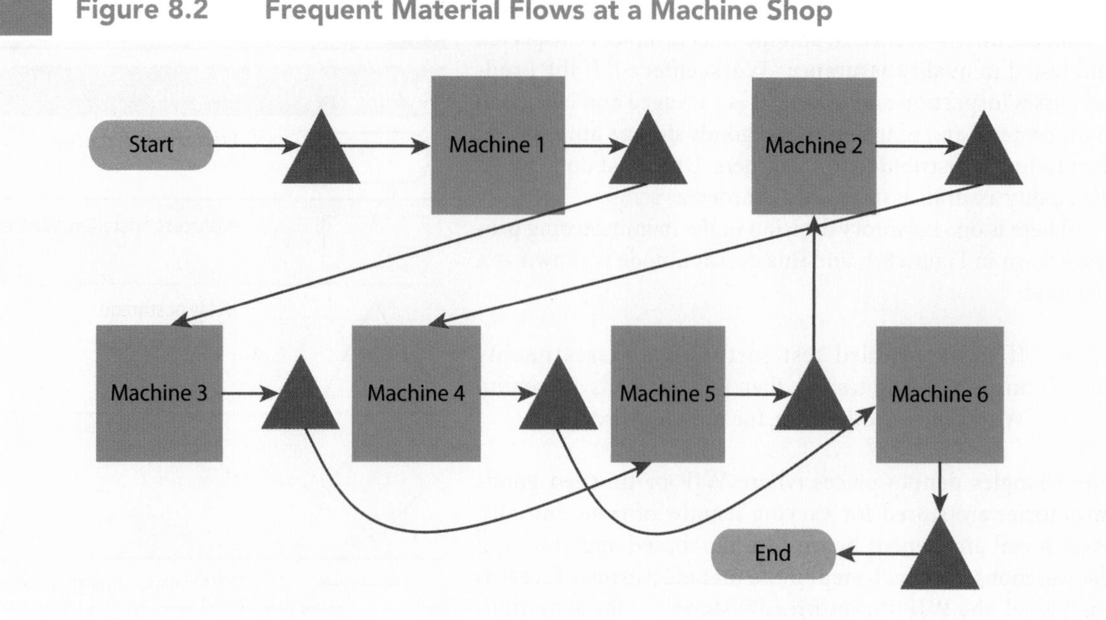

MATERIAL FLOW ANALYSIS

8.2 Analyze material flows and their impact on the organization

Material flow maps are important for understanding material flows and can serve as the foundation for analyzing flows into, within, and out of a process. When the initial flow map is complete, a number of items should become apparent—namely, where inventories are delayed or stored throughout the process, the paths that inventories follow as they wend their way through the process, and the sequence of activities that make up the process. It is then possible to measure travel distances and travel times, time spent in storage and in processing, and time spent waiting on materials. It is also possible to identify better routes for people, machinery, and materials throughout the facility and better placement of machines or departments. This information has implications for shop floor personnel assignments, personnel and machine scheduling, shop floor layout and storage requirements, and a host of other things such as employee training, information system requirements, supplier delivery scheduling, and distribution scheduling.

Referring to the test instrument manufacturing process shown in Figure 8.1, it can be seen that the flow is circular. However, a number of **material flow analysis** questions relating to effectiveness, quality, and productivity come to mind, and are listed below. Obviously, these questions vary based on the processes being analyzed.

material flow analysis When the initial material flow map is complete, a number of items should become apparent—namely, where inventories are delayed or stored throughout the process, the paths that inventories follow as they wend their way through the process, and the sequence of activities that make up the process. It is then possible to measure travel distances and travel times, time spent in storage and in processing, and time spent waiting on materials. It is also possible to identify better routes for people, machinery, and materials throughout the facility and better placement of machines or departments.

- How often are supplier deliveries made to the warehouse?
- How long are inventories stored in the warehouse?
- How often are inventories moved to the shop floor?
- Where do inventories tend to stack-up within the facility?
- Can purchased items bypass the warehouse and be delivered directly to the shop floor?
- Are any of the six processing areas acting as bottlenecks to the flow of materials?
- How long are packaged and labeled test instruments stored prior to distribution to customers from the shop floor storage area?
- How effective are the communications and delivery equipment between the warehouse and the shop floor storage areas?
- How often are test units discarded due to poor quality?
- Can poor-quality test units be repaired instead of discarded?
- What is the overall productivity of the manufacturing process?
- What is the actual manufacturing output versus the facility's design capacity?

Referring to Figure 8.2, the obvious flow problem is the sequencing and positioning of the machines. Even though many of the same questions shown here can be asked, additional questions regarding the machine shop layout could be as follows:

- How readily can the machines be moved to accommodate the most frequent sequencing of machines?
- How much floor space can be spared by moving the machines?
- Can material movement times be significantly reduced by moving the machines?
- Will a better layout improve flow time and productivity?

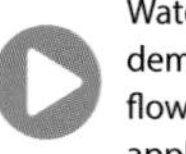

Watch a video demonstration of a material flow analysis software application

Answers to these questions can be found by collecting data such as activity times, wait times, machine inactivity times, units of inventory stored at various locations, production batch sizes, distances between activities, and the frequency and timing of inbound and outbound deliveries. These initial inquiries resulting from the flow mapping exercise serve as a starting point for analysis. The collected data can guide process assessment and improvement efforts. Once the data collection phase is complete, the participants in the analysis can compare the current state of the process to a desired state, and rank order the desired process changes based on cost, implementation time, and expected benefit. Process performance measures can then be instituted to track ongoing process improvements. While nothing beats actually observing existing processes, there are a number of software applications such as the one demonstrated in the video box that can aid material flow analyses.

Typical process changes might include decreasing process variability through use of standardized procedures or automation, cross-training workers to increase flexibility, hiring part-time workers, revising process layouts, use of fewer but more reliable suppliers, adding equipment to increase capacity at bottlenecked workcenters, and postponing final assembly until customer orders are received.

California-based natural food distributor Nature's Best undertook a massive material flow analysis to transition from a four-building, multitouch, long lead time distribution system to a one-building, agile, short lead time distribution system. The company went through the 18-month transition to improve customer service capabilities. "In order to maintain our service, we were deploying more and more people," says Brian McCarthy, senior VP of operations. Processing orders required an undesirable 18 touches before items made it onto trucks. Ultimately, Nature's Best personnel mapped out the interior design of a new building, repositioning all of its processes. They designed process spaces based on sales forecasts and performance data, and upgraded their warehouse management system.[4]

As materials, parts, and products flow through the manufacturing process, problems can occur that have a significant impact on the final product delivered to customers. Indeed, some managers are surprised when they discover that only a small percentage of total manufacturing lead time is spent adding value to products, a large amount of space is being used to store materials, and much of the equipment and workers on the shop floor are idle for long stretches of time. At a manufacturer of control panel buttons, for example, an analysis showed that while the actual manufacturing time had been reduced to just over two minutes, it was taking over 12 weeks to finally deliver product to customers! This equates to a ratio of value added time to total lead time of less than 1%.[5] One of the more popular and successful material flow analysis techniques involves the use of the Theory of Constraints, the next topic of discussion.

THE THEORY OF CONSTRAINTS

8.3 Apply the Theory of Constraints in an organization

Constraints in an organizational context are things that keep the firm from achieving its goals. Constraints can refer to physical things, such as material bottlenecks along the supply chain or on the manufacturing floor, untrained workers, or faulty equipment. Constraints can also refer to procedures and behavioral constraints, such as poorly designed training programs, a lack of preventive maintenance procedures, poor management decisions, or cultural

Figure 8.3 Bottleneck Flow in a Facility

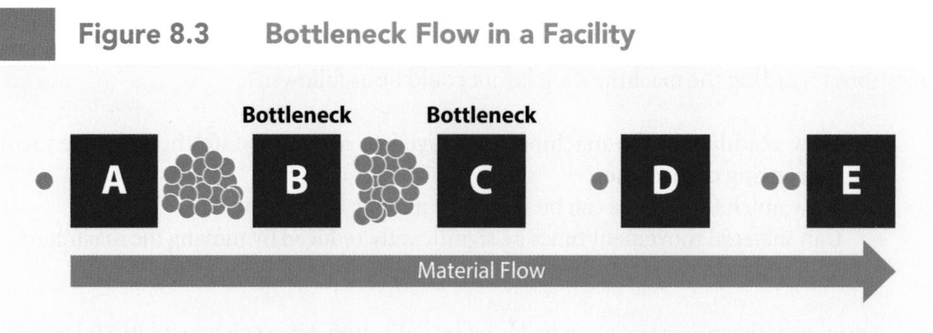

norms existing in the organization. A bottleneck is a constraint that restricts material flow (as illustrated in Figure 8.3), reduces capacity and throughput, increases order lead time, and negatively impacts customer service. Almost certainly, one or more bottlenecks can be found *in all organizations.* As one bottleneck is discovered and fixed, a second bottleneck surfaces and becomes the new primary constraint. Identifying and treating these process bottlenecks can be viewed as a continuous concern for most organizations.

Product quality can suffer when firms try to cut corners to make up for lost time as the result of a bottleneck. A host of other problems can also surface if bottlenecks are not identified and treated. Unscheduled overtime, higher inventory levels, frequent equipment breakdowns, and constant expediting of late orders (or jobs)—all of these create unnecessary costs and potential lost future sales from disgruntled customers.

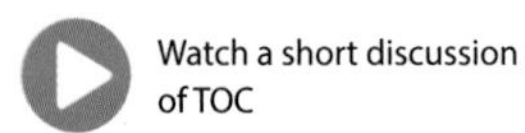

First introduced and briefly discussed in Chapter 4, identifying and improving constrained processes is the principal objective of the *Theory of Constraints* (TOC), and can be applied to all manufacturing, service, and administrative processes. The TOC has been written about and used in many business applications since the concept was first popularized by Eliyahu Goldratt in his 1984 book, *The Goal* (unfortunately, Dr. Goldratt died in 2011 at the age of 64).[6] Today, the TOC has come to be known as a philosophy of improvement that recognizes there will always be limitations to system performance, and that the limitations in many cases can be caused by a small number of process bottlenecks or constraints. Additionally, since identifying and reducing constraints can improve quality and reduce waste, TOC is often combined with the practices of lean and Six Sigma (the topics of Chapters 9 and 13). The Manufacturing Spotlight on the next page describes Automatic Spring Products' use of TOC.

Bottleneck activities can be found by creating time reports for various process activities for comparison purposes, or by simply looking for the telltale signs of a process bottleneck, such as inventory piling up, trucks waiting to be loaded or unloaded, jobs that have become backlogged, or queues of customers waiting to receive service. Successful managers can overcome constraints by:

- Increasing capacity at the constrained activity with better tools, workers, suppliers, or training/motivational methods
- Designing better material routes or layouts
- Avoiding having unconstrained resources doing unnecessary work
- Designing effective contingency plans or procedures
- Using performance measures that are tied to system-wide objectives
- Performing quality checks after each processing stage
- Performing routine preventive maintenance on equipment

TechOps, the maintenance unit of Delta Airlines, began implementing TOC in 2006. The result has been 20% faster engine overhauls, a 75% reduction in parts inventories, and a reduced total overhaul cost per engine of 13%.[7] In Arizona, semiconductor manufacturer Intel Corp. recently implemented TOC in its finished goods distribution center. Results could be seen within a few days—new methods created a faster and more predictable operation, resulting in average cycle time reductions of 68%, a WIP reduction of 65%, and a safer,

MANUFACTURING SPOTLIGHT

ASPC Sees Benefits With TOC

Michigan-based Automatic Spring Products Corp. (ASPC) makes springs and metal products for industrial customers. As the recession took hold in 2009, annual sales plummeted to $17 million, and ASPC's work force shrank to 110. By 2012, its employee count was 270, with sales exceeding $40 million. Today, things are going very well at ASPC, compared to the recession years.

iStock/Chinnasorn Pangcharoen

Through CEO Steven Moreland's leadership, the company implemented the Theory of Constraints (TOC), which resulted in significant savings, helping the company survive the recession and loss of major customers.

Today, ASPC uses both lean manufacturing and TOC. "Not everyone does that, but that's something we found works for our business model," Moreland explains. "TOC is a whole different way of looking at manufacturing, from the standpoint that there is always a bottleneck in every manufacturing plant," he adds. "If it breaks down, everything stops. Nothing can get through it," so the objective is managing the constraints.

TOC is best looked at as a focusing tool, according to Moreland. At ASPC, bottlenecks are found where "the most product must flow through one process," he says. If the heat-treating furnace is down, it prevents the company from reaching sales goals, since the company can't make up for the lost time. "Just getting incrementally better every single day is what gets me out of bed in the morning," says Moreland. "I can't wait to see what we're going to do today."[8]

less stressful environment. Since the changes were only adjustments of policies, measures, and behaviors, there were no implementation costs.[9]

THE DRUM, BUFFER, ROPE CONCEPT

The TOC can also be explained using the **drum, buffer, rope concept** (DBR), which was also introduced in Eliyahu Goldratt's books *The Goal* and *The Race*. An illustration of the DBR concept is shown in Figure 8.4. In the figure, the bottleneck process, Workcenter 3, is capacity constrained and thus sets the processing rate of the entire facility (50 units per day). This workcenter represents the drum that sets the pace (the beat of the drum) for the entire facility.

The buffer, between Workcenters 3 and 4, is additional completed Workcenter 3 inventory, allowed to sit in the buffer until it is needed. Inventory buffers, and in many cases additional service providers and workers, are used to ensure that the bottleneck resource can provide work to other downstream processes (in this case, Workcenter 4). Notice that Workcenters 1 and 2 have higher output capabilities than Workcenter 3. This means that no inventory buffers or safety stocks are required at these workcenters. Even if they experience machine breakdowns or other unscheduled downtime, they can eventually catch up with the constrained process. Downstream of the constrained process is Workcenter 4. If something halts production for a time at Workcenter 4, this is also OK, since output from Workcenter 3 will accumulate at the buffer. When Workcenter 4 is up and running again, it will quickly work through this accumulation because of its higher output capability.

The rope refers to the control or scheduling of work releases to the facility, which is derived according to the drum and the buffers. In the figure, the rope is the 50 units per day constrained production schedule. Because the output of the bottleneck process drives the output of the entire facility, organizations must work to increase capacity at the bottleneck process in order to increase the facility's overall capacity. If, at some future date, improvements have increased the output capability of Workcenter 3 to 75 units per day, the new constraint will become Workcenter 1, and the facility's output (the rope) will be 70 units per day. The DBR concept provides a basis for determining a production schedule that is realistic and protected from demand variabilities or stockouts. The steps in DBR production scheduling are:

drum, buffer, rope concept (DBR) A concept used to explain the TOC.

Figure 8.4 The Drum, Buffer, Rope Concept

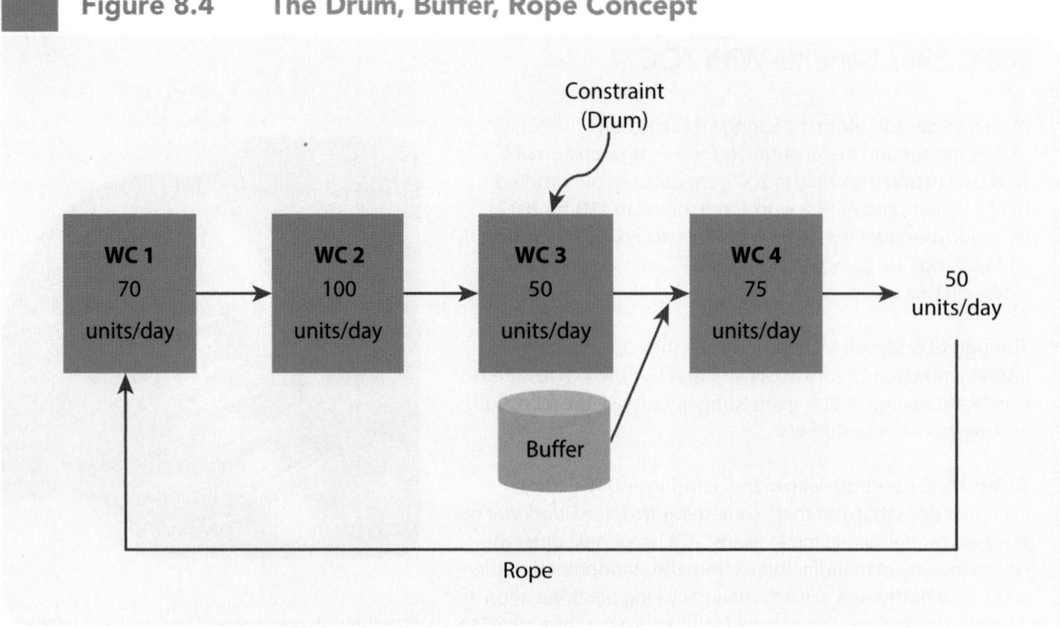

- Forecast the demand. This provides the ideal production rate objective.
- Identify the constrained resource(s) or bottleneck(s) in the system.
- Establish the production schedule in line with the most heavily constrained resource (the drum).
- Use inventory buffers at the critical bottlenecks to help ensure that desired production rates for the entire system can be achieved until the bottlenecks are improved.
- Synchronize the release of work at the constrained resources and the nonconstrained resources to ensure the right amounts of materials are available at all resources when needed, no unnecessary buffers are accumulating, and no processes are unduly impeding material flow.

The concepts of the TOC and DBR have been successfully applied in practice over the past 20+ years. In an extensive review of the TOC and DBR applications, Professors Mabin and Balderstone found published reports of over 100 uses of the applications by manufacturers and service organizations, including some of the world's largest and most recognizable companies as well as some small companies. Among all of the cases studied, no negative outcomes were ever found. The results from the implementations included improvements in revenue, output rate, profit, lead time, and inventory levels.[10] Today, the uses of TOC and DBR are as popular as ever.

MANUFACTURING FLEXIBILITY

8.4 Explain why manufacturing flexibility is important

manufacturing flexibility Refers to the ability of a manufacturing system to create different product types, change the order in how processes are operated, or change process capacities in response to predicted and unpredicted changes in demand.

As mentioned earlier, one objective of material flow management is increased flexibility to quickly alter production, product design, or delivery schedules. In situations where there are many competitors, and new technologies and innovative designs cause new products to be introduced frequently, demand for existing products becomes much more uncertain. This demand uncertainty makes **manufacturing flexibility** highly desirable. Manufacturing flexibility refers to the ability of a manufacturing system to create different product types, change the order in how processes are operated, or change process capacities in response to predicted and unpredicted changes in demand. Perhaps one of the better-known examples of flexibility is a Dell computer story. Dell has worked out a number of contingency plans to deal with potential internal and external supply interruptions. When a labor lockout idled 29 U.S. West Coast port facilities for 10 days in 2002, Dell used chartered air carriers to make round trips from its Asian parts suppliers to the United States, which kept Dell's manufacturing facilities up and running.[11]

Watch an FMS in action

Several terms have been used to describe manufacturing facilities when automation technologies are used to improve material flows and manufacturing flexibilities. A **flexible manufacturing system** (FMS) uses a central host computer, **computer numerically controlled machines** (CNC) and a plant-wide, automated material handling system equipped with automated conveyors, automated guided vehicles (AGVs), and automated storage and retrieval systems (AS/RS) to schedule small batches of products, route and store parts, and control machining operations among carefully laid-out assembly areas for a number of similar products. This system tries to combine the benefits of highly flexible machine shop processing with highly productive (and fast) repetitive processing.

flexible manufacturing system (FMS) Uses a central host computer, computer numerically controlled machines (CNC), and a plant-wide, automated material handling system equipped with automated conveyors, automated guided vehicles (AGVs), and automated storage and retrieval systems (AS/RS) to schedule small batches of products, route and store parts, and control machining operations among carefully laid-out assembly areas for a number of similar products. This system tries to combine the benefits of highly flexible machine shop processing with highly productive (and fast) repetitive processing.

The benefits of using an FMS include reductions in lead time, machining time, scrap, and piece cost, and the ability to quickly change product mix, routing, and machining sequence. FMS often goes hand in hand with **computer aided design** (CAD) systems, **computer assisted manufacturing** (CAM) systems, and group technology (GT) cells. Managing the entire system of interconnecting processes using a central integrated computer for planning, scheduling, and decision-making purposes is termed **computer integrated manufacturing** (CIM). The Manufacturing Spotlight below describes BAE Systems' CIM facility.

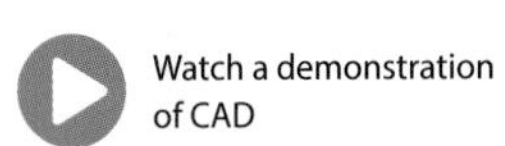
Watch a demonstration of CAD

CAD refers to the use of computer graphics applications in the product design process. Designers can pull up similar product designs stored in a computer database and modify them using light pens, joysticks, or similar devices. Designers can then rotate the product design three-dimensionally on a computer monitor, perform engineering design analyses,

MANUFACTURING SPOTLIGHT

BAE Systems' CIM Facility

In 2010, London-based BAE Systems opened a CIM facility to manufacture components for the F-35 combat aircraft. The planning for the facility began in 2006, to ensure that it could produce a high volume of titanium aircraft parts efficiently.

iStock/pilesasmiles

The CIM system uses two flexible manufacturing systems (FMS). Once an order is received, the information is passed to the FMS, which schedules the manufacture of the part by examining the current workload across each of eight machine tools. If one of the tools is free to accept the order, the FMS assigns the order. If not, the order is stored and then delivered to the next available machine.

Each FMS can store up to 1,000 cutting tools. Robot systems deliver cutting tools to each machine, and replace worn tools, which are then transferred to an area for refurbishment or disposal. When a machine receives a machining order, it checks to see if the right tools are available. If they are, the material is delivered to the machine. If not, the machine sends a message to the FMS, which determines if the needed tool is in its storage system. If it is, then the tool is robotically delivered to the machine. If the tool is unavailable, the FMS tells an operator to deliver one to the FMS. Robots then route the tool to the machine and the operations are performed, after which an operator unloads the part.

Machined parts are routed by the system to a deburring area and finally to a quality control station where a machine checks the parts' tolerances. Parts that meet specifications are then transferred to the aircraft production line.[12]

create material specifications, or cut the product in half to look inside the design. Designer creativity and productivity are greatly enhanced using CAD applications.

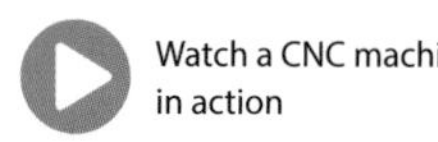

Watch a CNC machine in action

CAM refers to the use of computers in manufacturing processes. CAM applications include welding or painting robots, CNC machines (these are programmable machines, such as lathes, that are capable of storing machining steps for repetitively manufactured parts), automated conveyors, and automated, moving, overhead part racks.

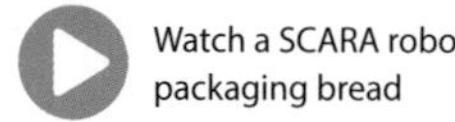

Watch a SCARA robot packaging bread

Today, one of the most highly regarded industrial robots is the Selective Compliance Assembly Robot Arm, or SCARA, developed in Japan over 45 years ago. The SCARA still remains the best robot for jobs involving point-to-point movements like dispensing, loading, picking and placing, assembling, and palletizing. "SCARAs are still the fastest robots," says Brian Jones, section manager of sales planning at Denso Robotics. "We make 4-axis SCARAs that perform a standard cycle in 0.29 seconds and within 20 microns of repeatability. That's impressive."[13]

Group technology cells refer to groups of manufacturing workstations that are dedicated to production of similar parts or part families, requiring the same processing equipment. The machines in each workstation are physically situated close together, and may be connected by automated material handling equipment. While this manufacturing strategy has existed since the 1950s, it has come into common use more recently due to the ability of computers to search through a database of product designs and process routings, and then cluster similarly processed parts into part families. There are a number of reported advantages. In a survey of 32 U.S. companies using GT cells, the five most commonly cited benefits were: (1) reduction of WIP inventories, (2) reduction of setup times, (3) reduction of manufacturing lead times, (4) reduction of material handling, and (5) improvement of output quality.[14]

MASS CUSTOMIZATION

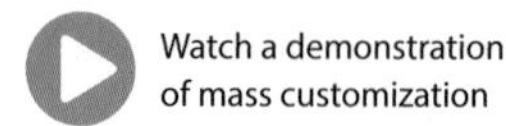

Watch a demonstration of mass customization

Generally speaking, manufacturing companies prefer product standardization because it enables use of automation to produce large quantities of identical product, resulting in lower purchasing and manufacturing costs, better equipment utilization, and a lower total cost per unit. Unfortunately, customers do not necessarily desire standardized products but may instead prefer customized products as long as the purchase price is comparable. Firms that can figure out how to offer customized products at relatively low prices can then find themselves with fewer competitors and potentially enjoy an advantage in the marketplace. Companies have been able to accomplish this using mass customization, previously discussed in Chapter 4. The idea is to design a product using standardized parts, while incorporating a degree of customized assembly, prior to delivery to customers.

Offering a number of finished product variations, and then delaying final assembly until a customer order is received, is a postponement strategy, and is a common practice of mass customization. These manufacturers mass produce parts and subassemblies, and negotiate large-volume purchases with suppliers to reduce costs. The customized final assembly uses only parts and components in stock. Numerous examples of mass customization can be found in both manufacturing and services. At Nike, for instance, customers can visit Nike.com and design a personalized pair of shoes that will be shipped directly to them within a few days. When purchasing a Dell computer, customers can specify the computer, keyboard, and monitor configuration they want by visiting Dell's website or by calling Dell's customer service number. At Toyota, customers can select from a number of options, interiors, and colors, and then order their car online.

computer numerically controlled machines (CNC) Programmable machines, such as lathes, that are capable of storing machining steps for repetitively manufactured parts.

computer aided design (CAD) Refers to the use of computer graphics applications in the product design process.

computer assisted manufacturing (CAM) Refers to the use of computers in manufacturing processes. CAM applications include welding or painting robots and CNC machines.

computer integrated manufacturing (CIM) Managing the entire system of interconnecting flexible manufacturing processes using a central integrated computer for planning, scheduling, and decision-making purposes.

LAYOUT DESIGN

8.5 Critique product- and process-focused, group technology, and project layouts

One of the more obvious characteristics impacting material flow, as shown back in Figure 8.2, is the layout of the facility. Well-designed manufacturing layouts can reduce product throughput time, which in turn reduces WIP inventory levels. Good layouts consider the placement of departments, workcenters, equipment, materials, and workers so that non-value-adding movements are reduced and the overall distances traveled within the facility for parts, components, products, and workers are reduced. Poor layout design can negatively impact employee morale and productivity, and can eventually lead to significant redesign costs as physical structures and heavy equipment are moved to accommodate layout design changes. There are a number of facility layout options to consider, depending on product customization requirements, output desired, funds available, and the product output mix. Several manufacturing facility layouts and their design considerations are discussed next.

iStock/RicAguiar

Assembly lines require workloads to be balanced so product flow can proceed smoothly and quickly.

PRODUCT-FOCUSED LAYOUTS

Product-focused layouts, also referred to as **assembly line layouts**, achieve high-volume output while making standardized products. Processing steps are standardized and grouped into relatively equal time lengths of work; these are then assigned to workcenters, permitting worker specializations to occur. Over time, workers become very proficient in their processing activities, further reducing average product lead times and increasing output levels. Typically, processing equipment and workers are dedicated to specific sets of tasks, and the products are very similar in design, requiring the same equipment arrangements and **setups**. (Many assembly lines process several models of the same product, requiring machine reprogramming and tooling changes, inventory changes, and processing activity changes, prior to the start of a new product model run. These activities are referred to collectively as a "setup.") Each unit of product typically follows the same sequence of processing steps, so the layout can utilize automated material handling equipment such as conveyors to transport products from one processing area to the next.

One of the most imitated assembly line systems in the world today is Toyota's automobile manufacturing system. Its assembly lines produce high volumes of automobiles, using very low setup times, with one of the lowest defect rates in the industry. The Toyota manufacturing facility in Kentucky, for example, produces about 2,000 vehicles per day on two assembly lines, or about one car every 30 seconds.[15]

Figure 8.5 shows a very simplified assembly line. Purchased parts are delivered to the line, where three workcenters perform a series of processing activities until the product is completed. The workcenters are located in close proximity to one another to facilitate faster WIP movements. The assembly tasks are divided as equally as possible for each workcenter, to balance work on the assembly line.

Balancing the line achieves a number of positive outcomes. By dividing the processing work equally, a fair work assignment is achieved for employees. It also reduces the likelihood and severity of bottlenecks, resulting in smoother product flow and higher potential product output levels (recall from the Theory of Constraints that the slowest workcenter will set the pace for the entire assembly line). Line balancing is based on the output levels desired, the work hours per day, the number of workers, and the assembly task times.

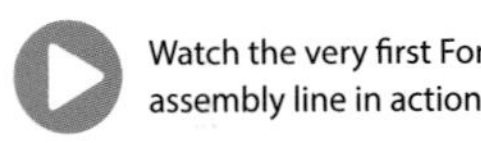
Watch the very first Ford assembly line in action

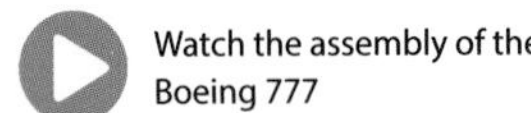
Watch the assembly of the Boeing 777

product focused layouts *See* Assembly line layouts.

assembly line layouts Enables high-volume output while making standardized products. Processing steps are standardized and grouped into relatively equal time lengths of work; these are then assigned to workers, permitting specializations to occur.

setups Many assembly lines process several models of the same product, requiring machine reprogramming and tooling changes, inventory changes, and processing activity changes, prior to the start of a new product model run. These activities are referred to collectively as a setup.

balancing the line Dividing the processing work equally to create an equitable work assignment for employees, reducing the likelihood and severity of bottlenecks, and resulting in smoother product flow and higher potential product output levels. Line balancing is based on the output levels desired, the work hours per day, the number of workers, and the assembly task times.

Figure 8.5 A Simple Assembly Line

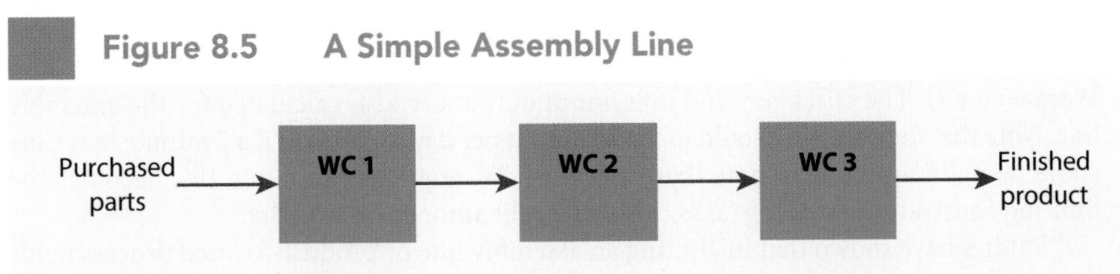

Assembly Line Balancing Steps

The sequence of steps required to balance an assembly line is relatively straightforward:

1. Specify the sequence of tasks to be performed, arranging the tasks in order, using a diagram where circles represent tasks and arrows represent the precedence relationships.
2. Determine the **takt time** (derived from the German word *taktzeit,* meaning literally "clock cycle"),[16] also referred to as the **cycle time**, using the formula:

$$\text{takt time} = \frac{\text{daily operating time}}{\text{desired output per day}}$$

The takt time (TT) establishes the desired pace of the assembly line, which is the maximum time each workcenter can spend on one unit, and also how often a unit must come off the end of the assembly line.

3. Determine the minimum number of workcenters (W_{min}) required to satisfy the takt time and the output requirement per day, using the formula:

$$W_{min} = \frac{\text{sum of all task times}}{\text{TT}}$$

4. Assign all of the tasks to workcenters, so that the sum of task times for each workcenter does not exceed the takt time. To minimize labor costs, the total number of workcenters should also be as close as possible to W_{min} found in Step 3. To minimize worker movements, avoid assigning tasks to workcenters that are not adjacent to one another.
5. Evaluate the efficiency of the assembly line using the formula:

$$\text{Efficiency} = \frac{\text{sum of all task times}}{(\text{\# workcenters} \times \text{TT})}$$

Note that (# workcenters × TT) represents the total labor time (assuming one worker per workcenter) needed to produce one unit of output (this includes labor work time and labor idle time).

6. If necessary, rebalance the line to maximize efficiency and output.

Example 8.1 shows an assembly line balancing problem and solution. In this example, a bicycle factory assembles a bicycle using eight assembly steps or tasks. The table shows that the task times vary from 1 to 7 minutes, with a total task time of 28 minutes. The precedence column shows that Task "a" must be completed first, followed by Tasks "b", "c", and "d". Tasks "b", "c", and "d" can be completed in any order; however, all three must be completed prior to the start of Task "e". Task "f" follows Task "e" and Tasks "g" and "h" are last and follow Task "f". The figure is constructed using these precedence relationships. The arrows in the figure indicate the assembly order and precedence, and the circled letters represent the tasks. To achieve a desired output of 60 units per day, the takt time must be 8 minutes, since the company operates 8 hours per day, or 480 minutes per day. The objective is then to group tasks so as not to exceed 8 minutes per unit per workcenter, and to try to group tasks so that the work is evenly distributed. The solution shown is just one potential assembly line balancing solution, since other solutions exist (such as grouping Tasks "a", "b", and "d" into Workcenter 1). The efficiency and maximum output are also calculated for the assembly line. Note that the company could increase output per day to 68 bikes if a 7 minute takt time could be maintained. Also note that since Task "e" requires 7 minutes, this becomes the limiting constraint, assuming tasks cannot be split among two workers.

Studies have shown that instituting an assembly line or product-focused process tends to increase worker injuries, boredom, absenteeism, turnover, and grievances, while lowering

takt time Derived from the German word *taktzeit*, meaning literally "clock cycle." *See* Cycle time.

cycle time A formula used to establish the desired pace of an assembly line, which is the maximum time each workcenter can spend on one unit, and also how often a unit must come off the end of the assembly line.

job satisfaction. For instance, repetition, high force exertion, and improper posture when using manufacturing tools can cause cumulative trauma disorders among assembly line workers. Swapping workers around in the middle of the day is sometimes done to reduce fatigue and injuries.[17] In a factory in the Netherlands, boiler manufacturer NefitFasto has employees walk around in circles, following a slow-moving assembly line, while performing all of the assembly work on each boiler. In seven minutes, a worker completes all of the assembly tasks, then starts again on another boiler. With seven workers, NefitFasto can make about 60 boilers per hour. "Standing all the time makes you more tired," says manager Theo Hendriks. "With this method, employees stay fresher and do their jobs better."[18]

Assembly Line Balancing Heuristics

For all but the simplest assembly lines, assigning tasks to workstations to maximize efficiency and productivity is a very complex problem. Typically, software-based **heuristic solutions** are used to balance most large assembly lines. A heuristic solution does not guarantee the best solution—it is a procedure that yields a reasonable solution in a relatively short period of time.

A great number of assembly line balancing heuristics have been proposed and tested over the years, and some have found their way into commercial software applications. For example, once a sequence of tasks has been specified, those tasks might then be assigned to workstations based on one of the following rules:

- Assign the largest remaining processing time first to a workcenter in sequential order, until the takt time is reached, then start a new workcenter. (Using this heuristic in Example 8.1 would have resulted in the same four workcenters.)
- Assign the largest remaining processing positional weight first (the weight is equal to the task processing time plus all of the processing times of tasks depending on it), until the takt time is reached, then start a new workcenter. (This heuristic would also have created the same four workcenters in Example 8.1.)
- Assign the task with the most number of following tasks first, in sequential order, until the takt time is reached, then start a new workcenter. (Again, this would have resulted in the same four workcenters.)
- Assign the task with the most number of immediate followers first, in sequential order, until the takt time is reached, then start a new workcenter. (Once again, this heuristic would not have changed any of the four workcenters in Example 8.1.)[19]

Group Technology Layouts

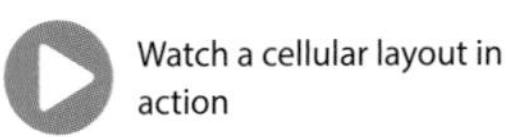
Watch a cellular layout in action

Group technology layouts, also referred to as **cellular layouts**, fall into the product-focused layout category as well. Parts and assemblies that are manufactured in the production facility and require the same processing equipment are identified and grouped into part families. Manufacturing "cells" or small assembly areas are then created to process these part families. Particularly if parts are needed frequently and in large quantities, it makes sense to create group technology layouts with equipment and workers dedicated to the production of these parts. The resulting layouts can then be balanced in a similar fashion to the methods shown in Example 8.1, and have the same advantages as assembly lines. The finished parts then are moved to the final assembly area or assembly line.

Figure 8.6 illustrates how part families can be identified, and how group technology layouts can be created. Manufactured parts are listed with their machining requirements. Parts are then grouped into families based on their common machining requirements. Cellular layouts are then created for these part families. The outputs from these manufacturing cells then go to the final assembly line.

Companies might use group technology layouts when reorganizing the shop floor after periodic expansions, to reduce material flow and inventory problems. For example, Electrical Box & Enclosures, Inc., a small, Alabama-based manufacturing company, started operations in 1988 with just a few machines. By 1997, the company had grown substantially, but haphazardly—while a few of its products accounted for over 60% of its total output, the firm was still laid out as a machine shop, with similar machines grouped in

heuristic solutions Procedures that yield a *reasonable solution* in a relatively short period of time.

group technology layouts *See* Cellular layouts.

cellular layouts Parts and assemblies that require the same processing equipment are identified and grouped into part families. Manufacturing "cells" or small assembly areas are then created to process these part families. Also referred to as group technology layouts or GT cells.

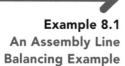

Example 8.1
An Assembly Line Balancing Example

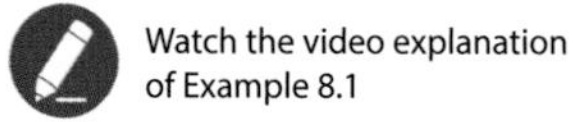

Watch the video explanation of Example 8.1

The Blakemaster Bicycle Company has decided to begin production of a new line of cruiser bikes, and has dedicated an area of its factory to a new production line. The processing activities, processing times, and precedence relationships are shown in the table below. Based on this information, a figure is constructed, with circles indicating the tasks, and arrows indicating the activity sequence and precedence. It works an 8-hour day, and the forecasted demand is 60 units per day. It wishes to balance the line.

Task	Time (min.)	Task Follows
a	4	—
b	3	a
c	6	a
d	1	a
e	7	b,c,d
f	2	e
g	2	f
h	3	f
Total	28	

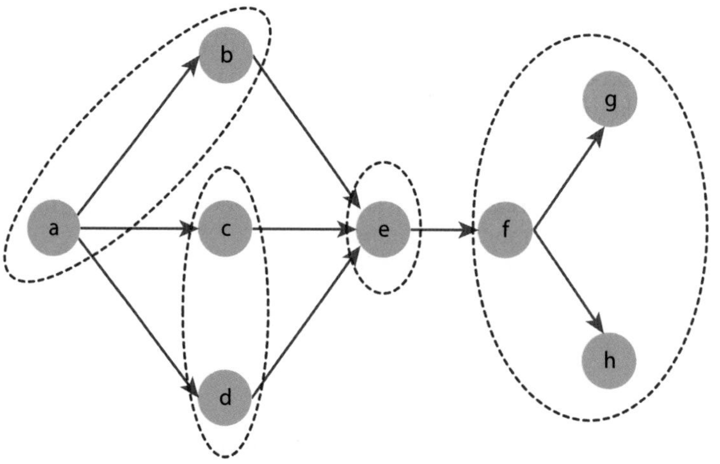

Solution:

The takt time is: $TT = \frac{480 \text{ min/day}}{60 \text{ units/day}} = 8$ minutes per unit. There must be *at least* 4 workcenters, since $W_{min} = \frac{28}{8} = 3.5$, or 4 workcenters. Grouping the activities while considering the processing sequence, task times, takt time, and proximities yields one potential solution: WC1: a,b; WC2: c,d; WC3: e; WC4: f,g,h. The dotted lines in the figure indicate the workcenters. With this balance, each workstation has 7 minutes of process time and 1 minute of idle time, as each unit is assembled (note that the pace of the line is 8 minutes per unit). The efficiency of the line is: $\text{Efficiency} = \frac{28}{8(4)} = 0.875$, or 87.5%. With output = 60 units/day, this equates to total work time of 60(28) = 1,680 minutes, or 28 labor hours/day; using 4 workers, this also means (32 – 28), or 4 hours of total labor idle time per day. Using the takt time formula, the maximum output/day $= \frac{480 \text{ min/day}}{7 \text{ units/day}} = 68$ units, if workers can maintain a 7-minute takt time (note that this is the minimum takt time).

Figure 8.6 Developing Cellular Layouts

Part	Lathe	Drill	Mill	Paint	Saw	Planer	Sander	Grinder	Buffer
001	X				X		X	X	
002		X	X						X
003	X			X		X			X
004			X	X				X	
005	X	X				X	X		
006				X	X		X		X
007			X				X	X	
008	X	X	X			X		X	
009				X	X		X		
010		X			X	X			X

Part Families (Cells)	Tools Required
1) 001,004, 010	Drill, Paint, Sander, Grinder, Buffer
2) 002,005,006,008	Lathe, Drill, Mill, Saw, Grinder, Buffer
3) 003,007,009	Paint, Saw, Planer, Sander, Buffer

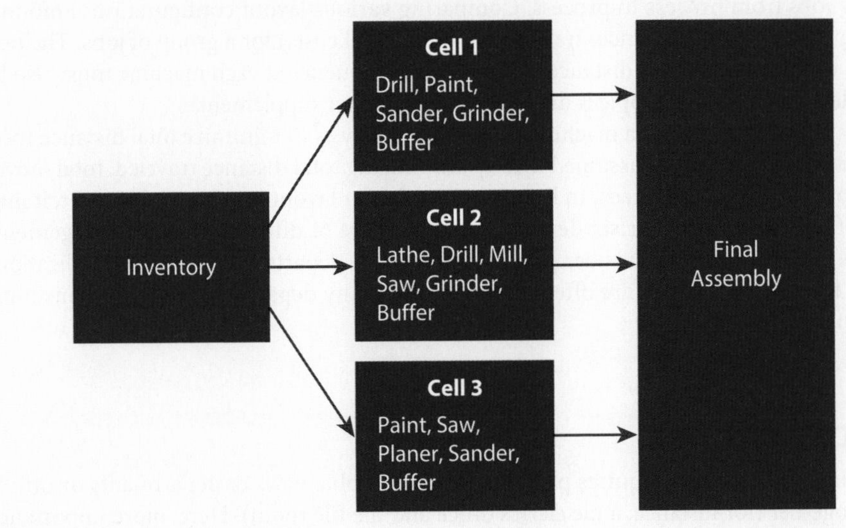

departments. As a result, material flow problems had surfaced, causing significant quality, lead time, and inventory problems. A plan was developed to design several group technology layouts around the most popular items, and the plan was in place by 1999. The resulting layout was able to achieve higher output, with 25% fewer employees, a 67% reduction in manufacturing lead times, and a 50% reduction in WIP inventories, with substantial improvements in quality.[20]

iStock/IPGGutenbergUKLtd

Most machine shops have similar equipment grouped together, to maximize flexibility.

PROCESS-FOCUSED LAYOUTS

Process-focused layouts are desirable when many different products are manufactured, requiring small output volumes or batch sizes. These layouts are designed for manufacturing flexibility, and are also called **intermittent process layouts** or **machine shop layouts**. In a typical week, some equipment may not be used at all, while other machines may be heavily utilized. Consequently, machines tend to be grouped by function in departments. Aside from machine shops, auto repair garages are also good examples of this type of production facility.

Due to the variable nature of demand, jobs are scheduled for processing and queued into the facility when they are received. For new jobs, this can result in significant wait times, depending on the amount of work already scheduled in the shop (note, for instance, how much longer it takes to get your car repaired when you show up at the repair shop at 10:00 a.m. instead of 8:00 a.m.). Different jobs require different processing steps within the facility, so parts, materials, and assemblies tend to be moving almost randomly within the shop. Thus, automated fixed-path material handling equipment, like conveyors or overhead racks, are not typically used. Instead, jobs are placed on pallets and moved with forklifts or manually in some other fashion. This type of material handling, combined with the queuing of jobs at various processing stages, creates relatively long lead times for jobs, along with higher WIP inventories, when compared to similar sized product-focused facilities. Process-focused facilities are built for processing flexibility but must sacrifice speed, production rate, and machine utilization, while resulting in high inventory carrying costs. Conversely, product-focused facilities are built to supply high volumes quickly, but sacrifice product flexibility in order to attain the high output levels.

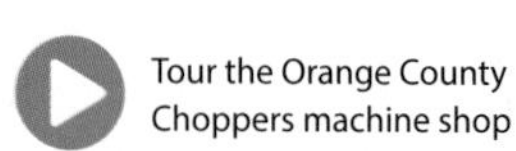

Tour the Orange County Choppers machine shop

To manage material flow in process-focused firms, the emphasis must first be on *placing the most frequently used departments close to one another*, so as to minimize lost time when moving jobs from process to process. Comparing various layout configurations amounts to comparing the total distances traveled (or total travel costs) for a group of jobs. The best layouts will minimize these distances or costs. Jobs in queues at each machine must also be scheduled effectively (this topic is discussed in the chapter supplement).

Example 8.2 illustrates a machine shop layout analysis to minimize total distance traveled per day (it is generally assumed that by minimizing total distance traveled, total movement costs are also minimized). In Example 8.2, a better layout was found; however, it may not be the best layout. (For six departments, there are 6! different layout arrangements possible, or 720 layouts to consider.) In cases with many departments, software applications to help find the best layout are often used, since so many department combinations must be evaluated.

process-focused layouts When similar processing equipment is departmentalized. These are desirable when many different products are manufactured, requiring small output volumes or batch sizes. These layouts are designed for manufacturing flexibility. Also referred to as intermittent process layouts or machine shop layouts.

intermittent process layouts *See* Process-focused layouts.

machine shop layouts *See* Process-focused layouts.

closeness desirability rating Used in office layouts. When department pairs are given numerical ratings based on their closeness desirability. The objective is to create a layout with the highest desirability rating.

OFFICE LAYOUTS

Designing office layouts requires placing certain desirable pairs of departments or offices closer together (for instance, a file clerk's office and the file room). Here, more importance is placed on the relationship between various offices than the number of trips between them. In a doctor's office, for example, it would be desirable to have the X-ray room *far away* from pediatrics. For each department pair, then, a **closeness desirability rating** can be specified, with the objective being to design a layout that maximizes an overall desirability rating for the entire office. Example 8.3 illustrates this concept. Note that to use this analysis, only office pairs sharing at least part of one wall are counted—otherwise, their desirability score is left out. It should also be noted that it might be desirable to use a combination of the analysis techniques illustrated in Examples 8.2 and 8.3 for a given layout problem; in this way, the evaluation team could consider the best layout from both distance traveled and closeness desirability perspectives.

Example 8.2
A Process-Focused Layout Analysis

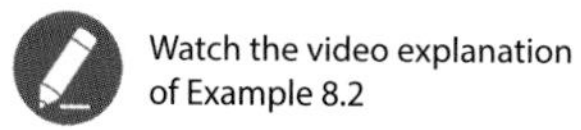

The Hayleyton Machine Shop has decided to analyze the job flow in its shop to see if a more effective layout can be designed to reduce average job lead time. It has six processing departments in the shop, positioned as shown here. The vertical distance between departments is 45 feet, while the horizontal distance is 60 feet. To move a job from Department B to Department E, for example, would require two horizontal moves (120 feet) and one vertical move (45 feet). For a typical day, the number of jobs moving from one department to the next is shown in the matrix here. Assume that diagonal moves are not possible.

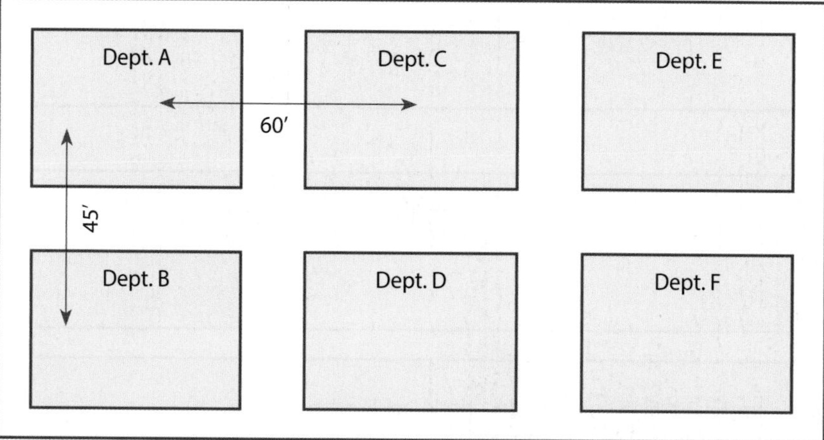

Interdepartmental Trips per Day						
	Dept. A	Dept. B	Dept. C	Dept. D	Dept. E	Dept. F
Dept. A	–	6	4	5	8	10
Dept. B	2	–	9	8	0	3
Dept. C	4	2	–	0	4	4
Dept. D	2	8	4	–	6	2
Dept. E	7	4	3	6	–	2
Dept. F	8	2	0	2	4	–

Multiplying the number of interdepartmental trips by the distances shown results in the following total distance matrix. Summing these results in a total distance traveled of 12,510 feet per day.

Total Distance Traveled per Day (feet)						
	Dept. A	Dept. B	Dept. C	Dept. D	Dept. E	Dept. F
Dept. A	-	270	240	525	960	1650
Dept. B	90	-	945	480	0	360
Dept. C	240	210	-	0	240	420
Dept. D	210	480	180	-	630	120
Dept. E	840	660	180	630	-	90
Dept. F	1320	240	0	120	180	-

When adding the distances traveled in both directions (A to B + B to A is 360 feet, for example), it can be seen that the following pairs of departments should be closer together: A–F, A–E, and B–C (other

(Continued)

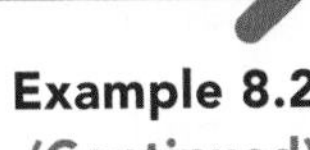

Example 8.2 (Continued)

departments, to a lesser degree, could also be placed closer to one another). Swapping departments A and C would put all three pairs of departments closer together, but it would also put other departments further apart, making the overall impact on total distance traveled less obvious. For each change, then, a new total distance must be calculated. The new layout would look like this:

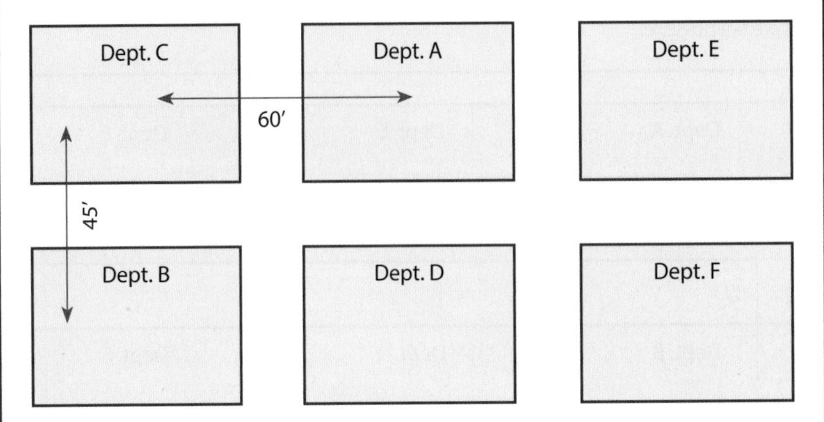

And the new total distance traveled matrix would look like this:

	Interdepartmental Trips per Day					
	Dept. A	Dept. B	Dept. C	Dept. D	Dept. E	Dept. F
Dept. A	–	630	240	225	480	1050
Dept. B	210	–	405	480	0	360
Dept. C	240	90	–	0	480	660
Dept. D	90	480	420	–	630	120
Dept. E	420	660	360	630	–	90
Dept. F	840	240	0	120	180	–

The total distance traveled in the revised layout would be 10,830 feet per day, an improvement of 1,680 feet per day, or about 13 percent. A large number of potentially good layouts could be designed and checked, and for this reason, a number of layout software applications are available, to reduce computation time.

RETAIL LAYOUTS

While all retail layouts utilize **servicescapes** to varying degrees, to create conditions that appeal to customers retailers are trying to attract, the ultimate goal of retail layouts is to maximize sales per customer. Successful retailers will combine their servicescapes and layouts to achieve high levels of sales.

servicescapes Describe the retail environment. This includes use of pleasant lighting, background music, and comfortable ambient temperatures. Other obvious servicescape items are well-placed signs, wide aisles, use of carpeting, pleasant wall colors, and "try-it-out" areas.

Servicescapes describe the retail environment, and this includes use of pleasant lighting, background music, and comfortable ambient temperatures. Other obvious servicescape items are well-placed signs, wide aisles, use of carpeting, pleasant wall colors, and "try-it-out" areas that are found in toy stores and music stores. Setting the right mood can have a big impact on repeat visits.

Good retail layouts expose customers to as many product choices as possible during their visits. As stated previously, a key objective is to *maximize sales per square foot of floor space.* This is why milk and eggs, two very common food shopping list items, are usually found at the

Example 8.3
An Office Layout Analysis Using a Closeness Desirability Rating

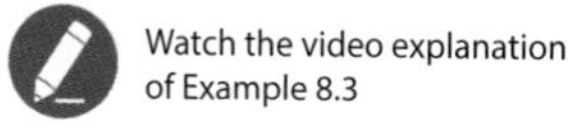

Watch the video explanation of Example 8.3

The Faith Consulting Company is leasing new office space and wants to design an office layout in which desirable office pairs are close together while undesirable pairs are far apart. Management has decided on a desirability scale of (–1 to 3), where –1 = undesirable, 0 = unimportant, 1 = slightly important, 2 = important, and 3 = very important. They have rated each set of office pairs, shown here, and wish to assess their current office layout and potentially find a better one.

Desirability Ratings

	B	C	D	E	F	G	H
A	2	0	–1	2	2	3	–1
B		0	2	1	1	0	3
C			2	2	0	0	1
D				1	–1	–1	3
E					3	1	2
F						3	1
G							0

Current Office Layout

File room (F)	Engineering offices (C)	Marketing offices (B)	Secretary and waiting area (A)
Purchasing (E)	President's office (D)	Conference room (H)	Copy room (G)

The closeness desirability score for the current layout = (A/B:2) + (A/H:–1) + (A/G:3) + (B/C:0) + (B/H:3) + (C/F:0) + (C/D:2) + (D/E:1) + (D/H:3) + (E/F:3) + (G/H:0) = 16. Note that no pairs are counted twice, and only pairs that have overlapping sides are counted. Note, for example, that F/D, E/H, and B/G were not counted, along with a number of other department pairs.

Placing the file room, F, next to the secretary's office, A, and moving the president's office, D, into the corner, results in the following layout:

New Office Layout

President's office (D)	Engineering offices (C)	Marketing offices (B)	Secretary and waiting area (A)
Purchasing (E)	Conference room (H)	File room (F)	Copy room (G)

(Continued)

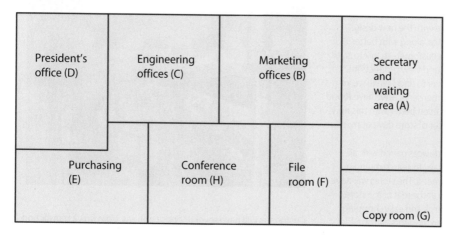

Example 8.3 (Continued)

The closeness desirability score for the new layout is: (A/B:2) + (A/F:2) + (A/G:3) + (B/C:0) + (B/H:3) + (B/F:1) + (C/D:2) + (C/E:2) + (C/H:1) + (D/E:1) + (E/H:2) + (H/F:1) + (F/G:3) = 23.

On the basis of this analysis, it can be concluded that the second layout is better; like the previous example, though, there are many potential layouts, so a number of those should be evaluated prior to selecting the most appropriate one.

back of grocery stores (as shown in Figure 8.7), and why candy, gum, and magazines (impulse items) are found in the checkout aisles. Another objective is to provide high levels of customer service, as described in the Service Spotlight below.

Several rules of thumb are typical considerations when planning a retail layout:

1. Space-out the high-demand items around the furthest reaches of the location.
2. Place high profit margin items and impulse items on end-aisle locations or at the storefront, to maximize exposure.
3. Within a product line, space-out popular models to maximize exposure to others.

More on retail layouts can be found in the final segment of this chapter.

PROJECT LAYOUTS

iStock/nightman1965

In project layouts, the product is stationary, while workers and equipment move in or out as needed.

Also called **fixed-position layouts**, **project layouts** are characterized by manufactured units that remain stationary (such as buildings and cruise ships), while workers and equipment move in and around the project depending on the construction work scheduled at that time. Effective project layouts must consider the scheduling of various processes (when building a house, the cement slab cannot be poured prior to the placement of underground utilities), the placing of materials needed for upcoming activities (staging areas are needed for materials and must be located close to projects), and the dynamic nature of projects (as time

SERVICE SPOTLIGHT

T-Mobile's New Retail Layout

T-Mobile USA, Inc., has unveiled a new store layout for nearly 400 stores across the United States. Its objective with the new design is to provide a better customer experience, along with better operating efficiencies. The layout allows customers to talk to sales representatives at private service desks and view products in clearly defined areas, making things easier to find. "While we've continually been honored for our customer service, we have found ways to make the shopping experience even better with this new design," says Debra Coates, senior director of store development.

The improved layout shows customers devices paired with all the relevant accessories, so they don't have to search multiple spots within the store to find what they need. The stores will have hardwood flooring, a messaging screen at the rear of the store, and an open environment, creating a quick and easy shopping experience. Information kiosks and video monitors will provide customers an interactive shopping experience.

Bloomberg/Contributor/Getty

Customers will have several service options, from quick transaction service counters to private service desks for long transactions.[21]

Figure 8.7 A Typical Customer Path Through a Grocery Store

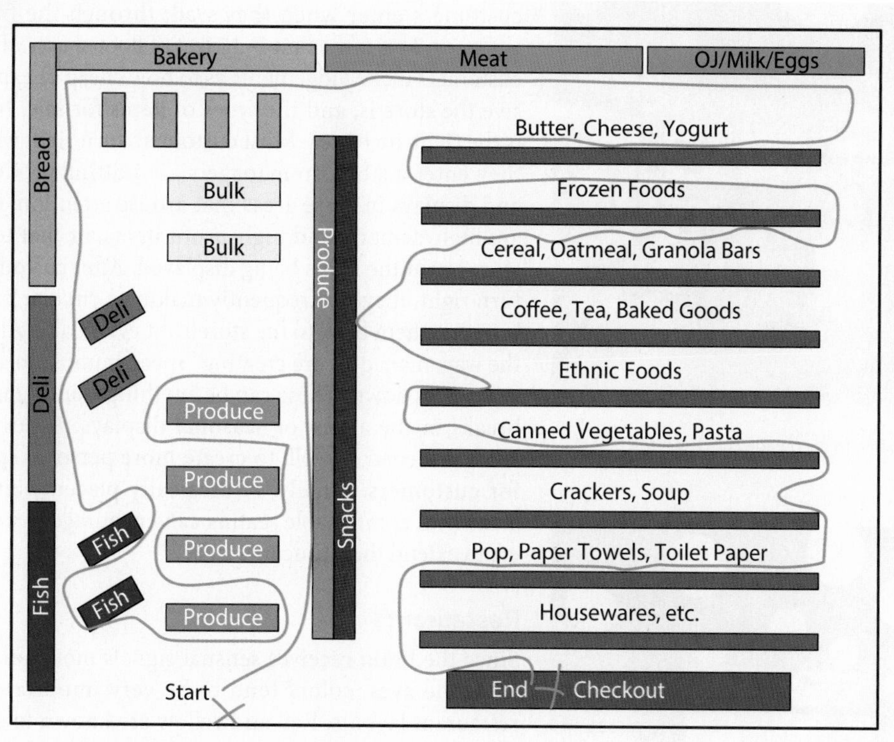

Source: Original image courtesy of Lindsey Evanoff, http://happyorhungry.com

progresses, some activities must be expedited to keep later activities from falling even further behind). Many of these project topics are discussed further in Chapter 12.

To reduce project lead times and total costs, some projects are now made on assembly lines. Sales of manufactured homes, for instance, are growing in the United States by about 5% per year. Frugal buyers are attracted to the low prices and quick availabilities of manufactured homes compared to traditionally built homes. "It was eight weeks from the time we signed the contract to the day we were ready to move in," says Dean Schaecher, a Boise, ID, home buyer. "Plus, it was built in a factory, so it could be inspected every step of the way, we knew exactly what our costs were, and it looks like a normal single-family home."[22] Additionally, many assemblies placed in projects are now constructed off-site on assembly lines and simply bolted or attached in place when they arrive on the project site. Examples are metal and wood framing and cabinetry in home constructions. This also tends to reduce costs while speeding up completion times.

fixed-position layouts Characterized by manufactured products that remain stationary (such as buildings and cruise ships), while workers and equipment move in and around the project depending on the construction work scheduled at that time. Also referred to as project layouts.

project layouts *See* Fixed-position layouts.

TRENDS IN LAYOUT DESIGN

8.6 Discuss some of the latest trends in layout design

Many of the layout trends reported on most frequently are concerned with retail shops and restaurants, and so these are reviewed here.

Retailing

Today, **visual merchandising** is changing the look and feel of retail layouts. End caps, at the end of each aisle, are making use of fixtures, lighting, and color to highlight products. Focal points are also being added in center-aisle locations, known as **micro-merchandising**, where product families are featured, sometimes using rounded front-edge shelving, to improve visual appeal. Aisle heights are also dropping in many stores, to allow customers to view other areas of the stores.[23]

visual merchandising Includes use of end caps at the end of each aisle, and making use of fixtures, lighting, and color to highlight products.

micro-merchandising Focal points that are added in center-aisle locations, where product families are featured, sometimes using rounded front-edge shelving, to improve visual appeal.

iStock/fiphoto

Retailers today are using visual merchandising to encourage customers to enter the store and to shop longer.

Bloomberg/Contributor/Getty

Dunkin' Donuts' new layout design features bright lighting and colors to attract customers.

Additionally, significant effort is being put into redesigning the threshold area, which is the first space customers enter when they walk through the front entrance. This is the first 5–15 feet of floor space, where customers make judgements as to how cheap or expensive the store is, and the types of items for sale. Next is the right-turn area. Most customers turn right when they enter a store, so managers are putting products and displays in these areas that arouse attention, that are high-demand and high-profit items, or that tell a story about the items being displayed. After customers turn right, they are frequently making a circular path, bringing them back to the storefront eventually. Along the way, managers are creating "speed bumps" to slow customers down. These can be anything from signage, breaks in the aisles, or seasonal displays. Aisles are being widened as well, to create more personal space for customers. Finally, strategically placed waiting areas with comfortable seating can encourage customers to extend their time in a store.[24]

Restaurants

Since the brain receives sensual signals most quickly from the eyes, colors tend to be very important in restaurant layouts. Red and yellow are known to subconsciously trigger hunger and excitement, and this is why a number of restaurant brands use these colors in their restaurants and logo designs.

Bright lighting can enhance speed of service and customer turnover, which can be useful for quick-serve restaurants and for boosting revenues. However, for many fast-casual restaurants seeking to create a different atmosphere, dim lighting tends to encourage customers to stay longer and enjoy themselves.

Another strategy in restaurant layouts is use of **sight lines**. Guests might get a view of the kitchen when ordering, which can create theater and freshness cues. "You need to have enough view to the back of the house so that it doesn't look like you're trying to hide something from the customers," says Dennis Lombardi, executive of food service strategies at Ohio-based consulting firm WD Partners. A redesigned layout at the Blimpie sandwich stores uses sight lines to allow customers to see meats sliced and sandwiches made. Blimpies' new layouts also feature a more open seating area to allow customers to feel a sense of community. "I want to create an atmosphere for them to feel welcomed in and not rushed out," says Bill Morris, owner of a redesigned Blimpie in Iowa.[25]

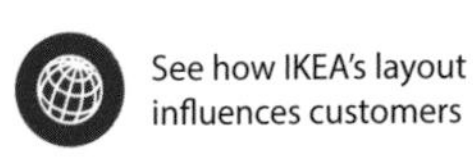

See how IKEA's layout influences customers

sight lines Used in many restaurant and retail layouts. Allow guests to get a view of the kitchen or other parts of the store.

Visit edge.sagepub.com/wisner to help you accomplish your coursework goals in an easy-to-use learning environment.

- Mobile-friendly eFlashcards
- Mobile-friendly practice quizzes
- A complete online action plan
- Chapter summaries with learning objectives
- Excel templates to assist with practice problems
- Original video case studies that demonstrate chapter concepts in action

SUMMARY

This chapter has expanded on the inventory management topics of Chapter 7, and presented a number of material flow management ideas important to operations management. Material flows can greatly impact the firm's costs and its ability to provide trading partners with timely, high-quality deliveries of product. In today's global economy, the flexibility to monitor process flows and rapidly adjust to changing demand patterns is a necessary competitive weapon, and can be achieved through application of the many material flow concepts discussed in this chapter. This chapter contained discussions of material flow mapping and analysis and manufacturing, retail, and office layouts. A number of layout concepts were also presented and discussed, including product- and process-focused layouts, group technology layouts, and project layouts. Finally, some trends in layout design were discussed.

KEY TERMS

Assembly line layouts, 223
Balancing the line, 223
Cellular layouts, 225
Closeness desirability rating, 228
Computer aided design (CAD), 221
Computer assisted manufacturing (CAM), 221
Computer integrated manufacturing (CIM), 221
Computer numerically controlled machines (CNC), 221
Cycle time, 224
Drum, buffer, rope concept (DBR), 219
Fixed-position layouts, 232
Flexible manufacturing system (FMS), 221
Group technology layouts, 225
Heuristic solutions, 225
Intermittent process layouts, 228
Machine shop layouts, 228
Manufacturing flexibility, 220
Material flow analysis, 216
Material flow mapping, 214
Micro-merchandising, 233
Process flowcharting, 214
Process-focused layouts, 228
Process mapping, 214
Product focused layouts, 223
Project layouts, 232
Servicescapes, 230
Setups, 223
Sight lines, 234
Takt time, 224
Value stream mapping, 214
Visual merchandising, 233

FORMULA REVIEW

Takt time (or cycle time): $TT = \frac{\text{daily operating time}}{TT}$, where TT = takt time

Minimum number of assembly line workcenters: $W_{min} = \frac{\text{sum of all task times}}{TT}$.

Assembly line efficiency: $\text{Efficiency} = \frac{\text{sum of all task times}}{(\#\text{workcenters} \times TT)}$.

SOLVED PROBLEMS

1. The following tasks must be arranged as an assembly line:

Task	Time (sec.)	Task Follows
a	14	—
b	23	—
c	19	a
d	11	b
e	17	c, d
f	28	e
Total	112	

a. Arrange the tasks using the precedence relationships, connected by flow arrows, as they would appear on the shop floor.

b. Assuming the facility is open 8 hours/day and desires an output of 800 units/day, determine the takt time and the minimum number of workcenters.

c. Balance the assembly line, determine the efficiency of the line, and determine the total labor work time and idle time per day, assuming one worker per workcenter.

d. Assuming one workcenter per task, what is the maximum output per day and the corresponding takt time and efficiency?

Answer:

a.

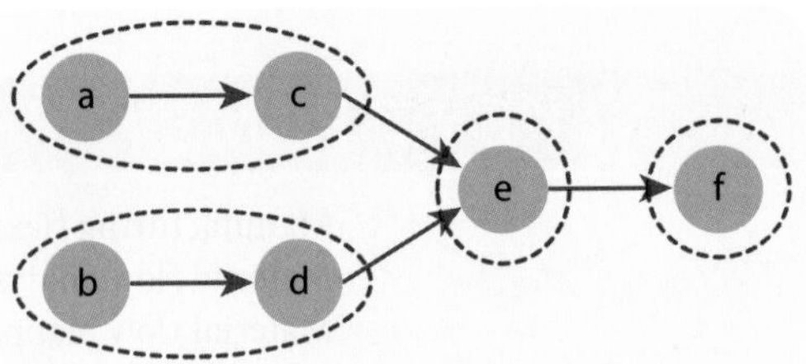

b.
$$TT = \frac{\text{daily operating time}}{\text{desired output per day}} = \frac{8(60)(60)}{800} = 36 \text{ sec/unit}$$

$$W_{min} = \frac{\text{sum of all task times}}{TT} = \frac{112}{36} = 3.1 \text{ or } 4 \text{ workcenters}$$

c. Workcenters are: (a,c), (b,d), (e), (f) shown as dotted circles in the figure.

$$\text{Efficiency} = \frac{\text{sum of all task times}}{(\#\,\text{workcenters} \times TT)} = \frac{112}{4(36)} = 0.778 = 77.8\%$$ Workers required = 4; labor time = 32 hours per day;

Total labor work time = [(800 units/day) (112 seconds/unit)]/[(60 seconds/minute) (60 minutes/hour)] = 24.89 hours/day. Thus, idle time = 32 hours – 24.89 hours = 7.11 hours/day.

d. With 6 workcenters, minimum takt time = 28 sec. (the longest task time). The maximum output is found using the takt time formula:

$$\text{Output/day} = \frac{\text{daily operating time}}{TT} = 8(60)(60)/28 = 1028.6 \text{ or } 1028 \text{ units.}$$

$$\text{Efficiency} = \frac{\text{sum of all task times}}{(\#\,\text{workcenters} \times TT)} = \frac{112}{6(28)} = 0.66.7 = 66.7\%$$

2. Determine the total movement cost per day, for the given process-focused facility, and then find a better layout.

Dept. A	Dept. C	Dept. E $2
Dept. B $1	Dept. D	Dept. F $1

A vertical, horizontal, or diagonal move between adjacent departments is $1, while a two-department move is $2, as shown above. For a typical day, the number of material movements from one department to the next (in both directions) is shown in the matrix that follows.

Trips/day	Dept. B	Dept. C	Dept. D	Dept. E	Dept. F
Dept. A	6	8	12	7	15
Dept. B	–	10	13	8	12
Dept. C	–	–	8	12	9
Dept. D	–	–	–	8	4
Dept. E	–	–	–	–	7

Answer:

The total cost matrix is shown as follows:

$/day	Dept. B	Dept. C	Dept. D	Dept. E	Dept. F
Dept. A	6	8	12	14	30
Dept. B	–	10	13	16	24
Dept. C	–	–	8	12	9
Dept. D	–	–	–	8	4
Dept. E	–	–	–	–	7

The total trip cost for the given layout is $181 per day. The two highest cost department pairs are (A/F) and (B/F). Thus, to reduce the layout cost, a logical move would be to swap departments C and F. The new total cost matrix would then be:

$/day	Dept. B	Dept. C	Dept. D	Dept. E	Dept. F
Dept. A	6	16	12	14	15
Dept. B	–	20	13	16	12
Dept. C	–	–	8	12	9
Dept. D	–	–	–	8	4
Dept. E	–	–	–	–	7

The change results in a total trip cost of $172, which is a savings of $9 per day, or about 5%. There could be other cheaper layouts, but 6! combinations would have to be checked to be sure.

3. Using the original layout shown in Problem 2, and the following desirability matrix, assess the current layout and try to find a better one. The scale used is: –1= undesirable, 0= unimportant, 1 = slightly important, 2 = important, and 3 = very important. If only corners are touching, then don't count the score.

Desirability Ratings

	Dept. B	Dept. C	Dept. D	Dept. E	Dept. F
A	1	0	2	2	1
B		0	–1	3	3
C			3	1	–1
D				0	2
E					1

Answer:

The desirability score for the original layout shown in Problem 2 is (A/B=1)+(A/C=0)+(B/D=–1)+(C/D=3)+(C/E=1)+(D/F=2)+(E/F=1) = 7. Based on the scores in the matrix, it would make sense to swap B and E, so that B/F and A/E can be counted and so that B/D won't be counted. The resulting layout desirability score would then be: (A/E=2)+(A/C=0)+(C/D=3)+(C/B=0)+(D/F=2)+(B/F=3) = 10. So this layout appears to be a significant improvement.

REVIEW QUESTIONS

1. What is the objective of material flow analysis?
2. What is a bottleneck?
3. Describe the Theory of Constraints (TOC).
4. What is the drum, buffer, rope (DBR) concept, and what does it have to do with the TOC?
5. What is manufacturing flexibility?
6. Explain the difference between a flexible manufacturing system and a computer integrated manufacturing system.
7. Provide an example of mass customization.
8. What type of manufacturing firm uses a product-focused layout? What are its objectives?
9. What is "takt time," and what is it used for?
10. What are the advantages and disadvantages of assembly line balancing?
11. What is a group technology layout?
12. What is a process-focused layout, and what would be an example of one?
13. What are the advantages and disadvantages of product-focused facilities compared to process-focused facilities?
14. What is the general objective when designing a process-focused layout?
15. What are the scheduling concerns at a product-focused facility and a process-focused facility?
16. What is a servicescape?
17. How do project layouts differ from product- and process-focused layouts?
18. What is visual merchandising and micro-merchandising?
19. What is a sight line, and how is it used to improve facility layouts?

DISCUSSION QUESTIONS

1. Why is it important to understand the flow of materials in an organization?
2. Construct a process map for a fast-food business, or a business of your choosing.
3. What are the process analysis questions that should be asked and answered for the map completed in Question 2?
4. How could the Theory of Constraints (TOC) be used at a neighborhood grocery store? For a basketball team?
5. Could the TOC be applied to management effectiveness?
6. Why is manufacturing flexibility a desirable characteristic? Is there an organization where this would not be desirable?
7. Describe how the Theory of Constraints could be used in a product-focused facility.
8. General Motors has a takt time of eight minutes per unit. What does this mean? If the GM plant operated 24/7, how many units would be produced in one year?
9. When, and for what type of facility, would a group technology layout be most appropriate?
10. Could a manufacturing facility layout be analyzed from a closeness desirability perspective? Would this be a good idea?
11. What could be the advantage of analyzing a layout from both a cost minimization and a closeness desirability perspective?
12. How could a servicescape be used in your classroom?
13. How could your university's bookstore use visual merchandising and micro-merchandising? Does your bookstore already use them?

EXERCISES AND PROJECTS

1. Go to a business with which you are familiar, and create a material/worker flow map. Then analyze the flows with the help of one of the managers at the facility.
2. Analyze your homework and study activities using the Theory of Constraints. Describe how you could improve this process by improving or eliminating a constraint.
3. Search online for three examples of mass customization not described in this text, and write a report describing these companies.

PROBLEMS

1. Use the tasks shown and their precedence relationships to create the flow diagram. Determine the takt time and the minimum number of workstations, assuming an 8-hour workday and a required output of 50 units per day.

Task	Time (min.)	Task Follows
a	2	—
b	1.5	a
c	5	a
d	3	a
e	1	b,c,d
f	2	e
Total	14.5	

2. Using the information from Problem 1, balance the line and determine the efficiency, the total labor time per day, the total work time per day, and the total idle time per day.
3. Also using the information from Problem 1, calculate minimum takt time and the corresponding output per day. What is the efficiency, total labor time, total work time, and total idle time per day?
4. If the company runs two shifts and operates 16 hours per day, determine the takt time in seconds per unit if the required output is 4,000 units per day.
5. The Mary Kay Bakery has decided to arrange its processes so that an assembly operation can be used to increase its baked goods output. The processing activities are shown below, with the arrows indicating the activity sequence and precedence. The desired output per day is 120 units. The bakery works one 8-hour shift per day. Balance the assembly line, using the information provided below. Calculate the takt time, the minimum number of workstations, and the line efficiency. Additionally, determine the total labor time, total work time, and total idle time per day.

Task	Time (min.)
a	2
b	1
c	3
d	3
e	3
f	2
g	2
h	3
Total	21 min.

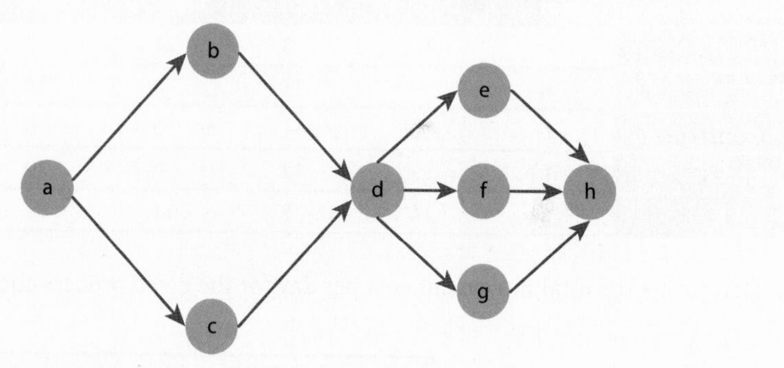

6. Using the information in Problem 5, determine the minimum takt time and the corresponding output per day. What is the new efficiency and the new work time and idle time per day?
7. Given a total task time of 48 minutes, a desired output of 80 units per day, and two 8-hour shifts per day, what is the takt time in minutes per unit? What is the minimum number of workcenters? If the assembly line is balanced with six workcenters, what is the efficiency?
8. Using the following assembly line information, construct a flow diagram using arrows to indicate sequence and precedence, calculate the takt time, calculate the minimum number of workcenters, balance the line, and finally, calculate the line efficiency. What is the total worker idle time per day? The desired output is 45 units per day. The factory is open for 8 hours per day.

Activity	Task Time (min.)	Immediate Predecessors
a	6	—
b	4	a
c	2	a
d	7	b
e	3	c
f	6	d,e

9. For the information given in Problem 8, what would be the minimum takt time, if the firm put one worker at each machine (i.e., used six workcenters)? What would be the corresponding output per day? What would be the efficiency? What would be the total worker idle time per day?

10. The Iarussi Real Estate Agency has decided to analyze the flow of employees in its office to see if a more effective layout can be designed to reduce total daily walking distance. It has five departments in the office, positioned as shown. Determine the total distance traveled per day for the given process-focused facility, and then find a better layout.

Dept. A	Dept. C	Dept. E
Dept. B	Dept. D	

(Horizontal distance: 30′; vertical distance: 25′)

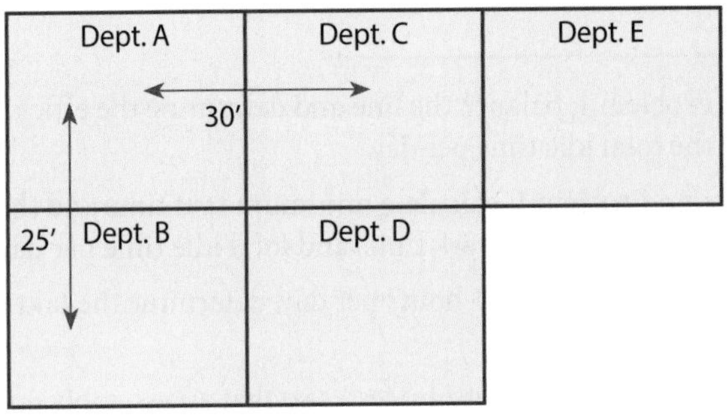

The vertical distance between departments is 25 feet, while the horizontal distance is 30 feet. To walk from Department A to Department D would then require a vertical move (25 feet) and a horizontal move (30 feet), assuming there are no hallways or diagonal movements. For a typical day, the number of employee movements from one department to the next is shown in the matrix below:

Trips/day	Dept. A	Dept. B	Dept. C	Dept. D	Dept. E
Dept. A	–	10	8	22	7
Dept. B	4	–	15	8	18
Dept. C	6	10	–	0	6
Dept. D	15	9	12	–	10
Dept. E	6	14	5	14	–

11. Determine the total movement cost per day for the given process-focused facility, and then find a better layout.

Dept. A	Dept. C	Dept. E
Dept. B	Dept. D	Dept. F

(Horizontal move: $1; vertical move: $1; diagonal move: $2)

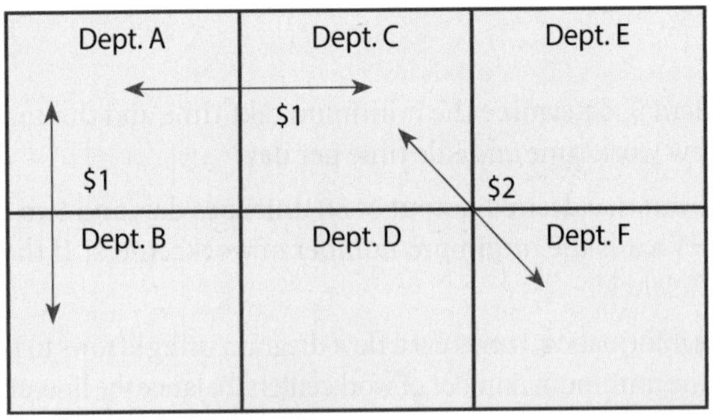

Each vertical or horizontal move between adjacent departments is $1, while a diagonal move is $2, as shown above. For a typical day, the number of material movements from one department to the next (in both directions) is shown in the matrix below:

Trips/day	Dept. B	Dept. C	Dept. D	Dept. E	Dept. F
Dept. A	22	18	16	27	13
Dept. B	—	12	0	12	17
Dept. C	—	—	8	17	21
Dept. D	—	—	—	24	0
Dept. E	—	—	—	—	17

12. For the office layout shown here, determine the closeness desirability rating using the following closeness desirability matrix. Treat the hallway as if it doesn't exist (i.e., the Production and Accounting Departments touch each other). The desirability scale used is: –1 = undesirable, 0 = unimportant, 1 = slightly important, 2 = important, and 3 = very important. Can you find a more desirable layout? How could you use both the total distance traveled and the closeness desirability in assessing the layout alternatives?

Management (1)	Production (2)	Engineering (3)	Reception (4)
Files (5)	Accounting (6)	Purchasing (7)	Sales (8)

Closeness Desirability Matrix

	(2)	(3)	(4)	(5)	(6)	(7)	(8)
(1)	2	2	–1	0	1	3	3
(2)		3	0	0	0	3	1
(3)			0	2	0	2	3
(4)				3	1	2	2
(5)					2	2	1
(6)						0	2
(7)							1

13. Determine the closeness desirability for the office layout and the desirability matrix shown below. The desirability scale is: –3 = undesirable, 0 = unimportant, 1 = slightly important, 2 = important, and 3 = very important. Assume that the department sides must overlap to count. Additionally, see if you can find a better layout.

Dept. A	Dept. C	Dept. D
Dept. B		

Closeness Desirability Matrix

	Dept. B	Dept. C	Dept. D
Dept. A	–3	2	1
Dept. B	–	2	2
Dept. C	–	–	0

14. For the office layout shown in Problem 13, assume a vertical move is 40 feet and horizontal move is 60 feet between adjacent departments. No diagonal movements are allowed. Using the daily trip information shown below, determine the current total footage traveled per day. Find a layout that is good from both a footage traveled basis and a closeness desirability basis.

Daily Trip Matrix (both directions)

Trips/day	Dept. B	Dept. C	Dept. D
Dept. A	20	32	28
Dept. B	–	26	42
Dept. C	–	–	18

15. For the following parts, determine part families and designate manufacturing cells for the part families. How many machines are required for your layout?

Part	Lathe	Drill	Mill	Paint	Saw	Planer	Sander	Grinder	Buffer
001	X				X		X	X	
002		X	X						X
003	X			X		X			X
004			X	X				X	
005	X	X				X	X		
006				X	X		X		X
007			X				X	X	
008	X	X	X			X		X	
009				X	X		X		
010		X			X	X			X

CASE STUDIES

CASE 1: The Chandler Hotel

Peter, a local business leader and entrepreneur from Peoria, IL, has recently purchased an old storefront building on the main street of the city. His plan is to open a boutique hotel in the building. On the first floor of the building there is enough room to have any six of the following guest services and hotel operations: reception, piano bar, business center, restrooms, coffee shop, pool, workout room, maintenance shop, and laundry. Guest services not located on the main floor will need to be located on the second floor of the building, along with two meeting rooms and additional restrooms.

Each of the services takes up about the same amount of space, and because of the support columns and beams for the building and its historical designation, the layout must be designed so that on the first and second floors, the six services or operations would be side by side and three deep, approximately, as shown in the figure here. Pete's goal is to have the space be inviting for the guests from the moment they walk into the hotel. He also wants to have operations that are logical for the guests. The hotel is on a corner lot, and there are windows across the front of the hotel and on one side.

Pete is pondering how to proceed with the layout of the first and second floors. He believes the first and second floor layouts may be the single most important factors in the future success of the hotel.

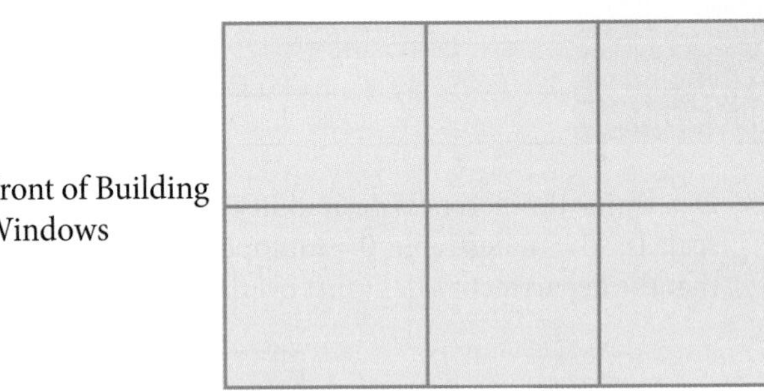

DISCUSSION QUESTIONS

1. What recommendations would you have for Pete regarding how to design the layout, and what services should be included for each floor? Explain your reasoning.

2. Develop a closeness desirability rating for each of the services contained in the layout on the first floor. Explain why you established the ratings that you did (see Example 8.3 in the chapter). Using your closeness desirability ratings, provide a layout and score for the first floor.

Note: Written by Jeffrey W. Fahrenwald, MBA, Rockford University, Rockford, IL. This case was prepared solely to provide material for class discussion. The author does not intend to illustrate either effective or ineffective handling of a managerial situation.

CASE 2: Material Flows at Third Midwest Bank

Third Midwest Bank is a regional bank with 10 locations and an online banking presence. The bank is a full-service bank that participates in the consumer lending and commercial lending markets and provides normal banking services for its individual and commercial customers. Recently, the president of the bank, Bob Thunderbird, hired a regional banking consulting firm to analyze banking operations. This was prompted by the upcoming implementation of a new ERP system for the bank. In order to properly implement the system, it was important for the bank to understand its current "as is" processes and to plan its "to be" processes, for when the ERP system was fully implemented.

Most of the material flows for the bank are materials related to bank transactions—paperwork, commercial paper, money, and information flows—related to the various types of transactions at the bank. These transactions include opening checking and savings accounts, savings and checking deposits or withdrawals, various types of loan applications and processing, mortgage lending and processing, and daily, weekly, monthly, and yearly closings of the books. Additionally, there are all the personnel, purchasing, and "bill paying" processes that a bank, like any other business, has to conduct. Every one of these processes will need to be mapped for the new ERP system.

To complicate matters, the same person can have various classifications for the bank and be involved in multiple material flows. For example, an employee of the bank can also have a savings and checking account at the bank, along with a mortgage.

Currently, the bank does not have a very good understanding of all of its material flows. There are reports that are produced daily and monthly that are not used in any meaningful way. The nightly closeouts of the tellers are well above industry average standards, and the bank has had some negative evaluations from regulators because of a lack of controls.

President Thunderbird believes employees of the bank are all working hard. Anyone who enters the bank branches will see people busy and not wasting time. However, employees spend a great deal of their time each day (up to 30%) "fixing" work they received from others so they can do their own jobs effectively. In other words, bank employees don't appear to be effectively handling the "handoffs," or work from one associate to another, which results in a great deal of rework, lost time, and productivity losses.

DISCUSSION QUESTIONS

1. What steps should be taken to clean up the bank's processes?
2. Should input from customers be included to create better processes? Why, or why not?
3. How should the changes made be monitored for success?

Note: Written by Jeffrey W. Fahrenwald, MBA, Rockford University, Rockford, IL. This case was prepared solely to provide material for class discussion. The author does not intend to illustrate either effective or ineffective handling of a managerial situation.

VIDEO CASE STUDY

Learn more about ***designing layouts*** from real organizations that use operations management techniques every day. Chris Bredesen is the Owner/Operating Partner at Rockefeller, a gastropub in Hermosa Beach, California. Restaurants take many factors into consideration when designing their layouts, including function, capacity, customer flow, and aesthetic. Watch this short interview to see how Rockefeller makes these decisions.

We knew there had to be a better way than simply responding first to the customers who screamed the loudest.

—**PATRICK CASEY,** chief process engineer, Xtek[1]

The biggest thing we can do for our customers' customers is to increase the velocity of information. With capabilities like tracking and geofencing, for instance, we can enable carriers to give shippers real-time answers to their most-important questions: Where is my load? When will it be there? Has it actually arrived? When did the truck depart?

—**BRIAN MCLAUGHLIN,** president, PeopleNet[2]

SUPPLEMENT: JOB SCHEDULING AND VEHICLE ROUTING

LEARNING OBJECTIVES

After completing this chapter supplement, you should be able to:

8S.1 Explain the concepts of job scheduling in both product- and process-focused systems

8S.2 Apply various machine-level dispatch rules

8S.3 Demonstrate several vehicle scheduling and routing heuristics

Master the content.

edge.sagepub.com/wisner

VEHICLE SCHEDULING AT AIRPORT LIMOUSINE SERVICES LTD.

Dispatchers at Hong Kong–based Airport Limousine Services Ltd. (ALS) had to take service information, communicate with chauffeurs, record statuses, dispatch orders, and make scheduling decisions, which began causing productivity and service quality problems as the company grew. Traffic congestion and flight delays caused even more problems. To deal with these challenges, ALS decided to use a fleet management system (FMS).

The Web-based application is used by ALS dispatchers as well as the company's travel agents. After midnight each day, the dispatcher uploads daily orders to the FMS. Once uploaded, a spreadsheet displays the orders so they can be edited. The FMS automatically connects airport transfer orders with real-time flight information and statuses. Each order is assigned to a vehicle for several hours. As orders commence, chauffeurs report back on their statuses—when they reach the pickup point, when the client is on board, and when they have reached their destinations. All of these statuses are updated into the FMS.

A FMS Gantt chart provides a view of the entire day. The Gantt chart rows are organized by vehicle and then the orders they are assigned, sorted by the pickup time. Thus, it is easy to see which vehicles are free. As new orders are received during the day, the FMS suggests the new vehicle assignments.

Prior to FMS deployment, ALS saw the lack of effective vehicle scheduling as a major bottleneck to business growth. After implementing the FMS, the company was able to greatly increase the number of customer orders accepted along with its vehicle utilization without any additional controllers or drivers. Approximately two more orders were handled per vehicle per day—a 40% improvement in utilization.[3]

INTRODUCTION

Job and vehicle scheduling are important flow management activities that can impact the firm's inventories and customer service capabilities. At process-focused facilities, once **jobs** (customer orders) have been accepted by a firm, they must be scheduled on specific machines according to some priority system. If poorly conceived priority systems are used, then jobs will not be completed in a timely fashion and other jobs in the queues will also finish behind schedule. Depending on the industry, the company, the software applications available, and the type of job, various priority scheduling systems are used.

In product-focused facilities, mixed-model sequencing is the primary issue, and these sequences can vary depending on the demand for the products and the time required for

jobs Customers' orders.

machine setups. Operations managers need to be aware of these scheduling techniques and any sequencing heuristics so that the most effective rules will be used. These scheduling rules are reviewed in this supplement.

For essentially the same reasons, vehicle scheduling and routing methods should be reviewed by operations managers—good vehicle schedules will mean lower in-transit inventories and more on-time deliveries. Given that fuel costs and traffic congestion continue to worsen, this adds yet another issue when considering vehicle schedules and routes. A number of the more popular vehicle scheduling heuristics are reviewed in this supplement.

JOB SCHEDULING

8S.1 Explain the concepts of job scheduling in both product- and process-focused systems

The scheduling of jobs in a facility is an important material flow management activity, since the timing of material purchases and estimates of the completion dates or delivery dates are based in large part on the upcoming schedule. Effective job scheduling can reduce queuing delays, inventory carrying costs, and job completion times, while increasing manufacturing capacity, employee productivity, and customer satisfaction. In many scheduling situations, there are trade-offs to be considered, such as finishing many smaller jobs instead of completing a few longer jobs. The scheduling techniques and concerns are substantially different for product-focused facilities compared to process-focused facilities. The scheduling techniques for both of these types of facilities are considered in the following sections.

JOB SCHEDULING IN PRODUCT-FOCUSED SYSTEMS

Product-focused or assembly line systems typically consist of automated or semiautomated equipment, with operators providing standardized processing to units of product as the units pass through the line. The scheduling objective is to keep the flow of goods smooth or consistent, so that equipment and labor utilization remain high. Due to the highly repetitive nature of these systems, the processing activity sequence and the balance of the line are designed when the system is originally designed and installed, so these are not scheduling issues. However, several other issues related to assembly line scheduling are discussed here.

epa bv/Alamy

Chrysler was able to save time and money when they discovered they could build the Jeep Compass, pictured here, on the same assembly line as the Dodge Caliber.

Shorter model production runs or lower lot sizes have the advantage of lower WIP inventories, which in turn create better shop flexibility. However, for short model runs, this requires more machine setups. If the time required to perform a setup is long, then model production runs must also be relatively long, which means greater WIP levels and higher carrying costs. Figure 8S.1 illustrates the lot size, flexibility, and setup time trade-off.

As shown in Figure 8S.1, using a short production run approach, the firm can satisfy greater demands for products A, B, and C over the same period of time with a small production run approach, with less time spent performing setups. This results in higher productivity, as well as greater **production flexibility**. Additionally, since the small production run approach requires smaller batches of purchased materials for each production run, the average WIP levels are lower, resulting in lower inventory carrying costs, provided suppliers can accommodate more deliveries with less product. For these reasons, the assembly line objective is to schedule short production runs; however, to do this, setup times must be short. Some companies have gone to great efforts to reduce setup times, including the purchase of

production flexibility The ability to change capabilities quickly to satisfy changing demands.

Figure 8S.1 Lot Size, Flexibility, and Setup Time Trade-off

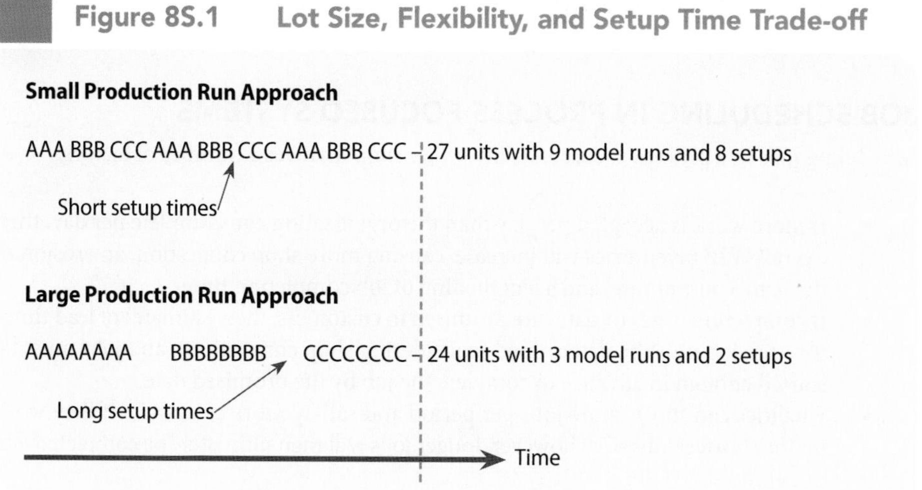

equipment that can automatically change tooling when different models are produced, as shown in the Emerson Network Power video.

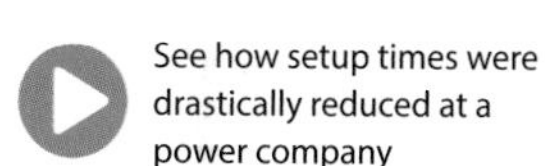

See how setup times were drastically reduced at a power company

Firms have also come to realize how much money can be saved when building multiple models on the same assembly line. When Chrysler began planning for building the Jeep Compass in 2007 on the same assembly line as its Dodge Caliber at its Belvidere plant in Illinois, the savings were immediately apparent to Frank Ewasyshyn, executive VP of manufacturing. "Thanks to Belvidere's ability to build multiple models off one assembly line, we expect Compass production to cost only 15 percent of the initial investment we made in the plant to build Dodge Caliber," he said.[4]

Aside from the production run size, the product model sequence is also a scheduling issue. Some product models may require longer and more costly setup activities, depending on the previous model produced on the line. Task times at various assembly stations can also vary substantially from model to model. Consequently, bottlenecks and line stoppages can occur, if model sequences and production run sizes are not communicated throughout the facility and to suppliers in advance. Product model sequencing, then, can significantly impact total setup time per day and production costs.

The demand for each product model obviously plays a role in how often a model production run is scheduled. This activity is referred to as **mixed-model assembly line sequencing**, and has been the topic of much research over the past 20 to 30 years. At Hyundai Motor Company, for example, its mixed-model sequencing activities are:

> Production schedules are determined from a master production schedule and then distributed to each plant's production planning department. The daily sequencing lists for the assembly lines are then developed using the following logic—given a daily production requirement for each model and assuming that lines are balanced, determine the sequence of model types for each assembly line that will smooth the demand for component parts and minimize any line balance delays. The models that have the closest to constant component usage rates are thus scheduled first, followed by models with more erratic component usage rates. Hyundai finds they must change the model sequence frequently as time passes, due to a host of unforeseen conditions such as defective parts or temporary insufficient capacity at a processing station.[5]

Since conditions on the manufacturing floor are constantly changing, model sequencing is not an exact science. A typical mixed-model assembly line involves multiple lot sizes, setup times, workcenter balancing variations, and varying model sequences; thus, the problem becomes intractable from a mathematical standpoint, and an optimal mixed-model sequence cannot be predetermined. Manufacturers are then left to make use of heuristic solutions that usually result in good sequencing patterns. Simulations have also been used

mixed-model assembly line sequencing When the demand for each product model determines how often a model production run is scheduled using one assembly line.

with some success to design assembly lines, along with determining a good work balance and mixed-model sequence.

JOB SCHEDULING IN PROCESS-FOCUSED SYSTEMS

Scheduling jobs in a process-focused facility or job shop involves a number of factors:

- If more work is accepted per day than the organization can complete per day, then overall WIP inventories will increase, causing more shop congestion, an erosion of the firm's output rate, and a lengthening of job completion times.
- If completion times or dates are promised to customers, then estimates of lead times for each job must be determined (considering shop congestion), and jobs must be started enough in advance to complete the job by the promised date.
- Facilities can finish more jobs per period and satisfy more customers if they work on the shortest jobs first; however, longer jobs will then ultimately be completed late or behind schedule.
- Some customers are more highly valued than others and may require earlier completion dates and be given processing priority in the shop, making it more difficult to estimate accurate completion dates for other jobs. And finally,
- Things go wrong on a daily basis, such as machine breakdowns, employee absences, poor raw-material quality, and processing errors, causing unforeseen delays in processing.

The job scheduling process thus includes *shop-wide control measures* such as input-output control techniques; *individual job control measures,* such as release rules and expediting; forward scheduling and Gantt chart scheduling; and, finally, *machine-level control measures,* such as sequencing or dispatching rules. These techniques are discussed in the following section.

Input-Output Control

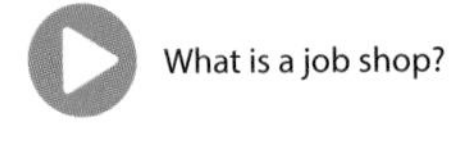

What is a job shop?

In many process-oriented facilities or **job shops**, determining the output capacity can be quite straightforward, and may be a matter of reviewing past daily job completion levels to arrive at a reasonable capacity estimate. Knowing this, **input-output control** (I/O) can be very simply applied:

- If current WIP levels are reasonable and product flow through the shop is steady, then the daily job acceptance or input rate should be set equal to the shop's daily output rate.
- If the shop is currently overloaded or heavily congested and WIP is increasing at several locations within the shop, then the shop's input rate should be less than the output rate, in order to reduce WIP levels.
- If the shop is currently underutilized and several workcenters are idle, then the shop's job input rate should be greater than the shop's job completion rate until ideal shop utilization is achieved.

In other words, as illustrated in Figure 8S.2, when I > O, WIP increases; when I < O, WIP decreases; when I = O, WIP stays constant. Over time, as technology enhancements and better flow management techniques increase overall job shop capacity, average input levels can be allowed to increase.

For most job shops, customer orders spend much of the time in queues at machines, waiting to be processed. If shops are heavily loaded, jobs may spend most of their total completion times waiting in queues, ultimately leading to lengthy completion times and customer dissatisfaction. Shops can reduce job inputs by either turning away new jobs, or by assigning completion dates considerably longer than the work is expected to take and then controlling when the jobs are released to the shop for processing. Unfortunately, neither of these alternatives is very appealing, which is why many machine shops and auto repair garages take on too much work, promise optimistic completion dates, and then invariably

job shops Process-oriented facilities or machine shops.

input-output control When I > O, WIP increases; when I < O, WIP decreases; when I = O, WIP stays constant. Used as a way to control shop congestion.

Figure 8S.2 Input-Output Control

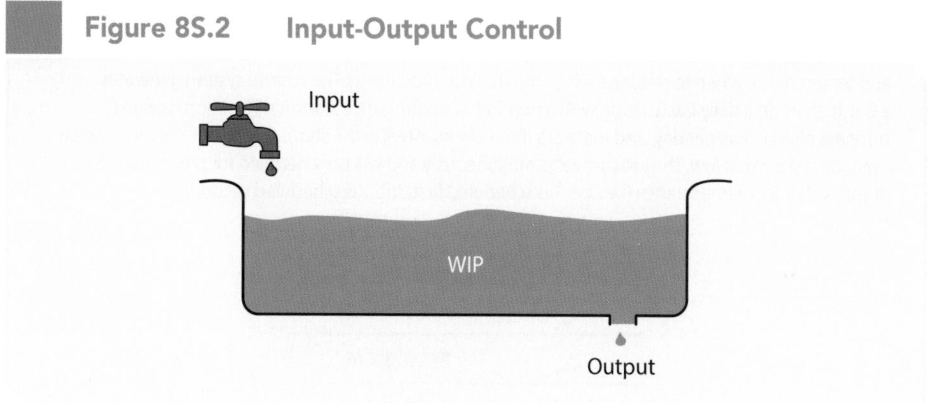

fall behind and finish after their completion promise dates. However, if I/O control combined with other shop floor control techniques are used to improve product flow, total queue time can be decreased, improving completion times and customer service capabilities.

Forward Scheduling and Gantt Chart Scheduling

For many job shops, **forward scheduling** is a tactic used to control shop loading, to estimate completion dates, and to determine when a job can be released, or started in the shop. Forward scheduling means to schedule jobs forward in time from their arrival date at the facility, taking into account current shop workloads. A **Gantt chart**, which is simply a timeline used for planning purposes, can be used with forward scheduling (or any other scheduling technique) to monitor and adjust the workloads at each workcenter, and to schedule downtime for maintenance activities, shift changes, operator days off, or other shop floor activities. A number of software applications are available today that create and change job schedules as new jobs are accepted. Ohio-based Xtek, a manufacturer of custom gears, found a system capable of scheduling each job differently. "I could schedule Job 1 from the due date back; Job 2 from today forward; and Job 3 from a mid-point based on machine constraints," says Patrick Casey, Xtek's chief process engineer.[6]

Example 8S.1 illustrates the use of forward loading and Gantt chart scheduling. The required process times and workcenter information are shown for the five jobs; the jobs are then scheduled on a Gantt chart using forward scheduling from time zero. In this example, the five jobs are prioritized in numerical order (Job 1 has a higher priority than Job 2, for example). Any number of priority systems could have been used to arrange the jobs in this order (priority systems are described further in the next section). When two jobs are waiting at the same machine to be processed, the highest-priority job goes first. The example also assumes zero movement time from one workcenter to the next. Expected completion dates for the jobs can be determined by looking at the ending times on the Gantt chart for each job. Job 1 can be completed by hour 8 (the end of day 1); Job 2 can be completed by hour 18 (during day 3); Job 3 can be completed by hour 4; Job 4 can be completed by hour 14; and Job 5 can be completed by hour 16. Note that use of the Gantt chart allows the scheduler to recognize, for instance, that Jobs 3 and 4 can be scheduled onto idle workcenters before they are needed by other, higher-priority jobs.

Gantt charts also allow shop managers to add "safety" hours to the completion estimates, based on their personal experiences with the equipment, employees, specific processing requirements, or the relative value of some customers. Workcenter A in Example 8S.1 is projected to be idle from hour 4 to hour 9. This idle time may be used to perform scheduled maintenance or for employees to spend time working on reducing job setup times.

Note in Example 8S.1 that while Job 2 had the second-highest priority, it still finished last among the group of jobs and had a relatively long queue time. This is simply the "nature of the beast" in job shop scheduling. Note that Job 2 had a lower priority than Job 1, and had to wait for Workcenter B to become available. Also note that Job 3 was able to start immediately at Workcenter B, since it required only one hour of processing and was expected to be

forward scheduling To schedule jobs forward in time from their arrival date at the facility, taking into account current shop workloads.

Gantt chart A timeline used for planning purposes that shows the time lengths and sequences of a project's task activities.

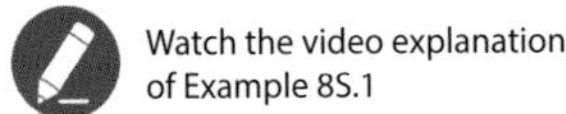

Example 8S.1
Forward Scheduling Jobs Using a Gantt Chart

Watch the video explanation of Example 8S.1

The Casey Machine Shop uses forward scheduling to determine job completion dates for its customers, and to determine when to release a job to the shop for processing. The control system generates a Gantt chart on a daily basis, along with a number of performance statistics. The shop is open for business eight hours per day, and there are three workcenters in the shop. Activity for the most recent five jobs is shown below. The jobs arrived simultaneously and will be scheduled for processing in numerical order of importance (i.e., Job 1 is scheduled first, Job 2 is scheduled second, etc.).

Job	Workcenter/Hours
1	A/2, B/4, C/2
2	B/3, A/3, C/6
3	B/1, C/3
4	A/2, C/1, B/5
5	C/3, A/3, B/1

Gantt Chart Scheduling

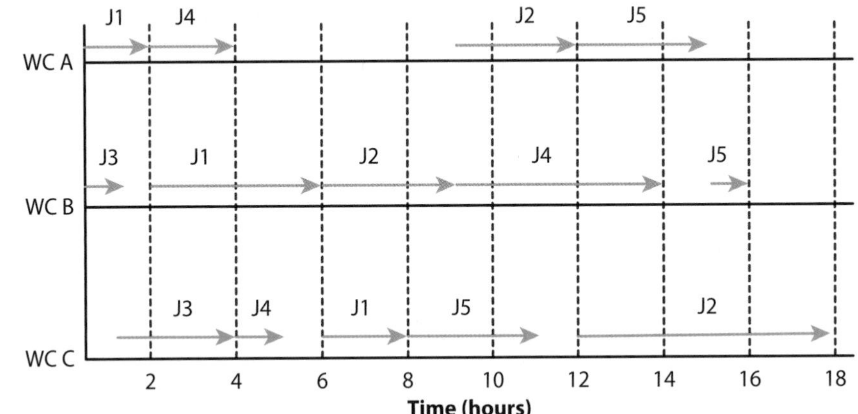

Job	Start Time	Completion Time	Queue Time
1	0 hrs.	8 hrs.	0 hrs.
2	0 hrs.	18 hrs.	6 hrs.
3	0 hrs.	4 hrs.	0 hrs.
4	0 hrs.	14 hrs.	6 hrs.
5	0 hrs.	16 hrs.	9 hrs.

Makespan = 18 hrs.

Average Flow time = (8+18+4+14+16)/5 = 12 hrs.

Average Queue time = (0+6+0+6+9)/5 = 4.2 hrs.

makespan The total elapsed time to complete a group of jobs.

average flow time Flow time begins when a job arrives at the shop, and ends when it leaves (averaged over a group of jobs).

average queue time Flow time minus process time (averaged over a group of jobs).

finished prior to Job 1's arrival. This illustrates the value of Gantt chart scheduling and workcenter loading, and is the method typically used in many shop floor control software applications.

The **makespan**, **average flow time**, and **average queue time** are also calculated and shown in Example 8S.1. These are job shop performance measures and are discussed in the following section; they are also defined in Table 8S.1.

Table 8S.1 Common Job Shop Performance Measures

Performance Measure	Description
Average Flow Time	Flow time begins when a job arrives at the shop, and ends when it leaves (averaged over a group of jobs).
Average Queue Time	Flow time minus process time (averaged over a group of jobs).
Average Job Lateness	Lateness is the difference between the completion date and the due date (if it finishes early, it is still "late"; averaged over a group of jobs).
Average Job Tardiness	Tardiness is the amount of time a job finishes beyond the due date (if it finishes early, tardiness is zero; averaged for a group of jobs).
Makespan	The total elapsed time to complete a group of jobs.

DISPATCH RULES

8S.2 Apply various machine-level dispatch rules

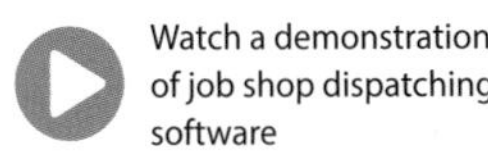
Watch a demonstration of job shop dispatching software

Dispatch rules allow machine operators to determine which job to process next from a queue of jobs waiting to be processed at a machine. Manufacturing managers and operators use dispatch rules to prioritize jobs and continually manage queues of work at each machine, since in practice, unforeseen circumstances might cause job priorities to change as the jobs make their way through all of the required processing activities. Typically, a shop floor supervisor will generate a job priority report for the day, using a shop floor control software application that considers all of the jobs currently on the shop floor in various stages of completion, those due to begin that day, the priorities of all of the jobs, and the dispatch rules being used. Jobs are thus scheduled at each machine for the day. As new jobs arrive and are released for processing, they are prioritized in real time in the control system, and queued along with the other jobs in the shop. Finally, throughout the day, machine operators must revise priorities and job processing sequences based on ever-changing conditions (a job may be pushed back in the queue, for instance, if the required materials or subassemblies have not yet arrived from a supplier or upstream workcenter).

A number of the more commonly cited dispatch rules are listed in Table 8S.2. Examining the performance of these dispatching rules has been the topic of much research using simulations of job shops under varying conditions.

In practice, simple dispatch rules concerned with each job's due date have been found to be the most popular, such as **earliest due date** (EDD) and **critical ratio** (CR). In simulation research, though, the **shortest process time** (SPT) rule worked the best in terms of minimizing average flow time, queue time, and makespan, although long jobs end up with low priorities, resulting in long queue times and tardy deliveries. In a number of studies, EDD and CR

dispatch rules Allow machine operators to determine which job to process next from a queue of jobs waiting to be processed at a machine. Manufacturing managers and operators use dispatch rules to prioritize jobs and continually manage queues of work at each machine.

earliest due date The job with the earliest due date is selected first.

critical ratio The job with the smallest ratio of (time until due date)/(remaining process time) is selected first.

shortest process time The job with the shortest process time is selected first.

minimum slack time per operation (MINSOP) The job with the minimum slack time per remaining operation is selected first. (Slack time is defined as time until due date minus remaining process time.)

Table 8S.2 Common Job Shop Dispatch Rules

Dispatch Rule	Description
Shortest Process Time (SPT)	The job with the shortest process time is processed first.
Earliest Due Date (EDD)	The job with the earliest due date is processed first.
Minimum Slack time per Operation (MINSOP)	The job with the minimum slack time per remaining operation is processed first. (Slack time is defined as time until due date minus remaining process time).
Critical Ratio (CR)	The job with the smallest ratio of (time until due date divided by remaining process time) is processed first.
First-Come-First-Served (FCFS)	The job arriving first at a workcenter is processed first.
Most-Important-Job-First	Jobs are prioritized based on the importance of the customer.

were also found to perform well in terms of **average job lateness** and **average job tardiness**. Interestingly, the **first-come-first-served** (FCFS) rule has been found to be quite popular in real job shops, even though under controlled conditions, this rule has never been shown to perform well using any performance measure. Perhaps its popularity is due to the perceived fairness attributed to FCFS processing. Understandably, the **most-important-job-first** rule was also found to be very popular in machine shops.[7] Some companies also use partial or combinations of the rules shown here. For instance, Taiwan-based Macronix International, a lithography company, uses a shortest-remaining-process-time dispatch rule combined with a remaining-time-until-due-date rule to reduce job completion times and completion time variances.[8] Example 8S.2 compares several dispatch rules using a single machine.

As expected, the SPT rule performed the best in terms of average flow time and queue time (which are associated with lower WIP inventory levels), while the EDD and CR rules looked to be the better for average lateness and average tardiness (which are associated with satisfied customers). While six jobs on one machine hardly make for a real-world example, they nevertheless illustrate the usefulness of these rules. Comparisons in practice require the processing of hundreds of jobs on multiple machines under frequently changing shop conditions.

Another complicating factor to consider when processing jobs at a machine is that setup times may be sequence-dependent. While different jobs may have significantly different setup times, some jobs may require the same setup activities. Consequently, an operator may want to group jobs together with the same or similar setup requirements, to reduce overall lost time due to machine setups. Obviously, sequencing jobs in this way would significantly alter all of the performance measures in Example 8S.2.

Finally, enough cannot be said regarding the *continuous variabilities* occurring in process-oriented manufacturing facilities. From one job to the next, and even one unit to the next, variabilities can occur in processing times and setup times due to changes in operators, operator fatigue, machine tool wear, supply interruptions, and last-minute changes in customer requirements, just to name a few. Thus, for any large group of jobs in a normal job shop setting, it is simply impossible to identify the optimal processing schedule. Processing jobs becomes an ongoing activity for managers and operators throughout the day—to effectively track the progress of all jobs while doing the best to satisfy customers and control costs. In many shops, there are **expeditors** whose job is to identify incoming material purchases and jobs on the shop floor that are behind schedule, and then do whatever is necessary to get purchased materials delivered and jobs completed by their due dates.

In this section we discussed managing internal material flows within the organization using various scheduling techniques. The next section focuses on the impact of vehicle scheduling and routing on material flows. This is a topic particularly important for supply chain participants who are trying to optimize material flow and integrate their efforts to create higher levels of customer satisfaction, while maintaining cost objectives.

average job lateness Lateness is the difference between the completion date and the due date (if it finishes early, it is still "late"; averaged over a group of jobs).

average job tardiness Tardiness is the amount of time a job finishes beyond the due date (if it finishes early, tardiness is zero; averaged for a group of jobs).

first-come-first-served The job arriving first at a workcenter is processed first.

most-important-job-first Jobs are prioritized based on the importance of the customer.

expeditors Shop floor employees who identify incoming material purchases and jobs on the shop floor that are behind schedule, and then do whatever is necessary to get purchased materials delivered and jobs completed by their due dates.

Example 8S.2 Comparing Dispatch Rules at a Single Machine

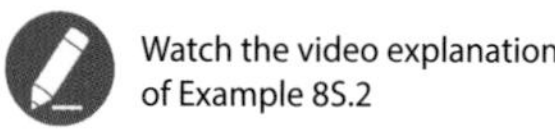

Watch the video explanation of Example 8S.2

Taylor, a business student working at his family's machine shop for the summer, decides to compare the use of several dispatch rules at the most bottlenecked machine in the shop. On the morning of his study, there were six jobs waiting to be processed at the machine. The estimated process times and job due dates are shown here. Taylor decides to compare SPT, EDD, and CR dispatching rules.

Job	Process Time (hrs.)	Due Date (hrs.)
A	8	24
B	2	36
C	6	8
D	4	12
E	10	24
F	5	6

SPT Dispatching:

Order	Completion Time	Queue Time	Lateness	Tardiness
B	2	0	34	0
D	6	2	6	0
F	11	6	5	5
C	17	11	9	9
A	25	17	1	1
E	35	25	11	11

Makespan = 35 hrs. (Note that the makespan will remain constant, regardless of the sequence, when using a single machine.)

Avg. Flow Time = (2+6+11+17+25+35)/6 = 16 hrs.

Avg. Queue Time = (0+2+6+11+17+25)/6 = 10.2 hrs.

Avg. Lateness = (34+6+5+9+1+11)/6 = 11 hrs.

Avg. Tardiness = (0+0+5+9+1+11)/6 = 4.3 hrs.

EDD Dispatching:

Order	Completion Time	Queue Time	Lateness	Tardiness
F	5	0	1	0
C	11	5	3	3
D	15	11	3	3
A	23	15	1	0
E	33	23	9	9
B	35	33	1	0

(*Note:* A and E had the same due date, so A was processed first because it had the lowest process time).

Avg. Flow Time = (5+11+15+23+33+35)/6 = 20.3 hrs.

Avg. Queue Time = (0+5+11+15+23+33)/6 = 14.5 hrs.

Avg. Lateness = (1+3+3+1+9+1)/6 = 3 hrs.

Avg. Tardiness = (0+3+3+0+9+0)/6 = 2.5 hrs.

CR Dispatching:

Critical Ratios: $A = \frac{24}{8} = 3, B = \frac{36}{2} = 18, C = \frac{8}{6} = 1.3, D = \frac{12}{4} = 3, E = \frac{24}{10} = 2.4, F = \frac{6}{5} = 1.2$

Order	Completion Time	Queue Time	Lateness	Tardiness
F	5	0	1	0
C	11	5	3	3
E	21	11	3	3
D	25	21	13	13
A	33	25	9	9
B	35	33	1	0

(*Note:* A and D had the same CR, so D was processed first because it had the lowest process time.)

(Continued)

Example 8S.2 (Continued)

Avg. Flow Time = (5+11+21+25+33+35)/6 = 21.7 hrs.

Avg. Queue Time = (0+5+11+21+25+33)/6 = 15.8 hrs.

Avg. Lateness = (1+3+3+13+9+1)/6 = 5 hrs.

Avg. Tardiness = (0+3+0+13+9+0)/6 = 4.2 hrs.

Ranking the performances of the dispatching rules:

Avg. Flow Time	Avg. Queue Time	Avg. Lateness	Avg. Tardiness
SPT/16.0	SPT/10.2	EDD/3	EDD/2.5
EDD/20.3	EDD/14.5	CR/5	CR/4.2
CR/21.7	CR/15.8	SPT/11	SPT/4.3

Based on his findings, Taylor recommends use of either the EDD or CR dispatching rule at this machine, to reduce average job lateness and tardiness.

VEHICLE SCHEDULING AND ROUTING

8S.3 Demonstrate several vehicle scheduling and routing heuristics

There are multiple objectives when considering vehicle scheduling and routing, including the minimization of costs (vehicle, personnel, and mileage), meeting customer delivery date requirements, maximizing driver productivity, and providing protection to the goods being transported. For services such as buses, taxis, and emergency vehicles, people are the things being transported; thus, the objective would be to minimize transportation time while maximizing safety.

iStock/bgwalker

The Pepsi Bottling Group of Denver takes advantage of the advanced communication technologies available today to become more efficient and prioritize high-volume customers on their delivery routes.

Today, communication technologies have allowed delivery companies to offer better service with fewer drivers and vehicles. For example, the Pepsi Bottling Group of Denver, CO, uses routing and scheduling software along with global positioning systems to optimally plan daily vehicle delivery routes so that its highest-volume customers receive priority service. Use of the system allowed it to improve delivery service while reducing driver overtime.[9]

For multiple pickups and deliveries, the scheduling and routing problem can be presented as a network of pickup and delivery points, as shown in Figure 8S.3. Node 1 represents the origination/destination point (as in the manufacturing or distribution facility), while nodes 2, 3, and 4 represent pickup and/or delivery points. The lines connecting the nodes can represent distance (such as shown here), cost, or time. The network represents a trip, or tour, consisting of a sequence of four stops (including the origination point).

For the simple case of one vehicle and the pickup/delivery points as shown in Figure 8S.3, with the vehicle starting and ending at the origination node, the situation is called the **traveling salesman problem**. For the small problem shown in Figure 8S.3, the idea is to find the best route that minimizes a time, mileage, or cost objective. For these nodes, there are three distinct tours to cover the pickup/delivery points: [1,2,3,4], [1,2,4,3], and [1,3,2,4]. (Note that [1,2,3,4] = [1,4,3,2], for instance.) The routing problem can also become more complicated

traveling salesman problem To find the best delivery route for one vehicle, which minimizes a time, mileage, or cost objective.

Figure 8S.3 A Vehicle Scheduling and Routing Network

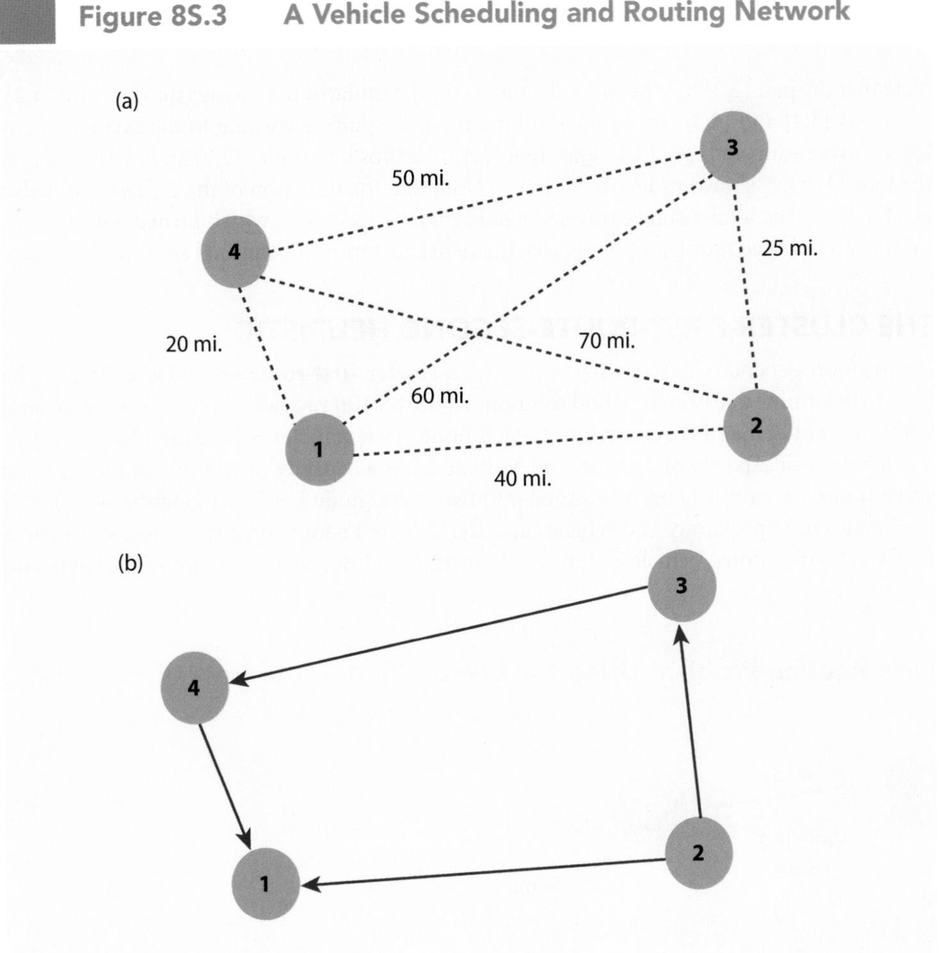

with the use of multiple vehicles, variable demands at each node, and multiple vehicle capacities. These more general problems are called **vehicle routing problems**. If specified pickup or delivery times exist, then the routing problem also becomes a scheduling problem.

For large real-world applications, there are simply too many route combinations to consider, and optimal solutions cannot be found; therefore, planners must use heuristics. Software applications are becoming very useful for these large-scale routing problems, and can create significant savings for the users. American Signature Furniture, a furniture manufacturer with its own delivery fleet, has reduced delivery vehicle mileage 15–20% by using one of these software applications. "This has enabled American Signature Furniture to streamline operations to reduce unnecessary fuel and resources. We now deliver more furniture each day while cutting costs," says Sonny Rice, senior business analyst at American Signature.[10] Three vehicle scheduling heuristics are described in the following sections.

vehicle routing problems Find the best delivery route with the use of multiple vehicles, variable demands at each node, and multiple vehicle capacities.

THE CLARK AND WRIGHT SAVINGS HEURISTIC

One of the most well-known heuristic methods for solving the traveling salesman problem is the **Clark and Wright savings heuristic**. The key to this procedure is the calculation of "savings" in miles (or cost), to combine two nodes into one tour, rather than have the vehicle return to the origination point and then head out to the next pickup/distribution point. The savings are calculated in this way for all paired combinations of delivery nodes, and the pairs are ranked from largest savings to smallest. The nodes for the entire tour are then linked according to this ranking. For the four nodes shown in Figure 8S.3, the following savings are calculated:

Clark and Wright savings heuristic One of the most well-known heuristic methods for solving the traveling salesman problem. The key to this procedure is the calculation of "savings" in miles (or cost), to combine two nodes into one tour, rather than have the vehicle return to the origination point and then head out to the next pickup/distribution point.

1) 1-2-1 and 1-3-1 (two trips) vs. 1-2-3-1 (one trip): savings is [(40×2) + (60×2)] – [40+25+60] = 75 miles.

2) 1-2-1 and 1-4-1 vs. 1-2-4-1: savings is [(40×2) + (20×2)] – [40+70+20] = –10 miles.
3) 1-3-1 and 1-4-1 vs. 1-3-4-1: savings is [(60×2) + (20×2)] – [60+50+20] = 30 miles.

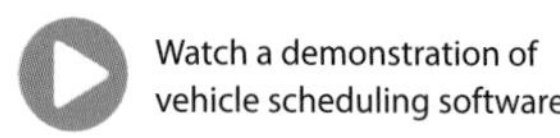

Note that the pair [2,3] has the same savings as [3,2]. Similarly, the savings for [2,4] and [4,2], as well as [3,4] and [4,3], are equal. Ranking the node pairs according to the savings calculated above results in [2,3], [3,4], and then [2,4]. We thus link nodes [2,3] and [3,4] to obtain the tour [1,2,3,4] shown in Figure 8S.3 (b). (Note that the direction of the arrows could also be [1,4,3,2].) The total distance traveled would then be 135 miles, which turned out to be the minimum distance tour (in other words, the heuristic found the optimal solution).

THE CLUSTER-FIRST-ROUTE-SECOND HEURISTIC

cluster-first-route-second heuristic For the more general vehicle routing problem, this heuristic can be used to determine a reasonably good solution.

For the more general vehicle routing problem, the **cluster-first-route-second heuristic** can be used to determine a reasonably good solution. Figure 8S.4(a) provides an eight-node problem, with different demand requirements at each node. Two vehicles will be used for the tours. Vehicle 1 has a capacity of 25 tons, and Vehicle 2 has a capacity of 18 tons. In Part (a), the seven nodes have initially been clustered into two tours (node 1 is the origination node), taking into account proximity and vehicle capacity. Vehicle 1's tour consists of three stops and a total weight of 18 tons. Vehicle 2's tour has four stops and also requires 18 tons. The Clark and

Figure 8S.4 Vehicle Routing Problem Using the Cluster-First-Route-Second Heuristic

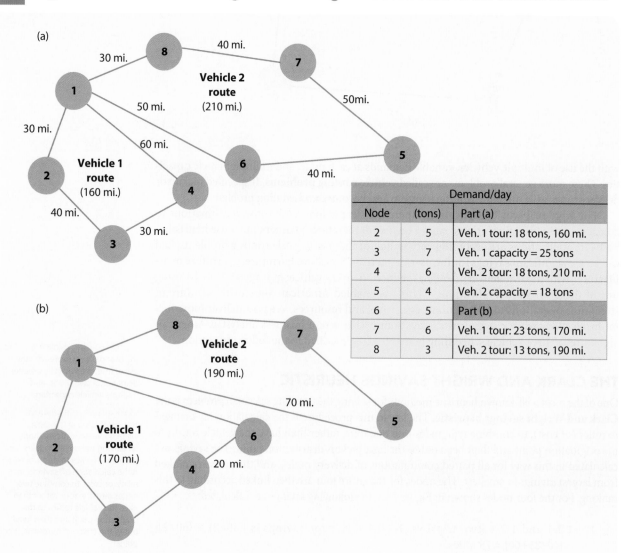

Demand/day		
Node	(tons)	Part (a)
2	5	Veh. 1 tour: 18 tons, 160 mi.
3	7	Veh. 1 capacity = 25 tons
4	6	Veh. 2 tour: 18 tons, 210 mi.
5	4	Veh. 2 capacity = 18 tons
6	5	Part (b)
7	6	Veh. 1 tour: 23 tons, 170 mi.
8	3	Veh. 2 tour: 13 tons, 190 mi.

Wright savings heuristic is used to construct the sequence for each tour, resulting in a Tour 1 distance of 160 miles and a Tour 2 distance of 210 miles, for a total distance of 370 miles.

The next step involves **tour improvement**, where one or more nodes are switched to another tour (in this case, the only other tour), so that vehicle capacities are not exceeded, and total distance of both tours is reduced. Since Vehicle 2 is already at capacity, it is only feasible to try switching one or more Tour 2 nodes to Tour 1 and Vehicle 1. Part (b) shows the revised solution. Here, node 6 was switched to Tour 1, adding 10 miles and 5 tons to the tour. Consequently, Tour 2's load was reduced 5 tons and the mileage was reduced 20 miles. The resulting total distance of both tours then became 360, a savings of 10 miles. No other nodes could be switched to Tour 1 due to the capacity limitation of Vehicle 1. Obviously, other factors such as geography, traffic flow, and customer value can enter into this solution, and tend to complicate the analysis.

THE CONCURRENT SCHEDULER APPROACH

For the vehicle scheduling problem, a simple heuristic called the **concurrent scheduler approach** can also be used. The steps are as follows:

1. Put the pickups and deliveries in order by their promised arrival times.
2. Assign Vehicle 1 to the earliest promised arrival time.
3. If possible, assign the next pickup/delivery to the closest idle vehicle; if all vehicles are busy, create a new vehicle schedule and assign the pickup/delivery to that vehicle. Repeat until all pickups/deliveries are scheduled.

tour improvement For the vehicle routing problem, when one or more nodes are switched to another tour, so that vehicle capacities are not exceeded, and total distance of both tours is reduced.

concurrent scheduler approach For the vehicle scheduling problem, this simple heuristic can also be used. The steps are to put the pickups and deliveries in order by their promised arrival times; assign Vehicle 1 to the earliest promised arrival time; if possible, assign the next pickup/delivery to the closest idle vehicle; if all vehicles are busy, create a new vehicle schedule and assign the pickup/delivery to that vehicle. Repeat until all pickups/deliveries are scheduled.

Example 8S.3 illustrates the concurrent scheduler approach. Vehicle 1 takes the first Customer. Vehicle 2 must take Customer 2, since Vehicle 1 will still be handling Customer 1. For Customer 4, both Vehicle 1 and Vehicle 2 will be available; however, since Vehicle 1 will be closer, it is assigned to Customer 4. The remaining customers are assigned to vehicles similarly. By the end of the day, three vehicles will be needed.

Other techniques exist for solving vehicle routing and scheduling problems, including use of dynamic programming, linear programming, and specialized algorithms.[11] Interested readers should look at some of the referenced articles for further discussions and appraisals of the techniques.

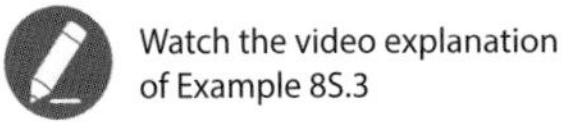

Example 8S.3 Using the Concurrent Scheduler Approach for Vehicle Deliveries

Watch the video explanation of Example 8S.3

Vicki's Delivery Express assigns pickups and deliveries to its vehicles and drivers based on each morning's list of required pickups and deliveries. Today, the current customer list is as follows (assume customers are listed in proximity to one another, i.e., Customer 3 is closer to Customer 4 than Customer 2 is):

Pickup/ Delivery	Promised Arrival Time	Completion Time	Vehicle Number
1	8:00 AM	8:45 AM	1
2	8:30 AM	9:15 AM	2 (Veh. 1 is busy)
3	9:00 AM	9:10 AM	1 (Veh. 1 is idle)
4	9:30 AM	10:00 AM	1 (Veh. 1 is closer)
5	9:45 AM	10:00 AM	2 (Veh. 1 is busy)
6	10:00 AM	10:45 AM	3 (Veh. 1 and 2 are busy)
7	10:30 AM	11:00 AM	2 (Veh. 2 is closer)
8	1:00 PM	2:00 PM	2 (Veh. 2 is closest)
9	1:30 PM	1:45 PM	3 (Veh. 3 is closer)
10	3:00 PM	4:30 PM	3 (Veh. 3 is closest)

(Continued)

Example 8S.3 (Continued)

Vehicle	Schedule	Start/End Times
1	1-3-4	7:45 AM/10:00 AM
2	2-5-7-8	8:15 AM/2:00 PM
3	6-9-10	9:45 AM/4:30 PM

To make the day's pickups and deliveries, Vicki assumes a 15-minute drive time to each customer. She schedules three vehicles for the times shown. As new customer requests are generated during the day, they are worked in to the existing schedule. Obviously, for small numbers of pickups and deliveries, part-time drivers must be used to avoid excessive idle time.

SUMMARY

Managing queues of jobs and pickups and deliveries of goods is an important consideration for operations managers, due to the impact on material flows, inventory carrying costs, and customer satisfaction. This supplement has presented and discussed the more popular job and vehicle scheduling techniques. Where appropriate, both qualitative and quantitative tools were explained and examples were provided. Understanding these concepts is necessary for understanding how various material flows impact the organization and its supply chains.

KEY TERMS

Average flow time, 250
Average job lateness, 252
Average job tardiness, 252
Average queue time, 250
Clark and Wright savings heuristic, 255
Cluster-first-route-second heuristic, 256
Concurrent scheduler approach, 257
Critical ratio, 251
Dispatch rules, 251
Earliest due date, 251
Expeditors, 252
First-come-first-served, 252
Forward scheduling, 249
Gantt chart, 249
Input-output control, 248
Jobs, 245
Job shops, 248
Makespan, 250
Minimum slack time per operation (MINSOP), 251
Mixed-model assembly line sequencing, 247
Most-important-job-first, 252
Production flexibility, 246
Shortest process time, 251
Tour improvement, 257
Traveling salesman problem, 254
Vehicle routing problems, 255

FORMULA REVIEW

Critical ratio = due date/process time.

Slack time = due date − process time.

Lateness = absolute value of (due date − completion time).

SOLVED PROBLEMS

1. Assume that all of the jobs shown here arrived at the same time. Use a Gantt chart and the critical ratio (CR) rule to determine the processing order. Determine the makespan, average flowtime, average queue time, average lateness, and average tardiness. Also assume that transfer times are zero.

Job	Est. Hours	Due Date (hrs.)
1	A/1, B/2, C/1	6
2	A/2, C/3, B/4	14
3	B/3, A/1, C/2	12
4	C/1, B/4	15
5	C/2, B/1, A/2	10

Answer:

The critical ratios are: Job 1—6/4 = 1.5; Job 2—14/9 = 1.56; Job 3—12/6 = 2; Job 4—15/5 = 3; Job 5—10/5 = 2. So, processing order is 1,2,5,3,4 (Jobs 3 and 5 had the same CR, but Job 5 had an earlier due date and lower processing time, so that one was scheduled first).

The Gantt chart:

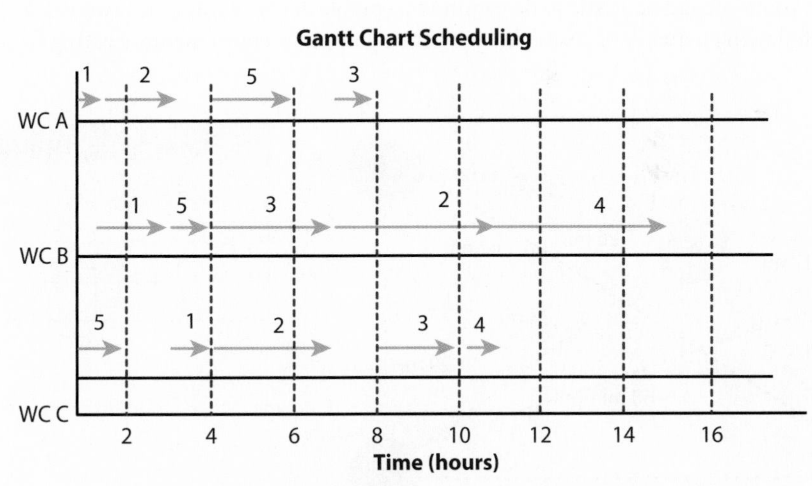

Job	Start Time	Completion Time	Queue Time	Tardiness	Lateness
1	0 hrs.	4 hrs.	0 hrs.	0 hrs.	2 hrs.
2	0 hrs.	11 hrs.	2 hrs.	0 hrs.	3 hrs.
3	0 hrs.	10 hrs.	4 hrs.	0 hrs.	2 hrs.
4	0 hrs.	15 hrs.	10 hrs.	0 hrs.	0 hrs.
5	0 hrs.	6 hrs.	1 hrs.	0 hrs.	4 hrs.

Makespan = 15 hrs.
Average flow time = (4+11+10+15+6)/5 = 9.2 hrs.
Average queue time = (0+2+4+10+1)/5 = 3.4 hrs.
Average tardiness = 0 hrs.
Average lateness = 11/5 = 2.2 hrs.

2. Use the Clark and Wright savings heuristic to determine an acceptable delivery route for the following network of customers, starting from location 1.

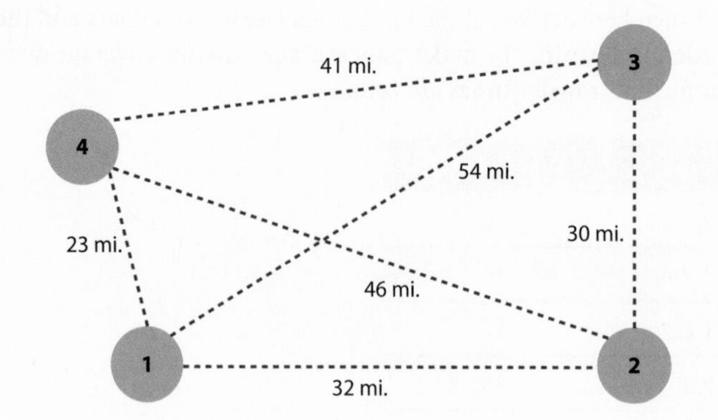

Answer:

1-2-3-1: 32(2)+54(2) – (32+30+54) = 56 mi.

1-3-4-1: 108+46 – (54+41+23) = 36 mi.

1-2-4-1: 64+46 – (32+46+23) = 9 mi.

So, starting with the nodes with the largest savings results in the tour: 1-2-3-4-1

3. Use the cluster-first-route-second heuristic to determine acceptable delivery routes for two trucks (5-ton and 8-ton capacities) and the following network of customers with their shipping requirements, starting from location 1.

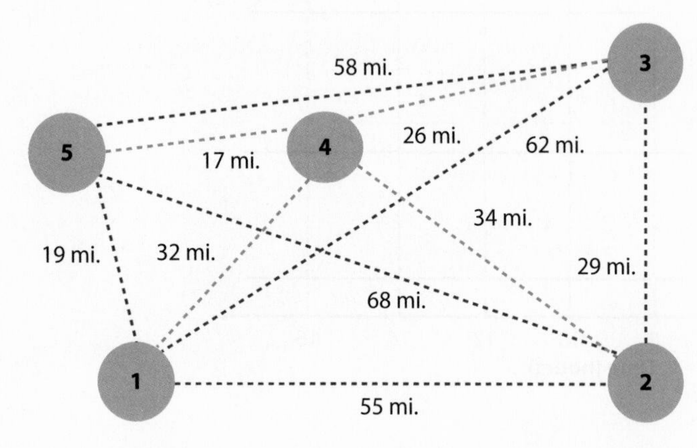

Node	Dem./day (tons)
2	2
3	4
4	2
5	3

Answer:

1) Clark-Wright savings:

1-2-3-1: 55(2)+62(2) – (55+29+62) = 88 mi.

1-2-4-1: 55(2)+32(2) – (55+34+32) = 53 mi.

1-2-5-1: 55(2)+19(2) – (55+68+19) = 6 mi.

1-3-4-1: 62(2)+32(2) - (62 +26+32) = 68 mi.

1-3-5-1: 62(2)+19(2) – (62+58+19) = 23 mi.

1-4-5-1: 32(2)+19(2) – (32+17+19) = 34 mi.

The tour with the largest savings is 1-2-3-1, and this is a total of 6 tons, so the 8-ton truck can handle this delivery and the trip is 146 miles. The 5-ton truck can then take the 1-4-5-1 route, with a 5-ton demand/day requirement and a trip of 68 miles. The total mileage is then 214 miles.

2) Route improvement: Other potential routes—1-3-4-1 (6 tons, 120 miles) and 1-2-5-1 (5 tons, 142 miles) = 262 miles (not as good); 1-2-4-1 (4 tons, 121 miles) and 1-3-5-1 (7 tons, 139 miles) = 260 miles (not as good); 1-2-3-4-1 (8 tons, 142 miles) and 1-5-1 (3 tons, 38 miles) = 180 miles (better); 1-2-4-5-1 (7 tons, 125 miles) and 1-3-1 (4 tons, 124 miles) = 249 miles (not as good).

So, the lowest mileage routes are Truck 1: 1-2-3-4-1 (8 tons) and Truck 2: 1-5-1 (3 tons), for a total of 180 miles.

4. Assuming that the customers are ranked in proximity to one another (i.e., Customer 4 is closer to Customer 3 than Customer 5 is), use the concurrent scheduler approach to assign deliveries to vehicles so that no deliveries are late and driving distance is minimized. Determine how many delivery vehicles are needed. Also, determine each vehicle's delivery schedule, the start time, and the finish time. Assume that drive time to each customer is 15 minutes.

Answer:

Delivery	Promised Arrival Time	Estimated Completion Time	Delivery Vehicle
1	8:30 AM	8:45 AM	1
2	8:45 AM	9:15 AM	2 (Veh. 1 busy)
3	9:00 AM	10:00 AM	1 (Veh. 2 busy)
4	9:30 AM	9:45 AM	2 (Veh. 1 busy)
5	10:00 AM	10:45PM	2 (Veh. 1 busy)
6	10:30 AM	11:00 AM	1 (Veh. 2 busy)
7	10:45 AM	11:30 PM	3 (Veh. 1 and 2 busy)
8	11:30 PM	12:15 PM	1 (Veh. 3 busy, Veh. 1 closer)
9	12:00 PM	1:00 PM	3 (Veh. 1 busy, Veh. 3 closer)
10	12:30 PM	12:45 PM	1 (Veh. 3 busy, Veh. 1 closer)
11	1:30 PM	2:15 PM	1 (Veh. 1 closest)
12	2:00 PM	3:00 PM	3 (Veh. 1 busy, Veh. 3 closer)
13	2:30 PM	3:30 PM	1 (Veh. 3 busy, Veh. 1 closer)

Vehicle	Schedule	Start/End Times
1	1-3-6-8-10-11-13	8:15AM – 3:30PM
2	2-4-5	8:30AM – 10:45AM
3	7-9-12	10:30AM – 3:00PM

REVIEW QUESTIONS

1. What are the job scheduling activities and objectives for assembly lines?
2. Define input-output control and describe how it is used in process-focused facilities.
3. What is forward scheduling, and why is it used?
4. What is a Gantt chart, and why is it used?
5. What are dispatch rules?

6. What does the traveling salesman problem refer to, and what is the solution objective? What heuristic is typically used to solve simple traveling salesman problems?
7. For large vehicle scheduling problems, which scheduling heuristic would most likely be used? Why?

DISCUSSION QUESTIONS

1. Which dispatch rule do you think is the best? Which one do you normally use when deciding which homework assignment to do next?
2. In dispatching terminology, if I am 20 minutes early for an appointment, I am late, but not tardy. Explain.
3. In many cases, the shortest-process-time dispatch rule works well. Why? What does it not do very well?

EXERCISES AND PROJECTS

1. Discuss the dispatch rules you typically use to schedule your homework assignments. Pick one day when you have multiple assignments and keep track of completion times, and then calculate average flow time and average queue time. Discuss and illustrate how the performance would change using different dispatch rules.
2. Visit a machine shop and find out how it normally dispatches jobs on its machines. Does it have an expeditor? Does it practice I/O control? Does it keep track of dispatch rule performance? Does it use dispatching software?

PROBLEMS

1. The Grebski Auto Repair Shop uses a shop floor control system based on forward scheduling to determine auto completion dates for its customers, and to determine when to release a car to the shop for repairing. The control system generates a Gantt chart on a daily basis, along with a number of statistics. The shop is open for business eight hours per day, and there are three repair centers in the shop. Activity to be scheduled for the next few days is shown here. The jobs are listed in order of customer arrival, and are scheduled for processing on a first-come-first-served basis. Job transfer times are zero. Determine what the due dates should be, along with the makespan, the average flowtime, and the average queue time.

Job	Repair Center/Est. Hours	Job	Repair Center/Est. Hours
1	A/1, B/3, C/2	4	A/3, C/2, B/2
2	A/2, C/3	5	C/1, B/4, A/2
3	B/1, A/2, C/1		

2. Using the information from Problem 1, and assuming that all of the automobiles arrived at the same time, use a Gantt chart and the shortest-process-time (SPT) rule to prioritize the jobs. Determine the due dates, the makespan, average flowtime, and average queue time. Assume that transfer times are zero. For ties, process the job with the lowest first repair center processing time first.

3. Assume that all of the jobs here arrived at the same time. Use a Gantt chart and the earliest due date (EDD) rule to prioritize the jobs. Determine the makespan, average flowtime, average queue time, average lateness, and average tardiness. Also assume that transfer times are zero.

Job	Est. Hours	Due Dates (hrs.)
1	A/2, B/1, C/2	15
2	A/1, C/3, B/2	9
3	B/1, A/2, C/3	10
4	C/2, B/3	8
5	C/1, B/3, A/1	12

4. Using the job information in Problem 3, construct a Gantt chart using the critical ratio (CR) rule to determine the job priority ranking. Assume all jobs arrived simultaneously. Determine the makespan, average flowtime, average queue time, average lateness, and average tardiness. Also assume that transfer times are zero. Which rule performed better, the EDD rule from Problem 3, or the CR rule? Explain.

5. Using the job information in Problem 3, construct a Gantt chart using the minimum slack per operation (MINSOP) rule to determine the job priority ranking. Assume all jobs arrived simultaneously. Determine the makespan, average flowtime, average queue time, average lateness, and average tardiness. Also assume that transfer times are zero.

6. Using the following information and assuming that all of the automobiles arrived at the same time, use a Gantt chart and the critical ratio (CR) rule to prioritize jobs for processing. Determine the makespan, average flowtime, average queue time, average lateness, and average tardiness. Also assume that transfer times are zero.

Job	Repair Center/Est. Hours	Due Date (hrs.)
1	A/1, B/3, C/2	8
2	A/2, C/3	15
3	B/1, A/2, C/1	7
4	A/3, C/2, B/2	20
5	C/1, B/4, A/2	16

7. Use the Clark and Wright savings heuristic to determine an acceptable delivery route for the following network of customers, starting from location 1. Assume that any diagonal trip must pass through location 5.

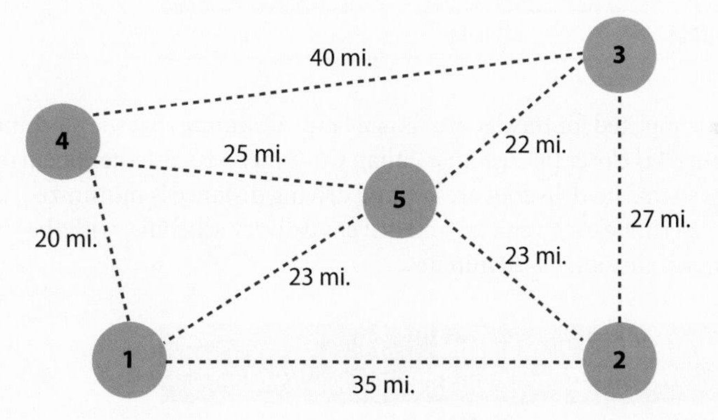

8. Use the cluster-first-route-second heuristic to determine acceptable total mileage delivery routes for two trucks (6-ton and 10-ton capacities) and the following network of customers with their shipping requirements, starting from location 1. Start with two tours: Tour 1—1-5-4-1 and Tour 2—1-2-3-1—then use the Clark and Wright savings heuristic to find an improvement on total distance traveled.

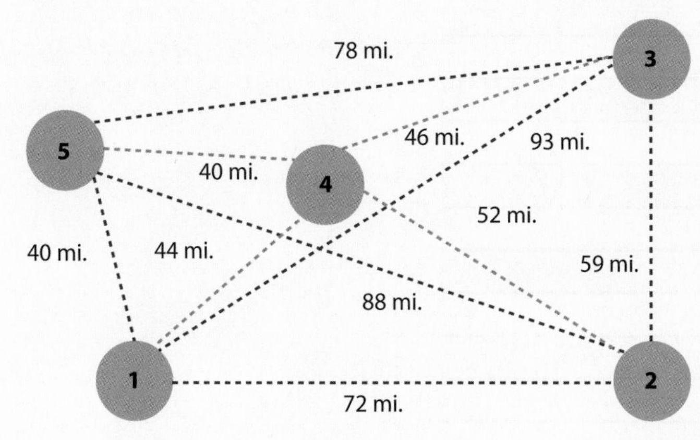

Node	Dem./day (tons)
2	3
3	3
4	4
5	2

9. Nikolai's Furniture Delivery business delivers to a set of customers as demand dictates. The current list of deliveries for the day is shown here. Assuming that the customers are ranked in proximity to one another (i.e., Customer 4 is closer to Customer 3 than Customer 5 is), use the concurrent scheduler approach to assign deliveries to vehicles so that no deliveries are late and driving distance is minimized. Determine how many delivery vehicles are needed. Also, determine each vehicle's delivery schedule, the start time, and the finish time. Assume that drive time to each customer is 15 minutes.

Delivery	Promised Arrival Time	Estimated Completion Time	Delivery Vehicle
1	9:00 AM	9:20 AM	
2	9:45 AM	10:15 AM	
3	10:00 AM	10:45 AM	
4	10:30 AM	11:00 AM	
5	10:45 AM	12:15 PM	
6	11:00 AM	11:45 AM	
7	11:30 AM	12:00 PM	
8	12:30 PM	2:00 PM	
9	1:00 PM	1:45 PM	
10	1:30 PM	2:30 PM	
11	2:30 PM	3:15 PM	
12	3:00 PM	4:00 PM	
13	3:30 PM	4:30 PM	

10. A listing of deliveries to be completed for the day are shown here. Assuming that the customers are ranked in proximity to one another (i.e., Customer 4 is closer to Customer 3 than Customer 5 is), use the concurrent scheduler approach to assign deliveries to vehicles so that no deliveries are late and driving distance is minimized. Determine how many delivery vehicles are needed. Also, determine each vehicle's and driver's delivery schedule, with the start time and the finish time. Assume that drive time to each customer is 20 minutes.

Delivery	Promised Arrival Time	Estimated Completion Time	Delivery Vehicle
1	8:30 AM	9:00 AM	
2	8:45 AM	9:30 AM	
3	9:30 AM	10:15 AM	
4	10:00 AM	10:30 AM	
5	10:15 AM	11:15AM	
6	10:30 AM	11:30 AM	
7	11:00 AM	12:00 PM	
8	11:30 PM	1:00 PM	
9	12:00 PM	12:45 PM	
10	12:30 PM	1:30 PM	
11	1:30 PM	2:15 PM	
12	1:45 PM	2:15 PM	
13	2:15 PM	3:30 PM	
14	3:00 PM	3:45 PM	
15	3:45 PM	4:15 PM	

CASE STUDIES

CASE 1: Fulfillment Center Issues

Direct Dosages is a prescription fulfillment center. It has its own pharmacy and processes prescriptions, then ships the medicines directly to patients' homes. Direct Dosages offers medicine at a reduced cost because of the volume it processes. Consequently, Direct Dosages' primary customers are the insurance companies, who benefit from the reduced prices. In addition, patients benefit from home delivery, an essential service for those extremely ill or disabled.

The Direct Dosages pharmacy is organized into five departments—order entry, order fulfillment, quality control, inventory, and packaging/shipping. Order entry inputs prescriptions received from doctors' offices and hospitals into Direct Dosages' database. The information includes the patient's name, address, type of medicine, quantity, dosage, doctor's name, and any special instructions. Order fulfillment pulls the prescriptions from the database and fills the orders. Quality control takes a sample of the orders processed each hour and ensures that the filled prescriptions contain no errors such as the wrong quantity, wrong medicine, and missing special instructions. If the order contains any errors, it is returned to order fulfillment. Filled prescriptions are sent to packaging/shipping either from order fulfillment or from quality control, if they have been selected for inspection. The function of the inventory department is to order and receive medications from the pharmaceutical companies and provide replenishment to order fulfillment and packaging/shipping for medicines, labels, bottles, and boxes when those departments request replenishment.

Because of its sequential process, Direct Dosages has been experiencing an increase in complaints about prescriptions not being processed in a timely manner. For example, new prescriptions are put in the queue with renewed prescriptions and are processed on a first-come-first-served basis. Patients who are renewing their prescriptions generally still have medication on hand. However, patients with new prescriptions do not yet have the needed medicines on hand; therefore, delays in fulfilling and shipping their prescriptions could adversely affect their health. In addition, Direct Dosages' departments' workloads are not balanced. Order entry is constantly busy, but packaging/shipping has idle periods while it waits on orders to be fulfilled and inspected. Also, because the order fulfillment process is labor intensive, there is more work in process (WIP) in this department at any given time. WIP in both quality control and packaging/shipping is relatively low.

DISCUSSION QUESTIONS

1. Based on the description of the workflow, is this a product-focused system or a process-focused system? Why?
2. Currently, Direct Dosages is using the first-come-first-served (FCFS) dispatch rule. What other dispatch rules may be more effective than FCFS? Explain the benefit of using a different dispatch rule.
3. In this situation, would input-output control be beneficial to implement? Explain why or why not.

Note: Written by Rick Bonsall, D. Mgt., McKendree University, Lebanon, IL. The people and company are fictional and any resemblance to any person or company is coincidental. This case was prepared solely to provide material for class discussion. The author does not intend to illustrate either effective or ineffective handling of a managerial situation.

CASE 2: Getting Around Campus

Vegas College was founded in the early 1800s, when the town was very small. Vegas was a small, private institution, and in the early years it had a small student population and just a few buildings. Getting from one building to another took a maximum of five minutes. As the college expanded during its first century, its footprint was still relatively small. Dormitories were close to the academic and administrative buildings. Students, faculty, and staff could easily park and walk from one facility to another.

When Vegas College was first founded, its benefactors donated a significant amount of land. However, during the first 50 years or so, there were some very hard times because of social and economic events such as the Great Depression and two world wars. Revenue hit extremely low points during those periods, and in order to keep the college open, the administration had to sell some of its land. The sale of land combined with the growth of the town around Vegas College resulted in it becoming landlocked. There was no longer available land adjacent to the current campus for expansion.

Eventually, economic conditions improved, and student enrollments increased. As it expanded its curriculum and degree programs, Vegas College grew into a university. Vegas University began to buy back some of the land it had sold years ago; however, it was still not enough to meet its expansion needs. Consequently, it began to build dormitories and administrative buildings wherever land was available in the local area. No longer could students, faculty, and staff easily walk to campus facilities. Something had to be done. Consequently, the university decided to provide transportation to and from its facilities.

Vegas University's Operations Department was tasked with developing and managing the campus bus service. The operations manager studied the layout of the extended campus and determined that there was no obvious, simple, circular route for the bus service. Furthermore, classes on Monday, Wednesday, and Friday were 50 minutes long, while classes on Tuesday and Thursday were 80 minutes long. Consequently, a single bus schedule would not accommodate the students' and faculty's daily transportation needs. The issue was further complicated by the need to get to sporting events, the dining facility, and the library. The operations manager was going to need to use a vehicle scheduling and routing method that addressed these issues.

DISCUSSION QUESTIONS

1. In the scenario described in the case, which of these three things should the operations manager consider when deciding on what approach to use: Solving the traveling salesman problem, addressing the problem in terms of capacity, or viewing the problem from a pickup and delivery perspective? Explain why you believe the operations manager should consider the problem a specific way.
2. Which of the three vehicle scheduling and routing methods would you recommend, and why: Clark and Wright savings heuristic, cluster-first-route-second heuristic, or concurrent scheduler approach?

Note: Written by Rick Bonsall, D. Mgt., McKendree University, Lebanon, IL. The people and company are fictional and any resemblance to any person or company is coincidental. This case was prepared solely to provide material for class discussion. The author does not intend to illustrate either effective or ineffective handling of a managerial situation.

CASE 3: Print Shop Scheduling Issues

Jerry Montana is the manager of a printing facility at the corporate headquarters of a major corporation. He was hired specifically to fix a number of issues in its print shop. While the print shop is an important function for the corporation, it is not its core business. Consequently, there had not been much emphasis on hiring qualified print shop managers in the past. Because of the current managerial issues, Janet Vogel, the VP of operations, is considering closing the print facility and outsourcing all the company's printing needs. However, based on the recommendations from her staff, she decided to hire a new and more qualified print shop manager and give him one year to fix the issues. If the issues are not resolved within the year, she will close the facility and outsource all printing needs.

The main issue in the print shop is scheduling. There has been a steady stream of complaints about missed deadlines. A significant portion of the job orders are from Marketing. Marketing routinely needs copies of proposals, contracts, and marketing materials. Because of the competitive nature of its business, the required turnaround time is often very short. Missed deadlines adversely affect Marketing's ability to close its deals. Since most of the deals are for millions of dollars, the print shop's failure to meet these internal customer expectations is having a significant impact on the corporation's revenues.

Other departments, in addition to Marketing, have many job orders for the print shop as well. Because their needs are primarily for internal meetings, the required turnaround time is not as short, when compared to Marketing. However, the departments generally do not give a lot of lead time for their requests. This exacerbates the issue of the print shop meeting its due dates.

Jerry decided that before he can determine how to resolve the scheduling issue he must first examine what services the print shop provides and how the shop is organized. The print shop provides only digital printing, and no offset, silk screen, or other types of printing. The items that can be digitally printed are booklets, brochures, calendars, flyers, envelopes, letterhead, notepads, business cards, labels, banners, posters, stickers, and tent cards. Jerry believes that the digital printing services are not a major issue, although there is setup time for the printers based on the type of job. Jerry believes that the root cause of missed deadlines centers on the other services provided—binding and finishing.

Finishing options include laminating, hole punching, cutting, folding, mounting, padding, collating, tabs, inserts, and vinyl covers. Depending on the job, some finishing services such as collating and inserts can be accomplished by the digital printers. Otherwise, those services must be done by hand. Binding services include coil binding, comb binding, tape binding, staples (any configuration), and ring binders. Most of the finishing and binding services must be done by hand; thus, they are very labor intensive and slow compared to the digital printing services.

Currently, the print shop is divided into four areas—digital printing, finishing, binding, and packaging. As Jerry observed the workflow through the day, he noticed several issues. The digital printing staff tended to do the short job runs before tackling any large job runs. Since the work orders for the short runs often had different requirements, the setup of the digital printers had to be redone for each job. Although the setup can be accomplished quickly, each day's accumulated setup time was significant.

The work in process (WIP) for each day was high. As the week progressed the WIP continued to increase. The digital print department completed work orders at a much faster pace than either finishing or binding could do because of the labor-intensive tasks. The workflow sequence of most work orders was digital printing, finishing, binding, and then packaging. Finishing and binding frequently became bottlenecks in the process. Packaging was where the finished work orders were shrink-wrapped and boxed. Generally, packaging could be accomplished quickly; thus, workers were frequently idle, waiting for jobs from binding.

DISCUSSION QUESTIONS

1. Based on the description of the workflow, is this a product-focused system or a process-focused system? Why?
2. Which dispatch rule do you believe would be the most effective in helping to reduce the number of missed deadlines? Explain why you selected the specific dispatch rule.
3. In this situation, would input-output control be beneficial to implement? Explain why or why not.

Note: Written by Rick Bonsall, D. Mgt., McKendree University, Lebanon, IL. The people and company are fictional and any resemblance to any person or company is coincidental. This case was prepared solely to provide material for class discussion. The author does not intend to illustrate either effective or ineffective handling of a managerial situation.

VIDEO CASE STUDY

Learn more about ***job scheduling*** from real organizations that use operations management techniques every day. Chris Bredesen is the Owner/Operating Partner at Rockefeller, a gastropub in Hermosa Beach, California. Rockefeller uses a number of techniques to schedule their employees and operating hours. Watch this short interview to find out why.

To be competitive, we have to look for every opportunity to improve efficiencies and productivity while increasing quality. Lean manufacturing principles have improved every aspect of our processes.

—**CYNTHIA FANNING,** product general manager, GE Appliances[1]

Beckett has a culture of lean thinking. From the front office to the assembly floor, we strive to find ways to improve our processes for greater efficiency, product quality and an enjoyable work environment.

—**KEVIN BECKETT,** president and CEO, R. W. Beckett[2]

LEAN SYSTEMS

9

LEARNING OBJECTIVES

After completing this chapter, you should be able to:

9.1 Summarize the history of the Toyota Production System
9.2 Identify the major elements of lean
9.3 Explain lean thinking applied to services
9.4 Describe how firms create and sustain a lean culture
9.5 Describe how lean methods create sustainable supply chains
9.6 Discuss several of the current trends in lean systems

Master the content.

edge.sagepub.com/wisner

COX MACHINE'S LEAN SUPPLY CHAIN

Kansas-based aerospace component manufacturer Cox Machine uses lean principles in its tightly managed supply chains. In 2007, Cox began standardizing and measuring its manufacturing system. This included a focus on operational excellence and traditional lean initiatives like 5S, kaizen events, and cellular layouts. Collectively, these practices are reducing cycle times, improving product flow, and reducing inventory levels. Cox's inventory turns increased from under four in 2007 to seven by 2013.

For Cox, lean practices start with the raw material supplier. The goal is to have the material delivered three days before a machining operation, which can be a constantly moving target due to fluctuations in forecasts and inventory levels. Cox has had the most success with suppliers that use the forecast that Cox provides, which is derived from the forecast that Cox's customer provides. After materials arrive and are inspected, Cox delivers it directly to a machine cell, avoiding a non-value-creating stop in the warehouse.

At the machine cell, Cox uses two or three machines to cut on the same job at the same time, reducing overall lead time for the job. It is shortened even further by having the cell operator deburr and inspect cell outputs, avoiding a second or third staging location and process. This takes several days' lead time out of each job.

Once a fabrication operation has been completed, Cox sends most of its product outside for coating. This involves chemical coating followed by primer. Many of the parts also require inspection. To reduce external lead times, Cox has entered into long-term agreements that help inspectors know what to expect. Cox also provides the forecasts to inspectors. The forecast includes special notation for parts that have not been run before, which allows inspectors to work on their internal planning ahead of time. When inspectors know what is coming, they can quote and meet shorter lead times.

Finally, by utilizing mutually beneficial shipping methods, advance shipping notices, and barcoding, Cox can help customers reduce their "dock-to-stock" times, which lowers finished goods inventories. Overall, Cox has reduced its average quoted lead time from sixteen weeks to four, and in many cases Cox can produce parts within a two-week lead time.[3]

INTRODUCTION

Today, the term **lean thinking** represents an important operating philosophy, central to the success of material flow management, which is one of the eight key supply chain processes discussed in Chapter 1. Lean organizations seek to simultaneously achieve the objectives of high quality, fast response, and low waste (and, hence, cost). Lean is also closely associated with Just-in-Time (JIT) management. While many may argue that Henry Ford and his company essentially invented JIT practices, the term *Just-in-Time* was originally associated with Toyota managers like Taiichi Ohno, along with his kanban system, encompassing continuous problem solving in order to eliminate waste and improve quality.

Use of the term *lean thinking* and its many pseudonyms (such as **lean systems**, **lean manufacturing**, **lean production**, or simply *lean*) has today almost entirely replaced use of

lean thinking An operating philosophy encompassing the objectives of high quality, fast response, and low waste within the organization and between supply chain trading partners. Also known as lean systems, lean manufacturing, lean production, and lean.

the term *JIT*. Lean systems are based on the **Toyota Production System** and seek to optimize use of time, human resources, and assets while improving productivity and quality. In the early 1980s, these practices started making their way to the Western world, first as JIT and then, today, as lean.

Eliminating waste is the most essential element in the use of lean systems. Excess inventories are considered a fundamental form of waste, and as inventories are reduced, problems with lead times, quality, supplier deliveries, and timing are typically uncovered. Eventually, these problems are remedied, resulting in higher levels of quality and customer service. As the drive to continuously reduce inventories and other forms of waste continues, the need to improve quality and lead times throughout the productive system follows (since excess inventories are typically kept as safety stock for times when supplier deliveries are late or quality problems are discovered). Thus, we find that becoming lean requires the firm also to employ quality improvement methods (which are discussed in Chapter 13).

A SHORT HISTORY OF LEAN AND THE TOYOTA PRODUCTION SYSTEM

9.1 Summarize the history of the Toyota Production System

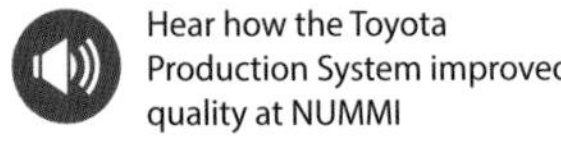

Hear how the Toyota Production System improved quality at NUMMI

The origins of lean are closely tied to Toyota and its Toyota Production System. Sakichi Toyoda founded the Toyoda Automatic Loom Works in 1926. In 1937, he sold his loom patents to finance an automobile manufacturing plant to compete with Ford and General Motors, which at the time accounted for over 90% of the vehicles manufactured in Japan. Sakichi's son Kiichiro Toyoda was named managing director of the new facility.[4]

Kiichiro spent a year in Detroit studying Ford's manufacturing system, among others, and then returned to Japan, where he adapted what he learned to the production of small quantities of automobiles, using small, frequently delivered batches of materials from suppliers. At the time, Ford's system in the United States was designed so that parts were fabricated in the plant, delivered directly to the assembly line, and then assembled onto a vehicle in very short order. Henry Ford had called this "flow production."[5]

Toyota Production System Seeks to optimize use of time, human resources, and assets, while improving productivity, quality, and customer service. It is based on the idea of reducing waste.

Eiji Toyoda, Sakichi's nephew, became the managing director of the renamed Toyoda Automotive Works in 1950. Eiji, too, traveled to Detroit to study Ford's automobile manufacturing system and was particularly impressed with its quality improvement activities. He was also impressed with Ford's *daily* automobile output of 7,000 cars, compared to Toyoda's cumulative *13-year* output to date of just 2,700 cars. Back in Japan, Eiji began implementing the flow production concepts he had seen at Ford, and this became a foundation element of what was later referred to as the Toyota Production System.

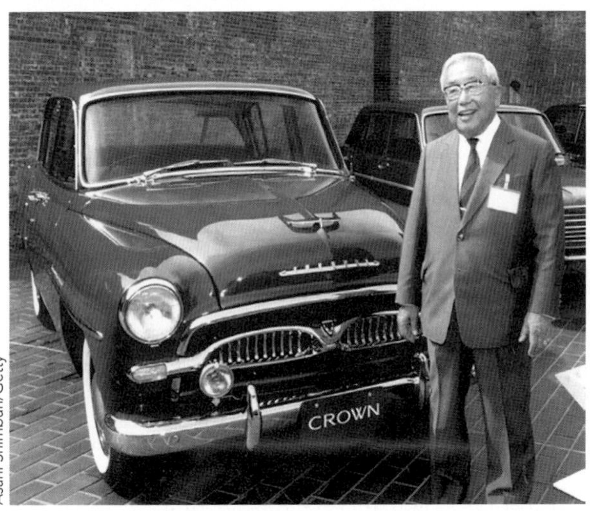

Asahi Shimbun/Getty

Eiji Toyoda, president of Toyota from 1967 to 1982, stands with an early model Toyota.

In 1957, the company was renamed the Toyota Company. After several car design failures in the United States, Toyota successfully introduced the good-looking, high-quality Corona in 1965, and by 1972, total U.S. sales had reached 1 million units.[6] In 1982, Eiji established Toyota Motor Sales USA, and finally in 1983, the global company became the Toyota Motor Corporation.

Taiichi Ohno, working at Toyota from the very beginning, expanded the concepts established by Kiichiro and Eiji by developing and refining methods to produce items only as they were needed for assembly. He, too, visited Detroit several times to observe automanufacturing techniques. After World War II, the destroyed Toyoda production facilities were rebuilt, with Taiichi playing a major role in establishing the low-batch production principles developed earlier. These principles proved quite valuable at the time, since postwar Japan was experiencing severe materials shortages.

Additionally, parts were produced only when needed by the next step in the production process. When a material movement or production signal or card (called a **kanban**) was used, the system became much more effective. This began to be called the kanban or JIT system within Toyota.

The final two notable people in the development of the Toyota Production System were Shigeo Shingo, a quality consultant hired by Toyota, and W. Edwards Deming, an American statistician who happened to be in Japan after the war helping to conduct the country's census. At the time, Deming was also attending professional engineering meetings in Japan to discuss his knowledge of statistical quality control techniques. In the 1950s, during further visits to Japan, Deming created his 14-point quality management guideline, and discussed these ideas with many Japanese manufacturing engineers and managers, including Toyota.

Shigeo Shingo developed the concept of **poka-yoke** in 1961, while he was employed as a consultant at Toyota. Poka-yoke means error- or mistake-proofing. The idea is to design processes so that mistakes or defects are prevented from occurring in the first place, and if they do occur, then further errors are prevented. These fail-safe mechanisms can be electrical, mechanical, visual, procedural, or any other method that prevents problems, errors, or defects, and they can be implemented anywhere in the organization.[7]

Early on, while Toyota was rapidly increasing its production, it was also experiencing quality problems that were impacting potential sales in the United States. To remedy this, Toyota implemented what it referred to as total quality control (TQC) in concert with its kanban system. This then became the final piece of the Toyota Production System, and was later refined and renamed total quality management (TQM). Interestingly, in the first quarter of 2007, Toyota sold more vehicles worldwide than General Motors, ending GM's 76-year reign as the world's largest automaker (today, GM and Toyota essentially share this title).[8]

Interestingly, the term *lean production* did not originate at Toyota. It was first used in a benchmarking study conducted by the International Motor Vehicle Program (IMVP) at the Massachusetts Institute of Technology. The IMVP conducted a global automobile quality and productivity benchmarking study that culminated in the book *The Machine That Changed the World* in 1990.[9] In the book, Dr. James Womack used the word *lean* to describe the Japanese plants in the benchmarking study (which included Toyota) when compared to their U.S. counterparts. These Japanese facilities used about half the manufacturing labor, half the space, and half the engineering hours to produce a new automobile model in half the time compared to U.S. automakers. They also used much less than half the average inventory levels to produce the same number of vehicles, with fewer defects. From this study, use of the term *lean* took off, and thus became associated with JIT, low inventories, less waste, and finally, the Toyota Production System.

LEAN PRACTICES

9.2 Identify the major elements of lean

The practices of lean have spread rapidly over the years among many manufacturers in numerous industries. In addition to manufacturing, lean practices are also frequently used in services, small businesses, and nonprofits. Implementing lean can start with something as simple as a watch. "Your first tool, if you're going to explore lean, probably should be a stopwatch so that you can just watch someone do what it is you need to do," explains lean practitioner Kevin Gingerich of Illinois-based Bosch Rexroth Linear Motion and Assembly Technologies. "You just time each piece of a manufacturing process or an assembly process, and you start to understand the wasted time involved."[10]

Many hospitals have implemented lean programs to improve employee productivity and patient flow (and thus reduce patient time at the hospital), and also to reduce materials costs. The Flinders Medical Centre in Australia used lean thinking to map patient flow in its emergency care area and was able to reduce emergency room congestion while reducing by 50% the number of people leaving without completing their care.[11] Small

kanban A material movement or production signal, or card.

poka-yoke Error- or mistake-proofing.

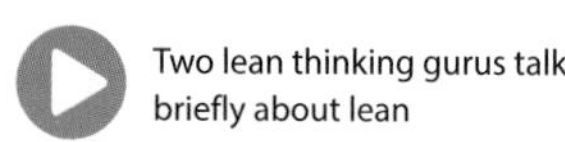
Two lean thinking gurus talk briefly about lean

businesses, too, can benefit—Mike Shanahan, co-owner of Connecticut-based small manufacturer Cadco Ltd., used lean thinking to reduce production lead times and to revise the layout of its facility. According to Shanahan, "The concept of lean is nothing like we thought it would be. It doesn't have to be complicated, unruly, or expensive. In my eyes, it's all about finding the simplest way to accomplish a task or an operation. And its success can be measured in small increments, astounding results, or something in between. Either way, it can be applied to almost any operation or any size."[12] And finally, the U.S. Navy used lean thinking to analyze its ordnance requisition process. It mapped the requisition process while measuring the touches and the process time for each step. As a result of several changes, it reduced its requisition cycle time by about 50%, and its backlog of orders also decreased.[13]

A number of good examples of using lean to improve supply chains also exist. The chapter-opening vignette describes Cox Machine's lean supply chain. The $20 billion global personal care product company Kimberly-Clark used lean thinking to reduce its North American network of 70 distribution centers to nine regional mega-centers. From 2006 to 2008, this leaner network resulted in 24 million fewer miles traveled between Kimberly-Clark distribution centers and client locations, saving millions of gallons of diesel fuel. Additionally, it actually reduced the average transit times to many of its customers.[14] Recently, Pennsylvania-based thermoform manufacturer McClarin Plastics offered lean certification classes to its employees, suppliers, and customers in order to lean out its supply chains. The goals were to reduce waste, supplier turnover, and manufacturing space and time. "This will bring everyone involved in a related supply chain together to learn how their performance affects others. The positive bottom line impact from the resulting relationships and understanding could be huge," explains Roger Kirk, vice president of marketing and engineering at McClarin.[15]

Many firms do not implement all of the lean activities, but rather select elements based on resources, product characteristics, customer needs, and supplier capabilities. Coffeehouse giant Starbucks has a VP of lean thinking who travels from region to region with his lean team, looking for ways to reduce the wasted movements of its baristas. This in turn gives

MANUFACTURING SPOTLIGHT Lean Systems at R. W. Beckett

Monty Rakusen/Getty

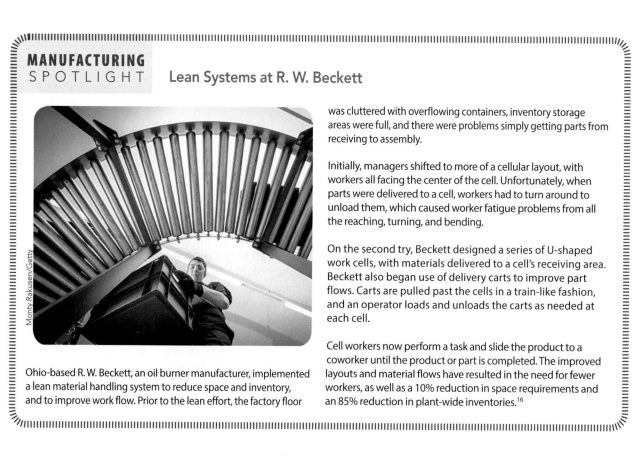

Ohio-based R. W. Beckett, an oil burner manufacturer, implemented a lean material handling system to reduce space and inventory, and to improve work flow. Prior to the lean effort, the factory floor was cluttered with overflowing containers, inventory storage areas were full, and there were problems simply getting parts from receiving to assembly.

Initially, managers shifted to more of a cellular layout, with workers all facing the center of the cell. Unfortunately, when parts were delivered to a cell, workers had to turn around to unload them, which caused worker fatigue problems from all the reaching, turning, and bending.

On the second try, Beckett designed a series of U-shaped work cells, with materials delivered to a cell's receiving area. Beckett also began use of delivery carts to improve part flows. Carts are pulled past the cells in a train-like fashion, and an operator loads and unloads the carts as needed at each cell.

Cell workers now perform a task and slide the product to a coworker until the product or part is completed. The improved layouts and material flows have resulted in the need for fewer workers, as well as a 10% reduction in space requirements and an 85% reduction in plant-wide inventories.[16]

baristas more time to interact with customers and improve the Starbucks experience. The results are streamlined operations, happier customers, and a better bottom line.[17]

THE ELEMENTS OF LEAN

Table 9.1 lists the major lean elements along with a short description of each element. Lean programs can vary significantly, based on a company's resource capabilities, product and process orientations, and past failures or successes with other improvement projects.

Waste Reduction

The desired outcome of waste reduction is value enhancement. Firms can reduce costs and add value to their goods and services by eliminating waste from their productive systems. Waste includes excess wait times, inventories, movements of people and materials, processing steps, and *any other non-value-adding activity*. Taiichi Ohno of Toyota described what he called the **seven wastes**, which have since been applied across many industries around the world, to identify and reduce waste. The seven wastes are listed and described in Table 9.2. The common term across the seven wastes is *excess*. Obviously, firms require some level of inventories, material and worker movements, and processing times, but the idea is to determine the *right* levels of these things and then decide how best to achieve them. The Manufacturing Spotlight on page 272 describes R. W. Beckett's lean efforts to reduce waste.

Using the Five-S's to Reduce Waste

One method used for waste reduction has been termed the **Five-S's**. The original Five-S's came from Toyota and were Japanese words relating to industrial housekeeping. The idea is that by implementing the Five-S's, the workplace will be cleaner, more organized, and safer, thereby reducing processing waste and improving productivity. California-based APL Logistics has been practicing lean and uses the Five-S's to improve safety and productivity in its warehouses. "The Five S's tell everyone that everything has a place. We have every kind of visual indicator of what you do for safety in our facility. When things are in order, it is easier for employees to find product. It is a more disciplined environment, which gives employees more pride in their job," says general manager Doug Tatum.[18] Table 9.3 lists and describes each of these terms, and presents equivalent S-terms used in the English version of the Five-S's (although the English Five-S's can vary based on company interpretations,

seven wastes Taiichi Ohno of Toyota described these, as they applied to the Toyota Production System, to identify and reduce waste. The common term across the seven wastes is *excess*.

Five-S's Came from Toyota and were Japanese words relating to industrial housekeeping. The idea is that by implementing the Five-S's, the workplace will be cleaner, more organized, and safer, thereby reducing processing waste and improving productivity.

Table 9.1 The Elements of Lean

Elements	Description
Waste reduction	The primary concern of lean; includes reducing excess inventories, material movements, production steps, scrap losses, rejects, and rework.
Lean supply chain relationships	Firms work with their suppliers and customers with the mutual goals of eliminating waste, improving speed, and improving quality. Key suppliers are considered partners, and close customer relationships are sought.
Lean layouts	WIP inventories are positioned close to each process, and layouts are designed to reduce movements of people and materials. Processes are positioned to allow smooth flow of work through the facility.
Inventory and setup time reduction	Inventories are reduced by reducing production batch sizes, setup times, and safety stocks. Tends to uncover processing problems, which are then managed and controlled.
Small batch scheduling	Firms produce frequent small batches of product, with frequent model changes to enable a level production schedule. Smaller, more frequent purchase orders are communicated to suppliers, and more frequent deliveries are offered to customers. Kanbans are used to pull WIP through the system.
Continuous improvement	As inventories are reduced, problems surface more quickly, causing the need for continual problem solving and process improvement. With lower safety stocks, quality levels must be high to avoid process shutdowns.
Workforce empowerment	Employees are cross-trained to add processing flexibility and to increase their ability to solve problems. Employees are trained to provide quality inspections as parts enter a process area. Employee roles are expanded, and they are given top management support and resources to identify and fix problems.

Table 9.2 The Seven Wastes

Wastes	Description
Overproducing	Production of unnecessary items to maintain high utilizations.
Waiting	Excess idle machine and operator time; materials experiencing excess wait time for processing.
Transportation	Excess movement of materials between processing steps; transporting items long distances using multiple handling steps.
Overprocessing	Non-value-adding manufacturing, handling, packaging, or inspection activities.
Excess inventory	Storage of excess raw materials, work-in-process, and finished goods.
Excess movement	Unnecessary movements of employees to complete a task.
Scrap and rework	Scrap materials and product rework activities due to poor-quality materials or processing.

Source: "Eleven-Step Recovery Plan: IE," by D. Cary, 2002, *IIE Solutions, 34*(2), pp. 43–48.

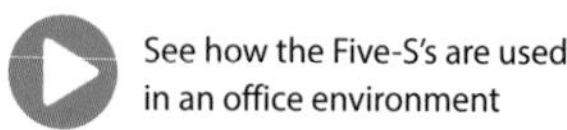

See how the Five-S's are used in an office environment

as seen in the Five S's video). The goals of the first two S-terms (sort and set in order) are to eliminate time spent searching for parts and tools, to avoid unnecessary movements, and to avoid using the wrong tools or parts. *Seiso*/sweep refers to proper workplace cleaning and maintenance, while *Seiketsu*/standardize seeks to reduce processing variabilities by eliminating nonstandard activities and resources. *Shitsuke*/self-discipline deals with forming and refining effective work habits.

The Five-S's can be employed in any service or manufacturing environment. Many lean efforts begin with implementation of the Five-S's. Firms can conduct a "waste hunt" using the Five-S's, then follow up with a "red-tag event" to remove or further evaluate all nonessential, red-tagged items. Some companies have also added a sixth-S, for safety, to assess the safety of work conditions and reduce the risk profile of the work area.[19]

LEAN SUPPLY CHAIN RELATIONSHIPS

If suppliers' delivery times are inconsistent or the quality of their goods does not meet specifications, then the buyer will likely carry safety stocks. Internally, extra work-in-process (WIP) inventories might be stored as a way to deal with temperamental processing equipment or other production problems. On the distribution side, firms hold stocks of finished goods in warehouses prior to shipment to customers, in some cases for months at a time, to avoid stockouts and maintain customer service levels. Holding these inbound, internal, and outbound inventories costs the firm money while not adding much, if any, value to the products or the firm; thus, they are considered wastes.

When a company, its suppliers, and its customers begin to work together to identify customer requirements, remove wastes, reduce costs, and improve quality and customer service, it marks the beginning of lean supply chain relationships. Using lean thinking with suppliers

Table 9.3 The Five-S's

Japanese S-Term	English Translation	English S-Term in Use
1. *Seiri*	Organization	Sort
2. *Seiton*	Tidiness	Set in order
3. *Seiso*	Purity	Sweep
4. *Seiketsu*	Cleanliness	Standardize
5. *Shitsuke*	Discipline	Self-discipline

Source: "Implementing 5S: To Promote Safety and Housekeeping," by J. Becker, 2001, *Professional Safety, 46*(8), pp. 29–31.

Figure 9.1 Relationship Between Order Quantity, Average Inventory, and Supplier Deliveries

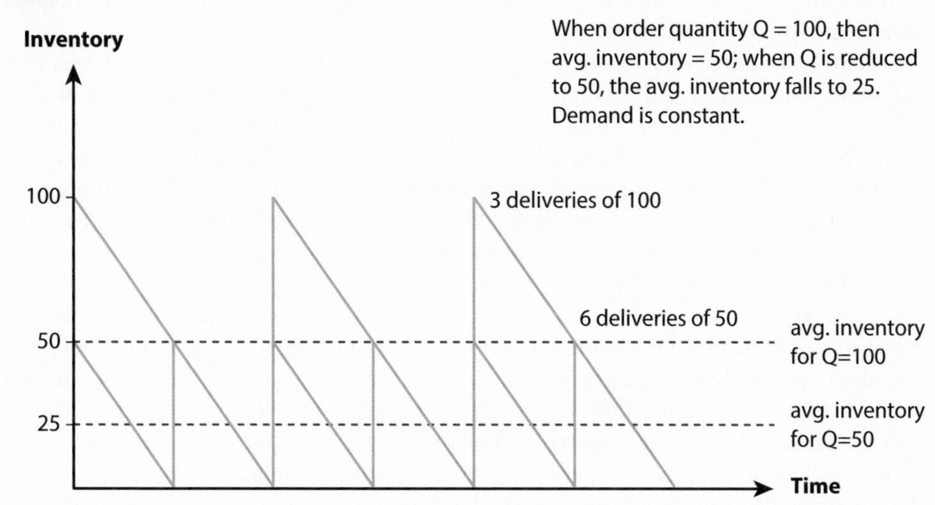

includes having them deliver smaller quantities, more frequently, to the point of use within the firm. As shown in Figure 9.1, reducing order quantities to half their original size reduces average inventory by 50%, but doubles the number of required deliveries. More frequent deliveries mean higher inbound transportation costs; to help reduce these costs, suppliers could distribute products from warehouses or production facilities located near the buyer. To entice suppliers to make these investments in warehouses or to simply deliver more frequently, buyers identify their best performing suppliers and give them a greater share of the total purchasing requirements. Making these small, frequent purchases from just a few suppliers, though, puts the firm in a position of greater dependence on these suppliers. It is therefore extremely important that deliveries always be on time, delivered to the right location, in the right quantities, and be of high quality, since existing inventories will be lower. This is why only the best suppliers are used.

Firms can also use lean thinking with their key customers. As customer relationships develop, the firm uses greater levels of capacity for a smaller number of large, steady customers. The firm locates production or warehousing facilities close to these customers and makes frequent small deliveries of finished products to the points of use within the customers' facilities, thus reducing transportation times and average inventory levels. Lean thinking with customers means determining how to give customers exactly what they want when they want it, while minimizing waste as much as possible. At MeadWestvaco's paper mill in Alabama, it uses customer feedback to influence plant investments that ultimately result in better product quality and acceptability. "Without question, customers are driving our business model," says Jack Goldfrank, coated board division president. The company conducts a customer survey every 18 months to assess product, service, reputation, practices, price, and value. The surveys allow it to determine where customers want improvements, and any trends that may exist.[20]

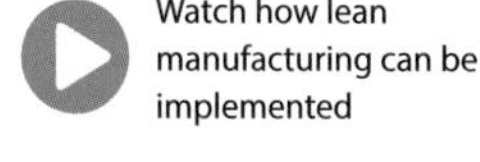

Lean Layouts

The primary design objective with lean layouts is to reduce wasted movements of workers, customers, and/or WIP, and to achieve smooth product flow through the facility. Constantly moving parts and people around

iStock/yoh4nn

Lean manufacturing layouts provide unobstructed lines of sight, with all inventories in containers at each workstation.

the production area add no value. Lean layouts allow people and materials to move only when and where they are needed, as quickly as possible. As discussed in Chapter 8, group technology layouts (also called cellular layouts) are often used as an example of layouts minimizing inventories and worker and part movements. Thus, these types of layouts would be considered lean.

Lean layouts are very visual, meaning that lines of visibility are unobstructed, making it easy for operators at one processing center to monitor work occurring at other centers. In lean manufacturing facilities, all purchased and WIP inventories are located on the production floor at their points of use, and the good visibility makes it easy to spot inventory buildups when machine breakdowns and bottlenecks occur. When these problems happen, they are spotted and fixed quickly. The relative closeness of the processing centers facilitates teamwork and joint problem solving, and requires less floor space than conventional production layouts.

Lean layouts allow problems to be tracked to their sources more quickly as well. As material and parts move from one processing center to the next, a quality problem, when found, can generally be traced to the previous work center, provided inspections are performed at each processing stage. In the United Kingdom, the British Aerospace Military Aircraft facility at Yorkshire was redesigned using lean concepts. One of the goals was to eliminate the non-value-added periods where components sat between processing stages. After rearranging the layout, some parts that had traveled 3 kilometers during processing moved only one-tenth of that distance. As a result, it was projected that productivity would increase by 20% and inventory levels would fall by 55%.[21]

Inventory and Setup Time Reduction

Excess inventories hide a number of purchasing, production, and quality problems within the organization. Once these problems are detected, they can be eliminated, improving product value and allowing the system to run more effectively at lower inventory levels. For example, reducing safety stocks of purchased materials will cause stockouts and potential manufacturing disruptions when late deliveries occur. Firms must then either find a way to resolve the delivery problem with the supplier or find a more reliable supplier. Either way, the end-result is a smoother-running supply chain with less inventory investment. The same story can be applied to production machinery. Properly maintained equipment breaks down less often, so less safety stock is needed to keep downstream processing areas fed with parts during machine breakdowns.

Another way to reduce inventory levels is to reduce purchase order quantities and production lot sizes. As shown in Figure 9.1, when order quantities and production lot sizes are cut in half, average inventories are also cut in half, assuming usage remains constant. Since reducing manufacturing lot sizes means increasing the number of **equipment setups**, and since setting up production equipment for the next production run takes valuable time, increasing the number of setups means the firm must find ways to reduce setup times. Once inventories have been reduced and the flow problems uncovered and resolved, the firm can reduce inventories still further, uncovering yet another set of problems to be resolved. With each of these inventory reduction iterations, the firm runs leaner, cheaper, faster, and with higher levels of product quality.

lean layouts Very visual layouts, meaning that lines of visibility are unobstructed, making it easy for operators at one processing center to monitor work occurring at other centers. In lean layouts, all purchased and WIP inventories are located on the production floor at their points of use, and the good visibility makes it easy to spot inventory buildups when machine breakdowns and bottlenecks occur.

equipment setup Setting up production equipment for the next production run.

SMED An abbreviation for single-minute (or single-digit) exchange of die.

SMED system A set of techniques that make it possible to perform equipment setup operations in a matter of minutes—ultimately, in the single-digit (less than 10 minute) range. This system was developed by Shigeo Shingo in Japan in the 1950s, and was applied at Toyota in the 1960s.

The SMED System

Lean manufacturers try to achieve **SMED**, which stands for single-minute exchange of die. The **SMED system** is a set of techniques that make it possible to perform equipment setup operations in a matter of minutes—ultimately, in the single-digit (less than 10 minute) range. This system was developed by Shigeo Shingo in Japan in the 1950s and used at Toyota in the 1960s. Back then, setup times were a big problem during the manufacturing of pressed steel car parts like doors. This originally required a machine down time of 12 to 36 hours when a multiton press needed to be reset for the production of another part. By applying the SMED system, the setup times were reduced dramatically. Depending on the process, setups in minutes may be very difficult, but if the SMED principles are followed, significant reductions in setup time can be obtained.

The SMED system consists essentially of three stages, as outlined here.[22]

Stage 1—Identify external setup tasks:

A number of setup activities can be performed externally (in other words, before machines are stopped for the product changeover). These include lining up the right people, preparing the parts and tools to be used for the next production run, making any tooling repairs, and then bringing the parts and tools to be used, as close as possible to the equipment. By performing these tasks externally, no actual clock-time time is lost, and setup times can be cut by as much as 30 to 50%.

Stage 2—Convert **internal setup activities** to **external setup activities**:

The key to successful implementation of Stage 2 is to look at each setup activity in a new light. Operators must brainstorm or re-examine setup tasks to see if any steps were mistakenly assumed to be internal (referring to setup time, which occurs while the machines are idle; these activities determine the actual setup clock time). They must try to identify ways to convert internal setup activities to external setup activities.

Stage 3—Streamline internal and external elements:

In this stage, all of the setup activities are continuously improved upon. This can be done by looking closely at each operations function and purpose very closely. Improvements can be divided into external and internal setup improvements. Approaches to accomplishing this include maintaining a visual and organized workplace; implementing parallel operations (performing multiple setup activities simultaneously); eliminating the need for adjustments; and automating activities.

The advantages of SMED, along with quicker setup times, are improved production flexibility, quicker delivery, better quality, and higher productivity. Through these benefits management will also see simpler and safer changeovers, less work-in-process inventory, and more standardized processes.

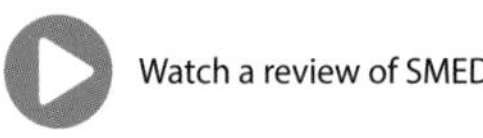

Small Batch Scheduling

As shown in Figure 9.1, small batch scheduling drives down costs by reducing system inventories. It also makes the firm more flexible to meet varying customer demands. Maintaining a set, level, small batch production schedule will also allow suppliers to anticipate and schedule their deliveries, resulting in fewer late deliveries. Texas-based National Coupling Co. has been practicing lean manufacturing since 2002, and today can produce about 1,500 coupling assemblies per week, with setups involving 60 to 80 product families. "With setups reduced to less than five minutes, we can maintain a high-velocity, high variability production line," says Ken Oberholz, vice president of operations. This flexibility allows the company to always make the right assemblies at the right time, with everything driven by customer requirements.[23]

Moving small production batches through a lean production facility is accomplished with the use of kanbans. When manufacturing cells need parts or materials, they use a kanban to signal their need for items from the upstream manufacturing cell, processing unit, or external supplier that is providing the needed material. In this way, nothing is provided until a downstream demand occurs. That is why a lean system is also known as a **pull system**. Ideally, parts are placed in standardized containers, and kanbans are used to control each container. Figure 9.2 illustrates how a kanban pull system works.

In Figure 9.2, when finished components are moved from Work cell B to the final assembly line, the following things occur:

1. The container holding finished parts in Work cell B's output area is emptied and a **production kanban** (a light, flag, or card) is used to tell Work cell B to begin processing more components to restock the empty container in its output area.

internal setup activities Setup activities occurring while the machines are idle. These activities contribute directly to the actual clock time of setups.

external setup activities Activities performed while the equipment is still making units of the previous item.

pull system When manufacturing cells need parts or materials, they use a kanban to signal their need for items from the upstream manufacturing cell, processing unit, or external supplier providing the needed material. In this way, nothing is provided until a downstream demand occurs.

production kanban A light, flag, or card that is used to tell the work cell to begin processing more components to restock the empty container in its output area.

Figure 9.2 A Kanban Pull System

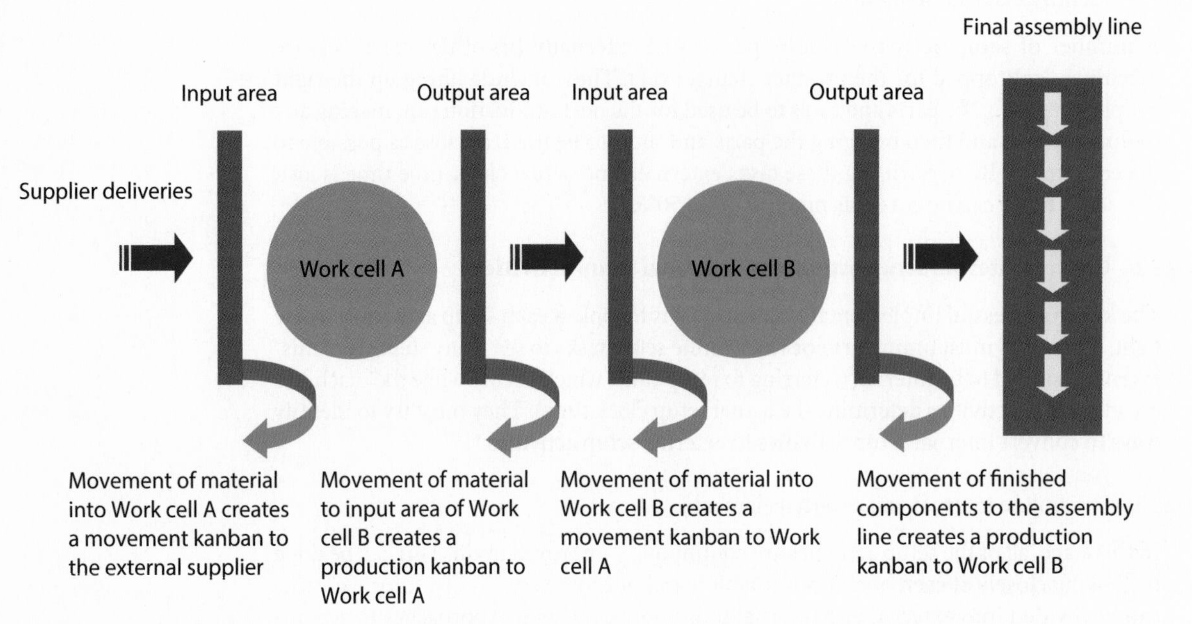
Final assembly line
Input area
Output area
Input area
Output area
Supplier deliveries
Work cell A
Work cell B
Movement of material into Work cell A creates a movement kanban to the external supplier
Movement of material to input area of Work cell B creates a production kanban to Work cell A
Movement of material into Work cell B creates a movement kanban to Work cell A
Movement of finished components to the assembly line creates a production kanban to Work cell B

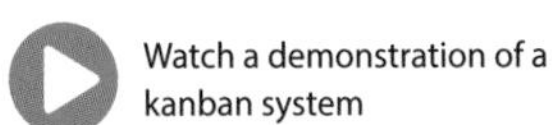
Watch a demonstration of a kanban system

2. During this stage, when parts are moved from Work cell B's input area to its processing area, the container holding these parts is emptied and a **withdrawal kanban** or movement kanban (a light, flag, or card) is used to indicate to Work cell A that more parts are needed. This authorizes a full container of parts to move from Work cell A's output area to Work cell B's input area, and the empty container is moved to Work cell A's output area.
3. As this movement occurs, a production kanban is used to authorize Work cell A to begin processing parts to restock its empty container in the output area.
4. Finally, as full containers of parts are emptied and used in Work cell A's processing area, the emptied containers in Work cell A's input area create a withdrawal kanban seen by the external supplier, who then restocks Work cell A's empty containers in the input area.

withdrawal kanban A light, flag, or card that is used to indicate to the upstream work cell that more parts are needed. This authorizes a full container of parts to move to the downstream work cell's input area. Also called a movement kanban.

iStock/Imageegaml

These shelves are holding standardized parts containers with kanban cards attached to the frames.

Thus, it can be seen that kanbans are used to control the flow of inventory through the facility. Inventories are not allowed to accumulate beyond the size of each container and the number of containers in the system. When containers are full, production stops until another production kanban is encountered. Kanbans these days don't have to be actual cards. At Franke Foodservice Systems, a Tennessee-based manufacturer of restaurant equipment, workers use cloud-based electronic kanbans—a practice becoming quite common. Their kanban application is integrated with materials data from two of the company's key suppliers, and more will eventually be added.[24]

Calculating the Number of Containers Needed

A simple relationship can be used to determine the number of containers needed for a lean production system:

$$K = \frac{DT(1+S)}{C},$$

Where:

K = the number of containers;

D = the demand rate of the assembly line;

T = the time for a container to make an entire circuit through the system, from being filled, moved, being emptied, and returned to be filled again;

C = the container size, in number of parts; and

S = the safety stock factor, from 0 to 100%.

Reducing inventory in a lean system occurs by reducing the number of containers in the system. Note that when the number of containers is reduced, the circuit time, T, for each container would also have to be reduced to enable the same demand to be met. This can be done by reducing setup time, processing time, wait time, move time, or some combination of these. Example 9.1 illustrates the calculation of containers in a lean system.

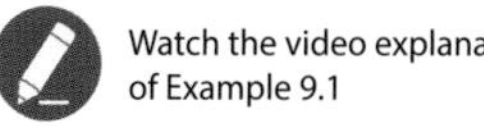

Example 9.1 Determining the Inventory Containers in a Lean System

Watch the video explanation of Example 9.1

The Bichsel Bicycle Co. was implementing lean throughout its factory, and needed to determine the number of containers at several of its work centers. In one such work center, the demand was 20 parts per hour and the containers they used for this part held 5 parts. If it normally took two hours for a full container to make a circuit through the work cell and back to its input side, and if it desired to carry 10% safety stock in the system, then the number of containers needed in the system would be:

$$K = \frac{DT(1+S)}{C} = \frac{20(2)(1.1)}{5} = 8.8 \text{ or } 9$$

The maximum inventory for this system would then be the total number of containers multiplied by the container size, or 9 × 5 = 45 units.

Continuous Improvement

As alluded to already, lean systems are never-ending works in progress. Compact layouts are designed to allow work to flow sequentially and quickly through the facility. Inventory is moved from supplier delivery vehicles to the shop floor, and placed in containers in designated work cell storage areas.

Purchase orders and production batches are small. In this system, problems often will surface, at least initially, as suppliers struggle to deliver frequently and on time, and as workers strive to maintain output levels while spending more time during the day, setting up machines for small production runs. To make the lean system work better, employees continuously seek ways to reduce supplier delivery and quality problems, and in the production area they solve movement problems, visibility problems, machine breakdown problems, machine setup problems, and internal quality problems.

In Japanese manufacturing facilities, this continuous improvement effort is known as **kaizen**. Kaizen comes from the Japanese words *kai* (change) and *Zen* (for the better). In U.S. firms, the **kaizen blitz** has become popular, and refers to typically a one-week improvement effort covering many areas at once and involving many workers in the firm.[25] The Manufacturing Spotlight "CertainTeed's Use of the Kaizen Blitz" describes the CertainTeed Corporation's use of a kaizen blitz to reduce energy costs.

kaizen A continuous improvement effort. Kaizen comes from the Japanese words *kai* (change) and *Zen* (for the better).

kaizen blitz Refers to typically a one-week improvement effort covering many areas at once and involving many workers in the firm.

workforce empowerment Managers support lean production efforts by providing subordinates with the skills, tools, time, empowerment, and other necessary resources to identify process problems and implement solutions. Managers create a culture in which workers are encouraged to speak out when problems exist.

Workforce Empowerment

Since lean systems depend so much on waste reduction and continuous improvement for their success, **workforce empowerment** must play a significant role in this process. Managers support lean production efforts by providing subordinates with the skills, tools, time, empowerment, and other necessary resources to identify process problems and implement solutions. Managers create a culture in which workers are encouraged to speak out when problems exist. At the Scania engine plant in Sweden, the facility is idled every

MANUFACTURING SPOTLIGHT

CertainTeed's Use of the Kaizen Blitz

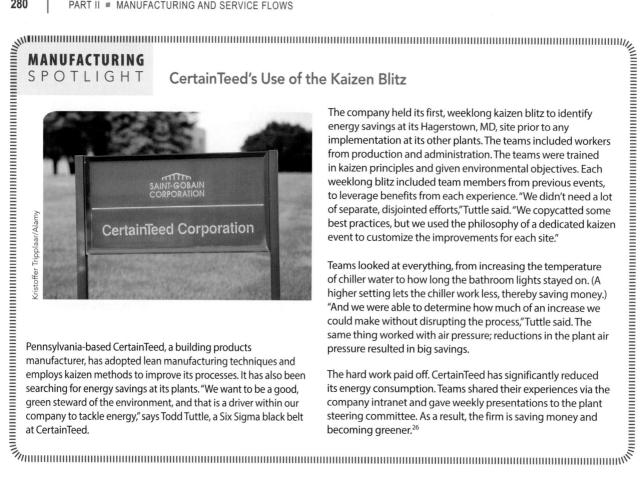

Kristoffer Tripplaar/Alamy

Pennsylvania-based CertainTeed, a building products manufacturer, has adopted lean manufacturing techniques and employs kaizen methods to improve its processes. It has also been searching for energy savings at its plants. "We want to be a good, green steward of the environment, and that is a driver within our company to tackle energy," says Todd Tuttle, a Six Sigma black belt at CertainTeed.

The company held its first, weeklong kaizen blitz to identify energy savings at its Hagerstown, MD, site prior to any implementation at its other plants. The teams included workers from production and administration. The teams were trained in kaizen principles and given environmental objectives. Each weeklong blitz included team members from previous events, to leverage benefits from each experience. "We didn't need a lot of separate, disjointed efforts," Tuttle said. "We copycatted some best practices, but we used the philosophy of a dedicated kaizen event to customize the improvements for each site."

Teams looked at everything, from increasing the temperature of chiller water to how long the bathroom lights stayed on. (A higher setting lets the chiller work less, thereby saving money.) "And we were able to determine how much of an increase we could make without disrupting the process," Tuttle said. The same thing worked with air pressure; reductions in the plant air pressure resulted in big savings.

The hard work paid off. CertainTeed has significantly reduced its energy consumption. Teams shared their experiences via the company intranet and gave weekly presentations to the plant steering committee. As a result, the firm is saving money and becoming greener.[26]

Wednesday at 8 a.m. for 26 minutes so every work team can hold an improvement meeting based on ideas on a whiteboard. Workers check the progress of each open idea, remove those that have been completed, and discuss new ones that were posted during the week. If additional resources or approvals are required, ideas move up to the whiteboard of the next level of management. All boards are public. Top management's whiteboard is placed in the middle of the plant, where everyone can see what is being worked on.[27]

LEAN THINKING IN SERVICES

9.3 Explain lean thinking applied to services

In many respects, services are like manufacturers—they have inventories, employees, procedures, locations, equipment, suppliers, and customers. In other words, various forms of waste can be identified and removed from most service processes. Lean practices are being used in banking, financial services, insurance, healthcare, utilities, retail, and government agencies to deliver high-quality, low-cost services to increasingly demanding customers. A number of lean service examples have already been provided throughout this chapter. **Lean services** focus on customer needs; they develop creative problem-solving abilities to improve and standardize processes to satisfy customers, while using tools for increasing quality, reducing waste, and improving service delivery. Several topics and tools used by lean services are discussed in the following section.

lean services Focus on customer needs; they develop creative problem-solving abilities to improve and standardize processes to satisfy customers, while using tools for increasing quality, reducing waste, and improving service delivery.

START WITH THE CUSTOMER

Spend time trying to identify what customers need. For example, service firms organize focus groups consisting of current and past customers to understand problems they might be having, what the company's strengths are, and what things customers want that the company is not providing. Here are some tips for planning and conducting a focus group:

1. Try to have a group of no more than eight to ten customers.
2. Develop a list of discussion topics ahead of time.
3. Determine the amount of time to be spent on each topic. (Good discussions usually require from one to two hours.)
4. Design questions in such a way that they encourage discussions. Don't ask questions that get short answers like "yes" or "true."
5. Start the session with an "ice breaker" that gets everyone talking. Make sure that everyone knows they are expected to contribute.
6. Have an experienced note taker attend. If possible, record the session on audio or video tape.
7. Afterward, review the notes, tape, or transcript, and summarize the major points, ranking them in terms of importance.[28]

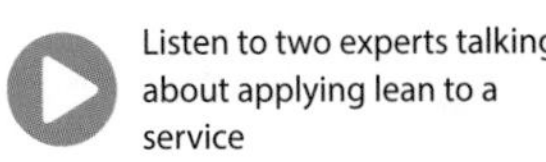

Listen to two experts talking about applying lean to a service

Additionally, companies can survey customers. Surveying customers regularly is a crucial part of running a successful business. Surveys can measure satisfaction with services provided, determine critical needs, and provide opportunities to build relationships with customers. Using this information to fill the needs of customers builds valuable loyalty and can create enthusiastic referrals. Here are some tips for creating good customer surveys:[29]

- Include open-ended questions to allow customers to give specific, actionable feedback. A rating is just not enough in some cases. For instance, if a customer responds with the highest rating, managers need to know why, so they can replicate that same experience with other customers.
- Design surveys to obtain truly candid, objective, and truthful customer responses. For example, using a 5-point scale with three or more positive rating points will bias the results. Distributing surveys to only seemingly satisfied or dissatisfied customers also leads to bias. Finally, making the survey too long (more than 5–7 questions) or the response scale too big (more than a 5-point scale) will create boredom, leading to low response rates or untruthful responses.
- Use surveys that get real information in real-time. Online surveys on company websites or placed in emails work much better than mailed surveys.
- Take actions on survey results. Call customers and resolve issues. Connect with customers. "Many companies never reach out to customers for feedback," says Bill Clerico, CEO of payment collection service WePay. "It sends a clear signal to customers that they don't often see—namely, that this company genuinely cares about their opinion and is acting on their feedback."
- Analyze and share the survey results with employees and customers. If the results are not positive, don't discard them and blame the methods. Embrace the feedback and do something about it.

process visibility Means that transactions and other activities in a process are known to users, and are performing accurately.

MAKE THE PROCESSES VISIBLE

Many service processes are complex with multiple decision points and take place inside a service provider's head (for example, call center representatives answering complicated healthcare-related questions). Lean involves the standardization of processes, so services must enable **process visibility** prior to any standardization efforts. Process visibility means that transactions and other activities in a process are known to users, and are performing accurately. Process visibility allows processes to be correctly aligned with key business goals. Business process monitoring helps provide such visibility, allowing organizations to proactively identify potential problems.

iStock/jazz42

Using sticky notes to describe workers' process steps makes processes visible to better enable process improvements.

One simple way to check process visibility is to try the *sticky note experiment*.[30] Find a team of service workers performing the same task, such as answering customer calls. Give each team member a different colored pad of

iStock/rpernell

ATMs have standardized and simplified a number of bank processes today.

sticky notes. Direct each team member to write the series of steps they take to do the work on their sticky notes. Once everyone is finished, have each person stick their series of notes in a row, on a whiteboard. In most cases, every row will be a different length, with different steps, in different sequences. If team members are doing the same work in different ways, then it is likely that customers aren't getting a consistent, high-quality service every time.

Another way to make service processes visible is to create process flow maps or value stream maps, similar to what was discussed and shown in Chapter 8 (and what will be discussed in Chapter 10, using customer flows). Once process steps have been identified and made visible, check sheets and time studies can be performed to identify problem areas or wastes in need of improvement. Steps in processes not adding value can be eliminated.

USE TECHNOLOGY

Automating service processes has become a widely used technique to standardize processes, while greatly decreasing service times and service costs. The purchase of books is a great example. A number of years ago, people drove to bookstores like Michigan-based mega bookstore Borders and perused books before purchasing. Then, Amazon entered the picture, allowing customers to search online and buy the same book cheaper than the Borders price. In 2011, after 40 years in business, Borders shut down and liquidated its assets, unable to create a successful blend of technology and service to attract customers.[31] New York–based Barnes & Noble has fared somewhat better—it sells books and its Nook e-reader online as well as in brick-and-mortar stores, and it has partnered with Microsoft and Samsung to offer other services. Still, it also appeared to be having some problems in 2014, in determining how to give customers what they want.[32]

The banking industry has also changed dramatically over the past 20 years, due to technology and the Internet. Customers obtain loans online, have their paychecks directly deposited into their accounts, pay bills online, and transfer money online. Additionally, customers use debit cards and obtain cash at ATMs. In fact, it is quite rare that customers actually visit an actual bank building these days. The four major U.S. **direct banks** (these are e-banks with no physical locations)—Ally Bank, Discover Bank, Capital One 360, and USAA, for example—are starting to outcompete their brick-and-mortar competitors, including big banks, large regionals, community banks, and credit unions. In a recent study by research firm TNS, direct banks stood out as the only category of banks to gain market share in the past decade among customers establishing or moving their primary banking relationships. The direct banks, which a decade ago attracted about 3.5% of new banking relationships, have since increased that share to about 8%.[33] Speed and convenience are the major selling points for these banks.

CREATING A LEAN CULTURE

9.4 Describe how firms create and sustain a lean culture

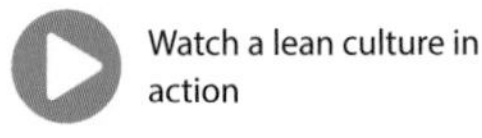
Watch a lean culture in action

As organizations implement lean practices, they often find that the most significant roadblock to further lean improvement relates to their lack of a **lean culture**. The root cause is often the organization's own bad habits. An organization's culture is tied closely to the individual behaviors of its leaders and other employees. To change bad habits, practice is the key factor. With enough practice, good habits can overcome the bad, and drive cultural change.

This is where many organizations fail in their lean transformations. They successfully implement a number of lean practices, but fail to make the activities become permanent, daily habits throughout the organization. The management side of the lean culture requires teaching others every day how to systematically strive toward the firm's lean transformation with action and overcoming obstacles. The activities of lifelong learning and improvement must be taught daily by the firm's leaders. Managers can get lost in the bad habit of classroom training followed by telling associates to go forth and improve. When this occurs in an organization, lean merely becomes a fad. Leaders must become the teachers in the organization, and this is what will drive the lean culture.[34]

direct banks E-banks, with no brick-and-mortar locations.

lean culture When organizations provide the leadership, training, communication, enthusiasm, and resources to employees over the long term, so they can continue a lean journey of finding and correcting problems.

Table 9.4 The 6-E's of Lean

E-Term	Description
Enlist	Seek assistance and cooperation from all of the staff.
Enable	Teach employees to take actions to continually improve their processes.
Engage	Keep employees involved in the process of change.
Excite	Encourage employees to stay active in finding and correcting problems.
Empower	Authorize employees to make changes happen in the areas they control.
Encourage	Inspire employees to tap into their creative and innovative capabilities, and frequently celebrate successes.

Source: Sedam, S. (2011, February). Creating a lean culture—builders speak out. *Professional Builder,* 1.

In 2013, Georgia-based Cbeyond Communications outsourced a number of IT services to India-based Tech Mahindra. While Cbeyond already had a strong lean culture, it wanted to spread this culture to Tech Mahindra. Its formula for implanting and sustaining a lean culture was the same formula used in Atlanta—daily meetings with managers and staff, real-time coaching and correction, regular root-cause analysis, and other lean exercises. Recognition of achievements happened frequently and was communicated throughout both organizations. A culture of lean thinking has continued to exist using a combination of continued leadership, vision, goals, and planning.[35]

Learning how to use lean thinking to improve quality, eliminate waste, and improve efficiencies will empower employees and keep them interested in a continuous emphasis on implementing lean. As Matt Collins, director of internal operations at Pennsylvania-based Keystone Custom Homes, puts it, "Discipline is key. Without it, lean stops after a company's managers sit around a table and brainstorm to create real answers to waste, yet the answers stay on a scratch pad and never make it to the field. Perhaps the biggest obstacle is a company's belief that it is already lean. Their premise is that lean is a status, not a process. Unless a company understands that lean is a never-ending journey, they will never be able to start down the path."[36]

Managers in many lean organizations use some form of the 6-E's to create and sustain a lean culture. These are shown in Table 9.4. Arizona-based furniture maker Pacific Manufacturing implemented a lean business model in 2005. Before long, with use of activities like 5S thinking, consolidating processes, cell layouts, teaching, and teamwork, the company was running smoothly and was able to weather the recession a few years later. Today, the lean culture is apparent throughout the company, and CEO Mark Erwin points to his engaged, enthused, and empowered staff as the primary reason for it. In response to the question, "What makes lean so successful at Pacific Manufacturing?" he emphasizes the three key management inputs of commitment, commitment, commitment, and employing the 6E's of lean.[37]

CAN COMPANIES BECOME TOO LEAN?

This is an interesting question, with a somewhat complex answer. In this chapter, lean practices have been portrayed in a very positive light. However, there are occasionally instances when lean organizations might wish they had more inventories or more suppliers. While these instances are rare, they can happen. Toyota, for example, got a wake-up call in March 2011, when an earthquake and tsunami hit northern Japan, causing a devastating loss of life and ruined businesses. Toyota had become the world's most successful automaker in part because of its lean operations. Over many years, it had taken excess inventories out of its operations, using JIT parts deliveries and a minimal number of suppliers. The disabling of a few of its key suppliers from the tsunami meant that assembly lines literally ground to a halt as far away as China and North America. Globally, Toyota's March 2011 production levels dropped by about 30%. It took six months for Toyota's suppliers to get back to delivering parts in the required volumes. Afterward, Toyota spread its purchases more evenly among its suppliers and asked the suppliers to maintain larger inventory buffers.[38]

MANUFACTURING SPOTLIGHT

Nike's Lean and Sustainable Supply Chain

iStock/shank ali

Footwear manufacturer Nike has been working with its contract manufacturers to train them in lean principles. This allows for more and quicker decision making by workers, through skill building, teamwork, and quality concepts. These traits have allowed Nike to build a more lean, green, empowered, and equitable supply chain.

Nike's corporate responsibility strategy has evolved from a risk management, philanthropic, compliance model to a long-term strategy focused on innovation and collaboration to prepare Nike to thrive in a sustainable economy. The company is increasing its focus on sustainable business and innovation (SB&I) to provide greater returns to its business, communities, factory workers, consumers, and the planet.

"Sustainability is key to Nike's growth and innovation," says Mark Parker, president and CEO. Recognizing the impacts of declining natural resources and the need to move to a low-carbon economy, Nike's goal is to achieve zero waste in the supply chain and have products and materials that can be continuously reused.

"The link between sustainability and Nike as a growth company has never been clearer," says Hannah Jones, vice president of SB&I. Today, the company is reducing waste and toxins and increasing its use of environmentally preferred materials throughout its product lines.[39]

During the recession of 2008 and 2009, a number of companies made significant cutbacks on labor, production, and material purchases. Coming out of the recession, some of these companies realized they had become too lean to handle the uptick of demand. "Some firms that made deep personnel cuts are now finding their teams are too lean to maintain quality service and meet increased customer demands," states Max Messmer, chair and CEO of California-based Robert Half International, a specialized staffing service.[40]

LEAN AND SUSTAINABLE SUPPLY CHAINS

9.5 Describe how lean methods create sustainable supply chains

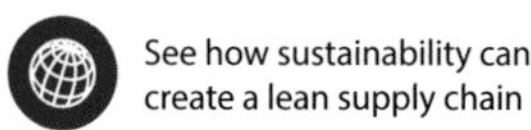
See how sustainability can create a lean supply chain

Since lean systems are concerned with eliminating waste throughout the firm and its supply chains, the linkage between lean and sustainability should seem clear. Adopting lean practices reduces waste and leads to improved environmental performance and profitability. Furthermore, lean systems increase the possibility that firms will adopt more advanced environmental management systems, leading to yet further performance improvements. Professors King and Lennox analyzed thousands of companies in the early 1990s and found ample evidence of this linkage between the concept of lean and the environment. They found that firms minimizing inventories and adopting quality standards were more likely to practice pollution prevention and also had lower toxic chemical emissions.[41]

Other examples in both manufacturing and services abound. Illinois-based Hospira, maker of pharmaceutical products, is not only dedicated to eliminating waste in all areas of production, but is also making headway on reducing the 2.4 billion pounds of waste that hospitals produce every year in the United States. As an example, Hospira developed and launched a new IV (intravenous) bag that produces 40–70% less waste than other flexible IV bags.[42] At New Jersey–based printing company Pictorial Offset Corp., management's desire to reduce waste led it to remove 300 chemical products from the plant and begin recycling corrugated and steel strapping waste. The firm has achieved a number of industry environmental firsts, including obtaining the quality-based ISO 9000 and environment-based ISO 14000 certifications simultaneously. It is also recognized as being **carbon-neutral** in part by planting 5,000 trees in New Jersey to offset the carbon footprint of its operations. These practices have also helped Pictorial Offset's sales—it has gained a number of new clients who sought out the printing firm because of its environmental reputation.[43]

carbon-neutral A description given to companies when they offset the carbon footprint of their operations by doing things like planting trees.

In the transportation industry, lean and sustainability go together well. According to John Tucker, marketing vice president at Datatrac Corp., "If you're not tracking each movement and have people running around out there and making three or four extra stops because things didn't get delivered or delivered correctly, that's wildly inefficient—you're consuming business resources, and you're becoming a hazard to the environment because you've logged, perhaps, three times more miles than you needed to in order for one shipment to be delivered."[44] Finally, the Manufacturing Spotlight on page 284 describes Nike Inc.'s lean and sustainable supply chain. According to Mark Parker, Nike president and CEO, "Making our business more sustainable benefits our consumers who expect products and experiences with low environmental impact, contract factory workers who will gain from more sustainable manufacturing, and our employees and shareholders who will be rewarded by a company that is prepared for the future."[45]

TRENDS IN LEAN SYSTEMS

9.6 Discuss several of the current trends in lean systems

While the lean practices have been around for decades, new and better ways of designing lean systems and using lean thinking can still be found. Technological changes have provided new opportunities for lean systems, and this is discussed in the following sections, along with an idea for applying lean principles in other areas of the firm.

ADDING INTELLIGENCE TO LEAN

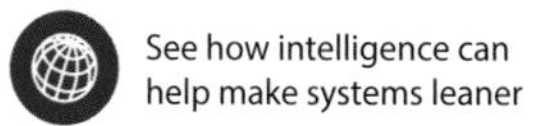
See how intelligence can help make systems leaner

Demand-pull systems are generally recognized as central to lean manufacturing, where material movement and production activities are controlled by kanban signals. Expanding on this idea, the use of big data, cloud computing, and mobile access have created multidomain pull systems that can apply to many operations processes. Adding intelligence to lean systems allows this expansion of the concept, and many are terming this capability **smart pull**. All functional domains of operations management, including quality, maintenance, time and attendance, material and production, and intelligence gathering, can be captured by the smart pull platform. This platform must have built-in machine integration capabilities for connecting to a wide variety of automation equipment and smart devices. The real-time data created by connected manufacturing processes can be used to actively monitor "traffic jams" in kanban loops and adjust parameters quickly; monitor situations and notify appropriate individuals when necessary; benchmark across facilities and globally deploy processes; utilize information from multiple events to determine optimal replenishment quantities and safety stock levels; and utilize RFID sensors to detect material consumption and remotely trigger supplier replenishments.[46]

California-based Apriso, a provider of manufacturing software solutions, launched a smart pull software product in 2013 that uses real-time process data to allow electronic kanbans to use seasonal order fluctuations, supplier performance, and employee knowledge to trigger more accurate order replenishment signals. "Recent advances in mobility, social media, and sensing technologies have completely changed the scope of what real-time data can be gathered. Combining this intelligence with the capability to quickly extract actionable insights enables highly efficient business processes to be formulated and executed just in time for dramatically improved responsiveness across manufacturing and supply chain operations," says James Mok, director of solution strategy and business development at Apriso.[47]

APPLYING LEAN THINKING TO OTHER DISCIPLINES

As discussed early in this chapter, lean thinking refers in large part to satisfying customer requirements quickly, while solving problems and minimizing waste. This philosophy is today being implemented not simply in operations, but across the organization. Brad Humphrey, president of Texas-based construction consulting firm Pinnacle Development Group, describes the application of lean to financial management for contractors. For companies to be financially successful, they need to prioritize expenditures while minimizing wasteful, personal, and non-business-related expenditures. His four lean principles for financial success are:

smart pull Adding intelligence to lean systems allows an expansion of the kanban concept.

- *Develop and manage your budget.* Set a budget, then review it weekly, noticing trends, receivables, and if departments are staying close to budget forecasts. If the budget appears to be off from what the needs are, the financial controller and senior leaders need to learn why the real numbers are too high or low.
- *Discipline yourself on what you will not spend.* Some contractors just can't help but buy that new shiny piece of equipment or upgrade their vehicles every year to the latest model. Others are tempted to spend money on worthwhile efforts, such as civic and community needs. These expenditures, if not managed carefully, can severely cripple cash flow needs within the business. Successful companies have set priorities each year for making donations.
- *Set "warning" signs for better financial management.* Top managers should be warned whenever finances are running in the wrong direction. Warning signs could include: cash flow amounts approaching the lower acceptable levels; purchases made outside of budgeted limits by personnel; costs of needed parts, materials, or services rising beyond past figures; and poor purchasing decisions that failed to leverage quantity discounts.
- *Problem-solve wasteful spending and emergency spending.* For example, a concrete contractor might receive some less-than-acceptable concrete material, and yet still use it and then order materials from the same provider again. This has future problems written all over it. Managers must think through root causes and implement solutions. Emergency spending is most often related to poor planning, poor organization, and poor preparation. Emergency spending is most often very expensive and increases costs needlessly.

Humphrey suggests some final thoughts for lean financial thinking: keep long-term success ahead of short-term expenditures; be "tight" with money, without being "Mr. Scrooge"; debt is a bad thing to own; and reward cost reduction ideas.[48]

Visit edge.sagepub.com/wisner to help you accomplish your coursework goals in an easy-to-use learning environment.

- Mobile-friendly eFlashcards
- Mobile-friendly practice quizzes
- A complete online action plan
- Chapter summaries with learning objectives
- Excel templates to assist with practice problems
- Original video case studies that demonstrate chapter concepts in action

SUMMARY

In this chapter, the topic of lean was explored, including a history of the Toyota Production System, which led to the concepts of Just-in-Time and most of the current lean practices. Lean organizations reduce waste by managing material flows so that inventories and lead times are reduced, which reduces costs and improves customer service. The primary lean elements are waste reduction, lean supply chain relationships, lean layouts, inventory and setup time reduction, small batch scheduling, continuous improvement, and workforce empowerment. Discussions of lean services, creating a lean culture, and lean's impact on the environment are also included.

KEY TERMS

Carbon-neutral, 284
Direct banks, 282
Equipment setups, 276
External setup activities, 277
Five-S's, 273
Internal setup activities, 277

Kaizen, 279
Kaizen blitz, 279
Kanban, 271
Lean culture, 282
Lean layouts, 276
Lean manufacturing, 269
Lean production, 269
Lean services, 280
Lean systems, 269
Lean thinking, 269
Poka-yoke, 271
Process visibility, 281
Production kanban, 277
Pull system, 269
Seven wastes, 273
Smart pull, 285
SMED, 276
SMED system, 276
Toyota Production System, 270
Withdrawal kanban, 278
Workforce empowerment, 279

FORMULA REVIEW

No. of containers in a lean system, $K = \frac{DT(1+S)}{C}$, where D = the demand rate of the assembly line; T = the time for a container to make an entire circuit through the system, from being filled, moved, being emptied, and returned to be filled again; C = the container size, in number of parts; and S = the safety stock factor, from 0 to 100%.

SOLVED PROBLEMS

1. The demand for a part at one work center is 70 parts/hr. The work center uses 12 containers, and each container for this part holds 10 parts. If the company wants to carry 5% excess safety stock in the system, calculate the time required for the containers to get through the system. Also, determine the maximum inventory for the system.

Answer:

No. of containers, $K = \frac{DT(1+S)}{C}$; solving for T, we have $T = \frac{C(K)}{D(1+S)} = \frac{10(12)}{70(1.05)} = 1.6$ hours. The maximum inventory is 10(12) = 120 units.

REVIEW QUESTIONS

1. What is lean thinking, and how is it different from JIT?
2. What does the Toyota Production System have to do with JIT and lean?
3. What is the most essential element of the lean philosophy? Why?
4. What person or people at Toyota is (are) most responsible for the development of the JIT concept?
5. How did the Toyota Production System get started?
6. What is poka-yoke, who developed the concept, and what do you think it has to do with lean?
7. What are the seven wastes?
8. What are the Five-S's, and from where did they originate?
9. What is SMED, and why would lean manufacturers want to achieve SMED?
10. What are kanbans, and why are they used in lean systems?
11. How is a kaizen blitz different from kaizen?
12. How are lean services different from lean manufacturers? How are they the same?
13. Why is process visibility important for an effective lean system?
14. Discuss the linkage between lean systems and sustainability.
15. How can a company create a lean culture?

DISCUSSION QUESTIONS

1. Discuss the seven wastes in terms of a business with which you are familiar.
2. Apply the Five-S's to improve how you could complete your daily chores or homework assignments.

3. Use an example to show how you could use lean thinking with a supplier and then with a customer.

4. Can a company be lean if its suppliers and customers are not practicing lean? Explain.

5. What are the advantages and disadvantages of making small, frequent purchases from just a few suppliers? How do we overcome the disadvantages?

6. Why should lean layouts be "visual"? How can this be accomplished?

7. Reducing production lot sizes and increasing equipment setups are common practices in most lean production settings. Why? How can this be accomplished?

8. How could your school implement lean practices? How could it sustain a lean culture?

EXERCISES AND PROJECTS

1. Search online and find a manufacturer and a service company, not mentioned in this chapter, that have implemented lean, and report on their experiences and results.

2. Go to a machine shop and tell it you are doing a report on SMED, and ask it if it is trying to reduce setup times and if it sees any advantage in SMED. Report on your findings.

3. Apply lean thinking to your school day and study habits, try it out, then write a report about it.

PROBLEMS

1. Boehm Compressors uses a lean production assembly line to make its compressors. In one assembly area, the demand is 100 parts per eight-hour day. It uses a container that holds eight parts. It typically takes about six hours to round-trip a container from one work center to the next and back again. It also desires to hold 15% safety stock of this part in the system.

   a) How many containers should Boehm Compressors be using?

   b) Calculate the maximum system inventory for this part.

   c) If it reduced the number of containers by one, how would this impact the required round-trip time, all else being constant?

2. A lean system has the following characteristics:

   Demand rate = 20 parts per hour; safety stock required = 5%; number of containers used = 14; lead time to replenish an order = 6 hours.

   a) Calculate the container size for the 14 containers.

   b) Calculate the maximum system inventories.

   c) If the required safety stock was changed to zero, what impact would this have on the container size?

3. A lean system uses 22 containers, each of which can hold 15 parts. The lead time required to round-trip one container through the system is normally four hours. The usual safety stock level is 10%.

   a) What is the maximum demand rate this system can accommodate?

   b) If demand is expected to be double the rate found in a) by the end of the year, what are all the ways the system can accommodate this change?

4. A manufacturing assembly line has a demand for a specific part of 1,200 parts per eight-hour day. It wants to design a lean system using containers. It takes about four hours to round-trip a container from one work center to the next and back again. It also wants to hold 10% safety stock of this part in its system.

   a) Design a container system. State each container's size and how many are needed.

   b) Calculate the maximum system inventory for this part.

CASE STUDIES

CASE 1: Natural Foods Grocer

Natural Foods Grocer is, as the name implies, a small, locally owned grocery store that sells only natural and organic foods. It is located in a city of about 200,000 people and is the only store of its kind in the city. Other local grocery stores have sections of organic food; however, no others stock exclusively natural and organic foods. The store was started by Sam and Wendy Raven, who became frustrated with the selections at other stores and decided to do something about it. Wendy has a background in nutrition and Sam has farmed for many years, so they know their products well, but neither came to the business with a background in retail or grocery. This led them to establish the store in a way that made sense to them, but that appears to be driving up costs compared to other stores in similar markets around the country. Currently, business traffic is strong, but margins are low.

The store is arranged with five cash registers in the front. The Ravens like to have at least four checkers scheduled at all times, with five scheduled at peak times. This leads to checkers standing around a good portion of their days when a register is not busy. Items in the store are organized by vendor. This makes stocking shelves very easy; however, if customers want to compare similar food items they may have to go to two or more aisles, and many times customers will simply leave an item in the wrong place after the comparison, if they decide not to purchase the item. Additionally, staff are often asked by customers to assist them in finding items if the customer doesn't know the vendor. The Ravens have printed out maps of the store, with each vendor listed with items the vendor carries to help customers find various items. Since items are stocked by vendor, if a vendor comes out with a new item the Ravens decide to stock, it may mean a great deal of movement of other items to fit the item on the shelf. Also, at this time, the Ravens mostly purchase items in large enough quantities to receive quantity discounts. Items on shelves are individually priced, so customers can quickly know the prices.

In an effort to save money when the store opened, used cash registers were purchased that are fairly manual by today's standards. The registers do not scan items, so cashiers must enter the prices of items into the register. This means when the store is busy and there are lines, cashiers, in an effort to hurry up, make more mistakes and actually slow down the time it takes to check out. In an effort to limit customer frustration regarding waits in line, the Ravens have mounted CRT screens above each line and broadcast short health food tips for the customers. The Ravens have been reading a number of trade publications lately, and in one, they came across an article about applying lean elements to a grocery store. Currently, they are considering adopting some of these techniques.

DISCUSSION QUESTIONS

1. If you were a customer, what would be your reaction to what Natural Foods management team has done so far to help address problems?
2. Which of the seven wastes, shown in Table 9.2, do you see evidence of in this case? Are there others you suspect are also present? Explain.
3. What are steps you would recommend the Ravens take to make their grocery operation more lean? Use Table 9.1 as a guide.

Note: Written by Jeffrey W. Fahrenwald, MBA, Rockford University, Rockford, IL. This case was prepared solely to provide material for class discussion. The author does not intend to illustrate either effective or ineffective handling of a managerial situation.

CASE 2: Applying Lean Principles at a University

Given the current economic realities of most U.S. states, public college and university budgets are being cut. University staff are being asked to do more with less. Historically, when budgets got tight, the universities were able to raise the cost of tuition to the students to cover any shortfall. This is becoming less of an option today, due to the already high cost of education and the amount of debt, in the form of student loans, the average college student is saddled with upon graduation. Universities are therefore looking for ways to cut costs while simultaneously improving the quality of the education. In some cases, universities have cut smaller programs; implemented larger teaching loads; delayed infrastructure improvements, maintenance, or major purchases; and increased class sizes. All of these changes in the long run will potentially make it more difficult to improve the quality of education a student receives.

At the same time, there is growing pressure from civic organizations, the U.S. Department of Education, and various state agencies for universities to do a better job demonstrating results. Taxpayers and politicians are looking for the universities to show quantifiable improvements and results.

You have been a consultant for the past 10 years working with organizations to implement lean techniques. You have a good understanding of the elements of lean—waste reduction, lean supply chain relationships, lean layouts, inventory and setup time reduction, small batch scheduling, continuous improvement, and workforce empowerment. You have been asked by the largest public university system in your state to recommend lean elements that should be applied to the university system.

DISCUSSION QUESTIONS

1. Which of the lean principles would you recommend as having the best chance of being successful in the university system? Why?
2. Which of the seven wastes of lean, shown in Table 9.2, would most likely be found in the university system? Cite several examples.
3. Can lean principles help universities become more efficient and effective in delivering a high-quality education? Why, or why not?

Note: Written by Jeffrey W. Fahrenwald, MBA, Rockford University, Rockford, IL. This case was prepared solely to provide material for class discussion. The author does not intend to illustrate either effective or ineffective handling of a managerial situation.

VIDEO CASE STUDY

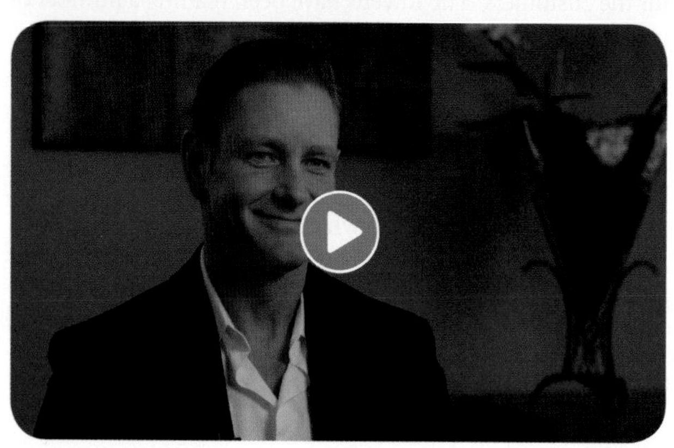

Learn more about ***lean systems*** from real organizations that use operations management techniques every day. Troy Ots is the Global Director of Production Operations and Design at Sage Publishing, an independent academic publisher in Thousand Oaks, California. For a company that manufactures many print products, developing and refining lean systems can make a big difference to their bottom line. Watch this short interview to find out how it's done.

When demand exceeds capacity, delays occur, patients wait unnecessarily, satisfaction declines and patient safety issues rise. However, in any capacity-constrained health-care system, the solution is not to ensure that capacity exceeds demand, in which case resources sit idle and are wasted. Rather, service capacity must be effectively matched to patient demand on a continuous and real-time basis.

—**THORN MAYER,** MD, CEO, BestPractices Inc., and medical director, NFL Players Association[1]

We expect to see more of America's casual chains join our many fine dining and independent restaurant clients by using their website to capture reservations and encourage repeat visits to their restaurants.

—**CHRIS PERSSON,** cofounder, Livebookings Ltd.[2]

MANAGING CUSTOMER AND WORK FLOWS

LEARNING OBJECTIVES

After completing this chapter, you should be able to:

10.1 Design a customer flow map and describe its benefits
10.2 Construct a service blueprint and explain its use
10.3 Describe how services manage capacity
10.4 Explain how customer queuing systems are designed and managed
10.5 Define work flow and describe how these flows are managed

Master the content.

edge.sagepub.com/wisner

THE MOOYAH GOGGLE TEST

Texas-based Mooyah Burgers & Fries, a small, fast-casual hamburger chain, has been giving some customers special goggles that track their eye movements from the restaurant's new wall graphics to its menu boards and anything else, from the time customers order until they leave. This new technology delves deeper into consumers' experiences than surveys or focus groups could.

Mooyah tested the tracking system at its two newest restaurants, which were designed with its latest ideas. The stores used vibrant colors and giant pictures, such as cows wearing sunglasses. Additionally, the two restaurants had made adjustments to the ordering process—there was more space in the queuing area and order sheets were available that customers could fill out while waiting in line.

One of the findings from the tests was that customers spent time observing all of the Mooyah employees, while waiting to pick up their orders. To management, this seemed like an ideal opportunity to train employees to entertain customers, so as to enhance their experiences at Mooyah. Management also learned something about the restaurant's wall graphics. Customers looked mostly at the bespectacled cows and the giant french fries pictures. Customers also noticed the graphics on the restaurant's bags showing how to open the bag to share their fries, and they also noticed signs near the menu boards advertising Mooyah's social network and website.

Management was satisfied with its menu boards after the tests, and is considering adding more food graphics on Mooyah's walls. When asked about the goggle system's value, Mooyah president Alan Hixon replied, "It's one of those things that's hard to monetize. It's alerting us to things we can do better, and over the long haul that should give guests a better experience. I'd say it's more of a brand-building tool than a sales-building tool."[3]

INTRODUCTION

For service companies, managing the flow of customers is an extremely important objective in terms of keeping customers satisfied and maintaining the firm's competitiveness. Readers should recall that flow management is one of the eight key supply chain processes. Customer flow describes how customers are physically processed through a facility, managed on an automated answering system or at a call center, or managed on an Internet site. When customer waiting lines or queues develop, this represents a real paradox for managers—on the one hand, queues of customers are good and represent potential purchases. On the other hand, long customer queues and long wait times are evidence of a flow problem, and will eventually result in angry customers and lost sales.

Since each customer is unique with different attitudes and perceptions, and may require a unique service or service delivery accommodation, managing these customer flows can be challenging. To help avoid customer flow problems, service managers can utilize the tools

Richard B. Levine/newscom

Overcrowded waiting areas indicate potential problems with appointment scheduling, queuing management, and service capacity.

described in the following sections. These tools include customer flow mapping, service delivery systems design, service capacity utilization, server scheduling, and customer queuing policies.

A discussion of work flows is also presented in the final segment of the chapter. Work flows occur as documents and information are passed among workers within an organization and between the firm and its trading partners. Managing the flow of this work as goods and services are created and delivered to customers can greatly impact an organization's costs, customer service, quality, and productivity. As one might expect, the use of software applications to help manage work flows has become quite common, and several of these are discussed.

CUSTOMER FLOW MAPPING

10.1 Design a customer flow map and describe its benefits

Somewhat similar to material flow maps, use of a **customer flow map** allows managers to visualize the flow of customers through a service delivery system, with the objective of identifying potential customer flow problems. Typically, these problems are characterized by long, unfair, or uncomfortable waits. Even when business is booming, however, as with a very popular restaurant or theme park, customer waits can still be managed effectively.

An example of a customer flow map at a quick-change lube shop is shown in Figure 10.1. After developing and analyzing the map of customer flows, and after talking to some of the customers, the lube shop manager identified several potential problem areas. The potential problems included customers not knowing where to put their car when pulling up to the shop; customers having to wait too long prior to speaking with an attendant; customers having nothing to do while waiting for their cars to be serviced; and customers being unable to see their car being serviced. Solutions to these problems might include:

customer flow map A visualization of the flow of customers through a service delivery system, with the objective of identifying potential customer flow problems.

- Better signage directing customers to the proper stall for oil changes and safety inspections;
- Use of a technician whose primary job is to greet customers and fill out the service orders;
- Design of a more comfortable waiting area (including a television, coffee machine, water machine, and magazine rack); and
- Installation of windows to view the garage from the waiting area.

Figure 10.1 Map of Customer Flows at Jaimie's Quick-Lube Shop

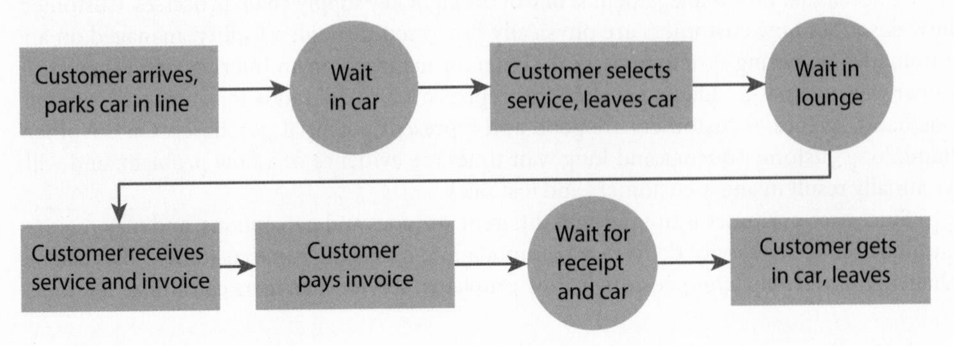

A queuing analysis might also be performed to determine waiting line characteristics, given the number of technicians employed at various times during the day (more on customer queuing analysis is covered later in this section). This information can then be used for better technician scheduling, promotional advertisements, and demand management techniques.

Texas-based Frost Bank, for example, changed its branch banks to make them more hospitable to customers, while also reducing wait times. A concierge counter serviced by an employee enables customers to get information as soon as they enter the bank. They provide full-service Internet terminals for their customers; for financial consultations, customers are shown to a waiting room with coffee, television, and the newspaper, while waiting to speak to an associate.[4]

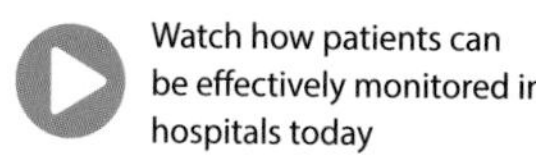
Watch how patients can be effectively monitored in hospitals today

Ruby Tuesday, a U.S. restaurant chain, uses business intelligence software to monitor things like customer wait times at each of its locations. When the system identified one of its restaurants with longer than normal wait times and service times, corporate managers used the system to look for clues to that store's specific problem. They found that this location was constantly running at full capacity due to an economic boom that had recently hit the area. The company made changes to improve kitchen and server productivities, and table turnover increased by 10%, which caused wait times to decrease.[5] The next section looks more closely at service delivery systems.

SERVICE DELIVERY SYSTEM DESIGN

10.2 Construct a service blueprint and explain its use

When analyzing existing service processes or designing new ones, service systems need to consider the objectives along with the desirable level of customer interaction for each process. In the lube shop described in Figure 10.1, it is unproductive and potentially unsafe to have customers in the work area, interacting with the technicians. Other potential problems at the shop appear to be occurring when customers cannot find someone to help them. When customers interact with company employees, both intentionally and unintentionally, these are referred to as **customer contact points**. Some service processes may require customer contact as illustrated in the lube shop example, when the customer first arrives and then when the invoice is paid. Other processes may work best with moderate or minimal customer contact, as when our customer watches the work being performed. Still other processes are best handled out of sight of the customer, as with the lube shop's bookkeeping and worker training procedures. Thus, it is advisable to assess the level of customer contact for service processes, with the objective of providing the right levels of contact. This technique is termed **service blueprinting**, and is discussed next.

SERVICE BLUEPRINTING

Service blueprinting, first introduced in Chapter 3, helps managers separate processes requiring customer contact from those not requiring customer contact. In this way, different forms of management control, personnel work methods, and tools can be employed to maximize both productivity and the level of customer service. The service blueprint is a representation of all activities constituting the service delivery process. Figure 10.2 illustrates an example of a service blueprint for the quick-change lube shop introduced in Figure 10.1.

In the figure, the rectangles represent activities occurring during the service, and the diamond represents a process decision. Based on management preference, customer flow, and process design, the lube service is divided into three contact levels: activities requiring direct customer contact, those requiring limited contact (visibility), and those requiring no customer contact. Each level suggests different management control techniques and layout considerations. At the direct customer contact level, employees interacting with customers need to be trained in sales and creating or maintaining good customer relations. Self-service strategies can also be employed, as in the waiting room at the lube shop. Consideration must also be given to signage, access, parking, and customer comfort items.

customer contact points Whenever customers interact with company employees, both intentionally and unintentionally.

service blueprinting A representation of all activities constituting the service delivery process. Assists in separating activities requiring customer contact from those not needing contact.

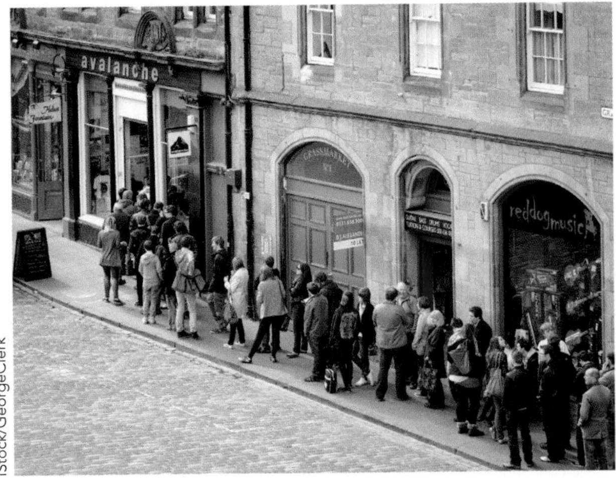

iStock/GeorgeClerk

Companies can reduce customer wait times using capacity management and demand management techniques.

At the indirect customer contact level, customers should be prevented from directly contacting company personnel or processes in these areas. In the lube shop scenario, a wall with a window prevents customers from speaking to technicians, while allowing customers to see the work being performed. Hiring and training procedures for this level should concentrate on identifying and developing personnel that are technically proficient at operating the necessary process equipment. These employees may have some minor interactions with customers; thus, it might be advisable to have them undergo some level of customer relationship training. Process automation may also be a consideration here, to increase productivity and service capacity.

Process automation can be troublesome, though, when used with customer contact activities. For example, some customers view automated self-service systems with great disdain, due to the learning that is required and because lower levels of personal service are provided. Most of us have encountered problems when trying to navigate self-service checkout stands, automated phone answering services, and in-store, automated product information kiosks. Shoppers at Trader Joe's, a U.S. discount store, find very little in the way of in-store technologies, and are treated to much more personal service and conversation than found at most of its competitors. On the other hand, automation that improves employee productivity without requiring a high degree of customer learning can be seen as a very positive thing by customers. The airline industry, for instance, appears to have adopted a good balance between expanded use of technology (online ticket purchases, airport check-in kiosks) and agents to serve customers personally.[6]

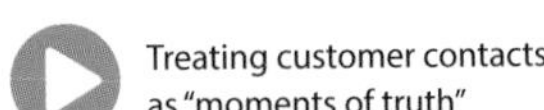

Figure 10.2 Service Blueprint for Jaimie's Quick-Change Lube Shop

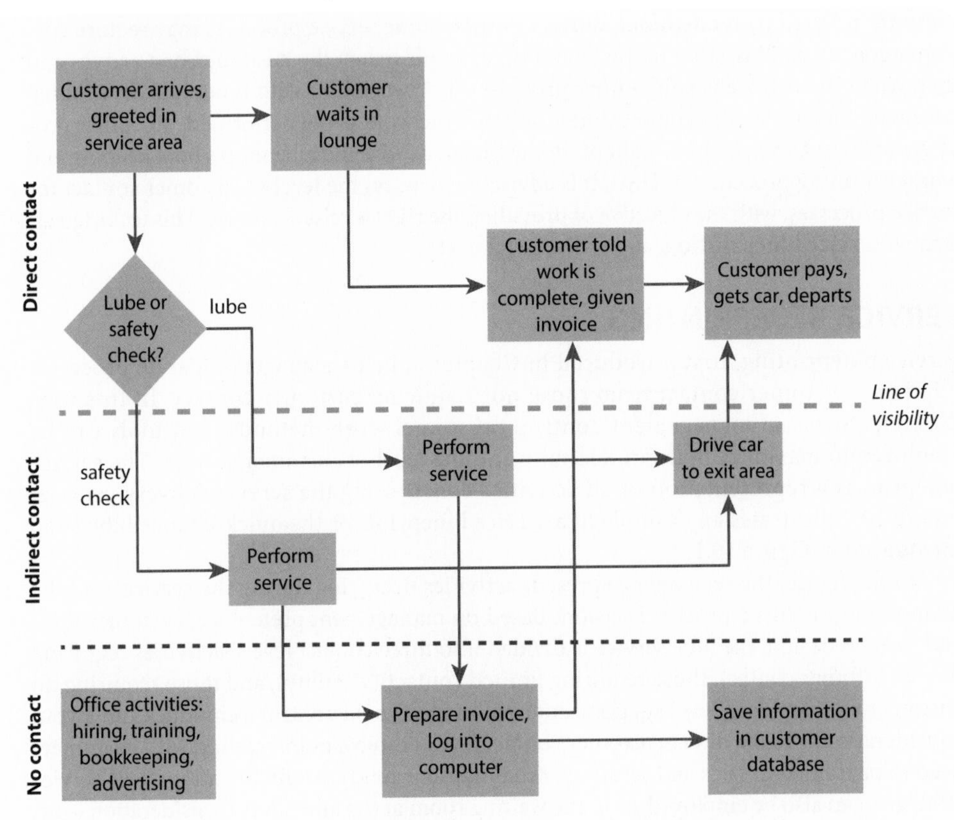

At the "no customer contact" level, customers must be completely separated from these process activities. In the lube shop example, some of these activities are shown. For example, hiring practices focus on identifying specialists in each of the activity areas, such as bookkeepers and other office personnel. Marketing practices in the lube shop might utilize a customer database to contact customers every 90 days for another oil change. Employee training sessions would also be conducted at this level. Information systems and other forms of office automation are typically heavily utilized to maximize backroom productivity.

The service blueprint, along with the customer flow map, allows management to obtain a complete picture of the service delivery system as is, along with providing ideas and designs for what it could be. The lube shop manager in Figures 10.1 and 10.2 should be able to use these tools to identify customer flow and service design problems, along with potential solutions. Useful statistics for the various service elements can be added to the customer flow map and service blueprint to complete the picture, such as average wait times, process capacities and costs, average throughput times, customer arrival patterns, queue lengths, and customer feedback. With this information, decisions can be made to modify design elements such as signage, service system layouts, hiring and training procedures, equipment, hardware and software used, and reports generated.

DEMAND VARIABILITY AND SERVICE CAPACITY UTILIZATION

10.3 Describe how services manage capacity

All customers hate waiting. To successfully manage customer relationships and to keep customers flowing through service processes, it is therefore absolutely essential that service firms know when customer visits are likely to peak, and how demand variations affect service capacity and customer wait times. Over time, bottlenecks will occasionally occur, as unexpected demand exceeds available service capacity, and it is up to management to reduce the likelihood of these occurrences with use of better capacity management and demand management techniques. While these topics were introduced in Chapters 4 and 6, this chapter will introduce a number of techniques to specifically address and enhance service capacity.

CAPACITY MANAGEMENT TECHNIQUES FOR SERVICES

A number of techniques are commonly employed in services to manage capacity, including use of effective employee scheduling, yield/revenue management, capacity sharing, employee cross-training, and self-service. Each of these techniques is shown in Table 10.1 and is discussed in the following section.

Table 10.1 Capacity Management Techniques for Services

Technique	Description
Employee scheduling	When the service capacity closely matches customer demand, this minimizes customer waits.
Yield/revenue management	Consists of a combination of overbooking, allocating capacity among customer segments, with use of differential pricing for the customer segments.
Capacity sharing	Finding other uses for capacity during periods of underutilization.
Employee cross-training	Cross-trained employees in an idle process can be moved temporarily to a busy process, temporarily adding additional capacity and reducing customer wait times.
Self-service	When services use customers as servers.

Employee Scheduling

Effective scheduling in services occurs when the number of employees scheduled (the service capacity) closely matches customer demand, resulting in minimal customer waits along with minimal employee idle time. Too little service capacity results in long customer wait times and lost sales, while excess capacity results in idle servers and high labor costs. An important consideration here is that excess service capacity is lost—it cannot be stored for use at a later time. A trade-off must then be considered by management—the cost of providing additional service capacity versus the cost of making customers wait. Employee scheduling can be difficult when demand varies considerably throughout the day, such as with restaurants, banks, hospital emergency rooms, and customer call centers. However, companies are getting better at scheduling through the use of improved demand forecasting techniques and simulation models.

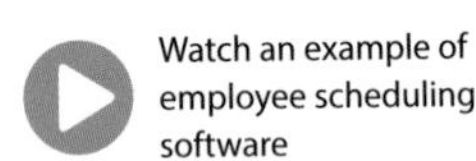
Watch an example of employee scheduling software

One approach to the scheduling problem begins with an hourly forecast of demand that can then be converted into staffing requirements for each day of the week. A workforce schedule is developed to match the staffing requirement as closely as possible. Excess staffing can be added based on the customer service level desired. For highly volatile demand situations, firms may opt to use standby or floating workers to better match service capacity and demand. Managers must also consider overtime costs, days-off requirements, and other labor contract requirements, which further complicate the scheduling problem. Example 10.1 illustrates the use of a simple workforce scheduling heuristic, which allows workers to have two consecutive days off each week.

In the example, the business owners can use the information provided and modify it to suit their scheduling preferences and customer service goals. For instance, Worker 3, a full-time employee, is not needed on Thursday. Alternately, the employee could be given Thursday and Friday off, leaving Worker 4 to work on Monday, Wednesday, and Friday, and Worker 5 to work on Friday. Worker 3 could also be given the original schedule and the

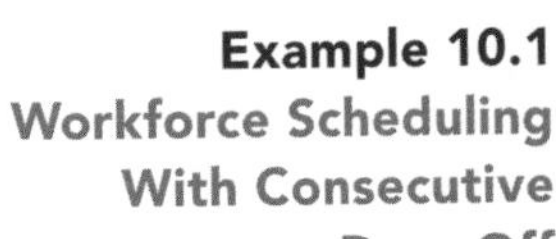

Example 10.1 Workforce Scheduling With Consecutive Days Off

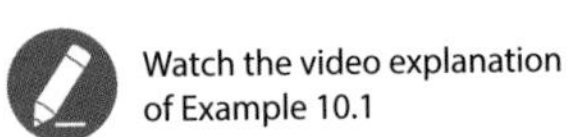
Watch the video explanation of Example 10.1

Chris and Nancy own a computer consulting business with three full-time employees and several part-timers. They need to develop a weekly schedule that allows all workers to have two consecutive days off per week, given the required staffing levels. After compiling the demand levels for the upcoming week, the worker requirements are as shown below. Assuming that the employees have no preference for which consecutive days they get off, the procedure is as follows:

1. Copy the daily requirements on the line for Worker 1; circle the lowest pair of daily requirements. For ties, choose the pair with the lowest daily requirement on an adjacent day. If a tie still exists, choose the first tied pair of days (for Worker 2 there are three equal pairs; however, the one circled below has lower requirements on adjacent days). Assign the noncircled days to Worker 1.
2. Subtract 1 from each of the noncircled days, then place the new daily requirements on the line for Worker 2. Repeat Step 1 for Worker 2 and then for the remaining workers, until no more workers are required.

	M	T	W	Th	F	S	Su
Requirements	4	3	4	2	3	1	2
Worker 1	4	3	4	2	3	(1	2)
Worker 2	3	2	3	1	(2	1)	2
Worker 3	2	1	2	0	2	(1	1)
Worker 4	1	(0	1)	0	1	1	1
Worker 5	0	0	1	0	0	0	0

Work schedule: Worker 1 has S/Su off; Worker 2 has F/S off; Worker 3 (a part-timer) has Th/S/Su off; Worker 4 (a part-timer) has T/W/Th off; and Worker 5 (a part-timer) works only on W.

company would have excess capacity on Thursday (perhaps the historic demand variance is high on Thursdays, making it desirable to have the excess capacity).

Part-time workers offer companies the flexibility to adjust capacity as needed. And, in today's labor market, retired workers make great part-timers. For years, the Rochester, NY, YMCA had trouble finding people willing to work during the morning shift, which started at 4:30 a.m. Today, its early crew includes mostly older employees. "They like it because it gives them more time to do the rest of the things they want," says Fernan Cepero, VP of human resources. Today, over 90% of the growth in the U.S. labor force is among workers over age 55.[7]

Yield/Revenue Management

Yield management, also called **revenue management**, refers to the process of selling portions of a fixed capacity to customers at varying prices, so as to maximize revenues. Industries commonly using yield management systems include airlines, passenger rail, hotels, cruise lines, and car rental agencies. American Airlines, with its Sabre computer reservation system, is typically given credit for developing the field of yield management after the airline industry's deregulation in 1978. The airline's yield management strategy was to allow some seats to be sold for low fares, to compete with the new startup carriers, while using differential prices for its remaining seats. **Differential pricing** refers to selling the same product to different customers for different prices. In 1992, American Airlines reported that use of its system resulted in an additional $1.4 billion in sales over a three-year period. Likewise, Hertz car rentals reported a 5% increase in average revenue per customer in 1995, using its revenue management system.[8] Recently, United Airlines posted a first quarter 2012 loss of $448 million—$286 million of that was blamed on "glitches" in its reservation and yield management systems. Reservation kiosks weren't working for a time, agents were overwhelmed, and seats went unsold or were sold at too low a price.[9]

Watch a discussion of yield management for airlines, hotels, and golf courses

The yield management strategy consists of a combination of overbooking and allocating capacity among customer segments, while using differential pricing for the customer segments. **Overbooking** refers to accepting more reservations than can be accommodated. For an airline, some customers will typically fail to show up for a flight; if the airline does not overbook, then the empty seats represent lost revenue on each flight. Historically, the argument for overbooking, for a number of industries, is very straightforward—companies that overbook make far more revenue than those that do not. The question then becomes not whether to overbook, but *how much* to overbook. Most airlines, for example, overbook a certain percentage of seats using proprietary computer algorithms. These computer systems will develop optimal overbooking policies for each flight, considering the costs of turning a reserved customer away, alternate flight arrangements, and empty seats. Example 10.2 illustrates the overbooking decision at a restaurant.

In Example 10.2, a zero overbooking policy (taking only 28 reservations) results in a total expected profit of $1,557. To find this total expected profit, the following calculations are made for each of the five no-show probabilities:

$$\begin{aligned}\text{Expected Net Profit} &= (\text{table profit} - \text{turnaway cost}) \times \text{no-show probability} \\ &= [(\text{tables filled} \times \text{profit per table}) - (\text{turnaways} \times \text{cost per turnaway})] \times \text{no-show probability}\end{aligned}$$

Then, each of the net profits is summed to find the total expected profit for a given number of reservations. Taking 29 reservations (overbooking by 1) means that if all customers show up, then one table of customers must be turned away. This scenario results in a higher expected profit in Example 10.2. Thus, based on the profit per table, the cost of turning away customers, and the probability of no-shows, it is concluded that the optimal policy is to overbook by 3 tables (taking 31 reservations). The expected profit generated is $1,638. If either the expected profit per table or the cost of turning away customers changes, Deborah should recalculate the expected profitabilities as shown here, to determine the new optimal overbooking policy.

Allocating fixed capacity to different customer groups is another concern in yield management. The decision here regards when to turn away one type of customer, while holding

yield management The process of selling portions of a fixed capacity to customers at varying prices, so as to maximize revenues.

revenue management *See* Yield management.

differential pricing Refers to selling the same product to different customers for different prices. Used in yield management.

overbooking Refers to accepting more reservations than can be accommodated, to maximize revenues.

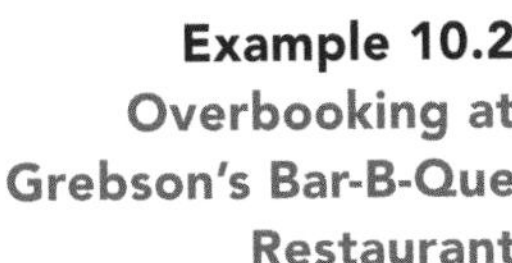

Example 10.2
Overbooking at Grebson's Bar-B-Que Restaurant

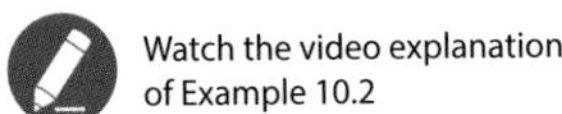

Watch the video explanation of Example 10.2

Deborah, the reservations manager at Grebson's Bar-B-Que, had compiled information from the recent reservation history of the restaurant, to determine the probability of no-shows, and hopefully, to determine the optimal overbooking policy to use. The restaurant's capacity is fixed at 28 tables. The information in the first table below shows the historic number of no-shows on a typical evening, along with the probability of occurrence. The question for Deborah is—how many reservations should she accept, given the probability of a no-show? The average profitability per table is $60 and the cost of lost goodwill due to turning away customers is estimated to be $30 per table. Since the expected profit is greater than the turn-away cost, it is therefore advisable to overbook.

The second table shows the outcomes for various overbooking policies, using the no-show occurrences. Given a no-show of 1 for instance, there will be one less table showing up for each number of reservations taken. Note that there is no reason to take reservations for more than 32 tables, since the worst case scenario (4 no-shows) would still fill the restaurant. Then, using these outcomes and their associated probabilities, the expected profit for each overbooking policy can be calculated, to determine the most desirable policy. The final tables show these calculations.

No-Shows	Probability
0	0.10
1	0.25
2	0.30
3	0.20
4	0.15

		Reservations/Showing Up				
No-Shows	**Probability**	**28**	**29**	**30**	**31**	**32**
0	0.10	28	29	30	31	32
1	0.25	27	28	29	30	31
2	0.30	26	27	28	29	30
3	0.20	25	26	27	28	29
4	0.15	24	25	26	27	28

Expected Profit with 28 Reservations					
No-Shows	0	1	2	3	4
Customers	28	27	26	25	24
Tables Filled	28	27	26	25	24
Profit ($)	1680	1620	1560	1500	1440
Turnaways	0	0	0	0	0
Cost ($)	0	0	0	0	0
Net Profit	1680	1620	1560	1500	1440
Probability	0.10	0.25	0.30	0.20	0.15
Expected Net	168	405	468	300	216
Total Expected Profit $1557					

Expected Profit with 29 Reservations					
No-Shows	0	1	2	3	4
Customers	29	28	27	26	25
Tables Filled	28	28	27	26	25
Profit ($)	1680	1680	1620	1560	1500
Turnaways	1	0	0	0	0
Cost ($)	30	0	0	0	0
Net Profit	1650	1680	1620	1560	1500
Probability	0.10	0.25	0.30	0.20	0.15
Expected Net	165	420	486	312	225
Total Expected Profit $1608					

Expected Profit with 30 Reservations					
No-Shows	0	1	2	3	4
Customers	30	29	28	27	26
Tables Filled	28	28	28	27	26
Profit ($)	1680	1680	1680	1620	1560
Turnaways	2	1	0	0	0
Cost ($)	60	30	0	0	0
Net Profit	1620	1650	1680	1620	1560
Probability	0.10	0.25	0.30	0.20	0.15
Expected Net	162	412.5	504	324	234
Total Expected Profit $1636.5					

Expected Profit with 31 Reservations					
No-Shows	0	1	2	3	4
Customers	31	30	29	28	27
Tables Filled	28	28	28	28	27
Profit ($)	1680	1680	1680	1680	1620
Turnaways	3	2	1	0	0
Cost ($)	90	60	30	0	0
Net Profit	1590	1620	1650	1680	1620
Probability	0.10	0.25	0.30	0.20	0.15
Expected Net	159	405	495	336	243
Total Expected Profit $1638					

(Continued)

Example 10.2 (Continued)

Expected Profit with 32 Reservations					
No-Shows	0	1	2	3	4
Customers	32	31	30	29	28
Tables Filled	28	28	28	28	28
Profit ($)	1680	1680	1680	1680	1680
Turnaways	4	3	2	1	0
Cost ($)	120	90	60	30	0
Net Profit	1560	1590	1620	1650	1680
Probability	0.10	0.25	0.30	0.20	0.15
Expected Net	156	397.5	486	330	252
Total Expected Profit $1621.5					

onto capacity with the hope that a higher revenue customer will arrive later. With airlines, for example, high-revenue frequent business travelers tend to make reservations close to the departure date, while low-revenue vacationers make reservations much further in advance. The airline must therefore decide at what point reservations for low-revenue customers will be shut down, in anticipation of incoming high-revenue passenger reservations. A simple approach is to assign a number of reservations for high-revenue customers, and another number for low-revenue customers.

Continuing with the airline example, the firm may decide to hold 75% of its seats for high-revenue customers and 25% for low-revenue customers. To keep from turning away high-revenue customers when their seat allocation is full, the airline might also decide to allow the low-revenue passenger seats to be sold to either class of passenger, on a first-come-first-served basis. Providing protection in this way to some seats for a particular class of passenger can also result in unused seats, which explains why customers can frequently find inexpensive travel accommodations at the last minute.

The final topic area of yield management is differential pricing. The idea here is to segment customers into different categories, so that high prices will be charged to customers willing to pay them, and low prices will be charged to customers who would not use the service at a higher price. As mentioned earlier, a typical full-service air carrier, for example, offers three classes of passenger service: first class, business class, and economy class, with designated seating. In many cases, economy class tickets for the same flight may cost only 10% of a first class ticket, and a third to half as much as a business class ticket. Additionally, as departure dates grow nearer, prices of all three classes will fluctuate based on the automated decisions from the yield management systems. This has resulted in very complicated fare structures for many airline companies.

Differential pricing—and, indeed, yield management in general—can be viewed as unfair by customers. In September 2000, for instance, some of the customers of online retailing giant Amazon.com began noticing they were paying different prices for DVD movies, based on their previous purchasing patterns. Customers started flooding Internet chat sites with complaints about the company. Amazon quickly issued statements that it was merely testing consumer response to various prices, cancelled its differential pricing policies, and refunded the differences charged to those who paid more for their DVDs.[10]

Capacity Sharing

Due to the high cost of many service delivery processes, firms are faced with finding other uses for capacity during periods of underutilization. Airlines, for instance, might share gates, baggage-handling equipment, and ground personnel. Air freight carriers, for example, might have capacity sharing agreements between various destinations, to reduce the amount of business turned away.[11] Capacity sharing in the passenger airline industry has come to be known as **code sharing**. Code sharing agreements among airlines can fall anywhere between outright mergers to arm's length agreements for sharing reservation systems or aircraft capacity, and they can be argued to be either pro-competitive by creating new services at lower costs, or anti-competitive by creating less capacity and higher fares. In 2010, Aeroflot Russian Airlines signed a code sharing agreement with Air France to create more passenger transport capacity between the two countries as well as nearby countries.[12]

In other examples of capacity sharing, resort hotels might lease large blocks of rooms to conventioneers during their off-seasons, while ski resorts might lease their properties out to concert promoters during the summer. Still other forms of capacity sharing allow services to make their capacities more flexible, and reduce the costs of overbooking. Hotels, for example, may enter into formal agreements to use one another's vacant rooms for customers when one property has no rooms available.

Cross-Training Employees

For services with multiple processes, employees in an idle process can be moved temporarily to a busy process, temporarily adding additional capacity and reducing customer wait times. This requires employees to be cross-trained on multiple service processes. The benefits are plainly evident in businesses like department stores and supermarkets. When lines at cash registers become long, for example, floor salespeople can be moved to idle registers until the customer queues are gone. Some managers, though, believe that temporarily transferring workers can result in a short-term loss of service quality as workers relearn the processes. In fact, researchers E. Pinker and R. Shumsky referred to service worker transfers as the potential creation of *consistent mediocrity*. They warned that flexible workers may not gain sufficient experience at each process to provide high-quality service to anyone, and what is gained in efficiency can be lost in service quality.[13]

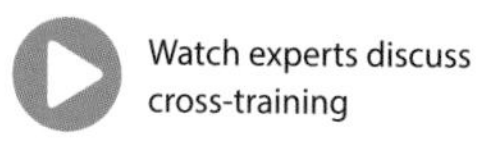
Watch experts discuss cross-training

Ken Bertam, president of Rhode Island–based manufacturer Herrick & White, would disagree. He explains that cross-training can help to even out workloads in the shop. "We take some of our senior people and train them internally in Access and AutoCAD. Now we have a half-dozen people who can work in either engineering or the shop. As engineering becomes busy and manufacturing slows, we bring them to engineering and they can help there. In some cases it works out well because they know what's happening up front. They've worked on the engineering aspect on some of the projects that are in the shop," says Bertram.[14]

code sharing Capacity sharing in the passenger airline industry.

Using Self-Service

Many services can use customers as servers, and in some cases, customers view this as a positive characteristic. Customers can customize services to fit their specific needs, potentially saving time as well as money, since firms generally understand that customers should be compensated for their work by offering them lower prices. Additionally, since customers use the service exactly when it is needed, service capacity becomes much more flexible. Proper customer training, however, can be difficult for some services—adequate signage and instructions must be available for customers at the self-service access points. Service providers must also be aware of all the potential mistakes that customers can make, and design steps to deal with customer mistakes when they occur.

Web-based technologies have enabled both customers and employees to obtain company information quickly, while reducing routine and time-consuming tasks for managers and service personnel. Many companies today use automated human resource systems that allow employees to track their own personnel, payroll, and tax records, for example, as well as download training and other employment documents. This frees up time for human resource personnel to perform more strategic activities, such as hiring and training.[15]

iStock/LighthouseBay

Self-service can be viewed as a positive thing by customers, provided the signage and instructions are user-friendly.

Andrew Geiger/2/Ocean/Corbis

Some ski resorts will open mountain biking trails in the summertime as a complementary service to allow them to operate year-round.

DEMAND MANAGEMENT TECHNIQUES IN SERVICES

The topic of demand management was introduced in Chapter 6, as a tool for managing demand when forecast errors caused potential product stockout or overstock situations. Similarly, when variable demand patterns cause service capacity and customer queuing problems that are partially aided by the use of capacity management techniques discussed in the preceding section, the firm can rely on demand management tactics to better manage available service capacity. A number of techniques may be used in order to manipulate demand, and in services, these include use of reservations, complementary services, demand sorting, and pricing policies and promotions. These techniques are summarized in Table 10.2 and are discussed further in the following sections.

Using Reservations

When service capacity is likely to be constrained, such as at a doctor's office or during peak dining hours at a restaurant, demand can be managed through use of a reservation system. Reservations can regulate customer arrivals and more evenly spread demand over a period of time, allowing more accurate employee scheduling and better utilization of available capacity. Use of reservation systems requires earlier planning on the part of customers and causes businesses to incur added expenses for their reservation systems and employee training. In the right applications, however, reservations are viewed as fair by customers and preferable to long waits for service.

Online reservation systems are already commonly used by customers for airline and hotel bookings, and corporate use of these systems is saving companies millions of travel dollars. California-based computer network and routing manufacturer Cisco Systems, for example, began using an online travel provider in the 1990s and estimates it saved $14 million on travel costs in 2004 alone.[16] More recently, online reservation systems have become popular for making dinner reservations.

complementary services
Service diversions that tend to better occupy the time of waiting customers, and be a source of additional revenues. For instance, a lounge area or bar may serve as a way to occupy customers who are waiting for a table at a restaurant.

Using Complementary Services

Service capacity problems may also be reduced through use of **complementary services**. For instance, a lounge area or bar may serve as a way to occupy customers who are waiting for a table at a restaurant. A restaurant, driving range, and pro shop can keep golfers occupied while waiting for their tee times. Movie theaters have video-game rooms to entertain moviegoers while waiting for a show to begin. These service

Table 10.2 Demand Management Techniques in Services

Technique	Description
Reservations	Reservations can regulate customer arrivals and more evenly spread demand over a period of time.
Complementary services	Offering diversions that occupy the time of waiting customers.
Demand sorting	Performing an initial sorting of customers when they enter the service system, to better direct them to the appropriate service processes or available servers, resulting in less overall wait time.
Pricing policies and promotions	Advertising promotions are commonly used with pricing changes to create changes in demand during off-seasons, holidays, evenings, and weekends.

diversions not only tend to better occupy the time of waiting customers, but they also can be a source of additional revenues. Seasonal services also develop complementary services to utilize capacity during characteristically slow periods of the year. Examples include an air-conditioning repair firm that also offers heater repair services, a snow ski resort that schedules mountain bike tours in the summer, and a ski boat retailer that also sells snow mobiles in the winter.

Using Demand Sorting

Sometimes, an initial "sorting" of customers can be performed as they first enter the service system, to better direct them to the appropriate service processes or available servers, resulting in less overall wait time. A city's motor vehicle department, for instance, may have a desk just inside the door to direct patrons to the appropriate service area, effectively reducing the occurrence of customers waiting in the wrong line. Automated answering services perform **demand sorting** by directing callers to select numbers for various services or information. And finally, airplane passengers can be sorted into groups based on seat assignments, in order to board them starting from the rear of the airplane, to reduce total boarding time. Demand sorting systems can also be based on things like customer importance, customer preference, or customer value. In Las Vegas, NV, for example, many restaurant buffets and resort shows have VIP lines, to allow high-value guests to avoid longer waits.

Using Pricing Policies and Promotions

For many services, lowering prices will increase customer purchases, while raising prices will reduce purchases. Reducing prices during slow-demand periods and/or increasing prices during periods of high demand can also smooth the demands placed on existing capacity and reduce customer flow problems. Nevada-based NV Energy, for instance, an electric utility, allows customers to participate in a peak-demand reduction program, which pays customers to let their electricity be turned off for a few minutes every hour during peak-usage periods. This allows NV Energy to better manage their electricity capacity, and avoid having to purchase electricity during these peak periods at high prices on the spot market from other electricity providers. Some restaurants offer reduced, early-bird dinner prices to encourage patrons to eat early. Similarly, movie theaters offer reduced-price matinees for showings during daytime hours.

Advertising promotions are commonly used with pricing changes to create even larger changes in demand during off-seasons, holidays, evenings, and weekends. Hotels and resorts may promote their facilities to conventions or for business meetings during seasonally slow months. Cell phone companies advertise their free weekend minutes; quick-change oil shops send out mailers promoting cheaper midweek prices; and grocery stores promote double-coupon savings days. All of these promotion and pricing strategies seek to make better use of available capacity, while reducing demand during peak usage periods. In turn, the firm is able to serve more customers with a given capacity and allow customers to wait shorter periods of time for their service, while improving overall productivity.

MANAGING CUSTOMER QUEUES

Explain how customer queuing systems are designed and managed

Even with the most adept management of service capacity and customer demand, long queues of customers will still occur from time to time. The dynamic properties of the service itself are to blame, here—customers arrive randomly and unexpectedly with varied requirements, while the service system's capacity varies based on the level of staffing and each server's processing capability. Sometimes, these two things just don't match up. With a little luck and some queuing management skills, though, service bottlenecks will occur infrequently and only for short periods of time. Customers will not wait long, however, in most situations before loudly complaining or simply leaving. In a survey of 3,000 consumers conducted by *Marketing Week* magazine, about 90% said they had given up on

demand sorting An initial "sorting" of customers performed as they first enter the service system, to better direct them to the appropriate service processes or available servers, resulting in less overall wait time.

SERVICE SPOTLIGHT

Cox Reduces Waits for the Cable Guy

Georgia-based Cox Communications recently launched an initiative to deal with the issue of waiting too long for the cable repair technician to arrive. Among subscription television companies, Cox had fallen behind in customer satisfaction according to the American Customer Satisfaction Index, prompting this initiative.

Kris Tripplaar/Sipa USA/newscom

Cox began using Time of Arrival (TOA), a cloud-based application from TOA Technologies. Every morning, the TOA system schedules routes based on technicians' skills and locations. When technicians arrive at a location, they register their arrival and expected completion times, and tasks to be performed. TOA then analyzes this information and predicts when workers will arrive at the next location. This allows Cox to more accurately schedule workers, and they now arrive within five minutes of their appointed times 98.5% of the time.

Additionally, instead of scheduling a second visit to complete an unexpectedly long job, repair technicians can report the situation to TOA, which either replans the rest of the worker's day or reassigns the next job to an idle worker, which allows workers to complete each job. This way, says Catherine Mitchell of Cox, "you can do the right thing in the home you're in and the rest of the company can figure out what's next, and you don't have to feel like you're letting anyone down."[17]

buying something because of a long queue, and 45% said this was the reason they preferred shopping online.[18]

Thus, it is up to management to address the trade-off in the cost of supplying greater levels of service capacity (more employees, more training, more automation, a larger facility) with the cost of making customers wait (loss of customers' current and future purchases, and negative word-of-mouth advertising). These days, companies are making use of software applications to cut down on queuing problems, as shown in the Service Spotlight above.

Since the cost of supplying additional service capacity can be high, it is important for companies to understand and make use of the psychological aspects of customer waiting and virtual queues. By addressing these issues, customers can become desensitized to the time spent waiting in queues, thus reducing the cost of customer waits. In turn, this will reduce the need for additional or reserve capacity throughout the service system. These topics are addressed next, followed by a discussion of the analysis and design of queuing systems.

THE PSYCHOLOGY OF WAITING

A number of approaches to dealing with waiting customers are addressed in a classic paper by David Maister, a consultant who studied the psychology of waiting in queues.[19] Two of Maister's observations he termed the **First** and **Second Laws of Service**:

> *First Law of Service: Satisfaction = perception – expectation*
>
> Customers start a service with expectations. If, after the service, they perceive the service as exceeding their initial expectations, they are satisfied. If their perceptions are that the service did not exceed expectations, they are dissatisfied.
>
> *Second Law of Service: It's hard to play catch-up ball*
>
> If the service begins well, it is easy to keep customers satisfied. Conversely, if customers become dissatisfied during the service, it is extremely difficult to turn things around.

First Law of Service Satisfaction = perception – expectation.

Second Law of Service It's hard to play catch-up ball.

The First Law of Service is interesting in that customer perceptions and expectations may not be based on reality, and can vary considerably from one customer to the next. Customer expectations are formed from previous experiences, advertisements, signs, and information from other people, while customer perceptions can be affected during the service encounter by a friendly server, mood music, pleasant surroundings, and a host of other things. One practice coming out of the First Law is to "under-promise and over-deliver." The Second Law is good to remember when trying to improve a service. Investments in service improvements might work best if placed at the initial contact or early stages of a service to make sure things get off to a good start.

Firms can manage both customer expectations and perceptions by observing and understanding how customers are affected when waiting for service. Waiting time management techniques resulting from Maister's queuing observations include keeping customers occupied, keeping customers informed, grouping customers together, and designing a fair waiting system.[20] These are briefly discussed next.

Why will people sometimes wait in long lines?

- *Keeping customers occupied.* One technique is to occupy people while they wait. Examples include having customers listen to music while they are on hold on the telephone, providing TVs to watch in waiting rooms, and placing mirrors next to elevators. Occupied customers feel more comfortable while waiting, and perceive their wait times to be shorter.
- *Keeping customers informed.* Waiting time uncertainty can produce anxiety and make the wait seem longer. Consequently, another common queue strategy is to keep customers informed of the approximate remaining wait time. City bus stops post arrival times for various bus routes; amusement parks post signs declaring the wait time remaining from that specific point in the queue; and city automobile license departments post the time remaining for customers in various queues. In Alaska, for example, people can view real-time web cameras at each of the state's motor vehicle department offices to see how busy an office is, prior to leaving their office or home.[21]
- *Designing a fair wait system.* Waits perceived as unfair can produce customer anxiety, and make the wait seem longer. Instead of using separate queues, organizations can use a multiple server "snake line" to increase the perception of fairness. Some retailers today are using electronic line management systems to move customers through queues more quickly and fairly. These systems feature display units located at each cashier station, along with lights and sound to direct customers to the next available cashier, eliminating congestion at cashier stations and the need for staff members to direct traffic.[22]
- *Grouping customers together.* Communicating with other customers can make the wait time seem shorter; many organizations have made an effort to design waiting areas conducive to conversation. Attention to how chairs, tables, sofas, and coffee pots are situated can help to spark conversations, providing yet another distraction to help pass the time.

Managing these customer perceptions is a form of demand management, and is as important as managing the actual waiting time. If customers perceive the wait to be less than or equal to their initial expectations, their overall service experience will be impacted in a positive way. On the other hand, a customer's perception that the wait time was too long may negatively affect the probability of future visits, regardless of the actual wait time.

USING VIRTUAL QUEUES

In spite of all efforts to reduce the actual and perceived waiting times for customers, there may still be periods of time when queuing problems persist. This may be particularly true for process capacities that are very difficult or expensive to expand. For these situations, a **virtual queue** concept can be employed. Restaurants located in malls, for instance, might provide customers with pagers, allowing the restaurant to track customers in a virtual queue while allowing them to walk around and shop while waiting for a table. The ice skating rink at Union Square, in San Francisco, recently launched a mobile phone app during the skating season, providing visitors with a virtual queue. The virtual queue enables patrons the freedom to explore the Union Square plaza while waiting for their turn to skate.[23]

virtual queue A computer-managed queue; allows restaurants located in malls, for instance, to provide customers with pagers, allowing the restaurant to track customers in a virtual queue while allowing them to walk around and shop while waiting for a table.

Walt Disney World, in Florida, was the first company to design and use a virtual queue concept for an amusement park. Its system, called FASTPASS™, was installed in five of the park's most popular attractions in 1999. Park-goers used their admission ticket to register at a ride they wanted to attend, and the park's computer system estimated their wait time and notified customers when to return. Customers' places were then held in a virtual queue. When guests returned at their designated times, they could immediately proceed to the attraction with no further waiting. Guests were overwhelmingly supportive of the concept, and Disney World found that people waited less time in queues, spent more money, and visited more attractions. FASTPASS™ is now used at all Disney amusement parks worldwide.[24]

THE ANALYSIS OF QUEUING SYSTEMS

When customers must be placed in queues, businesses have to design the most effective system for serving them. To develop an effective queuing system, managers need to know approximately how long customers must wait for service given a particular queuing system, as well as the impact that additional servers, configurations, and equipment will have on the waiting times. Managers must also know how long their customers are willing to wait for service before **reneging** (giving up and leaving the line), and how short the queue must be to avoid **balking** (not joining the queue in the first place, because it is too long). Designing an effective queuing system therefore requires the use of queuing models combined with actual observations. Obviously, managers using queuing system models do not know what actual demand over time will be, but they can use predictions of demand as the basis for initially designing queuing systems. Once queuing systems are in place, managers should collect data based on observations of actual demand and the resulting customer behavior, and then use that data to make adjustments to their queuing systems. These adjustments should help reduce waiting times, maximize queuing system performance, and increase customer satisfaction.

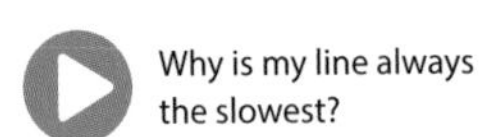

reneging When customers in a queue give up and leave the queue.

balking When customers don't join a queue because it is too long.

queue configuration Refers to the structure of the queue, i.e., multiple server, single queue, or multiple server, multiple queue.

Many queuing systems are complex and require computer simulations to adequately analyze and predict system characteristics. For these systems, readers are referred to one of the many detailed treatments of this topic such as R. Wolff's *Stochastic Modeling and the Theory of Queues*.[25] For a basic system with one queue and one or two servers, the analysis is rather straightforward and is discussed here. Given a demand source, a customer arrival rate, and a service process with a certain configuration and speed, queuing theory can estimate the average queue length, the number of people in the system, the average wait time, and the system utilization.

Figure 10.3 shows a basic queuing system with a one-queue, two-server **queue configuration**—in this case, a "snake-line." The other option would be to have one queue for each server. Customers might balk prior to entering the queue, if it appears too long.

Figure 10.3 A Basic Queuing System

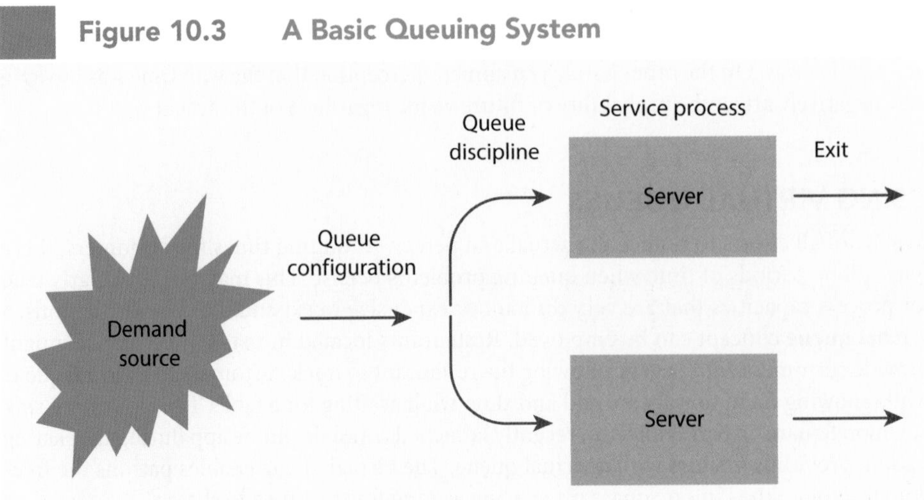

Customers are queued into and then selected from the system according to a queue discipline. The service process shows two servers in parallel. Once the entire service is completed, customers exit the system.

Customers arrive from the **demand source** according to an arrival pattern. Demand sources can contain a finite number or a very large (infinite) number of customers. For example, the demand source for an office candy machine might consist of exactly 10 customers (the 10 employees), whereas the demand source for a restaurant in a large city could be considered infinite.

The **arrival pattern** describes the time between customer arrivals, or the distribution of interarrival times. Research on this topic has found customer arrival times in many instances to be Poisson distributed. In other words, customers tend to arrive in groups, or one right after another, during specific periods of time. This is when a queuing system's design is most important, as during lunchtime or dinnertime at a restaurant. Using the Poisson distribution, the probability of n customers arriving within some time period t, is expressed as:

$$P_{n(t)} = \frac{(\lambda t)^n e^{-\lambda t}}{n!}$$

Where λ = average customer arrivals in time period t

t = number of time periods (usually 1)

n = number of customer arrivals of interest

e = natural log base (2.71828).

Example 10.3 illustrates the use of this formula.

demand source The pool of customers; it can contain a finite number or a very large (infinite) number of customers, and be homogenous or nonhomogenous.

arrival pattern Describes the time between customer arrivals, or the distribution of interarrival times.

jockeying When customers switch queues.

queue discipline Refers to the policy used to select the next customer in the queue for service.

queue segments Partitioning a queue; for example, an auto repair garage may have separate queues depending on the work to be performed, such as oil changes, tire repairs, or engine overhauls.

Queue Configuration

The queue configuration refers to the number and types of queues. A bank's teller window arrangement may have three bank tellers serving one continuous queue or snake line, for example. This arrangement is often seen as the most fair by customers, since it assures a first-come-first-served ordering policy and keeps line-switching or **jockeying** from occurring. A fast-food restaurant like McDonald's, for instance, may have a three-server, three-queue configuration. Entering customers must decide which queue to join; this can cause customer aggravation and jockeying to occur as queues slow down and speed up. Advantages of multiple queues, though, include the use of express lanes, the flexibility to select a server, and the appearance of smaller queues, which can reduce balking. Finally, a grocery store meat counter may have a customer-take-a-number queue, where entering customers select a number, guaranteeing them a place in line (another example of the virtual queue concept). These are three of the most common examples of queue configurations.

Queue Discipline

The **queue discipline** refers to the policy used to select the next customer in the queue for service. For people physically standing in a queue, the most popular queue discipline is the first-come-first-served (FCFS) policy. Other examples include the use of **queue segments**, or partitions. For example, an auto repair garage may have separate queues depending on the work to be performed, such as oil changes, tire repairs, or engine overhauls. Within each queue, though, it is most common to see the FCFS policy used. Hospital emergency rooms use a most-urgent-care-required priority system as a queue discipline, while nightclubs might use a most-important-customer-first or VIP type of queue discipline.

Rosa Betancourt/Alamy

VIP queues allow some people to cut into waiting lines, and can sometimes be viewed as an unfair queue discipline.

Example 10.3 Arrival Probabilities at Jeremiah's Quick-Change Lube Shop

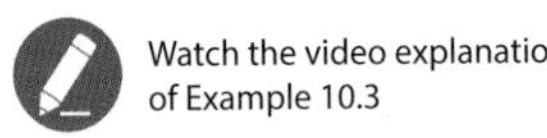

Watch the video explanation of Example 10.3

Jeremiah's Quick-Change Lube Shop can service an average of four cars per hour, and the owner wants to calculate the probability of various customer arrival rates. Given an average arrival rate of three customers per hour, he uses the Poisson distribution to calculate the probabilities of various customer arrivals per hour, shown here.

Number of arrivals, n	$P_n(\text{for } t = 1 \text{ hour}) = \frac{3^n e^{-3}}{n!}$	Cumulative probability
0	0.0498	0.0498
1	0.1494	0.1992
2	0.2240	0.4232
3	0.2240	0.6472
4	0.1680	0.8152

By summing the probabilities for each of the arrival rates, Jeremiah figures his shop can handle the demand per hour approximately 82% of the time. By subtracting this from 1.0, he sees that approximately 18% of the time, demand per hour will be greater than four customers, causing queues to develop.

This problem can also be solved using a spreadsheet, as shown here:

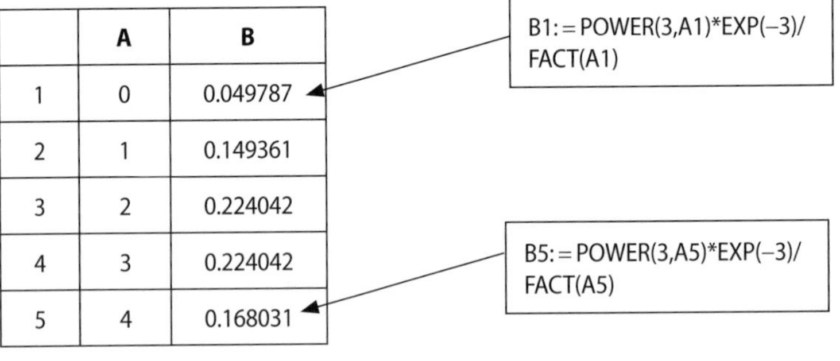

	A	B
1	0	0.049787
2	1	0.149361
3	2	0.224042
4	3	0.224042
5	4	0.168031

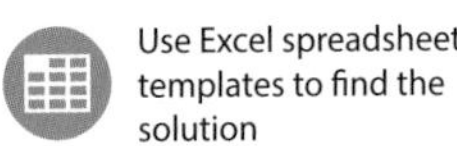

Use Excel spreadsheet templates to find the solution

Service Process

The service process consists of the servers, the process time distribution, the arrangement of servers, and the server management policies. For relatively easy and short service processes, such as haircuts, fast-food preparation, or making change at a cash register, service times have been shown to be exponentially distributed. Using parallel servers for a service (several bank tellers or cashiers) allows managers to quickly vary capacity as demand fluctuates, which generally requires service employees to be cross-trained, to enable capacity to vary at several service processes while minimizing server costs.

The servers themselves can have a significant impact on queue length. Some servers can make conversation, operate equipment, and serve customers simultaneously with little effort, while others may exhibit careless attitudes toward customers or be unable to do more than one thing at a time. Other factors include the willingness of customers to stand in the line, and the perceived quality of the service. These differences, along with variations in customer requirements, can cause service times to vary and greatly impact queue length and customer satisfaction.

Queuing System Operating Characteristics

For simple queuing system configurations with a few assumptions, operating characteristics can be determined and then applied by managers seeking to serve customers successfully while minimizing server costs. As stated earlier, managers can use these characteristics to design a potentially effective queuing system. However, they must also observe actual customer behavior after system implementation. Methods can then be employed to minimize customers' perceptions of waiting time, to maximize the firm's ability to provide adequate levels of customer service. More detailed and complicated services will require use of a system simulation to model the queuing system.

The simple one-server, one-queue service with the following assumptions leads to some very straightforward queuing characteristics:

- Customers arrive from an infinite population and their arrival rate is Poisson distributed.
- A single waiting line is used, with no balking or reneging allowed.
- The queue discipline is first-come-first-served (FCFS).
- One server is used, with exponentially distributed service times.
- The average service rate is greater than the average arrival rate.

The symbols and equations used to determine the queuing characteristics for a one-server, one-queue system are as follows:

λ = mean arrival rate

μ = mean service rate

ρ = mean server utilization = $\frac{\lambda}{\mu}$

L_q = mean number of customers in the queue = $\frac{\rho\lambda}{\mu-\lambda}$

L_s = mean number of customers in the system = $L_q + \rho$

W_q = mean waiting time in the queue = $\frac{L_q}{\lambda}$

W_s = mean waiting time in the system = $W_q + \frac{1}{\mu}$

P_0 = probability of zero customers in the system = $1 - \rho$

P_n = probability of *n*-customers in the system = $\rho^n(1 - \rho)$

Example 10.4 provides an application of these characteristics.

Example 10.4
Operating Characteristics at Stephen's Bookstore

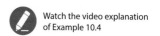

Watch the video explanation of Example 10.4

Stephen owns a small bookstore. Lately, he has wondered if people were waiting too long to buy a book. So he decides to observe customer arrivals and determine some operating characteristics. He finds that over the course of a typical day, he can serve 1 customer in about 3 minutes, and he normally gets about 100 customers in an 8-hour day. Using the standard assumptions, he calculates his store's queuing characteristics as:

$\lambda = 12.5$ customers per hour $\quad \mu = 20$ customers per hour

$\rho = \frac{12.5}{20} = 0.625$, or 62.5% utilization

$L_q = \frac{(.625)(12.5)}{20-12.5} = 1.04$ customers $\quad L_s = 1.04 + 0.625 = 1.7$ customers

$W_q = \frac{1.04}{12.5}$ hours × 60 min/hr = 5 minutes

W_s = 5 minutes + ($\frac{1}{20}$ hours × 60 min/hr) = 8 minutes

$P_{>1}$ = Probability of more than 1 customer in the system = $1 - (P_0 + P_1)$

$P_0 = 1 - 0.625 = 0.375$

$P_1 = (.625)(.375) = 0.234$

Thus, $P_{>1} = 1 - 0.609 = 0.391 = 39.1\%$

So, almost 40% of the time, at least one customer will be in line, waiting for service. Stephen must decide if this is acceptable.

MANAGING WORK FLOWS

10.5 Define work flow and describe how these flows are managed

The topic of work flow management is receiving substantial attention today, as software solution providers are developing applications to automate work flows. At its most basic level, **work flow** can generally be defined as:

> *The movement or transfer of work from the customer or demand source through the organization according to a set of procedures. Work may include documents, information, or tasks that are passed from one recipient to another for action.*

Work flow management visualized

In other words, work flow is the movement of tasks, information, and paperwork that accompany some service or manufacturing activity, until final delivery to the end recipient or user. Work flow normally comprises a number of logical, understood, or mandated steps that can involve a manual or machine activity. Automating the flow of work can greatly increase organizational productivity, and is thus today a very hot topic within automated information systems development. As a matter of fact, business process automation and the one-word term as it appears in many business periodicals—*work flow*—have today become almost synonymous. Consider, for instance, an automated teller machine, or ATM. This concept revolutionized the way banks managed money for bank depositors, greatly impacted the use of bank employees, and substantially changed the way customers interacted with their banks. More recently, Internet banking has further changed how customers interact with their banks and manage their flows of money.

work flow The movement or transfer of work from the customer or demand source through the organization according to a set of procedures. Work may include documents, information, or tasks that are passed from one recipient to another for action.

WORK FLOW ANALYSIS

Managers analyze work and its flows to determine how it adds value to the organization. Additionally, they consider how automation software might improve productivity and value to the organization. A work flow analysis should seek to find answers to the following questions:

SERVICE SPOTLIGHT

Peninsula Uses Dose Management Tool to Reduce Medication Errors

Maryland-based Peninsula Regional Medical Center began using a dose management tool in its central pharmacies in 2007 to improve work flow and reduce medication errors. A dose management application became necessary after Peninsula purchased a large oncology practice in 2007. After the purchase, chemotherapy infusions went from 10 to 40 per day.

With the dose management software application, the pharmacist enters the medication order into the pharmacy information system. When a technician is ready to process the order, the dose management tool prints an "in process" label. The technician then prepares the product. When the job is complete, the software notifies the pharmacist that the product needs verification. After the pharmacist verifies the product remotely, the system notifies the technician that the dose is ready to go and a final administration bar code is printed.

The dose management tool increased turnaround time in the pharmacy for the first three to six weeks, as the technicians initially resisted the new technology. "It is standardized work, and everybody had different ways of doing it before. We needed to get folks over that hump and used to using the system," said Dennis Killian, director of pharmacy services for Peninsula. Peninsula eventually realized a significant reduction in medication errors, since the dose management application could more easily detect errors.[26]

iStock/skynesher

1. Who requires the work, and how often is it required?
2. Does this work create value for the organization?
3. Who is performing the work?
4. How does the work travel through the organization?
5. Can the work be automated or simplified to improve value and productivity?

Work flow analysis can be used to tighten the connection between what the organization does, and what the internal users or external customers want. Delving into the questions stated here can help the firm achieve improvements by rethinking and redesigning various work processes. Analyzing work flows can help to identify work that can be eliminated or combined with other work to achieve improvements in cost and customer service. In the Service Spotlight on page 312, Peninsula Medical Center uses a work flow software application to reduce medication errors coming from its pharmacies.

Analyzing work flows in an organization can be a complicated task. Though most people understand how they perform their own tasks, they may not be able to identify the next step in a work flow process. Describing how work is currently accomplished and how it *should be* accomplished usually requires input from a number of people in several different departments. "You have to get people thinking about business processes," says Richard Kesner, CIO at Babson College. "And since most people think very narrowly about their work, that's actually not a small task."[27]

One common example would be a home loan application and approval process at a lending institution. Prior to the automated loan processes now typically in use at banks and other mortgage lenders, a customer's loan application would be delivered to the lending institution, where it was then distributed to a loan clerk. The clerk checked the loan for completeness and either returned it to the applicant for more information, rejected it based on unsatisfied loan requirements, or keyed the application into the company's loan document database and then forwarded the application to the next required approval clerk or loan officer. The next step in the process was then to confirm the applicant's risk level by reviewing his or her loan and repayment history, debt level, income, and other pertinent information. Verification forms would be mailed to employers and banks for completion. A loan decision would then be made by an underwriter or committee, and if approved, the funds would be made available and the loan would close. The loan process might have taken weeks to complete.

Today, the use of work flow process mapping has led to the automation of many office work flows. To continue with the example, within the past 10 to 15 years technologies have vastly streamlined the loan application and approval process. Loan officers can complete a mortgage application, for instance, and gain preapprovals quickly so that buyers can make an offer on a home. Software systems enable loan officers to pull credit reports, prequalify borrowers, submit applications, and receive underwriting decisions within just a few minutes in many cases. The mortgage lending process has been transformed from a manual one to a highly automated one, using improved process mapping and technology implementation at critical steps in the approval process to streamline the work flow. Technologies allow dozens of orders for title reports, for example, to be completed in the time it used to take for just one.[28]

WORK FLOWS WITHIN THE OFFICE

As described in the previous section, technology has greatly improved work flows for some organizations and processes. But according to David Alien, a management consultant in the United States and described by *Fast Company* magazine as "one of the most influential thinkers on productivity," technology can also increase work flow problems and make it harder for office workers to be productive. Sifting through dozens of unwanted emails each day to find the few important ones is one such example. Some of Alien's suggestions for taking control of daily office work include emptying email inboxes every 24 to 48 hours, doing tasks immediately if they will take less than two minutes to complete, categorizing to-do lists into various action categories, reviewing calendar and action lists daily, and finally, doing tasks based on the actions required, time and energy available, and the priority of the work.[29]

work flow analysis Identifying work that can be eliminated or combined with other work to achieve improvements in cost and customer service.

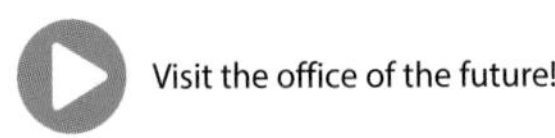

Care must also be taken not to think of office work flow management as simply the automation of current office practices. Rather, the overall objective of work flow management should be to redesign work processes so they become simpler, adaptive, seamless, or visible. Today, office work flows are often very complex, involving multiple parallel process paths with complex dependencies and decision trees or what-if scenarios. Office work flows also typically include use of Internet resources, desktop applications, networks, multiple servers, and email, phone, and fax communications. Thus, information systems and network managers are usually involved in developing work flow solutions that allow users to take the correct process steps in the correct sequence, with the proper documentation, all in a seamless fashion. For large office environments, these are not typically off-the-shelf solutions, but must be customized to create the outputs required.

Law firms, for example, are interested in managing case documents, court calendars, phone calls, emails, client contact information, invoices, and time sheets, as well as other documents, and are increasingly becoming paperless as new office management software is developed for both small and large law firms. Tools are being developed that allow office workers in these and other environments to use technologies to manage work flows without being overburdened by incompatibilities, training regimens, or security issues. In small office settings such as doctor and dentist offices, managing work flows can mean higher-quality patient care, fewer medication errors, lower costs, better staff interactions, and improved office productivity. The following section provides a discussion of work flow management among supply chain trading partners.

MANAGING WORK FLOWS ALONG A SUPPLY CHAIN

Sharing information and communicating quickly and effectively among supply chain partners is becoming a necessity today, as demand, capacity, supplies, technologies, and the competition undergo frequent and sometimes radical change. Nowhere is this more apparent than in the emergency services industry. Terrorist attacks, severe weather disasters, disease epidemics, and earthquakes tend to dramatically test the ability of various supply chains to manage work flows. For example, many of the current hospital supply chain management systems allow materials managers to identify products and equipment by department and analyze usage patterns. With this knowledge, they can create a list of supplies necessary for each type of disaster, as well as where those supplies are stored and who will deliver them. These systems efficiently process transactions, from the purchase order, to confirmation of receipt, to billing. Staff time is not consumed by counting and receiving supplies, and clinicians can focus instead on more valuable patient care and emergency response.[30]

The ability of companies to provide real-time information visibility to their trading partners has become a reality today with the use of sophisticated ERP systems, allowing firms to respond to exceptions, track partner performance, monitor shipments, and respond to order requests. The result is heightened readiness, lower safety stock levels, better customer service, and easier planning. When transactions happen at the warehouse for Lanier Worldwide, a distributor of copiers and related document management systems, the changes are reflected on its logistics visibility and control system within a matter of seconds.[31] Illinois-based Philips Lighting Electronics used the services of Zuken, a Japanese work flow systems consulting firm, to electronically link its engineering CAD systems with procurement to automate its internal supply chain. The result was the automation of its component selection process and data flow from engineering to procurement to manufacturing.[32]

Typical global companies today have many versions of different inventory control systems in various installations around the world, providing connectivity and visibility in varying degrees to the organization as a whole and its trading partners. Managing the flows of work with these systems is a very complex task, and there are a number of applications currently available that enable products and information to be shipped out and received throughout a supply chain.

supply chain event management Software that collects real-time data from multiple supply chain sources and converts it into information that gives business managers a good idea of how their supply chains are performing when problems occur.

Supply chain event management (SCEM) software collects real-time data from multiple supply chain sources and converts it into information that gives business managers a good idea of how their supply chains are performing. When a problem is identified, email, fax, and cell phone alerts are issued to relevant personnel, and recommendations are made regarding how to improve the situation. SCI Systems, an electronics manufacturer from Alabama, uses SeeChain to analyze the performance of its supply chain. "With SeeChain, we can manage supplier performance, react to demand changes, and more efficiently enhance our customers' business performance," says Vincent Melvin, SCI Systems' chief information officer.[33]

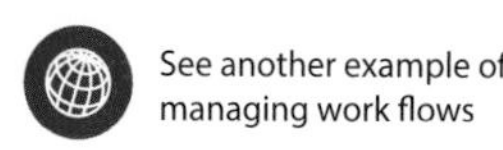
See another example of managing work flows

Effective use of technologies is allowing companies and their trading partners to organize work, exchange information, react to market changes, and in general, make better decisions more quickly. To be effective, however, firms must also consider the processes themselves and the cultural changes that ultimately accompany significant changes in how work is done.

SUMMARY

This chapter discussed the topics of customer and work flow management. Customer flows can be analyzed through use of flow maps and service blueprints, which allow managers to visualize how customers interact with, and travel through, a service system. Customer flow is impacted by service capacity, and this topic was presented, including the capacity management techniques of employee scheduling, yield management, employee cross-training, and self-service. Demand management strategies interact with service capacity to affect customer flow; therefore, this topic was also discussed. Queuing system design directly affects how customers are serviced, and several queuing systems were discussed, along with the impact that various queue management tactics have on the psychology of waiting. As services and products make their way through the organization to the customer, work flows are created that must also be managed effectively to maximize firm competitiveness. Finally, the concept of work flow was discussed, along with the impact technology has had on managing work flows.

KEY TERMS

Arrival pattern, 309
Balking, 308
Code sharing, 303
Complementary services, 304
Customer contact points, 295
Customer flow map, 294
Demand sorting, 305
Demand source, 309
Differential pricing, 299
First Law of Service, 306
Jockeying, 309
Overbooking, 299
Queue configuration, 308
Queue discipline, 309
Queue segments, 309
Reneging, 308
Revenue management, 299
Second Law of Service, 306
Service blueprinting, 295
Supply chain event management, 314
Virtual queue, 307
Work flow, 312
Work flow analysis, 313
Yield management, 299

FORMULA REVIEW

Expected net profit = (table profit – turnaway cost) × no-show probability
= [(tables filled × profit per table) – (turnaways × cost per turnaway)] × no-show probability.

Probability of n customers arriving within some time period *t* is $P_{n(t)} = \frac{(\lambda t)^n e^{-\lambda t}}{n!}$, where λ = average customer arrivals in time period *t*, *t* = number of time periods (usually 1), *n* = number of customer arrivals of interest, and *e* = natural log base (2.71828).

Mean server utilization, $\rho = \frac{\lambda}{\mu}$, where λ = mean arrival rate and μ = mean service rate.

Mean number of customers in the queue, $L_q = \frac{\rho\lambda}{\mu-\lambda}$.

Mean number of customers in the system, $L_s = L_q + \rho$.

Mean waiting time in the queue, $W_q = \frac{L_q}{\lambda}$.

Mean waiting time in the system, $W_s = W_q + \frac{1}{\mu}$.

Probability of zero customers in the system, $P_0 = 1 - \rho$.

Probability of *n* customers in the system, $P_n = \rho^n(1 - \rho)$.

SOLVED PROBLEMS

1. Determine a consecutive days off schedule using the following daily worker requirement, and use part-time workers if needed.

Answer:

	M	T	W	Th	F	S	Su
Requirements	5	3	4	4	2	5	5
Worker 1	5	3	4	(4)	(2)	5	5
Worker 2	4	(2)	(3)	4	2	4	4
Worker 3	3	2	3	(3)	(1)	3	3
Worker 4	2	(1)	(2)	3	1	2	2
Worker 5	1	1	2	2	(0)	(1)	1
Worker 6	0	0	1	1	0	1	0

The schedule requires 5 full-time workers and 1 part-timer.

2. Determine the optimal overbooking policy for a motel. The motel has 40 rooms. The historic number of no-shows for a typical day along with the probability of occurrence is shown below. The average profitability per room is $45, and the cost of lost goodwill due to overbooking is approximately $40.

		Reservations			
No-Shows	Probability	40	41	42	43
0	0.30	40	41	42	43
1	0.40	39	40	41	42
2	0.20	38	39	40	41
3	0.10	37	38	39	40

Note: No more than 3 over-bookings are needed since there are never more than 3 no-shows.

Answer:

Expected Profit with 40 Reservations				
No-Shows	0	1	2	3
Customers	40	39	38	37
Rooms Filled	40	39	38	37
Profit ($)	1800	1755	1710	1665
Turnaways	0	0	0	0
Cost ($)	0	0	0	0
Net Profit	1800	1755	1710	1665
Probability	0.3	0.4	0.2	0.1
Expected Net	540	702	342	167
Total Expected Profit $1751				

Expected Profit with 41 Reservations				
No-Shows	0	1	2	3
Customers	41	40	39	38
Rooms Filled	40	40	39	38
Profit ($)	1800	1800	1755	1710
Turnaways	1	0	0	0
Cost ($)	40	0	0	0
Net Profit	1760	1800	1755	1710
Probability	0.3	0.4	0.2	0.1
Expected Net	528	720	351	171
Total Expected Profit $1770				

Expected Profit with 42 Reservations				
No-Shows	0	1	2	3
Customers	42	41	40	39
Rooms Filled	40	40	40	39
Profit ($)	1800	1800	1800	1755
Turnaways	2	1	0	0
Cost ($)	80	40	0	0
Net Profit	1720	1760	1800	1755
Probability	0.3	0.4	0.2	0.1
Expected Net	516	704	360	176
Total Expected Profit $1756				

Expected Profit with 43 Reservations				
No-Shows	0	1	2	3
Customers	43	42	41	40
Rooms Filled	40	40	40	40
Profit ($)	1800	1800	1800	1800
Turnaways	3	2	1	0
Cost ($)	120	80	40	0
Net Profit	1680	1720	1760	1800
Probability	0.3	0.4	0.2	0.1
Expected Net	504	688	352	180
Total Expected Profit $1724				

The expected profits are maximized with 41 reservations or overbooking by 1 room.

3. Gillian's Bookstore can service an average of 10 customers per hour, and the owner wants to calculate the probability of various customer arrival rates.

   a. Given an average arrival rate of 4 customers per hour, she wants to use the Poisson distribution to calculate the probabilities of various customer arrivals per hour.

Answer:

Number of arrivals, n	$P_n(\text{for } t = 1 \text{ hour}) = \frac{4^n e^{-4}}{n!}$	Cumulative probability
0	0.0183	0.0183
1	0.0732	0.0915
2	0.1465	0.2380
3	0.1954	0.4334
4	0.1954	0.6288
5	0.1563	0.7851
6	0.1042	0.8893

   b. Determine how often more than 5 customers would show up in 1 hour.

Answer:

Sum the probabilities from 0–5 arrivals, then subtract from 1.

Yielding—1 – 0.7851 = 0.2149. So, about 21% of the time, more than 5 customers would arrive in 1 hour.

   c. Determine the queuing characteristics for this system, given that the store has one server.

Answer:

ρ = mean server utilization = $\frac{\lambda}{\mu} = 4/10 = 0.4$ or 40%

L_q = mean number of customers in the queue = $\frac{\rho\lambda}{\mu - \lambda} = \frac{.4(4)}{10-4} = 0.267$

L_s = mean number of customers in the system = $L_q + \rho = 0.267+0.4 = 0.467$

W_q = mean waiting time in the queue = $\frac{L_q}{\lambda} = 0.267/4 = 0.067$ hrs. = 4 min.

W_s = mean waiting time in the system = $W_q + \frac{1}{\mu} = 0.067+0.1 = 0.167$hrs. = 10 min.

P_0 = probability of zero customers in the system = $1 - \rho = 0.6$ or 60%

REVIEW QUESTIONS

1. What is the value in creating a customer flow map?
2. What is a customer contact point? Should firms try to minimize these?
3. What does service blueprinting have to do with customer contact points?
4. Explain the concept of "moments of truth."
5. How does employee scheduling impact service capacity? What other techniques are used to manage capacity in services?
6. What is the definition and objective of yield management? Give an example.
7. How important is overbooking in yield management?
8. Describe differential pricing and when it might be used.
9. What are the First and Second Laws of Service? How did they come about?
10. What are some things service firms can do to manage the psychological aspects of waiting to reduce customers' awareness of waiting in line?
11. What are the advantages of using virtual queues?
12. Define demand management, using examples.
13. What is meant by queue discipline?
14. Define the term *work* as it is used in the text, and then describe work flow.
15. Describe how work flow can be analyzed in organizations or supply chains.
16. How has technology changed the way work is managed in organizations today?
17. How have automated work flows tended to impact supply chains?

DISCUSSION QUESTIONS

1. Describe the customer contact points of a favorite restaurant, and discuss whether there should be fewer or more contact points.
2. Describe how differential pricing could be used at a hospital.
3. Describe some ways that services can manage or influence demand, using examples.
4. Use the First and Second Laws of Service in a real business example you can recall.
5. Describe all of the ways your doctor's office could use demand management.
6. What queue discipline is used when registering for classes at your school?
7. Why would a restaurant manager want to know the queuing characteristics of her restaurant?
8. Describe the work flow at your bank.
9. How could you analyze the work flow at your bank?
10. Describe how technology impacts work flow at your bank.

EXERCISES AND PROJECTS

1. Go to a restaurant and create a customer flow map, identifying any customer flow or associated problems. Create a service blueprint for the same restaurant and critique the restaurant, based on the flow map and service blueprint. Describe all of the moments of truth you encountered, and how they were handled by the servers.

2. Describe how movie theaters today use yield management and demand management techniques.

3. Spend an hour or two studying a queuing situation at Walmart on a busy Saturday. What are some queuing activities you notice? How are customers impacted by the psychology of waiting? Calculate some queuing system operating characteristics.

PROBLEMS

1. The manager at Tram's Candy Shop wants to determine a consecutive days off schedule for its workforce. Use the following daily worker requirement, and use part-time workers if needed.

	M	T	W	Th	F	S	Su
Requirement	6	4	5	4	3	2	2

2. Determine a consecutive days off schedule using the following daily worker requirement, and use part-time workers if needed.

	M	T	W	Th	F	S	Su
Requirement	12	13	15	10	17	9	6

3. Given the following information, determine the optimal overbooking policy for Talia's Beauty Salon. The salon's capacity is 8 patrons. The historic number of no-shows for a typical day along with the probability of occurrence is shown in the table. The average profitability per patron is $100 and the cost of lost goodwill per patron due to overbooking is approximately $50.

No-Shows	Probability
0	0.50
1	0.30
2	0.20

4. Given the following information, determine the optimal overbooking policy. The restaurant's capacity is 24 tables. The historic number of no-shows for a typical day along with the probability of occurrence is shown in the table below. The average profitability per table is $125, and the cost of lost goodwill per table due to overbooking is approximately $250.

No-Shows	Probability
0	0.25
1	0.45
2	0.20
3	0.10

5. What is the probability that exactly 10 customers will arrive in an hour when the mean arrival rate is 20 customers per hour and interarrival times are exponentially distributed?

6. Using the information in Problem 5, what is the probability that less than 5 customers will arrive in an hour?

7. Peggy's Car Wash can service an average of 12 cars per hour. Given an average arrival rate of 8 customers per hour, use the Poisson distribution to calculate the probability that the car wash can handle the demand. How often would the car wash demand exceed 10 cars per hour? 15 cars per hour?

8. What is the probability that *more than 2 customers* will arrive in an hour, when the mean arrival rate is 2 customers per hour and interarrival times are exponentially distributed?

9. Josh's Hot Dogs is a one-person hot dog stand, and normally gets about 10 customers per hour. Assuming that Josh can serve one customer in about 3 minutes, calculate the stand's queuing characteristics. What is the probability that there is more than one customer in the system, at any given time? Do you think Josh has an acceptable queuing system?

10. Change the arrival rate at Josh's Hot Dogs in Question 9 to 6 customers per hour. What impact does this have on the queuing characteristics? What is the probability that there is more than one customer in the system, at any given time? Do you think Josh has an acceptable queuing system?

11. Change the arrival rate at Josh's Hot Dogs in Question 9 to 14 customers per hour. What impact does this have on the queuing characteristics? What is the probability that there is more than one customer in the system, at any given time? Do you think Josh has an acceptable queuing system?

CASE STUDIES

CASE 1: Naturally Yours, Inc.

Naturally Yours, Inc., promotes itself as a natural and organic shopping experience for food, cosmetic beauty products, and nutrition products. Naturally Yours was started 25 years ago as a health store that supplied natural and organic ingredients that customers used as nutritional supplements in recipes and as medicinal interventions. As the national trend in healthy living increased, Naturally Yours began responding to customer requests and inquiries about alternatives in food and cosmetics. Presently, Naturally Yours has all of its operations in a large 30,000-square-foot building, after moving into a vacant department store five years earlier.

The nutrition and wellness department provides nutritional supplement products, wellness evaluations, personal health, and exercise consultations. The department has one small counter where health shakes are available for trial and purchase. The activity level in the nutrition and wellness department can be hectic, and when customers seek consultation at the one checkout area, it slows service significantly. Some customers from the organic grocery department move to the nutrition and wellness department when they are seeking information concerning ingredients on food labels, or are including food choices as part of their personal wellness efforts. Employees in the nutrition and wellness department are well trained in customer service and nutrition, including several staff with degrees or certifications in nutrition.

The organic grocery department has experienced significant growth and now represents over 60% of Naturally Yours' gross annual sales. The five checkout lines for grocery are in the front of the store and handle customers with grocery products, cosmetics, and nutrition supplements. Employees at the registers are trained in operating the registers and in basic customer service but do not have Naturally Yours training or credentials relative to natural and organic products.

In addition to riding the increased demand for natural and organic food products, Naturally Yours has carved out a niche by focusing on consumer awareness and demand for organic foods. This focus includes a "green movement" emphasis that covers all categories of raising, processing, and distributing to retail venues. The other movement that Naturally Yours has used to its advantage is "buying local," which is a worldwide trend. Naturally Yours supports local farmers, which assists in controlling transportation costs. Additionally, Naturally Yours has been partnering with suppliers that can adhere to its increasingly strict standards, which have been essential to its success as a leader in organic/natural foods retailing.

Naturally Yours' customer focus has been rewarded with an astounding first-time customer to return-customer ratio. Almost 68% of first-time shoppers become loyal customers as defined by return rates, longevity, and increased transaction amounts. Based on that data, Naturally Yours developed a strategy to get potential customers in the door. All of its promotional material focuses on people who are passionate about food (foodies), describing Naturally Yours products and its ability to search local and national suppliers for the best foods for its customers. Local and regional promotion campaigns proved very successful.

Naturally Yours has been studying the natural and organic grocery leader Whole Foods Market (WFM) and applying as much of the industry leader's differentiation within the store as possible. Naturally Yours is building sales in a new segment—convenience foods—appealing to a growing consumer interest area of healthy, convenient food selection. Naturally Yours is concerned that the sharp increase in new customers as a result of stealing customers from traditional groceries is going to level off and the competition in natural and organic food products is going to intensify. Naturally Yours is projecting the next competitive advantage opportunity for it will be on delivering excellent service throughout the shopping experience including product offerings, consultations, and convenience.

Natural/organic cosmetics is the newest addition to Naturally Yours' product line, and the cosmetics department carries both local and national brands. The plans for this department include adding a service counter and providing skin and beauty consultation services. Currently, the cosmetics department does not have a service counter, and customer questions are handled at the checkout facilities. Some customers engage employees stocking shelves in other departments or wait in line at the nutrition counter to ask questions, further adding to excessive wait times in checkout lines.

The three departments in food, cosmetics, and nutrition, along with the consultation services, are a strong competitive advantage for Naturally Yours. However, customers often complain about the long lines in general, the long lines as a result of customers asking questions at the checkout registers, and the overall waiting time in line. They also complain about not having access to knowledgeable staff for consultation before they enter the checkout line. The "low-hanging fruit" to improve customer satisfaction must focus on wait times.

DISCUSSION QUESTIONS

1. Based on the information provided in the case, how would you describe the structure of the wait lines?
2. What wait line calculations should be completed to determine the wait line performance at Naturally Yours? How will these calculations help Naturally Yours' improvement efforts?
3. Describe Naturally Yours' service system (lines and facilities) and then make recommendations for possible changes.
4. What other recommendations would you make to Naturally Yours to improve customer satisfaction?

Note: Written by Brian Hoyt, PhD, Ohio University, Athens, OH. The company is fictional and any resemblance to any company is coincidental. This case was prepared solely to provide material for class discussion. The author does not intend to illustrate either effective or ineffective handling of a managerial situation.

CASE 2: PJ Graphics

PJ Graphics started out as a marketing services firm that designed promotional print products and office promotional products (such as pens and coffee cups), with operations working from a home office. The company quickly grew to a full-line promotional solution and marketing services company with a full line of promotional item offerings (such as executive gifts, golf items, badges, lanyards, bags, and many others) that required a move to an office building, with a sales office and a purchasing office, along with room for inventory.

The next growth spurt was fueled by adding a profitable apparel and hats product line. The additional product line more than tripled revenues and also required a new work space that included a spirit wear store (shirts and hoodies for local school and community athletic teams and booster clubs). The new work space included a sales office, office space for the purchasing department, space for a graphic artist, a heat press and embroidery equipment room, inventory space, a sample product showroom, and the store.

PJ Graphics has hundreds of suppliers, with almost all products printed or embroidered with a custom-designed logo or message. The internal processes for estimates and orders, including shipping instructions, are not standardized, and with the addition of the spirit wear store have become cumbersome with increasing numbers of order errors. Estimates and orders are generated from email, fax, website, phone, and onsite walk-in traffic. Most estimates and orders are initiated internally from the sales department (using field sales and internal customer service staff), and overflow is handled by purchasing, graphic artists, and the retail store. Many repeat customers place subsequent orders with employees who processed their last order, adding more estimating and order placements from non–sales department staff. While some estimates can use standard supplier price lists, many quotes require accumulating product costs, design costs, print or decorating costs, and delivery/shipping costs that are custom to the order requirements.

Depending on the customer requirements and supplier, the base product order is placed with the supplier, and is then printed, embroidered, or decorated by the supplier, a third-party vendor, or in PJ Graphics' print/embroidery department. Logistics and shipping is arranged by PJ Graphics and could include drop shipping to third-party vendors for screen printing or finished goods drop shipping directly to the PJ Graphics' customer. Other orders from suppliers are finished at PJ Graphics and delivered or picked up on site. The increased volume of orders and increased expectations for service excellence highlight the need for PJ Graphics to organize its operation for continued success.

DISCUSSION QUESTIONS

1. Where should PJ Graphics start in improving operation flow, reducing errors, and increasing productivity?
2. If part of the process flow improvement included moving to a paperless system, what would you recommend as the first step for PJ Graphics to convert to a paperless work flow system?
3. Discuss the projected benefits for PJ Graphics if it improves work flow.

Note: Written by Professor Brian Hoyt, Ohio University. This case was prepared solely to provide material for class discussion. The author does not intend to illustrate either effective or ineffective handling of a managerial situation.

CASE 3: Sammie's

Sammie's is an all-in-one boutique, deli, and specialty ethnic grocery store shopping experience in a quaint New England beach town. Sammie's is located on the bottom floors of five historic buildings side by side taking up a block in the center of this small town. The upper floor of each building is high-end rental property for summer vacationers. The town is located on the famous Route 1 that travels along the Atlantic coastline of New England. Sammie's is on Route 1A, which is the original Route 1 before it was rerouted along the coast to avoid all the small towns and summer traffic. The town's population during the off season is just over 5,000 and explodes to over 50,000 during the summer, with many more traveling through on the scenic 1A route. Sammie's is a landmark, with decades of reviews profiling the shop's unique location, exotic foods, deli and coffee shop with outside seating looking out over the local harbor, souvenir shop, and local grocery store. To customers, Sammie's is a set of five different stores that are accessed only by leaving each store and reentering the next store from the sidewalk. Each store has its own canopy, and the deli/coffee shop has an extended temporary cover for summer dining.

Sammie's is planning to remodel the deli/coffee shop so it can serve dinner in addition to breakfast and lunch. Sammie's owners are also considering linking all the stores under one roof. Sammie's hired an architectural design firm to present a design that would connect all five buildings so that customers could move among the stores, and in particular provide a unique waiting experience for those waiting for the restaurant. The design calls for a single permanent canopy covering the entire sidewalk and outside dining area. In addition to the new restaurant revenue, this is an opportunity to improve the often noted "be ready to wait" notations in the summer travel reviews. Waiting areas, wait times, and cost reductions when sharing checkout responsibilities is an important improvement goal for the remodeled buildings. The remodeled space will also provide opportunities for the boutique jewelry store to expand its summer jewelry-making clinics for individuals and small groups. After a protracted battle with the City Council and planning department the design plans were finally approved.

DISCUSSION QUESTIONS

1. Identify several approaches for dealing with waiting customers that Sammie's should consider when it begins remodeling its service center to improve the waiting for service experience.
2. Sammie's managers have been discussing virtual queueing applications. Are there viable options for Sammie's?
3. With numerous independent competitors in each category (grocery, jewelry, souvenir, and deli) just down the road, Sammie's managers are concerned about customers reneging and balking in their wait lines. They are considering different wait line systems to address this concern. What recommendations can you make to help them decide?

Note: Written by Professor Brian Hoyt, Ohio University. This case was prepared solely to provide material for class discussion. The author does not intend to illustrate either effective or ineffective handling of a managerial situation.

VIDEO CASE STUDY

Learn more about ***managing work flows*** from real organizations that use operations management techniques every day. Amy Keelin and Christine Keelin are COO and CFO (respectively) at MPK Foods, a small family-owned company based in Duarte, California, that produces seasoning mixes sold to grocery stores. As a food product manufacturer, MPK's work flow operations are carefully coordinated to avoid contamination and preserve quality. Watch this short interview to learn how.

iStock/exipreess

The dynamics of business communication are shifting. Conversations that took place 10 years ago via face-to-face interaction requiring travel, or via phone, now happen via WebEx, video conferencing, and social media.

—**JOE GUSTAFSON,** CEO, Brainshark, Waltham, MA[1]

The key to good decision making is evaluating the available information—the data—and combining it with your own estimates of pluses and minuses. As an economist, I do this every day.

—**EMILY OSTER,** economist, Brown University, Providence, RI[2]

MANAGING INFORMATION FLOWS: MRP AND ERP

LEARNING OBJECTIVES

After completing this chapter, you should be able to:

11.1 Construct an information flow map
11.2 Explain the uses of MRP, DRP, and MRP II systems
11.3 Describe the historical developments and current use of ERP systems
11.4 Summarize the underlying principles of business process management
11.5 Recall three important trends in Enterprise Resource Planning

Master the content.

edge.sagepub.com/wisner

GALLUS BIOPHARMACEUTICALS USES RAPID IMPLEMENTATION FOR ITS ERP SYSTEM

Gallus BioPharmaceuticals (now part of North Carolina–based Patheon) took a faster, cheaper approach to ERP system implementation, partly out of necessity. In 2011, it acquired an existing facility from Johnson & Johnson and was given 120 days to transform Johnson & Johnson's IT infrastructure at the facility to Gallus's ERP system. "We have to track everything from preventative maintenance to cell-performance data," said Gallus CFO Steven Kasok.

Gallus management knew the 120-day implementation schedule was tight, particularly given the small size of the company's IT staff. The solution was to implement a simple, noncustomized system. Since there was no "cut-rate ERP" suitable for the biopharmaceutical industry, Gallus purchased EzPharma's ERP system for several million dollars, and saved costs on its implementation. It hired consultants to manage the system rollout, but used its own staff as much as possible and declined customization in almost all cases.

Since Gallus makes products for the commercial market, regulatory concerns are much greater than for other manufacturers. Aside from the one required regulatory software element, Gallus essentially implemented the ERP system straight out of the box. "The consultants would talk about [making changes in] the next phase. But I always said, 'This is the only phase,'" explained Kasok. "In an ideal world, we would have implemented just what we needed instead of what [Johnson & Johnson] already had," he said. "We did this as cost effectively as possible, and the return is a business that continues to run."[3]

INTRODUCTION

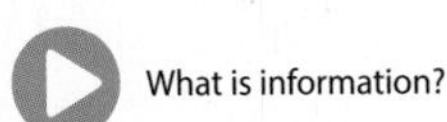

Managing information both inside the firm and extending outward to its trading partners is certainly one of the most crucial processes facing the firm today. The value of information and how it is used in the firm has already been introduced in a number of chapters in this text, from inventory to forecasting to customer service to capacity and to sustainability, to name just a few. Additionally, the technologies and software products for managing information are changing rapidly.

Most firms are swamped with all sorts of good and bad information, and a systematic effort to manage these flows of information will lead to a more effective organization. For instance, a group of researchers studying automobile supply chains found that information flow among trading partners was commonly withheld, masked, distorted, or just plain missing. And the cost of this lack of good information in terms of the bullwhip effect alone can be very high, perhaps adding as much as 20% to a firm's total costs.[4] The development of material requirements planning, manufacturing resource planning, and enterprise resource planning systems, along with other information systems such as customer relationship management, warehouse management, and manufacturing execution systems, have greatly facilitated planning and decision making for organizations.

To stay competitive, firms are becoming more global in nature, by building foreign manufacturing and retail facilities, creating global distribution networks, and partnering with foreign companies. This has created the need for global information visibility as well, to communicate system inventory levels, create more accurate forecasts, and reduce order cycle times, for example. These extended enterprises have created a huge volume of information, along with the corresponding need to better manage its flow and visibility.

As information technology changes, managers are further tempted to add to the layers of existing information with automated process management software applications such as business process management. This chapter will review the concept of information flow and the development of information system applications, as well as discuss how managers use these tools to manage the many flows of information.

THE CONCEPT OF INFORMATION FLOW

11.1 Construct an information flow map

Information and its flow can be thought of in the same manner as material and customer flows. In fact, supply chains consist of two equally important substructures—the physical item/customer flow system (which was discussed at length in Chapters 8 and 10), and the information flow system. The hub-and-spoke transportation networks operated by many airlines along with their centralized computer reservation systems provide a good example of the separate flows of physical items and information. Passengers and cargo are routed through airlines' primary hubs to reach their destinations. Computers linked to the airlines' reservation systems are located at travel agents, airline offices, and online travel sites, and communicate information to users regarding passengers and cargo.[5] Information thus has value just as materials do—it can be referred to as an asset, or more appropriately, an **intellectual asset**. Information technologies influence how information coordination takes place, reduces uncertainty, improves decision making, and promotes new coordination structures.

Most organizations have three key informational flows: **corporate information flow**, or the flow of information from the firm to its customers; **environmental information flow**, which is the flow from customers to the firm; and **internal information flow**, or information flow within the firm. These information flows are shown in Figure 11.1. In each case, managers must consider how information is captured, transformed, and exchanged, along with the interplay among the three flows, and the existing information capabilities of the local information system hardware and software. Here is a description, for example, of the key information flows at a bank:[6]

> Corporate websites, emailed monthly statements, and advertising generate corporate information flows, offering transaction opportunities to customers. In response, customers make deposits at ATMs and pay bills online, triggering transactions and generating environmental information flows. To support the transactions, internal information flows such as data processing, customer account updating, and reports creation occur, which is necessary for effective management of the new environmental information. Banking information technologies have today advanced so that most customers rarely visit their bank branches.

As with materials, the flow of information can be impeded or made to move faster, depending on the number of internal and external intermediaries and delays involved in the transfer of information. As the number of information processing locations increases, the flow of information slows, the likelihood of information distortions increase, and its value tends to decrease. Organizations can thus manage internal and external information flows by reducing the number of information processing locations. Dell Computer Corp. redesigned and better integrated its supply chain, for instance, by reducing non-value-adding information flows within its supply chain. Today, Dell's supply chain is leaner and faster, with information flowing very effectively from Dell's end-item sales locations to raw materials suppliers. The results are higher levels of quality and customization, and faster delivery times.[7]

intellectual asset When information has value it can be referred to as an intellectual asset.

corporate information flow The flow of information from the firm to its customers.

environmental information flow The flow from customers to the firm.

internal information flow Information flow within the firm.

Information velocity is a term used to describe how fast information flows from one process to another. Systems that handle e-commerce transactions such as Web servers require capabilities that allow for huge variations in information velocity without adversely impacting performance, such as during the Christmas buying season. In systems characterized by multiple human interactions and decision steps, or a lack of automation, information velocity and the information itself can be adversely impacted. Several years ago, for instance, a top manager for one of the major suppliers to the U.S. automobile industry remarked, "It takes two or more weeks for information from the automaker regarding the increase in the sales of a specific type of model that translates into materials requirements for our company, to get to us. This leaves us with about a week to manage our supply chain, leaving our inventory management ad hoc at best."[8]

Information volatility is another common term associated with information flow. Volatility refers to the uncertainty associated with information content, format, or timing. Spikes and lulls in daily webpage transactions, for instance, are associated with information volatility. This volatility can increase during holiday and seasonal periods, and firms must be able to accommodate this information volatility. Use of historical data and forecasting allows firms to plan for these times with extra system capacities.

Relationships with suppliers and customers are impacted by information and its availability, velocity, and volatility. The emergence of computers, computer networks, and software applications has given managers the ability to store, retrieve, process, and distribute very large amounts of information very quickly to users within the organization and among trading partners at a reasonable cost. Consequently, managers must consider how the flow of information impacts and adds value to the supply chain. As with the flow of materials, it becomes important, then, to map information flows to better understand and optimize their use and value. This topic is discussed next.

Information volatility can lead to poor decisions, stockouts, and damaged relationships with suppliers and customers.

INFORMATION FLOW MAPPING

Mapping information flows allows managers to identify how information is transmitted from one point to another both within the firm and externally, to suppliers and customers. Flow maps serve as a basis for analyzing information needs and the services necessary to align the firm's information collection and transfer capabilities with the information needs of its internal and external users. Mapping information flows involves a series of steps:[9]

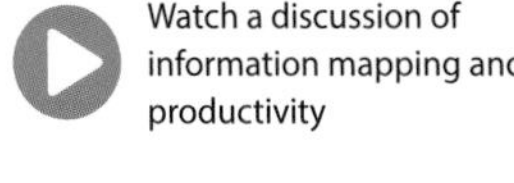

Watch a discussion of information mapping and productivity

1. Conduct an **information audit**. Determine current internal and external information users, and estimate their information requirements. The items of interest include knowledge of goods and services, the operating environments, information sources and system architectures, software applications, and other factors that influence use of information. The audit should uncover current information sources and uses.
2. Map the internal and external users' information flows. This will allow the analyst to see where redundancies or overlaps exist, and where information usage and sources can be eliminated, consolidated, or expanded.
3. Identify information needs that are currently not being satisfied. Discuss these potential needs with all internal and external users. Determine common informational needs and rank the needs based on the level of agreement regarding each information requirement. The analyst can then make suggestions for more optimal solutions for information flows.
4. Change information flows on the map as decisions to implement changes are made. These additions will make the design of the information flow map a dynamic process. Periodically revisit the flow map to identify better use of technologies, better flow arrangements, or new information requirements.

information velocity Describes how fast information flows from one process to another.

information volatility The uncertainty associated with information content, format, or timing.

information audit Determining the firm's current internal and external information users, and estimating their information requirements.

A basic information flow map is shown in Figure 11.1, presenting the internal and external informational flows of a manufacturer. In the flow map, it is seen that the manufacturer communicates corporate information or orders to suppliers through use of supplier websites, traditional purchase orders that are mailed or faxed to suppliers, bid requests, intermediaries such as foreign agents and shipment consolidators, and through existing supplier contracts. When suppliers act on these orders, these become environmental information flows or transactions. The manufacturer also communicates corporate information or offers to customers through use of the firm's website, media advertisements and promotions, field sales representatives, and distribution centers. Customers act on these offers by purchasing goods and services, and by creating environmental information flows or transactions.

The environmental information created by suppliers and customers is captured and processed using the firm's information system network and software applications. As indicated in the figure, information is transmitted to the manufacturer's supplier relationship management (SRM) and customer relationship management (CRM) software applications, where it is added to suppliers' and customers' information files. Internal information flows are created when supplier and customer information is analyzed and used to help identify new purchasing and product marketing strategies, to create performance reports, for interdepartmental communications, for product quality assessments and improvement efforts, and for a host of other decision support purposes. As needs for more information are discovered, the firm considers implementing other information system applications.

INFORMATION FLOW AMONG SUPPLY CHAIN TRADING PARTNERS

Watch a discussion of supply chains and information technology

In supply chains, trading partners are highly dependent on effective information support. Supply chain partners require information, for example, on current inventory levels, order and delivery status, production and forecast changes, and product design changes. The difficulty may be in how all this information is brought together, analyzed, and transmitted within the firm and to its trading partners. The Service Spotlight on page 329 describes information flow among Dart Transit's truck drivers, shippers, and customers. The integration of information flows along the supply chain is discussed further later in this chapter.

Figure 11.1 Information Flow Map for a Manufacturer

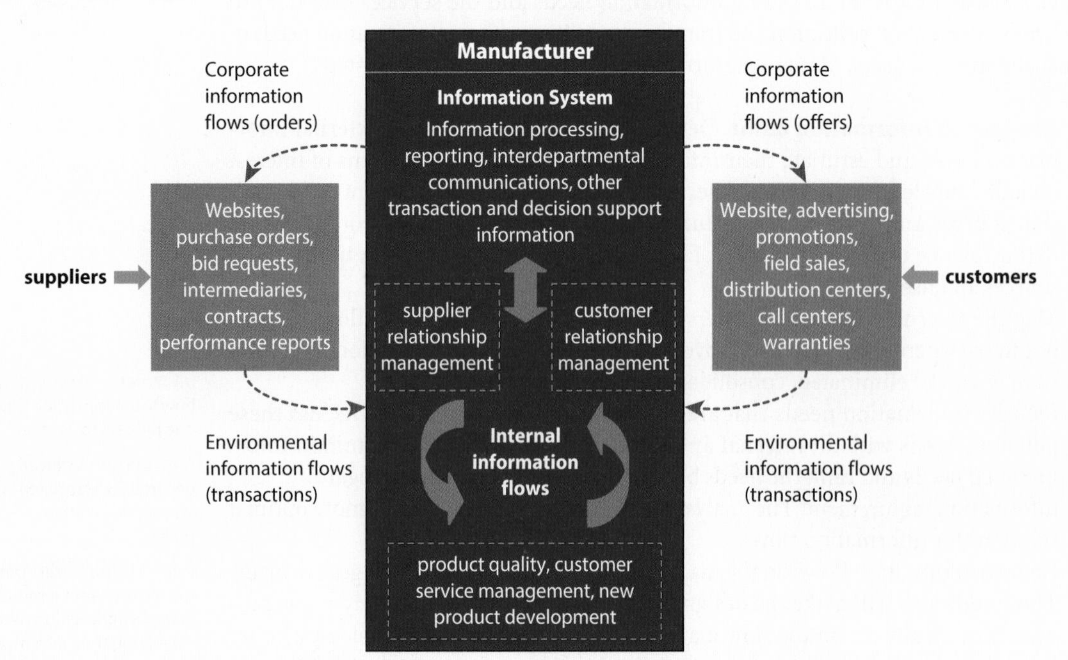

Dart Uses Technology to Schedule Drivers and Shipments

SERVICE SPOTLIGHT

iStock/Rcarner

Dart Transit Co., headquartered in Minnesota, is making better use of technology to attract more truck drivers and to make sure its drivers can return home each night. This means better load planning and scheduling. Its new plan is that every operator drives one 500-mile round-trip each day. Information flow among operators and Dart is constant, so everyone knows freight availability throughout the network and can plan when to arrive for pickups.

By putting tracking technologies on the trucks and making information available in real time, Dart is improving collaboration with shippers and customers, and better managing appointment times, drivers, and trucks. Dart is dedicating fleets of trucks to some customers, and then working with them to fill gaps in Dart's delivery routes using shipments from other customers. This requires a direct communication link with these customers. With its current systems, data pass directly between Dart's servers and that of its customers. Prior to this, the company was using a third-party network to exchange information, which took more time.[10]

Information flow problems are very common, for instance, in the construction industry. A construction project could involve a large number of companies, including architectural firms, construction companies, engineering firms, and independent subcontractors working closely in a time-sensitive environment. Large numbers of documents are passed among the companies, from technical drawings, legal contracts, and purchase orders to permits, build schedules, and delivery schedules. These projects tend to be paper intensive and can be slowed significantly by building code problems, labor availability, and late-supply deliveries. Initial project bids, for example, can be too low or high, depending on the availability and accuracy of information, leading to construction cost overruns or incomplete work. The timely sharing of information, reduction of errors and waste, and better use of information are all facilitated by use of information technologies in construction project management. The use of information system applications and the compatibility of communication tools as information flows within and among trading partners is thus an extremely important topic when considering supply chain performance, which is the topic of the next section.

DEPENDENT DEMAND INVENTORY MANAGEMENT

11.2 Explain the uses of MRP, DRP, and MRP II systems

When a manufacturer's finished product is purchased, this is considered the company's *independent demand*. Managing these finished product inventories was the topic of Chapter 7. Additionally, when a manufacturer's finished product is purchased, this creates an internal demand within the manufacturer for the raw materials, parts, and subassemblies that comprise the finished product. The quantities of parts required for these end-items are *dependent* on the external demand of the finished product. To manage these *dependent demand* items, most firms require some type of inventory system to identify when production orders and purchase orders need to be created, as well as the number of units to produce or purchase, in order to meet the demand for finished goods. This can be accomplished with the use of a material requirements planning system.

THE MATERIAL REQUIREMENTS PLANNING SYSTEM

material requirements planning (MRP) A software application that performs an analysis of the firm's existing internal conditions and determines the assembly and purchase requirements for a given product manufacturing schedule.

Figure 11.2 illustrates the inputs and outputs of a **material requirements planning (MRP)** system. The MRP system is a software application that has been widely available since the

This is the IBM 305 RAMAC, the first computer to run a very basic MRP system in the mid-1960s.

1970s—but can still be quite expensive today—for firms with many manufactured products and complicated product designs. Briefly, an MRP system performs an analysis of the firm's existing internal conditions and determines the assembly and purchase requirements for a given product manufacturing schedule. These systems have been extremely popular over the years, and have been touted by MRP software providers to provide better customer service, better demand responsiveness, lower inventory levels, and higher capacity utilization.

Aside from the cost of the software, there are potentially costly training and hardware expenditures, and implementation periods can take anywhere from a month or two to a year or two. And, as with any software application, the *garbage-in–garbage-out rule* applies. This means that in order for the MRP system to work properly, accurate and updated data must be made continuously available to the MRP. Otherwise, the system will produce inaccurate outputs, which are not worth much to the organization and can even be quite damaging in terms of stockouts or excess inventories. Companies might also need to change how they do things in order to accommodate the requirements of the MRP software. In fact, one of the primary reasons why MRP implementations fail is because companies simply underestimate the requirements of the MRP systems. MRP must be implemented as an entire system for it to successfully achieve its objectives of production and purchase order management.

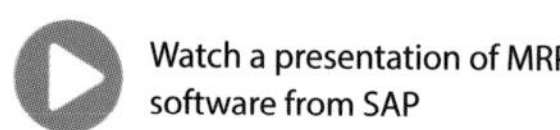

MRP Inputs

The direct MRP inputs are the master production schedule, current inventory and lead-time information, and bills of materials information. These are described in the following sections.

master production schedule Specifies which end-product is to be made, how many are required, and when they need to be completed. These usually take the form of a weekly production schedule. An input to the MRP.

Master Production Schedule

The **master production schedule** (MPS) specifies which *end-product* is to be made, how many are required, and when they need to be completed. These usually take the form of a

Figure 11.2 MRP System With Inputs and Outputs

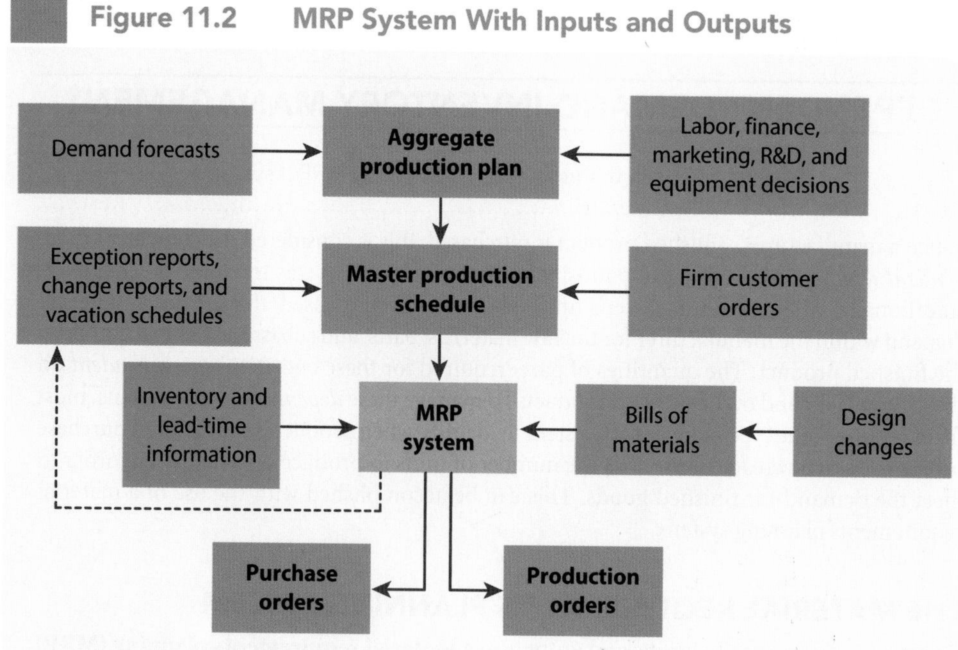

weekly production schedule, which then becomes an input to the MRP. The MPS is based on the aggregate production plan, existing or firm customer orders, and current information regarding the capacity of the manufacturing facility. Since workcenter capacities vary based on human resource deployment and equipment used, the MPS personnel must know how changes in human resources will likely vary over the coming months and year, and what equipment will be coming online or going out of use due to scheduled maintenance. Some of the newest automated manufacturing systems have MPS capabilities, but in many cases an office of MPS personnel with intimate knowledge of the firm's production characteristics performs the MPS activity.

As the capacity of the firm changes due to unforeseen changes in the workforce or production equipment, the MPS must then be revised. As customer orders come in from field salespeople and regional distribution centers, this information can be compared to existing MPS quantities, allowing for further revisions in the production schedule. These and other revisions to the MPS must be made far enough in advance for the production processes to respond. This requires the MPS to use a **frozen time fence**, or time period wherein no changes are allowed to the weekly production schedule. This time period is at least as long as the lead time required to purchase parts and assemble the finished product.

The aggregate production plan provides an annual production plan for each product family to the MPS personnel. The MPS personnel then break down or disaggregate the aggregate production plan, turning it into weekly production requirements for individual products (the MPS). Each week, the MPS extends its frozen weekly production schedule for the set frozen time period, and projects a working schedule for the remaining portion of the year. This is known as a **rolling production schedule**.

Inventory and Lead-Time Information

Other inputs to the MRP include accurate inventory and lead-time information for all raw material, work-in-progress, and finished goods. To provide accurate purchase and production orders, the MRP system must know the purchasing lead times for all incoming parts, and the assembly lead times for each assembled item on the shop floor. The system must also know the current number of each purchased part, assembled component, and finished product on the shop floor and in the warehouse. This information can be particularly problematic, since as suppliers are replaced, as product designs change, as shrinkage occurs, and as items move into and out of the warehouse and production facility, then lead times and inventory levels change. If these changes are not updated in the MRP system as soon as they occur, then the MRP becomes subject to the garbage-in–garbage-out rule. In many companies this is an ongoing problem, causing periods when the MRP system must be shut down and information updated.

Bill of Materials

For each end-product on the MPS, a **bill of materials** (BOM) exists. Simply put, the BOM is a *recipe* for that product. It indicates all of the raw materials, parts, and assemblies required to manufacture the product. It also indicates how many of each part are required, the parts that go into each assembly, and the order of assembly. The simplest form a BOM can take is the **product structure diagram**, shown in Figure 11.3.

The MRP then breaks down or *explodes* the BOM, determining the parts and processing required at each level of the BOM. The requirements for the Level 0 item (the finished product) are determined first, by subtracting the current inventory on hand of the finished product from production required by the MPS. The Level 1 item requirements are determined next in the same fashion, and this progresses until all of the item levels are completed. For instance, when viewing Figure 11.3, it can be seen that for a net requirement of 50 tables, the company must make 50 top assemblies and 100 skirt assemblies, and it must purchase 200 legs. (The "4" in parentheses under "legs" signifies that 4 legs are required for *each* table; similarly, 2 skirt assemblies are required for *each* table, and 2 corner brackets are required for *each* skirt assembly, for a total of 4 corner brackets for each table.)

The BOM, along with item lead-time information, can be used to determine the minimum lead time or frozen time fence for a product, as discussed earlier. The lead times for all of the items in the BOM in Figure 11.3 are shown. Using a time line and a bottom-up

frozen time fence Time period wherein no changes are allowed to the weekly production schedule. This time period is at least as long as the lead time required to purchase parts and assemble the finished product.

rolling production schedule Each week, the MPS extends its frozen weekly production schedule for the set frozen time period, and projects a working schedule for the remaining portion of the year.

bill of materials The BOM is a *recipe* for that product. It indicates all of the raw materials, parts, and assemblies required to manufacture the product. It also indicates how many of each part are required, the parts that go into each assembly, and the order of assembly.

product structure diagram The simplest form a BOM can take.

Figure 11.3 Product Structure Diagram for a Table

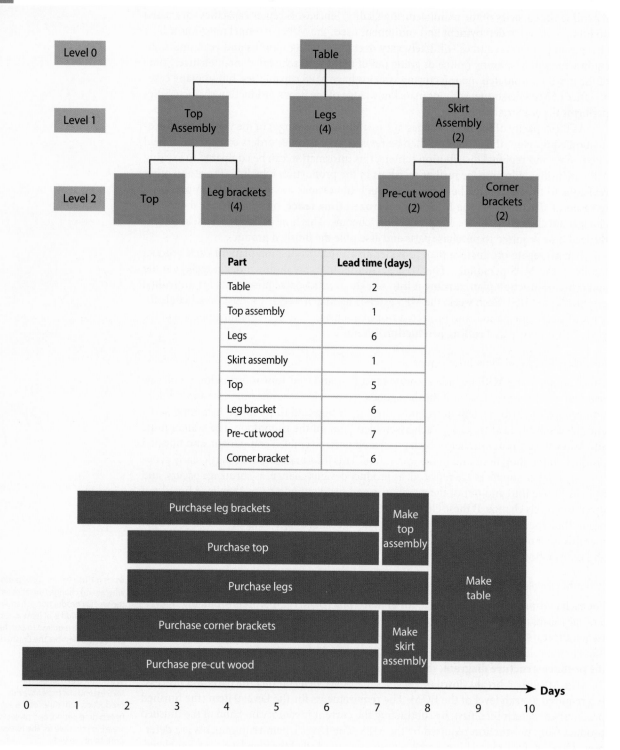

Part	Lead time (days)
Table	2
Top assembly	1
Legs	6
Skirt assembly	1
Top	5
Leg bracket	6
Pre-cut wood	7
Corner bracket	6

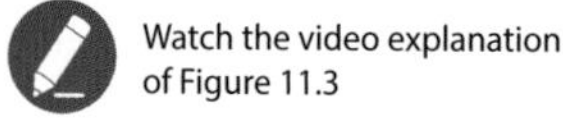
Watch the video explanation of Figure 11.3

approach, it can be seen that it will take eight days to finish a skirt assembly: the precut wood is purchased at time 0, and the corner brackets are purchased at time 1; both pars are available at time 7, and it takes one more period to finish the skirt assembly. The top assembly can also be finished in the same eight days. At time 2, the legs can be purchased. The final table assembly will take two additional days, for a total purchase and production lead time of ten days. The frozen time fence for this table should then be at least ten days, and possibly longer if the purchase order and production lead times are subject to any variabilities. Note that purchases are delayed as long as possible to minimize inventory carrying costs. Increases in the MPS within this frozen time period would require expediting, and cost the firm additional money.

MRP Outputs

The outputs of the MRP consist of the purchase orders, production orders, and workcenter capacity feedback information, which are sent to MPS personnel in the form of missed due dates, changes to process capacities, and other information impacting the production facility's ability to make product. The purchase orders and production orders are read directly from the MRP's *planned order release* computations for each item in the BOM. These computations determine the feasibility of the MPS. Computing the planned order releases for each item in the BOM follows.

The MRP Part Records

Each item in the BOM must be associated with a *part record*, as shown in Table 11.1. Since eight items appear in the table BOM shown in Figure 11.3, then eight part records must be created in the MRP system for this product. Table 11.1 shows the calculations of the planned order releases for the eight parts, including the finished table. Note that each part record contains 10 days—the frozen time period. The rule to remember when following the generation of numbers in the part records of Table 11.1 is:

> The planned order releases of the assembled part (also called the "parent item") determine the gross requirements of the constituent parts (the "children items").

The Level 0 Part Record

The first part record completed must always be the Level 0 item, or finished product (in this case, a table). The gross requirements entries for the Level 0 item are the MPS quantities for the frozen time period. Any current or starting inventories are shown in the space prior to period 1, in the projected on-hand inventory row. If production orders are already in progress, then their scheduled deliveries are shown in the scheduled receipts row (in this case, 10 units are shown as scheduled receipts for day 1). The end-of-period projected on-hand inventory can be calculated as the sum of the previous period's ending inventory, the scheduled receipts for the current period, and any completed planned order releases, minus the gross requirements for the current period. For period 1, the projected on-hand inventory would then be 30 + 10 – 10 = 30 tables. For period 3, the projected on-hand inventory is initially projected to be 20 – 20 = 0 tables. However, since the safety stock requirement (or SS) is 15 tables, the net requirement is 15. The required lot size, though, is 10, meaning that only multiples of 10 tables can be made.

Thus, in period 1, a planned order release for 20 tables is created, which will be completed by period 3 (the lead time, or LT, is stated as 2 days). In period 3, the updated projected on-hand inventory is then 20 tables. In the current period (period 1), none of these 20 tables is already in progress; thus, the order is not shown as a scheduled receipt in period 3. In similar fashion, planned order releases are also generated in periods 3, 6, 7, and 8.

The Skirt Assembly Part Record—Level 1

Once the planned order releases of the table have been calculated, the gross requirements for the skirt assembly (as well as the other two Level 1 items) can be determined. Since two skirt assemblies are required for each table (shown on the BOM), the gross requirements for skirt assemblies are twice that of the planned order releases for tables (recall the parent–child rule mentioned earlier). The projected on-hand inventories are then determined, and when this number falls below zero (in this case, no safety stock is required) a planned order release must be generated. For skirt assemblies, the lot size is lot-for-lot (LFL), meaning that just enough to maintain zero inventories is assembled whenever an order is placed. Planned order releases are generated in periods 2, 5, 6, and 7.

Table 11.1 MRP Part Records for the Table in Figure 11.3

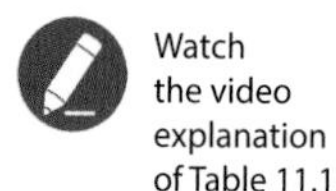

Watch the video explanation of Table 11.1

Table – Level 0		1	2	3	4	5	6	7	8	9	10
Gross Requirements		10	10	20	0	20	0	0	20	10	15
Scheduled Receipts		10									
Projected On-Hand Inventory	30	30	20	20	20	20	20	20	20	20	15
Net Requirements				15		15			15	5	10
Planned Order Releases		20		20			20	10	10		

Q = 10; LT = 2; SS = 15

x2 x2 x2 x2 x2

Skirt Assembly – Level 1		1	2	3	4	5	6	7	8	9	10
Gross Requirements		40	0	40	0	0	40	20	20	0	0
Scheduled Receipts		20									
Projected On-Hand Inventory	25	5	5	0	0	0	0	0	0	0	0
Net Requirements				35			40	20	20		
Planned Order Releases			35			40	20	20			

Q = LFL; LT = 1; SS = 0

x2 x2 x2 x2

Corner Bracket – Level 2		1	2	3	4	5	6	7	8	9	10
Gross Requirements		0	70	0	0	80	40	40	0	0	0
Scheduled Receipts				60	60						
Projected On-Hand Inventory	90	90	20	80	140	60	20	10	10	10	10
Net Requirements								30			
Planned Order Releases		30									

Q = 30; LT = 6; SS = 10

x2 x2 x2 x2

Pre-cut Wood – Level 2		1	2	3	4	5	6	7	8	9	10
Gross Requirements		0	70	0	0	80	40	40	0	0	0
Scheduled Receipts					150	50					
Projected On-Hand Inventory	92	92	22	22	172	142	102	62	62	62	62
Net Requirements											
Planned Order Releases											

Q = 50; LT = 7; SS = 20

x4 x4 x4 x4 x4

Legs – Level 1		1	2	3	4	5	6	7	8	9	10
Gross Requirements		80	0	80	0	0	80	40	40	0	0
Scheduled Receipts											
Projected On-Hand Inventory	300	220	220	140	140	140	60	120	80	0	0
Net Requirements								20			
Planned Order Releases		100									

Q = 100; LT = 6; SS = 40

Table – Level 0		1	2	3	4	5	6	7	8	9	10
Gross Requirements		10	10	20	0	20	0	0	20	10	15
Scheduled Receipts		10									
Projected On-Hand Inventory	30	30	20	20	20	20	20	20	20	20	15
Net Requirements				15		15			15	5	10
Planned Order Releases		20		20			20	10	10		

Q = 10; LT = 2; SS = 15

×1 ×1 ×1 x1 x1

Top Assembly – Level 1		1	2	3	4	5	6	7	8	9	10
Gross Requirements		20	0	20	0	0	20	10	10	0	0
Scheduled Receipts		10									
Projected On-Hand Inventory	10	0	0	0	0	0	0	0	0	0	0
Net Requirements				20			20	10	10		
Planned Order Releases			20			20	10	10			

Q = LFL; LT = 1; SS = 0

x4 x4 x4 x4

Leg Bracket – Level 2		1	2	3	4	5	6	7	8	9	10
Gross Requirements		0	80	0	0	80	40	40	0	0	0
Scheduled Receipts				50	50	50					
Projected On-Hand Inventory	100	100	20	70	120	90	50	60	60	60	60
Net Requirements								10			
Planned Order Releases		50									

Q = 50; LT = 6; SS = 20

x1 x1 x1 x1

Top – Level 2		1	2	3	4	5	6	7	8	9	10
Gross Requirements		0	20	0	0	20	10	10	0	0	0
Scheduled Receipts					30						
Projected On-Hand Inventory	30	30	10	10	40	20	10	40	40	40	40
Net Requirements								10			
Planned Order Releases			40								

Q = 40; LT = 5; SS = 10

The Corner Bracket and Pre-cut Wood Part Records—Level 2

Note from the BOM that two of each of these parts is needed to make the skirt assembly. Consequently, each planned order release for the skirt assembly is multiplied by 2, to determine the gross requirements for both of these parts. After completing the part records, it is found that a planned order release for corner brackets is needed in period 1 (this is a purchase order), and no planned order releases are need for precut wood.

The Leg Part Record—Level 1

The BOM states that four legs are required to assemble each table. Thus, each planned order release for tables is multiplied by 4 to determine the gross requirements for legs. When the part record is complete, it is found that a net requirement of 20 exists in period 7, requiring a planned order release of 100 in period 1 (note that a safety stock of 40 and order multiples of 100 are required for legs).

The Top Assembly Part Record—Level 1

The top assembly gross requirements are generated from the table planned order releases. To maintain the projected on-hand inventory levels at 0, four planned order releases are needed in periods 2, 5, 6, and 7.

The Leg Bracket Part Record—Level 2

Four leg brackets are required for each top assembly. Thus, the planned order releases for the top assembly are multiplied by 4 to generate the leg bracket gross requirements. To maintain the safety stock at 20 units, a net requirement of 10 units is needed in period 7. Since the lot size is 50, a planned order release of 50 is generated in period 1 (the lead time is 6 days).

The Top Part Record—Level 2

One top is required for each top assembly; thus, the top assembly planned order releases directly translate into the top gross requirements. A planned order release of 40 is generated in period 2.

The outputs of the MRP can now be seen in Table 11.1. The table assembly workcenter is told when to assemble tables, and how many are needed. The skirt assembly and top assembly workcenters are also told when and how many assemblies to make. Finally, the buyers in the firm are told when to purchase corner brackets, precut wood, legs, leg brackets, and tops, and how many to purchase.

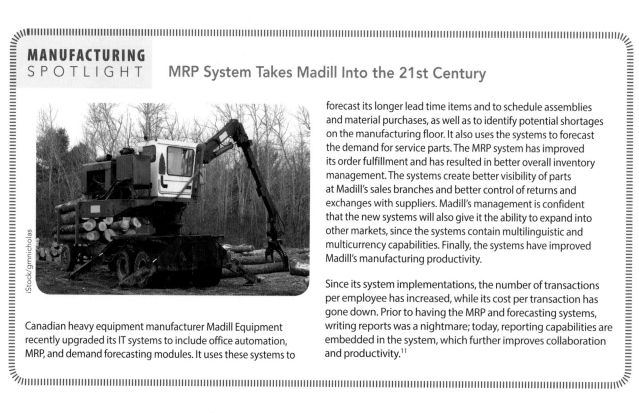

If it had turned out, for example, that more precut wood was needed in period 6, then there would not be enough remaining time to generate a purchase (the purchase lead time is 7 days). In this case, a precut wood purchase would have to be expedited and an exception report would be generated and transmitted to the MPS personnel, so that upcoming table production quantities could be revised. Alternately, a shift of production floor personnel or equipment might be made, to accommodate the additional capacity requirements. The Manufacturing Spotlight "MPR Systems Takes Madill Into the 21st Century" describes use of an MRP system at Madill, a Canadian heavy equipment manufacturer.

MANUFACTURING SPOTLIGHT

MRP System Takes Madill Into the 21st Century

iStock/gmnicholas

Canadian heavy equipment manufacturer Madill Equipment recently upgraded its IT systems to include office automation, MRP, and demand forecasting modules. It uses these systems to forecast its longer lead time items and to schedule assemblies and material purchases, as well as to identify potential shortages on the manufacturing floor. It also uses the systems to forecast the demand for service parts. The MRP system has improved its order fulfillment and has resulted in better overall inventory management. The systems create better visibility of parts at Madill's sales branches and better control of returns and exchanges with suppliers. Madill's management is confident that the new systems will also give it the ability to expand into other markets, since the systems contain multilinguistic and multicurrency capabilities. Finally, the systems have improved Madill's manufacturing productivity.

Since its system implementations, the number of transactions per employee has increased, while its cost per transaction has gone down. Prior to having the MRP and forecasting systems, writing reports was a nightmare; today, reporting capabilities are embedded in the system, which further improves collaboration and productivity.[11]

THE DISTRIBUTION REQUIREMENTS PLANNING SYSTEM

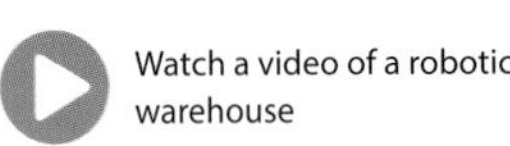
Watch a video of a robotic warehouse

The **distribution requirements planning** (DRP) **system** allows a firm's distribution centers to communicate firm orders to the MRP. As retailers and other customers order goods from a manufacturer, orders are filled from a distribution center. Eventually, the distribution center's reorder point (ROP) for each item is reached, and an order is transmitted to the factory. A planning system is needed to manage the movements of stock into and out of each of these facilities, to avoid stockouts or excess stock situations in factories and distribution centers, and to plan ahead for delivery vehicle and distribution center capacities.

According to a study by ProLogis Global Solutions, creating a network that can meet customer demands while minimizing costs is the number one challenge facing supply chain executives.[12] DRP systems at distribution centers connected to MRP systems at the factory are essentially creating customer-driven or supply chain pull-oriented systems, which is what lean systems seek to create (as discussed in Chapter 9). Today, many fully implemented enterprise resource planning (ERP) systems (discussed later in this chapter) contain MRP and DRP modules.

The *DRP record* is very similar to the MRP part record. The demand profile at each distribution center is translated into a demand forecast for each period, and this replaces the gross requirements used in the MRP. The forecasted requirements are subtracted from the distribution center's on-hand inventories and planned receipts. Net requirements are generated as safety stock levels are reached, and based on the delivery lead times, planned shipping quantities are generated (similar to the planned order releases in the MRP). The planned shipping quantities for all of the firm's distribution centers are then aggregated into one set of time-phased requirements for the manufacturing facility. A DRP record is shown in Table 11.2.

The DRP planned shipping quantities are very important sources of information for the manufacturing facility. The MPS scheduling function can use the information to adjust future MPS quantities to better meet actual demand. It also allows the firm's top planners to compare the information used in preparing the aggregate production plan to the various marketplace demand characteristics throughout the year, as well as to indicate the firm's ability to satisfy demand. And finally, when inventories are in short supply due to unforeseen changes in overall demand, material availability, or manufacturing capacity, the DRP can be used to inform warehouses when shipments will be arriving, and for allocating units among the firm's distribution centers.

distribution requirements planning system Allows a firm's distribution centers to communicate firm orders to the MRP. As retailers and other customers order goods from a manufacturer, orders are filled from a distribution center. Eventually, the distribution center's reorder point (ROP) for each item is reached, and an order is transmitted to the factory. The DRP system is needed to manage the movements of stock into and out of each of these facilities.

Ideally, finished goods arrive on distributor and retailer loading docks at precisely the right time and right quantity. As with many other supply chain management strategies, Walmart is leading the way, by providing its suppliers point-of-sale (POS) data for each store, updated several times daily, to allow suppliers to adjust their shipments and manufacturing efforts based on what is actually selling and where.

Table 11.2 Distribution Center DRP Record

Distribution Center No. 6											
Product: Table		1	2	3	4	5	6	7	8	9	10
Forecast Requirements		2	4	3	6	5	4	8	0	3	5
Shipments In-Transit			30								
Projected On-Hand Inventory	6	4	30	27	21	16	12	4	4	31	26
Net Requirements										2	
Planned Shipments								30			

Q = 30; LT = 2; SS = 3

Projected order to be communicated to the factory MRP system

THE MANUFACTURING RESOURCE PLANNING SYSTEM

Once MRP and DRP systems became operational and users saw the benefits of this information for planning, purchasing, and manufacturing control purposes, a desire by personnel in various functional areas of the firm was created beginning in the 1980s, to use the MRP as a planning tool on a much larger scale. The initial expansion of the MRP was for capacity requirements planning purposes. If cost information could be attached to each of the BOMs, then the projected financial requirements to achieve the aggregate production plan could be determined. Marketing personnel might use the MRP system to determine the manufacturing requirements for a planned promotional campaign. Human resource personnel could use the MRP system to generate the projected labor requirements for the firm's short- and long-term expansion plans. Shop floor managers could use the MRP system for overtime planning and worker scheduling purposes. Manufacturing engineers could use the system to help plan facility expansions. The desire to perform these look-ahead activities or use what-if scenarios for planning purposes was the impetus for the development of the **manufacturing resource planning (MRP II) system**.

Today, most MRP II systems have a simulation capability to allow managers to perform what-if analyses and gain an understanding of likely outcomes when capacity or production timing decisions are made. Other software modules are also included with MRP II systems, enabling various functional area personnel to interact with the MRP II system using a central database. Production, marketing, human resource, and finance personnel would then work together to develop a feasible aggregate plan based on available funds, equipment, advertising plans, and labor. In this way, all functional areas have a vested interest in achieving the aggregate plan. Starting in the early 1990s in the United States, and continuing today, many MRP II systems were integrated into system-wide ERP applications. However, the functionality of MRP II systems remains, whether it is a stand-alone system or part of a larger ERP system.

manufacturing resource planning (MRP II) system Today, most MRP II systems have a simulation capability to allow managers to perform what-if analyses and gain an understanding of likely outcomes when capacity or production timing decisions are made. Other software modules are also included with MRP II systems, enabling various functional area personnel to interact with the MRP II system using a central database. Production, marketing, human resource, and finance personnel would then work together to develop a feasible aggregate plan based on available funds, equipment, advertising plans, and labor.

The Capacity Requirements Planning Function

One of the most important features of the MRP II is the **capacity requirements planning** capability. Given MPS quantities, the planned order releases from the MRP, the current shop workload, part routing information, and processing and purchasing lead times, the short-range capacity requirements can be developed for the entire production facility. Initially, the MPS may be found to be infeasible given the shop's current workload and the capacity of each workcenter. If this is the case, the choices are either to increase capacity or reduce or delay the MPS. The MRP II system generates **load reports** for each workcenter for a series of time periods. These load reports compare the required capacity for the given MPS with the projected available capacity. Given this information, production managers can determine if workloads need to be shifted to later periods, overtime needs to be scheduled, or work needs to be contracted out. Ultimately, a feasible production schedule and capacity plan is decided upon.

capacity requirements planning Given MPS quantities, the planned order releases from the MRP, the current shop workload, part routing information, and processing and purchasing lead times, the short-range capacity requirements can be developed for the entire production facility. Initially, the MPS may be found to be infeasible given the shop's current workload and the capacity of each workcenter. If this is the case, the choices are either to increase capacity or reduce or delay the MPS.

load reports Compare the required capacity for the given MPS with the projected available capacity. Given this information, production managers can determine if workloads need to be shifted to later periods, overtime needs to be scheduled, or work needs to be contracted out.

As the actual work begins, reports generated by the MRP II system aid in monitoring the progress of work and allow managers to adjust capacities to keep the flow of work on schedule. However, even when a feasible schedule is indicated by the load reports, variabilities in processing times and parts deliveries can still cause production system delays and bottlenecks, requiring further capacity adjustments or expediting, or simply resulting in some late production orders. The capacity requirements planning capability also allows firms to assure timely planned deliveries to key customers.

Extension of MRP II

MRP II systems have found applications in large-scale services that require complex scheduling of materials and workers, and have a need to perform analyses of market alternatives, for example. Large resort/hotel complexes are one such example. MRP II systems can be used for tracking food supplies at a number of the resort's restaurants, for growth and hiring plans, and to analyze the impact a large concert or convention would have on the resort's hotel rooms, restaurants, and other amenities. Foxwoods Resort and Casino in Connecticut has 29 food and beverage outlets, 11 casino service outlets, 5 restaurant service outlets, 5 casino lounges, and 5 production kitchens requiring 3,700 food and beverage items, in its sprawling 4.7 million square foot facility. At one time, the foodservice processes were all controlled manually, which negatively impacted productivity, speed, consistency, and accuracy. In January 2005, Foxwoods went live with an automated food and beverage inventory and recipe control process to better manage its foodservice operations. Its system collects POS data and feeds it to its ERP system, which generates purchase orders, monitors inventories, executes requisitions and transfers, manages production, maintains recipes, and provides food costing analyses.[13]

THE EVOLUTION AND USE OF ENTERPRISE RESOURCE PLANNING SYSTEMS

11.3 Describe the historical developments and current use of ERP systems

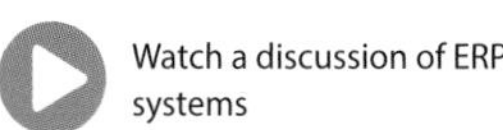

Having information available in real time can reduce uncertainties and lead times, and improve material and product tracking as well. Unfortunately, information is not always easily accessible or reliable, and can become extremely complicated as the number of production facilities, products, parts, suppliers, distribution centers, customers, and interactions increases. Added to these problems is the existence of arms-length trading relationships and a general lack of trust in many supply chains, and even within a single organization, making the idea of information sharing and process integration somewhat unrealistic. Today, organizations are realizing that information sharing among departments and extending to trading partners is ultimately beneficial to end-consumers, and thus to the supply chain constituents.

Along with this realization has been the growth of MRP II systems, which allowed functional area personnel to interact with the system, obtain real-time information, and perform what-if analyses using a shared database within the corporate unit. While still in

Figure 11.4 The Enterprise Resource Planning (ERP) System

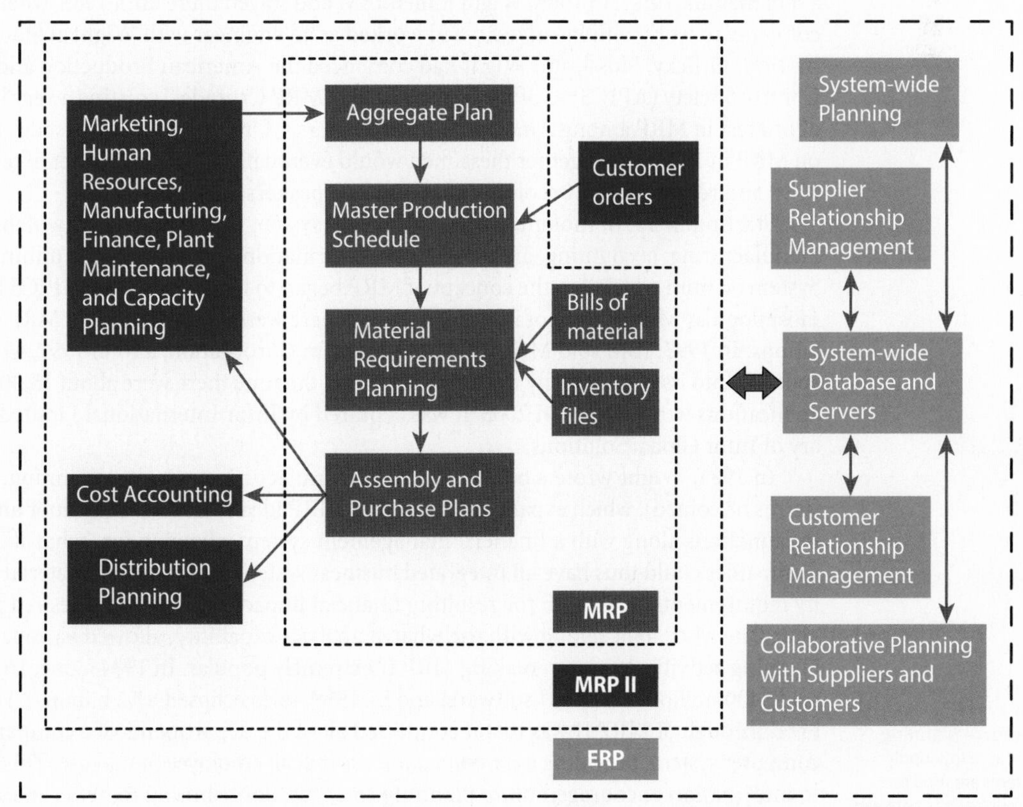

widespread use across the globe, many of these MRP II applications are evolving today into corporate-wide **enterprise resource planning (ERP) systems**. In many supply chains, ERP systems are used to automate communications between suppliers and buyers. The umbrella term *enterprise resource planning* was actually coined in a 1990 report by Gartner, Inc., a provider of research, analysis, and consultancy services for the global information technology industry. Deloitte Consulting, though, provided one of the more comprehensive definitions of ERP in a 1999 news story:

> ERP is a packaged business software system that lets a company automate and integrate the majority of its business processes, share common data and practices across the enterprise, and produce and access information in a real time environment.[14]

Figure 11.4 illustrates the ERP system, showing how each of the older planning system approaches fit in with the ERP. The following section describes the historical developments of these systems.

NOTABLE HISTORICAL DEVELOPMENTS LEADING UP TO ERP

While there were several MRP-type systems in use dating from the early 1960s, computing power at that time was such that these systems were extremely basic. As mentioned earlier, the first MRP applications were run on the IBM 305 and IBM 650 RAMAC (Random Access Method of Accounting and Control) system, and could do only the most basic net change material requirement calculations. In 1961, at the J. I. Case tractor manufacturing facility in Racine, WI, IBM employees Ted Musial and Gene Thomas, Case employees Joe Orlicky and A. R. Brani, along with other IBM and Case employees, designed and installed the first continuous net change MRP system, using the IBM 305 and 650 RAMAC.[15]

The people perhaps most responsible for developing and advancing the concepts of MRP were Joe Orlicky, George Plossl, and Oliver Wight. Orlicky left Case and moved to IBM in 1962. He later met Wight, who was working at the Connecticut-based Stanley Works, a tool manufacturer. In 1965, Wight joined IBM and stayed there until 1968, when he left the company to work with Plossl, who had worked as an engineer with Wight at Stanley Works. By 1971, Orlicky, Plossl, and Wight had convinced the American Production and Inventory Control Society (APICS) to officially launch the "MRP Crusade," creating a very high degree of interest in MRP among American manufacturers.[16] Orlicky wrote the first definitive book on MRP in 1975, and together these men would eventually author a number of textbooks on MRP and related topics, becoming sought-after speakers and consultants.[17]

Starting in 1978, though, with IBM's MRP system called MAPICS (which stands for manufacturing, accounting, and production information control system) running on IBM's System 36 mini computer, the concept of MRP began to really take off. MAPICS became the most popular MRP system of its time. By 1981, there were a reported 8,000 MRP implementations. In 1993, IBM sold MAPICS to the Marcam Corporation, and in 1997, MAPICS was spun off into its own publicly traded company; at the time there were about 15,000 MAPICS applications worldwide.[18] In 2005, it was acquired by Infor International Limited, a subsidiary of Infor Global Solutions.

In 1981, Wight wrote a book describing manufacturing resource planning, or MRP II (terms he coined), which expanded the original MRP idea to include shop floor and accounting functions along with a financial management system, allowing for "what-if" analyses.[19] Companies could thus have an integrated business system that provided material and capacity requirements along with the resulting financial impact, when given a desired production plan. The MRP logic, along with the what-if analysis capability, allowed various functional planning activities to occur, making MRP II extremely popular. In 1984 alone, 16 companies sold $400 million in MRP II software, and by 1989, sales eclipsed $1.2 billion.[20] The primary breakthrough of MRP II was that it connected all of the departments of a company into one computer system, providing a *common database* that all employees could use. This easy access to information encouraged more planning to occur, contributing to better manufacturing control and investment decisions. The weakness of MRP II was that it linked departments

enterprise resource planning (ERP) systems In many supply chains, ERP systems are used to automate communications between suppliers and buyers.

within one unit; it lacked the capability to link the operations of an organization's foreign units with its domestic units. Additionally, MRP II could not interface with a firm's suppliers or customers. For these reasons, enterprise-wide applications began to be developed.

In 1972, five former IBM systems analysts founded SAP (Systemanalyse und Programmentwicklung, or Systems Analysis and Program Development), in Mannheim, Germany. Their vision was to develop software that enabled users to process data interactively in real time, using a computer screen as the focal point of data processing. Their first product was financial accounting software in 1973, which later came to be known as the R/1 System ("R" stands for real-time data processing). In 1979, SAP released its R/2 System for mainframes, and in 1992 it introduced its R/3 client-server software system. SAP continued to add packages to its system over the years, including materials management, asset accounting, cost accounting, personnel management, plant maintenance, and production planning and control applications. By 1993, SAP had a global customer base of 3,500 companies; had 15 global subsidiary companies; and was selling software in 14 different languages. By 2005, some 12 million users were working each day with over 25 SAP business software applications in 120 countries. Today, SAP is the world's fourth-largest software maker and the largest ERP software provider, with about 25% of the global ERP market.[21] SAP's largest competitor, Oracle, has been very busy acquiring the competition. It has spent many billions of dollars buying out more than a dozen companies, including PeopleSoft, JD Edwards, Siebel Systems, Retek, and Profit Logic. The ERP market is today growing at about 7% per year, with worldwide annual sales by 2020 expected to eclipse $41 billion.[22]

Today, SAP and Oracle account for about 36% of the ERP software market.

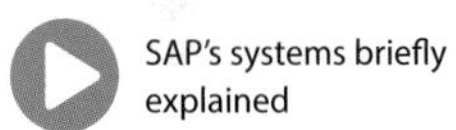
SAP's systems briefly explained

Thus, during the 1990s as computer speed and technologies advanced, ERP systems were developed as bundled suites of applications that could be run on client-servers, allowing greater scalability, support for more concurrent users, and lower-cost hardware. Many of these systems today still use the original MRP-based net requirements and order release capabilities, along with the planning capabilities of the MRP II systems, which is why Figure 11.4 shows ERP to be encompassing both of these earlier systems. In many companies with extensive existing or **legacy systems**, ERP vendors will connect these applications as well as provide other custom applications, allowing the ERP system to become a central information repository and a data distribution facility for all departments and far-flung units in an organization.

As the move toward lower inventories, shorter lead times, and lean manufacturing continues, ERP systems are focusing more on providing real-time information visibility across all of the organization's global business units and ultimately among trading partners, tracking various performance metrics, and facilitating collaboration through customer relationship management, supplier relationship management, and quality management software applications.

Actually, the idea of integrating processes with supply chain trading partners in real time, using ERP system applications such as supplier relationship management, warehouse management, transportation management, and customer relationship management modules, was the topic of a 2000 report by Gartner (recall it coined the original ERP term), wherein it sought to create the next label for planning systems: "ERP II." On the other hand, AMR Research favors the new labels "enterprise commerce management" or "ECM."[23] Whatever the moniker employed, the concept of real-time integration of outward-facing applications such as CRM and SRM into internally focused or back-office ERP applications is the vision that many companies as well as software providers are adopting and promoting today. The result is that companies must face the reality that their original ERP investments are going to require further investments in "add-ons," or other applications, to make real-time supply chain information sharing and collaboration occur. (Add-on applications are discussed later in this chapter.) This also means that most enterprise systems are, or soon will be, considered **best-of-breed systems**, with applications purchased from multiple vendors over time. Consequently, application compatibility has become a big concern for many ERP system owners.

legacy systems Extensive, earlier-existing information systems.

best-of-breed systems Applications purchased from multiple vendors over time.

SERVICE SPOTLIGHT

Service Shop Implements Cloud ERP

Australia-based Headland Machinery recently found it needed a solution for its project management problems. As the business expanded, Headland's management team found it increasingly difficult to assign and manage projects to its growing service workforce. At one point Headland was using three systems simultaneously in order to gain organizational efficiencies. With a service team of field engineers, and office staff who all required access to the database, Headland was finding it difficult to manage customer data, schedule service calls, automate maintenance, or streamline billing. The situation was reducing productivity and creating miscommunications.

iStock/coffeeyu

In 2011, Headland implemented NetSuite's cloud ERP system for its Australian operations and its foreign sister company, Aotea Machinery. The ERP solution provided a single, comprehensive, real-time view of its projects. Its system handles Headland's scheduling of maintenance and repair work, project installations, and breakdown support, with greater accuracy, faster response, and better problem resolution.

The system manages all account services through a single dashboard view via the Internet, with all backups, upgrades, and installations completed automatically. Mobile integration allows access via smartphone, tablet, and laptop, so field users can accept jobs, invoice from the field, and log travel times. Workforce automation capabilities create more efficient planning, scheduling, and administration for a streamlined work flow.[24]

CLOUD-BASED ERP SYSTEMS

Traditional ERP systems are installed and maintained on location, and in large multinational companies this is still predominantly the case. For small- to medium-sized organizations, though, with only a small number of users and only a few IT personnel, **cloud-based ERP systems** are preferred. Cloud ERP, also referred to as an SaaS or a software-as-a-service system, is delivered purely through a Web browser via an Internet connection. In the cloud ERP model, the software supplier houses and manages the software, and user companies pay a subscription fee per user for the software—typically on a monthly basis. Employees can thus remotely access their business data through any device with online capabilities. Cloud ERP systems remove the need for businesses to own and maintain the software and data on their own computers. Security can also be much better with cloud systems. Most of the largest providers offer rigorous security, disaster recovery, and backup procedures that are cost-prohibitive for many on-site ERP systems. Several of the best-selling systems are from NetSuite, Sage, Microsoft Dynamics, SAP, and Oracle. The Service Spotlight above describes Headland Machinery's use of a cloud ERP.

The cost of ERP systems has come down substantially in recent years with the development of cloud-based systems, greater levels of competition, and cheaper hardware, but it can still be expensive. A moderately sized company with 50 concurrent users might pay about $500,000 in licensing and maintenance fees, consulting and customization costs, and equipment upgrade and personnel costs. Annual upgrade and customization costs can run another 20% per year.[25] A similar sized, cloud-based system might cost $100,000 per year in user fees, so as the company grows, the purchased system starts to look better. For small companies, though, with a few users, a cloud-based system might cost several thousand dollars in upfront cost, and a few hundred to a few thousand dollars per month.[26]

cloud-based ERP systems Also referred to as an SaaS or a software-as-a-service system; is delivered purely through a Web browser via an Internet connection. In the cloud ERP model, the software supplier houses and manages the software, and user companies pay a subscription fee per user for the software—typically on a monthly basis.

THE BENEFITS AND SHORTCOMINGS OF ERP SYSTEMS

The shortcomings of ERP systems can be seen in Table 11.3. For many companies leading up to the end of 1999, ERP implementation was seen as a solution to the Y2K issues that were thought to exist on many information systems at the time. This urgency to beat the Y2K deadline resulted in implementations that were less than ideal, leaving companies and their untrained employees unprepared to properly utilize the various ERP applications purchased. Consequently, many did not realize the full potential of these systems, and at the time, the systems themselves were blamed for many of the problems. This lack of preparedness also led to a second wave of implementations later, in an attempt to more fully optimize the original (and expensive) ERP investments.

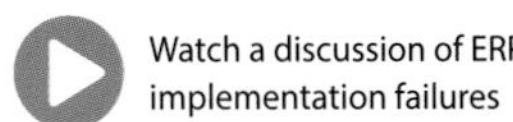
Watch a discussion of ERP implementation failures

A number of high-profile ERP failures have been noted over the past 20 years. In fact, in a study of 64 Fortune 500 companies, 25% responded that they suffered from a drop in performance when their ERP systems went live.[27] In another study that tracked ERP implementations since 1994, more than half exceeded their budgets and did not meet time lines, and nearly one-third had been completely abandoned in progress.[28] Examples include Hershey Foods. After spending $112 million to install ERP modules supplied by SAP, Manugistics, and Siebel, Hershey decided to "go live" with all three systems at once, just prior to the busy 1999 Halloween season, a full 18 months earlier than the original plan. Consequently, Hershey was unable to effectively fill orders for both the Halloween and Christmas seasons that year due to system failures, resulting in a 12% decline in 1999 revenues.[29]

In the fall of 1999, Whirlpool also blamed lengthy shipping delays on difficulties associated with its new ERP implementation. Most experts agree, though, that failures are the result of poor training. "Very rarely are there instances when it's the ERP system itself—the actual software—that fails," says Jim Shepherd, of Boston-based AMR Research. "Blaming the failure on a system implementation has become a convenient excuse for companies that have missed their quarter-end [earnings] target."[30]

With ERP systems, customer service representatives can become far more active with customers. When customers make an inquiry, then customer credit ratings, purchase and return histories, and letters received and sent can be quickly retrieved. What resources should be assigned to this inquiry? Will the customer likely pay on time? Can we interest them in other products? Can orders be filled and shipped as requested? These are questions that customer service personnel must deal with every day while using an ERP system, and they can affect customer lifetime purchases as well as the firm's reputation.

Warehouse workers who used to track inventory levels on scraps of paper must instead put accurate inventory levels into the ERP system and keep them updated *all the time*. If they fail to do this, the customer service reps may see erroneously low inventory levels in the system and tell customers the product they want is stocked out. Responsibility, information visibility, communication ease, and adequate system training are all necessary when organizations implement ERP.[31]

As alluded to earlier, the implementation requirements for on-site ERP systems can be difficult. ERP's shared database becomes the one source of "truth" for the organization. No longer will the finance department have one set of numbers while purchasing, sales, and marketing have others; and all revenue contributions for the various business units will immediately be known to everyone, since all are using the same system. During the implementation period, which can last up to two years, firms often discover that one or more of their important processes is not supported by the ERP software. At this point, either the firm must change to accommodate the software (which may mean substantial changes to the culture of the firm, its mission, its processes, and/or its people), or the firm must modify the software to fit the processes, which slows down the implementation process considerably, adds customization and training costs to the total ERP bill, makes future upgrades more difficult, and may introduce bugs into the system.

While there is certainly no shortage of "hype" from ERP suppliers concerning the expected benefits from ERP implementations, a number of benefits have been identified by a majority of ERP users, and these are listed in

Table 11.3 ERP Shortcomings

- Large initial and add-on expense
- Significant training expense
- Inventory records must be accurate, continuously updated, and communicated to users
- Long implementation periods
- Processes must change to accommodate software
- Software customizations might be required

Table 11.4 ERP Benefits[32]

- Improved decision making
- Improved financial management
- Improved customer service and retention
- Faster, more accurate transactions
- Staffing reduction
- Cycle time reduction
- Improved inventory/asset management
- Reduced logistics cost
- Improved warehouse management
- Enhanced demand forecasting
- Deployment speed (cloud)
- Ease of expansion/upgrades/flexibility (cloud)
- Reduced cost (cloud)

Table 11.4. Some of these are associated with cloud systems. A number of these benefits occur at various time periods during the post-implementation phase.

Directly after implementation and for a period of perhaps one year, companies familiarize themselves with the ERP system and the process changes that have occurred. This can be referred to as the **stabilize phase**, and it is during this time that many users may develop the opinion that the ERP system was a failure because initial expectations have not yet materialized. For approximately the next two years (the **synthesize phase**), companies seek organizational improvements by improving processes, adding complementary software applications, mastering the ERP system, and gaining additional support for the system. After three years, the ERP system along with its users have reached a level of maturity where system optimization is most likely to occur, also termed the **synergize phase.**[33] One final note regarding ERP systems and benefits is worthy of mention here: Poorly managed organizations with many deeply rooted problems are unlikely to suddenly rise to the occasion after implementing an ERP system. Long-term firm success lies more in the collective knowledge and experience of the employees than in the information systems used by the firm.

As with the notable failures described briefly in this section, there have certainly been many notable ERP system successes. The Colgate-Palmolive Company, a multibillion-dollar global consumer products corporation, implemented SAP's R/3 system in 1993 and eventually was able to reduce finished inventory levels by 50% and cut order receipt-to-delivery time for its top 50 customers from 12 to 5 days.[34] In 2000, Marathon Oil Corp., a multibillion-dollar integrated energy company headquartered in Houston, TX, wanted to fold its major business processes into one central information system, so it chose SAP to provide its core ERP system. Heeding the warnings from the many high-profile failures at the time, Marathon was able to successfully go live with a global implementation of eight enterprise application modules in a record 13 months. A few years later, the Marathon ERP implementation team offered several lessons they learned from their implementation process:[35]

- Plan the work and work the plan. Use sound project management techniques.
- It is all about the people. Make sure they are fully involved throughout the entire project.
- Support has to include the CEO's sponsorship and visible involvement.
- Make change management an integral discipline in the project.
- Do not give in to the lure of tweaking this and that. Minimize the customization of code. It will only add time and cost.
- Transfer the full spectrum of ownership. Make sure the users have the knowledge to use the new tools, the responsibility to make them work right, and the vision to capitalize quickly on new capabilities.

stabilize phase Directly after ERP implementation, and for a period of perhaps one year, companies familiarize themselves with the system and the process changes that have occurred.

synthesize phase One year after implementing ERP, companies seek organizational improvements by improving processes, adding complementary software applications, mastering the ERP system, and gaining additional support for the system.

synergize phase Three years after implementing ERP, the system along with its users have reached a level of maturity where system optimization is most likely to occur.

application add-ons ERP system customizations.

ADDING APPLICATIONS TO THE ERP

To reduce implementation and familiarization time, organizations today are quite likely to start small, investing in a basic ERP system to combine with or replace an existing MRP, MRP II, or some other legacy system. Later, as users gain familiarity with the capabilities of the system, customizations are desired in the form of **application add-ons**, listed in Table 11.5.

Additionally, as products, markets, and the competition change, businesses look for modules to serve these changing needs, and vendors today are likely to have a suitable and compatible application to sell them. For instance, after the global conglomerate Colgate-Palmolive Co. implemented its ERP system, it later added a vendor managed inventory application, and then also implemented supply network planning modules in all of its manufacturing and distribution facilities. Finally, it added production planning,

Table 11.5 ERP Application Add-Ons

Application Add-On	Description
Financial Management Module	Includes general ledger, accounts receivable/payable, fixed assets, cash management, financial statement preparation, cost control, and budgeting applications.
Production Management Module	Communicates the manufacturing plan from the ERP to the shop floor. It also sends actual production data from the shop floor back to the ERP.
Logistics Management Module	A family of logistics-oriented software applications including transportation management systems, warehouse management systems, and returns management systems.

scheduling, and demand planning modules and integrated them with its warehouse management software.[36]

ERP suppliers want their products to become the foundations of firms' planning system infrastructures, by making the ERP system a central information repository, with the ability to connect legacy applications, other business systems, and future add-on applications in the areas of production and distribution, finance, sales and marketing, human resources, and other industry-specific applications. "The packaged application gives you a starting point," says Larry Ferrere, VP of marketing at Vastera Inc., an ERP application supplier. "There's no need to reinvent the wheel," he says. "Users can focus on coding objects specific to their business processes."[37]

In most ERP systems, a number of different modules are being used including finance, marketing/sales, human resources/payroll, production, logistics, inventory/purchasing, quality control, plant maintenance, project management, banking, and decision support. The finance, production, and logistics modules are the most commonly used and are discussed in the following sections.

Financial Management Module

The financial management module is one of the more vital modules in any ERP system, incorporating applications such as general ledger, accounts receivable/payable, fixed assets, cash management, financial statement preparation, cost control, and budgeting. In many cases, ERP financial management capabilities also include activity-based costing, product life cycle costing, stock purchases, continuous internal audit capabilities, financial ratio analysis, profitability analysis, and balanced scorecards for performance monitoring purposes. Many of these systems also incorporate pattern recognition capabilities that enable the recognition of fraud. With these technologies, accountants and other finance professionals have moved from being the traditional scorekeepers to today's decision makers.

Globalization, competition, mergers and acquisitions, and outsourcing have all contributed to the need for efficiency improvements through cost reductions, process performance and quality improvements, and faster delivery times to improve customer service. Consequently, enterprises are requiring financial and other types of decisions to be made quickly and frequently. Thus, finance needs access to information in real time across all business units and departments to support rapid decision making. Additionally, the right kind of information must be collected and analyzed to avoid making ineffective organizational decisions.

The accounting scandals at companies like Enron, WorldCom, and Arthur Andersen led in part to the 2002 U.S. Sarbanes-Oxley Act (SOA), a corporate accountability law with oversight by the Securities and Exchange Commission. Thus, a host of ERP financial management modules now contain sections that address SOA compliance, drastically cutting the time required to keep up with the SOA financial rules through automation of accounting processes.[38]

Production Management Module

Also termed a **manufacturing execution system (MES) module**, this ERP system add-on has long been sought as a way to tie management planning to the manufacturing floor. Manufacturers using shop floor control systems realize the value of these automated systems in eliminating paperwork, scheduling production, and managing work-in-process inventories. The problem has been in making shop floor data accessible to ERP systems in real time. Taking orders and generating production plans at the global enterprise level cannot be accomplished effectively if the people doing these jobs can't determine, in real time, what's happening at every facility around the world. When shop floor personnel are forced to manually input manufacturing data into an ERP system, and in some cases when the MES is not adequately integrated into the ERP, shop floor data input errors can cause a whole host of planning and execution problems (the good ol' garbage-in–garbage-out problem).

MES software communicates the manufacturing plan from the ERP to the shop floor. Then, as products are manufactured, the MES sends actual production data from the shop floor back to the ERP. This feedback is necessary to ensure that the right amount of materials are being purchased, the right amount of product is being produced, and customer due dates are being met. MES applications automate the recording and transmission of data, reducing errors and the time to transfer information. Electronic records of shop floor activities are created and placed on a database for use in planning and decision making at the ERP level. "Using a standard MES will give us an IT infrastructure that promotes agility by streamlining the process of getting plans to the plant floor, as well as delivering the production information needed to make critical decisions at the corporate level," says Geir Einset, director of operations at Elcoteq, a Finland-based telecommunications manufacturer.[39]

As with any software implementation, there can be problems associated with implementation time, user training, and customization cost. But when the application must be integrated with an existing ERP system, compatibility and configuration problems must also be overcome. Another consideration is whether or not to implement an entire system-wide MES at once, or in piecemeal fashion (to reduce cost and implementation time). According to Mark Roache, associate director of IT consulting services at KMI, not fully implementing an MES can mean loss of some essential functions. "MES is one of those things in which if you complete 80 percent of what you said you were going to do, the remaining 20 percent is where all the value was," Roache says.[40]

manufacturing execution system (MES) module An ERP system add-on, ties management planning to the manufacturing floor. It communicates the manufacturing plan from the ERP to the shop floor. Then, as products are manufactured, the MES sends actual production data from the shop floor back to the ERP.

Logistics Management Module

Also termed **logistics execution suites**, these are blanket terms for a family of logistics-oriented software applications including transportation management systems, warehouse management systems, and returns management systems. Companies are finding significant benefits from integrating their basic ERP systems with logistics execution suites. These systems provide "a networked view of the world," says Tillman Estes, SAP's director of business development for supply chain execution. "It will include everyone from order routing and transportation planning and execution to event management, the consumer, and everything in-between," he adds.[41]

logistics execution suites A blanket term for a family of logistics-oriented software applications including transportation management systems, warehouse management systems, and returns management systems. Companies are finding significant benefits from integrating their basic ERP systems with logistics execution suites. These systems provide "a networked view of the world."

Transportation Management System

Transportation management system (TMS) applications allow firms, for instance, to select the best mix of transportation service and pricing, to determine the best use of containers or truck trailers, to better manage transportation contracts, to rank transportation options, to clear customs, to track product movements, and to monitor carrier performance. Rhodes International, a Utah-based frozen bread dough manufacturer, uses its TMS to build its truckload shipments, determine shipment routings, and track them once they leave its warehouses.[42] With these systems, visibility and security are very important. Shippers, governments, and customers want to know where the goods are, which means real-time information about an item's location during warehousing and delivery to the final destination is required. Consequently, information may need to be provided by the manufacturer, third-party logistics providers, agents, freight forwarders, and others as products move through global supply chains.

transportation management system Allows firms, for instance, to select the best mix of transportation service and pricing, to determine the best use of containers or truck trailers, to better manage transportation contracts, to rank transportation options, to clear customs, to track product movements, and to monitor carrier performance.

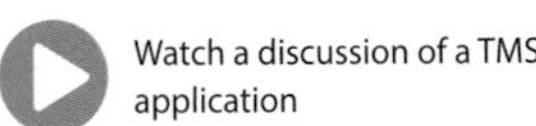
Watch a discussion of a TMS application

The desire to secure national borders against unwanted shipments has increased due to terrorist concerns, causing a number of governments to more closely regulate the flow of goods across its borders. This has added further risk of transportation delays, as companies deal with an added layer of bureaucracy and reporting at various border entry sites. Thus, many TMS software applications today have added capabilities for customs declaration, calculation and payment of tariffs, duties and duty drawbacks, and advanced filing of shipment manifests.

Warehouse Management System

When a TMS is coupled with a **warehouse management system** (WMS), supply chain effectiveness is even further enhanced. For example, a company might use its TMS to forecast throughput volumes based on data provided by the WMS and then report back the most efficient mode of shipping. The WMS could then determine warehouse item picks based on TMS shipping requirements. One result might be that one fully loaded truck instead of two partially loaded trucks would be dispatched for a delivery. Warehouse management systems track and control the flow of goods from the receiving dock of a distribution center until the item is loaded for outbound shipment to the customer. Radio frequency identification tags placed on products and pallets within the distribution center play a central role in controlling the flow of goods. The goals of a WMS include reducing distribution center labor costs, streamlining the flow of goods, reducing the time products spend in the distribution center, managing distribution center capacity, reducing paperwork, and managing the cross-docking process.

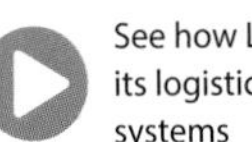
See how Lennox integrates its logistics management systems

Michigan-based furniture maker Haworth completed a $14 million rollout of its TMS and WMS in 2004, resulting in greatly reduced freight costs and greater warehouse worker efficiencies. The TMS considers customer orders, factory schedules, carrier rates and availability, and shipping costs, then produces an optimum, lowest-cost delivery plan. Plans are updated every 15 minutes, and there is an automated system that lets Haworth negotiate deliveries with its carriers. Its WMS tracks finished goods from Haworth's three distribution centers to the customer sites. Acting on shipping plans from the TMS, the WMS directs the movement of goods based on real-time data on space, equipment, inventory, and personnel.[43]

Returns Management System

Reverse logistics, discussed further in Chapter 15, is the process of returning finished products for replacement, repair, or cash, and is a necessary and costly supply chain management activity. Some studies have found that about 20% of products are returned, and that it adds approximately $1.50 in costs for every $1 of merchandise returned.[44] **Returns management systems** (RMS) are thus being created to provide global visibility, standardization, and documentation of product returns, while minimizing reverse logistics costs. In addition to managing returns, the RMS can also be designed to handle returnable assets such as pallets, platforms, and containers.

In many cases, returns capabilities are built into WMS applications. Some companies use their WMS to facilitate the returns process before the original product is even shipped. "Many direct-to-consumer companies will have the WMS create a return label when they are printing out the initial paper work," says Noah Dixon, industry strategy leader at RedPrairie, a Wisconsin-based logistics system provider. "A residential customer can then go to a shipper like FedEx, UPS, or the post office and use that label to process the return."[45] Product recalls can also be handled using the RMS in combination with the WMS. A WMS with lot and serial number tracking capability, for example, allows a company to bring back only units of product that have been identified with a particular defect.

warehouse management system Tracks and controls the flow of goods from the receiving dock of a distribution center until the item is loaded for outbound shipment to the customer.

returns management systems Systems that provide global visibility, standardization, and documentation of product returns, while minimizing reverse logistics costs. In addition to managing returns, the RMS can also be designed to handle returnable assets such as pallets, platforms, and containers.

INTEGRATING ERP WITH SUPPLY CHAIN TRADING PARTNERS

Taking the reader back now to a core idea of supply chain management—to share information, to communicate, and to collaborate on processes so that customers get what they want, when they want it, at the desired levels of quality and price—technology is enabling this to happen more effectively and efficiently than ever before. Here's a very simple example—shifting to shared enterprise applications will eliminate manual rekeying of data as information passes from one firm to the next; and this problem is very common among many trading partners today. This sort of redundant activity is one of the more obvious areas for cost savings when considering the integration of enterprise applications. More specifically, the term **enterprise application integration** refers to the use of plans, methods, and tools designed to modernize, consolidate, integrate, and coordinate computer applications.[46]

By their very nature, ERP applications are interactive. Many add-on applications require process data and other information to be shared both internally among departments and units, and externally with the firm's suppliers and/or its customers. This creates the need for internal integration between various applications and the ERP, and for external integration of applications connected to trading partners' ERP systems. To accomplish this in real time would greatly speed up the manufacturing and delivery processes, and reduce errors and redundant activities. Consequently, many organizations are investing in internal and external application integration software, also called **middleware**, along with other integration solutions. Several of these are discussed in the following segments.

Internal Enterprise Application Integration

As companies invest in various enterprise applications they find they need to share information between these and other existing applications. If not managed correctly, this can become a time-consuming and expensive process. One way to avoid problems is to purchase a suite of application modules in one package from one supplier, covering a wide range of applications such as MES, WMS, TMS, and RMS. In this way, the integration capabilities are already designed into the applications.

When applications are purchased from different vendors, the user usually has to tie the applications together using integration middleware. Haworth, mentioned earlier, used eGate Integrator, an integration tool from SeeBeyond Technology Corp. of California, to tie together its TMS and WMS applications. The software passes customer orders, shipping plans, and shipping notifications between the two applications and Haworth's other systems. Oracle developed Fusion Middleware to integrate, for instance, computer automated design (CAD) system information and the ERP. Even small manufacturers might have 10 or 15 different manufacturing systems, and every time a change is made to a bill of materials, all of the systems have to reflect the change.[47]

Another way to achieve application integration, particularly when the applications are purchased at different times from different suppliers, is to use third-party **Web services**. Web services let applications communicate with one another without the need for custom coding, eliminating barriers caused by incompatible hardware, software, and operating systems. This allows companies to achieve internal integration when varied applications have been added to ERP systems over time. Web services can also be used to achieve integration between trading partner ERP systems.[48]

enterprise application integration Refers to the use of plans, methods, and tools designed to modernize, consolidate, integrate, and coordinate computer applications.

middleware Internal and external application integration software.

Web services Third-party services that let applications communicate with one another without the need for custom coding, eliminating barriers caused by incompatible hardware, software, and operating systems. This allows companies to achieve internal integration when varied applications have been added to ERP systems over time.

External Enterprise Application Integration

In a very basic supply chain interaction, information flow is from purchase order, to inventory control, to shipping, to receiving, and then to accounts payable. Prior to the emergence of ERP and the latest data exchange technologies, communications involved phone conversations, faxes, and emails between buyers and suppliers. Today, a buyer's ERP communications can be translated by a middleware application into the supplier's ERP system, and vice versa. The buyer's ERP system can generate an order and transmit to the ERP system of the supplier, and then receive order confirmations, shipping notices, and invoices from the supplier's system. Middleware thus acts as an information broker in the integrated supply chain.

Canada-based Mark Anthony Group, owner of Mike's Hard Lemonade, is a great example of the use of externally integrated information systems. It owns no facilities—rather, it contracts out the manufacturing, bottling, and distribution processes. It has designed its own integration platform, or middleware, based on Microsoft's Biztalk and installed by Sunaptic Solutions. This gives it the ability to monitor inventory levels, distribution patterns, and product formulas, using a number of information system applications of Mark Anthony and its partners.[49]

Another method for integrating trading partner processes and applications is through use of a **Web portal**. This is a website that provides secure access to data, applications, and services to business partners. Portals support multiple languages, platforms, and software content. "A Web-based front end will allow you to enable your suppliers with a tool to give you advance ship notification. It will allow them to drop ship for you, store inventory for you, and ship orders to your warehouses. And that Web-based front end, because it is integrated, can be part of your logistics network now," says Tom Kozenski, product marketing leader at Georgia-based software maker RedPrairie. "BMW uses portals, and they have upward of 3,500 suppliers that are doing vendor managed inventory and exchanging forecasts, production planning, and inventory," he adds.[50]

Care must be taken, however, to avoid overreliance on automated, shared processes. A good relationship with a supplier, for example, can be put at risk if process integration causes less frequent face-to-face or telephone communications. In other words, software applications cannot replace relationship-building activities. World-class supply chains have built their success on employees who communicate with trading partner employees, not just software applications with data exchange capabilities.

AUTOMATING PROCESS MANAGEMENT

11.4 Summarize the underlying principles of business process management

The term **business process management** (BPM) has come to be recognized today as automated process management and all of the software applications now available that assist firms in managing and automating business processes. BPM is also commonly used in coordination with many ERP applications, and is discussed in the following section.

Web portal A website that provides secure access to data, applications, and services to business partners. Portals support multiple languages, platforms, and software content.

business process management Has come to be recognized today as automated process management and all of the software applications now available that assist firms in managing and automating business processes.

Skandia Saves Costs With BPM

SERVICE SPOTLIGHT

Alistair & Jan Campbell/UK City/Corbis

In the United Kingdom, global insurance company Skandia utilized a BPM application to streamline its handling of customer correspondence. Originally, staff would log incoming correspondence into a database, which was then distributed to departments and eventually transferred to a number of end-user systems. Using BPM, Skandia centralized its processes into a single system. This removed a large number of labor-intensive tasks, which allowed employees to spend more time helping customers, solving problems, and selling product.

The improvements saved Skandia about £250,000 per year and increased business volume, resulting in no job losses from its centralization effort. Additionally, Skandia expected to save £150,000 annually on paper, printing, and storage. A further benefit was improved workforce satisfaction.

Today, the staff feel more engaged. The improvements allow workers to spend more time helping customers and using email and the phone. In this case, Skandia's experiences support the idea that BPM can work for smaller projects as well as for larger, business-wide projects.[51]

BUSINESS PROCESS MANAGEMENT

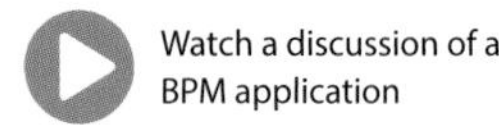
Watch a discussion of a BPM application

Recall from Chapter 1 that a process, simply put, is a sequence of activities designed to achieve a specific outcome. The processes of a business are what the business does; they are responsible for making the business successful; they are how the business responds to its customers' requirements. Managers, most certainly, should be very interested in carefully designing, assessing, and improving these processes, so that customers get the best-quality goods and services when they want them, at the prices they are willing to pay.

Without this continuous effort to manage key business processes, a company would eventually lose its competitive position to businesses that are more proactive with respect to ever-changing customer requirements. BPM offers a structured, standardized, analytical approach to this effort. The objectives of BPM are to see how a business operates its processes, improves them, and ensures that they continue to operate effectively in the future. Additionally, and as described in the Service Spotlight on page 349, BPM seeks to automate many processes, reduce paperwork, and make information more accessible so that employees are more productive and work is accomplished more quickly. The underlying principles of BPM include:[52]

- Processes must be adequately mapped and documented;
- Key processes should focus on customers;
- Procedures should be documented to ensure consistency and repeatability of quality performance;
- Measurement activities should assess individual processes;
- Process management should be based on a continuous approach to optimization through problem solving; and
- Process management should be inspired by best practices to ensure that superior competitiveness is achieved.

Specifically, as shown in Figure 11.5, BPM activities should include identifying all core processes, mapping or modeling the processes, monitoring performance, identifying problems, selecting improvement activities, and finally implementing new process designs. BPM applications bring real-time visibility, accountability, and reporting capabilities to the management of processes. When integrated with ERP systems and associated applications, BPM gives managers the power to see how processes are performing across the entire organization, identify process strengths and weaknesses, and allow good process designs to become better.

Today, use of BPM software solutions is becoming widespread across all industries. In many cases, companies purchase BPM software to improve their regulatory compliance and customer service processes. BPM applications enable businesses to design and optimize business processes using tools such as modeling and simulation, performance monitoring, and reporting features. Additionally, implementation times can be greatly reduced using an off-the-shelf BPM application. Examples include automatic correspondence processing templates used by mutual fund companies, enabling them to preconfigure letter text, integrate addresses, and print, fax, mail, or email customer correspondence; healthcare provider templates for scheduling, financial counseling, registration, claims processing, and payment processing; mortgage-lending templates for loan condition fulfillment, appraisals, and broker communications; and call center applications that enable firms to obtain customer information quickly from a number of other applications, and integrate with computer telephony, digital call recording, and the Internet.[53]

Utah-based O. C. Tanner, distributor of employee recognition goods and services, selected a BPM application to track and maintain its highly customized employee recognition programs. It was able to reduce the time to get a new customer onstream from 12 days to 7, as well as make the entire process completely visible. North Carolina–based Blue Rhino, distributor of barbecue grill propane tanks, implemented automated control of its financial transactions. It was able to reduce the time required to perform audits.[54] Canada-based Cambrian Credit Union installed BPM software to automate its loan processes. The software allows underwriters and other employees to add comments, supporting documents, and other materials as needed. The credit union improved its loan processing rates from 650 per month, prior to BPM, to 800 loans per month, after implementation.[55]

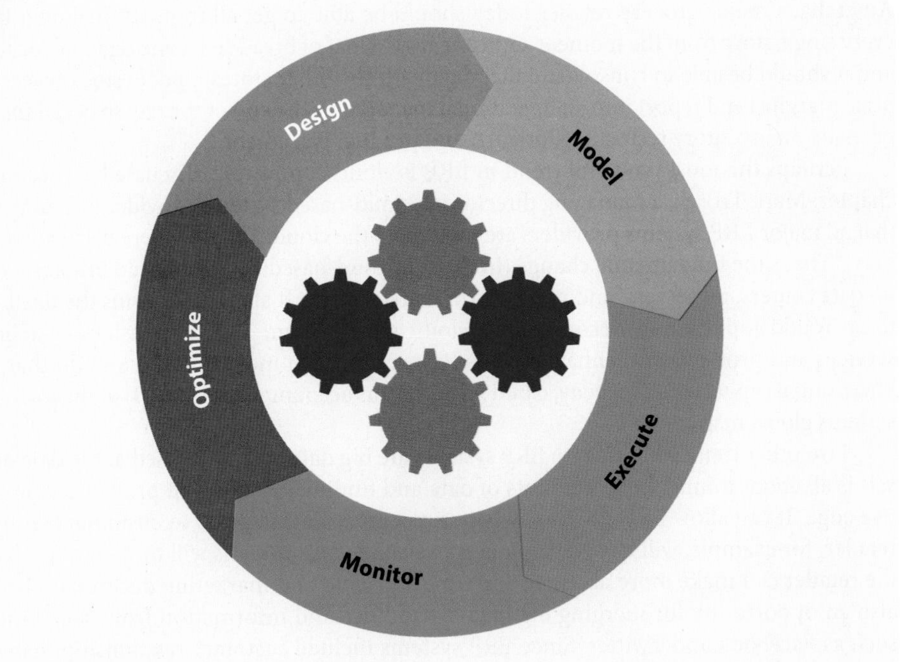

Figure 11.5 BPM Activities

Most recently, companies are looking to BPM applications as a means for encouraging the sharing of ERP system information. Customers, trading partners, and employees in geographically dispersed units are requiring real-time access to key processes of the organization. BPM solutions that can integrate with ERP systems and other enterprise applications and allow the access of key process information create a much more agile organization—one that can react very quickly to changes in the firm's external and internal environments. CEOs and other managers can use BPM to view and manipulate hundreds of predefined reports in real time, or create new ones. GAF Materials, a New Jersey–based roofing and building materials manufacturer, uses its enterprise-wide BPM tool to allow supply chain, sales, distribution, and finance departments to work from the same forecast. "Once we've determined our sales forecast, the BPM solution can give us all the SCM information required to meet that forecast, including capacity, raw materials, expenses, costs to deliver, and budgeting needs," says Rick Stevenson, director of supply chain planning and business intelligence.[56]

TRENDS IN ENTERPRISE RESOURCE PLANNING

11.5 Recall three important trends in Enterprise Resource Planning

In the years since the start of the recent global recession, businesses have had to adapt and evolve their operations to remain competitive and profitable. One area changing radically in the face of this new business environment is ERP. ERP systems have been largely characterized by companies rolling out large, in-house systems from technology giants like SAP and Oracle. The complexity of ERP systems meant that they tended to be big, expensive, and difficult or time-consuming to implement.

Today, though, ERP systems are beginning to become more flexible and responsive to allow businesses to adapt quickly to meet changing customer needs. ERP is also becoming more responsive to the needs of business managers, delivering accurate information to decision makers in a timely fashion. "People have had to really focus on what their customers want," says Peter Ryan, technology partner at Deloitte Consulting. "ERP has gone that way as well. Fundamentally it's about the customer, but it's also about getting the right information at the right time on the right device to the right people in terms of the people servicing the customer."[57]

Cloud computing, social media, big data, and sustainability add-on applications are keeping ERP relevant. According to Elaine Tan of the Institute of Chartered Accountants, Australia, a major grocery retailer today should be able to get all transactional data from every single store from the moment someone buys a loaf of bread from one regional location, and it should be able to consolidate that data with the other stores, update stock levels and price margins, and report it to an operational manager by the end of the day so decisions can be made on inventory restocking, pricing, and product placement.

Perhaps the most powerful trend in ERP is cloud computing, discussed earlier in the chapter. Mark Troselj, a managing director for cloud-based systems provider Netsuite, says that all major ERP systems providers are moving to the cloud. “That’s where it’s headed,” he says. “That’s the fundamental change [in ERP].” Cloud-based ERP means no infrastructure, no data centers, no servers, and no platform management. It also allows firms the flexibility to easily add applications. According to Deloitte’s Peter Ryan, “It allows businesses to bring services and products and enhancements to market much more quickly, and do that at a lower initial capital cost.”[58] Today, cloud ERP systems account for about 70% of the total ERP systems global market.[59]

Two other trends that tie into ERP systems are big data and social media. Big data analysis is all about mining huge amounts of data and finding insights that provide a competitive edge. It can allow ERP systems to better recognize and respond to customer trends. A retailer, for example, will have data on every sale. Big data analysis will find sales trends, so the retailer can make more accurate and timely pricing and marketing decisions. There is also an opportunity for merging big data capabilities and information from social media such as Facebook and Twitter. Since ERP systems include customer relationship management applications, it becomes a low-cost way of getting a lot of customer-oriented analyses to managers, to allow a better understanding of customers and their needs.

Finally, sustainability applications are pairing with ERP systems to enable supply chains to implement and track sustainability initiatives. The information required to track a supply chain’s environmental footprint is substantial. Ensuring regulatory compliance and customer reporting requirements involves an integration among supply chain management, contract management, bills of materials and routings, and multisite/intercompany transactions. These data reside within ERP, so ERP is the natural place to manage supply chain sustainability. Environmental performance measurements must be analyzed with other performance indicators to gauge business success, and ERP is the platform used by senior executives to accomplish this task. Today, ERP system add-ons, both in-house and in the cloud, to enable supply chain carbon footprint tracking are becoming available.

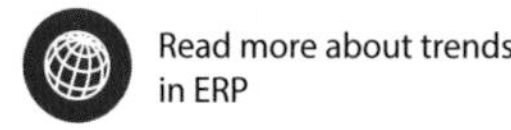
Read more about trends in ERP

SAGE edge™

Visit edge.sagepub.com/wisner to help you accomplish your coursework goals in an easy-to-use learning environment.

- Mobile-friendly eFlashcards
- Mobile-friendly practice quizzes
- A complete online action plan
- Chapter summaries with learning objectives
- Excel templates to assist with practice problems
- Original video case studies that demonstrate chapter concepts in action

SUMMARY

This chapter has presented a detailed discussion of managing information flow, a topic that can impact a firm’s ability to track customers, inventories, and suppliers. Managers must be aware of the types of information the firm requires and then decide how best to manage this information, both inside and outside the firm. Systems like MRP, MRP II, and ERP have played key roles in managing enterprise information, along with the many system modules that typically accompany most enterprise applications. Advances in information system technologies have allowed process management to become automated today, which has decreased costs while improving productivity and customer service. Some of the more recent advances in ERP systems are cloud systems, the use of big data analysis, and environmental ERP applications.

KEY TERMS

Application add-ons, 344
Best-of-breed systems, 341
Bill of materials, 331
Business process management, 349
Capacity requirements planning, 338
Cloud-based ERP systems, 342
Corporate information flow, 326
Distribution requirements planning system, 337
Enterprise application integration, 348
Enterprise resource planning (ER) systems, 340
Environmental information flow, 326
Frozen time fence, 331
Information audit, 327
Information velocity, 327
Information volatility, 327
Intellectual asset, 326
Internal information flow, 326
Legacy systems, 341
Load reports, 338
Logistics execution suites, 346
Manufacturing execution system (MES) module, 346
Manufacturing resource planning (MRP II), 338
Master production schedule, 330
Material requirements planning (MRP), 329
Middleware, 348
Product structure diagram, 331
Returns management systems, 347
Rolling production schedule, 331
Stabilize phase, 344
Synergize phase, 344
Synthesize phase, 344
Transportation management system, 346 Warehouse management system, 347
Web portal, 349
Web services, 348

FORMULA REVIEW

Projected on-hand inventory = (the previous period's ending inventory + the scheduled receipts for the current period + any completed planned order releases) – the gross requirements for the current period.

Net requirement = number of units needed to keep the projected on-hand inventory at either zero or the required safety stock.

SOLVED PROBLEMS

1. Complete the following MRP part record:

Part A		1	2	3	4	5	6	7	8	9	10
Gross Requirements		32	16	34	40	51	26	19	42	34	29
Scheduled Receipts			24								
Projected On-Hand Inventory	56	24	32	5	5	5	5	5	5	5	5
Net Requirements				7	40	51	26	19	42	34	29
Planned Order Releases		7	40	51	26	19	42	34	29		

Q = LFL, LT = 2, SS = 5

Answer:

The completed portion of the part record is shown in orange. Explanation—the projected on-hand inventory controls when things need to happen. In this case, the goal is never to let the end-of-period inventory be less than 5 units (the safety stock). The period 1–ending inventory is 56 – 32 = 24. In period 2, the end-of-period inventory is 24 + 24 – 16 = 32. Then, in period 3, the inventory is projected to be less than 0, so an order must be planned. The net requirement for period 3 is 7, since 32 + 7 – 34 = 5 (the safety stock). Thus, a planned order release must be made in period 1, since the lead time = 2 periods. Since LFL order quantities are used, the planned order release for period 1 = net requirement of 7 in period 3. The remaining projected on-hand inventories, net requirements, and planned order releases are calculated similarly.

2. Given the following, calculate the minimum lead time to make a chair:

Part	Lead Time
Chair	2
Leg Assembly	3
Legs	4
Hardware	3
Seat	4

Chair
Leg Ass'ly
Seat
Legs (4)
Hardware

Answer:

The legs and hardware can be purchased simultaneously, in 4 days. Then the leg assembly can be completed in another 3 days. During this same 7-day period, the seat can be purchased. Finally, the leg assembly and seat can be made into a chair in 2 days. Total minimum lead time is 9 days.

3. Using the information in Problem 2, complete the following part records.

Chair		1	2	3	4	5	6	7	8	9	10
Gross Requirements		16	8	9	12	14	11	6	18	12	10
Scheduled Receipts		5									
Projected On-Hand Inventory	22	11	3	3	3	3	3	3	3	3	3
Net Requirements				9	12	14	11	6	18	12	10
Planned Order Releases		9	12	14	11	6	18	12	10		

Q = LFL, LT = 2, SS = 3

Leg Assembly		1	2	3	4	5	6	7	8	9	10
Gross Requirements		9	12	14	11	6	18	12	10		
Scheduled Receipts		20									
Projected On-Hand Inventory	40	51	39	25	14	28	10	18	28	28	28
Net Requirements						2		12	2		
Planned Order Releases			20		20	20					

Q = 20, LT = 3, SS = 10

Legs		1	2	3	4	5	6	7	8	9	10
Gross Requirements			80		80	80					
Scheduled Receipts		100									
Projected On-Hand Inventory	100	100	120	120	40	60	60	60	60	60	60
Net Requirements						60					
Planned Order Releases		100									

Q = 50, LT = 4, SS = 20

Answer:

The completed part record information is shown in orange. The projected on-hand inventory is always the end-of-period amount, and is calculated as the (previous period amount) + (any current-period scheduled receipts) – (gross requirements). The net requirement is always the amount needed to be added to the previous-period projected on-hand inventory so that the current end-of-period inventory will be either 0 or the required safety stock. The planned order releases are always multiples of Q needed to satisfy the net requirement. When Q = LFL, then the planned order releases will always be equal to the net requirements. When Q is a fixed quantity, then Q will not necessarily be equal to the net requirement. The planned order releases are what is needed to be either purchased or assembled in that period.

REVIEW QUESTIONS

1. Why is information considered an intellectual asset?
2. Define the three key informational flows in most organizations.
3. Define information velocity and describe its importance to and impact on the firm.
4. Define information volatility and describe its importance to and impact on the firm.
5. What is information flow mapping used for, and what roles do information audits play in flow mapping?
6. Define dependent demand.
7. In just a few sentences, explain what the MRP is, and what it does.
8. Where do the production numbers in the MPS come from?
9. What is a frozen time period or time fence in the MPS?
10. What is a rolling production schedule in the MPS?
11. Why is accurate inventory and lead-time information so important to the MRP?
12. What is a bill of materials (BOM), and why is it important to the MRP?
13. What is the MRP part record rule?
14. What does the DRP do, and how does it fit in with the MRP?
15. Why are the DRP planned shipping quantities so important?
16. What were the drivers behind the development of MRP II?
17. How does the MRP II system perform capacity requirements planning?
18. What is ERP, and how is it different from MRP II?
19. Describe the historical developments leading up to today's ERP systems.
20. What are cloud-based ERP systems, and why do firms use them?
21. Why have ERP implementations often failed in the past?
22. What are the benefits of an ERP system?
23. What is a best-of-breed ERP system? Are there any problems with this type of system?
24. Describe the three post-implementation phases for ERP system users.
25. What are ERP system application add-ons, and which ones are the most popular?
26. What do logistics management systems consist of, and why are they considered so important to firms that use them?
27. What are RMS's, and how are they used?
28. What does enterprise application integration refer to, and how is this accomplished?
29. How is internal application integration accomplished?
30. How is external application integration typically accomplished?
31. What is business process management (BPM), and how is it accomplished?
32. Can BPM solutions be integrated with the ERP?
33. What are some of the trends today, in ERP system applications?

DISCUSSION QUESTIONS

1. Describe the key information flows that might occur at Amazon.com.
2. Design an information flow map for a specific type of firm other than the one shown in Figure 11.1.
3. Describe several ways that various functional groups or departments in a firm might use an MRP II system.
4. Provide an example of how MRP II can be used in a service, such as a school.
5. Would it be a good idea to combine a TMS with a WMS? Why?
6. Would it be a good idea to combine BPM solutions with an ERP system? Why?

EXERCISES AND PROJECTS

1. Select a firm or department with processes you can monitor, such as your place of employment. Perform an information audit and state your findings in a report. Construct an information flow map as part of your report.
2. Find online a recent example of a firm's experiences when implementing its ERP system. Write a report of the firm's ERP system, its customizations, and its experiences.
3. Write a report about sustainable ERP and cite several examples of firms using these applications.

PROBLEMS

Use the table and figure here to answer Problems 1 and 2.

Part	Lead Time (days)
A	2
B	4
C	3
D	3

Part A
Part B (2)
Part D
Part C (4)

1. Determine the minimum number of days to make a complete Part A, starting with no current inventories.
2. Determine the quantities of Parts B, C, and D required to make 50 Part A.

Use the table and figure here to answer Problems 3 and 4.

Part	Lead Time (days)
A	2
B	4
C	3
D	3
E	2

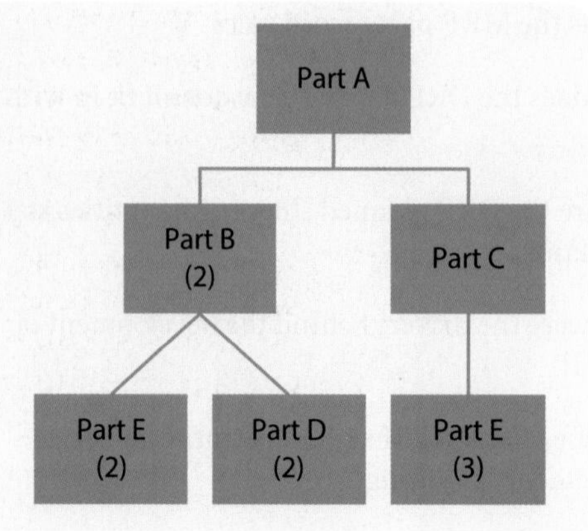

3. Determine the minimum number of days to make Part A, starting with no current inventories.
4. Determine the quantities of all parts required to make 100 Part A.
5. Complete the following MRP part record (note the lot size, lead time, and safety stock).

Part A		1	2	3	4	5	6	7	8	9	10
Gross Requirements		15	26	14	20	16	0	10	12	16	19
Scheduled Receipts		20									
Projected On-Hand Inventory	40										
Net Requirements											
Planned Order Releases											

Q = 20, LT = 3, SS = 4

6. Complete the following MRP part record (note the lot size, lead time, and safety stock).

Part A		1	2	3	4	5	6	7	8	9	10
Gross Requirements		12	4	22	15	19	10	15	12	19	24
Scheduled Receipts		10									
Projected On-Hand Inventory	16										
Net Requirements											
Planned Order Releases											

Q = LFL, LT = 2, SS = 6

7. Complete the following MRP part record (note the lot size, lead time, and safety stock).

Part A		1	2	3	4	5	6	7	8	9	10
Gross Requirements		15	10	20	25	30	20	25	15	20	25
Scheduled Receipts		25									
Projected On-Hand Inventory	30										
Net Requirements											
Planned Order Releases											

Q = LFL, LT = 3, SS = 0

8. Complete the following MRP part record (note the lot size, lead time, and safety stock).

Part A		1	2	3	4	5	6	7	8	9	10
Gross Requirements		45	36	40	19	42	86	29	45	60	32
Scheduled Receipts		35		70							
Projected On-Hand Inventory	105										
Net Requirements											
Planned Order Releases											

Q = 35, LT = 3, SS = 30

9. Given the information shown here, complete the part records for all four parts. Use LFL order quantities for all parts. No safety stocks are required, and there are no scheduled receipts.

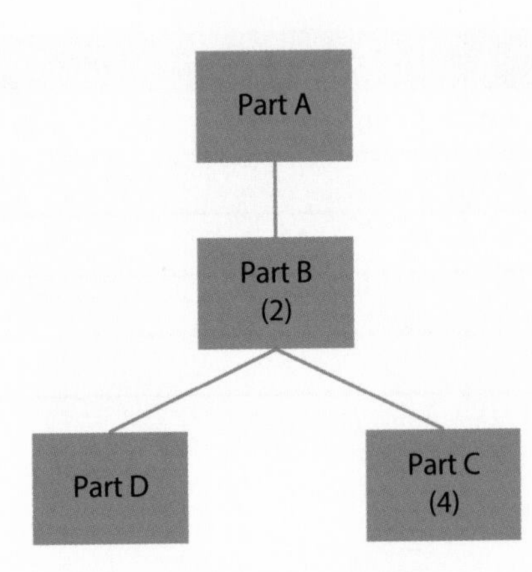

Part	Lead time (days)	Beginning Inventory
A	2	12
B	4	40
C	1	65
D	3	30

10. Given the information shown here, complete the part records for all parts. Also:

a. Determine the minimum lead time to make Part A, starting with no current inventories.

b. Determine the amounts of each part required to make 100 Part A's, starting with no current inventories.

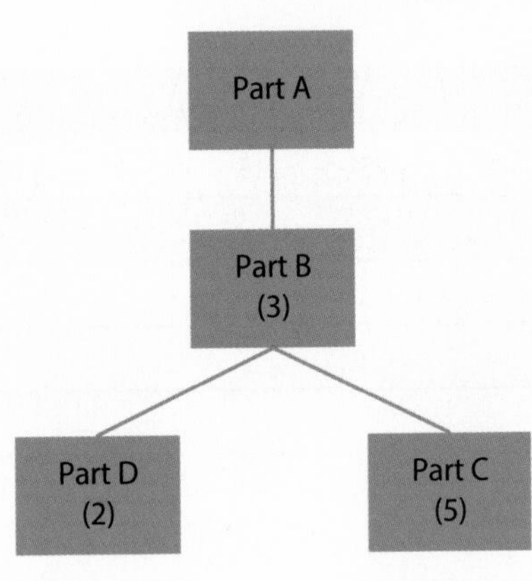

Part	Lead time (days)	Beginning Inventory	Order Quantity	Safety Stock
A	3	40	LFL	4
B	1	80	LFL	12
C	1	300	25	20
D	2	225	25	10

11. Using the product structure diagram and the other information on the opposite page, complete the part records for each of the six items. Note that Part D appears in two places, but must be combined into one part record, and also note there are no scheduled receipts. Also, list the purchase and production plans for the eight periods.

12. Using the information in Problem 11, determine the minimum lead time to make Parts A, B, and C, assuming no current inventories. If 100 Part A's are required, how many of each of the other parts are required, assuming no current inventories?

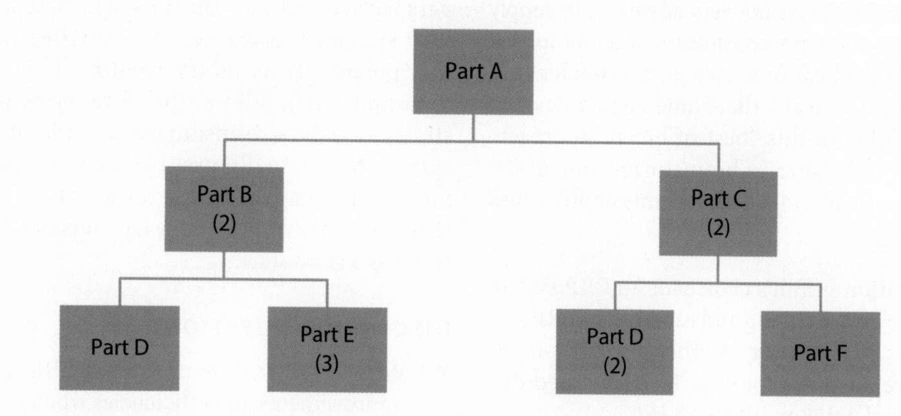

Part	Lead time (days)	Beginning Inventory	Order Quantity	Safety Stock
A	2	20	LFL	5
B	3	30	10	5
C	1	20	25	0
D	2	90	12	5
E	1	62	50	0
F	2	46	LFL	10

	Periods							
Part A	**1**	**2**	**3**	**4**	**5**	**6**	**7**	**8**
Gross Req.	5	3	6	8	4	10	5	2

CASE STUDIES

CASE 1: ERP System Implementation Decisions at T40 Enterprises

This was the project Bill had been waiting for since he graduated with his BA in supply chain management and a minor in information technology: the management of an ERP system implementation. He knew from his coursework that a number of crucial decisions had to be made in the planning stages, and he was considering how to proceed. He was staring at a to-do list of some of the key decisions that he had to make.

Bill had started to map out the information flows at T40 Enterprises—an important step prior to any system implementation. It was critical to understand what information was exchanged with which processes and between which functions. It had been a while since such a process mapping exercise was done, so Bill was proud to uncover significant process improvements and efficiencies.

With these optimized processes in place, Bill was looking for an appropriate ERP system vendor that would be able to represent T40's processes in its system. Unfortunately, however, there was no perfect match out there. He therefore had to either modify T40's internal processes to match how the ERP system was handling these processes, or he had to modify the vendor's standard ERP solution to match T40's processes. Both approaches had advantages and disadvantages, and the decision was not an easy one to make. He thus jotted on his to-do list to brainstorm and note down pros and cons for either approach.

Another dilemma he faced as he researched the different system vendors was that all of them had their pluses and minuses. For example, while one ERP system vendor had great expertise, and therefore had sophisticated processes in warehouse management, it was not very advanced in supply management. Bill was therefore considering whether to pick and choose the best applications from each provider, and then integrate them. He heard that some companies had been quite successful with this "best-of-breed" approach, but he also wanted to be sure to brainstorm some of the potential disadvantages for T40. This became another task on his to-do list.

A further consideration in Bill's choice for an ERP system vendor was whether one of the big and established ERP system vendors would be better, or whether a smaller-niche player may be more advantageous for T40. He noted this down as an additional point on his to-do-list.

These were quite a lot of important decisions that Bill had to make. However, he did not want to stop here. He also already wanted to think about the next steps in the ERP system implementation, once a vendor had been chosen. One issue that he had to decide on was whether to implement the system with a so-called "big bang" or with a phased-in approach. The "big bang" approach would entail implementing all components and modules of the ERP system, and then going live with all of them at the same time. This would mean that all departments and functions would have the new system at the same time. The phased-in approach would mean that the going live would commence with one function—for example, accounting. After accounting had been working with the new system for a while, the second function would follow, and so on. The choice was not straightforward, so he noted this issue on his to-do list as well.

One last issue Bill wanted to think about was how to go about introducing the new system to the users. He knew that the success of an ERP system not only depended on a successful implementation from an information systems perspective, but also on the users' satisfaction with the ERP system. If users were not satisfied with the system, they potentially would try avoiding it, or their productivity would suffer. Bill was therefore trying to come up with strategies of how to ensure users would be happy with the system, and actually use it to be more productive. This formed the last task on his to-do list for now. Obviously, there were many more issues to consider, but Bill thought this was a good start.

DISCUSSION QUESTIONS

1. Why was Bill able to uncover significant process improvements and efficiencies when mapping out the company's processes as a preparatory step to the ERP system implementation?
2. Think about Bill's decision whether to modify T40's internal processes to match how the ERP system was handling these processes or to modify the vendor's standard ERP solution to match T40's processes. What are some advantages and disadvantages of these approaches?
3. What are disadvantages of a "best-of-breed" approach?
4. What are advantages and disadvantages of contracting with a big and established ERP system vendor?
5. What should Bill consider when making the decision whether to implement the ERP system with a "big bang" or with a phased-in approach?
6. What are strategies to ensure users are happy with the system and actually use it to be more productive?

Note: Written by Tobias Schoenherr, PhD, Michigan State University. This case was prepared solely to provide material for class discussion. The author does not intend to illustrate either effective or ineffective handling of a managerial situation.

CASE 2: Process Efficiencies at Lansing Corp.

Andrew had a big task ahead of him: He was charged to develop a case for process efficiencies to be gained through the ERP system implementation that was scheduled to be carried out early next year. His supervisor explained to him the importance of the task, since the new ERP system was going to be a significant change from the old legacy system that had been in place, and he was expecting resistance from some user groups. He therefore wanted to be prepared and do everything to make sure his coworkers shared the same excitement about the system as he did. His intention was that with function-specific cases and demonstrations of benefits, derived from the new system, people would be more likely to buy into the ERP system.

His supervisor asked him to start with a case on how the processing of purchase orders could be facilitated, leading to less work overall for individuals associated with the process. His supervisor described to him the current process as follows. When purchasing wants to issue a purchase order (PO) to one of its suppliers, it has to do so in its function-specific purchasing system. Once all the data are entered, the PO is finalized and the system prints five copies of the document, which are forwarded to the following departments: manufacturing operations (to let them know that materials have been ordered, so they can schedule shifts accordingly), receiving (to let them know that they should be expecting a delivery), inventory control (to let them know that their request for replenishment has been fulfilled), accounting (to let them know that an invoice is to be expected from the supplier), and last but not least, the supplier itself. These documents were sent via company mail. Once received by the departments, the information from the document was entered into their respective computer system (i.e., the manufacturing system, the inventory control system, etc.).

A common issue that had been of concern with the current process was that data were incorrectly entered into the function-specific systems, and thus inaccurate information was used to make decisions. This would be avoided with an integrated ERP system, as would be the cumbersome printing, mailing, and reentering of information. In addition, information would be conveyed instantaneously, without any delay, as was currently the case. These were just some benefits that the system would bring about, all focusing on efficiencies. But these were also the obvious gains. It was Andrew's task now to identify additional process efficiencies that would be enabled with the ERP system, specifically focusing on the PO process.

DISCUSSION QUESTIONS

1. What benefits could the ERP system provide for how the receiving of materials is managed? Think about the efficiencies in the receiving department, and efficiencies possible for other departments that may be involved after the products are received.

2. What would be some other processes whose efficiencies could be improved via the ERP system, and how would this be accomplished?

Note: Written by Tobias Schoenherr, PhD, Michigan State University. This case was prepared solely to provide material for class discussion. The author does not intend to illustrate either effective or ineffective handling of a managerial situation.

CASE 3: The Success of an ERP System Implementation at Beta Corp.: Was This a Mistake?

Amy, who was responsible for Beta Corp.'s information technology infrastructure, was walking briskly to her office. She just got off the phone with Kevin, one of the current summer interns, who had prepared a report on the ERP system implementation and its outcomes. Amy oversaw this project earlier this year. She was very proud of her accomplishments, so she was eager to read the report and look over the improvements she was able to facilitate with her ERP system implementation. The implementation happened without any major glitches; the transition from the old legacy system to the new ERP system was smooth, and internal users had successfully been trained in the new system. What Amy was now looking for in the report was evidence for the significant process efficiencies that she expected from the implementation. This was, after all, the real test of whether the implementation of the new system had been successful.

Amy arrived at her office, and with excitement she sat down to look over the report. The smile on her face quickly changed, however, to a concerned and somewhat confused frown. She was glancing over the executive summary of the report, which was anything other than good. She flipped back to the title page to make sure that this was indeed the report she had asked Kevin to prepare, and that it was actually about the ERP system implementation she had overseen. It was. "What happened?" Amy asked out loud.

The overall results in the report were disappointing. While the system seemed to be functioning fine, overall productivity measures were down on a number of dimensions, such as orders processed, invoices paid, and scheduled production. These were exactly the dimensions that Amy had hoped would improve with the ERP system, due to its integrative nature and its ability to communicate and share information easily between functions. Was the ERP system implementation a mistake? Did she do anything wrong? Why were these dimensions not improving, but in fact deteriorating? She picked up the phone to call Kevin into her office, since he had prepared the report. Maybe he could provide her some insight into why this was happening.

DISCUSSION QUESTIONS

1. What might be some reasons why productivity measures decreased?

2. What could Amy have done to prevent this decline in performance?

3. What would be good measures to assess the success of an ERP system?

Note: Written by Tobias Schoenherr,, PhD, Michigan State University. This case was prepared solely to provide material for class discussion. The author does not intend to illustrate either effective or ineffective handling of a managerial situation.

VIDEO CASE STUDY

Learn more about ***managing information*** from real organizations that use operations management techniques every day. Craig Nielsen is a Principal at Digital Benefit Advisors, a national employee benefits firm. It is of the utmost importance for Digital Benefit Advisors to keep detailed and confidential records of their clients' information. Watch this short interview to find out how they do it.

If you don't spend at least 40 percent of your time planning, then it's time to look for another gig.

—**ROB BLACK,** president, Project Masters, Inc.[1]

Operations keeps the lights on, strategy provides a light at the end of the tunnel, but project management is the train engine that moves the organization forward.

—**JOY GUMZ,** senior director, Project Auditors LLC[2]

MANAGING PROJECTS

LEARNING OBJECTIVES

After completing this chapter, you should be able to:

12.1 Describe the primary concerns and objectives of project management
12.2 Develop a work breakdown structure and a Gantt chart
12.3 Understand and discuss the Critical Path Method and the Program Evaluation and Review Technique
12.4 Perform project crashing
12.5 Identify and manage project risks
12.6 Discuss the advantages and disadvantages of cloud-based project management applications

Master the content.

edge.sagepub.com/wisner

SCOTTISHPOWER RENEWABLES TO BUILD WORLD'S LARGEST TIDAL ENERGY PROJECT

The largest tidal energy project ever built will be located near the island of Islay, which is located off the west coast of Scotland. Planned by ScottishPower Renewables, the 10-megawatt project will harness the power of the sea in the fast-moving currents of the Sound of Islay. "With around a quarter of Europe's potential tidal energy resource and a tenth of the wave capacity, Scotland's seas have unrivalled potential to generate green energy, create new, low carbon jobs and bring billions of pounds of investment to Scotland," says John Swinney, Scotland's finance secretary.

The energy project will utilize 10 tidal turbines (similar to what is shown in the image), each producing 1 megawatt of electricity. The turbines will be built by Norway-based Hammerfest Strm, which has been operating a prototype in Norway for over six years. The electricity generated will be used primarily by Diageo, one of the largest distillers on the island of Islay. "Alongside energy saving measures, wave and tidal energy will have a critical role to play in helping Scotland reduce climate emissions and phase out polluting coal and nuclear power," says Richard Dixon, director of the environmental conservation group WWF Scotland.

The Scottish government is opposed to any new nuclear power plants in Scotland, and has a goal of providing 80% of electricity demand using renewables by 2020. By comparison, in 2009, only 27% of electric power in Scotland came from renewables.[3]

INTRODUCTION

Project management is concerned primarily with the successful planning, scheduling, and controlling of project resources. Projects occur all the time in all organizations, from the relatively quick and simple (such as finding a suitable supplier) to the extremely complex and time consuming (such as designing a new model of automobile). Unfortunately, if these projects are mismanaged, the outcome can be project failures, resulting in excess costs and time, and/or poor performance. The ability to lead a diverse and geographically dispersed project team in achieving project goals is becoming increasingly important. This chapter reviews all of the necessary tools and topics to help project managers make the right decisions, at the right time, for the right costs.

While project management techniques have been around for quite some time, environmental conditions today require project managers to more carefully assess risk and

Watch a video about the Channel Tunnel

Watch a video about the Hong Kong International Airport

Watch a video about the International Space Station

Watch a video about the Three Gorges

Watch a video about the Antilla Tower

Table 12.1 Examples of Large and Expensive Projects

Project Name	Description
Channel Tunnel	A 31-mile undersea tunnel connecting England and France, it began in 1988 and was completed in 1994 for a cost of $21 billion, which was 80% more than the original projected cost.[5]
Hong Kong International Airport (HKIA)	Begun in 1991, HKIA was built on an island off the coast of Hong Kong. It is the most expensive airport ever built, at a cost of $20 billion. It was completed in 1998 and handles over 63 million passengers per year.[6]
International Space Station (ISS)	The most expensive project ever built, the ISS involves a collaboration of hundreds of companies and 15 nations. The initial module was put into orbit in 2000, and the most recent addition was made in 2011. So far, the United States has spent about $75 billion on the 925,000-pound, 357-foot ISS. Total costs for the project exceed $100 billion.[7]
Three Gorges Dam	This 7,660-foot long hydroelectric dam was built across the Yangtze River from 1994 until 2006 at a cost of $26 billion. It was fully operational in 2012, with a capacity of 22,500 megawatts.[8]
Antilla Tower	This $1.8-billion, 27-story home, owned by billionaire Mukesh Ambani, was completed in 2010 in Mumbai, India. The building has three helipads, six floors of parking, guest suites, a theater, a temple, and a ballroom. The building also requires hundreds of staff to operate.[9]

security, and consequently develop failure probabilities and contingency plans for many projects. Additionally, technological advances such as cloud-based computing and open source software have allowed for better project planning options and reduced costs for many companies.

This chapter will show managers how to construct Gantt charts, use the critical path method (CPM) to identify critical activities, and determine when project crashing makes the most sense. These and other project management techniques will allow managers to predict and potentially negotiate more realistic completion dates and project costs. When projects are completed on time and under budget, while meeting their performance requirements, everyone wins.

PROJECT MANAGEMENT DEFINED

12.1 Describe the primary concerns and objectives of project management

First, let's answer the question: What is a **project**? According to the Project Management Institute, it is "a temporary group activity designed to produce a unique product, service or result."[4] Projects have a defined beginning and end, with specific tasks, objectives, and assigned resources. They are not routine activities, and involve a group of skilled professionals (such as designers, engineers, and construction workers) accomplishing a set of operations and activities. The group of workers is brought together specifically for this one project, such as building a tunnel, bridge, or skyscraper; programming a software application; or bringing relief supplies to the victims of a natural disaster. Examples of some of the largest, most expensive projects ever undertaken are shown in Table 12.1.

project A temporary group activity designed to produce a unique product, service, or result. Projects have a defined beginning and end, with specific tasks, objectives, and assigned resources.

managing projects The planning, scheduling, and controlling of resources (such as capital, people, materials, and equipment) to meet the specific goals (such as completion date, budgeted cost, and required performance) of the project.

Managing projects, then, is the planning, scheduling, and controlling of resources (such as capital, people, materials, and equipment) to meet the specific goals (such as completion date, budgeted cost, and required performance) of the project. Project goals are usually tied to the client's requirements such as when the project needs to be completed, how the completed project will perform, and what constitutes completion. The primary trade-offs in projects always involve cost, time, and performance. Spending more money or reducing performance requirements can save time, for example. Balancing these competing objectives is often the most challenging task for the project manager.

Throughout this chapter, projects will be treated generically, even though projects are indeed different, as shown in Table 12.1. A project to bring relief supplies to the 1.3 million displaced survivors of the southern Haiti earthquake of 2010, for instance, was obviously very different from the project to develop Apple's MacBook Pro computer. However, both of these projects required skillful managers and workers, as well as the right resources for successful project completion.

PROJECT PLANNING AND THE GANTT CHART

12.2 Develop a work breakdown structure and a Gantt chart

The planning phase is probably the single most significant contributor to successful project completion. No doubt, many of you have heard of the 7-Ps of planning: Prior-Proper-Planning-Prevents-Perilously-Poor-Performance (or another similar version). This certainly holds true for the planning of projects. For example, according to research done by Connecticut-based Meta Group, poor project planning is to blame for the failure of one-third of new software projects.[10] Furthermore, according to the industry publication *IEEE Software*, two of the top three deadliest sins of project management are (1) not planning at all, and (2) failure to plan for risk.[11] Finally, according to Rob Black, president of Project Masters, Inc., "Almost every reason for failure is due to poor planning."[12]

During the initial planning phase of a project, all of the project's independent tasks should be defined as much as possible, so that time and cost estimates and resource assignments can be made, and then control systems can be designed. The set of task descriptions is termed a **work breakdown structure** (WBS). It looks similar to a manufacturing bill of materials, and is shown in Figure 12.1 for a fictional park maintenance project. Specifically, the WBS is a hierarchical listing that starts with the finished project, and then segments the work into more basic work packages or tasks. Successive levels identify increasingly detailed or basic activities that make up the higher-level work.

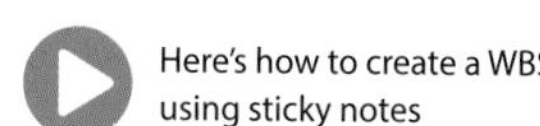

work breakdown structure All of the project's independent tasks, defined as much as possible.

Figure 12.1 Park Maintenance Project Work Breakdown Structure

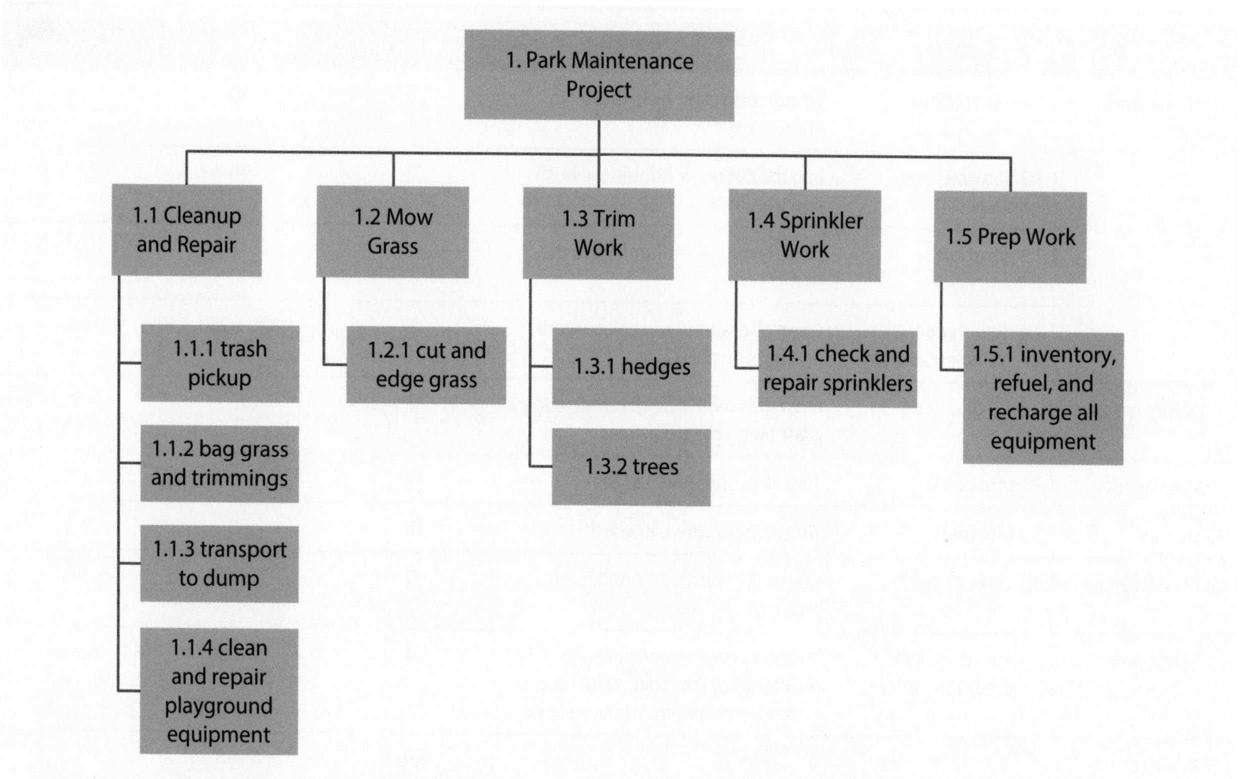

When the WBS is complete, the organization can more easily determine the time estimates for each activity, assign tasks to workers, and calculate the projected costs. This can be accomplished using a table describing each task and the accompanying activities, shown in Table 12.2. The total cost for the park maintenance project comes to just over $900, and this could be used as a starting place for bidding or negotiating purposes.

THE GANTT CHART

At first glance, it appears the park maintenance project could be completed in perhaps eight hours if several workers are used. To get a better picture, though, the project manager might construct a **Gantt chart**, which shows the time lengths and sequences of the task activities. The Gantt chart was invented by Henry L. Gantt (1861–1919), a mechanical engineer who early in his career worked with Frederick Taylor in developing the ideas behind scientific management at Midvale Steel and Bethlehem Steel. Gantt designed his charts so that production managers could quickly determine if work was ahead of or behind schedule. He described the use of his chart in a 1919 book, *Organizing for Work*.[13] Figure 12.2 shows a Gantt chart for the fictional park maintenance project shown in the WBS.

Here are some best practices for project planning

Along the horizontal axis is a timeline (in this case, the time units are hours). Associated with each activity is a bar showing the activity start and finish times, thus allowing workers to quickly see activity times and sequences. Using the precedence and activity duration information in Table 12.2, the Gantt chart for the park maintenance project is constructed in Figure 12.2. Based on the completed Gantt chart for the project, it appears that 14 hours instead of 8 would be needed to complete all of the park maintenance activities, due to the required sequencing of the activities.

Gantt chart A timeline used for planning purposes that shows the time lengths and sequences of a project's task activities.

Another issue is the assignment of workers to the project. While at least part of this decision relies on management judgment or preference, the Gantt chart can be used for this decision—one worker could do the activities in Task 1.5, for example, in Figure 12.2, while

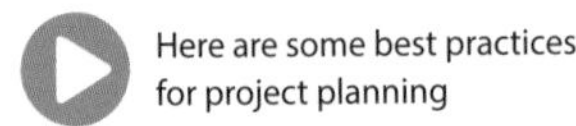

Table 12.2 Time, Cost, and Precedence Information for the Park Maintenance Project

Task	Activity	Description	Duration (hrs.)	Cost ($15/hr.)	Precedence
1.1 Clean and repair	1.1.1 trash pickup	Empty trash cans, pick up litter in entire park	2	30	1.5
	1.1.2 bag grass and trimmings	Bag the cut grass; bundle the bush and tree limbs	2	30	1.2.1, 1.3
	1.1.3 transport	Haul trash/grass/trimmings to the dump	1	15	1.1.1, 1.1.2
	1.1.4 clean/repair playground equipment	Clean all equipment; replace worn and missing parts	8	120 + 250	1.5
1.2 Mow grass	1.2.1 cut grass; edge grass	Mow grass with riding mower; edge grass along concrete areas	5	75	1.1.1
1.3 Trim work	1.3.1 trim hedges	Trim all bushes and hedges	4	60	1.5
	1.3.2 trim trees	Trim all trees where needed	6	90	1.5
1.4 Sprinklers	1.4.1 check/repair	Check all sprinklers/bubblers and repair where needed	5	75 + 50	1.5
1.5 Prep work	1.5.1 inventory, fuel/charge equipment	Inventory equipment/parts; do maintenance if needed; refuel and recharge equipment where needed	4	60 + 50	None
			Total	**$905**	

Figure 12.2 The Gantt Chart for Park Maintenance Project

Task	Activity
1.5 Prep work	Inventory, fuel and charge equipment
1.3 Trim work	Trim hedges
	Trim trees
1.4 Sprinklers	Check/repair
1.1 Cleanup/repair	Trash pickup
	Bag grass/trimmings
	Transport
	Clean/repair playground equip.
1.2 Mow grass	Cut/edge grass

0 2 4 6 8 10 12 14
Time, hours

also picking up the trash, cutting/edging the grass, bagging the grass, and hauling trash to the dump. Additionally, it appears that four more workers will be needed to perform Tasks 1.3 and 1.4, and to clean and repair the playground equipment. It may also be possible to have one worker trim hedges and then check and repair sprinklers, without going over the 14-hour time estimate. Thus, for simple projects, Gantt charts are low cost, simple to construct, and easy to understand. But what about building a house? A high-rise? Or a dam? For highly complex projects like these and the ones shown in Table 12.1, planning involves many hundreds or thousands of hours and complex task considerations. In these cases, while a WBS is still used, project managers need a tool that more adequately considers task interdependencies and precedence relationships. PERT and CPM, the two most widely used and computerized project management techniques, are preferred for these types of projects, and are discussed next.

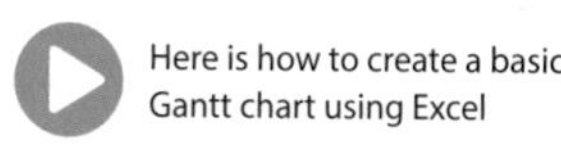

Here is how to create a basic Gantt chart using Excel

THE CPM AND PERT PROJECT MANAGEMENT TECHNIQUES

12.3 Understand and discuss the Critical Path Method and the Program Evaluation and Review Technique

The best-known project management techniques are the **Critical Path Method** (CPM) and the **Program Evaluation and Review Technique** (PERT). Both techniques were developed independently at about the same time in the late 1950s. This is considered the start of modern project management. Mathematicians Morgan Walker of DuPont and James Kelly of Remington Rand are generally credited with developing the CPM method. DuPont had purchased one of the first UNIVAC computers, built by a division of Remington Rand, and wanted to see if it could be used for planning, scheduling, and estimating activities. Walker and Kelly developed the algorithms that became one of the first-ever computer applications. The company Booz Allen Hamilton developed PERT for the U.S. Navy. The PERT method was later applied to the U.S. Polaris missile project, and is credited with taking two years off the originally projected completion time.[14]

While some of the details of CPM and PERT are different, both seek to accomplish the same thing: to determine the *longest sequence* of activities that, when linked together, determine the completion time for the entire project. This is termed the **critical path**. A delay in any of the critical path activities will likely delay the entire project. Therefore, critical path activities must be managed closely, to allow projects to finish on time. Some projects may have multiple critical paths, and during the life of a project, noncritical path activities

Critical Path Method A method developed in the 1950s to determine a project's longest sequence of activities that, when linked together, determine the completion time for the entire project.

Program Evaluation and Review Technique *See* Critical Path Method.

critical path The longest sequence of activities that, when linked together, determine the completion time for the entire project. A delay in any of the critical path activities will delay the entire project. Therefore, critical path activities must be managed closely, to allow projects to finish on time.

might become critical if they experience lengthy delays. In the following discussion, the comments and steps apply to both PERT and CPM, so no further distinction will be made between the two.

To begin, the following steps are required:

1. Identify all of the project's activities, and the time required to complete each activity.
2. Determine the sequential relationships among all of the activities. (Note that Steps 1 and 2 were discussed earlier for the WBS.)
3. Construct an activity network using the information contained in Steps 1 and 2.
4. Determine the critical path (the longest-time path through the network).
5. Determine the early start/early finish schedule and the late start/late finish schedule. For each activity in the project, the early start, early finish, late start, and late finish times must be calculated. The difference between the early start and late start times or the early finish and late finish times is defined as the **slack time**.

slack time The difference between the early start and late start times or the early finish and late finish times.

Example 12.1 illustrates the steps in constructing an activity network for the earlier-described park maintenance project.

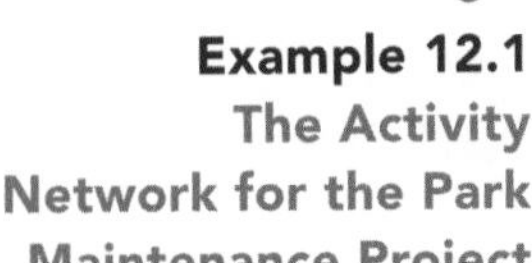

Example 12.1 The Activity Network for the Park Maintenance Project

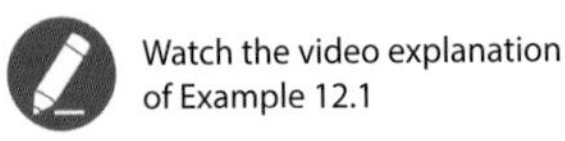

Activity	Time (hrs.)	Immediate Predecessor(s)
1.1.1	2	1.5.1
1.1.2	2	1.2.1, 1.3.1, 1.3.2
1.1.3	1	1.1.1, 1.1.2
1.1.4	8	1.5.1
1.2.1	5	1.1.1
1.3.1	4	1.5.1
1.3.2	6	1.5.1
1.4.1	5	1.5.1
1.5.1	4	none

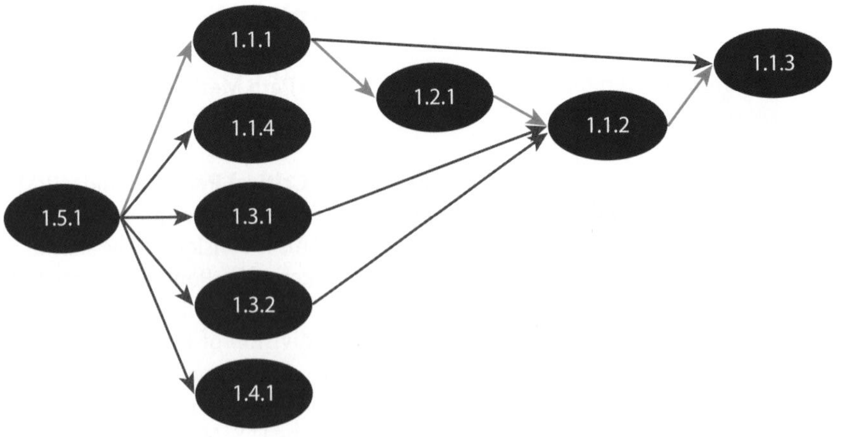

Constructing the activity network:

The ovals represent the activities and the arrows represent the activity sequence and predecessors. Activities 1.1.1, 1.1.4, 1.3.1, 1.3.2, and 1.4.1 cannot begin until 1.5.1 is completed. Similarly, 1.1.2 cannot begin until 1.2.1, 1.3.1, and 1.3.2 are completed. Note that 1.1.3, 1.1.4, and 1.4.1 are all path-ending activities.

DETERMINING THE CRITICAL PATH

The critical path of a project is the longest set of activities in a project. This is important, since these activities will most likely determine the total time to complete the entire project. Viewing the activity network for the park maintenance project in Example 12.1, the six possible activity paths are:

(1) 1.5.1—1.1.1—1.1.3
(2) 1.5.1—1.1.1—1.2.1—1.1.2—1.1.3
(3) 1.5.1—1.1.4
(4) 1.5.1—1.3.1—1.1.2—1.1.3
(5) 1.5.1—1.3.2—1.1.2—1.1.3, and
(6) 1.5.1—1.4.1.

Summing the activity times, the six activity path completion times are: (1) 7; (2) 14; (3) 12; (4) 11; (5) 13; and (6) 9. Thus, the critical path is Path 2, with a completion time of 14 hours, which is shown in orange in the activity network in Example 12.1. Activities on the critical path are referred to as **critical activities**, since these activities determine a project's completion time. These five activities must be managed closely to ensure that delays in these activities are minimized so the project can be completed on time.

critical activities Activities on the critical path.

DETERMINING THE EARLY/LATE START AND EARLY/LATE FINISH SCHEDULES

For all of the activities not on the critical path, there are potential slack times between an activity's completion and the next scheduled activity. Slack times tell the project manager how long an activity can be delayed without affecting the overall project's completion time. An early start schedule shows how early an activity can be started, and a late start schedule shows how late an activity can be started without delaying project completion. As shown in Example 12.2, the early/late start and early/late finish schedules and the activity slack hours are shown. Note that the slack time is calculated as (late start – early start) or (late finish – early finish) time.

All critical path activities have slack times of zero. A number of other activities, though, such as Activity 1.3.2 shown in Example 12.2, can have low slack times, and should also be monitored closely to ensure that delays do not create new critical paths and push back the completion of the entire project.

Referring to Example 12.2, to calculate the activity slack times for the park maintenance project, the early and late, start and finish times are filled in starting with the first activity—1.5.1, with a starting time of 0. It is also easiest if the critical path activity boxes are completed first. The early start time for 1.5.1 is 0, and the early finish time is 4 hours. Since 1.5.1 is a critical path activity, the late start and late finish times are also 0 and 4 hours. Similarly, Activity 1.1.1, a critical path activity with an activity time of 2 hours, must begin at 4 hours (early and late start times) and finish at 6 hours (early and late finish times). Activities 1.2.1, 1.1.2, and 1.1.3 are all completed similarly, resulting in no slack times for these activities and a project completion time of 14 hours. Next, the early start time for 1.1.4, 1.3.1, 1.3.2, and 1.4.1 is 4 hours, since that is when Activity 1.5.1 finishes. Activity 1.1.4 is an ending activity, so it can have a late finish time of 14 hours with a late start time of 6 hours. Activity 1.4.1 is also an ending activity, and therefore has a late finish time of 14 hours with a late start time of 9 hours. Once the early and late, start and finish times are known, the slack times can be calculated.

Up to this point, we have assumed that all activity times are known and constant. In the real world, however, most activities have varying completion times depending on a number of factors. Supplier deliveries can be late, machines break down, workers get sick, and the weather gets bad. These unexpected difficulties can cause many delays in a large project, so time variabilities should be considered during the planning phase. Accounting for these time variabilities is considered in the next section.

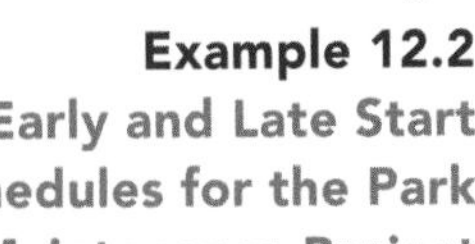

Example 12.2
Early and Late Start Schedules for the Park Maintenance Project

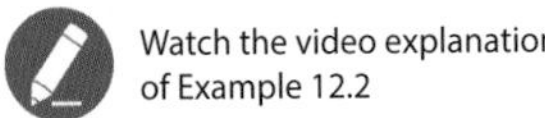

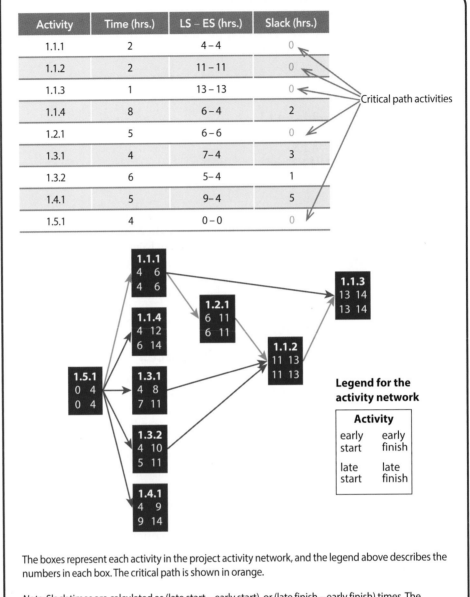

Activity	Time (hrs.)	LS – ES (hrs.)	Slack (hrs.)
1.1.1	2	4 – 4	0
1.1.2	2	11 – 11	0
1.1.3	1	13 – 13	0
1.1.4	8	6 – 4	2
1.2.1	5	6 – 6	0
1.3.1	4	7– 4	3
1.3.2	6	5– 4	1
1.4.1	5	9– 4	5
1.5.1	4	0 – 0	0

Critical path activities

1.1.1 4 6 4 6
1.1.4 4 12 6 14
1.5.1 0 4 0 4
1.3.1 4 8 7 11
1.3.2 4 10 5 11
1.4.1 4 9 9 14
1.2.1 6 11 6 11
1.1.2 11 13 11 13
1.1.3 13 14 13 14

Legend for the activity network

Activity	
early start	early finish
late start	late finish

The boxes represent each activity in the project activity network, and the legend above describes the numbers in each box. The critical path is shown in orange.

Note: Slack times are calculated as (late start – early start), or (late finish – early finish) times. The critical path activities have zero slack.

USING THREE TIME ESTIMATES FOR PROJECT ACTIVITIES

Borrowing from PERT, we can employ a beta distribution (which is commonly used to describe uncertainties or random variations) based on three time estimates to complete each activity. The three activity time estimates are defined as follows:

optimistic completion time The time to complete the activity if everything goes according to plan (the probability should be very low that the activity can be completed in less time).

pessimistic completion time The maximum completion time for an activity, given that everything goes wrong (the probability should be very low that the activity can be completed in a longer time).

most likely completion time The best estimate of completion time for an activity, given normal conditions.

> **Optimistic completion time** (a). The time to complete the activity if everything goes according to plan (the probability should be very low that the activity can be completed in less time).
>
> **Pessimistic completion time** (b). The maximum completion time for an activity, given that everything goes wrong (the probability should be very low that the activity can be completed in a longer time).
>
> **Most likely completion time** (m). The best estimate of completion time for an activity, given normal conditions.

To determine the **expected activity completion time**, t, the beta distribution weights are used with the three time estimates as follows:

$$t = (a + 4m + b)/6$$

To calculate one particular **activity completion time variance**, σ_A^2, the following equation is used:[15]

$$\sigma_A^2 = [(b - a)/6]^2$$

Example 12.3 illustrates the calculation of expected times and variances for the park maintenance project.

expected activity completion time The beta distribution weights are used with the three time estimates as follows: $t = (a + 4m + b)/6$.

activity completion time variance The following equation is used for the variance: $\sigma_A^2 = [(b - a)/6]^2$.

Calculating the Probability of Completion by a Given Time

The original CPM determined that 14 hours would be needed to complete the park maintenance project. Using the expected activity times generated in Example 12.3, the expected completion time for the project then becomes 14.41 hours. Given the variances shown in Example 12.3 associated with each activity, though, it may very well take longer than 14.41 hours to complete. The time variations of activities on the critical path are particularly noteworthy, since these could delay the entire project.

Again borrowing from PERT, the variance of the project's completion time is found by summing the variances of the critical path activities, or:

$$\sigma_P^2 = \Sigma(\text{critical path activity variances})$$

For the park maintenance project shown in Example 12.3, this is:

$$\sigma_P^2 = 0.063 + 0.028 + 0.004 + 0.444 + 0.007 = 0.546$$

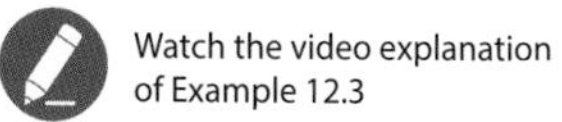

Example 12.3
Expected Times and Variances for the Park Maintenance Project

Watch the video explanation of Example 12.3

Activity	Optimistic a	Most likely m	Pessimistic b	Expected t	Variance σ_A^2
1.1.1	1.5	2	3	2.08	0.063
1.1.2	1.5	2	2.5	2.0	0.028
1.1.3	0.8	1	1.2	1.0	0.004
1.1.4	5	8	10	7.83	0.694
1.2.1	4	5	8	5.33	0.444
1.3.1	3	4	6	4.16	0.25
1.3.2	3.5	6	10	6.25	1.174
1.4.1	4	5	7	5.17	0.25
1.5.1	3.5	4	4.5	4.0	0.007

Critical path variances

The original activity times for the park maintenance project from Examples 12.1 and 12.2 are shown above as the most likely times, m. The expected times and the variances are calculated as shown in the chapter. For Activity 1.1.1, $t = (a + 4m + b)/6 = (1.5 + 8 + 3)/6 = 2.08$, and the variance $= [(b - a)/6]^2 = (1.5/6)^2 = 0.063$. Note that as the spread between the optimistic and pessimistic completion times increases, the variance also increases. The expected completion time for the park project is then the sum of the critical path activity expected times, or $2.08 + 2 + 1 + 5.33 + 4 = 14.41$ hours.

Note: The critical path activity variances are shown in orange.

With a standard deviation of:

$$\sigma_p = \sqrt{\sigma_p^2} = \sqrt{0.546} = 0.739 \text{ hours}.$$

If we now assume that project completion times are normally distributed around the expected project completion time, then the normal curve Z-table can be used to find the **probability of completing a project by a given time** (this implies a 50% probability of completing the park maintenance project in less than 14.41 hours and 50% probability of completing the project in more than 14.41 hours). Use the standard normal equation to find Z:

$$Z = (\text{desired completion date} - \text{expected completion date}) / \sigma_P .$$

Example 12.4 illustrates this concept.

Calculating the Required Completion With a Stated Probability

On the other hand, it might be preferable to determine how long a project is likely to take if we desire a high level of confidence in our completion time estimate. This may prove useful, for instance, if we are negotiating a due date with a client. In this case, start first with the Z-table—find the Z associated with a high probability (say, 99%), then use the standard normal equation to find the corresponding due date. Solving this equation for the due date yields:

$$\text{desired completion date} = (Z\sigma_P) + \text{expected completion date} .$$

Example 12.5 illustrates this concept.

probability of completing a project by a given time Use the standard normal equation to find Z, where Z = (desired completion date − expected completion date) / σ_p. Then use the Z table to determine the probability.

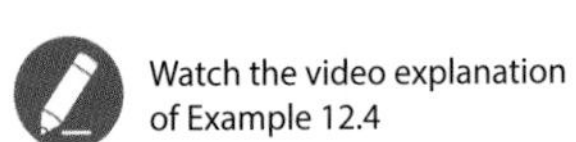

Example 12.4
Determining the Probability of Completing the Park Maintenance Project Within 15 Hours

Watch the video explanation of Example 12.4

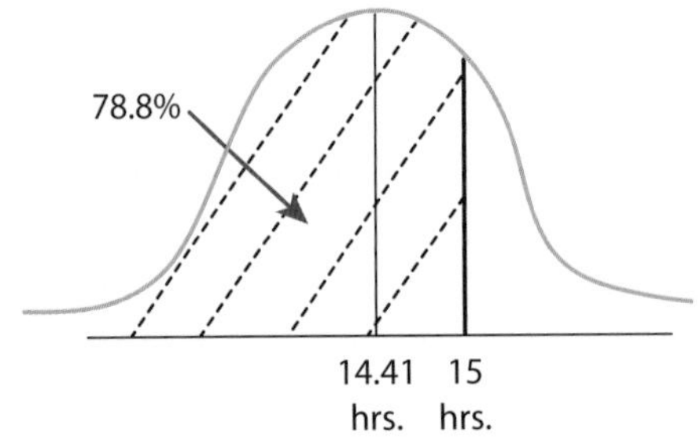

If it is desired to complete the project within 15 hours, the Z formula yields:

Z = (desired completion time − expected completion time)/σ_p = (15 − 14.41) / 0.739 = 0.8. Referring to the Z-table in Appendix A, a Z value of 0.8 above the mean indicates a probability of 0.788. Thus, there is a 78.8% probability that the park maintenance project can be finished in 15 hours.

MONITORING THE VARIABILITIES OF NONCRITICAL ACTIVITIES

If activities not on the critical path have relatively high variabilities, then these could potentially delay the entire project's completion date. Consider, for example, Path 5 from Example 12.1, consisting of Activity 1.3.2, which has a high variance (1.174) and only 1 hour of slack time, as shown in Example 12.2. It also has a pessimistic completion time of 10 hours. It then would appear somewhat likely that Activity 1.3.2 will experience delays, causing the park project to miss its projected completion time, even though it is not a critical activity. Thus, project managers must keep in close contact with these noncritical activities to monitor their progress and ensure they do not get behind schedule.

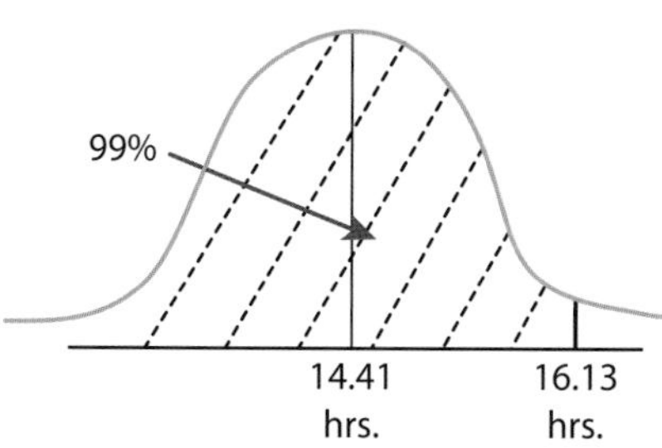

If it is desired to state a completion time with a 99% level of confidence, the Z formula yields:

Desired completion time = $Z\sigma_P$ + expected completion time, or 2.33(.739) + 14.41 = 16.13 hours. (Referring to the Z-table in Appendix A, a 99% level of confidence corresponds to a Z value of 2.33. Thus, we would be 99% sure we could complete the project in 16.13 hours.)

Example 12.5
Determining the Completion Hours for the Park Maintenance Project With a 99% Confidence Level

Watch the video explanation of Example 12.5

PROJECT TRADE-OFFS AND CRASHING

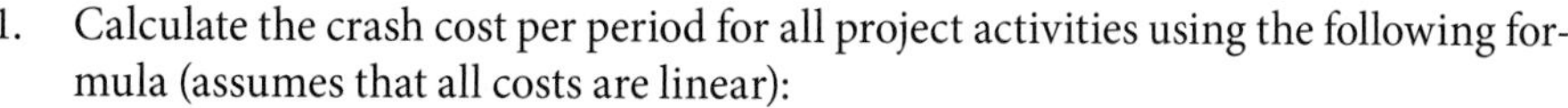

The project manager can often reduce a project's completion time by assigning more resources to it—more workers or overtime can be used, or more equipment can be assigned to the project. All of these resources come at a cost, and this is referred to as the time–cost trade-off in project management. Reducing a project's completion time by using more resources is called **project crashing**. Each activity in a project has a normal completion time and cost, and some activities can have a shortest possible time for completion (the **crash time**) with an associated higher cost (the **crash cost**). Some activities, though, such as drive times, may not be able to be shortened.

Project managers interested in shortening a project want to know which activities can be crashed, and what the crash costs will be, so that project crashing can be done at the lowest possible additional cost. Managers also realize that crashing an activity on the critical path might then cause another activity path to become the critical path and hence control the length of the project. Thus, project crashing must consider the impacts on all project activities and paths in the network. The following three-step procedure can be used for crashing activity times while keeping down crash costs:

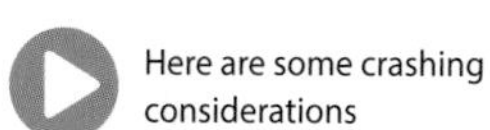
Here are some crashing considerations

1. Calculate the crash cost per period for all project activities using the following formula (assumes that all costs are linear):

$$\text{Crash cost per period} = \frac{(\text{crash cost} - \text{normal cost})}{(\text{normal time} - \text{crash time})}$$

   Table 12.3 shows the normal times and crash times and their costs for the park maintenance project.

2. Determine the desired completion time and the critical path (using the normal time estimates). If the critical path time is longer than the desired completion time, and there is more than one critical path, select one arbitrarily. Pick the activity on the critical path with the lowest crash cost per period (if there are multiple activities with the lowest crash cost per period, select one arbitrarily that has not already been crashed to the maximum extent possible). Crash this activity until the desired time savings have been achieved or until no further crash time exists for that activity.
3. Reduce the length of the crashed path, and update the project cost. Return to Step 2 until the desired project completion time has been achieved. Note that to determine

project crashing Reducing a project's completion time by using more resources.

crash time The shortest possible time for activity completion.

crash cost The cost to achieve the crash time.

the minimum project completion time, it would be necessary to compare the crash times for all the activity paths on the project activity network.

Example 12.6 illustrates activity crashing with the park maintenance project.

Table 12.3 Normal and Crash Times and Costs for the Park Maintenance Project

Activity	Normal Time (hrs.)	Normal Cost ($)	Crash Time (hrs.)	Crash Cost ($)	Crash Cost per Hour ($)
1.1.1	2	30	1	60	30
1.1.2	2	30	1	60	30
1.1.3	1	15	1	15	—
1.1.4	8	370	2	730	60
1.2.1	5	75	3	135	30
1.3.1	4	60	1	240	60
1.3.2	6	90	2	270	45
1.4.1	5	125	2.5	200	30
1.5.1	4	110	2	170	30
		$905			

The crash cost per hour is calculated as:

$$\text{Crash cost per hour} = \frac{(\text{crash cost} - \text{normal cost})}{(\text{normal time} - \text{crash time})}$$

Note: The crash cost per hour for the critical path activities are shown in orange.

MANAGING PROJECT RISK

12.5 Identify and manage project risks

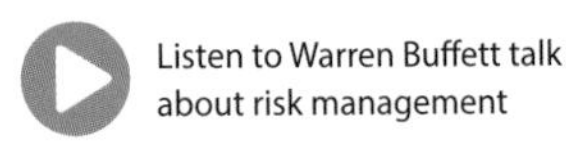

Listen to Warren Buffett talk about risk management

Project risk is a major concern in all projects, and can be defined as "unexpected events that can cause missed project completion times or cost overruns." Project managers must try to identify potential risks, assess their likelihood of occurrence, and then develop plans to mitigate project risks, along with contingency plans to deal with the risks when they do occur.

Unforeseen events, combined with a lack of risk management plans, can prove extremely expensive The Channel Tunnel project's large cost overruns mentioned in Table 12.1 is one such project. Also recall, in Chapter 6, our discussion of the MGM Mirage's CityCenter project—a $9 billion multiple resort/casino complex that had made no contingency plans for an economic downturn that occurred right in the middle of the project's construction. The Service Spotlight on page 378 describes project risk management at the 2012 Olympic Park in London.

Generally speaking, there are five categories of project management risks:

project risk Unexpected events that can cause missed project completion times or cost overruns.

external risks Risks outside of company control, which can cause project delays.

cost risks Risks that are mostly within company control, such as cost overruns by suppliers and subcontractors, design changes occurring during the project, and poor estimates of activity costs.

1. **External risks**. Outside of company control. Examples include changes in economic conditions, government regulatory changes, legal developments, weather disruptions, and new products or competitors in the marketplace.
2. **Cost risks**. Mostly within company control. Examples are cost overruns by suppliers and subcontractors, design changes occurring during the project, and poor estimates of activity costs.

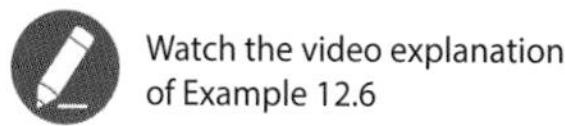

Example 12.6
Crashing Activities in the Park Maintenance Project

Watch the video explanation of Example 12.6

City management has decided it needs the park maintenance project completed in 11 hours instead of the 14-hour normal completion time. Additionally, it needs to know the new total cost of the project. In the table below, the critical path activities and crash costs per hour are shown in orange. It is seen that all critical path activities with available crash hours have the same crash cost per hour. So Activity 1.5.1 is selected, since it has 2 crash hours available, and it belongs in all activity paths. Thus, all pathways will be reduced simultaneously.

Activity	Normal Time (hrs.)	Crashed Time (hrs.)	Crash Cost ($)	Crash Cost per Day ($)
1.1.1	2	1	1	30
1.1.2	2→1	1	1	30
1.1.3	1	1	0	—
1.1.4	8	2	6	60
1.2.1	5	3	2	30
1.3.1	4	1	3	60
1.3.2	6	2	4	45
1.4.1	5	2.5	2.5	30
1.5.1	4→2	2	2	30

The two crash hours will reduce the Activity 1.5.1 normal time to two hours, and add an additional cost of $60 to the project. The resulting critical path time then becomes 12 hours. Activity 1.1.2 is selected next, since it belongs to multiple paths and has a crash time available of one hour. This activity is crashed, making the Activity 1.1.2 normal time one hour, which adds $30 to the project's total cost. The new normal times are shown in orange, above. Referring to Example 12.1, the activity paths and normal times are shown below:

Path	Length (hrs.)
1.5.1—1.1.1—1.1.3	5
1.5.1—1.1.1—1.2.1—1.1.2—1.1.3	11
1.5.1—1.1.4	10
1.5.1—1.3.1—1.1.2—1.1.3	8
1.5.1—1.3.2—1.1.2—1.1.3	10
1.5.1—1.4.1	7

Thus, it is seen that there is still one critical path, it has a crashed time of 11 hours, and the total project cost is now $905 + $90 = $995. The project could still easily be crashed one more hour, by crashing Activity 1.1.1 for one hour, at a cost of $30.

3. **Schedule risks**. Mostly within company control. Examples include unrealistic activity time estimations, inaccurate technical and operational requirements, and insufficient resources.
4. **Technology risks**. Can be either inside or outside of company control. Examples include use of unfamiliar technology or software, failures or breakdowns of technology and software, and software integration problems.
5. **Operational risks**. Within company control. Examples include incorrect activity scheduling, poor forecasting, poor supplier selection, lack of communication among key personnel, and inadequate production design or ramp-up.

schedule risks Unrealistic activity time estimations, inaccurate technical and operational requirements, and insufficient resources, which cause project delays.

technology risks Failures or breakdowns of technology and software, and software integration problems, which can delay projects.

operational risks Incorrect activity scheduling, poor forecasting, poor supplier selection, lack of communication among key personnel, or inadequate production design or ramp-up, which can cause project delays.

SERVICE SPOTLIGHT

Project Risk Management at London's Olympic Park

Construction of the 2012 Olympic Park in London serves as a model of good project risk management. By October 2011, a total of 68 million hours had been worked at the site since the project began in 2005, with only 114 injuries and eight events considered dangerous.

iStock/Johnny Greig

To achieve that type of performance, the government agency charged with staging the games adopted several health and safety risk management approaches. During construction of the Olympic Park, contractors, designers, and construction coordinators were required to monitor and submit monthly reports on their firms' health and safety risk performances. Communications with workers about lessons learned from incidents also were important parts of the risk management program. For example, health and safety requirements associated with various tasks each day were included in daily activity briefings.

An example of risk management at the site was the potential for materials falling off the construction trucks being used. To minimize this risk, a traffic management plan was implemented to ensure that trucks and pedestrians were kept apart. Additionally, drilling into concrete to secure seats in the Olympic Stadium presented several risks to workers, including hand–arm vibrations and exposure to noise. Consequently, an apparatus was developed to hold the drills that otherwise would have been held by hand. This reduced both the amount of hand–arm vibrations and noise.[16]

IDENTIFYING RISKS

Early in the project's planning stages, the project team must spend time brainstorming and researching potential risks and their likelihood of occurrence. Risks can then be assessed and resources assigned to manage these risks. In evaluating each potential risk, management should assess the likelihood of occurrence, the severity of the impact on the project, and the risk's controllability. A risk assessment score could then be calculated using the variables mentioned here, to assist in ranking the risks. Example 12.7 illustrates the risk assessment score.

Based on the risk assessment, the firm can begin monitoring the highest-scoring risks while devising plans to mitigate and then minimize their impact if they do come to fruition. Risk levels should be updated periodically during the planning phases, and then while the project is being completed. If risks are considered high, the firm may wish to drop the project, if possible. It may need to assemble a risk management team for large and potentially costly projects.

MITIGATION AND CONTINGENCY PLANS

For each identified risk, managers should consider two actions: a plan to reduce or mitigate the risk, and a contingency plan to implement if the event occurs. For the firm in Example 12.7, managers might consider using several different forecasting techniques, looking at historical forecasting error levels, or negotiating a guaranteed contract with the customer to make the forecast unimportant. They might want to finalize contracts with their labor unions, and find more reliable suppliers. These would be examples of **risk mitigation plans**.

When designing contingency plans, managers should consider moderate and worst-case scenarios. Well-designed contingency plans can keep the devastating impacts of risk events from happening. For the firm, again, in Example 12.7: Managers should consider the consequences of forecasting too high, as well as too low, and plan how to deal with these outcomes. Perhaps identifying a substitute labor force and backup suppliers would also be good ideas. Detailed contingency plan guidelines or instructions should be compiled and communicated to the necessary personnel. As the project goes forward, these plans must be revisited and revised as conditions dictate.

risk mitigation plans Actions taken to reduce project risk.

Example 12.7
Assessing Project Risks

Watch the video explanation of Example 12.7

The Meana Engineering Co. had recently begun planning a relatively large project and had identified five potential risks it wanted to assess and rank. The risks and their assessments are shown here:

Risk	Likelihood	Severity	Controllability	Total
Legal aspects	7	3	2	12
Supplier deliveries	5	7	4	16
Labor strike	3	9	4	16
Software bugs	3	4	2	9
Inaccurate forecast	5	4	8	17

A 10-point scale is used, where 1 = very low level of concern and 10 = very high level of concern. The scores are added (assuming all three assessment variables are equally weighted) to obtain a total score for each risk. Inaccurate forecasting, labor strike, and supplier deliveries are given relatively high levels of risk, while legal aspects are assessed at lower risk, with software bugs having the lowest risk.

Over time, as projects are planned and completed, the firm can develop profiles for certain types of risks and projects. It will know which risks are important, how mitigation efforts fared, and which contingency plans had the most success. This knowledge will help to reduce project failures and cost or time overruns.

TRENDS IN PRODUCT MANAGEMENT

12.6 Discuss the advantages and disadvantages of cloud-based project management applications

This chapter has discussed project management tools using a small-park maintenance project as the example. For large or complex projects and projects with far-flung and international participants, firms use **project management software** and cloud-based systems. Employees and subcontractors can access the projects online and make changes or receive updates easily.

project management software Software designed to track a project's progress.

SERVICE SPOTLIGHT

Ajasa Switches to Use of MS Project

Tony Williamson, CEO of Minnesota-based Ajasa Technologies, formerly used Excel spreadsheets to track the firm's projects. "That was just horrendous," explains Williamson. "It was one huge spreadsheet. You'd open it up and somebody would have it locked; you'd save a copy and somebody else would come in and save another copy over yours." Ajasa now relies on MS Project. Williamson partly credits this change with increasing the firm's annual revenues to more than $35 million.

Ajasa's employees and subcontractors (some of which are in foreign countries) can access a project through a central server and adjust projected times for tasks, for example. Project managers can monitor multiple projects and estimate the times suppliers should need to complete a task. Users have varied access levels, so project managers can view budgets, for instance, while suppliers can't.

Ajasa used MS Project, for example, to manage a large-scale electronic money transfer project for a bank that wanted to convert its 12 regions into one automated clearinghouse. The project took five years to complete, and none of the bank's 81 million daily transactions was disrupted. MS Project allowed Ajasa to see scheduling conflicts upfront and successfully balance the workload and costs for the project.[17]

The ability of project management software to track a project's progress is perhaps one of its biggest advantages. The experiences of Ajasa Technologies, with its use of project management software, are shown in the Service Spotlight "Ajasa Switches to Use of MS Project."

Complex projects can be tricky, with many tasks—each having its own completion problem, due date, and subcontractor. Team-member tasks, revisions, quality considerations, and costs must continually be tracked and updated or reprogrammed. The project manager needs to communicate and collaborate with team members effectively as well. Additionally, project management software can identify potential problems more quickly; clarify the project's scope and personnel responsibilities; optimize resources; and ensure payment for completed work in an effective manner. All of these requirements can be handled with any one of a number of good project management software solutions. Users must remember, though, that use of project management software doesn't guarantee projects will be completed on time or within budget constraints. The software is only as good as the people using it and the data put into it.

For small businesses with relatively less complex projects, free or **open source software** products are also available. Some project management software can cost as much as $20,000, which is simply out of many small companies' budget ranges. The free software products have the basic project management tools like Gantt charts and critical path determinations, but do not offer capabilities such as risk management, or services like technical support, detailed documentation, and customization capabilities.

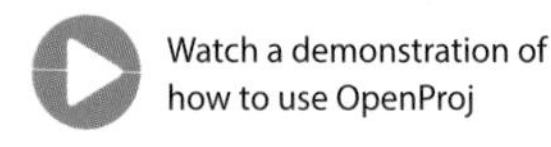
Watch a demonstration of how to use OpenProj

There are some notable exceptions: OpenProj, for example, a free, open source solution owned by California-based Serena Software, is considered one of the most sophisticated project management software solutions ever provided in open source format. It is compatible with other software products and operating systems, and is used in over 100 countries. GanttProject is another freeware example—it is considered an easy-to-use program for any manager with a desire to keep up with ongoing projects and staff.[18]

CLOUD-BASED PROJECT MANAGEMENT

Cloud computing can be defined as the access and delivery of information technology resources including software, operating systems, and servers on an as-needed basis, for a subscription price or fee. For instance, suppose your project team has a job opportunity to build a database from JPEG images of archived government documents. Each image must first be converted to PDF format, and then to searchable text using optical character recognition (OCR). The job completion time has a requirement of two weeks. Do you take the job? After some quick calculations, the team determines it will take about 30 seconds per page to make the conversions. With your firm's server and the number of images to convert, this means 139 days to complete the job! The options are to somehow buy or rent and then configure 30 servers (high risk), turn the job down (and risk losing future jobs), or look for a commercial cloud computing solution that could get the job done. This was a real scenario—the firm in question was able to find a cloud service that did the required computing in less than a day for about $300.[19]

The example above illustrates the computing power and capabilities of cloud applications, which give smaller firms the ability to compete with large firms without having to make large capital investments in information systems. Instead, firms can use whatever computing resources they need, as often or as seldom as needed, and pay only for what they use. Another example is a mandate by the U.S. government's Office of Management and Budget (OMB). In an effort to reduce the government's carbon footprint by eliminating about 40% of existing data centers, the OMB directed all federal agencies in 2010 to begin moving all information technology requirements to the cloud whenever reliable, secure, cost-effective cloud solutions could be found.[20]

open source software Free software for small businesses with relatively less complex projects.

cloud computing Access and delivery of information technology resources including software, operating systems, and servers on an as-needed basis, for a subscription price or fee.

Regarding project management software, a 2012 *InformationWeek* magazine survey found that about 60% of the business managers responding said their firms had dedicated project management offices using commercial, purchased project management software. The rest were using a mix of simple tools like spreadsheets and/or cloud applications. Some managers in the survey were reluctant to use cloud applications due to worries about data security, availability, or hidden fees and cost escalations.[21] Questions regarding security, though, while very common regarding the cloud, are for the most part unfounded. All cloud sites use either 128-bit or 256-bit data encryption. At the 128-bit level, it would take modern-day computers literally forever to cycle through all the possible decryption keys. Compared to most home computers connected to the Internet, cloud systems are more secure.

One example of a **cloud-based project management solution** is HyperOffice. The Maryland-based firm has about 300,000 users and targets small- to medium-sized businesses. The product has collaboration features, an interactive Gantt chart, and most other features required by small-business managers. "I can set up projects and tasks of any duration, and anyone in my group can be informed when their task is due or when another task is complete and theirs can begin," says David Marlatt of DNM Architect. For firms with 50 users, the cost is roughly $3,500 per year, which includes all of the necessary setup and support.[22] For large global firms with many hundreds of users, cloud systems most likely would not offer a cost advantage over purchased software.

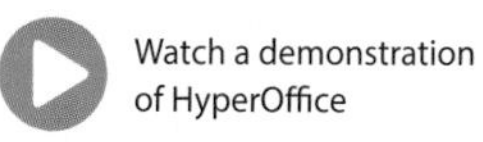
Watch a demonstration of HyperOffice

cloud-based project management solution Project management software available in the cloud.

SAGE edge™

Visit edge.sagepub.com/wisner to help you accomplish your coursework goals in an easy-to-use learning environment.

- Mobile-friendly eFlashcards
- Mobile-friendly practice quizzes
- A complete online action plan
- Chapter summaries with learning objectives
- Excel templates to assist with practice problems
- Original video case studies that demonstrate chapter concepts in action

SUMMARY

Project management is an important element in a manager's tool set today. Successful project managers not only need behavioral skills to deal effectively with diverse work groups and global partners, but also the ability to manage the planning and execution of many simultaneous complex project activities. This chapter has reviewed the essentials of project management, from creating a work breakdown structure and Gantt chart, to use of the critical path method, to completion probability estimates, to project crashing, to project risk analysis, to cloud-based software. In all projects, the objective is to correctly complete project activities on time and within budget constraints. The tools outlined in this chapter will help managers in these efforts. A number of videos reinforcing the tools presented in the chapter were also provided.

KEY TERMS

Activity completion time variance, 373
Cloud-based project management solution, 381
Cloud computing, 380
Cost risks, 376
Crash cost, 375
Crash time, 375
Critical activities, 371
Critical path, 369
Critical Path Method, 369
Expected activity completion time, 373
External risks, 376
Gantt chart, 368
Managing projects, 366
Most likely completion time, 372
Open source software, 380
Operational risks, 377
Optimistic completion time, 372
Pessimistic completion time, 372
Probability of completing a project by a given time, 374
Program Evaluation and Review Technique, 369
Project, 366
Project crashing, 375
Project management software, 379

Project risk, 376
Risk mitigation plans, 378
Schedule risks, 377
Slack time, 370
Technology risks, 377
Work breakdown structure, 367

FORMULA REVIEW

Expected activity completion time: $t = (a + 4m + b)/6$, where a = optimistic completion time, m = most likely completion time, and b = pessimistic completion time.

Activity completion time variance: $\sigma_A^2 = [(b-a)/6]^2$, where a,b are defined as above.

Variance of the project's completion time: $\sigma_p^2 = \Sigma$ (critical path activity variances).

Probability of completing a project by a given time: (1) use the standard normal equation to find Z, where Z = (desired completion date – expected completion date) / σ_p; and (2) look up Z in a Z-table to find the probability.

Project completion time associated with a high level of confidence: (1) start first with the Z-table—find the Z associated with a high probability (say, 99%); (2) use the standard normal equation to find the corresponding due date—desired completion date = $(Z\sigma_p)$ + expected completion date.

$$\text{Crash cost per period} = \frac{(\text{crash cost} - \text{normal cost})}{(\text{normal time} - \text{crash time})}$$

where crash cost = cost to achieve the crash time, and crash time = the shortest possible time for activity completion.

SOLVED PROBLEMS

1. For the following project, construct a Gantt chart for the activities shown:

Activity	Predecessor(s)	Duration (days)
A	—	1
B	A	2
C	A	3
D	B	2
E	B,C	1
F	E	1

Based on your Gantt chart, what are the days to completion?

Answer:

Activity	0–1	1–2	2–3	3–4	4–5	5–6
A	■					
B		■	■			
C		■	■	■		
D				■	■	
E					■	
F						■

Time 0 1 2 3 4 5 6

The expected days to completion are 6.

2. Using the project in Problem 1, construct the project network and list all of the possible activity paths. Determine the critical path(s). What are the critical path days to completion?

Answer:

The project network is constructed using the predecessor list. Activity A has no predecessor, so A is first; both B and C are preceded by A, so they are next; D is preceded by B, so it follows B; E is preceded by both B and C; and finally, F is preceded by E, to complete the network. Note that the arrows show the precedence.

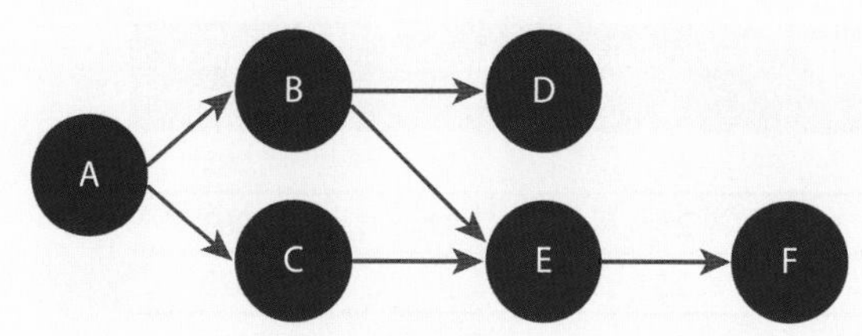

The possible activity paths are then: A-B-D, A-B-E-F, and A-C-E-F

The activity path times are: A-B-D = 5 days; A-B-E-F = 5 days; A-C-E-F = 6 days. The critical path is: A-C-E-F, with 6 days to completion.

3. Using the project in Problem 1, determine the ES, EF, LS, LF, and slack times for each activity.

Answer:

Activity	Time	LS – ES (hrs.)	Slack (hrs.)
A	1	0–0	0
B	2	2–1	1
C	3	1–1	0
D	2	4–3	1
E	1	4–4	0
F	1	5–5	0

The key here is to construct the project network boxes first, and fill in the ES/LS and EF/LF times for the critical path activities. Then determine the ES/LS and EF/LF times for the noncritical path activities. Note the critical path activities have no slack.

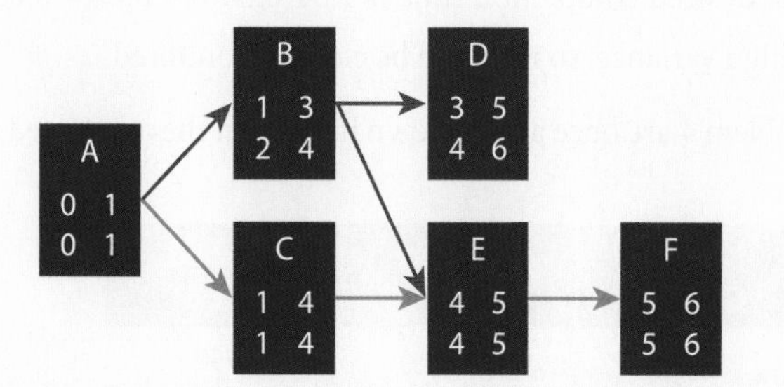

4. The project in Problem 1 is shown here with three time estimates.

Activity	Optimistic	Most Likely	Pessimistic
A	0.5	1	2.0
B	1	2	2.5
C	2.5	3	3.5
D	1	2	3
E	0.9	1	1.1
F	0.5	1	1.5

a. Calculate the expected completion times and completion time variances for each activity.

b. What are the expected days to completion now?

Answer:

a. (See table below)

Activity	Optimistic a	Most Likely m	Pessimistic b	Expected t	Variance σ_A^2
A	0.5	1	2	1.08	0.063
B	1	2	2.5	1.92	0.063
C	2.5	3	3.5	3	0.028
D	1	2	3	2	0.111
E	0.9	1	1.1	1	0.001
F	0.5	1	1.5	1	0.028

b. The expected completion time for the project is the sum of the critical path expected activity times, or 1.08 + 3 + 1 + 1 = 6.08 days.

5. Using the data from Problem 4, calculate the variance and standard deviation of the project's completion time. Also:

a. What is the probability that the project can be completed in 6.5 days?

b. What would be the completion days, if we needed a 95% confidence level?

c. Which noncritical activities should be monitored closely? Why?

Answer:

The variance of the project's completion time is the sum of the critical path activity variances, or: (0.063 + 0.028 + 0.001 + 0.028) = 0.12

The standard deviation of the completion time is then $\sqrt{0.12} = 0.346$ days.

a. Using the Z-table, we need to find the Z = (desired completion time – expected completion time) / σ_p or (6.5 – 6.08)/0.346 = 1.21. Thus, the probability is 0.8849, or about 88% chance of completing the project in 6.5 days.

b. Finding the Z associated with a 95% probability, we get 1.64 from the Z-table. Using the Z formula, 1.64 = (DCT – 6.08)/0.346, so the desired completion time is 1.64(0.346) + 6.08 = 6.65 days.

c. Activity D has a relatively high variance, so it should be closely monitored.

6. The project activities from Problem 4 are once again shown here, with the associated activity costs, crashed time, and crash costs.

Activity	Normal Time	Normal Cost ($)	Crashed Time	Crashed Cost ($)
A	1	500	0.5	750
B	2	1,500	1.5	2,000
C	3	2,000	2.5	2,750
D	2	1,000	1.0	2,000
E	1	300	1	300
F	1	600	0.5	1,100

a. Calculate the crash costs per day.

b. It is desired to complete the project in 5 days. Crash the necessary activities and determine the total costs, including the crash costs.

c. What are the *minimum* completion days, and what is the total crash cost?

Answer:

a. (See table here)

Activity	Normal Time (hrs)	Normal Cost ($)	Crashed Time (hrs)	Crashed Cost ($)	Crashed Cost per Day ($)
A	1	500	0.5	750	500
B	2	1,500	1.5	2,000	1,000
C	3	2,000	2.5	2,750	1,500
D	2	1,000	1.0	2,000	1,000
E	1	300	1.0	300	—
F	1	600	0.5	1,100	1,000

b. It is desired to reduce the project completion time by one day. Activity A is on the critical path and has the lowest crash cost per day. So we crash Activity A by the maximum time (0.5 days) at a cost of $250. An additional 0.5 days is needed, so Activity F is crashed for the 0.5 days, at a cost of $500. The new total project cost is then $5,900 + $750 = $6,650. A-C-E-F is still the critical path at 5 days.

c. The activity paths and their associated crash times are:

A-B-D = 3.0 days, A-B-E-F = 3.5 days, and A-C-E-F = 4.5 days, so 4.5 days is the minimum project time, with a total cost of $5,900 + $1,500 = $7,400.

7. An entrepreneur wished to assess the risks associated with opening a new business in another country. She estimated the risks as (where 1 = low concern, 10 = extreme concern):

Risk	Likelihood of Occurrence	Severity of Impact	Controllability
Taxation issues	5	4	4
Legal issues	6	5	8
Labor issues	4	8	2
Political issues	6	5	8
Supplier issues	4	7	3

The owner decided to weigh the risks equally. Rank the five risks in terms of their total risk scores.

Answer:

Summing the risks, we find the following:

Taxation issues = 13, Legal issues = 19, Labor issues = 14, Political issues = 19, and Supplier issues = 14. So the legal and political issues appear to be the highest risks.

REVIEW QUESTIONS

1. What is a project?
2. Explain the importance of project planning.
3. What is a work breakdown structure, and what are its benefits?
4. What is a Gantt chart, and what are its benefits?
5. What do both CPM and PERT try to do?
6. What is the critical path? Why is it so important for successful project management?
7. What are critical activities? What is slack time?
8. What is project crashing? Crash time? Crash cost? When would you need to do project crashing?
9. What is project risk, and what are the categories of project risk? Are these major considerations? If so, why?
10. What is risk mitigation? How is this related to contingency planning?

DISCUSSION QUESTIONS

1. Can noncritical activities become critical? If so, how?
2. Why is it important to determine early and late, start and finish schedules?
3. What are the benefits of using three time estimates for project activities? When would you want to do this?
4. How can activity time variances cause problems for project managers?
5. When would you want to buy your own project management software, and when would you want to use open source or cloud-based project management applications?

EXERCISES AND PROJECTS

1. Find information on a large project similar to those listed in Table 12.1 and write a report, describing as many elements of the project as possible.
2. Consider a typical week of your studies this semester to be a project, and create a work breakdown structure for it. Calculate the expected activity completion times and variances.

PROBLEMS

1. For the following project, construct a Gantt chart.

Activity	Predecessor(s)	Duration (days)	Activity	Predecessor(s)	Duration (days)
A	—	1	E	B	3
B	A	3	F	C,D	1
C	A	2	G	F	2
D	A	4	H	E,G	4

Based on your Gantt chart, what are the days to completion?

2. Using the project in Problem 1, construct the project network and list all of the possible pathways to completion. Determine the critical path(s). What are the critical path days to completion?

3. For the following project, construct a Gantt chart.

Activity	Predecessor(s)	Duration (days)	Activity	Predecessor(s)	Duration (days)
A	—	3	D	A,B	3
B	—	4	E	B,C	1
C	—	2	F	D,E	3

Based on your Gantt chart, what are the days to completion?

4. Using the project in Problem 3, construct the project network and list all of the possible pathways to completion. Determine the critical path(s). What are the critical path days to completion?

5. For the following project, construct a Gantt chart.

Activity	Predecessor(s)	Duration (days)	Activity	Predecessor(s)	Duration (days)
A	—	2	E	C,D	4
B	—	1	F	E	2
C	A	3	G	D	3
D	B	1	H	G	2

Based on your Gantt chart, what are the days to completion?

6. Using the project in Problem 5, construct the project network and list all of the possible pathways to completion. Determine the critical path(s). What are the critical path days to completion?
7. Using the project in Problem 5, determine the ES, EF, LS, LF, and slack times for each activity.

Use the project information below and the critical path activities from Problem 6 to answer the next five problems:

Activity	Optimistic	Most Likely	Pessimistic	Activity	Optimistic	Most Likely	Pessimistic
A	1.5	2	2.3	E	2.5	4	6
B	1	1	1	F	1.5	2	4.5
C	2	3	4	G	2	3	6.5
D	0.5	1	2.5	H	1	2	3.5

8. Calculate the expected completion times and completion time variances for each activity.
9. What are the expected days to completion?
10. Calculate the variance and standard deviation of the project's expected completion time.
11. What is the probability that the project can be completed in 14 days?
12. What would be the desired completion days, if you needed a 98% confidence level? Which noncritical activities should be monitored closely? Why?

Use the project activities shown below with the associated activity costs, crash time, and crash costs, to answer the next three problems.

Activity	Normal Time	Normal Cost ($)	Crash Time	Crash Cost ($)
A	2	1,000	1.5	1,250
B	1	200	1	0
C	3	2,200	1.5	2,600
D	1	850	0.5	1,080
E	4	3,000	2	3,800
F	2	1,500	1.5	1,550
G	3	2,500	2	2,750
H	2	2,700	0.5	3,900

13. Calculate the crash costs per day.
14. The critical path is A-C-E-F, and it is desired to complete the project in 10 days. Crash the necessary activities and determine the total costs, including the minimum crash costs.
15. Using the activity paths from Problem 6, what are the minimum completion days, and what is the total project cost?
16. The Mejza Travel Agency was thinking of expanding to open offices in European countries and wanted to assess and rank various risks. The risks and their assessments (where 1 = low concern and 10 = high concern) are shown below:

Risk	Likelihood	Severity	Controllability
Taxation issues	8	2	8
Land value	3	7	5
Labor issues	6	9	3
Political issues	2	8	6
Technological issues	3	7	4

The agency owners decided that the risks should be weighted equally. Rank the five risks in terms of their total risk scores.

CASE STUDIES

CASE 1: The Move

Jeff is COO for a $30 million, technology-based organization called MRO Supply. MRO Supply is located in the Upper Midwest of the United States. It is 4 p.m. on a Monday in January, and he just received a call from Paul, a friend who happens to run the office of the local electrical utility provider. He informs Jeff that the owner of the building where MRO Supply, a company of 50 associates, is located has not yet paid, and is unlikely to pay the utility bills for the building; therefore, on February 20, power in the building will be turned off. The owner has not paid the electrical bill for over 12 months. MRO Supply is one of about 40 tenants in the building. Unfortunately, even if MRO Supply and the other tenants pay the past-due bills (which is *very* unlikely), the owner of the building would still not pay going forward. Also, since the tenants are not responsible for the building, it is not even clear the utility could accept direct payment from these parties.

Jeff thus has about 30 days to relocate MRO Supply. MRO Supply is a "virtual distribution company" for the U.S. government, meaning it purchases items for government organizations and has them delivered directly from the manufacturer to the government users. This is all done electronically, so the company is heavily IT based. Jeff believes it is possible to successfully relocate the company within 30 days without having any downtime or interruption of customer service. The only other option would be to go out of business. If he executes the move effectively and communicates well with the organization's employees, it should be possible not to have anyone quit during this time. If the move is not handled and communicated well, Jeff will likely lose 15% of his workforce due to fears the company could close.

MRO Supply is located in a town of about 200,000 people, and all the employees live within 20 miles of the business. Therefore, it is not realistic to think about moving a long distance from where the business is currently located. Also, it is the desire of the owners of the company to stay in town. Jeff has calculated he needs about 20,000 square feet of space, with parking for 50. Ideally, he would also like room for potential expansion. He believes there are about 10 locations in the area that would fit their needs. All locations would need some amount of remodeling. He has contacts with three general contractors who could do the remodeling if they have the time, but it is not clear at this point if any could get the work done in the time frame needed. Jeff needs to be able to move all the employees and servers, and to be able to have the office set up and functioning by February 20.

The owners have asked Jeff to develop a plan to successfully move the company. They want him to develop two alternative locations from which they may choose. They expect his plan to have a budget, specific steps he and others are going to take, responsibilities for tasks, and a strategy not to have customer service decline during the time leading up to and through the move. Jeff has four main managers (Logistics, Purchasing, Customer Service, and Supplier Development) who report to him, and two additional managers (IT and Finance) at his level, on whom he can rely. Jeff estimates that in order to accomplish this move, everyone's workload will increase by about 20%. Given the short time frame it is not possible to hire anyone new, so he has to expedite the move without any additional headcount. He will need to have specialized movers transport IT equipment and perhaps other movers for everything else the company decides to take as part of the move.

In Jeff's favor, he has a great group of employees who are committed to the organization. MRO Supply's customers all deal with the organization via phone or email, and are located throughout the Midwest and Japan. MRO Supply's supplier network is located throughout the United States and Japan. A typical order cycle is the following: An RFQ from the customer is received and sent to one to three vendors for a quote; when quotes are received, the best quote is sent to the customer, who reviews it and if acceptable sends an order for the item(s); an order is then sent to the vendor, who ships directly to the customer or to a consolidation warehouse if the order needs to be consolidated. The process normally takes five working days. MRO Supply receives on average about 300 RFQs a day, which is about capacity with the current workforce working eight hours a day.

DISCUSSION QUESTIONS

1. What are the first steps Jeff should take to address this problem?
2. What are the main project tasks that need to be addressed?
3. What are the risks related to this project?
4. What steps, if any, could Jeff take to minimize these risks?

Note: Written by Jeffrey W. Fahrenwald, MBA, Rockford University, Rockford, IL. This case was prepared solely to provide material for class discussion. The author does not intend to illustrate either effective or ineffective handling of a managerial situation.

CASE 2: Transforming a Community

Mike lives in a region that has historically been rated one of the least livable in the country for a region of its size (about 500,000 people). Recently, a group of people (mostly business leaders) from the region have joined together and formed a steering committee that will oversee a regional transformation, with a goal of moving the region from one of the worst to one of the top 25 places to live in the United States in 10 years. Mike has been hired to be executive director of this effort.

The first thing Mike did was recruit other community members to make a case for change. After the case for change was presented and accepted by community leaders, community visioning sessions were held. These visioning sessions led to the development of a community vision that had the wide support of area citizens, business owners, and political leaders.

The results of the visioning sessions identified 11 focus areas that needed to be addressed if the community were to be transformed. These focus areas included:

- Safety (lowering crime)
- Healthy lifestyles (lowering obesity levels and improving fitness)
- Education (raising educational levels and lowering dropout rates)
- Economy and jobs (creating and attracting more and better-paying jobs)
- Planning (being able to reach measurable results)
- Funding and alignment (having the community pulling in the same direction)
- Physical infrastructure (improving transportation, roads, and other forms of infrastructure)
- Families and neighborhoods (creating great places for people to live and visit)
- Leadership and youth (developing leaders for now and the future)
- Arts and recreation (making the area a great place to "play")
- Connectedness (ensuring the region is connected to other regions in the area)

Groups of people in the community have been recruited to develop a plan to address each of the focus areas listed above. The groups have further identified local organizations (both public and private) that have knowledge and/or ownership of something related to each of the focus areas. The steering committee recognizes the large size and scope of the task, and is looking at potential ways to manage the transformation.

DISCUSSION QUESTIONS

1. Is this regional transformation a good candidate for project management and project management techniques? Why, or why not?
2. What are the disadvantages and risks in using project management tools and techniques to help move the transformation along?
3. What direction does Mike need to give to the leaders of the various focus areas if he decides to manage this as a large project?

Note: Written by Jeffrey W. Fahrenwald, MBA, Rockford University, Rockford, IL. This case was prepared solely to provide material for class discussion. The author does not intend to illustrate either effective or ineffective handling of a managerial situation.

VIDEO CASE STUDY

Learn more about ***managing projects*** from real organizations that use operations management techniques every day. Chris Fultz is the Director of the Program Management Office for Rolls-Royce's defense business in Indianapolis, Indiana. For a company that produces highly technical and potentially hazardous products, it is essential for project managers at to be highly skilled and supported. Watch this short interview to find out more.

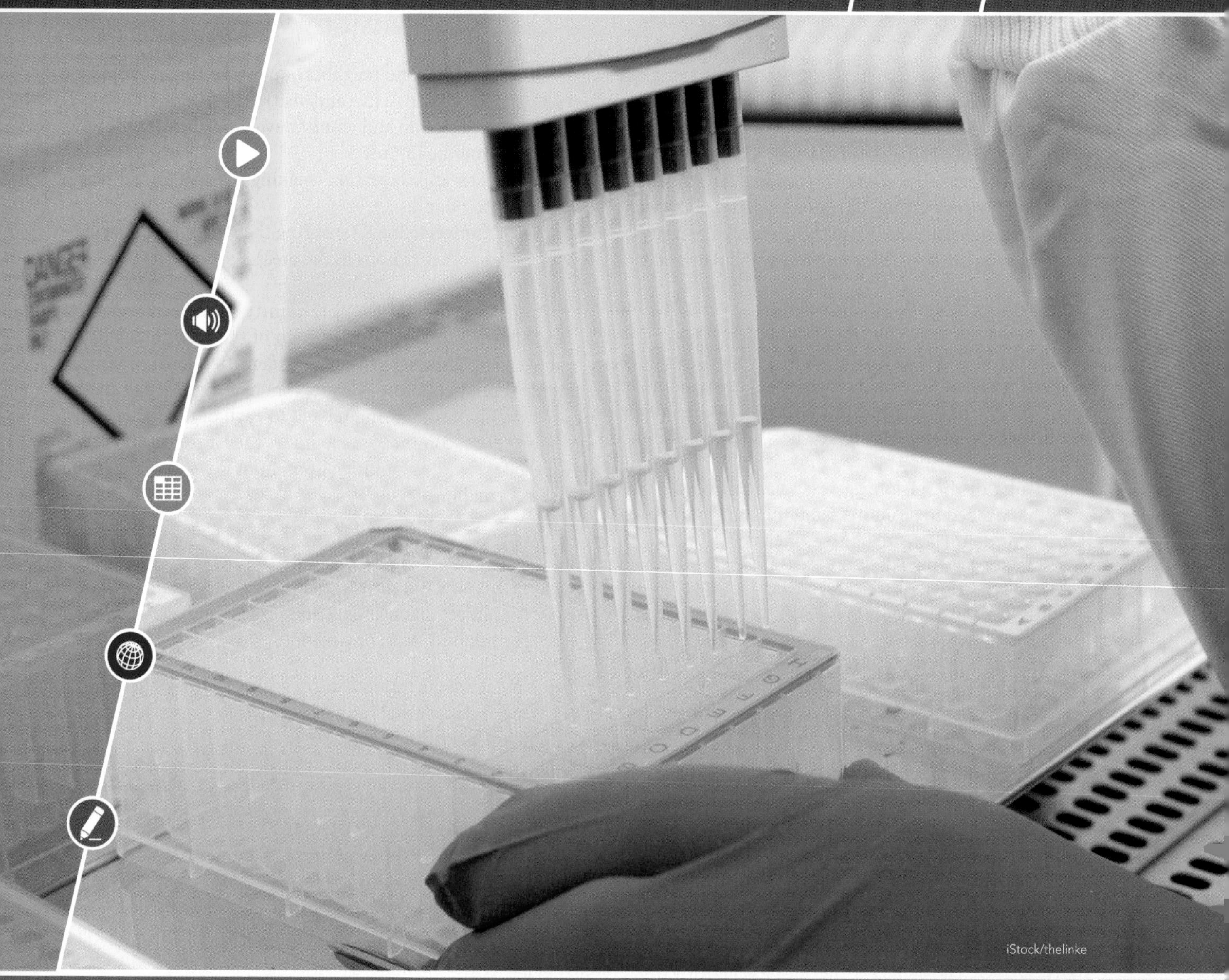
iStock/thelinke

The big myth is that Six Sigma is about quality control and statistics. It is that—but it's a helluva lot more. Ultimately, it drives leadership to be better by providing tools to think through tough issues. At Six Sigma's core is an idea that can turn a company inside out, focusing the organization outward on the customer.

—**JACK WELCH,** former chairman and CEO, General Electric[1]

Doing things right the first time adds nothing to the cost of your product or service. Doing things wrong is what costs money.

—**PHILIP CROSBY,** noted author and quality expert[2]

The definition of insanity is "Doing what you have always done and expecting a different result."

—**ALBERT EINSTEIN**[3]

SIX SIGMA QUALITY MANAGEMENT

13

LEARNING OBJECTIVES

After completing this chapter, you should be able to:

13.1 Discuss the origins of Six Sigma
13.2 Identify the linkages between lean programs and Six Sigma
13.3 Summarize the notable contributions to Six Sigma
13.4 Apply the various statistical tools of Six Sigma
13.5 Explain the new applications of Six Sigma

Master the content.

edge.sagepub.com/wisner

LOUISIANA STATE POLICE CRIME LAB USES SIX SIGMA TO IMPROVE PRODUCTIVITY

Historically, Louisiana's crime rates have been significantly higher than the U.S. national average. This fact contributed to a large backlog of DNA evidence to be analyzed at the Louisiana State Police Crime Lab (LSPCL) in 2008. Consequently, something needed to be done to improve the lab's productivity. The goal of the LSPCL was to utilize a scientific approach to improve lab productivity and reduce case backlogs. The decision was made to apply Six Sigma techniques in this effort. The lab chose to use Six Sigma's DMAIC methodology as its guiding principle, described below:

DEFINE: The problem was excessive case turnaround times and a high level of case backlogs.

MEASURE: The LSPCL decided to measure the actual physical movements of people and evidence throughout the lab. For a typical case, this resulted in a total of 12,687 feet travelled, or about 106 minutes of travel time. In one year, one lab employee might process 400 cases, resulting in hundreds of hours of lost time due to walking and moving evidence.

ANALYZE: To investigate potential causes of excessive time required to process a case, a pilot study consisting of five days of laboratory operations was conducted, with four support technicians and three DNA analysts performing the required lab work. A number of routing and bottleneck issues were identified during the study.

IMPROVE: Over a dozen improvements were implemented as a result of the pilot study. Lab processes and equipment were relocated to reduce movement waste, workstations were redesigned, barcoded labels replaced the old manual labelling, lab doors were removed to speed operations within lab spaces, all unnecessary procedural steps were removed, and an hourly master schedule was implemented for analysts.

CONTROL: Daily production meetings were implemented to ensure that all processes and people were functioning as required.

The results after six months of operation were impressive. The average DNA analysis time was reduced by 50%, from 258 days to 129 days. This resulted in a doubling of the lab's productivity, from 40 to 80 cases per week.[4]

INTRODUCTION

As discussed in previous chapters, customers today make goods and services purchase decisions based mostly on price, quality, and customer service. This makes it necessary for firms to implement strategies emphasizing speed, innovation, integration, quality, and efficiency. **Six Sigma** is a quality philosophy that helps to achieve these strategic initiatives, while at the same time resolving trade-offs that can exist when simultaneously pursuing the goals of low price, high quality, and fast response.

Six Sigma A quality philosophy that helps to achieve a firm's strategic initiatives, while at the same time resolving trade-offs that can exist when simultaneously pursuing the goals of low price, high quality, and fast response. It is a statistics-based decision-making framework designed to make significant quality improvements in value-adding processes.

Quality assessment and improvement is a necessary companion to lean production, the topic of Chapter 9. As lean systems begin to eliminate waste and shrink inventories, then problems with bottlenecked processes, poor quality, and delivery timing are typically uncovered both in production and with inbound and outbound goods. Using the tools of Six Sigma, these problems can be remedied, resulting in higher levels of quality and customer service. Thus, as the drive to reduce inventory and waste continues, the need to continually improve quality throughout the production system also continues. Six Sigma stresses a long-term commitment to identifying customer expectations and excelling in meeting and exceeding those expectations. Since environmental changes (such as the most recent global recession) along with changes in technology and competition cause customer expectations to change, firms must then commit to a program of continual reassessment and improvement; this, too, is an integral part of Six Sigma. This chapter discusses the Six Sigma philosophy as well as the tools used in Six Sigma improvement efforts. The next section describes the historical developments of Six Sigma.

THE ORIGINS OF SIX SIGMA

13.1 Discuss the origins of Six Sigma

Watch Jack Welch discussing Six Sigma

Six Sigma was pioneered by global communications company Motorola in 1987, and is a statistics-based decision-making framework designed to make significant quality improvements in value-adding processes. (In 2011, Motorola was split into two publicly traded companies—Motorola Mobility and Motorola Solutions.) Six Sigma is actually a registered trademark of Motorola and is always used with uppercase S's. In the 1980s, a senior staff engineer at Motorola named Mikel Harry formed a team of engineers to experiment with problem solving using statistical analyses, and this became the foundation for Six Sigma. Richard Schroeder, at the time the vice president of customer service at Motorola, heard about Harry's work, and also applied the methodology to his work at Motorola. Soon, both groups were announcing large reductions in errors and related costs. Ultimately, both men left Motorola and formed the Six Sigma Academy. In 2005, the firm was acquired by a number of investors and renamed SSA & Company, and is based in New York City. Today, the firm concentrates on showing companies how they can combine lean and Six Sigma to achieve exceptional results (a topic discussed later in this chapter).[5]

General Electric was the first large-scale adopter and advocate of Six Sigma after Motorola, and is considered by most experts to have been responsible for Six Sigma's rapidly achieved high profile. On GE's website it prominently states: "Today's competitive environment leaves no room for error. We must delight our customers and relentlessly look for new ways to exceed their expectations. This is why Six Sigma Quality has become a part of our culture."[6] Please see the video of GE's former chairman and CEO, Jack Welch, discussing Six Sigma.

The goal of quality perfection is represented by the term *Six Sigma*. Statistically speaking, Six Sigma refers to the likelihood that 99.99966% of the time, a process sample average will fall below a control limit placed six standard deviations (or sigmas) above the true process mean, assuming the process is in control with normally distributed data. This represents the goal of having a defect occur in a process only 0.00034% of the time, or 3.4 times out of every million measurement opportunities—very close to perfection. Table 13.1 shows the Six Sigma levels for various **defects per million opportunities (DPMO)**, using the Six Sigma methodology.

Today, many organizations practice Six Sigma, including such early adopters as Honeywell, General Electric, and Dow Chemical. More recently, companies such as Caterpillar, Dell, Boeing, and Bechtel have found success using Six Sigma. Over a recent 20-year period of study, use of Six Sigma saved Fortune 500 companies an estimated $427 billion, according to research published in *iSixSigma Magazine*. "Our data also showed that corporate-wide Six Sigma deployments save an average of 2% of total revenue per year," said Michael Marx, research manager for iSixSigma. As an indicator of its success, Marx added, "About 53 percent of Fortune 500 companies are currently using Six Sigma—and that figure rises to 82 percent when you look at just the Fortune 100."[7]

defects per million opportunities (DPMO)
A standard performance metric used in Six Sigma.

Table 13.1 Six Sigma Levels

Sigma Level (Standard Deviations Above the Mean)	Defects per Million Opportunities (DPMO)	Percent of Defect-Free Output
2	308,537	69.15
2.5	158,686	84.13
3	66,807	93.32
3.5	22,750	97.73
4	6,210	99.38
4.5	1,350	99.865
5	233	99.977
5.5	32	99.9968
6	3.4	99.99966

In 1999, Ford Motor Company became the first U.S. automaker to adopt Six Sigma. Automobile manufacturing provides a great example of the need for Six Sigma thinking. Since automobiles have roughly 20,000 **opportunities for a defect to occur (OFD)**, and assuming an automobile company operates at a 5 sigma level (233 DPMO), this would equate to about five defects for each car produced. Improving to the 6 sigma operating level would mean about one defect for every 15 automobiles produced—a huge improvement. Calculating the DPMO can be accomplished using the following formula:

$$\text{DPMO} = \frac{\text{number of defects}}{(\text{OFD per unit})(\text{number of units})} \times 1{,}000{,}000$$

Example 13.1 illustrates the calculation of DPMO and the use of Table 13.1.

Companies continue to use Six Sigma programs to generate cost savings or increased sales through process improvements. In fact, Motorola at one time stated that its savings from the use of Six Sigma had exceeded $17 billion.[8] This type of outcome is possible as firms identify customer requirements, uncover all of the opportunities for errors or defects to occur, review performance against Six Sigma performance standards, and then take the actions necessary to achieve those standards. The most successful projects meet strategic business objectives, reduce product and service variations to optimal levels, and produce a product or service that satisfies the customer.

opportunities for a defect to occur (OFD) It is used in the DPMO calculation, and refers to the maximum number of defects that can occur per unit.

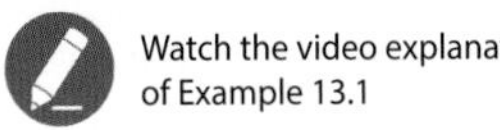

Example 13.1
Calculating the DPMO and Six Sigma Defect Level for Luke's Speedy Deliveries

Watch the video explanation of Example 13.1

Luke, the owner of Luke's Speedy Deliveries, a home delivery service, keeps track of customer complaints. For each delivery, there are three possible types of complaint: a late delivery, a poorly handled delivery, or an incorrect delivery. Each week, Luke calculates the rate of delivery "defects" for all deliveries, and then uses this information to determine his company's Six Sigma quality level. During the past week, the company made 620 deliveries. The drivers received 16 late delivery complaints, 19 poorly handled delivery complaints, and 5 incorrect delivery complaints.

Luke's defects per million opportunities, or DPMO, is:

$$\text{DPMO} = \frac{\text{number of defects}}{(\text{OFD per unit})(\text{number of units})} \times 1{,}000{,}000$$

$$\frac{40}{(3)(620)} \times 1{,}000{,}000 = 21{,}505 \text{ defective deliveries per million.}$$

Using Table 13.1, this reveals a Six Sigma level of slightly better than 3.5.

Watch managers discussing their Six Sigma experiences

Like all improvement programs, Six Sigma cannot guarantee continued or even initial business success. Poor management decisions and investments, and a company culture not conducive to change, can undermine even the best Six Sigma intentions. Ironically, Six Sigma originator Motorola struggled financially for a number of years and was forced to lay off tens of thousands of workers from 2000 to 2007.[9] Camera and film maker Polaroid, another early user of Six Sigma, filed for Chapter 11 bankruptcy protection in 2001, and the following year sold its name and all assets to a subsidiary of the Illinois-based Bank One Corp.[10]

COMPARING SIX SIGMA AND LEAN

13.2 Identify the linkages between lean programs and Six Sigma

The Six Sigma and lean philosophies actually have many similarities. For lean practices to be successful (allowing the firm to operate with low inventories), purchased parts and assemblies, work-in-process, and finished goods must all meet or exceed quality requirements. Also, recall from Chapter 9 that one of the elements of lean is continuous improvement—these are areas where the practice of Six Sigma can be put to good use in a lean system. In many cases, firms are pursuing both of these initiatives simultaneously. The Avery Point Group, an executive search firm headquartered in Connecticut, does a sampling every year of Internet job postings, and finds that about half of the companies seeking candidates with either Six Sigma or lean skill sets want the other skill set as well.[11]

Over the long term, successful companies must offer high-quality goods at reasonable prices, while providing acceptable levels of customer service. Rearranging factory floor layouts and reducing batch sizes and setup times, for example, will reduce manufacturing lead times and inventory levels, providing better delivery performance and lower cost. These are lean production initiatives. Using statistical quality control charts to monitor processes, creating long-term relationships with high-quality suppliers, and reducing delivery problems,

SERVICE SPOTLIGHT

Cedars-Sinai Uses Lean Six Sigma to Improve Hand Hygiene

California-based Cedars-Sinai Hospital uses Lean Six Sigma to improve hand hygiene, a particularly troublesome problem. To be effective, hand hygiene needs to be incorporated into the daily schedules of all staff having contact with patients. When initially mapping the workflow processes, managers learned that personnel were not using many of the hand sanitizers, since they were not readily accessible. Staff had to look for them, which interrupted their workflow and reduced use of the hand sanitizers.

The solution involved developing a three-phase Lean Six Sigma program. Phase 1 involved strategic placement of hand sanitizers, based on a study of staff movements throughout the hospital. Each staff member's workflow was tracked, and hand sanitizers were placed accordingly throughout the hospital.

Phase 2 focused on raising awareness. Hand-hygiene messages were placed on elevator doors and other busy areas, and computer screen savers were designed that discussed the importance of hand hygiene. Hand hygiene was also a key topic during orientation of new employees.

Phase 3 was to sustain the hand-washing compliance. Cedars-Sinai began using secret shoppers to observe whether

iStock/nano

hand-hygiene rules were being followed. Wireless monitoring wrist badges worn by those entering and leaving patient rooms also began to be used (the badges record hand-washing activity).

Cedars-Sinai's strategy is to achieve success incrementally. It is finding compliance in specific units and then spreading that success throughout the entire hospital.[12]

fall under the Six Sigma umbrella of activities. This explains how the two concepts can work together to achieve better overall firm performance. Lean is all about reducing waste, while Six Sigma is all about improving quality—which, in turn, reduces waste.

LEAN SIX SIGMA

A term is now being used to describe the melding of lean and Six Sigma practices—**Lean Six Sigma**, or occasionally just Lean Six. In 2009, for example, the U.S. Navy commissioned the nuclear aircraft carrier USS *George H. W. Bush,* built by global security company Northrop Grumman, using lean manufacturing and Six Sigma extensively to improve quality, reduce costs, and shorten cycle time.[13]

After the dot-com bust of 2001, many companies began considering implementing some form of lean or Six Sigma, or a combination approach. Four companies in particular that had implemented both lean and Six Sigma after 2001 were studied by *Electronic Business* magazine in 2006—Canada-based Celestica; ON Semiconductor, headquartered in Arizona; California-based Solectron; and Xerox, headquartered in Connecticut. All four firms were healthier in 2006 than in 2001, and three claimed their business turnaround was a direct result of their Lean Six Sigma approach.[14] Today, more than 20% of U.S. hospitals use some form of Lean Six Sigma; Cedars-Sinai's experiences with Lean Six Sigma are presented in the Service Spotlight on page 394.

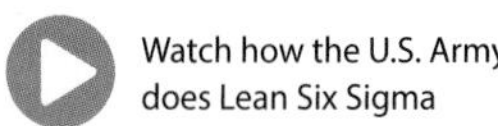

Watch how the U.S. Army does Lean Six Sigma

THE ELEMENTS OF SIX SIGMA

13.3 Summarize the notable contributions to Six Sigma

The philosophy and tools of Six Sigma are borrowed from a number of resources, including quality professionals such as W. Edwards Deming, Philip Crosby, and Joseph Juran; the Malcolm Baldrige National Quality Award and the International Organization for Standardization's ISO 9000 and 14000 families of standards; the Motorola and General Electric practices relating to Six Sigma; and statistical process control techniques originally developed by Walter Shewhart (the topic of the Chapter 13 Supplement). From these resources, a number of commonly used elements emerge that are collectively known today as Six Sigma. A few of the quality resources are discussed next, followed by a discussion of the qualitative and quantitative elements of Six Sigma.

DEMING'S QUALITY CONTRIBUTIONS

W. Edwards **Deming's Theory of Management**, as explained in his book *Out of the Crisis,* states that since managers are responsible for creating the systems that make organizations work, they must also be held responsible for the organization's problems. Thus, only management can fix problems, through application of the right tools, resources, encouragement, commitment, and cultural change. Deming's Theory of Management was the centerpiece of his teachings around the world (Deming died in 1993) and includes his 14 Points for Management, shown in Table 13.2.[15]

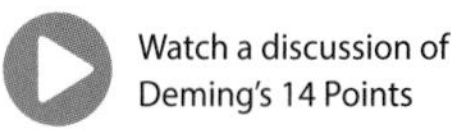

In 1950, Deming was invited to Japan by the Union of Japanese Scientists and Engineers. He gave an eight-day lecture on quality control in Tokyo, followed by a one-day course for top management. Deming taught the basics of statistical quality control plainly and thoroughly to executives, managers, and engineers. His teachings made a deep impression on the participants and provided a great impetus to quality control in Japan, which was in its infancy at the time. In appreciation of these and other efforts in Japan by Deming, the Deming Prize was established in 1951 and has become one of the highest awards for quality management in the world. The award is given to approximately four or five companies per year.[16]

Deming's 14 Points for Management, shown in Table 13.2, are all related to Six Sigma principles, covering the qualitative as well as quantitative aspects of quality management. He was convinced that high quality was the outcome of an all-encompassing philosophy geared toward personal and organizational growth. He argued that growth occurred through top management vision, support, and value placed on all employees and suppliers. Value is

Lean Six Sigma Also known as Lean Six. Refers to the combination practice of lean with Six Sigma.

Deming's Theory of Management Since managers are responsible for creating the systems that make organizations work, they must also be held responsible for the organization's problems. Thus, only management can fix problems, through application of the right tools, resources, encouragement, commitment, and cultural change.

Table 13.2 Deming's 14 Points for Management

1. Create constancy of purpose for improvement of product and service.	Define values, mission, and vision to provide long-term direction for management and employees. Invest in innovation, training, and research.
2. Adopt the new philosophy.	Adversarial management–worker relationships and quota systems do not work in today's work environment. Management must create cooperative relationships aimed at increasing quality and customer satisfaction.
3. Cease dependence on mass inspection.	Inspecting products does not create value or prevent poor quality. Workers must use statistical process control to improve quality.
4. End the practice of awarding business on the basis of price tag alone.	Purchases should not be based on low cost; buyers should develop long-term relationships with a few good suppliers.
5. Constantly improve the production and service system.	Significant quality improvement comes from continual incremental improvements that reduce variation and eliminate common causes.
6. Institute training.	Managers need to learn how the company works. Employees should receive adequate job training and statistical process control training.
7. Adopt and institute leadership.	Managers are leaders, not supervisors. They help, coach, encourage, and provide guidance to employees.
8. Drive out fear.	A supportive organization will drive out fear of reprisal, failure, change, the unknown, and loss of control. Fear causes short-term thinking.
9. Break down barriers between departments.	Cross-functional teams focus workers, break down departmental barriers, and allow workers to see the big picture.
10. Eliminate slogans, exhortations, and targets for the workforce.	Slogans and motivational programs are aimed at the wrong people. They don't help workers do a better job. They cause worker frustration and resentment.
11. Eliminate numerical quotas for workers and managers.	Quotas are short-term thinking and cause fear. Numerical goals have no value unless methods are in place that will allow them to be achieved.
12. Remove barriers that rob people of pride of workmanship.	Barriers are performance and merit ratings. Workers have become a commodity. Workers are given boring tasks with no proper tools, and performance is appraised by supervisors who know nothing about the job. Managers won't act on worker suggestions. This must change.
13. Encourage education and self-improvement for everyone.	All employees should be encouraged to further broaden their skills and improve through continuing education.
14. Take action to accomplish the transformation.	Management must have the courage to break with tradition and explain to a critical mass of people that the changes will involve everyone. Management must speak with one voice.

demonstrated through investments in training, equipment, continuing education, support for finding and fixing problems, and teamwork both within the firm and with its suppliers. Use of statistical methods, elimination of "inspected-in" quality policies, and elimination of decisions based solely on cost are also required to improve quality.

Today, Deming's work lives on through the Deming Institute, a nonprofit organization he founded to foster greater understanding of Deming's principles and vision. The institute provides conferences, seminars, and training materials to managers seeking to make use of Deming's philosophies.[17]

CROSBY'S QUALITY CONTRIBUTIONS

Philip Crosby, a former vice president of quality at the New York–based manufacturer ITT Corporation, was a highly sought-after quality consultant during the latter part of his life and wrote 14 books concerning quality, most notably *Quality Is Free* and *Quality Without Tears* (he died in 2001).[18] His studies of quality improvement programs, as discussed in *Quality Is Free*, were that these programs invariably more than paid for themselves. In *Quality Without Tears*, Crosby discussed his Four Absolutes of Quality, shown in Table 13.3. Companies like IBM and General Motors benefited greatly from implementing Crosby's ideas.

Table 13.3 Crosby's Four Absolutes of Quality

1. The definition of quality is conformance to requirements.	Adopt a do-it-right-the-first-time attitude. Never sell a faulty product to a customer.
2. The system of quality is prevention.	Use SPC as part of the prevention system. Make corrective changes when problems occur. Take preventive action.
3. The performance standard is zero defects.	Insist on zero defects from suppliers and workers. Education, training, and commitment will eliminate defects.
4. The measure of quality is the price of nonconformance.	The price of nonconformance is the cost of poor quality. Implementing a prevention program will eliminate this.

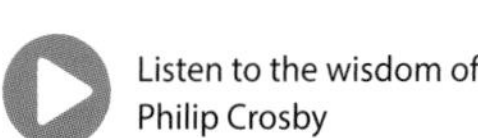
Listen to the wisdom of Philip Crosby

In his many years as a quality improvement consultant, Crosby is credited with enforcing the message "Do things right the first time" and introducing the importance of striving for zero defects. He also became well known for acquainting professionals with the following theories: The price of nonconformance is a measure of poor quality; prevention is a means to eliminate quality problems; leadership is a requirement to make progress; teamwork is the principle for work; and customer requirements define the standard of quality performance. Crosby emphasized a commitment to quality improvement by top management, development of a defect prevention system, employee education and training, and continuous assessment—all quite similar to Deming's ideas. Crosby's Quality College, the educational division of his consultancy, began in 1979. It taught over 100,000 managers and executives worldwide about various quality concepts, prior to Crosby's death in 2001.[19]

JURAN'S QUALITY CONTRIBUTIONS

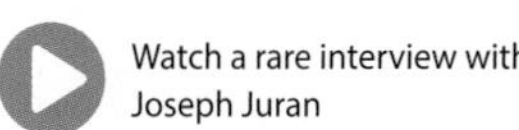
Watch a rare interview with Joseph Juran

Joseph Juran, founder of the Juran Institute, helped to write and develop the *Quality Control Handbook* in 1951 (it is now in its sixth edition)[20] and wrote a number of other books on quality as well. Born in 1904, Juran remained an active lecturer right up until his death in 2008 at the age of 103. He also remained active by overseeing the Juran Foundation. "My job of contributing to the welfare of my fellow man," Juran wrote, "is the great unfinished business."[21]

Like Deming, Juran helped to engineer the Japanese quality revolution that started in the 1950s. Juran, similar to both Crosby and Deming, strived to introduce new types of thinking about quality to business managers and employees, but Juran's beliefs varied somewhat from those of Crosby and Deming. He is recognized as the person who brought the human element to quality improvement. He believed that for managers to listen, the message had to be spoken in dollars. For workers to listen, the topics had to be about specific things. So he discussed the costs of poor quality to get the attention of managers, and then discussed statistical quality control methods with workers.

Juran's recommendations focused on his Quality Trilogy, described in Table 13.4. In his dealings with companies, Juran found that most had given a high priority to quality control but paid little attention to quality planning and improvement. Thus, while both Japanese and U.S. businesses had been using quality control techniques since the 1950s, Japan's overall quality levels grew faster than those of the United States because Japanese business managers placed a greater emphasis on quality planning and improvement.

Many characteristics of the Deming, Crosby, and Juran quality philosophies are quite similar. All three focus on top management commitment, the need for continuous improvement efforts, training, and the use of statistical methods for quality control purposes.

Baldrige Quality Award Signed into law on August 20, 1987. The objectives of the award are to stimulate firms to improve quality and productivity, to recognize firms for their quality achievements, to establish criteria and guidelines so that organizations can independently evaluate their quality improvement efforts, and to provide examples and guidance to those companies wanting to learn how to manage and improve quality and productivity.

THE MALCOLM BALDRIGE NATIONAL QUALITY AWARD

The **Baldrige Quality Award** was signed into law on August 20, 1987, and is named in honor of then–U.S. president Ronald Reagan's secretary of commerce, who helped draft an

Table 13.4 Juran's Quality Trilogy

1. Quality planning	The process of preparing to meet quality goals. Identify internal and external customers, determine their needs, and develop products that satisfy those needs. Managers set short- and long-term goals, establish priorities, and compare results to previous plans.
2. Quality control	The process of meeting quality goals during operations. Determine what to control, establish measurements and standards of performance, measure performance, interpret the difference between the actual measure and the standard, and take action if necessary.
3. Quality improvement	The process of achieving greater levels of quality performance. Show the need for improvement, identify projects for improvement, organize support for the projects, diagnose causes, implement remedies for the causes, and provide control to maintain improvements.

Peter Yates/Getty

Cadillac quality chief Rosetta Riley is shown here holding the Malcolm Baldrige Award. The coveted Baldrige Award indicates a high level of quality for the award recipients.

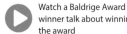

early version of the award, and who was tragically killed in a rodeo calf-roping accident one month before the award was enacted. The objectives of the award (which is given only to U.S. firms) are to stimulate firms to improve quality and productivity, to recognize firms for their quality achievements, to establish criteria and guidelines so that organizations can independently evaluate their quality improvement efforts, and to provide examples and guidance to those companies wanting to learn how to manage and improve quality and productivity.

The Baldrige Award is managed by the U.S. Commerce Department's National Institute of Standards and Technology (NIST). It is presented by the president of the United States in November of each year to U.S. companies in six categories: small business, service, manufacturing, education, healthcare, and nonprofit. Applicants are judged in seven areas: leadership; strategic planning; customer focus; measurement, analysis, and knowledge management; workforce focus; operations focus; and results. Up to three awards can be given annually to companies in each of the six categories.

Watch a Baldrige Award winner talk about winning the award

Through 2015, there have been over 1,600 applications filed, with 102 organizations winning the award. Seven organizations have won the award twice: Solectron (1991 and 1997), the Ritz-Carlton Hotel Company (1992 and 1999), Texas Nameplate Company (1998 and 2004), Sunny Fresh Foods (1999 and 2005), MEDRAD (2003 and 2010), MESA Products (2006 and 2012), and Midway USA (2009 and 2015). Four winners were Fortune 500 companies: Motorola (1988), Federal Express Corp. (1990), Eastman Chemical Co. (1993), and Solectron Corp. (1991 and 1997). Nearly all 50 states have their own versions of the Baldrige Award, and internationally there are over 100 quality awards that have used the Baldrige Award as a model. As of 2012, only state award winners are eligible to apply for the Baldrige Award.[22]

All award applications receive approximately 1,000 hours of review by quality professional volunteers, and are awarded performance scores in the seven categorical areas listed in this section. Finalists are visited by teams of examiners wherein information is clarified and performance is reassessed. The winners are then selected from this group. All organizations are encouraged by NIST to obtain a copy of the Baldrige Award criteria and perform self-assessments using the form and its point-scoring guidelines. Completing a self-assessment using the Baldrige Award criteria identifies the firm's strengths and weaknesses and can aid in implementing quality improvement initiatives. To date, many thousands of firms have requested copies of the official application and scoring guidelines.[23]

K&N—Only the Second Restaurant to Win the Baldrige Award

SERVICE SPOTLIGHT

K&N won the Baldrige Award in 2010 and was only the second restaurant company to win the award. Texas-based K&N includes four Rudy's Country Store and Bar-B-Q units and four Mighty Fine Burgers, Fries, and Shakes units. The company began operations in 1993, and today it employs over 500 people. Its North Austin Rudy's unit is so popular, it ranks number one out of 67,000 Texas restaurants in food sales per square foot.

Co-owner Ken Schiller says his company's success is due to its focus on its customers and its employees. "Our team members are the face that our guests see every day," Schiller says. Their biggest challenge is attracting and employing what he terms "A-players." To attract and retain these people, K&N provides excellent benefits: Employees are considered full time at 30 hours per week; they are offered health insurance, with K&N paying 90% of the cost; and they get a company matching 401(k) retirement account. All new employees spend 10 hours in K&N's foundations class, learning about the K&N culture. "We focus on delighting guests, and we believe that if we keep that focus, that the profits take care of themselves," explains Schiller.[24]

THE ISO 9000 AND 14000 FAMILIES OF MANAGEMENT STANDARDS

In 1946, delegates from 25 countries met in London and decided to create a new international organization, with the objective "to facilitate the international coordination and unification of industrial standards." The new organization, called the International Organization for Standardization, or ISO, officially began operations on February 23, 1947. Located in Geneva, Switzerland, the ISO as of 2015 has 162 member countries and has published more than 19,500 international standards covering almost all aspects of technology and business.[25]

ISO standards are developed in response to market demand, and are based on consensus among the member countries. This ensures widespread applicability of the standards. ISO considers evolving technologies and member interests by requiring a review of its standards at least every five years to decide whether they should be maintained, updated, or withdrawn. In this way, ISO standards retain their position as state of the art.

Developing consensus for ISO standards on an international scale is a major undertaking. In all, there are some 3,000 ISO technical groups with approximately 50,000 experts participating annually to develop ISO standards. Examples include standards for agriculture and construction, mechanical engineering, medical devices, and information technology developments, such as the digital coding of audio-visual signals for multimedia applications.

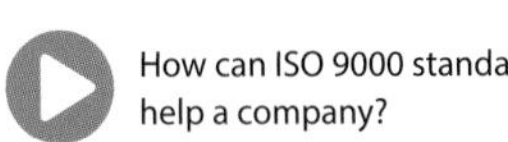

How can ISO 9000 standards help a company?

In 1987, ISO adopted the **ISO 9000** series of five international quality standards, and has revised them several times over the years. These standards have proven to be ISO's most popular, and have been adopted in the United States by the American National Standards Institute (ANSI) and the American Society for Quality (ASQ). The standards apply to all types of businesses. In many cases worldwide, companies will not buy from suppliers who do not possess an ISO 9000 certification. The most recently adopted ISO 9000 standard is ISO 19011 (it provides guidance on internal and external audits of quality management systems).

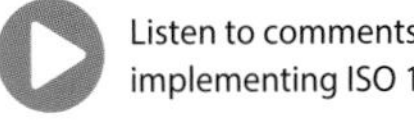

Listen to comments about implementing ISO 14001

After the rapid acceptance of ISO 9000 and the increase of environmental awareness around the world, ISO considered the need for international environmental management standards. It formed an environmental advisory group in 1991, which eventually led to the adoption of the **ISO 14000** family of international environmental management standards in 1997. Several of the most recently adopted ISO 14000 standards are the ISO 14064 standard for greenhouse gas accounting and verification, and the ISO 14065 standard, which provides the requirements for the accreditation of agencies that carry out these activities. These standards will help organizations address climate change and support emissions trading schemes.

Today, the ISO 9000 and 14000 families of certifications are the most widely used standards of ISO, with more than a million organizations in 178 countries holding one or both types of certifications. The standards that have earned the ISO 9000 and ISO 14000 families a worldwide reputation are known as "generic management system standards," meaning that the same standards can be applied to any type of organization. "Generic" also means that no

ISO standards Developed by the International Organization for Standardization in response to market demand, and are based on consensus among the member countries.

ISO 9000 A series of five international quality standards, adopted by ISO in 1987. The most popular standard adopted.

ISO 14000 A family of international environmental management standards, adopted by ISO in 1997.

matter what the organization's scope of activity, if it wants to establish a quality management system or an environmental management system, then relevant standards of the ISO 9000 or ISO 14000 families can provide the requirements.

THE DMAIC IMPROVEMENT CYCLE

The **DMAIC improvement cycle**, an important element of Six Sigma, consists of a sequence of five steps necessary to drive process improvements. These are described in Table 13.5. The cycle can be applied to any process or project, both in services and manufacturing firms. The improvement cycle begins with identifying customer requirements and then seeks to analyze and modify processes or projects to meet those requirements.

The DMAIC improvement cycle allows organizations to systematically monitor and improve processes that are tied to customer requirements. By concentrating on these processes, firms can make significant improvements in quality and customer satisfaction. (Recall the chapter-opening vignette discussed using the DMAIC cycle.) The University of Toledo Medical Center in Ohio used the DMAIC cycle in conjunction with a Six Sigma project to improve its kidney transplant process. As a direct result of the project, transplant patients began receiving transplants more quickly, saving lives.[26]

SIX SIGMA TRAINING LEVELS

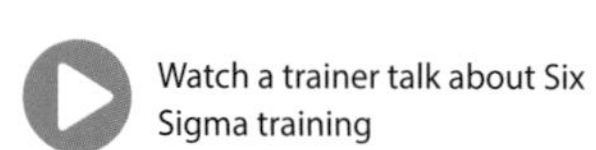
Watch a trainer talk about Six Sigma training

A number of organizations offer various training courses and certifications in Six Sigma methods, and the somewhat standardized training levels are summarized in Table 13.6. Global manufacturing giant GE began using Six Sigma in the 1980s, and today, GE employees are still receiving training in the strategy, tools, and techniques of Six Sigma.

At GE's Lighting Solutions division, for example, its website states, "Our success with Six Sigma has exceeded the most optimistic predictions. Across GE Lighting Solutions, our associates embrace Six Sigma's customer-focused, data-driven philosophy and apply it to everything we do. We build on these successes by sharing best practices across all of our businesses, putting the full power of Six Sigma behind our quest for better, faster customer solutions."[27]

DMAIC improvement cycle An important element of Six Sigma. Consists of a sequence of five steps necessary to drive process improvements (design, measure, analyze, improve, control).

critical-to-quality characteristics CTQ characteristics. Customer requirements deemed to be critical to achieving customer satisfaction.

Six Sigma training is becoming widespread, particularly evidenced by the high demand and salaries for workers with Master Black Belts (MBB) and Black Belts (BB). Year after year, salary surveys show it pays to get Six Sigma training. In the United States, workers with any level of Six Sigma training in 2012 earned $16,826 more on average than those without any Six Sigma training. Particularly notable is the large benefit for Master Black Belt training. In

Table 13.5 The DMAIC Improvement Cycle

Element	Description
Define	Identify customers and their requirements deemed to be critical to achieving customer satisfaction (also known as **critical-to-quality characteristics,** or CTQ characteristics). Identify any gaps between the CTQ characteristics and process outputs. Where gaps exist, create Six Sigma projects to close the gaps.
Measure	Determine how to measure performance for each process where a gap exists and prepare a data collection plan. Use check sheets to organize the data.
Analyze	Analyze the performance data collected. Use Pareto charts and fishbone diagrams to help identify the causes of the poor process performance.
Improve	Design and implement an improvement plan to remove the causes of poor performance. This may require modifying, redesigning, or reengineering the process. Document the improvement effort and confirm, with additional monitoring, that the process gaps have been significantly reduced or eliminated.
Control	Continue to monitor the process to ensure that performance levels are maintained. Design and use quality control charts to continuously monitor and control the process. If performance gaps once again appear, repeat Steps 1–5.

Table 13.6 Six Sigma Training Levels

Training Levels	Description
Yellow Belt	Has a basic understanding of the Six Sigma methodology and the tools within the DMAIC problem-solving process, including process mapping, cause-and-effect tools, simple data analysis, and process improvement and control methods.
Green Belt	Is a trained team member allowed to work on small, carefully defined Six Sigma projects, requiring less than full-time commitment. Has enhanced problem-solving skills, and can gather data and execute project experiments. Typically spends 25% of their time on Six Sigma projects.
Black Belt	Has a thorough knowledge of Six Sigma philosophies and principles. Exhibits team leadership, understands team dynamics, and assigns team members with roles and responsibilities. Has a complete understanding of the DMAIC process and a basic knowledge of lean concepts. Has knowledge of and can use advanced statistics, coaches successful project teams, and provides group assessments. Identifies projects and selects project team members, acts as an internal consultant, mentors Green Belts and project teams and provides feedback to management.
Master Black Belt	Has a proven mastery of process variability reduction, waste reduction, and growth principles, and can effectively train at all levels. Challenges conventional wisdom and provides guidance and knowledge to lead and change organizations using Six Sigma. Directs Black and Green Belts on the performance of their Six Sigma projects and also provides guidance and direction to management teams regarding the technical proficiency of Black Belt candidates, the selection of projects, and the overall health of a Six Sigma program.

Source: Six Sigma belts, executives, and champions –what does it all mean? http://asq.org/learn-about-quality/six-sigma/overview/belts-executives-champions.html

2012, for example, the premium for MBBs over holders of the BB was $25,583.[28] Several of the useful tools of Six Sigma are discussed next.

THE TOOLS OF SIX SIGMA

13.4 Apply the various statistical tools of Six Sigma

PROCESS MAPS

Also called **process diagrams** or **flow diagrams**, this tool is the necessary first step when evaluating any manufacturing or service process. As described in several previous chapters, **process maps** use rectangles representing process action elements and ovals representing wait periods, connected by arrows to show the flow of products or customers through the process. Once a process or series of processes is mapped, potential problem areas can be identified and further evaluated for things like excess inventories, wait times, or capacity problems. An example of a customer flow diagram for a restaurant is shown in Figure 13.1. Using the diagram, restaurant managers can observe process activities and wait times, looking for potential problems requiring further analysis.

process diagrams Also called process maps or flow diagrams. A necessary first step when evaluating any manufacturing or service process. They use rectangles representing process action elements and ovals representing wait periods, connected by arrows to show the flow of products or customers through the process.

flow diagrams *See* Process diagrams.

process maps *See* Process diagrams.

check sheets Allow users to determine frequencies for specific problems. Managers make a list of potential problem areas based on their observations, then direct employees to keep counts of each problem occurrence for a period of time.

Pareto charts Attributed in part to the work of Vilfredo Pareto, a noted 19th-century Italian economist and mathematician. It is a chart showing the magnitudes of problems, from biggest to smallest.

CHECK SHEETS

Check sheets allow users to determine frequencies for specific problems. For the restaurant example shown in Figure 13.1, managers could make a list of potential problem areas based on their observations, then direct employees to keep counts of each problem occurrence on check sheets for a given period of time (long enough to allow for true problem level determinations). At the end of the data collection period, the problem occurrences are tallied and problem areas are evaluated. Figure 13.2 shows a check sheet that could be used in a restaurant.

PARETO CHARTS

Pareto charts, useful for many applications, are attributed in part to the work of Vilfredo Pareto, a noted 19th-century Italian economist and mathematician. In 1906, Pareto described the unequal distribution of wealth in his country, observing that 20% of the people owned

Figure 13.1 Process Map of Customer Flow at a Restaurant

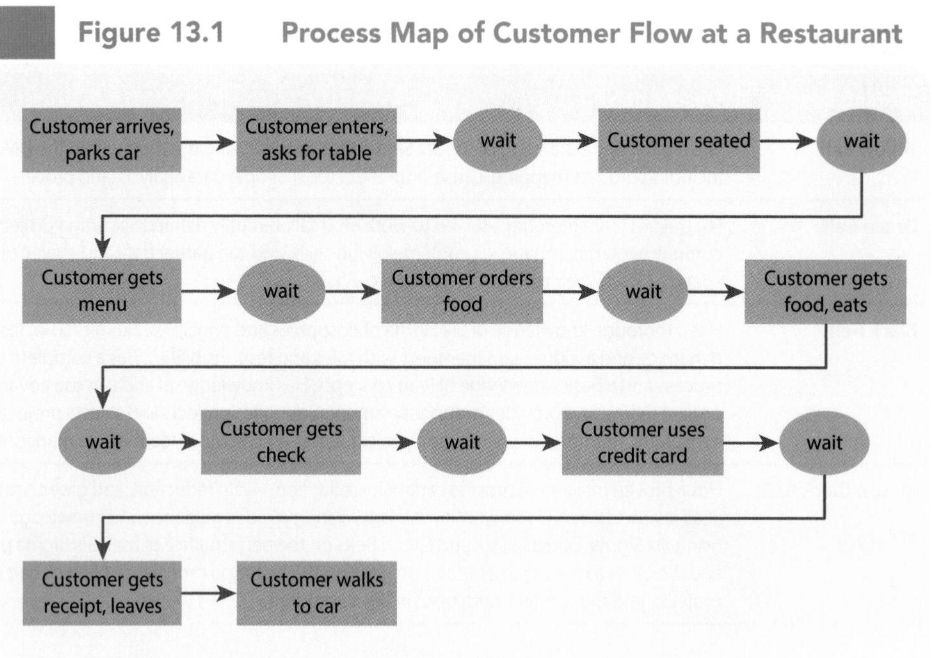

Pareto Principle Refers to Juran's thinking that 20% of something is typically responsible for 80% of the results. Also known as the 80/20 Rule.

about 80% of the wealth. In quality improvement efforts, Pareto charts show the magnitude of problems, arranged from largest to smallest. Decades later, Joseph Juran described what he called the **Pareto Principle**, referring to his experience that 20% of something is typically responsible for 80% of the results. Eventually, this idea became widely known as the Pareto Principle, or the 80/20 Rule.[29] Applied to quality improvement, this refers to the common

Figure 13.2 Restaurant Problem Check Sheet

Problem	Mon.	Tues.	Wed.	Thurs.	Fri.	Sat.	Sun.	Sub-Totals	% of Total
long wait	𝍸 /	𝍸	𝍸 ///	𝍸 /	𝍸 ////	𝍸 𝍸	////	**48**	**26.5**
cold food		//	/	/	///	//		**9**	**5.0**
bad food	//	/	///		/	////		**11**	**6.1**
wrong food	𝍸	//	/	//	𝍸	///	/	**19**	**10.5**
bad server	𝍸 /	///	𝍸	/	𝍸 /	//	/	**24**	**13.3**
bad table		/	//		/	///	/	**8**	**4.4**
room temp.			//	///	𝍸	𝍸		**15**	**8.3**
too expensive	/	//	/	/	///	///		**11**	**6.1**
no parking			//		𝍸	𝍸 //		**14**	**7.7**
wrong change	𝍸 /	/	////		////	///		**18**	**9.9**
other		/	//			/		**4**	**2.2**
Totals	**26**	**18**	**31**	**14**	**42**	**43**	**7**	**181**	**100**

Figure 13.3 Pareto Chart For Restaurant Problems

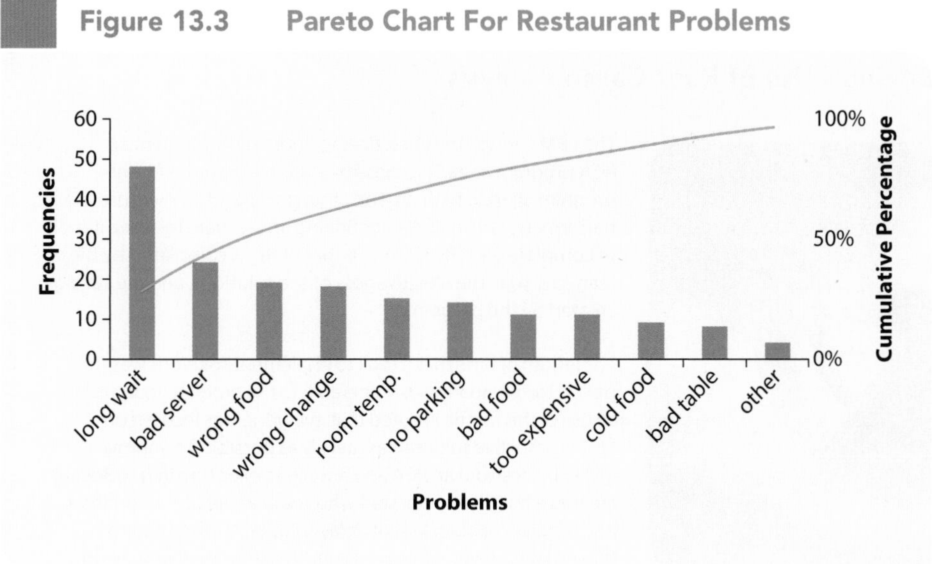

observation that a few of a firm's problems account for most of the problem occurrences. In other words, firms should fix the few biggest problems first.

Pareto charts present data in an organized fashion, showing process problems or defects from most to least severe, along with the cumulative percentage of problem occurrences contributed by each problem. It makes sense when utilizing a firm's scarce resources to work on solving the most severe problems first. As shown in Figure 13.3, the *long wait* restaurant problem identified in the Figure 13.2 check sheet is the most severe problem, and should be the subject of initial improvement efforts. (Note that, in this case, the two biggest of the 10 problems accounted for about 40% of the occurrences.)

CAUSE-AND-EFFECT DIAGRAMS

Once a significant problem has been identified, **cause-and-effect diagrams** (also called **fishbone diagrams** or **Ishikawa diagrams**) can be used to aid in brainstorming the causes of the problem. Figure 13.4 illustrates a cause-and-effect diagram for the most severe *long wait* problem identified in Figure 13.3. The problem is shown at the right side of the fishbone diagram. Each of the four diagonals of the diagram represents a potential group of causes. The four groups of causes shown, Material, Machine, Methods, and Manpower—also known as the **4 Ms**—are the standard classifications used for identifying problem causes. In most cases, problem causes will be found in one or more of these four areas.

Typically, Six Sigma team members will gather to brainstorm the potential causes for a problem within these four areas (also referred to as **root cause analysis**). In Figure 13.4, each branch on one of the four diagonals represents one potential cause. Subcauses are also part of the brainstorming process, and are shown as smaller branches attached to each of the primary causes. Asking the question "why?" in response to each potential cause will uncover the potential subcauses. Breaking a problem down into its potential causes and subcauses in this way allows workers to then return to the site of the original problem to determine the relative significance of each cause and subcause, using more specific check-lists and Pareto charts once again. Eventually, the firm identifies the primary root causes of a problem, and can take appropriate steps to eliminate them until most or all of the problem's impact disappears. The Manufacturing Spotlight on page 404 describes Boeing's very successful root cause analysis group.

A detailed cause-and-effect diagram can be a very powerful tool for use in Six Sigma improvement efforts. Without its use, workers and managers risk trying to eliminate causes that have little to do with the problem at hand, or working on causes that are minor compared to other, more significant problem causes. Once most of a problem's causes are identified and

cause-and-effect diagrams Also called fishbone diagrams or Ishikawa diagrams. They are used in brainstorming the causes of the problem. The problem is shown at the right side of the fishbone diagram, with four diagonals of the diagram representing a potential group of causes.

fishbone diagrams *See* Cause-and-effect diagrams.

Ishikawa diagrams *See* Cause-and-effect diagrams.

4 Ms The four groups of causes—Material, Machine, Methods, and Manpower—used in cause-and-effect diagrams.

root cause analysis Brainstorming the potential causes for a problem within the 4 Ms. Each branch on one of the four diagonals represents one potential cause. Subcauses are also part of the brainstorming process and are shown as smaller branches attached to each of the primary causes. Asking the question "why?" in response to each potential cause will uncover the potential subcauses. Breaking a problem down into its causes and subcauses will lead to problem solutions.

MANUFACTURING SPOTLIGHT

Boeing's Use of Root Cause Analysis

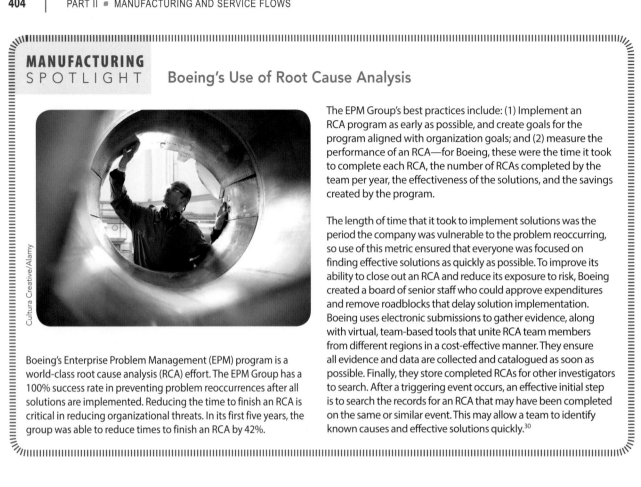

Cultura Creative/Alamy

Boeing's Enterprise Problem Management (EPM) program is a world-class root cause analysis (RCA) effort. The EPM Group has a 100% success rate in preventing problem reoccurrences after all solutions are implemented. Reducing the time to finish an RCA is critical in reducing organizational threats. In its first five years, the group was able to reduce times to finish an RCA by 42%.

The EPM Group's best practices include: (1) Implement an RCA program as early as possible, and create goals for the program aligned with organization goals; and (2) measure the performance of an RCA—for Boeing, these were the time it took to complete each RCA, the number of RCAs completed by the team per year, the effectiveness of the solutions, and the savings created by the program.

The length of time that it took to implement solutions was the period the company was vulnerable to the problem reoccurring, so use of this metric ensured that everyone was focused on finding effective solutions as quickly as possible. To improve its ability to close out an RCA and reduce its exposure to risk, Boeing created a board of senior staff who could approve expenditures and remove roadblocks that delay solution implementation. Boeing uses electronic submissions to gather evidence, along with virtual, team-based tools that unite RCA team members from different regions in a cost-effective manner. They ensure all evidence and data are collected and catalogued as soon as possible. Finally, they store completed RCAs for other investigators to search. After a triggering event occurs, an effective initial step is to search the records for an RCA that may have been completed on the same or similar event. This may allow a team to identify known causes and effective solutions quickly.[30]

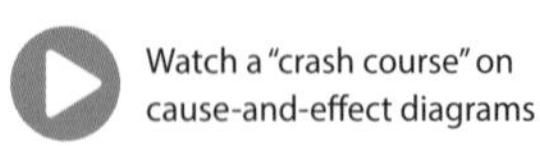
Watch a "crash course" on cause-and-effect diagrams

eliminated, the problem itself should be back under control. At this point, firms can design and begin using statistical process control charts, discussed in the following chapter supplement.

TRENDS IN SIX SIGMA

13.5 Explain the new applications of Six Sigma

Although the philosophy and practices of Six Sigma have been in use for over 25 years, new applications of Six Sigma are constantly being discussed and published in research journals and trade publications. Two of the most recent applications are presented here.

SIX SIGMA AND REVENUE MANAGEMENT

Read more about trends in Six Sigma

One approach for optimizing revenues in an organization is to offer the right service to customers at the right time, for the right price. When applied to perishable services such as airline seats or hotel rooms, this is referred to as **revenue management** or **yield management** (a topic discussed in Chapter 10). Applying Six Sigma to revenue management allows the firm to reduce costs while maximizing revenues, which will further improve profits.

In revenue management, the problem of when to offer a service, to whom, and how much to charge is addressed. If an unrented hotel room or empty airline seat is considered a defect, then Six Sigma can be used to seek out the root causes of the defects, eliminate them, and ultimately improve a firm's financial performance. Six Sigma can also support revenue managers in making correct forecasting, overbooking, and market segmentation decisions. Specifically, the DMAIC improvement cycle can be used to improve revenue management. Currently, major hotel chains such as Starwood Hotels and Resorts Worldwide are experimenting with this approach.

revenue management Offering the right service to customers at the right time, for the right price. Also referred to as yield management.

yield management *See* Revenue management.

Figure 13.4 Cause-and-Effect Diagram for the Long Wait Problem

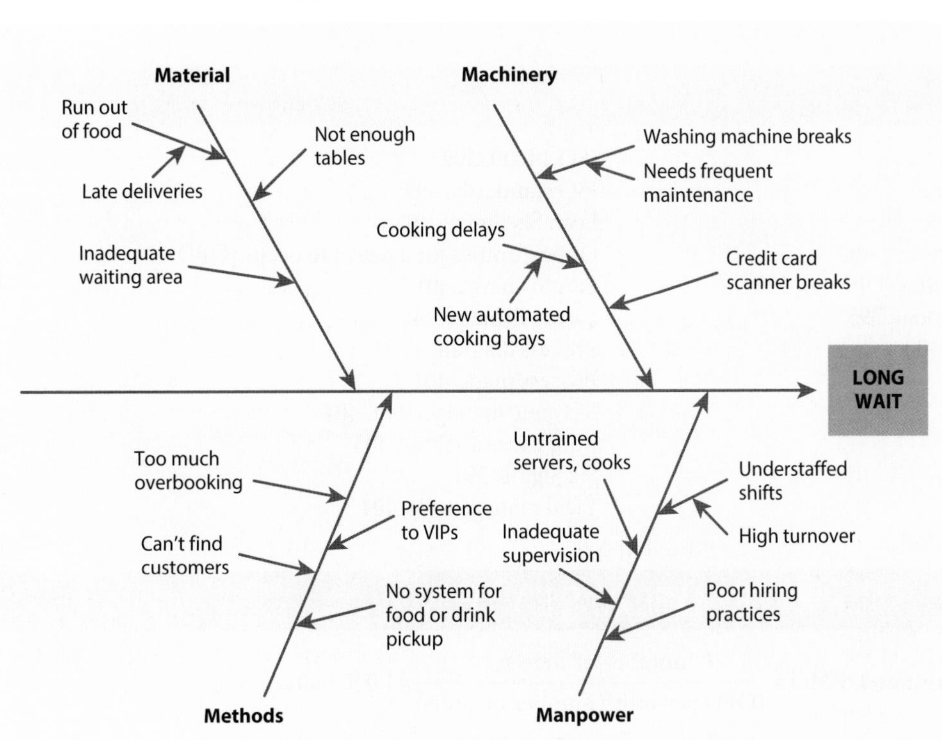

SIX SIGMA AND THE THEORY OF CONSTRAINTS

Using the Theory of Constraints (TOC) to identify bottlenecks (as described in Chapter 8), while using Six Sigma to improve the bottleneck processes, provides a potent combination for quickly finding root causes and improving capacities in organizations. A U.S. mining company has been experimenting with this combination (it refers to it as "6TOC") to keep costs down while maximizing capacity. In one case, it used Six Sigma to improve its truck hauling bottleneck by studying how rock was hauled and dumped into the primary crusher. Ultimately, it was able to lower the truck hauling cycle times, which increased production and delayed the purchase of another truck and the hiring of another driver.[31]

Visit edge.sagepub.com/wisner to help you accomplish your coursework goals in an easy-to-use learning environment.

- Mobile-friendly eFlashcards
- Mobile-friendly practice quizzes
- A complete online action plan
- Chapter summaries with learning objectives
- Excel templates to assist with practice problems
- Original video case studies that demonstrate chapter concepts in action

SUMMARY

In operations management, the use of Six Sigma to manage quality can provide firms with a distinct competitive advantage. This chapter provided a discussion of the philosophy, tools, and contributors to Six Sigma. A discussion of lean and Six Sigma was also included, since lean systems require the use of Six Sigma quality improvement methods and

tools. A number of important Six Sigma practices have been reviewed in this chapter that will aid the firm in its quality improvement efforts. Regardless of whether the firm is a manufacturer or a service, these tools can be utilized to assess current practices and processes, leading to continuous quality improvement.

KEY TERMS

Baldrige Quality Award, 397
Cause-and-effect diagrams, 403
Check sheets, 401
Critical-to-quality characteristics, 400
Defects per million opportunities (DPMO), 392
Deming's Theory of Management, 395
DMAIC improvement cycle, 400
Fishbone diagrams, 403
Flow diagrams, 401
4 Ms, 403
Ishikawa diagrams, 403
ISO 9000, 399
ISO 14000, 399
ISO standards, 399
Lean Six Sigma, 395
Opportunities for a defect to occur (OFD), 393
Pareto charts, 401
Pareto Principle, 402
Process diagrams, 401
Process maps, 401
Revenue management, 404
Root cause analysis, 403
Six Sigma, 391
Yield management, 404

FORMULA REVIEW

Defects per million opportunities, DPMO $= \frac{\text{number of defects}}{(\text{OFD per unit})(\text{number of units})} \times 1{,}000{,}000$

where OFD = opportunities for a defect to occur.

SOLVED PROBLEMS

Vickie and Todd make dog treats for their Internet order business, Good Boys Bakery. They want to track quality, so they decide to calculate their defects per million opportunities, or DPMO, each month. For each bag of dog treats they sell, there are four possible defects or customer complaints: a food complaint, a delivery timing complaint, an incorrect order, or a damaged order. During the past month, Good Boys filled 340 orders. It received eight complaints. Calculate the DPMO and determine the approximate Six Sigma level.

Answer:

$$\text{Good Boys DPMO} = \frac{\text{number of defects}}{(\text{OFD per unit})(\text{number of units})} \times 1{,}000{,}000$$

$$= \frac{8}{(4)(340)} \times 1{,}000{,}000 = 5{,}882 \text{ defects per million}$$

Using Table 13.1, this reveals a Six Sigma level of slightly better than 4.

REVIEW QUESTIONS

1. Describe Six Sigma's origins.
2. What is the reason for using the name *Six Sigma*?
3. What is DPMO, and why would a company calculate it?
4. What does Six Sigma have to do with lean? What is Lean Six Sigma?
5. Describe Deming's Theory of Management, and how it can be used to improve quality.
6. What is the Deming Prize? What companies can receive it?
7. What was the reasoning behind Crosby's belief that quality is free?

8. How did Juran discuss quality differently among management and then among workers?
9. What are the two most widely used ISO standards, and why are they so popular? Can they be used by any type of organization? Are ISO standards primarily about quality?
10. What is the DMAIC improvement cycle, and when would you use it?
11. What are critical-to-quality characteristics, and how are they used in Six Sigma?
12. Why are Six Sigma efforts tied to customer requirements?
13. How is a Black Belt different from a Master Black Belt in Six Sigma training?
14. What is the purpose of using a process diagram?
15. What are check sheets, and how are they used?
16. What are Pareto charts, and why are they useful in quality improvement efforts?

DISCUSSION QUESTIONS

1. Do you think a Six Sigma level of 4 is good? Explain.
2. Do you agree with Deming's Theory of Management? Explain.
3. Why do you suppose the Baldrige Quality Award is given only to U.S. organizations?
4. How could a company benefit from using the Baldrige Award application without actually applying for the award?
5. Apply the DMAIC improvement cycle to the improvement of the dining hall at a university.
6. Do you think Six Sigma training is necessary? Explain.
7. Construct a cause-and-effect diagram for the following problem: The university course registration process is too long. Brainstorm some potential causes.

EXERCISES AND PROJECTS

1. Using the Baldrige Award's seven performance categories, assess the company where you are employed. Do you think the company could improve? Explain your reasoning. Use your university or your most recent job if you are not currently employed.
2. Construct a flow diagram of the registration process at your university. What areas would you investigate further in order to identify problems? Use the DMAIC cycle to outline how you could solve one of the problems identified in your flow diagram.

PROBLEMS

1. Stan and Laurie Eakins, owners of Eakins Boat Rentals, want to start analyzing their company's quality. For each boat rental, there are four types of customer complaint: (a) boat not operating properly, (b) wrong-size boat, (c) uncomfortable boat, and (d) boat breaks during operation. During the past week, the company rented 104 boats. Eakins received a total of 12 complaints.
   a. What is the company's DPMO for the past week?
   b. What is the Six Sigma operating level?
2. If a product has 162 parts, the company has produced 10,000 units, and so far has had 1,100 customer complaints about quality, what is its probable DPMO? What is its Six Sigma operating level?
3. A company currently has produced 1,425,000 units, with a total defect level of 4,280. Each unit has a potential of 294 defects.
   a. What is the company's DPMO?
   b. What is its Six Sigma operating level?
   c. The company's goal is to reach a Six Sigma operating level of 6 for the next 1,000,000 units. What would its defect level have to be to achieve this goal?
4. A machine operator has produced 500 units of a particular part, and has stated he has only had 4 units fail to meet the company's one design specification. Is this good from a Six Sigma standpoint?

CASE STUDIES

CASE 1: The Mobile Surgical Kit Design Division

A large manufacturer and distributor of surgical medical supplies has been testing the use of a 3-D printer to produce a surgical kit that it will use to launch a new division. The Mobile Surgical Kit Design (MSKD) division is projected to be operational in one year and will focus on two markets. One segment is the ambulatory surgical centers that do not have easy access to traditional supply chains, can't hold adequate inventory levels, or have custom items in the surgical kits. Field trials in this segment were conducted with military triage and surgical sites close to conflicts, and medical units in third world countries or large refugee communities without adequate medical facilities. Both applications are often disconnected from regular supply chain systems and do not have the resources to stockpile inventory. The second segment will target medical/surgical facilities with low volume needs for custom surgical kits. Customers in this segment often pay premiums for custom surgical kits that are not inventoried at any level of the supply chain. Both segments have a need for surgical tools that deviate from standard tools in size and configuration as required by the dynamic environment in which the surgery is performed, including battle fields, remote villages, and temporary ambulatory medical offices.

The new division will launch with a surgical kit product line that can be produced on site. Customers will contract with MSKD to send engineering and production teams that will produce kits on site as needed. The second stage for MSKD will be to bundle the 3-D printer, the design and production processes, and a mobile production pod, and sell the entire unit to customers as a product with after-sales maintenance services. The second stage will also include licensing or partnerships with a 3-D printer manufacturer. The 3-D printed surgical kit will include a Kelly hemostat, needle driver, tissue forceps, retractor, scalpel handle, and Metzenbaum scissors. This is a functional surgical kit that can be produced on the 3-D printer.

The operations manager has requested additional resources to train all employees in Six Sigma methodologies rather than using a corporate model with a separate quality department. The level of quality for the 3-D printed products is critical to meeting customer requirements and establishing a competitive advantage, as this exploding field of 3-D printing brings in new competitors. The OM will need to submit a separate proposal for startup costs. The new division will start with 60 employees, including departments in sales and customer service, engineering (including field service technicians), manufacturing, logistics, and administration (including support staff, maintenance, accounting, and marketing not provided by corporate).

DISCUSSION QUESTIONS

1. Do you think it is a good idea to include a Six Sigma program in the division's startup plan? Why, or why not? What should the rationale be in the proposal to corporate?
2. Describe what you think the outcomes of the employee quality training program will look like, including the number and color of Six Sigma belts the teams should achieve after training. Discuss the possible makeup of the quality improvement teams.
3. The division manager will have to add information in the job descriptions for the human resources department, so that candidates for positions at the facility have adequate skills, knowledge, and experiences in preparation for Six Sigma training. Generate a list of skills and competencies that are important foundations for employees who will be immediately engaged in a Six Sigma training program.

Note: Written by Brian Hoyt, PhD, Ohio University, Athens, OH. This case was prepared solely to provide material for class discussion. The author does not intend to illustrate either effective or ineffective handling of a managerial situation.

CASE 2: Special Event Apparel

Special Event Apparel (SEA) is a fast-growing "pop up" retailer specializing in custom-printed T-shirts on college campuses. SEA started out as a business idea of three college students—Andrew, a criminal justice major; Mitchell, an information systems major; and Allison, a special education major. The business started with a need for uniform T-shirts for their intramural sand volleyball team. The three students wanted something different than the plain shirts bought at a department store and marked up with permanent markers, or the university-issued colored shirts with heat-pressed numbers. Their frustration in finding a business that could handle custom art on athletic apparel delivered before the start of the intramural season was the stimulus for Special Event Apparel.

The company grew organically from word of mouth (it always had the coolest uniforms in the league), and when orders for shirts expanded to other leagues (basketball, flag football, soccer, whiffle ball, and many others) they quickly learned how to work with apparel suppliers and screen printers to handle a larger volume of orders. Andrew and Mitchell did all the graphic design work and Allison took care of working with suppliers, including purchasing shirts, scheduling, screen print work, and carriers to drop-ship completed orders to customers on campus. As the business grew, the trio hired friends and roommates as sales representatives, customer service representatives, purchasing agents, and a business manager/accountant. The business also expanded into applications beyond intramural athletics and included student associations, special events such as concerts, and other campus events.

The outlook was bright, as revenue and profits were increasing each semester. While this quick success was encouraging, the number of business errors was increasing at an alarming rate. Orders consistently had sizing errors (not enough of one size or too many of another); style errors (wrong shirts or shorts); errors with colors, designs, and screen printing; and, finally, partial orders delivered and late back orders. A particularly embarrassing issue was the numerous spelling errors on team names, event names, or text included on the shirts.

Until recently, SEA experienced a very unusual response to the errors. SEA was such a creative organization that many of the errors had a "cult-like" following, and shirts were worn as if they were collectables. However, with the upcoming price increases, SEA recognized that the next business activity for the owners was to improve the company's operations.

Allison had recently been introduced to Six Sigma use in school systems through an elective business class. She suggested to the other two owners that she could lead an effort to address the operational inefficiencies that produced the growing number of order errors. Additionally, an investor contacted them and proposed investing a large amount of capital in SEA to expand to other campuses as a franchised operation. One condition was that SEA improve its operations.

DISCUSSION QUESTIONS

1. Why would potential franchisees be concerned with a business concept that is so out of control?
2. What quality tools should Allison use to identify the problems in SEA processes? How would she use them?
3. If a completed Pareto chart identified the largest problem area to be errors in information submitted to vendors (spelling, sizes, approved graphics, etc.), what tool would move the cause analysis forward?

Note: Written by Brian Hoyt, PhD, Ohio University, Athens, OH. This case was prepared solely to provide material for class discussion. The author does not intend to illustrate either effective or ineffective handling of a managerial situation.

CASE 3: Integrated Marketers

Integrated Marketers (IM) provides promotional products that focus on supporting clients' integrated marketing efforts. IM is a full-service promotional company that offers a full array of customizable promotional items, apparel, and logo/brand designing. Its services include graphic design, apparel embroidery and heat press, and "company store" fulfillment. It specializes in event promotion, company store design and fulfillment, and team apparel.

Product lines for IM are categorized as apparel and promotional items. Apparel is a popular promotional tool for company uniforms, athletic teams, and special events, and these items make up a large percentage of IM's revenue and continue to be a strong profit margin category. Promotional items are categorized into groups by promotion objective: integrated marketing tools and special event items. Integrated marketing tools are threaded with other marketing efforts and campaigns the customer has interacted with and are intended to inspire some type of customer action or intent to purchase. Promotional items frequently used as integrated marketing items include pens and office items, executive gifts, tools and hardware, lanyards, and computer accessories. Special event items are marketing tools intended to increase attention, exposure, and recall. Promotional items frequently used for special events include golf accessories, signage, automotive items, awards and recognition items, home use items, stress balls, and bags.

Integrated Marketers started 15 years ago serving small businesses and individuals with promotional products and customer apparel, but has steadily developed a more diverse customer base by adding product lines and services such as embroidery and graphic design. Broader product lines in promotional items and apparel were marketed to larger corporate accounts. Orders and contracts increased with school systems, medical centers, business associations, public utilities, financial institutions, and other organizations with multiple sites and larger employee and customer bases. Growth has been increasing steadily with the addition of these larger customers, accompanied by a corresponding growth in staff. In the last three years, IM has experienced more rapid growth in accounts and sales revenues while employee numbers have been relatively stable. While this growth was expected with the expanded product lines and changing customer base, the control of internal systems is lagging behind. The owner of IM recognizes that a shortage of personnel contributes to work systems appearing out of control. Performance measures also point to a need to repair existing work systems. Sales are up but profit margins are going down with cost drivers unidentified. IM has received complaints about errors in quotes, ordering, and production. Poor cash flow is an additional performance measure that adds pressure to the situation, caused in part by the increase of accounts receivables. The number of accounts that are not paying on time or not paying at all is increasing at an alarming rate. The external sales staff don't consider this to be within their domain, and the inside sales and operations staffs are so busy that no one has time to address the situation. IM is examining all of its work systems by first prioritizing the impact the system has on potential sales and cost contribution. Some of the work systems being reviewed include the customer quoting and ordering system (email, fax, phone, on site), purchasing (from apparel and promotional item vendors), accounts receivable, and sales and marketing (customer relationship management and analysis, sales planning, segmentation, pricing strategies).

One employee, the most recent hire, has experience in process improvement and Six Sigma applications, and has been assigned as team leader to prioritize improvement efforts and to begin on work system improvement. The team leader will be using a Six Sigma improvement approach consisting of five steps to direct process improvement: define, measure, analyze, improve, and control. After meeting with all employees and using project prioritizing matrix methods, the first system they will address is the accounts receivable (AR) system.

The team moved through the Define stage and determined critical internal customer satisfaction quality characteristics such as reducing average days of receivables, reducing average cost in receivables, and reducing the percent of uncollectable accounts. The collected information on industry standards and cash flow impacted whether the receivables were reduced. Activities in the Measure stage included putting together check sheets to collect AR data from the existing accounting software database. Accounts receivable data were collected from the past two years and first categorized by type of account using the affinity diagram quality tool. Account categories included entertainment and gaming (such as Bingo), government agencies, public schools, banks, medical facilities, not-for-profit organizations, private community groups, faith-based organizations, public utilities, and small businesses. The data were also used to calculate average days (30, 60, 90, 120+), average $, total $, and $ as a % of revenue. The initial data mining revealed some alarming numbers: The total $ in account receivables for each of the last two years was almost 10% of total revenue, and approaching $2,000,000 annually; additionally, almost 90% of receivables were not collected, amounting to .081% of total revenues or approximately $162,000. These numbers certainly reveal why there is a cash flow crunch, but it requires a specific intervention to realize a system improvement.

Growth projections for the industry are healthy, but growth for IM will be contingent on how well it can improve its accounts receivable work system performance. The improvement team needs to begin the Analyze stage and then Improve and Control right away.

QUESTIONS

1. Which quality tool will be useful to see Integrated Marketer's accounts receivable work system's performance over time? What is the purpose of that quality tool?
2. Identify and describe a quality tool that Integrated Marketer can use to focus its efforts toward improving the accounts receivable work system.
3. How can Integrated Marketer be assured that it is working on the "biggest problem area" before a system improvement trial?
4. How will Integrated Marketer know if its improvement attempt actually made a difference on the accounts receivable work system?

Note: Written by Brian Hoyt, PhD, Ohio University, Athens, OH. This case was prepared solely to provide material for class discussion. The author does not intend to illustrate either effective or ineffective handling of a managerial situation.

VIDEO CASE STUDY

Learn more about ***quality control*** from real organizations that use operations management techniques every day. Jim Biafore is the Senior Director at Beefsteak, a restaurant in Washington, D.C. Beefsteak prides itself on offering fresh, healthy, high-quality dishes on a consistent basis. Watch this short interview to learn how they do it.

I am continually surprised at how often shop owners tell me they would like to do data collection for SPC, but they are "just too small" a shop or they "can't afford all that fancy equipment." There seems to be a mistaken perception out there that (1) SPC is a lot more complicated than it is and (2) you need expensive hardware and a sophisticated computerized system just to get into it.

—**GEORGE SCHUETZ,** director of precision gages, Mahr Federal[1]

Inserting garbage data into the most elegant of calculations will result in nonsensical analysis and decisions. Getting enough of the right data, at the right time, to the right people is the constantly evolving challenge that must be met. Technology now facilitates the real-time flow of this information. The technology can be implemented and process improvements achieved only if an enterprise is willing to make the investment.

—**BRANDON THEISS,** Master Black Belt, American Standard Brands[2]

SUPPLEMENT: STATISTICAL QUALITY CONTROL 13S

LEARNING OBJECTIVES

After completing this chapter supplement, you should be able to:

13S.1 Describe the types of process variations and the measurements required for quality control purposes
13S.2 Construct the process control charts for variable data
13S.3 Construct the process control chart for attribute data
13S.4 Calculate the process capability index and show how it is used
13S.5 Explain how acceptance sampling is used

Master the content.
edge.sagepub.com/wisner

IMPROVING BRICKS WITH STATISTICAL PROCESS CONTROL

For the South Carolina–based Palmetto Brick Company, making high-quality, long-lasting bricks at a fair price has been a company value passed down through four generations. One way the Anderson family, the owners of the company, have accomplished this is through use of statistical process control (SPC) software to monitor the brick-making processes.

Clay, the primary material used in bricks, presents a range of characteristics that must be closely monitored. Colors and sizes must also be carefully monitored, and SPC allows Palmetto to catch problems while they can still be corrected. Once bricks are fired, it becomes too late to fix anything, and any product not meeting specifications must be thrown out.

Some of the activities where quality measurements are taken for control chart purposes include raw material blends; extruded brick sizes; brick moisture levels; visual checks for color, consistency, and chippage; fired brick sizes; and saturation coefficients.

Process operators enter sample data into the software application, and real-time feedback is displayed on the monitors: A green light indicates a problem-free condition, a yellow light means there is a trend indicating a potential problem that may lead to defects, and a red light indicates an out-of-control situation requiring immediate action. The software displays all of the required control charts, as well as process capability numbers. Data analyses can also be generated.

Palmetto's attention to quality has helped it to stay successful all these years. Today, it makes 150 million bricks per year, and guarantees them for 150 years.[3]

INTRODUCTION

The final step in most Six Sigma or quality improvement efforts is to employ **statistical quality control** (SQC), also called **statistical process control** (SPC). Once a problem is identified, analyzed, improved, and deemed to be under control, workers gather process performance data, create **control charts** to monitor process performance, and then begin collecting and plotting sample measurements in a continuous fashion. These SQC activities allow workers to take corrective steps quickly if the control charts indicate the start of an out-of-control situation. It is important to note that SQC techniques will be useless unless the process is *already under control*. Out-of-control processes must be analyzed and improved using the tools described in Chapter 13 (check sheets, Pareto charts, and fishbone diagrams).

The formal practice of statistical quality control dates back to 1924, when Walter A. Shewhart of Bell Laboratories described a control chart for the first time. It was then used at Western Electric in Illinois to successfully study fuses and controls.[4] Control charts are graphic

statistical quality control *See* Statistical process control.

statistical process control Once a problem is identified, analyzed, fixed, and deemed to be under control, workers gather process performance data, create control charts to monitor process performance, and then begin collecting and plotting sample measurements in a continuous fashion. These activities allow workers to take corrective steps quickly if the control charts indicate the start of an out-of-control situation.

control charts Allow managers to monitor samples of process performance.

Figure 13S.1 Control Chart Images

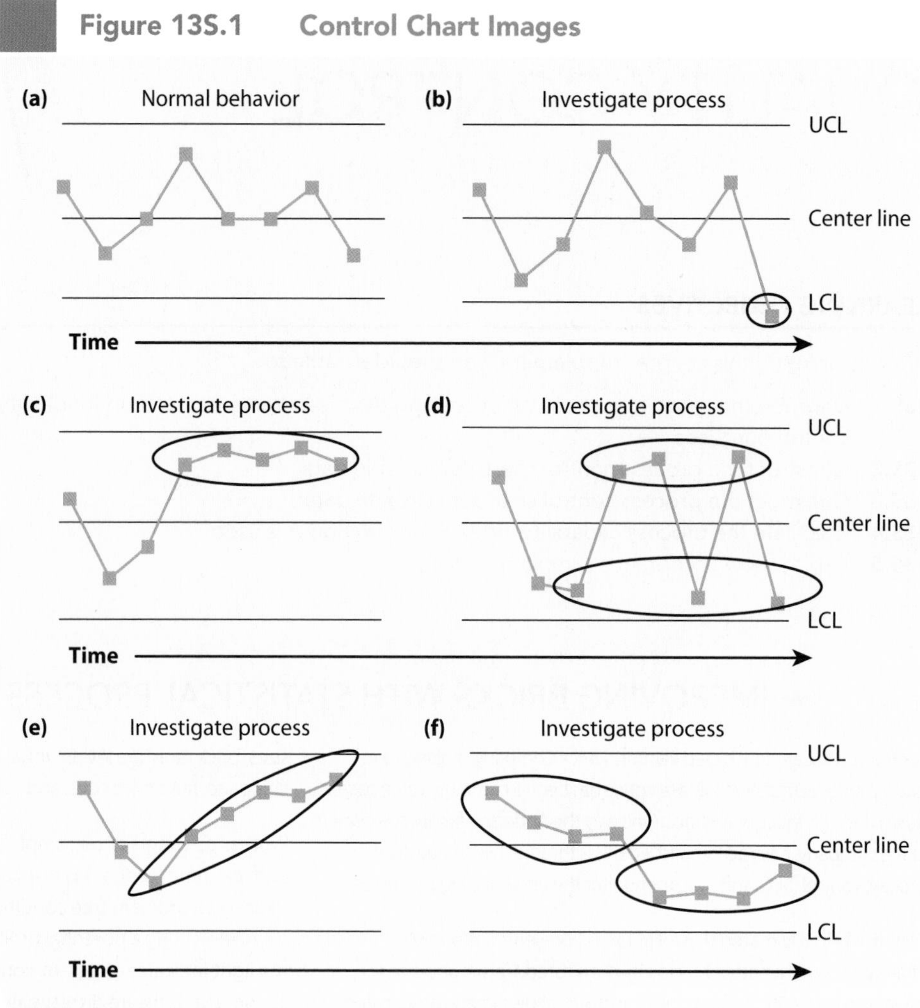

Watch a general discussion of control charts

representations of process performance over time, showing the desired measurement (the center line of the control chart) and the process's upper and lower **control limits** (typically designed as ± 3 standard deviations from the mean or center line). This visual aid makes it very easy for operators to design control charts, plot data, and compare performance over time.

If the process performance sample measurements fall within the acceptable control limits and appear *normally distributed* around the desired measurement (the center line of the control chart), the process is said to be in *statistical control* and is permitted to continue. Sample measurements continue to be collected over time and plotted on the control chart. When a sample plot falls out of the acceptable limits, or when the plots no longer appear normally distributed above and below the desired measurement, the process is then considered *out of control* (interpreting control charts is somewhat of an art). When this happens, process problems and their root causes are identified and the causes are eliminated, as described in Chapter 13. Control chart plots can then resume once the process is considered back under statistical control.

PROCESS VARIATIONS

control limits Used in control charts, based on an assumption that the sampling distribution is normal, and that the control limits are typically ±3.0 standard deviations from the population mean, which contains 99.73% of the sampling distribution.

13S.1 Describe the types of process variations and the measurements required for quality control purposes

Figure 13S.1 shows an acceptable control chart, (a), along with several other control charts considered out of control. As shown in chart (b), if one data point falls above or below the control limits, the process should be investigated for poor performance causes. As shown in chart (c), if five or more consecutive data points fall above or below the center line, the process should be investigated. In chart (d), the data points appear to be erratic, and not close to the center line. In chart (e), if there is an upward or downward trend in the data points, the process should be investigated. And finally, in chart (f), there is a noticeable shift in the data points, indicating a process problem.

The final step is to determine if the process is capable of meeting customer requirements. SQC methods have been used successfully in a wide range of industries for many years. The supplement-opening Manufacturing Spotlight describes their use in the making of bricks. The remaining portion of this supplement will describe the tools of SQC for several types of data.

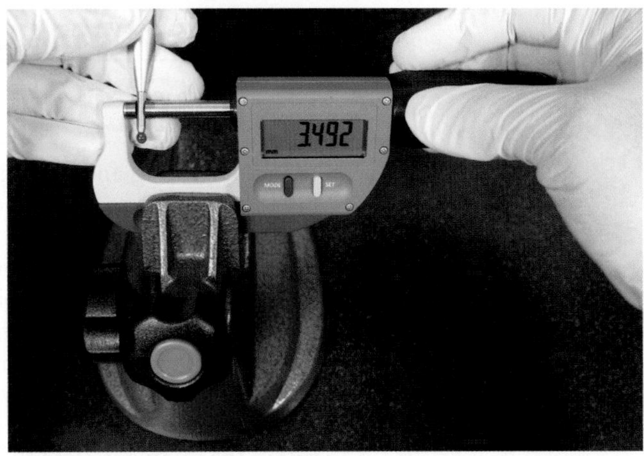

iStock/PoonsakBoonmak

A digital micrometer such as the one shown is accurate to within 1 micron, or 1 millionth of a meter.

All processes exhibit variations in performance, regardless of the care taken to ensure accuracy. Process measurement variations are unavoidable. They are unavoidable because every physical measurement has some uncertainty. Using extreme care, a chemical analyst, for example, can only obtain a substance weight within the accuracy of a balance. For example, most four-place analytical balances are accurate to ± 0.0001 grams. Thus, the analyst can measure a 1.0000-gram weight to an accuracy of ± 0.0001 grams. For this reason, use of SPC is warranted to monitor all process performance, from precise measures such as these, to the monitoring of service times at a restaurant, to the paint color of an automobile. The types of variations and their control are discussed next.

MEASUREMENT VARIATIONS

Variations in process measurements can be either **natural variations** or **assignable variations**. All process measurements are affected by these variations; environmental noise or natural variations are to be expected. When *only the natural variations are present* (such as variations in humidity caused by changing weather conditions or variations in driving time caused by highway traffic patterns), the process is in statistical control. These natural variations are typically accepted as uncontrollable. Assignable variations, on the other hand, are those that can be traced to a specific "fixable" cause (such as the causes and subcauses shown in Figure 13.4). These assignable variations are created by causes that can be identified and eliminated, and this is the objective of statistical process control.

natural variations Uncontrollable process variations, such as variations in humidity caused by changing weather conditions or variations in driving time caused by highway traffic patterns.

assignable variations Process variations that can be traced to a specific "fixable" cause. These assignable variations are created by causes that can be identified and eliminated, and this is the objective of statistical process control.

DATA SAMPLES

Because of the presence of variations in all process measures, and because sample sizes greater than one more closely describe actual process performance, data samples are collected and the sample measures are then plotted on control charts. Sample measures can be classified as either **variable data** or **attribute data**, and each requires a different type of control chart. Variable data are continuous, such as weight, time, and length (as in the weight of a box of cereal, the time to serve a customer, or the length of a steel rod). Attribute data indicate the presence of some attribute such as color, satisfaction, workability, or beauty (for instance, determining whether or not a car was painted the right color, if a customer liked the meal, or if the lightbulb worked).

Variable data samples are collected to determine the means of the sample measures (for instance, an average of 12.04 ounces in a sample of four boxes of cereal), whereas attribute data samples are collected to determine the percent defectives within each sample (for instance, 10% of the customers in a sample size of 20 did not like their meal). The two types of control charts used with these data are discussed next.

variable data Continuous process data, such as weight, time, and length (as in the weight of a box of cereal, the time to serve a customer, or the length of a steel rod).

attribute data Yes/no or pass/fail process data that indicate the presence of some attribute such as color, satisfaction, workability, or beauty (for instance, determining whether or not a car was painted the right color, if a customer liked the meal, or if the lightbulb worked).

PROCESS CONTROL FOR VARIABLE DATA

13S.2 Construct the process control charts for variable data

When measuring and plotting variable process data, two types of control charts are needed: the **$\bar{x}$ chart** and the **R chart**. The $\bar{x}$ chart is used to track the central tendency of the sample means, while the R chart is used to track sample ranges, or the variation of the measurements within each sample. A perfect process would have sample means equal to the desired measure and sample ranges equal to zero (no variation). To assess whether or not a variable data process is in control, then, it is necessary to view *both of these charts in unison*. Note that a sample's mean might look fine, even though several of the measures making up the sample might vary widely from the desired measure, making the sample's range very high. It could also be the case that the sample's range looked fine (the range within the sample is close to zero), even though all of the measures were far from the desired measure, making the sample's mean look bad. For variable data, then, *both* the $\bar{x}$ chart and the R chart must show that the samples are in control before the process itself is considered in control.

CONSTRUCTING THE $\bar{x}$ CHART AND THE R CHART

The first step in constructing any control chart is to gather data (provided the process is already in control using the Six Sigma methods described in Chapter 13). Typically, about 25 or 30 samples of size 5–10 are collected over a period of time. Then, for each sample, the mean, $\bar{x}$, and the range, R, are calculated. Next, the *mean of all the sample means*, $\bar{\bar{x}}$, and the *mean of the sample ranges*, $\bar{R}$, are calculated. The $\bar{\bar{x}}$ and $\bar{R}$ measures are used as the center lines (the desired measures) for their respective control charts. Example 13S.1 illustrates the calculation of the center lines of the $\bar{x}$ chart and the R chart. The formulas used to calculate the center lines, $\bar{\bar{x}}$ and $\bar{R}$, are:

$$\bar{\bar{x}} = \frac{\Sigma_{i=1}^{k} \bar{x}_i}{k} \text{ and } \bar{R} = \frac{\Sigma_{i=1}^{k} R_i}{k},$$

where k indicates the number of samples and i indicates the specific sample.

As shown in Example 13S.1, $\bar{\bar{x}} = 11.97$ and $\bar{R} = 0.39$. If these measures are acceptable to the Rich Soup Co., then they can be used to construct the control charts (it is very important to note that if the process is currently out of control, the data will be completely unacceptable for designing control charts, and this will become evident once the data are plotted). These means are also used to calculate the **upper control limits** (UCL) and **lower control limits** (LCL) for the two control charts. Control limits are typically established as three standard deviations above and below the population mean, such that 99.7% of the sample plots fall within these limits. The formulas are:

$$UCL_{\bar{x}} = \bar{\bar{x}} + A_2\bar{R} \text{ and } LCL_{\bar{x}} = \bar{\bar{x}} - A_2\bar{R}$$

$$UCL_R = D_4\bar{R} \text{ and } LCL_R = D_3\bar{R},$$

where A_2, D_3, and D_4 are constants based on the size of each sample, n, and are shown in Table 13S.1 (the constants shown are based on an assumption that the sampling distribution is normal, and that the control limits are ±3.0 standard deviations from the population mean, which contains 99.73% of the sampling distribution).

Example 13S.2 illustrates how to calculate $\bar{x}$, $\bar{\bar{x}}$, R, and $\bar{R}$ for the Rich Soup Co. using a spreadsheet.

$\bar{x}$ chart For variable data, used to track the central tendency of the sample means.

R chart For variable data, it is used to track sample ranges, or the variation of the measurements within each sample.

$\bar{x}$ For variable data, the mean of a sample's measurements.

R For variable data, it is the difference between the largest and the smallest measurement in one sample.

$\bar{\bar{x}}$ The center line of the $\bar{x}$ chart.

$\bar{R}$ The center line of the R chart.

upper control limits A line that is three standard deviations above the mean, so that 99.7% of the sample plots fall inside this limit.

lower control limits A line that is three standard deviations below the mean, so that 99.7% of the sample plots fall inside this limit.

Example 13S.1
Variable Data for Soup Cans at the Rich Soup Co.

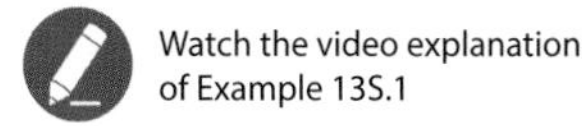

Watch the video explanation of Example 13S.1

The Rich Soup Co. has collected process data in order to construct control charts to use in its 12-ounce canning facility. It collected 20 samples of size 4, each hour over a 20-hour period. The data are shown below for each sample:

	Samples					
Hour	1	2	3	4	$\bar{x}$	R
1	12	12.2	11.7	11.6	11.88	0.6
2	11.5	11.7	11.6	12.3	11.78	0.8
3	11.9	12.2	12.1	12	12.05	0.3
4	12.1	11.8	12.1	11.7	11.93	0.4
5	12.2	12.3	11.7	11.9	12.03	0.6
6	12.1	11.9	12.3	12.2	12.13	0.4
7	12	11.7	11.6	12.1	11.85	0.5
8	12	12.1	12.2	12.3	12.15	0.3
9	11.8	11.9	12	12	11.93	0.2
10	12.1	11.9	11.8	11.7	11.88	0.3
11	12.1	12	12.1	11.9	12.03	0.2
12	11.9	11.9	11.7	11.8	11.83	0.2
13	12	12	11.8	12.1	11.98	0.3
14	12.1	11.9	12	11.7	11.93	0.4
15	12	12	11.7	11.2	11.73	0.8
16	12.1	12	12	11.9	12.00	0.2
17	12.1	12.2	12	11.9	12.05	0.3
18	12.2	12	11.7	11.8	11.93	0.5
19	12	12.1	12.3	12	12.10	0.3
20	12	12.2	11.9	12	12.03	0.3
Means					**11.97**	**0.39**

Using the data in Example 13S.1 and Table 13S.1 for a sample size of 4, the upper and lower control limits can be determined for both the $\bar{x}$ chart and the R chart:

$$\mathrm{UCL}_{\bar{x}} = \bar{\bar{x}} + A_2\bar{R} = 11.97 + 0.729(0.39) = 12.25$$

$$\mathrm{LCL}_{\bar{x}} = \bar{\bar{x}} - A_2\bar{R} = 11.97 - 0.729(0.39) = 11.69$$

and

$$\mathrm{UCL}_{\mathrm{R}} = D_4\bar{R} = 2.282(0.39) = 0.89$$

$$\mathrm{LCL}_{\mathrm{R}} = D_3\bar{R} = 0(0.39) = 0$$

Table 13S.1 Constants for Computing

Control Chart Limits (±3σ)			
Sample Size, *n*	Mean Factor, A_2	UCL, D_4	LCL, D_3
2	1.88	3.268	0
3	1.023	2.574	0
4	0.729	2.282	0
5	0.577	2.115	0
6	0.483	2.004	0
7	0.419	1.924	0.076
8	0.373	1.864	0.136
9	0.337	1.816	0.184
10	0.308	1.777	0.223

Example 13S.2 Spreadsheet Calculations for the Rich Soup Co. Data

Use Excel spreadsheet templates to find the solution

	A	B	C	D	E	F	G
1	**Hour**	**1**	**2**	**3**	**4**	$\bar{x}$	***R***
2	1	12	12.2	11.7	11.6	11.88	0.6
3	2	11.5	11.7	11.6	12.3	11.78	0.8
4	3	11.9	12.2	12.1	12	12.05	0.3
5	4	12.1	11.8	12.1	11.7	11.93	0.4
6	5	12.2	12.3	11.7	11.9	12.03	0.6
7	6	12.1	11.9	12.3	12.2	12.13	0.4
8	7	12	11.7	11.6	12.1	11.85	0.5
9	8	12	12.1	12.2	12.3	12.15	0.3
10	9	11.8	11.9	12	12	11.93	0.2
11	10	12.1	11.9	11.8	11.7	11.88	0.4
12	11	12.1	12	12.1	11.9	12.03	0.2
13	12	11.9	11.9	11.7	11.8	11.83	0.2
14	13	12	12	11.8	12.1	11.98	0.3
15	14	12.1	11.9	12	11.7	11.93	0.4
16	15	12	12	11.7	11.2	11.73	0.8
17	16	12.1	12	12	11.9	12.00	0.2
18	17	12.1	12.2	12	11.9	12.05	0.3
19	18	12.2	12	11.7	11.8	11.93	0.5
20	19	12	12.1	12.3	12	12.10	0.3
21	20	12	12.2	11.9	12	12.03	0.3
22						11.96	0.39

F2: = AVERAGE(B2:E2)

G4: = MAX(B4:E4) – MIN(B4:E4)

F22: = AVERAGE (F2:F21)

G22: = AVERAGE (G2:G21)

Next, the means and control limits are used to construct the two variable data control charts. In Figures 13S.2 and 13S.3, the sample means and ranges from Example 13S.1 are plotted on the two variable data control charts, showing the center lines and the control limits. From these plots, it appears that the process is in statistical control, so the Rich Soup Co. can begin using these charts to monitor the canning process. Note that if the process was shown to be out of control on either chart, the control charts would not be useful and would be discarded until problems and their causes were identified and eliminated, and the process was once again in statistical control.

Once a good set of control charts has been created and samples from the process are being statistically monitored, the following steps should be followed:

1. Collect samples of size 4–5 periodically (the period depends on the process being monitored).
2. Plot the sample means and ranges on the control charts while monitoring the process.
3. When the process is trending out of control, use check sheets, Pareto charts, and fishbone diagrams to investigate causes and eliminate assignable process variations.
4. Continuously repeat Steps 1–3.

PROCESS CONTROL FOR ATTRIBUTE DATA

13S.3 Construct the process control chart for attribute data

When collecting attribute data regarding the performance of a process, the use of $\bar{x}$ and R charts no longer apply. In these cases, either **P charts**, which monitor the *percent defective* in each sample, or **C charts**, which count the *number of defects* per unit of output, are used. Each of these is discussed next.

P charts Control charts for attribute data, which monitor the *percent defective* in each sample.

C charts Control charts for attribute data that count the *number of defects* per unit of output.

Figure 13S.2 $\bar{x}$ **Chart for the Rich Soup Co.**

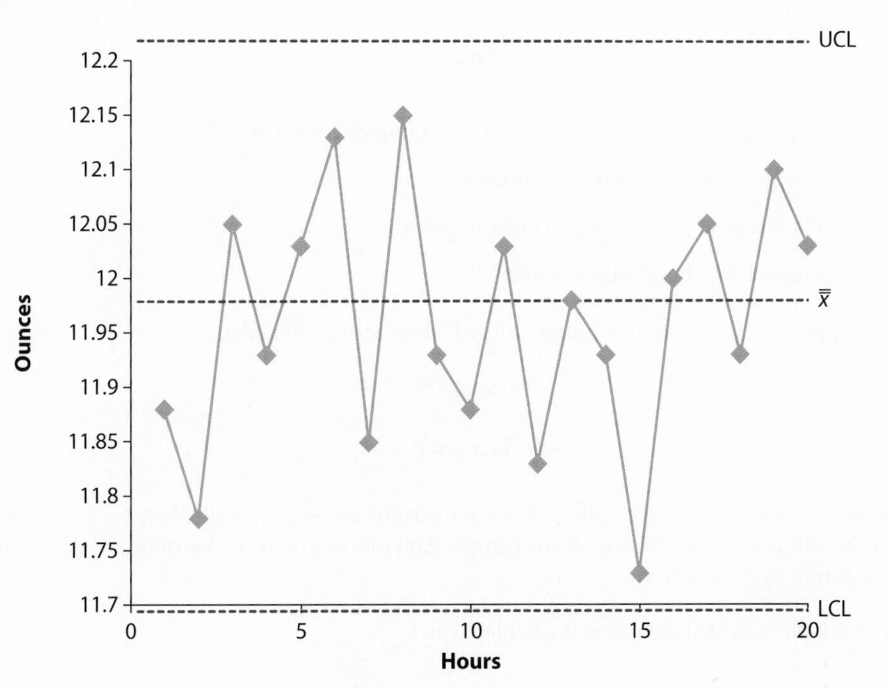

Note: To plot the $\bar{x}$ data using a spreadsheet, highlight the $\bar{x}$ data column, then click on Insert, Line, and any 2-D Line.

Figure 13S.3 R Chart for the Rich Soup Co.

Use Excel spreadsheet templates to practice

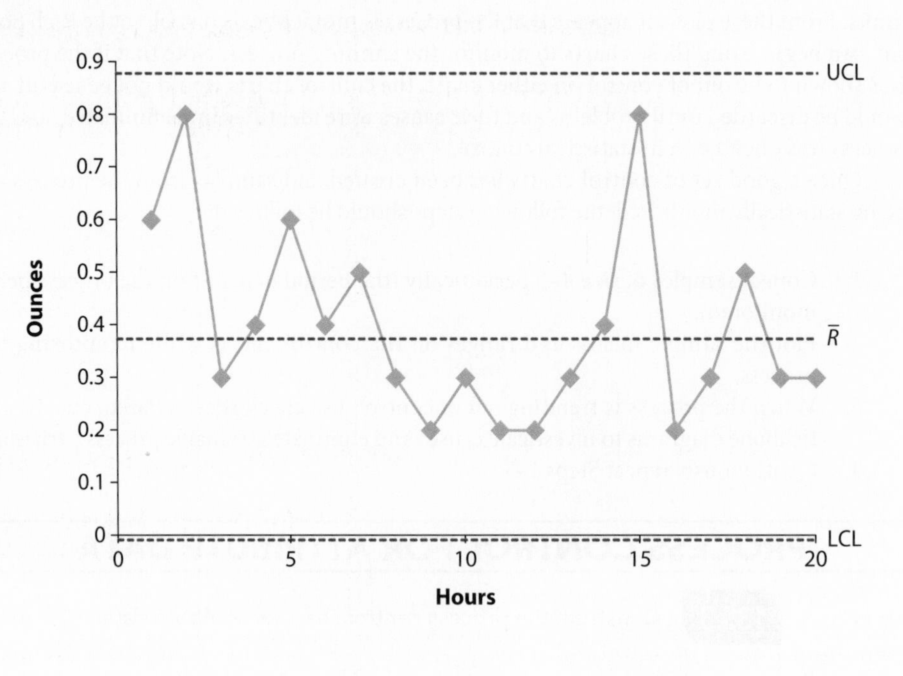

Note: To plot the R data using a spreadsheet, highlight the R data column, then click on Insert, Line, and any 2-D Line.

USING AND CONSTRUCTING P CHARTS

The P chart is the most commonly used attribute control chart. If large sample sizes are used when collecting data, the samples can be assumed to be normally distributed. The following formula is used to calculate the center line, $\overline{P}$, for the P chart:

$$\overline{P} = \frac{\sum_{i=1}^{k} P_i}{k},$$

where $\overline{P}$ is the mean percent defective for all samples collected,

k represents the number of samples,

P is the percent defective in one sample, and

i represents the specific sample.

The upper and lower control limits for the P chart are calculated as:

$$\text{UCL}_p = \sqrt{\frac{(\overline{P})(1-\overline{P})}{n}} + z\sigma_p$$

$$\text{LCL}_p = \overline{P} - z\sigma_p$$

where z is the number of standard deviations from the mean (recall when $z = 3$, the control limits will contain 99.73% of all the sample data plots), and σ_p is the standard deviation of the sampling distribution.

The sample standard deviation is calculated as:

$$\sigma_p = \sqrt{\frac{(\overline{P})(1-\overline{P})}{n}},$$

where n is the size of each sample.

Jacob & Lillie's Cakery Co. makes cupcakes, and the co-owners have decided to begin monitoring their quality using a P chart. So, over the past 30 days, they have collected and assessed 100 cupcakes each day. The chart below shows the percent defectives for each sample and the overall average percent defective, or $\overline{P}$.

Day	Percent Defective	Day	Percent Defective	Day	Percent Defective
1	0.01	11	0.02	21	0.02
2	0.02	12	0.03	22	0
3	0	13	0	23	0.01
4	0.03	14	0.04	24	0.02
5	0	15	0.01	25	0.01
6	0.01	16	0.04	26	0.03
7	0.04	17	0	27	0
8	0	18	0	28	0.02
9	0	19	0.01	29	0.01
10	0.02	20	0.03	30	0
				$\overline{P}$	**0.014**

Note: The $\overline{P}$ can be calculated using a spreadsheet, by using the *average* function for the 30% defectives. The σ_P can also be calculated using the SQRT function.

Example 13S.3
Attribute Data for Jacob & Lillie's Cakery Co.

Watch the video explanation of Example 13S.3

Use Excel spreadsheet templates to find the solution

Example 13S.3 provides the data used to determine $\overline{P}$, σ_P, and the control limits for the P chart.

As shown in Example 13S.3, $\overline{P} = 0.014$. Calculating σ_P yields:

$$\sigma_P = \sqrt{\frac{(\overline{P})(1-\overline{P})}{n}} = \sqrt{\frac{(0.014)(0.986)}{100}} = 0.012\,.$$

Next, the control limits can be calculated (assuming the desired z is 3):

$$UCL_P = \overline{P} + z\sigma_P = 0.014 + 3(0.012) = 0.05, \text{ and}$$

$$LCL_P = \overline{P} - z\sigma_P = 0.014 - 3(0.012) = 0.$$

Note, here, that the LCL is truncated at 0, since there cannot be a negative fraction defective.

Figure 13S.4 shows the P chart for Jacob & Lillie's Cakery Co., with the fraction defectives plotted from Example 13S.3. Viewing the chart, it can be seen that while a few data points are close to the upper control limit, the process still appears to be in control, since the data points are randomly dispersed around the center line, inside the control limits, and about half the data points are on each side of the center line. Thus, the company can begin using this control chart to monitor its cupcake quality. Note that a number of data points fall on the lower control limit. Should this be considered a problem? No, since these points indicate a sample with zero defective cupcakes.

Figure 13S.4 P Chart for Jacob & Lillie's Cakery Co.

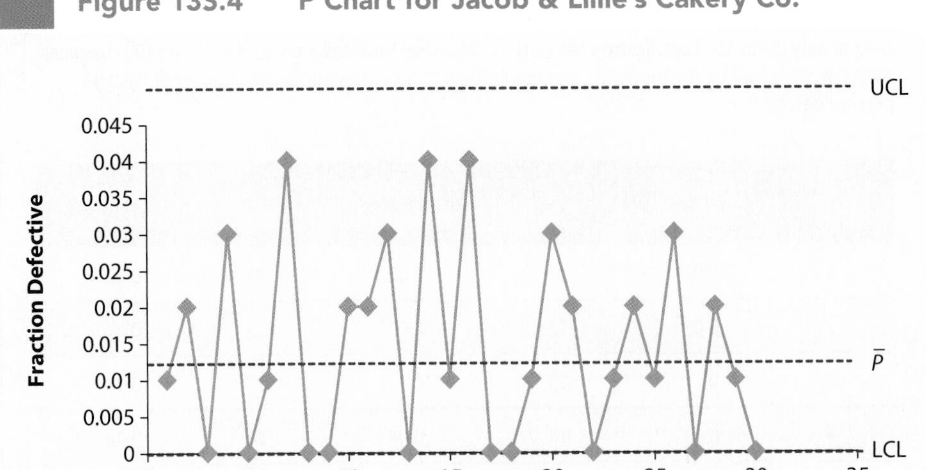

Use Excel spreadsheet templates to practice

Note: The P chart can be created using a spreadsheet, by highlighting the percent defectives, then clicking on Insert, Line, and any 2-D Line.

USING C CHARTS

When multiple errors can occur in a process resulting in a defective unit, then we can use C charts to control the *number* of defects per unit of output. C charts are useful when a number of mistakes or errors can occur per unit of output, but they occur infrequently. Examples can include a hotel stay, a printed textbook, or a construction project. The control limits for C charts are based on the assumption of a Poisson probability distribution of the item of interest (commonly used when defects are infrequent). In this case, the distribution variance is equal to its mean. For C charts, then,

$$\bar{c} = \text{mean errors per unit of measure (and also the sample variance),}$$

$$\sqrt{\bar{c}} = \text{sample standard deviation, and}$$

$$\bar{c} \pm 3\sqrt{\bar{c}} = \text{control limits.}$$

Example 13S.4 can be used to illustrate the calculation of the C chart's control limits. In the example, the units of measure are days; thus, the average daily defects are 29.1 (the center

Example 13S.4 Monitoring Editorial Defects at the Elizabeth Publishing Co.

Watch the video explanation of Example 13S.4

The editorial assistants are monitored for defects in the firm's printed work on a monthly basis. Over the past 30 days, a total of 872 editorial mistakes were found. Computing the center line and control limits reveals:

$$\bar{c} = \frac{872}{30} = 29.1 \text{ mistakes per day; with the}$$

$$UCL_c = 29.1 + 3\sqrt{29.1} = 45.3 \text{ and } LCL_c = 29.1 - 3\sqrt{291} = 12.9.$$

The daily defects can then be monitored similarly to the P chart in Figure 13S.3.

line and also the variance). The upper and lower control limits are 45.3 and 12.9, respectively. The Elizabeth Publishing Co. can now use the C chart center line and control limits based on the 30-day error data to monitor its daily editorial error rate.

PROCESS CAPABILITY

13S.4 Calculate the process capability index and show how it is used

Operations managers and production personnel are particularly interested in **process capability**, and they perform analyses to help them predict how well a process will meet customer requirements and design specifications. When design specifications change, in-control and capable processes may suddenly be unable to produce acceptable product. Process capability is a measure of the ability of a process to consistently produce a product or service within design specifications. For example, a 1-liter water container might be designed to hold 1.0 liters with a tolerance of ± 0.05 liters. Thus, the design specification would be a water container filled with 0.95 to 1.05 liters of water. A filling machine similar to the one shown here would then be designed to operate within this specification.

Once a process, such as a water filling machine, is found to be in control using the tools discussed earlier, it can be periodically tested to see if it is capable of performing within the required design specifications (the specifications, for example, could require tighter limits than the ± 3 standard deviation limits used in earlier examples). If a process is not capable of meeting design specifications, management has some options. One option would be to leave the process as is and use inspection to catch any units not meeting specifications. This could cause potential quality problems when some poor quality units are missed, and also create increased inspection costs. Customer complaints would also likely increase. Another option is to relax design specifications to match the process capability, which would also reduce product quality and customer satisfaction. A third option is to improve the process capability through process redesign and more detailed problem-solving activities.

iStock/Avatar 023

Automatic liquid filling machines such as the one shown are accurate to ± 5%, depending on the fill size and type of liquid.

Figure 13S.5 shows five possible process capability situations that can occur. In situation (a), the process is easily capable of meeting design specifications because the current process variations are much tighter than the design specifications. In situation (b), the process comfortably meets design specifications because the current process variations are less than the design specifications. In situation (c), the process variations are equal to the design specifications, so most of the time the process will be capable of meeting requirements; however, there occasionally may be failures. Situation (d) shows that the process is not capable of meeting the design specifications (the current process variations are greater than the design specifications). Even though this process may be in control, the process will create defective output, resulting in scrap, rework, and dissatisfied customers. In situation (e), the process is capable of meeting the lower specification; however, some of the output will not meet the upper specification (even though the specification range is greater than the current process variation range, the process mean is off-center and is certainly out of control). The processes in (c), (d), and (e) are all in need of improvement. As shown in the figures, process capability studies aid in the understanding of process variation by comparing actual processes to the way they were designed to work.

process capability A measure of the ability of a process to consistently produce a product or service within design specifications.

Figure 13S.5 Process Capability Situations

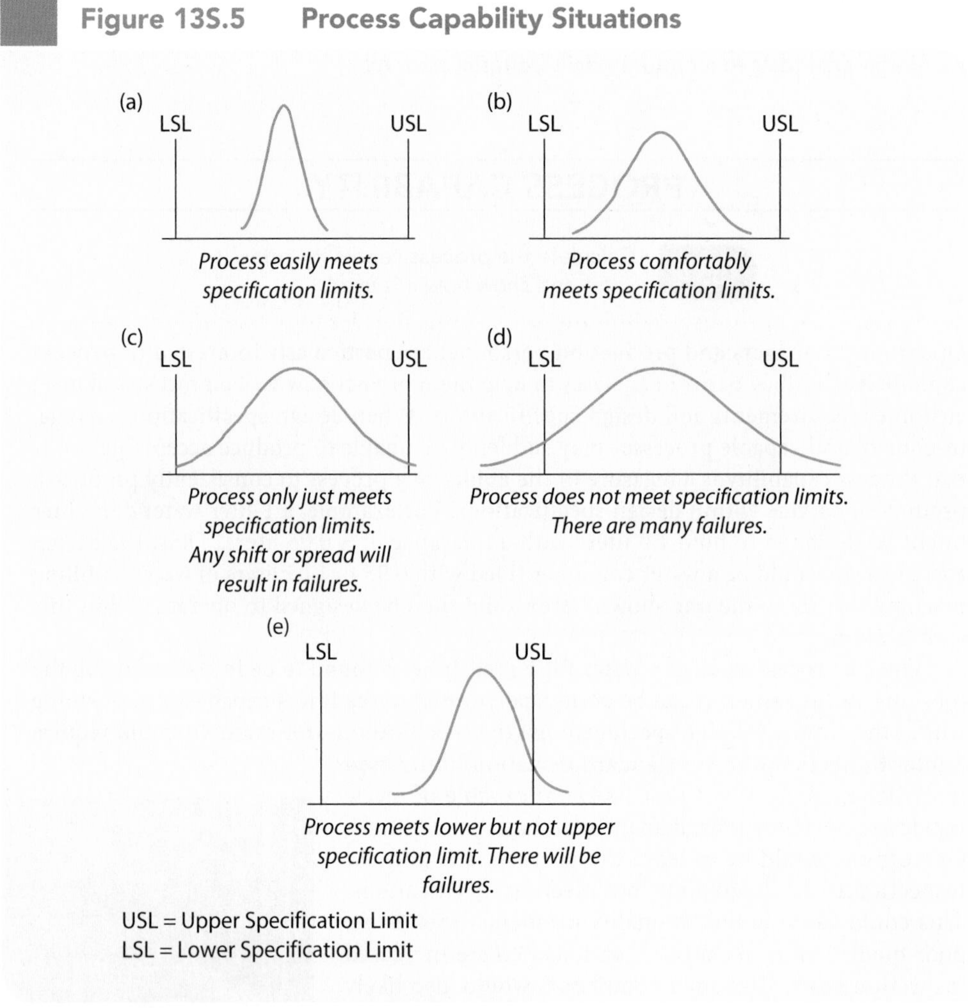
(a)
LSL
USL
Process easily meets specification limits.
(b)
LSL
USL
Process comfortably meets specification limits.
(c)
LSL
USL
Process only just meets specification limits. Any shift or spread will result in failures.
(d)
LSL
USL
Process does not meet specification limits. There are many failures.
(e)
LSL
USL
Process meets lower but not upper specification limit. There will be failures.
USL = Upper Specification Limit
LSL = Lower Specification Limit

PROCESS CAPABILITY INDEX

The **process capability index** (C_{pk}) shows whether or not the process mean has shifted away from the design target and is off-center. Calculating the index shows how well a process is performing. It can be calculated as the smaller of two numbers, as follows:

$$C_{pk} = \text{Min}\left[\frac{\bar{\bar{x}} - LSL}{3\sigma} \; or \; \frac{USL - \bar{\bar{x}}}{3\sigma}\right]$$

where:

USL, LSL = upper and lower design specification limits

3σ = three times the actual process standard deviation

$\bar{\bar{x}}$ = the process mean or center line of the $\bar{x}$ chart.

process capability index Shows whether the process mean has shifted away from the design target and is off-center.

When comparing the numerator to the denominator in the equations shown here, if the C_{pk} is greater than 1.0, then the process is deemed capable of meeting the design specifications. In other words, if the design limits in the numerators are larger than three times the *actual* process standard deviation in the denominator (both above and below the process mean), then the process is capable of meeting the design specifications. This would be similar to situations (a) and (b) in Figure 13S.5. However, the process mean could be shifted closer to one of the specification limits, and this would be the case if $\bar{\bar{x}}$, after collecting new samples, has moved closer to one of the limits. This would be indicated by one of the

Example 13S.5 Calculating the Process Capability Index

Watch the video explanation of Example 13S.5

Referring back to the Rich Soup Co. in Example 13S.1, recall that the control charts were designed as $\bar{\bar{x}} = 11.97$, with the UCL = 12.25 and LCL = 11.69. Now, suppose these limits were then made to be the specification limits. After a significant production period, new data were collected and the new $\bar{\bar{x}}$ was found to be 12.04, with a $\sigma = 0.01$. The C_{pk} would then be calculated as:

$$C_{pk} = \min\left[\frac{\bar{\bar{x}} - LSL}{3\sigma} \text{ or } \frac{USL - \bar{\bar{x}}}{3\sigma}\right] = \min\left[\frac{12.04 - 11.69}{3(0.01)} \text{ or } \frac{12.25 - 12.04}{3(0.01)}\right]$$

$$= \min(11.67 \text{ or } 7) = 7.$$

Since the $C_{pk} > 1.0$, the process is deemed to be easily within the specification limits, as with (a) in Figure 13S.5. Since the two numbers are not equal, though, the process mean has shifted—in this case toward the UCL.

Alternately, if the $\sigma = 0.08$, the C_{pk} would be:

$$C_{pk} = \min\left[\frac{12.04 - 11.69}{3(0.08)} \text{ or } \frac{12.25 - 12.04}{3(0.08)}\right] = \min(1.46 \text{ or } 0.875) = 0.875.$$

Now the $C_{pk} < 1.0$, which means the actual process variation exceeds the UCL in this case. The process no longer meets specifications, and would look similar to part (e) in Figure 13S.5.

calculations in the C_{pk} formula being less than 1.0, which is similar to (e) in Figure 13S.5. Example 13S.5 provides an example using the process capability index.

Process capability calculations will help organizations identify process problems so that process solutions can be implemented, which will ultimately reduce the costs of poorly performing processes.

ACCEPTANCE SAMPLING

13S.5 Explain how acceptance sampling is used

acceptance sampling When shipments of a product are received from suppliers, or before goods are shipped out to customers, samples can be taken from the shipment and compared to a quality acceptance standard. The quality of the sample is then assumed to represent the quality of the entire shipment.

When shipments of a product are received from suppliers, or before goods are shipped out to customers, samples can be taken from the shipment and compared to a quality acceptance standard. The quality of the sample is then assumed to represent the quality of the entire shipment. (Particularly when shipments contain many units of product, sampling is far less time consuming than testing every unit to determine the overall quality of an incoming or outgoing shipment.) Ideally, if trusted strategic alliance members within a supply chain are using Six Sigma quality improvement tools to build quality into the goods they provide, acceptance sampling can eventually be eliminated and used only when new suppliers furnish goods to the firm. In these situations, **acceptance sampling** can be used to determine whether or not a shipment will be accepted or returned to the supplier.

iStock/ndoeljindoel

For large shipments such as the one shown here, acceptance sampling methods are normally used.

SAMPLING PLAN

One topic that arises is how big to make the test sample, and what sort of sampling plan to use. One way to ensure that the quality of the sample represents the quality of the entire shipment is to make the sample size equal to the size of the shipment (in other words, examine every unit). Since in many cases this is impractical (for very large shipments, for example), firms must assume the risk of incorrectly judging the quality of the shipment based on the size of the sample: The smaller the sample size, the greater the risk of incorrectly judging a shipment's quality.

Some sampling plans call for a single sample—a set number of units are randomly taken from each shipment and tested. If units fail, they are designated as bad, and the entire shipment is accepted if the number of bad units found meets an acceptance standard. If the sample exceeds a rejection standard, then the entire shipment is rejected. Another type of plan is double sampling. If a first sample exceeds the maximum allowable number of bad units in order to be deemed acceptable, then another sample is taken and checked. The idea is to reduce the inherent risk in testing less than 100% of the shipment.

SAMPLING RISK

There is a cost to both the supplier and buyer when incorrect quality assessments are made. When a buyer rejects a shipment of high-quality goods because the sample quality level *did not* meet its acceptance standard, this is termed **producer's risk**. When this happens, it is caused by what is termed a **type-I error**. Conversely, when a buyer accepts a shipment of low-quality goods because the sample *did* meet its acceptance standard, this is termed **consumer's risk** and is the result of a **type-II error**. Obviously, trading partners wish to avoid or minimize the occurrence of both of these outcomes. To minimize type-I and type-II errors, buyers and sellers must derive an acceptable sampling plan by agreeing on unacceptable defect levels and a sample size big enough to result in minimal numbers of type-I and type-II errors. Over time, as the number of errors decline, sample sizes can be reduced.

producer's risk When a buyer rejects a shipment of high-quality goods because the sample quality level *did not* meet its acceptance standard.

type-I error When producer's risk occurs in acceptance sampling.

consumer's risk When a buyer accepts a shipment of low-quality goods because the sample *did* meet its acceptance standard.

type-II error When consumer's risk occurs in acceptance sampling.

operating characteristic curve An S-shaped curve used to illustrate the probability of accepting a shipment as a function of the shipment's quality.

USE OF OPERATING CHARACTERISTICS CURVES

As described previously, different sampling plans will provide different capabilities of determining correct quality assessments. Checking every unit will always correctly determine a shipment's quality. As the sample size decreases, though, the producer's and consumer's risk increases. The **operating characteristic** (OC) **curve**, shown in Figure 13S.6, is used to illustrate the probability of accepting a shipment as a function of the shipment's quality.

The first thing to notice about the OC curve in Figure 13S.6 is its S-shape. As the percent nonconforming in a sample increases, the probability of acceptance decreases, but not in a linear fashion. Typically, the binomial distribution is used to obtain probabilities

Figure 13S.6 Operating Characteristic Curve

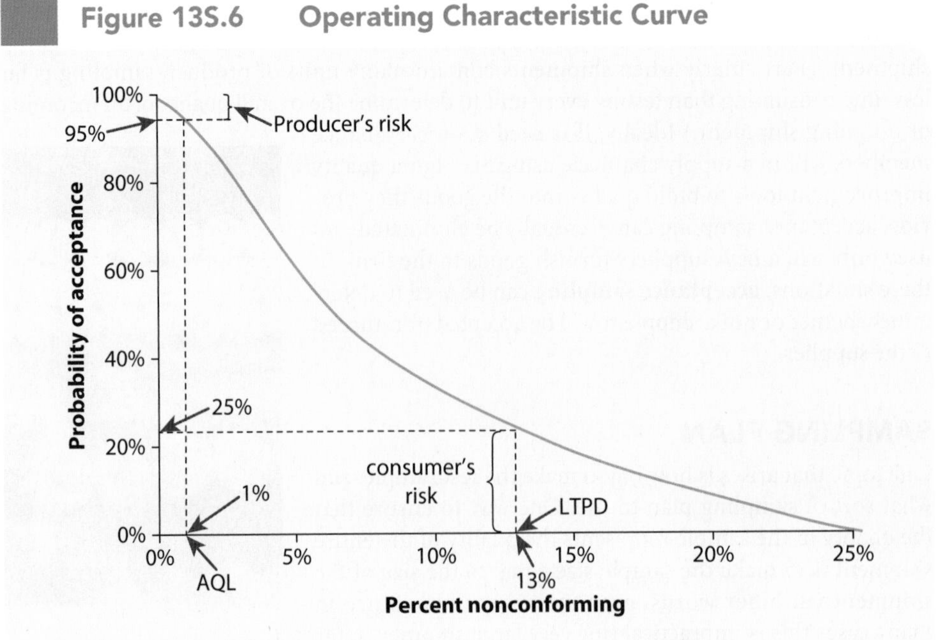

of accepting a shipment with varying levels of defectives. The actual shape of the OC curve depends on the consumer's willingness to accept a shipment based on the percent nonconforming in a sample, as well as the size of the sample. As shown on the particular OC curve in the figure, there is about a 95% probability of accepting a shipment with 1% defective items. This also means there is a 5% probability of rejecting that same shipment (producer's risk). Additionally, as shown in the figure, there is about a 25% probability of accepting a shipment with 13% defective items.

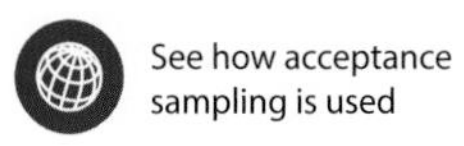
See how acceptance sampling is used

If the consumer is willing to accept a shipment with 1% or fewer defectives, this is termed the **acceptable quality level**, or AQL. Additionally, if the consumer considers shipments with greater than 13% defectives to be completely unacceptable, then this is termed the **lot tolerance percent defectives**, or LTPD. This defines the upper limit of percent defectives a consumer is willing to tolerate. If the consumer wants to ensure that it will accept these poor quality shipments no more than 25% of the time, this is shown on Figure 13S.6 as the consumer's risk.

acceptable quality level The percentage of defects the consumer is willing to accept.

lot tolerance percent defectives Defines the upper limit of percent defectives a consumer is willing to tolerate.

Visit edge.sagepub.com/wisner to help you accomplish your coursework goals in an easy-to-use learning environment.

- Mobile-friendly eFlashcards
- Mobile-friendly practice quizzes
- A complete online action plan
- Chapter summaries with learning objectives
- Excel templates to assist with practice problems
- Original video case studies that demonstrate chapter concepts in action

SUMMARY

This supplement described many of the tools used in statistical process control. The two basic types of data are variable data and attribute data. Each type of data requires a different type of data sample and control chart, and each of these was discussed. Additionally, readers were shown the basics of constructing control charts. Processes can be deemed to be capable, and this topic was examined, along with calculating process capability indexes. Finally, the topics of acceptance sampling and operating characteristics curves were discussed.

KEY TERMS

Acceptable quality level, 427
Acceptance sampling, 425
Assignable variations, 415
Attribute data, 415
C charts, 420
Consumer's risk, 426
Control charts, 413
Control limits, 414
Lot tolerance percent defectives, 427
Lower control limits, 416
Natural variations, 415
Operating characteristic curve, 426
P charts, 420
Process capability, 423
Process capability index, 424
Producer's risk, 426
R, 416
$\overline{R}$, 416
R chart, 416
Statistical process control, 413
Statistical quality control, 413
Type-I error, 426
Type-II error, 426
Upper control limits, 416
Variable data, 415
$\overline{x}$, 416
$\overline{x}$ chart, 416
$\overline{\overline{x}}$, 416

FORMULA REVIEW

Center line of the $\bar{x}$ chart, $\bar{\bar{x}} = \frac{\sum_{i=1}^{k} \bar{x}_i}{k}$, where k indicates the number of samples, $\bar{x}$ is the mean of each sample, and i indicates the specific sample.

Center line of the R chart, $\bar{R} = \frac{\sum_{i=1}^{k} R_i}{k}$, where k indicates the number of samples, R is the range within each sample, and i indicates the specific sample.

Lower control limit for the $\bar{x}$ chart, $LCL_{\bar{x}} = \bar{\bar{x}} - A_2\bar{R}$, where A_2, D_3, and D_4 are constants obtained from Table 13S.1.

Lower control limit for the R chart, $LCL_R = D_3\bar{R}$

Upper control limit for the $\bar{x}$ chart, $UCL_x = \bar{\bar{x}} + A_2\bar{R}$

Upper control limit for the R chart, $UCL_R = D_4\bar{R}$

Center line for the P chart, $\bar{P} = \frac{\sum_{i=1}^{k} P_i}{k}$, where P_i is the percent defective for each sample, i, and k is the number of samples.

Lower control limits for the P chart, $LCL_P = \bar{P} - z\sigma_P$, where z is the number of standard deviations from the mean and σ_P is the sample standard deviation.

Upper control limit for the P chart, $UCL_P = \sqrt{\frac{(\bar{P})(1-\bar{P})}{n}} + z\sigma_P$

Sample standard deviation, $\sigma_p = \bar{P}$, where n is the size of each sample.

Sample standard deviation for the C chart $= \sqrt{\bar{c}}$, where $\bar{c}$ = mean errors per unit.

Upper and lower control limits for the C chart $= \bar{c} \pm 3\sqrt{\bar{c}}$

Process capability index, $C_{pk} = \min\left[\frac{\bar{\bar{x}} - LSL}{3\sigma} \text{ or } \frac{USL - \bar{\bar{x}}}{3\sigma}\right]$

where USL, LSL = upper and lower specification limits, 3σ = three times the actual process standard deviation, and $\bar{\bar{x}}$ = the process mean or center line of the $\bar{x}$ chart.

SOLVED PROBLEMS

1. Use the following variable data set to answer the following questions:

	Sample					
Day	1	2	3	4	$\bar{x}$	R
1	14.1	13.2	12.7	10.6	12.7	3.5
2	13.5	11.7	12.6	14.3	13.0	2.6
3	12.9	13.2	12.8	12.6	12.9	0.6
4	12.9	12.8	13.1	11.2	12.5	1.9
5	12.4	13.3	12.1	13.9	12.9	1.8

a. Find the sample means and ranges for the data set.

b. Calculate the center lines for the two control charts.

c. Calculate the upper and lower control limits for the two control charts.

d. Plot the data. Does the process appear to be in control? Why, or why not?

Answer:

a. See the $\bar{x}$ and R columns in orange. To calculate $\bar{x}$, the measures in each sample are summed, then divided by 4. To calculate R, the difference between the largest and smallest measure in each sample is calculated.

b. $\bar{\bar{x}}$ is found by calculating the mean of the sample means (summing the $\bar{x}$ and dividing by 5). $\bar{\bar{x}} = 12.8$. $\bar{R}$ is found by calculating the mean of the ranges for the samples. $\bar{R} = 2.1$.

c. $UCL_{\bar{x}} = \bar{\bar{x}} + A_2\bar{R} = 12.8 + 0.729(2.1) = 14.33$; note that A_2, D_3, and D_4 are found in Table 13S.1, for a sample size of 4.

$LCL_{\bar{x}} = \bar{\bar{x}} - A_2\bar{R} = 12.8 - 0.729(2.1) = 11.26$.

$UCL_R = D_4\bar{R} = 2.282(2.1) = 4.79$.

$LCL_R = D_3\bar{R} = 0(2.1) = 0$.

d. $\bar{x}$ chart:

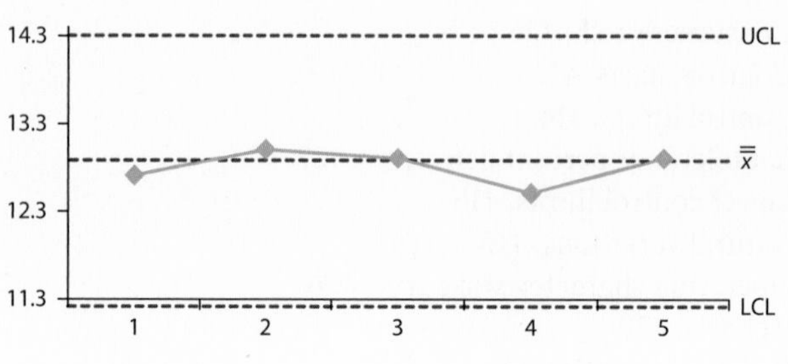

R chart:

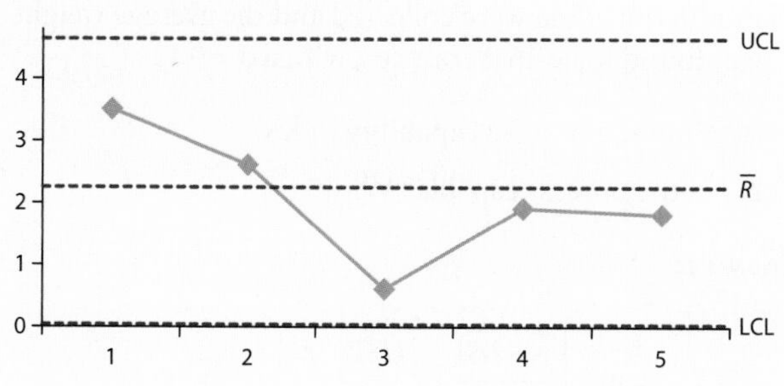

Although there are only five data points, it appears that the process is in control—no points fall outside the control limits, and the points fall close to the center lines, with no patterns.

2. Use the following attribute data to answer the following questions. Each day, 20 patrons were asked if they enjoyed their dinner. The number responding "no" was tracked for 10 days.

Day	No. of No's	Day	No. of No's
1	3	6	3
2	0	7	0
3	1	8	2
4	7	9	1
5	2	10	4

a. Calculate $\overline{P}$.

b. Calculate σ_P.

c. Calculate the upper and lower control limits for the P chart, using z = 3.

d. Plot the data. Does the process appear to be in control?

Answer:

a. Calculate the percent defectives for each sample:

Day	% Defective	Day	% Defective
1	0.15	6	0.15
2	0	7	0
3	0.05	8	0.10
4	0.35	9	0.05
5	0.10	10	0.20

$\overline{P}$ is the average percent defective = 0.115 or 11.5%

b. $\sigma_p = \sqrt{\frac{\overline{P}(1-\overline{P})}{n}} = \sqrt{\frac{(.115)(.885)}{20}} = 0.071$

c. $\text{UCL}_\text{P} = \overline{P} + z\sigma_\text{P} = 0.115 = 3(0.071) = 0.329$

$\text{LCL}_\text{P} = \overline{P} - z\sigma_p = 0.105 - 3(.071) = 0.0$ (truncated at 0.0).

d. P chart:

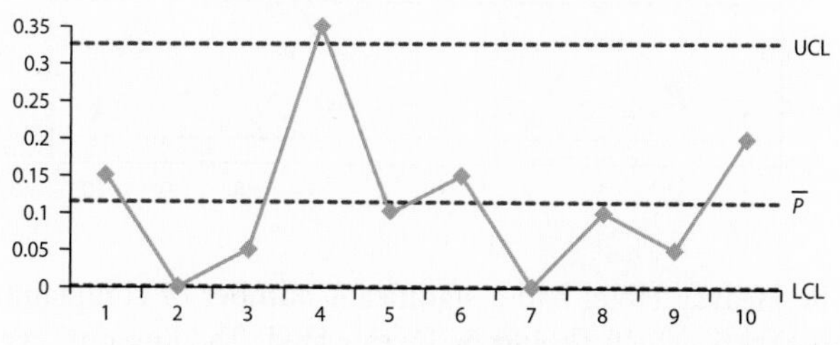

The data in the P chart show the process possibly to be out of control—data point 4 is above the UCL. This has to be investigated, even though the following six data points appear to be OK. The process might need to be shut down while problems are analyzed and alleviated.

3. For the past 10 days, the Heavey Hotel has tallied the total complaints from customers. The findings are shown in the data set here:

Day	No. of Complaints	Day	No. of Complaints
1	18	6	13
2	6	7	10
3	12	8	20
4	3	9	16
5	24	10	4

a. Calculate $\overline{C}$.

b. Calculate the sample standard deviation for the C chart.

c. Calculate the upper and lower control limits for the C chart.

d. Plot the data on a C chart. Does the hotel appear to be in control?

Answer:

a. The total complaints for the 10 days are 126. Thus, $\overline{C} = 12.6$.

b. $\sqrt{\overline{c}} = \sqrt{12.6} = 3.55$.

c. $UCL_c = \bar{c} + 3\sqrt{\bar{c}} = 12.6 + 3(3.55) = 23.25.$

d. $LCL_c = \bar{c} - 3\sqrt{\bar{c}} = 12.6 - 3(3.55) = 1.95.$

e. The C chart:

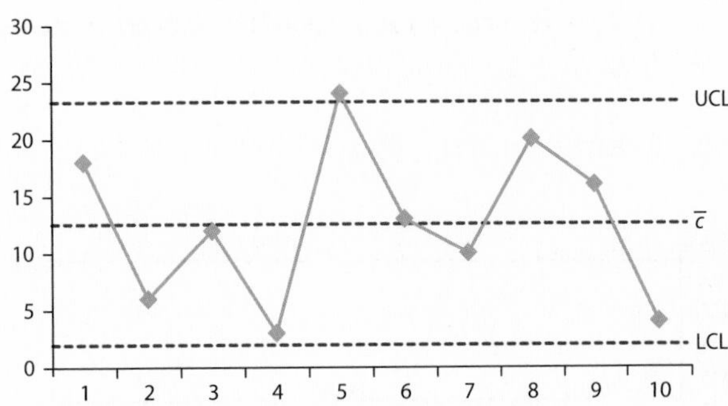

The Heavey Hotel had a significant number of complaints on Day 5, which should be investigated. The low numbers on Days 4 and 10 are not problematic—actually, the hotel's management may want to investigate and repeat what they did on those days.

4. The specification limits for the weight of a 16-ounce jar of pickles is set at 16 ± 0.5 ounces. After a period of production, data were collected and the average weight was found to be 16.05 ounces, with a $\sigma = 0.12$.

   a. Find the process capability index.

   b. Is the process capable? Why?

Answer:

a. $$C_{pk} = \min\left[\frac{\bar{\bar{x}} - LSL}{3\sigma} \text{ or } \frac{USL - \bar{\bar{x}}}{3\sigma}\right]$$

$$= \min\left[\frac{16.05 - 15.5}{3(0.12)} \text{ or } \frac{16.5 - 16.05}{3(0.12)}\right]$$

$$= \min\,[1.53 \text{ or } 1.25].$$

b. Since the $C_{pk} > 1.0$, the process is deemed to be easily within the specification limits. Since both numbers are not equal, though, the process mean has shifted, in this case toward the UCL.

REVIEW QUESTIONS

1. Who is generally credited with the formal beginning of statistical quality control? When did this take place?
2. What does it mean when a process is said to be "in control" or "out of control"?
3. What are the two types of process variations, and which one does statistical process control seek to eliminate? What can be done with the other one?
4. Describe "variable data," and explain why two types of control charts are needed to ensure that these types of processes are under control.
5. How are the upper and lower control limits normally constructed?
6. When would management want to use a C chart instead of a P chart?
7. Why do firms calculate process capability indexes?
8. What is acceptance sampling, and what are the risks of using it?
9. What are operating characteristics curves, and how are they generated? What do they show?

DISCUSSION QUESTIONS

1. Why must samples of data be collected? Why not just take one measurement and plot that?
2. Can a process exhibit sample measurement plots that are all inside the control limits and still be considered out of control? Explain.
3. What are some variable data and attribute data that could be collected to track the quality of education at your university?
4. Why is it important to use a good set of control charts? What if the control charts are not a good set?
5. Explain how P charts can be used in a manufacturing facility.
6. Why must attribute data samples be large?
7. Why is it that P charts do not usually look symmetrical around the center line?
8. Can a process mean be "off-center," yet still be capable? Explain.
9. Can a process be considered in statistical control, yet also be considered incapable? Explain.
10. When would you want to test 100% of a supplier's shipment for the required quality level, instead of a sample?

EXERCISES AND PROJECTS

1. Find online two examples of organizations using control charts, and describe their use. Make one example a manufacturing company, and the other a service company.
2. Pick a stock on one of the major exchanges. Collect the daily stock prices and then determine the weekly average price (so each data point will have five prices), for eight weeks. Create the two control charts for this variable data, and plot the eight data points. Describe what you find.

PROBLEMS

Use the following seven samples, taken on seven consecutive days at Nik and Aubrey's Deli, to answer the next two problems. Five random customer wait times were measured each day.

Day	Wait Time (min.)
1	2.5, 3, 1.5, 3, 4
2	2, 4.5, 3.5, 2, 4
3	1.5, 5, 3.5, 2, 2.5
4	3, 3.5, 5, 2.5, 2
5	2, 5.5, 2.5, 3, 1.5
6	2.5, 3.5, 4, 2, 2.5
7	3.5, 1.5, 2, 4, 2

1. Calculate the $\bar{x}$, $\bar{\bar{x}}$, R, and $\bar{R}$ for the samples.
2. Find the 3-sigma UCL and LCL for the mean and range charts. Plot the data. Does the deli wait time process look to be in statistical control? Why, or why not?

Use the following sample information, obtained by taking four doughnuts per hour for 12 hours from the McNulty Bakery doughnut process and weighing them, for the next two problems.

Hour	Weight (gms)	Hour	Weight (gms)
1	110, 105, 98, 100	7	89, 102, 101, 99
2	79, 102, 100, 104	8	100, 101, 98, 96
3	100, 102, 100, 96	9	98, 95, 101, 100
4	94, 98, 99, 101	10	99, 100, 97, 102
5	98, 104, 97, 100	11	102, 97, 100, 101
6	104, 97, 99, 100	12	98, 100, 100, 97

3. Calculate the, $\bar{x}$, $\bar{\bar{x}}$, R, and $\bar{R}$ for the samples.
4. Find the 3-sigma UCL and LCL for the mean and range charts. Plot the data. Does the process look to be in statistical control. Why, or why not?
5. Using a spreadsheet, repeat Problem 3 and then create the line charts for the $\bar{x}$ data and the R data.
6. After collecting and measuring a number of pizza delivery time samples, Lindi's Pizzeria finds the mean of all the samples to be 27.4 minutes, with an average sample range of 5.2 minutes. It tracked four deliveries per hour for 18 hours to obtain its samples.
   a. Is this an example of variable or attribute sampling data?
   b. Find the UCL and LCL for both the $\bar{x}$ and R charts.

Use the information provided here for the next two problems:

Ten customers per hour were asked by the cashier at the JCWiz Sushi Bar if they liked their meal, and the percent who said "no" are shown in the following table, for a 12-hour period.

Hour	Percent Defective	Hour	Percent Defective
1	0	7	0.1
2	0.2	8	0
3	0.4	9	0
4	0.1	10	0.2
5	0.1	11	0
6	0.2	12	0.1

7. Determine $\overline{P}$ and σ_p.

8. Determine the 3-sigma UCL and LCL. Plot the percent defectives for each sample. Does customer satisfaction appear to be in statistical control? How could Lindi's improve the analysis?

9. Using a spreadsheet, repeat Problem 7 and create the line chart for the percent defective data.

Use the information here for the next two problems:

Error-checkers at the Whole Life Insurance Company checked 100 online applications per day for errors in the applications. The number of defective applications are shown here, for a 10-day period.

Day	Number Defective	Day	Number Defective
1	6	6	2
2	2	7	0
3	8	8	5
4	4	9	6
5	10	10	4

10. Determine $\overline{P}$ and σ_p.

11. Determine the 3-sigma UCL and LCL. Plot the percent defectives for each sample. Does the online application process appear to be in statistical control? Why, or why not?

12. Mary Jane's Steakhouse tracks customer complaints every day and then follows up with its customers to resolve problems. For the past 30 days, it received a total of 22 various complaints from unhappy customers. Using this information, calculate:

    a. $\overline{C}$

    b. The 3-sigma control limits

Use the following information for the next two problems:

Over a 10-day period, a manufacturing company has counted the number of units not meeting design specifications. The findings are shown below.

Day	No. of Rejects	Day	No. of Rejects
1	4	6	5
2	2	7	1
3	6	8	2
4	1	9	10
5	5	10	8

13. Calculate $\overline{C}$ and the sample standard deviation for the C chart.

14. Calculate the upper and lower control limits for the C chart. Plot the data on a C chart. Does the manufacturing process appear to be in control? Why, or why not?

15. Jallo Tooling Co. has an automated lathe, and the owners want to determine the tool's capability for machining a part's diameter to a specification of 7.620 ± 0.002 centimeters. After a trial run period, the lathe produced a sample mean of 7.621 centimeters, with a standard deviation of 0.001 centimeter. Calculate the C_{pk} for this lathe, and decide if Jallo Tooling is able to produce this part.

16. A machine shop produces parts for the automobile industry, and one part has a design specification of 4.000 inches in length, with a tolerance of ± 0.003 inches. The machining center operator making the part checks the output of each piece, and after 20 pieces finds the average part length to be 4.001 inches, with a $\sigma = 0.002$ inches.

    a. What is the capability index for this part?

    b. Is the current process capable? Why?

17. Tan Bearings Co. has been making a bearing with a diameter of 2.00 centimeters and a standard deviation of 0.01 centimeters. A new customer has a design requirement for a bearing with a diameter specification of 1.98 centimeters and a tolerance of ± 0.055 centimeters.

    a. Determine the C_{pk}.

    b. Can Tan Bearings successfully make this bearing? Why?

CASE STUDIES

CASE 1: Public Health and Product Safety Concerns

Companies seldom produce all the raw materials that go into their final product. Many rely on suppliers to provide them with the materials they'll use to produce their product lines. One example of this is flooring. One of the biggest sellers is resilient flooring. Resilient flooring comes in many materials—cork, wood, vinyl, asphalt, and linoleum. As with many industries, flooring made outside of the United States is less expensive for retailers to purchase. One example of this is laminate flooring, and China is a major producer of laminate flooring.

The potential health issue with laminate flooring is the amount of formaldehyde it contains. The formaldehyde comes from the adhesives that bind the layers of wood or plastic that compose the laminate wood. Over time, the formaldehyde is emitted into the air. In sufficient quantities, formaldehyde can cause respiratory, skin, and neurological health issues.

In 2015, laminate wood from several different retailers was tested and found to be high in formaldehyde. Accusations were made that the retailers should have known about the dangerously high levels of formaldehyde in the Chinese-manufactured laminate wood. Some of the Chinese laminate wood had from 6 to 20 times the allowable level. Once the story came to light, the companies affected recalled the product. Their negligence was investigated by the Environmental Protection Agency (EPA) and the Department of Justice (DOJ).

The consequences were severe. One company, Lumber Liquidators, was fined $10 million. In addition, because of the news, its stock dropped approximately 70%. This could have been avoided if companies had procedures in place to test the laminate wood provided by its suppliers. Testing would have revealed a startling difference between American-made laminate wood and Chinese laminate wood. American-made laminate wood, which was tested at the same time as the Chinese laminate wood, contained acceptable levels of formaldehyde.

DISCUSSION QUESTIONS

1. Considering the large quantities of laminate wood in a shipment, what type of sampling should the flooring retailers have used to enable them to determine if the laminate wood from different suppliers met minimum specifications?

2. Explain the difference between producer's risk and consumer's risk. Which type of error applies to each type of risk? Which type is described in the case?

Note: Written by Rick Bonsall, D. Mgt., McKendree University, Lebanon, IL. This case was prepared solely to provide material for class discussion. The author does not intend to illustrate either effective or ineffective handling of a managerial situation.

Sources:

1. Roche, J. A. (2015). Lumber Liquidators has reached a $10 million settlement with the DOJ, and the stock is soaring. *Business Insider*, http://www.businessinsider.com/lumber-liquidators-reaches-settlement-with-doj-2015-10

2. Flooring market analysis by product (soft coverings, resilient flooring, non-resilient flooring, seamless flooring), by application (residential, commercial, industry), and segment forecasts to 2020. (2014). Grand View Research, http://www.grandviewresearch.com/industry-analysis/flooring-market-analysis

3. Update on formaldehyde. (2013). Consumer Product Safety Commission, https://www.cpsc.gov/PageFiles/121919/AN%20UPDATE%20ON%20FORMALDEHYDE%20final%200113.pdf

4. Abrams, R. (2015, November 5). Lumber Liquidators names a longtime director as chief. *New York Times, Business Day.*

CASE 2: Statistical Process Control at the Jones Corporation

The Jones Corporation had been doing well for years. It felt it was the best in its industry. Henry Jones, the CEO, decided that the corporation needed to achieve an award of national significance that was recognized across industries as a top-tier award. Thus, Henry decided that his company would apply for the Malcom Baldrige National Quality Award. Since the Baldrige Award criteria focus on results, the Jones Corporation would need to review its processes and document its results in order to demonstrate that it deserved to be selected as a Baldrige award recipient.

Jones and his staff reviewed the criteria categories: leadership, strategic planning, customer focus, measurement, analysis, and knowledge management, workforce focus, operational focus, and results. A "champion" was selected from the Jones Corporation for each of the seven categories. Arthur Hopkins was assigned to operational focus and Bill Marley was assigned to customer focus. Both champions knew that their departments needed to collect data and analyze them in order to determine the performance results. They believed that the key to earning the award was to demonstrate that the processes within each of their departments were in statistical control. Furthermore, they needed to demonstrate that they had the tools needed to continuously monitor the processes, and to determine which processes required corrective actions to remain in control.

The Jones Corporation was a manufacturing company; therefore, Arthur knew that his department would be collecting variable data. These data would include information such as the time it took to assemble a unit of product, and the control limits of various products. Since Bill's responsibility was to ensure the corporation had the proper level of customer focus, his department would be collecting attribute data. They would be monitoring and analyzing the customers' satisfaction levels in multiple areas such as frequency of meetings, ease of doing business, listens to customers' needs, and provides cost-effective solutions. Some of the data collection was already being done and analyzed on a routine basis. However, there were areas that they had never measured before; therefore, staff would need to develop and employ the proper tools to support statistical process control.

DISCUSSION QUESTIONS

1. What type of charts would Arthur's staff use to monitor and analyze the variable data? Explain what each chart is designed to track.

2. What type of charts would Bill's staff use to monitor and analyze the attribute data? Explain what each chart is designed to track.

3. Explain what is determined by collecting variable data samples and attribute data samples.

Note: Written by Rick Bonsall, D. Mgt., McKendree University, Lebanon, IL. The people and company are fictional and any resemblance to any person or company is coincidental. This case was prepared solely to provide material for class discussion. The author does not intend to illustrate either effective or ineffective handling of a managerial situation.

Source:

1. 2013–2014 business/nonprofit criteria now available, http://www.nist.gov/baldrige/bus_np_criteria.cfm

CASE 3: Takata's Airbag Quality Problem

Consumers around the world rely on manufacturers to build safe products. The bigger the company, the more consumers trust it to deliver on their expectations concerning safety. Statistical quality control (SQC) enables all companies, large and small, to ensure their processes are capable of meeting consumers' expectations. Is it possible that a defective product could slip through and be sold and delivered to a consumer? The answer is yes. However, it is a reasonable assumption that the quantity of defective units will not be in the millions.

In April 2013, Takata announced that its airbags, which are used by many of the leading automobile brands, had defective inflator and propellant devices. The defects could result in metal fragments shooting into drivers during a crash. As early as 2002, Takata reported that its Mexico plant had a defect rate six to eight times acceptable quality levels. This implies that Takata used some type of SQC; consequently, it was able to determine that defects existed and at what level. However, there is no indication that the out-of-control process was ever corrected.

Approximately 34 million vehicles are possibly affected within the United States. Worldwide, another 7 million are estimated to be affected. Whatever the size of the airbag recall, it is quickly taking a backseat to the number of injuries and deaths associated with the defective airbags. Unconfirmed reports put the number of injuries at 105 and the current death toll at 8.

Obviously, the human cost from these defects is immeasurable. There is also a powerful economic effect on Takata, which controls 22% of the worldwide airbag market, as costs continue to increase as additional cars are recalled. Takata will take a huge financial loss. That is in addition to fines being placed on the company. The National Highway Traffic Safety Administration (NTHSA) imposed a record civil penalty of $200 million. A few months later, Takata was fined an additional $14,000 a day for not cooperating with a national safety investigation. Although the final cost to replace an airbag differs with brands, it can cost from $1,000 to $1,500 per airbag to be replaced. If the number of vehicles mentioned above all need replacement airbags, the cost will be astronomical.

Honda, Takata's biggest customer, dropped Takata as its supplier of airbag inflators. This is a significant blow to Takata. Although it sells other equipment such as seatbelts, steering wheels, electronics, and child seats, airbags make up approximately 40% of its business. The consequences of Takata's poor quality testing continue to pile up. Nissan and Toyota also dropped Takata as their supplier. Following suit, Ford and Mazda joined the other major automobile manufacturers and dropped Takata as a supplier of airbag inflators for all future cars. Although they have not yet dropped Takata, Fuji Heavy Industries Limited (maker of Subaru) and Mitsubishi are deciding if they will do the same.

The financial cost for Takata is growing. Its market share for airbag inflators may drop from 22% to 5% by 2020. To make matters worse, Takata's competitors, Daicel Corporation, Autoliv Incorporate, and TRW Automotive, will fill the void left by the cancellations. Because of its apparent lack of—or adherence to—statistical process control, Takata could end up going out of business, or at least becoming a much smaller company. Within just three days of its announcement, its stock declined 39%. Takata reduced its profit forecast by a mammoth 75%.

DISCUSSION QUESTIONS

1. What process or activity should Takata have employed to enable it to determine there was such a high defect rate with its airbag inflators?
2. Based on the narrative, which type of data, variable or attribute, should Takata have collected and analyzed in order to determine if its process was in control? Explain why you selected the specific data type.
3. Based on your response to Question 2, what type of charts would it use to monitor and analyze the data?
4. What is the current financial condition of Takata?

Note: Written by Rick Bonsall, D. Mgt., McKendree University, Lebanon, IL. This case was prepared solely to provide material for class discussion. The author does not intend to illustrate either effective or ineffective handling of a managerial situation.

Sources:

1. Teen driver's death linked to Takata air bag problems. (2015, November 3). CBS News, http://www.cbsnews.com/news/is-your-takata-air-bag-under-recall/
2. Addady, M. (2015). Ford dumps Takata after massive airbag recall. *Fortune*, http://fortune.com/2015/11/23/ford-dumps-takata-airbag/
3. Nissan joins Toyota, Honda in dropping Takata airbag inflators. (2015, July 15). *Automotive News*, http://www.autonews.com/article/20151107/OEM01/151109845/nissan-joins-toyota-honda-in-dropping-takata-airbag-inflators

VIDEO CASE STUDY

Learn more about ***statistical quality control*** from real organizations that use operations management techniques every day. Jim Biafore is the Senior Director at Beefsteak, a restaurant in Washington, D.C. Like many businesses, Beefsteak regularly measures and evaluates the effectiveness of their products and services to ensure that they are meeting their own standards of quality. Watch this short interview to learn how.

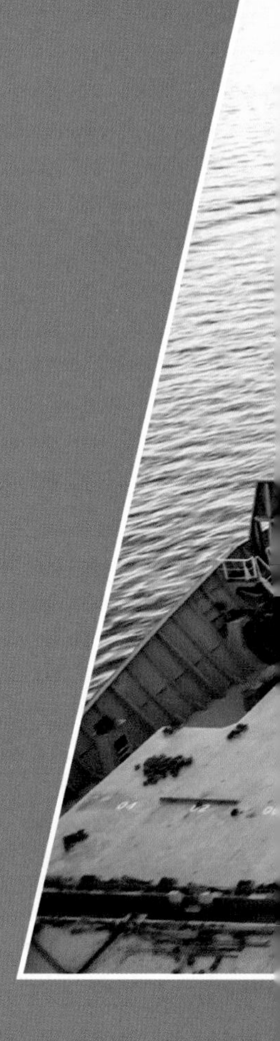

PART III

SUPPLY CHAIN PROCESSES

iStock/Getty/Teradat Santivivut

At the end of the day, the companies we polled realize that spend management is the fastest, most efficient way to accelerate bottom-line results while continuing to deliver for customers and create value for their organizations, and they are using it to transform procurement into a key competitive advantage so that they can emerge stronger from the downturn.

—**HARI CANDADAI,** director of solutions marketing, Ariba, Inc.[1]

An important re-engineering principle is that companies should focus on their core competence and outsource everything else.

—**BILL GATES,** founder, Microsoft[2]

GLOBAL SUPPLY MANAGEMENT

LEARNING OBJECTIVES

After completing this chapter, you should be able to:

14.1 Explain the strategic importance of supply management
14.2 Review the six-step process of the purchasing cycle
14.3 Perform the calculations in the break-even analysis for make-or-buy decisions
14.4 Discuss the opportunities and challenges of global sourcing
14.5 Explain the benefits of supply base rationalization
14.6 Summarize the approaches used in managing supplier relationships
14.7 Describe the issues and benefits of ethical and sustainable sourcing
14.8 Discuss how e-procurement systems assist firms in streamlining purchasing activities
14.9 Compare current strategies used for improving supplier performance

Master the content.

edge.sagepub.com/wisner

THE PRACTICE OF NEARSHORING

Nearshoring refers to the use of suppliers near or in the buyer's home country. Recently, many U.S. companies have been revising their outsourcing strategies to include suppliers in the United States or nearby countries. One reason was the Fukushima earthquake and tsunami in 2011. It created severe supply chain problems for the companies doing business with Japanese manufacturers. U.S. buyers began using more nearshoring following this incident. The beneficiaries of this change have been suppliers in the United States, Mexico, and countries in South and Central America having low-cost labor and an existing supply chain infrastructure.

In 2004, an earthquake off the coast of Indonesia also created a tsunami, killing over 100,000 people and impacting supply chains operating in the affected areas. In the recent past, escalating fuel prices made doing business with distant suppliers significantly more expensive. Another factor driving sourcing for U.S. buyers is speed to market. This is particularly true for perishable goods, where shippers are seeking to get their products on store shelves quickly. Added to all of this is the increase in labor costs in Asia, combined with a decrease in wages in the United States.

Company strategies also support the trend of nearshoring. In 2009, for example, GE announced it was bringing the manufacturing of water heaters back to the United States. The following year, GE said it would also bring washer and dryer manufacturing back to the United States. Another major U.S. manufacturer, Caterpillar, announced it would source excavators from plants in Texas and Georgia. By locating production for U.S. markets in the United States, Caterpillar was able to free up capacity at its Japanese plants to serve the growing Asian markets.

Chris Painter, CEO of Transfreight, comments, "When combined with the fact that manufacturing cost advantage is continuing to diminish in key offshore manufacturing regions, we believe there is the potential for a [dramatic] move toward increased local sourcing and manufacturing products destined for the North American market within North America. It's a matter of finding the right balance where you can achieve the lowest possible cost with an acceptable level of risk. We believe companies that focus on supply chain nimbleness and built-in adaptability will be best positioned to optimize this balance."[3]

INTRODUCTION

At first glance, purchasing materials, services, and other items for a business might seem simple—you go to a retailer or an online supplier and buy things. Purchasing goods and services for business purposes, though—also referred to as **commercial buying**—is far more involved; in fact, it is considered a very important business process.

commercial buying Purchasing goods and services for business purposes.

Organizations use multiple terms to describe the process of purchasing. The Institute for Supply Management (ISM), a nonprofit organization dedicated to the education of purchasing professionals, defines **purchasing** as "a major function of an organization that is responsible for acquisition of required materials, services, and equipment." **Procurement** refers to "specifications development, value analysis, supplier market research, negotiation, buying activities, contract administration, inventory control, traffic, receiving and stores," whereas **sourcing** is defined as "the entire purchasing process or cycle," which includes writing purchase specifications, searching for and selecting suppliers, negotiating the purchase price, and evaluating a supplier's performance. Finally, **supply management** is defined by ISM as "the identification, acquisition, access, positioning and management of resources the organization needs or potentially needs in the attainment of its strategic objectives."[4]

These definitions suggest that the term *purchasing* simply describes the act of buying goods and services, while the other three are more strategic, and include finding the most appropriate suppliers and then ensuring that these suppliers perform effectively for the organization. To guarantee continued supplier performance, many organizations today are creating long-lasting, win–win supplier relationships, which have also become important aspects of supply management. In fact, supplier relationship management is one of the eight key supply chain processes discussed in Chapter 1. Finally, the Internet has enabled buyers to locate foreign suppliers more easily. This has created more competition, and in many cases reduced costs and improved the quality of purchased goods, thus bringing about the term *global supply management*. The following sections cover the basics of global supply management, including the influence of technology on the buying process, supply base rationalization, ethical and sustainable sourcing, and building supplier relationships.

purchasing Acquisition of required materials, services, and equipment.

procurement Specifications development, value analysis, supplier market research, negotiation, buying activities, contract administration, inventory control, traffic, receiving, and stores.

sourcing The entire purchasing process or cycle, including writing purchase specifications, searching for and selecting suppliers, negotiating the purchase price, and evaluating a supplier's performance.

supply management The identification, acquisition, access, positioning, and management of resources the organization needs or potentially needs in the attainment of its strategic objectives.

purchase spend Money the firm spends on goods and services.

spend management Use of smart purchasing practices to reduce purchase spend.

THE STRATEGIC ROLE OF SUPPLY MANAGEMENT

14.1 Explain the strategic importance of supply management

Supply management personnel meet the ongoing needs of an organization by purchasing specific items, sometimes in very large quantities, to be delivered on required dates to specific locations. U.S. manufacturers, for example, spend over half of each sales dollar on materials purchases. The term **purchase spend** refers to money the firm spends on goods and services. Table 14.1 provides material spend data for 2009–2013 for U.S. manufacturers.[5]

Supply management personnel also buy services including equipment maintenance, employee healthcare, and transportation. Thus, a company's costs and profitability can be significantly impacted if supply management departments effectively and efficiently manage material and service purchases. A large organization with annual sales of $1 billion, for instance, might spend $500 million on purchases. Through smart purchasing, a procurement manager could save the firm 10% of its annual purchase spend, or in this example, $50 million. This is one example of **spend management**. In other words, since purchase spend is part of costs of goods sold, any spend reduction directly improves the firm's profit before taxes. For this

Table 14.1 U.S. Manufacturing Cost of Materials as a Percent of Shipment Value (000's)

Year	Total Cost of Materials ($)	Total Value of Shipments ($)	Percentage
2013	3,456,983,065	5,846,767,820	59.13
2011	3,240,477,063	5,498,599,159	58.93
2010	2,763,128,338	4,916,646,802	56.20
2009	2,426,171,049	4,419,501,476	54.90

Note: Data for 2012 are unavailable.

reason, supply managers are today viewed as important strategic members of the firm. During the recent economic recession starting in 2009, spend management was one of the most basic strategies for helping companies stay profitable in a terrible market.

Watch a discussion of spend management

In today's marketplace, reducing purchase spend is still seen as an important way to maximize profits. Starting in 2014, for example, Nissan and alliance partner Renault began standardizing their use of items such as steering wheels, side mirrors, and door handles across their model lineups to cut costs. The effort was part of a strategy of using common components to maximize economies of scale. By sharing more parts, the company aims to cut purchasing costs 20 to 30%.[6]

Due to the sheer volume of purchases at many firms, an important part of the supply management process is developing long-term beneficial relationships with suppliers. In many instances, working with a supplier means much more than negotiating price reductions. A supplier's use of technology, its production and delivery capabilities, as well as new product development plans are often shared with the buying organization. In turn, the organization might share its future product designs and demand forecasts. Thus, a supply management department is seen as the "driver" in its supply chains to improve quality and delivery timing while holding down costs, which hopefully encourages suppliers to manage *their* suppliers in the same way. Global electronics manufacturer Flextronics, for example, does about 90% of its purchasing with just 10% of its suppliers. This increases Flextronics' purchasing leverage with these suppliers due to its high volumes of purchased parts. There are also other benefits. "Consolidating our spend provides us with the ability to work more closely with a core group of suppliers," says Bob Cusick, chief procurement officer. "This assists in developing more partnerships and provides Flextronics with clearer insight into suppliers' products, market changes and new technologies."[7]

Specifically, the objectives of supply management are to:

1. Maintain an uninterrupted flow of goods and services to the organization, at the desired customer service levels;
2. Minimize the investment in inventory to free up capital for other projects;
3. Ensure the required levels of purchased item quality;
4. Search for and develop best-in-class suppliers;
5. Standardize goods and services purchased whenever possible to reduce costs;
6. Purchase the required goods and services at the lowest total cost of ownership;
7. Achieve good working relationships with other functional areas of the organization;
8. Accomplish supply objectives at the lowest possible operating costs; and
9. Seek ways to improve the organization's competitive position.[8]

Further discussions of these topics are contained in the following sections.

THE PURCHASING CYCLE

14.2 Review the six-step process of the purchasing cycle

The **purchasing cycle** can be broken down to a six-step process. The first three steps involve *preparing for* the acquisition of goods and services, and are generally done together to assess the current situation. The final steps involve the actual acquisition of goods and services.

purchasing cycle A six-step process—the first three steps involve *preparing for* the acquisition of goods and services, and are generally done together to assess the current situation. The final steps involve the actual acquisition of goods and services.

CONDUCTING AN INTERNAL ASSESSMENT

Purchases are commonly divided into general **spend categories**, each with common characteristics such as raw materials, customized items, standardized items, and services, and then each of these general categories may be further subdivided. For example, the Schindler Group, a global provider of elevators and escalators, has two primary spend categories—production materials and nonproduction materials and services. Its production materials category is broken down into cars, doors, machines, mechanics, electromechanical components, electronic assemblies, spares, and other. Its nonproduction

spend categories Purchases are commonly divided into categories with common characteristics such as raw materials, customized items, standardized items, and services, and then each of these general categories may be further subdivided.

materials and services category is further divided into eight subcategories.[9] Supply management personnel understand and may specialize in the spend categories and subcategories, including the demand histories, design specifications, and current suppliers of the various purchased items.

Buyers also identify the users of the purchased items, manage existing supplier relationships, as well as search for other potential suppliers. Additionally, marketing personnel need to understand the impact purchases might have on product completion dates; logistics personnel are notified of purchased goods specifications, such as size and weight, for shipping purposes; and finance personnel need to know the magnitude of the spend.

ASSESSING THE MARKET

Purchasing specialists make assessments of risks and opportunities in the external environment. For example, an assessment of the bargaining power of the firm in relation to its suppliers should be made, based on the volume of purchases it normally makes and the number and size of its current and potential suppliers. Some spend categories may be characterized by a large number of competitive suppliers, while others may have a few large suppliers that dominate the market.

Noncritical, low-risk **functional goods**, such as office supplies, are highly standardized and easily substituted, and thus can be easily and cheaply purchased with simple contracts or **procurement cards** or **p-cards** (these are low-limit corporate bank cards designed to streamline the purchasing and payment process). On the other hand, unique items with customized specifications are considered to be high risk and high cost for the buying firm. These are termed **innovative goods**. Backup suppliers might be identified to reduce the risk of supply interruptions. In its Brazil facility, for example, Swedish truck maker Volvo Group buys many of the components and parts that go into the manufacture of its trucks (today, China's Geely Holdings owns the Volvo Car Corp.). At its manufacturing site, Volvo has specialized production processes it views as critical to its competitive advantage. Volvo has suppliers that make items for its production processes, which have the potential to shut down the production line if the items are not available. Consequently, Volvo purchases additional safety stocks of these items to avoid disruptions in supply.[10]

functional goods Noncritical, low-risk goods such as office supplies, which are highly standardized and easily substituted, and thus can be easily and cheaply purchased.

procurement cards Low-limit corporate bank cards designed to streamline the purchasing and payment process.

p-cards *See* Procurement cards.

innovative goods Unique items with customized specifications that are considered to be high risk and high cost for the buying firm.

COLLECTING SUPPLIER INFORMATION

When supply management personnel have analyzed the market and the type of purchase required, they must assess their current and potential suppliers. This information will then

SERVICE SPOTLIGHT

Areva's Program for Locating Suppliers

French energy company Areva has started a new program to locate suppliers for its critical equipment needs, and has proved very successful in locating and ensuring supplier diversity. Every three months there is a global meeting of procurement personnel where information is shared on procurement lessons learned from all of Areva's current projects. Topics covered include overall supplier performance, product quality, and cost. This information is then taken back to each project for use as needed. The supplier program also includes coordinating efforts to locate and visit suppliers with a global presence. It is advantageous that Areva suppliers have facilities in multiple countries so they can supply "locally" to Areva's many global projects. Finally, Areva enters into long-term agreements with suppliers like Japan Steel Works to ensure the supply of several highly critical products or materials.[11]

iStock/SusanChiang

be used in the competitive bidding process or negotiating process. In **competitive bidding**, the contract is usually awarded to the *lowest-priced bidder* determined to be *responsive* and *responsible* by the buyer. A responsive bid is one that conforms to the invitation to bid, and a responsible bid is one that is capable and willing to perform the work as specified (see more on the bidding process on page 444).

Supply managers and buyers may use a number of sources of information in their supplier assessments, including:

- On-file records of suppliers used in the past,
- Supplier directories,
- Online and printed catalogs,
- Trade magazines,
- Supplier websites, and
- Sales presentations.

Supplier information is used to narrow the list of available suppliers to the ones who meet the organization's purchasing criteria. Less time will be spent finding suppliers for functional goods, while a great deal of time and energy will be used when searching for suppliers of innovative goods. For example, if an organization is developing a new product, it wants to ensure all parts, components, and materials purchased will meet the design specifications at a reasonable cost from reliable suppliers. The Service Spotlight on page 442 describes Areva's methods for locating suppliers.

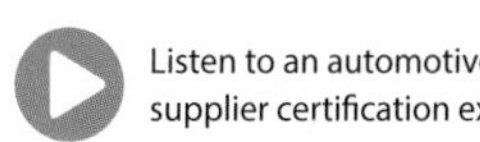
Listen to an automotive supplier certification expert

competitive bidding A process wherein a contract is usually awarded to the *lowest-priced bidder* determined to be *responsive* and *responsible* by the buyer. A responsive bid is one that conforms to the invitation to bid, and a responsible bid is one that is capable and willing to perform the work as specified.

sourcing strategy A plan for managing the supply of purchased items, which is linked to spend analysis and goals, and tied to corporate and supply chain strategies.

supply base The list of suppliers the firm is currently using.

supplier certification program A formal process for approving a supplier. Supplier certification often takes place before a supplier is allowed to quote prices or receive an order.

DEVELOPING THE SOURCING STRATEGY

Supply management personnel should have a full understanding of the type of purchase they are making and the supply market. If the supply market is competitive, then good prices and terms would be expected. If, on the other hand, the market is not competitive, the sourcing strategy might include seeking ways to collaborate with suppliers to obtain some service benefits, in lieu of negotiating better prices.

Purchasing personnel can then develop their **sourcing strategy**—a plan for managing the supply of purchased items, which is linked to their analysis and goals and tied to corporate and supply chain strategies. It might be necessary, for example, to reduce the size of the firm's **supply base** (the list of suppliers the firm is currently using), devise a program to further develop some of its current suppliers, or implement a **supplier certification program** for those suppliers that provide strategic items. Supplier certification often takes place before a supplier is allowed to quote prices or receive an order. A cross-functional team from the buying firm might visit the supplier's facilities and observe its equipment, personnel, facilities, and quality systems in order to ensure they meet the buying firm's requirements. Industry-wide certifications such as ISO 9000 and 14000 might also be used for supplier certifications.[12]

Particularly in light of the garment factory collapse in Bangladesh that killed 1,127 workers in 2013 (the factory had made clothing for Benetton, J. C. Penney, and others), companies purchasing from foreign manufacturers should incorporate plant visits in their certification programs. According to the Council of Fashion Designers of America president Diane von Furstenberg, "What happened in Bangladesh is a tragedy and a harsh reminder that it is our obligation as designers to make sure our factories are a safe place to work and that the workers are respected. I also encourage you to have your production team visit directly with your supplier partners to see firsthand the working conditions and treatment of workers. There are third-party vendors who can audit and inspect for you. It is important to know who you work with and to ensure safety and fairness in the workplace."[13]

Mamunur Rashid/Alamy

The Rana Plaza building in Bangladesh collapsed in 2013, killing 1,127 garment workers and potentially harming the reputations of companies associated with the garment factory.

SOLICITING AND EVALUATING BIDS

Supply management personnel can obtain pricing information and proposals for work from suppliers in a number of ways, including verbal quotes, a request for information, a request for quote, a request for proposal, or an invitation to bid. These are described in Table 14.2.

Evaluating competitive bids for products may include calculating the **total cost of ownership** (TCO), a relatively common method for comparing competing price quotes. This is a projected cost estimate that includes the initial acquisition costs, the estimated lifetime operating and maintenance costs, and the end-of-life salvage and disposition costs. To compare the TCOs for a product offered by several suppliers, it is necessary to determine all of the cash outflows and inflows over the expected lifetime of each supplier's product, and then calculate the net present values:

$$\text{TCO} = \text{NPV(salvage value)} - \text{purchase cost} - \text{NPV(operating + maintenance costs)},$$

where the NPV factors are calculated as $(1+d)^{-\text{Year}}$, with d = annual discount rate.

Note that other costs may be included in the TCO such as leasing, warranty, downtime, and insurance costs. Failure to address and accurately estimate these lifetime cash flows can lead to bad purchase decisions. Table 14.3 describes these costs in greater detail, and Example 14.1 provides a TCO example.

total cost of ownership (TCO) A relatively common method for comparing competing price quotes. This is a projected cost estimate that includes the initial acquisition costs, the estimated lifetime operating and maintenance costs, and the end-of-life salvage and disposition costs.

statement of work In response to a request for a price quote, a supplier often attaches this document, describing exactly what will be done and how.

NOTIFYING THE SELECTED SUPPLIER AND IMPLEMENTING THE CONTRACT

Based on their evaluations, supply management personnel award the contract to the preferred supplier. If the supplier is new to the firm, a communication plan is developed to

Table 14.2 Obtaining Pricing Information and Plans From Suppliers

Verbal quotes	Requested for low-cost, non critical purchases. The buyer selects a supplier and a verbal agreement is made regarding price, the number of units to be purchased, and the delivery requirements.
Request for information (RFI)	Requested to collect information on price, product design, timing, and other terms of interest. The supplier information is non-binding but allows buyer to prepare budgets, determine the total purchase cost for a new good or service, or help the firm prepare a more detailed request for quote.
Request for quote (RFQ)	Used when the purchasing specifications can be clearly stated, for relatively small purchases. Purchasing personnel send an inquiry form to one or more potential suppliers. Suppliers submit price quotes based on specified quantities or services. The RFQ is not binding unless specified, and it may be used as the starting point for negotiations.
Invitation to bid (IFB)	Similar to the RFQ, but can entail high costs and complex services. A number of suppliers will be asked to bid. The opening and closing dates of the bid and the basis for awarding a contract are communicated to the potential suppliers. Generally, the contract is awarded to the low-priced bidder meeting all of the requirements; however, bidders might also be told that bids will be used as a starting point for further negotiations.
Request for proposal (RFP)	A formal request for pricing, services, and plans, which is used for complex and critical purchases. Typically, it is requested from buyers who are not sure what they want. It allows suppliers to develop product and service specifications based on their own knowledge of the materials, processes, and technologies needed. A supplier's **statement of work** is typically attached, describing exactly what will be done and how. An RFP is most commonly used as a starting point to negotiate a contract.

Table 14.3 Total Cost of Ownership Cash Flows

Acquisition costs	• Supplier visits and product assessment costs • Purchase price + taxes + financing costs • Transportation costs
Ownership costs	• Fuel + energy costs • Maintenance + repair costs • Warranty costs • Training costs • Insurance costs
End-of-life costs	• Salvage value • Disposal costs

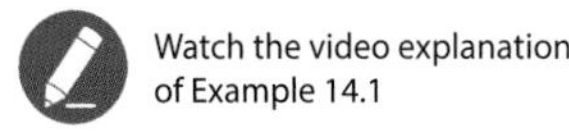

Example 14.1
Total Cost of Ownership Analysis for a Generator

Watch the video explanation of Example 14.1

The Del Construction Co. wants to purchase a 10,000-watt diesel generator. It has looked at two models—the Carol 902 and the Ricker 9100. The projected cash flows for each are shown here:

Supplier	Purchase Price ($)	Annual Operating and Maintenance Costs ($000) Yr.1	Yr.2	Yr.3	Yr.4	Yr.5	Salvage Value ($)
Carol	−6750	−16	−16	−16	−16	−16	+1000
Ricker	−5475	−18	−18	−18	−18	−18	+500
NPV factor	0	.909	.826	.751	.683	.621	.621

NPV(Carol) = −6750 − 16,000(.909) − 16,000(.826) − 16,000(.751) − 16,000(.683) − 16,000(.621) + 1,000(.621) = **−$66,769**

NPV(Ricker) = −5475 − 18,000(.909) − 18,000(.826) − 18,000(.751) − 18,000(.683) − 18,000(.621) + 500(.621) = **−$73,385**

The purchase costs and the annual operating and maintenance costs are shown above as negative cash flows, while the salvage values are positive cash flows. Using an annual discount of 10% yields the NPV factors above, calculated as: $(1+.1)^{-Year}$. Summing the 5-year cash flows yields the NPVs shown above for the two generators. As shown here, even though the original purchase price is considerably lower for the Ricker generator, the higher annual operating and maintenance costs, along with the lower salvage value, make the Ricker generator ultimately more costly. Given this analysis, Del should select the Carol generator.

notify warehousing, accounts payable, customer service, and users in the firm so computer programs can be modified and any required user training can be started.

Supplier and product performance is usually tracked throughout the life of the contract. This information is then reported to user groups and senior executives on a periodic basis. Eventually, the supply base might change along with products purchased, if poor performance is found. Lessons learned from each sourcing project should also be recorded and communicated to avoid problems in the future.

THE MAKE-OR-BUY DECISION

14.3 Perform the calculations in the break-even analysis for make-or-buy decisions

As discussed in Chapters 1 and 4, outsourcing refers to buying goods and services while ceasing to make them in-house, and this is one aspect of the **make-or-buy decision**. In recent years, the trend has been moving toward more outsourcing combined with the creation of lasting supplier relationships, which allows firms to concentrate more resources on their internal competencies. Some outsourcing has been with foreign suppliers with low labor costs, although this is beginning to change, as discussed in the chapter-opening Manufacturing Spotlight on **nearshoring**. The make-or-buy decision is a strategic one that can impact an organization's competitive position. Aerospace contractor Lockheed Martin outsources the maintenance of its global manufacturing equipment to enable better efficiencies and to further support its competitive strategy. The maintenance supplier provides Lockheed with diagnostic help, preventive maintenance, field service, training, and spare parts.[14] The reasons for outsourcing a good or service are shown in Table 14.4, and the reasons favoring making items in-house are listed in Table 14.5.

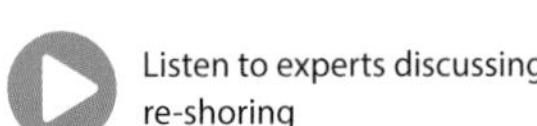

Listen to experts discussing re-shoring

A furniture store, for example, might consider outsourcing its delivery service instead of using its own vehicles and employees. However, if the delivery service provider is managed poorly, this arrangement could result in poor customer service and lost future business when the outside delivery service misses delivery times and damages furniture during its deliveries. For this reason, firms might decide only to outsource noncore activities (note the chapter-opening quote of Bill Gates). According to Rob Davis, head of business development at Virginia-based Diakon Logistics, ongoing engagement with an outsourcing partner is also a must. "Outsourcing isn't wiping one's hands clean of a situation," says Davis. "It requires partnership and involvement and communication about what's going on and what the client wants done. The value of outsourcing is having an expert come in and say, 'This is what I think we should do,' but it's still the client's responsibility to make the decision of what they do and to have the left hand talk to the right hand."[15]

make-or-buy decision A strategic decision regarding whether the firm will purchase, make in-house, or do some combination of the two. In recent years, the trend has been moving toward more outsourcing combined with the creation of lasting supplier relationships.

nearshoring Purchasing goods and services closer to the country of the buyer.

insourcing *See* Backsourcing.

backsourcing *See* Insourcing.

Conversely, **insourcing** refers to using internal resources to make goods and services that previously were outsourced. This practice is also sometimes referred to as **backsourcing**, and occasionally re-shoring (if the firm had previously outsourced to a foreign supplier). If the furniture store mentioned above outsourced its delivery service and sold its delivery truck, then found its transportation provider was doing a poor job of delivering

Table 14.4 Reasons for Outsourcing

Reason	Explanation
Lower cost	Reducing cost is an important reason for outsourcing, especially for generic items supplied by firms specializing in these items. The quantity needed by the buyer may be too small to justify investing in production equipment. Some foreign suppliers may also offer a cost advantage because of lower labor and/or materials costs.
Insufficient capacity	A firm may be producing near capacity, making it impossible to produce the items in-house without additional production equipment and personnel. The firm may also wish to outsource items to free up capacity to focus on producing other, more vital items.
Lack of technology or expertise	The firm may not have the necessary technologies or expertise to manufacture an item. Alternately, suppliers might hold the patents to a technology, thus precluding the make option.
Better quality	Purchased components may be superior in quality because suppliers have better technologies, processes, and skilled labor.

Table 14.5 Reasons for Producing In-House

Reason	Explanation
Protect proprietary technologies	A firm may have developed a technology, product, or process that needs to be protected to maintain a competitive advantage. Firms risk revealing their proprietary items when outsourcing or co-sourcing to suppliers.
No competent supplier	If no suppliers are available to produce an item, the firm may be forced to make it in-house. The firm may opt to produce the item in the short term, while using supplier development strategies to help suppliers create the capabilities to eventually produce it.
Better quality control	If the firm has the capability, the make option allows for the most control over product design, manufacturing, labor usage, and other activities to ensure that high-quality goods and services are made.
Use of idle capacity	A short-term solution for a firm with idle capacity is to use it to make goods and services. It avoids the layoff of skilled workers, and when business picks up, the firm can outsource these items to produce more strategic items.
Control of lead time and logistics	The make option provides better control of product lead time as well as logistics costs, since management would control all phases of design, manufacturing, and distribution. If these are desired competitive elements for the firm, then in many cases the items will not be outsourced.
Lower cost	If technology, capacity, and labor skills are available, the make option may be more economical, particularly if large quantities of the item are needed on a continuing basis. Although the make option can have a high fixed cost due to initial capital investments, it could have a lower unit cost, since it avoids supplier price markups and creates economies of scale.

furniture, it might then decide to purchase another vehicle, hire a driver, and insource the delivery service. In 2012, U.S. president Barak Obama even sounded off on insourcing. After meeting with several business leaders from the tech and manufacturing sectors at the White House to get input on how best to insource work that went to India, China, and other low-cost locations, he said, "You've heard of outsourcing. Well, these companies are insourcing. That's exactly the kind of commitment to country that we need—especially right now, when we're in a make-or-break moment for the middle class and those aspiring to get to the middle class here in the United States."[16] In a spectacular turnabout, General Motors is hiring 3,000 IT people who previously worked for Hewlett-Packard on GM projects. GM plans to insource about 90% of the work that had previously been outsourced to HP.[17]

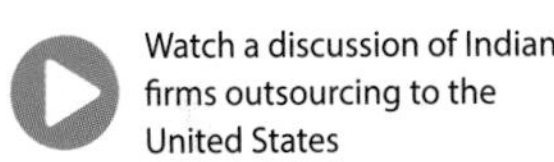
Watch a discussion of Indian firms outsourcing to the United States

Finally, the make-or-buy decision is not always an either-or option. Firms might decide to continue making some of their required units in-house while outsourcing the rest to suppliers—this is referred to as **co-sourcing**. In some co-sourcing arrangements, external workers are used for heavy demand periods, or to provide a particular expertise that internal staff lack. The next section describes the make-or-buy break-even analysis.

THE MAKE-OR-BUY BREAK-EVEN ANALYSIS

While cost is rarely the only consideration used in strategic sourcing decisions, the break-even analysis is a desirable sourcing tool when cost is a primary consideration. The assumptions for the analysis are that the fixed cost and variable cost per unit remain constant. (While this topic was covered in Chapter 4, it is worth revisiting the break-even analysis used in the make-or-buy decision here.)

co-sourcing Continuing to make some required units in-house while outsourcing the rest to suppliers.

To calculate the break-even point, the total cost of making is set equal to the total cost of buying, as shown here:

$$\text{Make cost} = \text{Buy cost}$$

$$F_m + V_m(x) = F_b + V_b(x)$$

where:

F_m = Manufacturing fixed cost, F_b = Buying fixed cost

V_m = Manufacturing variable cost/unit, V_b = Buying variable cost/unit

x = Units manufactured or purchased.

Solving the equation for x provides the break-even point. Small required quantities means the firm should buy (the lower fixed cost dominates), while large required quantities means the firm should make the item (the lower variable cost dominates). Example 14.2 presents a break-even analysis for the make-or-buy decision.

GLOBAL SOURCING

14.4 Discuss the opportunities and challenges of global sourcing

In recent years, the growth of international agreements promoting free trade has provided opportunities for many firms to expand their supply bases to include foreign suppliers. As shown in Table 14.6, world and North American merchandise imports, which shrank dramatically during the 2008–2010 global economic crisis, have rebounded substantially and are now many trillions of dollars annually.[18] In 2013, the world's top four merchandise importing countries were the United States ($2.3 trillion), China ($1.9 trillion), Germany ($1.2 trillion), and Japan ($0.8 trillion). Imports are projected to continue growing at about 2–3% per year in developed countries, and over 6% per year among developing economies.

While this level of **global sourcing** provides many opportunities for companies to further improve product quality, cost, and delivery performance, it also poses unique challenges for supply management personnel. In a recent survey of companies by *World Trade* magazine, 77% reported doing at least some of their purchasing internationally. Of those companies sourcing globally, about 79% said the primary benefit was lower cost, while about 61% said the biggest problem was late deliveries. Interestingly, about 45% of the respondents said they planned to start bringing sourcing closer to home.[19] (Recall the chapter-opening vignette on nearshoring.)

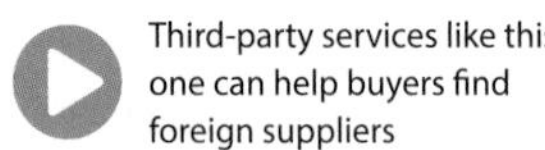
Third-party services like this one can help buyers find foreign suppliers

global sourcing Purchasing items internationally.

import broker A service that performs import transactions for a fee. Import brokers do not take title to the goods. Instead, ownership passes directly from the seller to the buyer.

import merchant A service that buys and takes title to international goods and then resells them to the buyer.

Successful global sourcing requires the skills to deal with foreign company executives and other employees (who may not speak English), long distances and other logistics problems, import/export regulations, tax issues, political problems, and a number of other issues not typically encountered with domestic sourcing. For these reasons, an **import broker**, who performs import transactions for a fee, can be used. Import brokers do not take title to the goods. Instead, ownership passes directly from the seller to the buyer. Supply management personnel can also buy foreign goods from an **import merchant**, who buys and takes title to the goods and then resells them to the buyer.

Table 14.6 World and North American Merchandise Imports (trillion $)

Year	World Imports	North American Imports
2013	18.155	3.195
2012	17.850	3.192
2011	17.779	3.090
2010	15.076	2.508

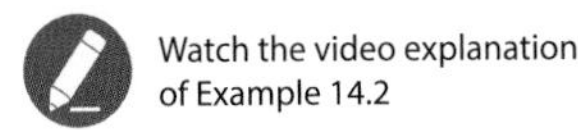

Example 14.2
A Make-or-Buy Break-Even Analysis

Watch the video explanation of Example 14.2

The Pearson Kayak Manufacturing Co. is considering whether or not to make a key part for one of its kayak models. Its projected total requirement for the part is 15,000 units, and a trusted supplier can make the part for \$25 per unit. John, the owner, estimates that the purchase contract will cost \$250 to prepare, and if Pearson made the part in-house, an additional investment in equipment would cost \$30,000; the variable cost for the part would be \$14 per unit. John wants to know if Pearson should make or buy the part. Performing the analysis:

$$F_m + V_m(x) = F_b + V_b(x)$$

$$\$30{,}000 + \$14(x) = \$250 + \$25(x)$$

Collecting terms yields: \$29,750 = \$11(x), or x = 2,705 units.

Since it needs 15,000 parts, and this is greater than the break-even point, the decision is to *make the part*. If it needs less than 2,705 units, it would want to purchase the part. As a check, John calculates the total cost of 15,000 units for each alternative:

Make cost = \$30,000 + 14(15,000) = \$240,000, and the Buy cost = \$250 + \$25(15,000) = \$375,250.

The figure provided here shows the break-even point more clearly:

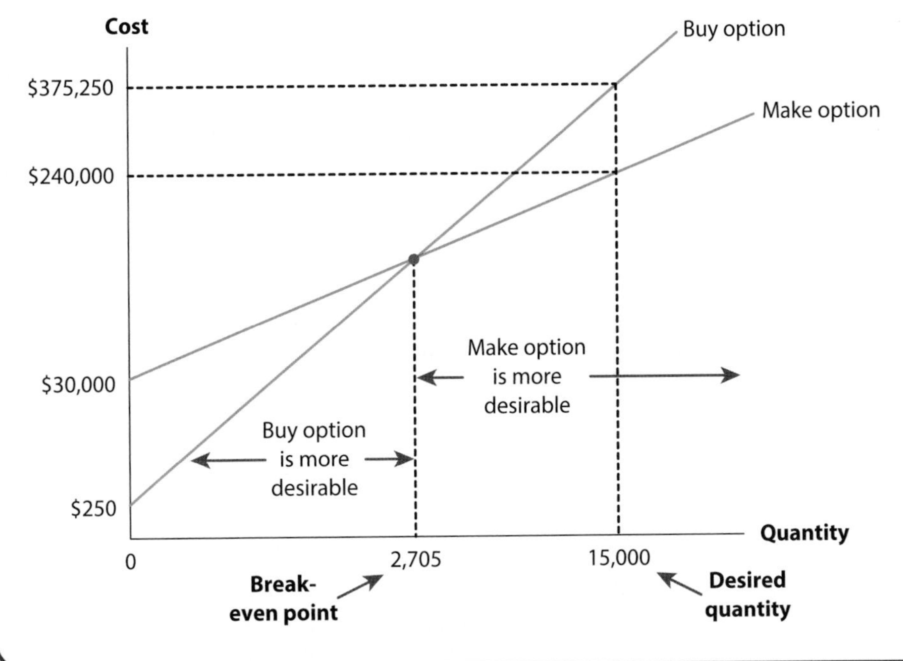

THE IMPACTS OF TARIFFS AND TRADE AGREEMENTS

There are a number of international trading arrangements designed to reduce tariffs and trade barriers among various countries. A **tariff** is a tax or customs fee, and is frequently applied to imported goods. Tariffs are designed to raise money for governments and can also be protectionist in nature. For example, a country with farmers growing bananas may impose a high tariff on imported bananas to protect its domestic growers. Obviously, protectionist tariffs can reduce trade, which can also reduce the potential size of a firm's supply base and can even promote poor-quality domestic production and trade wars.

Which is better—free trade or protectionism? Watch the debate.

tariff A tax or customs fee imposed by a government on imported goods to protect local industries and/or raise revenue.

In the United States, the first tariffs were imposed on imported goods in 1790 as a way to help pay for the Revolutionary War and further fund the U.S. government. These taxes were generally in the 5–15% range, and funded over 90% of the U.S. budget. Over time, politicians successfully argued for higher import tariffs to help protect goods that were manufactured by struggling U.S. industries. For example, in 1848, a 45% tariff was imposed on imported wool products to help wool producers in the United States. Consequently, this caused other countries to retaliate against U.S. exports, which tended to hurt many mature U.S. industries, such as cotton. Today, protectionist policies are becoming less popular in the United States—less than one-third of imported goods are taxed, with tariffs generally in the 1–2% range, and fund only about 1% of the U.S. budget.[20]

After World War II, the United States helped to form the General Agreement on Tariffs and Trade (GATT, 1947) to reduce global tariffs and promote trade among member countries. In 1995, GATT was replaced by the World Trade Organization (WTO), headquartered in Switzerland. A number of free trade agreements have sprung up since World War II, some of which are listed in Table 14.7.[21]

In free trade agreements, firms can sell and purchase from firms in member countries with little or no tariffs or trade barriers. This allows firms to grow their supply bases and potentially find products at lower prices and better quality. The United States, as of 2016, has free trade agreements with 20 countries: Australia, Bahrain, Canada, Chile, Colombia, Costa Rica, Dominican Republic, El Salvador, Guatemala, Honduras, Israel, Jordan, Korea, Mexico, Morocco, Nicaragua, Oman, Panama, Peru, and Singapore.[22] The Spotlight on OM Trends on page 451 describes Mexico's strong growth in foreign trade, enabled in part by its use of free trade agreements.

CHALLENGES FOR GLOBAL SOURCING

In the United States, global sourcing has grown, in part due to improvements in communication and transportation technologies, reduction of international trade barriers, and deregulation of the transportation industry. However, global sourcing challenges remain, including the time and costs involved in selecting foreign suppliers and dealing with tariffs; U.S. customs clearance; currency exchange rates; and political, cultural, labor, infrastructure, and legal problems.

Unlike dealing with domestic suppliers, the costs involved in identifying, selecting, and evaluating foreign suppliers can be prohibitive. Additionally, if the supplier is in a distant location, then logistical issues may render delivery lead time unacceptable, especially for perishable goods. (Note the 2015 U.S. west coast shipping ports clogged for a number of months due to dock worker strikes and slowdowns.) Foreign purchases must deal with potentially complex shipping terms. The International Chamber of Commerce created a

Table 14.7 Global Trade Agreements

European Union (EU)	Started May 1950; and was originally comprised of Belgium, France, Luxembourg, Italy, the Netherlands, and Germany. Currently, the EU has 28 member countries. The primary trade goal of the EU is to create a single market for goods and services, allowing member countries to better compete with markets like the United States.
Association of Southeast Asian Nations (ASEAN)	Created in August 1967; and is comprised of the 10 countries in the Southeast Asian region: Brunei, Cambodia, Indonesia, Laos, Malaysia, Myanmar, Philippines, Singapore, Thailand, and Vietnam. The primary objective is to support economic growth, social progress, and cultural development in the region.
Southern Common Market (MERCOSUR)	Agreement in March 1991 among Argentina, Brazil, Paraguay, and Uruguay. Goal was to form a common market based on economic and political cooperation. In July 2012 Venezuela became a member and Paraguay was suspended.
North American Free Trade Agreement (NAFTA)	Started January 1, 1994. Removed trade barriers among the United States, Canada, and Mexico. Many tariffs were eliminated, with an immediate effect, while others were phased out over periods ranging from 5-15 years.
Common Market for Eastern and Southern Africa (COMESA)	Began in December 1994 with a strategy of economic prosperity through regional trade integration. Currently, there are 19 member countries, with a total population of over 400 million.

The Growth of Foreign Trade in Mexico

SPOTLIGHT ON **OM TRENDS**

The recent global recession has tested commitments to keep countries' borders open, as politicians have created trade barriers for short-term economic gains. This is a fair summary of the current state of global trade. But not in Mexico, one of the greatest defenders of free trade in the world. Recently, Felipe Calderón, Mexico's president from 2006 to 2012, made a public statement in favor of free trade. It was also a criticism of some of Mexico's trading partners. These include the United States, where several protectionist measures are being debated, and two Latin American countries that have recently enacted protectionist policies.

Mexico is one of the most open of the world's leading economies. In 2010, foreign trade accounted for almost 60% of its GDP, compared with 48% for China, 22% for the United States, and 19% for Brazil. Furthermore, by 2017, Mexican foreign trade will comprise almost 85% of GDP, according to estimates. Mexico's foreign trade has been boosted by its proximity to the United States; the NAFTA trade agreement among Mexico, Canada, and the United States; its large number of other free trade agreements; and its supply of skilled and semiskilled labor. Some 110,000 engineers graduated in 2010, more than double the number in 1999. Consequently, Mexico has become ever more efficient and skills-rich. The country now even exports cars to China.[23]

uniform set of rules, called **incoterms** (International Commercial Terms), for international transactions of goods with respect to shipping costs, risks, and responsibilities of the buyer, seller, and shipper.

Global sourcing can also involve **countertrade**, in which goods or services of domestic firms are exchanged for goods or services—and in some cases currency—from foreign firms. This type of arrangement is sometimes used by countries where there is a shortage of exchangeable currency (such as the Russian ruble) and a surplus of tradable goods (such as Russian oil). A specific example of this involves China and Russia. China is financing the East Siberia–Pacific Ocean oil pipeline to the tune of $25 billion, and in return, Russia is delivering 110 million barrels of oil annually to China for a 20-year period.[24]

Countertrade transactions are more complicated than currency transactions because goods are frequently exchanged for goods. Countertrade activities include barter, offsets, and counterpurchases. **Barter** is the exchange of goods or services without involving currency. An **offset** is an exchange for industrial goods or services as a condition of a military-related export. It is commonly used in the aerospace and defense sectors. A **counterpurchase** is an arrangement whereby an exporter agrees to sell goods or services to a foreign importer for currency, while simultaneously agreeing to buy goods or services from that same foreign importer.

SUPPLY BASE RATIONALIZATION

14.5 Explain the benefits of supply base rationalization

A common sourcing activity is to reduce purchases from marginal or poor-performing suppliers while increasing purchases from more desirable, top-performing suppliers. Firms doing this are practicing **supply base rationalization**, also referred to as **supply base reduction** or **supply base optimization**. Indeed, activities aimed at fostering buyer–supplier relationships to increase the performance and value of suppliers are simply easier when fewer suppliers are involved. Additionally, use of fewer suppliers means larger purchases for each supplier—this should result in lower overall prices due to quantity discounts offered by many suppliers. Thus, supply base rationalization programs have multiple benefits—reduced purchase prices due to quantity discounts, fewer suppliers to manage, more frequent collaborations between buyer and supplier, and greater overall levels of quality and delivery reliability—since only the best suppliers remain in the supply base.

Aside from having ties to supply chain management, supplier relationships, purchasing costs, and product quality, supply base rationalization is also consistent with ethical and sustainable sourcing efforts—firms may desire to interact more frequently and closely with

incoterms (International Commercial Terms) A uniform set of rules created by the International Chamber of Commerce for international transactions of goods with respect to shipping costs, risks, and responsibilities of the buyer, seller, and shipper.

countertrade When goods or services of domestic firms are exchanged for goods or services, and in some cases currency, from foreign firms.

barter The exchange of goods or services without involving currency.

offset An exchange for industrial goods or services as a condition of a military-related export. It is commonly used in the aerospace and defense sectors.

counterpurchase An arrangement whereby an exporter agrees to sell goods or services to a foreign importer for currency, while simultaneously agreeing to buy goods or services from that same foreign importer.

supply base rationalization Reducing purchases from marginal or poor-performing suppliers while increasing purchases from more desirable, top-performing suppliers.

supply base reduction *See* Supply base rationalization.

supply base optimization *See* Supply base rationalization.

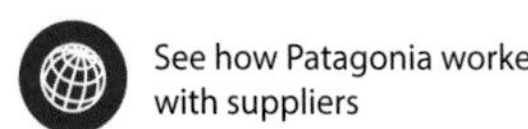
See how Patagonia worked with suppliers

suppliers exhibiting ethical and sustainable purchasing habits (a topic discussed later in the chapter). Firms may wish to rationalize their supply bases using ethical and sustainable business practices as two of their screening criteria.

At automaker Ford, Paul Wood, manager of global purchasing, describes the company's sourcing framework: "The framework is designed to develop long-term, closer relationships with significantly fewer suppliers. The theory is that developing closer relationships will result in better quality, lower cost, and improved innovation." The project began with Ford identifying 20 items that accounted for a large portion of Ford's annual purchase spend. "We saw that for each of these items, we might have seven, eight, nine or even more different suppliers. We want to reduce this to three or four suppliers who will supply 100 percent of that commodity." Thus, the remaining suppliers benefit from increased business, and Ford benefits from shared innovation, increased quality, and lower cost.[25]

Supply base rationalization is a straightforward, simple sourcing strategy, and is often the initial supply chain management effort, usually preceding the formation of long-term buyer–supplier strategic relationships. Particularly when economic times are tough, reducing purchasing spend tends to sit atop buyers' agendas, which can lead to sourcing from low-cost countries and pose significant risks to corporations when foreign suppliers conceal ethical and quality problems. To help corporate buyers, the UK fair trade organization Tradecraft has produced a number of guidelines, reports, and online tools to show how ethical purchasing can be done in ways to benefit both parties.[26] The next section discusses the benefits of supplier relationship management.

SUPPLIER RELATIONSHIP MANAGEMENT

14.6 Summarize the approaches used in managing supplier relationships

Due to the increasing number of items that firms outsource, as discussed earlier, the performance of a firm's supply base has a growing impact on its reputation. Thus, supply management professionals must spend more time than ever before managing relationships with suppliers, rather than simply making one-time purchases of goods and services.

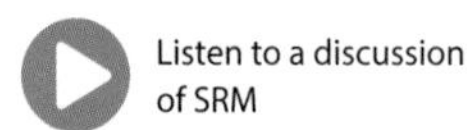
Listen to a discussion of SRM

Supplier relationship management (SRM), according to global consultant Accenture, "encompasses a broad suite of capabilities that facilitate collaboration, sourcing, transaction execution and performance monitoring between an organization and its trading partners."[27] In a nutshell, SRM involves streamlining the processes and communication between a buyer and supplier, using software applications that enable these processes to be managed more efficiently and effectively. SRM software automates the exchange of information among several layers of relationships that can be complex and time consuming.

Obviously, not all suppliers are considered critical or key, and thus not much time is required to build relationships with these suppliers. Relationship depth with suppliers actually runs along a continuum, from arm's-length relationships at one end of the spectrum, to strategic alliances or partnerships at the other end. Managing relationships with strategic alliance suppliers provides the most benefit for the firm, and this topic is discussed next.

STRATEGIC ALLIANCE SUPPLIER RELATIONSHIPS

An ongoing supplier relationship may be considered a **strategic alliance** or **key supplier relationship** if the relationship has been beneficial and the two parties see a reason to work together more often and share more information. The reasons for strengthening a buyer–supplier relationship can include:

- A shared desire to improve quality;
- A greater possibility for price reductions and profit improvements;
- The supplier's desire for further sales growth to the buyer;
- A mutual desire to work together using new technologies or to develop new products; and
- The purchasing firm's desire to insure against supply disruptions.

supplier relationship management Encompasses a broad suite of capabilities that facilitate collaboration, sourcing, transaction execution, and performance monitoring between an organization and its trading partners.

strategic alliance An ongoing supplier relationship that has been beneficial and the two parties see a reason to work together more often and share more information.

key supplier relationship *See* Strategic alliance.

Strategic alliances are seen as a means to build stronger, more extensive ties between buyers and suppliers, with the overall objectives of lowering costs and improving quality and customer service. Initiatives are designed to create "win–win" relationships, which together can add value for the respective companies. In a strategic alliance partnership the buying firm would pay the supplier promptly, include the supplier on problem-solving teams, and guarantee a certain percent of its business to that supplier. In return, the supplier would deliver product as promised, respond promptly to concerns of the buyer, and offer input to improve the buyer's business.

Strategic alliances tend to come about when a service or good is strategically important to a firm's success. The partners share information on their long-term strategies and frequently work together as a team to seek out problems and solve them, both from the buyer's and the supplier's perspective. There is a general understanding that process improvements will ultimately benefit both parties. More elaborate mechanisms are put in place to facilitate the alliance, including early supplier involvement in the development of new goods and services. In this case, key suppliers are members of the buyer's new product/service design team, which allows the buyer to take advantage of new proprietary technologies owned by the supplier and to shorten the design cycle, which can give the buying firm a competitive advantage. As part of the new product development team, the supplier also has opportunities to sell more product to the buyer.

The Clorox Company, for example, found that a supplier of trigger sprayers was packing too few to a box to efficiently feed its production line. The sheer number of boxes had increased Clorox's disposal costs. The purchasing department went to the supplier, a long-time partner, and asked it to ship in bulk containers of 5,000 sprayers each, rather than the 500-count corrugated boxes, emphasizing that both sides would save money. The supplier found pallet-sized bulk boxes that were large enough to ship the required quantities, could be reused up to 10 times, and could protect the sprayers. Clorox tested the new shipping boxes and determined it could change its production loading system to accommodate the new packaging successfully. Both sides experienced cost benefits due to lower labor costs and disposal fees for Clorox, and lower distribution costs for the supplier.[28]

Vendor Managed Inventory

Vendor managed inventory (VMI) is a strategic alliance–based approach to controlling inventory and reducing costs. Buyers provide inventory information to a key supplier, including historical usage, current inventory levels, minimum and maximum stock levels, sales forecasts, and upcoming promotions. The supplier then takes on the responsibility and risk for planning, managing, and monitoring the replenishment of inventory at the buyer's facility. Buyers benefit from faster order-processing times, fewer stockouts, and lower inventory management and ordering costs. Suppliers benefit from having guaranteed future purchases, and a reduced variance in purchase quantities caused by a buyer's erratic forecasting (recall discussions of the bullwhip effect in Chapter 7). Milk, bread, eggs, and other fresh product are delivered daily to convenience stores using VMI, for example, to keep the shelves full, the product fresh, and the paperwork simple.

Chicago-based Lawson Products, a supplier of maintenance and repair products, offers a very sophisticated version of VMI. For example, a typical Lawson sales rep would arrive at a customer's site and then be responsible for stocking products, along with counting inventory and ordering. "We become an extension of the customer's location and a highly trusted partner—almost as if an employee," says CEO Michael DeCata. The sales reps are often so savvy that they know to reorder on a drawer that's still two-thirds full, and not reorder on the drawer that's nearly empty, because they are so familiar with the frequency at which the inventory turns over. "What we aspire to is—you will never call us, because the stuff will always be there," DeCata explains. "There's no next-day service. It's there, when you need it, before your mechanic reaches into the drawer. It's a very high bar, but it's what we aspire to."[29]

A more advanced form of VMI is **supplier co-location**. A full-time supplier representative resides in the buying firm's purchasing department, holding a dual position as both buyer and supplier representative. This person may also contribute to the buying

vendor managed inventory (VMI). A strategic alliance–based approach to controlling inventory and reducing costs. Buyers provide inventory information to a key supplier including historical usage, current inventory levels, minimum and maximum stock levels, sales forecasts, and upcoming promotions. The supplier then takes on the responsibility and risk for planning, managing, and monitoring the replenishment of inventory at the buyer's facility.

supplier co-location A more advanced form of VMI. A full-time supplier representative resides in the buying firm's purchasing department, holding a dual position as both buyer and supplier representative. This person may also contribute to the buying firm's new product development and value engineering/value analysis teams by suggesting modifications or alternate components during the product design phase that are unknown to the engineering or design personnel.

firm's new product development and value engineering/value analysis teams by suggesting modifications or alternate components during the product design phase that are unknown to the engineering or design personnel. The supplier benefits from continued sales, more opportunities to participate in new project designs, and the supply of new products to the buyer.

SRM SOFTWARE

Many organizations are investing in SRM software modules due to the wealth of information that can be derived from these systems. SRM software can organize supplier information and allow the firm to quickly identify, for example, all current suppliers for an item, performance rankings of all suppliers, and similar purchased items. According to global software developer SAS, an effective SRM solution "provides real supplier intelligence—the ability to understand and predict the value of supplier relationships—through an enterprisewide, integrated view of a company's suppliers and the commodities or services they provide. It enables businesses to collect, analyze and leverage all aspects of their supplier data and purchasing history, providing vital insights into the supply base and purchasing history."[30]

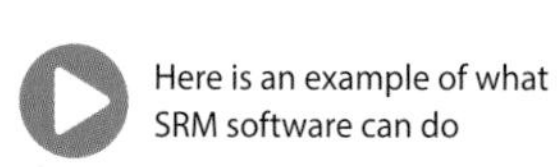

Here is an example of what SRM software can do

There are two types of SRM software applications: transactional and analytic. **Transactional SRM** enables an organization to track supplier interactions such as order planning, order payments, and returns. Transactional SRM tends to focus on short-term reporting and is event driven, focusing on questions such as: What did we buy yesterday? What supplier did we buy from? What was the cost of the purchase? On the other hand, **analytic SRM** allows the company to analyze the firm's supply base. The analysis provides answers to questions such as: Which suppliers should the company develop long-term relationships with? Which suppliers would make the company more profitable? Analytic SRM enables more long-term supply base planning.

One of the more recent SRM software developments is the use of **cloud-based SRM** services. This occurs when an SRM software supplier offers customers the ability to use the supplier's SRM software through an Internet portal, for a subscription or usage fee. Particularly for small companies, SRM cloud solutions are a ready-to-use combination of software and preconfigured content at a relatively low price. These applications are available "out of the box," and allow very rapid deployment with little required training. For example, California-based Ketera Contract Management charges $1,000 per month for up to 15 users to use its SRM solution.[31]

transactional SRM Software that enables an organization to track supplier interactions such as order planning, order payments, and returns. Transactional SRM tends to focus on short-term reporting and is event driven, focusing on such questions as: What did we buy yesterday? What supplier did we buy from? What was the cost of the purchase?

analytic SRM Software that allows the company to analyze the firm's supply base. The analysis provides answers to questions such as: With which suppliers should the company develop long-term relationships? Which suppliers would make the company more profitable? Analytic SRM enables long-term supply base planning.

cloud-based SRM A service offered by an SRM software supplier. Customers use the supplier's SRM software through an Internet portal, for a subscription or usage fee.

ethical sourcing Bringing about positive social change through organizational buying behaviors. Includes promoting diversity by intentionally buying from small firms, ethnic minority businesses, and women-owned enterprises; discontinuing purchases from firms that use child labor or other unacceptable labor practices; and sourcing from firms with good labor treatment or environmental protection reputations.

ETHICAL AND SUSTAINABLE SOURCING

14.7 Describe the issues and benefits of ethical and sustainable sourcing

Ethical sourcing can be defined as "bringing about positive social change through organizational buying behaviors."[32] Ethical sourcing practices include promoting diversity by intentionally buying from small firms, ethnic minority businesses, and women-owned enterprises; discontinuing purchases from firms that use child labor or other unacceptable labor practices; and sourcing from firms with good labor treatment or environmental protection reputations. Supply managers and corporate executives play central roles in promoting ethical sourcing by creating a supportive organizational culture, developing policies that support the firm's desire to practice ethical sourcing, communicating these policies to trading partners, and then implementing the ethical sourcing plans. Massachusetts-based athletic footwear retailer Reebok launched its ethical sourcing program in the early 1990s. It emphasizes the roles played by supplier factory managers in maintaining quality workplace conditions. Reebok also tries to collaborate with its competitors in establishing common human rights guidelines, since they all might be buying merchandise from the same factories.[33]

Purchasing goods from suppliers in developing countries can be risky since human rights, animal rights, safety, and environmental abuses can become associated with the firm's foreign suppliers, leading to negative publicity, product boycotts, a tarnished

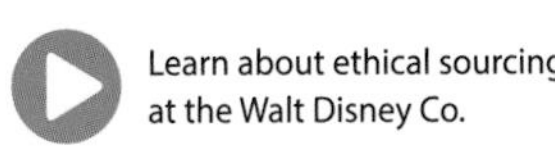
Learn about ethical sourcing at the Walt Disney Co.

company image, brand degradation, and ultimately lower sales and profits. This very thing happened to running-gear manufacturer Nike in the mid-1990s when it contracted with Pakistani factories to make footballs. Unknown to Nike, much of the work was subcontracted to local villagers, where children as young as 10 were drawn into the production process. Since that time, Nike has worked hard to improve its purchasing practices. Use of ethical sourcing practices is more difficult than it sounds. Modern supply chains can include suppliers in many countries with varied labor issues, wages, and living conditions. Nike's global supply chain, for instance, employs some 800,000 workers in 52 countries.[34]

The purchase of fair trade products is a recent sourcing activity that is becoming popular as firms seek to demonstrate a more ethical approach to purchasing. A fair trade product, as defined in Chapter 2, is a product manufactured or grown by a disadvantaged producer in a developing country that receives a fair price for its goods. The term *fair trade* most often refers to farming products such as coffee, cocoa, sugar, bananas, and cotton that are produced in developing countries and exported to large firms in developed countries. Agencies such as the Fairtrade Foundation, Fairtrade Labelling Organizations International, and the World Fair Trade Organization seek out and certify these types of products as being "fair trade products."[35] Leading retailers offer items for sale that are designated as fair trade products. In the United Kingdom, for example, consumers can purchase fair trade rubber gloves with the knowledge that Sri Lankan rubber farmers are benefitting from a fair price, technical support, and help with buying farming equipment.

Alex Segre/Alamy

A number of fair trade–certified products can easily be found in most grocery stores.

SUSTAINABLE SOURCING

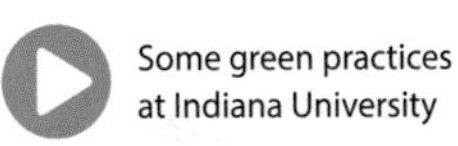
Some green practices at Indiana University

Protecting the Earth's environment has been a subject of concern for many years, and more recently it has become a popular topic of debate as politicians and voters discuss the impacts of global warming. Awards such as the Goldman Environmental Prize, which began in 1990, have served as a support mechanism for environmental reform, providing global publicity for specific environmental problems. Businesses today are also discovering that significant additional profits can be realized from acting in environmentally responsible ways.

Growing out of this environmental awareness was the idea of **green purchasing**. Green purchasing is a practice aimed at ensuring that purchased products or materials meet environmental objectives of the organization such as waste reduction, hazardous material elimination, recycling, remanufacturing, and material reuse. According to the globally recognized Institute for Supply Management, green purchasing is defined as "making environmentally conscious decisions throughout the purchasing process, beginning with product and process design, and through product disposal."[37] Companies like California-based healthcare provider Kaiser Permanente and beer producer Anheuser-Busch have been recognized as corporate trailblazers in green purchasing. In 2001, Kaiser Permanente formed an environmental stewardship council focusing on green buildings, green purchasing, and environmentally sustainable operations. Anheuser-Busch, for example, worked with its suppliers to reduce the lid diameter of four types of cans, saving 17.5 million pounds of aluminum as well as reducing the energy needed to produce and transport the cans.[38]

green purchasing Making environmentally conscious decisions throughout the purchasing process, beginning with product and process design, and through product disposal.

Sustainability, initially introduced in Chapter 1, is a broad term that includes green purchasing as well as some aspects of social responsibility and financial performance. It can be defined as "the ability to meet the needs of current supply chain members without hindering the ability to meet the needs of future generations in terms of economic, environmental, and social challenges." For businesses and their trading partners, sustainability is seen today as doing the right things in ways that make economic sense. **Sustainable sourcing** is one activity, then, within the larger umbrella term of sustainability—it includes green purchasing,

sustainable sourcing A process of purchasing goods and services that takes into account the long-term impact on people, profits, and the planet.

SERVICE SPOTLIGHT

Bon Appétit's Sustainable Initiatives

California-based Bon Appétit manages more than 400 cafeterias for corporations and universities across the United States and outlines sustainability initiatives in its contract proposals.

iStock/stevecolieimages

Bon Appétit currently recycles 40% of its organic waste across the United States through composting or donating food scraps to be used as pig food. It uses on-site gardens when possible, then sends the rest to an off-site composter. Used fryer oil goes to a biodiesel company. In some locations, it gives compost to its Farm-to-Fork farmer partners, and then turns around and buys their harvests, creating a closed-loop relationship between Bon Appétit and many of its suppliers.

In 1999, Bon Appétit launched its Farm-to-Fork program, an initiative requiring its chefs to buy at least 20% of their ingredients locally. The small family farms the company supports have a smaller negative impact on the land because they avoid chemical inputs in favor of compost, use of cover crops, and diversity.

In 2007, Bon Appétit implemented its Low Carbon Diet Program to encourage its chefs to think about how their food choices help reduce CO_2 emissions. For instance, meat and dairy are especially high in carbon because cows, sheep, and goats emit methane. To reduce this, Bon Appétit has reduced beef and cheese purchases.[36]

some form of financial benefit, as well as some aspects of ethical sourcing. Very simply, it has been defined as "a process of purchasing goods and services that takes into account the long-term impact on people, profits, and the planet."[39] The Service Spotlight above describes a number of sustainable sourcing initiatives at Bon Appétit.

To make sustainable sourcing a reality, companies must rely upon close, collaborative relationships with their key suppliers and customers. Palm oil, a vegetable oil used in many food and cosmetic products, is one example—consumer goods companies like Kraft, Unilever, and Nestlé all desire to purchase sustainable palm oil. Consequently, the World Wildlife Fund and Unilever formed the Roundtable for Sustainable Palm Oil to create sustainable practices for palm oil cultivation, to work with the growers, and ultimately to certify palm oil producers. Today, certified sustainable palm oil producers get paid higher prices for their palm oil from companies like Kraft and Nestlé, which in turn charge higher prices for their sustainable consumer products—prices that many consumers are willing to pay.[40]

Governments, cities, and leading businesses are now getting involved, to set some clear targets for organizations to achieve. In 2005, UK prime minister Tony Blair set up a business-led group called the Sustainable Procurement Task Force (SPTF) to examine how funds could be spent in a sustainable manner. The aim of the group was to show how sustainable purchases could benefit organizations, help society, boost the economy, and support the natural environment.[41] Seattle, WA, has been practicing sustainable purchasing for many years. The city's Green Purchasing Program promotes use of goods, materials, and services that help to reduce greenhouse gas emissions. Purchasing contracts also mandate 100% recycled paper for duplex document production and toxin-free chemicals in products the city buys.[42]

Firms, their supply chains, and government agencies alike realize that every purchase has a global environmental impact, and with careful sourcing, money can be saved. Collection, transport, manufacturing, and scrapping of raw materials and finished products require the use of fossil fuels; products purchased from distant suppliers require greater amounts of fuel for transportation; products transported via ship or rail use less fuel than do trucks or airlines; plant-based products generally have a smaller environmental impact than petroleum-based products; factories powered by solar or wind equipment have smaller environmental impacts than factories powered by oil or coal; and energy-efficient products consume less energy.

E-PROCUREMENT SYSTEMS

14.8 Discuss how e-procurement systems assist firms in streamlining purchasing activities

Many firms are looking for ways to streamline paper-based purchasing activities, where possible, through use of Internet purchasing, also referred to as **e-purchasing** or **e-procurement**. Supply management professionals assess, select, and manage suppliers from all over the world. To assist in these activities, software companies have developed SRM software, as described earlier, and e-procurement tools. E-procurement tools are used primarily for smaller purchases such as maintenance, repair, and operating (MRO) supplies (office supplies and spare parts, for example).

A number of benefits have been associated with e-purchasing, which include:

- Elimination of paperwork;
- Reduced time between recognition of need and receipt of an order;
- Reduced errors in ordering and order fulfillment;
- Reduced overhead costs; and
- More free time to strategically manage the supply base.[43]

REVERSE AUCTIONS

In recent years, firms have become more involved in using **reverse auctions**, a form of e-purchasing, principally as a way to reduce purchase spend. Reverse auctions work best for common catalogue item purchases, where specifications are very well defined. John Deere, for example, saves money on vehicle signs, forged steel tools, and corrugated packaging through use of reverse auctions.[44] In reverse auctions, the buying firm controls the bidding process either through proprietary software developed in-house or through a third party. All potential bidders (suppliers) are prequalified before the purchase requirements are released and the bidding begins. Suppliers may then log onto a designated website and place their offers, while watching all the bids as they come in, and may reduce their own bids until the close of the auction.

The supplier submitting the lowest bid meeting the specifications is generally selected. Aside from the benefit of getting low prices, when using a third-party reverse auction website service, such as California-based Ariba, the buyer can utilize a vast pool of prequalified domestic and foreign suppliers, further improving the potential for low prices and even better product quality. Actor William Shatner has popularized Priceline.com's reverse auction site for many years, for purchasing airline tickets, hotel stays, and rental cars.

Government agencies also frequently use reverse auctions. Maricopa County, CA, for example, conducted a reverse auction in 2013 to obtain health benefits for county employees. The county first narrowed the field down to a short list of vendors, and then conducted a reverse auction. The result was a high-quality benefits package and multimillion-dollar savings for the county and taxpayers.[45]

e-MARKETPLACES

Online marketplaces, also called **e-marketplaces**, are Internet locations where buyers and sellers meet to trade goods, services, and information. Most B2B e-marketplaces serve two functions: They allow companies to more easily find buyers or suppliers, and they provide an efficient network for negotiating, settlement, and delivery of goods. Currently, e-marketplaces exist for many industries. A quick search in a global e-marketplace directory, for example, revealed 781 e-marketplaces in 40 industries.[46]

E-marketplaces can be structured similar to e-Bay, where the website is a neutral third party bringing together buyers and suppliers. An example of this for B2B transactions is the site www.buyerzone.com. In many cases, though, an e-marketplace is set up by a consortium of buyers seeking to combine their purchasing power to obtain lower unit costs through

e-purchasing *See* E-procurement.

e-procurement Purchasing goods and services over the Internet.

reverse auctions A bidding process controlled by the buyer, wherein all potential bidders (suppliers) are prequalified before the purchase requirements are released and the bidding begins. Suppliers may then log onto a designated website and place their offers, while watching all the bids as they come in, and may reduce their own bids until the close of the auction. The supplier submitting the lowest bid meeting the specifications is generally selected.

e-marketplaces Online marketplaces where buyers and sellers meet to trade goods, services, and information.

MANUFACTURING SPOTLIGHT Xerox Uses Social Media to Engage Its Customers

Kristoffer Tripplaar/Alamy

Document technology company Xerox understands the customer service benefits that come about when its staff communicate with customers using social media. Xerox began using social media in 2009 and has a global presence on all of the major social media platforms. It tracks social media performance by monitoring every mention of the brand and how often customers can be engaged in conversations.

Xerox has a formal training program for its staff for use of social media. One class teaches employees how to start engaging customers using social media in a way that is transparent and genuine. More advanced classes help employees develop tactics for improving customer service and identifying profitable uses of social media. In general, Xerox uses social media to listen, engage, and provide support to customers.

Xerox also tries to organize its social media efforts around advertising campaigns. A recent trade show in Germany is one example. While Xerox was not the biggest exhibitor, its social media efforts at creating a buzz around what it was doing at the trade show gained it more social mentions than any other vendor at the show.[47]

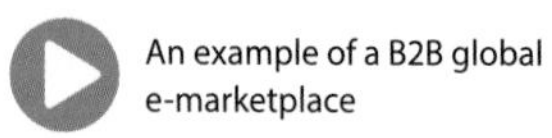
An example of a B2B global e-marketplace

quantity discounts. In 2000, for example, General Motors, Ford, Chrysler, Nissan, Renault, and Peugeot formed an e-marketplace company called Covisint, with the aim of finding lower supplier prices for extremely large purchases of common automotive items used by all of the companies (the company has since expanded its business model).[48] Alternately, an e-marketplace can be formed by a group of suppliers seeking to make their combined product offerings attractive to buyers at favorable terms. One example is United Raw Material Solutions (www.urms.com), which is a consortium of many suppliers in various industries. Finally, e-marketplaces can be a private marketplace set up, for instance, by a large buyer for its suppliers, or by a large supplier for its buyers.

SOCIAL MEDIA

Social media include blogs, discussion boards, online video, podcasting, social networks, and wikis. In a recent survey, the top five social media sites were Facebook, YouTube, Twitter, Yahoo! Answers, and Pinterest.[49] Company managers or owners might use Facebook, for instance, to generate new demand by showcasing completed jobs and communicating how the company supports specific causes.

For several years now, many consumers have been using search engines and social media prior to making a purchase. In fact, according to a survey by GroupM Search, about 40% of consumers who first used Internet searches were then further motivated to use social media prior to making a purchase decision.[50] Unfortunately, businesses have not been as quick to use social media, particularly for B2B sales or purchases. Only now are B2B businesses beginning to explore the use of social media to manage existing customers and seek out new ones. In interviews with over 3,000 corporate executives in May 2012, only 52% said they believed that social media were important to their businesses, and executives were struggling to articulate a vision for how they wanted to use social media.[51]

Companies like Xerox, though, described in the Manufacturing Spotlight above, have found success in using social media. In yet another survey, conducted by Sagefrog Marketing Group in 2012, the most popular B2B marketing tactics were all related to online efforts: website development, email marketing, social media, and search engine optimization.[52]

social media Include blogs, discussion boards, online video, podcasting, social networks, and wikis.

TRENDS IN GLOBAL SUPPLY MANAGEMENT

14.9 Compare current strategies used for improving supplier performance

Today, measuring and tracking supplier performance is an important component of the buyer–supplier relationship. Both informal and formal means are used to evaluate suppliers, although informal evaluations tend to be more common among small organizations. Informally, supply personnel may approach internal product users who maintain contacts with suppliers to gather their performance assessments. Supply managers may also talk to people outside the organization at conferences or professional meetings to see if their impressions of the supplier are on target. Some examples of the formal performance measurement and supplier reward systems are discussed next.

SUPPLIER PERFORMANCE RATING SYSTEMS

Many supply management departments develop internal surveys to evaluate their suppliers' performance in key areas using a rating system. For example, suppliers might be rated on:

- Product and service quality,
- Delivery and order lead time performance,
- Total cost performance,
- Customer service and support management, and
- Product and technology contribution.

Different data collection techniques can be used to evaluate suppliers. Some firms may simply choose to note whether or not expectations were met for each key area. Other companies may develop more detailed evaluation forms where each area has specific performance items that are measured. One example is scoring key areas using a numbering system (0 to 100) and then assigning an overall letter grade. The firm might alternately weight each item based on importance, and then tabulate an overall weighted score.

Chrysler uses a **supplier scorecard** to track supplier performance, based on five criteria: delivery, quality, cost, warranty, and partnership. In 2011, its scorecard was revised for the third time in three years, which underscores the importance it places on good supplier performance. In 2013, Vari-Form was rated one of Chrysler's top-performing suppliers, with delivery and quality scores above 95%.[53] Scorecards are commonly used to rate supplier performance and to compare competing suppliers. In many cases, feedback from these scorecards is an input to the supplier's own quality improvement system. A generic weighted scorecard is shown and described in Example 14.3.

SUPPLIER PERFORMANCE MEETINGS

Company and supplier representatives may meet annually to discuss the supplier's performance. The annual performance meeting is used as a vehicle to provide suppliers a report of their performance, exchange experiences and results, address ways to improve performance, and then develop an action plan for the following year. Suppliers that have not met performance expectations may be placed on a probationary status, with specific goals and a plan for improvement. Probationary suppliers that have not performed well may no longer be used. Minnesota-based Hearth & Home Technologies has supplier management teams using scorecards, and annual supplier meetings to connect senior management with suppliers and to manage supplier performance. The procurement staff keep a 12-month rolling average score for each supplier, and use these scores to categorize suppliers as preferred, approved, or conditional. Annual meetings are then used to drive quality and cost improvements to the suppliers.[54]

supplier scorecard Used by buyers to track supplier performance.

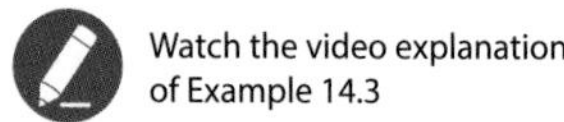

Example 14.3
Weighted Supplier Scorecard

Watch the video explanation of Example 14.3

Supplier Name: The Donohue Co. Item: 8″ Gate Valve					
Performance Criteria	Weight	Actual	Ideal	Rating (0–10)	Weighted Score
On-Time Deliveries	20%	100%	100%	10	2
Price	10%	$1,250	$900	7.2	0.72
Product Availability	10%	100%	100%	10	1
Customer Service	20%	80%	100%	8	1.6
Product Quality	25%	95%	100%	9.5	2.375
Order Lead time	10%	10 days	7 days	7	0.7
Warranty	5%	5 yrs.	5 yrs.	10	0.5
				Total Score	8.895

The Donohue Co. performance was rated using seven performance criteria. Notice that the weights sum to 100%. The actual performance is shown for each criterion and compared to the buyer's ideal or desired performance, to obtain the rating. In this case, the rating scale used is 1–10. For the Price criterion, the rating is found as: 900/1,250 = 0.72 × 10 = 7.2. The weighted score is then calculated as the (weight) × (rating) for each criterion. The total score is found by summing the criterion scores.

SUPPLIER RECOGNITIONS AND AWARDS

The buying organization may also give awards to suppliers with a demonstrated high level of performance, to serve as motivation to continue performing well and to seek further improvements. An annual meeting with suppliers, for example, can be used to hand out the awards, which may include a certificate for "best-in-class" or "most improved."

The Texas Instruments Supplier Excellence Awards have been in use for almost 30 years. Texas Instruments uses the award as a key vehicle for communicating supplier requirements and for defining supplier excellence. "We have a supplier base of more than 14,000 companies," says Rob Simpson, VP of worldwide procurement. "And having a company-wide definition of what makes a top supplier is critical for communicating and improving our standards and quantifying our ever-increasing expectations."[55] Northrop Grumman's Aerospace Systems sector honored 74 companies from the United States, Canada, and Turkey with its annual supplier awards for 2013. Northrop Grumman provides awards to suppliers that achieve distinction in product quality, on-time delivery, customer satisfaction, and robust, lean processes. "Achieving excellence in any endeavor is difficult, but consider how tough it is when we're challenged to do more with less and to keep doing it better," said Lisa Kohl, vice president, global supply chain, Northrop Grumman Aerospace Systems. "Northrop Grumman has set a very high standard and it's our privilege to honor those suppliers that exceed it."[56]

SUMMARY

This chapter discussed a number of issues involved in the purchase of goods and services in an organization. Because of the degree of outsourcing occurring globally, and the need to remain competitive during tough economic times, the process of supply management has become increasingly strategic. Firms spend 50% or more of their sales dollars on direct and indirect materials, services, and capital equipment. During new product development, supplier representatives often serve as members of a cross-functional team, and their input is highly valued in terms of minimizing costs or improving quality. Additionally, with the help of SRM software, supply management professionals today are able to spend more time managing their supply bases. Supply base reduction, strategic sourcing, supplier development and certification programs, and supplier partnering are some of the initiatives implemented by organizations to manage their suppliers more effectively. Supply management must also be aware of opportunities to improve supply chain effectiveness, as well as detect threats that could potentially disrupt supply. For example, ethical and sustainable sourcing is now viewed not only as necessary, but a good way for firms to improve competitiveness. As discussed throughout this chapter, worldwide events play a bigger role than ever in the complexity of supply management.

KEY TERMS

Analytic SRM, 454
Backsourcing, 446
Barter, 451
Cloud-based SRM, 454
Commercial buying, 439
Competitive bidding, 443
Co-sourcing, 447
Counterpurchase, 451
Countertrade, 451
E-marketplaces, 457
E-procurement, 457
E-purchasing, 457
Ethical sourcing, 454
Functional goods, 442
Global sourcing, 448 Green purchasing, 455
Import broker, 448
Import merchant, 448
Incoterms, 451
Innovative goods, 442
Insourcing, 446
Key supplier relationship, 452
Make-or-buy decision, 446
Nearshoring, 446
Offset, 451
P-cards, 442
Procurement, 440
Procurement cards, 442
Purchase spend, 440
Purchasing, 440
Purchasing cycle, 441
Reverse auctions, 457
Social media, 458
Sourcing, 440
Sourcing strategy, 443
Spend categories, 441
Spend management, 440
Statement of work, 444
Strategic alliance, 452
Supplier certification program, 443
Supplier co-location, 453
Supplier relationship management, 452
Supplier scorecard, 459
Supply base, 443
Supply base optimization, 451
Supply base rationalization, 451
Supply base reduction, 451
Supply management, 440
Sustainable sourcing, 455
Tariff, 449
Total cost of ownership (TCO), 444
Transactional SRM, 454
Vendor managed inventory (VMI), 453

FORMULA REVIEW

Total cost of ownership = NPV(salvage value) – Purchase cost – NPV(operating + maintenance costs), where NPV factors are calculated as $(1+d)^{-Year}$, with d = annual discount rate.

Break-even point is found by setting Make cost = Buy cost, or: $F_m + V_m(x) = F_b + V_b(x)$, where: F_m = Manufacturing fixed cost, F_b = Buying fixed cost, V_m = Manufacturing variable cost/unit, V_b = Buying variable cost/unit, x = Units manufactured or purchased.

SOLVED PROBLEMS

1. Hathaway Oil was evaluating compressor suppliers, and wanted to calculate the total cost of ownership for two competing models. It used the following data for comparison. Assume an 8% per year discount rate. Which model should be purchased?

   Model A: purchase cost = \$42,000; operating cost = \$8,000/year; maintenance cost = \$1,000/year; estimated life = 7 years; salvage value = \$15,000.

   Model B: purchase cost = \$48,000; operating cost = \$7,500/year; maintenance cost = \$800/year; estimated life = 7 years; salvage value = \$18,000.

Answer:

	Time 0	Year 1	Year 2	Year 3	Year 4	Year 5	Year 6	Year 7	Total
Model A	–42,000	–9,000	–9,000	–9,000	–9,000	–9,000	–9,000	–9,000+15,000	–\$80,109
Model B	–48,000	–8,300	–8,300	–8,300	–8,300	–8,300	–8,300	–8,300+18,000	–\$80,716
NPV factor	1	0.926	0.857	0.794	0.735	0.681	0.630	0.583	

Based on the calculations, Model A would be slightly preferred.

2. Deem Inc. was trying to decide if it should continue making ear buds or outsource to a supplier. Its fixed costs to make them in-house were \$150,000, and the variable costs were \$3 per unit. One of its suppliers made a similar product for \$7 per unit.
   a. Calculate the break-even point.
   b. If Deem needed 20,000 units, what should it do?

Answer:

a. $F_m + V_m(x) = F_b + V_b(x)$; 150,000 + 3X = 7X; 150,000 = 4X. The break-even point, X = 37,500 units.

b. Since it needs fewer than 37,500 units, it should outsource ear buds.

REVIEW QUESTIONS

1. What is a p-card, and when would you use it?
2. How is competitive bidding used in purchasing?
3. What is a supply base?
4. Describe the total cost of ownership and how it is used.
5. What is outsourcing? Insourcing? Backsourcing? Co-sourcing? Nearshoring? When might you use these?
6. When would a break-even analysis be used by supply management?
7. What is a tariff? How might tariffs be used to support protectionist policies?
8. What is free trade? What are some examples of free trade agreements? Why are they formed?
9. What is countertrade? Is barter a form of countertrade? Why would firms use barter?

10. What is supply base rationalization? Can this be a good practice? Explain.
11. Is supplier relationship management all about software? Explain.
12. What are strategic alliance suppliers?
13. What is early supplier involvement, and how can this be beneficial to both buyer and supplier?
14. What is the difference between transactional and analytic SRM?
15. What is ethical sourcing? Sustainable sourcing? Green sourcing? How are they different?
16. What is a fair trade product?
17. What is an e-marketplace? How do businesses use them?
18. What is a reverse auction? When would you want to use it?
19. How can businesses use social media to buy and sell products?
20. What are supplier scorecards? How are they used?

DISCUSSION QUESTIONS

1. How has the Internet changed purchasing? Use an example.
2. Give some examples of fair trade products. Does Starbucks use fair trade coffee? Why? What certification agencies are being used today?
3. When would supply base rationalization be a bad idea?
4. Why aren't all suppliers "strategic suppliers"?

EXERCISES AND PROJECTS

1. List all of the social media sites you can find. Search for compressors for sale on social media, and see how many companies use social media to sell compressors.
2. Make arguments for outsourcing/offshoring, and backsourcing/re-shoring. Use companies in your discussions.
3. Report on two companies that use supplier scorecards to track supplier performance. Compare the two scorecards.

PROBLEMS

1. The Elizabeth Candies Co. is considering the purchase of a new robotic palletizer and is comparing two suppliers—the Schibrowski Co. and the Rogers Co. The Schibrowski robot system costs \$84,000, with a projected annual operating cost and maintenance cost of \$22,000. Its salvage value is \$30,000 after 7 years. The Rogers system costs \$102,000 with a projected annual operating and maintenance cost of \$19,000 and a salvage value of \$36,000 after 7 years. Which system is preferred if the cash flows are discounted annually at 12%?

2. Find the net present values of the following potential purchases and projected cash flows, discounted at 6% annually:

   Machine A: Purchase price = \$32,000; salvage value after 8 years = \$8,000; annual operating and maintenance cost = \$3600.

   Machine B: Purchase price = \$28,000; salvage value after 8 years = \$10,000; annual operating and maintenance cost = \$4,300.

   Which purchase would be preferred?

3. An ice cream machine has an initial cost of \$22,000. In Year 4, it will require major maintenance at a cost of \$4,000. Each year, it is projected to generate \$5,000 in net revenues for the company. The annual operating cost for the machine is \$800, and it has a salvage value of \$1,500 in Year 8. What is the net present value for this machine, using a 7% annual discount rate?

4. The Velcu Manufacturing Co. is considering outsourcing one of its standard parts to free up capacity for other, more important items. It makes the part for \$22, and requires 12,000 of the parts per year, with a fixed cost contribution of \$5,000 per year. Greg, the supply manager, has identified two capable suppliers that make the part—the Spens Co. sells the product for \$19, but requires an upfront, one-time contractual and transportation fee of \$4,000. The Perkins Co.'s

cost is $19.50 per unit, with no other fees. Determine the break-even points, graph the three alternatives, and show which alternative is preferred for the supply of 12,000 units per year.

5. Your firm can make a product in-house for $1.25 total cost per unit using equipment that would cost $30,000. Your firm could alternately purchase the same item for $1.65 per unit. Indicate the range of units where purchasing would be preferred, and the range where making the product in-house would be preferred.

6. Your firm is contemplating making a part in-house, for use in a product your company manufactures. Currently, your company buys the part for $26 from a reliable supplier. The required quantity is 12,000 parts over the expected life of the product your company sells. One alternative would be to purchase a semiautomated machine at a cost of $38,000, which could make the part for $20. A second alternative would be to buy a fully automated machining center for $95,000 which could make the part for $17. Over what range would each alternative be preferred? What should your company do?

7. A weighted supplier scorecard is shown below. Determine the total weighted score for the supplier. Use a 10-point scale. Note that excellent = 10.

Supplier Name: The Naylor Co. Item: Office Supplies					
Performance Criteria	Weight	Actual	Ideal	Rating (0–10)	Weighted Score
On-time deliveries	20%	80%	100%		
Pricing	25%	Excellent	Excellent		
Availability	5%	100%	100%		
Customer service	30%	75%	100%		
Quality	10%	100%	100%		
Order leadtime	10%	5 days	2 days		

8. A weighted scorecard is used to compare three suppliers for a product. Determine the total weighted scores for the suppliers, and which supplier would be preferred. Use a 10-point scale. Note that excellent = 10, good = 8, fair = 6, poor = 4.

Performance Criteria	Weight	Ideal	Supplier A	Supplier B	Supplier C
On-time performance	30%	100%	92%	98%	96%
Pricing	25%	$25	$28	$26	$25
Customer service	25%	Excellent	Excellent	Good	Fair
Meets quality check	10%	100%	96%	100%	100%
Order change request	10%	Excellent	Fair	Good	Poor

9. A weighted scorecard is used to compare three suppliers for a product, using a 10-point scale. Determine the total weighted scores for the suppliers, and which supplier would be preferred.

Performance Criteria	Weight	Supplier A Performance	Supplier B Performance	Supplier C Performance
On-time performance	23%	8.6	9.2	10
Pricing	28%	10	8.7	8.3
Customer service	20%	9	8	10
Meets quality check	15%	9.2	10	9.4
Supplier contributions	14%	9	8	8

CASE STUDIES

CASE 1: Reverse Auctions at Acme Corporation

Deborah, chief purchasing officer of Acme Corporation, just poured herself a fresh cup of coffee, as she was reviewing the usage statistics of Acme's newly implemented reverse auction system. She had done everything she could to educate potential users about the benefits of this type of e-procurement, but to her surprise, only a fraction of her staff had been using this tool to source products or services. She was convinced of the tool's usefulness, and thought she had conveyed her passion about the approach to her staff as well. Looking at the statistics, this apparently was not the case.

While reverse auctions (RAs) had been around for almost two decades, Acme buyers had been wary of the approach due to the negative publicity the tool had received. In RAs, which are initiated by the buying company, prequalified suppliers are invited to submit their bids online on a request for quotation (provided to them earlier). Once the auction event commences, suppliers are able to see the current lowest bid (but not the company's name). In order to win the business, lower bids have to be submitted (hence the term *reverse*). RAs usually only last between 30 and 60 minutes. Suppliers are able to submit multiple bids, should their previously submitted offer be underbid. The event closes once no lower bids are received within a certain timeframe (usually a few minutes).

Since some very competitive scenarios can ensue, RAs have been portrayed as a tool to achieve significant price reductions, with penalties potentially paid later on, in terms of poorer quality and lack of relationship commitment. A term that had been commonly used was that suppliers were being "squeezed" for their profit margins. This is where the negative perception of the tool came from. Additional user resentment came also from the first experiences at another division of Acme. It turned out that in these auctions, which were run by one of Smith's colleagues, no suppliers were willing to bid on the request for quotation. It may have been due to the suppliers simply not wanting to participate in the event, or the fact that the item put up for bid was a custom-made assembly that would become an integral part of Acme's final product. Was this item perhaps too complex to be put up for bid in RA? In any case, this unsuccessful event a few years ago did not help user perceptions of the tool for Deborah's division. However, significant advances had been made in RAs' applications since then, and best practices had been documented, so that Deborah felt it would be prudent to try the approach again. This is why she spearheaded the implementation in her division, and had her staff trained in the tool. She was a firm supporter of the approach, but she was also cautious in that it should only be applied when appropriate.

In an attempt to illustrate to her staff on when RAs would be most appropriate, she was looking for a set of key characteristics to aid in this effort. Thinking back to her prior experiences with RAs, one key characteristic she identified was to have at least three qualified suppliers that are willing and capable to bid on the business. With fewer than three suppliers, the competitive dynamics would likely not result in the intended outcome. She was also thinking about the types of items that would be ideal candidates for RAs. Based on the less-than-successful experience with the custom-made assembly auctioned by another division, she noted that the items in the auction should be ideally very standard, as opposed to custom-designed or custom-engineered. "There must be more characteristics that would speak in favor of an RA," Deborah was thinking to herself, but she could not come up with any more. "This would be a good project for our new hire in the purchasing department," she contemplated, and sent an email to the new hire to come up with as many characteristics as possible, which would speak in favor of a reverse auction. She had high hopes for the new hire to provide some guidance for her team, so that RAs would be more readily used.

DISCUSSION QUESTIONS

1. What are advantages and disadvantages of RAs?
2. The negative perception of RAs was, in some part, substantiated, due to buyers using the tool to their advantage, without regard for the supplier. Brainstorm successful strategies to use that won't harm the buyer–supplier relationship when applying RAs.
3. Imagine you are the new hire who received Deborah's request to come up with as many characteristics as possible that would speak in favor of RAs. Please list additional potential characteristics that would make the situation more amenable for RAs, and explain how they may facilitate the successful use of this new tool.

Note: Written by Tobias Schoenherr, Michigan State University. This case was prepared solely to provide material for class discussion. The author does not intend to illustrate either effective or ineffective handling of a managerial situation.

CASE 2: WPA Products and the Challenge to Address Child Labor

Ken, chief purchasing officer at WPA Products., was pacing up and down his office. He just got off the phone with Burt, a good friend of his who was working as the VP for purchasing at Great Goods Import (GGI). Ken and Burt, who knew each other from college, ended up going through a similar career path, and both were now in executive positions at import/export companies. Burt was telling Ken about allegations being made against GGI, which was about one of their major suppliers in Bangladesh using child labor. Burt was on his way to the airport to visit the supplier and get a better picture of the situation. Since Ken was doing business with similar suppliers in the same region, Burt thought he would alert Ken.

Both had been talking about the dangers of this happening, and understood the challenges well. They knew that even if they did their due diligence and everything they could to prevent child labor from being used, they still couldn't totally control the issue. After all, it is an issue at the supplier, and not at their companies. However, they knew that if the issue was going to be publicized, their firms would have to carry a lot of the blame and criticism as well, and potentially damage their reputations. This could also result in lost sales for other products.

Burt or his staff had been visiting the supplier on a regular basis to ensure that fair labor practices were employed. This was also clearly spelled out in their supply contracts. Nevertheless, child labor was apparently being employed by this supplier. Could they have done more, in addition to having it spelled out in the contract, and during the regular control visits? What is their responsibility for preventing use of child labor for their products? How can they be sure that no child labor is being used? These were some questions that Burt was considering as he drove to the airport. He had also shared these questions with Ken, and was planning on calling him once he got to his hotel in Dhaka, so that they could bring together their thoughts.

DISCUSSION QUESTIONS

1. Why should Ken or Burt be concerned about the use of child labor at one of their suppliers? Why is it also their problem?
2. What are additional ways that Ken or Burt can help prevent child labor?
3. Why is it so challenging a task to prevent child labor?

Note: Written by Tobias Schoenherr, Michigan State University. This case was prepared solely to provide material for class discussion. The author does not intend to illustrate either effective or ineffective handling of a managerial situation.

CASE 3: Global Sourcing and Risk Management at ABC Corp.

As Randy was starting out the day and looking through the new emails in his inbox on Monday morning, a new message from his supervisor popped up with high importance. The text read as follows: "Randy, I know you have been getting some top-notch education in supply management, and I would greatly appreciate your insight into a real dilemma that we are currently facing. We have been sourcing our bearing assembly for the 456 Model from Mumbai Manufacturing Inc. (MMI) for the last two years, and we have been real pleased with their performance. However, recently, their deliveries have been getting increasingly unpredictable, due to delays in transit. We need to seriously reevaluate our decision to source globally from MMI. Could you please look into this further? It would be great if you can get back to me by the end of the day with some preliminary thoughts." Randy knew he had his work cut out for him.

MMI had been a long-standing partner of ABC Corp., and was recently awarded the bearing assembly for the 456 Model. The decision to go with MMI was primarily based on the prior relationship ABC had with MMI, as well as MMI winning one of the coveted supplier awards from ABC four years ago, distinguishing it as a quality supplier. MMI was proud of this distinction, especially coming from a country such as India, and has been trying to keep up the good work. However, factors outside of its control were straining the relationship, such as the unpredictability of deliveries, as mentioned in the note by Randy's supervisor. With ABC's focus on lean and close-to-zero inventories, unpredictable deliveries were not acceptable.

As Randy looked into reasons for the delays in transit, he was quite surprised by the variety of causes. Several times it was due to the cargo ship having to deviate from its normal route due to bad weather, and in one instance the cause was a pirate threat in the waters the vessel was planning to traverse. There were clearly a lot more risks involved, when compared to a domestic supplier (implying a shorter, but not necessarily less risky, transportation proposition). In order to gauge the feasibility of the relationship with MMI, Randy started to jot down other risk factors that may impede a timely delivery.

DISCUSSION QUESTIONS

1. What are additional risk factors that may impede a timely delivery from an overseas supplier?
2. In general, what risk factors would speak against global sourcing?
3. What would be some strategies going forward? Is global sourcing still feasible, given the unpredictability of deliveries and the focus on lean at ABC?

Note: Written by Tobias Schoenherr, Michigan State University. This case was prepared solely to provide material for class discussion. The author does not intend to illustrate either effective or ineffective handling of a managerial situation.

VIDEO CASE STUDY

Learn more about ***managing global supply chains*** from real organizations that use operations management techniques every day. Stewart Newbold is the Director of Operations at ThinkFoodGroup, the company behind chef José Andrés's restaurants, hotels, food products, media ventures, educational initiatives, and philanthropy. A wide-reaching and diversified organization, ThinkFoodGroup regularly manages their suppliers on a global scale. Watch this short interview to find out how they do it.

iStock/ronniechua

Market access is one of the top factors in a company's site location decision. Manufacturers want to get raw materials in and finished products out efficiently and quickly.

—**RONALD W. DEBARR,** CEO, Northeast Ohio Trade & Economic Consortium[1]

Trucking is not a business where money just rolls through the door. Everybody knows what they need to do: lower empty miles, minimize fuel, maximize revenue per truck.

—**DONALD BROUGHTON,** trucking analyst, Avondale Partners[2]

As companies strive to wring every cent out of their logistics costs, they're increasingly taking a hard look at their reverse logistics practices. And no wonder— they may find a motherlode waiting to be mined.

—**LESLIE HANSEN HARPS,** president, Leslie Harps & Company[3]

LOCATION, LOGISTICS, AND PRODUCT RETURNS

15

LEARNING OBJECTIVES

After completing this chapter, you should be able to:

15.1 Utilize location analysis techniques to compare the attractiveness of potential manufacturing or service locations
15.2 Compare the five modes of transportation
15.3 Discuss warehouse risk pooling and use of the square root rule
15.4 Describe the benefits of returns management
15.5 Discuss the environmental benefits of logistics sustainability

Master the content.

edge.sagepub.com/wisner

NAFTA AND THE I-35 CORRIDOR

The North American Free Trade Agreement (NAFTA) links over 400 million workers producing $17 trillion worth of goods and services in the United States, Canada, and Mexico. Trade among the three countries has dramatically grown from $290 billion in 1993 (the year NAFTA was implemented) to $1.1 trillion in 2012.

A number of areas in the United States are proving to be attractive to businesses seeking import and export opportunities in Canada and Mexico. The Interstate 35 corridor, for example, stretches from Laredo, TX (on the U.S.–Mexico border), to Duluth, MN, which is close to the Canadian border. Additionally, cities like Kansas City, MO, are attracting manufacturers that want to be close to the I-35 corridor.

The Kansas-based Coleman Co. opened a 1.1-million-square-foot facility in Kansas City, due in part to access to I-35. Missouri-based Variform, an automotive supplier, built a 36,000-square-foot production facility in Liberty, MO, due to its proximity to I-35. The plant supplies a Ford plant in Kansas City, and has plans also to supply a Ford plant in Mexico.

In 2009, Kansas City Southern Railroad and Kansas City Southern de Mexico launched a dedicated intermodal service between Kansas City and several Mexican destinations. The area is becoming a key intermodal shipping lane and an alternative to the more congested Chicago shipping lanes among the northeastern United States, the Midwest, and Mexico. Additionally, the third-largest trucking hub in the country is located in the Kansas City area, with facilities operated by dozens of trucking companies.

The state of Nebraska is also well situated for manufacturers to take advantage of trade with Canada and Mexico. The state's geographic position helps attract distribution operations for companies doing business with Mexico and Canada using both rail and the I-35 corridor. One product example is distillers' grain, a by-product of ethanol. Nebraska producers can ship distillers' grain by train to Mexico, where it is used as feed for livestock and poultry. BNSF Railway and Union Pacific move the product between Nebraska, Canada, and Mexico. Additionally, the U.S. Route 81 highway connects York, NE, and Interstate 35, where product can also be transported to Canada and Mexico.[4]

INTRODUCTION

Whenever a good or service is purchased, the seller is expected to deliver the product as promised. The delivery process is a great opportunity for a company to create goodwill with the customer (by delivering as promised) or risk losing that customer's business (by delivering late). To meet delivery expectations, some companies might locate warehouses in the vicinity with ample inventories so there would always be enough supply on hand. Today, though, this expensive approach is widely avoided, as companies have adopted lean practices (as discussed in Chapter 9). Companies are also planning and forecasting collaboratively, as discussed in Chapter 6, to improve forecast accuracies and

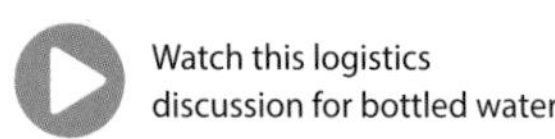
Watch this logistics discussion for bottled water

product delivery times. As a result, organizations are improving their supply chains by reducing order lead times and inventories; locating manufacturing, retail, and distribution centers close to customers; and using various transportation alternatives to achieve lower costs and better customer service. Software applications also play a role in logistics by making shipments visible to trading partners. All of these activities demonstrate the valued role of logistics management.

While there are many definitions of logistics, the Council of Logistics Management (now part of the Council of Supply Chain Management Professionals) defines **logistics** as:

> the process of planning, implementing, and controlling the efficient, effective flow and storage of goods, services, and related information from point of origin to point of consumption for the purpose of conforming to customer requirements.[5]

The important elements of this definition are the flow of goods (or transportation), storage, and meeting customer requirements. This includes all inbound, outbound, internal, and external item movements, including product returns. Simply put, logistics means having the right stuff, in the right location, at the right time. For this reason, location plays a significant role in logistics management.

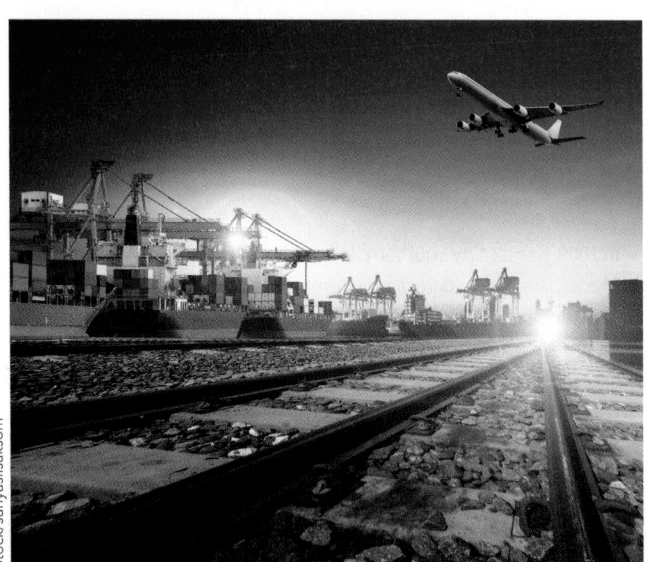
iStock/suriyasilsaksom

Logistics activities are responsible for getting products where they need to be, when the customer wants them.

Logistics personnel make sure goods and services are received correctly from suppliers, moved and stored correctly within the company, and distributed correctly to customers. Logistics creates value throughout the order fulfillment process (recall this is one of the key supply chain processes described in Chapter 1). Inventories are placed where and when they are needed to meet internal and external customer requirements. Logistics managers are responsible for seeing that purchased items arrive at the right time to start a manufacturing process; for raw material and work-in-process storage; for finished goods storage at warehouses and distribution centers; and for making sure customers receive their orders on time. This can be done on a regional, national, and global scale, and can become extremely complex if product movements require dealing with a developing country's poor transportation infrastructure. Thus, **logistics management** combines warehouse location planning, transportation management, and product returns management with the goal of meeting customer service requirements at the lowest possible cost. To accomplish this goal, companies must have an effective logistics strategy, along with a good network of facilities and information capabilities.

This chapter begins with a discussion of location planning and analysis and its impact on logistics decisions, followed by a description of the transportation planning process. The following sections will then discuss the activities involved in warehousing and product returns management. The chapter concludes with a discussion of logistics sustainability.

logistics The process of planning, implementing, and controlling the efficient, effective flow and storage of goods, services, and related information from point of origin to point of consumption for the purpose of conforming to customer requirements.

logistics management Combines warehouse location planning, transportation management, and product returns management with the goal of meeting customer service requirements at the lowest possible cost.

MANUFACTURING AND SERVICE LOCATION STRATEGIES

15.1 Utilize location analysis techniques to compare the attractiveness of potential manufacturing or service locations

Facility location is an important (and often expensive) decision affecting the firm's ability to receive and distribute goods, and to serve customers in cost-effective ways. The locations of production facilities, offices, warehouses, and retail sites affect the efficient flow

iStock/toddmedia

Ford's Kansas City assembly plant is one of the world's largest plants, covering 1,200 acres with 4.7 million square feet of floor space. It makes over 400,000 automobiles per year.

of goods to and from these facilities. Once a decision on locating a facility is made, inbound and outbound transportation arrangements can then be determined. Thus, facility locations have long-lasting impacts on a firm's many supply chains and become an integral part of the firm's logistics strategy. Additionally, with increased globalization and investments in faster transportation and communications technologies, companies are able to locate facilities most anywhere in the world—close to suppliers, close to customers, or somewhere in between.

It might appear that easy access to global markets, the large number of domestic and foreign suppliers, and affordable communications systems make the role of location less important as a source of competitive advantage. On the contrary, just the opposite is true. Ease of access, ample suppliers, and readily available communications mean that many small businesses can compete on the global stage. This has made location decisions even more important for firms desiring to keep their customers happy. Additionally, numerous successful business clusters such as California's Silicon Valley, New York's Wall Street, and Milan's fashion industry show that location is still a very important consideration.

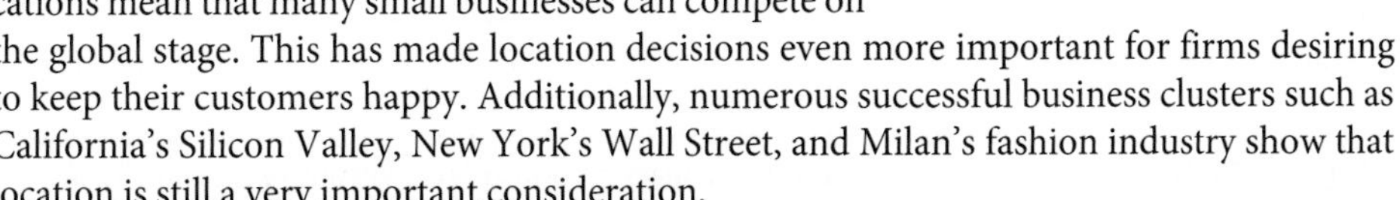

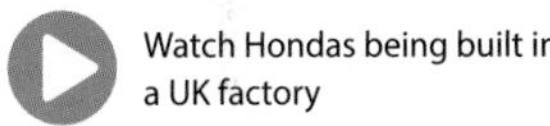

Watch Hondas being built in a UK factory

Location decisions involve identifying the markets to be served by the facility, researching potential locations, and then selecting a site that best meets the company's location requirements. For example, Honda's global location strategy of building cost-effective manufacturing facilities in areas that best meet its requirements as well as those of its local customers has served the company well. Honda's "localization" manufacturing strategy is to start small—build autonomous plants that are self-contained, employ locals, and then build cars as local demand increases. This approach has allowed the company to stay flexible, innovative, efficient, and profitable. Honda was the first Japanese automaker to build a manufacturing facility in the United States—the Accord was produced in a 1-million-square-foot plant in Marysville, OH, in 1982. By 2010, the plant's size was almost four times bigger, and Honda had added eight additional manufacturing facilities in six states.[6] Several factors influencing the location decision are discussed next.

LOCATION CONSIDERATIONS

As mentioned previously, there are three general considerations involved in location decisions—the market to be served, the potential locations available to serve the market, and then the site selection based on company requirements and each potential site's assessment. Manufacturing and warehousing facilities have more location flexibility since goods can be transported anywhere, while services generally must be located within the market served. As shown in Table 15.1, a number of factors can impact where organizations tend to locate facilities. These are discussed in the following sections.

Currency Exchange Rate and Stability

Watch the grand opening of the first McDonald's in Moscow

One factor that impacts business cost and, consequently, location attractiveness for global companies is the value and stability of a country's currency. All organizations doing business internationally will be subjected to the risk of currency exchange rate fluctuation. If a country's currency is valued poorly on the international market, firms with facilities in that country may find it very difficult to take profits out of the country or make payments in local currencies to foreign suppliers. For example, when McDonald's first started opening restaurants in Russia in the 1990s, it built an office tower in Moscow using Russian rubles and then rented office space to multinational companies seeking to do business in Russia, in order to turn Russian profits into hard currency.[7]

location decisions Decisions that involve the market to be served, the potential locations available to serve the market, and then the site selection based on company requirements and each potential site's assessment.

Table 15.1 Important Considerations in the Location Decision

Currency Exchange Rate and Stability	Countries with low-value currencies make it difficult to take profits out of the country.
Labor Issues	Labor availability, productivity, and education; labor union presence and wages and benefits; and labor laws are all key factors in making facility location decisions
Land Availability and Cost	Suburban locations can reduce cost; however it may be difficult to find labor, and transportation systems may be undeveloped.
National Competitiveness	The institutions, policies, and factors that determine the level of productivity and hence competitiveness of a country, are considered.
Proximity to Markets	Locating close to customers reduces delivery times, and is a common strategy for both manufacturers and service providers.
Proximity to Suppliers	Locating close to suppliers can mean faster supplier deliveries and lower inbound transportation costs.
Quality of Life	When companies transfer employees to new locations, they are often interested in the impact on employee well-being.
Regional Trade Agreements	These agreements impact import/export duties and restrictions. As of 2016, there were 625 regional trade agreements around the world.
Taxes and Incentives	Local, state, and national taxes can negatively impact location attractiveness, while foreign trade zones and import duties can have the opposite effect.

Labor Issues

Issues such as labor availability, productivity, education, and skill; labor union presence and wages and benefits; and labor laws are all key factors in making facility location decisions. Countries like Mexico and China have long competed by offering cheap labor, but today they find their competitive advantage dwindling as labor and transportation costs escalate, and as other countries like Vietnam offer even lower labor costs. The apparel industry, for example, which depends heavily on cheap labor, is beginning to shift production from Southern China to Vietnam because of the extremely competitive labor cost there.

While labor cost continues to be an important location factor, competitive advantage is also impacted by labor education and skill set. India is probably one of the best examples—it offers a large workforce that is well educated, skilled, readily adaptable, experienced in Western business practices and technologies, and with a high level of fluency in English that few of its low-cost competitors can match. This makes the country ideal for engineering, IT, banking, and other services requiring a highly educated workforce. According to Sriram Prakash, a senior manager at Deloitte U.K., "The three top criteria for selecting a location are cost, availability of skill and scalability." Prakash says India still has the advantage in terms of scalability, or the ability to accommodate a growing amount of work.[8]

Land Availability and Cost

Outlying or suburban locations can be attractive because of the lower acreage cost and wider range of choices compared to citywide locations. Outlying locations, though, may have difficulty finding an available workforce or a developed transportation network. Most service locations cannot use outlying locations since it would mean a severe loss of customers. As mentioned earlier, when Honda first decided to set up a factory in the United States, it selected Marysville, a small town about 40 miles from Columbus, OH, a major population center. Affordable land near the highway was readily available, and Honda could draw its workforce from Columbus and several closer communities. Similarly, when

Honda built its assembly plant in Alabama, the site was located in Lincoln, 40 miles east of the large city of Birmingham.

National Competitiveness

While a nation's competitiveness might be defined in a number of ways, the World Economic Forum (a nonprofit international organization committed to improving the world, headquartered in Geneva, Switzerland) defines a nation's competitiveness as "the set of institutions, policies, and factors that determine the level of productivity of a country. The level of productivity, in turn, sets the level of prosperity that can be earned by an economy."[9] Thus, **national competitiveness** is highly impacted by a country's productivity, or its ability to transform inputs into outputs.

The Global Competitiveness Report, prepared each year by the World Economic Forum, provides detailed assessments of the productive potential of nations. The annual report ranks 140 countries (as of 2015) in terms of a weighted 12-factor competitiveness index, including such things as innovation, financing, infrastructure, workforce education and health, and technology. For 2015, the top 10 countries in the report, in order, were: Switzerland, Singapore, the United States, Germany, the Netherlands, Japan, Hong Kong, Finland, Sweden, and the United Kingdom.[10] Countries with high competitiveness rankings could potentially be better candidates for a facility location, compared to less competitive countries.

Watch a discussion of the Global Competitiveness Report

Proximity to Markets

Interestingly, a survey of foreign manufacturers in China found that a large portion of these businesses were located in China to gain access to local markets, rather than for export reasons.[11] Similarly, as discussed earlier in the chapter, a number of Japanese automobile manufacturers have built assembly plants in the United States to be close to the U.S. automobile market. In the service industry, proximity to customers is even more critical. Few customers will frequent a remotely located gas station, fast-food restaurant, or supermarket if another, more accessible alternative is available. The Manufacturing Spotlight below describes East Penn's decision to locate a battery manufacturing facility in China to better serve its customers.

national competitiveness The set of institutions, policies, and factors that determine the level of productivity of a country. The level of productivity, in turn, sets the level of prosperity that can be earned by an economy.

MANUFACTURING SPOTLIGHT

East Penn's Wujiang Facility

Pennsylvania-based battery maker East Penn Manufacturing Co. was founded in 1946, and since then, it has expanded rapidly. Today, East Penn has 100 warehouses, distribution centers, and subsidiaries in the United States and Canada, along with joint ventures in Austria, Brazil, India, and Mexico. In 2006, East Penn located its first Chinese battery recycling and manufacturing facility in Wujiang.

In the mid-1990s, East Penn began selling its products in China through distributors and resellers. As sales increased, the demand for after-sales service also grew, so East Penn decided it needed to locate there, to better serve its customers. East Penn ultimately chose to locate in the Wujiang Economic Development Zone, since it was given tax and customs fees reductions. The facility will eventually provide after-sales services throughout the Asia–Pacific region. The company has sent employees from its U.S. headquarters to train Chinese staff, and some have traveled to Pennsylvania for further training.

China's growing economy and its desire for clean energy offer many opportunities for companies like East Penn. In addition to world-class transportation, communications, and utility systems, China wants to attract U.S. brands and technical products such as industrial batteries. Today, East Penn's Chinese facility is well positioned to benefit from that demand.[12]

iStock/Baloncici

Proximity to Suppliers

Many manufacturing firms prefer locations close to suppliers for quick material availability and inbound transportation cost reasons. The proximity of suppliers has an impact on delivery timing and, consequently, the effectiveness of the supply chain. For example, Japanese electronics manufacturers are finding that China is a good place to locate manufacturing facilities due to the high percentage of components that are made in China. In contrast, Arkansas-based American Railcar Inc. tends to use only U.S. suppliers when making railcars, in order to better control its inbound shipments and because of the stringent transportation safety regulations. In 2011, Caterpillar announced plans to move some production from Japan to Athens, GA, in part to be close to its base of suppliers.[13]

Quality of Life

While **quality of life** means different things to different people, companies often consider the impact on employee well-being when transferring employees to a new facility location. In a survey conducted among a cross-section of Americans a few years ago, people were asked to define quality of life. The most common response was along the lines of "getting good things, living well, and enjoying peace, security, and happiness."[14] To aid companies seeking locations with a good quality of life, a number of indexes have been developed over the years, and there are some commonalities regarding the factors measured in these indexes, which include the following: material well-being; health; political stability, freedom, and security; family and community well-being; climate and air quality; and job security.[15] For example, the top five countries listed in Numbeo's Quality of Life Index of 2015 were: Switzerland, Germany, Sweden, the United States, and Finland.[16]

When Human Identification Technologies of Redlands, CA, searched for a location to open a lab for 100 forensic science employees, it eventually decided on Kirksville, a town of 18,000 in Missouri, specifically for quality of life reasons. Kirksville offers a nationally recognized university and a premier facility for training osteopathic physicians. Additionally, the area's public school system has received national awards for excellence. In fact, the CEO was so impressed with the area he moved his family there.[17]

Regional Trade Agreements

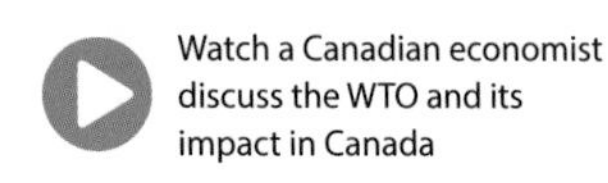
Watch a Canadian economist discuss the WTO and its impact in Canada

The **World Trade Organization** (WTO), based in Geneva, Switzerland, helps to negotiate and enforce regional trade agreements.[18] Its goal is to ensure that producers, importers, and exporters can conduct trade smoothly. These trade agreements, some of which were discussed in Chapter 14, can greatly impact the attractiveness of locations, and the flows of goods and services. The WTO is a nonprofit international body with 162 member countries, as of 2015. Trade disputes can arise when one member country believes another is violating a trade agreement negotiated within the WTO. For instance, in July 2013, Japan and Russia were trying to resolve a dispute involving a claim by Japan that Russia was charging a recycling fee on imported automobiles, which was inconsistent with several trade agreements between the two countries.[19] One recent free trade agreement for the United States is with Panama. With the expansion of the Panama Canal, that country's economy is booming. Prior to 2012 (when the agreement went into effect), import tariffs for U.S. goods ranged from 7–260%. The agreement eliminates tariffs and other trade barriers for the U.S. exports. As U.S. firms see their sales in Panama increasing, they will eventually consider locating regional facilities there.[20]

quality of life Material well-being; health; political stability, freedom, and security; family and community well-being; climate and air quality; and job security.

World Trade Organization A nonprofit organization based in Geneva, Switzerland. It helps to negotiate and enforce regional trade agreements. Its goal is to ensure that producers, importers, and exporters can conduct trade smoothly.

Taxes and Incentives

The level of local, regional, and national taxes—along with any monetary incentives that might be offered to businesses—are important location considerations. At the federal level, a tariff is a tax imposed by the government on imported goods to protect local industries and/or raise revenue. Thus, countries with high tariffs would discourage companies from importing goods into the country, and consequently provide encouragement for companies to set up factories within the country to sell domestically. To encourage foreign trade, many governments have set up **foreign trade zones** where parts and materials can be imported duty-free as long as the imports are used as inputs to the local production of goods that are eventually exported. If the goods are sold domestically, duties are paid as soon as the goods leave the free trade zones. Outside the United States, foreign trade zones are also referred to as **free trade zones**.

Nevada, considered a business-friendly state in the United States, does not have a corporate income tax, state personal income tax, corporate franchise tax, or inventory tax. Companies such as Amazon.com have taken advantage of this by setting up large distribution centers in Nevada. According to an annual survey of over 500 CEOs across the United States in 2015, the top five business-friendly states were Texas, Florida, North Carolina, Tennessee, and Georgia. On the other hand, the states with the worst climate for businesses were California, New York, and Illinois.[21]

Zuma/Alamy

Amazon.com's Fernley, NV, 750,000-square-foot fulfillment center operates 24 hours per day, 365 days per year.

LOCATION ANALYSIS TECHNIQUES

Two of the more basic techniques that organizations use to assist in making location decisions are described here: the weighted-factor rating technique and the center-of-gravity technique. While a number of other location analysis techniques exist, such as mathematical programming models, simulation models, and network planning models, these are beyond the scope of this text, and interested readers are referred to several textbooks on this topic.[22]

The Weighted-Factor Rating Technique

The **weighted-factor rating technique**, similar to the weighted supplier scorecard in Chapter 14, can be used to compare the attractiveness of potential manufacturing or service locations along a number of quantitative and qualitative dimensions. Analyzing potential facility locations using this approach involves the following steps:

1. Identify all factors considered important to the facility location decision.
2. Assign a weight to each factor in terms of its relative importance (typically, the weights sum to 1).
3. Assign a performance score to each factor, for each location considered. Scores can be assigned quantitatively or qualitatively. For example, if the factor is *labor availability*, scores can be based on the sizes of each location's available workforce; if the factor is *quality of life*, a more qualitative approach might be used. Typical scoring systems might vary from 1 to 10 or 1 to 100.
4. Multiply each factor score by its weight, and sum the weighted scores for each potential location.
5. Select the location with the highest total weighted score.

The weighted-factor score is thus calculated as:

$$S_A = \Sigma\, w_i F_i$$

where

S_A = weighted-factor score for location A;

w_i = weight used for factor i;

F_i = factor i.

foreign trade zones To encourage trade, governments establish areas where parts and materials can be imported duty-free as long as the imports are used as inputs to the local production of goods that are eventually exported; also called free trade zones outside the United States.

free trade zones *See* Foreign trade zones.

weighted-factor rating technique An analysis method that can be used to compare the attractiveness of potential manufacturing or service locations along a number of quantitative and qualitative dimensions.

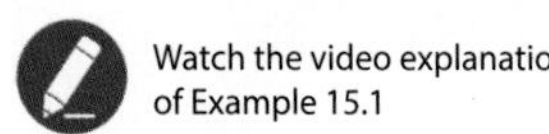

Example 15.1
The Weighted-Factor Rating Technique

Watch the video explanation of Example 15.1

The following five factors have been identified as necessary for analyzing three potential distribution center locations—Los Angeles, Las Vegas, and Phoenix. An analysis team has determined the important location factors, weights, and scores to be used in the analysis, and these are shown here.

Location Factor	Weight	Los Angeles	Las Vegas	Phoenix
Land/construction costs	0.20	64	92	100
Skilled labor availability	0.15	100	78	82
Distance to market	0.30	100	88	70
Taxes/incentives	0.25	68	85	100
Quality of life	0.10	94	87	100

The Analysis

For each factor, the best location was given the maximum score of 100 by the evaluation team, and the other two were scaled downward from the best performance. For the Land/Construction Cost factor, for example, Phoenix had the lowest projected cost and was awarded 100 points (using a 1–100 scale). Las Vegas had a somewhat higher cost, while the Los Angeles cost was considerably higher. Phoenix scored the highest on three of the factors, while Los Angeles scored the highest on the other two. Calculating the total scores reveals:

Los Angeles = 0.2(64) + 0.15(100) + 0.3(100) + 0.25(68) + 0.1(94) = 84.2

Las Vegas = 0.2(92) + 0.15(78) + 0.3(88) + 0.25(85) + 0.1(87) = 86.5

Phoenix = 0.2(100) + 0.15(82) + 0.3(70) + 0.25(100) + 0.1(100) = **88.3**

Since Phoenix has the highest score, it is the recommended location.

Note that the factors, the weights, and the total scores can be highly influenced from bias on the part of the analyst; therefore, a location analysis team should be used when analyzing and selecting facility locations. The team should include representatives from marketing, purchasing, production, finance, and logistics, along with representatives from any key suppliers and customers impacted by the location. Example 15.1 illustrates the weighted-factor rating technique.

The Center-of-Gravity Technique

Another common method used in locating a single facility is the **center-of-gravity technique**, also referred to as the **centroid method**. This technique finds a central location that tends to minimize the total transportation costs between the proposed facility and any number of markets the proposed facility will serve. (This method assumes that transportation costs vary directly with distance, and no special shipping costs are considered.) The analysis requires the shipping volume for each market and the (X,Y) coordinate distances from a given point of origin. For example, an organization's logistics department may want to determine the lowest transportation cost location for a distribution center, which will serve several markets. The center-of-gravity X and Y coordinates can be found using:

center-of-gravity technique Graphically finds a central location that tends to minimize the total transportation costs between the proposed facility and any number of markets the proposed facility will serve. (This method assumes that transportation costs vary directly with distance, and no special shipping costs are considered.) Also referred to as the centroid method.

centroid method *See* center-of-gravity technique.

$$C_x = \frac{\Sigma(V_i d_{xi})}{\Sigma V_i} \text{ and } C_y = \frac{\Sigma(V_i d_{yi})}{\Sigma V_i}$$

where:

C_x = X coordinate of the center-of-gravity location;

C_y = Y coordinate of the center-of-gravity location;

V_i = Volume of shipments required by market i;

d_{xi} = X coordinate distance to market i from the coordinate grid origin; and

d_{yi} = Y coordinate distance to market i from the coordinate grid origin.

The advantage of the center-of-gravity technique is that it is relatively easy to use once market demand and grid locations are determined. Only an approximate location is possible, though, when using the center-of-gravity method, since the calculated coordinate location may be infeasible (it may be in the middle of a lake or highway, for example). The next step, then, would be to find the closest *feasible* location—an available plot of land, for example, which provides easy access to transportation and labor. Example 15.2 provides a sample problem and solution for a proposed distribution center.

LOCATION ANALYSIS SOFTWARE

A number of location analysis software solutions are also used when businesses have more specific location needs, and two of the solutions available are discussed here. Connecticut-based Pitney Bowes, an e-commerce solution provider, offers its AnySite® platform to provide data to optimize a site location. AnySite performs predictive analytics and modeling for business location selection decisions. U.S. health club operator 24 Hour Fitness, for example, spends several million dollars to launch every new site. It needs insightful data and analysis to forecast site performance over a long-term horizon to avoid the costly mistake of a poor-performing facility. The AnySite platform allowed 24 Hour Fitness to expand its evaluation to include not only demographic data, but also the psychographics and behaviors most relevant to its industry. When assessing locations for new facilities, 24 Hour Fitness relies on AnySite to analyze markets, forecast member potential, and pinpoint pockets of opportunity.[23]

Massachusetts-based Caliper, a provider of geographic information systems and transportation software, offers its desktop Maptitude solution to analyze and understand how geography affects a business. Maptitude allows businesses to visualize data in new and different ways, and to unearth geographic patterns hidden in company data. CKE Restaurant Holdings, owner of Hardee's and Carl's Jr. fast-food restaurants, uses Maptitude to delineate its franchise territories and provide its franchisees with market maps highlighting existing restaurant proximities, competitor locations, and target areas for future growth. CKE's franchisees use Maptitude to easily comprehend the complex components of their specific markets. Previously, when evaluating trade areas for a new franchise, CKE relied on individual variables such as basic census characteristics, competition, and activity generators. The data were spread across various platforms and software products throughout the organization. It was difficult to get a clear picture of those market areas with the highest probability for success. CKE uses Maptitude to create a development "blueprint" for future restaurant development.[24]

TRANSPORTATION PLANNING

15.2 Compare the five modes of transportation

transportation planning Involves matching one or more modes of transportation with the types of items to be shipped, the needs of shippers and customers, and the laws governing transportation. Selecting one or more transportation modes is a function of how fast things must be delivered; the size, weight, and value of the items to be shipped; the transportation modes available; and the funds available to pay for transportation.

Transportation planning involves matching one or more modes of transportation with the types of items to be shipped, the needs of shippers and customers, and the laws governing transportation. One objective of transportation planning is to design transportation systems to successfully fulfill customer orders. Selecting transportation modes is a function of how fast things must be delivered; the size, weight, and value of the items to be shipped;

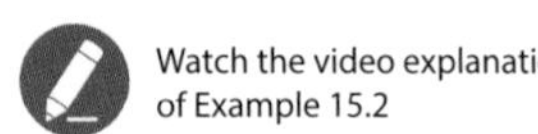

Example 15.2
The Center-of-Gravity Technique

Watch the video explanation of Example 15.2

The Stanley Company has four markets it wishes to serve with a centrally located distribution center. Below is a grid system that was overlaid on a map of the area containing the four markets. The *(X,Y)* coordinates in kilometers for the four markets are: M1 = (200, 860); M2 = (800, 625); M3 = (300, 325); and M4 = (720, 280).

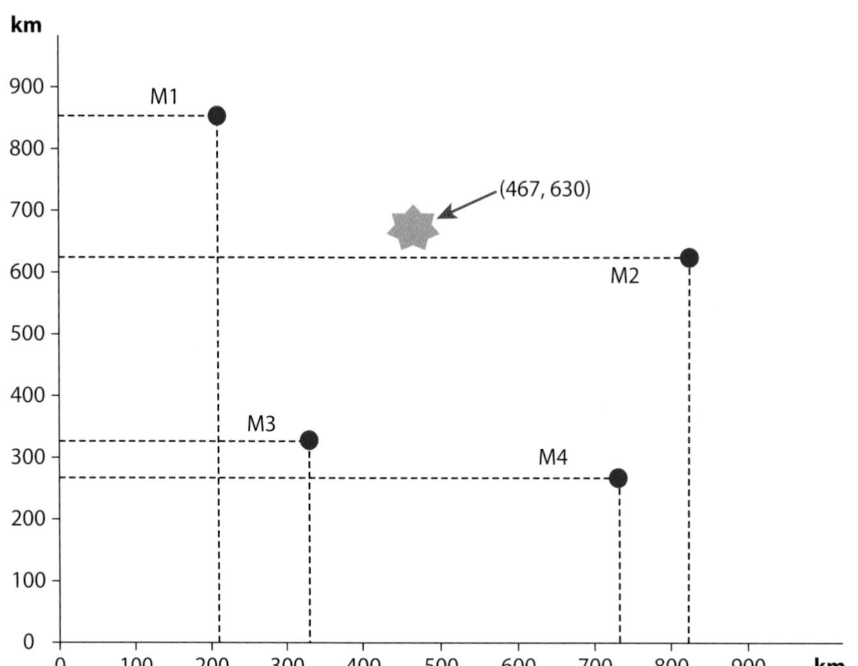

The projected annual demand for each of the markets is:

$V_1 = 4000$ units, $V_2 = 3100$ units, $V_3 = 1600$ units, and $V_4 = 1200$ units.

Finding the center-of-gravity location for the distribution center:

$$C_x = \frac{\Sigma(V_i d_{xi})}{\Sigma V_i} = \frac{(4000 \times 200) + (3100 \times 800) + (1600 \times 300) + (1200 \times 720)}{9900} = 467 \text{ km, and}$$

$$C_y = \frac{\Sigma(V_i d_{yi})}{\Sigma V_i} = \frac{(4000 \times 860) + (3100 \times 625) + (1600 \times 325) + (1200 \times 280)}{9900} = 630 \text{ km}$$

The *(X,Y)* coordinate of the proposed distribution center is then (467, 630), which is shown in the grid map above. Note that the center-of-gravity location is closer to markets M1 and M2. This is due to the higher demand in these markets.

the transportation modes available; and the funds available to pay for transportation. The following section describes the five most common modes of transportation.

MODES OF TRANSPORTATION

There are five basic **modes of transportation**: truck, rail, air, water, and pipeline carriers. These modes and the amount of freight they haul each year in the United States are shown in Table 15.2. In 2012, the U.S. transportation system moved approximately 17 billion tons of freight, valued at \$12 trillion.[25] Note the dominance of trucking among the five modes and the relative high value of shipments carried by air freight, when compared to its small tonnage hauled. Each of these modes offers distinct advantages to customers, and their selection depends on a number of factors, as mentioned previously. Discussions of each of the modes follow.

modes of transportation Air, rail, truck, water, and pipeline carriers.

Table 15.2 2012 U.S. Domestic Freight Hauled

Mode	Tons (millions)	% of Total	Value (billion $)	% of Total
Truck	12,973	77.2	10,531	88.0
Rail	1,855	11.0	400	3.3
Pipeline	1,421	8.5	699	5.8
Water	542	3.2	170	1.4
Air	3	.02	163	1.4
Total	16,794		11,963	

Source: U.S. Bureau of Transportation Statistics, www.rita.dot.gov

Truck

Trucks (also referred to as **motor carriers**) travel the United States on over 4 million miles of highway, and are the most flexible mode of transportation. As shown in Table 15.2, trucks account for the vast majority of U.S. freight hauled. Trucks have low fixed and variable costs relative to other modes, and can compete favorably with rail and air, particularly for distances shorter than 1,000 miles.

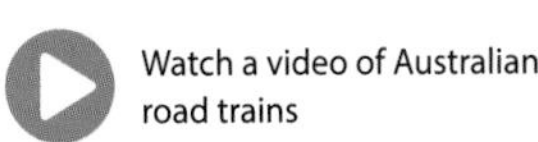
Watch a video of Australian road trains

motor carriers Trucks.

less-than-truckload carriers Trucks that move small packages or shipments taking up less than one truckload. The shipping fees are higher per hundred weight (cwt) than TL fees, since the carrier must consolidate smaller shipments into one truckload, then break the truckload back down into individual shipments at the destination for individual deliveries.

truckload carriers Trucks that move shipments taking up an entire truckload.

rail carriers A designated mode of transportation. Rail service tends to be relatively slow and inflexible; however, rail carriers charge less than air and motor carriers.

The primary disadvantages for trucks are weather and traffic problems. The tragic collapse of the eight-lane Minneapolis, MN, I-35 West Bridge over the Mississippi River in August 2007 killed 13 people and provided a painful reminder of the importance of transportation infrastructure. Per day, more than 140,000 vehicles, including approximately 5,700 commercial vehicles, used this bridge—Minnesota's busiest. In 2005, the bridge was inspected and received a low safety rating, indicating that it should have been either repaired or replaced.[26]

Trucks can be classified as **less-than-truckload** (LTL) **carriers** or **truckload** (TL) **carriers.** LTL carriers move small packages or shipments that take up less than one truckload, and the shipping fees are higher per hundred weight (cwt) than TL fees, since the carrier must consolidate smaller shipments into one truckload, then break the truckload back down into individual shipments at the destination for individual deliveries. However, for small-item shippers, using LTL carriers is still a much less expensive alternative than using a TL carrier.

The LTL industry in the United States is made up of a small number of large, national LTL carriers. The top five U.S. LTL carriers are FedEx Freight, Con-Way Freight, YRC Freight, UPS Freight, and Old Dominion Freight Line. In contrast, there are over 30,000 TL carriers in the United States (most are one- or two-truck companies privately owned by the drivers).

Rail

Rail carriers compete most favorably when the distance is long and the shipments are heavy or bulky. At one time in the United States, rail carriers transported the majority of goods shipped; however, since World War II, their share of the transportation market has steadily fallen. As of 2012, seven Class I (or national) railroads, 21 regional railroads, and 510 local railroads used over 140,000 miles of privately owned and maintained railroad tracks in the United States.[27] Rail service tends to be relatively slow and inflexible; however, rail carriers charge less than air and motor carriers. To better compete, railroads have begun purchasing trucking companies and can thus offer point-to-point pickup and delivery

iStock/pamspix

On February 18, 2006, an Australian-built Mack truck pulled 113 semitrailers, 4,837 feet long, for the record of the longest road train (multiple loaded trailers) ever pulled. Most road trains, though, consist of three to four trailers, similar to the one shown here.

iStock/Nikada

The Chinese Shanghai Maglev is generally considered to be the fastest regularly scheduled high-speed rail.

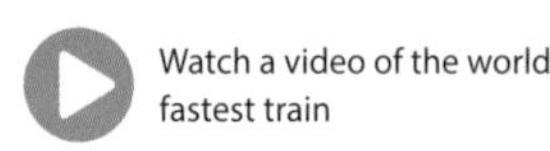

Watch a video of the world's fastest train

service using trucks and flatcars that carry the truck trailers (known as **trailer-on-flatcar service** or TOFC service, a form of intermodal transportation discussed later in this chapter).

One of the trends in passenger rail transportation is the use of **high-speed trains**. While there is no official definition of the term, high-speed rail usually refers to a type of rail transportation that operates significantly faster than traditional rail traffic, using specialized trains and dedicated tracks. Today, they are operated in the United States by Amtrak along the northeast corridor (Boston–New York–Washington, DC). Bombardier Inc., a Montreal-based transportation and aerospace company, designed and manufactured Amtrak's Acela Express, an electric high-speed train. These trains can make the Washington, DC–Boston trip in about 6.5 hours, averaging approximately 70 miles per hour, although top speeds can reach 120 miles per hour (other slower trains and lack of straight-line track have tended to reduce the average speeds).[28] There are several other projects attempting to get started in the United States, but so far, the high cost is creating quite a bit of opposition.

In comparison, the Chinese Shanghai Maglev, shown in the photo on this page, has a top operating speed of 431kph (268mph), and is generally regarded as the fastest high-speed train. In Europe, one of the most modern high-speed trains, the AGV Italo, began service in 2012 and has a maximum operational speed of 360kph (224mph). The Japanese high-speed Shinkansen bullet trains have carried millions of passengers for years on an extensive network of track.[29]

Air

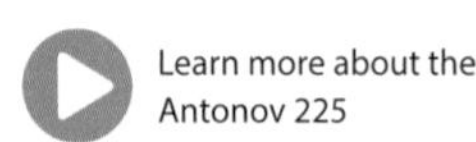

Learn more about the Antonov 225

Transporting goods using **air carriers** is very expensive relative to other modes, but also very fast—particularly for long distances. As shown in Table 15.2, the amount of freight hauled is very small relative to other modes, since airlines cannot carry extremely heavy or bulky cargo (an exception is the world's largest commercial cargo airliner, the Ukrainian-built Antonov 225, which can carry a payload more than twice the weight of what a Boeing 747 freighter can carry).[30] For light, high-value goods that need to travel long distances quickly, air transportation is the best of the modal alternatives. The Manufacturing Spotlight on the next page describes one of the newest and fastest passenger airliners.

Although the incidence of shipment damage is quite low and schedule frequency is good, air transportation is limited in terms of geographic coverage. Most small cities in the United States, for example, do not have airports or regularly scheduled air service; therefore, air transportation service must be combined with trucks for these locations. As of 2013, there were 503 commercial airports in the United States.

Approximately half of the goods transported by air are carried by freight-only airlines like FedEx, the world's largest air cargo airline. This represents a significant change since the late 1960s, when most air cargo was hauled by passenger airlines.

Water

Shipping goods by **water carrier** is very inexpensive but also very slow and inflexible. There are several types of water transportation, including inland waterway, lake, coastal and intercoastal ocean, and global deep-sea carriers. Most of the inland waterway transportation is used to haul heavy, bulky, low-value materials such as coal, grain, and sand, and competes primarily with rail and pipeline carriers. Inland water transport is obviously limited to areas accessible by water, and hence growth in this area of transportation is limited. Like rail and air transportation, water carriers are sometimes paired with motor carriers to enable door-to-door pickup and delivery service.

In the United States, Mississippi River barges are used to transport over 7 million tons of commodities each year worth about $2.8 billion, but a lengthy drought over much of the country is placing much of this hauling in jeopardy. The U.S. Army Corps of Engineers has been dredging the middle Mississippi in an attempt to maintain a 9-foot-deep channel,

trailer-on-flatcar service An intermodal form of transportation using trucks and rail carrier flatcars that carry the truck trailers. Also called piggyback service.

high-speed trains Usually refers to a type of rail transportation that operates significantly faster than traditional rail traffic, using specialized trains and dedicated tracks.

air carriers A very expensive mode of transportation, but also very fast—particularly for long distances.

water carrier A very inexpensive transportation mode, and also very slow and inflexible. There are several types of water transportation, including inland waterway, lake, coastal and intercoastal ocean, and global deep-sea carriers.

MANUFACTURING SPOTLIGHT

Boeing's 787 Dreamliner Begins Operating

The Boeing 787 Dreamliner is the first airplane to combine long-distance capabilities and mid-size capacity, allowing airlines to fly longer nonstop routes more quickly, which is preferred by travelers. The 787 set two world records for speed and distance for the airplane's weight class when it departed from Seattle in 2011 and flew 10,710 miles nonstop to Dhaka, Bangladesh. After a 2-hour refueling, the airplane continued around the world, returning to Seattle in a record time of 42 hours and 27 minutes. The airplane is 20% more fuel efficient than similarly sized airplanes.

iStock/Tokarsky

Aside from performance, the 787 improves the passenger experience with an innovative interior design, shown here. Boeing studied the psychological experiences of passengers during commercial flights, and these experiences were then integrated into cabin design. A broad entryway welcomes passengers into the spacious cabin. Vaulted ceilings give the space a sense of openness. Other interior features include larger windows and blue-sky lighting effects. The nearly vertical cabin sidewalls provide more room and personal space. The cabin is pressurized to an altitude of 6,000 feet, which translates to a better flight experience. Finally, enhanced gust suppression technology senses turbulence and commands wing control surfaces to counter it, which greatly smooths the ride and reduces dangers of motion sickness.[31]

which is what most barges need to navigate the river. At the start of 2013, some analysts were fearful that eventually the river would need to be closed to traffic entirely.[32]

There have been developments in **deep-sea transportation** that have made water transportation cheaper and more desirable, even with the slow transportation times. The development and use of supertankers and containerships have added a new dimension to water transportation. Many of today's oil supertankers are more than 1,200 feet long (that's four U.S. football fields) and carry over 2 million barrels of oil. The largest oil supertanker was the *Seawise Giant*, measuring 1,500 feet in length and able to carry more than 560,000 tons, or 4 million barrels of oil.[33] With these ships, oil-producing nations can today cheaply ship large quantities of oil around the globe anywhere demand exists. Even small shippers can ship items overseas cheaply because of the ability to consolidate small shipments in containers that are placed on board containerships.

iStock/KiraVolkov

Mississippi River barges may have to curtail operations if the river depth cannot be kept at greater than 9 feet.

Shipping containers allow most any packaged product to be shipped overseas, and add an element of protection to the cargo. **Containerships** carry the majority of the world´s water-transported manufactured goods, and they can carry more than 10,000 standard 20-foot equivalent containers (these are normally 20 feet in length, 8.5 feet high, and 8 feet wide), holding up to 52,000 pounds each, with a total containership value sometimes as high as $300 million. At any given time, there are approximately 5 to 6 million containers being shipped between countries using containerships.[34]

deep-sea transportation The use of oil supertankers and containerships.

containerships Carry the majority of the world´s water-transported manufactured goods; can carry more than 10,000 standard 20-foot equivalent containers.

pipeline carriers A very specialized mode of transportation; once the initial investment of the pipeline is recovered, there is very little additional maintenance cost, so long-term pipeline transportation tends to be very inexpensive. Pipelines can haul materials that are only in a liquid or gaseous state, and so the growth potential for pipelines is limited.

Pipeline

Pipeline carriers are very specialized with respect to the products they can carry; however, once the initial investment of the pipeline is recovered, there is very little additional maintenance cost, so long-term pipeline transportation tends to be very inexpensive. Pipelines

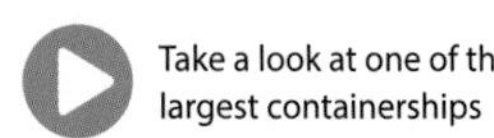
Take a look at one of the largest containerships

can haul materials that are only in a liquid or gaseous state, and so the growth potential for pipelines is limited. One of the items pipelines haul is coal, and they do this by first pulverizing coal into small particles, then suspending it in water to form **coal slurry**. When the coal slurry reaches its destination, the coal and water are separated. Other items transported include water, oil, gasoline, and natural gas. The continuous nature of pipeline flow is what makes it unique—once the product reaches its destination, it is continuously available.

Pipelines are today being constructed to haul large quantities of natural gas and oil from desolate areas to existing processing facilities hundreds and even thousands of miles away. In 2012, Gazprom, the Russian government–owned gas giant, along with a number of other European companies, completed the world's longest (759 miles) subsea gas pipeline, linking Russian gas fields with Germany and other European markets using a Baltic Sea route. Today, the renamed company, Nord Stream AG, transports about 1,900 billion cubic feet of gas per year through the pipeline.[35] So long as the world remains dependent on energy products such as coal, oil, and natural gas, there will be a need for pipeline transportation.

INTERMODAL TRANSPORTATION

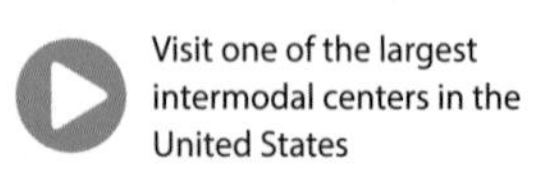
Visit one of the largest intermodal centers in the United States

Intermodal transportation, or the use of combinations of the transportation modes, makes the movement of goods much more convenient and efficient. Intermodal transportation actually dates back to the 18th century, prior to the railways. Wood containers were used for shipping coal on canal barges in England in the 1780s. The coal containers were then transferred to horse-drawn carriages. Wooden coal containers were also used on railways starting in the 1830s on the Liverpool and Manchester Railway.[36]

coal slurry Pulverized coal particles, suspended in water.

intermodal transportation The use of combinations of the transportation modes, such as TOFC and COFC.

container-on-flatcar (COFC) A form of intermodal transportation. It uses containers and rail carrier flatcars that carry the containers; also called piggyback service.

piggyback service A type of intermodal transportation service, such as TOFC and COFC.

ROROs Roll-on–roll-off containerships.These allow truck trailers, automobiles, heavy equipment, and specialty cargo to be directly driven on and off the ship into secured below-deck garages, without the use of cranes.

Most large intermodal transportation companies today such as J. B. Hunt, Schneider, and FedEx offer one-stop, door-to-door shipping capabilities—they transport shippers' goods by determining the best intermodal transportation and warehousing arrangements to meet customer requirements as cheaply as possible. Here is a transportation example using a number of intermodal combinations:

> A manufacturing company packs a standard 8-foot container for shipment to an overseas customer. The container is sealed and hauled by a motor carrier for transport to a nearby rail terminal. The container is then loaded onto a flatcar and double-stacked with another container where it is then transported to a seaport on the U.S. west coast. Upon arrival, the container is placed aboard a containership and transported to Japan. In Japan, the container is loaded onto another motor carrier for transport to its final destination, where it finally is unpacked. In this example, goods were only packed and unpacked one time. The container was used in three modes of transportation and remained sealed until the final destination when customs authorities unsealed, examined, and accepted the goods.

Nick Suydam/Alamy

Trains routinely carry double-stacked containers on flatcars, destined for coastal ports and container ships.

The above example highlights a number of intermodal transportation combinations. The most common are truck trailer-on-flatcar (TOFC) and **container-on-flatcar (COFC)**, also called **piggyback service**. The same containers can be placed on board containerships and freight airliners. These combinations attempt to combine the flexibility of motor carriers with the economy of rail and/or water carriers. The BNSF Railway, headquartered in Texas, operates one of the largest railroad networks in North America, and moves more intermodal traffic than any other rail system in the world today. Intermodal combinations account for about half of the number of units transported by BNSF.[37]

Another example of intermodal transportation are **ROROs**, or *roll-on–roll-off* containerships. These allow truck trailers, automobiles, heavy equipment, and specialty cargo to be directly driven on and off the ship, into secured below-deck

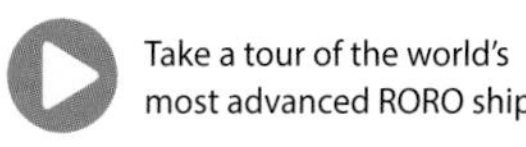

Take a tour of the world's most advanced RORO ship

garages, without the use of cranes. The New Jersey–based Atlantic Container Line operates the largest and most versatile RORO containerships in the world, capable of carrying a wide variety of oversized cargo. Its RORO vessels are some of the most flexible ships operating today—its G-3 vessels can carry 1,000 automobiles, plus 1,850 standard 20-foot containers.[38]

TRANSPORTATION SECURITY

Transportation security refers to the safeguarding of transportation systems to ensure safe travels for the general public and the safe and lawful transport of goods. In the United States, particularly with airlines, it has become a very important issue since September 11, 2001. Congress passed the Aviation and Transportation Security Act on November 19, 2001, creating a large organization (the Transportation Security Administration, or TSA) to oversee transportation security. Today, TSA oversees security at all U.S. airports. In addition, the Department of Homeland Security (DHS) was created in 2003 to provide overall national security leadership.

Some recent activities have resulted from this heightened emphasis on transportation security in the United States. TSA has had numerous agency chiefs since 9/11, and has spent more than $12 billion to improve security on airplanes and in airports. One of the latest DHS initiatives was the outfitting of advanced imaging technology (AIT) scanners in U.S. airports since 2010. These AITs use millimeter wave technology to generate images reflected from the bodies being scanned.[39] An even newer initiative is to use biometric screening. Precertified members use their biometrics (fingerprint and iris) to verify their identity, allowing them expedited security screenings at major U.S. airports.[40] Additionally, 100% of the air cargo on commercial passenger aircraft must be prescreened, according to the Improving America's Security Act of 2007.[41] Finally, DHS scans 98% of imported cargo for radiation, and U.S. Customs and Border Protection prescreens U.S.-bound containers at 58 seaports around the world.[42]

Other forms of U.S. transportation have taken a backseat to the airlines when it comes to security concerns and funding. As of the end of 2013, TSA had over 55,000 full-time workers, most of whom were passenger and baggage screeners in the Aviation Security program. By contrast, fewer than 700 workers were involved in surface transportation security. In recent years, TSA has received around $5.7 billion in mandatory and discretionary appropriations, which—together with spending authority from offsetting collections—gives the agency an annual budget of more than $7 billion. In the 2015 TSA budget, Aviation Security measures accounted for 79% of the total.[43]

WAREHOUSING MANAGEMENT

15.3 Discuss warehouse risk pooling and use of the square root rule

Warehousing, a primary concern of logistics, provides a very strategic supply chain service. It enables firms to store their purchases, work-in-progress, and finished goods, as well as perform breakbulk and assembly activities, while allowing faster and more frequent deliveries of finished products to customers. Ideally, these activities result in better customer service. The use of warehouses is generally increasing in the United States—as disposable incomes among consumers have increased over the years, it has increased demand for goods. These goods must then move through various distribution systems. Not only is the number of warehouses growing, but they're getting larger and more sophisticated as well. About 10 years ago in the United States, the average warehouse size was approximately 250,000 square feet. Today, 400,000-foot warehouses are becoming more prevalent (that's almost five soccer fields). These large warehouses are typically automated as well.

In many cases, warehouses aren't used to store things, but rather to receive bulk shipments, break them down, repackage various items into outgoing orders, and then distribute these orders to a manufacturing location or retail center. These activities are collectively referred to as **crossdocking**. In this case, the warehouse is more accurately described as a **distribution center**. Firms locate warehouses closer to suppliers, closer to customers, or to more centralized locations, depending on the storage objectives and customer service

transportation security The safeguarding of transportation systems to ensure safe travels for the general public and the safe and lawful transport of goods.

crossdocking When distribution centers receive bulk shipments, break them down, repackage various items into outgoing orders, and then distribute these orders to a manufacturing location or retail center.

distribution center Warehouses that aren't used to store things, but rather perform crossdocking activities.

iStock/Solidago

Walmart operates over 40 regional distribution centers to supply its retail stores, such as this one in St. George, Utah. Each has over 1 million square feet of floor space and employs about 1,000 workers.

requirements. So warehouses are very much in use—some just to store things and others to provide efficient throughput of goods. Also, with the growing use of e-retailers like Amazon, distribution centers are essentially the store—customers demand quick fulfillment, and so in many cases the distribution centers are located close to groups of customers. "Investing in your warehouse is not just about cost reduction anymore," explains Mitch Rosenberg, VP of marketing at Massachusetts-based Kiva Systems. "Twenty-first century consumers are different than their 20th century predecessors, so the warehouse must also be able to contribute to a positive customer experience."[44] The following sections discuss a number of warehousing issues, including the types of warehouses, risk pooling, warehouse location, and lean warehousing.

THE IMPORTANCE AND TYPES OF WAREHOUSES

Tour one of Amazon's distribution centers on a busy day

Firms hold inventories for a number of reasons, as explained in Chapter 7. Purchasing managers order raw materials, parts, and assemblies, which are typically shipped to a warehouse located close to the buyer, and then transferred to the buyer's operations as needed. In a retail setting, a distribution center might be regionally located, with the retailer receiving bulk orders from many suppliers, then breaking these down (termed **breakbulk** activities) and reassembling outgoing orders for delivery to each retail location.

Conversely, firms may operate **consolidation warehouses** to collect large numbers of LTL shipments from nearby suppliers, where these are then consolidated and transported in TL quantities to a manufacturing facility located at some distance from the consolidation center. The use of consolidation warehouses and distribution centers allows firms to realize both purchase economies and transportation economies. Firms can buy goods in bulk at lower unit costs, and then ship these goods at TL rates either to a distribution center or directly to a manufacturing location. They can also purchase and move small-quantity purchases at LTL rates to nearby consolidation warehouses.

Private Warehouses

The term **private warehouses** refers to warehouses that are owned by the firm storing the goods. For firms with large volumes of goods to store or transfer, private warehouses represent an opportunity to reduce the costs of warehouse leasing. United Parcel Service, Walmart, and Sears Holding Corp., for example, are three of the largest private warehouse operators in North America.[45] Besides the long-term cost benefit that private warehouses can provide, another consideration is the level of control provided by private warehouses. Firms can decide what to store, what to process, what types of security to provide, and what types of equipment to use at their warehouses. Private warehousing can also enable a company to better utilize its workforce and expertise in terms of transportation and warehousing activities. Finally, private warehouses can generate income and tax advantages through leasing of excess capacity and/or asset depreciation. For these reasons, private warehousing accounts for the vast majority of overall warehouse space in the United States.[46]

Owning warehouses, though, can be a significant financial risk and loss of flexibility for the firm. The costs to build, equip, and then operate a warehouse can be very high, and most small- to moderate-sized firms simply cannot afford private warehouses. Private warehouses also bind firms to locations that may not prove optimal as time passes. Warehouse size or capacity is also somewhat inflexible, at least in the short term. Another problem can be insurance. Insurance companies, in many cases, do not like insuring goods in private warehouses, simply because security levels can be meager or nonexistent, creating a significant concern regarding fires or thefts of goods.

breakbulk When bulk orders are received at a distribution center from many suppliers, then broken down for outgoing shipments.

consolidation warehouses Warehouses that collect large numbers of LTL shipments from nearby suppliers, and then consolidate and transport the items in TL quantities to a manufacturing facility located at some distance from the warehouse.

private warehouses Warehouses that are owned by the firm storing the goods.

public warehouses For-profit organizations that provide a wide range of light manufacturing, warehousing, and distribution services to other companies.

Public Warehouses

As the name implies, **public warehouses** are for-profit organizations that provide a wide range of light manufacturing, warehousing, and distribution services to other companies. These services include the following:

- *Breakbulk.* Large-quantity shipments are broken down so that items can be combined into specific customer orders, and then shipped out.
- *Repackaging.* After breakbulk, items are repackaged for specific customer orders. Public warehouse personnel can also provide product packaging and labeling services.
- *Light assembly.* Some public warehouses provide final assembly operations to satisfy customer requests and to create customized final products.
- *Incoming and outgoing product quality inspections.*
- *Material handling, equipment maintenance, and documentation services.*
- *Short- and long-term storage.*

Public warehouses provide the short-term flexibility and investment cost savings that private warehouses simply cannot offer. If demand changes, or the firm's product mix changes, the use of public warehouses allows the firm to quickly change warehouse locations or space requirements. Public warehouses allow firms to test market areas and withdraw quickly if demand does not materialize as expected. The relative cost for firms to use a public warehouse can also be very small if the space requirements are minimal.

One of the main disadvantages associated with public warehouses is the lack of control provided to the goods owners. Other potential problems include lack of communications with warehouse personnel, lack of specialized services or capacity at the desired locations, and lack of care and security that might be given to products.

Firms might find it advantageous to use public warehouses in some locations and private warehouses in others. For large, established markets and relatively mature products, large firms may decide that owning and operating a warehouse makes the most sense, whereas the same firm may lease space and pay for services at public warehouses in developing markets or low-demand areas. During the recent economic downturn, use of public warehousing and other transportation services grew tremendously as shippers sought to reduce their costs. New Jersey–based Ultra Logistics, for example, grew significantly during the recession for precisely this reason. It typically handles more than 40,000 truckloads of goods per year for clients such as Kraft Foods, Con-Agra, Anheuser-Busch, and L'Oréal.[47]

RISK POOLING

One of the more important decisions regarding private warehouses is where to locate them. This decision will affect the number of warehouses needed, required capacities, system safety stock and inventory levels, customer service levels, and warehousing system costs. For a given market area, as the number of warehouses used by one company increases, the system becomes more *decentralized.* In a decentralized warehousing system, responsiveness and delivery service levels will increase, since goods can be delivered more quickly to customers; however, warehousing system operating and inventory costs will also increase. Other costs that come into play here are outgoing transportation costs to customers, and the transportation costs associated with the incoming deliveries of goods to each warehouse. Thus, the trade-off between costs and customer service must be carefully considered as a company makes its warehouse location decisions. This brings up the very important topic of risk pooling.

Risk pooling describes the relationship among the number of warehouses, system inventories, and customer service, and it can be explained intuitively as follows:

> When market demand is random, it is very likely that higher-than-average demand from some customers will be offset by lower-than-average demand from other customers. Thus, as the number of customers served by a single warehouse increases, demand variabilities will tend to offset one another more often, reducing the overall demand variance and the likelihood of stockouts. Consequently, as the number of customers served by a warehouse increases, the amount of safety stock required to guard against stockouts decreases. In other words, the more *centralized* a warehousing system becomes (fewer warehouses), the *lower the safety stock* required to achieve a given system-wide customer service level (recall from Chapter 7 that as stockouts decrease, customer service levels increase).

risk pooling Explains the relationship between the number of warehouses, system inventories, and customer service—when market demand is random, it is very likely that higher-than-average demand from some customers will be offset by lower-than-average demand from other customers. Thus, as the number of customers served by a single warehouse increases, demand variabilities will tend to offset one another more often, reducing the overall demand variance and the likelihood of stockouts.

As mentioned previously, risk pooling assumes that higher-than-average demand in one market area tends to be offset by lower-than-average demand in another, provided both areas are served by the same warehouse. In smaller market areas served by decentralized warehouses, this may not hold true, and warehouses would then require relatively higher levels of safety stock. This is why a smaller number of large, centralized warehouses serving large market areas require lower overall system inventories, compared to a larger number of small, decentralized warehouses serving the same markets.

A good illustration of this principle occurred in Europe after the formation of the European Union in 1993. Prior to that time, European logistics systems were formed along national lines. Each country's distribution system operated independently of the others, requiring company warehouses to be located in each country. With the arrival of a single European market in 1993, these distribution systems no longer made economic sense. For instance, Becton Dickinson, an American manufacturer of diagnostics equipment, was burdened in Europe in the early 1990s with a very inefficient and costly distribution system. Its inventory carrying costs were high, while its stockouts were numerous. After the formation of the European Union, the company closed its distribution centers in Sweden, France, Germany, and Belgium, and shifted all of its distribution operations to a single, new, automated center in Belgium. In less than a year, average stock levels were down 45%, and stockouts were reduced by 75%. Other companies in Europe had similar results.[48]

square root rule Used in risk pooling; as the number of warehouses in a system changes, the system inventory required is equal to the original system inventory times the ratio of the square root of the new number of warehouses to the square root of the original number of warehouses.

The effect of risk pooling can be estimated numerically by the **square root rule**, which suggests that as the number of warehouses in a system changes, the system inventory required is equal to the original system inventory times the ratio of the square root of the new number of warehouses to the square root of the original number of warehouses.[49] The square root rule is formulated as:

$$S_2 = \frac{\sqrt{N_2}}{\sqrt{N_1}}(S_1)$$

where

S_1 = total system stock of boots for the N_1 warehouses;

S_2 = total system stock of boots for the N_2 warehouses;

N_1 = number of warehouses in the original system; and

N_2 = number of warehouses in the proposed system.

Example 15.3
Risk Pooling at Mengwasser's Boot Barn

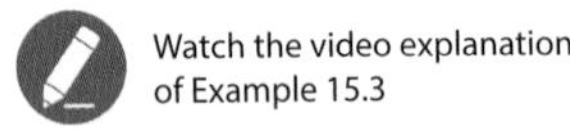

Watch the video explanation of Example 15.3

Mengwasser's Boot Barn currently owns two warehouses in Portland and Phoenix to store its boots before shipping them out to various retail customers across the western United States. The owner is considering changing to one centralized warehouse in Las Vegas to service all of Mengwasser's retail customers, and is curious to know the impact this will have on its system inventories. Mengwasser's current average inventory level is approximately 6,000 boots at each warehouse. It has found that this level of stock will result in warehouse stockouts approximately 1% of the time. Using the square root rule, the new average inventory level needed at the central Las Vegas warehouse to maintain the same low level of stockouts is:

$$S_2 = \frac{\sqrt{N_2}}{\sqrt{N_1}}(S_1) = \frac{\sqrt{1}}{\sqrt{2}}(12{,}000) = \frac{1}{1.415}(12{,}000) = 8{,}485 \text{ boots},$$

Comparing the two requirements, the inventory reduction is:

$$\frac{(12000 - 8485)}{12000} = 29.3\%$$

Of course, Mengwasser's will now have to consider the impact this will have on transportation costs and delivery times.

A simple illustration of risk pooling is shown in Example 15.3. In the example, reducing the number of warehouses in a system from two to one causes a reduction in average inventory of approximately 29% (since less safety stock is required).

LEAN WAREHOUSING

As firms develop their supply chain management capabilities, items will be moving more quickly through inbound and outbound warehouses and distribution centers. This creates the need for **lean warehousing**. Some examples of these lean capabilities include the following:

- *Greater emphasis on crossdocking.* Warehouse employees receive shipments, perform breakbulk, then repackage items quickly into outgoing shipments. Far fewer goods will be stored for any appreciable time, and average warehouse inventory levels will decrease while the number of stockkeeping units will increase.
- *Reduced lot sizes and shipping quantities.* Inbound and/or outbound shipping quantities are likely to be smaller and more frequent, containing mixed quantities of goods and thus requiring more handling.
- *A commitment to customers and service quality.* Warehouse employees must perform warehouse activities so as to meet the requirements of their inbound suppliers and outbound customers.
- *Increased automation.* To improve handling speed and reliability, more warehouse activities will become automated, from scanner/bar code computer tracking systems, to warehouse management software applications, to automated storage and retrieval systems.
- *Increased assembly operations.* As more firms implement lean systems and mass customization, warehouses will be called upon to perform final assembly operations to meet specific customer requirements. This will change the skill set requirements of warehouse employees, along with equipment requirements.

Watch a short video on crossdocking

Most distribution centers today have adopted many of these concepts. Indiana-based Prime Distribution Services (PDS) offers distribution services to suppliers in club-store grocery supply chains. It offers warehousing, crossdocking, packaging, and freight consolidation to suppliers who are looking to increase speed and reduce costs as much as possible to compete in the extremely low-profit-margin grocery industry. Consequently, PDS distribution capabilities have had to evolve to survive. The company recently combined several distribution centers into a single 1.2-million-square-foot heavily automated facility that provides greater control over inventory, more responsive order management, and easier building of mixed item pallets.[50]

RETURNS MANAGEMENT

15.4 Describe the benefits of returns management

Returns management (also known as **reverse logistics**) refers to the reverse flow of goods *from customers to sellers* in a supply chain occurring when goods are returned. The entire returns management cycle is occasionally referred to as the 3-Rs, which stands for returns, refurbish, and recycle. In other words, returns management refers to the movement, storage, and processing of returned goods—a potentially costly undertaking. How costly? According to the Reverse Logistics Association, annual product returns in the United States amount to approximately $150 to $200 billion, or about 6% of total U.S. annual retail sales. It has also been estimated that supply chain costs associated with reverse logistics average between 7–10% of the costs of goods sold.[51]

Recall that returns management was described as one of the eight key supply chain processes in Chapter 1. Returns are increasing today because of the growth of Internet shopping, free shipping/return policies, direct-to-store shipments, and direct-to-home shipments. When manufacturers use cheap and untested foreign suppliers, this also can cause a

lean warehousing Using techniques that move items more quickly through inbound and outbound warehouses and distribution centers.

returns management The movement, storage, and processing of returned goods. Also known as reverse logistics.

reverse logistics *See* Returns management.

high number of product recalls and returned goods. In 2007, for example, California-based Mattel, the world's largest toymaker, recalled 2 million Chinese-made toys because they were covered with paint containing a high lead content. After an investigation, it was found that one of Mattel's trusted toy suppliers had subcontracted work to unauthorized suppliers.[52]

Besides the significant impact on costs, as stated previously, returns also can have a direct negative impact on the environment, customer service, the firm's reputation, and profitability if not managed properly. "Reverse logistics is all about damage control and making the process as customer-friendly as possible," says Lou Cerny, vice president of Sedlak Management Consultants. "You've already disappointed the customer once, now you have to close the loop as soon as possible."[53]

See another example of returns management

Many firms hire companies specializing in returns management to ensure its items and customers are managed correctly. Texas-based computer maker Dell Inc., known for its supply chain management capabilities, has set its sights on creating the same sort of reputation for its product returns. It has contracted with GENCO Supply Chain Solutions to manage Dell's testing, repairing, and remanufacturing services. Texas-based InteliSol will provide part harvesting and other recovery services for Dell within the same returns management facility.[54]

THE IMPACT OF PRODUCT RETURNS ON THE COMPANY

Product returns can represent significant challenges for companies. In many cases, reverse logistics activities are seen simply as an unwanted cost of doing business. Problems include the inability of information systems to handle returns or monitor reverse product flows, the lack of worker training in product returns procedures, little or no identification on returned packages, the need for adequate inspection and testing of returns, and the placing of potentially damaged returned products back into sales stocks. A poor returns management system can affect the entire supply chain financially and can have a negative impact on how a consumer views a product brand, potentially impacting future sales. A recent report by global business consulting company Accenture found that reverse logistics costs four to five times more than forward logistics, and on average requires 12 times as many processing steps. Their findings, though, also suggest that reverse logistics represents a huge source of untapped value for a company.[55]

Tribune Content Agency LLC/Alamy

This GameStop factory in Grapevine, TX, repairs video games and hardware that customers have traded for new games and hardware. GameStop then resells the refurbished items.

From a marketing perspective, a well-managed returns process can create goodwill and enhance customers' perceptions of product quality and purchase risk. From a quality perspective, product failure and returns information can be used by quality personnel in root cause analyses and by design personnel to reduce future design errors (the number one reason for a product return is a defective or damaged item). From a logistics perspective, returned products can still create value as original products, refurbished products, or repair parts. This also tends to reduce disposal costs. Thus, while 46% of companies report losing money on product returns, about 8% actually report making money. Online shoe merchant Zappos has a very high return rate (about 35%) but views this as a competitive advantage. It provides free returns, no questions asked, but also boasts very high repurchase rates from its customers.[56]

TRENDS IN LOGISTICS

15.5 Discuss the environmental benefits of logistics sustainability

Today, firms are facing growing pressure from suppliers, customers, employees, and regulatory agencies to improve environmental performance. A related concern is that an enormous portion of the world's oil reserves are consumed to move goods around the globe. A study

Going Green Is Saving Green for Wright & Filippis

SERVICE SPOTLIGHT

Len Collection/Alamy

Since 2010, Michigan-based Wright & Filippis, a medical equipment supplier, has made several changes to improve sustainability in its logistics systems. One example is with its fleet of delivery trucks—they are being converted to propane gas for fuel. While management had already converted the company's forklifts to propane, the CEO took a taxi ride one day and learned it was using propane, which prompted the firm to begin its truck fuel conversions.

Wright & Filippis soon learned that converting its delivery trucks meant more than just environmental sustainability: The fuel burns cheaper and engines last longer, while incurring less total maintenance cost. Prior to the conversion, for instance, oil changes were done every three months; now it's every five to six months. Using nine delivery trucks, the firm estimates it is saving $27,000 per year and wasting less labor time refueling, all while reducing CO_2 emissions.[57]

in 2009 found that about 71% of the global oil demand was for transportation. In the United States, that translates to 6,400 gallons of oil used *every second* for the transportation sector, which amounts to more CO_2 emissions than any nation's *entire economy,* except China.[58] Managers are realizing the impact of transportation on their firms' carbon footprints and costs, and are beginning to do something about it. The Service Spotlight above describes the efforts of a medical supply company to improve its logistics sustainability performance. Politicians are also taking note of voter sentiment and beginning to enact more stringent environmental protection laws regarding transportation.

In trucking, the big energy wastes come from trucks returning from their deliveries empty, termed **empty miles**, engine idling, and several maintenance issues. Washington, DC–based Trucking Efficiency, a combined effort of the Carbon War Room and the North American Council for Freight Efficiency, aims to drastically improve efficiencies of the North American trucking industry. It offers reports assessing current technologies, best practices, tire pressure systems, idle reduction solutions, maintenance suggestions, and other technologies in progress. It also offers workshops bringing together industry leaders and technology experts to facilitate shared learning.[59]

Arkansas-based Tyson Foods is always looking for ways to replace empty miles with revenue miles, as long as they don't interfere with its delivery needs. Recently, Tyson teamed with the Coca-Cola Company to use empty, refrigerated Tyson trucks to make deliveries to Coke customers, which reduced empty miles without sacrificing Coke's customer service or truck availability at Tyson plants.[60] Schneider National, headquartered in Wisconsin, uses Omnitracs' Trailer Tracks software combined with solar and cellular power to keep track of its 44,000 intermodal shipping containers and truck trailers. The technology allows Schneider to pinpoint the exact locations of empty containers and trailers, which improves dispatching performance and reduces driver wait times and empty miles.[61]

Actually, a number of nonprofit organizations have been formed to help firms with their **logistics sustainability** efforts. In the United States, the Environmental Protection Agency launched SmartWay in 2004; it is a voluntary partnership that helps companies improve their transportation capabilities—to move more ton-miles of freight with lower emissions and less energy, at a lower cost. SmartWay gives its partners a set of EPA-tested tools to make informed transportation choices. It helps them measure, benchmark, and report carbon emissions, and to improve supply-chain efficiencies and environmental performance. SmartWay helps its partners exchange performance data and accelerate adoption of advanced technologies and operational practices. Since 2004, SmartWay partners have

empty miles Refers to trucks returning from their deliveries empty.

logistics sustainability The efforts of transportation companies to reduce carbon emissions, and improve supply-chain efficiencies and environmental performance.

eliminated 51.6 million metric tons of CO_2 and 37,000 tons of particulate matter. It has saved 120.7 million barrels of oil and $16.8 billion in fuel costs. This equals taking more than 10 million cars off the road for an entire year. Since 2004, some 3,000 of the nation's shippers, logistics companies, and truck, rail, barge, and multimodal carriers have registered with SmartWay. SmartWay carriers now account for 22% of all trucking miles, and SmartWay is actively working to expand to all freight modes.[62]

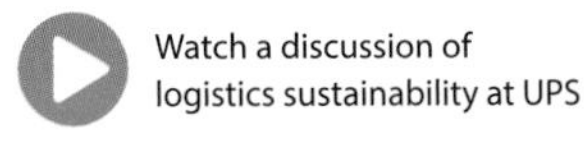
Watch a discussion of logistics sustainability at UPS

UPS is aiming to become a leader in carbon emissions reduction from transportation by 2020. In 2013, its carbon emissions decreased 1.5% from 2012, even though global shipping volumes increased 3.9%. In 2013, UPS increased use of natural gas vehicles across the United States, and added 249 heavy-duty tractors fueled by liquefied natural gas (LNG). The company expected to deploy more than 1,000 LNG tractors by the end of 2014. In 2013, UPS's alternative fuel and advanced technology vehicles worldwide logged 55 million miles and avoided the use of 5.8 million gallons of gasoline and diesel fuel. The company reports that these savings put it well on its way to reaching a goal of driving 1 billion miles in alternative fuel and advanced technology vehicles by the end of 2017.[63]

PRODUCT RETURNS AND SUSTAINABILITY

The environmental impacts from product returns can be reduced through activities such as recycling, reusing materials and products, or the refurbishing of used products. Retailers have discovered that in many cases, the best option for a returned item may simply be to recycle it or throw it out rather than incur the supply chain costs for the item's journey back to a manufacturer. That is precisely the thinking behind New Jersey–based 3PL Yusen Logistics' decision to open a reverse logistics facility in Northwest Arkansas where it offers a number of services related to returned goods, which ultimately reduces their environmental impacts. Services at the facility include sorting, testing, repairing, repackaging, part harvesting, and recycling.[64]

While organizations might still be tempted to use landfills for product and material disposal, landfills have become much more expensive to use. Local, state, and federal governments are imposing stricter rules and higher costs regarding the use of landfills. These changes have led to innovative ways of dealing with used products or product waste. According to Gary Cullen, chief operating officer of 4PRL LLC, the reverse logistics arm of consultants The Georgetowne Group, "Much efficiency can be found in near-sourcing third party service providers who specialize in redeployment, repair, reuse, recycling, reclamation, and resale. This appears to be a successful business model in today's fuel conscious and green minded environment." Cullen contends that these 3PL providers are typically targeted close to the originator of equipment being returned, reused, or recycled, which has many additional benefits. "A closer country allows for use of cheaper modes of transportation as well as less overall time and movement," says Cullen. "The goal for nearsourced reverse logistics operations is to reduce movement and handling, and being able to find service providers in the country with the lowest wage and processing costs. Combine this with the improving of your environmental image and you have a 'win–win' for your clients, consumers, and shareholders."[65]

SAGE edge™

Visit edge.sagepub.com/wisner to help you accomplish your coursework goals in an easy-to-use learning environment.

- Mobile-friendly eFlashcards
- Mobile-friendly practice quizzes
- A complete online action plan
- Chapter summaries with learning objectives
- Excel templates to assist with practice problems
- Original video case studies that demonstrate chapter concepts in action

SUMMARY

This chapter has provided a comprehensive view of logistics, from the impacts of location on logistics cost to the various modes of transportation, and including discussions of warehousing, returns management, and logistics sustainability. Several quantitative tools to aid logistics decision making were also illustrated. Logistics allows companies to provide high levels of customer service, but this comes at a cost—higher inventories, more warehouses, and faster transportation. Good logistics managers find the right combinations of these elements to satisfy customers while minimizing costs and the impacts on the environment. It is a balancing act that can mean more profits and a competitive advantage for the firm when performed correctly.

KEY TERMS

Air carriers, 480
Breakbulk, 484
Center-of-gravity technique, 476
Centroid method, 476
Coal slurry, 482
Consolidation warehouses, 484
Container-on-flatcar (COFC), 482
Containerships, 481
Crossdocking, 483
Deep-sea transportation, 481
Distribution center, 483
Empty miles, 489
Foreign trade zones, 475
Free trade zones, 475
High-speed trains, 480
Intermodal transportation, 482
Lean warehousing, 487
Less-than-truckload carriers, 479
Location decisions, 471
Logistics, 470
Logistics management, 470
Logistics sustainability, 489
Modes of transportation, 478
Motor carriers, 479
National competitiveness, 473
Piggyback service, 482
Pipeline carriers, 481
Private warehouses, 484
Public warehouses, 484
Quality of life, 474
Rail carriers, 479
Returns management, 487
Reverse logistics, 487
Risk pooling, 485
ROROs, 482
Square root rule, 486
Trailer-on-flatcar service, 480
Transportation planning, 477
Transportation security, 483
Truckload carriers, 479
Water carrier, 480
Weighted-factor rating technique, 475
World Trade Organization, 474

FORMULA REVIEW

The weighted-factor score for location analysis: $S_A = \Sigma\, w_i F_i$, where S_A = weighted-factor score for location A; w_i = weight used for the factor *i*; and F_i = factor *i*.

The center-of-gravity location coordinates, X and Y: $C_x = \dfrac{\Sigma(V_i d_{xi})}{\Sigma V_i}$ and $C_y = \dfrac{\Sigma(V_i d_{yi})}{\Sigma V_i}$, where C_x = *X* coordinate of the center-of-gravity location; C_y = *Y* coordinate of the center-of-gravity location; V_i = Volume of shipments required by market *i*; d_{xi} = *X* coordinate distance to market *i* from the coordinate grid origin; and d_{yi} = *Y* coordinate distance to market *i* from the coordinate grid origin.

The warehouse square root rule: $S_2 = \dfrac{\sqrt{N_2}}{\sqrt{N_1}}(S_1)$ where S_1 = total system stock for the N_1 warehouses; S_2 = total system stock for the N_2 warehouses; N_1 = number of warehouses in the original system; and N_2 = number of warehouses in the proposed system.

SOLVED PROBLEMS

1. Cody Mufflers wanted to locate a new muffler shop in the southwest region of the United States. The following potential locations, factors, and weights were decided upon:

Location Factor	Weight	San Diego	Las Vegas	Albuquerque
Lease/Construction Costs	0.15	57	82	100
Proximity to Major Street	0.20	100	90	84
Population in Area	0.30	89	100	75
Taxes/Incentives	0.20	74	79	100
Other Competitors in Area	0.15	86	72	100

Answer:

Sabrena, the shop owner, calculated the scores as follows:

$$\text{San Diego} = 0.15(57) + 0.20(100) + 0.30(89) + 0.20(74) + 0.15(86) = 82.95$$

$$\text{Las Vegas} = 0.15(82) + 0.20(90) + 0.30(100) + 0.20(79) + 0.15(72) = 86.90$$

$$\text{Albuquerque} = 0.15(100) + 0.20(84) + 0.30(75) + 0.20(100) + 0.15(100) = 89.30$$

Based on these calculations, Cody Mufflers decides to locate in Albuquerque.

2. Vellenga Warehousing desired to locate a central warehouse to serve five Arizona markets. Placed on a grid system, its five markets had coordinates and demand as shown below. Determine the center-of-gravity coordinates.

Location Coordinates (miles)	Demand (units)
(25, 20)	8,500
(140, 25)	25,000
(180, 100)	18,000
(120, 250)	12,500
(225, 185)	6,500

Answer:

Note that a graph is not necessary to calculate the center-of-gravity coordinates; however, it might prove useful as a visualization aid.

$$C_x = \frac{\Sigma(V_i d_{xi})}{\Sigma V_i} = \frac{(8500\times 25)+(25000\times 140)+(18000\times 180)+(12500\times 120)+(6500\times 225)}{(8500+25000+18000+12500+6500)} = \frac{9915000}{70500} = 140.6 \text{ miles}$$

$$C_y = \frac{\Sigma(V_i d_{yi})}{\Sigma V_i} = \frac{(8500\times 20)+(25000\times 25)+(18000\times 100)+(12500\times 250)+(6500\times 185)}{70500} = \frac{6922500}{70500} = 98.2 \text{ miles.}$$

3. Freeman Classic Car Sales wants to better centralize its warehouses from six to three. It currently has approximately 1,250 cars in its six warehouses. What should be its new total number of cars, to keep its current service level?

Answer:

$$S_2 = \frac{\sqrt{N_2}}{\sqrt{N_1}}(S_1) = \frac{\sqrt{3}}{\sqrt{6}}(1250) = 884 \text{ cars.}$$

REVIEW QUESTIONS

1. Define logistics. How is it different from transportation?
2. What are the activities and the goal of logistics management?
3. What are the steps in a facility location decision, and how does facility location impact logistics?
4. How do locations for manufacturing facilities differ from service locations?
5. What are the factors that impact a firm's location decision?
6. What is the World Trade Organization's role in regional trade agreements?
7. What are tariffs, and why would a country want to use them?
8. Why should the weighted-factor rating technique be performed by a team of analysts, instead of one analyst? What should the weights sum to?
9. What are the assumptions of the center-of-gravity technique? What types of organizations might use this technique?
10. What are the five modes of transportation, and which is the most flexible?
11. What is a real-time location system, and why do railroads use them?
12. What type of vessel hauls the most on-water cargo?
13. Define intermodal transportation and describe two variations of intermodal service.
14. Why is transportation security considered so important in the United States? Which mode of transportation is most impacted by security concerns?
15. What is the difference between a warehouse and a distribution center? Which one performs more crossdocking?
16. Describe the differences between a public and a private warehouse. Could either of these be a consolidation warehouse?
17. Describe the idea of risk pooling and how it relates to warehouse location.
18. Describe the three warehouse location strategies.
19. What does the concept of lean warehousing refer to?
20. What is returns management, and in what ways can this be a benefit to the firm?
21. Describe how a firm would practice logistics sustainability.

DISCUSSION QUESTIONS

1. Discuss which location factors would impact where you would buy a house.
2. Why might a country's competitiveness impact a firm's decision to locate a facility in that country?
3. When might a firm desire to locate close to its suppliers? Its customers? Somewhere in-between? What are the impacts on cost and customer service?
4. How can a nation's trade agreements with other countries impact a firm's willingness to open new locations in those countries?
5. Why is the tonnage hauled by rail decreasing in the United States? What are the railroads doing to counteract this trend?
6. Do you think it is beneficial for a company to practice logistics sustainability? Why, or why not?

EXERCISES AND PROJECTS

1. Write a report about manufacturing in the United States in the right-to-work states. Discuss the impact on employment and any current trends.
2. Research one of the more recent foreign Walmart locations and the reasons stated for its location. What impact did it have on local businesses? On employment?
3. What is the current status of high-speed rail in the United States since this text was published? Describe the ongoing projects.

PROBLEMS

1. The following factors are being used to evaluate three potential country locations for the Zampino Manufacturing Co. Perform the analysis using a 100-point scale, and select the best location, using the weights and scores shown.

Location Factor	Weight	United States	Mexico	Canada
Land Availability	0.15	85	75	100
National Competitiveness	0.15	100	65	85
Quality of Life	0.30	90	80	100
Labor Availability	0.25	70	100	72
Transportation Infrastr.	0.10	100	82	90

2. Pollard Car Refurbishing Centers wants to add a center in the U.S. southwest. The location factors, weights, and potential locations are shown below. Select the preferred location using a 100-point scale.

Location Factor	Weight	El Paso	Albuquerque	Tucson
Garage Availability/Cost	0.20	80	85	70
Area Population	0.25	60	75	75
Quality of Life	0.15	60	100	80
Labor Availability	0.25	100	85	80
Parts Availability	0.15	100	80	90

3. Jack wants to go to college and has several places in mind. He has listed the important factors and their weights, then performed enough research to determine the relative scores for the institutions using a 100-point scale. Which school would he favor?

Location Factor	Weight	University of Arizona	UCLA	University of Colorado
School Reputation	0.15	80	100	85
Majors He Might Select	0.25	90	100	100
Tuition Cost	0.20	100	60	75
Living Cost	0.15	100	60	80
Geographic Quality	0.15	80	100	90
Student Organizations	0.10	85	100	90

4. There are three markets to be served by Faith Distributing Co. The company desires to centrally locate the facility to minimize transportation costs. The (X,Y) coordinates in kilometers to the center of each market from a grid overlaying the markets are: M1 = (30,52); M2 = (120,25); and M3 = (45,125). The forecasted demands over the next five years for each market are: M1 = 125,000 units; M2 = 80,000 units; and M3 = 45,000 units. Using the center-of-gravity technique, find the COG and create a grid map showing the three markets and the COG location.

5. The Ferris Company has three markets it wishes to serve with a centrally located manufacturing site. It has placed approximations of each market on a grid system, as shown on the opposite page. All three markets are approximately the same size. Determine the center-of-gravity coordinates for the manufacturing site.

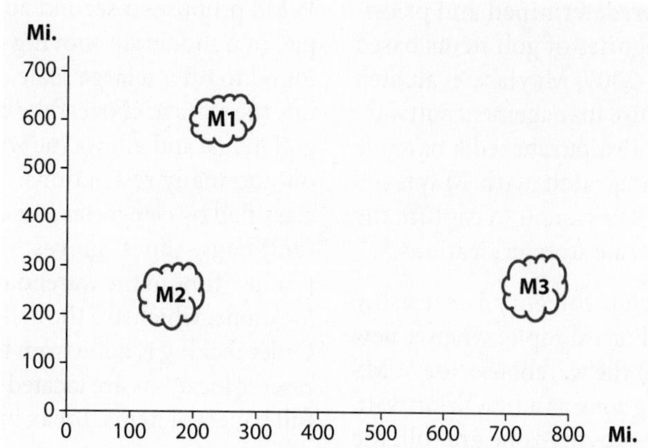

6. A parts supplier has three industrial customers located in southern California. It wishes to build a centralized distribution center to serve the three customers. The locations of the three customers and their part volume requirements are shown below. Use the center-of-gravity method to determine the location for the distribution center.

Customer	Location Coordinates, mi.(x,y)	Parts/Year
1	(180, 60)	10,000
2	(40, 90)	12,500
3	(84, 125)	4,600

7. Michelle's Fine Furniture desires to increase its warehouses from two to three in its market areas, and the manager wants to know the impact this will have on its system inventories. The current average inventory level is approximately 3,000 units at each of the two warehouses. Use the square root rule to calculate the new inventory level needed to maintain the same level of stockouts.

8. Using the information in Problem 7, if Michelle's preferred instead to go with one centrally located warehouse, how would this impact system inventories?

9. For the following warehouse system information, determine the average inventory levels required to maintain the same customer service levels.

   Current system: 6 warehouses with 5,000 units at each warehouse.

   a. The new system will have 3 warehouses.

   b. The new system will have 10 warehouses.

10. Meltoni's Tires wants to switch to a more decentralized warehousing system. It currently has one central warehouse, with 4,000 tires. If it goes to a four warehouse system, what would be the impact on inventory, given that it wishes to maintain the same stockout levels?

CASE STUDIES

CASE 1: Golf Equipment Warehousing Operations at Mayfare

As a leading global manufacturer of golf clubs, bags, and clothing, Mayfare Golf keeps close tabs on its warehouse operations to know exactly what's coming in and going out, when items are moving, and at what cost. If Mayfare's computer system says there are 100 Z-Drivers in the warehouse, then Mayfare expects them to be there. Its reputation could suffer if any items became stocked out. Mayfare began its warehousing operations for golf items in January 2009, as part of its U.S. golf equipment subsidiary in Thailand.

Communicating with golf item suppliers simultaneously in several locations in Asia is no easy task. It is a challenging exercise, but one that is critical in the golf item supply chain. Mayfare's primary business strategy is providing outstanding golf products and customer service at a reasonable cost. Warehousing therefore becomes a vital part of delivering the company vision. This means putting in place the right logistical infrastructure to support Mayfare's customer service requirements and to provide visibility to its supply chain members.

Each zone in the warehouse is predetermined and prioritized for storage of specific categories of golf items based on movement requirements. In 2009, Mayfare evaluated and purchased a leading warehouse management software system (WMS) application and also purchased a barcode application. The WMS was integrated with Mayfare's enterprise resource planning (ERP) system to capture the inventory movements and to allocate storage locations.

The storage location for each club category is set using item movement requirements. For example, when a new "hot" model of golf club arrives at the warehouse, the WMS assigns storage in the fast-moving zone as a first priority. If, however, all locations in the fast-moving zone are full, the WMS proposes a second zone—which could be, for example, in a moderate-moving zone nearby. This method was found to offer a large scale of operating flexibility to facilitate the storage of overflow cargoes of different categories of golf items, and allows the warehouse to operate easily without too many restrictions. Apart from this, storage is also classified by categories like clubs, golf balls, and accessories (golf bags, shoes, gloves, etc.). To accommodate smooth product flow in the warehouse, one product is located in two locations, which are the active bin and the reserve location. Order picking is done from the active bin at floor level, while reserve locations are located on higher shelves and store only full pallets of items. Break bulk is performed when needed.

A Challenging Period for Sport Goods Warehousing Operations

When the company launches new golf products, all department managers join together to discuss the product introduction plans, and any challenging concerns and proposals are raised. One proposal, for example, was to obtain demand forecasts from key customers like major department stores in advance, to plan the distribution of new items effectively. Another issue discussed recently was a complaint from key customers—the frequent wrong order picking of golf products. Most warehouse workers are familiar with products that have been packaged in cartons and can easily recognize the product names from carton labels. However, golf clubs are put in clear plastic bags. Clubs under the same model name could have either steel or graphite shafts. Clubs could also be either right-handed or left-handed, and these two issues caused a significant amount of wrong order picking. To avoid any inventory discrepancies, warehouse workers are required to perform cycle counts every morning and reconcile the physical inventory with the inventory record in the ERP. This helps to trace wrong order picking and improves inventory accuracy.

The handling of incoming cargo at the warehouse was another serious concern. In many cases, the packages were loose cargo to be unloaded from containers or trucks. This required an uneven and sometimes sizeable labor force to unload the cargo. Additionally, in many cases the pallet configuration (the packaged quantity) for each product on each pallet was not identical. In other words, Product A may be packaged in 24 per box on some pallets and 30 per box on other pallets. This nonstandardized pallet configuration became a significant burden for warehouse workers, to reconfigure pallets for storage at the warehouse.

Finally, the operators wanted personal computers with the ERP system and the WMS to be installed for their use at the warehouse. It would then be the duty of the inventory controllers at the warehouse to input both inbound and outbound information into the ERP system while also keying the same information into the WMS.

DISCUSSION QUESTIONS

1. Identify all of the operational problems of this case, and discuss the seriousness of each problem.
2. What preventive actions can be implemented for wrong order picking?
3. What could be done to improve the inventory handling problem and the warehouse computing problem?
4. If you were the warehouse manager of the company, what would you do to further streamline the operational flow and design of the warehousing operations found in this case?

Note: Written by Watcharapoj (Jack) Sapsanguanboon, Professor, Graduate School of Management and Innovation, King Mongkut's University of Technology, Thailand. This case was prepared solely to provide material for class discussion. The author has disguised names and other identifying information to protect confidentiality and does not intend to illustrate either effective or ineffective handling of a managerial situation.

CASE 2: The Challenge of Selecting the Best Mode of Transportation

Henry had gone straight from his undergraduate degree to working on his MBA. Because his work experience was limited, he was excited to get an internship at Watterstrom Logistics. Several weeks into his internship Henry decided this was the field for him. His manager assigned Henry a project to help him better understand the importance of selecting the best mode of transportation for Watterstrom's clients' products. Henry was to report back and explain what he learned.

Henry knew that logistics has a powerful effect on a company's balance sheet. Henry's initial research showed the best mode of transportation often depends on the industry using it. Industries that deal in bulk products such as corn, soybeans, wheat, cement, crude oil, and coal must decide which mode of transportation is best. That decision is often based on the distance over which the shipment must be moved. Trucks have a cost advantage for short distances up to 500 miles; consequently, they function primarily as the short haul option. As the distance increases, rail has a cost advantage over trucks; however, barges have the greatest cost advantage if a waterway connects the point of origin and the destination.

Watterstrom Logistics provided shipping services to all industries; the grain industry was Watterstrom's main client base. Henry discovered that for the grain industry there are three grain supply chains: export of bulk grain, bulk grain for the domestic market, and export of containerized specialty grain products. Since barges are the least expensive mode of transportation, the critical factors are the shipment origin/destination and their proximities to navigable waterways. In the United States, most grain production is located near the Mississippi River or the waterways that feed into it. The importance of waterways to the grain industry is evident in the fact that four of the top ten barge companies are owned by grain companies (ADM, ConAgra, Cargill, and Bunge).[1]

Henry wondered (assuming the origin and destination can be accessed by water, rail, or roads) what other than cost could be a driving factor? Although single barges haul cargo, they usually are cabled together in what is called a 15-barge tow. The capacity of a 15-barge tow is 22,500 tons.[2] Henry wondered how this compared to the capacity of rail cars and semitrucks. He found that just as barges are cabled together to create a larger capacity system, the same is done with rail cars. The standard is a 100-car train whose hauling capacity is 11,200 tons.[2] Thus, it takes two 100-car trains to match a 15-barge tow. Semitrucks are a third option for meeting shipping needs. A single semitruck can haul 26 tons.[2] Henry realized a drawback of semitrucks is they are a single shipping system, unlike barges or rail cars, which are combined to create a larger shipping system. To equal the cargo capacity of either a 15-barge tow or two 100-car trains, approximately 870 semitrucks would be required.[2]

Examining the aforementioned facts and based on the assumption that the origin and destination can be accessed by water, rail, or roads, Henry decided that barges were the best transportation option. However, even if the assumption stands, there are other factors that the supply chain manager must consider. Henry discovered that in 2012 there was a drought that caused the water levels on the Mississippi to drop. A barge usually runs 12 feet deep. Early in 2012, the Mississippi was at the 20-foot level—a level that can easily accommodate a fully loaded barge. However, because of the drought and the coinciding drop in the level of the river, barges were restricted to a 9-foot draft. Because of the lower draft, cargo loads had to be much less—approximately 600 tons less per barge. Consequently, approximately 40% of the normal tonnage capacity was lost capacity. During the two-month period of December 2011 and January 2012, before the drought hit, 7 million tons of farm products were shipped by barge. In addition, there were 3.8 million tons of coal and about 700,000 tons of crude.[3] The shipping needs for these industries were still the same despite the drought; however, the cargo capacity of the waterway system was insufficient to carry the load. To put this in perspective, to cover the lost tonnage of a single barge, Watterstrom Logistics would need 24 trucks. Rail would appear to be a viable option to cover the lost tonnage for farm product shipments. However, the cost was an additional 30 to 35 cents per bushel to ship by rail. The increased cost to ship the lost tonnage (7 million tons) of farm products by rail would be $30–$35 million.[3] Henry realized that in addition to cost he had to factor in possible delays due to weather and the hauling capacity of a specific mode of transportation.

DISCUSSION QUESTIONS

1. What is the benefit of intermodal transportation for this case?
2. Which mode of transportation do you think has the most potential for problems? Why?
3. Which mode of transportation is the most flexible? The least flexible? Why?
4. Examining all the modes of transportation and the major issues with waterways, should Watterstrom's supply chain manager even consider barges? Why, or why not?

Note: Written by Rick Bonsall, D. Mgt., McKendree University, Lebanon, IL. The people and company are fictional and any resemblance to any person or company is coincidental. This case was prepared solely to provide material for class discussion. The author does not intend to illustrate either effective or ineffective handling of a managerial situation.

Sources:

1. The transportation of grain, http://www.envisionfreight.com/value/pdf/Grain.pdf
2. Iowa Department of Transportation. (2014). http://www.envisionfreight.com/value/?id=illustration
3. Salter, J., & Suhr, J. (2012). Drought threatens to close Mississippi to barges. *The Oakland Press*, http://www.envisionfreight.com/value/pdf/Grain.pdf

CASE 3: Location as an Enabler for Sustainability

John is the supply chain manager at Nishimura Fulfillment and Distribution Services. Nishimura is expanding rapidly and developing plans to open operations in six emerging markets. The company maintains its own transportation fleet, barges, rail cars, and semitrucks. It is concerned about the environment, and thus wants to improve its sustainability results.

Since its fulfillment and distribution centers will be at the selected locations for at least 10 years, Nishimura believes that location selection is one of the most critical decisions to make. Therefore, it assigned John to develop a proposal on how to address location selection and sustainability.

John discovered that for all locations, whether domestic or worldwide, factors such as labor, land availability and cost, proximity to markets, and proximity to suppliers, taxes, and incentives were key considerations. When locating outside the home country, currency exchange and stability as well as national competitiveness were examined.

Because of Nishimura's corporate values, senior management wanted to ensure sustainability was addressed. Logistics sustainability is defined as "the efforts of transportation companies to reduce carbon emissions, and improve supply chain efficiencies and environmental performance." Therefore, one key to sustainability was reducing fuel consumption. Nishimura's fulfillment and distribution centers deal in tons of cargo. Its fleet's fuel consumption was tremendous. Pollution was also a concern. John discovered that these two sustainability issues could be addressed by utilizing state-of-the art technology such as more fuel-efficient engines; however, the cost may be prohibitive when upgrading Nishimura's large transportation fleet.

John's analysis determined that location selection could help reduce these sustainability concerns. Instead of focusing on either proximity to markets or suppliers, a more balanced assessment could significantly reduce fuel consumption and pollution. Examining the transportation needs from a long-term perspective would enable a more efficient use of transportation options. The Council of Logistics defines logistics as "the process of planning the efficient, effective flow of goods from point of origin to point of consumption." Armed with this knowledge, John recognized that Nishimura must utilize all the tools of logistics management to address not only the best cost per shipment, but all the concerns associated with freight transportation, such as fuel consumption and pollution. Therefore, John planned to recommend that the location selection process include sustainability as a major factor. His recommendation would include factoring in fuel consumption and pollution to prove how, in the long term, location selection would reduce these issues.

DISCUSSION QUESTIONS

1. Instead of focusing only on the best cost alternative for their shipping, companies can use a combination of modes. What is the term that describes this action? What would be required to make it efficient and effective? Could this be a consideration for Nishimura?
2. What are the supply chain environmental challenges in this case? What are some examples of tools, programs, or partnerships that Nishimura can use to enhance logistics sustainability?
3. What are some issues with barge, rail, and truck transportation systems that affect sustainability?
4. Two common location analysis techniques are the weighted-factor rating technique and the center-of-gravity technique. Which technique would be best to use based on the argument that sustainability must be a major consideration? Why?

Note: Written by Rick Bonsall, D. Mgt., McKendree University, Lebanon, IL. The people and company are fictional and any resemblance to any person or company is coincidental. This case was prepared solely to provide material for class discussion. The author does not intend to illustrate either effective or ineffective handling of a managerial situation.

CASE 4: Apple's Location Strategy

"Location, location, location" is an operations management phrase spoken over and over. It signifies how important selecting the location of manufacturing facilities or retail stores is to the success of a business. Apple is very concerned about the location of its retail stores. Clearly, its retail stores are a critical channel for supplying both goods and services to its customers.

Apple opened its first retail store in the United States in 2001.[1] Since then, Apple has grown the number of its retail stores in the United States and expanded the retail store strategy throughout the world. By 2014, Apple had 255 retail stores in 44 states in the United States, and 169 retail stores in 14 foreign countries.[2] Apple is very particular about the type of retail location it requires. Management puts a premium on high-traffic locations with eye-catching architecture. To ensure a high volume of traffic, Apple looks for specific transportation modes such as subways and buses, and heavily traveled streets. Its New York store in the Upper West Side is renowned for its architecture. It has ground-floor stone walls 45 feet tall and a glass roof.[1] Furthermore, it concentrates on upscale, quality shopping venues. Apple's emphasis on upscale locations serves as a means for drawing quality labor and Apple customers. Although proximity to suppliers is often a consideration for companies in determining location, Apple is more interested in proximity to markets. This weight on proximity to markets correlates to its emphasis on upscale shopping venues.

The success of this location selection strategy is clearly evident in Apple's retail store growth. However, there may be a more telling sign. Microsoft started opening retail stores in 2009, eight years after Apple. Its overarching location selection strategy is to locate retail stores next to Apple's.[3] Although Microsoft still needs to select the specific spot, its location selection process has been shortened by following Apple's lead. Microsoft has retail stores located in 37 states (38, if you include Puerto Rico) and one foreign country—Canada. In 2015, it planned to open an additional retail store in Sydney, Australia. Microsoft's state and country selections match quite closely with Apple's, which is further evidence of the same location selection process.[4,5]

DISCUSSION QUESTIONS

1. Describe the selection criteria used by Apple.
2. Did Microsoft make the correct decision by adopting Apple's location strategy? Explain your answer.
3. Microsoft started its retail store strategy eight years after Apple. Why do you think it has nearly caught up with Apple in the number of states served by its retail stores?

Note: Written by Rick Bonsall, D. Mgt., McKendree University, Lebanon, IL. This case was prepared solely to provide material for class discussion. The author does not intend to illustrate either effective or ineffective handling of a managerial situation.

Sources:

1. LaVallee, A. (2009). Apple's "significant store" strategy. *Wall Street Journal*, http://blogs.wsj.com/digits/2009/11/12/apples-significant-store-strategy/
2. Apple's retail expansion is about how it can emerge from its own shadow. (2014). MarketWatch, http://blogs.marketwatch.com/behindthestorefront/
3. Wingfield, N. (2009). Microsoft retail fail? They laughed at Apple, too. *Wall Street Journal*, http://blogs.wsj.com/digits/2009/10/15/microsoft-retail-fail-they-laughed-at-apple-too/
4. Microsoft store locations, http://www.microsoft.com/en-us/store/locations
5. Apple retail stores, United States, http://www.apple.com/retail/storelist/

VIDEO CASE STUDY

Learn more about ***logistics*** from real organizations that use operations management techniques every day. Amy Keelin and Christine Keelin are COO and CFO (respectively) at MPK Foods, a small family-owned company based in Duarte, California, that produces seasoning mixes sold to grocery stores. Logistics decisions can greatly affect whether a company is able to deliver its good or services on time. Watch this short interview to learn how MPK makes those decisions.

iStock/claudiodivizia

Everyone wants better visibility throughout their supply chains, but the level of integration across supply chains to get that visibility is getting harder.

—**DAVID CAHN,** VP, corporate product strategy, CDC Software[1]

Creating a better world requires teamwork, partnerships, and collaboration, as we need an entire army of companies to work together to build a better world within the next few decades. This means corporations must embrace the benefits of cooperating with one another.

—**SIMON MAINWARING,** award-winning branding consultant, advertising creative director, and social media specialist[2]

INTEGRATING PROCESSES ALONG THE SUPPLY CHAIN

16

LEARNING OBJECTIVES

After completing this chapter, you should be able to:

16.1 Discuss the importance of process integration in managing supply chains
16.2 Summarize the obstacles to successful process integration
16.3 Describe the issues associated with supply chain risk and security
16.4 Describe the important trends in process integration

PROCESS INTEGRATION IS A COMPLEX UNDERTAKING AT IBM

IBM's supply chains include hundreds of thousands of suppliers for the many products it makes, including mainframe computers, servers, software, and spare parts. For supply chains of this size and complexity, process integration is no small task. Essentially, process integration at IBM has matured as the company evolved.

Initially, IBM let each business unit within the company run itself, including managing its supply chains. Later, as IBM became more of a global enterprise, supply chain integration became much more complex. Today, nothing is done locally—all supply chain processes are fully integrated on a global basis, from purchasing to manufacturing to logistics.

Originally, purchased goods arrived at one production site and finished products came out on the other end, and everything was managed on site. Now that IBM's global supply chains are more complex, the movements of goods, the processes, and communications are managed within and across all supply chains, using business analytics. IBM's integrated supply chains can handle orders for a new mainframe computer, software, service orders, and orders for spare parts using the same corporate worldwide system.

IBM managers need to know how supply chains are performing, so any problems can receive attention. IBM realizes that its ability to perform depends on the information given to its suppliers, so they can contribute to IBM's overall success. "Collaboration with our suppliers and business partners is very important to us today," says Mike Ray, IBM's VP of business integration. "In the old days, relationships with suppliers were almost adversarial at times. The buyer never gave much information to the supplier and the supplier wouldn't communicate much either. This led to many problems because of mismatches on requirements. What we learned is that everyone engaged in the supply chain, whether it is the buyer, or the supplier, or the logistics provider, needs visibility and information."

IBM also extends its integration efforts to sustainability initiatives, to achieve cost savings. It calls this its Green Sigma tool. It creates facility efficiencies using instrumentation with analytics to measure energy usage. Several years ago, IBM reduced overall energy usage across its business units by 10% and has continued to lower energy usage by 5% annually. This service is also made available to its suppliers and customers.[3]

INTRODUCTION

As first discussed in Chapter 1 and mentioned throughout the text, the network of companies making parts, supplies, and eventually finished goods and services available to customers, including the processes involved in purchasing, production, and logistics, is called a supply chain. Typically, a firm has multiple supply chains (one for each item produced) consisting of suppliers, customers, and the internal departments and personnel involved. The primary goal in supply chain management is to manage these processes to create value for the goods and services provided to customers, which in turn benefits the firm, its customers, and its suppliers.

To maximize value, firms in a supply chain must integrate process activities with their trading partners. The term **process integration** means sharing information, collaborating, and coordinating resources to jointly manage a process. Recall that the eight key supply chain processes discussed in Chapter 1 became the foundation for many of the chapters in this textbook, with the objective being to integrate these processes with suppliers and customers. While this text has discussed these processes and other issues concerning production, purchasing, and logistics, the idea that processes must be coordinated and shared or integrated among supply chain members to maximize value has only been briefly mentioned thus far. This chapter discusses process integration in detail.

iStock/mattjeacock

Process integration is a challenging, yet necessary, component of supply chain management.

For many firms, process integration can be a significant problem—employees and their managers may be more accustomed to "protecting turf" than coordinating activities with another company's personnel. Even information sharing among personnel inside the firm can be problematic. In fact, a recent survey of human resource managers and business executives found internal process integration to be one of the most challenging activities to implement and sustain.[4] Furthermore, since internal process integration between departments is considered to be a necessary foundation for successful external integration between trading partners, then problems with internal process integration would make external process integration even more difficult to achieve. This chapter discusses the key business processes requiring integration, the impact of integration on the bullwhip effect, the importance of process integration in supply chain management, and issues of supply chain risk and security that come about as information is shared.

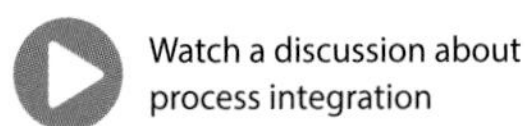

Watch a discussion about process integration

Supply chain process integration can be an extremely difficult task because it requires proper training and preparedness, willing and competent trading partners, trust, compatible information systems, and potentially a change in one or more organizational cultures. However, the benefits of collaboration and information sharing among companies in a supply chain can be significant: reduced supply chain costs, greater flexibility to respond to market changes, fewer process problems (and, hence, less need for safety stock), higher quality levels, reduced time to market, and better utilization of resources. A model representing the steps recommended for process integration is discussed next.

THE SUPPLY CHAIN PROCESS INTEGRATION MODEL

16.1 Discuss the importance of process integration in managing supply chains

Figure 16.1 presents the supply chain process integration model, starting with the identification of key trading partners, development of supply chain strategies, aligning key process objectives with supply chain strategies, developing external supply chain performance measures for each key process, integrating key processes with supply chain partners, and then reevaluating the integration model periodically. Each of the elements in the model is discussed next.

process integration Sharing information, collaborating, and coordinating resources to jointly manage a process.

key trading partners Trusted suppliers that provide a substantial share of the firm's purchased goods and services; and satisfied customers who buy a significant portion of the firm's products.

IDENTIFY KEY TRADING PARTNERS

For each of the firm's goods and services produced, it is important to identify the critical or **key trading partners** that will eventually enable the successful sale and delivery of

Figure 16.1 Supply Chain Process Integration Model

Identify key trading partners
Establish supply chain strategies
Align key process objectives with supply chain strategies
Develop performance measures for each integrated process
Assess and improve external process integration
Re-evaluate annually or as required

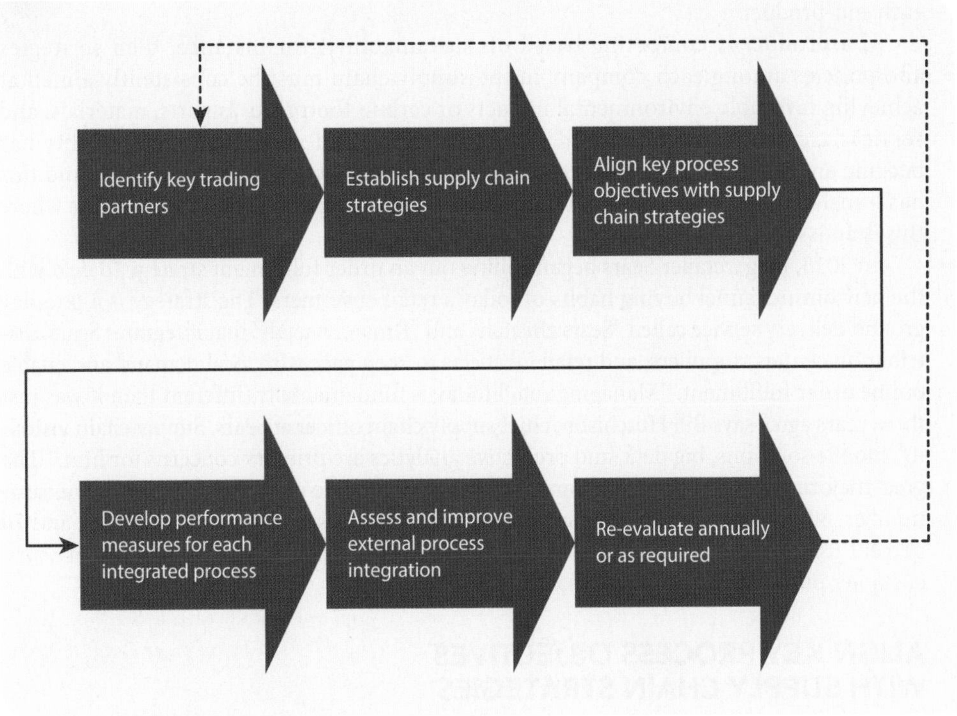

end-products to the final customers. Over time, companies create these trading partners through long-term, successful business dealings—trusted suppliers that provide a substantial share of the firm's purchased goods and services, and satisfied customers who buy a significant portion of the firm's products. Identifying the key suppliers and customers allows the firm to concentrate its time and resources on managing important process links with these companies, enabling the larger supply chain to perform better (i.e., the suppliers' suppliers and the customers' customers). Including nonessential businesses will prove counterproductive in terms of successful supply chain management. In a landmark supply chain paper written in 1998, the authors defined key trading partners as "all those autonomous companies or strategic business units who actually perform operational and/or managerial activities in the business processes designed to produce a specific output for a particular customer or market."[5]

Watch how an organization worked with its trading partners to improve the supply chain

Depending on where within a supply chain a firm is physically located (close to its suppliers, close to its markets, or somewhere in between), the structure of the network of key trading partners will vary. Identifying the network of key trading partners for each of the firm's goods and services is something that should be done to help the firm decide which businesses to include in its process integration efforts. Coordinating processes with its key suppliers was seen as so important to IBM, for example, that in 2006 it moved its global procurement headquarters to Shenzhen, China, from the United States.[6]

ESTABLISH SUPPLY CHAIN STRATEGIES

Management should identify the appropriate supply chain strategies associated with each of their firm's goods and services. Some end-products, for example, may be competing primarily based on quality, while others rely more on price, customer service, or sustainability to attract customers (as discussed in Chapter 2). The end-product strategy should translate into policies for each company in the supply chain regarding the designs of the parts and components to be manufactured; the parts, services, and supplies to be purchased; the suppliers used; the manufacturing processes employed; the logistics systems to be used; the warranty and return services offered; and the amount of outsourcing employed. In each of these areas, policies should be geared toward supporting the overall supply chain strategy for each end-product.

If a product is competing based on sustainability, for instance, then strategies and policies among each company in the supply chain must be consistently aimed at achieving favorable environmental impacts or carbon footprints as parts, materials, and services are produced and moved along toward the end-customer. Sustainability has become an important issue today as organizations seek better ways to compete, and this has translated into sustainability requirements for all companies in supply chains where this is an issue.

In 2015, megaretailer Sears began rolling out an order fulfillment strategy to deal with the new omnichannel buying habits of today's retail customers. The strategy is a one-day ground delivery service called "Sears cheetah" and "Kmart cheetah" that integrates Sears' distribution centers, suppliers, and retail locations to keep pace with local demand and enable online order fulfillment. "Managing retail today is fundamentally different than it was just three years ago," says Bill Hutchison, chief supply chain officer at Sears. Supply chain visibility, mobile solutions, big data, and predictive analytics are primary concerns for him. "The great majority of our customers shop online before coming to our stores," he says. "The same number, 80 percent, rely on their social networks when researching new products, and 70 percent use their smart phones for shopping the store." Today, the vast majority of Sears' customer purchases are influenced online.[7]

ALIGN KEY PROCESS OBJECTIVES WITH SUPPLY CHAIN STRATEGIES

Following discussions with the firm's key customers and suppliers, the primary supply chain strategies can be identified for each of the firm's products. Managers then need to identify the important processes contributing to successful goods and services and align process objectives to ensure that resources and efforts are effectively deployed within each firm and aligned with the correct supply chain strategy. If the end-product competes using a low-cost strategy, for example, then purchased items and other resources should also seek to maintain low costs. Key suppliers should also be on board with the same low-cost initiatives (hence the need for process integration).

Chapter 1 reviewed the eight important supply chain business processes, and these are again shown in Table 16.1. Discussions of each of these processes can be found throughout the text; therefore, only brief descriptions are provided here. Recall that a **process** can be defined as a set of activities designed to utilize inputs to produce a good or service for an internal or external customer.

process A set of activities designed to utilize inputs to produce a good or service for an internal or external customer.

Customer Relationship Management

The **customer relationship management process** provides the firm with the structure for developing and managing customer relationships. As discussed in Chapters 5 and 10, key customers are identified, their needs are determined, and then goods and services are developed to meet their needs. Over time, relationships with these key customers are solidified through the sharing of information; the formation of cross-company teams to improve product design, delivery, quality, and cost; and the development of shared goals.

customer relationship management process Provides the firm with the structure for developing and managing customer relationships. Key customers are identified, their needs are determined, and then goods and services are developed to meet their needs. Over time, relationships with these key customers are solidified through the sharing of information; the formation of cross-company teams to improve product design, delivery, quality, and cost; and the development of shared goals.

Customer Service Management

As discussed in Chapter 5, the **customer service management process** is what provides information to customers and manages all product and service agreements between the firm and its customers. Information can be offered through a number of communication channels including websites, personal interactions, information system linkages, and printed media. Objectives and policies are developed to ensure proper distribution of goods and services to customers, to adequately respond to product and delivery complaints, and to utilize the most effective means of communication. The process also includes methods for monitoring and reporting customer service performance.

customer service management process Providing information to customers and managing all product and service agreements between the firm and its customers.

Table 16.1 The Eight Key Supply Chain Processes

Process	Description	Associated Activities
Customer relationship management	Creating and maintaining customer relationships	Identify and categorize key customers; tailor goods and services to meet the needs of customer groups.
Customer service management	Interacting with customers to maintain customer satisfaction	Manage product and service agreements with customers; design and implement customer response procedures.
Demand management	Balancing customer demand with supply capabilities	Forecast demand; plan or adjust capacity to meet demand; develop contingency plans for imbalances.
Order fulfillment	Satisfying customer orders	Design distribution network to deliver products on time.
Manufacturing flow management	Making products to satisfy target markets	Design manufaturing processes to create products customers want.
Supplier relationship management	Creating and maintaining supplier relationships	Identify key suppliers; establish formal relationships; further develop key suppliers.
Product development and commercialization	Develop new products frequently and get them to market effectively	Develop sources for new ideas; develop cross-functional product teams, including customers and suppliers.
Returns management	Managing product returns and disposal effectively	Develop guidelines for returns and disposal; develop returns network.

Source: The Global Supply Chain Forum, The Ohio State University, www.fisher.osu.edu/centers/scm

Demand Management

The **demand management process**, as discussed in Chapter 6, balances customer demand and the firm's production capabilities. The specific demand management activities include forecasting demand and then utilizing techniques to vary capacity and demand within the purchasing, production, and distribution functions. Forecasts are used to predict demand requirements, and can be made more accurate using a collaborative planning approach with customers. A number of effective techniques exist to smooth demand variabilities and increase or decrease capacity when disparities exist between demand and supply.

Watch an organization discuss how it manages customer orders

demand management process Balancing customer demand and the firm's production capabilities. The specific demand management activities include forecasting demand and then utilizing techniques to vary capacity and demand within the purchasing, production, and distribution functions.

Order Fulfillment

The **order fulfillment process** is the set of activities that allows the firm to fill customer orders while providing the required levels of customer service at the lowest possible cost. Thus, the order fulfillment process must integrate the firm's marketing, production, and logistics plans to be effective. As discussed in Chapter 15, order fulfillment issues include the location of suppliers, the modes of inbound and outbound transportation used, and the location of production facilities and distribution centers. The order fulfillment process must integrate closely with customer relationship management, customer service management, supplier relationship management, and returns management to ensure that customer requirements are being met.

order fulfillment process The set of activities that allows the firm to fill customer orders while providing the required levels of customer service at the lowest possible cost.

Manufacturing Flow Management

As discussed in Chapter 8, the **manufacturing flow management process** is the set of activities responsible for making the actual product, establishing the manufacturing flexibility required to adequately serve the markets, and designing the production system to meet order

manufacturing flow management process The set of activities responsible for making the actual product, establishing the manufacturing flexibility required to adequately serve the markets, and designing the production system to meet order lead-time requirements.

MANUFACTURING SPOTLIGHT

Sanyuan Foods Integrates Its Milk Supply Chain

Lou Linwei/Alamy

In 2008, a Chinese milk scandal involved melamine, a chemical used in fertilizers. It was used to increase the milk's protein levels so it could be sold at a higher price. Twenty Chinese milk producers used it in 2008, sickening 300,000 infants and killing 6. The Sanlu Group, for example, knew that its milk suppliers added melamine to the milk used in its baby formula, but continued to distribute it for months after the discovery. Sanlu was ultimately shut down.

The lack of accountability and integration proved fatal to Sanlu and its supply chain members. Sanlu received complaints about its formula as early as December 2007, yet did nothing about it. Operators, managers, and owners at various points in Sanlu's supply chain allowed the tainted milk to be produced and distributed to reduce quickly rising costs in the Chinese milk industry.

In comparison, Sanyuan Foods' highly integrated supply chain guaranteed the quality of its milk products and kept it successful. Sanyuan maintained caution while expanding its supply chain beyond northern China. This strategy allowed it to focus more attention on its trading partners. The company created secure milk sources by using dairy farms run with strict quality-control systems for animal feed procurement, veterinary care, milking, and delivery of milk to processing plants. Sanyuan directly participated in the establishment of these quality-management systems.[8]

lead-time requirements. As customers and their requirements change, the supply chain and the manufacturing flow process must also change, to maintain competitiveness. As was shown in Chapter 9, the flexibility and rapid response requirements in many supply chains result in the firm's use of lean systems in order to continue to meet customer requirements.

Manufacturing flow characteristics also impact supplier requirements. For instance, as manufacturing batch sizes and lead-time requirements are reduced, supplier deliveries must become smaller and more frequent, potentially causing supplier interactions and supplier relationships to change.

Supplier Relationship Management

The supplier relationship management process defines how the firm manages its relationships with suppliers. As was discussed in Chapter 14, firms in actively managed supply chains seek out small numbers of the best-performing suppliers and establish ongoing, mutually beneficial, close relationships with these suppliers in order to meet cost, quality, and customer service objectives for key materials, products, and services. For other, nonessential items, firms may use reverse auctions, bid arrangements, or catalogues to select suppliers. Activities in this process include screening and selecting suppliers, negotiating product and service agreements, monitoring supplier performance, and interacting with suppliers for new product design and development purposes. As discussed in the Manufacturing Spotlight above, the Chinese company Sanyuan Foods used close relationships with its supply chain trading partners to avoid problems in the 2008 melamine milk scandal in that country.

Product Development and Commercialization

Product design and development was discussed in Chapter 3. As defined in Chapter 1, the product development and commercialization process is responsible for developing new products to meet changing customer requirements and then getting these products to market quickly. This process can become integrated when customers and suppliers are involved with the firm in new product development, to ensure that products conform to customers' needs and purchased items meet manufacturing requirements. Activities in the product development and commercialization process include methods and incentives for generating new product ideas; the formation of new product development teams; assessing and selecting new product ideas; determining marketing channels and rolling out the products; and, finally, assessing the success of each new product.

Returns Management

The returns management process, discussed in Chapter 15, can be extremely beneficial for supply chain management in terms of maintaining acceptable levels of customer service and identifying product improvement opportunities. Returns management activities include proper reconditioning, recycling, or disposal of goods; warranty repairs; and collecting returns data. Returns management personnel frequently communicate with customers, as well as personnel from customer relationship management, during the returns process.

One of the goals of returns management is to reduce returns. This is accomplished by communicating return and repair information to product development personnel, suppliers, and other potential contributors to any returns problems, to guide the improvement of future product and purchased item designs.

For each of the eight processes identified previously, objectives or goals must be developed to help guide the firm toward its integration goals. Additionally, consistent objectives within each functional area of the firm can help integrate processes internally, as well as focus efforts and firm resources toward attaining the supply chain strategy. For instance, if the supply chain strategy is to compete using low pricing, marketing objectives for the customer relationship management process might be to find cheaper delivery alternatives, develop vendor-managed inventory accounts, and automate the customer order process. Production objectives might be to develop bulk packaging solutions consistent with the modes of transportation and distribution systems used, to increase mass production capabilities, and to identify the lowest total cost manufacturing sites for specific products. Purchasing objectives might be to identify the cheapest materials and components that meet specifications and to utilize reverse auctions whenever possible. Firms should similarly progress through each of the key processes using teams of employees from each function to develop process objectives.

DEVELOP PERFORMANCE MEASURES FOR EACH INTEGRATED PROCESS

Firms should develop performance measures to monitor integrations with trading partners in each of the key supply chain process areas discussed previously. Teams consisting of representatives from all primary trading partners should be created to design and discuss these measures, to maintain consistencies with the supply chain strategies for each product.

In highly integrated supply chains, trading partners monitor a number of performance measures that are *averaged across the member firms* for each key supply chain process, resulting in an overall picture of supply chain performance. Inbound and outbound logistics costs, for example, have come under much greater scrutiny over the past few years because of rising fuel costs. High fuel prices have increased the pressure on trading partners to find cheaper ways to transport goods in a timely fashion, and this can be particularly problematic for global supply chains. While the topic of performance measures was discussed initially in Chapter 2, a number of other traditional supply chain integration performance measures are described in Table 16.2.

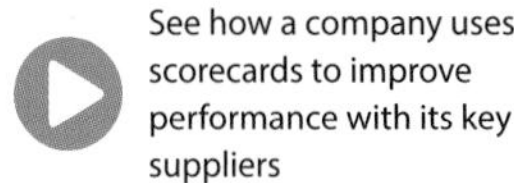

See how a company uses scorecards to improve performance with its key suppliers

The SCOR Model

One method for integrating supply chains and measuring performance is the Supply Chain Operations Reference (SCOR®) model developed in 1996 by supply chain consulting firms Pittiglio, Rabin, Todd & McGrath and AMR Research. These firms also founded the Texas-based Supply Chain Council, a nonprofit global organization with a current membership of over 1,000 profit and nonprofit organizations on six continents. In 2014, the Supply Chain Council merged with APICS, the global professional association for supply chain and operations management, to form the APICS Supply Chain Council. The purpose of the Supply Chain Council is to manage the SCOR model, while providing education opportunities for its members.[9]

SCOR model Helps to integrate the operations of supply chain members by linking the delivery operations of the seller to the sourcing operations of the buyer.

The **SCOR model** helps to integrate the operations of supply chain members by linking the delivery operations of the seller to the sourcing operations of the buyer. Starting in 2013, members could obtain a professional certification in knowledge and methods of the SCOR

Table 16.2 Supply Chain Performance Measures

Performance Measure	Description
Total supply chain management costs	The costs to process orders, purchase materials, purchase energy, comply with environmental regulations, manage inventories and returns, and manage supply chain finance, planning, and information systems. Leading supply chains spend an average of 4 to 5% of sales on supply chain management costs. The average company spends about 5 to 6%.
Supply chain cash-to-cash cycle time	The average number of days between paying for raw materials and getting paid for product, for the supply chain trading partners (calculated by inventory days of supply + days of sales outstanding – average payment period for material). This measure shows the impact of lower inventories on the speed of cash moving through firms and the supply chain. The best supply chains have an average cash-to-cash cycle time of about 30 days, which is far less than the average company.
Supply chain production flexibility	The average time required for supply chain members to provide an unplanned, sustainable 20% increase in production. The ability for the supply chain to quickly react to unexpected demand spikes while still maintaining financial targets provides tremendous competitive advantage. One common supply chain practice is to maintain stocks of component parts locally for supply chain customers to quickly respond to unexpected demand increases. Average production flexibility for best-in-class supply chains is from one to two weeks.
Supply chain delivery performance	The average percentage of orders that are filled on or before the requested delivery date. In the top-performing supply chains, delivery dates are being met from 94 to 100% of the time. For other firms, delivery performance is approximately 70 to 80%.
Supply chain perfect order fulfillment performance	The average percentage of orders that arrive on time, complete, and damage-free. This is quickly becoming the standard for delivery performance and represents a significant source of competitive advantage for top-performing supply chains.
Supply chain e-business performance	The average percentage of electronic orders received for all supply chain members. In 1998, only about 2% of all firms' purchase orders were made over the Internet. By 2007, for example, office supply retailer Staples said that 90% of their orders came in electronically. Additionally, use of e-procurement can save up to 90% of the administrative costs of ordering.[10] Today, supply chain companies are investing heavily in e-based order-receipt systems and marketing strategies.
Supply chain environmental performance	The percentage of supply chain trading partners that have become ISO 14000 certified; the percentage of supply chain trading partners that have created a director of environmental sustainability; the average percentage of environmental goals met; the average number of policies adopted to reduce greenhouse gas emissions; and the average percentage of carbon footprints that have been offset by sound environmental practices.

Source: Adapted from Geary, S., and Zonnenburg, J. P. (2000, July). What it means to be best in class. *Supply Chain Management Review*, July 2000: 42–50.

model, termed a SCOR-P certification. Also new for 2013, the SCOR model's 11th revision has added a new process category, ENABLE, as shown in the model in Figure 16.2.[11]

The SCOR model is used as a supply chain management diagnostic, benchmarking, and process improvement tool by manufacturing and service firms in a variety of industries around the globe. Some of the notable firms to have success using the SCOR model include Intel, IBM, 3M, Cisco, Siemens, and Bayer. Striving for the best telecommunications supply chain, Alcatel (now Alcatel-Lucent), for example, used SCOR metrics following the economic downturn of 2001 to measure and benchmark its performance. Major improvements were realized in delivery performance, sourcing cycle time, supply chain management cost, and inventory days of supply.[12] Cisco set out to revamp its supply chain in 2005 using the SCOR model as a way to monitor its growing global footprint. It eventually appointed a vice president responsible for the SCOR model's functions.[13] In 2010, German semiconductor manufacturer Infineon used the SCOR model to build an agile and adaptable supply chain. Hundreds of employees, customers, suppliers, and production partners were involved in the 18-month project. Results included improved flexibility and reduction of total finished goods inventory levels, leading to improved shareholder confidence and stock price.[14]

The SCOR model separates supply chain operations into six process categories—plan, source, make, deliver, return, and enable, as described in Table 16.3.[15]

Figure 16.2 The SCOR Model Processes and Linkages

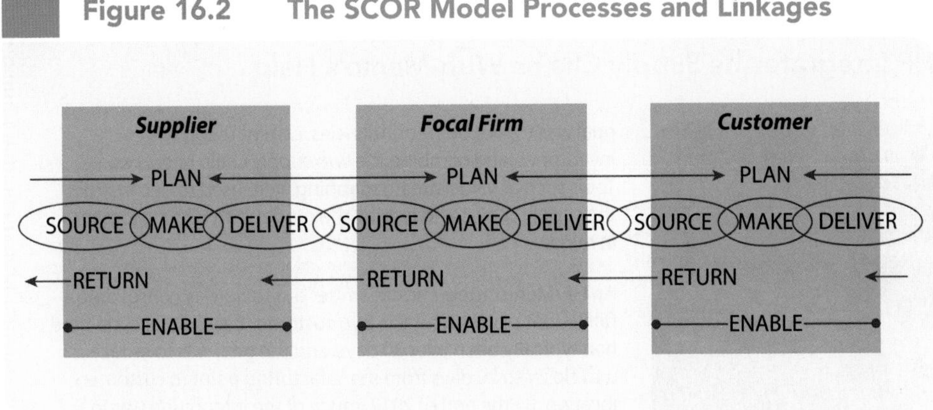

Implementing the SCOR model is no simple task. It requires a significant investment of time, and open communications within the firm and among supply chain partners. However, the firms that use the model find it very beneficial. For instance, Joe Williams, director of global productivity at Mead Johnson Nutritionals, a division of Bristol-Myers Squibb, says the SCOR model is playing a big role in helping its unit measure its supply chain performance against other companies. But getting those measurements "is a big job," he says. "SCOR is definitive in some respects and open to interpretation in others."

The SCOR model is designed to enable effective communication, performance measurement, and integration of processes among supply chain members. A standardized reference model helps management focus on management issues, serving internal and external customers, and instigating improvements along the supply chain. Using the SCOR software,

Table 16.3 SCOR Model Process Categories

Category	Description
Plan	Demand and supply planning that includes balancing resources with requirements; establishing/communicating plans for the supply chain; and managing supply chain performance, data collection, inventories, capital assets, transportation, and regulatory requirements.
Source	Sourcing products including scheduling deliveries and receiving, verifying, and transferring product; authorizing supplier payments; identifying and selecting suppliers and assessing supplier performance; managing incoming inventories and supplier agreements.
Make	Production execution including scheduling production activities, producing, testing, packaging, and releasing product for delivery; managing work in process, equipment, and facilities.
Deliver	Order, warehouse, and transportation management for all products, including all ordering steps from order inquiries and quotes to routing shipments and selecting carriers; warehouse management from receiving and picking to loading and shipping product; invoicing customers; managing finished product inventories and import/export requirements.
Return	Returns of purchased materials to suppliers and receipt of finished goods returns from customers, including authorizing and scheduling returns; receiving, verifying, and disposition of defective or excess products; return replacement or credit; and managing return inventories.
Enable	The processes associated with establishing, maintaining, and monitoring information, relationships, resources, assets, compliance, and contracts required to operate supply chains. Enable processes support the design and management of the planning and execution processes of supply chains.

MANUFACTURING SPOTLIGHT

HP Integrates Its Supply Chains With Menlo's Help

iStock/JasonDoiy

When computer maker HP acquired networking equipment company 3Com in 2009, the two companies' supply chains had to be integrated, both internally and externally. The company had to combine two different supply chains that were managing similar inventories and markets, and using very different strategies.

To assist with integration efforts, HP partnered with Menlo Logistics, a third-party logistics provider. The goal was to root out redundancies, eliminate surplus inventories, and combine the two supply chain networks. Tools such as value stream mapping were used to deconstruct the supply chains and rethink the model with HP's customers in mind.

An HP/Menlo integration team set out to quickly consolidate a fulfillment platform for the two customer bases. Total cycle time had typically been over 30 days, and the goal was to reduce it to closer to 20 days from manufacturing point to customer location. By the end of 2012, much of the integration was in place worldwide and working as planned. HP was successfully meeting the needs of different customer groups, and doing so with less time and cost.

Today, the new HP supply chain is a combination of the best of both companies' supply chains, one that has been optimized to grow the business. The supply chain has been consolidated and centralized, resulting in a streamlined operation that uses standardized processes across all regions. The whole integration effort was a collaboration, with Menlo and other 3PLs, allowing HP to deliver value for customers. This collaborative approach allowed HP to build trust in its supply chain that far exceeded initial expectations.[16]

virtually any supply chain can be configured, evaluated, and benchmarked against best practices, leading to continuous improvements and sustainable competitive advantage for the supply chain's participating members.

ASSESS AND IMPROVE EXTERNAL PROCESS INTEGRATION

Watch a discussion of tips for managing suppliers

Over time, organizations eliminate poor-performing suppliers as well as unprofitable customers, while concentrating their efforts on developing beneficial relationships with the remaining high-performing suppliers and high-profit customers. Building, maintaining, and strengthening these relationships is accomplished with process integration. As process integration matures among supply chain partners, supply chain performance improves and everyone benefits.

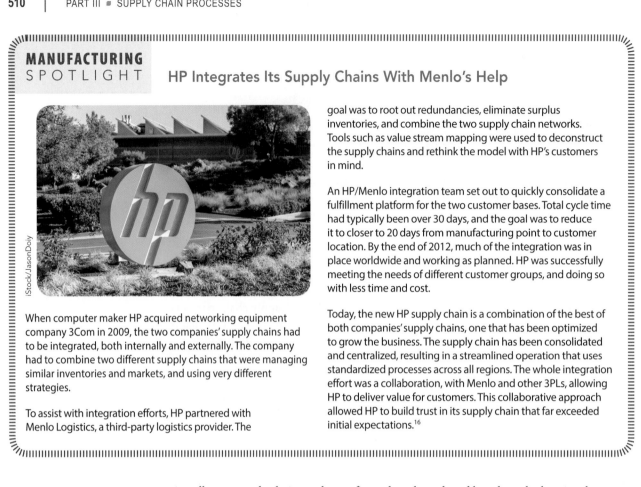

Supply chain members must be willing to share sales and forecast information, along with information on new products, capacity expansion plans, new technologies, and new marketing campaigns, in order to ultimately satisfy end-customers and maximize profits. Focusing on process integration will enable firms to collaborate and share information. The Manufacturing Spotlight above, for example, describes HP's efforts to integrate two separate supply chains when it purchased 3Com in 2009.

Teams formed to design and organize process performance measures should be viewed as a key resource for process integration. These teams can set and revise supply chain process objectives, and the type of information that must be shared to achieve the objectives. Once the performance metrics are designed for each process, they can be monitored to identify any integration problems or competitive weaknesses. Firms should jointly assess their levels of process performance and integration, and collaborate on methods to improve both. How important is process integration to improving supply chain performance? A McKinsey and Company "Supply Chain Champions" study was conducted to determine a number of characteristics of successful consumer goods supply chains. It plotted the performance of 40 leading packaged goods companies, and then correlated the success of these leaders with various supply chain attributes. Supply chain collaboration surfaced as the leading success factor.[17]

The way information is communicated plays an extremely important role in process integration. Today, connecting buyers and suppliers via the Internet is one important way that supply chains are becoming integrated. Generally termed **knowledge–management solutions**, these Internet applications enable real-time collaboration and flow of information among supply chain partners—the ability to "see" into suppliers' and customers' operations, collect supply chain data, and make faster decisions. "Today's competitive landscape is defined by companies that are best-in-class in managing their extended end-to-end supply chain," says Lorenzo Martinelli, executive vice president of E2Open, a California-based provider of supply chain management software.[18]

Supply chain communication and Internet technologies support the flow of goods and information among companies, the negotiation and execution of contracts, the management of supply and demand problems, making/executing orders, and the handling of financial settlements, all with a high level of security. California-based home textile retailer Anna's Linens uses an Internet portal solution to communicate with over 100 of its key suppliers and distributors. The system has enabled Anna's to make opportunistic purchases from other retail closures and immediately interpret global trends using real-time visibility within its supply chains.[19]

REEVALUATE THE INTEGRATION EFFORTS AS REQUIRED

In light of the fast-paced changes occurring with communication technologies and new products, new suppliers, and new markets, trading partners should revisit their integration model periodically to identify any changes and to assess the impact these changes are having on integration efforts. New suppliers may have entered the scene with better capabilities, more distribution choices, and better resources. Or perhaps the firm may be redesigning an older product, requiring different purchased components or supplier capabilities. The firm might also be moving into a new foreign market, potentially requiring an entirely different supply chain using a different competitive strategy. These examples are common and should cause firms to reevaluate their supply chain strategies, objectives, processes, performance measures, and integration levels.

The growing importance of global trade for the Canadian economy, for example, has made it extremely important for Canadian firms to reevaluate their supply chains often. For example, Canada's west coast container port traffic increased almost six-fold from 1990 to 2010. Rather than continuing with the standard strategy of manufacturing and sourcing in low-cost China, firms are now using a mix of strategies among opportunities in Canada, the United States, Europe, Mexico, and China. They are paying attention to lead-time variability, logistics costs, and on-time shipments when making their global manufacturing and sourcing decisions.[20]

OBSTACLES TO PROCESS INTEGRATION

16.2 Summarize the obstacles to successful process integration

A number of factors can impede process integration along supply chains, causing loss of visibility, information distortion, longer cycle times, stockouts, and the bullwhip effect, resulting in higher overall costs and lower customer satisfaction. Managers must try to identify these obstacles and take steps to eliminate them, to create more competitive supply chains. Table 16.4 summarizes these obstacles. Each of these is discussed next.

knowledge–management solutions Internet applications that enable real-time collaboration and flow of information among supply chain partners; the ability to "see" into suppliers' and customers' operations, collect supply chain data, and make faster decisions.

THE SILO MENTALITY

Too often, firms fail to consider the impacts of their actions on their supply chains and on long-term competitiveness and profitability. An "I win, you lose" **silo mentality** can occasionally be evidenced when using hard negotiations with the hungriest suppliers, paying little attention to the after-sale needs of customers, or assigning few resources toward developing new goods and services. Particularly with firms involved in global supply chains, silo mentalities can crop up as a result of cultural differences. The UK auto firm

silo mentality An "I win, you lose" attitude, as evidenced when using hard negotiations with the hungriest suppliers, paying little attention to the after-sale needs of customers, or assigning few resources toward developing new goods and services.

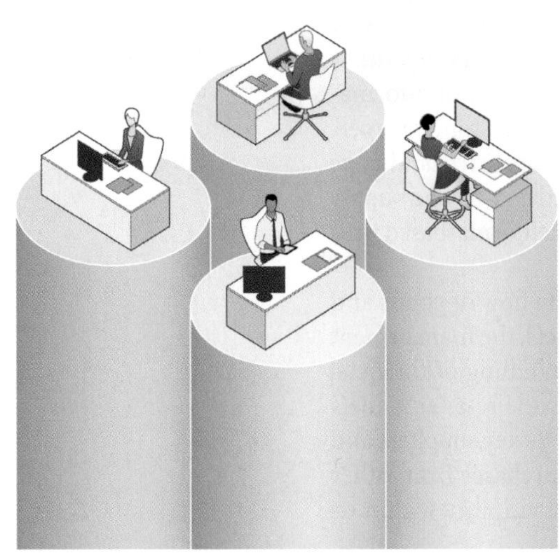

iStock/mathisworks

Operating with a silo mentality, disregarding the impact of a firm's decisions on other members of its supply chain, can lead to negative effects on the firm's competitiveness and profitability.

Rover is a case in point. In the 1980s, Rover formed a partnership with Japan-based Honda to provide products for its new model program. The arrogance of Rover managers and a lack of a learning culture at Rover prevented it from realizing any benefits from the partnership. Later, when the German firm BMW bought Rover, communications with German managers and political infighting were even worse. The managerial problems that surfaced with Chrysler and Daimler-Benz, leading to dissolution of that partnership, were similar.[21]

Eventually, lack of collaboration will create quality, cost, and customer service problems that are detrimental to supply chains. In fact, Wayne Bourne, vice president of logistics and transportation at electronics retailer Best Buy, noted in an interview that the most significant obstacle to overcome in supply chain management was the silo mentality that exists in companies.[22]

Internally, the silo effect might be found between personnel of different departments. The transportation manager, for instance, may be trying to minimize total annual transportation costs against the wishes of the firm's sales department. Delivery inconsistencies caused by use of the cheapest transportation providers might be causing the firm's retail customers to experience shortages, which deteriorate customer service levels. To overcome these and other silo mentalities, managers must strive to align supply chain goals and their own companies' goals and incentives. Functional decisions must be made while considering the impact on a firm's overall profits and those of their supply chain members. Performance reviews of managers should include the ability of their department to integrate processes internally and externally, and in meeting overall supply chain goals.

Outside the firm, managers must work to educate their suppliers and customers regarding the overall impact of their firms' actions on their supply chains. This should be an important part of the supply chain relationship management process. Additionally, suppliers should be annually evaluated and potentially replaced if their performance

Table 16.4 Obstacles to Process Integration

Silo mentality	Failing to see the big picture; acting only in regards to the firm itself.
Lack of information visibility	The inability to easily share or retrieve trading partner information in real time, as needed by supply chain partners.
Lack of trust	Unwillingness to share information due to a fear that the other party will take an unfair advantage or use the information unethically.
Lack of knowledge	Lack of process skills or knowledge regarding the long-term benefits of SCM.
Activities causing the bullwhip effect	
Demand forecast updating	Using varying customer orders to create and update forecasts, production schedules, and purchase requirements.
Order batching	Ordering large quantities of goods from suppliers on an infrequent basis to reduce order and transportation costs.
Price fluctuations	Offering price discounts to buyers, causing erratic buying patterns.
Rationing and shortage gaming	Allocating short product supplies to buyers, causing buyers to increase future orders beyond what they really need.

vis-à-vis supply chain objectives does not improve. California-based Sutter Health, a network of physicians, hospitals, and other healthcare providers, has long believed integration among all departments is the best and most efficient way to deliver care to patients. In fact, in a study by Dartmouth Medical School's Center for the Evaluative Clinical Sciences, Sutter's physicians, hospitals, home care, and hospice services were found to represent a national integration benchmark.[23]

LACK OF INFORMATION VISIBILITY

Lack of **information visibility** along the supply chain is also cited as a common process integration problem. Information visibility can be defined as the sharing of data in real time required to manage the flow of goods and services between suppliers and customers. In geographically dispersed supply chains, information visibility is particularly important. New product safety standards, trade agreements, and security mandates are changing almost daily, making information visibility critical for importers and shippers. "*Visibility* is not just about watching stuff happen," says Melissa Irmen, vice president of products and strategy for North Carolina–based *Integration* Point, a provider of global trade and regulatory compliance solutions. "Things are changing so fast, and to have connectivity to all partners is just critical."[24] In many cases, IT systems are to blame. In a survey of 1,500 pharmaceutical manufacturers, for instance, only one-third thought that their IT systems were providing adequate information visibility, even though most already had spent millions on ERP systems and other technologies.[25]

iStock/johnshepherd

Information visibility is crucial for the success of geographically dispersed supply chains. A lack of visibility can cause all kinds of supply chain problems.

If trading partners have to carve out data from their information systems and then send them to one another, where they then have to be uploaded to other systems prior to being shared and evaluated, the extra time can mean higher inventories, higher costs, longer response times, and lost customers. This is the primary problem that supply chain software producers are working to overcome today. Most of these software applications allow users to share data using third-party business applications with process integration capabilities. Keeping track of cargo containers for ocean carriers is one such area where supply chain visibility is creating big improvements for the parties involved. For every 100 incoming containers at ports, for instance, only about 45 go out loaded, leaving revenue-generating backhauls on the table. Better supply chain visibility in this case can lead to a better match of loads and containers.

Watch a discussion of visibility in the drug supply chain

RFID (radio frequency identification) technology can add tremendous real-time information visibility capabilities to supply chains. Users can determine the exact location of any product, anywhere in a supply chain, at any time. Furthermore, RFID tags can capture more accurate, specific, and timely data than barcodes, while reducing or eliminating data collection labor time and errors. When a shipment of roses, for example, drops below a safe temperature, an RFID system can alert dispatchers to send them to a closer destination. "When you have bad data, you make bad decisions," says Kaushal Vyas, director of product development at Georgia-based Infor, a business software provider. "You must be able to source and mine data from all the different places in real time, so you can focus on the exceptions that you need to manage in order to boost your performance."[26]

LACK OF TRUST

Successful process integration among trading partners requires trust, and as with the silo mentality and lack of information visibility, the lack of trust is seen as a major stumbling block in successful supply chain management. Trust develops over time among trading

information visibility The sharing of data in real time required to manage the flow of goods and services between suppliers and customers.

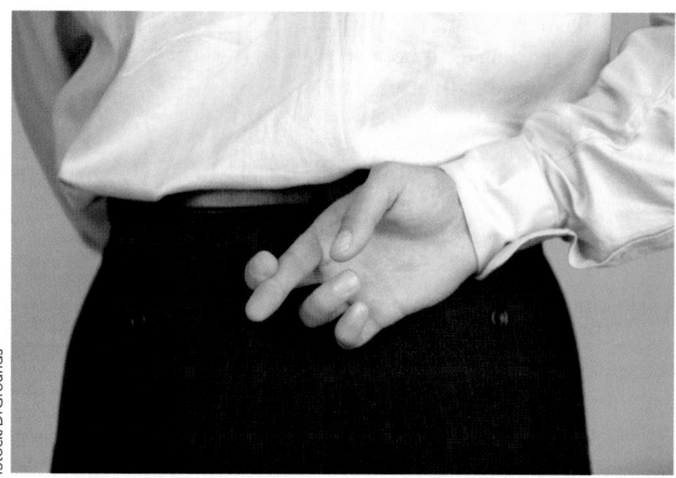
iStock/DrGrounds

Building trust with supply chain trading partners can take time, but it is a worthwhile investment. A lack of trust can seriously impede supply chain success.

partners, as each participant follows through on promises made to the other businesses. Even though this sounds cliché, relationships employing trust result in a win–win, or win–win–win, situation for the participants. Boeing's 787 Dreamliner, for example, had initial orders for 710 airplanes from 50 companies when it first debuted. Playing a central role in these orders were Boeing's 70 supplier–partners, which were supplying close to 70% of the airplane's parts and assemblies. The trust underlying the partnerships was clearly evident in the fact that Boeing also relied on these suppliers to perform detailed engineering and testing of many of the components supplied for the airliner.[27]

Unfortunately, old-fashioned company practices and purchasing habits don't change overnight. Until managers understand that it is in their firms' best interests to trust one another and collaborate, supply chain success will be an uphill battle. The Mayo Clinic builds a collaborative culture by hiring professionals with collaborative attitudes and a common set of deeply held values regarding care for patients. At computing giant IBM, CEO Sam Palmisano transformed an extremely hierarchical culture based on individualism to one of collaboration by organizing online, town hall–type meetings involving tens of thousands of IBM employees and dozens of trading partners. IBM reinforces collaboration with "thanks awards," which are T-shirts, backpacks, and other similar gear, emblazoned with the IBM logo and given by IBM employees.[28]

While the sharing of information among supply chain partners is growing in acceptance, many companies still have a long way to go. "We are early in the cycle, maybe in the second inning," says David Smith, head of human performance practice at Accenture, a global technology services consulting firm. "Companies are beginning to attack it. Very few are getting it right."[29]

LACK OF KNOWLEDGE

Companies have been slowly moving toward process integration for years, and it is just within the past few years that technology has caught up with this vision, enabling process integration across extended supply chains. Getting a network of firms and their employees to work together successfully, though, requires managers to use subtle persuasion and education to get their own firms and their trading partners to do the right things. The cultural, trust, and process knowledge differences in firms are such that firms successfully managing their supply chains must spend significant amounts of time influencing and increasing the capabilities of their own employees, as well as those of their trading partners.

collaborative education Training trading partner employees.

Training trading partner employees is known as **collaborative education**, and can result in faster process integration and, ultimately, more successful supply chains. As technologies change, as outsourcing increases, and as supply chains are expanded to foreign suppliers and markets, the pressure to extend software and management training to trading partners increases. As Rick Behrens, senior manager of supplier development at Boeing Company's Integrated Defense Systems unit, explains, "We look at our suppliers as an extension of Boeing. So, since we invest heavily in training and education of our employees, why wouldn't we invest in education and development for our suppliers?" Farm and construction equipment manufacturer John Deere, for example, has established a global learning and development center specifically for training its key suppliers.[30]

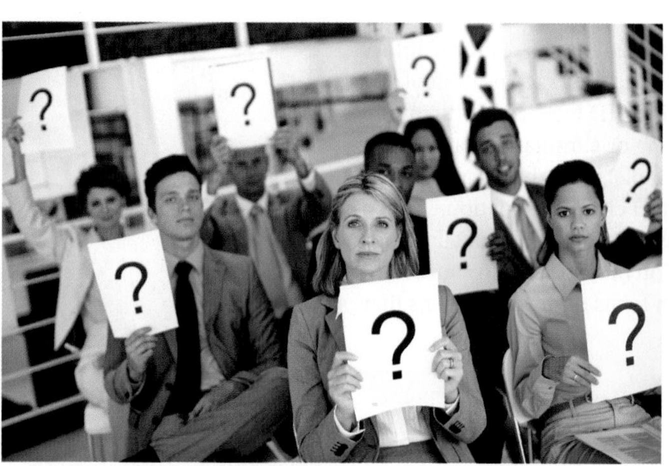

iStock/laflor

Process integration can only be done successfully if employees receive adequate training and education.

Change and information sharing can be threatening to people; they may fear losing control or losing their jobs, particularly if outsourcing accompanies process integration. Additionally, as firms construct their supply chain information infrastructures, they may find themselves with multiple ERP systems, a mainframe manufacturing application, and desktop analysis and design software that all need to be integrated both internally and externally. Managers have to realize that people using the systems must be involved early on in terms of the purchase decision, the implementation process, and with training.

For all organizations, successful process integration requires a regimen of ongoing training. When education and training are curtailed, innovation cannot occur, and innovation fuels competitiveness. Poor decision making and other human errors can have a rippling effect in supply chains, causing loss of confidence and trust, and a magnification of the error and correction costs. Industry trade shows, conferences, and expos can be valuable sources of learning, exchanging ideas, and gathering new information about process integration.

ACTIVITIES CAUSING THE BULLWHIP EFFECT

As discussed in Chapter 7 of this textbook, the bullwhip effect can be a pervasive and expensive problem along supply chains, and is caused by a number of factors that trading partners can control. Recall that even though end-item demand may be relatively constant, forecasts of demand by suppliers, combined with additions of safety stock to their production schedules to account for forecast errors, create larger and larger orders to suppliers as we move back up a supply chain, causing what is termed the *bullwhip effect*. These amplified orders cause problems with capacity planning, inventory control, and workforce and production scheduling, and they ultimately result in lower levels of customer service, greater overall levels of safety stock, and higher total supply chain costs. In some early research on the bullwhip effect, four major causes of the bullwhip effect were identified.[31] The causes of the bullwhip effect and the methods used to counteract them are discussed in the following sections.

Demand Forecast Updating

When a buyer places an order, the supplier might use that information as a predictor of future demand. Based on this information, suppliers update their demand forecasts and the corresponding orders they place with their own suppliers. If lead times vary between the time orders are placed and deliveries are made, then safety stocks also grow and are included in any future orders, which in turn cause the bullwhip effect for other suppliers' orders further up the supply chain. The bullwhip effect in this case is caused by frequent **demand forecast updating**.

One solution to this problem is for the buyer to make its actual demand data available to its suppliers. Better yet, if all point-of-sale data are made available to the upstream suppliers, all supply chain members can then update their demand forecasts less frequently, using actual demand data. This real demand information also tends to reduce safety stocks among supply chain members, generating even less variability in supply chain orders. Thus, the importance of supply chain information visibility can again be seen.

Using the same forecasting techniques and buying practices over time also tends to smooth demand variabilities and hence safety stock among supply chain members. Reducing the length of the supply chain can also lessen the bullwhip effect by reducing the number of occasions where forecasts are calculated and safety stocks are added. Examples of this are Drugstore.com, Amazon.com, and other firms that bypass distributors and resellers and sell directly to consumers. These companies can see actual end-customer demand, resulting in much more stable and accurate forecasts.

demand forecast updating When a buyer places an order, the supplier might use that information as a predictor of future demand. Based on this information, suppliers update their demand forecasts and the corresponding orders they place with their own suppliers. If lead times vary between the time orders are placed and deliveries are made, then safety stocks also grow and are included in any future orders, which in turn, cause the bullwhip effect for other suppliers' orders further up the supply chain.

Order Batching

In a typical buyer–supplier scenario, customer demand draws down existing inventories until a reorder point is reached wherein the buyer places an order with the supplier. Inventory levels, prior delivery performance, or the desire to order full truckloads or container loads of materials may cause orders to be placed at varying time intervals. For example, the supplier receives an order from a customer; then, at some future time period, another order is received from the same customer, for a quantity much different in size from the prior order. This type of random **order batching** creates demand variabilities that cause the use of safety stock by the supplier, creating a bullwhip effect.

Another type of order batching can occur when salespeople need to fill end-of-quarter or end-of-year sales quotas, or when buyers desire to fully spend budget allocations at the end of their fiscal year. These erratic surges in year-end production and buying also create the bullwhip effect. If the timing of these surges is the same for many of the firm's customers, the bullwhip effect can be severe.

Using information visibility and more frequent and smaller order sizes will tend to reduce the order batching problem. When suppliers know that large orders are occurring because of the need to spend budgeted monies, for instance, they will not revise forecasts based on this information. Furthermore, when using automated or computer-assisted order systems, order costs are reduced, allowing firms to order more frequently. To counteract the need to order full truckloads or container loads of an item, firms can order smaller quantities of a variety of items from a supplier, or use a freight forwarder to consolidate small shipments, to avoid the high unit cost of transporting at less-than-truckload or less-than-container load quantities.

order batching Inventory levels, prior delivery performance, or the desire to order full truckloads or container loads of materials may cause orders to be placed at random or varying time intervals, which creates order variances.

forward buying When buyers "stock up" to take advantage of discounted prices, causing order and order timing variances. Also known as stockpiling.

everyday low pricing (EDLP) When manufacturers reduce the forward buying of their customers by offering uniform wholesale prices, instead of occasional discounted prices.

rationing Can occur when total demand exceeds a supplier's finished goods available. When this happens, the supplier might allocate units of product in proportion to what buyers ordered.

shortage gaming When buyers figure out that rationing is occurring, they inflate their orders to satisfy their real needs.

Price Fluctuations

When suppliers offer special promotions, quantity discounts, or other special pricing discounts, these pricing fluctuations result in significant **forward buying** activities on the part of buyers, who "stock up" to take advantage of discounted prices. Forward buying occurs between retailers and consumers, between distributors and retailers, and between manufacturers and distributors due to pricing promotions at each stage in a supply chain, and all of these contribute to erratic buying patterns, lower forecast accuracies, and consequently, the bullwhip effect. If these pricing promotions become commonplace, customers will stop buying when prices are undiscounted and buy only when the discount prices are offered, even further contributing to the bullwhip effect. To deal with these demand fluctuations, manufacturers must vary capacity by scheduling overtime and undertime for employees, finding places to store stockpiles of inventory, and dealing with higher levels of inventory shrinkage as inventories are held for longer periods.

The fairly obvious way to reduce bullwhip problems caused by fluctuating prices is to eliminate occasional price discounting among the supply chain's members, and instead use an **everyday low pricing** (EDLP) strategy. Manufacturers can reduce the forward buying of their customers by offering uniform wholesale prices. Many retailers have adopted this notion of EDLP, while eliminating promotions that cause forward buying. Similarly, buyers can negotiate with their own suppliers to offer EDLP as a way to curtail promotions.

Rationing and Shortage Gaming

Rationing can occur when total demand exceeds a supplier's finished goods available. When this happens, the supplier might allocate units of product in proportion to what buyers ordered. In other words, if a supplier has finished units equal to 75% of its total demand, buyers are allocated 75% of what they ordered. Unfortunately, when buyers figure out what's happening, they inflate their orders to satisfy their real needs. This strategy is known as **shortage gaming**. Of course, this further exacerbates the supply problem, as the supplier and, in turn, its suppliers, struggles to keep up with these higher demand levels. When, on the other hand, production capacity eventually equals demand and orders are filled completely, orders suddenly drop to less than normal levels as the buying firms try to unload their excess inventories. This has occurred occasionally in the United States and elsewhere around the world—for instance, with gasoline supplies. As soon as consumers think a shortage is looming, demand suddenly increases as

Richard Naude/Alamy

Employing an everyday low price (EDLP) strategy allows retailers to offer wholesale prices, reducing the need for promotions that cause forward buying.

people top off their tanks and otherwise try to stockpile gasoline, which itself creates a deeper shortage. When these types of shortages occur due to shortage gaming, suppliers can no longer discern their customers' true demands, and this can result in unnecessary additions to production capacity, warehouse space, and transportation investments.

One way to eliminate shortage gaming is for sellers to allocate short supplies based on the demand histories of their customers. In that way, customers are essentially not allowed to exaggerate orders. And once again, the sharing of capacity and inventory information between a manufacturer and its customers can also help to eliminate customers' fears regarding shortages and eliminate gaming. Also, sharing future order plans with suppliers allows suppliers to increase capacity if needed, thus avoiding a rationing situation.

Martin Shields/Alamy

Consumers line up to top off their tanks when a gas shortage occurs, creating even greater shortages.

Thus, it is seen that a number of actions on the part of buyers and suppliers tend to cause the bullwhip effect. When trading partners use the strategies discussed previously to reduce the bullwhip effect, the growth of information sharing, collaboration, and process integration occurs among trading partners. Firms that strive to share data, forecasts, plans, and other information can significantly reduce the bullwhip effect.

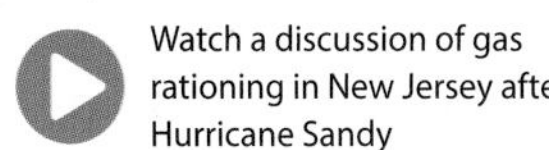
Watch a discussion of gas rationing in New Jersey after Hurricane Sandy

MANAGING SUPPLY CHAIN RISK AND SECURITY

16.3 Describe the issues associated with supply chain risk and security

As supply chains grow to include more foreign sources and markets, there is a corresponding increase in supply chain disruptions caused by weather and traffic delays, infrastructural problems, political problems, and the fears of unlawful or terrorist-related activities.

Panjiva Analyzes Supply Chain Risk

SERVICE SPOTLIGHT

iStock/Saklakova

One afternoon in November 2008, the owner of China Top Industries, a shoe factory in China, gathered his workers and made a surprise announcement—the factory was closing immediately. He then promptly left the factory, leaving behind a mountain of debt. The closure came as a shock to the company's 2,000 employees as well as its American customers, who were suddenly left with a huge hole in their supply chains.

In New York City, though, one person had seen it coming. Josh Green, the CEO of Panjiva, a company providing analyses on foreign suppliers for the apparel industry, had predicted problems with China Top. "On October 1st, according to our data, [China Top] had had a drop-off in output," Green said. "So we had a good indicator a full month ahead."

Using a set of software applications, Panjiva offers clients detailed assessments of supply chain risk. The firm sifts through mountains of information to develop detailed analyses of firms' quality, social responsibility, and financial health. In the past, company managers had not been actively managing supply chain risks. Today, though, most managers perceive their firm's risk of a disruption growing.

One of the keys to Panjiva's assessments are data on supplier shipments. The company determines which suppliers shipped on time, how loyal their customers were, and whether their output was suddenly decreasing, which can indicate problems. "What these guys are doing is absolutely revolutionary," said Jonathan Glick, owner of the investment firm Edge Ideas.[32]

For example, in just the last few years there have been political upheavals, riots, and wars in Egypt, Syria, and Libya; the BP oil well disaster along the U.S. Gulf Coast region; drug wars in Mexico; earthquakes in Chile, China, Japan, and Haiti; Australian wildfires and floods; and numerous airplane crashes and suicide bombs. Besides the obvious and unfortunate impact on life, these events also add elements of greater financial, reputation, and delivery risk to global supply chains, creating a need for better planning and security.

Therefore, while use of global supply chains may have resulted in cheaper labor and material costs, better product quality, and greater market coverage, it also can result in higher security costs and risk, potentially leading to lower profits and customer service levels. Managing risk and security along supply chains is discussed in detail in the following section.

SUPPLY CHAIN RISK

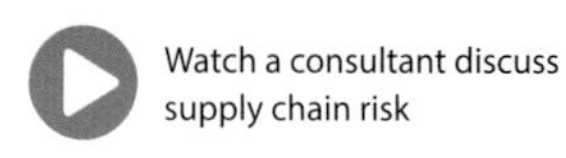
Watch a consultant discuss supply chain risk

In a study commissioned by Rhode Island–based commercial insurer Factory Mutual Insurance Co., the three biggest threats facing companies, according to 500 North American and European company executives, were competition, supply chain disruptions, and property-related risks.[33] In yet another study by global management consulting company Accenture, 73% of the responding companies had experienced recent supply chain disruptions, and over half had said the impact on customer service was moderate to significant. These and other studies point to the fact that as more and more firms penetrate new and emerging markets, **supply chain risk** is increasing. Specifically, supply chain risk refers to interruptions in the supply of goods and services in a supply chain caused by quality and safety challenges, supply shortages, legal issues, security problems, regulatory and environmental compliance, weather and natural disasters, or terrorism. In all supply chains, there is always some element of risk. One firm, New York–based Panjiva, helps firms reduce the risk in their supply chains, and is described in the Service Spotlight "Panjiva Analyzes Supply Chain Risk."

As the global economy heats up, risk management appears to be an even greater concern than ever before to managers. "Clearly, risk mitigation is a high priority for every corporate we speak with. In the U.S., even though the economy may be picking up, this still remains the hot button with virtually all of our clients," says Craig Weeks, managing director of global transaction services at Citibank.[34] A number of steps have been suggested for managing supply chain risk, and several good examples exist that highlight successful supply chain risk management. Table 16.5 describes these risk management activities, and they are discussed next.

supply chain risk Interruptions in the supply of goods and services in a supply chain caused by quality and safety challenges, supply shortages, legal issues, security problems, regulatory and environmental compliance, weather and natural disasters, or terrorism.

Increase Safety Stocks and Forward Buying

If the firm fears a supply disruption, it may choose to carry some level of additional safety stock to provide the desired product until a suitable substitute source can be found. If the purchased item is scarce, if the supply disruption is likely to be lengthy, or if the firm fears

Table 16.5 Activities for Managing Supply Chain Risk

Risk Management Activity	Comments
Increase safety stocks and forward buying	Can be costly. A stopgap alternative.
Identify backup suppliers and logistics services	Requires additional time and relationship building.
Diversify the supply base	Suppliers from geographically dispersed markets can minimize the impacts of disruptions.
Utilize a supply chain IT system	Collecting and sharing information with supply chain partners can reduce disruptions.
Develop a formal risk management program	Identifies potential disruptions and the appropriate responses.

Source: Field, A. (2006, December 18). How "free" is free trade? *Journal of Commerce*, 1 -3; Kline, J. (2007). Managing emerging market risk. *Logistics Management*, 46(5), 41 -44; Swaminathan, J., & Tomlin, B. (2007). How to avoid the risk management pitfalls. *Supply Chain Management Review*, 11(5), 34 -43.

continued and lengthy price increases, it may decide to purchase large quantities of product, also known as **stockpiling** or forward buying. Safety stocks and forward buying should only be viewed as temporary solutions, however, since they can both dramatically increase inventory carrying costs, particularly for firms with large numbers of purchased items. Also, as described earlier, this can cause the bullwhip effect.

In some cases, though, stockpiling may be viewed as the only short-term solution for managing risk. In 2006, many organizations opted to stockpile the influenza drug Tamiflu to prepare for a potential avian influenza pandemic, since shortages of the drug worldwide had already been experienced. In the United States, for example, 300 firms along with the government had already been engaged in significant stockpiling of Tamiflu by the summer of 2006.[35]

Identify Backup Suppliers and Logistics Services

Another very simple strategy for guaranteeing a continuous supply of purchased items and logistics services is to identify suppliers, transportation and warehousing services, and other third-party services to use in case the preferred supplier or service becomes unavailable. The disadvantage of this strategy is that it requires additional time to find and qualify sources and to build value-enhancing relationships. Additionally, it may tend to damage relationships with existing trading partners. The backup source may also see limited value in the relationship if it is providing only a small percentage of total demand; its price for the goods or services will also likely be higher. Additionally, use of multiple sources may allow proprietary designs or technologies to be copied, creating yet additional risk.

Backup or **emergency sourcing**, though, may be a sound strategy in specific cases. During the 2002 U.S. West Coast dockworker strikes, airfreight capacity quickly ran out, causing freight rates to skyrocket and firms to be unable to quickly move freight. Companies that had already entered into contracts for emergency airfreight service were able to maintain operations during the port disruptions.[36] Sainsbury's, a UK supermarket chain, uses multiple suppliers for the many products it buys as part of its business continuity plan, established in response to events such as the Irish Republican Army's bombing campaigns in the 1990s, the Y2K computer bug, the 2001 fuel shortage, and the foot-and-mouth disease outbreaks in the United Kingdom. Additionally, Sainsbury's works closely with key suppliers to ensure that they, too, have business continuity plans.[37]

Diversify the Supply Base

Madagascar, the one-time provider of half of the world's vanilla supply, saw Cyclone Hudah destroy 30% of its vanilla bean vines in 2000. Additionally, a political problem in Madagascar caused its primary port to be closed for many weeks in 2002. These two events caused vanilla prices to skyrocket for an extended period of time until growers in other countries could increase their outputs. Buyers with vanilla supplier contracts in multiple countries were able to avoid some of this pricing problem. Eventually, the market for vanilla became more diversified, creating a situation whereby vanilla buyers today have more vanilla sources outside of Madagascar.[38] In another example, an earthquake in Japan in 2007 halted automobile production at a number of the country's car plants because they were all buying piston rings from Riken, which had sustained damage from the earthquake.[39]

In the examples above, concentrating purchases with one supplier was seen as increasing supply risk, while purchasing the same or similar products from geographically dispersed suppliers spread the risk of supply disruptions from political upheavals, weather-related disasters, and other widespread supply problems. Buyers, though, must consider the impact of a geographically dispersed supply base on other supply chain risks. While potentially reducing the risk associated with geographical supply disruptions, the use of suppliers in multiple countries exposes buyers to additional political, customs clearance, exchange rate, and security risks.

Utilize a Supply Chain IT System

As firms expand their supply chains, they find customs clearance requirements and paperwork becoming more detailed and complicated. Complying with these regulations requires

stockpiling *See* Forward buying.

emergency sourcing Use of backup suppliers.

information and data visibility among supply chain participants, and involvement by all key supply chain partners. Accurate data transmissions can help to reduce stockouts and the bullwhip effect caused by forecasting and order inaccuracies, and late deliveries, which also pose significant risk and cost to supply chains.

Information systems should be designed to help mitigate supply chain risk. As stated by Julian Thomas, head of the supply chain advisory department at the global auditing and advisory firm KPMG, "Risk should be on the agenda and as you build your systems, you need to put in place systems to monitor and evaluate risk continuously."[40] Farm and ranch equipment retailer Tractor Supply, headquartered in Tennessee, is a good example of a firm making use of information technologies to support flexible and quick decision making to reduce risk. For example, it uses an on-demand transportation management system (TMS), an ERP system, and a voice-picking solution for its distribution centers. "In 2005, transportation capacity was really tight after Hurricane Katrina hit, but the way our TMS is configured we have the ability to escalate carrier service from low-cost to high-cost providers and sometimes when all the carriers in a market were taken, we had to take carriers in from another market," says Mike Graham, vice president of logistics at Tractor Supply. "We also have the flexibility within our DC network to react quickly if there is an event and move stores from one DC to another."[41]

Develop a Formal Risk Management Program

By far the most proactive risk management activity is to create a **formal risk management plan** encompassing the firm and its trading partners. Risk management becomes an executive-level priority. Potential risks are identified and prioritized, and appropriate responses are designed to minimize the disruption to supply chains. Additionally, mechanisms are developed to recover quickly, efficiently, with minimal damage to the firm's reputation and customer satisfaction. Finally, performance measures are developed to monitor the firm's ongoing risk management capabilities.

A supply chain risk management office can be created to oversee and coordinate the firm's risk management efforts. The risk manager provides guidance and support to department managers, is the interface between the firm and its trading partners, and possesses the knowledge to adequately identify, prioritize, and provide a plan to reduce risks. In 2005, Tractor Supply, for example, developed a disaster recovery plan as part of its overall risk management strategy. One year later, its Waco, TX, distribution center was struck by a tornado in the evening, leaving two to three inches of water standing in the facility and product scattered across the landscape for miles. By the time logistics VP Mike Graham made it to his office the next day, plans were already in place to repair the damage, and within several hours all of the customers served by the Waco distribution center were linked to other facilities. "We did not miss a delivery the following week and May is actually a peak season for us," said Graham.[42]

Richard Sharman, a partner in KPMG's risk advisory services group, offers his advice for developing risk management plans: "Companies almost need to ask themselves the stupid questions to think about the full spectrum of business risks, and how they would manage them," he says. Another consideration is to "Know your partner. There is no substitute for that," says Brian Joseph, a partner at global business consultant PricewaterhouseCoopers.[43] When outsourcing to firms in foreign locales, it is also necessary to have adequate quality controls in place, and require suppliers to report periodically to the firm to ensure its products are meeting design requirements.

formal risk management plan The most proactive risk management activity; risk management becomes an executive-level priority. Potential risks are identified and prioritized, and appropriate responses are designed to minimize the disruption to supply chains. Additionally, mechanisms are developed to recover quickly, efficiently, with minimal damage to the firm's reputation and customer satisfaction. Finally, performance measures are developed to monitor the firm's ongoing risk management capabilities.

SUPPLY CHAIN SECURITY

supply chain security management Concerned with reducing the risk of intentionally created disruptions in supply chain operations including product and information theft and activities seeking to endanger personnel or sabotage supply chain infrastructure.

As supply chains become more global and technologically complex, so does the need to secure them. **Supply chain security management** is concerned with reducing the risk of intentionally created disruptions in supply chain operations, including product and information theft and activities seeking to endanger personnel or sabotage supply chain infrastructure. The crash of Pan Am Flight 103 in Lockerbie, Scotland, in 1988 not only tragically illustrated the weaknesses of airline security systems at the time, but it also exposed the dependency of entire supply chains on each member's own security capabilities. In this incident, it was not Pan

Am's security processes that failed in permitting the bomb onto Flight 103. Instead, it was Malta Airlines' security system that originally allowed the luggage carrying a bomb into its baggage handling system. After the Malta Airlines flight, the luggage was then transferred to Pan Am Flight 103. In the United States, the attacks of September 11, 2001, were a wakeup call to many businesses to begin assessing their needs for supply chain security systems. Prior to that time, most executives were aware that their operations might be vulnerable to security problems; however, most firms (as well as government agencies) chose to put off improving security practices.[44]

iStock/Maica

A global supply chain is only as secure as its weakest link.

The notion that a supply chain is only as secure as its weakest link is illustrated in the Pan Am example. It is therefore necessary today for firms to manage not only their own security but the security practices of their supply chain partners as well. Eventually, as supply chains and relationships with trading partners mature, security management will be recognized as an important supply chain process. Supply chain security, though, is an extremely complex problem—security activities begin at the factory where goods are packaged and loaded, and then include the logistics companies transporting goods to ports, the port terminals and customs workers, the ocean carriers, the destination ports and customs workers, additional transportation companies, distribution centers and workers, and the final delivery companies.

Security management collaboration should include, for example, contractual requirements for secure systems, "standards of care" for movement and storage of products as they move along the supply chain, and the use of law enforcement officials or consultants in security planning, training, and incident investigation. Table 16.6 describes four increasing levels of supply chain security system preparedness, and these are discussed in the following sections.

Basic Initiatives

Watch discussion of port and shipping container security issues

At their most basic level, security systems should include procedures and policies for securing offices, manufacturing plants, warehouses, and other physical facilities; additionally, they should provide security for personnel, computing systems, and freight shipments. Managers should consider use of security badges and guards, conducting background checks on applicants, using antivirus software and passwords, and using shipment-tracking technologies.

Today, cargo theft is one of the biggest problems facing global supply chains, and some of the basic security approaches can be used to reduce this threat. Existing technologies and lack of downside risk have enabled thieves to be more sophisticated and daring than ever before. Stolen goods can be moved to a warehouse, offloaded, repackaged, remanifested,

Table 16.6 Supply Chain Security System Response

Level of Security System Response	Description
Basic initiatives	Physical security measures; personnel security; standard risk assessment; basic computing security; continuity plan; freight protection.
Reactive initiatives	Larger security organization; C-TPAT compliance; supply base analysis; supply continuity plan; limited training.
Proactive initiatives	Director of security; personnel with military or government experience; formal security risk assessment; advanced computing security; participation in security groups.
Advanced initiatives	Customer/supplier collaboration; learning from the past; formal security strategy; supply chain drills, simulations, exercises; emergency control center.

Source: Rice, J. (2007, May 1). Rethinking supply chain security. *Logistics Management.*

and placed on another vehicle before the theft is even discovered and reported.[45] Walmart represents a very good example of a network of complex global supply chains—its systems process over 11 million data transfers daily, and its annual worldwide product losses top $3 billion.[46]

Reactive Initiatives

Reactive security initiatives represent a somewhat deeper commitment to the idea of security management compared to basic initiatives, but still lack any significant efforts to organize a cohesive and firm-wide plan for security management. Many firms in this category, for example, implemented security systems in response to the 9/11 terrorist attacks. These initiatives include assessing suppliers' security practices, developing continuity plans for various events, and implementing specific training and education programs.

C-TPAT, or Customs-Trade Partnership Against Terrorism, refers to a partnership among U.S. Customs, the International Cargo Security Council (a U.S. nonprofit association of companies and individuals involved in transportation), and Pinkerton (a global security advising company), whereby companies agree to improve security in their supply chain in return for "fast lane" border crossings. Additionally, U.S. Customs and Border Protection personnel state that nonparticipants are six times more likely to receive a security-related container inspection at U.S. border crossings.[47] The U.S. government is currently working with other countries to implement similar programs.

Proactive Initiatives

Proactive security initiatives venture outside the firm to include suppliers and customers, and also include a more formalized approach to security management within the firm. Security activities occurring among firms in this category include the creation of an executive-level position such as director of corporate security; the hiring of former military, intelligence, or law enforcement personnel with security management experience; a formal and comprehensive approach to assess the firm's exposure to security risks; the use of cyberintrusion detection systems and other advanced information security practices; and the development of freight security plans in collaboration with logistics service providers. Home Depot, for example, uses a computer risk modeling approach to assess its supply chains' vulnerabilities and then design appropriate security measures. "We look at 35 global risk elements and one of those is threat of terrorism," explains Benjamin Cook, senior manager for global trade service for Home Depot. "We use that technique to help us roll out a strategy that is most appropriate to the country we are sourcing from."[48]

Advanced Initiatives

Firms with advanced security management systems are recognized as industry leaders with respect to their security initiatives. **Advanced security initiatives** include full collaboration with key suppliers and customers in developing quick recovery and continuity plans for supply chain disruptions; considerations of the past security failures of other firms in developing a more comprehensive and effective security system; the design of a complete supply chain security management plan that is implemented by all key trading partners; and the use of an emergency control center to manage responses to unexpected supply chain disruptions.

Industry security leaders like Michigan-based Dow Chemical see supply chain security simply as good business. As Henry Ward, director of transportation security and safety at Dow, stated, "We view security as one of the steps we take to make sure we remain a reliable supplier of goods to the marketplace." Dow's efforts to improve supply chain visibility and security led to a 50% improvement in the time it took to identify and resolve transit problems, and a 20% inventory reduction at receiving terminals. Dow uses RFID and a global positioning system to track large intermodal containers as they move from North America to Asia. Dow sees collaboration with governments and supply chain partners as crucial to its success. "We take an integrated approach to supply chain security, which means we look at it holistically," said Ward.[49]

reactive security initiatives A somewhat deeper commitment to the idea of security management compared to basic initiatives, but they still lack any significant efforts to organize a cohesive and firm-wide plan for security management.

proactive security initiatives Ventures outside the firm to include suppliers and customers, and also include a more formalized approach to security management within the firm.

advanced security initiatives Include full collaboration with key suppliers and customers in developing quick recovery and continuity plans for supply chain disruptions; considerations of the past security failures of other firms in developing a more comprehensive and effective security system; the design of a complete supply chain security management plan that is implemented by all key trading partners; and the use of an emergency control center to manage responses to unexpected supply chain disruptions.

TRENDS IN PROCESS INTEGRATION

16.4 Describe the important trends in process integration

Process integration, among departments within the firm and externally between the firm and its trading partners, is being tremendously impacted these days by technology. Management recognizes, now, that internal process integration can be improved through use of social technologies. Business research firm Gartner predicts that over 50% of large firms will have internal Facebook-like collaborative networks by 2016, and many of these organizations will consider their networks as essential as email or phones. Some of the other important internal integration trends include:[50]

- Collaboration managers are rolling out internal collaboration software with continual feedback cycles that integrate with cultural change agents and project champions, to ensure high usage.
- More cross-system IT integration or middleware is being created, with continued growth of tablets to further enable employees to consume, create, and share content.
- Collaboration is becoming embedded into existing business processes such as customer relationship management and enterprise resource planning.
- The number of cloud services employed across organizations continues to grow, which likely means that integration projects are piling up for the IT groups.
- Cloud and mobile computing are allowing company personnel to implement data analytics and to mine social media data to enable quicker and better decision making.

Business process integration is also impacted to a large degree by new technologies. In fact, the term **B2B process integration** today refers primarily to integration software and cloud platforms. In a recent survey of high-tech companies, Canadian software company OpenText found that 79% exchanged transactions with their trading partners electronically, 58% said their B2B process integrations had improved supply chain visibility and thus reduced purchasing costs, and 42% said they processed invoices in real time with their trading partners.[51] For many organizations, IBM has become one of the preferred B2B integration platform providers. Its integration product can automate the complete "buy-sell-ship-pay" processes that involve a range of documents and transactions. The integration capabilities include not just the buyers and sellers of the goods or services, but also banks and third-party logistics companies. Its solution automates these processes and provides visibility into data and processes shared with external entities.[52]

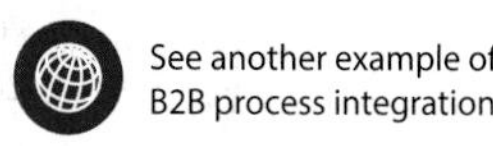
See another example of B2B process integration

B2B process integration Refers primarily to integration software and cloud platforms.

SAGE edge™

Visit edge.sagepub.com/wisner to help you accomplish your coursework goals in an easy-to-use learning environment.

- Mobile-friendly eFlashcards
- Mobile-friendly practice quizzes
- A complete online action plan
- Chapter summaries with learning objectives
- Excel templates to assist with practice problems
- Original video case studies that demonstrate chapter concepts in action

SUMMARY

In this chapter, the topic of integrating processes among the firm and its supply chain partners was discussed, including the steps required to achieve effective process integration, the advantages of doing this, and the obstacles to overcome. While process integration is considered the primary means to achieving successful supply chain management, it is the

one thing firms struggle with most when setting out to manage their supply chains. Without the proper support, training, tools, trust, and preparedness, process integration most likely will be impossible ever fully to achieve.

The supply chain integration model provides the framework for integrating processes with trading partners, and this model served as the foundation for the chapter. The role played by performance measures in assessing and improving integration was also discussed. Additionally, a discussion of supply chain risk and security management outlined the need for firms and their trading partners to collaborate in developing effective strategies for assessing the risk of supply chain disruptions, and implementing solutions. Finally, the current trend with the use of technology in process integration was discussed.

KEY TERMS

Advanced security initiatives, 522
B2B process integration, 523
Collaborative education, 514
Customer relationship management process, 504
Customer service management process, 504
Demand forecast updating, 515
Demand management process, 505
Emergency sourcing, 519
Everyday low pricing (EDLP), 516
Formal risk management plan, 520
Forward buying, 516
Information visibility, 513
Key trading partners, 502
Knowledge-management solutions, 511
Manufacturing flow management process, 505
Order batching, 516
Order fulfillment process, 505
Proactive security initiatives, 522
Process, 504
Process integration, 502
Rationing, 516
Reactive security initiatives, 522
SCOR model, 507
Shortage gaming, 516
Silo mentality, 511
Stockpiling, 519
Supply chain risk, 518
Supply chain security management, 520

REVIEW QUESTIONS

1. What does process integration mean, and what does it have to do with supply chain management?
2. What makes process integration difficult to achieve?
3. What are the basic supply chain strategies?
4. What is a key trading partner?
5. What are the eight key supply chain business processes, and why are they important when managing supply chains?
6. What is the difference between the customer service management process and the customer relationship management process?
7. What are knowledge-management solutions, and how can they support a firm's supply chain integration efforts? Give some examples.
8. Why is lack of trust an obstacle to supply chain management? How can companies overcome this obstacle?
9. Why is visibility so important when integrating processes?
10. Define the bullwhip effect and describe how it impacts supply chain integration, or how integration impacts the bullwhip effect.
11. What are the things firms must overcome to minimize the bullwhip effect?
12. What is forward buying? Is this a good thing to do?
13. Define shortage gaming and describe when firms would do this.
14. Why should reducing the length of the supply chain also reduce the bullwhip effect?
15. What is everyday low pricing, and how does it impact the bullwhip effect?
16. What is the difference between supply chain risk management and supply chain security management? Which do you think is most important?
17. What types of supply chains are most likely to be impacted by risk and security problems? Why?
18. What is the difference between reactive and proactive supply chain security initiatives?

DISCUSSION QUESTIONS

1. Describe some supply chain (external) performance measures for several of the eight key supply chain business processes, assuming the overall strategy is superior customer service. What if the overall strategy is sustainability?
2. What do you think is the biggest obstacle to successful supply chain management? Why?
3. List some steps or initiatives firms can take to reduce supply chain risk and increase security.
4. Do you think Kmart's supply chain is integrated as well as Walmart's? Why, or why not?
5. Describe the various supply chain risk issues at McDonald's, a bank, and an airline. How could these companies reduce risk?
6. Describe the various supply chain security issues at McDonald's, a bank, and an airline. How could these companies improve security?

EXERCISES AND PROJECTS

1. Research and write a paper on supply chain security issues before and after September 11, 2001.
2. Pick a large, publicly held corporation and discuss its supply chain management strategies, its trading partners, and the success it attributes to its supply chain management efforts.

CASE STUDIES

CASE 1: External Integration—Necessary, but Not Sufficient?

For the past year, Allyson had been responsible for driving better integration between her company, Gamma Corporation, and both its suppliers and customers. She had been tasked with this external integration initiative by Robert Bird, the president of the company, who recognized that Gamma was not doing everything it could to leverage the strengths of its external partners. However, over the course of the year, Allyson was able to establish key linkages and communication channels between Gamma and its external partners. The additional information she was able to obtain via these channels was significant, and she was now looking forward to seeing the bottom-line impact her efforts have had.

When Allyson started the project, she was easily convinced of the case for better external integration, as the benefits were apparent. For example, integrating with customers would enable the company to obtain a better understanding of customers' wants and needs, thus being able to offer more tailored and innovative solutions. This seemed especially valuable since Gamma had missed some key market opportunities in the past, as competitors were able to enter new markets more quickly and accommodate changing customer tastes more expeditiously. Establishing closer bonds and sharing information with suppliers also seemed to be warranted. With such more integrated linkages, forecasting could be enhanced, enabling Gamma to communicate demand predictions continuously to suppliers. This would enable suppliers to plan more effectively and with less uncertainty for Gamma's needs, saving them valuable resources. On the flipside, Gamma was hoping to build on the suppliers' knowledge in their particular area of expertise. This was especially crucial in areas where Gamma did not have sufficient research and development prowess to be able to be at the leading edge. Overall, the benefits to be derived via external integration seemed tremendous, so Allyson was certain to see some significant improvements manifest due to her efforts.

She was therefore looking forward to the meeting Mr. Bird had requested with her. She walked full of energy and excitement into the president's front office, and let his administrative assistant know that she had an appointment with him. The assistant asked her to have a seat, since she was a bit early. She must have sensed Allyson's excitement, and thought she would better let her know. With a muted voice, she said, "Well, I just wanted to let you know that Mr. Bird has not been in a good mood this morning, and I believe it might be because of the project you had been working on." Allyson was confused, and asked whether she thought it was indeed about her project. The assistant quietly nodded her head.

Allyson was stunned. She had been working on this project so hard for the last year, and she was able to obtain so much valuable information from both customers and suppliers. Why, then, should this not have manifested in improved bottom-line performance impacts?

It was a good thing that the assistant warned Allyson of Mr. Bird's mood, since the meeting ended up not being very pleasant. Her efforts throughout the last year indeed did not help Gamma on any of its key performance indicators, such as increased sales (Allyson had hoped that this would increase due to better knowledge of customer needs and wants) or innovation performance (Allyson had hoped that this would increase due to suppliers offering ideas for product improvements). Why didn't these expectations materialize?

Allyson took the afternoon off to clear her mind and to think about what might have happened. She was clearly able to gather some invaluable information through her external integration efforts with customers and suppliers. She was sure of that, since she saw the information and intelligence gathered via the improved communication channels between Gamma and its external partners. The information obtained clearly included key pieces of information of how to slightly change Gamma's product offerings to make its products more appealing to its customers and to further differentiate from the competition. This should have yielded higher sales. In addition, information obtained from suppliers included suggestions for how to tweak Gamma's specifications so as to enhance the performance of its delivered components, contributing to the products' innovativeness.

Allyson dug deeper into the issues on the following day. Why didn't the valuable intelligence she was able to obtain help Gamma to increase its performance? She started out by looking into what happened to the information. Once the better communication and information sharing channels were established, she had passed the gathered information on to the appropriate departments, but then moved on to the next department to improve their external integration with external partners. She thought that the "enabled" departments would put the information to best use, and then also do their best to keep up the integration linkages. But when looking into it further, now, it turned out that her assumptions were mistaken. While communication channels were still being used and valuable information was being exchanged, *it did not seem to actually reach the person who would be able to use it internally.* "Seriously?" she asked out loud. "External integration seems to work, but we are failing due to a lack of integration internally?" This may indeed have been the culprit behind the unrealized improvement in performance due to external integration, and she was determined to find the root cause for it and correct it.

DISCUSSION QUESTIONS

1. Why is internal integration so important (maybe even more important than external integration)?
2. Why do you think there are so many challenges associated with internal integration?
3. How can internal integration be achieved?

Note: Written by Tobias Schoenherr, PhD, Michigan State University. This case was prepared solely to provide material for class discussion. The author does not intend to illustrate either effective or ineffective handling of a managerial situation.

CASE 2: Risk Management at Alpha Inc.

With globalization offering many opportunities, challenges were surely also not absent. Alpha Inc. had to realize this when one of its suppliers, SCorp., was unable to deliver for four weeks last year. This got Alpha into a significant predicament, since the company itself had to default on several of its outstanding orders, due to the missing input materials from SCorp. Alpha was therefore seriously considering its current risk management strategies, specifically as they relate to the assurance of supply.

Alpha couldn't really blame SCorp. for not delivering, since the breakdown was out of its control: SCorp. was one of the companies that had been significantly damaged by the earthquake that struck northern Italy, where SCorp.'s main manufacturing facilities were located. SCorp. did everything it could to get up to speed quickly, but it was still down for four weeks. During this time, Alpha was trying to source the products from alternate suppliers—which, however, did not have any additional capacity left on such short notice. Many of them also would not have been able to produce Alpha's products due to the tight engineering specifications required by Alpha. These difficulties were largely unanticipated, which made Alpha realize the need for better risk management.

Alpha recognized that what exacerbated the situation was its single-source strategy. This was done in an effort to consolidate the supply base, and to foster closer relationships with the remaining suppliers. This objective was certainly achieved—Alpha had a great relationship with SCorp., and had become one of its premium customers. Therefore, from this perspective, the assurance of supply seemed to be safe. In addition, the possibility of an earthquake occurring in this particular region of Italy had been judged minimal, and thus no further thought was devoted to it. However, this event made Alpha now realize that a more comprehensive risk management approach was needed, also in instances where one would not expect anything to go wrong.

DISCUSSION QUESTIONS

1. What risk mitigation strategies might Alpha want to explore in order to reduce the risk of similar repercussions in the future?

2. What additional risks might be worth considering in global supply chains?
3. Why has risk management become especially important in the last one or two decades?

Note: Written by Tobias Schoenherr, PhD, Michigan State University. This case was prepared solely to provide material for class discussion. The author does not intend to illustrate either effective or ineffective handling of a managerial situation.

CASE 3: Supplier Integration at International Lighting Corp.

Something had to change. International Lighting Corp. (ILC) just lost another new product introduction race to one of its fiercest competitors, Midwest Lamp Manufacturing (MLM). The industry had been tinkering with a new type of bulb for car headlamps that would illuminate the road in a brighter light, yet not be distracting to drivers on the other side of the road. While it was only a matter of weeks in which ILC lost the race of the new product introduction to MLM, the timing can be very significant in the automotive supply industry. This happened even though ILC thought it had done all of its homework to be in a good position, almost doubling its expenditures for research and development (R&D). The effort, however, was apparently without success. What went wrong? This was the question that Felix was tasked to answer.

Felix started to compare ILC to MLM, the competitor that was able to introduce the new bulbs earlier, to identify what it did differently. He found that it could not be due to a lack of internal company resources devoted to the project. On this dimension, ILC was far superior compared to MLM, at least when measured based on the R&D budget. This was puzzling to Felix. How was MLM able to beat ILC to market despite its lower level of resources to foster innovation?

After a day of reading and comparing the companies' two supply chains, Felix thought he might have found the answer. He came across a press release by one of MLM's suppliers, priding itself on helping MLM bring this new type of bulb to market expeditiously and successfully. According to the press release, the supplier seemed to have played a major part in helping MLM develop the product.

This was unlike the approach ILC had been taking in its new product development efforts. ILC usually started by doing all the R&D, design, and testing in-house. This was done because of its fears of suppliers leaking confidential information in this critical development phase, its desire for control, and also its confidence in its own capabilities (especially recently; after all, the R&D budget had been increased so significantly). Only once the product had been developed was it shared with suppliers. This, however, sometimes resulted in the supplier sending the item back with the explanation that it does not have the capabilities to manufacture these items to these specifications. While the suppliers then often made suggestions on how to modify the products, this resulted in a significant delay in the final roll-out of the product. Could this have been one of the reasons why ILC failed to beat MLM again? It clearly seemed that integrating with suppliers early on in the new product development process worked out successfully for MLM.

DISCUSSION QUESTIONS

1. Why can supplier integration into a company's new product development be so valuable?
2. What incentives may a company provide in order to obtain the best ideas from suppliers?
3. What are some potential downsides of supplier integration for a company's new product development?

Note: Written by Tobias Schoenherr, PhD, Michigan State University. This case was prepared solely to provide material for class discussion. The author does not intend to illustrate either effective or ineffective handling of a managerial situation.

VIDEO CASE STUDY

Learn more about ***managing supply chain risk*** from real organizations that use operations management techniques every day. Craig Nielsen is a Principal at Digital Benefit Advisors, a national employee benefits firm. Offering a new product or service introduces significant risk for benefits agencies, and it is their responsibility to manage that risk for their clients. Watch this short interview to learn how Digital Benefits Advisors does this.

/ APPENDIX A /

Z VALUES FOR AREAS UNDER THE NORMAL CURVE

This table gives the area under the curve to the left of x, for various Z scores, or the number of standard deviations from the mean. For example, in the figure, if $Z = 1.96$, the value .97500 found in the body of the table is the total shaded area to the left of x.

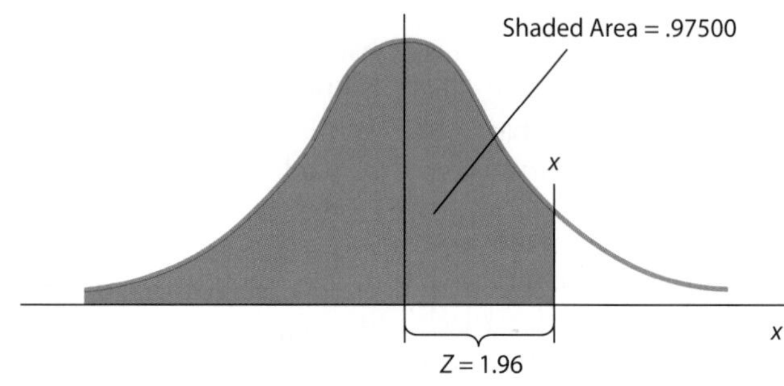

Z	00	.01	.02	.03	.04	.05	.06	.07	.08	.09
.0	.50000	.50399	.50798	.51197	.51595	.51994	.52392	.52790	.53188	.53586
.1	.53983	.54380	.54776	.55172	.55567	.55962	.56356	.56749	.57142	.57535
.2	.57926	.58317	.58706	.59095	.59483	.59871	.60257	.60642	.61026	.61409
.3	.61791	.62172	.62552	.62930	.63307	.63683	.64058	.64431	.64803	.65173
.4	.65542	.65910	.66276	.66640	.67003	.67364	.67724	.68082	.68439	.68793
.5	.69146	.69497	.69847	.70194	.70540	.70884	.71226	.71566	.71904	.72240
.6	.72575	.72907	.73237	.73536	.73891	.74215	.74537	.74857	.75175	.75490
.7	.75804	.76115	.76424	.76730	.77035	.77337	.77637	.77935	.78230	.78524
.8	.78814	.79103	.79389	.79673	.79955	.80234	.80511	.80785	.81057	.81327
.9	.81594	.81859	.82121	.82381	.82639	.82894	.83147	.83398	.83646	.83891
1.0	.84134	.84375	.84614	.84849	.85083	.85314	.85543	.85769	.85993	.86241
1.1	.86433	.86650	.86864	.87076	.87286	.87493	.87698	.87900	.88100	.88298
1.2	.88493	.88686	.88877	.89065	.89251	.89435	.89617	.89796	.89973	.90147
1.3	.90320	.90490	.90658	.90824	.90988	.91149	.91309	.91466	.91621	.91774
1.4	.91924	.92073	.92220	.92364	.92507	.92647	.92785	.92922	.93056	.93189
1.5	.93319	.93448	.93574	.93699	.93822	.93943	.94062	.94179	.94295	.94408

Z	00	.01	.02	.03	.04	.05	.06	.07	.08	.09
1.6	.94520	.94630	.94738	.94845	.94950	.95053	.95154	.95254	.95352	.95449
1.7	.95543	.95637	.95728	.95818	.95907	.95994	.96080	.96164	.96246	.96327
1.8	.96407	.96485	.96562	.96638	.96712	.96784	.96856	.96926	.96995	.97062
1.9	.97128	.97193	.97257	.97320	.97381	.97441	.97500	.97558	.97615	.97670
2.0	.97725	.97784	.97831	.97882	.97932	.97982	.98030	.98077	.98124	.98169
2.1	.98214	.98257	.98300	.98341	.98382	.98422	.98461	.98500	.98537	.98574
2.2	.98610	.98645	.98679	.98713	.98745	.98778	.98809	.98840	.98870	.98899
2.3	.98928	.98956	.98983	.99010	.99036	.99061	.99086	.99111	.99134	.99158
2.4	.99180	.99202	.99224	.99245	.99266	.99286	.99305	.99324	.99343	.99361
2.5	.99379	.99396	.99413	.99430	.99446	.99461	.99477	.99492	.99506	.99520
2.6	.99534	.99547	.99560	.99573	.99585	.99598	.99606	.99621	.99632	.99643
2.7	.99653	.99664	.99674	.99683	.99693	.99702	.99711	.99720	.99728	.99736
2.8	.99744	.99752	.99760	.99767	.99774	.99781	.99788	.99795	.99801	.99807
2.9	.99813	.99819	.99825	.99831	.99836	.99841	.99846	.99851	.99856	.99861
3.0	.99865	.99869	.99874	.99878	.99882	.99886	.99889	.99893	.99896	.99900
3.1	.99903	.99906	.99910	.99913	.99916	.99918	.99921	.99924	.99926	.99929
3.2	.99931	.99934	.99936	.99938	.99940	.99942	.99944	.99946	.99948	.99950
3.3	.99952	.99953	.99955	.99957	.99958	.99960	.99961	.99962	.99964	.99965
3.4	.99966	.99968	.99969	.99970	.99971	.99972	.99973	.99974	.99975	.99976
3.5	.99977	.99978	.99978	.99979	.99980	.99981	.99981	.99982	.99983	.99983
3.6	.99984	.99985	.99985	.99986	.99986	.99987	.99987	.99988	.99988	.99989
3.7	.99989	.99990	.99990	.99990	.99991	.99991	.99992	.99992	.99992	.99992
3.8	.99993	.99993	.99993	.99994	.99994	.99994	.99994	.99995	.99995	.99995
3.9	.99995	.99995	.99996	.99996	.99996	.99996	.99996	.99996	.99997	.99997

/ APPENDIX B /

SOLUTIONS TO ODD-NUMBERED PROBLEMS

PART I—DEVELOPING OPERATIONS STRATEGIES

CHAPTER 2 — CORPORATE STRATEGY, PERFORMANCE, AND SUSTAINABILITY

PROBLEMS

1. 1st month—labor prod = 1320/2900 = 0.46 cust/labor$; mat'l. prod = 1320/860 = 1.53 cust/mat'l$; energy prod = 1320/185 = 7.14 cust/energy$; lease prod = 1320/1500 = 0.88 cust/lease$
   2nd month—labor prod = 1500/3000 = 0.5 cust/labor$; mat'l. prod = 1500/800 = 1.88 cust/mat'l$; energy prod = 1500/200 = 7.5 cust/energy$; lease prod = 1500/1500 = 1.0 cust/lease$

3

	March	April	May	June
Labor prod	3.84	4.04	4.03	4.16
Growth		5.2%	–0.25%	3.2%

5. Labor prod = (325000 × 1249)/(6400 × 15) = 4228.4

   Mat'l. prod = (325000 × 1249)/40625000 = 9992

   Utility prod = (325000 × 1249)/4400 = 92,255.7

   Total prod = (325000 × 1249)/(6400 × 15 + 40625000 + 4400) = 9.97

7. Single-factor productivities

   2014: Labor productivity = $66,000 sales/$10,800 = 6.11 sales $ per labor $;

   lease productivity = $66,000/$24,000 = 2.75 sales $ per lease $.

   2015: Labor productivity = $69,500 sales/$11,600 = 5.99 sales $ per labor $;

   lease productivity = $69,500/$24,500 = 2.84 sales $ per lease $.

   Multiple-factor productivities

   2014: $66,000 sales/[$10,800 + $24,000] = 1.90 sales $ per input $.

   2015: $69,500 sales/[$11,600 + $24,500] = 1.93 sales $ per input $.

Labor productivity grew from 2014 to 2015 by (5.99 – 6.11)/6.11 = –0.02 or –2%. The lease productivity grew by (2.84 – 2.75)/2.75 = 0.033 or 3.3%. The multiple-factor productivity grew by (1.93 – 1.90)/1.90 = 0.016 or 1.6%. Ultra management should look into why labor cost grew faster than ski revenue from 2014 to 2015.

9. Net profit margin = 94153/1450627 = 6.49%

   Current ratio = 327176/86904 = 3.76

   Inventory turnover = 675860/163465 = 4.13

   Purchasing efficiency = 675860/600000 = 113%

11. Net profit margin = 1745286/10187125 = 17.13%

    Current ratio = 12427000/2432804 = 5.11

    Inventory turnover = 4325219/209398 = 20.66

CHAPTER 3 — PRODUCT DESIGN AND DEVELOPMENT

1. Note – Year 1 NPV = $\frac{(130{,}000)}{(1+.1)^1}$

Year	Cash in-flows	NPV
1	$130,000	$118,182
2	250,000	206,612
3	300,000	225,394
4	100,000	68,301
	Totals	$618,489
	Investment	500,000
	Total Value	**$118,489**

3. $\text{IRR} - \$500{,}000 = \frac{130{,}000}{1+\text{IRR}} + \frac{250{,}000}{(1+\text{IRR})^2} + \frac{300{,}000}{(1+\text{IRR})^3} + \frac{100{,}000}{(1+\text{IRR})^4}$

   1) Guess 12% – $\frac{130{,}000}{1.12} + \frac{250{,}000}{1.2544} + \frac{300{,}000}{1.4049} + \frac{100{,}000}{1.5735} = \$592{,}461$

   2) Guess 15% – $\frac{130{,}000}{1.15} + \frac{250{,}000}{1.3225} + \frac{300{,}000}{1.5209} + \frac{100{,}000}{1.7490} = \$556{,}507$

   3) Guess 18% – $\frac{130{,}000}{1.18} + \frac{250{,}000}{1.3924} + \frac{300{,}000}{1.6430} + \frac{100{,}000}{1.9388} = \$523{,}887$

   4) Guess 20% – $\frac{130{,}000}{1.2} + \frac{250{,}000}{1.44} + \frac{300{,}000}{1.728} + \frac{100{,}000}{2.0736} = \$503{,}781$

   So, the IRR is slightly more than 20%.

5.

Year	Projected Cash In-Flows$_1$ ($)	NPV$_1$	Projected Cash In-Flows$_2$ ($)	NPV$_2$
1	138,000	$123,214	112,000	$100,000
2	225,000	179,369	188,000	149,872
3	240,000	170,827	154,000	109,614
4	55,000	34,953	86,000	54,655
	Total	$508,363	Total	$414,141
	Investment	325,000		285,000
	Total value	**$183,363**		**$129,141**

Project 1 should receive the funding.

7. Proj. a. Students could do this the long way, or realize that this is an annuity, and use the formula:

$$NPV = 26{,}000\left[\frac{1-(1+.08)^{-10}}{.08}\right] + 2500/(1.08)^{10} - 185{,}000 = \$174{,}462 + 1158 - 185{,}000$$

$$= -\$9{,}380$$

$$\text{Proj. b. } NPV = 6{,}000\left[\frac{1-(1+.08)^{-25}}{.08}\right] - 82{,}000 = \$64{,}049 - 82{,}000 = -\ \$17{,}951$$

$$\text{Proj. c. } NPV = 80{,}000\left[\frac{1-(1+.08)^{-4}}{.08}\right] + 16{,}000/(1.08)^{4} - 249{,}000 = \$264{,}970 + 11760 - 249{,}000$$

$$= \$27{,}730$$

Project c returns the only positive NPV, so it would be the best.

9. Solving using Excel:

   Using the function NPV (0.1, B3:B7) – 845000, we get $171,237.10

   Using the function IRR (B2:B7), where the B column are the cash flows, we get 21.09%.

CHAPTER 4 — PROCESS DESIGN AND CAPACITY MANAGEMENT

1. August—115/140 = 82.1%

   September—132/180 = 73.3%

3. [5500/ (50 × 5)]/25 = 88%

5. $Util._1 = 9500/12000 = 79.2\%$

   $Util._2 = 10500/12000 = 87.5\%$

   Growth = (87.5 – 79.2)/79.2 = 10.5%

7. This is a Theory of Constraints question. The assembly process can make 15 units/day. Process 1 is the biggest bottleneck, followed by Process 3.

9. a. Current capacity is 4 units per day. Stages 1 and 3 are bottlenecks relative to stage 2.

   b. Stage 1 needs 3 machines and operators. Stage 2 needs 2 machines and operators. Stage 3 needs 4 machines and operators.

11.

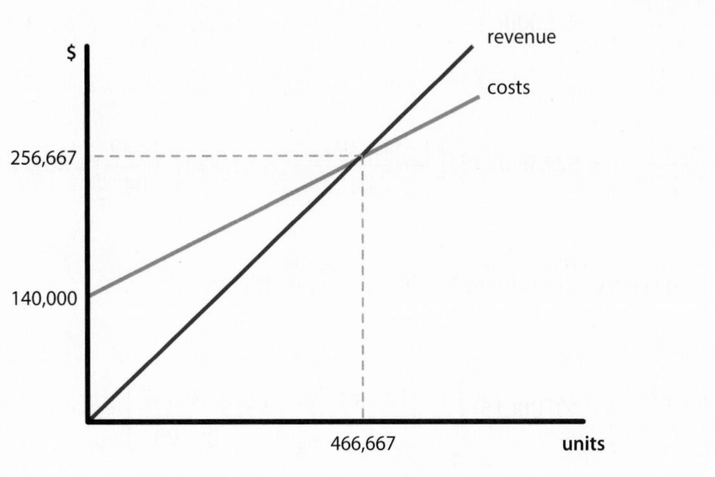

13. Make = Buy; 140,000 + 0.25X = 0.35X; break-even = 1,400,000 units; so it would take 1400000/250000 = 5.6 years for them to break even if they made instead of bought.

15. 1,400,000(0.35) = $490,000

17. Revenues = costs; 29X = 18(5000); X = 3103.4, or 3104 units.
    Make = buy; 30,000 + 12X = 18X; 6X = 30,000; X = 5000 units.

CHAPTER 5 — CUSTOMER RELATIONSHIPS AND CUSTOMER SERVICE

1. a. $$\text{A: NPV}_A = P\left[\frac{1-(1+i)^{-n}}{i}\right] = \$108{,}000(.18)\left[\frac{1-(1+.04)^{-6}}{.04}\right] = \$19{,}440\left[\frac{0.210}{.04}\right] = \$102{,}060$$

$$\text{B: NPV}_B = P\left[\frac{1-(1+i)^{-n}}{i}\right] = \$82{,}000(.22)\left[\frac{1-(1+.04)^{-15}}{.04}\right] = \$18{,}040\left[\frac{0.445}{.04}\right] = \$200{,}695$$

$$\text{C: NPV}_C = P\left[\frac{1-(1+i)^{-n}}{i}\right] = \$29{,}000(.31)\left[\frac{1-(1+.04)^{-26}}{.04}\right] = \$8{,}990\left[\frac{0.639}{.04}\right] = \$143{,}695$$

   b. Customer B has the highest value, but all are high-value customers and might only be segmented by product purchase history, not profitability.

3. $$\text{A: NPV}_A = P\left[\frac{1-(1+i)^{-n}}{i}\right] = \$108{,}000(.09)\left[\frac{1-(1+.04)^{-6}}{.04}\right] = \$9{,}720\left[\frac{0.210}{.04}\right] = \$51{,}030$$

$$\text{B: NPV}_B = P\left[\frac{1-(1+i)^{-n}}{i}\right] = \$82{,}000(.11)\left[\frac{1-(1+.04)^{-15}}{.04}\right] = \$9{,}020\left[\frac{0.445}{.04}\right] = \$100{,}348$$

$$\text{C: NPV}_C = P\left[\frac{1-(1+i)^{-n}}{i}\right] = \$29{,}000(.15)\left[\frac{1-(1+.04)^{-26}}{.04}\right] = \$4{,}350\left[\frac{0.639}{.04}\right] = \$69{,}491$$

No, nothing changed relative to problem 1—the ranking is still B, C, A.

5. $$\text{A: NPV}_A = P\left[\frac{1-(1+i)^{-n}}{i}\right] = \$3500(.15)\left[\frac{1-(1+.08)^{-10}}{.08}\right] = \$525\left[\frac{0.537}{.08}\right] = \$3523$$

$$\text{B: NPV}_B = P\left[\frac{1-(1+i)^{-n}}{i}\right] = \$4000(.14)\left[\frac{1-(1+.08)^{-8}}{.08}\right] = \$560\left[\frac{0.460}{.08}\right] = \$3218$$

7. Solve the following first: $\$560\left[\frac{X}{.08}\right] = \$3523$; solving: X = 0.503

Then solve: $1-(1+.08)^{-X} = 0.503$; or $(1+.08)^{-X} = 0.497$; try 10: 0.463; try 9: .500; try 9.2: 0.493

Try 9.15: 0.495; so the expected lifetime of customer B would have to be about 9.15 years.

PART II—MANUFACTURING AND SERVICE FLOWS

CHAPTER 6 — DEMAND MANAGEMENT, FORECASTING AND AGGREGATE PLANNING

1.

Period	Demand (units)	SMA Forecast
1	22	
2	16	
3	25	
4	27	21
5	19	22.7
6	28	23.7
7	22	24.7
8		23

3.

Period	Demand (units)	Exp. Sm. Forecast
1	22	22
2	16	22
3	25	20.2
4	27	21.64
5	19	23.25
6	28	21.98
7	22	23.79
8		23.25

5. Using LINEST function in Excel, returns: Y = 0.643X + 20.14

Using CORREL function in Excel returns: R = 0.322, which is not very good. $R^2 = 0.1039$.

So, no, the technique is not very good.

7.

Month	Demand (units)	Forecast 1 (units)	error	APE	Forecast 2 (units)	error	APE
January	1200	1086	114	9.5	1421	–221	18.4
February	1160	1120	40	3.4	1082	78	6.7
March	1232	1090	142	11.5	1141	91	7.4
April	1095	1240	–145	13.2	995	100	9.1
May	1250	1326	–76	6.1	1185	65	5.2
June	1310	1140	170	13.0	1243	67	5.1
July	1190	1092	98	8.2	1072	118	9.9
August	1265	1141	124	9.8	1342	77	6.1
MAD			113.6			**102.1**	
MAPE				9.3			**8.5**

The 2nd forecast is better—lower MAD, MAPE.

9.

Period	Demand (units)	WMA	error	Exp. Sm.	error
1	1081			1081	
2	1655			1081	
3	1422			1224.5	
4	1387	1423.7	–36.7	1273.9	113.1
5	1291	1451.1	–160.1	1302.2	–11.2
6	1386	1346	40	1299.4	86.6
7	1224	1357.7	–133.7	1321.1	–97.1
8	1166	1286	–120	1296.8	–130.8
MAD			98.1		**87.8**

The exponential smoothing forecast has a lower MAD, so it is a better forecast.

11. The correlation coefficient is 0.3244. "Sort of" correlated.

13. The exponential smoothing forecast is better, since it has a lower MAD. Note that only the 9 months were compared for both forecasts.

Month	Umbrella Sales (units)	3-pd WMA Forecast	Abs. Error	Exp. Sm. Forecast	Abs. Error
January	1420			1420.0	
February	1380			1420.0	
March	1440			1408.0	
April	1635	1418.0	217.0	1417.6	217.4
May	1744	1525.5	218.5	1482.8	261.2
June	1486	1650.5	164.5	1561.2	75.2
July	1208	1593.2	385.2	1538.6	330.6
August	1145	1398.6	253.6	1439.4	294.4
September	1337	1232.1	104.9	1351.1	14.1
October	1388	1253.6	134.4	1346.9	41.1
November	1456	1324.1	131.9	1359.2	96.8
December	1684	1411.8	272.2	1388.2	295.8
MAD			**209.1**		**180.7**

15.

Month	Level Strategy Wages	Hiring	Purch.	Holding	Shortage	Chase Strategy Wages	Hiring	Layoff	Purch.
Jan.	4 × 160 × 30 = 19200	16000	38,700		1420	19200 + 7200	16000		60000
Feb.	19200		38,700		840	14400		1000	30000
Mar.	19200		38,700		660	14400			36000
Apr.	19200		38,700	420		9600		1000	22500
May	19200		38,700	2000		9600			15000
June	19200		38,700	3680		9600			13500
July	19200		38,700	5460		4800		1000	12000
Aug.	19200		38,700	6740		9600	4000		19500
Sept.	19200		38,700	7920		9600			21000
Oct.	19200		38,700	8100		14400	4000		36000
Nov.	19200		38,700	5180		19200 + 7200 + 3000	4000 + 8 × 2000 = 20000		82500
Dec.	19200		38,700	160		48000	24000		114000
Totals	230,400	16000	464,400	39660	2920	199,800	68000	3000	462,000
Grand Totals				$753,380				**$732,800**	

Month	Mixed Strategy Wages	Hiring	Layoff	Purch.	Holding	Shortage
Jan.	19200	16000		42000		1200
Feb.	19200			42000		400
Mar.	19200			42000		
Apr.	9600		2000	17100		360
May	9600			17100		220
June	9600			17100	6	
July	9600			17700	120	
Aug.	9600			17700	84	
Sept.	9600			17700	18	
Oct.	19200 + 7200 + 4720	8000+ 12000		77700	852	
Nov.	31120			77700	756	
Dec.	31120			77700	30	
Totals	208,560	36000	2000	463,500	1866	2180
Grand Total:					**$714,106**	

CHAPTER 7 — INDEPENDENT DEMAND INVENTORY MANAGEMENT SYSTEMS

1. $EOQ = \sqrt{\frac{2SD}{iC}} = \sqrt{\frac{2(20)(10000)}{.4(0.20)}} = \sqrt{5,000,000} = 2236$

3. $\frac{QiC}{2} = \frac{2236(.4).2}{2} = \$89.44 \text{ TIC} = (\$89.45)2 = \$178.90$

5. $d(L) = \frac{10000}{365}(2) = 55$; Policy is to order 2236 hot dogs whenever there are 55 left in stock, or every 81 days.

7. EOQ = 5000; Annual OC = \$200; ICC = \$200; TIC = \$400; 2 orders; 182.5 days; ROP = 55; Order 5000 hot dogs every 182 days.

9. $EOQ_1 = \sqrt{\frac{2(25)(1200)}{.24(62)}} = 63.5$; $EOQ_2 = \sqrt{\frac{2(25)(1200)}{.24(57)}} = 66.2$; $EOQ_3 = \sqrt{\frac{2(25)(1200)}{.24(54)}} = 68$

   Only EOQ_1 is valid.

11. $EOQ_1 = \sqrt{\frac{2(25)(10000)}{.25(1)}} = 1414$; $EOQ_2 = \sqrt{\frac{2(25)(10000)}{.25(.95)}} = 1451$(increase to 5000)

    $$T_1 = O_1 + I_1 + P_1 = \frac{10000(25)}{1414} + \frac{1414(0.25)(1)}{2} + 10000(1) = 176.80 + 176.75 + 10000 = 10,353.55$$

$$T_2 = O_2 + I_2 + P_2 = \frac{10000(25)}{5000} + \frac{5000(0.25).95}{2} + 10000(.95) = 50 + 593.75 + 9500 = 10{,}143.75$$

Yes, take the discount.

13. ROP = d(L) + zσ = 10(7) + 1.65(4) = 76.6

15. $ROP = \bar{d}(\bar{L}) + z\sqrt{\bar{L}\sigma_d^2 + \bar{d}^2\sigma_L^2} = 3(18) + 2.06(\sqrt{18(25) + 9(36)} = 54 + 2.06(27.8) = 111.3$

The safety stock is 57.3.

17. t = EOQ/d = 1265/(8000/365) = 57.7 or 58 days

19. Q = 10(40) + 1.76(17) – 81 = 348.9 or 349 units.

21. $IDS = \frac{(Avg.\ Inventory\ \$)}{(Annualized\ COGS/365)} = 150{,}500/(895{,}000/365) = 61.4\text{days}$

$DRO = \frac{(Avg.\ Receivables\ \$)}{(Annualized\ Credit\ Revenues/365)} = 26000/(68000/365) = 139.6\text{days}$

$DPO = \frac{(Avg.\ Payables\ \$)}{(Annualized\ Materials\ Costs/365)} = 158{,}000/(1{,}050{,}000/365) = 54.9\text{days}$

C2C = (inventory days of supply + days of receivables outstanding) – days of payables outstanding = 61.4 + 139.6 – 54.9 = 146.1 days

The IDS is high, which means high carrying cost; the DRO is very high which is bad—it is taking too long to get paid; the DPO is high which is bad—this will hurt the firm's credit; C2C is high which is also bad, for the reasons already stated.

CHAPTER 8 — MATERIAL FLOW ANALYSIS AND FACILITY LAYOUTS

1. Takt = 480/50 = 9.6 min; Min # workstations = 14.5/9.6 = 2

3. With 6 workers, min takt time = 5; output = 480/5 = 96 units/day; efficiency = 14.5/(6(5)) = 48.3%
Total labor time = 48 hrs/day; total work time = 23.2 hrs/day; total idle time = 24.8 hrs/day

5. Takt time = 480/120 = 4 min; Min # WS = 19/4 = 5

   WS1: a,b; WS2: c; WS3: d; WS4: e; WS5: f,g; WS6: h (a couple of others also work)

   Efficiency = 19/(6(4)) = 79.2%; Tot lab time = 48hrs/day; tot work time = 120(19) = 38hrs/day

   Tot idle time = 48 – 38 = 10 hrs/day

7. Takt time = 960/80 = 12 min/unit; Min # WC = 48/12 = 4; Efficiency = 48/(72) = 66.7%

9. Min takt time = 7 min (the max task time)

   Output = 480/7 = 68.6 = 68 units/day

   Efficiency = 28/6(7) = 66.67%

   Total labor time = 48 hrs/day; work time = 68(28)/60 = 31.73 hrs/day;

   Idle time = 48 – 31.73 = 16.3 hrs/day

11.

Cost/day	Dept. B	Dept. C	Dept. D	Dept. E	Dept. F
Dept. A	22	18	32	54	39
Dept. B	—	24	0	36	34
Dept. C	—	—	8	17	42
Dept. D	—	—	—	48	0
Dept. E	—	—	—	—	17

Total daily cost = \$391; try switching C and E to make A and E closer and D and E closer.

Cost/day	Dept. B	Dept. C	Dept. D	Dept. E	Dept. F
Dept. A	22	36	32	27	39
Dept. B	—	24	0	36	34
Dept. C	—	—	16	17	21
Dept. D	—	—	—	24	0
Dept. E	—	—	—	—	34

New total daily cost = \$362, a savings of \$29 or 7.4%. Other layouts will also work.

13. The scores are: (A, B) = −3, (A, C) = 2, (C, D) = 0, for a total score of −1. Try swapping B and D. The new scores would be: (A, D) = 1, (A, C) = 2, (C, B) = 2, for a total score of 5.

15. Try to arrange 3 or 4 part families.

Part Families (Cells)	Tools Required
1) 001,005, 007,008	Lathe, Drill, Mill, Saw, Planer, Sander, Grinder
2) 002,006,009, 010	Drill, Mill, Paint, Saw, Planer, Sander, Buffer
3) 003,004	Lathe, Mill, Paint, Planer, Grinder, Buffer

This arrangement requires 20 machines.

CHAPTER 8S — JOB SCHEDULING AND VEHICLE ROUTING

1.

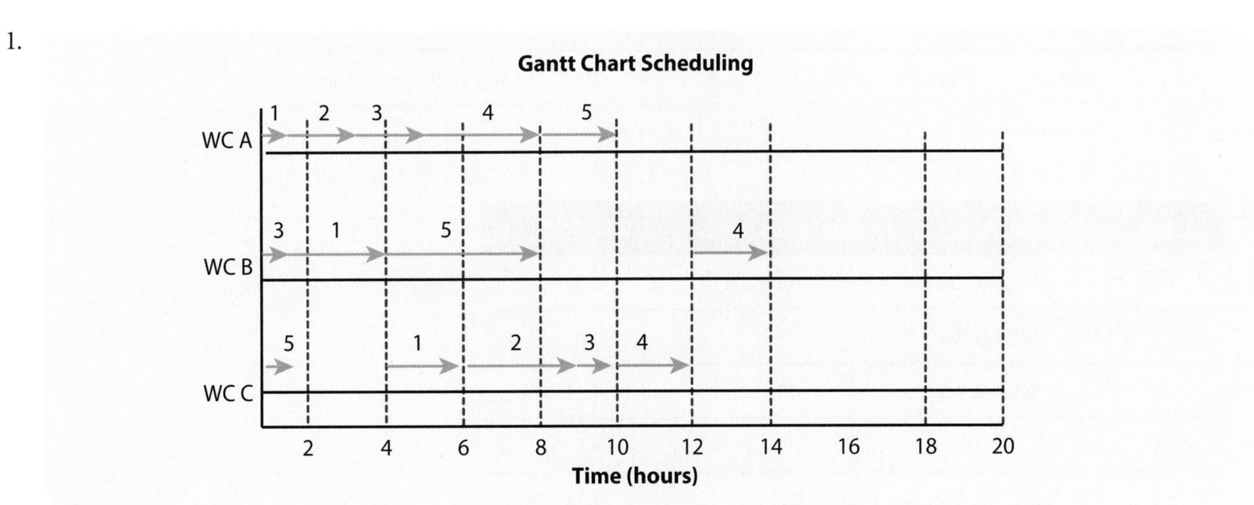

Jobs	Due date	FT	QT	
1	6 hrs	6 hrs	0	Makespan = 14 hrs
2	9 hrs	9 hrs	4 hrs	Avg. flowtime = 9.8 hrs
3	10 hrs	10 hrs	6 hrs	Avg. queue time = 4 hrs.
4	14 hrs	14 hrs	7 hrs	
5	10 hrs	10 hrs	3 hrs	

3. EDD priority = 4, 2, 3, 5, 1

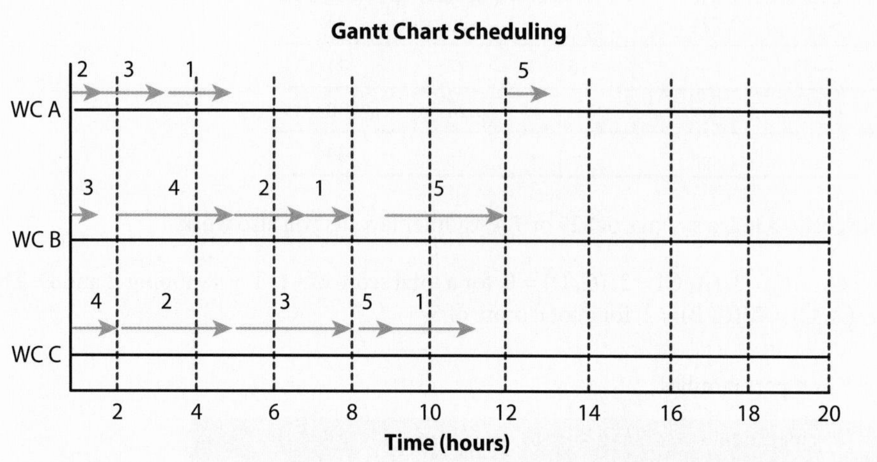

Jobs	Due date	FT	QT	Late	Tardy	
4	8 hrs	5 hrs	0 hrs	3	0	Makespan = 13 hrs
2	9 hrs	7 hrs	1 hrs	2	0	Avg. flowtime = 8.8 hrs
3	10 hrs	8 hrs	2 hrs	2	0	Avg. queue time = 3.4 hrs.
5	12 hrs	13 hrs	8 hrs	1	1	Avg. lateness = 2.4 hrs.
1	15 hrs	11 hrs	6 hrs	4	0	Avg. tardiness = 0.2 hrs.

5.

Job	Est. Hours	Due Dates (hrs.)	MINSOP
1	A/2, B/1, C/2	15	3.33
2	A/1, C/3, B/2	9	1.0
3	B/1, A/2, C/3	10	1.33
4	C/2, B/3	8	1.5
5	C/1, B/3, A/1	12	2.33

Job priority ranking—2, 3, 4, 5, 1

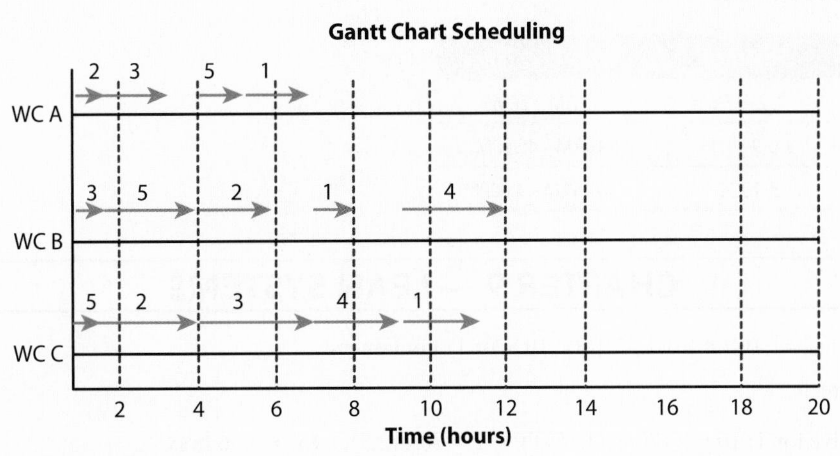

Jobs	Due date	FT	QT	Late	Tardy	
2	9 hrs	6 hrs	0 hrs	3	0	Makespan = 12 hrs
3	10 hrs	7 hrs	1 hrs	3	0	Avg. flowtime = 8.2 hrs
4	8 hrs	12 hrs	7 hrs	4	4	Avg. queue time = 2.8 hrs.
5	12 hrs	5 hrs	0 hrs	7	0	Avg. lateness = 4.2 hrs.
1	15 hrs	11 hrs	6 hrs	4	0	Avg. tardiness = 0.8 hrs.

7. For the 5 nodes shown, the following savings are calculated:

   1) 1-2-1 and 1-3-5-1 (two trips) vs. 1-2-3-5-1 (one trip): savings is $[(35 \times 2) + (45 \times 2)] - [35 + 27 + 45] = 53$ miles
   2) 1-2-1 and 1-4-1 vs. 1-2-5-4-1: savings is $[(70 + 40)] - [(35 + 48 + 20)] = 7$ miles
   3) 1-4-1 and 1-3-5-1 vs. 1-4-3-5-1: savings is: $[(40 + 90)] - [20 + 40 + 45] = 25$ miles

So, combining trips 1 & 3, we get 1-2-3-5-4-1 as the shortest trip (129 miles).

9.

Delivery	Promised Arrival Time	Estimated Completion Time	Delivery Vehicle
1	9:00 AM	9:20 AM	1
2	9:45 AM	10:15 AM	1
3	10:00 AM	10:45 AM	2 (veh. 1 busy)
4	10:30 AM	11:00 AM	1 (veh. 2 busy)
5	10:45 AM	12:15PM	3 (veh. 1,2 busy)
6	11:00 AM	11:45 AM	2 (veh. 1,3 busy)
7	11:30 AM	12:00 PM	1(veh. 2,3 busy)
8	12:30 PM	2:00 PM	1 (veh.1 closest)
9	1:00 PM	1:45 PM	2 (veh. 1 busy)
10	1:30 PM	2:30 PM	3 (veh. 1,2 busy)
11	2:30 PM	3:15 PM	2 (veh. 3 busy)
12	3:00 PM	4:00 PM	3 (veh. 2 busy)
13	3:30 PM	4:30 PM	2 (veh. 3 busy)

Shown in orange above. Also:

Vehicle	Schedule	Start/End Times
1	1-2-4-7-8	9AM – 2PM
2	3-6-9-11-13	10AM – 4:30PM
3	5-10-12	10:45AM – 4:00PM

CHAPTER 9 — LEAN SYSTEMS

1. a) K = (DT(1+S))/C = [(100/8)(6)(1.15)]/8 = 10.8, or 11 containers.
   b) 11(8) = 88 parts
   c) Use K = 10, solve for T: 10 = [(100/8)(1.15)T]/8; T = 80/(12.5)(1.15) = 5.56 hrs

3. a) D = CK/T(1+S) = 15(22)/4(1.10) = 75 parts/hr.
   b) The C could double to 30 parts; the K could double to 44 containers; the T could shrink to 2 hours.

CHAPTER 10 — MANAGING CUSTOMER AND WORK FLOWS

1.

	M	T	W	Th	F	S	Su
Requirement	6	4	5	4	3	2	2
Worker 1	6	4	5	4	3	2	2
Worker 2	5	3	4	3	2	2	2
Worker 3	4	2	3	2	2	2	1
Worker 4	3	1	2	1	1	2	1
Worker 5	2	0	1	1	1	1	0
Worker 6	1	0	1	0	0	0	0

Requires 5 full-time workers and 1 part-time worker.

3.

Expected Profit With 8 Reservations			
No-Shows	0	1	2
Customers	8	7	6
Tables Filled	8	7	6
Profit ($)	800	700	600
Turnaways	0	0	0
Cost ($)	0	0	0
Net Profit	800	700	600
Probability	0.5	0.3	0.2
Expected Net	400	210	120
Total Expected Profit $730			

Expected Profit With 10 Reservations			
No-Shows	0	1	2
Customers	10	9	8
Tables Filled	8	8	8
Profit ($)	800	800	800
Turnaways	2	1	0
Cost ($)	100	50	0
Net Profit	700	750	800
Probability	0.5	0.3	0.2
Expected Net	350	225	160
Total Expected Profit $755			

Expected Profit With 9 Reservations			
No-Shows	0	1	2
Customers	9	8	7
Tables Filled	8	8	7
Profit ($)	800	800	700
Turnaways	1	0	0
Cost ($)	50	0	0
Net Profit	750	800	700
Probability	0.5	0.3	0.2
Expected Net	375	240	140
Total Expected Profit $755			

The optimal overbooking policy is both 1 and 2 for the salon.

5. $Pn(t) = \dfrac{(\lambda t)^n e^{-\lambda t}}{n!} = 20^{10} e^{-20} / 10! = 0.006$; less than 1% chance.

7. Use $Pn(t) = \dfrac{(\lambda t)^n e^{-\lambda t}}{n!} = 8^n e^{-8}/n!$ for n from 0 to 12, then sum probabilities:

n	Prob.	*n*	Prob.	*n*	Prob.
0	0.0003	5	0.0916	10	0.0993
1	0.0027	6	0.1221	11	0.0722
2	0.0107	7	0.1396	12	0.0481
3	0.0286	8	0.1396		
4	0.0573	9	0.1241		

Sum = 0.9362; so 94% of the time, they will get 12 or fewer cars/hour arriving, so yes, they can handle the demand.

9. $\lambda = 10$ customers per hour; $\mu = 20$ customers per hour

$\rho = 10/20 = 0.5$ or 50% utilization

$L_q = \dfrac{\rho\lambda}{\mu-\lambda}$ customers $= 0.5(10)/(20 - 10) = 0.5$; $L_s = L_q + \rho = .5 + 0.5 = 1$ customer

$W_q = \dfrac{L_q}{\lambda} = 0.5/10 = .05$ hours × 60 min/hr = 3 minutes

$W_s = W_q + \dfrac{1}{\mu} = 3$ min + 1/20 cust/hr (hours × 60 min/hr) = 6 minutes

P > 1 = Probability of more than 1 customer in the system = 1 – (P0 + P1)

$P0 = 1 - \rho = 0.5$

$P1 = \rho(1 - \rho) = 0.25$

Thus P > 1 = 1 – 0.75 = 25%

This looks reasonable.

11. $\lambda = 14$ customers per hour; $\mu = 20$ customers per hour

$\rho = 14/20 = 0.7$ or 70% utilization

$L_q = \dfrac{\rho\lambda}{\mu-\lambda}$ customers $= 0.7(14)/(20-14) = 1.63$; $Ls = L_q + \rho = 1.63 + 0.7 = 2.33$ customers

$W_q = \dfrac{L_q}{\lambda} = 1.63/14 = .117$ hours $\times$ 60 min/hr = 7 minutes

$W_s = W_q + \dfrac{1}{\mu} = 7$ min + 1/20 cust/hr (hours $\times$ 60 min/hr) = 10 minutes

$P > 1$ = Probability of more than 1 customer in the system $= 1 - (P0 + P1)$

$P0 = 1 - \rho = 0.3$

$P1 = \rho(1 - \rho) = 0.21$

Thus $P > 1 = 1 - 0.51 = 49\%$

This will probably not work—the wait time is too long.

CHAPTER 11 — MANAGING INFORMATION FLOWS: MRP AND ERP

1. Purchase both C and D—max time is 3 days. Make B—4 more days. Make A—2 more days. So minimum leadtime is 9 days.

3. Purchase E and D—max lead time is 3 days. So Part B can be finished in 3 + 4 = 7 days.

   Part C can be finished in 2 + 3 = 5 days, so Part A can be finished in 7 + 2 = 9 days

5. Answers are in orange.

Part A		1	2	3	4	5	6	7	8	9	10
Gross Requirements		15	26	14	20	16	0	10	12	16	19
Scheduled Receipts		20									
Projected On-Hand Inventory	40	45	19	5	5	9	9	19	7	11	12
Net Requirements					19	15		5		13	
Planned Order Releases		20	20		20		20	20			

Q = 20, LT = 3, SS = 4

7. Answers are in orange.

Part A		1	2	3	4	5	6	7	8	9	10
Gross Requirements		15	10	20	25	30	20	25	15	20	25
Scheduled Receipts		25									
Projected On-Hand Inventory	30	40	30	10	0	0	0	0	0	0	0

Net Requirements				15	30	20	25	15	20	25
Planned Order Releases	15	30	20	25	15	20	25			

Q = LFL, LT = 3, SS = 0

9.

Part A		1	2	3	4	5	6	7	8
Gross Requirements		4	3	5	3	7	6	9	4
Scheduled Receipts									
Projected On-Hand Inventory	12	6	3						
Net Requirements				2	3	7	6	9	4
Planned Order Releases		2	3	7	6	9	4		

Part B		1	2	3	4	5	6	7	8
Gross Requirements		4	6	14	12	18	8		
Scheduled Receipts									
Projected On-Hand Inventory	40	36	30	16	4				
Net Requirements						14	8		
Planned Order Releases		14	8						

Part C		1	2	3	4	5	6	7	8
Gross Requirements		56	32						
Scheduled Receipts									
Projected On-Hand Inventory	65	9							
Net Requirements			23						
Planned Order Releases		23							

Part D		1	2	3	4	5	6	7	8
Gross Requirements		14	8						
Scheduled Receipts									
Projected On-Hand Inventory	30	16	8						
Net Requirements									
Planned Order Releases									

11.

Part A		1	2	3	4	5	6	7	8
Gross Requirements		5	3	6	8	4	10	5	2
Scheduled Receipts									
Projected On-Hand Inventory	20	15	12	6	5	5	5	5	5
Net Requirements					7	4	10	5	2
Planned Order Releases			7	4	10	5	2		

Part B		1	2	3	4	5	6	7	8
Gross Requirements			14	8	20	10	4		
Scheduled Receipts									
Projected On-Hand Inventory	30	30	16	8	8	8	14		
Net Requirements					17	7	1		
Planned Order Releases		20	10	10					

Part E		1	2	3	4	5	6	7	8
Gross Requirements		60	30	30					
Scheduled Receipts									
Projected On-Hand Inventory	62	2	0	0					
Net Requirements			28	30					
Planned Order Releases		28	30						

Part C		1	2	3	4	5	6	7	8
Gross Requirements			14	8	20	10	4		
Scheduled Receipts									
Projected On-Hand Inventory	20	20	6	23	3	18	14		
Net Requirements				2		7			
Planned Order Releases			25		25				

Part D		1	2	3	4	5	6	7	8
Gross Requirements		20	60	10	50				
Scheduled Receipts									
Projected On-Hand Inventory	90	70	10	12	10				
Net Requirements				5	43				
Planned Order Releases		12	48						

Part F		1	2	3	4	5	6	7	8
Gross Requirements			25		25				
Scheduled Receipts									
Projected On-Hand Inventory	46	46	21	21	10				
Net Requirements					14				
Planned Order Releases			14						

Need to buy D, E, F in the amounts days shown on the Planned Order Releases.

Need to make A, B, C in the amounts and days shown on the POR's.

CHAPTER 12 — MANAGING PROJECTS

1.

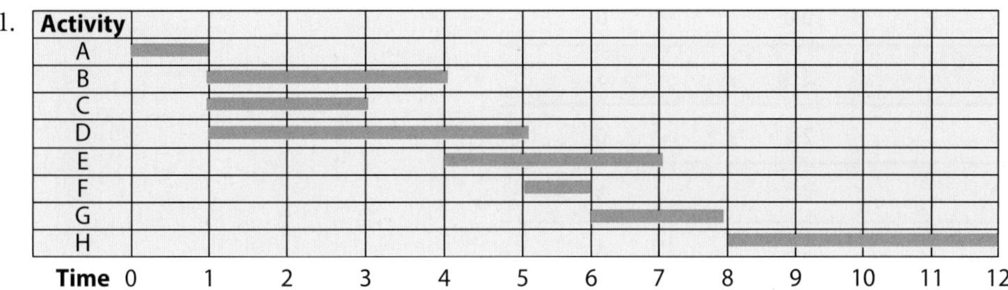

There are 12 days to completion.

3.

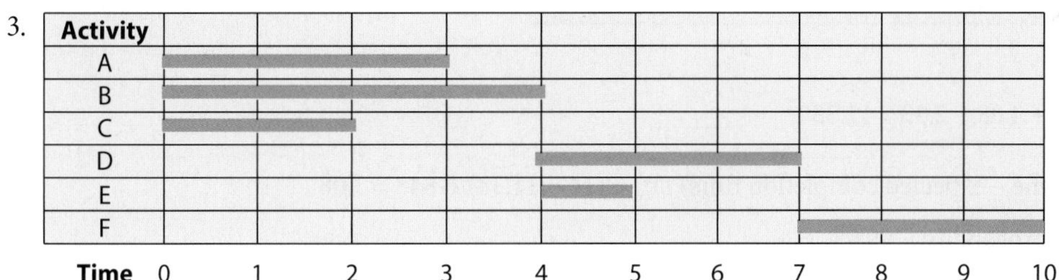

There are 10 days to completion.

5.

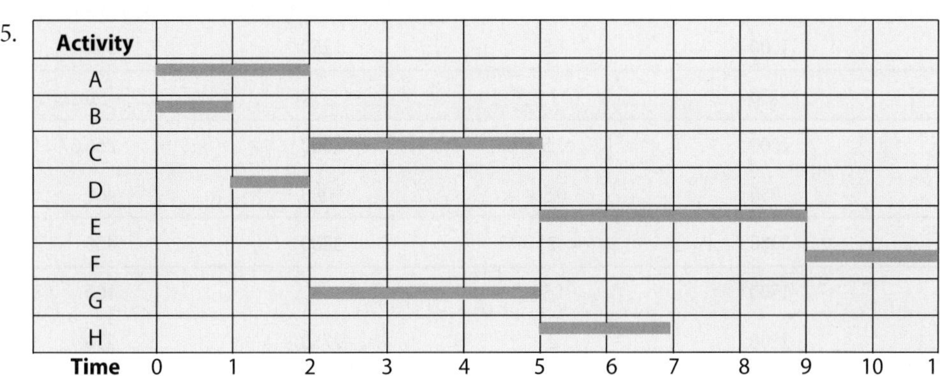

There are 11 days to completion.

7.

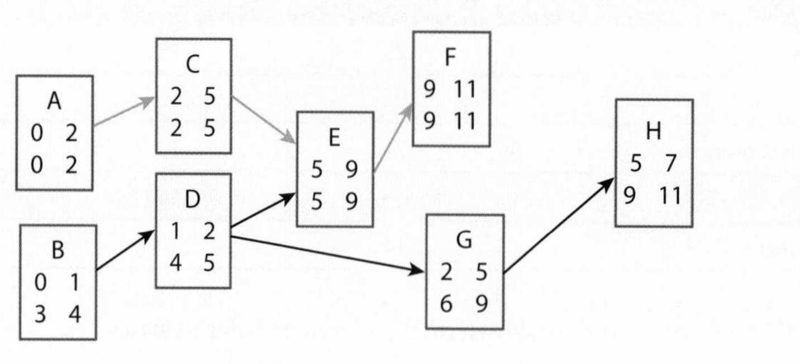

Activity	Time	LS - ES (hrs.)	Slack (hrs.)
A	2	0-0	0
B	1	3-0	3
C	3	2-2	0
D	1	4-1	3
E	4	5-5	0
F	2	9-9	0
G	3	6-2	4
H	2	9-5	4

9. A + C + E + F = 1.97 + 3.0 + 4.08 + 2.33 = 11.38

11. Z = (desired completion time – expected completion time) / σ_p = (14 – 11.38)/0.848 = 3.08

    From Z-table: 0.99896, so probability is 99.9%.

13. $\text{Crash cost / day} = \frac{(\text{crash cost} - \text{normal cost})}{(\text{normal time} - \text{crash time})}$

Activity	Normal time	Normal cost ($)	Crash time	Crash cost ($)	Crash cost/day($)
A	2	1000	1.5	1250	500
B	1	200	1	0	0
C	3	2200	1.5	2600	266.67
D	1	850	0.5	1080	460
E	4	3000	2	3800	400
F	2	1500	1.5	1550	100
G	3	2500	2	2750	250
H	2	2700	0.5	3900	800

15. The possible activity paths are then: A-C-E-F (6.5 days), B-D-E-F (5 days), and B-D-G-H (4 days), so ACEF is the critical path and the total cost is \$13950 + 1500 = \$15450.

CHAPTER 13 — SIX SIGMA QUALITY MANAGEMENT

1. a. DPMO = (number of defects)/ ((OFD per unit)(number of units)) × 1,000,000
   = 12 × 1000000/(4 × 104) = 28,846

   b. Using Table 13.1, this is a Six Sigma operating level between 3 and 3.5.

3. a. DPMO = 4280 × 1000000/(294 × 1425000) = 10.2
   b. Between 5.5 and 6.
   c. 3.4 = D × 1000000/(294 × 1000000), or 3.4(294) = D, so Defects = 1000.

CHAPTER 13S — STATISTICAL QUALITY CONTROL

1.

Day	Wait Time (min.)	$\overline{X}$	R
1	2.5, 3, 1.5, 3, 4	2.8	2.5
2	2, 4.5, 3.5, 2, 4	3.2	2.5
3	1.5, 5, 3.5, 2, 2.5	2.9	3.5
4	3, 3.5, 5, 2.5, 2	3.2	3
5	2, 5.5, 2.5, 3, 1.5	2.9	4
6	2.5, 3.5, 4, 2, 2.5	2.9	2
7	3.5, 1.5, 2, 4, 2	2.6	2.5

$\overline{\overline{x}} = 2.93$; $\overline{R} = 2.86$

3.

Hour	Weight (gms)	$\overline{X}$	R	Hour	Weight (gms)	$\overline{X}$	R
1	110, 105, 98, 100	103.3	7	7	89, 102, 101, 99	97.8	13
2	79, 102, 100, 104	96.3	25	8	100, 101, 98, 96	98.8	5
3	100, 102, 100, 96	99.5	6	9	98, 95, 101, 100	98.5	6
4	94, 98, 99, 101	98	7	10	99, 100, 97, 102	99.5	5
5	98, 104, 97, 100	99.8	7	11	102, 97, 100, 101	100	5
6	104, 97, 99, 100	100	7	12	98, 100, 100, 97	98.8	3

$\overline{\overline{x}} = 99.2$

$\overline{R} = 8$

5.

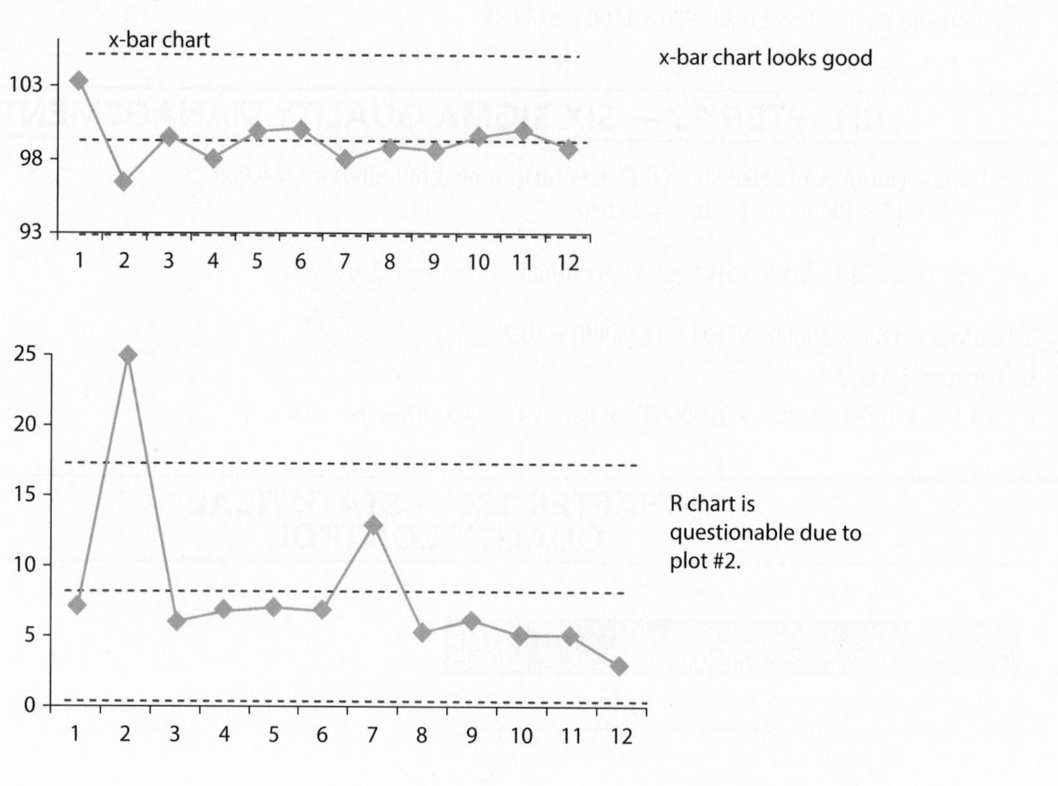

Charts above were created using Excel.

7. $\overline{p} = 1.4/12 = 0.117$ or 11.7%

$$\sigma_p = \sqrt{\frac{.177(.883)}{10}} = 0.102$$

9.

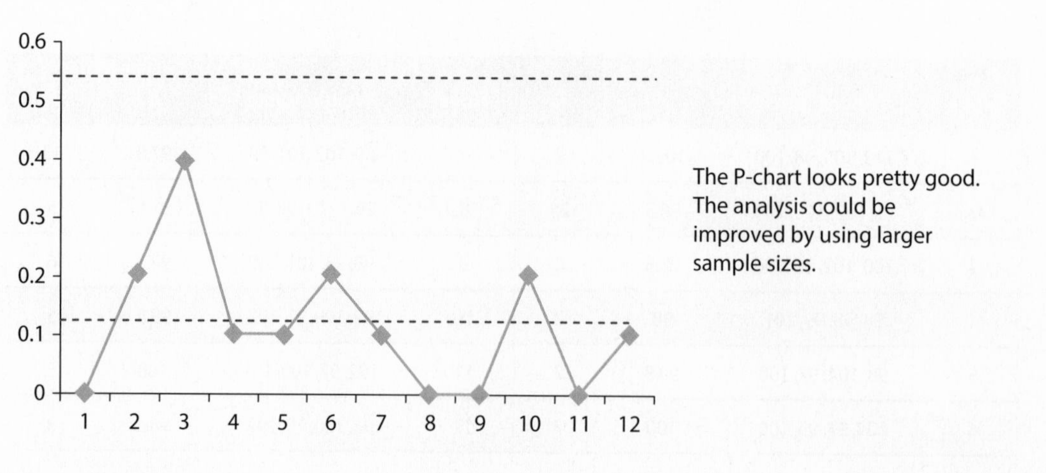

Chart above was made using Excel.

11. $UCL = .047 + 3(.021) = 0.11$

$LCL = 0$

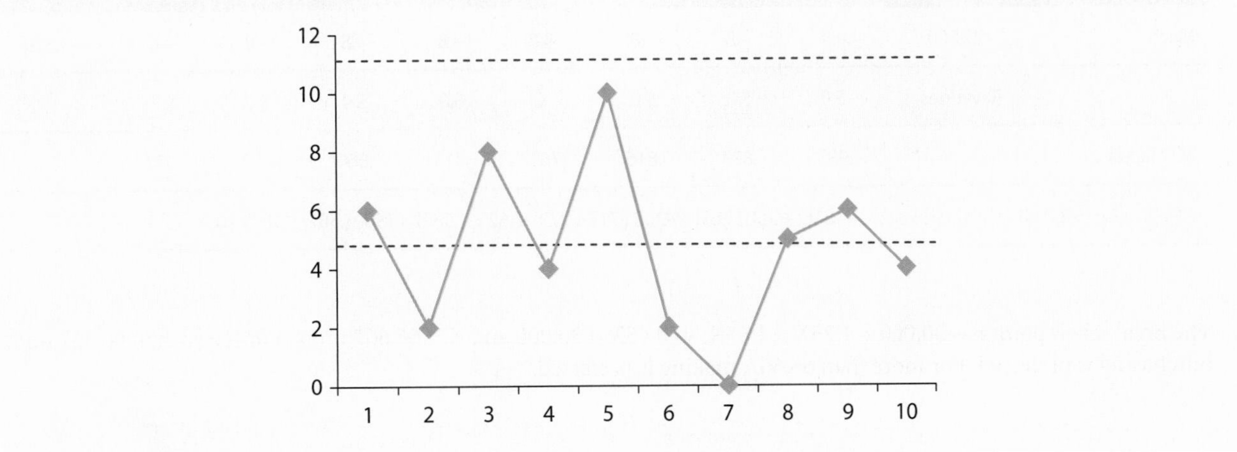

The chart looks questionable, since the plots are not close to the center line. Plot 5 is also close to the UCL; but still in control.

13. $\bar{c} = 44/10 = 4.4$

$\sqrt{\bar{c}} = 2.1$

15. $C_{pk} = \text{Min}\left[\frac{\bar{\bar{x}} - LSL}{3\sigma} \text{ or } \frac{USL - \bar{\bar{x}}}{3\sigma}\right] = \text{Min}\left[\frac{7.621 - 7.618}{.003} \text{ or } \frac{7.622 - 7.621}{.003}\right] = \text{Min}(1 \text{ or } .33) = .33$

Since the C_{pk} is less than 1, process is not capable.

17. a. $C_{pk} = \text{Min}\left[\frac{2.0 - 1.945}{.03} \text{ or } \frac{2.015 - 2.0}{.03}\right] = \text{Min}(2.5 \text{ or } 1.17) = 1.17$

b. Yes, since the index is > 1.

PART III—MANAGING SUPPLY CHAINS

CHAPTER 14 — GLOBAL SUPPLY MANAGEMENT

1.

Supplier	Purchase Price ($)	Annual Oper. & Maint. Costs ($000) Yr.1	Yr.2	Yr.3	Yr.4	Yr.5	Yr.6	Yr.7	Salvage Value ($)
Schibr.	−84,000	−22	−22	−22	−22	−22	−22	−22	+30,000
Rogers	−102,000	−19	−19	−19	−19	−19	−19	−19	+36,000
NPV factor	0	.892	.797	.712	.636	.567	.507	.452	
NPV(Schibr.) = −84000 − 22000 (.892 + .797 + .712 + .636 + .567 + .507 + .452) + 30000 (.452) = −$170,826									
NPV(Rogers) = −102000 − 19000 (.892 + .797 + .712 + .636 + .567 + .507 + .452) + 36000 (.452) = −172,520									

The Schibrowski company is slightly preferred.

3.

	Purchase Price ($)	Annual Oper. & Maint. Costs ($000)								Salvage Value ($)
		Yr.1	Yr.2	Yr.3	Yr.4	Yr.5	Yr.6	Yr.7	Yr.8	
Mach	−22,000	−.8	−.8	−.8	−4.8	−.8	−.8	−.8	−.8	+1,500
	Revenues	5.0	5.0	5.0	5.0	5.0	5.0	5.0	5.0	
NPV factor		.935	.873	.816	.763	.713	.666	.623	.582	
NPV(Mach) = −22000 + 4200 (.935 + .873 + .816) + 200 (.763) + 4200 (.713 + .666 + .623 + .582) + 1500 (.582) = $899.20										

5. The break-even point is—30,000 + 1.25X = 1.65X; so 0.45X = 30,000 and X = 66,667 units. For fewer than 66,667 units, purchasing is preferred. For more than 66,667, making is preferred.

7.

Performance Criteria	Weight	Actual	Ideal	Rating (0–10)	Weighted Score
On-Time Deliveries	20%	80%	100%	8	1.6
Pricing	25%	Excellent	Excellent	10	2.5
Availability	5%	100%	100%	10	.5
Customer Service	30%	75%	100%	7.5	2.25
Quality	10%	100%	100%	10	1
Order Leadtime	10%	5 days	2 days	4	.4

Answers are shown in orange above. The total weighted score is 8.25.

9.

Performance Criteria	Weight	Supplier A Perf.	Score A	Supplier B Perf.	Score B	Supplier C Perf.	Score C
On-Time Performance	23%	8.6	1.98	9.2	2.12	10	2.3
Pricing	28%	10	2.8	8.7	2.44	8.3	2.32
Customer Service	20%	9	1.8	8	1.6	10	2
Meets Quality Check	15%	9.2	1.38	10	1.5	9.4	1.41
Supplier Contributions	14%	9	1.26	8	1.12	8	1.12
Total Weighted Score			9.22		8.78		9.15

So, Supplier A is preferred.

CHAPTER 15 — LOCATION, LOGISTICS, AND PRODUCT RETURNS

1.

Location Factor	Weight	U.S.	Mexico	Canada
Land Availability	0.15	85	75	100
National Competitiveness	0.15	100	65	85
Quality of Life	0.30	90	80	100
Labor Availability	0.25	70	100	72
Transportation Infrastr.	0.10	100	82	90
Weighted Scores		82.25	78.2	**84.75**

Canada has the highest score, and is therefore preferred.

3.

Location Factor	Weight	U. of Arizona	UCLA	U. of Colorado
School Reputation	0.15	80	100	85
Majors He Might Select	0.25	90	100	100
Tuition Cost	0.20	100	60	75
Living Cost	0.15	100	60	80
Geographic Quality	0.15	80	100	90
Student Organizations	0.10	85	100	90
Weighted Scores		**90**	86	87.25

University of Arizona has the highest score, and is therefore preferred.

5. Let's make the markets = 1 unit.

   Then $C_x = 225(1) + 150(1) + 750(1)/3 = 375$, and $C_y = 600 + 240 + 250/3 = 363$

7. $S_2 = \frac{\sqrt{N_2}}{\sqrt{N_1}}(S_1) = \frac{\sqrt{3}}{\sqrt{2}}(6000) = 7348$ units or 2449 per warehouse

9. a. $S_2 = \frac{\sqrt{N_2}}{\sqrt{N_1}}(S_1) = \frac{\sqrt{3}}{\sqrt{6}}(30{,}000) = 21{,}213$ units or 7071 units per warehouse

   b. $S_2 = \frac{\sqrt{N_2}}{\sqrt{N_1}}(S_1) = \frac{\sqrt{10}}{\sqrt{6}}(30{,}000) = 38{,}730$ units or 3873 per warehouse

/ NOTES /

Chapter 1

1. Alpern, P. (2010). Bringing digital sense to a global enterprise. *IndustryWeek, 259*(12), 44.
2. Gilmore, D. (2008, October 23). Supply chain news: The 10 best quotes from CSCMP 2008. *SupplyChainDigest,* http://www.scdigest.com/assets/FirstThoughts/08-10-23.php
3. Polischuk, T. (2010). When Walmart speaks. *Package Printing, 57*(11), 20.
4. See Boeing's organizational chart, https://www.google.com/search?q=famous+company+organizational+chart s&tbm=isch&tbo=u&source=univ&sa=X&ved=0CB0QsARqFQoTCPin-dLVrsgCFQ2ZiAodfksL6g&biw=1680&bih=882#imgrc=hHL9U8zNjCc4yM%3A
5. Brochner, J. (2010). Innovation and ancient Roman facilities management. *Journal of Facilities Management 8*(4), 246.
6. Business operations manager. *U.S. News & World Report,* http://money.usnews.com/careers/best-jobs/business-operations-manager
7. Evans, J., & Lindsay, W. (2002). *The management and control of quality.* (5th ed.). Mason: South-Western, 2002.
8. Devane, T. (2004). *Integrating lean Six Sigma and high-performance organizations: Leading the charge toward dramatic, rapid, and sustainable improvement.* San Francisco: Pfeiffer.
9. Watson, R., & Leson, K. (2011). On the clock. *Quality Progress, 44*(3), 44–51.
10. Oliver, R., & Webber, M. (1992). Supply chain management: Logistics catches up with strategy. *Outlook* (1982). Cited in M. Christopher, M. (1992). *Logistics: The strategic issues.* London, England: Chapman & Hall, 63–75.
11. Blanchard, D. (2012). How to manage a global supply chain. *IndustryWeek, 261*(8), 30.
12. Taylor, P. (2013, October 15). Benefits of outsourcing come under scrutiny. FT.com, 1; Hamm, S. (2004, October 4). Is outsourcing on the outs? *BusinessWeek,* 42.
13. Ovanessoff, A., & Purdy, M. (2011). Global competition 2021: Key capabilities for emerging opportunities *Strategy and Leadership, 39*(5), 46.
14. Croxton, K., Garcia-Dastugue, S., Lambert, D., & Rogers, D. (2001). The supply chain management processes. *International Journal of Logistics Management, 12*(2), 13–36.
15. Myron, D. (2011). CRM recovers with low-cost options. *Customer Relationship Management, 15*(8), 4.
16. See Correia, J., Dharmasthira, Y., & Pang, C. (2013). Market share analysis: Customer relationship management software, worldwide, 2012, http://my.gartner.com
17. See Aho, K. (2013, July 18). 2013 customer service hall of fame, http://money.msn.com
18. Craig, M. (2011). TransLink and the 2010 Olympic winter games. *Institute of Transportation Engineers, 81*(1), 56–60.
19. The cult of the dabbawala. (2008, July 10). *The Economist,* www.economist.com; Pathak, G. (2010). Delivering the nation: The dabbawalas of Mumbai. *Journal of South Asian Studies, 33*(2), 235–257.
20. Hickey, K. (2006). Data warehouses integrate supply chains. *World Trade, 19*(2), 42.
21. Bremner, B., Edmondson, G., Dawson, C., Welch, D., & Kerwin, K. (2004, October 4). Nissan's boss: Carlos Ghosn saved Japan's no. 2 carmaker. Now he's taking on the world. *BusinessWeek.*
22. Petersen, J., & Kumar, V. (2010, April 1). Can product returns make you money? *MIT Sloan Management Review,* http://sloanreview.mit.edu/the-magazine/2010-spring/51316/can-product-returns-make-you-money/#1
23. Bustillo, M. (2010, December 27). Retailers loosen up on returns. *Wall Street Journal,* B1.
24. Encyclopedia of business. (2nd ed.), http://www.referenceforbusiness.com/management/Sc-Str/Service-Industry.html
25. Ciccatelli, A. (2013). Customer service is key to Phone.com's success. *Customer, 31*(7), 28.
26. Castro, K., & Pitta, D. (2012). Relationship development for services: An empirical test. *The Journal of Product and Brand Management, 21*(2), 126–131.
27. Iconic brands combine to create full-service restaurant company. (2010). *Franchising World, 42*(5), 91; Betts, P., & Nakamoto, M. (2010, April 9). Solar impulse takes flight toward the impossible. *Financial Times,* 17; Scholtes, S. (2009, September 17). Capco eyes North America expansion. *Financial Times,* 27.
28. Ford, H., & Crowther, S. (1922). *My Life and work.* Garden City, NY: Garden City Publishing.
29. Six Sigma saves billions of dollars. (2010). *ASQ Six Sigma Forum Magazine, 9*(4), 40.
30. Kwak, Y. (2011). A brief history of project management. In Morris, P. W. G., Pinto, J. K., & Söderlund, J. (Eds.). (2011). *The Oxford handbook of project management.* Oxford, England: Oxford University Press.
31. Japan: Nissan publishes 2011 sustainability report. (2011, June 28). *Just—Auto Global News,* 1.

Chapter 2

1. Strauss, L. (2011). Lead, have a clear strategy, delegate. *Barron's, 91*(31), 35–36.
2. GE traces the key to sustainable growth with its 2010 citizenship report. (2011, August 12). *Economics Week,* 504.
3. Liveris, A. (2011). Ethics as a strategy. *Leadership Excellence, 28*(2), 17.
4. See www.missionstatements.com
5. Ibid.
6. Back from the brink. (2006, June). *Chief Executive,* 36–39. Also see De, M. (2006, November 3). Ex-leader of computer associates gets 12-year sentence and fine. *New York Times.*
7. See www.redbox.com/history
8. U.S. executives remain bullish on American manufacturing, study finds. (2014, October 23), http://www.bcg.com/media/pressreleasedetails.aspx?id=tcm:12-168578
9. Hughes, J., & Schlangenstein, M. (2010, December 8). Southwest loses on-time bragging rights as 2010 ranking slips. Bloomberg.com.
10. See who made the 2015 Global RepTrak® 100, http://www.reputationinstitute.com/research/Global-RepTrak-100
11. The 2014 customer service hall of fame. (2014, July 19), http://www.usatoday.com/story/money/business/2014/07/19/customer-service-hall-of-fame/12690983/
12. Hsieh, T. (2010). *Delivering happiness: A path to profits, passion, and purpose.* New York: Hachette Book Group.
13. Polaroid Z2300 instant digital camera, http://www.polaroid.com/products/Z2300-instant-camera
14. Raynor, M. (2011). Disruptive innovation: The Southwest Airlines case revisited. *Strategy & Leadership, 39*(4), 31–34.
15. Adams, B. (2003). Performance measures and profitability factors of successful African-American entrepreneurs: An exploratory study. *Journal of American Academy of Business, 2*(2), 418–424.
16. Levenson, A., & Faber, T. (2009). Count on productivity gains. *HRMagazine, 54*(6), 68–74.
17. Poirier, C., Swink, M., & Quinn, F. (2009). Progress despite the downturn. *Supply Chain Management Review, 13*(7), 26.
18. Biederman, D. (2010, May 10). The customer is king, again. *Journal of Commerce,* 1.
19. See, for instance, Chapman, L. (2012, February 16). Where is Obama's windfall profits tax on the oil and gas industry? http://www.huffingtonpost.com/lloyd-chapman/oil-gas-windfall-tax_b_1280253.html
20. Wilson, J. (2014, October 19). BHP Billiton leads miners' retreat from supersizing. FT.com, 1.
21. Triplett, J. (1999). The Solow productivity paradox: What do computers do to productivity? *The Canadian Journal of Economics, 32*(2), 309–334.
22. Nancheria, A. (2010). Superior customer service boosts market performance. *T + D, 64*(6), 24.
23. Henschen, D. (2008, November 24). Decision time. *InformationWeek,* 33–40; and Global Workplace Solutions corporate website: www.globalwps.com
24. See Sustainability, www.walmartstores.com/sustainability; and The sustainability consortium, www.sustinabilityconsortium.org
25. Debusk, G., & Crabtree, A. (2006). Does the balanced scorecard improve performance? *Management Accounting Quarterly, 8*(1), 133–143.
26. See, for example, DeBusk, G., & Crabtree, A. (2006). Does the balanced scorecard improve performance? *Management Accounting Quarterly, 8*(1), 44–48; Kaplan, R. S., & Norton, D. P. (1992). The balanced scorecard—measures that drive performance. *Harvard Business Review, 70*(1), 71–79; Lester, T. (2004, October 6). Measure for measure, the balanced scorecard remains a widely used management tool. *Financial Times,* 6; and Lawson, R., Stratton, W., & Hatch, T. (2007). Scorecarding in the public sector: Fad or tool of choice? *Government Finance Review, 23*(3), 48–52.
27. Lester, T. Measure for measure, the balanced scorecard remains a widely used management tool. *Financial Times,* 6.
28. Bacon, J. (2014, April 2). What's your chief marketing officer really thinking? *Marketing Week* (online), 1.
29. Moore, K., Eyestone, K., & Coddington, D. (2013). The big deal about big data. *Healthcare Financial Management, 67*(8), 60–68.
30. Gustafson, M. (2014). Big data and agriculture. *AgriMarketing, 52*(2), 24–27.
31. McAfee, A., & Brynjolfsson, E. (2012, October). Big data: The management revolution. *Harvard Business Review,* 60–70.
32. Gustafson, M. (2014). Big data and agriculture. *AgriMarketing, 52*(2), 24–27.
33. Schwartz, M. (2013, February 26). HP launches big data security products, threat research. *InformationWeek* (online), 1.
34. Virtustream and skilled analysts to offer enterprise big data cloud solutions. (2013, March 16). *Marketing Weekly Solutions,* 3 05.
35. Jack, A. (2011, December 15). Charity begins at the office. *Financial Times,* 16.
36. Ethical sourcing: coffee, http://www.starbucks.com/responsibility/sourcing/coffee
37. See, for example, Androich, A. (2007, July/August). Get your green on. *Real Screen,* 14; Watson, T. (2000, November 7). Environmental pioneer dies. *USA Today,* 24A.
38. Pinchot, G. (1908). *The conservation of natural resources.* Washington, DC: U.S. Department of Agriculture. (Farmers' Bulletin, 327); also see Beatley, T. (2009). Sustainability 3.0 building tomorrow's Earth-friendly communities. *Planning, 75*(5), 16–22.
39. Watkins, E. (2011, April 7). Hersha Hospitality Management helps clean the world. *Lodging Hospitality,* 1.
40. Case study: Kroger tackles sustainability one lonely orange at a time. (2014). *PR News, 70*(38), 1.
41. Rogers, D. (2011). Sustainability is free—the case for doing the right thing. *Supply Chain Management Review, 15*(6), 10–17.
42. A new view that links quality and social responsibility. *Journal for Quality and Participation, 34*(3), 34–35.
43. AlSagheer, A. (2011). Six Sigma for sustainability in multinational organizations. *Journal of Business Case Studies, 7*(3), 7–15.

Chapter 3

1. 30 best creative, design & marketing quotes, http://www.slideshare.net/mijkdemijk/30-best-creative-design-marketing-quotes
2. A genius departs: Steve Jobs. (2011). *The Economist, 401*(8754), 81.
3. Design quotes, http://www.lukew.com/quotes
4. Cebrzynski, G. (2008). Market-testing new products earns A-plus from national chains. *Nation's Restaurant News, 42*(37), 37–40.
5. See, for instance, Bajarin, T. (2012, May 7). 6 reasons Apple is so successful. *Time,* http://techland.time.com/2012/05/07/six-reasons-why-apple-is-successful
6. See, for instance, Going global, www.toyota.com/esq/pdf/hwt-going-global.pdf
7. Ten things we know to be true, https://www.google.com/intl/en/about/company/philosophy
8. See, for example, A timeline: The Blockbuster life cycle. (2011, April 7), http://www.forbes.com/2010/05/18/blockbuster-netflix-coinstar-markets-bankruptcy-coinstar_slide_14.html; and for Netflix, see About Netflix, https://pr.netflix.com/WebClient/loginPageSalesNetWorksAction.do?contentGroupId=10477&contentGroup=Company+Timeline
9. Thilmany, J. (2003). Birth of a new product. *Mechanical Engineering, 125*(10), 52–54.
10. Morris, T., & Pinnington, A. (1998). Evaluating strategic fit in professional service firms. *Human Resource Management Journal, 8*(4), 76–80.
11. Frohlich, T. C. (2014, March 3). Worst product flops of all time, http://247wallst.com/special-report/2014/03/03/worst-product-flops-of-all-time/#ixzz40YNLz7If

12. Levick, R. (2013, January 31). Spotlight on outsourcing: Boeing scrambles as Toyota triumphs, http://www.forbes.com/sites/richardlevick/2013/01/30/spotlight-on-outsourcing-boeing-scrambles-as-toyota-triumphs
13. Denning, S. (2013, January 21). What went wrong at Boeing? http://www.forbes.com/sites/stevedenning/2013/01/21/what-went-wrong-at-boeing
14. Anthes, G. (2008, August 11). The new face of R&D. *Computerworld*, 32–33; and King, A., & Lakhani, K. (2013). Using open innovation to identify the best ideas. *MIT Sloan Management Review, 55*(1), 41–48.
15. King, A., & Lakhani, K. (2013). Using open innovation to identify the best ideas.
16. Carr, D. (2012, January 6). SAS's year of living socially. *InformationWeek* (online), 1.
17. Dynamatic buys German auto component maker. (2012, January 9). *Accord Fintech*, 1.
18. Zegler, J. (2012). 2012 new product development survey. *Beverage Industry, 103*(1), 56–63.
19. Penenberg, A. (2011, September). They have hacked your brain. *Fast Company*, 85–92.
20. A key to services innovation: Services blueprinting. (2008, January 30), http:// http://research.wpcarey.asu.edu/marketing/a-key-to-service-innovation-services-blueprinting/
21. Alpern, P. (2011). Breaking down manufacturing walls with 3-D simulation. *IndustryWeek, 260*(1), 44.
22. A taste of the science behind Sam's Sales. (2010, June/July). *Retailing Today*, 13–14.
23. Lammers, D. (2008). Freescale taking RCP to pilot production stage. *Semiconductor International, 31*(8), 17–18.
24. DeLuna, J. (2010, December). Boeing to ramp-up 777 production rate. *Airfinance Journal*, 1.
25. Liddle, A. (2008). Dunkin' tests order kiosks to minimize service "bottlenecks." *Nation's Restaurant News, 42*(10), 20.
26. Winner, R., Pennell, J., Bertrand, H., & Slusarczuk, M. (1988). The role of concurrent engineering in weapons system acquisition. Institute for Defense Analyses, R-338.
27. A discussion of the history of concurrent engineering and the sashimi system can be found in Umemoto, K., Endo, A., & Machado, M. (2004). From Sashimi to Zen-In: The evolution of concurrent engineering at Fuji Xerox. *Journal of Knowledge Management, 8*(4), 89–99.
28. Ibid.
29. Ziemke, M., & Spann, M. (1991). Warning: Don't be half-hearted in your efforts to employ concurrent engineering. *Industrial Engineer, 23*(2), 45–49.
30. Ellram, L., Tate, W., & Carter, C. (2007). Product-process-supply chain: An integrative approach to three-dimensional concurrent engineering. *International Journal of Physical Distribution & Logistics Management, 37*(4), 305–324.
31. Cure for offshoring: The design side of product development. (2010). *Machine Design, 82*(18), 32–34.
32. Ray, J. (2010, June 11). Sustainable product design is much more than just good PR. FT.com, 1.
33. Barnes, G. (2013). Packaging's first role: Protect the product. *Dairy Foods, 114*(2), 59–60.
34. Thomason, B., & Marquis, C. (2010, September/October). Leadership and the first and last mile of sustainability. *Ivey Business Journal* (online), 1.
35. Gustafson, M. (2011). Tomorrow's technology—today! *AgriMarketing, 49*(8), 2011: 22–25.
36. Sustainability: Coke launches recycling push. (2009, September 17). *Marketing Week*, 5.
37. Sibley, A. (2011, October). Thought leader: An unconventional approach to sustainability. *New Zealand Management*, 18–19.
38. Trends analyzed for this industry, http://www.plunkettresearch.com/wireless-cellphone-rfid-market-research/industry-trends
39. Forcinio, H. (2014). Eight trends to watch in 2014. *Pharmaceutical Technology, 38*(3), 80–83.
40. Henkes, T. (2014). Strategic packaging trends shape new market opportunities. *Flexible Packaging, 16*(1), 34–36.
41. Sullivan, C., & Horwitz-Benett, B. (2014, May). Workplace design trends: Make way for the Millenials. *Building Design & Construction*, 1.
42. Sullivan, C., & Horwitz-Benett, B. (2014, May). Workplace design trends.
43. 2015 Edison award winners, http://www.edisonawards.com/winners2015.php

Chapter 4

1. Business quotes of the week archives, http://www.rm-improve.com/Index/quote.html
2. Shacklett, M. (2014). Painting supply chain green. *World Trade, 27*(5), 14–19.
3. Snel, A. (2011). FoD. *Nation's Restaurant News, 45*(16), 20.
4. Sampson, W. (2012). Mass customization meets regional partnerships. *CabinetMaker, 26*(11), 36–39.
5. Zeiger, A. (1999). Customization nation. *Incentive, 173*(5), 35–40.
6. See, for example, Choi, C. (2014, May 19). Burger King ditches "have it your way" slogan after 40 years. *HuffPost Business*, http://www.huffingtonpost.com/2014/05/19/burger-king-slogan_n_5353576.html
7. Clark, N. (2012, January 11). Twelve trends for 2012. *Marketing*, 26–28.
8. Clarke, R. (2012). Using data to transform healthcare delivery. *Healthcare Financial Management*, 66(3), 66–70.
9. See, for example, Ross, S. (2015, November 10). McDonald's vs. Burger King: Comparing business models, http://www.investopedia.com/articles/markets/111015/mcdonalds-vs-burger-king-comparing-business-models.asp; Wong, V. (2014, March 25). How the average McDonald's makes twice as much as Burger King, http://www.businessweek.com/articles/2014-03-25/how-the-average-mcdonald-s-makes-twice-as-much-as-burger-king; and Matthews, C. (2014, January 23). 3 reasons Wendy's is eating McDonald's lunch, http://business.time.com/2014/01/23/mcdonalds-and-wendys-battle-in-fast-food-wars/
10. See, for example, Flow charts: Understanding and communicating how a process works, http://www.mindtools.com/pages/article/newTMC_97.htm
11. See, for example, Burgess, R. (1998). Avoiding supply chain management failure: Lessons from business process re-engineering. *The International Journal of Logistics Management, 9*(1), 15–23; Hammer, M., & Champy, J. (1993). *Re-engineering the corporation: A manifesto for business revolution*. New York: Harper Business; and Morris, D., & Brandon, J. (1993). *Re-engineering your business*. New York: McGraw-Hill.
12. See, for example, Davenport, T. (1996). Why reengineering failed: The fad that forgot people. *Fast Company, 1*(1).
13. Under control. (2011, September 5). *The Engineer*, 38–44.
14. King, J. (2012). Rebirth of re-engineering. *Computerworld, 46*(16), 21–25.
15. LaBarre, O. (2011, October). In a class by herself. *Bank Systems & Technology*, 29.
16. Drickhamer, D. (2004). Don't fool yourself with metrics. *IndustryWeek, 253*(10), 85.
17. Thilmany, J. (2003). Birth of a new product. *Mechanical Engineering, 125*(10), 52–54.
18. Cangemi, M. (2012). The real benefits of continuous monitoring. *Financial Executive, 28*(4), 35–38.
19. Rio all-suite hotel and casino, Wikipedia.org/wiki/Rio_All_Suite_Hotel_and_Casino
20. Berzon, A. (2009, October 12). Fontainebleau in Las Vegas likely to get low-ball bids. *Wall Street Journal*, B1.
21. 40% of flood-hit Japan firms to shrink Thai ops: Poll. (2012, February 6). *Asia Pulse*, 1; Phillips, M. (2012, February 6). For some U.S. manufacturers, time to head home. *BusinessWeek*, 1.
22. See, for example, Goss, J. (2014, December 16). Henry Ford and the assembly line, http://history1900s.about.com/od/1910s/a/Ford—Assembly-Line
23. Eliyahu M. Goldratt, renowned business "guru" and author of international best-selling business novel "The Goal," dies at age 70. (2011, June 24). *PR Newswire*, 1.
24. Gorbach, G. (2009). Moving toward manufacturing sustainability. *Plant Engineering, 63*(3), 14.
25. Coca-Cola Enterprises and Cranfield join forces to unlock the future of sustainable manufacturing. (2015, March 26). *Progressive Digital Media Packaging News*, 1.
26. Gould, J. (2009). Sustainable workplace design creates innovation opportunities. *Buildings, 103*(7), 60–62.
27. Zegler, J. (2012). Facilities go beyond green. *Beverage Industry, 103*(7), 67.

Chapter 5

1. Leonard, K. (2011). 10 ways to rearchitect your contact center: CRM. *Customer Relationship Management, 15*(11), 17–23.
2. 40 eye-opening customer service quotes. (2014, March 4), Forbes.com, http://www.forbes.com/sites/ekaterinawalter/2014/03/04/40-eye-opening-customer-service-quotes/
3. Sam Walton quotes, http://thinkexist.com/quotes/sam_walton/
4. Hoff, J. (2010). Customer-centric service. *Electrical Apparatus, 63*(9), 5.
5. See, for example: Gartner says customer relationship management software market grew 13.3 percent. (2015, May 19). 2015 Gartner press release, http://www.gartner.com/newsroom/id/3056118
6. Interested readers can go to the ACSI website at www.theacsi.org for more information about the ACSI.
7. Dyché, J. (2002). *The CRM handbook: A business guide to customer relationship management*. Upper Saddle River, NJ: Addison-Wesley.
8. Bergeron, B. (2002). *Essentials of CRM: A guide to customer relationship management*. New York: John Wiley & Sons.
9. E-business disaster: Why an ambitious and expensive project failed. (2009). *Strategic Direction, 25*(5), 21–22.
10. Dickie, J. Fueling the CRM engine. (2007). *Customer Relationship Management, 11*(4), 10.
11. Goldenberg, B. (2010). Your people are half the battle. *Customer Relationship Management, 14*(4), 6.
12. NMA @ 10: Secrets of success. (2005, June 16). *New Media Age*, 18.
13. Customer service. Entrepreneur.com, http://www.entrepreneur.com/encyclopedia/customer-service
14. Johnson, J., Wood, D., Wardlow, D., & Murphy, P., Jr. (1999). *Contemporary logistics*. Upper Saddle River, NJ: Prentice-Hall, Inc.
15. 10 tips to soothe stressed guests. (2010, December 16). *Restaurant Hospitality*, 1.
16. Bligh, P., & Turk, D. (2004). *CRM unplugged: Releasing CRM's strategic value*. Hoboken, NJ: John-Wiley & Sons.
17. Winer, R. (2001). A framework for customer relationship management. *California Management Review, 43*(4), 89–105.
18. Kotler, P. (2000). *Marketing management*. Upper Saddle River, NJ: Prentice Hall.
19. Vergara, D. (2009). Get a little closer. *Target Marketing, 32*(5), 30–31.
20. Winer, R. (2001). A framework for customer relationship management. *California Management Review, 43*(4), 89–105. Also see Hughes, A. M. How to compute your customer lifetime value. Database Marketing Institute, www.dbmarketing.com/articles
21. Collieer, S. (2007). Another way to look at "member value." *Credit Union Magazine 73*(1), 9A.
22. Shanmuganathan, P., Stone, M., & Foss, B. (2004). Ethnic banking in the United States. *LIMRA's MarketFacts Quarterly, 23*(4), 22–28.
23. Marjo, J. (2004). What women want: Gender-based marketing is a risky business, but it's a risk companies can't afford not to take. *CMA Management, 77*(8), 18.
24. Lyons, D (2004). Too much information. *Forbes, 174*(12), 110.
25. Schlosser, J. (2004). Cashing in on the new world of me. *Fortune, 150*(12), 244–249.
26. See, for instance, Snyder, P. (2004). Wanted: Standards for viral marketing. *Brandweek, 45*(26), 21; and Dunne, D. (2004). Bottom-up branding. *Marketing, 109*(22), 10.
27. Raley's selects Revionics Social Commerce solution. (2014, January 19). *Wireless News*, 1
28. Bannan, K. (2013). How EMC integrated social media to drive engagement. *B to B, 98*(2), 36.
29. Chan, J. (2005). Toward a unified view of customer relationship management. *Journal of American Academy of Business, 6*(1), 32–39.
30. Musico, C. (2009). Making the grade: CRN. *Customer Relationship Management, 13*(7), 22–27.
31. Keough, J. (2008). Thoughts on "firing" customers. *Industrial Distribution, 97*(10), 7.
32. Bowman, J. (2004, November 5). The advertising lag. *Media*, 11.
33. Derrick, S. (2004, October). How to get from A to B. *Revolution*, 56–60.
34. Medienhaus closes 40 percent more business using Siebel sales. (2004, November 8). *Business Wire*.
35. DMA releases 2010 response rate trend report. (2010, June 15). DMA press release, http://www.the-dma.org/cgi/dispannouncements?article=1451
36. Bhote, K. (1996). *Beyond customer satisfaction to customer loyalty: The key to greater profitability*. New York: AMA Membership Publications Division.
37. Krell, E. (2004, September). The 2004 CRM Elite: Six companies that set out to get measurable results, then met or surpassed their expectations. DestinationCRM.com, http://www.destinationcrm.com/Articles/Editorial/Magazine-Features/The-2004-CRM-Elite-43751.aspx
38. Fisher, C. (2003). Why do lay people believe that satisfaction and performance are correlated? Possible sources of a commonsense theory. *Journal of Organizational Behavior, 24*(6), 753.
39. Rauch, M. (2005). Motivating the masses. *Incentive, 179*(2), 26–29.
40. Barsky, J., Frame, C., & McDougal, J. (2004). Variety of strategies help improve hotel employee satisfaction. *Hotel and Motel Management, 219*(21), 8–9.
41. Special report: Big Mac's makeover—McDonald's turned around. (2004). *The Economist, 373*(8397), 88.
42. Parseghian, P. (2010). Bern's Steak House. *Nation's Restaurant News, 44*(2), 8.
43. Berry, L. (1995). *On great service. New York:* The Free Press.
44. Farber, B., & Wycoff, J. (1991). Customer service: Evolution and revolution. *Sales and Marketing Management, 143*(5), 44–49.
45. Alban, O. (2004). Optimizing customer experiences: Bridging front-office contact centers and back-office departments. *Customer Inter@ction Solutions, 22*(12), 50–53.
46. NMA OUTSOURCING: Customer call centres. (2004, October 28). *New Media Age*, 10.
47. Smith, D., & Tanner, L. (2004). Will utilities plug in? *Electric Perspectives, 29*(2), 22–29.
48. Nationwide chief explains offshore rejection. (2004). *Supply management, 9*(20), 38.

49. Thibodeau, P. (2004). Offshoring fuels IT hiring boom in India. *Computerworld, 38*(42), 8.
50. Virtual call center. Techtarget.com, http://searchcrm.techtarget.com/definition/virtual-call-center
51. Garber, A. (2004). No mystery: Shopping the "shops' gains in popularity. *Nation's Restaurant News, 38*(50), 39–41.
52. Home Improvement Research Institute. (2015, March 5). HIRI/IHS global insight up 4.0% in 2014, expecting 5.7% sales growth in 2015. Press release, https://www.hiri.org/?page=Media [Sage: don't know what this goes with]

Chapter 6

1. Fulcher, J. (2009). Unilever betting on "demand sensing" to weather volatile market conditions. *Manufacturing Business Technology, 27*(5), 7.
2. Emily Procter qutoes, http://www.brainyquote.com/quotes/quotes/e/emilyproct421109.html#645KOLcuoGC4ifoK.99
3. Weist, J., Huff, K., & McMillan, K. (2009). Give nurses the right tools and labor costs go down. *Healthcare Financial Management, 63*(4), 82–90.
4. Hackett research alert: Despite prospect of harsh punishment by Wall Street, most companies fail when forecasting earnings & sales. (2008, February 11). *Business & Finance Week*, 154.
5. Nokia feels the squeeze from shortage. (2003, November 13). *Off the Record Research.*
6. Lambert, D. M. (2004, September). The essential supply chain management processes. *Supply Chain Management Review*, 21.
7. Apple: 600,000 iPhone preorders crashed systems. (2010, June 16, 2010). ZDNet, www.zdnet.com/blog/btl/apple-600000-iphone-preorders-crashed-systems/35899?tag=mantle_skin;content
8. O'Leary, C. (2007). A red carpet reception? *Mergers and Acquisitions, 42*(11), 66–71.
9. Zegler, J. (2012). 2012 new product development survey. *Beverage Industry, 103*(1), 56–60, 62, 64–66.
10. Apartment demand weakened by financial crisis but holding up in Q2. (2008). *Mortgage Banking, 69*(1), 144.
11. Goldfisher, K. (1992). Modified Delphi: A concept for new product forecasting. *The Journal of Business Forecasting, 11*(4), 10.
12. Elliott, G., Jiang, F., Redding, G., & Stening, B. (2010). The Chinese business environment in the next decade: Report from a Delphi study. *Asian Business & Management, 9*(4), 459–480.
13. Costa-Font, M., Serra, T., Gil, M., & Gras, A. (2009). Explaining low farm-gate prices in the Catalan wine sector. *International Journal of Wine Business Research, 21*(2), 169–184.
14. 2011 Tōhoku earthquake and tsunami, http://en.wikipedia.org/wiki/2011_T%C5%8Dhoku_earthquake_and_tsunami
15. Gardner, E. (2006). Exponential smoothing: The state of the art—part II. *International Journal of Forecasting, 22*(4), 637–666.
16. Focus on forecasting and inventory strategy. (2009). *IndustryWeek, 258*(9), 1.
17. CPFR guidelines and resources, www.gs1us.org
18. Supply Chain Management Terms and Glossaries—Council of Supply Chain Management Professionals; available from http://cscmp.org/digital/glossary/document.pdf.
19. Berry, J. (2013, May 31). What is collaborative planning, forecasting, and replenishment (CPFR)? SocialSupplyChains.com, http://www.socialsupplychains.com/what-is-collaborative-planning-forecasting-and-replenishment-cpfr/
20. Katz, J. (2010). Forecasts demand change. *Industry Week, 259*(5), 26–29.
21. Crum, C., & Palmatier, G. E. (2004, January/February). Demand collaboration: What's holding us back? *Supply Chain Management Review*, 54–61.
22. Smith, L. (2006). West Marine: A CPFR success story. *Supply Chain Management Review, 10*(2), 29–36.
23. Bruno-Britz, M. (2009). Sticking to the schedule. *Bank Systems & Technology, 47*(1), 1.
24. Speizer, I. (2009). An on-demand workforce. *Workforce Management, 88*(11), 45–49.

Chapter 7

1. Business quotes about inventory, https://www.google.com/search?q=business+quotes+about+inventory&biw=1680&bih=890&tbm=isch&tbo=u&source=univ&sa=X&ei=v5-JVdbgHsTWoATJmanIBQ&ved=0CDgQsAQ&dpr=1
2. Silver, E. (2008). Inventory management: An overview, Canadian publications, practical applications and suggestions for future research. *INFOR, 46*(1), 15–27.
3. McCrea, B. (2010). WMS update: Rolling inventory. *Logistics Management, 49*(11), 34–37.
4. See http://www.spr.doe.gov/dir/dir.html; http://www.eia.gov/tools/faqs/faq.cfm?id=33&t=6; http://en.wikipedia.org/wiki/Strategic_Petroleum_Reserve_(United_States); and Blumenthal, R. (2005). Oil's well that ends well—if the U.S. goes easy on crude. *Barron's, 85*(12), 12.
5. Gupta, M. (2011). The state of the p-card. *Government Procurement, 18*(6), 1.
6. Aastrup, J., & Kotzab, H. (2010). Forty years of out-of-stock research—and shelves are still empty. *International Review of Retail, Distribution & Consumer Research, 20*(1), 147–164. Also see http://en.wikipedia.org/wiki/Stockout#cite_note-6
7. Koch, C. (2000). The big payoff. *CIO, 14*(1), 100–112.
8. Jacoby, D. (2010). The oil price "bullwhip": Problem, cost, response. *Oil & Gas Journal, 108*(11), 20–25.
9. An interesting discussion of the formulation of the lead time demand standard deviation can be found in Ballou, R. (1985). *Business logistics management.* Englewood Cliffs, NJ: Prentice-Hall, 388.
10. Different take on inventory management. (2011, November/December). *Process Engineering*, 12.
11. Brown, M. (2011). Inventory optimization: Show me the money. *Supply Chain Management Review, 15*(4), 47–49.
12. Jusko, J. (2010). Better metrics, better results. *IndustryWeek, 259*(8), 16.
13. Yokl, R. (2005). Less is more when storing inventory. *Hospital Materials Management, 30*(8), 2–3.
14. Bolstorff, P. (2003, December). Measuring the impact of supply chain performance. *Logistics Today*, 6.

Chapter 8

1. Leveraging lean designs. (2009). *IndustryWeek, 258*(8), 1.
2. Sampson, W. (2012). Going lean. *CabinetMaker+FDM, 26*(3), 22–27.
3. Katz, J. (2010). Value propositions. *IndustryWeek, 259*(10), 1.
4. Loudin, A. (2010, June 10). The right recipe. *Food Logistics*, 16–18.
5. Meczes, R. (2005, Spring). Make the right move. *Works Management*, 40–44.
6. For more information on Dr. Goldratt, see the AGI Goldratt Institute: www.goldratt.com
7. Canaday, H. (2009). Leaning out time in engine shops. *Air Transport World, 46*(4), 71–74.
8. Daly, P. (2012). Spring-loaded continuous improvement. *Grand Rapids Business Journal, 30*(22), 1.
9. See the Theory of Constraints International Certification Organization success stories at www.tocico.org
10. Mabin, V., & Balderstone, S. (2003). The performance of the theory of constraints methodology: Analysis and discussion of successful TOC applications. *International Journal of Operations & Production Management, 23*(6), 568–595.
11. Breen, B. (2004, November). Living in Dell time. *Fast Company*, 86–92.
12. Wilson, D. (2011, April 25). Manufacturing technology: Hard work. *The Engineer*, 33.
13. Nunes, J. (2005). SCARA robots: Still speedy and dependable. *Robotics World, 23*(3), 4–5.
14. Adil, G., & Rajamani, D. (2000). The trade-off between intracell and intercell moves in group technology cell formation. *Journal of Manufacturing Systems, 19*(5), 305–317.
15. Toyota factory tour in Georgetown, KY, http://www.factorytour.com/tours/toyota.cfm
16. Definition found at Vorne Industrial Displays & Productivity Tools website, www.vorne.com
17. Key, W. (1994). Assembly-line job satisfaction and productivity. *Industrial Engineering, 26*(11), 44–45.
18. Marsh, P. (2001, August 1). The delicate touch of the assembly line: The art of manufacturing, Part II. *Financial Times*, 11.
19. Goncalves, J., & de Almeida, J. (2002). A hybrid genetic algorithm for assembly line balancing. *Journal of Heuristics, 8*(6), 629–642.
20. Meller, R., & DeShazo, R. (2002). Manufacturing system design case study: Multi-channel manufacturing at Electrical Box & Enclosures. *Journal of Manufacturing, 20*(6), 445–457.
21. Wireless communication companies; T-Mobile USA unveils new global design retail stores. (2011, October 14). *Economics Week*, 899.
22. Sales of manufactured homes climb 29 percent in Idaho. (2010, November 22). Oregonlive.com, www.oregonlive.com
23. Store profit specialists, www.discoverdbr.com/visualmerchandisingtrends
24. Khan, H. (2014, March 19). How to create retail store interiors that get people to purchase your products, www.shopify.com/blog/12927757
25. Avant, M. (2014, June). Mind over matter. *QSR Magazine*, www.qsrmagazine.com/store/mind-over-matter

Chapter 8 Supplement

1. Custom job shop says APS package offered simple solution to complex problems. (2004). *MSI, 22*(12), 38.
2. Leavitt, W. (2009). Fleets online. *Fleet Owner, 104*(5), 82.
3. Chun, A. (2011). Optimizing limousine service with AI. *AI Magazine, 32*(2), 27–41.
4. Karuppan, C. (2006). Labor flexibility: Too much of a good thing? *Industrial Management, 48*(5), 13–18.
5. Duplaga, E., Hahn, C., & Hur, D. (1996). Mixed-model assembly line sequencing at Hyundai Motor Company. *Production and Inventory Management Journal, 37*(3), 20–26.
6. Custom job shop says APS package offered simple solution to complex problems. (2004). *MSI, 22*, 38.
7. For detailed discussions of dispatch rule performance, see, for example, McKay, K., Safayeni, F., & Buzacott, J. (1988). Job shop scheduling theory: What is relevant? *Interfaces, 18*(4), 84–90; Panwalker, S., & Iskander, W. (1977). A survey of scheduling rules. *Operations Research, 25*(1), 45–61; and Wisner, J., & Siferd, S. (1995). A survey of U.S. manufacturing practices in make-to-order machine shops. *Production and Inventory Management Journal, 36*(1), 1–7.
8. Ying-Jen, C., Su, Y., Ming-Shing, H., & Wang, I. (2000). Real-time dispatching reduces cycle time. *Semconductor International, 23*(3), 109–112.
9. Deierlein, B. (2005). Going wireless. *Beverage World, 124*(1756), 48.
10. Mobile resource management cuts costs; saves fuel. (2009, May 13). *Material Handling Management*, 1.
11. *Arunapuram*, S., *Mathur*, K., & *Solow*, D. (2003). Vehicle routing and scheduling with full truckloads. *Transportation Science, 37*(2), 170; Doll, L. (1980). Quick and dirty vehicle routing procedure. *Interfaces, 10*, 84–85; Dreyfus, S. (1969). An appraisal of some shortest-path algorithms. *Operations Research, 17*, 395–412; Pollack, M., & Weibenson, W. (1960, March/April). Solution of the shortest-route problem—a review. *Operations Research*, 224–230; Currie, R., & Salhi, S. (2003). Exact and heuristic methods for a full-load, multi-terminal, vehicle scheduling problem with backhauling and time windows. *The Journal of the Operational Research Society, 54*(4), 390; and Toth, P., & Vigo, D. (Eds.). (2002). *The vehicle routing problem.* Philadelphia, PA: SIAM.

Chapter 9

1. Wheeler, C. (2014, February 24). Lean manufacturing quotes for education and inspiration. The Mobile Workplace Power blog, http://www.newcastlesys.com/blog/bid/337009/Lean-Manufacturing-Quotes-for-Education-and-Inspiration#sthash.sxZHqJxD.dpuf
2. Lazerick, C. (2010, April 1). Lean thinking in lean times. *Material Handling Management*, 1.
3. Beason, M. (2013). Lean machining—integrating the supply chain. *Manufacturing Engineering, 151*(2), 75–79.
4. For histories of lean and the Toyota Production System, see, for instance, Becker, R. (2001). Learning to think lean: Lean manufacturing and the Toyota Production System. *Automotive Manufacturing & Production, 113*(6), 64–65; and Dahlgaard, J., & Dahlgaard-Park, S. (2006). Lean production, Six Sigma quality, TQM and company culture. *TQM Magazine, 18*(3), 263–277.
5. A brief history of lean, http://www.lean.org/WhatsLean/History.cfm
6. Arndorfer, J., Atkinson, C., Bloom, J., & Cardona, M. (2005). The biggest moments in the last 75 years of advertising history. *Advertising Age, 76*(13), 12–15.
7. Manivannan, S. (2006). Error-proofing enhances quality. *Manufacturing Engineering, 137*(5), 99–105.
8. Nakamoto, M., & Reed, J. (2007, April 24). Toyota claims global top spot from GM. FT.com, 1.
9. Womack, J., Jones, D., & Roos, D. (1990). *The machine that changed the world.* New York: Maxwell MacMillan International.
10. Waurzyniak, P. (2009). Lean automation. *Manufacturing Engineering, 142*(2), 65–71.
11. Ben-Tovim, D., Bassham, J., Bolch, D., & Martin, M. (2007). Lean thinking across a hospital: Redesigning care at the Flinders Medical Centre. *Australian Health Review, 31*(1), 10–15.
12. A small company makes big gains implementing lean. (2006). *Management Services, 50*(3), 28–31.
13. Roughead, G. (2009). Featured company: U.S. Navy. *ASQ Six Sigma Forum Magazine, 8*(3), 40.
14. Albright, D., & Lo, A. (2009). Transportation management's role in supply chain excellence. *Logistics Management, 48*(10), 44.
15. Taking lean beyond the plant floor. (2008). *IndustryWeek, 257*(8), 15.
16. Lazerick, C. (2010, April 1). Lean thinking in lean times. *Material Handling Management*, 1.
17. Jargon, J. (2009, August 4). Latest Starbucks buzzword: "Lean" Japanese techniques. *Wall Street Journal*, A1.

18. Kempfer, L. (2007). The safety mosaic. *Material Handling Management, 62*(4), 44–45.
19. Tool for productivity, quality, throughput, safety. (2006). *Management Services, 50*(3), 16–18; Becker, J. (2001). Implementing 5S: To promote safety and housekeeping. *Professional Safety, 46*(8), 29–31.
20. Shaw, M. (2004). Customers drive end-product attributes, technology choices at MeadWestvaco Mill. *Pulp Paper, 78*(1), 40.
21. Varley, P. (1999). All-inclusive deal. *Supply Management, 4*(21), 40–41.
22. What is SMED and why is it important? http://www.leanaccountants.com/2011/12/what-is-smed-and-why-is-it-important.html; and SMED, http://www.makigami.info/cms/smed
23. Going deep with a four-way valve. (2009). *Manufacturing Engineering, 142*(5), 39–42.
24. Michel, R. (2009). Cloud computing moves toward the factory. *Manufacturing Business Technology, 27*(5), 10.
25. Chakravorty, S., & Franza, R. (2012). Kaizen blitz. *Industrial Engineer, 44*(4), 28–33.
26. Hughes, M. (2010). Kaizen means ka-ching! *Industrial Engineer, 42*(2), 50–52.
27. Robinson, A., & Shroeder, D. (2009). The role of front-line ideas in lean performance improvement. *The Quality Management Journal, 16*(4), 27–40.
28. Strategies for introducing change and evaluating effectiveness in your safety and health program. (2005, January). *Safety Compliance Letter*, 7–11.
29. Rogers, J. (2012, February 27). Customer surveys: 5 things you need to know. *The Huffington Post*, 1.
30. Ross, K. (2013, December 13). Lean is even more important in services than manufacturing. *IndustryWeek*, 1.
31. Noguchi, Y. (2011, August 10). Why Borders failed while Barnes & Noble survived, http://www.npr.org/2011/07/19/138514209/why-borders-failed-while-barnes-and-noble-survived
32. Trachtenberg, J. (2014, June 26). Barnes & Noble to split retail stores, nook digital business, http://online.wsj.com/articles/barnes-noble-to-split-into-two-companies-1403699838
33. Lindorff, D. (2013, March 1). Online banks outgrowing brick-and-mortar rivals, http://www.americanbanker.com/magazine/123_3/market-share-for-direct-banks-is-higher-than-ever-1056784-1.html
34. See Vincent, C. (2014). Kata culture. *AQ Six Sigma Forum Magazine, 13*(3), 30–31; The coaching kata, http://www-personal.umich.edu/~mrother/Homepage.html
35. Expert answers. (2014). *Quality Progress, 47*(9), 87–89.
36. Sedam, S. (2011, February). Creating a lean culture—builders speak out. *Professional Builder*, 1.
37. Lewis, J. (2012). What makes lean successful? *CabinetMaker + FDM, 26*(6), 18–22.
38. Marchese, K., & Lam, B. (2014, June 13). How to build an anticipatory supply chain. *IndustryWeek*, 1.
39. Nike reveals global strategy for creating a more sustainable business. (2010, January 30). *Entertainment Close-Up*, 1.
40. CFOs plan slight increase in financial hiring in first quarter. (2011). *Business Credit, 113*(1), 2.
41. King, A., & Lenox, M. (2001). Lean and green? An empirical examination of the relationship between lean production and environmental performance. *Production and Operations Management, 10*(3), 244–256.
42. Blanchard, D. (2006). Diagnosis: Green and lean. *IndustryWeek, 255*(9), 13.
43. Smith, M. (2007). Going green drives sales. *Printing Impressions, 49*(10), 60–61.
44. McCue, D. (2012). Technology and sustainability: When lean and green converge. *World Trade, 25*(10), 26–30.
45. Nike reveals global strategy for creating a more sustainable business. (2010, January 30). *Entertainment Close-Up*, 1.
46. Thomas, F. (2014, October 6). Beyond lean: Adding intelligence to unlock the power of smart pull. *Industrial Maintenance & Plant Operation*, 1.
47. Apriso launches industry's first smart pull manufacturing solution. (2013, June 25). *Business Wire*, 1.
48. Humphrey, B. (2014, June 17). Lean financial management, Part 1. ForConstructionPros.com, 1.

Chapter 10

1. Mayer, T., & Kirk, J. (2012). The business case for patient flow. *Healthcare Executive, 27*(4), 50–53.
2. Livebookings, Inc. Bonefish Grill enters into agreement with Livebookings to build online reservation system. (2010, October 2). *Marketing Weekly News*, 131.
3. Brandau, M. (2009). The eyes have it: Mooyah tracks guests' perceptions. *Nation's Restaurant News, 43*(37), 6, 14.
4. Schneider, I. (2004). Here today . . . everywhere tomorrow. *Bank Systems and Technology, 41*(11), 47–50.
5. Levinson, M. (2005). The brains behind the big, bad burger and other tales of business intelligence. *CIO, 18*(11), 1.
6. Gelsomino, J. (2004, October). True tales of customer-centric retailing. *Chain Store Age*, 44A.
7. Lytle, T. (2012). Benefits for older workers. *HRMagazine, 57*(3), 53–58.
8. Wirtz, J., Kimes, S., Theng, J., & Patterson, P. (2003). Revenue management: Resolving potential customer conflicts. *Journal of Revenue and Pricing Management, 2*(3), 216–223.
9. Laing, J. (2012). On the runway, ready for takeoff. *Barron's, 92*(19), 23–24.
10. Cox, J. (2001). Can differential prices be fair? *The Journal of Product and Brand Management, 10*(4/5), 264–275.
11. Armbruster, W. (2003, July 7). With Oliver Evans, executive VP of Cargo, Swiss International Airlines. *Journal of Commerce*, 1.
12. Companies & markets. (2010, March 26). *Russia & CIS Business & Investment Weekly*, 1.
13. Pinker, E., & Shumsky, R. (2000). The efficiency-quality trade-off of cross-trained workers. *Manufacturing and Service Operations Management, 2*(1), 32–48.
14. Forth, K. (2009). Project managing for success. *FDM, 81*(8), 20–23.
15. Weatherly, L. (2005). HR technology: Leveraging the shift to self-service—it's time to go strategic. *HR Magazine, 50*(3), A1–A11.
16. Atkinson, W. (2005). Travel spend flies onto procurement radar. *Purchasing, 134*(10), 18–19.
17. Nash, K. (2010). No wait for the cable guy. *CIO, 23*(17), 1.
18. Handley, L. (March 17, 2011). Shopping: Time to brush up on your floor play? *Marketing Week*, 20–22.
19. Maister, D. (1985). The psychology of waiting lines. In J. Czepiel, M. Solomon, & C. Suprenant (Eds.), *The service encounter* (pp. 113–123). Lexington, MA: D.C. Heath & Co.
20. Ibid.
21. Benoit, T. (2005, August 13). Opinion: Maine learns to drive. *Knight Ridder Tribune Business News*, 1.
22. Castro, B. (2004). Line up customers and sales. *Chain Store Age, 80*(6), 85.
23. The Safeway holiday ice rink in Union Square. (2013, December 21). *Journal of Transportation*, 39.
24. Dickson, D., Ford, R., & Laval, B. (2005). Managing real and virtual waits in hospitality and service organizations. *Cornell Hotel and Restaurant Administration Quarterly, 46*(1), 52–68.
25. Wolff, R. (1989). *Stochastic modeling and the theory of queues*. Englewood Cliffs, NJ: Prentice-Hall.
26. Blank, C. (2011). Dose management tools improve workflow, reduce medication errors. *Drug Topics, 155*(10), 20.
27. Liebmann, L. (1996, February 5). Managing workflow—chart your gameplan. *Communications Week*, 43.
28. O'Neill, D. (2003). Electronic orders—critical technology to fulfill the mortgage origination process. *Mortgage Banking, 63*(5), 83–84.
29. A five-step process for managing workflow and boosting your performance output. (2005). *IOMA's Report on Managing Training & Development, 5*(4), 4–6.
30. Wyatt, J. (2003). Code red: Ready to roll. *Health Management Technology, 24*(11), 26.
31. Michel, R. (2005). Reaching beyond the four walls. *Modern Materials Handling, 60*(7), 43.
32. Sullivan, L. (2003, October 13). Philips cuts costs by aligning procurement, engineering. *EBN*, 1.
33. Mann, P. (2002). Tweak the supply chain. *MSI, 20*(2), 57–58.

Chapter 11

1. Kho, N. (2011). On the road to improved information experiences. *EContent, 34*(5), 22–26.
2. Emily Oster quotes, http://www.brainyquote.com/quotes/quotes/e/emilyoster554579.html
3. Overby, S. (2012). ERP on speed. *CIO, 25*(9), 1.
4. Childerhouse, P., Hermiz, R., Mason-Jones, R., Popp, A., & Towill, D. (2003). Information flow in automotive supply chains—identifying and learning to overcome barriers to change. *Industrial Management & Data Systems, 103*(7), 491–502.
5. Lewis, I., & Talayevsky, A. (2004). Improving the interorganizational supply chain through optimization of information flows. *Journal of Enterprise Information, 17*(3), 229–238.
6. Lejeune, A., & Roehl, T. (2003). Hard and soft ways to create value from information flows: Lessons from the Canadian Financial Services Industry. *Canadian Journal of Administrative Sciences, 20*(1), 35–53.
7. Krovi, R., Chandra, A., & Rajagopalan, B. (2003). Information flow parameters for managing organizational processes. *Communications of the ACM, 46*(2), 77–82.
8. Ibid.
9. Based in part on Hibberd, B., & Evatt, A. (2004). Mapping information flows: A practical guide. *Information Management Journal, 38*(1), 58.
10. Andel, T. (2011, October 13). Managing your information supply chain. *Material Handling & Logistics*, 1.
11. Madill equipment: CA. (2008). *CA Magazine, 141*(1), 32–33.
12. Trunick, P. (2005). How to design a cost-effective DC. *Logistics Today, 46*(5), 42–44.
13. Snyder, D. (2005). Foxwoods sees the wonder of a strong back office thanks to EatecNetX. *Nation's Restaurant News, 39*(26), S26–27.
14. Mabert, V., (2007). The early road to material requirements planning. *Journal of Operations Management, 25*, 346–356.
15. Orlicky, J. (1973). Net change material requirements planning. *IBM System Journal, 1*, www.ibm.com. The author is most appreciative of discussions held with Gene Thomas regarding the history of MRP, and his role in its development.
16. Waddell, B. (2005). MRP on the rocks, www.evolvingexcellence.com; Waddell, B., "MRP R.I.P.," www.bestmanufacturingpractices.com
17. See, for example, Plossl, G., & Wight, O. (1967). *Production and inventory control: Principles and techniques*. New York: Prentice-Hall; and Orlicky, J. (1975). *Material requirements planning: The new way of life in production and inventory management*. New York: McGraw-Hill; Wight, O. (1982). *The executive's guide to successful MRPII*. Hoboken, NJ: John Wiley & Sons.
18. MAPICS, Inc. History, http://www.fundinguniverse.com/company-histories/mapics-inc-history/
19. Wight, O. (1981). *Manufacturing resource planning: MRP II: Unlocking America's productivity potential*. Boston, MA: CBI Publishing Co.
20. Hopp, W., & Spearman, M. (2004). To pull or not to pull: What is the question? *Manufacturing & Service Operations Management, 6*(2), 133–148.
21. SAP: A 43-year history of success, www.sap.com/company/history.epx
22. SAP offers surprisingly strong outlook. (2006, January 25); and Oracle details postmerger plans. (2006, January 18). ZDNet News, www.news.zdnet.com. Also see: Global ERP software market is expected to reach $41.69 billion by 2020, http://www.prnewswire.com/news-releases/global-erp-software-market-is-expected-to-reach—4169-billion-by-2020-498133891.html
23. Burns, M. (2011). What does an ERP system cost?, http://www.camagazine.com/archives/print-edition/2011/aug/columns/camagazine50480.aspx
24. Case study: Headland Machinery addresses business pain points with NetSuite ERP/CRM solution. (2014, May). *Manufacturers' Monthly*, 1.
25. Enterprise resource planning. *Darwin Magazine Executive Guides*, www.darwinmag.com/technology/enterprise/erp/index/htm
26. Chan. W. (2013). How much does an ERP system cost? http://www.calsoft.com/blogs/how-much-does-an-erp-system-cost
27. Enterprise resource planning.
28. Stapleton, G., & Rezak, C. (2004). Change management underpins a successful ERP implementation at Marathon Oil. *Journal of Organizational Excellence, 23*(4), 15–22.
29. Koch, C. (2002, November 15). Hershey's bittersweet lesson. *CIO*, www.cio.com
30. Wheatley, M. (2000, June 1). ERP training stinks. *CIO*, www.cio.com
31. Enterprise resource planning.
32. See, for example, Hawking, P., Stein, A., & Foster, S. (2004). Revisiting ERP systems: Benefit realization. *Proceedings of the 37th Hawaii International Conference on System Sciences*, 1 -8; McCrea, B. (2011). Putting the spotlight on ERP. *Logistics Management*, 50(6), 32 -35; and Brown, G. (2013). Your IT strategy & cloud computing: Where does it fit? http://www.randgroup.com/insights/your-it-strategy-and-cloud-computing-where-does-it-fit
33. Hawking, Stein, & Foster. (2004). Revisiting ERP systems.
34. Wang, B., & Nah, F. (2001). "ERP + E-Business = A new vision of enterprise system. In S. Dasgupta (Ed.), *Managing Internet technologies in organizations: Challenges and opportunities* (2001). Hershey, PA: Idea Group Publishing.
35. Stapleton, G., & Rezak, C. (2004). Change management underpins a successful ERP implementation at Marathon Oil.
36. ERP + E-Business = A new vision of enterprise system.
37. Radding, A. (1999, April 5). ERP—more than an application. *InformationWeek*, 1A.
38. Ruderman, G. (2004). Relieve the burden of regulatory compliance. *MSI, 22*(6), 34–37.
39. Fulcher, J. (2006). Global execution. *Manufacturing Business Technology, 24*(3), 38.
40. Russell, R. (2004). Manufacturing execution systems: Moving to the next level. *Pharmaceutical Technology, 28*(1), 38–43.
41. Zuckerman, A. (2005). What's working (and what isn't) in integrated supply chain technology. *World Trade, 18*(6), 50–54.
42. Ibid.

43. Anthes, G. (2004). Refurnishing the supply chain. *Computerworld, 38*(23), 39–40.
44. Coia, A. (2005). Smoothing reverse flow. *Frontline Solutions, 6*(5), 34–36.
45. Trebilcock, B. (2004). Managing returns with WMS. *Modern Materials Handling, 59*(10), 33–36.
46. Mendoza, L., Perez, M., & Griman, A. (2006). Critical success factors for managing systems integration. *Information Systems Management, 23*(2), 56–75.
47. Production engineering—production software: The hub of the matter. (2006, January 30). *The Engineer*, 36–38.
48. Tom, K. (2005). Execution software's virtual company. *Frontline Solutions, 6*(6), 26.
49. Stoller, J. (2004). Navigating the inter-application zone. *CMA Management, 78*(7), 32–35.
50. Tom, K. (2005). Execution software's virtual company. *Frontline Solutions, 6*(6), 26.
51. Pritchard, S. (2009, November 2). Did IT work? BPM is finally aligning business and IT. FT.com, 1.
52. Lee, R., & Dale, B. (1998). Business process management: A review and evaluation. *Business Process Management Journal, 4*(3S), 214–223.
53. Puccinelli, R. (2005). BPM templates. *KM World, 14*(1), S4–5.
54. Lamont, J. (2006). BPM: From the user's perspective. *KM World, 15*(1), 14–15.
55. Britt, P. (2005). How to get there from here. *Bank Systems & Technology, 42*(12), 39.
56. Leahy, T. (2005). Solutions for supply chain woes. *Business Finance, 11*(9), 37–39.
57. Power, B. (2014). Enterprise resource planning comes of age. *Charter, 85*(1), 30–31.
58. Ibid.
59. See, for example, Columbus, L. (2015). Five catalysts accelerating cloud ERP growth in 2015, www.forbes.com/sites/louiscolumbus/2015/01/27/five-catalysts-accelerating-cloud-erp-growth-in-2015

Chapter 12

1. Black, R. (2005). Proper planning can help project managers avoid raging fires. *Computing Canada, 31*(16), 30.
2. Meier, J. Project management quotes, http://sourcesofinsight.com/project-management-quotes
3. Bolger, A. (2011, March 17). Holyrod approves world's largest tidal energy project. FT.com, 1.
4. Olsen, R., (1971). Can project management be defined? http://www.pmi.org/learning/project-management-defined-concept-1950
5. Krystek, L. (2011). The channel tunnel, http://www.unmuseum.org/7wonders/chunnel.htm
6. Hong Kong International Airport, http://en.wikipedia.org/wiki/Hong_Kong_International_Airport; HKIA fact sheets, http://www.hongkongairport.com/eng/media/facts-figures/facts-sheets.html
7. Garcia, M. About the space station: Facts and figures, http://www.nasa.gov/mission_pages/station/main/onthestation/facts_and_figures.html; Ten surprising facts about the international space station, http://www.pbs.org/spacestation/station/issfactsheet.htm; Smith, M. (2014). NASA IG: ISS cost U.S. $75 billion so far, estimates of future costs overly optimistic, http://www.spacepolicyonline.com/news/nasa-ig-iss-cost-u-s-75-billion-so-far-estimates-of-future-costs-overly-optimistic
8. Three Gorges Dam, http://en.wikipedia.org/wiki/Three_Gorges_Dam
9. The $1 billion Antilia, Mumbai, India, http://www.cbsnews.com/media/10-of-the-worlds-most-expensive-homes/8/
10. King, J. (1997). Poor planning kills projects, pushes costs up. *Computerworld, 31*(38), 6.
11. McConnell, S. (2001, September/October). The nine deadly sins of project planning. *IEEE Software*, 5–7.
12. Black, R. (2005). Proper planning can help project managers avoid raging fires.
13. Henry Gantt's legacy to management is the Gantt chart, http://www.ganttchart.com/history.html; Gantt charts, http://www.vectorstudy.com/management-theories/gantt-charts
14. Critical path method, www.referenceforbusiness.com/encyclopedia/Cos-Des/Critical-Path-Method.html
15. The variance formula is based the idea that 6 standard deviations separate both ends of the beta distribution (or ± 3 standard deviations from the mean). Then, since $(b - a) = 6$ standard deviations, we have $(b - a)/6 =$ standard deviation, and then $[(b - a)/6]^2 =$ variance.
16. Veysey, S. (2011). Olympic Park a risk management model. *Business Insurance, 45*(47), 4, 28.
17. Smith, S. (2011). Juggling it all. *Back Enterprise, 42*(1), 34–35.
18. Margea, R., & Margea, C. (2011). Open source approach to project management tools. *Informatica Economica, 15*(1), 196–206.
19. Opiola, J., & Lockwood, S. (2012). Getting clear about the cloud. *Public Manager, 41*(2), 10–12.
20. Ibid.
21. Quagliata, K. (2012, June 6). Buyer's guide: SaaS project management tools. *InformationWeek* (online), 1.
22. Business news: HyperOffice beefs up its online project management application. (2010, November 13). *Marketing Weekly News*, 700; Businesses, www.hyperoffice.com/pricing

Chapter 13

1. Welch, J., & Byrne, J. (2003). *Jack: Straight from the gut.* Grand Central Publishing.
2. Crosby, P. (1979). *Quality is free: The art of making quality certain.* New York: McGraw-Hill.
3. Operational excellence & leadership quotes, http://www.operational-excellence-consulting.com/opex-articles/opex-quotes.html
4. Melinda, R., & Kupferschmid, T. (2011). Louisiana state crime laboratory: Increasing efficiency of forensic DNAD casework using lean Six Sigma tools. *Management Services, 55*(4), 20–24.
5. Phillips, E. (2002). Six Sigma: The breakthrough management strategy revolutionizing the world's top corporations. *Consulting to Management, 13*(4), 57–69. Also see the SSA & Co. website: www.ssaandco.com
6. What is Six Sigma? http://www.ge.com/en/company/companyinfo/quality/whatis.htm
7. Report finds Six Sigma has saved Fortune 500 $427B, http://www.reliableplant.com/Read/4285/report-finds-six-sigma-has-saved-fortune-500-$427b
8. Blanchard, D. (2006). Diagnosis: Green and lean. *IndustryWeek, 255*(9), 13.
9. Phillips, E. (2002). Six Sigma: The breakthrough management strategy revolutionizing the world's top corporations. *Consulting to Management, 13*(4), 57–59.
10. Business brief--Primary PDC Inc.: Joint bankruptcy plan filed to dissolve former Polaroid. (2003, January 17). *Wall Street Journal*, B-3.
11. Lean is crushing Six Sigma. (2010). *Manufacturing Engineering, 144*(4), 19–20.
12. Buell, J. (2010). Lean Six Sigma and patient safety. *Healthcare Executive, 25*(2), 26–35.
13. See, for example, Brodshy, R. (2009). Deep-sixing waste. *Government Executive, 41*(12), 19–20; Kucner, R. (2009). Staying seaworthy. *Six Sigma Forum Magazine, 8*(2), 25–31; and Westervelt, R. (2009). Clariant rebuilds momentum. *Chemical Week, 171*(10), 41.
14. Harbert, T. (2006). Lean, mean, Six Sigma machines. *Electronic Business, 32*(6), 38–42.
15. Deming, W. (1986). *Out of the crisis.* Cambridge, MA: MIT Press
16. The Deming Prize and development of quality control/management in Japan, https://www.juse.or.jp/deming_en/award/03.html
17. About the institute, www.deming.org
18. Crosby, P. (1979). Quality is free: The art of making quality certain. New York: McGraw-Hill (1979); and Crosby, P. (1984). *Quality without tears.* New York: McGraw-Hill.
19. Johnson, K. (2001). Philip B. Crosby's mark on quality. *Quality Progress, 34*(10), 25–30.
20. Juran, J., & De Feo, J. (2010). *Juran's quality handbook.* New York: McGraw-Hill.
21. Butman, J., & Roessner, J. *An immigrant's gift: The life of quality pioneer Joseph M. Juran.* PBS documentary video, produced by Howland Blackiston, copyright 1997, WoodsEnd, Inc.
22. U.S. Secretary of Commerce Penny Pritzker announces four recipients of 2015 Baldrige Award, http://www.nist.gov/baldrige/award_recipients/index.cfm
23. About us, who we are, www.nist.gov/baldrige/about/
24. Ruggless, R. (2010). K&N wins Baldrige Award. *Nation's Restaurant News, 44*(26), 4.
25. About ISO, http://www.iso.org/iso/home/about.htm
26. Franchetti, M. (2009). Perfect match. *ASQ Six Sigma Forum Magazine, 8*(4), 10–17.
27. GE's redesigned plant makes everything faster for you, http://www.gelighting.com/LightingWeb/na/resources/document-library/#q=six%20sigma&fq=&sortParam=&p=1&pageSize=50
28. Rewards for Master Black Belts. (2013). *Quality Progress, 46*(12), 52–53.
29. Reh, J. Pareto's principle—the 80–20 rule, http://management.about.com/cs/generalmanagement/a/Pareto081202.htm
30. Hall, M. (2010). A solution for IT. *Industrial Engineer, 42*(5), 47–52.
31. Creasy, T. (2014). Rock solid. *Quality Progress, 47*(12), 44–51.

Chapter 13 Supplement

1. Schuetz, G. (2014). Gaging for SPC: Now even simpler. *Modern Machine Shop, 87*(6), 62–64.
2. Theiss, B. (2011). Numbers are not enough. *Industrial Engineer, 43*(9), 28–33.
3. Control your process. (2009). *Ceramic Industry, 159*(2), 30–32; About us: History & legacy, www.palmettobrick.com/about/default.aspx
4. Torbeck, L. (2011). Statistics in the service of quality. *Pharmaceutical Technology, 35*(6), 34–35.

Chapter 14

1. Spend management takes center stage. (2009, September 19). *Marketing Weekly News*, 58.
2. Bill Gates quotes, http://www.mytopbusinessideas.com/bill-gates-quotes/
3. McCue, D. (2012). Sourcing focuses on home—nearly. *World Trade, 25*(5), 20–27.
4. The Institute for Supply Management, www.ism.ws
5. See the U.S. Census Bureau, *Annual survey of manufactures*, at http://www.census.gov/econ/census07/www/get_data.html
6. Greimel, H. (2015). Nissan vehicles to use common visible parts. *Automotive News, 89*(6658), 16.
7. Carbone, J. (2009). Flextronics focuses more spend with fewer suppliers. *Purchasing, 138*(12), 30–32.
8. Johnson, P., & Flynn, A. (2015). *Purchasing and supply management* (15th ed.). (pp. 46–49). Boston: McGraw-Hill Irwin.
9. See the Schindler website, www.schindler.com
10. Linder, A., & Majander, U. (2004). *Transfer of export process from customer to supplier: The case of Volvo do Brasil* (Master's thesis). Gothenburg University, Sweden.
11. Silva, T. (2009). Identifying, cultivating, and qualifying suppliers. *Nuclear Plant Journal, 27*(3), 32–35.
12. ISO 9000—quality management, http://www.iso.org/iso/iso_9000
13. Ang, K. (2013). More accidents hit Cambodian plants. *Women's Wear Daily, 205*(104), 1.
14. Maintenance outsourcing as a global strategy. (2009). *IndustryWeek, 258*(5), 22.
15. McCue, D. (2014). Outsourcing still on the rise. *World Trade, 27*(12), 19–21.
16. McDougall, P. (2012, January 13). Obama's insourcing call falls on deft ears. *InformationWeek* (online), 1.
17. Murphy, C. (2012, October 19). Why GM's hiring 3,000 IT pros from HP. *InformationWeek* (online), 1.
18. Members and observers, https://www.wto.org/english/thewto_e/whatis_e/tif_e/org6_e.htm
19. International sourcing: Offshore or near-shore? (2009). *World Trade, 22*(5), 46–48.
20. See, for instance, Episodes of protectionism in U.S. history. (2010, October 8). *Wall Street Journal* (online); Irwin, D. (1998). Changes in U.S. tariffs: The role of import prices and commercial policies. (1998). *The American Economic Review, 88*(4), 1015–1026.
21. See, for example, Hornbeck, J. F. (2004, February 13). CRS report for Congress—NAFTA at ten: Lessons from recent studies, www.aseansec.org; Klonsky, J., & Hanson, S. (2012). Mercosur: South America's fractious trade bloc, http://www.cfr.org/trade/mercosur-south-americas-fractious-trade-bloc/p12762
22. Free trade agreements, www.ustr.gov/trade-agreements/free-trade-agreements
23. Rathbone, J. (2012, June 18). Free trade: Way ahead is openness, not protectionism. FT.com, 1.
24. China secures oil supplies from Russia and Brazil. (2009, March). *Trade Finance*, 1.
25. Morrissey, H. (2006). Be a top flight customer. *Supply Management, 11*(7), 30.
26. Gooch, F. (2008). Playing fair in hard times. *Supply Management, 13*(24), 42–44.
27. Ellinor, R. (2005). Study shows SRM leaders. *Supply Management, 10*(25), 10.
28. Clorox's efforts trigger comprehensive savings. (2003, April). *WasteWise Update*, 10.
29. Wells, A. (2014, November 6, 2014). Lawson Products takes business to the next level. *Industrial Distribution*, 1.
30. SAP supplier relationship management, http://www.sap.com/solution/lob/procurement/software/srm/index.html
31. Hannon, D. (2010). On the hunt for contract management software under $100K. *Purchasing, 139*(1), 1.
32. Worthington, I., Ram, M., Boyal, H., & Shah, M. (2008). Researching the drivers of socially responsible purchasing: A cross-national study of supplier diversity initiatives. *Journal of Business Ethics, 79*(3), 319–331.
33. Berthiaume, D. (2006, January). Reebok's sourcing strategy places ethics first. *Chain Store Age*, 32A.
34. Boggan, S. (2001, October 20). Nike admits mistakes over child labor. *Independent/UK*, www.independent.co.uk; Levenson, E. (2008, November 17). Citizen Nike. CNNMoney.com, www.cnnmoney.com/2008
35. Murray, S. (2006, June 13). Confusion reigns over labeling fair trade products. *Financial Times*, 2. Also see About fairtrade, www.fairtrade.net; and About WFTO, http://www.wfto.com
36. Sullivan, D. (2012). Serving up sustainable food service options. *BioCycle, 53*(4), 32–36.
37. Institute for Supply Management, www.ism.ws

38. Turner, M., & Houston, P. (2009). Going green? Start with sourcing. *Supply Chain Management Review, 13*(2), 14–20.
39. Mulani, N. (2008). Sustainable sourcing: Do good while doing well. *Logistics Management, 47*(7), 25–26.
40. Lim, S. (2009, July 15). Backers don't buy "friendly" palm oil. *Wall Street Journal*, C14.
41. Ellinor, R. (2007). Costing the Earth. *Supply Management, 12*(2), 24.
42. Kuranko, C. (2008). The green standard. *The American City & County, 123*(9), 40–43.
43. Adapted from Leenders, M. R., Fearon, H. E., Flynn, A. E., & Johnson, F. P. (2002). *Purchasing and supply management* (12th ed.). (p. 140). New York: McGraw-Hill.
44. Smock, D. (2001, September 6, 2001). Deere takes a giant leap. *Purchasing*, 1.
45. Tillman, F. (2014). Capitalize on reverse auctions. *Public Management, 96*(6), 25.
46. eMarket Services, www.emarketservices.com/start/eMarket-Directory/index.html
47. Valentine, M. (2012, July 19). Business talk in social circles. *Marketing Week*, 43–46.
48. Muller, J. (2012, June 27). Covisint didn't die; it just went to the cloud. Forbes.com, 1.
49. Countdown: Top 10 most popular social media sites. (2012, June 8). *Dayton Business Journal*, 1.
50. Consumers combine search, social media for purchasing decisions. (2011, February 24). *InformationWeek* (online), 1.
51. CEOs value social media more than others in c-suite. (2012). *PR News, 68*(23), 1.
52. Sagefrog Marketing Group, LLC; Philadelphia and Princeton marketing agency releases B2B marketing survey results. (2012, August 11). *Marketing Weekly News*, 86.
53. Mayne, E. (2011). Chrysler tweaks supplier scorecard. *Ward's Auto World, 47*(7), 6; Chrysler group names Vari-Form as a top-performing supplier finalist for 2013. (2014, July 22). *Manufacturing Close-Up*, 1.
54. How to monitor supplier performance. (2007). *Purchasing, 136*(15), 54.
55. Awards programs lift supplier performance to new heights. (2009). *Purchasing, 138*(6), 57–59.
56. Northrup Grumman recognizes top suppliers. (2014, September 10). *Manufacturing Close-Up*, 1.

Chapter 15

1. Krizner, K. (2012). Logistics solutions further inland. *World Trade, 25*(11), 43–45.
2. Schulz, J. (2013, April 10). Logistics management's top 50 less-than-truckload & truckload trucking companies. *SupplyChain, 247*, 1–4.
3. Found in Harps, L. (2002, January). Getting started in reverse logistics. *Inbound Logistics*, 1.
4. Krizner, K. (2010). The NAFTA attraction. *World Trade, 23*(8), 45–47; Sergie, M. NAFTA's economic impac, http://www.cfr.org/trade/naftas-economic-impact/p15790
5. Digital glossary, www.cscmp.org/digital/glossary
6. See, for example, Horovitz, B. (1983, April 4). Honda not so simple anymore. *IndustryWeek*, 45; Honda chooses Indiana for US$400 mil. factory. (2006, June 28), https://www.ihs.com/country-industry-forecasting.html?ID=106599218; Johnson, K. (2014, August 9). Honda's global strategy—go local. *Washington Post*, 1.
7. Knobel, B. (1993, June 2). Side order of real estate: McDonald's opens an office tower to help it turn a profit in Moscow. *Los Angeles Times*, 1.
8. Gunn, M. (2010). Where in the world? *Insurance and Technology, 35*(5), 26.
9. The Global Competitiveness Report 2014–2015, http://reports.weforum.org/global-competitiveness-report-2014-2015/#=
10. Ibid.
11. The RightSite Team. (2010, April 6). Balancing market access and supplier proximity, http://rightsite.asia/en/article/balancing-market-access-and-supplier-proximity
12. Hulme, V. (2010). East Penn in China. *China Business Review, 37*(3), 53–55.
13. Hannon, D. (2010). American railcar uses TMS to shine light on inbound supply chain. *Purchasing, 139*(3), 13–14; Caterpillar, Inc.: Caterpillar expands operations in United States. (2012, March 2). *Economics Week*, 266.
14. Rabianski, J. (2007). Employee quality of life in corporate location decisions. *Journal of Corporate Real Estate, 9*(1), 50–63.
15. The Economist Intelligence Unit's Quality-of-Life Index, http://www.economist.com/media/pdf/QUALITY_OF_LIFE.pdf
16. Quality of Life Index for Country 2015, http://www.numbeo.com/quality-of-life/rankings_by_country.jsp?title=2015
17. Kirksville: Small town, widespread collaboration, hard-working employees. (2009). *Pharmaceutical Executive, 29*(5), B10.
18. What is the WTO? https://www.wto.org/english/thewto_e/whatis_e/whatis_e
19. Russian federation—recycling fee on motor vehicles, https://www.wto.org/english/tratop_e/dispu_e/cases_e/ds463_e.htm
20. Trunick, P. (2012). New opportunities in exporting. *World Trade, 25*(10), 44–46.
21. 2015 best and worst state rankings, http://chiefexecutive.net/2015-best-worst-states-business/
22. Eiselt, H., & Marianov, V. (Eds.). (2011). *Foundations of location analysis*. New York: Springer; Barros, A. (1998). *Discrete and fractional programming techniques for location models*. New York: Springer; and Drezner, Z. (Ed.). (1995). *Facility location: A survey of applications and methods*. New York: Springer.
23. Case study: 24 hour fitness, http://www.pitneybowes.com/content/dam/pitneybowes/us/en/legacy/docs/us/software/industry-pages/Retail/Location-Analysis-Strategy/PDFs/24-Hour-Fitness-Case-Study.pdf
24. How CKE grew their business with maptitude, http://www.caliper.com/map-software/case-studies/how-cke-grew-their-business-with-maptitude.htm
25. Freight data and statistics, http://www.rita.dot.gov/bts/sites/rita.dot.gov.bts/files/subject_areas/freight_transportation/index.html
26. Swift currents, debris slow recovery effort. (2007, August 13), www.npr.org
27. Railroad classes, https://en.wikipedia.org/wiki/Railroad_classes
28. Acela express, USA, www.railway-technology.com/projects/amtrak/
29. Japanese bullet trains—40 years at the forefront. (2007, September 3), http://www.railway-technology.com/features/feature1216
30. Boeing freighter family, http://www.boeing.com/commercial/freighters/; AN-225 Mriya super heavy transport, http://www.antonov.com/aircraft/transport-aircraft/an-225-mriya
31. Emery, B. (2010). Innovation in commercial aircraft: The 787 Dreamliner cabin. *Research Technology Management, 53*(6), 24–29; Boeing 787 Dreamliner sets speed, distance records. (2011, December 9). *Asia Pulse*, 1.
32. Sanbum, J. (2013, January 4). Mississippi River could close to barge traffic within days. *TIME Business & Money* (online), www.business.time.com/2013/01/04
33. Singhj, B. (1999, July 11). The world's biggest ship. *The India Tribune* (online), www.tribuneindia.com/1999/99jul11/sunday/head3.htm
34. Container ship, en.wikipedia.org/wiki/Container_ship
35. Zolfagharifard, E. (2010, May 4). Oil and gas: In from the cold. *The Engineer*, 18; Nord stream, http://en.wikipedia.org/wiki/Nord_Stream
36. What is intermodal? http://www.proficienttransport.com/history.html
37. BNSF website: www.bnsf.com
38. Atlantic Container Line website: www.aclcargo.com
39. DHS rolls out airport body scanners. (2010, March 5). *InformationWeek* (online), 1.
40. CLEAR to work with TSA to strengthen airport security. (2014, September 29). *Airline Industry Information*, 1.
41. Karp, A. (2009). Cargo screenings: "Serious challenges." *Air Transport World, 46*(6), 45–47.
42. Edmonson, R. (2009, July 22). DHS scans 98 percent of imports for radiation. *Journal of Commerce*, 1.
43. This week. (2010, March 29). *Journal of Commerce*, 1; The transportation security administration and the aviation-security fee. (2013, December 10), http://budget.house.gov/news/documentsingle.aspx?DocumentID=364049; Chotiner, K. (2015). DHS sets out FY 2016 budget needs. *Jane's Airport Review, 27*(3), 1.
44. Shaklett, M. (2011). The 21st century warehouse. *World Trade, 24*(3), 18–25.
45. Kator, C. (2006). Warehouse giants. *Modern Materials Handling, 61*(12), 31.
46. Feare, T. (2001). Jazzing up the warehouse. *Modern Materials Handling, 56*(7), 71–72.
47. Biederman, D. (2010, March 8). 3PLs put pedal to the metal. *Journal of Commerce*, 1.
48. Brown, M. (1997, June). The slow boat to Europe. *Management Today*, 83–86.
49. Maister, D. (1976). Centralization of inventories and the "square root law." *International Journal of Physical Distribution and Materials Management, 6*(3), 124–134.
50. Trebilcock, B. (2010). Distribution evolution at PDS. *Modern Materials Handling, 65*(2), 14–15.
51. Rogers, D., Lambke, R., & Benardino, J. (2013). Taking control of reverse logistics. *Logistics Management, 52*(5), 52–62.
52. Lawrence, D. (2007, August 31). China issues food, toy recall rules to tighten safety. Bloomberg.com News, www.bloomberg.com/apps/news?pid=20601080&sid=asUaOAct_vrc&refer=asia. Also see Wisner, J. (2011). The Chinese-made toy recalls at Mattel, Inc. *Business Case Journal, 18*(1), 16–30.
53. Rogers, L. (2009). Going in reverse to move forward. *Modern Materials Handling, 64*(9), 28.
54. Gallagher, T. (2009, July 22). GENCO contracts for Dell remanufacturing. *Journal of Commerce*, 1.
55. Blanchard, D. (2009). Moving ahead by mastering the reverse supply chain. *IndustryWeek, 258*(6), 58.
56. Martinez, R. (2010). Best practices in "returns management." *Multichannel Merchant, 26*(12), 29.
57. Andel, T. (2012, February 15). Savings along the road to sustainability. *Material Handling & Logistics*, 1.
58. Fawley, E., (2011, June 11). Energy 101: Oil, http://fresh-energy.org/2011/11/energy-101-oil/; Bielak, A. Breaking down the blueprint: Energy efficiency and energy security, http://t4america.org/blog/2009/06/03/breaking-down-the-blueprint-energy-efficiency-and-energy-security
59. Trucking efficiency website: www.truckingefficiency.org
60. Ask what if. (2012). *World Trade, 25*(12), 18–20.
61. Schneider National installs container, trailer tracking. (2013, July 1). *Fleet Owner*, 1.
62. SmartWay, www.epa.gov/smartway
63. Andel, T. (2014, August 1). Logistics companies celebrate sustainability. *Material Handling & Logistics*, 1.
64. Sustainability at sea and in northwest Arkansas. (2009, June/July). *Retailing Today*, 24–25.
65. Burnson, P. (2013). Reverse logistics: Closing the global supply chain loop. *Logistics Management, 52*(2), 34–35.

Chapter 16

1. Krizner, K. (2010). Supply chain visibility and efficiency gets a boost. *World Trade, 23*(1), 22–26.
2. Collaboration quotes, http://www.brainyquote.com/quotes/keywords/collaboration.html#U1CeKQkvjrqocjK1.99
3. Shacklett, M. (2012). IBM evolves a globally integrated supply chain. *World Trade, 25*(5), 32–35.
4. Blanchard, D. (2006). Too many supply chains are failing to integrate. *IndustryWeek, 255*(11), 45–46; Talent management must mesh with business goals for post-recession success. (2010). *HR Focus, 87*(1), 8.
5. Lambert, D., Cooper, M., & Pagh, J. (1998). Supply chain management: Implementation issues and research opportunities. *International Journal of Logistics Management, 9*(2), 1–19.
6. Siu, S. (2007, January 8). CargoSmart Ltd. *Journal of Commerce*, 1.
7. Burnson, P. (2015). Sears plays it cool. *Logistics Management, 54*(2), 24–26.
8. DeLaurentis, T. (2009). Ethical supply chain management. *The Chinese Business Review, 36*(3), 38–41.
9. Interested readers can visit www.supply-chain.org for more information about the Supply Chain Council.
10. Varmazis, M. (2007). What to look for in online office supply catalogs. *Purchasing, 136*(11), 33.
11. McCrea, B. (2012). Certification: The career enhancer. *Supply Chain Management Review, 16*(4), S3–S11; SCOR model enhances how supply chains are enabled. (2012, December 4). *Material Handling & Logistics*, 1.
12. Taken from the online proceedings of the Supply-Chain World–Latin America 2002 conference, Mexico City, Mexico (www.supplychainworld.org/la2002/program.html).
13. Harbert, T. (2009). Why the leaders love value chain management. *Supply Chain Management Review, 13*(8), 12–16.
14. SCC names supply chain excellence winners. (2010, November 1). *Material Handling & Logistics*, 1.
15. SCOR framework, http://www.apics.org/sites/apics-supply-chain-council/frameworks/scor
16. Healy, T. (2014). How they did it: HP meets the challenge of a supply chain merger. *Supply Chain Management Review, 18*(6), 10–19.
17. Duffy, M. (2009). Is supply chain the cure for rising healthcare costs? *Supply Chain Management Review, 13*(6), 1.
18. DiBenedetto, B. (2007, May 21). Thinking lean. *Journal of Commerce*, 1.
19. Wilson, M. (2010). A blanket solution. *Chain Store Age, 86*(1), 39.
20. Canadian firms rethinking logistics business models, new report shows. (2011). *Canadian Transportation Logistics, 114*(3), 8–9, 26.
21. Lester, T. (2007, June 29). Masters of collaboration—how well do U.K. businesses work together? *Financial Times*, 8.
22. Trunick, P. (2002). It's crunch time. *Transportation & Distribution, 43*(1), 5–6.
23. Robert Reed on hospital–physician integration. (2010). *Healthcare Financial Management, 64*(6), 30.
24. Biederman, D. (2010, April 5). Visibility into compliance. *Journal of Commerce*, 1.
25. Geller, S. (2007). The pharmaceutical industry looks to reduce waste by getting lean. *Pharmaceutical Technology, 31*(3), 130.
26. Field, A. (2007, May 7). Sound the alarm. *Journal of Commerce*, 1.
27. Avery, S. (2007). At Boeing, supplier collaboration takes off. *Purchasing, 136*(13), 1.
28. Maccoby, M. (2006). Creating collaboration. *Research Technology Management, 49*(6), 60–62.

29. Roberts, B. (2007). Counting on collaboration. *HR Magazine, 52*(10), 47–51.
30. Maylett, T., & Vitasek, K. (2007). For closer collaboration, try education. *Supply Chain Management Review, 11*(1), 58.
31. Lee, H., Padmanabhan, V., & Whang, S. (1997). The bullwhip effect in supply chains. *Sloan Management Review, 38*(3), 93–102; Lee, H. (2010). Taming the bullwhip. *Journal of Supply Chain Management, 46*(1), 7.
32. Risen, C. (2009). Managing supply chain risk by monitoring Chinese sourcing capacity. *World Trade, 22*(2), 44–46.
33. Hofmann, M. (2007). Financial executives rate top challenges through 2009. *Business Insurance, 41*(21), 4–5.
34. O'Connell, O. (2010, April). America's trade & supply chain: Lessons learned. *Trade Finance,* 1.
35. Esola, L. (2006). Employers questioned on pandemic drug plan. *Business Insurance, 40*(49), 4–5.
36. Swaminathan, J., & Tomlin, B. (2007). How to avoid the risk management pitfalls. *Supply Chain Management Review, 11*(5), 34–43.
37. Supply disruption discussed. (2003). *Business Insurance, 37*(22), 17.
38. Swaminathan, J., & Tomlin, B. (2007). How to avoid the risk management pitfalls. *Supply Chain Management Review, 11*(5), 34–43.
39. Tieman, R. (2007, September 10). It's about common sense. *Financial Times*, 5.
40. Ibid.
41. Flexing supply chain muscle. (2007). *Chain Store Age, 83*(9), 10A.
42. Ibid.
43. Felsted, A. (2007, September 10). Lessons from Barbie world. *Financial Times*, 1.
44. Rice, J. (2007). Rethinking security. *Logistics Management, 46*(5), 28.
45. Anderson, B. (2007). Prevent cargo theft. *Logistics Today, 48*(5), 37–38.
46. McCourt, M. (2007). Supply chains: Get a global view and find the weakest link. *Security, 44*(8), 8.
47. See, for example, www.cargosecurity.com/ncsc/education-CTPAT.asp
48. Terreri, A. (2006). How do you balance shipment speed with a secure supply chain? *World Trade 19*(11), 18–22.
49. Michel, R. (2006). Profit from secure supply chains. *Manufacturing Business Technology, 24*(11), 1.
50. Hase, A. (2013, December 20). What's next for business collaboration? Six trends emerging in 2014, http://www.mindlinksoft.com/blog/bid/72586/What-s-next-for-business-collaboration-Six-Trends-emerging-in-2014
51. Morley, M. (2015, March 8). Did you know that 80% of high tech companies are "high adopters" of B2B integration technologies? http://www.gxsblogs.com/morleym/2015/03/did-you-know-that-80-of-high-tech-companies-are-high-adopters-of-b2b-integration-technologies.html
52. B2B integration, http://www-03.ibm.com/software/products/en/category/b2b-integration

GLOSSARY

4 Ms The four groups of causes—Material, Machine, Methods, and Manpower—used in cause-and-effect diagrams.

ABC inventory classification An approach used to help companies manage their independent demand inventories. The idea is to pay closer attention to items accounting for a larger percentage of the firm's annual spend. The Class A items (the most important) represent about 20% of inventory SKUs and account for perhaps 80% of the firm's annual spend.

Acceptable quality level The percentage of defects the consumer is willing to accept.

Acceptance sampling When shipments of a product are received from suppliers, or before goods are shipped out to customers, samples can be taken from the shipment and compared to a quality acceptance standard. The quality of the sample is then assumed to represent the quality of the entire shipment.

Activity completion time variance The following equation is used for the variance: $\sigma_A^2 = [(b - a)/6]^2$.

Advanced security initiatives Include full collaboration with key suppliers and customers in developing quick recovery and continuity plans for supply chain disruptions; considerations of the past security failures of other firms in developing a more comprehensive and effective security system; the design of a complete supply chain security management plan that is implemented by all key trading partners; and the use of an emergency control center to manage responses to unexpected supply chain disruptions.

Aggregate planning Planning that occurs when firms consider their long-term business plans (such as new market expansion), forecast the intermediate- and long-term demand for their end-products, then translate this information into production, capacity, human resource, purchasing, logistics, and financial plans three to 18 months into the future.

Air carriers A very expensive mode of transportation, but also very fast—particularly for long distances.

Analytic SRM Software that allows the company to analyze the firm's supply base. The analysis provides answers to questions such as: With which suppliers should the company develop long-term relationships? Which suppliers would make the company more profitable? Analytic SRM enables long-term supply base planning.

Anticipation inventories These are held so that demand can be met during periods of expected high demand.

Application add-ons ERP system customizations.

Approach to analytics Knowing what to do with all of the customer information available to the firm.

Arrival pattern Describes the time between customer arrivals, or the distribution of interarrival times.

Assemble-to-order processes Processes that make use of mass customization and thus assemble products once orders are received.

Assembly line layouts Enables high-volume output while making standardized products. Processing steps are standardized and grouped into relatively equal time lengths of work; these are then assigned to workers, permitting specializations to occur.

Assembly line processes Processes that produce high output volumes, with low unit prices, but with little production flexibility.

Assignable variations Process variations that can be traced to a specific "fixable" cause. These assignable variations are created by causes that can be identified and eliminated, and this is the objective of statistical process control.

Associative forecasts Quantitative forecasting techniques that assume that one or more factors (independent variables) are related to demand, and therefore can be used to predict future demand.

Attribute data Yes/no or pass/fail process data that indicate the presence of some attribute such as color, satisfaction, workability, or beauty (for instance, determining whether or not a car was painted the right color, if a customer liked the meal, or if the lightbulb worked).

Average flow time Flow time begins when a job arrives at the shop, and ends when it leaves (averaged over a group of jobs).

Average job lateness Lateness is the difference between the completion date and the due date (if it finishes early, it is still "late"; averaged over a group of jobs).

Average job tardiness Tardiness is the amount of time a job finishes beyond the due date (if it finishes early, tardiness is zero; averaged for a group of jobs).

Average queue time Flow time minus process time (averaged over a group of jobs).

B2B process integration Refers primarily to integration software and cloud platforms.

Backsourcing *See* Insourcing.

Balanced scorecard Developed by Drs. Robert Kaplan and David Norton, a performance scorecard using 20 to 30 performance measures, balanced across four categories.

Balancing the line Dividing the processing work equally to create an equitable work assignment for employees, reducing the likelihood and severity of bottlenecks, and resulting in smoother product flow and higher potential product output levels. Line balancing is based on the output levels desired, the work hours per day, the number of workers, and the assembly task times.

Baldrige Quality Award Signed into law on August 20, 1987. The objectives of the award are to stimulate firms to improve quality and productivity, to recognize firms for their quality achievements, to establish criteria and guidelines so that organizations can independently evaluate their quality improvement efforts, and to provide examples and guidance to those companies wanting to learn how to manage and improve quality and productivity.

Balking When customers don't join a queue because it is too long.

Barter The exchange of goods or services without involving currency.

Basic operations activities Purchasing, storage, transformation, distribution, and product returns.

Basic research Discovering new phenomena or new ways of looking at things.

Batch processes Processes allowing moderate customization and higher output volume. Batch production occurs when a limited number of units are created stage by stage over a series of workstations.

Benchmarking The practice of copying what others do best.

Best-of-breed systems Applications purchased from multiple vendors over time.

Big data Large volumes of data collected using information technologies from a number of sources including social networks, website clicks, emails, sales information, insurance information, billing information, and warranty information, just to name a few.

Big data analytics When organizations analyze a huge array of data using predictive modeling techniques to help pinpoint problems or opportunities to create value.

Bill of materials The BOM is a *recipe* for that product. It indicates all of the raw materials, parts, and assemblies required to manufacture the product. It also indicates how many of each part are required, the parts that go into each assembly, and the order of assembly.

Bottleneck A constraint caused by a process, tool, or person that limits the output of a system.

Breakbulk When bulk orders are received at a distribution center from many suppliers, then broken down for outgoing shipments.

Break-even analysis When cost trade-offs are analyzed among the various options to determine which option is best.

Break-even point The point in a break-even analysis where total revenues equal total costs.

Bullwhip effect Forecasts of demand combined with additions of safety stock that tend to amplify purchases from suppliers. As suppliers then make forecasts and also add safety stock, inventories become still more amplified as we move back up the supply chain. This inventory amplification problem can add significant costs to the supply chain.

Business cycle Refers to economic fluctuations (recessions or expansions), which are actually not very predictable. Recent business cycles in the United States have been affected by various global events.

Business ethics The application of ethical principles to business situations.

Business process integration The sharing and coordination of key processes between companies in a supply chain.

Business process management Has come to be recognized today as automated process management and all of the software applications now available that assist firms in managing and automating business processes.

Business process reengineering The fundamental rethinking and redesign of business processes to improve efficiency and effectiveness.

C charts Control charts for attribute data that count the *number of defects* per unit of output.

Capacity The maximum amount of goods and/or services that a system can produce over a set period of time.

Capacity requirements planning Given MPS quantities, the planned order releases from the MRP, the current shop workload, part routing information, and processing and purchasing lead times, the short-range capacity requirements can be developed for the entire production facility. Initially, the MPS may be found to be infeasible given the shop's current workload and the capacity of each workcenter. If this is the case, the choices are either to increase capacity or reduce or delay the MPS.

Capacity sharing The distribution of capacity among companies when additions to capacity are expensive and when demand is highly variable.

Capacity utilization The amount of effective capacity actually used.

Carbon-neutral A description given to companies when they offset the carbon footprint of their operations by doing things like planting trees.

Cash-to-cash cycle time An inventory performance measure indicating how long cash is tied up in the main cash-producing and cash-consuming areas of receivables, payables, and inventory.

Causal variable A predictor of the dependent variable demand.

Cause-and-effect diagrams Also called fishbone diagrams or Ishikawa diagrams. They are used in brainstorming the causes of the problem. The problem is shown at the right side of the fishbone diagram, with four diagonals of the diagram representing a potential group of causes.

Cellular layouts Parts and assemblies that require the same processing equipment are identified and grouped into part families. Manufacturing "cells" or small assembly areas are then created to process these part families. Also referred to as group technology layouts or GT cells.

Center-of-gravity technique Graphically finds a central location that tends to minimize the total transportation costs between the proposed facility and any number of markets the proposed facility will serve. (This method assumes that transportation costs vary directly with distance, and no special shipping costs are considered.) Also referred to as the centroid method.

Centroid method *See* Center-of-gravity technique.

Check sheets Allow users to determine frequencies for specific problems. Managers make a list of potential problem areas based on their observations, then direct employees to keep counts of each problem occurrence for a period of time.

Clark and Wright savings heuristic One of the most well-known heuristic methods for solving the traveling salesman problem. The key to this procedure is the calculation of "savings" in miles (or cost), to combine two nodes into one tour, rather than have the vehicle return to the origination point and then head out to the next pickup/ distribution point.

Closeness desirability rating Used in office layouts. When department pairs are given numerical ratings based on their closeness desirability. The objective is to create a layout with the highest desirability rating.

Cloud computing Access and delivery of information technology resources including software, operating systems, and servers on an as-needed basis, for a subscription price or fee.

Cloud-based ERP systems Also referred to as an SaaS or a software-as-a-service system; is delivered purely through a Web browser via an Internet connection. In the cloud ERP model, the software supplier houses and manages the software, and user companies pay a subscription fee per user for the software—typically on a monthly basis.

Cloud-based project management solution Project management software available in the cloud.

Cloud-based SRM A service offered by an SRM software supplier. Customers use the supplier's SRM software through an Internet portal, for a subscription or usage fee.

Cluster-first-route-second heuristic For the more general vehicle routing problem, this heuristic can be used to determine a reasonably good solution.

Coal slurry Pulverized coal particles, suspended in water.

Code sharing Capacity sharing in the passenger airline industry.

Collaborative education Training trading partner employees.

Collaborative planning, forecasting, and replenishment Information shared between suppliers and retailers aids in planning, forecasting, and satisfying customer demands through shared information. This allows for continuous updating of inventory and upcoming requirements, resulting in less safety stock.

Commercial buying Purchasing goods and services for business purposes.

Competitive bidding A process wherein a contract is usually awarded to the *lowest-priced bidder* determined to be *responsive* and *responsible* by the buyer. A responsive bid is one that conforms to the invitation to bid, and a responsible bid is one that is capable and willing to perform the work as specified.

Complementary services Service diversions that tend to better occupy the time of waiting customers, and be a source of additional revenues. For instance, a lounge area or bar may serve as a way to occupy customers who are waiting for a table at a restaurant.

Computer aided design (CAD) Refers to the use of computer graphics applications in the product design process.

Computer assisted manufacturing (CAM) Refers to the use of computers in manufacturing processes. CAM applications include welding or painting robots and CNC machines.

Computer integrated manufacturing (CIM) Managing the entire system of interconnecting flexible manufacturing processes using a central integrated computer for planning, scheduling, and decision-making purposes.

Computer numerically controlled machines (CNC) Programmable machines, such as lathes, that are capable of storing machining steps for repetitively manufactured parts.

Concurrent engineering Designing the manufacturing process or service delivery system simultaneously with the design of the product.

Concurrent scheduler approach For the vehicle scheduling problem, this simple heuristic can also be used. The steps are to put the pickups and deliveries in order by their promised arrival times; assign Vehicle 1 to the earliest promised arrival time; if possible, assign the next pickup/delivery to the closest idle vehicle; if all vehicles are busy, create a new vehicle schedule and assign the pickup/delivery to that vehicle. Repeat until all pickups/deliveries are scheduled.

Consolidation warehouses Warehouses that collect large numbers of LTL shipments from nearby suppliers, and then consolidate and transport the items in TL quantities to a manufacturing facility located at some distance from the warehouse.

Consumer surveys When marketing departments and others develop surveys and use focus groups to gather consumer opinions of existing products and new product ideas to generate a forecast.

Consumer's risk When a buyer accepts a shipment of low-quality goods because the sample *did* meet its acceptance standard.

Container-on-flatcar (COFC) A form of intermodal transportation. It uses containers and rail carrier flatcars that carry the containers; also called piggyback service.

Containerships Carry the majority of the world´s water-transported manufactured goods; can carry more than 10,000 standard 20-foot equivalent containers.

Contingency plans Insurance-type activities that are performed to protect the firm and its customers for times when actual demand varies significantly from the forecast. For example, airlines offer to pay customers to take a later flight when seats are overbooked and too many customers show up for the flight; retailers hold safety stocks of high-demand items; resorts have lists of part-time, on-call workers who can fill in on a moment's notice when demand is greater than expected.

Contingent workers Part-time and temporary workers.

Continuous processes Processes with almost no product variety and equipment that is highly automated and dedicated to one task. The product flow is continuous.

Contract manufacturers Firms that custom manufacture parts or products for other firms, under the buying firm's label or brand.

Contract services Firms that provide custom services for other firms, such as services for housekeeping, maintenance, and landscaping at a hotel.

Control charts Allow managers to monitor samples of process performance.

Control limits Used in control charts, based on an assumption that the sampling distribution is normal, and that the control limits are typically ± 3.0 standard deviations from the population mean, which contains 99.73% of the sampling distribution.

Core competencies The collective capabilities or skill sets possessed by the firm that distinguish it from its competitors.

Corporate information flow The flow of information from the firm to its customers.

Corporate social responsibility The practice of business ethics.

Co-sourcing Continuing to make some required units in-house while outsourcing the rest to suppliers.

Cost risks Risks that are mostly within company control, such as cost overruns by suppliers and subcontractors, design changes occurring during the project, and poor estimates of activity costs.

Counterpurchase An arrangement whereby an exporter agrees to sell goods or services to a foreign importer for currency, while simultaneously agreeing to buy goods or services from that same foreign importer.

Countertrade When goods or services of domestic firms are exchanged for goods or services, and in some cases currency, from foreign firms.

Crash cost The cost to achieve the crash time.

Crash time The shortest possible time for activity completion.

Critical activities Activities on the critical path.

Critical path The longest sequence of activities that, when linked together, determine the completion time for the entire project. A delay in any of the critical path activities will delay the entire project. Therefore, critical path activities must be managed closely, to allow projects to finish on time.

Critical Path Method A method developed in the 1950s to determine a project's longest sequence of activities that, when linked together, determine the completion time for the entire project.

Critical ratio The job with the smallest ratio of (time until due date)/(remaining process time) is selected first.

Critical-to-quality characteristics CTQ characteristics Customer requirements deemed to be critical to achieving customer satisfaction.

CRM applications Software applications used in managing customer relationships.

Crossdocking When distribution centers receive bulk shipments, break them down, repackage various items into outgoing orders, and then distribute these orders to a manufacturing location or retail center.

Customer communities Using company websites and social networks to facilitate communication or the exchange of ideas between customers and company personnel.

Customer contact The amount or percentage of time customers are in contact with the service system while the service is being provided.

Customer contact centers Allows integration of all of the methods customers can use to contact a business, including telephone, mail, comment cards, email, website messages, and chat rooms.

Customer contact points Whenever customers interact with company employees, both intentionally and unintentionally.

Customer flow map A visualization of the flow of customers through a service delivery system, with the objective of identifying potential customer flow problems.

Customer lifetime value The net present value of the customer's lifetime projected profits.

Customer loyalty programs Rewarding repeat customers with discounts, credits, cash, and prizes.

Customer participation approach Use of self-service.

Customer relationship management Managing the firm's customer base so they remain satisfied and continue to purchase goods and services.

Customer relationship management process Provides the firm with the structure for developing and managing customer relationships. Key customers are identified, their needs are determined, and then goods and services are developed to meet their needs. Over time, relationships with these key customers are solidified through the sharing of information; the formation of cross-company teams to improve product design, delivery, quality, and cost; and the development of shared goals.

Customer relationship process The infrastructure that motivates valuable customers to remain loyal and buy again.

Customer segmentation Grouping customers so the company can design specific initiatives to satisfy the groups and provide personalized services to the most profitable groups.

Customer service departments Create and maintain an emphasis on service quality, and add a sense of formality to the firm's customer service strategy.

Customer service failure Occurs when any of the customer service activities is neglected or performed poorly.

Customer service management Attending to customer needs before, during, and after the sale.

Customer service management process Providing information to customers and managing all product and service agreements between the firm and its customers.

Customer service pilot project Enables management to assess the impact of an initiative on customer satisfaction, the real costs involved, and the changes in organizational structure required, prior to any organizational customer service strategy rollout.

Customer service process The design and delivery of high-value customer service activities.

Customer service teams Can consist of executives, department managers, design engineers, and other personnel, to react to a significant customer service problem.

Cycle inventories Created when the firm purchases or produces a quantity large enough to last until the next purchase or production period.

Cycle time A formula used to establish the desired pace of an assembly line, which is the maximum time each workcenter can spend on one unit, and also how often a unit must come off the end of the assembly line.

Cyclical variations Demand patterns that occur every several years and are influenced by macroeconomic and political factors.

Dashboards Web-based scorecards.

Days of receivables outstanding An inventory performance measure that indicates the average number of days it takes a company to collect what is owed to it after a credit sale has been completed.

Days payable outstanding An inventory performance measure that tells about how long it takes a company to pay its creditors, such as suppliers.

Deep-sea transportation The use of oil supertankers and containerships.

Defects per million opportunities DPMO A standard performance metric used in Six Sigma.

Delphi method Developed by the RAND Corporation in the 1950s, a series of questionnaires are used to establish a forecast consensus among a group of experts for situations when relevant data are not readily accessible.

Demand forecast updating When a buyer places an order, the supplier might use that information as a predictor of future demand. Based on this information, suppliers update their demand forecasts and the corresponding orders they place with their own suppliers. If lead times vary between the time orders are placed and deliveries are made, then safety stocks also grow and are included in any future orders, which in turn, cause the bullwhip effect for other suppliers' orders further up the supply chain.

Demand management The process that balances customer requirements with supply chain capabilities.

Demand management process Balancing customer demand and the firm's production capabilities. The specific demand management activities include forecasting demand and then utilizing techniques to vary capacity and demand within the purchasing, production, and distribution functions.

Demand sorting An initial "sorting" of customers performed as they first enter the service system, to better direct them to the appropriate service processes or available servers, resulting in less overall wait time.

Demand source The pool of customers; it can contain a finite number or a very large (infinite) number of customers, and be homogenous or nonhomogenous.

Deming's Theory of Management Since managers are responsible for creating the systems that make organizations work, they must also be held responsible for the organization's problems. Thus, only management can fix problems, through application of the right tools, resources, encouragement, commitment, and cultural change.

Dependent demand Parts that are required to build end-items and are *dependent* on the external demand of the finished product.

Design capacity A maximum sustainable output per period.

Design for manufacture and assembly Software applications that consolidate parts and essentially simplify product designs, thus reducing assembly cost. The software helps designers examine alternate material, part, and process choices to judge the cost of design and material trade-offs.

Differential pricing Refers to selling the same product to different customers for different prices. Used in yield management.

Direct banks E-banks, with no brick-and-mortar locations.

Direct mail When a hard-copy marketing communication is sent to potential customers' addresses.

Diseconomies of scale When too much size and capacity lead to increases in unit costs.

Dispatch rules Allow machine operators to determine which job to process next from a queue of jobs waiting to be processed at a machine. Manufacturing managers and operators use dispatch rules to prioritize jobs and continually manage queues of work at each machine.

Distribution center Warehouses that aren't used to store things, but rather perform crossdocking activities.

Distribution requirements planning system Allows a firm's distribution centers to communicate firm orders to the MRP. As retailers and other customers order goods from a manufacturer, orders are filled from a distribution center. Eventually, the distribution center's reorder point (ROP) for each item is reached, and an order is transmitted to the factory. The DRP system is needed to manage the movements of stock into and out of each of these facilities.

DMAIC improvement cycle An important element of Six Sigma. Consists of a sequence of five steps necessary to drive process improvements (design, measure, analyze, improve, control).

Drum, buffer, rope concept (DBR) A concept used to explain the TOC.

Earliest due date The job with the earliest due date is selected first.

Early supplier involvement The practice of inviting supplier representatives to participate on new product design teams.

Economic order quantity The order quantity that will minimize the sum of the annual inventory holding cost and the annual order cost.

Economies of scale Conditions that are created when purchasing and manufacturing in bulk to reduce per-unit costs.

Effective capacity or best operating level Once a production facility is completed, this lower maximum sustainable throughput will most likely be achieved, due to demand fluctuations, equipment breakdowns, worker inconsistencies, and other unforeseen circumstances.

E-marketplaces Online marketplaces where buyers and sellers meet to trade goods, services, and information.

Emergency sourcing Use of backup suppliers.

Empty miles Refers to trucks returning from their deliveries empty.

Enterprise application integration Refers to the use of plans, methods, and tools designed to modernize, consolidate, integrate, and coordinate computer applications.

Enterprise resource planning (ERP) A multimodule software application for managing a firm's functional activities, suppliers, and customers.

Enterprise resource planning (ERP) systems In many supply chains, ERP systems are used to automate communications between suppliers and buyers.

Environmental information flow The flow from customers to the firm.

E-procurement Purchasing goods and services over the Internet.

E-purchasing *See* E-procurement.

Equipment setups Setting up production equipment for the next production run.

Ethical sourcing Bringing about positive social change through organizational buying behaviors. Includes promoting diversity by intentionally buying from small firms, ethnic minority businesses, and women-owned enterprises; discontinuing purchases from firms that use child labor or other unacceptable labor practices; and sourcing from firms with good labor treatment or environmental protection reputations.

Everyday low pricing (EDLP) When manufacturers reduce the forward buying of their customers by offering uniform wholesale prices, instead of occasional discounted prices.

Expected activity completion time The beta distribution weights are used with the three time estimates as follows: $t = (a + 4m + b)/6$.

Expeditors Shop floor employees who identify incoming material purchases and jobs on the shop floor that are behind schedule, and then do whatever is necessary to get purchased materials delivered and jobs completed by their due dates.

Exponential smoothing forecast A slightly more sophisticated form of weighted moving average forecast, in which the forecast for the next period is the current period's forecast adjusted by a weighted difference between the current period's actual data and forecast. This approach requires fewer calculations than the weighted moving average forecast because only two data points are needed.

External customer service audits Identifying changes in the service requirements of customers and determining the firm's current customer service performance and that of its competitors.

External risks Risks outside of company control, which can cause project delays.

External setup activities Activities performed while the equipment is still making units of the previous item.

Fair trade products Products that are manufactured or grown by a disadvantaged producer in a developing country who received a fair price for the goods.

False positive blocking When spam-blockers incorrectly identify an email as spam and block it.

Finished goods Completed products ready for delivery to customers.

First Law of Service Satisfaction = perception – expectation.

First-come-first-served The job arriving first at a workcenter is processed first.

First-tier customers The firm's most valued direct customers.

First-tier suppliers The firm's primary goods and service suppliers.

Fishbone diagrams *See* Cause-and-effect diagrams.

Five-S's Came from Toyota and were Japanese words relating to industrial housekeeping. The idea is that by implementing the Five-S's, the workplace will be cleaner, more organized, and safer, thereby reducing processing waste and improving productivity.

Fixed-position layouts Characterized by manufactured products that remain stationary (such as buildings and cruise ships), while workers and equipment move in and around the project depending on the construction work scheduled at that time. Also referred to as project layouts.

Flexible manufacturing system (FMS) Uses a central host computer, computer numerically controlled machines (CNC), and a plant-wide, automated material handling system equipped with automated conveyors, automated guided vehicles (AGVs), and automated storage and retrieval systems (AS/RS) to schedule small batches of products, route and store parts, and control machining operations among carefully laid-out assembly areas for a number of similar products. This system tries to combine the benefits of highly flexible machine shop processing with highly productive (and fast) repetitive processing.

Flow diagrams *See* Process diagrams.

Flow management Making the product or service and managing production inventories.

Focus groups Assembled groups of customers giving their opinions regarding various proposed program initiatives.

Forecast bias A type of forecast error that occurs when a forecast has a tendency to be either consistently higher or lower than the actual demand.

Forecast error For a given time period, it is simply the difference between the actual demand and the forecast for that period.

Foreign trade zones To encourage trade, governments establish areas where parts and materials can be imported duty-free as long as the imports are used as inputs to the local production of goods that are eventually exported; also called free trade zones outside the United States.

Formal risk management plan The most proactive risk management activity; risk management becomes an executive-level priority. Potential risks are identified and prioritized, and appropriate responses are designed to minimize the disruption to supply chains. Additionally, mechanisms are developed to recover quickly, efficiently, with minimal damage to the firm's reputation and customer satisfaction. Finally, performance measures are developed to monitor the firm's ongoing risk management capabilities.

Forward buying When buyers "stock up" to take advantage of discounted prices, causing order and order timing variances. Also known as stockpiling.

Forward scheduling To schedule jobs forward in time from their arrival date at the facility, taking into account current shop workloads.

Free trade zones *See* Foreign trade zones.

Frozen time fence Time period wherein no changes are allowed to the weekly production schedule. This time period is at least as long as the lead time required to purchase parts and assemble the finished product.

Functional goods Noncritical, low-risk goods such as office supplies, which are highly standardized and easily substituted, and thus can be easily and cheaply purchased.

Gantt chart A timeline used for planning purposes that shows the time lengths and sequences of a project's task activities.

Global sourcing Purchasing items internationally.

Good Any tangible product, like an automobile.

Goods–service package The explicit service, implicit service, facilitating goods, and the supporting facility.

Green purchasing Making environmentally conscious decisions throughout the purchasing process, beginning with product and process design, and through product disposal.

Group technology layouts *See* Cellular layouts.

Happy-productive worker hypothesis Overall job satisfaction is a critical link to employee performance and customer service performance.

Hedge inventories Used when companies stockpile inventories to protect against price increases or supply shortages.

Heuristic solutions Procedures that yield a *reasonable solution* in a relatively short period of time.

High-quality customer service Using the four basic service principles—reliability, recovery, fairness, and wow factor.

High-speed trains Usually refers to a type of rail transportation that operates significantly faster than traditional rail traffic, using specialized trains and dedicated tracks.

House of quality Part of quality function deployment, it shows the relationships among customer requirements, product attributes, and design specifications. It helps evaluate how competitive the product will be, and is used as a benchmarking evaluation tool of the product against its competitors.

Import broker A service that performs import transactions for a fee. Import brokers do not take title to the goods. Instead, ownership passes directly from the seller to the buyer.

Import merchant A service that buys and takes title to international goods and then resells them to the buyer.

Incoterms (International Commercial Terms). A uniform set of rules created by the International Chamber of Commerce for international transactions of goods with respect to shipping costs, risks, and responsibilities of the buyer, seller, and shipper.

Independent demand The external demand for a firm's finished products.

Information audit Determining the firm's current internal and external information users, and estimating their information requirements.

Information velocity Describes how fast information flows from one process to another.

Information visibility The sharing of data in real time required to manage the flow of goods and services between suppliers and customers.

Information volatility The uncertainty associated with information content, format, or timing.

Innovative goods Unique items with customized specifications that are considered to be high risk and high cost for the buying firm.

Input-output control When I > O, WIP increases; when I < O, WIP decreases; when I = O, WIP stays constant. Used as a way to control shop congestion.

Insourcing *See* Backsourcing.

Intellectual asset When information has value it can be referred to as an intellectual asset.

Intermittent process layouts *See* Process-focused layouts.

Intermodal transportation The use of combinations of the transportation modes, such as TOFC and COFC.

Internal customer service audit Reviewing the firm's current customer service measures, policies, and practices.

Internal information flow Information flow within the firm.

Internal rate of return The discount rate that makes a project's net present value equal to its investment cost.

Internal setup activities Setup activities occurring while the machines are idle. These activities contribute directly to the actual clock time of setups.

Inventory carrying costs The costs associated with storing inventories.

Inventory days of supply An inventory performance measure that tells management how long inventory is held before it is sold.

Inventory management performance Measures of how well companies are creating good customer service while keeping inventories low.

Ishikawa diagrams *See* Cause-and-effect diagrams.

ISO 9000 A series of five international quality standards, adopted by ISO in 1987. The most popular standard adopted.

ISO 14000 A family of international environmental management standards, adopted by ISO in 1997.

ISO standards Developed by the International Organization for Standardization in response to market demand, and are based on consensus among the member countries.

Job shops Process-oriented facilities or machine shops. where similar processing equipment or specialties are housed, offering custom products or services. Output volumes are low, unit prices are high, waiting time is long, and production flexibility to accommodate customer requirements is high.

Jobs Customers' orders.

Jockeying When customers switch queues.

Jury of executive opinion A forecasting technique that uses a group of senior executives who are knowledgeable about the firm's products, markets, competitors, and the general business environment to develop a demand forecast.

Just-in-Time Systems in which supplies and assemblies are "pulled" through the system when and where they are needed.

Kaizen A continuous improvement effort. Kaizen comes from the Japanese words *kai* (change) and *Zen* (for the better).

Kaizen blitz Refers to typically a one-week improvement effort covering many areas at once and involving many workers in the firm.

Kanban A material movement or production signal, or card.

Key supplier relationship *See* Strategic alliance.

Key trading partners Trusted suppliers that provide a substantial share of the firm's purchased goods and services; and satisfied customers who buy a significant portion of the firm's products.

Knowledge–management solutions Internet applications that enable real-time collaboration and flow of information among supply chain partners; the ability to "see" into suppliers' and customers' operations, collect supply chain data, and make faster decisions.

Lean culture When organizations provide the leadership, training, communication, enthusiasm, and resources to employees over the long term, so they can continue a lean journey of finding and correcting problems.

Lean layouts Very visual layouts, meaning that lines of visibility are unobstructed, making it easy for operators at one processing center to monitor work occurring at other centers. In lean layouts, all purchased and WIP inventories are located on the production floor at their points of use, and the good visibility makes it easy to spot inventory buildups when machine breakdowns and bottlenecks occur.

Lean manufacturing *See* Lean thinking.

Lean production *See* Lean thinking.

Lean services Focus on customer needs; they develop creative problem-solving abilities to improve and standardize processes to satisfy customers, while using tools for increasing quality, reducing waste, and improving service delivery.

Lean Six Sigma Also known as Lean Six. Refers to the combination practice of lean with Six Sigma.

Lean systems *See* Lean thinking.

Lean thinking An operating philosophy encompassing the objectives of high quality, fast response, and low waste within the organization and between supply chain trading partners. Also known as lean systems, lean manufacturing, lean production, and lean.

Lean warehousing Using techniques that move items more quickly through inbound and outbound warehouses and distribution centers.

Legacy systems Extensive, earlier-existing information systems.

Less-than-truckload carriers Trucks that move small packages or shipments taking up less than one truckload. The shipping fees are higher per hundred weight (cwt) than TL fees, since the carrier must consolidate smaller shipments into one truckload, then break the truckload back down into individual shipments at the destination for individual deliveries.

Life cycle assessments Cradle-to-grave analyses of products' environmental impacts, including assessments of the carbon footprint, energy usage, air acidification impact, and water contamination profile.

Linear trend forecast A linear regression forecast, where one variable is time (the independent variable) and the other variable is the actual data (such as demand).

Load reports Compare the required capacity for the given MPS with the projected available capacity. Given this information, production managers can determine if workloads need to be shifted to later periods, overtime needs to be scheduled, or work needs to be contracted out.

Location decisions Decisions that involve the market to be served, the potential locations available to serve the market, and then the site selection based on company requirements and each potential site's assessment.

Logistics execution suites A blanket term for a family of logistics-oriented software applications including transportation management systems, warehouse management systems, and returns management systems. Companies are finding significant benefits from integrating their basic ERP systems with logistics execution suites. These systems provide "a networked view of the world."

Logistics management Combines warehouse location planning, transportation management, and product returns management with the goal of meeting customer service requirements at the lowest possible cost.

Logistics sustainability The efforts of transportation companies to reduce carbon emissions, and improve supply-chain efficiencies and environmental performance.

Logistics The process of planning, implementing, and controlling the efficient, effective flow and storage of goods, services, and related information from point of origin to point of consumption for the purpose of conforming to customer requirements.

Lot tolerance percent defectives Defines the upper limit of percent defectives a consumer is willing to tolerate.

Lower control limits A line that is three standard deviations below the mean, so that 99.7% of the sample plots fall inside this limit.

Machine shop layouts *See* Process-focused layouts.

Maintenance, repair, and operating supplies Purchased items consumed in-house or used to support manufacturing and service processes.

Make versus buy analysis A specific type of break-even analysis where the firm is considering two alternatives—making a product in-house or buying it from suppliers.

Make-or-buy decision A strategic decision regarding whether the firm will purchase, make in-house, or do some combination of the two. In recent years, the trend has been moving toward more outsourcing combined with the creation of lasting supplier relationships.

Makespan The total elapsed time to complete a group of jobs.

Make-to-order processes Processes that create custom products from job shops, projects, and some batch facilities.

Make-to-stock processes Processes that create stock products in anticipation of demand.

Managing projects The planning, scheduling, and controlling of resources (such as capital, people, materials, and equipment) to meet the specific goals (such as completion date, budgeted cost, and required performance) of the project.

Manufacturing execution system module An ERP system add-on, ties management planning to the manufacturing floor. It communicates the manufacturing plan from the ERP to the shop floor. Then, as products are manufactured, the MES sends actual production data from the shop floor back to the ERP.

Manufacturing flexibility Refers to the ability of a manufacturing system to create different product types, change the order in how processes are operated, or change process capacities in response to predicted and unpredicted changes in demand.

Manufacturing flow management process The set of activities responsible for making the actual product, establishing the manufacturing flexibility required to adequately serve the markets, and designing the production system to meet order lead-time requirements.

Manufacturing resource planning Software systems that were designed to allow firms to perform forward-looking *what-if analyses* of plant capacities.

manufacturing resource planning (MRP II) system Today, most MRP II systems have a simulation capability to allow managers to perform what-if analyses and gain an understanding of likely outcomes when capacity or production timing decisions are made. Other software modules are also included with MRP II systems, enabling various functional area personnel to interact with the MRP II system using a central database. Production, marketing, human resource, and finance personnel would then work together to develop a feasible aggregate plan based on available funds, equipment, advertising plans, and labor.

Mass customization process A hybrid process combining several aspects of the job shop and assembly line processes to create high volume production of customized products.

Master production schedule Specifies which end-product is to be made, how many are required, and when they need to be completed. These usually take the form of a weekly production schedule. An input to the MRP.

Material flow analysis When the initial material flow map is complete, a number of items should become apparent—namely, where inventories are delayed or stored throughout the process, the paths that inventories follow as they wend their way through the process, and the sequence of activities that make up the process. It is then possible to measure travel distances and travel times, time spent in storage and in processing, and time spent waiting on materials. It is also possible to identify better routes for people, machinery, and materials throughout the facility and better placement of machines or departments.

Material flow mapping A method for identifying the current sequence of activities making up the process, to understand material flows. The objective is to identify and evaluate or eliminate the activities that are not adding value, and then improve the remaining process activities.

Material requirements planning (MRP) Software applications that were developed to try to balance part purchases and plant capacities with production requirements.

Mean absolute deviation The most common method for comparing forecasting techniques; it averages the absolute value of the errors over a given period of time.

Mean absolute percentage error This method provides an estimate of the magnitude of forecast error. The monthly absolute forecast error divided by actual demand is summed, then divided by the number of months used in the forecast and multiplied by 100 to derive an average percentage deviation.

Micro-merchandising Focal points that are added in center-aisle locations, where product families are featured, sometimes using rounded front-edge shelving, to improve visual appeal.

Middleware Internal and external application integration software.

Minimum slack time per operation (MINSOP) The job with the minimum slack time per remaining operation is selected first. (Slack time is defined as time until due date minus remaining process time.)

Mission statement A statement that provides direction for the firm's strategic plan. It might include descriptions of its goods and services, the processes it employs, the markets where it competes, its potential customers, and its distinctive competencies.

Mixed-model assembly line sequencing When the demand for each product model determines how often a model production run is scheduled using one assembly line.

Modes of transportation Air, rail, truck, water, and pipeline carriers.

Most likely completion time The best estimate of completion time for an activity, given normal conditions.

Most-important-job-first Jobs are prioritized based on the importance of the customer.

Motor carriers Trucks.

Multiple regression forecasting A regression forecast that is used when there are several independent variables used together, to predict the dependent variable (i.e., demand).

Multiple-factor productivity A ratio of outputs to multiple inputs.

Mystery shoppers Professionals who pose as customers to assess the customer service performance of employees.

National competitiveness The set of institutions, policies, and factors that determine the level of productivity of a country. The level of productivity, in turn, sets the level of prosperity that can be earned by an economy.

Natural variations Uncontrollable process variations, such as variations in humidity caused by changing weather conditions or variations in driving time caused by highway traffic patterns.

Nearshoring Purchasing goods and services closer to the country of the buyer.

Neighborhood marketing Identifying customers based on geography, where customer segments can be viewed as having similar income levels or ethnic traits.

Net present value The sum of a stream of future cash flows, discounted using the firm's desired discount rate.

Neuroscience Exploring the subconscious minds of consumers to uncover new product ideas.

Niche segmentation A type of segmentation that groups customers with similar needs, geographical locations, buying attitudes, or buying habits.

Offset An exchange for industrial goods or services as a condition of a military-related export. It is commonly used in the aerospace and defense sectors.

Open innovation Collaborating with universities, suppliers, customers, and others to generate product ideas.

Open source software Free software for small businesses with relatively less complex projects.

Operating characteristic curve An S-shaped curve used to illustrate the probability of accepting a shipment as a function of the shipment's quality.

Operational risks Incorrect activity scheduling, poor forecasting, poor supplier selection, lack of communication among key personnel, or inadequate production design or ramp-up, which can cause project delays.

Operations The set of activities associated with purchasing, making, delivering, and returning (or recycling) goods and services.

Operations management The effective planning, organizing, and controlling of the many value-creating activities of the firm.

Operations strategies The set of decisions made within the operations function to support the overall mission and strategy of the firm.

Opportunities for a defect to occur OFD It is used in the DPMO calculation, and refers to the maximum number of defects that can occur per unit.

Optimal review period Used for the periodic review model. It is found by dividing the EOQ by the average daily demand.

Optimistic completion time The time to complete the activity if everything goes according to plan (the probability should be very low that the activity can be completed in less time).

Order batching Inventory levels, prior delivery performance, or the desire to order full truckloads or container loads of materials may cause orders to be placed at random or varying time intervals, which creates order variances.

Order costs The administrative costs associated with purchasing items.

Order cycle The time from initiation of the customer order until the product or service is delivered to the customer.

Order fulfillment process The on-time delivery of goods and services to customers, including the set of activities that allows the firm to fill customer orders while providing the required levels of customer service at the lowest possible cost.

Order lead time The time from order receipt to delivery to the customer.

Outsourcing Buying goods and services from suppliers instead of making them in-house.

Outsourcing customer service Using a third-party customer service provider.

Overbooking Refers to accepting more reservations than can be accommodated, to maximize revenues.

P charts Control charts for attribute data, which monitor the *percent defective* in each sample.

Pareto charts Attributed in part to the work of Vilfredo Pareto, a noted 19th-century Italian economist and mathematician. It is a chart showing the magnitudes of problems, from biggest to smallest.

Pareto Principle Refers to Juran's thinking that 20% of something is typically responsible for 80% of the results. Also known as the 80/20 Rule.

P-cards *See* Procurement cards.

Performance measures Criteria that tell managers how the company is doing, and what needs to be fixed to enable the firm to accomplish its objectives.

Periodic review model Assuming variable demand, this model uses a variable order quantity at fixed reorder periods. Requires higher safety stock levels than the reorder point models.

Pessimistic completion time The maximum completion time for an activity, given that everything goes wrong (the probability should be very low that the activity can be completed in a longer time).

Piggyback service A type of intermodal transportation service, such as TOFC and COFC.

Pilot manufacturing After the design-build-test phase is successfully completed, the product is manufactured on a limited basis to determine if the production equipment can reliably manufacture the good, and if full-scale production is possible.

Pipeline carriers A very specialized mode of transportation; once the initial investment of the pipeline is recovered, there is very little additional maintenance cost, so long-term pipeline transportation tends to be very inexpensive. Pipelines can haul materials that are only in a liquid or gaseous state, and so the growth potential for pipelines is limited.

Poka-yoke Error- or mistake-proofing.

Postponement A mass customization term, occurring when the final assembly is postponed until the specific customer orders are received.

Post-transaction customer service elements The customer service elements occurring after the product or service has been sold.

Pre-transaction customer service elements The customer service elements occurring within the firm prior to, or apart from, the sale of goods and services.

Private warehouses Warehouses that are owned by the firm storing the goods.

Proactive security initiatives Ventures outside the firm to include suppliers and customers, and also include a more formalized approach to security management within the firm.

Probabilistic demand and lead time reorder point model When variable demand and variable lead time exist, the model says to order the EOQ whenever the inventory on-hand reaches the reorder point level.

Probabilistic demand reorder point model When variable demand exists, this model assumes the purchase lead time to be constant; however, the time between orders would vary. The model says to order the EOQ whenever the inventory on-hand reaches the reorder point level.

Probability of completing a project by a given time Use the standard normal equation to find Z, where Z = (desired completion date – expected completion date) / σ_P. Then use the Z table to determine the probability.

Process capability A measure of the ability of a process to consistently produce a product or service within design specifications.

Process capability index Shows whether the process mean has shifted away from the design target and is off-center.

Process diagrams Also called process maps or flow diagrams. A necessary first step when evaluating any manufacturing or service process. They use rectangles representing process action elements and ovals representing wait periods, connected by arrows to show the flow of products or customers through the process.

Process flowchart or process map A diagram showing the sequence of steps involved in a process, used to help users understand how a process works and where problems might be found.

Process flowcharting *See* Material flow mapping.

Process integration Sharing information, collaborating, and coordinating resources to jointly manage a process.

Process mapping *See* Material flow mapping.

Process maps *See* Process diagrams.

Process visibility Means that transactions and other activities in a process are known to users, and are performing accurately.

Processes Methods for getting work done. Processes consist of a series of steps that turn inputs into outputs.

Process-focused layouts When similar processing equipment is departmentalized. These are desirable when many different products are manufactured, requiring small output volumes or batch sizes. These layouts are designed for manufacturing flexibility. Also referred to as intermittent process layouts or machine shop layouts.

Procurement Specifications development, value analysis, supplier market research, negotiation, buying activities, contract administration, inventory control, traffic, receiving, and stores.

Procurement cards Low-limit corporate bank cards designed to streamline the purchasing and payment process.

Producer's risk When a buyer rejects a ship1ment of high-quality goods because the sample quality level *did not* meet its acceptance standard.

Product design The process of making decisions about the characteristics, features, and performance of a company's product.

Product development and commercialization Designing and producing new products that customers want, and doing it frequently and efficiently.

Product family Consists of different products that share similar characteristics, components, or manufacturing processes.

Product focused layouts *See* Assembly line layouts.

Product structure diagram The simplest form a BOM can take.

Production flexibility The ability to change capabilities quickly to satisfy changing demands.

Production kanban A light, flag, or card that is used to tell the work cell to begin processing more components to restock the empty container in its output area.

Production planning strategies Sets of activities in operations management for meeting the aggregate plan. These consist of the chase, level, and mixed strategies.

Productivity growth rate A calculation of the change in productivity from one period to the next, divided by the original productivity.

Profitable customer A customer who yields a higher revenue stream than the company's cost of attracting, selling, and servicing that customer.

Program Evaluation and Review Technique *See* Critical Path Method.

Project A temporary group activity designed to produce a unique product, service, or result. Projects have a defined beginning and end, with specific tasks, objectives, and assigned resources.

Project crashing Reducing a project's completion time by using more resources.

Project layouts *See* Fixed-position layouts.

Project management software Software designed to track a project's progress.

Project management The planning, scheduling, and controlling of resources to meet the specific goals of a project.

Project process A type of job shop process where one unique product is manufactured requiring one unique set of processes.

Project risk Unexpected events that can cause missed project completion times or cost overruns.

Public warehouses For-profit organizations that provide a wide range of light manufacturing, warehousing, and distribution services to other companies.

Pull system When manufacturing cells need parts or materials, they use a kanban to signal their need for items from the upstream manufacturing cell, processing unit, or external supplier providing the needed material. In this way, nothing is provided until a downstream demand occurs.

Purchase cost The actual cost of the items bought from suppliers.

Purchase spend Money the firm spends on goods and services.

Purchasing Acquisition of required materials, services, and equipment.

Purchasing cycle A six-step process—the first three steps involve *preparing for* the acquisition of goods and services, and are generally done together to assess the current situation. The final steps involve the actual acquisition of goods and services.

Qualitative forecasting techniques Forecasts that are based on guesswork, intuition, or opinions, and are generally used when data are unavailable or too old to be of much use.

Quality function deployment A method that helps companies create designs that are more customer-focused.

Quality of life Material well-being; health; political stability, freedom, and security; family and community well-being; climate and air quality; and job security.

Quantitative forecasting techniques Forecasts that make use of mathematical models and relevant historical data to generate forecasts. The quantitative methods can be further divided into two groups: time series and associative models.

Quantity discount model An extension of the EOQ to be used when the purchase price is allowed to vary—for instance, when quantity discounts are offered by a supplier.

Queue configuration Refers to the structure of the queue, i.e., multiple server, single queue, or multiple server, multiple queue.

Queue discipline Refers to the policy used to select the next customer in the queue for service.

Queue segments Partitioning a queue; for example, an auto repair garage may have separate queues depending on the work to be performed, such as oil changes, tire repairs, or engine overhauls.

$\bar{R}$ The center line of the R chart

R For variable data, it is the difference between the largest and the smallest measurement in one sample.

R chart For variable data, it is used to track sample ranges, or the variation of the measurements within each sample.

Radio frequency identification A small, data storage device that allows data to be read at a distance, without requiring line-of-sight scanning.

Rail carriers A designated mode of transportation. Rail service tends to be relatively slow and inflexible; however, rail carriers charge less than air and motor carriers.

Random variations Demand variations due to unexpected events such as natural disasters (hurricanes, tornadoes, fire), strikes, and wars. Random variations are what cause even the best forecasts to contain error.

Rationing Can occur when total demand exceeds a supplier's finished goods available. When this happens, the supplier might allocate units of product in proportion to what buyers ordered.

Raw materials Purchased parts and materials that are delivered by suppliers and used in the manufacture of finished products or services.

Reactive security initiatives A somewhat deeper commitment to the idea of security management compared to basic initiatives, but they still lack any significant efforts to organize a cohesive and firm-wide plan for security management.

Reneging When customers in a queue give up and leave the queue.

Reorder point The inventory on-hand needed to satisfy demand during the order lead time period.

Returns management systems Systems that provide global visibility, standardization, and documentation of product returns, while minimizing reverse logistics costs. In addition to managing returns, the RMS can also be designed to handle returnable assets such as pallets, platforms, and containers.

Returns management The movement, storage, and processing of returned goods. Also known as reverse logistics.

Revenue management Offering the right service to customers at the right time, for the right price. Also referred to as yield management.

Reverse auctions A bidding process controlled by the buyer, wherein all potential bidders (suppliers) are prequalified before the purchase requirements are released and the bidding begins. Suppliers may then log onto a designated website and place their offers, while watching all the bids as they come in, and may reduce their own bids until the close of the auction. The supplier submitting the lowest bid meeting the specifications is generally selected.

Reverse logistics *See* Returns management.

Rights and duties Some actions are simply right, without any regard to the consequences.

Risk mitigation plans Actions taken to reduce project risk.

Risk pooling Explains the relationship between the number of warehouses, system inventories, and customer service—when market demand is random, it is very likely that higher-than-average demand from some customers will be offset by lower-than-average demand from other customers. Thus, as the number of customers served by a single warehouse increases, demand variabilities will tend to offset one another more often, reducing the overall demand variance and the likelihood of stockouts.

Robust model Refers to the flatness of the total inventory cost curve, which means the EOQ model can be used in a variety of situations.

Rolling production schedule Each week, the MPS extends its frozen weekly production schedule for the set frozen time period, and projects a working schedule for the remaining portion of the year.

Root cause analysis Brainstorming the potential causes for a problem within the 4 Ms. Each branch on one of the four diagonals represents one potential cause. Subcauses are also part of the brainstorming process and are shown as smaller branches attached to each of the primary causes. Asking the question "why?" in response to each potential cause will uncover the potential subcauses. Breaking a problem down into its causes and subcauses will lead to problem solutions.

ROROs Roll-on–roll-off containerships. These allow truck trailers, automobiles, heavy equipment, and specialty cargo to be directly driven on and off the ship into secured below-deck garages, without the use of cranes.

Running sum of forecast error Provides a measure of forecast bias. When the RSFE is positive, it means the forecast is generally underestimating demand. When it is negative, the RSFE indicates an overestimating demand situation.

Safety stocks These inventories are held to satisfy demand when delivery or production problems occur, or when demand is higher than expected.

Sales force estimates When field sales personnel provide estimates of future customer demand. These forecasts may be politically motivated or based on performance expectations.

Sample coefficient of determination R^2, it is a measure of the variation in the dependent variable that can be explained by the independent variable. Simply put, it is a measure of how good the regression line fits the data. The value of R^2 falls between 0 and 1. As the value of R^2 approaches 1, it indicates that variations in the dependent variable and the regression line (the forecast) are closely related.

Sample correlation coefficient R, it is a measure of the strength and direction of the relationship between the independent variable and the dependent variable. It ranges from -1 to $+1$; if the value of R is positive, it means *increases* in the independent variable result in *increases* in the dependent variable.

Sashimi system An early Japanese version of concurrent engineering.

Schedule risks Unrealistic activity time estimations, inaccurate technical and operational requirements, and insufficient resources, which cause project delays.

SCOR model Helps to integrate the operations of supply chain members by linking the delivery operations of the seller to the sourcing operations of the buyer.

Scorecarding Using some form of balanced scorecard.

Seasonal variations Demand patterns that repeat over a consistent interval such as days, weeks, months, or seasons.

Second Law of Service It's hard to play catch-up ball.

Service An intangible product such as the delivery of automobiles to the dealership, or the repair of automobiles once they are sold.

Service blueprinting A flowcharting method, used when designing and evaluating a new service or improving an existing service. It lays out the direct and indirect activities occurring between the service provider and the customer, and the noncontact activities that don't involve the customer.

Service level The percentage of time the firm does not want to stockout during the order lead time period, or the area under the demand distribution that is covered by, or to the left of, the ROP.

Service recovery An equitable compensation or arrangement to compensate for a service failure.

Servicescapes Describe the retail environment. This includes use of pleasant lighting, background music, and comfortable ambient temperatures. Other obvious servicescape items are well-placed signs, wide aisles, use of carpeting, pleasant wall colors, and "try-it-out" areas.

Setups Many assembly lines process several models of the same product, requiring machine reprogramming and tooling changes, inventory changes, and processing activity changes, prior to the start of a new product model run. These activities are referred to collectively as a setup.

Seven wastes Taiichi Ohno of Toyota described these, as they applied to the Toyota Production System, to identify and reduce waste. The common term across the seven wastes is *excess*.

Shortage gaming When buyers figure out that rationing is occurring, they inflate their orders to satisfy their real needs.

Shortest process time The job with the shortest process time is selected first.

Sight lines Used in many restaurant and retail layouts. Allow guests to get a view of the kitchen or other parts of the store.

Silo mentality An "I win, you lose" attitude, as evidenced when using hard negotiations with the hungriest suppliers, paying little attention to the after-sale needs of customers, or assigning few resources toward developing new goods and services.

Simple linear regression forecasts A causal variable is identified, which is a predictor of demand. Linear regression is used to identify the causal relationship and the forecast equation.

Simple moving average forecast A technique that uses recent historical demand to generate a forecast and is fairly reliable when the demand is stable over time.

Single-factor productivity A ratio of outputs to one input.

Six Sigma A quality philosophy that helps to achieve a firm's strategic initiatives, while at the same time resolving trade-offs that can exist when simultaneously pursuing the goals of low price, high quality, and fast response. It is a statistics-based decision-making framework designed to make significant quality improvements in value-adding processes.

Slack time The difference between the early start and late start times or the early finish and late finish times.

Smart pull Adding intelligence to lean systems allows an expansion of the kanban concept.

SMED An abbreviation for single-minute (or single-digit) exchange of die.

SMED system A set of techniques that make it possible to perform equipment setup operations in a matter of minutes—ultimately, in the single-digit (less than 10 minute) range. This system was developed by Shigeo Shingo in Japan in the 1950s, and was applied at Toyota in the 1960s.

Smoothing constant A weight used in the exponential smoothing forecast. The weight must be between 0 and 1.

Social media Include blogs, discussion boards, online video, podcasting, social networks, and wikis.

Sourcing The entire purchasing process or cycle, including writing purchase specifications, searching for and selecting suppliers, negotiating the purchase price, and evaluating a supplier's performance.

Sourcing strategy A plan for managing the supply of purchased items, which is linked to spend analysis and goals, and tied to corporate and supply chain strategies.

Spend categories Purchases are commonly divided into categories with common characteristics such as raw materials, customized items, standardized items, and services, and then each of these general categories may be further subdivided.

Spend management Use of smart purchasing practices to reduce purchase spend.

Square root rule Used in risk pooling; as the number of warehouses in a system changes, the system inventory required is equal to the original system inventory times the ratio of the square root of the new number of warehouses to the square root of the original number of warehouses.

Stabilize phase Directly after ERP implementation, and for a period of perhaps one year, companies familiarize themselves with the system and the process changes that have occurred.

Statement of work In response to a request for a price quote, a supplier often attaches this document, describing exactly what will be done and how.

Statistical process control Once a problem is identified, analyzed, fixed, and deemed to be under control, workers gather process performance data, create control charts to monitor process performance, and then begin collecting and plotting sample measurements in a continuous fashion. These activities allow workers to take corrective steps quickly if the control charts indicate the start of an out-of-control situation.

Statistical quality control *See* Statistical process control.

Stockout costs Encountered when the internal or external demand for items cannot be met.

Stockpiling *See* Forward buying.

Strategic alliance An ongoing supplier relationship that has been beneficial and the two parties see a reason to work together more often and share more information.

Strategic fit The alignment of product designs with the operational capabilities and policies of the firm (*internal fit*) and with the condition of the market and desires of customers (*external fit*).

Strategic planning The process of determining a firm's long-term goals, plans, and policies.

Strategy A description of how the firm intends to compete, or provide value to its customers, both now and into the future.

Strategy trade-offs When doing more of one activity requires doing less of something else, creating the need for a compromise.

Supplier certification program A formal process for approving a supplier. Supplier certification often takes place before a supplier is allowed to quote prices or receive an order.

Supplier co-location A more advanced form of VMI A full-time supplier representative resides in the buying firm's purchasing department, holding a dual position as both buyer and supplier representative. This person may also contribute to the buying firm's new product development and value engineering/value analysis teams by suggesting modifications or alternate components during the product design phase that are unknown to the engineering or design personnel.

Supplier relationship management Encompasses a broad suite of capabilities that facilitate collaboration, sourcing, transaction execution, and performance monitoring between an organization and its trading partners.

Supplier scorecard Used by buyers to track supplier performance.

Supply base The list of suppliers the firm is currently using.

Supply base optimization *See* Supply base rationalization.

Supply base rationalization Reducing purchases from marginal or poor-performing suppliers while increasing purchases from more desirable, top-performing suppliers.

Supply base reduction *See* Supply base rationalization.

Supply chain The network of companies eventually making goods and services available to consumers, including all of the functions enabling the purchasing, production, delivery, and recycling of materials, components, and end-goods.

Supply chain event management Software that collects real-time data from multiple supply chain sources and converts it into information that gives business managers a good idea of how their supply chains are performing when problems occur.

Supply chain management The integration of key business processes concerning the flow of materials from raw material suppliers to the final customer.

Supply chain risk Interruptions in the supply of goods and services in a supply chain caused by quality and safety challenges, supply shortages, legal issues, security problems, regulatory and environmental compliance, weather and natural disasters, or terrorism.

Supply chain security management Concerned with reducing the risk of intentionally created disruptions in supply chain operations including product and information theft and activities seeking to endanger personnel or sabotage supply chain infrastructure.

Supply management The identification, acquisition, access, positioning, and management of resources the organization needs or potentially needs in the attainment of its strategic objectives.

Sustainability The ability to meet the needs of current supply chain members without hindering the ability to meet the needs of future generations in terms of economic, environmental, and social challenges.

Sustainable processes Processes that provide outputs for the organization in an environmentally acceptable manner.

Sustainable product and process design The incorporation of sustainability elements into the design, operation, and disposal stages for goods and services. Improves the economic, environmental, and social/ethical performance of products, processes, manufacturers, and services.

Sustainable sourcing A process of purchasing goods and services that takes into account the long-term impact on people, profits, and the planet.

Synergise phase Three years after implementing ERP, the system along with its users have reached a level of maturity where system optimization is most likely to occur.

Synergize phase One year after implementing ERP, companies seek organizational improvements by improving processes, adding complementary software applications, mastering the ERP system, and gaining additional support for the system.

Takt time Derived from the German word *taktzeit*, meaning literally "clock cycle." *See* Cycle time.

Target inventory level The order-up-to level when using the periodic review model.

Tariff A tax or customs fee imposed by a government on imported goods to protect local industries and/or raise revenue.

Technology risks Failures or breakdowns of technology and software, and software integration problems, which can delay projects.

Telemarketing When salespeople use the telephone to identify potential new customers.

The three competitive dimensions Cost, quality, and customer service.

Theory of Constraints A general philosophy stating that a system is only as good or strong as its weakest part.

Third-party logistics services Outside agents that move items domestically or into foreign locations.

Three-dimensional concurrent engineering The simultaneous design of the product, the process, and the supply chain.

Time series forecasts Quantitative forecasting techniques based on the assumption that the future is an extension of the past; thus, historical demand can be used to predict future demand.

Total annual inventory costs The sum of the annual inventory carrying costs, order costs, stockout costs, and purchase costs.

Total cost of ownership (TCO) A relatively common method for comparing competing price quotes. This is a projected cost estimate that includes the initial acquisition costs, the estimated lifetime operating and maintenance costs, and the end-of-life salvage and disposition costs.

Total quality management A philosophy that seeks to improve quality continuously to please customers, reduce costs, and ultimately create competitive advantage for the firm.

Tour improvement For the vehicle routing problem, when one or more nodes are switched to another tour, so that vehicle capacities are not exceeded, and total distance of both tours is reduced.

Toyota Production System Seeks to optimize use of time, human resources, and assets, while improving productivity, quality, and customer service. It is based on the idea of reducing waste.

Tracking signal Used for determining if the RSFE is within acceptable limits. It can also be used as a running check on the accuracy of a forecasting technique.

Trailer-on-flatcar service An intermodal form of transportation using trucks and rail carrier flatcars that carry the truck trailers. Also called piggyback service.

Transaction elements of customer service The customer service elements occurring during the order cycle.

Transactional SRM Software that enables an organization to track supplier interactions such as order planning, order payments, and returns. Transactional SRM tends to focus on short-term reporting and is event driven, focusing on such questions as: What did we buy yesterday? What supplier did we buy from? What was the cost of the purchase?

Transportation inventories These inventories are owned by the firm and are in-transit either in-bound to the firm or out-bound to the firm's customers.

Transportation management system Allows firms, for instance, to select the best mix of transportation service and pricing, to determine the best use of containers or truck trailers, to better manage transportation contracts, to rank transportation options, to clear customs, to track product movements, and to monitor carrier performance.

Transportation planning Involves matching one or more modes of transportation with the types of items to be shipped, the needs of shippers and customers, and the laws governing transportation. Selecting one or more transportation modes is a function of how fast things must be delivered; the size, weight, and value of the items to be shipped; the transportation modes available; and the funds available to pay for transportation.

Transportation security The safeguarding of transportation systems to ensure safe travels for the general public and the safe and lawful transport of goods.

Traveling salesman problem To find the best delivery route for one vehicle, which minimizes a time, mileage, or cost objective.

Trend variations Demand variations caused by gradually increasing or decreasing movements over time, due to factors such as population growth and age, cultural changes, and income shifts.

Triple bottom line A firm's efforts to provide social, environmental, and economic benefits to stakeholders. Also referred to as the "three P's," which stands for *people, planet,* and *profit*.

Truckload carriers Trucks that move shipments taking up an entire truckload.

Type-I error When producer's risk occurs in acceptance sampling.

Type-II error When consumer's risk occurs in acceptance sampling.

Upper control limits A line that is three standard deviations above the mean, so that 99.7% of the sample plots fall inside this limit.

Utilitarianism An ethical act that creates the greatest good for the greatest number of people.

Value engineering Reducing a new product's cost through use of readily available parts instead of custom-designed parts, and use of cheaper materials and simpler designs, provided the changes have no effect on the product's use or performance.

Value stream mapping *See* Material flow mapping.

Variable data Continuous process data, such as weight, time, and length (as in the weight of a box of cereal, the time to serve a customer, or the length of a steel rod).

Vehicle routing problems Find the best delivery route with the use of multiple vehicles, variable demands at each node, and multiple vehicle capacities.

Vendor managed inventory (VMI) A strategic alliance–based approach to controlling inventory and reducing costs. Buyers provide inventory information to a key supplier including historical usage, current inventory levels, minimum and maximum stock levels, sales forecasts, and upcoming promotions. The supplier then takes on the responsibility and risk for planning, managing, and monitoring the replenishment of inventory at the buyer's facility.

Versioning Personalizing catalogues to appeal to individuals or very small market niche segments.

Viral marketing Direct online information sharing between the company and its customers.

Virtual call center Locating the organization's call center agents anywhere, while the center is managed as a single entity.

Virtual queue A computer-managed queue; allows restaurants located in malls, for instance, to provide customers with pagers, allowing the restaurant to track customers in a virtual queue while allowing them to walk around and shop while waiting for a table.

Visual merchandising Includes use of end caps at the end of each aisle, and making use of fixtures, lighting, and color to highlight products.

Warehouse management system Tracks and controls the flow of goods from the receiving dock of a distribution center until the item is loaded for outbound shipment to the customer.

Water carrier A very inexpensive transportation mode, and also very slow and inflexible. There are several types of water transportation, including inland waterway, lake, coastal and intercoastal ocean, and global deep-sea carriers.

Web portal A website that provides secure access to data, applications, and services to business partners. Portals support multiple languages, platforms, and software content.

Web services Third-party services that let applications communicate with one another without the need for custom coding, eliminating barriers caused by incompatible hardware, software, and operating systems. This allows companies to achieve internal integration when varied applications have been added to ERP systems over time.

Web-based customer service Enabling information to be provided to customers about the company's goods and services in the field, as well as marketing information, training, logistics information, diagnostic information, and collaborative planning initiatives.

Weighted moving average forecast Similar to simple moving average forecast; however, it allows the user to weight the more recent periods more heavily to take into consideration recent changes in the data. This forecast is the weighted average of the *n*-period observations, using varied weights.

Weighted-factor rating technique An analysis method that can be used to compare the attractiveness of potential manufacturing or service locations along a number of quantitative and qualitative dimensions.

Withdrawal kanban A light, flag, or card that is used to indicate to the upstream work cell that more parts are needed. This authorizes a full container of parts to move to the downstream work cell's input area. Also called a movement kanban.

Work breakdown structure All of the project's independent tasks, defined as much as possible.

Work flow The movement or transfer of work from the customer or demand source through the organization according to a set of procedures. Work may include documents, information, or tasks that are passed from one recipient to another for action.

Work flow analysis Identifying work that can be eliminated or combined with other work to achieve improvements in cost and customer service.

Workforce empowerment Managers support lean production efforts by providing subordinates with the skills, tools, time, empowerment, and other necessary resources to identify process problems and implement solutions. Managers create a culture in which workers are encouraged to speak out when problems exist.

Work-in-process Items in some intermediate stage of processing by the firm.

World Trade Organization A nonprofit organization based in Geneva, Switzerland. It helps to negotiate and enforce regional trade agreements. Its goal is to ensure that producers, importers, and exporters can conduct trade smoothly.

$\bar{x}$ For variable data, the mean of a sample's measurements.

$\bar{\bar{x}}$ The center line of the $\bar{x}$ chart

$\bar{x}$ chart For variable data, used to track the central tendency of the sample means.

Yield management The process of selling portions of a fixed capacity to customers at varying prices, so as to maximize revenues.

COMPANY INDEX

P

R

S

T

U

V

W

X

Y

Z

AUTHOR INDEX

SUBJECT INDEX

A

B

C

D

E

Q

R

S

T

U

V

W

X

Y